Western Philosophy

D1245668

BLACKWELL PHILOSOPHY ANTHOLOGIES

Each volume in this outstanding series provides an authoritative and comprehensive collection of the essential primary readings from philosophy's main fields of study. Designed to complement the *Blackwell Companions to Philosophy* series, each volume represents an unparalleled resource in its own right, and will provide the ideal platform for course use.

Western Philosophy
An Anthology

Second edition

Edited by
John Cottingham

Blackwell
Publishing

Editorial material and organization © 1996, 2008 by Blackwell Publishing Ltd

BLACKWELL PUBLISHING
350 Main Street, Malden, MA 02148–5020, USA
9600 Garsington Road, Oxford OX4 2DQ, UK
550 Swanston Street, Carlton, Victoria 3053, Australia

First edition published 1996 by Blackwell Publishers Ltd
Second edition published 2008 by Blackwell Publishing Ltd

10 2013

Library of Congress Cataloging-in-Publication Data

Western philosophy : an anthology / edited by John Cottingham. – 2nd ed.
p. cm. – (Blackwell philosophy anthologies)
Includes bibliographical references and index.
ISBN 978-1-4051-2477-5 (hardcover : alk. paper) – ISBN 978-1-4051-2478-2 (pbk. : alk. paper)
1. Philosophy–Introductions. I. Cottingham, John, 1943–
BD21.W43 2008
190–dc22

2007025829

A catalogue record for this title is available from the British Library.

Set in 10.5/12.5pt Minion
by SPi Publisher Services, Pondicherry, India
Printed and bound in Singapore
by COS Printers Pte Ltd

The publisher's policy is to use permanent paper from mills that operate a sustainable forestry
policy, and which has been manufactured from pulp processed using acid-free and elementary
chlorine-free practices. Furthermore, the publisher ensures that the text paper and cover board
used have met acceptable environmental accreditation standards.

For further information on
Blackwell Publishing, visit our website:
www.blackwellpublishing.com

John Cottingham's
Western Philosophy: An Anthology
Praise for the first edition

'It is difficult to imagine how this volume could be improved upon as the very best historically based anthology of the essential philosophical writings. Cottingham's commentary and introductions are extremely clear and helpful. It will provide an ideal text for an excellent introductory course in philosophy'. **Christopher Hookway, University of Sheffield**

'This volume is a superb resource for beginning students and their teachers. Not only is it an excellent anthology – a comprehensive, well-chosen, well-edited collection of classic texts, from Plato to Sartre, Aristotle to Rawls – it is also a perspicuous systematic presentation of the subject, owing to the editor's skilful provision of introductory material and notes. Judiciously annotated lists of supplementary readings further enhance the value of this outstanding volume.' **Vere Chappell, University of Massachusetts**

'In this anthology the highly respected philosopher John Cottingham has assembled 100 classic selections from Plato to Parfit. Done with care and considerable expertise the result is arguably the best single-volume introduction to the writings of Western philosophy.' **John Haldane, University of St Andrews**

'A truly outstanding collection. An excellent course book which doubles as a solid reference volume. The clarity of the commentary makes these classic readings vivid and accessible to students.' **George Graham, University of Alabama**

'By providing the means to appreciate philosophy as *the* great historical odyssey of the human intellect, this ambitious anthology makes philosophy come alive for students and general readers alike.' **David Cooper, University of Durham**

For JCC and family,
and In Memoriam VXG

Contents

Preface

An anthology can serve many different purposes. Anthologies of poetry usually leave readers to make their own way, sampling the flowers arranged for their delight. With philosophy things are rather different. Many of the arguments of the great philosophers rest on a daunting array of presuppositions and concealed premises, and careful guidance is needed if many readers are not to be overwhelmed. The texts included in this volume, and the linking passages of introduction and commentary, offer a guided tour through the main branches of the subject, introducing the ideas in sequence, and uncovering the main outlines of that complex interplay of arguments which forms the Western philosophical tradition. The central aim, as with all anthologies, is to put the reader in touch with the texts themselves. Those embarking on the subject can sometimes find it hard even to grasp just what philosophy is, and there is no better way of discovering than to read the writings of the great philosophers at first hand. This volume is designed to present some of the most important extracts from those writings in a way that will enable the individual to achieve a clear overview of how the subject developed, and how the most important theories fit into the overall picture. It is, I hope, a book which individuals will be able to keep by them, for pleasure and profit, as they set out on the quest for philosophical understanding.

The book also has the more specific aim of being serviceable to university students undertaking a formal course of study in philosophy. Philosophy is a wide-ranging subject, and there is no single template for an ideal introductory course (and even if there were, philosophy departments worth their salt would not wish to grind out exactly the same syllabus year after year). There are many ways into philosophy, and no good reason why one particular branch of the subject should always form the chosen route. One of the objects of this book is to provide, within the compass of a single volume, a set of key introductory materials for the widest possible range of courses, covering all the main branches of the subject (or at least all those suitable for teaching at a basic undergraduate level). Fundamental issues in epistemology are dealt with in Part I ('Knowledge and Certainty'). Part II ('Being and Reality') is concerned with general metaphysics and ontology, and Part III ('Language and Meaning') deals with central philosophical concerns about how language is related to thought and to the world. The philosophy of mind is covered in Part IV ('Mind and Body'), and the important issues of personal identity and the freedom of the will receive separate treatment in Part V ('The Self and Freedom'). The philosophy of religion and the philosophy of science are dealt with in Part VI ('God and Religion') and Part VII ('Science and Method') respectively. The next two parts deal with moral philosophy: Part VIII ('Morality and the Good Life') tackles theoretical and systematic issues in normative ethics, while Part IX ('Problems in Ethics') covers a selection of key issues in applied moral philosophy. Part X ('Authority and the State') and Part XI ('Beauty and Art') deal respectively with political philosophy and aesthetics, and, to conclude the volume, Part XII ('Human Life and its Meaning') covers some of the various ways in which great thinkers, ancient and modern, have tackled the old puzzle of what significance, if any, attaches to human existence.

Although the first three parts of the volume are devoted to epistemology, metaphysics and philosophy of language, traditionally considered as having a 'foundational' role in philosophy, the issues raised here are among the most demanding in the book, and there is no compelling reason why any given introductory course should have to begin with them. Each part of the volume is intended to be self-contained, and students and teachers are invited to work on the various parts of the book in any order they see fit, or indeed to concentrate on any particular part or parts in isolation. That said, given the nature of philosophy there is inevitably a fair amount of overlap between the topics raised in various parts; where this happens footnotes are provided to draw attention to connections with relevant texts or commentary in other parts of the volume.

The passages of introduction and commentary which link the extracts have been kept as concise and clear as possible. They are, of course, no substitute for the interpretations and evaluations which lecturers and instructors will themselves wish to provide. This book is designed to be serviceable for both teachers and students, not to eliminate the need for hard work by either group. So what is provided here is a basic scaffolding on which courses can be constructed, and a supportive framework for those coming to the texts for the first time. There is always a danger of oversimplification when writing with the principal aim of helping the student reader. Philosophy is not an easy subject, and spoon-feeding is often counterproductive; in the end there is no alternative to readers wrestling with the arguments for themselves. But without a clear initial overview, the whole philosophical enterprise can seem dauntingly obscure. Qualifications, objections, reinterpretations – these can always be added later; but if there is no initial understanding, the enthusiasm for making these further efforts will simply ebb away before any progress has been made.

These points notwithstanding, there may still be some who may have certain reservations about the very idea of introducing students to philosophy by way of an anthology, as opposed to through the intensive study of complete texts. Those who (like the present writer) were taught by this latter method will know that it has a very great deal to recommend it. Nevertheless, the vast expansion in numbers in tertiary education during the late twentieth century has required many philosophy teachers to rethink their approach. This has been particularly true in the United Kingdom. A typical annual philosophy intake in most British universities used to comprise a relatively small number of students who, even in their first year, could be taught in specialized classes and tutorials. But nowadays introductory classes can run to hundreds, and for groups of this size no library, however well equipped, can furnish enough copies of books and articles to support the traditional tutorial system based on the weekly reading list. Many teachers in Britain have thus had to accept what their counterparts in North America and elsewhere have long taken as given: the need for a single compendious volume of readings which will supply the materials for an entire introductory course in philosophy. Such volumes do not, of course, preclude students from reading more widely (as every good teacher will want to encourage them to do); but they at least ensure that some of the basic textual materials are to hand.

Although the volume is a stout one, the constraints of space are nevertheless such that many hard choices have been necessary. To begin with, this is a collection based on 'classic' texts, and this means that only a relatively small percentage of the extracts are taken from the work of philosophers from the recent past. To have given a representative selection of today's proliferating philosophical theories and debates would have required virtually an entire volume corresponding to each of the divisions of the present book. The classic materials featured here are nevertheless designed to provide a good base for understanding more recent developments, and the commentary accompanying each part of the volume often includes brief glances forward to later theories. Even within the terms of its chosen framework, however, the selection presented here cannot make any claim to completeness: the schema of twelve extracts in each of the twelve parts yields that pleasingly duodecimal aggregate traditionally termed a 'gross' (which gives the book a considerably wider scope than most recent anthologies); but I am well aware of the very many candidates for inclusion that have had to be omitted. If specialists, turning to their chosen authors, are shocked by the brevity of the extracts, or the severity of the abridgements, I can only plead that they bear in mind that nothing in the present project is designed to stop students going on to make a more detailed and thorough study of the authors represented here. On the contrary, it is my earnest hope that students who might have been overwhelmed by stern injunctions to read 'all or nothing' will be sufficiently excited by some of the extracts here to turn to the full texts, and to the suggestions for further reading which are provided at the end of each Part.

As well as the abridging noted in the previous paragraph, in preparing the extracts for inclusion in this volume I have not hesitated to modify spelling, punctuation and layout to make the material more readily accessible to the modern reader. It is of course vital that critical editions should preserve the original texts for scholarly use, but the aims of an anthology such as this are rather different; and since so many long-dead Greek, Latin, French and German writers are in any case presented here in modern English translations, it seemed over-exacting to insist on antiquated spelling and grammar just for those philosophers who wrote in English. I did indeed at one point consider 'translating' the extracts from such writers as Locke and Hume (that is, providing completely new modern English versions), but in the end (despite the urgings of some colleagues) resisted this radical measure, contenting myself instead with a few minor modifications of phrasing in places where the original was so antique that it might pose a major obstacle to the modern student reader. Some will feel I have not gone far enough; others will no doubt express outrage that a single comma has been altered. Bearing in mind, as always, the readership for whom this book is intended, I have tried to follow an Aristotelian mean between opposing culinary vices: my aim has been to avoid making the fare either blandly over-processed or harshly indigestible.

As for the principles of selection, since it would be impossibly ponderous to defend each decision, chapter and verse, I will simply observe that one overarching aim has been to try to make sure that the materials within each Part of the volume hang together as far as possible; rather than leaving readers to sink or swim, as is often done, I have tried to guide them through the extracts, linking the ideas together, so that by the end of each Part they should be able to move towards achieving a coherent, if necessarily schematic, overview of the relevant branch of the subject. Further details of the plan of the book may be found in the 'Advice to Readers and Format of the Volume' (pp. xxxiv–xxxvi, below).

I am very grateful to the publishers and individual authors and translators named in the footnotes at the start of each extract for permission to reproduce the materials indicated. Further details are given in the Acknowledgements (pp. xxii–xxxiii, below). (In a number of cases, the translations from the original Greek, Latin, French and German texts are my own.) As noted above, for the purposes of the present volume it has been necessary to abridge some of the extracts, and in the interests of clarity or consistency I have sometimes modified the original spelling and punctuation, and made occasional minor changes in phrasing. Further details may be found in the footnotes accompanying each extract. Finally, I should like to acknowledge here the wealth of helpful advice I have received from friends and colleagues in the course of preparing this volume. I am especially grateful to John Ackrill, John Andrews, Doug Buchanan, Edmund Burke, Harley Cahen, Enrique Chávez-Arvizo, Max de Gaynesford, Hanjo Glock, John Haldane, Brad Hooker, Andrew Mason, Richard Norman, David Oderberg, Derek Parfit, Harry Parkinson, John Preston, Michael Proudfoot, Steve Smith, Sandy Stewart, Jim Stone, Mark Tebbit and Rosemary Wright. I am greatly indebted to Enrique Chávez-Arvizo for checking the 'Notes on the Philosophers', and for preparing the index.

Preface to the second edition

The original edition of 1996 contained ten Parts of ten extracts each. All the material that appeared in the first edition has been retained in full, but the volume has been substantially enlarged for this second edition.

In the first place, each of the existing Parts now contains two additional extracts, bringing the total number of extracts per Part to twelve instead of ten. The decision to use more modern material for these further extracts was relatively easy, not just because many philosophers and students find a special excitement in more recent developments, but also because philosophy is a living and constantly evolving subject, and it is important for those studying the Western philosophical tradition to be aware that it continues to develop. The roots and trunk of the old plant are immensely valuable in themselves, but also because they put forth fresh shoots. That said, the selection of the new, more recent, materials was far from easy, since unlike the great classics of the past, they have yet to prove their enduring worth; what is more, today's philosophers are notoriously at odds about the relative importance of the proliferating current trends in the subject. I cannot hope to please everyone, but I have tried to select pieces that, firstly, will give some sense of where each of the respective branches of the subject is going, and, secondly, will stand some comparison with their august predecessors – either because since publication they have already achieved something of the status of instant classics, or else because they are at least worthy representatives of distinctive strands of philosophical inquiry that seem likely to endure.

As well as augmenting the existing Parts of the volume, I have also included two completely new Parts, each of twelve items, which (as noted above in the main Preface) brings the total number of extracts in the book as a whole to 144, in place of the original hundred. Dividing the spoils equally between 'theoretical' and 'practical' philosophy (to use a classification commonly employed in Philosophy departments in continental Europe), I have devoted these two new sections of the book to Philosophy of Language, and to the Meaning of Life respectively. The former is a subject that forms a vitally important part of the Western philosophical tradition, and one that many readers of the first edition expressed a strong interest in seeing included in any revised volume; the latter relates to one of philosophy's oldest and most weighty preoccupations, eclipsed under the restrictive conception of philosophical inquiry that became fashionable around the middle of the twentieth century, but now happily reinstated.

I am most grateful to those many philosophical colleagues from around the world who were kind enough to let me know that they found the first edition of the book useful, and I am heavily indebted to a large number of friends and colleagues for invaluable suggestions about the composition of this new edition, and/or for comments on the new material. Particular thanks are due to Michaela Baker, Jonathan Dancy, Max de Gaynesford, Brian Feltham, Philip Goff, Brad Hooker, John Hyman, Ward Jones, Seán MacGiollarnath, David Oderberg, John Preston, Severin Schroeder, Philip Stratton-Lake, Daniel Whiting and Andrew Williams. Emma Borg was kind enough to cast an expert eye over the draft of Part III, and made many valuable suggestions for improvement, and Joseph Jedwab kindly did the same for Part VI, and Andrew Williams for Part X. I have a special debt to Javier Kalhat, whose judicious advice was an enormous help to me, and who also provided unstinting assistance in hunting down the relevant materials and making suggestions for abridgement. Bryan Weaver provided much appreciated help with the additions to Part IX. Finally, I should like to express my thanks to Nick Bellorini, the Commissioning Editor at Blackwell Publishers, for encouraging me to produce this second edition, and to all the members of the editorial and production team for their hard work and efficiency.

JC
Reading, England
April 2007

Acknowledgements

The editor and publishers wish to thank the following who have kindly given permission for the use of copyright material.

Part I   Knowledge and Certainty

4 René Descartes, Meditation I and part of II, pp. 12–17 from *Meditations on First Philosophy* [*Meditationes de prima philosophia*, 1641], trans. John Cottingham (Cambridge: Cambridge University Press, 1986). © 1986 by Cambridge University Press. Reprinted by permission of Cambridge University Press.

6 Gottfried Wilhelm Leibniz, paras 44–53 from (ed. and trans.) Peter Remnant and Jonathan Bennett, *New Essays on Human Understanding* [*Nouveaux essais sur l'entendement humain, c.*1704; first pub. 1765] (Cambridge: Cambridge University Press, 1981). © 1981 by Cambridge University Press. Reprinted by permission of Cambridge University Press.

8 Immanuel Kant, extracts from 'Introduction', Sections 1 and 2 (B1–5); 'Transcendental Logic', Section 1 (B74–5); 'Transcendental Analytic', Book I, Chapter 2; 'Transition to the Transcendental Deduction of the Categories' (B124–6) from *Critique of Pure Reason* [*Kritik der reinen Vernunft*, 1781; 2nd edn 1787], trans. (with minor modifications) N. Kemp Smith (2nd edn) (London: Macmillan, 1933). Translation © The Estate of Norman Kemp Smith 1929, 1933, 2003. Reprinted by permission of Palgrave Macmillan.

10 G. E. Moore, 'A Defence of Common Sense' [1925], extracts from G. H. Muirhead (ed.), *Part I. Contemporary British Philosophy*, second series (London: Allen & Unwin, 1925).

11 Wilfred Sellars, 'The Myth of the Given', first presented as part of a lecture series given at the University of London in 1956, under the title 'The Myth of the Given: Three Lectures on Empiricism and the Philosophy of Mind'. First published in *The Foundations of Science and the Concepts of Psychoanalysis*, Minnesota Studies in the Philosophy of Science, vol. I, H. Feigl and M. Scriven (eds.) (Minneapolis, MN: University of Minnesota Press, 1956). © 1956 by University of Minnesota Press. Reprinted by permission of University of Minnesota Press.

12 Edmund Gettier, 'Is Justified True Belief Knowledge?', pp. 121–3 from *Analysis*, vol. 23 (1963). © 1963 by Edmund L. Gettier. Reprinted by permission of the author.

Part II   Being and Reality

2 Aristotle, Chapter 5 (2a11–4b19), pp. 5–12 from *Categories* [*Kategoriai, c.*330 BC], trans. J. L. Ackrill (Oxford: Clarendon, 1963). © 1963 by Oxford University Press. Reprinted by permission of Oxford University Press.

3 René Descartes, Part I, articles 51, 52, 54, 63; Part II, articles 1, 2, 3, 4, 21, 22, 23, 36, 64 from *Principles of Philosophy* [*Principia Philosophiae*, 1644], pp. 210–11, 215, 223–5, 232, 240, 247 from *The Philosophical Writings of Descartes*, vol. I, trans. J. Cottingham, R. Stoothoff and D. Murdoch (Cambridge: Cambridge University Press, 1985). © 1985 by Cambridge University Press. Reprinted by permission of Cambridge University Press.

5 Gottfried Wilhelm Leibniz, *New System of Nature and the Communication of Substances* [*Système nouveau de la nature et de la communication des substances*, 1695], pp. 115–25 (with omissions) from *Philosophical Writings*, trans. G. H. R. Parkinson and M. Morris (London: Dent, 1973). © 1973. Reprinted by permission of Everyman's Library, an imprint of Alfred A. Knopf.

9 Martin Heidegger, §§ 1, 2, 3, 4, 15, 26, 29, pp. 21, 25, 31, 32–5, 95–8, 160–1, 172–4 from *Being and Time* [*Sein und Zeit*, 1927], trans. J. Macquarrie and E. Robinson (New York: Harper and Row, 1962). Translation © 1962 by Blackwell Publishing Ltd. Reprinted by permission of HarperCollins Publishers and Blackwell Publishing Ltd.

10 Rudolf Carnap, 'The Elimination of Metaphysics through Logical Analysis of Language' [*Überwindung der Metaphysik durch Logische Analyse der Sprache*, 1932], pp. 60–80 (abridged) from A. J. Ayer (ed.), *Logical Positivism* (New York: Free Press, 1959). First published in *Erkenntnis*, vol. II, trans. Arthur Pap. © 1959 by The Free Press. Abridged with permission of The Free Press, a Division of Simon & Schuster, Inc.

11 W. V. O. Quine, 'On What There Is', pp. 21–38 (abridged) from *The Review of Metaphysics*, vol. 2, (1948). © 1948 by *The Review of Metaphysics*. Reprinted with permission of *The Review of Metaphysics*.

12 Derek Parfit, 'The Puzzle of Reality: Why Does the Universe Exist?', pp. 3–5. (abridged) from *Times Literary Supplement*, 3 July, 1992. © 1992 by Derek Parfit. Reprinted by permission of the author and *Times Literary Supplement*.

Part III   Language and Meaning

4 René Descartes, extract from Part V of *Discourse on the Method* [*Discours de la méthode*, 1637], from pp. 139–40 of *The Philosophical Writings of Descartes*, vol. I trans. John Cottingham, R. Stoothoff and D. Murdoch (Cambridge: Cambridge University Press, 1985). © 1985 by Cambridge University Press. Reprinted by permission of Cambridge University Press.

8 Gottlob Frege, 'Sense and Reference', from the article 'Sense and Reference' [*Sinn und Bedeutung*, 1892], pp. 56–62 from the English version in Peter Geach and Max

Black (eds), *Translations from the Philosophical Writings of Gottlob Frege* (Oxford: Blackwell, 1952). © 1952 by Blackwell Publishing Ltd. Reprinted by permission of Blackwell Publishing Ltd.

9 Bertrand Russell, extracts from Chapter 16 from *Introduction to Mathematical Philosophy* (London: Allen & Unwin, 1919).

10 J. L. Austin, 'Performative Utterances' [*Proceedings of the Aristotelian Society,* Supplementary Volume 32 (1957–8).] © 1957 by *Proceedings of the Aristotelian Society.* Reprinted by permission of The Aristotelian Society.

11 Paul Grice, 'Logic and Conversation', originally delivered as part of the William James lectures at Harvard University in 1967, pp. 43–58 (abridged) from *Syntax and Semantics*, vol. III (New York: Academic Press, 1973). © 1973. Reprinted by permission of Elsevier.

12 Saul Kripke, pp. 26, 27, 48–9, 57, 96, 127–33 from *Naming and Necessity* (Oxford: Blackwell, 1980). © 1972, 1980 by Saul A. Kripke. Reprinted by permission of Harvard University Press and Blackwell Publishing Ltd.

Part IV   Mind and Body

2 Aristotle, extracts from Book I, chapters 1 and 4; Book II, Chapters 1–3, *De Anima* [c. 325 bc], pp. 1–16 from D. W. Hamlyn (ed. and trans.), *Aristotle's De Anima,* (Oxford: Clarendon, 1968). © 1968 by Oxford University Press. Reprinted by permission of Oxford University Press.

4 René Descartes, pp. 17–19 and 51–9 (with omissions) from *Meditations on First Philosophy* [*Meditationes de Prima Philosophia*, 1641], trans. John Cottingham (Cambridge: Cambridge University Press, 1986, rev. edn 1996). © 1986 by Cambridge University Press. Reprinted by permission of Cambridge University Press.

9 Franz Brentano, extracts from Book II, Chapter 1 from Linda L. McAlister (ed. and trans.), *Psychology from an Empirical Standpoint* [*Psychologie vom empirischen Standpunkt*, 1874] (London: Routledge, 1974). © 1974. Reprinted by permission of Taylor & Francis Books UK.

10 Gilbert Ryle, extracts from chapters 1 and 7 from *The Concept of Mind* (London: Hutchinson, 1949). © 1949. Reprinted by permission of the Principal, Fellows, and Scholars of Hertford College in the University of Oxford and Taylor & Francis Books UK.

11 Hilary Putnam, 'Psychological Predicates', (abridged) from W. H. Capitan and D. D. Merrill (eds), *Art, Mind, and Religion* (Pittsburgh: University of Pittsburgh Press, 1967). © 1967. Reprinted by permission of the University of Pittsburgh Press.

12 Thomas Nagel, 'What is it Like to be a Bat?' pp. 435–50 (abridged) from *Philosophical Review* LXXXIII, 4 (October 1974). © 1974 by Thomas Nagel. Reprinted by permission of the author.

Part V   The Self and Freedom

4 Sigmund Freud, extracts from chapters 17 and 18 in *Introductory Lectures on Psychoanalysis* [*Vorlesungen zur Einführung in die Psychoanalyse*, 1916–17], trans. J. Riviere (London: Allen & Unwin, 1922).

5 Derek Parfit, extracts from sections 95 and 96, pp. 279–87 in *Reasons and Persons* (Oxford: Oxford University Press, 1984; reprinted 1987). © 1984 by Derek Parfit. Reprinted by permission of Oxford University Press.

6 Charles Taylor, pp. 46–52 from *Sources of the Self: The Making of Modern Identity*, (Cambridge: Cambridge University Press, 1989). © 1989 by Charles Taylor. Reprinted by permission of Cambridge University Press and Harvard University Press.

10 Jean-Paul Sartre, extracts (abridged) from Part IV, chapter 1, sections i and iii, pp. 433–7, 440–1, 553–6 in *Being and Nothingness* [1943], trans. H. E. Barnes (London: Methuen, 1957). © 1957. Reprinted by permission of Taylor & Francis Books UK and Philosophical Library, New York.

11 P. F. Strawson, 'Freedom and Resentment' [1962] pp. 5–13 from *Freedom and Resentment and Other Essays* (London: Methuen, 1974). © 1974 by P. F. Strawson. Reprinted by permission of Taylor & Francis Books UK.

12 Harry G. Frankfurt, 'Alternate Possibilities and Moral Responsibility,' pp. 829–39 (abridged) from *The Journal of Philosophy* Vol. 66 (1969). © 1969 by Harry G. Frankfurt. Reprinted by permission of the author and *Journal of Philosophy*.

Part VI God and Religion

3 René Descartes, *Meditations on First Philosophy* [*Meditationes de Prima Philosophia*, 1641], from the *Third Meditation*, trans. J. Cottingham (Cambridge: Cambridge University Press, 1986). © 1986 by Cambridge University Press. Reprinted by permission of Cambridge University Press.

5 Gottfried Wilhelm Leibniz, Part I, §§ 7–15, 19–26 (with omissions) from *Theodicy: Essays on the Goodness of God, the Liberty of Man and the Origin of Evil* [*Essais de théodicée sur la bonté de Dieu, la liberté de l'homme et l'origine du mal*, 1710], trans. E. M. Huggard (London: Routledge, 1951). © 1951. Reprinted by permission of Taylor & Francis Books UK.

8 Søren Kierkegaard, extracts from pp. 26–35 and 177–82 (with minor modifications) in *Concluding Unscientific Postscript* [1846], trans. D. F. Swenson (Princeton, NJ: Princeton University Press, 1941). © 1941 by Princeton University Press, 1969 renewed. Reprinted by permission of Princeton University Press.

10 John Wisdom, 'Gods' pp. 185–206 (considerably abridged) from *Proceedings of the Aristotelian Society* XLV [1944–5]. © 1945 by *Proceedings of the Aristotelian Society*. Reprinted by permission of The Aristotelian Society.

11 Robert M. Adams, Section I from 'Moral Arguments for Theistic Belief'. Originally published in C. F. Delaney (ed.), *Rationality and Religious Belief* (Notre Dame: University of Notre Dame Press, 1979). © 1979 by the University of Notre Dame. Reprinted by permission of University of Notre Dame Press.

12 Alvin Plantinga, 'Is Belief in God Properly Basic?', pp. 41–51 (abridged) from *Noûs*, 15 (1981). © 1981 by *Noûs*. Reprinted by permission of Blackwell Publishing Ltd.

Part VII Science and Method

1 Aristotle, 'Physics' [c.325 bc], Book II, Chapter 3 and Chapter 8 (extracts); translation taken (with adaptations) from Aristotle, *Physica*, trans. R. P. Hardie

and R. K. Gaye (Oxford: Clarendon Press, 1930). © 1930 by Oxford University Press. Reprinted by permission of Oxford University Press.

3 René Descartes, extracts from Parts v and vi from *Discourse on the Method* [*Discourse de la Méthode*, 1637], pp. 131–4 and 142–4 from John Cottingham, R. Stoothoff and D. Murdoch (eds. and trans.), *The Philosophical Writings of Descartes* (Cambridge: Cambridge University Press, 1985). © 1985 by Cambridge University Press. Reprinted by permission of Cambridge University Press.

4 George Berkeley, §§ 1–5, 11, 17–18, 26–8, 35–41, 52–3, 58, 67, 71–2 from *On Motion* [*De Motu*, 1721], from A. A. Luce and T. E. Jessop (eds), *The Works of George Berkeley*, trans. A. A. Luce (London: Nelson, 1948–51). © 1948.

7 Immanuel Kant, 'Analogies of Experience: Second Analogy', B 233–42 from *Critique of Pure Reason* [*Kritik der reinen Vernunft*, 1781; 2nd edn 1787], pp. 218–24 (with omissions and minor modifications) from N. Kemp Smith (ed.), *Immanuel Kant's Critique of Pure Reason* (London: Macmillan, 1929, repr. 1965). Translation © The estate of Norman Kemp Smith 1929, 1933, 2003. Reprinted by permission of Palgrave Macmillan.

9 Karl Popper, 'Conjectures and Refutations', from 'Science: Conjectures and Refutations'; lecture delivered in 1953 and originally published under the title 'Philosophy of Science: A Personal Report', Chapter 1 (abridged) from *Conjectures and Refutations* (London: Routledge, 1963; 3rd edn 1969). © 1969 by Karl Popper. Reprinted by permission of The Estate of Sir Karl Popper.

10 Carl G. Hempel, 'Explanation in Science and in History', pp. 7–33 (abridged) from R. G. Colodny (ed.) *Frontiers of Science and Philosophy* (London and Pittsburgh: Allen & Unwin and University of Pittsburgh Press, 1962). © 1962. Reprinted by permission of the University of Pittsburgh Press.

11 Grover Maxwell, 'The Ontological Status of Theoretical Entities', pp. 3–15 (abridged) from Herbert Feigl and Grover Maxwell (eds), *Scientific Explanation, Space, and Time*, vol. 3, *Minnesota Studies in the Philosophy of Science* (Minneapolis: University of Minnesota Press, 1962). © 1962 by University of Minnesota Press. Reprinted by permission of University of Minnesota Press.

12 Thomas S. Kuhn, Chapters 2, 6, 7, 8, 9 and 10, pp. 10–11, 64–5, 76–7, 81–3, 93–5, 112, 117–18 from *The Structure of Scientific Revolutions* [1962] (2nd edn, Chicago: University of Chicago Press, 1970). © 1970 by Thomas S. Kuhn. Reprinted by permission of the University of Chicago Press.

Part VIII Morality and the Good Life

5 Immanuel Kant, extracts from Chapters 1 and 2 from *Groundwork of the Metaphysic of Morals* [*Grundlegung zur Metaphysik der Sitten*, 1785], translated from H. J. Paton, *The Moral Law* (London: Hutchinson, 1948). © 1948. Reprinted by permission of Taylor & Francis Books UK.

8 Friedrich Nietzsche, §§ 26, 29, 32, 33, 39, 186, 201, 203 from *Beyond Good and Evil* [*Jenseits von Gut und Böse*, 1886], trans. W. Kaufmann (New York: Random House, 1966). © 1966 by Random House, Inc. Used by permission of Random House, Inc.

9 W. D. Ross, Chapter II from 'What Makes Right Acts Right?', pp. 16–24 (with omissions) from *The Right and the Good* (Oxford: Clarendon, 1930). © 1930 by Oxford University Press. Reprinted by permission of Oxford University Press.

10 John Rawls, 'The Main Idea of the Theory of Justice' and 'The Original Position and Justification,' pp. 10–13, 15–18 from *A Theory of Justice* (Cambridge, Mass.: The Belknap Press of Harvard University Press, 1971). © 1971, 1999 by the President and Fellows of Harvard College. Reprinted by permission of Harvard University Press.

11 Alasdair Macintyre, extracts from Chapter 6, pp. 62–8 and Chapter 15, pp. 216–24. *After Virtue: A Study in Moral Theory* (London: Duckworth, 1981; 2nd edn 1985). © 1981, 1984 by University of Notre Dame. Reprinted by permission of University of Notre Dame Press and Gerald Duckworth & Co Ltd.

12 Bernard Williams, excerpts from Chapter 8 'Knowledge, Science, Convergence', pp. 135–55 from *Ethics and the Limits of Philosophy* (London: Collins/Fontana, 1985). © 1985 by Bernard Williams. Reprinted by permission of Taylor & Francis Books UK.

Part IX   Problems in Ethics

1 Aristotle, *Politics* [*Politika*, c.330 bc], Book I, Chapters 3–7 (1253b1–1255b40), (with omissions) from W. D. Ross (ed.) *The Works of Aristotle*, vol. X, trans. B. Jowett (Oxford: Clarendon, 1921). © 1921 by Oxford University Press. Reprinted by permission of Oxford University Press.

8 Aldo Leopold, 'The Land Ethic', pp. 201–26 (abridged) from *A Sand County Almanac: And Sketches Here and There* (Oxford: Oxford University Press, 1949; repr. 1977), © 1949 by Oxford University Press, Inc. Reprinted by permission of Oxford University Press, Inc.

9 Judith Jarvis Thomson, 'A Defense of Abortion', pp. 47–66 (abridged) from *Philosophy and Public Affairs* (Fall 1971). © 1971 by *Philosophy and Public Affairs*. Reprinted by permission of Blackwell Publishing Ltd.

10 Peter Singer, 'Famine, Affluence, and Morality', pp. 229–43 (abridged) from *Philosophy and Public Affairs*, 1, no. 3 (Spring 1972). © 1972 by *Philosophy and Public Affairs*. Reprinted by permission of Blackwell Publishing Ltd.

11 James Rachels, 'Active and Passive Euthanasia', originally published in the *New England Journal of Medicine* (1975), pp. 78–80. © 1975 by the Massachusetts Medical Society. All rights reserved. Reprinted by permission of the Massachusetts Medical Society.

12 Leon R. Kass, 'The Wisdom of Repugnance', pp. 17–26 (abridged) from *The New Republic*, 2 June (1997). © 1997 by Leon Kass. Reprinted by permission of the author.

Part X   Authority and the State

2 Thomas Aquinas, 'On Princely Government,' [1265–7], pp. 3–13, Book I, chapters 1 and 2 from A. P. D'Entrèves, *Aquinas: Selected Political Writings*, trans. J. G. Dawson (Oxford: Blackwell, 1948). © 1948 by Blackwell Publishing Ltd. Reprinted by permission of Blackwell Publishing Ltd.

6 Jean-Jacques Rousseau, extracts from Book I, chapters 6, 7, 8; Book II, chapters 1, 3, 4; Book IV, chapter 2, pp. 13–16; 17–19; 23–4; 26–7; 28–9; 30–1; 105–6 from *The Social Contract and Discourses* [*Du contrat social*, 1762], trans. G. D. H. Cole

(London: Dent, 1955). © 1913. Reprinted by permission of Everyman's Library, an imprint of Alfred A. Knopf.

7 G. W. F. Hegel, extracts from §§ 142, 156–9, 182–3, 185, 187–8, 257–61, addition to 261, 273, 279, 281, 308, 316–18 in *Philosophy of Right* [*Grundlinien der Philosophie des Rechts*, 1821], trans. T. M. Knox (Oxford: Clarendon, 1942). © 1942 by Oxford University Press. Reprinted by permission of Oxford University Press.

8 Karl Marx and Friedrich Engels, pp. 44–8, 61, 82–7 (with omissions and minor modifications) from *Die deutsche Ideologie* [*The German Ideology*, composed 1845–7; first published 1932], trans. S. Ryazanskaya (London: Lawrence and Wishart, 1965). © 1975 by Lawrence and Wishart. Reprinted by permission of Lawrence and Wishart Ltd.

10 Robert Nozick, chapter 7, section 1, pp. 149–63 (with omissions) from *Anarchy, State and Utopia* (Oxford: Blackwell, 1974). © 1974 by Basic Books, Inc. Reprinted by permission of Blackwell Publishing Ltd.

11 David Gauthier, 'Why Contractarianism?', pp. 65ff. (abridged) from Peter Vallentyne (ed.), *Contractarianism and Rational Choice* (Cambridge: Cambridge University Press, 1991). © 1991 by Cambridge University Press. Reprinted by permission of Cambridge University Press.

12 Ronald Dworkin, 'Why Liberals Should Care about Equality', pp. 205–13 (abridged), from Ronald Dworkin, *A Matter of Principle* (Cambridge, Mass.: Harvard University Press, 1985). © 1985 by Ronald Dworkin. Reprinted by permission of Harvard University Press and Oxford University Press.

Part XI Beauty and Art

2 Aristotle, *Poetics* [*Peri Poetikes*, c.325 bc], extracts from Chapters 4, 6, 7, 8, 9, 10, 11, 25 from W. D. Ross (ed.), *The Works of Aristotle*, trans. I. Bywater, with minor modifications (Oxford: Clarendon Press, 1924). © 1924 by Oxford University Press. Reprinted by permission of Oxford University Press.

5 Immanuel Kant, Part I, Book I, §§ 1–7, pp. 41–53 (with omissions) from *Critique of Judgement* [*Kritik der Urteilskraft*, 1790], trans. J. C. Meredith (Oxford: Clarendon, 1928). © 1928 by Oxford University Press. Reprinted by permission of Oxford University Press.

6 Arthur Schopenhauer, 'On Aesthetics', volume II, Chapter 19, §§ 205–10, 212–13, 218 (with omissions and a few minor modifications) from *Parerga and Paralipomena* [1851], trans. E. F. J. Payne (Oxford: Clarendon, 1974). © 1974 by Oxford University Press. Reprinted by permission of Oxford University Press.

7 Friedrich Nietzsche, Sections 1 and 2 from *The Birth of Tragedy and the Case of Wagner* [*Die Geburt der Tragödie*, 1872], trans. W. Kaufmann (New York: Random House, 1967). © 1967 by Walter Kaufmann. Used by permission of Random House, Inc.

8 Leo Tolstoy, Chapter 1 and part of Chapter 2, pp. 1–10 from *What is Art?* [*Shto Takoy Iskoostvo*, 1896], trans. Aylmer Maude (London: Brotherhood Publishing, 1898).

9 Jean-Paul Sartre, 'Imagination and Art', pp. 211–17 from *L'imaginaire: Psychologie phénoménologique de l'imagination* [1940], translated as *The Psychology of Imagination* (London: Rider, 1950). © 1950. Reprinted by permission of Taylor & Francis Books UK.

10 Ludwig Wittgenstein, 'Lectures on Aesthetics' [1938], I, §§ 17–26; II, §§ 1–12, 16–19, 35–8; IV §§ 1–3. pp. 6–8, 11–15, 17–18, 28–30 from L. Wittgenstein, *Lectures and Conversations on Aesthetics, Psychology and Religious Belief*, ed. C. Barrett (Oxford: Blackwell, 1978). © 1966 by Blackwell Publishing Ltd. Reprinted by permission of Blackwell Publishing Ltd.

11 Frank Sibley, 'Aesthetic Concepts', pp. 421–50 (abridged) from *Philosophical Review* 68 (1959). © 1959 by Cornell University Press. All rights reserved. Reprinted by permission of the current publisher, Duke University Press.

12 Nelson Goodman, pp. 3–9, 31–8 (abridged) from *The Languages of Art* (Oxford: Oxford University Press, 1969). © 1976 by Nelson Goodman. Reprinted by permission of Hackett Publishing Company, Inc.

Part XII   Human Life and its Meaning

7 Friedrich Nietzsche, extracts from *Thus Spake Zarathustra* [*Also Sprach Zarathustra*, 1891], Part I. English version based on the translation of Thomas Common (6th edn, London: Routledge, 1906), with modifications.

8 Bertrand Russell, 'A Free Man's Worship', (1903). Reprinted in *Collected Papers*, Volume 12 (London: Routledge, 1985). © 1985 by The Bertrand Russell Peace Foundation Ltd. Reprinted by permission of The Bertrand Russell Peace Foundation and Taylor & Francis Books UK.

9 Albert Camus, pp. 107–11 from *The Myth of Sisyphus* (London: Penguin, 1955). Translation © Justin O'Brien, 1955. Reprinted by permission of Penguin Books Ltd and Knopf, a division of Random House, Inc.

10 Thomas Nagel, 'The Absurd', from *Journal of Philosophy* vol. LXIII, no. 20 (1971). © 1971 by Thomas Nagel. Reprinted by permission of the author and *Journal of Philosophy*.

11 William Lane Craig, 'The Absurdity of Life without God', Chapter 2, pp. 57–75 (abridged) from *Reasonable Faith, Christian Truth and Apologetics* [1984] (revised edn, Wheaton, Ill.: Crossway Books, 1994). © 1994. Used by permission of Crossway Books, a division of Good News Publishers, Wheaton, IL 60187, USA, www.crossway.com

12 Robert Nozick, 'Philosophy's Life', Ch. 26, pp. 297–302 from *The Examined Life: Philosophical Meditations* (New York: Simon and Schuster, 1989). © 1989 by Robert Nozick. Reprinted by permission of Simon & Schuster Adult Publishing Group and Georges Borchardt, Inc., on behalf of the author.

Every effort has been made to trace all the copyright holders, but if any have been inadvertently overlooked the publishers will be pleased to make the necessary arrangement at the first opportunity.

Advice to Readers and Format of the Volume

Socrates of Athens famously declared that 'the unexamined life is not worth living', and his motto aptly explains the impulse to philosophize. Taking nothing for granted, philosophy probes and questions the fundamental presuppositions of every area of human inquiry. Although, in the modern academic world, it is studied in courses put on by professionalized departments, and although many of its contemporary practitioners employ a daunting array of technical terminology, philosophy can never quite fit the model of a tightly specialized discipline, like biochemistry or musicology. For part of the job of the philosopher is to keep at a certain critical distance from current doctrines, whether in the sciences or the arts, and to examine instead how the various elements in our worldview clash, or fit together. Some philosophers have tried to incorporate the results of these inquiries into a grand synoptic view of the nature of reality and our human relationship to it. Others have mistrusted system-building, and seen their primary role as one of clarification, or the removal of obstacles along the road to truth. But all have shared the Socratic vision of using the human intellect to challenge comfortable preconceptions, insisting that every aspect of human theory and practice be subjected to continuing critical scrutiny.

There are many ways of approaching philosophy, but sooner or later every student will have to come to terms with the great canonical classics by the founding fathers of the subject, including Plato and Aristotle, Descartes and Locke, Hume and Kant – works in which the fundamental problems of philosophy were defined and shaped. The main subject matter of the present volume consists in carefully chosen extracts from the writings of these and other 'classic' philosophical authors. Though most of the texts included here predate the twentieth century, it would be quite wrong to pigeonhole them as belonging merely to the 'history' of the subject. For philosophy has a unique relationship to its past. On the one hand it does not entirely match the pattern of 'progressive' scientific disciplines, which ruthlessly abandon old theories as new discoveries are made and better systems are developed; but on the other hand it is quite different from those antiquarian disciplines which aim to immerse themselves in the ideas of the past 'for their own sake'. Rather, philosophers conduct their researches in a kind of perpetual living dialogue with the protagonists of the past; each new philosophical movement gains vitality and meaning by drawing on, and reacting against, previous approaches. In presenting the views of the great canonical thinkers this volume aims to serve not just as an introduction to the 'history' of the subject, but as an introduction to philosophy itself.

Though this is a collection based on extracts from philosophical 'classics', it should certainly not be treated as an anthology of 'sacred texts', or definitive pronouncements by unquestioned authorities. It is integral to the very idea of philosophy that every philosophical doctrine, without exception, is there to be scrutinized and challenged. A good philosophy student will never rest content with knowing what the great philosophers said, but will want to form a considered and critical view of whether their arguments are justified, and what issues, if any, they illuminate. Most of the ideas contained in this book have been subject to endless analysis and discussion by generations of commentators, but they still have power to speak to us afresh, provided we approach them open-mindedly, and without undue reverence. Though it raises problems of its own, there is a lot to be said for Descartes's famous observation that in philosophy the natural light of reason within each of us is a better guide to the truth than past authority. Philosophy is, of course, part of a continuing tradition, and there is much to be gained from seeing how that tradition originated and developed. But the principal object of studying the materials in this book is not to pay homage to past genius, but to enrich one's understanding of central problems that are as pressing today as they have always been – problems about knowledge, truth and reality, the nature of the mind, the basis of right action, and the best way to live. These questions help to mark out the territory of philosophy as an academic discipline, but in a wider sense they define the human predicament itself; they will surely continue to be with us for as long as humanity endures.

Format of the volume

- The book is divided into twelve Parts, each covering a principal branch of philosophy.
- Each of the twelve main Parts of the book is intended to be more or less self-contained, so they do not have to be studied in any particular order (indeed many readers may decide, depending on their interests, to focus on a particular Part or Parts, and perhaps to skip some Parts entirely).
- Each of the twelve Parts presents, in chronological order, a selection of twelve extracts from key texts which have shaped the nature and development of the relevant branch of philosophical thinking.
- The extracts are introduced and linked together by a concise philosophical commentary which sets out to explain the principal issues raised in the readings, and to focus attention on the most important concepts and arguments involved.
- Within each Part of the volume, the passages of linking commentary form a continuous narrative designed to guide the reader through the texts. The reader will find that philosophical issues arising from a particular text are often picked up in the introduction to a subsequent text.

- In each Part of the volume, after the extracts and commentary, specimen questions are provided to help readers assess their philosophical grasp of the materials.
- Detailed suggestions for further reading are provided in special annotated bibliographies to be found at the end of each Part of the volume.
- Biographical and philosophical information on the authors of the extracts is contained in a separate table ('Notes on the Philosophers') at the end of the volume.
- When each new extract is introduced, a footnote is provided giving details of the source from which it is taken. The original title and date of publication or composition are always indicated [in square brackets].
- Explanatory footnotes have been added at various points, elucidating possibly obscure references or terminology, or providing cross-references to other parts of the volume. All such footnotes are by the Editor, except where they are preceded by an asterisk (*), in which case they appeared in the original work from which the extract is taken.

PART I
Knowledge and Certainty

Knowledge and Certainty
Introduction

Philosophy has always aimed to go beyond our ordinary, unreflective awareness of things. The philosopher typically subjects our everyday convictions to careful logical scrutiny, exposing inconsistencies and misconceptions, and attempting to arrive at a critical standpoint which will enable us to discard what is confused, and to supply a solid rational justification for what is retained. Using the tools of reason, of logical analysis and conceptual clarification, philosophy tries to replace what is doubtful and uncertain with something more coherent and stable. The goal, in short, is to move beyond mere belief, towards systematic knowledge and understanding.

We all realize, in our reflective moments, that many of our beliefs are liable to be mistaken. And even when our beliefs happen to be true, we can often appreciate that this is not much more than a lucky accident – we could equally well have been wrong. But what is the difference between mere belief, and the more stable and reliable kind of cognition that is entitled to be called knowledge, or true understanding? What do we mean by such understanding: how can it be defined, what are its origins, and how is it to be achieved? This fundamental set of questions forms the subject matter of that branch of philosophy known as the theory of knowledge, or *epistemology* (from the Greek word *episteme*, meaning 'knowledge' or 'understanding'). From the seventeenth century onwards, epistemology has been at or near the centre of philosophical inquiry. But, as with so many other areas of philosophy, much of the framework for subsequent developments comes from the ideas of the classical Greek thinkers, and of Plato in particular.

1 Innate Knowledge: Plato, *Meno**

Our first extract, from the *Meno* (*c*.385 BC), begins with Meno taunting Socrates for his role as a stingray or 'torpedo-fish', paralysing his victims by relentlessly attacking their confused and inconsistent beliefs. But it ends showing Socrates in a more positive role, more like that of the 'midwife',[1] using careful and systematic questioning to draw out, from the minds of his pupils, the seeds of true and reliable knowledge. From its own inner resources, the mind, suitably guided, can reach a genuine understanding of the truth. We have within us 'true thoughts which only need to be awakened into knowledge by putting questions'. This notion is graphically expressed in terms of the poetic idea of the soul's immortality: it 'remembers' or 'recollects' truths it knew in a previous existence. The point is made through a detailed mathematical example. By careful questioning Socrates is able to get the slave boy to recognize that the way to construct a square double in area to a given square is to use the diagonal of the given square as a base.

Though readers may feel that Socrates is 'leading' the boy in the direction he wants, it should be clear that the result of the exchange is quite different from what happens in 'spoon-feeding', where the learner simply accepts what the teacher imparts. For after his exchange with Socrates, once the areas have been drawn in, and various attempted solutions discarded as wrong, the boy is able to 'see for himself' that the square drawn on the diagonal does, and indeed must, produce the right answer. The choice of a mathematical example to illustrate the theory of the mind's innate cognitive powers is no accident. For Plato, mathematical understanding is an example of the kind of reliable cognition which takes us beyond the unsatisfactory world of everyday appearances towards a realm of more permanent and secure truths. As will become apparent, this notion, together with the doctrine of innate knowledge, plays a key role in the subsequent development of the philosophy of knowledge.

MENO: Socrates, I used to be told, before I knew you, that you were always doubting yourself and making others doubt; and now you are casting your spells over me, and I am simply getting bewitched and enchanted, and am at my wits' end. And if I may venture to make a jest upon you, you seem to me both in your appearance and in your power over others to be very like the flat torpedo fish, who torpifies those who come near him and touch him, as you have now torpified me, I think. For my soul and my tongue are really torpid, and I do not know how to answer you; and though I have been delivered of an infinite variety of speeches about virtue before now, and to many persons – and very good ones they were, as I thought – at this moment I cannot even say what virtue is. And I think that you are very wise in not voyaging and going away from home, for if you did in other places as you do in Athens, you would be cast into prison as a magician.

SOCRATES: You are a rogue, Meno, and had all but caught me.

MENO: What do you mean, Socrates?

SOCRATES: I can tell why you made a simile about me.

MENO: Why?

SOCRATES: In order that I might make another simile about you. For I know that all pretty young gentlemen like to have pretty similes made about them – as well they may – but I shall not return the compliment. As to my being a torpedo, if the

---

* Plato, *Meno* [*Menon*, *c*.380 BC], 79e–86c. Trans. B. Jowett, in *The Dialogues of Plato* (Oxford: Clarendon, 1892), vol. II, pp. 39–47; diagrams added for this anthology.
[1] The comparison is found in a later Platonic dialogue, the *Theaetetus*.

torpedo is torpid as well as the cause of torpidity in others, then indeed I am a torpedo, but not otherwise; for I perplex others, not because I am clear, but because I am utterly perplexed myself. And now I know not what virtue is, and you seem to be in the same case, although you did once perhaps know before you touched me. However, I have no objection to join with you in the enquiry.

MENO: And how will you enquire, Socrates, into that which you do not know? What will you put forth as the subject of enquiry? And if you find what you want, how will you ever know that this is the thing which you did not know?

SOCRATES: I know, Meno, what you mean; but just see what a tiresome dispute you are introducing. You argue that a man cannot enquire either about that which he knows, or about that which he does not know; for if he knows, he has no need to enquire; and if not, he cannot; for he does not know the very subject about which he is to enquire?

MENO: Well, Socrates, and is not the argument sound?

SOCRATES: I think not.

MENO: Why not?

SOCRATES: I will tell you why: I have heard from certain wise men and women who spoke of things divine that –

MENO: What did they say?

SOCRATES: They spoke of a glorious truth, as I conceive.

MENO: What was it? and who were they?

SOCRATES: Some of them were priests and priestesses, who had studied how they might be able to give a reason of their profession: there have been poets also, who spoke of these things by inspiration, like Pindar, and many others who were inspired. And they say – mark, now, and see whether their words are true – they say that the soul of man is immortal, and at one time has an end, which is termed dying, and at another time is born again, but is never destroyed. And the moral is, that a man ought to live always in perfect holiness. 'For in the ninth year Persephone sends the souls of those from whom she has received the penalty of ancient crimes back again from beneath into the light of the sun above, and these are they who become noble kings and mighty men and great in wisdom and are called saintly heroes in after ages.' The soul, then, as being immortal, and having been born again many times, and having seen all things that exist, whether in this world or in the world below, has knowledge of them all; and it is no wonder that she should be able to call to remembrance all that she ever knew about virtue, and about everything; for as all nature is akin, and the soul has learned all things, there is no difficulty in her eliciting or as men say learning, out of a single recollection all the rest, if a man is strenuous and does not faint; for all enquiry and all learning is but recollection. And therefore we ought not to listen to this sophistical argument about the impossibility of enquiry for it will make us idle, and is sweet only to the sluggard; but the other saying will make us active and inquisitive. In that confiding, I will gladly enquire with you, into the nature of virtue.

MENO: Yes, Socrates; but what do you mean by saying that we do not learn, and that what we call learning is only a process of recollection? Can you teach me how this is?

SOCRATES: I told you, Meno, just now that you were a rogue, and now you ask whether I can teach you, when I am saying that there is no teaching, but only recollection; and thus you imagine that you will involve me in a contradiction.

MENO: Indeed, Socrates, I protest that I had no such intention. I only asked the question from habit; but if you can prove to me that what you say is true, I wish that you would.

SOCRATES: It will be no easy matter, but I will try to please you to the utmost of my power. Suppose that you call one of your numerous attendants, that I may demonstrate on him.

MENO: Certainly. Come hither, boy.

SOCRATES: He is Greek, and speaks Greek, does he not?

MENO: Yes, indeed; he was born in the house.

SOCRATES: Attend now to the questions which I ask him, and observe whether he learns of me or only remembers.

MENO: I will.

SOCRATES: Tell me, boy, do you know that a figure like this is a square [figure 1]?

BOY: I do.

SOCRATES: And you know that a square figure has these four lines equal?

BOY: Certainly.

SOCRATES: And these lines which I have drawn through the middle of the square are also equal?

BOY: Yes.

SOCRATES: A square may be any size?

BOY: Certainly.

SOCRATES: And if one side of the figure be of two feet, and the other side be of two feet, how much will the whole be? Let me explain: if in one direction the space was of two feet, and in the other direction of one foot, the whole would be of two feet taken once?

BOY: Yes.

SOCRATES: But since this side is also of two feet, there are twice two feet?

BOY: There are.

SOCRATES: Then the square is of twice two feet?

BOY: Yes.

SOCRATES: And how many are twice two feet? count and tell me.

BOY: Four, Socrates.

SOCRATES: And might there not be another square twice as large as this, and having like this the lines equal?

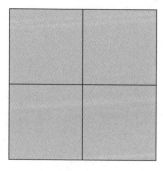

Figure 1

BOY: Yes.

SOCRATES: And of how many feet will that be?

BOY: Of eight feet.

SOCRATES: And now try and tell me the length of the line which forms the side of that double square: this is two feet – what will that be?

BOY: Clearly, Socrates, it will be double.

SOCRATES: Do you observe, Meno, that I am not teaching the boy anything, but only asking him questions; and now he fancies that he knows how long a line is necessary in order to produce a figure of eight square feet; does he not?

MENO: Yes.

SOCRATES: And does he really know?

MENO: Certainly not.

SOCRATES: He only guesses that because the square is double, the line is double.

MENO: True.

SOCRATES: Observe him while he recalls the steps in regular order. [To the Boy] Tell me, boy, do you assert that a double space comes from a double line? Remember that I am not speaking of an oblong, but of a figure equal every way, and twice the size of this – that is to say of eight feet; and I want to know whether you still say that a double square comes from a double line?

BOY: Yes.

SOCRATES: But does not this line become doubled if we add another such line here [figure 2]?

BOY: Certainly.

SOCRATES: And four such lines will make a space containing eight feet?

BOY: Yes.

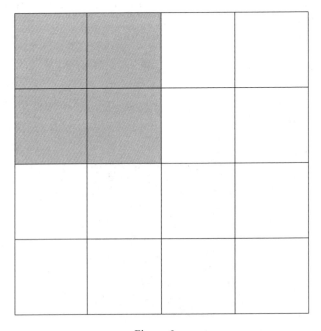

Figure 2

SOCRATES: Let us describe such a figure: Would you not say that this is the figure of eight feet?

BOY: Yes.

SOCRATES: And are there not these four divisions in the figure, each of which is equal to the figure of four feet?

BOY: True.

SOCRATES: And is not that four times four?

BOY: Certainly.

SOCRATES: And four times is not double?

BOY: No, indeed.

SOCRATES: But how much?

BOY: Four times as much.

SOCRATES: Therefore the double line, boy, has given a space, not twice, but four times as much.

BOY: True.

SOCRATES: Four times four are sixteen – are they not?

BOY: Yes.

SOCRATES: What line would give you a space of eight feet, as this gives one of sixteen feet; – do you see?

BOY: Yes.

SOCRATES: And the space of four feet is made from this half line?

BOY: Yes.

SOCRATES: Good; and is not a space of eight feet twice the size of this, and half the size of the other?

BOY: Certainly.

SOCRATES: Such a space, then, will be made out of a line greater than this one, and less than that one?

BOY: Yes; I think so.

SOCRATES: Very good; I like to hear you say what you think. And now tell me, is not this a line of two feet and that of four?

BOY: Yes.

SOCRATES: Then the line which forms the side of eight feet now ought to be more than this line of two feet, and less than the other of four feet?

BOY: It ought.

SOCRATES: Try and see if you can tell me how much it will be.

BOY: Three feet.

SOCRATES: Then if we add a half to this line of two, that will be the line of three. Here are two and there is one; and on the other side, here are two also and there is one: and that makes the figure of which you speak [figure 3]?

BOY: Yes.

SOCRATES: But if there are three feet this way and three feet that way, the whole space will be three times three feet?

BOY: *That* is evident.

SOCRATES: And how much are three times three feet?

BOY: Nine.

SOCRATES: And how much is the double of four?

BOY: Eight.

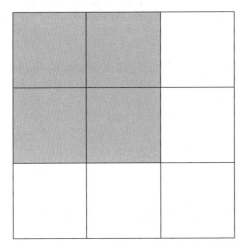

Figure 3

SOCRATES: Then the figure of eight is not made out of a line of three?

BOY: No.

SOCRATES: But from what line? – tell me exactly; and if you would rather not reckon, try and show me the line.

BOY: Indeed, Socrates, I do not know.

SOCRATES: Do you see, Meno, what advances he has made in his power of recollection? He did not know at first, and he does not know now, what is the side of a figure of eight feet: but then he thought that he knew, and answered confidently as if he knew, and had no difficulty; now he has a difficulty, and neither knows nor fancies that he knows.

MENO: True.

SOCRATES: Is he not better off in knowing his ignorance?

MENO: I think that he is.

SOCRATES: If we have made him doubt, and given him the 'torpedo's shock', have we done him any harm?

MENO: I think not.

SOCRATES: We have certainly, as would seem, assisted him in some degree to the discovery of the truth; and now he will wish to remedy his ignorance, but then he would have been ready to tell all the world again and again that the double space should have a double side.

MENO: True.

SOCRATES: But do you suppose that he would ever have enquired into or learned what he fancied that he knew, though he was really ignorant of it, until he had fallen into perplexity under the idea that he did not know, and had desired to know?

MENO: I think not, Socrates.

SOCRATES: Then he was the better for the torpedo's touch?

MENO: I think so.

SOCRATES: Mark now the farther development. I shall only ask him, and not teach him, and he shall share the enquiry with me: and do you watch and see if you find me telling or explaining anything to him, instead of eliciting his opinion. Tell me, boy, is not this a square of four feet which I have drawn [figure 4]?

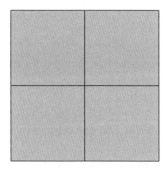

Figure 4

BOY: Yes.
SOCRATES: And now I add another square equal to the former one?
BOY: Yes.
SOCRATES: And a third, which is equal to either of them?
BOY: Yes.
SOCRATES: Suppose that we fill up the vacant corner?
BOY: Very good.
SOCRATES: Here, then, there are four equal spaces [figure 5]?
BOY: Yes.
SOCRATES: And how many times larger is this space than this other?
BOY: Four times.
SOCRATES: But it ought to have been twice only, as you will remember.
BOY: True.

Figure 5

SOCRATES: And does not this line, reaching from corner to corner, bisect each of these spaces [figure 6]?

BOY: Yes.

SOCRATES: And are there not here four equal lines which contain this space?

BOY: There are.

SOCRATES: Look and see how much this space is.

BOY: I do not understand.

SOCRATES: Has not each interior line cut off half of the four spaces?

BOY: Yes.

SOCRATES: And how many such spaces are there in this section [the section marked out by the diagonal lines]?

BOY: Four.

SOCRATES: And how many in this? [the original shaded square]

BOY: Two.

SOCRATES: And four is how many times two?

BOY: Twice.

SOCRATES: And this space is of how many feet?

BOY: Of eight feet.

SOCRATES: And from what line do you get this figure?

BOY: From this.

SOCRATES: That is, from the line which extends from corner to corner of the figure of four feet?

BOY: Yes.

SOCRATES: And that is the line which the learned call the diagonal. And if this is the proper name, then you, Meno's slave, are prepared to affirm that the double space is the square of the diagonal?

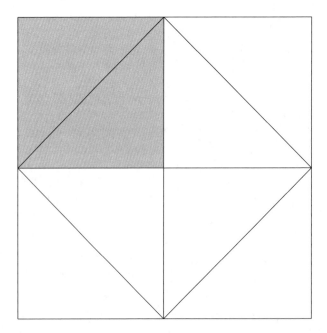

Figure 6

BOY: Certainly, Socrates.

SOCRATES: What do you say of him, Meno? Were not all these answers given out of his own head?

MENO: Yes, they were all his own.

SOCRATES: And yet, as we were just now saying, he did not know?

MENO: True.

SOCRATES: But still he had in him those notions of his – had he not?

MENO: Yes.

SOCRATES: Then he who does not know may still have true notions of that which he does not know?

MENO: He has.

SOCRATES: And at present these notions have just been stirred up in him, as in a dream; but if he were frequently asked the same questions, in different forms, he would know as well as anyone at last?

MENO: I dare say.

SOCRATES: Without anyone teaching him he will recover his knowledge for himself if he is only asked questions?

MENO: Yes.

SOCRATES: And this spontaneous recovery of knowledge in him is recollection?

MENO: True.

SOCRATES: And this knowledge which he now has must he not either have acquired or always possessed?

MENO: Yes.

SOCRATES: But if he always possessed this knowledge he would always have known; or if he has acquired the knowledge he could not have acquired it in this life, unless he has been taught geometry; for he may be made to do the same with all geometry and every other branch of knowledge? Now, has anyone ever taught him all this? You must know about him, if, as you say, he was born and bred in your house.

MENO: And I am certain that no one ever did teach him.

SOCRATES: And yet he has the knowledge?

MENO: The fact, Socrates, is undeniable.

SOCRATES: But if he did not acquire the knowledge in this life, then he must have had and learned it at some other time?

MENO: Clearly he must.

SOCRATES: Which must have been the time when he was not a man?

MENO: Yes.

SOCRATES: And if there have been always true thoughts in him, both at the time when he was and was not a man, which only need to be awakened into knowledge by putting questions to him, his soul must have always possessed this knowledge, for he always either was or was not a man?

MENO: Obviously.

SOCRATES: And if the truth of all things always existed in the soul, then the soul is immortal. Wherefore be of good cheer, and try to recollect what you do not know, or rather what you do not remember.

MENO: I feel, somehow, that I like what you are saying.

SOCRATES: And I, Meno, like what I am saying. Some things I have said of which I am not altogether confident. But that we shall be better and braver and less helpless if we think that we ought to enquire, than we should have been if we indulged in the idle fancy that there was no knowing and no use in seeking to know what we do not know; – that is a theme upon which I am ready to fight, in word and deed, to the utmost of my power.

2   Knowledge versus Opinion: Plato, *Republic**

The distinction between knowledge and mere true belief (or opinion) has already emerged in the previous extract. Socrates there talked of 'true opinions which can be aroused by questioning and turned into knowledge'. But what is the difference between the two? As Socrates points out later in the *Meno*, it does not seem to lie in degree of usefulness, for the person who has a correct belief about the way to get to Larissa is just as good a guide as one who has knowledge. But knowledge, he goes on to explain, confers a plus: 'True opinions are fine and useful as long as they stay with us; but they do not stay, and they depart from the mind. So they are not of great value until you fasten them down by working out the reason why. This process, Meno my friend, is recollection, as we agreed earlier. Once they are fastened, they become knowledge and then they are more permanent. Hence knowledge is a finer and better thing than true opinion, since it is secured by a chain' (*Meno*, 98a 1–5). What is suggested here is that one who has knowledge is able to back up his opinion by providing a justification, or an explanatory account. Only when opinion is secured by a rational account, only when one can explain *why* a given belief is correct, is that belief entitled to the accolade 'knowledge'.

So far the Platonic account of knowledge seems straightforward enough. But elsewhere the distinction between knowledge and belief is explained in a way which seems to carry far more complex implications about the nature of reality. The most famous of these passages is in Plato's best-known work, the *Republic* (*c.*380 BC), where

he gives an account of the true philosophers, the lovers of knowledge and wisdom (who alone, Plato maintains, are fitted to rule the state). In the course of the argument, knowledge and opinion are said to be different powers or faculties, from which the (questionable) inference is drawn that they must have different objects. The ordinary everyday objects of opinion can be said to be what they are (beautiful, or large, or heavy or whatever) only in a qualified sense; Plato puts this by saying that such objects are somewhere in between what *is* and what *is not*. But true knowledge, being more stable and permanent, must relate to what really *is* – to objects that count as beautiful or large or heavy in an utterly unqualified and unrestricted way. Thus Plato introduces what have come to be known as the Forms – eternal, unchanging, absolute realities, which are the true objects of knowledge. These absolute realities cannot be grasped via the senses, but are objects of pure understanding: the contrast throughout the following passage is between particular visible manifestations or examples of beauty (or justice or whatever), and the abstract notion of 'the Beautiful itself' which belongs to a higher order of reality and which is apprehended by the intellect alone. As Plato puts it, 'those who are able to see the many beautiful [objects], and who yet neither see absolute beauty…who see the many just [objects] and not absolute justice …may be said to have opinion but not knowledge'. As with all of the *Republic*, the argument is presented as a dialogue between Socrates and a sparring partner (in this case, Glaucon). Socrates, talking in the first person, speaks first.

---

* Plato, *Republic* [*Politeia*, *c.*380 BC], Bk V, 474b–483e. Trans. B. Jowett, in *The Dialogues of Plato* (Oxford: Clarendon, 1892), vol. III, pp. 171–9.

I think we must explain whom we mean when we say that philosophers are to rule the State ... Some natures ought to study philosophy and to be leaders in the State, and others who are not born to be philosophers are meant to be followers rather than leaders.

Then now for a definition, he said.

Follow me, I said, and I hope that I may in some way or other be able to give you a satisfactory explanation.

Proceed.

I dare say that you remember, and therefore I need not remind you, that a lover, if he is worthy of the name, ought to show his love not to some one part of that which he loves, but to the whole.

I really do not understand, and therefore beg of you to assist my memory.

Another person, I said, might fairly reply as you do; but a man of pleasure like yourself ought to know that all who are in the flower of youth do somehow or other raise a pang or emotion in a lover's breast, and are thought by him to be worthy of his affectionate regards. Is not this a way which you have with the fair: one has a snub nose, and you praise his charming face; the hook-nose of another has, you say, a royal look; while he who is neither snub nor hooked has the grace of regularity: the dark visage is manly, the fair are children of the gods; and as to the sweet 'honey pale', as they are called, what is the very name but the invention of a lover who talks in diminutives, and is not averse to paleness if appearing on the cheek of youth? In a word, there is no excuse which you will not make, and nothing which you will not say, in order not to lose a single flower that blooms in the spring-time of youth.

If you make me an authority in matters of love, for the sake of the argument, I assent.

And what do you say of lovers of wine? Do you not see them doing the same? They are glad of any pretext of drinking any wine.

Very good.

And the same is true of ambitious men; if they cannot command an army, they are willing to command a file; and if they cannot be honoured by really great and important persons, they are glad to be honoured by lesser and meaner people, – but honour of some kind they must have.

Exactly.

Once more let me ask: Does he who desires any class of goods, desire the whole class or a part only?

The whole.

And may we not say of the philosopher that he is a lover, not of a part of wisdom only, but of the whole?

Yes, of the whole.

And he who dislikes learning, especially in youth, when he has no power of judging what is good and what is not, such a one we maintain not to be a philosopher or a lover of knowledge, just as he who refuses his food is not hungry, and may be said to have a bad appetite and not a good one?

Very true, he said.

Whereas he who has a taste for every sort of knowledge, and who is curious to learn and is never satisfied, may be justly termed a philosopher? Am I not right?

Glaucon said: If curiosity makes a philosopher, you will find many a strange being will have a title to the name. All the lovers of sights have a delight in learning, and must therefore be included. Musical amateurs, too, are a folk strangely out of place among philosophers, for they are the last persons in the world who would come to anything like a philosophical discussion, if they could help, while they run about at the Dionysiac festivals as if they had let out their ears to hear every chorus; whether the performance is in town or country – that makes no difference – they are there. Now are we to maintain that all these and any who have similar tastes, as well as the professors of quite minor arts, are philosophers?

Certainly not, I replied; they are only an imitation.

He said: Who then are the true philosophers?

Those, I said, who are lovers of the vision of truth.

That is also good, he said; but I should like to know what you mean.

To another, I replied, I might have a difficulty in explaining; but I am sure that you will admit a proposition which I am about to make.

What is the proposition?

That since beauty is the opposite of ugliness, they are two?

Certainly.

And inasmuch as they are two, each of them is one?

True again.

And of just and unjust, good and evil, and of every other class, the same remark holds: taken singly, each of them is one; but from the various combinations of them with actions and things and with one another, they are seen in all sorts of lights and appear many?

Very true.

And this is the distinction which I draw between the sight-loving, art-loving, practical class and those of whom I am speaking, and who are alone worthy of the name of philosophers.

How do you distinguish them? he said.

The lovers of sounds and sights, I replied, are, as I conceive, fond of fine tones and colours and forms and all the artificial products that are made out of them, but their mind is incapable of seeing or loving absolute beauty.

True, he replied.

Few are they who are able to attain to the sight of this.

Very true.

And he who, having a sense of beautiful things has no sense of absolute beauty, or who, if another lead him to a knowledge of that beauty is unable to follow – of such a one I ask, Is he awake or in a dream only? Reflect: is not the dreamer, sleeping or waking, one who likens dissimilar things, who puts the copy in the place of the real object?

I should certainly say that such a one was dreaming.

But take the case of the other, who recognizes the existence of absolute beauty and is able to distinguish the idea from the objects which participate in the idea, neither putting the objects in the place of the idea nor the idea in the place of the objects – is he a dreamer, or is he awake?

He is wide awake.

And may we not say that the mind of the one who knows has knowledge, and that the mind of the other, who opines only, has opinion?

Certainly.

But suppose that the latter should quarrel with us and dispute our statement, can we administer any soothing cordial or advice to him, without revealing to him that there is sad disorder in his wits?

We must certainly offer him some good advice, he replied.

Come, then, and let us think of something to say to him. Shall we begin by assuring him that he is welcome to any knowledge which he may have, and that we are rejoiced at his having it? But we should like to ask him a question: Does he who has knowledge know something or nothing? (You must answer for him.)

I answer that he knows something.

Something that is or is not?

Something that is; for how can that which is not ever be known?

And are we assured, after looking at the matter from many points of view, that absolute being is or may be absolutely known, but that the utterly non-existent is utterly unknown?

Nothing can be more certain.

Good. But if there be anything which is of such a nature as to be and not to be, that will have a place intermediate between pure being and the absolute negation of being?

Yes, between them.

And, as knowledge corresponded to being and ignorance of necessity to not-being, for that intermediate between being and not-being there has to be discovered a corresponding intermediate between ignorance and knowledge, if there be such?

Certainly.

Do we admit the existence of opinion?

Undoubtedly.

As being the same with knowledge, or another faculty?

Another faculty.

Then opinion and knowledge have to do with different kinds of matter corresponding to this difference of faculties?

Yes.

And knowledge is relative to being and knows being. But before I proceed further I will make a division.

What division?

I will begin by placing faculties in a class by themselves: they are powers in us, and in all other things, by which we do as we do. Sight and hearing, for example, I should call faculties. Have I clearly explained the class which I mean?

Yes, I quite understand.

Then let me tell you my view about them. I do not see them, and therefore the distinctions of figure, colour, and the like, which enable me to discern the differences of some things, do not apply to them. In speaking of a faculty I think only of its sphere and its result; and that which has the same sphere and the same result I call the same faculty, but that which has another sphere and another result I call different. Would that be your way of speaking?

Yes.

And will you be so very good as to answer one more question? Would you say that knowledge is a faculty, or in what class would you place it?

Certainly knowledge is a faculty, and the mightiest of all faculties.

And is opinion also a faculty?

Certainly, he said; for opinion is that with which we are able to form an opinion.

And yet you were acknowledging a little while ago that knowledge is not the same as opinion?

Why, yes, he said: how can any reasonable being ever identify that which is infallible with that which errs?

An excellent answer, proving, I said, that we are quite conscious of a distinction between them.

Yes.

Then knowledge and opinion having distinct powers have also distinct spheres or subject-matters?

That is certain.

Being is the sphere or subject-matter of knowledge, and knowledge is to know the nature of being?

Yes.

And opinion is to have an opinion?

Yes.

And do we know what we opine? or is the subject-matter of opinion the same as the subject-matter of knowledge?

Nay, he replied, that has been already disproven; if difference in faculty implies difference in the sphere or subject-matter, and if, as we were saying, opinion and knowledge are distinct faculties, then the sphere of knowledge and of opinion cannot be the same.

Then if being is the subject-matter of knowledge, something else must be the subject-matter of opinion?

Yes, something else.

Well then, is not-being the subject-matter of opinion? or, rather, how can there be an opinion at all about not-being? Reflect: when a man has an opinion, has he not an opinion about something? Can he have an opinion which is an opinion about nothing?

Impossible.

He who has an opinion has an opinion about some one thing?

Yes.

And not-being is not one thing but, properly speaking, nothing?

True.

Of not-being, ignorance was assumed to be the necessary correlative; of being, knowledge?

True, he said.

Then opinion is not concerned either with being or with not-being?

Not with either.

And can therefore neither be ignorance nor knowledge?

That seems to be true.

But is opinion to be sought without and beyond either of them, in a greater clearness than knowledge, or in a greater darkness than ignorance?

In neither.

Then I suppose that opinion appears to you to be darker than knowledge, but lighter than ignorance?

Both; and in no small degree.

And also to be within and between them?

Yes.

Then you would infer that opinion is intermediate?

No question.

But were we not saying before, that if anything appeared to be of a sort which is and is not at the same time, that sort of thing would appear also to lie in the interval between pure being and absolute not-being; and that the corresponding faculty is neither knowledge nor ignorance, but will be found in the interval between them?

True.

And in that interval there has now been discovered something which we call opinion?

There has.

Then what remains to be discovered is the object which partakes equally of the nature of being and not-being, and cannot rightly be termed either, pure and simple; this unknown term, when discovered, we may truly call the subject of opinion, and assign each to their proper faculty, the extremes to the faculties of the extremes and the mean to the faculty of the mean.

True.

This being premised, I would ask the gentleman who is of the opinion that there is no absolute or unchangeable idea of beauty – in whose opinion the beautiful is the manifold – he, I say, your lover of beautiful sights, who cannot bear to be told that the beautiful is one, and the just is one, or that anything is one – to him I would appeal, saying, Will you be so very kind, sir, as to tell us whether, of all these beautiful things, there is one which will not be found ugly; or of the just, which will not be found unjust; or of the holy, which will not also be unholy?

No, he replied; the beautiful will in some point of view be found ugly; and the same is true of the rest.

And may not the many which are doubles be also halves? – doubles, that is, of one thing, and halves of another?

Quite true.

And things great and small, heavy and light, as they are termed, will not be denoted by these any more than by the opposite names?

True; both these and the opposite names will always attach to all of them.

And can any one of those many things which are called by particular names be said to be this rather than not to be this?

He replied: They are like the punning riddles which are asked at feasts or the children's puzzle about the eunuch aiming at the bat, with what he hit him, as they say in the puzzle, and upon what the bat was sitting.[1] The individual objects of which I am speaking are also a riddle, and have a double sense: nor can you fix them in your mind, either as being or not-being, or both, or neither.

Then what will you do with them? I said. Can they have a better place than between being and not-being? For they are clearly not in greater darkness or negation than not-being, or more full of light and existence than being.

That is quite true, he said.

---

[1] A man who was not a man (a eunuch) threw a stone that was not a stone (a pumice-stone) at a bird that was not a bird (a bat) sitting on a twig that was not a twig (a reed).

Thus then we seem to have discovered that the many ideas which the multitude entertain about the beautiful and about all other things are tossing about in some region which is half-way between pure being and pure not-being?

We have.

Yes; and we had before agreed that anything of this kind which we might find was to be described as matter of opinion, and not as matter of knowledge; being the intermediate flux which is caught and detained by the intermediate faculty.

Quite true.

Then those who see the many beautiful, and who yet neither see absolute beauty, nor can follow any guide who points the way thither; who see the many just, and not absolute justice, and the like, – such persons may be said to have opinion but not knowledge?

That is certain.

But those who see the absolute and eternal and immutable may be said to know, and not to have opinion only?

Neither can that be denied.

The one love and embrace the subjects of knowledge, the other those of opinion? The latter are the same, as I dare say you will remember, who listened to sweet sounds and gazed upon fair colours, but would not tolerate the existence of absolute beauty.

Yes, I remember.

Shall we then be guilty of any impropriety in calling them lovers of opinion rather than lovers of wisdom, and will they be very angry with us for thus describing them?

I shall tell them not to be angry; no man should be angry at what is true.

But those who love the truth in each thing are to be called lovers of wisdom and not lovers of opinion.

Assuredly.

3   Demonstrative Knowledge and its Starting-points: Aristotle, *Posterior Analytics**

Readers of the preceding extracts may feel inclined to agree with Plato that knowledge is superior to mere opinion, and that it needs to go beyond the particular to some more abstract level of rational justification; but they may also feel sceptical both about the notion of *innate* sources of knowledge (put forward in the *Meno*), and also about the sharp contrast (in the *Republic*) between the visible and the intelli-gible realms, which seems to downgrade the role of ordinary sensory information as a source of knowledge. The following extract from Aristotle puts pressure on both these Platonic ideas.

In his views on knowledge, Aristotle accepted the Platonic idea that what is known must have a certain stability, and immunity from change and fluctuation. Genuine scientific knowledge, it is asserted in the following extracts from the

---

* Aristotle, *Posterior Analytics* [*Analytica Hystera*, c.330 BC], extracts from Bk I, ch. 1 (71a1–4), ch. 2 (71b9–25), ch. 4 (73a21–5), ch. 8 (75b21–36); Bk II, ch. 19 (99b20–110b12). Translation by John Cottingham.

Posterior Analytics, is of that which 'cannot be otherwise'; it concerns 'eternal truths', not particulars. Aristotle also lays out a normative framework for such knowledge: it must proceed from self-evident premises, or starting-points, and it must advance by rigorous logical steps from premises to conclusion. Notice that there are two requirements here. The second, that the conclusion should follow from the premises, is the requirement of deductive validity in argument ('deductive' because the conclusions follow inevitably from the premises from which they are logically *deduced*). Aristotle, in his famous theory of the *syllogism*, had drawn up a procedure for testing the validity of arguments (a syllogism is a standard pattern of formal valid argument, such as 'all *A*s are *B*, all *B*s are *C*, therefore all *A*s are *C*'). But validity alone does not suffice to produce knowledge. The syllogism 'All planets are stars, all stars are square, therefore all planets are square' is perfectly valid – the conclusion follows inescapably from the premises – but it is worthless as a contribution to scientific knowledge, since the premises, or starting-points of the argument, are false. So Aristotle insists that what is required for deductive knowledge,

in addition to the logical validity of the relevant argument patterns, is that the starting points themselves should be self-evidently true.

Plato, as we have seen (extract 1), believed that the mind has innate knowledge of certain self-evident truths. But Aristotle questions the suggestion that the starting-points for knowledge have to be innate, stressing instead the crucial role of sense-perception in providing the raw materials of knowledge. Knowledge must involve going beyond particular instances, and grasping universal truths, but this need not, according to Aristotle, imply the existence of abstract Forms over and above particular objects and groups of objects. Rather, knowledge develops naturally from sense-perception, since the human mind has the capacity for noticing and remembering general similarities which underlie the flux of sensory experience. This faculty for grasping the universal in the particular is called by Aristotle *nous* or 'intuition' (though he does not succeed in making it clear just how the results of intuition are supposed to have the self-evidence and certainty needed to serve as the starting-points for scientific demonstration).

All teaching and all intellectual learning arises from pre-existing knowledge. This is evident if we look at all the examples. For the mathematical sciences are acquired in this way, as is each of the other arts. The same goes for arguments – both syllogistic and inductive, for both produce instruction by means of what we are already aware of ...

We consider we have scientific knowledge or understanding of something ... whenever we consider we know that the cause of the item in question is its cause, and that it is not possible for it to be otherwise. So it is clear that having scientific knowledge is something of this sort. For both those who do and those who do not have knowledge think that they are in this situation, the latter merely believing it, while the former are actually in it. Hence scientific knowledge relates to that which cannot be otherwise.

We shall discuss later whether there is also another way of knowing. But we can state now that there is knowledge through demonstration. By demonstration I mean a scientific syllogism, and by this I mean one whose possession constitutes scientific knowledge.

If knowledge is indeed what we have just proposed, demonstrative knowledge must necessarily depend on premises which are true, primary, immediate, and better known than, and prior to and causes of, the conclusion ... Without such conditions there can be syllogisms, but not be a demonstration, since it will not produce scientific knowledge ...

Since it is impossible for that of which there is knowledge to be otherwise, that which is known through demonstrative knowledge must be necessary. Demonstrative knowledge is the knowledge we have in virtue of having a demonstration. A demonstration therefore is a syllogistic deduction from necessary premises...

It is evident that if the premises of a syllogism are universal, then the conclusion of such a demonstration – demonstration in the strict sense – must also be an eternal truth. So there can be no demonstration with respect to perishable things, nor any scientific knowledge of them strictly speaking but only in the accidental sense; for in such cases the attribute does not belong to the subject universally, but only at a particular time and in some respect... Demonstrations and knowledge of things that occur often, such as eclipses of the moon, do hold good permanently in so far as they relate to events of a certain kind; but in so far as they do not hold good permanently, they are [not universal but merely] particular. And so in other cases...

We have said that it is not possible to achieve scientific knowledge through demonstration unless we know the premises that are primary and immediate... With regard to these starting-points, it would be strange if we possessed them all along, since then we would possess knowledge superior to demonstration without being aware of it. But if, by contrast, we acquire them, and did not possess them earlier, how would we come to know them and learn them in the absence of any pre-existing knowledge? That is impossible, as we said earlier with regard to demonstration.[1] Thus it is clearly impossible either for us to possess them all along, or for us to acquire them if we are ignorant and have no predisposition for knowledge. So we must already have some capacity...

This capacity evidently belongs to all animals, since they have an innate power of discernment – what we call *sense-perception*. Though it is innate, there are some animals in which the sense-impression persists, while in others it does not. For the latter group... there is no knowledge outside the act of perceiving; but others can retain something in the mind after perceiving it. And when this happens frequently, we get a difference arising as a result of the retention, some come to develop a *logos*[2] and others do not.

Thus from sense-perception there arises memory; and when there is repeated memory of the same thing, there arises *experience* (for though there are many memories, they make up a single experience). And from experience – the whole universal now established in the mind (the *one* distinct from the *many*, whatever is *one and the same* in all the many instances) – there arises the starting-point of a skill, or of scientific knowledge (skill if it concerns what merely comes to be, scientific knowledge if it concerns what *is*).

Thus these dispositions are neither innate in a determinate form, nor on the other hand do they arise from other higher states of knowledge, but they come about from sense-perception. It happens just as in battle when there is a rout: if one man stands fast, another does, and then another, until a position of strength is reached. The mind is so constituted as to be capable of this.

Let us now restate the account we have just given, which was not very clear. When one of the undifferentiated particular things 'stands fast', a primitive universal is in the mind; for although what one perceives is the particular thing, the perception is *of* a universal – for example of a *man*, not of Callias, the particular individual. Again,

---

[1] Compare the first sentence of this extract.
[2] A (rational) account or general concept.

a stand is made in these primitive universals, and the process continues until the ultimate universal concepts stand (for example, such and such a species of animal is a step towards the general kind *animal*, and so on). So clearly it is [not by deduction but] by induction that we have to get to know the starting-points.

Concerning the intellectual faculties by which we reach the truth, some are always true, while others, such as opinion and reasoning, admit of falsehood; scientific knowledge and intuition (*nous*) are always true. No other kind of thought except intuition is more accurate than scientific knowledge, and the starting-points are more knowable than the demonstrations which proceed from them...Hence there cannot be scientific knowledge of the starting-points; and since nothing can be more true than scientific knowledge except intuition, it is intuition that grasps the starting-points.

4 New Foundations for Knowledge: René Descartes, *Meditations**

Both in Plato's search for eternal, unchanging objects of knowledge, and in Aristotle's definition of true knowledge as being of that which cannot be otherwise, we can see the idea that what qualifies as knowledge must have a certain stability. Many centuries later, at the start of what is known as the 'early modern' period, this theme was taken up, though in a very different way, by René Descartes, whose writings had a profound effect on the subsequent development of philosophy in general and epistemology in particular.

Descartes became struck by the instability and unreliability of many of the accepted doctrines he had been taught as a student. In his *Discourse on the Method (Discours de la méthode)* published anonymously in 1637, he remarked of the philosophy he had learnt at school that despite having been taught for many centuries, it contained 'no point that was not disputed and hence doubtful'. And as for other sciences, in so far as they borrowed their principles from philosophy, 'nothing solid could be built on such shaky foundations'. In his masterpiece, the *Meditations on First Philosophy*, published in Latin in 1641, Descartes records his determination to sweep away all previously accepted opinions,

and start afresh. His project is nothing less than the reconstruction of knowledge from the foundations upwards. To pursue this goal, he devises a systematic method of doubt: anything that can be called into question, for any reason whatever, will be discarded. Previous beliefs acquired via the senses are all jettisoned, on the grounds that the senses have sometimes proved unreliable. Even such straightforward beliefs as 'I am now sitting by the fire' are doubted, on the grounds that I might be dreaming; and the argument is then broadened to question whether I can know for certain that anything external to the mind really exists. The argument next turns to the abstract propositions of mathematics, which seem to be immune from the previous doubts since their truth does not depend on whether their objects actually exist; but even these are called into question by the thought that an all-powerful God might make me go wrong 'every time I add two and three'. To reinforce all the doubts, an imaginary scenario is introduced of a 'malicious demon of the utmost power who employs all his energies to deceive me'. Finally, at the start of the Second Meditation, the meditator reaches his 'Archimedian point'. No matter how much he is deceived, there is one truth that

---

* René Descartes, *Meditations on First Philosophy* [*Meditationes de prima philosophia*, 1641], Meditation I and part of II. Trans. J. Cottingham (Cambridge: Cambridge University Press, 1986; rev. edn 1996), pp. 12–17.

cannot be doubted: '*I am, I exist*, is certain, every time it is conceived in the mind.' This, elsewhere expressed in the famous formula 'I am thinking therefore I exist' (in French, *je pense donc je suis*, or, in Latin, *cogito ergo sum*) is the first principle of Descartes's new philosophy.

 ## What can be called into doubt

Some years ago I was struck by the large number of falsehoods that I had accepted as true in my childhood, and by the highly doubtful nature of the whole edifice that I had subsequently based on them. I realized that it was necessary, once in the course of my life, to demolish everything completely and start again right from the foundations if I wanted to establish anything at all in the sciences that was stable and likely to last. But the task looked an enormous one, and I began to wait until I should reach a mature enough age to ensure that no subsequent time of life would be more suitable for tackling such inquiries. This led me to put the project off for so long that I would now be to blame if by pondering over it any further I wasted the time still left for carrying it out. So today I have expressly rid my mind of all worries and arranged for myself a clear stretch of free time. I am here quite alone, and at last I will devote myself sincerely and without reservation to the general demolition of my opinions.

But to accomplish this, it will not be necessary for me to show that all my opinions are false, which is something I could perhaps never manage. Reason now leads me to think that I should hold back my assent from opinions which are not completely certain and indubitable just as carefully as I do from those which are patently false. So, for the purpose of rejecting all my opinions, it will be enough if I find in each of them at least some reason for doubt. And to do this I will not need to run through them all individually, which would be an endless task. Once the foundations of a building are undermined, anything built on them collapses of its own accord; so I will go straight for the basic principles on which all my former beliefs rested.

Whatever I have up till now accepted as most true I have acquired either from the senses or through the senses. But from time to time I have found that the senses deceive, and it is prudent never to trust completely those who have deceived us even once.

Yet although the senses occasionally deceive us with respect to objects which are very small or in the distance, there are many other beliefs about which doubt is quite impossible, even though they are derived from the senses – for example, that I am here, sitting by the fire, wearing a winter dressing-gown holding this piece of paper in my hands, and so on. Again, how could it be denied that these hands or this whole body are mine? Unless perhaps I were to liken myself to madmen, whose brains are so damaged by the persistent vapours of melancholia that they firmly maintain they are kings when they are paupers, or say they are dressed in purple when they are naked, or that their heads are made of earthenware, or that they are pumpkins, or made of glass. But such people are insane, and I would be thought equally mad if I took anything from them as a model for myself.

A brilliant piece of reasoning! As if I were not a man who sleeps at night, and regularly has all the same experiences while asleep as madmen do when awake – indeed sometimes even more improbable ones. How often, asleep at night, am I convinced of just such familiar events – that I am here in my dressing-gown, sitting by the fire – when in fact I am lying undressed in bed! Yet at the moment my eyes are certainly wide awake when I look at this piece of paper; I shake my head and it is not asleep; as I stretch out and feel my hand I do so deliberately, and I know what I am doing. All this would not happen with such distinctness to someone asleep. Indeed! As if I did not remember other occasions when I have been tricked by exactly similar thoughts while asleep! As I think about this more carefully, I see plainly that there are never any sure signs by means of which being awake can be distinguished from being asleep. The result is that I begin to feel dazed, and this very feeling only reinforces the notion that I may be asleep.

Suppose then that I am dreaming, and that these particulars – that my eyes are open, that I am moving my head and stretching out my hands are not true. Perhaps, indeed, I do not even have such hands or such a body at all. None the less, it must surely be admitted that the visions which come in sleep are like paintings, which must have been fashioned in the likeness of things that are real, and hence that at least these general kinds of things – eyes, head, hands and the body as a whole – are things which are not imaginary but are real and exist. For even when painters try to create sirens and satyrs with the most extraordinary bodies, they cannot give them natures which are new in all respects; they simply jumble up the limbs of different animals. Or if perhaps they manage to think up something so new that nothing remotely similar has ever been seen before – something which is therefore completely fictitious and unreal – at least the colours used in the composition must be real. By similar reasoning, although these general kinds of things – eyes, head, hands and so on – could be imaginary, it must at least be admitted that certain other even simpler and more universal things are real. These are as it were the real colours from which we form all the images of things, whether true or false, that occur in our thought.

This class appears to include corporeal nature in general, and its extension; the shape of extended things; the quantity, or size and number of these things; the place in which they may exist, the time through which they may endure, and so on.

So a reasonable conclusion from this might be that physics, astronomy, medicine, and all other disciplines which depend on the study of composite things, are doubtful; while arithmetic, geometry and other subjects of this kind, which deal only with the simplest and most general things, regardless of whether they really exist in nature or not, contain something certain and indubitable. For whether I am awake or asleep, two and three added together are five, and a square has no more than four sides. It seems impossible that such transparent truths should incur any suspicion of being false.

And yet firmly rooted in my mind is the long-standing opinion that there is an omnipotent God who made me the kind of creature that I am. How do I know that he has not brought it about that there is no earth, no sky, no extended thing, no shape, no size, no place, while at the same time ensuring that all these things appear to me to exist just as they do now? What is more, since I sometimes believe that others go astray in cases where they think they have the most perfect knowledge, may I not similarly go wrong every time I add two and three or count the sides of a square, or in some even simpler matter, if that is imaginable? But perhaps God would not have allowed me to be deceived in this way, since he is said to be supremely good. But if it were inconsistent with his goodness to have created me such that I am deceived all the time, it would seem equally foreign to his goodness to allow me to be deceived even occasionally; yet this last assertion cannot be made.

Perhaps there may be some who would prefer to deny the existence of so powerful a God rather than believe that everything else is uncertain. Let us not argue with them, but grant them that everything said about God is a fiction. According to their supposition, then, I have arrived at my present state by fate or chance or a continuous chain of events, or by some other means; yet since deception and error seem to be imperfections, the less powerful they make my original cause, the more likely it is that I am so imperfect as to be deceived all the time. I have no answer to these arguments, but am finally compelled to admit that there is not one of my former beliefs about which a doubt may not properly be raised; and this is not a flippant or ill-considered conclusion, but is based on powerful and well thought-out reasons. So in future I must withhold my assent from these former beliefs just as carefully as I would from obvious falsehoods, if I want to discover any certainty.

But it is not enough merely to have noticed this; I must make an effort to remember it. My habitual opinions keep coming back, and, despite my wishes, they capture my belief, which is as it were bound over to them as a result of long occupation and the law of custom. I shall never get out of the habit of confidently assenting to these opinions, so long as I suppose them to be what in fact that they are, namely highly probable opinions – opinions which, despite the fact that they are in a sense doubtful, as has just been shown, it is still much more reasonable to believe than to deny. In view of this, I think it will be a good plan to turn my will in completely the opposite direction and deceive myself, by pretending for a time that these former opinions are utterly false and imaginary. I shall do this until the weight of preconceived opinion is counterbalanced and the distorting influence of habit no longer prevents my judgement from perceiving things correctly. In the meantime, I know that no danger or error will result from my plan, and that I cannot possibly go too far in my distrustful attitude. This is because the task now in hand does not involve action but merely the acquisition of knowledge.

I will suppose therefore that not God, who is supremely good and the source of truth, but rather some malicious demon of the utmost power and cunning has employed all his energies in order to deceive me. I shall think that the sky, the air, the earth, colours, shapes, sounds and all external things are merely the delusions of dreams which he has devised to ensnare my judgement. I shall consider myself as not having hands or eyes, or flesh, or blood or senses, but as falsely believing that I have all these things. I shall stubbornly and firmly persist in this meditation; and, even if it is not in my power to know any truth, I shall at least do what is in my power, that is, resolutely guard against assenting to any falsehoods, so that the deceiver, however powerful and cunning he may be, will be unable to impose on me in the slightest degree. But this is an arduous undertaking, and a kind of laziness brings me back to normal life. I am like a prisoner who is enjoying an imaginary freedom while asleep; as he begins to suspect that he is asleep, he dreads being woken up, and goes along with the pleasant illusion as long as he can. In the same way, I happily slide back into my old opinions and dread being shaken out of them, for fear that my peaceful sleep may be followed by hard labour when I wake, and that I shall have to toil not in the light, but amid the inextricable darkness of the problems I have now raised.

[So ends the First Meditation. In the opening of the Second Meditation, which follows, Descartes's meditator struggles to escape from the morass of doubt into which he has fallen.]

So serious are the doubts into which I have been thrown as a result of yesterday's meditation that I can neither put them out of my mind nor see any way of resolving them. It feels as if I have fallen unexpectedly into a deep whirlpool which tumbles me around so that I can neither stand on the bottom nor swim up to the top. Nevertheless I will make an effort and once more attempt the same path which I started on yesterday. Anything which admits of the slightest doubt I will set aside just as if I had found it to be wholly false; and I will proceed in this way until I recognize something certain, or, if nothing else, until I at least recognize for certain that there is no certainty. Archimedes used to demand just one firm and immovable point in order to shift the entire earth; so I too can hope for great things if I manage to find just one thing, however slight, that is certain and unshakeable.

I will suppose then, that everything I see is spurious. I will believe that my memory tells me lies, and that none of the things that it reports ever happened. I have no senses. Body, shape, extension, movement and place are chimeras. So what remains true? Perhaps just the one fact that nothing is certain.

Yet apart from everything I have just listed, how do I know that there is not something else which does not allow even the slightest occasion for doubt? Is there not a God, or whatever I may call him, who puts into me the thoughts I am now having? But why do I think this, since I myself may perhaps be the author of these thoughts? In that case am not I, at least, something? But I have just said that I have no senses and no body. This is the sticking point: what follows from this? Am I not so bound up with a body and with senses that I cannot exist without them? But I have convinced myself that there is absolutely nothing in the world, no sky, no earth, no minds, no bodies. Does it now follow that I too do not exist?

No: if I convinced myself of something then I certainly existed. But there is a deceiver of supreme power and cunning who is deliberately and constantly deceiving me. In that case I too undoubtedly exist, if he is deceiving me; and let him deceive me as much as he can, he will never bring it about that I am nothing so long as I think that I am something. So after considering everything very thoroughly, I must finally conclude that this proposition, *I am, I exist*, is necessarily true whenever it is put forward by me or conceived in my mind.

5 The Senses as the Basis of Knowledge: John Locke, *Essay concerning Human Understanding**

One of the striking features of Descartes's approach to knowledge was its 'internal' starting-point. 'I resolved one day to pursue my studies within myself', he wrote in the *Discourse*; and in the above extract from the *Meditations* we see him carrying out the strategy of leading the mind away from the outside world, away from the external senses, and focusing on the meditator's inner awareness of his own existence. This very private beginning may not seem a promising start for the construction of an objective system of knowledge. But what Descartes does

---

* John Locke, *An Essay concerning Human Understanding* [1690], extracts (with omissions) from Bk I, ch. 2, §§ 1–5 and 12–16; Bk II, ch. 1, §§ 1–5; spelling and punctuation revised. There are many available editions of the *Essay*, of which the most definitive is the critical edition of P. H. Nidditch (Oxford: Clarendon, 1975); cf. pp. 48–58.

in the subsequent Meditations is to rely on the innate ideas with which he claims the mind is furnished. Chief of these is the idea of infinite perfection, which Descartes uses as the basis for a (controversial) proof that an infinite and perfect being, God, must really exist. And having established the existence of God, he then uses the other innate ideas, especially those of mathematics, as the foundations for his new scientific system. As he put in the *Discourse*, 'I noticed certain laws which God has so ordained in nature, and of which he has implanted such notions in our minds, that after adequate reflection we cannot doubt that they are exactly observed in everything that exists or occurs in the world'.

Descartes's appeal to innate ideas had a long ancestry (for its origins in Plato, see extract 1, above). But towards the end of the seventeenth century, in his *Essay concerning Human Understanding* (1690), John Locke launched a massive broadside against the doctrine of innateness, arguing instead that the senses are the primary source of all knowledge. He compares the mind to a *tabula rasa*, a blank sheet or 'white paper devoid of all characters', and then asks 'whence has it all the materials of reason and knowledge?'. To his own question he then supplies the famous reply, 'in one word, from *experience*'. On this *empiricist* conception (as it has come to be known, from the Greek word *empeiria*, 'experience'), observation via the senses, plus the mind's subsequent reflection on the data so acquired, constitutes the basis of all the knowledge we have, or can have.

Locke argues that the reasoning traditionally employed to support the doctrine of innate ideas is wholly inadequate. Innatists typically appeal to 'universal assent' – that there are certain fundamental truths accepted by everyone; but Locke objects, first, that even if universal assent were established it would not prove innateness; and second that, in any case, these supposedly innate principles are 'so far from having a universal assent that there are a great part of mankind to whom they are not so much as known'. He cites the cases of 'idiots and children'. With regard to the abstract principles of logic and mathematics (often thought to be prime candidates for innately implanted principles), Locke observes that many people go through their entire lives without thinking of them at all: 'a great part of illiterate people and savages pass many years even of their rational age, without even thinking on this and the like general propositions'. Locke then proceeds to set out his own account of how we come to knowledge of general propositions: the senses first 'let in particular ideas', and furnish the 'yet empty cabinet' (the image here is of the mind as a chamber that is entirely empty until the data from the senses enter it); the mind then gets to work on these materials, abstracting from the particular and learning the use of 'general names'. Here and elsewhere Locke does not deny that human beings have innate *capacities*, but he argues that a capacity to come to know *X* is not at all the same as innate knowledge of *X*. If it were, then one would have to say, absurdly, that we have innate knowledge of everything we learn in life.[1] His uncompromising conclusion is that the human mind does not have the 'least glimmering' of any ideas which it does not receive either from sensation or subsequent reflection.

 It is an established opinion amongst some men, that there are in the understanding certain *innate principles*; some primary notions . . . characters, as it were stamped upon the mind of man, which the soul receives in its very first being; and brings into the world with it. It would be sufficient to convince unprejudiced readers of the falseness of this supposition, if I should only show . . . how men, barely by the use of their natural faculties, may attain to all the knowledge they have, without the help of any innate impressions; and may arrive at certainty, without any such original notions or principles. For I imagine any one will easily grant that it would be impertinent to

---

[1] In later sections of the *Essay*, Locke proceeds to argue equally vigorously that there are no innate moral or practical principles, any more than there are innate logical and mathematical principles, and that observed divergences in religious belief and practice rule out the idea of a universal innate idea of God.

suppose the ideas of colours [to be] innate in a creature to whom God hath given sight, and a power to receive them by the eyes from external objects; and no less unreasonable would it be to attribute several truths to the impressions of nature, and innate characters, when we may observe in ourselves faculties, fit to attain as easy and certain knowledge of them as if they were originally imprinted on the mind...

There is nothing more commonly taken for granted, than that there are certain principles both *speculative* and *practical* (for they speak of both) universally agreed upon by all mankind: which, therefore they argue, must needs be the constant impressions which the souls of men receive in their first beings, and which they bring into the world with them, as necessarily and really as they do any of their inherent faculties.

This argument, drawn from universal consent, has this misfortune in it: that if it were true in matter of fact, that there were certain truths wherein all mankind agreed, it would not prove them innate, if there can be any other way shown how men may come to that universal agreement in the things they do consent in; which I presume may be done.

But, which is worse, this argument of universal consent, which is made use of to prove innate principles, seems to me a demonstration that there are none such: because there are none to which all mankind give a universal assent. I shall begin with the speculative, and instance... *Whatsoever is, is*; and *It is impossible for the same thing to be, and not to be*, which of all others I think have the most allowed title to innate... But yet I take liberty to say that these propositions are so far from having a universal assent that there are a great part of mankind to whom they are not so much as known.

For, first it is evident that all *children*, and *idiots*, have not the least apprehension or thought of them: and the want of that is enough to destroy that universal assent, which must needs be the necessary concomitant of all innate truths: it seeming to me near a contradiction to say that there are truths imprinted on the soul which it perceives or understands not; imprinting, if it signify any thing, being nothing else but the making certain truths to be perceived. For to imprint any thing on the mind without the mind's perceiving it seems to me hardly intelligible. If therefore children and idiots have souls, have minds, with those impressions upon them, they must unavoidably perceive them, and necessarily know and assent to these truths – which since they do not, it is evident that there are no such impressions. For if they are not notions naturally imprinted, how can they be innate? And if they are notions imprinted, how can they be unknown?

To say a notion is imprinted on the mind, and yet at the same time to say that the mind is ignorant of it, and never yet took notice of it, is to make this impression nothing. No proposition can be said to be in the mind which it never yet knew, which it was never yet conscious of. For if any *one* may, then, by the same reason, *all* propositions that are true, and the mind is capable ever of assenting to, may be said to be in the mind, and to be imprinted: since if any one can be said to be in the mind which it never yet knew, it must be only because it is *capable* of knowing it – and so the mind is, of all truths it ever shall know. Nay, thus truths may be imprinted on the mind, which it never did, nor ever shall know: for a man may live long, and die at last in ignorance of many truths, which his mind was capable of knowing, and that with certainty. So that if the *capacity* of knowing be the natural impression contended for, all the truths a man ever comes to know will, by this account, be, every one of them, innate; and this great point will amount to no more, but only to a very improper way of speaking; which whilst it pretends to assert the contrary, says nothing different from those who deny innate principles. For nobody, I think, ever denied that the mind was capable of knowing several truths.

The capacity, they say, is innate, the knowledge acquired. But then to what end such contest for certain innate maxims? If truths can be imprinted on the understanding without being perceived, I can see no difference there can be between any truths the mind is capable of knowing in respect of their original [their origins]. They must all be innate, or all adventitious [coming from outside]: in vain shall a man go about to distinguish them. He therefore that talks of innate notions in the understanding cannot (if he intend thereby any distinct sort of truths) mean such truths to be in the understanding as it never perceived, and is yet wholly ignorant of. For if these words ('to be in the understanding') have any propriety, they signify to be understood. So that 'to be in the understanding' and 'not to be understood'; 'to be in the mind' and 'never to be perceived', is all one, as to say, anything is, and is not, in the mind or understanding. If therefore these two propositions, *Whatsoever is, is*; and *It is impossible for the same thing to be and not to be*, are by nature imprinted, children cannot be ignorant of them: infants, and all that have souls must necessarily have them in their understandings, know the truth of them, and assent to it.

To avoid this, it is usually answered that all men know and *assent* to them *when they come to the use of reason*, and this is enough to prove them innate. I answer:

Doubtful expressions, that have scarce any signification, go for clear reasons to those who, being prepossessed, take not the pains to examine even what they themselves say. For to apply this answer with any tolerable sense to our present purpose, it must signify one of these two things: either that as soon as men come to the use of reason, these supposed native inscriptions come to be known and observed by them; or else, that the use and exercise of men's reasons assists them in the discovery of these principles, and certainly makes them known to them.

If they mean that by the *use of reason* men may discover these principles, and that this is sufficient to prove them innate, their way of arguing will stand thus: that whatever truths reason can certainly discover to us, and make us firmly assent to, those are all naturally imprinted on the mind; since that universal assent, which is made the mark of them, amounts to no more but this – that by the use of reason, we are capable to come to a certain knowledge of, and assent to them. And by this means there will be no difference between the maxims of the mathematicians and theorems they deduce from them: all must be equally allowed innate, they being all discoveries made by the use of reason, and truths that a rational creature may certainly come to know, if he apply his thoughts rightly that way...

If by knowing and assenting to them *when they come to the use of reason* be meant that this is the time when they come to be taken notice of by the mind – and that as soon as children come to the use of reason, they come also to know and assent to these maxims – this also is false, and frivolous. *First*, it is false. Because it is evident these maxims are not in the mind so early as the use of reason; and therefore the coming to the use of reason is falsely assigned as the time of their discovery. How many instances of the use of reason may we observe in children, a long time before they have any knowledge of this maxim *that it is impossible for the same thing to be and not to be*?

A great part of illiterate people, and savages, pass many years, even of their rational age, without ever thinking on this, and the like general propositions. I grant men come not to the knowledge of these general and more abstract truths, which are thought innate, till they come to the use of reason; and I add, *nor then neither.* Which is so, because till after they come to the use of reason, those general abstract ideas are not framed in the mind, about which those general maxims are, which are mistaken for innate principles; but [they] are indeed discoveries made ... and brought into the mind by the same way, and discovered by the same steps, as several other propositions, which nobody was ever so extravagant as to suppose innate ... I allow therefore a necessity that men should come to the use of reason, before they get the knowledge of those general truths: but deny that men's coming to the use of reason is the time of their discovery.

In the mean time, it is observable that this saying, that men know and assent to these maxims *when they come to the use of reason,* amounts in reality of fact to no more but this: that they are never known nor taken notice of before the use of reason, but may possibly be assented to sometime after, during a man's life; but when, is uncertain. And so may all other knowable truths, as well as these, which therefore have no advantage, nor distinction from others, by this note of being known when we come to the use of reason; nor are thereby proved to be innate, but quite the contrary.

But *secondly,* were it true that the precise time of their being known and assented to were *when men come to the use of reason,* neither would that prove them innate ... All that can with any truth be meant by this proposition, that men *assent to them when they come to the use of reason,* is no more but this, that the making of general abstract ideas and the understanding of general names, being a concomitant of the rational faculty, and growing up with it, children commonly get not those general ideas nor learn the names that stand for them till (having for a good while exercised their reason about familiar and more particular ideas) they are, by their ordinary discourse and actions with others, acknowledged to be capable of rational conversation. If assenting to these maxims *when men come to the use of reason* can be true in any other sense, I desire it may be shown; or at least, how in this or any other sense it proves them innate.

The senses at first let in particular ideas and furnish the yet empty cabinet; and the mind by degrees growing familiar with some of them, they are lodged in the memory, and names got to them. Afterwards the mind, proceeding farther, abstracts them, and by degrees learns the use of general names. In this manner the mind comes to be furnished with ideas and language, the materials about which to exercise its discursive faculty; and the use of reason becomes daily more visible, as these materials, that give it employment, increase. But though the having of general ideas and the use of general words and reason usually grow together, yet I see not how this any way proves them innate. The knowledge of some truths, I confess, is very early in the mind; but in a way that shows them not to be innate. For, if we will observe, we shall find it still to be about ideas not innate, but acquired – it being about those first, which are imprinted by external things, with which infants have earliest to do, and which make the most frequent impressions on their senses. In ideas thus got, the mind discovers that some agree, and others differ, probably as soon as it has any use of memory; as soon as it is able to retain and receive distinct ideas. But whether it be then, or no, this is certain: it does so long before it has the use of words, or comes to that which we commonly call the *use of reason*. For a child knows as certainly, before it can speak, the difference between the ideas of sweet and bitter (i.e. that sweet is not bitter) as it knows afterwards (when it comes to speak) that wormwood and sugar-plums are not the same thing.

A child knows not that three and four are equal to seven, till he comes to be able to count to seven, and has got the name and idea of equality; and then upon the explaining those words, he presently assents to, or rather perceives the truth of, that proposition. But neither does he then readily assent because it is an innate truth, nor was his assent wanting, till then, because he wanted the use of reason; but the truth of it appears to him, as soon as he has settled in his mind the clear and distinct ideas that these names stand for; and then he knows the truth of that proposition upon the same grounds, and by the same means, that he knew before that a rod and cherry are not the same thing...

[At the start of Book II of the *Essay,* Locke gives his own view on the origin of ideas.]

Every man being conscious to himself that he thinks, and that which his mind is employed about while thinking, being the ideas that are there, it is past doubt that men have in their minds several ideas, such as are those expressed by the words, *whiteness, hardness, sweetness, thinking, motion, man, elephant, army, drunkenness* and others. It is in the first place to be inquired: How he comes by them?...

Let us suppose the mind to be, as we say, white paper, void of all characters, without any ideas. How comes it to be furnished? Whence comes it by that vast store, which the busy and boundless fancy of man has painted on it, with an almost endless variety? When has it all the materials of reason and knowledge? To this I answer, in one word, from *experience*. In that all our knowledge is founded, and from that it ultimately derives itself. Our observation employed either about external sensible objects, or about the internal operations of our minds perceived and reflected on by ourselves, is that which supplies our understandings with all the materials of thinking. These two are the fountains of knowledge, from whence all the ideas we have, or can naturally have, do spring.

First, our *senses*, conversant about particular sensible objects, do convey into the mind several distinct *perceptions* of things, according to the various ways wherein those objects do affect them. And thus we come by those ideas we have of *yellow, white, heat, cold, soft, hard, bitter, sweet,* and all those which we call sensible qualities, which when I say the senses convey into the mind, I mean, they, from external objects, convey into the mind what produces there those *perceptions.* This great source of most of the ideas we have, depending wholly upon our senses, and derived by them to the understanding, I call *sensation.*

Secondly, the other fountain from which experience furnishes the understanding with ideas is the *perception of the operations of our own minds* within us, as it is employed about the ideas it has got. Which operations, when the soul comes to reflect on and consider, do furnish the understanding with another set of ideas, which could not be had from things without [outside]. And such are *perception, thinking, doubting, believing, reasoning, knowing, willing,* and all the different acting of our own minds; which we, being conscious of, and observing in ourselves, do from these receive into our understandings as distinct ideas, as we do from bodies affecting our senses. This source of ideas every man has wholly in himself; and though it be not sense, as having nothing to do with external objects, yet it is very like it, and might properly enough be called internal sense. But as I call the other *sensation*, so I call this *reflection*, the ideas it affords being such only as the mind gets by reflecting on its own operations within itself. By *reflection* then . . . I would be understood to mean that notice which the mind takes of its own operations, and the manner of them, by reason whereof there come to be ideas of these operations in the understanding. These two, I say, viz. external material things, as the objects of *sensation*, and the operations of our own minds within, as the objects of *reflection*, are, to me, the only originals from whence all our ideas take their beginnings . . .

The understanding seems to me not to have the least glimmering of any ideas which it does receive from one of these two. External objects furnish the mind with the ideas of sensible qualities, which are all those different perceptions they produce in us; and the mind furnishes the understanding with ideas of its own operations.

6 Innate Knowledge Defended: Gottfried Leibniz, *New Essays on Human Understanding**

Locke's attack on the theory of innate knowledge provoked a comprehensive response from the German philosopher Gottfried Leibniz, in his *New Essays on Human Understanding* (*Nouveaux Essais sur l'entendement humain*), written in French and completed in 1704 (but not published until 1765, some fifty years after the author's death). Leibniz agrees with Locke that sensory stimulation is necessary for the acquisition of knowledge. But he argues that it is not, by itself, sufficient. The senses merely elicit or activate what is already in a certain sense present within us – 'living fires or flashes of light hidden inside us but made visible by the stimulation of the senses, as sparks can be struck from a steel'. Leibniz goes on to cite the necessary truths of mathematics as support for his version of the theory of innateness: the truth of such propositions 'does not depend on instances, nor consequently on the testimony of the senses'. Readers may well see a parallel here with the earlier arguments of Plato in the *Meno* (extract 1, above). Although sensory

stimulation (the drawing of a visible diagram in the sand) *helped* the slave boy to see the result concerning the square on the diagonal, the *truth* of the proposition in question does not in any way depend on such experiments or observations or 'instances'; it can be demonstrated quite independently of experience. Reflection on the universal and necessary nature of truths of this kind leads Leibniz to the conclusion that proof of necessary truths such as those of mathematics 'can only come from inner principles'.

Locke, as is clear from our previous passage (extract 5), had objected that if such truths were indeed imprinted in the mind from birth, one would surely expect young children to be aware of them – which in many cases they patently are not. To this Leibniz replies that although present in the mind, such principles are not like notices conspicuously posted on a 'notice board': it often needs diligent attention for us to achieve the kind of explicit awareness that makes us recognize their truth. Against Locke's image of

---

* G. W. Leibniz, *New Essays on Human Understanding* [*Nouveaux essais sur l'entendement humain, c.*1704; first pub. 1765]. Trans. and ed. Peter Remnant and Jonathan Bennett (Cambridge: Cambridge University Press, 1981), paras 44–53.

the mind as a *tabula rasa* or blank sheet, Leibniz compares the mind to a block of marble – one that is not homogenous but already veined in a certain pattern: the sculptor's blows (corresponding to the stimulation of the senses) are certainly necessary, but they serve to uncover a shape that is already present in the structure of the stone. There follows an interesting discussion of the way in which the cognitive activities of the human mind seem to transcend entirely the straightforward 'stimulus-response' capacities of animals. The beasts, as Leibniz puts it, are like 'simple empirics': their awareness of things is limited to *particular* sensory images and impressions. Humans, by contrast, 'are capable of demonstrative knowledge' – that is, they can use their reason to establish universal and logically necessary truths (like those of mathematics). Leibniz's innatism thus proclaims the power of human reason to achieve knowledge that goes wholly beyond what can be derived from sensory data: 'What shows the existence of inner sources of necessary truths is also what distinguishes man from beast.'

 The *Essay on the Understanding*, produced by an illustrious Englishman, is one of the finest and most admired works of the age. Since I have thought at length about the same subject and about most of the topics which are dealt with in it, I have decided to comment upon it. I thought that this would be a good opportunity to publish something entitled *New Essays on the Understanding* and to gain a more favourable reception for my thoughts by putting them in such good company. I thought too that I might benefit from someone else's labour, not only to lessen mine (since it is easier to follow the thread of a good author than to do everything by one's own efforts), but also to add something to what he has produced for us, which is always easier than to start from the beginning. It is true that my opinions frequently differ from his, but far from denying the merit of this famous writer I testify in his favour by showing where and why I differ from him, when I find that on certain significant points I have to prevent his authority from prevailing over reason.

Indeed, although the author of the *Essay* says hundreds of fine things which I applaud, our systems are very different. His is closer to Aristotle and mine to Plato, although each of us parts company at many points from the teachings of both of these ancient writers. He is more popular whereas I am sometimes forced to be a little more esoteric and abstract – which is no advantage for me, particularly when writing in a living language. However, I think that by using two speakers, one of whom presents opinions drawn from that author's *Essay* and the other adds my comments, the confrontation will be more to the reader's taste than a dry commentary from which he would have to be continually turning back to the author's book in order to understand mine. Nevertheless it would be well to compare our writings from time to time, and to judge of his opinions only from his own book even though I have usually retained its wording. I am afraid that the obligation to follow the thread, when commenting on someone else's treatise, has shut out any hope of my attaining to the charms of which dialogue is capable; but I hope that the matter will make up for the shortcomings of the manner.

Our disagreements concern points of some importance. There is the question whether the soul in itself is completely blank like a writing tablet on which nothing has as yet been written – a *tabula rasa* – as Aristotle and the author of the *Essay* maintain, and whether everything which is inscribed there comes solely from the senses and experience; or whether the soul inherently contains the sources of various notions and doctrines, which external objects merely rouse up on suitable occasions, as I believe and as do Plato . . . and all those who understand in this sense the passage in St Paul where he says that God's law is written in our hearts (Romans, 2: 15). The Stoics call these sources 'Prolepses', that is fundamental assumptions or things taken for granted in advance. Mathematicians call them common notions or *koinai ennoiai*. Modern philosophers give them other fine names . . . 'seeds of eternity' and also *zopyra* – meaning living fires or flashes of light hidden inside us but made visible by the stimulation of the senses, as sparks can be struck from a steel. And we have reason to believe that these flashes reveal something divine and eternal: this appears especially in the case of necessary truths. That raises another question, namely whether all truths depend on experience, that is on induction and instances, or if some of them have some other foundation. For if some events can be foreseen before any test has been made of them, it is obvious that we contribute something from our side. Although the senses are necessary for all our actual knowledge, they are not sufficient to provide it all, since they never give us anything but instances, that is particular or singular truths. But however many instances confirm a general truth, they do not suffice to establish its universal necessity; for it does not follow that what has happened will always happen in the same way. For instance, the Greeks and Romans and all the other nations on earth always found that within the passage of twenty-four hours day turns into night and night into day. But they would have been mistaken if they had believed that the same rule holds everywhere, since the contrary was observed during a stay in Novaya Zemlya. And anyone who believed that it is a necessary and eternal truth at least in our latitudes would also be mistaken, since we must recognize that neither the earth nor even the sun exist necessarily, and that there may come a time when this beautiful star no longer exists, at least in its present form, nor its whole system.

From this it appears that necessary truths, such as we find in pure mathematics and particularly in arithmetic and geometry, must have principles whose proof does not depend on instances nor, consequently, on the testimony of the senses, even though without the senses it would never occur to us to think of them. This distinction must be thoroughly observed, and Euclid understood that so well that he demonstrates by reason things that experience and sense-images make very evident. Logic also abounds in such truths, and so do metaphysics and ethics, together with their respective products, natural theology and natural jurisprudence; and so the proof of them can only come from inner principles, which are described as innate.

It would indeed be wrong to think that we can easily read these eternal laws of reason in the soul, as the Praetor's edict can be read on his notice-board, without effort or inquiry; but it is enough that they can be discovered within us by dint of attention: the senses provide the occasion, and successful experiments also serve to corroborate reason, somewhat as checks in arithmetic help us to avoid errors of calculation in long chains of reasoning.

It is in this same respect that man's knowledge differs from that of beasts: beasts are sheer empirics and are guided entirely by instances. While men are capable of demonstrative knowledge, beasts, so far as one can judge, never manage to form necessary propositions, since the faculty by which they make sequences is something lower than the reason which is to be found in men. The sequences of beasts are just like those of simple empirics who maintain that what has happened once will happen again in a case which is similar in the respects that they are impressed by, although that does not enable them to judge whether the same reasons are at work. That is what makes it so easy for men to ensnare beasts, and so easy for simple empirics to make mistakes. Even people made cunning by age and experience are not proof against this when they trust too much to their past experience; as has happened to various people engaged in civil or military affairs, through their not taking sufficiently to heart that the world changes and that men become cleverer and find hundreds of new tricks – whereas the deer and hares of our time are not becoming craftier than those of long ago. The sequences of beasts are only a shadow of reasoning, that is, they are nothing but a connection in the imagination – a passage from one image to another; for when a new situation appears similar to its predecessor, it is expected to have the same concomitant features as before, as though things were linked in reality just because their images are linked in the memory. It is true, moreover, that reason counsels us to expect ordinarily that what we find in the future will conform to long experience of the past; but even so, this is no necessary and infallible truth, and it can fail us when we least expect it to, if there is a change in the reasons which have been maintaining it. This is why the wisest men do not trust it so implicitly that they neglect to probe somewhat, where possible, into the reason for such regularities, in order to know when they will have to allow exceptions. For only reason is capable of establishing reliable rules, of making up the deficiencies of those which have proved unreliable by allowing exceptions to them, and lastly of finding unbreakable links in the cogency of necessary inferences. This last often provides a way of foreseeing events without having to experience sensible links between images, as beasts must. Thus what shows the existence of inner sources of necessary truths is also what distinguishes man from beast.

Perhaps our gifted author will not entirely disagree with my view. For after devoting the whole of his first book to rejecting innate illumination, understood in a certain sense, he nevertheless admits at the start of his second book, and from there on, that ideas which do not originate in sensation come from reflection. But reflection is nothing but attention to what is within us, and the senses do not give us what we carry with us already. In view of this, can it be denied that there is a great deal that is innate in our minds, since we are innate to ourselves, so to speak, and since we include Being, Unity, Substance, Duration, Change, Action, Perception, Pleasure, and hosts of other objects of our intellectual ideas? And since these objects are immediately related to our understanding and always present to it (although our distractions and needs prevent us being always aware of them), is it any wonder that we say that these ideas, along with what depends on them are innate in us? I have also used the analogy of a veined block of marble, as opposed to an entirely homogeneous block of marble, or to a blank tablet – what the philosophers call a *tabula rasa*. For if the soul were like such a blank tablet then truths would be in us as the shape of Hercules is in a piece of marble when the marble is entirely neutral as to whether it assumes this shape or some other. However, if there were veins in the block which marked out the shape of Hercules rather than other shapes, then that block would be more determined to that shape and Hercules would be innate in it, in a way, even though labour would be required to expose the veins and to polish them into clarity, removing everything that prevents their being seen. This is how ideas and truths are innate in us – as inclinations, dispositions, tendencies, or natural potentialities, and not as actions; although these potentialities are always accompanied by certain actions, often insensible ones, which correspond to them.

Our gifted author seems to claim that there is nothing *potential* in us, in fact nothing of which we are not always actually aware. But he cannot hold strictly to this; otherwise his position would be too paradoxical, since, again, we are not always aware of our acquired dispositions or of the contents of our memory, and they do not even come to our aid whenever we need them, though often they come readily to mind when some idle circumstance reminds us of them, as when hearing the opening words of a song is enough to bring back the rest. So on other occasions he limits his thesis to the statement that there is nothing in us of which we have not at least previously been aware. But no one can establish by reason alone how far our past and now perhaps forgotten awarenesses may have extended, especially if we accept the Platonists' doctrine of recollection which, though sheer myth, is entirely consistent with unadorned reason. And furthermore, why must we acquire everything through awareness of outer things and not be able to unearth anything from within ourselves? Is our soul in itself so empty that unless it borrows images from outside it is nothing? I am sure that our judicious author could not approve of such a view. Where could tablets be found which were completely uniform? Will a perfectly homogeneous and even surface ever be seen? So why could we not also provide ourselves with objects of thought from our own depths, if we take the trouble to dig there? Which leads me to believe that fundamentally his view on this question is not different from my own or rather from the common view, especially since he recognizes two sources of our knowledge, the senses and reflection.

7   Scepticism versus Human Nature: David Hume, *Enquiry concerning Human Understanding**

The debate between Locke and Leibniz over the sources of knowledge exerted a strong influence on the philosophy of the eighteenth century. The famous Scottish philosopher David Hume came down firmly on the side of Locke. Sense experience, he argued, must be the basis of all knowledge concerning matters of fact or existence. Yet the work of Descartes, as we have seen from the above extract (no. 4), had shown, or seemed to show, that any attempt to base knowledge on sensory experience was wrong-headed, since a series of sceptical arguments could be mounted to call the reliability of the senses into doubt. In our next extract, from Section XII of An Enquiry

concerning Human Understanding (1748), Hume provided a systematic critique of much philosophical scepticism.

First Hume targets the kind of scepticism 'much inculcated by Descartes' – the kind of radical doubt entertained as a first step, prior to any science or philosophy. It is impossible, Hume argues, for us consistently to entertain this kind of universal doubt, and even if we could do so, the doubts raised would be entirely incurable. Next Hume targets the kind of scepticism that operates at a later stage, 'consequent to science and enquiry' – the kind which uses the supposed results of science and philosophy to cast doubt on our

---

* David Hume, *An Enquiry concerning Human Understanding* [1748], Section XII; abridged, with modified spelling, punctuation and grammar. There are many editions of this work, including that by Tom L. Beauchamp (Oxford: Oxford University Press, 1999), which contains a helpful introduction for students.

ordinary beliefs about the nature of the world around us. Here Hume draws attention to the power of human nature as against abstract philosophical reasoning: men are carried 'by a natural instinct to repose faith in their senses'. Hume proceeds to develop this theme, by pointing out that 'nature is always too strong for principle'. We are bound, when we leave the philosophy class and resume the 'occupations of common life', to be entirely immune to the abstract reasonings of the extreme sceptics or 'Pyrrhonians':[1] they will 'vanish like smoke' when put in opposition to the 'more powerful principles of our nature'. Finally, Hume goes on to allow the merits of 'mitigated'

or limited scepticism, which warns us against too readily accepting wild and extravagant doctrines. There is a place for philosophy here, in showing us how to think sensibly, and avoid dogmatism. But we can only do this by 'limiting our enquiries to such subjects as are best adapted to the narrow capacity of human understanding'; we must realize (as Hume argues elsewhere) that all our beliefs about matters of fact and existence must be 'founded entirely upon experience'.[2] Hume here sets up what was to become a highly influential conception of knowledge as something that can operate only within the bounds determined by our nature as human beings.

 There is not a greater number of philosophical reasonings, displayed upon any subject, than those which prove the existence of a Deity, and refute the fallacies of atheists; and yet the most religious philosophers still dispute whether any man can be so blinded as to be a speculative atheist. How shall we reconcile these contradictions? The knights-errant, who wandered about to clear the world of dragons and giants, never entertained the least doubt with regard to the existence of these monsters.

The *sceptic* is another enemy of religion, who naturally provokes the indignation of all divines and graver philosophers; though it is certain that no man ever met with any such absurd creature, or conversed with a man who had no opinion or principle concerning any subject, either of action or speculation. This begets a very natural question: What is meant by a sceptic? And how far it is possible to push these philosophical principles of doubt and uncertainty?

There is a species of scepticism, *antecedent* to all study and philosophy, which is much inculcated by Descartes and others as a sovereign preservative against error and precipitate judgement. It recommends a universal doubt, not only of all our former opinions and principles, but also of our very faculties; of whose veracity, say they, we must assure ourselves, by a chain of reasoning, deduced from some original principle which cannot possibly be fallacious or deceitful. But neither is there any such original principle which has a prerogative above others, that are self-evident and convincing; nor, if there were, could we advance a step beyond it, but by the use of those very faculties of which we are supposed to be already diffident. The Cartesian doubt, therefore, were it ever possible to be attained by any human creature (as it plainly is not) would be entirely incurable; and no reasoning could ever bring us to a state of assurance and conviction upon any subject.

It must, however, be confessed that this species of scepticism, when more moderate, may be understood in a very reasonable sense, and is a necessary preparative to the study of philosophy, by preserving a proper impartiality in our judgements, and weaning our mind from all those prejudices, which we may have imbibed from

---

[1] After the ancient Greek philosopher Pyrrho of Elis (*c.*365–275 BC) who argued that knowledge of the nature of things is utterly unattainable, and advocated total suspension of belief.

[2] For this thesis, and Hume's rejection of speculative philosophy which goes beyond these limits, see below, Part II, extract 7.

education or rash opinion. To begin with clear and self-evident principles, to advance by timorous and sure steps, to review frequently our conclusions, and examine accurately all their consequences (though by these means we shall make both a slow and a short progress in our systems) are the only methods by which we can ever hope to reach truth, and attain a proper stability and certainty in our determinations.

There is another species of scepticism, *consequent* to science and enquiry, when men are supposed to have discovered either the absolute fallaciousness of their mental faculties, or their unfitness to reach any fixed determination in all those curious subjects of speculation about which they are commonly employed. Even our very senses are brought into dispute by a certain species of philosophers; and the maxims of common life are subjected to the same doubt as the most profound principles or conclusions of metaphysics and theology. As these paradoxical tenets (if they may be called tenets) are to be met with in some philosophers, and the refutation of them in several, they naturally excite our curiosity, and make us enquire into the arguments, on which they may be founded.

I need not insist upon the more trite topics, employed by the sceptics in all ages, against the evidence of *sense*; such as those which are derived from the imperfection and fallaciousness of our organs, on numberless occasions; the crooked appearance of an oar in water; the various aspects of objects, according to their different distances; the double images which arise from pressing one eye; with many other appearances of a like nature. These sceptical topics, indeed, are only sufficient to prove that the senses alone are not implicitly to be depended on; but that we must correct their evidence by reason, and by considerations, derived from the nature of the medium, the distance of the object, and the disposition of the organ, in order to render them, within their sphere, the proper criteria of truth and falsehood. There are other more profound arguments against the senses, which admit not of so easy a solution.

It seems evident that men are carried, by a natural instinct or prepossession, to repose faith in their senses; and that, without any reasoning, or even almost before the use of reason, we always suppose an external universe, which depends not on our perception, but would exist, though we and every sensible creature were absent or annihilated. Even the animal creation are governed by a like opinion, and preserve this belief of external objects in all their thoughts, designs and actions.

It seems also evident that when men follow this blind and powerful instinct of nature, they always suppose the very images, presented by the senses, to be the external objects, and never entertain any suspicion that the one are nothing but representations of the other. This very table, which we see white, and which we feel hard, is believed to exist, independent of our perception, and to be something external to our mind, which perceives it. Our presence bestows not being on it: our absence does not annihilate it. It preserves its existence uniform and entire, independent of the situation of intelligent beings who perceive or contemplate it.

But this universal and primary opinion of all men is soon destroyed by the slightest philosophy, which teaches us that nothing can ever be present to the mind but an image or perception, and that the senses are only the inlets, through which these images are conveyed, without being able to produce any immediate intercourse between the mind and the object. The table, which we see, seems to diminish, as we remove farther from it; but the real table, which exists independent of us, suffers no alteration: it was, therefore, nothing but its image, which was present to the mind.

These are the obvious dictates of reason; and no man, who reflects, ever doubted that the existences, which we consider, when we say, *this house* and *that tree*, are nothing but perceptions in the mind,[1] and fleeting copies or representations of other existences, which remain uniform and independent.

So far, then, are we necessitated by reasoning to contradict or depart from the primary instincts of nature, and to embrace a new system with regard to the evidence of our senses. But here philosophy finds herself extremely embarrassed, when she would justify this new system, and obviate the cavils and objections of the sceptics. She can no longer plead the infallible and irresistible instinct of nature: for that led us to a quite different system, which is acknowledged fallible and even erroneous. And to justify this pretended philosophical system, by a chain of clear and convincing argument, or even any appearance of argument, exceeds the power of all human capacity...

The great subverter of *Pyrrhonism* or the excessive principles of scepticism is action, and employment, and the occupations of common life. These principles may flourish and triumph in the schools, where it is, indeed, difficult, if not impossible, to refute them. But as soon as they leave the shade, and by the presence of the real objects, which actuate our passions and sentiments, are put in opposition to the more powerful principles of our nature, they vanish like smoke, and leave the most determined sceptic in the same condition as other mortals.

The sceptic, therefore, had better keep within his proper sphere, and display those *philosophical* objections, which arise from more profound researches. Here he seems to have ample matter of triumph; while he justly insists, that all our evidence for any matter of fact, which lies beyond the testimony of sense or memory, is derived entirely from the relation of cause and effect; that we have no other idea of this relation than that of two objects, which have been frequently *conjoined* together; that we have no argument to convince us, that objects, which have, in our experience, been frequently conjoined, will likewise, in other instances, be conjoined in the same manner; and that nothing leads us to this inference but custom or a certain instinct of our nature;[2] which it is indeed difficult to resist, but which, like other instincts, may be fallacious and deceitful. While the sceptic insists upon these topics, he shows his force, or rather, indeed, his own and our weakness; and seems, for the time at least, to destroy all assurance and conviction. These arguments might be displayed at greater length, if any durable good or benefit to society could ever be expected to result from them.

For here is the chief and most confounding objection to *excessive* scepticism, that no durable good can ever result from it, while it remains in its full force and vigour. We need only ask such a sceptic, *What his meaning is? And what he proposes by all these curious researches?* He is immediately at a loss, and knows not what to answer. A Copernican or Ptolemaic, who supports each his different system of astronomy, may hope to produce a conviction, which will remain constant and durable, with his

---

[1] Compare Berkeley's theory that nothing exists outside the mind: see below, Part II, extract 6.
[2] Compare Hume's own discussion of these matters in Part II, extract 7, and Part VI, extracts 5 and 6, below.

audience. A Stoic or Epicurean displays principles which may not be durable, but which have an effect on conduct and behaviour. But a Pyrrhonian cannot expect that his philosophy will have any constant influence on the mind, or, if it had, that its influence would be beneficial to society. On the contrary, he must acknowledge, if he will acknowledge anything, that all human life must perish, were his principles universally and steadily to prevail. All discourse, all action would immediately cease; and men remain in a total lethargy, till the necessities of nature, unsatisfied, put an end to their miserable existence. It is true; so fatal an event is very little to be dreaded. Nature is always too strong for principle. And though a Pyrrhonian may throw himself or others into a momentary amazement and confusion by his profound reasonings, the first and most trivial event in life will put to flight all his doubts and scruples, and leave him the same, in every point of action and speculation, with the philosophers of every other sect, or with those who never concerned themselves in any philosophical researches. When he awakes from his dream, he will be the first to join in the laugh against himself, and to confess that all his objections are mere amusement, and can have no other tendency than to show the whimsical condition of mankind, who must act and reason and believe – though they are not able, by their most diligent enquiry, to satisfy themselves concerning the foundation of these operations, or to remove the objections which may be raised against them.

There is indeed a more *mitigated* scepticism ... which may be both durable and useful, and which may in part be the result of this Pyrrhonism, or *excessive* scepticism, when its undistinguished doubts are in some measure corrected by common sense and reflection. The greater part of mankind are naturally apt to be affirmative and dogmatical in their opinions ... But could such dogmatical reasoners become sensible of the strange infirmities of human understanding, even in its more perfect state ... such a reflection would naturally inspire them with more modesty and reserve, and diminish their fond opinion of themselves ...

Another species of mitigated scepticism which may be of advantage to mankind, and which may be the natural result of Pyrrhonian doubts and scruples, is the limitation of our enquiries to such subjects as best adapted to the narrow capacity of human understanding. The imagination of man is naturally sublime, delighted with whatever is remote and extraordinary, and running without control into the most distant parts of space and time in order to avoid the objects which custom has rendered too familiar to it. A correct judgement observes a contrary method, and avoiding all distant and high enquiries, confines itself to common life, and to such subjects as fall under daily practice and experience, leaving the more sublime topics to the embellishment of poets and orators, or to the arts or priests and politicians. To bring us to so salutary a determination, nothing can be more serviceable than to be once thoroughly convinced of the force of the Pyrrhonian doubt, and of the impossibility that anything but the strong power of natural instinct could free us from it ... This narrow limitation, indeed, of our inquiries is in every respect so reasonable that it suffices to make the slightest examination into the natural powers of the human mind, and to compare them with their objects, in order to recommend it to us. We shall then find what are the proper subjects of science and enquiry.

8   Experience and Understanding: Immanuel Kant, *Critique of Pure Reason**

The history of the theory of knowledge is sometimes presented as a battle between two opposing camps of philosophers – *empiricists* (from the Greek, *empeiria*, 'experience'), who believe sensory experience is the basis of all knowledge, and *rationalists* (from the Latin, *ratio*, 'reason'), who believe the inner light of reason enables us to acquire knowledge that is independent of experience. The contrast can be overdone, and it easily leads to oversimplifications; but we can, none the less, discern empiricist elements in the above extracts from Aristotle and Locke, while the selections from Plato and Descartes reveal a distrust of the senses that is characteristic of the 'rationalist' outlook. Leibniz, as the above extract (no. 6) shows, stressed the importance of sensory stimulus for the mind, but nevertheless insisted on the innateness of a 'host of objects of our intellectual ideas'. In his monumental work the *Critique of Pure Reason*, published in 1781, the celebrated German philosopher Immanuel Kant attempted to resolve some of these tensions.

Kant's views on knowledge were strongly influenced by David Hume, whom he credited with having roused him from his 'dogmatic slumbers'. Kant's fundamental thesis is that the only possible objects of human knowledge are phenomena – the empirically observable objects of the world around us. 'Nothing is really given us,' he argued, 'except perception and the empirical advance from this to other possible perceptions.'[1] He is thus deeply suspicious of the claims of 'rationalist' philosophers of knowledge to describe a reality going wholly beyond the observable world. But he is equally critical of Locke's thesis that knowledge arises from the 'empty cabinet' of the mind being furnished with sense impressions. As he puts it at the start of the extracts quoted below, 'although all our knowledge begins with experience, it does not follow that it all arises out of experience'. According to Kant, the mind, in experiencing the world, necessarily interprets it or processes it in terms of a certain structure: it comes to the world already armed with 'concepts of the understanding'. These concepts are described by Kant as *a priori*, meaning prior to, or independent of, experience. But Kant takes a crucially different route from previous innatists who had suggested that the mind was simply endowed (by God, as Descartes maintained, or from a previous existence, as Plato had it) with a range of nonempirical concepts and truths. Instead, Kant argues that all the concepts of the understanding are derived from certain fundamental categories which are *presupposed* by experience. Categories such as the categories of substance and causality are fundamental preconditions for our being able to experience the world at all. Kant thus offers a compromise between, or rather a synthesis of, empiricist and rationalist approaches to knowledge. Knowledge involves a kind of fusion of 'intuitions' (sensory representations) on the one hand, and the concepts of the understanding on the other. As he puts it below, in what has become a much-quoted slogan, 'thoughts without content are empty, intuitions without concepts are blind'.

The distinction between pure and empirical knowledge

There can be no doubt that all our knowledge begins with experience. For how would our faculty of knowledge be awakened into action unless the objects affecting our senses produced representations, and also aroused the activity of our understanding

---

* Immanuel Kant, *Critique of Pure Reason* [*Kritik der reinen Vernunft*, 1781; 2nd edn 1787]. Trans. N. Kemp Smith (2nd edn, London: Macmillan, 1933); with minor modifications. The extracts printed here are from the Introduction, Sections 1 and 2 (B1–5); the 'Transcendental Logic', Section 1 (B74–5); and from the 'Transcendental Analytic', Bk I, ch. 2 ('Transition to the Transcendental Deduction of the Categories'), B124–6.

[1] *Critique of Pure Reason*, A493, B521.

to compare these representations? How, furthermore, could our knowledge be awakened unless our understanding, by combining or separating these representations, worked up the raw material of the sensible impressions into that knowledge of objects which is called experience? In the order of time, therefore, we have no knowledge antecedent to experience, and with experience all our knowledge begins.

But though all our knowledge *begins* with experience, it does not follow that it all *arises out of* experience. For it may well be that even our empirical knowledge is made up of what we receive through impressions, and of what our own faculty of knowledge supplies from itself (sensible impressions serving merely as the occasion). If our faculty of knowledge makes any such addition, it may be that we are not in a position to distinguish it from the raw material until with long-practised attention we have become skilled to do so.

This then is a question which at least calls for further examination, and does not permit any off-hand answer: is there any knowledge that is in this way independent of experience, and even of all impressions of the senses? Such knowledge is called *a priori* and is distinguished from the *empirical*, which has its sources *a posteriori* (that is, in experience).

The expression *a priori* does not however indicate precisely enough the full meaning of our question. For it has been customary to say, even of much knowledge that is derived from empirical sources, that we have it, or are capable of having it, *a priori*; what this is taken to mean is that we do not derive it immediately from experience, but from a universal rule – a rule which is itself borrowed from experience. Thus we might say of a man who undermined the foundations of a house that he might have known *a priori* that it would fall (that is, he need not have waited for the experience of its actually falling). But still he could not know this completely *a priori*. For he had first to learn through experience that bodies are heavy, and therefore fall when their supports are withdrawn.

In what follows, therefore, we shall understand by *a priori* knowledge not knowledge independent of this or that experience, but knowledge absolutely independent of all experience. Opposed to it is empirical knowledge, which is knowledge possible only *a posteriori* (that is, through experience). *A priori* modes of knowledge are called 'pure' when there is no admixture of anything empirical. Thus, for instance, the proposition 'every change has a cause', although an *a priori* proposition, is not a pure proposition, since 'alteration' is a concept which can be derived only from experience.

We are in possession of certain modes of *a priori* knowledge, and even the common understanding is never without them

What we require here is a criterion by which to distinguish with certainty between pure and empirical knowledge. Experience teaches us that a thing is so and so, but not that it cannot be otherwise. First, then, if we have a proposition which is thought of as *necessary*, it is an *a priori* judgement; and if in addition it is not derived from any proposition except one also having the validity of a necessary judgement, it is an absolutely *a priori* judgement. Secondly, experience never confers on its judgements true or strict, but only assumed and comparative universality, through induction.[1]

---

[1] See below, Part VII, extract 5.

We can properly only say, therefore, that so far as we have hitherto observed there is no exception to this or that rule. If, then, a judgement is thought with strict universality, in such a manner that no exception is allowed as possible, it is not derived from experience, but is valid absolutely *a priori*. Empirical universality, by contrast, is only an arbitrary extension of a validity holding in *most* cases to one which holds in all (for instance, in the proposition 'all bodies are heavy'). When, on the other hand, strict universality is essential to a judgement, this involves a special source of knowledge, namely a faculty of *a priori* knowledge. Necessity and strict universality are thus sure criteria of *a priori* knowledge, and are inseparable from each other...

Now it is easy to show that there are actually in human knowledge judgements which are necessary and in the strictest sense universal, and which are therefore pure *a priori* judgements. If an example from the sciences is asked for, we have only to look to any of the propositions of mathematics. If we seek an example from the understanding in its quite ordinary employment, the proposition 'every change *must* have a cause' will serve our purpose. Here the very concept of a cause so manifestly contains the concept of necessary connection with an effect, and of the strict universality of this rule, that the concept would be altogether lost if we tried to derive it (as Hume did)[1] from a repeated association of that which happens with that which precedes... Even without appealing to such examples, it is possible to show that pure *a priori* principles are indispensable for the possibility of experience, and so to prove their existence *a priori*. For how could experience get its certainty if all the rules whereby it proceeds were always themselves empirical and therefore contingent? Such rules could hardly be regarded as first principles...

The idea of a transcendental logic

Our knowledge springs from two fundamental sources of the mind; the first is the capacity of receiving representations (the ability to receive impressions), the second is the power to know an object through these representations (spontaneity in the production of concepts). Through the first, an object is *given* to us; through the second, the object is *thought* in relation to that representation... Intuition and concepts constitute, therefore, the elements of all our knowledge, so that neither concepts without an intuition in some way corresponding to them, nor intuitions without concepts, can yield knowledge. Both may be either pure or empirical. When they contain sensation (which presupposes the actual presence of the object) they are empirical. When there is no mingling of sensation with the representation, they are pure. Sensation may be called the *material* of sensible knowledge. Pure intuition, therefore, contains only the *form* under which something is intuited; the pure concept only the form of an object in general. Pure intuitions or pure concepts are possible only *a priori*; empirical intuitions and empirical concepts only *a posteriori*.

If the *receptivity* of our mind, its power of receiving representations in so far as it is in any way affected, is to be called 'sensibility', then the mind's power of producing representations from itself, the *spontaneity* of knowledge, should be called 'understanding'. Our nature is so constituted that our intuitions can never be other than

[1] See below, Part VII, extract 6.

sensible; that is, it contains only the mode in which we are affected by objects. The faculty, on the other hand, which enables us to *think* the object of sensible intuition is the understanding. To neither of these powers may a preference be given over the other. Without sensibility, no object would be given to us; without understanding, no object would be thought. Thoughts without content are empty; intuitions without concepts are blind. It is therefore just as necessary to make our concepts sensible, that is, to add the object to them in intuition, as to make our intuitions intelligible, that is to bring them under concepts. These two powers or capacities cannot exchange their functions. The understanding can intuit nothing, the senses can think nothing. Only through their union can knowledge arise...

Transition to the transcendental deduction of the categories

...There are only two conditions under which the knowledge of an object is possible, first *intuition*, through which it is given, though only as appearance; and second, the *concept* (corresponding to this intuition) through which an object is thought. It is evident that the first condition, whereby objects can be intuited, does actually lie *a priori* in the mind as the formal ground of the objects. All appearances necessarily agree with this formal condition of sensibility, since only through it can they appear, that is, be empirically intuited and given. The question now arises whether *a priori* concepts do not also serve as antecedent conditions, needed if anything can be, not just intuited, but thought of as an object in general. In that case, all empirical knowledge of objects would necessarily conform to such concepts, because only by presupposing them in this way is anything capable of being an object of experience. Now all experience does indeed contain, in addition to the intuition of the senses through which something is given, a *concept* of an object as thereby given or appearing. Concepts of objects in general thus underlie all empirical knowledge as its *a priori* conditions. The objective validity of the categories as *a priori* concepts rests, therefore, on the fact that (so far as the form of thought is concerned) it is only through them that experience becomes possible. They relate of necessity and *a priori* to the objects of experience, since only by means of them can any object of experience be thought.

9   From Sense-certainty to Self-consciousness: Georg Hegel, *Phenomenology of Spirit**

In standard courses on the theory of knowledge in the 'analytic' tradition which today dominates Anglo-American philosophy, it has often been the custom to move swiftly on from Kant to the twentieth century, with only the briefest of passing references to what happened in between. The principal casualty of such an approach is the Hegelian movement, which in fact exerted an enormous influence even in Britain and America during the nineteenth and early twentieth century. Georg

* G. W. F. Hegel, *Phänomenologie des Geistes* [1807], English version adapted from Hegel, *The Phenomenology of Mind*, trans. J. B. Baillie (London: Sonnenschein, 1910), extracts from Preface, Introduction, Section A, Parts I, II, III, and Section B, Part IV (pp. 21–3, 25, 90–1, 104–5, 110–11, 113–14, 125–6, 129, 164–5).

Wilhelm Friedrich Hegel is a notoriously hard writer to understand, and his high-flown and abstract style makes his ideas particularly difficult to summarize, or to present in excerpts. But for any overview of the theory of knowledge that is not to be radically defective, it is essential to make some attempt to come to terms with his unique contribution.

In his *Phenomenology of Spirit* (1807) Hegel introduces a dynamic and essentially historical perspective into what had hitherto been a supposedly static and timeless framework for understanding the nature of knowledge. Hegel conceives of the world in terms of a progressive movement of Mind or Spirit (*Geist*) towards full self-realization as self-conscious awareness. Hegel uses the term 'the Absolute' to refer to the resulting reality, manifested in culmination of the process towards self-fulfilment: 'Of the Absolute it must be said that it is essentially a result, that only in the end is it what it truly is.' Here and in the first of the extracts that follow, Hegel firmly rejects the notion that knowledge can be constructed from timelessly valid 'fundamental propositions' or 'first principles', emphasizing instead that knowledge comes about via a *process* – what he calls a gradual development of knowing or a 'coming to be of knowledge'. Truth, for Hegel, is the eventual and distant culmination of an arduous and lengthy gestation process undergone by mind or spirit – a process which is, moreover, not a simple linear progression, but a perpetual dialectical struggle.

By the term 'dialectical', Hegel means to convey the idea that any given stage in the mind's ascent to truth is likely to be beset with tensions and paradoxes: for any given thesis, analysis will reveal confusions and contradictions which will generate an antithesis – the opposite of the original thesis. But the confrontation between thesis and antithesis in turn leads to fresh tensions, thus bringing about the formulation of a synthesis, which attempts to resolve the previous contradictions, while incorporating the insights they contained into a new and deeper perspective. But the synthesis will itself then be subject to further dialectical tensions: the process repeats itself endlessly in the upward struggle towards the truth.[1]

This dynamic process is clearly at work in the account Hegel gives of the actual development of human knowledge. We begin with what he calls *sense certainty* – the direct and immediate acquaintance, via the senses, with particular objects. But although this may seem a 'rich' and fruitful kind of knowledge, it is in fact nothing more than a coming up against a set of raw materials – a mere barrage of uninterpreted impressions. If any genuine cognitive grasp of the world is to be achieved, we must go beyond mere sense-certainty to *perception*: we must transcend isolated particulars, and apprehend things in a more systematic way, as having universal properties (to put it crudely, we have to go beyond just pointing at some immediately present item, and proceed to make some judgement like 'here is a yellow, round tennis ball'). Yet here again there will be tensions – for example the tension between our conception of objects as having a unity, and the various quite different properties (yellowness, roundness and so on) which we ascribe to them on the basis of our various modes of conscious awareness (sight, hearing, taste and so on). And so this stage too is transcended, giving way to what Hegel calls *understanding*, a conception which involves recognizing what Hegel calls 'Force' – something with permanent causal powers which underlies the various manifested properties of things. Here we reach something which is 'completely set free from thought', and exists 'in and for itself' (again, very crudely: the tennis ball has the power to bounce, to resist pressure, to break a window, and so on). Yet even this stage of understanding is now subjected to further analysis which reveals the need for a higher stage of knowledge which Hegel calls *self-consciousness*: in order to understand objects as having causal powers, we must interact with them as purposive, self-conscious agents. True knowledge of the world is thus available only to self-conscious subjects who are aware of themselves, of their active causal participation in the world around them. With *self-consciousness*, we have 'passed into the native land of truth, into that kingdom where it is at home'.

---

[1] Though the terms 'thesis', 'antithesis' and 'synthesis' are handy labels for referring to the structure of Hegel's dialectic, it should be noted that they are not used by Hegel himself. Moreover, not all of Hegel's translations and sequences have this 'three-step' development, though it is characteristic of many of them.

Knowledge is only real and can only be set forth fully in the form of science, in the form of system. Further, a so-called fundamental proposition or first principle of philosophy, even if it is true, is yet none the less false, just because and in so far as it is merely a fundamental proposition, merely a first principle. It is for that reason easily refuted. The refutation consists in bringing out its defective character; and it *is* defective because it is merely the universal, merely a principle, the beginning. If the refutation is complete and thorough, it is derived and developed from the nature of the principle itself, and not accomplished by bringing in from elsewhere other counter-assurances and chance fancies. It would be strictly the development of the principle, and thus the completion of its deficiency, were it not that it misunderstands its own purport by taking account solely of the negative aspect of what it seeks to do, and is not conscious of the positive character of its process and result. The really positive working out of the beginning is at the same time just as much the very reverse: it is a negative attitude towards the principle we start from. Negative, that is to say, in its one-sided form, which consists in being primarily immediate, a mere purpose. It may therefore be regarded as a refutation of what constitutes the basis of the system; but more correctly it should be looked at as a demonstration that the *basis* or principle of the system is in point of fact merely its *beginning*.

That the truth is only realized in the form of system, that substance is essentially subject, is expressed in the idea which represents the Absolute as Spirit (*Geist*) – the grandest conception of all, and one which is due to modern times and its religion. Spirit is the only reality. It is the inner being of the world, that which essentially is, and is *per se*. It assumes objective determinate form, and enters into relations with itself – it is externality (otherness) and exists for self. Yet in this determination, and in its otherness, it is still one with itself, it is self-contained and self-complete, in itself and for itself at once. The self-containedness, however, is first something known by us, it is implicit in its nature (*an sich*); it is spiritual substance. It has to become self-contained for itself, on its own account. It must get knowledge of spirit, and must be conscious of itself as spirit. This means it must be presented to itself as an object, but at the same time straightaway annul and transcend this objective form. It must be its own object in which it finds itself reflected. So far as its spiritual content is produced by its own activity, it is only *we*, the thinkers, who know spirit to be for itself, to be objective to itself; but in so far as spirit knows itself to be for itself, then this self-production, this pure notion, is the sphere and element in which its objectification takes effect, and where it gets its existential form. In this way it is in its existence aware of itself as an object in which its own self is reflected. Mind which, when thus developed, knows itself to be mind, is science. Science is its realization and the kingdom it sets up for itself is its own native element...

It is this process by which science in general comes about, this gradual development of knowing, that is set forth here in the *Phenomenology of Spirit*. Knowing, as it is found at the start, mind in its immediate and primitive stage, is without the essential nature of the mind, is sense-consciousness. To get the length of genuine knowledge, or produce the element where science is found – the pure conception of science itself – a long and laborious journey must be undertaken. This process towards science, as regards the content it will bring to light and the forms it will assume in the course of its progress, will not be what is primarily imagined by leading the unscientific consciousness up to the level of science. It will be something different too from establishing and laying the foundations of science; and certainly something else than the sort of ecstatic enthusiasm which starts straight off with absolute knowledge, as if shot out of a pistol, and makes short work of other points of view simply by explaining that it is to take no notice of them...

The knowledge which is at the outset, or immediately, our object, can be nothing else but just that which is immediate knowledge, knowledge of the immediate, of what *is*. We have, in dealing with it, to proceed, in an immediate way, to accept what is given, not altering anything in it as it is presented before us, and keeping mere apprehension from conceptual comprehension.

The concrete content, which *sense-certainty* furnishes, makes it at first sight appear to be the richest kind of knowledge, to be even a knowledge of endless wealth... Besides that, it seems to be the truest, the most authentic knowledge: for it has not as yet lost anything from the object; it has the object before itself in its entirety and completeness. This bare fact of certainty, however, is really the most abstract and the poorest kind of truth. It merely says regarding what it knows: it *is*; and its truth contains solely the being of the fact it knows...

Immediate certainty does not make the truth its own, for truth is something universal, whereas certainty wants to deal with the This. *Perception*, on the other hand, takes what exists (for it) to be a universal... It is a universal, and the object is a universal. The principle of universality has arisen and come into being for us, who are tracing the course of experience. And our process of apprehending what perception is, therefore, is no longer a contingent series of acts of apprehension, as is the case with sense-certainty, but a logically necessitated process...

Let us now see what sort of experience consciousness forms in the course of its actual perception. We, who are analysing this process, find this experience already contained in the development (just given) of the object, and of the attitude of consciousness towards it. The experience will be merely the development of the contradictions that appear there... The object which I apprehend presents itself as purely one and single. But in addition, I am aware of the *property* in it, a property which is universal, thereby transcending the particularity of the object...

To begin with, then, I am aware of the thing as a 'one', and have to keep it fixed in this true character as one. If in the course of perceiving, something crops up contradicting that, then I must take it to be due to my reflection. Now, in perception, various different properties also turn up, which seem to be properties of the thing. But the thing is a 'one'; and we are aware in ourselves that this diversity, by which the thing ceases to be a unity, arises in us. This thing, then, is, in point of fact, merely white to *our* eyes, *also* sharp to *our* tongue, and *also* cubical to *our* feeling, and so on. The entire diversity of these aspects comes not from the thing, but from us; and we find them falling apart thus from one another, because the organs they affect are quite distinct (the eye is entirely distinct from the tongue, and so on). We are consequently the universal medium where such elements get dissociated, and exist each by themselves. By the fact, then, that we regard the characteristic of being a universal medium as *our* reflection, *we* preserve and maintain the self-sameness and truth of the thing, its being a 'one'...

Consciousness has found 'seeing' and 'hearing' etc., pass away in the dialectic process of sense-experience, and has, at the stage of perception, arrived at thoughts which it brings together in the first instance as the unconditioned universal. This unconditioned element, if it were taken as inert essence, bare and simple, would itself be nothing but the one-sided extreme of being-for-itself; for the non-essential world would then stand over against it. But if this was how it was related to the latter, it would itself be unessential, and consciousness would not have been disentangled from the deceptions of perception; whereas this universal has turned out to be something that has passed beyond such conditioned, separate existence, and returned to itself.

But this unconditioned universal, which henceforward is the true object of consciousness, is still *object* of consciousness; consciousness has not yet grasped its *principle* or *notion* as such. There is an essential distinction between the two which must be grasped. On the one hand, consciousness is aware that the object has passed from its relation to another back into itself, and thereby become 'notion', inherently and in itself; but on the other hand consciousness is not yet the notion explicitly or *for itself*, and consequently it does not know itself in the reflected object. *We* (who are analysing an experience) found this object arise through the process of consciousness in such a way that consciousness is implicated and involved in the development of the object... But because in this movement consciousness had as its content merely the objective entity, and not consciousness as such, the result has to be given an objective significance for consciousness. Consciousness, however, still withdraws from what has arisen, so that the latter in objective form is the essential reality for consciousness...

It is *understanding* to which the concept of Force belongs, that is, properly speaking the principle which supports the different moments in so far as they are different... Force is the unconditioned universal which is *in itself* just what it is for something else (or that which holds the difference within itself) – for it is nothing else than *existence-for-an-other*. Hence, for Force to be what it truly is, it has to be completely set free from thought, and put forward as the substantial reality of these differences – that is, first the substance as the entire force existing in and for itself, and then its differences as substantial entities, or as moments subsisting each on its own account. Force as such, force as driven back within itself, is thus by itself an excluding unity, for which the unfolding of the elements or differences is another thing subsisting separately; and thus there are set up two sides, distinct and independent. But force is also the whole, or it remains what, in its very conception it is...

In the kinds of certainty hitherto considered, the truth for consciousness is something other than consciousness itself. The conception of this truth, however, vanishes in the course of our experience of it. What the object immediately was *in itself* – whether mere being, in *sense-certainty*, a concrete thing, in *perception*, or force, in the case of *understanding* – turns out in truth to be no such thing. But instead, this inherent nature proves to be a way in which it is for another. The abstract conception of the object gives way before the actual concrete object, or the first immediate idea is cancelled in the course of experience. Mere certainty has vanished in favour of truth.

There has now arisen, however, what was not established in the case of these previous relationships, viz. a certainty that is on a par with its truth. For certainty is to itself its own object, and consciousness is to itself the truth. Otherness is, of course, also found there – consciousness makes a distinction. But what is distinguished is of such a kind that consciousness, at the same time, holds there is no distinction made. If we call the movement of knowledge 'conception', and knowledge as simple movement of Ego, the 'object', we say that not only for us (tracing the process) but likewise for knowledge itself, the object corresponds to the conception. Or if we call 'conception' what the object is in itself, and 'object' what the object is as object, or for another, it is clear that being 'in itself' and being 'for another' are here the same. For the inherent being is consciousness; yet it is still just as much that for which the other (what it is 'in itself') is. And it is *for* consciousness that the inherent nature of the object and its 'being for another' are one and the same. Ego is the content of the relation, and itself the process of relating. It is Ego itself which is opposed to another and, at the same time, reaches out beyond this other, which other is none the less taken to be only itself.

With *self-consciousness*, then, we have now passed into the native land of truth, into that kingdom where it is at home. We have to see how the form or attitude of self-consciousness in the first instance appears. When we consider this new form of and type of knowledge, the knowledge of self in its relation to that which preceded, namely the knowledge of another, we find indeed that this latter has vanished, but that its moments have at the same time been preserved. The loss consists in this, that those moments are here present as they are implicitly, as they are in themselves. The being which 'meaning' dealt with – particularity [in *sense-certainty*], and the universality of *perception* opposed to it, and also the inner region of *understanding* – these are no longer present as substantial elements, but as moments of *self-consciousness*, that is, as abstractions or differences which are of no account for consciousness itself – not really differences at all, but elements that ultimately disappear.

10   Against Scepticism: G. E. Moore, *A Defence of Common Sense**

In the writings of Kant, and even more in Hegel, we can see the style and language of philosophy becoming increasingly technical, with a consequent loss of the transparency and directness at which many of its earlier practitioners had aimed. In our own time, the writings of Hegel and his followers, in particular, have often been accused of being at best hard to follow, and at worst verging on the rankly unintelligible. At the start of the twentieth century, with the rise of the so-called 'analytic' movement, there was something of a revulsion against philosophical obscurantism, and a move towards a more down-to-earth approach. As far as the philosophy of knowledge is concerned, one important influence was the work of George Edward Moore, widely regarded as one of the founders of the analytical philosophy which now predominates in the English-speaking world.

In his famous essay 'A Defence of Common Sense' (1925), Moore pours a cold douche on the tortuous agonizings of many past philosophers

* G. E. Moore, 'A Defence of Common Sense' [1925], extracts from Part I. First published in *Contemporary British Philosophy*, 2nd series, ed. G. H. Muirhead (London: Allen & Unwin, 1925); repr. in G. E. Moore, *Selected Writings*, ed. T. Baldwin (London: Routledge, 1993).

about the possibility of genuine knowledge. He lists a number of basic 'truisms' of which he insists he is entitled to be quite certain – for example the proposition that the earth exists, and existed for a large number of years before he was born. (Remember that Descartes, in the *Meditations* (extract 4, above), had used his method of doubt – the dreaming argument, the hypothesis of a malicious deceiver – to call into question just such apparently obvious beliefs as the belief in an external world.) For Moore, such plain common-sense beliefs are just known to be true, and any philosopher who maintains the contrary is sooner or later bound to be trapped in inconsistency.

We can see here something of an echo of Hume's scathing attacks against the wilder kinds of philosophical scepticism. But whereas Hume (extract 7, above) had pointed to our irresistibly strong human beliefs as being too strong for the sceptic to subvert, Moore suggests that what is wrong with philosophical scepticism is that it is inevitably trapped in a self-refuting paradox. The very fact that some philosophers have called into question the existence of the earth, for example, shows that the existence of the earth cannot be denied 'for when I speak of "philosophers" I mean, of course, as we all do, exclusively philosophers who have been human beings, with human bodies that have lived on the earth'.

The argument is not entirely convincing as it stands, since there is surely nothing to prevent the sceptic presenting his or her position in a more guarded way that avoids commitment to the supposed common-sense view (Descartes, indeed, aimed to do just that). Moore none the less succeeds in raising the interesting thought that the philosopher's job might be not so much to propound high-flown theories as to remove the confusions and mistakes of previous theorists. The idea was taken up in a more sophisticated way by the famous Austrian philosopher Ludwig Wittgenstein, who argued in *On Certainty* (first published in 1969, eighteen years after his death) that the basic propositions instanced by Moore form part of a fundamental framework that is unavoidable if it is even to make sense to raise questions about what we know: 'I did not get my picture of the world by satisfying myself of its correctness. No: it is the inherited background against which I distinguish between true and false...All testing, all confirmation and disconfirmation of a hypothesis, takes place within a system. And this system is not a more or less arbitrary and doubtful point of departure for all our arguments; no, it belongs to the essence of what we call an argument. The system is not so much the point of departure as the element within which arguments have their life...I should like to say Moore does not *know* what he asserts he knows, but it stands fast for him, as also for me; regarding it as absolutely solid is part of our *method* of doubt and enquiry.'[1] Whatever judgement one passes on Moore's approach, it continues to provoke important questions about the relationship between philosophical theorizing about knowledge and the seemingly unshakeable everyday beliefs which we all share.

In what follows I have merely tried to state, one by one, some of the most important points in which my philosophical position differs from positions which have been taken up by *some* other philosophers... I am going to begin by enunciating, under the heading (1), a whole long list of propositions, which may seem, at first sight, such obvious truisms as not to be worth stating: they are, in fact, a set of propositions, every one of which (in my own opinion) I *know*, with certainty, to be true...

   (1) The propositions to be included in this list are the following. There exists at present a living human body, which is *my* body. This body was born at a certain time in the past, and has existed continuously ever since, though not without undergoing changes; it was, for instance, much smaller when it was born, and for some time afterwards, than it is now. Ever since it was born, it has been either in contact with or

[1] Ludwig Wittgenstein, *On Certainty* [*Über Gewissheit*] (Oxford: Blackwell, 1977), §§ 94, 105, 150.

not far from the surface of the earth; and, at every moment since it was born, there have also existed many other things, having shape and size in three dimensions (in the same familiar sense in which it has), from which it has been *at various distances* (in the familiar sense in which it is now at a distance both from that mantelpiece and from that bookcase, and at a greater distance from the bookcase than it is from the mantelpiece); also there have (very often, at all events) existed some other things of this kind with which it was *in contact* (in the familiar sense in which it is now in contact with the pen I am holding in my right hand and with some of the clothes I am wearing). Among the things which have, in this sense, formed part of its environment (i.e., have been either in contact with it, or at *some* distance from it, however *great*) there have, at every moment since its birth, been large numbers of other living human bodies, each of which has like it, (*a*) at some time been born, (*b*) continued to exist from some time after birth, (*c*) been, at every moment of its life after birth, either in contact with or not far from the surface of the earth; and many of these bodies have already died and ceased to exist. But the earth had existed also for many years before my body was born; and for many of these years, also, large numbers of human bodies had, at every moment, been alive upon it; and many of these bodies had died and ceased to exist before it was born. Finally (to come to a different class of propositions), I am a human being, and I have, at different times since my body was born, had many different experiences, of each of many different kinds: e.g., I have often perceived both my own body and other things which formed part of its environment, including other human bodies; I have not only perceived things of this kind, but have also observed facts about them, such as, for instance, the fact, which I am now observing, that that mantelpiece is at present nearer to my body than that bookcase; I have been aware of other facts, which I was not at the time observing, such as, for instance, the fact, of which I am now aware, that my body existed yesterday and was then also for some time nearer to that mantelpiece than to that bookcase; I have had expectations with regard to the future, and many beliefs of other kinds, both true and false; I have thought of imaginary things and persons and incidents, in the reality of which I did not believe; I have had dreams; and I have had feelings of many different kinds. And, just as my body has been the body of a human being, namely myself, who has, during his lifetime, had many experiences of each of these (and other) different kinds; so, in the case of very many of the other human bodies which have lived upon the earth, each has been the body of a different human being, who has, during the lifetime of that body, had many different experiences of each of these (and other) different kinds.

(2) I now come to [a] single truism which, as will be seen, could not be stated except by reference to the whole list of truisms, just given in (1). This truism also (in my own opinion) I *know*, with certainty, to be true; and it is as follows: ... Each of us (meaning by 'us', very many human beings of the class defined) has frequently *known*, with regard to himself or *his* body and the time at which he knew it, everything which, in writing down my list of propositions in (1), I was claiming to know about myself or my body and the time at which I wrote that proposition down ... Just as *I* knew (when I wrote it down) 'There exists at present a living human body which is my body', so each of us has frequently known with regard to himself at some other time the different but corresponding proposition, which *he* could *then* have properly expressed by, 'There exists *at present* a human body which is my body'; ... and so on, in the case of *each* of the propositions enumerated in (1) ...

In what I have just said, I have assumed that there is some meaning which is *the* ordinary or popular meaning of such expressions as 'The earth has existed for many years past'. And this, I am afraid, is an assumption which some philosophers are capable of disputing. They seem to think that the question 'Do you believe that the earth has existed for many years past?' is not a plain question, such as should be met either by a plain 'Yes' or 'No', or by a plain 'I can't make up my mind', but is the sort of question which can be properly met by: 'It all depends on what you mean by "the earth" and "exists" and "years"'... It seems to me that such a view is as profoundly mistaken as any view can be. Such an expression as 'The earth has existed for many years past' is the very type of an unambiguous expression, the meaning of which we all understand. Anyone who takes a contrary view must, I suppose, be confusing the question whether we understand its meaning (which we all certainly do) with the entirely different question whether we *know what it means*, in the sense that we are able to *give a correct analysis* of its meaning. The question what is the correct analysis of *the* proposition meant *on any occasion*... by 'The earth has existed for many years past' is, it seems to me, a profoundly difficult question, and one to which, as I shall presently urge, no one knows the answer. But to hold that we do not know what, in certain respects, is the analysis of what we understand by such an expression, is an entirely different thing from holding that we do not understand the expression. It is obvious that we cannot even raise the question how what we do understand by it is to be analysed, unless we do understand it. So soon, therefore, as we know that a person who uses such an expression is using it in its ordinary sense, we understand his meaning. So that in explaining that I was using the expressions used in (1) in their ordinary sense (those of them which have an ordinary sense, which is not the case with quite all of them), I have done all that is required to make my meaning clear.

But now, assuming that the expressions which I have used to express (2) are understood, I think, as I have said, that many philosophers have really held views incompatible with (2). And the philosophers who have done so may, I think, be divided into two main groups [A and B respectively]...

A. ... Some philosophers, belonging to this group, have held that no propositions belonging to *any* of the classes in (2) are wholly true, while others have only held this with regard to *some* of the classes in (2)... All such views, whether incompatible with *all* of the propositions in (1), or only with *some* of them, seem to me to be quite certainly false; and I think the following points are specially deserving of notice with regard to them.

(*a*) If *any* of the classes of propositions in (2) is such that no proposition of that class is true, then no philosopher has ever existed, and therefore none can ever have held with regard to any such class, that no proposition belonging to it is true. In other words, the proposition that some propositions belonging to each of these classes are true is a proposition which has the peculiarity, that, if any philosopher has ever denied it, it follows from the fact that he has denied it, that he must have been wrong in denying it. For when I speak of 'philosophers' I mean, of course (as we all do), exclusively philosophers who have been human beings, with human bodies that have lived upon the earth, and who have at different times had many different experiences. If, therefore, there have been any philosophers, there have been human beings of this class; and if there have been human beings of this class, all the rest of what is asserted in (1) is certainly true too. Any view, therefore, incompatible with the proposition that many propositions corresponding to each of the propositions in (1) are true, can only be true, on the hypothesis that no philosopher has ever held any such view. It follows, therefore, that, in considering whether this proposition is true, I cannot consistently regard the fact that many philosophers, whom I respect, have, to the best of my belief, held views incompatible with it, as having any weight at all against it. Since, if I know that they have held such views, I am, *ipso facto*, knowing that they were mistaken; and, if I have no reason to believe that the proposition in question is true, I have still less reason to believe that they have held views incompatible with it; since I am more certain that they have existed and held *some* views, i.e., that the proposition in question is true, than that they have held any views incompatible with it.

(*b*) It is, of course, the case that all philosophers who have held such views have repeatedly, even in their philosophical works, expressed other views inconsistent with them: i.e., no philosopher has ever been able to hold such views consistently. One way in which they have betrayed this inconsistency, is by alluding to the existence of other philosophers. Another way is by alluding to the existence of the human race, and in particular by using 'we' in the sense in which I have already constantly used it, in which any philosopher who asserts that 'we' do so and so, e.g., that '*we* sometimes believe propositions that are not true', is asserting not only that he himself has done the thing in question, but that *very many other human beings, who have had bodies and lived upon the earth*, have done the same. The fact is, of course, that all philosophers have belonged to the class of human beings which exists only if (2) be true: that is to say, to the class of human beings who have frequently *known* propositions corresponding to each of the propositions in (1). In holding views incompatible with the proposition that propositions of all these classes are true, they have, therefore, been holding views inconsistent with propositions which they themselves *knew* to be true; and it was, therefore, only to be expected that they should sometimes betray their knowledge of such propositions. The strange thing is that philosophers should have been able to hold sincerely, as part of their philosophical creed, propositions inconsistent with what they themselves *knew* to be true; and yet, so far as I can make out, this has really frequently happened...

B. This view, which is usually considered a much more modest view than A, has, I think, the defect that, unlike A, it really is self-contradictory, i.e., entails both of two mutually incompatible propositions. Most philosophers who have held this view, have held, I think, that though each of us knows propositions corresponding to *some* of the propositions in (1), namely to those which merely assert that I myself have had in the past experiences of certain kinds at many different times, yet none of us knows *for certain* any propositions either of the type which assert the existence of *material things* or of the type which assert the existence of *other* selves, beside myself, and that *they* also have had experiences. They admit that we do in fact *believe* propositions of both these types, and that they *may* be true: some would even say that we know them to be highly probable; but they deny that we ever know them, *for certain*, to be true. Some of them have spoken of such beliefs as 'beliefs of Common Sense', expressing thereby their conviction that beliefs of this kind are very commonly entertained by mankind: but they are convinced that these things are, in all cases, only *believed*, not known for certain; and some have expressed this by saying that they are matters of Faith, not of Knowledge.

Now the remarkable thing which those who take this view have not, I think, in general duly appreciated, is that, in each case, the philosopher who takes it is making an assertion about 'us' – that is to say, not merely about himself, but about *many other human beings as well*. When he says 'No human being has ever *known* of the existence of other human beings', he is saying: 'There have been many other human beings beside myself, and none of them (including myself) has ever known the existence of other human beings'. If he says: 'These beliefs are beliefs of Common Sense, but they are not matters of *knowledge*', he is saying: 'There have been many other human beings, beside myself, who have shared these beliefs, but neither I nor any of the rest have ever known them to be true'. In other words, he asserts with confidence that these beliefs *are* beliefs of Common Sense, and seems often to fail to notice that, *if* they are, they must be true; since the proposition that they are beliefs of Common Sense . . . logically entails the proposition that many human beings, beside the philosopher himself, have had human bodies, which lived upon the earth, and have had various experiences, including beliefs of this kind. This is why this position, as contrasted with positions of group A, seems to me to be self-contradictory. Its difference from A consists in the fact that it is making a proposition about *human knowledge* in general, and therefore is actually asserting the existence of many human beings, whereas philosophers of group A in stating their position are not doing this: they are only contradicting *other* things which they hold. It is true that a philosopher who says 'There have existed many human beings beside myself, and none of us has ever known the existence of any human beings beside himself', is only contradicting himself if what he holds is 'There have *certainly* existed many human beings beside myself' or, in other words, 'I know that there have existed other human beings beside myself'. But this, it seems to me, is what such philosophers have in fact been generally doing. They seem to me constantly to betray the fact that they regard the proposition that those beliefs *are* beliefs of Common Sense, or the proposition that they themselves are not the only members of the human race, as not merely true, but *certainly* true; and *certainly* true it cannot be, unless one member, at least, of the human race, namely themselves, has *known* the very things which that member is declaring that no human being has ever known.

Nevertheless, my position that I *know*, with certainty, to be true all of the propositions in (1), is certainly not a position, the denial of which entails both of two incompatible propositions. If I do *know* all these propositions to be true, then, I think, it is quite certain that other human beings also have known corresponding propositions: that is to say (2) also is true, and I know it to be true. But do I really *know* all the propositions in (1) to be true? Isn't it possible that I merely believe them? Or know them to be highly probable? In answer to this question, I think I have nothing better to say than that it seems to me that I *do* know them, with certainty. It is, indeed, obvious that, in the case of most of them, I do not know them *directly*: that is to say, I only know them because, in the past, I have known to be true *other* propositions which were evidence for them. If, for instance, I do know that the earth had existed for many years before I was born, I certainly only know this because I have known other things in the past which were evidence for it. And I certainly do not know exactly what the evidence was. Yet all this seems to me to be no good reason for doubting that I do know it. We are all, I think, in this strange position that we do *know* many things, with regard to which we *know* further that we must have had evidence for them, and yet we do not know *how* we know them, i.e., we do not know what the evidence was. If there is any 'we', and if we know that there is, this must be so: for that there is a 'we', is one of the things in question. And that I do know that there is a 'we', that is to say, that many other human beings, with human bodies, have lived upon the earth, it seems to me that I do know, for certain.

If this first point in my philosophical position, namely my belief in (2), is to be given any name, which has actually been used by philosophers in classifying the positions of other philosophers, it would have, I think, to be expressed by saying that I am one of those philosophers who have held that the 'Common Sense view of the world' is, in certain fundamental features, *wholly* true. But it must be remembered that, according to me, all philosophers, without exception, have agreed with me in holding this: and that the real difference, which is commonly expressed in this way, is only a difference between those philosophers, who have *also* held views inconsistent with these features in 'the Common Sense view of the world', and those who have not.

The features in question (namely, propositions of any of the classes defined in defining (2)) are all of them features, which have this peculiar property – namely, that *if we know that they are features in the 'Common Sense view of the world', it follows that they are true*: it is self-contradictory to maintain that *we* know them to be features in the Common Sense view, and that yet they are not true; since to say that *we* know this, is to say that they are true. And many of them also have the further peculiar property that, *if they are features in the Common Sense view of the world (whether we know this or not), it follows that they are true*, since to say that there is a 'Common Sense view of the world' is to say that they are true. The phrases 'Common Sense view of the world' or 'Common Sense beliefs' (as used by philosophers) are, of course, extraordinarily vague; and, for all I know, there may be many propositions which may be properly called features in 'the Common Sense view of the world' or 'Common Sense beliefs', which are not true, and which deserve to be mentioned with the contempt with which some philosophers speak of 'Common Sense beliefs'. But to speak with contempt of those 'Common Sense beliefs' which I have mentioned is quite certainly the height of absurdity. And there are, of course, enormous numbers of other features in the Common Sense view of the world which, if these are true, are quite certainly true too: e.g., that there have lived upon the surface of the earth not only human beings, but also many different species of plants and animals, etc., etc.

11   Does Empirical Knowledge have a Foundation? Wilfrid Sellars, *The Myth of the Given**

The latter half of the twentieth century saw a resurgence of interest in the problem of the foundations of knowledge, a problem that had figured prominently in the thought of René Des- cartes in the seventeenth century (see extract 4, above). Our next excerpt, from a highly influen- tial paper by the American philosopher Wilfrid Sellars, takes as its target the idea that all our

* First presented as part of a lecture series given at the University of London in 1956, under the title 'The Myth of the Given: Three Lectures on Empiricism and the Philosophy of Mind'. First published in H. Feigl and M. Scriven (eds), *The Foundations of Science and the Concepts of Psychoanalysis*, Minnesota Studies in the Philosophy of Science, vol. 1 (Minneapolis: University of Minnesota Press, 1956).

knowledge must be derived or inferred from certain basic authoritative statements, knowledge of which is 'non-inferential' – that is, these statements are not themselves inferred from any other statements. As paradigms of such supposedly authoritative statements Sellars instances, on the one hand, basic analytic statements such as 'two plus two makes four', and, on the other hand, simple reports of immediate sensory experience, for example 'this is red'. (This follows a long tradition concerning the two fundamental types of proposition on which all our knowledge is supposed to be based; compare for example David Hume, Part II, extract 7, below).

Knowledge, on the model Sellars is about to attack, is like a complex edifice whose whole weight rests ultimately on its foundations. In the case of empirical knowledge, what supposedly makes the foundations secure is that, at the level of basic sensory experience, I am confronted with a datum (e.g. an impression of redness) that directly validates my speech-act when I declare 'this is red'. As Sellars puts it, 'one is committed to a stratum of authoritative nonverbal episodes ("awareness") the authority of which accrues to a superstructure of *verbal actions*, provided that the expressions occurring in these actions are properly *used*. These self-authenticating episodes would constitute the tortoise on which stands the elephant on which rests the edifice of empirical knowledge...'

It looks deceptively simple: when I see the red apple, there is an experiential datum – a 'given', and it is this that confers authority on my statement 'this is red'.[1] But Sellars acutely argues that under scrutiny this idea – the 'myth of the given' as he calls it – turns out to be highly problematic.

For the correctness of my judgement about this apple's being red depends on a whole network of complex linguistic rules about the standard conditions for the appropriate use of the predicate 'red' (roughly, something counts as red only if it would be called 'red' by a normal English-speaking observer in normal light). So the picture of what is 'given' somehow validating my knowledge in isolation must be wrong. It is, Sellars argues, 'a matter of simple logic, that one couldn't have observational knowledge of *any* fact unless one knew many *other* things as well'.

Sellars's work is part of a reaction against the atomistic models of knowledge found for example in Hume (in the eighteenth century) and in the logical positivists (earlier in the twentieth),[2] in favour of a more 'holistic' or systematic conception (compare Hegel, extract 9 above). It also follows the lead of Wittgenstein in rejecting first-personal accounts of the basis of knowledge, and acknowledging instead its fundamentally social or inter-personal nature.[3] But if the 'myth of the given' is abandoned, are we not left with knowledge as a mere network of interlinked statements, each depending on some other statement, without any direct 'point of contact' with an actual mind-independent reality? One might fear this would leave us with the picture referred to at the close of the extract, of 'a great Hegelian serpent of knowledge with its tail in its mouth (Where does it begin?).' Sellars ends by suggesting, plausibly, that neither of these two models is satisfactory (the 'myth of the given', on the one hand, and the 'serpent' of mere systematic coherence on the other); but exactly how to construct a more adequate model for the human epistemic enterprise is still a matter of fierce philosophical debate.

One of the forms taken by the Myth of the Given is the idea that there is, indeed *must be*, a structure of particular matter of fact such that (*a*) each fact can not only be noninferentially known to be the case, but presupposes no other knowledge either of particular matter of fact, or of general truths; and (*b*) such that the noninferential knowledge of facts belonging to this structure constitutes the ultimate court of appeals for all factual claims – particular and general – about the world. It is

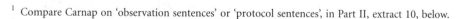

---

[1] Compare Carnap on 'observation sentences' or 'protocol sentences', in Part II, extract 10, below.

[2] Compare Part I, extracts 5 and 7, and Part II, extracts 7 and 10.

[3] See Ludwig Wittgenstein, *Philosophical Investigations* [1953], §§ 243–315. Compare also Part III, extract 2, below.

important to note that I characterized the knowledge of fact belonging to this stratum as not only noninferential, but as presupposing no knowledge of other matter of fact, whether particular or general. It might be thought that this is a redundancy, that knowledge (not belief or conviction, but knowledge) which logically presupposes knowledge of other facts *must* be inferential. This, however, as I hope to show, is itself an episode in the Myth.

Now, the idea of such a privileged stratum of fact is a familiar one, though not without its difficulties. Knowledge pertaining to this level is *noninferential*, yet it is, after all, *knowledge*. It is *ultimate*, yet it has *authority*. The attempt to make a consistent picture of these two requirements has traditionally taken the following form:

> Statements pertaining to this level, in order to 'express knowledge' must not only be made, but, so to speak, must be worthy of being made, *credible*, that is, in the sense of worthy of credence. Furthermore, and this is a crucial point, they must be made in a way which *involves* this credibility. For where there is no connection between the making of a statement and its authority, the assertion may express *conviction*, but it can scarcely be said to express knowledge.

The authority – the credibility – of statements pertaining to this level cannot exhaustively consist in the fact that they are supported by *other* statements, for in that case all *knowledge* pertaining to this level would have to be inferential, which not only contradicts the hypo-thesis, but flies in the face of good sense. The conclusion seems inevitable that if some statements pertaining to this level are to express *noninferential* knowledge, they must have a credibility which is not a matter of being supported by other statements. Now there does seem to be a class of statements which fill at least part of this bill, namely such statements as would be said to *report observations,* thus, 'This is red.' These statements, candidly made, have authority. Yet they are not expressions of inference. How, then, is this authority to be understood?

Clearly, the argument continues, it springs from the fact that they are made in just the circumstances in which they are made, as is indicated by the fact that they characteristically, though not necessarily or without exception, involve those so-called token-reflexive expres-sions which, in addition to the tenses of verbs, serve to connect the circumstances in which a statement is made with its sense...

It would appear, then, that there are two ways in which a sentence token can have credibility: (1) The authority may accrue to it, so to speak, from above, that is, as being a token[1] of a sentence type all the tokens of which, in a certain use, have credibility, e.g. '2 + 2 = 4.' In this case, let us say that token credibility is inherited from type authority. (2) The credibility may accrue to it from the fact that it came to exist in a certain way in a certain set of circumstances, e.g. 'This is red.' Here token credibility is not derived from type credibility.

Now the credibility of *some* sentence types appears to be *intrinsic* – at least in the limited sense that it is not derived from other sentences, type or token. This is, or seems to be, the case with certain sentences used to make analytic statements. The credibility of *some* sentence types accrues to them by virtue of their logical relations to other sentence types, thus by virtue of the fact that they are logical consequences of more basic sentences. It would seem obvious, however, that the credibility of empirical sentence types cannot be traced without remainder to the credibility of other sentence types. And since no empirical sentence type appears to have *intrinsic* credibility, this means that credibility must accrue to *some* empirical sentence types by virtue of their logical relations to certain sentence tokens, and, indeed, to sentence tokens the authority of which is not derived, in its turn, from the authority of sentence types.

The picture we get is that of their being two *ultimate* modes of credibility: (1) The intrinsic credibility of analytic sentences, which accrues to tokens as being tokens of such a type; (2) the credibility of such tokens as 'express observations', a credibility which flows from tokens to types.

---

[1] An instance. Thus each individual dollar bill is a *token* of a certain type of currency of a given value.

Let us explore this picture, which is common to all traditional empiricisms, a bit further. How is the authority of such sentence tokens as 'express observational knowledge' to be understood? It has been tempting to suppose that in spite of the obvious differences which exist between 'observation reports' and 'analytic statements', there is an essential similarity between the ways in which they come by their authority. Thus, it has been claimed, not without plausibility, that whereas *ordinary* empirical statements can be *correctly* made without being true, observation reports resemble analytic statements in that being correctly made is a sufficient as well as necessary condition of their truth. And it has been inferred from this – somewhat hastily, I believe – that 'correctly making' the report 'This is green' is a matter of 'following the rules for the use of "this", "is" and "green"'. Three comments are immediately necessary:

(1) First a brief remark about the term 'report'. In ordinary usage a report is a report made *by* someone *to* someone. To make a report is to *do* something. In the literature of epistemology, however, the word 'report' or '*Konstatierung*'[1] has acquired a technical use in which a sentence token can play a reporting role (*a*) without being an *overt* verbal performance, and (*b*) without having the character of being 'by someone to someone' – even oneself. There is, of course, such a thing as 'talking to oneself'... but, as I shall be emphasizing in the closing stages of my argument, it is important not to suppose that all 'covert' verbal episodes are of this kind.

(2) My second comment is that while *we* shall not assume that because 'reports' *in the ordinary sense* are *actions*, 'reports' in the sense of *Konstatierungen* are also actions, the line of thought we are considering treats them as such. In other words, it interprets the correctness of *Konstatierungen as* analogous to the rightness of actions. Let me emphasize, however, that not all *ought* is *ought to do*, nor all correctness the correctness of *actions*.

(3) My third comment is that if the expression 'following a rule' is taken seriously, and is not weakened beyond all recognition into the bare notion of exhibiting a uniformity – in which case the lightning–thunder sequence would 'follow a rule' – then it is the knowledge or belief that the circumstances are of a certain kind, and not the mere fact that they *are* of this kind, which contributes to bringing about the action.

In the light of these remarks it is clear that if observation reports are construed as *actions*, *if* their correctness is interpreted as the correctness of an *action*, and if the authority of an observation report is construed as the fact that making it is 'following a rule' in the proper sense of this phrase, *then* we are face to face with givenness in its most straightforward form. For these stipulations commit one to the idea that the authority of *Konstatierungen* rests on nonverbal episodes of awareness – awareness that something is the case, e.g. *that this is green* – which nonverbal episodes have an intrinsic authority (they are, so to speak, 'self-authenticating') which the verbal performances (the *Konstatierungen*) properly performed 'express'. One is committed to a stratum of authoritative nonverbal episodes ('awareness') the authority of which accrues to a superstructure of *verbal actions*, provided that the expressions occurring in these actions are properly *used*. These self-authenticating episodes would constitute

---

[1] German term, meaning a declaration or declarative act.

the tortoise on which stands the elephant on which rests the edifice of empirical knowledge...

But what is the alternative? We might begin by trying something like the following: An overt or covert token of 'This is green' in the presence of a green item is a *Konstatierung* and expresses observational knowledge if and only if it is a manifestation of a tendency to produce overt or covert tokens of 'This is green' – given a certain set – if and only if a green object is being looked at in standard conditions. Clearly on this interpretation the occurrence of such tokens of 'This is green' would be 'following a rule' only in the sense that they are instances of a uniformity, a uniformity differing from the lightning–thunder case in that it is an acquired causal characteristic of the language user. Clearly the above suggestion... won't do as it stands. Let us see, however, if it can't be revised to fit the criteria I have been using for 'expressing observational knowledge'...

[We] have seen that to be the expression of knowledge, a report must not only *have* authority, this authority must *in some sense* be recognized by the person whose report it is. And this is a steep hurdle indeed. For if the authority of the report 'This is green' lies in the fact that the existence of green items appropriately related to the perceiver can be inferred from the occurrence of such reports, it follows that only a person who is able to draw this inference, and therefore who has not only the concept *green*, but also the concept of uttering 'This is green' – indeed, the concept of certain conditions of perception, those which would correctly be called 'standard conditions' – could be in a position to token 'This is green' in recognition of its authority. In other words, for a *Konstatierung* 'This is green' to 'express observational knowledge', not only must it be a *symptom or sign* of the presence of a green object in standard conditions, but the perceiver must know that tokens of 'This is green' are symptoms of the presence of green objects in conditions which are standard for visual perception.

Now it might be thought that there is something obviously absurd in the idea that before a token uttered by, say, Jones could be the expression of observational knowledge, Jones would have to know that overt verbal episodes of this kind are reliable indicators of the existence, suitably related to the speaker, of green objects. I do not think that it is. Indeed, I think that something very like it is true. The point I wish to make now, however, is that if it *is* true, then it follows, as a matter of simple logic, that one couldn't have observational knowledge of *any* fact unless one knew many *other* things as well. And let me emphasize that the point is not taken care of by distinguishing between *knowing how* and *knowing that*, and admitting that observational knowledge requires a lot of 'know how'. For the point is specifically that observational knowledge of any particular fact, e.g. that this is green, presupposes that one knows general facts of the form *X is a reliable symptom of Y*. And to admit this requires an abandonment of the traditional empiricist idea that observational knowledge 'stands on its own feet'. Indeed, the suggestion would be anathema to traditional empiricists for the obvious reason that by making observational knowledge *presuppose* knowledge of general facts of the form *X is a reliable symptom of Y*, it runs counter to the idea that we come to know general facts of this form only *after* we have come to know by observation a number of particular facts which support the hypothesis that X is a symptom of Y.

And it might be thought that there is an obvious regress in the view we are examining. Does it not tell us that observational knowledge at time t presupposes knowledge of the form *X is a reliable symptom of Y*, which presupposes prior observational knowledge, which presupposes other knowledge of the form *X is a reliable symptom of Y*, which presupposes still other, and prior, observational knowledge, and so on? This charge, however, rests on too simple, indeed a radically mistaken, conception of what one is saying of Jones when one says that he *knows* that p. It is not just that the objection supposes that knowing is an *episode*; for clearly there are episodes which we can correctly characterize as knowings, in particular, *observings*. The essential point is that in characterizing an episode or a state as that of *knowing*, we are not giving an empirical description of that episode or state; we are placing it in the logical space of reasons, of justifying and being able to justify what one says.

Thus all that the view I am defending requires is that no tokening by S *now* of 'This is green' is to count as 'expressing observational knowledge' unless it is also correct to say of S that he *now* knows the appropriate fact of the form *X is a reliable symptom of Y*, namely that (and again I oversimplify) utterances of 'This is green' are reliable indicators of the presence of green objects in standard conditions of perception. And while the correctness of this statement about Jones requires that Jones could *now* cite prior particular facts as evidence for the idea that these utterances *are* reliable indicators, it requires only that it is correct to say that Jones *now* knows, thus remembers, that these particular facts did obtain. It does not require that it be correct to say that at the time these facts did obtain he *then knew* them to obtain. And the regress disappears...

The idea that observation 'strictly and properly so-called' is constituted by certain self-authenticating nonverbal episodes, the authority of which is transmitted to verbal and quasi-verbal performances when these performances are made 'in conformity with the semantical rules of the language', is, of course, the heart of the Myth of the Given. For the *given*, in epistemological tradition, is what is *taken* by these self-authenticating episodes. These 'takings' are, so to speak, the unmoved movers of empirical knowledge, the 'knowings in presence' which are presupposed by all other knowledge, both the knowledge of general truths and the knowledge 'in absence' of other particular matters of fact. Such is the framework in which traditional empiricism makes its characteristic claim that the perceptually given is the foundation of empirical knowledge.

If I reject the framework of traditional empiricism, it is not because I want to say that empirical knowledge has no foundation. For to put it this way is to suggest that it is really 'empirical knowledge so-called', and to put it in a box with rumours and hoaxes. There is clearly *some* point to the picture of human knowledge as resting on a level of propositions – observation reports – which do not rest on other propositions in the same way as other propositions rest on them. On the other hand, I do wish to insist that the metaphor of 'foundation' is misleading in that it keeps us from seeing that if there is a logical dimension in which other empirical propositions rest on observation reports, there is another logical dimension in which the latter rest on the former.

Above all, the picture is misleading because of its static character. One seems forced to choose between the picture of an elephant which rests on a tortoise (What supports the tortoise?) and the picture of a great Hegelian serpent of knowledge with its tail in its mouth (Where does it begin?). Neither will do. For empirical knowledge, like its sophisticated extension, science, is rational, not because it has *a foundation* but because it is a self-correcting enterprise which can put *any* claim in jeopardy, though not *all* at once.

12   The Conditions for Knowledge: Edmund Gettier, *Is Justified True Belief Knowledge?**

The final extract in our survey of accounts of knowledge in the Western philosophical tradition takes us full circle back to an issue first raised by Plato: what exactly are the conditions that distinguish genuine knowledge from mere belief or opinion? For me to *believe* something, even with utter conviction, is clearly not on its own sufficient for me to count as having knowledge: my belief must, in addition, be *true*. (Thus, countless people used to believe the earth was fixed and immoveable, but since this belief was false, it could never qualify as knowledge.) But the truth of a belief, though necessary, is still not sufficient for its counting as knowledge. I may, being an incurable optimist, believe it will be fine weather for my holiday, and my belief may in fact turn out to be true; but this would not entitle one to say I *knew* it would be fine: knowledge normally requires some *basis* or evidence for its truth (a notion prefigured in Plato's suggestion that knowledge is better than true opinion since it is 'secured by a chain' of reasoning or justification: see introduction to extract 2, above).

The above considerations suggest that a plausible analysis of someone's having knowledge involves three elements: first, their having a belief; second, their belief's being true; and third, their having some reason or justification for their belief. Various more or less elaborate versions of this 'justified true belief' account of knowledge were widely explored by twentieth-century epistemologists, and until the publication of Edmund Gettier's paper the consensus was that

something along these lines was correct. But Gettier's short but ingenious argument destroyed that consensus by producing cases where the knowledge claim fails, despite the three standard conditions being met. A person, argues Gettier, may be justified in a belief (or have good evidence for it, or have the right to be sure about it); and what is more the belief may indeed be true; and yet these conditions are not enough to constitute a case of knowledge.

Gettier's examples (which are concisely set out in the extract below) hinge on somewhat unusual chains of coincidence, where a belief the agent is perfectly justified in holding just happens to be true for reasons unknown to the agent. Nonetheless, his cases provide counterexamples to the standard accounts of knowledge that are extremely difficult to circumvent. In response to the 'Gettier problem', some philosophers have attempted (with disputed success) to revise the standard definition of knowledge (for example, by introducing the idea that to count as knowledge a belief must be *caused* in a certain way by the states of affairs to which it refers); while others have questioned the whole attempt to define knowledge in terms of necessary and sufficient conditions. The debate continues, and illustrates something we shall find many times in the remaining parts of this volume: how complex a task it can be to achieve a clear philosophical understanding of the fundamental concepts we need in order to make sense of reality and our relationship to it.

 Various attempts have been made in recent years to state necessary and sufficient conditions for someone's knowing a given proposition. The attempts have often been such that they can be stated in a form similar to the following:[1]

---

* Originally published in *Analysis*, 23 (1963), pp. 121–3; reprinted with minor changes of layout.

[1] *Plato seems to be considering some such definition at *Theaetetus* 201, and perhaps accepting one at *Meno* 98. [See above, extract 1.]

(a) S knows that P if and only if
    (i)   P is true,
    (ii) S believes that P, and
    (iii) S is justified in believing that P.

For example, Chisholm has held that the following gives the necessary and sufficient conditions for knowledge:[2]

(b) S knows that P if and only if
    (i)   S accepts P,
    (ii) S has adequate evidence for P,
    (iii) P is true.

Ayer has stated the necessary and sufficient conditions for knowledge as follows:[3]

(c) S knows that P if and only if
    (i)   P is true,
    (ii) S is sure that P is true, and
    (iii) S has the right to be sure that P is true.

I shall argue that (a) is false in that the conditions stated therein do not constitute a *sufficient* condition for the truth of the proposition that S knows that P. The same argument will show that (b) and (c) fail if 'has adequate evidence for' or 'has the right to be sure that' is substituted for 'is justified in believing that' throughout.

I shall begin by noting two points. First, in that sense of 'justified' in which S's being justified in believing P is a necessary condition of S's knowing that P, it is possible for a person to be justified in believing a proposition which is in fact false. Second, for any proposition P, if S is justified in believing P, and P entails Q, and S deduces Q from P and accepts Q as a result of this deduction, then S is justified in believing Q. Keeping these two points in mind, I shall now present two cases in which the conditions stated in (a) are true for some proposition, though it is at the same time false that the person in question knows that proposition.

Case 1

Suppose that Smith and Jones have applied for a certain job. And suppose that Smith has strong evidence for the following conjunctive proposition:

(d) Jones is the man who will get the job, and Jones has ten coins in his pocket.

Smith's evidence for (d) might be that the president of the company assured him that Jones would in the end be selected, and that he, Smith, had counted the coins in Jones's pocket ten minutes ago. Proposition (d) entails:

---

[2] *Roderick M. Chisholm, *Perceiving: A Philosophical Study* (Ithaca, NY: Cornell University Press, 1957), p. 16.

[3] *A. J. Ayer, *The Problem of Knowledge* (London: Penguin, 1976).

(*e*) The man who will get the job has ten coins in his pocket.

Let us suppose that Smith sees the entailment from (*d*) to (*e*) and accepts (*e*) on the grounds of (*d*), for which he has strong evidence. In this case, Smith is clearly justified in believing that (*e*) is true.

But imagine, further, that unknown to Smith, he himself, not Jones, will get the job. And, also, unknown to Smith, he himself has ten coins in his pocket. Proposition (*e*) is then true, though proposition (*d*), from which Smith inferred (*e*), is false. In our example, then, all of the following are true:

(i)   (*e*) is true,
(ii) Smith believes that (*e*) is true, and
(iii) Smith is justified in believing that (*e*) is true.

But it is equally clear that Smith does not know that (*e*) is true; for (*e*) is true in virtue of the number of coins in Smith's pocket, while Smith does not know how many coins are in Smith's pocket, and bases his belief in (*e*) on a count of the coins in Jones's pocket, whom he falsely believes to be the man who will get the job.

Case 2

Let us suppose that Smith has strong evidence for the following proposition:

(*f*) Jones owns a Ford

Smith's evidence might be that Jones has at all times in the past within Smith's memory owned a car, and always a Ford, and that Jones has just offered Smith a ride while driving a Ford. Let us imagine, now, that Smith has another friend, Brown, of whose whereabouts he is totally ignorant. Smith selects three place names quite at random and constructs the following three propositions:

(*g*) Either Jones owns a Ford, or Brown is in Boston.
(*h*) Either Jones owns a Ford, or Brown is in Barcelona.
(*j*) Either Jones owns a Ford, or Brown is in Brest-Litovsk.

Each of these propositions is entailed by (*f*). Imagine that Smith realizes the entailment of each of these propositions he has constructed by (*f*), and proceeds to accept (*g*), (*h*) and (*j*) on the basis of (*f*). Smith has correctly inferred (*g*), (*h*) and (*j*) from a proposition for which he has strong evidence. Smith is therefore completely justified in believing each of these three propositions. Smith, of course, has no idea where Brown is.

But imagine now that two further conditions hold. First, Jones does *not* own a Ford, but is at present driving a rented car. And second, by the sheerest coincidence, and entirely unknown to Smith, the place mentioned in proposition (*h*) happens really to be the place where Brown is. If these two conditions hold, then Smith does not know that (*h*) is true, even though

(i) (*h*) *is* true,
(ii) Smith does believe that (*h*) is true, and
(iii) Smith is justified in believing that (*h*) is true.

These two examples show that definition (*a*) does not state a *sufficient* condition for someone's knowing a given proposition. The same cases, with appropriate changes, will suffice to show that neither definition (*b*) nor definition (*c*) do so either.

Specimen Questions

1   Why does Plato maintain, in the *Meno*, that what we call learning is really *recollection*?

2   Explain Plato's contrast, in the *Republic*, between examples of visible beauty and 'the beautiful itself'. Why does he believe true knowledge must relate to the latter, not the former?

3   What does Aristotle mean by 'demonstrative knowledge'? How does he think we grasp the starting-points for such knowledge?

4   What arguments does Descartes use to cast doubt on his previous beliefs? Is he right to claim that the proposition 'I exist' has a special kind of certainty?

5   What are Locke's main arguments against the doctrine of innate knowledge? Do you find them compelling?

6   Why does Leibniz believe that knowledge of the principles of logic and mathematics cannot be derived from experience?

7   Explain Hume's attitude to scepticism, and his reasons for thinking excessive doubt is ultimately pointless.

8   How does Kant's theory of knowledge involve a synthesis of rationalist and empiricist elements?

9   Explain the importance of the idea of a historical process in Hegel's conception of knowledge.

10   Why did G. E. Moore maintain there are a large number of basic truisms which we simply know, and which it is absurd to doubt? Was he correct?

11   What does Sellars mean by the 'myth of the given'? Should it be abandoned?

12   Set out the standard, 'justified true belief' account of knowledge, and explain how Gettier's examples undermine it. Can the standard account be repaired?

Suggestions for Further Reading

A comprehensive reference work containing articles on all the philosophers included in this Part is J. Dancy and E. Sosa (eds), *A Companion to Epistemology* (Oxford: Blackwell, 1993).

Plato

Plato, *Meno*. A modern translation available in paperback is by W. K. C. Guthrie (Harmondsworth: Penguin, 1956).

Plato, *Republic*. Many translations are available, including F. M. Cornford (Oxford: Oxford University Press, 1941) and H. P. D. Lee (Harmondsworth: Penguin, 1955).

General introductions to Plato's thought include J. C. Gosling, *Plato* (London: Routledge, 1973), and A. E. Taylor, *Plato: The Man and his Work* (5th edn, London: Methuen, 1948).

For a stimulating discussion of the interchange between Socrates and Meno, see T. Irwin, *Plato's Ethics* (Oxford: Oxford University Press, 1995), ch. 9.

There is an excellent account of Plato's views on knowledge in J. Annas, *An Introduction to Plato's Republic* (Oxford: Oxford University Press, 1980).

The nature of knowledge is discussed in many other works of Plato, especially the *Theaetetus*. A good starting-point is F. M. Cornford, *Plato's Theory of Knowledge* (London: Routledge, 1960). See also I. M. Crombie, *An Examination of Plato's Doctrines*, vol. II (London: Routledge, 1963); N. P. White, *Plato on Knowledge and Reality* (Indianapolis: Hackett, 1976); R. Kraut (ed.), *The Cambridge Companion to Plato* (Cambridge: Cambridge University Press, 1991), esp. chs 6, 9.

Aristotle

Aristotle, *Posterior Analytics*. There is a version of the complete text translated and edited by J. Barnes (Oxford: Clarendon, 1975).

An excellent introduction to Aristotle's thought, including numerous extracts from key texts, is J. L. Ackrill, *Aristotle the Philosopher* (Oxford: Oxford University Press, 1981).

See also D. J. Allen, *The Philosophy of Aristotle* (Oxford: Oxford University Press, 1952); J. Barnes, *Aristotle* (Oxford: Oxford University Press, 1982); W. D. Ross, *Aristotle* (London: Methuen, 1949).

For a more detailed study of Aristotle's views on knowledge, see C. C. W. Taylor, 'Aristotle's Epistemology', in S. Everson (ed.), *Epistemology* (Cambridge: Cambridge University Press, 1990).

See also J. Barnes, M. Schofield and R. Sorabji (eds), *Articles on Aristotle* (London: Duckworth, 1975–9), vols 1 and 4; J. Barnes (ed.), *The Cambridge Companion to Aristotle* (Cambridge: Cambridge University Press, 1995).

Descartes

Descartes, René, *Meditations on First Philosophy* [*Meditationes de prima philosophia*, 1641], trans. J. Cottingham (Cambridge: Cambridge University Press, 1986; rev. edn 1996).

A general introduction to Descartes's philosophy is J. Cottingham, *Descartes* (Oxford: Blackwell, 1986).

See also A. Kenny, *Descartes* (New York: Random House, 1968); B. Williams, *Descartes: The Project of Pure Inquiry* (Harmondsworth: Penguin, 1979); M. Wilson, *Descartes* (London: Routledge, 1978).

For a more detailed discussion of some of Descartes's views on knowledge, see E. M. Curley, *Descartes against the Sceptics* (Oxford: Blackwell, 1978). A collection of essays on these and other aspects of Descartes's philosophy is J. Cottingham (ed.), *The Cambridge Companion to Descartes* (Cambridge: Cambridge University Press, 1993).

Locke

Locke, John, *An Essay concerning Human Understanding* [1689], ed. P. H. Nidditch (Oxford: Clarendon, 1975).

An excellent introduction to Locke's philosophy is E. J. Lowe, *Locke* (London: Routledge, 2005); also recommended is R. S. Woolhouse, *Locke* (Brighton: Harvester, 1983).

See also R. I. Aaron, *John Locke* (3rd edn, Oxford: Clarendon, 1971); J. D. Mabbott, *John Locke* (London: Macmillan, 1973).

See also the valuable collection of essays in I. Tipton (ed.), *Locke and Human Understanding* (Oxford: Oxford University Press, 1977).

An influential critical study of Locke and other 'empiricist' philosophers is J. Bennett, *Locke, Berkeley, Hume* (Oxford: Oxford University Press, 1971).

Leibniz

Leibniz, G. F. W., *New Essays on Human Understanding* [*Nouveaux essais sur l'entendement humain, c.*1704; first pub. 1765], ed. and trans. P. Remnant and J. Bennett (Cambridge: Cambridge University Press, 1981).

Many of Leibniz's other important works are translated in Leibniz, *Philosophical Writings*, ed. G. H. R. Parkinson (rev. edn, London: Dent, 1973). See also G. W. Leibniz, *Philosophical Texts*, ed. R. S. Woolhouse and R. Franks (Oxford: Oxford University Press, 1998), which contains a helpful introduction for students.

A useful introduction is N. Rescher, *The Philosophy of Leibniz* (Englewood Cliffs, NJ: Prentice-Hall, 1968).

See also C. D. Broad, *Leibniz: An Introduction*, ed. C. Lewy (rev. edn, Cambridge: Cambridge University Press, 1975).

For a general account of the philosophy of Leibniz and other 'rationalist' thinkers, see J. Cottingham, *The Rationalists* (Oxford: Oxford University Press, 1988).

For a valuable account of the Locke–Leibniz debate, see N. Jolley, *Leibniz and Locke: A Study of the New Essays* (Oxford: Oxford University Press, 1984).

Hume

Hume, D., *An Enquiry concerning Human Understanding* [1748], ed. Tom L. Beauchamp (Oxford: Oxford University Press, 1999).

A clear basic introduction to Hume's thought is D. Macnabb, *David Hume* (2nd edn, Oxford: Blackwell, 1966).

See also T. Penelhum, *Hume* (New York: St Martin's, 1975); N. Kemp Smith, *The Philosophy of David Hume* (London: Macmillan, 1941).

For a more detailed account of the Humean philosophy see B. Stroud, *Hume* (London: Routledge, 1977); D. Pears, *Hume's System* (Oxford: Oxford University Press, 1990).

See also D. F. Norton (ed.), *The Cambridge Companion to Hume* (Cambridge: Cambridge University Press, 1994), chs 1 and 4.

Kant

Kant, I., *Critique of Pure Reason* [1781; 2nd edn 1787], trans. N. Kemp Smith (New York: St Martin's, 1986).

For a sound summary of Kant's arguments see R. Scruton, *Kant* (Oxford: Oxford University Press, 1982).

For a general introductory survey of the philosophical tradition to which Kant belongs, see J. Cottingham, *Rationalism* (London: Granada, 1984).

For detailed analysis and criticism of Kant's arguments see R. C. S. Walker, *Kant* (London: Routledge, 1978); J. F. Bennett, *Kant's Analytic* (Cambridge: Cambridge University Press, 1966); P. F. Strawson, *The Bounds of Sense* (London: Methuen, 1966); P. Guyer, *Kant and the Claims of Knowledge* (Cambridge: Cambridge University Press, 1987).

A valuable collection of essays is P. Guyer (ed.), *The Cambridge Companion to Kant* (Cambridge: Cambridge University Press, 1992). See esp. introduction and ch. 2.

Hegel

Hegel, G. W. F., *The Phenomenology of Mind* [1807], trans. J. B. Baillie (London: Sonnenschein, 1910). A more recent version is available in paperback as Hegel, *The Phenomenology of Spirit*, trans. A. V. Miller (Oxford: Clarendon, 1977).

For a clear and accessible introduction to this difficult work, see R. Norman, *Hegel's Phenomenology* (London: Sussex University Press, 1976).

A valuable and influential account of Hegel's thought is C. Taylor, *Hegel* (Cambridge: Cambridge University Press, 1975).

For a useful collection of essays on all aspects of Hegel's philosophy, see F. C. Beiser (ed.), *The Cambridge Companion to Hegel* (Cambridge: Cambridge University Press, 1993). See esp. ch. 2 (by R. Pippin, on the structure of the *Phenomenology of Spirit*) and ch. 5 (by M. Forster, on Hegel's dialectic).

Moore

Moore, G. E., 'A Defence of Common Sense' [1925], in G. H. Muirhead (ed.), *Contemporary British Philosophy*, 2nd series (London: Allen & Unwin, 1925). Reprinted with other important essays in G. E. Moore, *Selected Writings*, ed. T. Baldwin (London: Routledge, 1993).

A valuable critical study of Moore is T. Baldwin, *G. E. Moore* (London: Routledge, 1990).

See also B. Stroud, *The Significance of Philosophical Scepticism* (Oxford: Clarendon, 1984); L. Wittgenstein, *On Certainty* (Oxford: Blackwell, 1969); A. Stroll, *Moore and Wittgenstein on Certainty* (Oxford: Oxford University Press, 1994).

Sellars

The full text of Sellars's paper may be found in his *Science, Perception and Reality* (London: Routledge, 1963).

A concise introduction to the problems of 'foundationalism' is the article so entitled by William Alston in Dancy and Sosa (eds), *A Companion to Epistemology*.

For a detailed treatment of many of the issues, see L. Bonjour, *The Structure of Empirical Knowledge* (Cambridge, Mass.: Harvard University Press, 1985).

For some brilliant (but quite complex) reflections on some of the issues raised by Sellars's paper, see John McDowell, *Mind and World* (Cambridge, Mass.: Harvard University Press, 1994).

Gettier

A useful exposition of the 'Gettier problem' is Paul Moser's article so entitled in Dancy and Sosa (eds), *A Companion to Epistemology*.

Moser's own solution, developing a fourth condition for knowledge (knowledge is justified true belief *sustained by the collective totality of truths*) appears in his *Knowledge and Evidence* (Cambridge: Cambridge University Press, 1989).

For a different but related approach, see D. M. Armstrong, *Belief, Truth and Knowledge* (Cambridge: Cambridge University Press, 1973).

For a 'causal' approach, focusing on the way knowledge is produced, see A. I. Goldman, *Epistemology and Cognition* (Cambridge, MA: Harvard University Press, 1986). For the idea that to count as knowledge a belief must 'track the truth', see R. Nozick, *Philosophical Explanations* (Oxford: Clarendon, 1981).

PART II
Being and Reality

Being and Reality
Introduction

One of the oldest aspirations of philosophy has been to inquire into the ultimate nature of reality. The phrase sounds impressive enough, but what does it mean? Nowadays most people would say that investigating what there is, or what the world is like, is the job of the scientist, not the philosopher. But in earlier times the two roles were not clearly separated. When the writers of the Middle Ages described Aristotle as a philosopher (indeed he was known as *The* Philosopher), they were thinking partly of his accounts of the natural world, his physics, biology and so on. But Aristotle also aimed to investigate the nature of 'being *qua* being', or being as such; he wanted to analyse the basic notions that are involved in our understanding of the world. The book in which he presents this idea of a general study of being is called the *Metaphysics*. The term originally derives from the position to which the book was assigned by early Greek editors of Aristotle, who placed it *after* his various writings on physics (in Greek *meta ta physica*, 'after the physics'). But since the Greek preposition *meta* can also mean 'beyond', the term 'metaphysics' came to be used as an apt label for philosophical inquiry that goes *beyond* the particular sciences and asks very general questions about the nature of reality and the ultimate conceptual categories in terms of which we are to understand it. The history of metaphysics is the history of various fundamental theories about 'ontology' or being, and it is some of the most influential of these theories that form the subject matter of this part of the volume.

1 The Allegory of the Cave: Plato, *Republic* *

Though the systematic study of metaphysics was inaugurated by Aristotle, metaphysical theorizing did not begin with him. A variety of different theories about the ultimate nature of the world had been developed by those earlier Greek philosophers known as the 'Presocratics'; and Aristotle's own teacher, Plato, was famous for his theory of Forms, an account of a realm of abstract reality to be apprehended by the intellect – a realm 'above and beyond' the ordinary world of particular objects that we perceive by the senses. Plato's metaphysics is intimately linked to his theory of knowledge (see Part I, introduction to extract 2, above); he believed that in order to attain genuine knowledge we need go beyond the changing world of day-to-day *particulars* and grasp the timeless and unchanging *universals* of which ordinary objects are imperfect instances (thus, a particular beautiful object is only beautiful in a limited and passing way – a mere copy of the Form of Beauty, the 'beautiful itself').

In our first extract, from the *Republic* (written in the early fourth century BC), Plato compares the noblest Form, the Form of the Good, to the sun: just as the sun makes ordinary objects visible, so the Form of the Good is the source of the intelligibility and reality of the Forms. Next, in the simile of the 'Divided Line', Plato suggests that ordinary everyday objects stand in the same relationship to the Forms as shadows do to their originals. And finally, in his famous allegory of the Cave, Plato compares the gradual ascent of the mind towards the Forms with a journey from darkness to light.

Within the cave (the ordinary world of the five senses), most of us are like chained prisoners watching shadows thrown by a fire. We adopt our opinions second-hand, manipulated and controlled by others. But even if we get free and look around the cave for ourselves, we are still only operating within the ordinary visible world, the world of particular objects. We need to struggle upwards, out of the cave, into the higher world of universals, grasped not by the senses but by the intellect. Our eyes dazzled by the brightness, we first can look only at reflections in pools (perhaps corresponding to mathematical objects, which help the mind to move away from particulars and towards abstract universals); but eventually we will be able to turn our eyes to the light of the stars and finally the Sun itself. The heavenly bodies here stand for the Forms, and the Sun represents the ultimate source of truth, the Form of the Good. In the upper world of Plato's parable, we are not dealing with ordinary visible light; illumination comes instead at an intellectual level, from the supreme Form which 'is the controlling source of all reality and understanding'. As always, Plato presents his argument in dialogue form: Socrates (representing Plato's own views) speaks first; the respondent is Glaucon.

Let me remind you of what I have mentioned in the course of this discussion, and at many other times.

What?

The old story, that there are many beautiful and many good things, and so of all the other things which we describe and define – to all of them the term 'many' is applied.

True, he said.

And there is an absolute beauty and an absolute good, and of other things to which the term 'many' is applied there is an absolute; for they can be brought under a single idea which is called the essence of each.

Very true.

The many, as we say, are seen but not known, and the ideas are known but not seen.

* Plato, *Republic* [*Politeia*, c.380 BC], 507b1–517c6. Trans. B. Jowett, in *The Dialogues of Plato* (Oxford: Clarendon, 1892), vol. III, pp. 207–17; with minor modifications.

Exactly.

And what is the organ with which we see the visible things?

The sight, he said.

And with the hearing, I said, we hear, and with the other senses perceive the other objects of sense?

True.

But have you remarked that sight is by far the most costly and complex piece of workmanship which the artificer of the senses ever contrived?

No, I never have, he said.

Then reflect: has the ear or voice need of any third or additional nature in order that the one may be able to hear and the other to be heard?

Nothing of the sort.

No, indeed, I replied; and the same is true of most, if not all, the other senses – you would not say that any of them requires such an addition?

Certainly not.

But you see that without the addition of some other nature there is no seeing or being seen?

How do you mean?

Sight being, as I conceive, in the eyes, and he who has eyes wanting to see; colour being also present in them, still unless there be a third nature specially adapted to the purpose, the owner of the eyes will see nothing and the colours will be invisible.

Of what nature are you speaking?

Of that which you term light, I replied.

True, he said.

Noble, then, is the bond which links together sight and visibility, and great beyond other bonds by no small difference of nature; for light is their bond, and light is no ignoble thing.

Nay, he said, the reverse of ignoble.

And which, I said, of the gods in heaven would you say was the lord of this element? Whose is that light which makes the eye to see perfectly and the visible to appear?

You mean the sun, as you and all mankind say.

May not the relation of sight to this deity be described as follows?

How?

Neither sight nor the eye in which sight resides is the sun?

No.

Yet of all the organs of sense the eye is the most like the sun?

By far the most like.

And the power which the eye possesses is a sort of effluence which is dispensed from the sun?

Exactly.

Then the sun is not sight, but the author of sight who is recognized by sight?

True, he said.

And this is he whom I call the child of the good, whom the good begat in his own likeness, to be in the visible world, in relation to sight and the things of sight, what the good is in the intellectual world in relation to mind and the things of mind?

Will you be a little more explicit? he said.

Why, you know, I said, that the eyes, when a person directs them towards objects on which the light of day is no longer shining, but the moon and stars only, see dimly, and are nearly blind; they seem to have no clearness of vision in them?

Very true.

But when they are directed towards objects on which the visible sun shines, they see clearly and there is sight in them?

Certainly.

And the soul is like the eye: when resting upon that on which truth and being shine, the soul perceives and understands, and is radiant with intelligence; but when turned towards the twilight of becoming and perishing, then she has opinion only, and goes blinking about, and is first of one opinion and then of another, and seems to have no intelligence?

Just so.

Now, that which imparts truth to the known and the power of knowing to the knower is what I would have you term the idea of good, and this you will deem to be the cause of science, and of truth in so far as the latter becomes the subject of knowledge; beautiful too, as are both truth and knowledge, you will be right in esteeming this other nature as more beautiful than either; and, as in the previous instance, light and sight may be truly said to be like the sun, and yet not to be the sun, so in this other sphere, science and truth may be deemed to be like the good, but not the good; the good has a place of honour yet higher.

What a wonder of beauty that must be, he said, which is the author of science and truth, and yet surpasses them in beauty; for you surely cannot mean to say that pleasure is the good?

God forbid, I replied; but may I ask you to consider the image in another point of view?

In what point of view?

You would say, would you not, that the sun is not only the author of visibility in all visible things, but of generation and nourishment and growth, though he himself is not generation?

Certainly.

In like manner the good may be said to be not only the author of knowledge to all things known, but of their being and essence, and yet the good is not essence, but far exceeds essence in dignity and power.

Glaucon said, with a ludicrous earnestness: By the light of heaven, how amazing!

Yes, I said, and the exaggeration may be set down to you; for you made me utter my fancies.

And pray continue to utter them; at any rate let us hear if there is anything more to be said about the similitude of the sun.

Yes, I said, there is a great deal more.

Then omit nothing, however slight.

I will do my best, I said; but I should think that a great deal will have to be omitted.

I hope not, he said.

You have to imagine, then, that there are two ruling powers, and that one of them is set over the intellectual world, the other over the visible ... May I suppose that you have this distinction of the visible and intelligible fixed in your mind?

I have.

Now take a line which has been cut into two unequal parts, and divide each of them again in the same proportion, and suppose the two main divisions to answer, one to the visible and the other to the intelligible, and then compare the subdivisions in respect of their clearness and want of clearness, and you will find that the first section in the realm of the visible consists of images. And by images I mean, in the first place, shadows, and in the second place, reflections in water and in solid, smooth and polished bodies and the like: Do you understand?

Yes, I understand.

Imagine, now, the other section, of which this is only the resemblance, to include the animals which we see, and everything that grows or is made.

Very good.

Would you not admit that both the sections of this division have different degrees of truth, and that the copy is to the original as the realm of opinion is to the realm of knowledge?

Most undoubtedly.

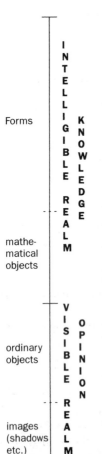

Next proceed to consider the manner in which the realm of the intellectual is to be divided.

In what manner?

Thus: – There are two subdivisions, in the lower of which the soul uses the figures given by the former division as images; the enquiry can only be hypothetical, and instead of going upwards to a principle descends to the other end; in the higher of the two, the soul passes out of hypotheses, and goes up to a principle which is above hypotheses, making no use of images as in the former case, but proceeding only in and through the ideas themselves.

I do not quite understand your meaning, he said.

Then I will try again; you will understand me better when I have made some preliminary remarks. You are aware that students of geometry, arithmetic, and the kindred sciences assume the odd and the even and the figures and three kinds of angles and the like in their several branches of science; these are their hypotheses, which they and everybody are supposed to know, and therefore they do not deign to give any account of them either to themselves or others; but they begin with them, and go on until they arrive at last, and in a consistent manner, at their conclusion?

Yes, he said, I know.

And do you not know also that although they make use of the visible forms and reason about them, they are thinking not of these, but of the ideals which they resemble; not of the figures which they draw, but of the absolute square and the absolute diameter, and so on – the forms which they draw or make, and which have shadows and reflections in water of their own, are converted by them into images, but they are really seeking to behold the things themselves, which can only be seen with the eye of the mind?

That is true.

And of this kind I spoke as the intelligible, although in the search after it the soul is compelled to use hypotheses; not ascending to a first principle, because she is unable to rise above the region of hypothesis, but employing the objects of which the shadows below are resemblances in their turn as images, they having in relation to the shadows and reflections of them a greater distinctness, and therefore a higher value.

I understand, he said, that you are speaking of the province of geometry and the sister arts.

And when I speak of the other division of the intelligible, you will understand me to speak of that other sort of knowledge which reason herself attains by the power of dialectic, using the hypotheses not as first principles, but only as hypotheses – that is to say, as steps and points of departure into a world which is above hypotheses, in order that she may soar beyond them to the first principle of the whole; and clinging to this and then to that which depends on this, by successive steps she descends again without the aid of any sensible object, from ideas, through ideas, and in ideas she ends.

I understand you, he replied; not perfectly, for you seem to me to be describing a task which is really tremendous; but, at any rate, I understand you to say that knowledge and being, which the science of dialectic contemplates, are clearer than the notions of the arts, as they are termed, which proceed from hypotheses only: these are also contemplated by the understanding, and not by the senses: yet, because they start from hypotheses and do not ascend to a principle, those who contemplate them appear to you not to exercise the higher reason upon them, although when a first principle is added to them they are cognizable by the higher reason. And the habit which is concerned with geometry and the cognate sciences I suppose that you would term understanding and not reason, as being intermediate between opinion and reason.

You have quite conceived my meaning, I said; and now, corresponding to these four divisions, let there be four faculties in the soul – reason answering to the highest, understanding to the second, faith (or conviction) to the third, and perception of shadows to the last – and let there be a scale of them, and let us suppose that the several faculties have clearness in the same degree that their objects have truth.

I understand, he replied, and give my assent, and accept your arrangement.

And now, I said, let me show in a figure how far our nature is enlightened or unenlightened. Behold! human beings living in an underground cave, which has a mouth open towards the light and reaching all along the cave; here they have been from their childhood, and have their legs and necks chained so that they cannot move, and can only see before them, being prevented by the chains from turning round their heads. Above and behind them a fire is blazing at a distance, and between the fire and the prisoners there is a raised way; and you will see, if you look, a low wall built along the way, like the screen which marionette players have in front of them, over which they show the puppets.

I see.

And do you see, I said, men passing along the wall carrying all sorts of vessels, and statues and figures of animals made of wood and stone and various materials, which appear over the wall? Some of them are talking, others silent.

You have shown me a strange image, and they are strange prisoners.

Like ourselves, I replied; and they see only their own shadows, or the shadows of one another, which the fire throws on the opposite wall of the cave?

True, he said; how could they see anything but the shadows if they were never allowed to move their heads?

And of the objects which are being carried in like manner they would only see the shadows?

Yes, he said.

And if they were able to converse with one another, would they not suppose that they were naming what was actually before them?

Very true.

And suppose further that the prison had an echo which came from the other side, would they not be sure to fancy when one of the passers-by spoke that the voice which they heard came from the passing shadow?

No question, he replied.

To them, I said, the truth would be literally nothing but the shadows of the images.

That is certain.

And now look again, and see what will naturally follow if the prisoners are released and disabused of their error. At first, when any of them is liberated and compelled suddenly to stand up and turn his neck round and walk and look towards the light, he will suffer sharp pains; the glare will distress him, and he will be unable to see the realities of which in his former state he had seen the shadows; and then conceive some one saying to him, that what he saw before was an illusion, but that now, when he is approaching nearer to being and his eye is turned towards more real existence, he has a clearer vision, – what will be his reply? And you may further imagine that his instructor is pointing to the objects as they pass and requiring him to name them, – will he not be perplexed? Will he not fancy that the shadows which he formerly saw are truer than the objects which are now shown to him?

Far truer.

And if he is compelled to look straight at the light, will he not have a pain in his eyes which will make him turn away to take refuge in the objects of vision which he can see, and which he will conceive to be in reality clearer than the things which are now being shown to him?

True, he said.

And suppose once more, that he is reluctantly dragged up a steep and rugged ascent, and held fast until he is forced into the presence of the sun himself, is he not likely to be pained and irritated? When he approaches the light his eyes will be dazzled, and he will not be able to see anything at all of what are now called realities.

Not all in a moment, he said.

He will require to grow accustomed to the sight of the upper world. And first he will see the shadows best, next the reflections of men and other objects in the water, and then the objects themselves; then he will gaze upon the light of the moon and the stars and the spangled heaven and he will see the sky and the stars by night better than the sun or the light of the sun by day?

Certainly.

Last of all he will be able to see the sun, and not mere reflections of him in the water, but he will see him in his own proper place, and not in another; and he will contemplate him as he is.

Certainly.

He will then proceed to argue that this is he who gives the season and the years, and is the guardian of all that is in the visible world, and in a certain way the cause of all things which he and his fellows have been accustomed to behold?

Clearly, he said, he would first see the sun and then reason about him.

And when he remembered his old habitation, and the wisdom of the cave and his fellow prisoners, do you not suppose that he would felicitate himself on the change, and pity them?

Certainly, he would.

And if they were in the habit of conferring honours among themselves on those who were quickest to observe the passing shadows and to remark which of them went before, and which followed after, and which were together; and who were therefore best able to draw conclusions as to the future, do you think that he would care for such honours and glories, or envy the possessors of them? Would he not say with Homer, 'Better to be the poor servant of a poor master', and to endure anything, rather than think as they do and live after their manner?

Yes, he said, I think that he would rather suffer anything than entertain these false notions and live in this miserable manner.

Imagine once more, I said, such a one coming suddenly out of the sun to be replaced in his old situation; would he not be certain to have his eyes full of darkness?

To be sure, he said.

And if there were a contest, and he had to compete in measuring the shadows with the prisoners who had never moved out of the cave, while his sight was still weak, and before his eyes had become steady (and the time which would be needed to acquire this new habit of sight might be very considerable), would he not be ridiculous? Men would say of him that up he went and down he came without his eyes; and that it was better not even to think of ascending; and if any one tried to loose another and lead him up to the light, let them only catch the offender, and they would put him to death.

No question, he said.

This entire allegory, I said, you may now append, dear Glaucon, to the previous argument; the prison-house is the world of sight, the light of the fire is the sun, and you will not misapprehend me if you interpret the journey upwards to be the ascent of the soul into the intellectual world according to my poor belief, which, at your desire, I have expressed – whether rightly or wrongly God knows. But, whether true or false, my opinion is that in the world of knowledge the idea of good appears last of all, and is seen only with an effort; and, when seen, is also inferred to be the universal author of all things beautiful and right, parent of light and of the lord of light in this visible world, and the immediate source of reason and truth in the intellectual; and that this is the power upon which he who would act rationally either in public or private life must have his eye fixed.

I agree, he said, as far as I am able to understand you.

2   Individual Substance: Aristotle, *Categories**

Aristotle's approach to the nature of reality is more robustly down-to-earth than Plato's. He accepts the need to identify something stable and enduring in a world of constant change; but he rejects the notion of universal Forms or essences in the Platonic sense of items with a reality of their own distinct from particular instances of things. For Aristotle, the ultimate units of being are individual substances – for example a particular man, or a particular horse.

Aristotle arrives at this view by linking the concept of a substance with the grammatical notion of a *subject*. In the sentence 'Bucephalus is strong', Bucephalus (the famous war-horse of Alexander the Great) is the subject, and 'strong' the predicate: we may say that strength is *predicated* of the subject; the quality of strength is to be found in this horse. The subject, Bucephalus, by contrast, exists in its own right: it does not have to exist *in* something else.

In the extract that follows, Aristotle points out that 'a substance, numerically one and the same, is able to receive contraries. For example, an individual man, one and the same, becomes pale at one time and dark at another.' Of course, not *all* the properties of an individual can change: if a horse sprouted horns and chewed the cud it would cease to be a horse altogether. So in addition to the *accidental* or contingent properties (like being fat, or healthy, or fast or lame) that may change from day to day, or year to year, substances have *essential* characteristics which make them the kinds of thing they are. But these universal essences, for Aristotle, have no independent reality in their own right: they simply exist *in* the particular substances of which they are instances. So while Plato puts universals higher in the order of being (particular horses are but pale copies of the Form of Horse), Aristotle reverses the order: it is individual substances (like a particular horse) that exist independently; equine properties or 'predicates' (for example, being a quadruped, having a mane, being strong, and so on) cannot exist independently, but only *in* a particular subject.

 A *substance* – that which is called a substance most strictly, primarily and most of all – is that which is neither said of a subject nor in a subject:[1] for example, the individual man, or the individual horse. The species in which the things primarily called substances are, are called *secondary substances*, as also are the genera of these species. For example, the individual man belongs in a species, man, and animal is a genus of the species; so these – both man and animal – are called secondary substances.

It is clear from what has been said that if something is said of a subject both its name and its definition are necessarily predicated of the subject. For example, man is said of a subject, the individual man, and the name is of course predicated (since you will be predicating man of the individual man), and also the definition of man will be predicated of the individual man (since the individual man is also a man). Thus both the name and the definition will be predicated of the subject. But as for things which are in a subject, in most cases neither the name nor the definition is predicated of the subject. In some cases there is nothing to prevent the name from being predicated of the subject, but it is impossible for the definition to be predicated. For example, white,

* Aristotle, *Categories* [*Kategoriai*, *c.*330 BC], ch. 5 (2a11–4b19). Trans. J. L. Ackrill (Oxford: Clarendon, 1963), pp. 5–12.

[1] 'In a subject': in the sentence 'Socrates is bald', the attribute of baldness is *in* the subject (Socrates). 'Said *of* a subject': in the sentence 'Socrates is a man', what is *said of* Socrates is the species to which he belongs. Aristotle is about to argue that the individual subject (e.g. Socrates) is the basic or primary substance. Species and genus (e.g. man, animal) are substances only in a secondary sense, since they would not exist at all if individuals did not exist.

which is in a subject (the body), is predicated of the subject; for a body is called white. But the definition of white will never be predicated of the body.

All the other things are either said of the primary substances as subjects or in them as subjects. This is clear from an examination of cases. For example, animal is predicated of man and therefore also of the individual man; for were it predicated of none of the individual men it would not be predicated of man at all. Again, colour is in body and therefore also in an individual body; for were it not in some individual body it would not be in body at all. Thus all the other things are either said of the primary substances as subjects or in them as subjects. So if the primary substances did not exist it would be impossible for any of the other things to exist.

Of the secondary substances the species is more a substance than the genus, since it is nearer to the primary substance. For if one is to say of the primary substance what it is, it will be more informative and apt to give the species than the genus. For example, it would be more informative to say of the individual man that he is a man than that he is an animal (since the one is more distinctive of the individual man while the other is more general); and more informative to say of the individual tree that it is a tree than that it is a plant. Further, it is because the primary substances are subjects for all the other things and all the other things are predicated of them or are in them, that they are called substances most of all. But as the primary substances stand to the other things, so the species stands to the genus: the species is a subject for the genus (for the genera are predicated of the species but the species are not predicated reciprocally of the genera). Hence for this reason too the species is more a substance than the genus.

But of the species themselves – those which are not genera – one is no more a substance than another: it is no more apt to say of the individual man that he is a man than to say of the individual horse that it is a horse. And similarly of the primary substances one is no more a substance than another: the individual man is no more a substance than the individual ox.

It is reasonable that, after the primary substances, their species and genera should be the only other things called (secondary) substances. For only they, of things predicated, reveal the primary substance. For if one is to say of the individual man what he is, it will be in place to give the species or the genus (though more informative to give man than animal); but to give any of the other things would be out of place – for example, to say 'white' or 'runs' or anything like that. So it is reasonable that these should be the only other things called substances. Further, it is because the primary substances are subjects for everything else that they are called substances most strictly. But as the primary substances stand to everything else, so the species and genera of the primary substances stand to all the rest: all the rest are predicated of these. For if you will call the individual man grammatical it follows that you will call both a man and an animal grammatical; and similarly in other cases.

It is a characteristic common to every substance not to be in a subject. For a primary substance is neither said of a subject nor in a subject. And as for secondary substances, it is obvious at once that they are not in a subject. For man is said of the individual man as subject but is not in a subject: man is not *in* the individual man. Similarly, animal also is said of the individual man as subject but animal is not *in* the individual man. Further, while there is nothing to prevent the name of what is in a subject from being sometimes predicated of the subject, it is impossible for the definition to be predicated. But the definition of the secondary substances, as well as the name, is predicated of the subject: you will predicate the definition of man of the individual man, and also that of animal. No substance, therefore, is in a subject.

This is not, however, peculiar to substance; the differentia also is not in a subject. For footed and two-footed are said of man as subject but are not in a subject; neither two-footed nor footed is *in* man. Moreover, the definition of the differentia is predicated of that of which the differentia is said. For example, if footed is said of man the definition of footed will also be predicated of man; for man is footed.

We need not be disturbed by any fear that we may be forced to say that the parts of a substance, being in a subject (the whole substance), are not substances. For when we spoke of things *in a subject* we did not mean things belonging in something as *parts*.

It is a characteristic of substances and differentiae that all things called from them are so called synonymously. For all the predicates from them are predicated either of the individuals or of the species. (For from a primary substance there is no predicate, since it is said of no subject; and as for secondary substances, the species is predicated of the individual, the genus both of the species and of the individual. Similarly, differentiae too are predicated both of the species and of the individuals.) And the primary substances admit the definition of the species and of the genera, and the species admits that of the genus; for everything said of what is predicated will be said of the subject also. Similarly, both the species and the individuals admit the definition of the differentiae. But synonymous things were precisely those with both the name in common and the same definition. Hence all the things called from substances and differentiae are so called synonymously.

Every substance seems to signify a certain 'this'. As regards the primary substances, it is indisputably true that each of them signifies a certain 'this'; for the thing revealed is individual and numerically one. But as regards the secondary substances, though it appears from the form of the name – when one speaks of man or animal – that a secondary substance likewise signifies a certain 'this', this is not really true; rather, it signifies a certain qualification, for the subject is not, as the primary substance is, one, but man and animal are said of many things.

However, it does not signify simply a certain qualification, as white does. White signifies nothing but a qualification, whereas the species and the genus mark off the qualification of substance – they signify substance of a certain qualification. (One draws a wider boundary with the genus than with the species, for in speaking of animal one takes in more than in speaking of man.)

Another characteristic of substances is that there is nothing contrary to them. For what would be contrary to a primary substance? For example, there is nothing contrary to an individual man, nor yet is there anything contrary to man or to animal. This, however, is not peculiar to substance but holds of many other things also, for example, of quantity. For there is nothing contrary to four foot or to ten or to anything of this kind – unless someone were to say that many is contrary to few or large to small; but still there is nothing contrary to any *definite* quantity.

Substance, it seems, does not admit of a more and a less. I do not mean that one substance is not more a substance than another (we have said that it is), but that any given substance is not called more, or less, that which it is. For example, if this substance is a man, it will not be more a man or less a man either than itself or than another man. For one man is not more a man than another, as one pale thing is more pale than another and one beautiful thing more beautiful than another. Again, a thing is called more, or less, such-and-such than itself; for example, the body that is pale is called more pale now than before, and the one that is hot is called more, or less, hot. Substance, however, is not spoken of thus. For a man is not called more a man now than before, nor is anything else that is a substance. Thus substance does not admit of a more and a less.

It seems most distinctive of substance that what is numerically one and the same is able to receive contraries. In no other case could one bring forward anything, numerically one, which is able to receive contraries. For example, a colour which is numerically one and the same will not be black and white, nor will numerically one and the same action be bad and good; and similarly with everything else that is not substance. A substance, however, numerically one and the same, is able to receive contraries. For example, an individual man – one and the same – becomes pale at one time and dark at another, and hot and cold, and bad and good. Nothing like this is to be seen in any other case.

But perhaps someone might object and say that statements and beliefs are like this. For the same statement seems to be both true and false. Suppose, for example, that the statement that somebody is sitting is true; after he has got up this same statement will be false. Similarly with beliefs. Suppose you believe truly that somebody is sitting; after he has got up you will believe falsely if you hold the same belief about him. However, even if we were to grant this, there is still a difference in the *way* contraries are received. For in the case of substances it is by themselves changing that they are able to receive contraries. For what has become cold instead of hot, or dark instead of pale, or good instead of bad, has changed (has altered); similarly in other cases too it is by itself undergoing change that each thing is able to receive contraries. Statements and beliefs, on the other hand, themselves remain completely unchangeable in every way; it is because the *actual thing* changes that the contrary comes to belong to them. For the statement that somebody is sitting remains the same; it is because of a change in the actual thing that it comes to be true at one time and false at another. Similarly with beliefs. Hence at least the *way* in which it is able to receive contraries – through a change in itself – would be distinctive of substance, even if we were to grant that beliefs and statements are able to receive contraries. However, this is not true. For it is not because they themselves receive anything that statements and beliefs are said to be able to receive contraries, but because of what has happened to something else. For it is because the actual thing exists or does not exist that the statement is said to be true or false, not because it is able itself to receive contraries. No statement or belief is changed at all by anything. So since nothing happens in them, they are not able to receive contraries. A substance, on the other hand, is said to be able to receive contraries, because it itself receives contraries. For it receives sickness and health, and paleness and darkness; and because it itself receives the various things of this kind it is said to be able to receive contraries. It is, therefore, distinctive of substance that what is numerically one and the same is able to receive contraries. This brings to an end our discussion of substance.

3   Supreme Being and Created Things: René Descartes, *Principles of Philosophy* *

The notion of a substance played a key role in the metaphysical thought of the Middle Ages. As we have seen, Aristotle conceived of a substance as an individual subject enduring through change, and having independent existence. In the thirteenth century, the celebrated philosopher and theologian St Thomas Aquinas, taking his cue from Aristotle, defined a substance as an *ens per se existens* – an 'entity existing *through itself*' (independently, or in its own right).[1] But if the idea of an independent being is construed in the strongest possible sense, as something whose existence is entirely self-sufficient, then one might conclude that the term 'substance' should strictly speaking be reserved for God alone (since, according to standard Christian doctrine, He alone is the eternal source of all being, and the existence of everything else is dependent on Him). And this is precisely the line taken several centuries later by René Descartes, at the start of the following extract from the *Principles of Philosophy* (*Principia Philosophiae*, published in Latin in 1644).

God, according to Descartes, is the sole substance in the strict sense; created things can count as substances only in a secondary sense. But in his account of created things, Descartes makes a striking departure from the framework for understanding reality which Aristotle had offered. The Cartesian[2] framework for explaining the physical world offers a radically new 'ontology' – a radically new conception of what there is. As we saw in the previous extract, Aristotle grouped individual substances together as belonging to natural kinds (*species* and *genera*); and among 'scholastic' medieval philosophers (those who followed a broadly Aristotelian approach), a great deal of energy was spent in classifying natural phenomena, and explaining

the way things behaved in terms of the essential characteristics of the natural kind to which they were taken to belong. (The traditional classificatory scheme involved four principal elements, earth, water, air and fire, each made up of different combinations of the four qualities, Cold, Wet, Dry and Hot.) Ushering in the scientific revolution of the seventeenth century, Descartes argues that to understand natural phenomena we need instead to adopt a mathematical approach. What matters for explanation in physics are not differences in 'kind' but a quantitative analysis, expressible in terms of strict mathematical laws. Hence we find, in place of the traditional plurality of individual substances belonging to various natural kinds, just one essential kind of matter: the whole universe is composed of a single 'extended stuff', and all phenomena are to be explained quantitatively, in terms of the size, shape and motion of its particles.

Descartes's account of the world thus conceives of matter as a single extended body, indefinitely modifiable as to its dimensions, and dependent only on the supreme substance, God, for its existence and the movement of its parts. Finally, to complete the picture, there are, in addition to the creator and the physical world, created minds or souls: individual centres of consciousness, whose existence, Descartes maintains, does not require anything material (for more on this notion of the immaterial mind, compare Part IV, extract 4, below). Descartes's ontology thus gives us three categories of substance: first, substance in the strict sense – the independent, self-sufficient creator, God; second, extended substance, or matter; and third 'thinking substance' – the category to which created minds belong.

---

* René Descartes, *Principles of Philosophy* [*Principia Philosophiae*, 1644], Part I, articles 51, 52, 54, 63; Part II, articles 1, 2, 3, 4, 21, 22, 23, 36, 64. Trans. J. Cottingham, R. Stoothoff and D. Murdoch, in *The Philosophical Writings of Descartes*, vol. I (Cambridge: Cambridge University Press, 1985), pp. 210–11, 215, 223–5, 232, 240, 247.

[1] Thomas Aquinas, *Sententia super Metaphysicam* [1269–72], IV, 1, 540–3.

[2] Cartesian: belonging to Descartes (from 'Cartesius', the Latin version of his name).

What is meant by 'substance' – a term which does not apply univocally to God and his creatures.

In the case of those items which we regard as things or modes of things, it is worthwhile examining each of them separately. By *substance* we can understand nothing other than a thing which exists in such a way as to depend on no other thing for its existence. And there is only one substance which can be understood to depend on no other thing whatsoever, namely God. In the case of all other substances, we perceive that they can exist only with the help of God's concurrence. Hence the term 'substance' does not apply *univocally*, as they say in the Schools, to God and to other things; that is, there is no distinctly intelligible meaning of the term which is common to God and his creatures. In the case of created things, some are of such a nature that they cannot exist without other things, while some need only the ordinary concurrence of God in order to exist.[1] We make this distinction by calling the latter 'substances' and the former 'qualities' or 'attributes' of those substances.

The term 'substance' applies univocally to mind and to body. How a substance itself is known.

But as for corporeal substance and mind (or created thinking substance), these can be understood to fall under this common concept: things that need only the concurrence of God in order to exist. However, we cannot initially become aware of a substance merely through its being an existing thing, since this alone does not of itself have any effect on us. We can, however, easily come to know a substance by one of its attributes, in virtue of the common notion that nothingness possesses no attributes, that is to say, no properties or qualities. Thus, if we perceive the presence of some attribute, we can infer that there must also be present an existing thing or substance to which it may be attributed.

To each substance there belongs one principal attribute; in the case of mind, this is thought, and in the case of body it is extension.

A substance may indeed be known through any attribute at all; but each substance has one principal property which constitutes its nature and essence, and to which all its other properties are referred. Thus extension in length, breadth and depth constitutes the nature of corporeal substance; and thought constitutes the nature of thinking substance. Everything else which can be attributed to body presupposes extension, and is merely a mode of an extended thing; and similarly, whatever we find in the mind is simply one of the various modes of thinking. For example, shape is unintelligible except in an extended thing; and motion is unintelligible except as motion in an extended space; while imagination, sensation and will are intelligible only in a thinking thing. By contrast, it is possible to understand extension without shape or movement, and thought without imagination or sensation, and so on; and this is quite clear to anyone who gives the matter his attention.

---

[1] Concurrence: the continuous conserving power of God necessary to keep things in existence.

How we can have clear and distinct notions of thinking substance and of corporeal substance, and also of God.

Thus we can easily have two clear and distinct notions or ideas, one of created thinking substance, and the other of corporeal substance, provided we are careful to distinguish all the attributes of thought from the attributes of extension. We can also have a clear and distinct idea of uncreated and independent thinking substance, that is of God. Here we must simply avoid supposing that the idea adequately represents everything which is to be found in God; and we must not invent any additional features, but concentrate only on what is really contained in the idea and on what we clearly perceive to belong to the nature of a supremely perfect being. And certainly no one can deny that we possess such an idea of God, unless he reckons that there is absolutely no knowledge of God to be found in the minds of men . . .

How thought and extension may be distinctly recognized as constituting the nature of mind and of body.

Thought and extension can be regarded as constituting the natures of intelligent substance and corporeal substance; they must then be considered as nothing else but thinking substance itself and extended substance itself – that is, as mind and body. In this way we will have a very clear and distinct understanding of them. Indeed, it is much easier for us to have an understanding of extended substance or thinking substance than it is for us to understand substance on its own, leaving out the fact that it thinks or is extended. For we have some difficulty in abstracting the notion of substance from the notions of thought and extension, since the distinction between these notions and the notion of substance itself is merely a conceptual distinction. A concept is not any more distinct because we include less in it; its distinctness simply depends on our carefully distinguishing what we do include in it from everything else . . .

The arguments that lead to the certain knowledge of the existence of material things.

Everyone is quite convinced of the existence of material things. But earlier on we cast doubt on this belief and counted it as one of the preconceived opinions of our childhood.[1] So it is necessary for us to investigate next the arguments by which the existence of material things may be known with certainty. Now, all our sensations undoubtedly come to us from something that is distinct from our mind. For it is not in our power to make ourselves have one sensation rather than another; this is obviously dependent on the thing that is acting on our senses. Admittedly one can raise the question of whether this thing is God or something different from God. But we have sensory awareness of, or rather as a result of sensory stimulation we have a clear and distinct perception of, some kind of matter, which is extended in length, breadth and depth, and has various differently shaped and variously moving parts

---

[1] Compare the doubts raised in the First Meditation: see above, Part I, extract 4.

which give rise to our various sensations of colours, smells, pain and so on. And if God were himself immediately producing in our mind the idea of such extended matter, or even if he were causing the idea to be produced by something which lacked extension, shape and motion, there would be no way of avoiding the conclusion that he should be regarded as a deceiver. For we have a clear understanding of this matter as something that is quite different from God and from ourselves or our mind; and we appear to see clearly that the idea of it comes to us from things located outside ourselves which it wholly resembles. And we have already noted that it is quite inconsistent with the nature of God that he should be a deceiver. The unavoidable conclusion, then, is that there exists something extended in length, breadth and depth and possessing all the properties which we clearly perceive to belong to an extended thing. And it is this extended thing that we call 'body' or 'matter'.

The basis for our knowledge that the human body is closely conjoined with the mind.

By the same token, the conclusion that there is a particular body that is more closely conjoined with our mind than any other body follows from our clear awareness that pain and other sensations come to us quite unexpectedly. The mind is aware that these sensations do not come from itself alone, and that they cannot belong to it simply in virtue of its being a thinking thing; instead, they can belong to it only in virtue of its being joined to something other than itself which is extended and movable, namely what we call the human body. But this is not the place for a detailed explanation of its nature.

Sensory perception does not show us what really exists in things, but merely shows us what is beneficial or harmful to man's composite nature.

It will be enough, for the present, to note that sensory perceptions are related exclusively to this combination of the human body and mind.[1] They normally tell us of the benefit or harm that external bodies may do to this combination, and do not, except occasionally and accidentally, show us what external bodies are like in themselves. If we bear this in mind we will easily lay aside the preconceived opinions acquired from the senses, and in this connection make use of the intellect alone, carefully attending to the ideas implanted in it by nature.

The nature of body consists not in weight, hardness, colour, or the like, but simply in extension.

If we do this, we shall perceive that the nature of matter, or body considered in general, consists not in its being something which is hard or heavy or coloured, or

---

[1] For more on Descartes's view of the human being as combination of incorporeal mind and extended body, see below, Part IV, extract 4.

which affects the senses in any way, but simply in its being something which is extended in length, breadth and depth. For as regards hardness, our sensation tells us no more than that the parts of a hard body resist the motion of our hands when they come into contact with them. If, whenever our hands moved in a given direction, all the bodies in that area were to move away at the same speed as that of our approaching hands, we should never have any sensation of hardness. And since it is quite unintelligible to suppose that, if bodies did move away in this fashion, they would thereby lose their bodily nature, it follows that this nature cannot consist in hardness. By the same reasoning it can be shown that weight, colour, and all other such qualities that are perceived by the senses as being in corporeal matter, can be removed from it, while the matter itself remains intact; it thus follows that its nature does not depend on any of these qualities . . .

The extension of the world is indefinite.

What is more we recognize that this world, that is, the whole universe of corporeal substance, has no limits to its extension. For no matter where we imagine the boundaries to be, there are always some indefinitely extended spaces beyond them, which we not only imagine but also perceive to be imaginable in a true fashion, that is, real. And it follows that these spaces contain corporeal substance which is indefinitely extended. For, as has already been shown very fully, the idea of the extension which we conceive to be in a given space is exactly the same as the idea of corporeal substance.

Similarly, the earth and the heavens are composed of one and the same matter; and there cannot be a plurality of worlds.

It can also easily be gathered from this that celestial matter is no different from terrestrial matter.[1] And even if there were an infinite number of worlds, the matter of which they were composed would have to be identical; hence, there cannot in fact be a plurality of worlds, but only one. For we very clearly understand that the matter whose nature consists simply in its being an extended substance already occupies absolutely all the imaginable space in which the alleged additional worlds would have to be located; and we cannot find within us an idea of any other sort of matter.

All the variety in matter, all the diversity of its forms, depends on motion.

The matter existing in the entire universe is thus one and the same, and it is always recognized as matter simply in virtue of its being extended. All the properties which we clearly perceive in it are reducible to its divisibility and consequent mobility in respect of its parts, and its resulting capacity to be affected in all the ways which we perceive as being derivable from the movement of the parts. If the division into parts

---

[1] Descartes here rejects the traditional doctrine of a radical difference between 'sublunary' or terrestrial phenomena and the incorruptible world of the heavens.

occurs simply in our thought, there is no resulting change; any variation in matter or diversity in its many forms depends on motion. This seems to have been widely recognized by the philosophers, since they have stated that nature is the principle of motion and rest. And what they meant by 'nature' in this context is what causes all corporeal things to take on the characteristics of which we are aware in experience...

God is the primary cause of motion; and he always preserves the same quantity of motion in the universe.

After this consideration of the nature of motion, we must look at its cause. This is in fact twofold: first, there is the universal and primary cause – the general cause of all the motions in the world; and second there is the particular cause which produces in an individual piece of matter some motion which it previously lacked. Now as far as the general cause is concerned, it seems clear to me that this is no other than God himself. In the beginning in his omnipotence he created matter along with its motion and rest; and now, merely by his regular concurrence, he preserves the same amount of motion and rest in the material universe as he put there in the beginning. Admittedly motion is simply a mode of the matter which is moved. But nevertheless it has a certain determinate quantity; and this, we easily understand, may be constant in the universe as a whole while varying in any given part. Thus if one part of matter moves twice as fast as another which is twice as large, we must consider that there is the same quantity of motion in each part; and if one part slows down, we must suppose that some other part of equal size speeds up by the same amount. For we understand that God's perfection involves not only his being immutable in himself, but also his operating in a manner that is always utterly constant and immutable. Now there are some changes whose occurrence is guaranteed either by our own plain experience or by divine revelation, and either our perception or our faith shows us that these take place without any change in the creator; but apart from these we should not suppose that any other changes occur in God's works, in case this suggests some inconstancy in God. Thus, God imparted various motions to the parts of matter when he first created them, and he now preserves all this matter in the same way, and by the same process by which he originally created it; and it follows from what we have said that this fact alone makes it most reasonable to think that God likewise always preserves the same quantity of motion in matter...

The only principles which I accept, or require, in physics are those of geometry and pure mathematics; these principles explain all natural phenomena, and enable us to provide quite certain demonstrations regarding them.

I will not here add anything about shapes or about the countless different kinds of motions that can be derived from the infinite variety of different shapes. These matters will be quite clear in themselves when the time comes for me to deal with them. I am assuming that my readers know the basic elements of geometry already, or have sufficient mental aptitude to understand mathematical demonstrations.

For I freely acknowledge that I recognize no matter in corporeal things apart from that which the geometers call quantity, and take as the object of their demonstrations, i.e. that to which every kind of division, shape and motion is applicable. Moreover, my consideration of such matter involves absolutely nothing apart from these divisions, shapes and motions; and even with regard to these, I will admit as true only what has been deduced from indubitable common notions so evidently that it is fit to be considered as a mathematical demonstration.

4   Qualities and Ideas: John Locke, *Essay concerning Human Understanding**

A consequence of the new 'mathematicized' physics of Descartes was that a certain gap opened up between the quantitative description of the world put forward by the scientist and the 'common sense' world revealed by the five senses – the world of colours, smells, tastes, sounds and textures. Descartes had pointed out that nothing reaches the brain from the outside world except various 'local motions' transmitted via the sense organs; and he concluded that 'the properties in external objects to which we apply the terms "light", "colour", "smell", "taste", "sound", "heat" and "cold"... are so far as we can see simply various dispositions in the shapes, sizes, positions and movements of their parts that make them able to set up various kinds of motions in our nerves, which then produce all the various sensations in our soul'.[1] Taking up this theme, the English philosopher John Locke made a radical distinction between *primary* and *secondary* qualities of things. Primary qualities such as shape, he argues in the following extract from the *Essay concerning Human Understanding* (which appeared at the end of 1689[2]), are 'utterly inseparable from the Body in whatsoever state it be'. Descartes, as we have seen, took being extended in three dimensions as the essential characteristic of matter; Locke's list of the basic or primary qualities of matter comprises 'solidity, extension, figure [i.e. shape] and mobility'.

Now as far as our ordinary idea of the objects around us is concerned, we normally conceive of them as having many other qualities in addition to those on Locke's list – the marigold has a striking colour, the pineapple a characteristic taste, the perfume a distinctive aroma, and so on. But such qualities are, for Locke, merely *powers* which objects have to produce various sensations in us by means of their primary qualities (here Locke again owes much to his illustrious French predecessor: compare the sentence from Descartes quoted in the previous paragraph). The upshot is that when we conceive of an object as having shape, for example, there is, as Locke puts it, a 'resemblance' between our idea of the object and how it really is: '[the] patterns do really exist in the Bodies themselves'. But when we call an object 'sweet' or 'blue', 'there is nothing like our ideas existing in the bodies themselves'.

The real physical world thus turns out to be, for Locke, very different in nature from how we often naïvely suppose it to be. A kind of veil interposes itself between our human sensory awareness of the world on the one hand, and, on the other, the world as it 'really is' – the world of corpuscular physics consisting simply of solid, extended, moving particles. Some readers may feel that this distinction between appearance and reality is indeed forced on us by the discoveries

---

* John Locke, *An Essay concerning Human Understanding* [1690], Bk II, ch. 8, §§ 7–22 inclusive; punctuation, spelling and layout adapted. Several editions are available; the standard critical edition by P. H. Nidditch (Oxford: Clarendon, 1975) preserves the original formatting (pp. 134–43).

[1] Descartes, *Principles of Philosophy* [1644], Part IV, article 198.

[2] Though the date on the title page of the first edition is 1690.

of science. But we need to be on our guard. Does science actually show us that a marigold is not 'really' coloured? Indeed, on Locke's own account, if the redness of a rose is a 'power' to produce certain sensations in us, does this not imply that the flower does genuinely possess that power? Finally if a metaphysical veil is to be drawn between *some* of our ideas and how things really are 'out there', one might begin to ask whether *any* of our ideas can support the notion of 'what really exists in the bodies themselves' (for more on this, see extract 6, below).

To discover the nature of our *ideas* the better, and to discourse of them intelligibly, it will be convenient to distinguish them, as they are ideas or perceptions in our minds, and as they are modifications of matter in the bodies that cause such perceptions in us; that so we may not think (as perhaps usually is done) that they are exactly the images and resemblances of something inherent in the subject; most of those [ideas] of sensation being in the mind no more the likeness of something existing without [outside] us, than the names, that stand for them, are the likeness of our *ideas*, which yet upon hearing, they are apt to excite in us.

Whatsoever the mind perceives in itself, or is the immediate object of perception, thought, or understanding, that I call *idea*; and the power to produce any idea in our mind, I call *quality* of the subject wherein that power is. Thus a snowball having the power to produce in us the *ideas* of *white, cold*, and *round*, the powers to produce those *ideas* in us, as they are in the snowball, I call *qualities*; and as they are sensations, or perceptions, in our understandings, I call them *ideas*. Which ideas, if I speak of sometimes as in the things themselves, I would be understood to mean those qualities in the objects which produce them in us.

Qualities thus considered in bodies are, first such as are utterly inseparable from the body, in what estate soever it be; such as in all the alterations and changes it suffers, all the force can be used upon it, it constantly keeps; and such as sense constantly finds in every particle of matter, which has bulk enough to be perceived, and the mind finds inseparable from every particle of matter, though less than to make itself singly be perceived by our senses. E.g., take a grain of wheat, divide it into two parts, each part has still *solidity, extension, figure*, and *mobility*; divide it again, and it retains still the same qualities; and so divide it on, till the parts become insensible, they must retain still each of them all those qualities. For division (which is all that a mill, or pestle, or any other body, does upon another, in reducing it to insensible parts) can never take away either solidity, extension, figure, or mobility from any body, but only makes two, or more distinct separate masses of matter, of that which was but one before, all which distinct masses, reckoned as so many distinct bodies, after division make a certain number. These I call *original* or *primary qualities* of body, which I think we may observe to produce simple *ideas* in us, viz. solidity, extension, figure, motion, or rest, and number.

Secondly, such *qualities*, which in truth are nothing in the objects themselves, but powers to produce various sensations in us by their *primary qualities*, i.e. by the bulk, figure, texture, and motion of their insensible parts, as colours, sounds, tastes, etc., these I call *secondary qualities*. To these might be added a third sort which are allowed to be barely powers though they are as much real qualities in the subject, as those which I to comply with the common way of speaking call *qualities*, but for distinction *secondary qualities*. For the power in fire to produce a new colour, or consistency in wax or clay by its primary qualities, is as much a quality in fire, as the power it has to produce in me a new *idea* or sensation of warmth or burning, which I felt not before, by the same primary qualities, viz. the bulk, texture, and motion of its insensible parts.

The next thing to be considered, is how *bodies* produce *ideas* in us, and that is manifestly *by impulse*, the only way which we can conceive bodies operate in.

If then external objects be not united to our minds, when they produce *ideas* in it; and yet we perceive these original *qualities* in such of them as singly fall under our senses, it is evident, that some motion must be thence continued by our nerves, or animal spirits,[1] by some parts of our bodies, to the brains or the seat of sensation, there to produce in our minds the particular ideas we have of them. And since the extension, figure, number, and motion of bodies of an observable bigness, may be perceived at a distance by the sight, it is evident some singly imperceptible bodies must come from them to the eyes, and thereby convey to the brain some *motion*, which produces these *ideas*, which we have of them in us.

After the same manner that the *ideas* of these original qualities are produced in us, we may conceive that the *ideas of secondary qualities* are also produced, viz. *by the operation of insensible particles on our senses*. For it [is] manifest that there are bodies, and good store of bodies, each whereof is so small that we cannot, by any of our senses, discover either their bulk, figure, or motion, as is evident in the particles of the air and water, and others extremely smaller than those – perhaps as much smaller than the particles of air, or water, as the particles of air or water are smaller than peas or hailstones. Let us suppose at present that the different motions and figures, bulk, and number of such particles, affecting the several organs of our senses, produce in us those different sensations which we have from the colours and smells of bodies; e.g. that a violet, by the impulse of such insensible particles of matter of peculiar figures and bulks, and in different degrees and modifications of their motions, causes the *ideas* of the blue colour, and sweet scent of that flower to be produced in our minds – it being no more impossible to conceive, that God should annex such ideas to such motions, with which they have no similitude, than that he should annex the idea of pain to the motion of a piece of steel dividing our flesh, with which that idea has no resemblance.

What I have said concerning *colours* and *smells* may be understood also of *tastes* and *sounds, and other [similar] sensible qualities*; which, whatever reality we, by mistake, attribute to them, are in truth nothing in the objects themselves but powers to produce various sensations in us, and *depend on those primary qualities*, viz. bulk, figure, texture, and motion of parts; as I have said.

From whence I think it is easy to draw this observation, that the *ideas of primary qualities* of bodies *are resemblances* of them, and their patterns do really exist in the bodies themselves; but the *ideas produced* in us *by these secondary qualities, have no resemblance* of them at all. There is nothing like our *ideas* existing in the bodies themselves. They are, in the bodies we denominate from them, only a power to produce those sensations in us. And what is sweet, blue, or warm in *idea* is but the certain bulk, figure, and motion of the insensible parts in the bodies themselves, which we call so.

Flame is denominated *hot* and *light*; snow *white* and *cold* and manna *white* and *sweet*, from the *ideas* they produce in us. Which qualities are commonly thought to be

---

[1] 'Animal spirits': a fine gas or vapour supposed to be the vehicle for the transmission of nerve-impulses.

the same in those bodies that those *ideas* are in us, the one the perfect resemblance of the other, as they are in a mirror; and it would by most men be judged very extravagant if one should say otherwise. And yet he that will consider that the same fire, that at one distance produces in us the sensation of *warmth*, does, at a nearer approach, produce in us the far different sensation of *pain*, ought to bethink himself what reason he has to say that his *idea* of *warmth*, which was produced in him by the fire, is actually *in* the fire; and his *idea* of *pain*, which the same fire produced in him the same way, is *not* in the fire. Why is whiteness and coldness in snow, and pain not, when it produces the one and the other *idea* in us; and can do neither but by the bulk, figure, number, and motion of its solid parts?

The particular *bulk, number, figure, and motion of the parts* of fire, or snow, are *really in them*, whether anyone's senses perceive them or no; and therefore they may be called *real qualities*, because they really exist in those bodies. But *light, heat, whiteness*, or *coldness*, are no more *really in them* than *sickness* or *pain* is *in* manna. Take away the sensation of them; let not the eyes see light, or colours, nor the ears hear sounds; let the palate not taste, nor the nose smell, and all colours, tastes, odours, and sounds, as they are such particular *ideas*, vanish and cease, and are reduced to their causes, i.e. bulk, figure, and motion of parts.

A piece of manna[1] of a sensible bulk is able to produce in us the *idea* of a round or square figure; and, by being removed from one place to another, the *idea* of motion. This *idea* of motion represents it as it really is in the manna moving. A circle or square are the same, whether in *idea* or existence – in the mind, or in the manna. And this, [that] both *motion and figure are really in the manna*, whether we take notice of them or no, this everybody is ready to agree to. Besides, manna, by the bulk, figure, texture, and motion of its parts, has a power to produce the sensations of sickness, and sometimes of acute pains, or gripings in us. That these *ideas* of *sickness* and *pain* are not *in* the manna, but effects of its operations on us, and are nowhere when we feel them not – this also every one readily agrees to. And yet men are hardly to be brought to think that *sweetness and whiteness are not really in manna*; which are but the effects of the operations of manna, by the motion, size, and figure of its particles on the eyes and palate; as the pain and sickness caused by manna are confessedly nothing but the effects of its operations on the stomach and guts, by the size, motion, and figure of its insensible parts (for by nothing else can a body operate, as has been proved). As if it could not operate on the eyes and palate, and thereby produce in the mind particular distinct *ideas*, which in itself it has not, as well as we allow it can operate on the guts and stomach, and thereby produce distinct *ideas*, which in itself it has not. These *ideas* being all effects of the operations of manna on several parts of our bodies, by the size, figure, number, and motion of its parts, why those produced by the eyes and palate should rather be thought to be really in the manna, than those produced by the stomach and guts; or why the pain and sickness, *ideas* that are the effects of manna, should be thought to be nowhere, when they are not felt; and yet the sweetness and whiteness, effects of the same manna on other parts of the body, by ways equally as unknown, should be thought to exist in the manna, when they are not seen nor tasted, would need some reason to explain.

---

[1] Plant extract used in the seventeenth century as a laxative.

Let us consider the red and white colours in porphyry. Hinder light but from striking on it, and its colours vanish; it no longer produces any such ideas in us. Upon the return of light, it produces these appearances on us again. Can any one think any real alterations are made in the porphyry by the presence or absence of light; and that those ideas of whiteness and redness, are really in porphyry in the light, when it is plain *it has no colour in the dark*? It has, indeed, such a configuration of particles, both night and day, as are apt by the rays of light rebounding from some parts of that hard stone, to produce in us the idea of redness, and from others the idea of whiteness. But whiteness or redness are not in it at any time, but such a texture that has the power to produce such a sensation in us.

Pound an almond, and the clear white *colour* will be altered into a dirty one, and the sweet *taste* into an oily one. What real alteration can the beating of the pestle make in any body, but an alteration of the *texture* of it?

Ideas being thus distinguished and understood, we may be able to give an account, how the same water, at the same time, may produce the idea of cold by one hand, and of heat by the other: Whereas it is impossible, that the same water, if those ideas were really in it, should at the same time be both hot and cold. For if we imagine *warmth*, as it is *in our hands*, to be *nothing but a certain sort and degree of motion in the minute particles of our nerves, or animal spirits*, we may understand how it is possible that the same water may at the same time produce the sensation of heat in one hand, and cold in the other; which yet figure never does, that never producing the idea of a square by one hand, which has produced the idea of a globe by another. But if the sensation of heat and cold be nothing but the increase or diminution of the motion of the minute parts of our bodies, caused by the corpuscles of any other body, it is easy to be understood: that if that motion be greater in one hand than in the other, if a body be applied to the two hands, which has in its minute particles a greater motion than in those of one of the hands, and a less than in those of the other, it will increase the motion of the one hand and lessen it in the other, and so cause the different sensations of heat and cold that depend thereon.

I have, in what just goes before, been engaged in physical enquiries a little farther than, perhaps, I intended. But it being necessary to make the nature of sensation a little understood, and to make the differences between the *qualities in bodies* and the *ideas produced by them in the mind* to be distinctly conceived, without which it were impossible to discourse intelligibly of them; I hope, I shall be pardoned this little excursion into natural philosophy, it being necessary in our present enquiry, to distinguish the primary, and *real qualities* of bodies, which are always in them (viz. solidity, extension, figure, number, and motion, or rest), and are sometimes perceived by us (viz. when the bodies they are in are big enough singly to be discerned), from those *secondary* and *imputed qualities*, which are but the powers of several combinations of those primary ones, when they operate without being distinctly discerned; whereby we also may come to know what *ideas* are, and what are not, resemblances of something really existing in the bodies we denominate from them.

5   Substance, Life and Activity: Gottfried Leibniz, *New System**

Although Locke (see previous extract) characterized the material world in terms of the 'primary qualities' of things, he did make sporadic use of the traditional Aristotelian label 'substance', while none the less voicing some reservations about exactly what it meant. If we describe a particle as round and hard, what does it mean to add that it is a *substance* that is round and hard? 'If anyone will examine himself concerning his notion of pure substance in general,' Locke observed, 'he will find he has no other idea of it at all, but only a supposition of he knows not what *support* of such qualities which are capable of producing ideas in us.'[1]

Once this troubling question had been asked, it was not long before some philosophers were suggesting that the notion of substance might be abandoned altogether (see extract 7, below). Others, however, continued to defend the concept of substance as being of the greatest importance. The German philosopher Gottfried Leibniz, a keen supporter of the new mathematical and corpuscular physics that flourished during the latter seventeenth century, came to the conclusion that the notion of substance provided essential metaphysical underpinning for a complete understanding of reality. In his *New System*, published in French in 1695, Leibniz argues that a purely mathematical account of the world, in terms of extension (size and shape) must be deficient. First, Leibniz insists that we need in our account of reality to recognize the essential *unity* of things: the world cannot be a mere collection of arbitrary heaps or piles of stuff – 'an accumulation of parts *ad infinitum*'; sooner or later we must acknowledge some ultimate units – what Leibniz calls 'metaphysical atoms'. And second, Leibniz maintains that size and shape alone cannot explain the *activity* and

power found in the universe: 'extended mass is not of itself enough, and use must also be made of the notion of *force* which is fully intelligible, although it falls within the sphere of metaphysics'.

Now as we have seen (extract 3 above), Descartes had explained motion by invoking the creative power and continuous conserving action of the supreme substance, God; but Leibniz argues that in favouring this 'solution' the supporters of Descartes were simply 'falling back on a miracle'. Instead, Leibniz offers a metaphysical picture of the world such that activity and energy are involved at the deepest level in the ultimate individual units of being. Reality is composed of an infinite plurality of 'metaphysical points' or 'atoms of substance' (what Leibniz was later to call 'monads'). 'It is only unities which are real and absolutely without parts, which can be the sources of actions, and as it were the ultimate elements into which substantial things can be analysed.' Leibniz makes it clear that the rational souls of human beings are the most important examples of such individual units of substance, or spontaneous centres of activity (and he thinks this notion underpins our independence and freedom). But even the humblest of bodies are made up of metaphysical units which have something 'soul-like' about them: 'Each simple substance has relations which express all the others, and consequently it is a perpetual living mirror of the universe.' So, far from the 'dead' world of extended matter posited by Descartes, Leibnizian metaphysics presents a universe whose ultimate constituents are in some sense 'animated' or 'alive', containing within themselves the source of their activity, and internally ordered in such a way as to ensure the harmonious operation of the universe as a whole.

---

* Gottfried Wilhelm Leibniz, *New System of Nature and the Communication of Substances* [*Système nouveau de la nature et de la communication des substances*, 1695]. Trans. G. H. R. Parkinson and M. Morris, in Leibniz, *Philosophical Writings* (London: Dent, 1973), pp. 115–25; with omissions.
[1] *Essay concerning Human Understanding*, Bk II, ch. xxiii, § 2.

Although I am one of those who have done much work on mathematics, I have constantly meditated on philosophy from my youth up, for it has always seemed to me that in philosophy there was a way of establishing something solid by means of clear proofs. I had travelled far into the world of the Scholastics,[1] when mathematics and modern writers[2] lured me out again, while still a young man. I was charmed with their beautiful way of explaining nature mechanically, and scorned, with justice, the method of those who only make use of forms or faculties, from which we learn nothing. But later, when I tried to get to the bottom of the actual principles of mechanics in order to give an explanation of the laws of nature which are known through experience, I became aware that the consideration of an *extended mass* is not of itself enough, and that use must also be made of the notion of *force*, which is fully intelligible, although it falls within the sphere of metaphysics. It seemed to me also that the opinion of those who transform or degrade the lower animals into mere machines,[3] although it seems possible, is improbable, and even against the order of things.

At first, when I had freed myself from the yoke of Aristotle, I had believed in the void and atoms, for it is this which best satisfies the imagination. But returning to this view after much meditation, I perceived that it is impossible to find *the principles of a true unity* in matter alone, or in what is merely passive, since everything in it is but a collection or accumulation of parts *ad infinitum*. Now a multiplicity can be real only if it is made up *of true unities* which come from elsewhere and are altogether different from mathematical points, which are nothing but extremities of the extended and modifications out of which it is certain that nothing *continuous* could be compounded. Therefore, to find these *real unities*, I was constrained to have recourse to what might be called a *real and animating point* or to an atom of substance which must embrace some element of form or of activity in order to make a complete being. It was thus necessary to recall and in a manner to rehabilitate *substantial forms*, which are so much decried today, but in a way which makes them intelligible and separates the use which must be made of them from their previous abuse. I found then that their nature consists of force and that from this there follows something analogous to feeling and to appetite; and that therefore it was necessary to form a conception of them resembling our ordinary notion of *souls*. But just as the soul must not be used to explain the detail of the economy of the animal's body, so I judged in the same way that these forms ought not to be used to explain the particular problems of nature, although they are necessary to establish true general principles. Aristotle calls them *first entelechies*; I call them, more intelligibly perhaps, *primitive forces*, which contain not only the *act*, or the fulfilment of possibility, but also an original *activity*.

I saw that these forms and these souls must be indivisible like our mind ... But this truth revived the great difficulties about the origin and duration of souls and forms. For since every *simple substance* which possesses a true unity can have its beginning and end by miracle alone, it follows that they could not begin except by creation, nor come to an end except by annihilation. Thus (with the exception of such souls as God still wills to create expressly) I was obliged to recognize that the constitutive forms of substance must have been created with the world and that they go on subsisting always ...

---

[1] Advocates of the traditional philosophy, based on Aristotle.
[2] Leibniz refers to Descartes and his followers.
[3] See Part IV, extract 4, below.

Nevertheless I deemed that we ought not to mix without distinction or to confuse with other forms or souls, *minds* or rational souls, which are of a superior order and have incomparably more perfection than those forms embedded in matter which, on my view, are to be found everywhere, since in comparison with these others, minds or rational souls are little gods, made in the image of God, and having in them some glimmering of divine light. This is why God governs minds as a prince governs his subjects, or as a father cares for his children; whereas he disposes of other substances as an engineer handles his machines. Thus minds have special laws which set them above the revolutions of matter, by the very order God has introduced into them; and it may truly be said that all the rest are made for them alone, the very revolutions being arranged for the felicity of the virtuous and the punishment of the wicked...

But there still remained the more important question of what becomes of these souls or forms at the death of the animal, or at the destruction of the individual unit of organized substance. This question is the more awkward, inasmuch as it seems unreasonable that souls should remain useless in a chaos of confused matter. This ultimately made me decide that there was only one sensible thing to believe; that is to maintain the conservation not only of the soul but also of the animal itself and of its organic machine; even though the destruction of its grosser parts has reduced it to such smallness that it evades our senses, just as it did before birth. Moreover, nobody can mark precisely the true time of death, which may for a long time pass for a mere suspension of observable actions, and fundamentally is never anything else but that in the case of simple animals; witness the *resuscitations* of flies which have been drowned and then buried under powdered chalk, and several similar instances, which make us realize that there might be other resuscitations, and in cases which were much further gone, if men were in a position to readjust the machine... It is therefore natural that since an animal has always been living and organized... it should also always continue to be so. And since there is thus no first birth or entirely new generation of the animal it follows that it will suffer no final extinction or complete death, in the strict metaphysical sense...

But rational souls obey much more exalted laws, and are immune from anything which could make them lose the status of citizens of the society of minds, since God has so provided that no changes of matter could make them lose the moral qualities of their personality. And it may be said with truth that everything tends to the perfection not only of the universe in general, but also of these created things in particular, who are destined for so high a degree of happiness that the universe becomes concerned in it by virtue of the divine goodness which is communicated to each created being, in so far as sovereign wisdom can permit...

I am as willing as any man to give the moderns their due but I think they have carried reform too far, among other things in confusing the natural with the artificial, through not having had sufficiently exalted ideas of the majesty of Nature. They conceive that the difference between her machines and ours is but the difference between the great and the small. This recently led a very clever man to remark that when looking at Nature from near at hand she appears less admirable than we thought, being no more than a workman's shop. I believe that this does not give a sufficiently just idea, or one sufficiently worthy of her, and there is no system except mine which properly exhibits the immense distance which really lies between the least productions and mechanisms of Divine wisdom and the greatest achievements of the skill of a limited mind. This difference is one not merely of degree, but of kind also. It must be recognized that Nature's machines possess a truly infinite number of organs, and are so well protected and armed against all accidents that it is not possible to destroy them. A natural machine still remains a machine in its least parts, and, what is more, it always remains the very same machine that it was, being merely transformed by the different foldings it receives, and being sometimes stretched, sometimes contracted and as it were concentrated, when we think that it is destroyed.

Furthermore, by means of the soul or form, there is a true unity which corresponds to what is called the *I* in us; a thing which could not occur in artificial machines, nor in the simple mass of matter, however organized it may be. This can only be regarded as like an army or a flock, or like a pond full of fish, or a watch made up of springs and wheels. Yet if there were no true *substantial unities*, there would be nothing real or substantial in the collection. It was this that [has led some philosophers to] abandon Descartes and to adopt Democritus's theory of atoms, in order to find a true unity. But *atoms of matter* are contrary to reason, besides the fact that they also are composed of parts, since the invincible attachment of one part to another (granted that this could be reasonably conceived or supposed) would not destroy their diversity. It is only *atoms of substance*, that is to say unities which are real and absolutely without parts, which can be the sources of actions, and the absolute first principles of the composition of things, and as it were the ultimate elements into which substantial things can be analysed. They might be called *metaphysical points*; there is about them *something vital* and a kind of *perception*, and *mathematical points* are their *points of view* for expressing the universe. But when corporeal substances are contracted all their organs constitute for us but a *physical point*. Thus physical points are indivisible in appearance only: mathematical points are exact, but they are nothing but modalities. It is only metaphysical points, or points of substance (constituted by forms or souls), which are both exact and real; and without them there would be nothing real, since without true unities there would be no plurality.

Once I had established these things, I thought I had reached port; but when I set myself to reflect on the union of the soul with the body, I seemed to be cast back again into the open sea. For I could find no way of explaining how the body causes something to happen in the soul, or vice versa, nor how one created substance can communicate with another. M. Descartes left the field at this stage, as far as we can gather from his writings; but his disciples, realizing that the common opinion is inconceivable, maintained that we are aware of the qualities of bodies because God produces thoughts in the soul on the occasion of the movements of matter; and when our soul wishes to move the body in its turn, they deemed that it is God that moves it for the soul. And as the communication of motion seemed to them likewise inconceivable, they maintained that God gives motion to a body on the occasion of the motion of another body. This is what they call *the System of occasional causes*, which has become very fashionable owing to the fine reflections of the author of the *Recherche de la Vérité*.[1]

It must be admitted that they have gone a great way in regard to this problem by showing what cannot possibly take place; but their explanation of what does in fact occur does not remove the difficulty. It is quite true that in the strict metaphysical

---

[1] Nicolas Malebranche. See Part IV, extract 6, below.

sense there is no real influence exerted by one created substance on another, and that all things, with all their realities, are continually produced by the power of God: but to solve these problems it is not enough to make use of the general cause, and to drag in what is called the *deus ex machina*.[1] For when this is done without giving any further explanation in terms of the order of secondary causes, this is properly speaking to fall back on miracle. In philosophy, we must attempt to give an explanation showing in what way things are brought about by the Divine wisdom, in conformity with the notion of the subject in question.

Being thus constrained to grant that it is impossible for the soul or for any other true substance to receive anything from without, except by Divine omnipotence, I was insensibly led to adopt a view which surprised me, but which seems inevitable, and which does in fact possess very great advantages and considerable beauties. This view is that we must say that God first created the soul, and every other real unity, in such a way that everything in it must spring from within itself, by a perfect *spontaneity* with regard to itself, and yet in a perfect *conformity* with things outside. And thus, since our internal sensations (those, that is to say, which are in the soul itself and not in the brain or in the subtle parts of the body) are but phenomena dependent upon external entities, or rather are really appearances, and, as it were, well-ordered dreams, these internal perceptions within the soul itself must arise in it from its own original constitution, that is to say through the natural representative ability (capable of expressing entities outside itself in relation to its organs) with which it has been endowed since its creation, and which constitutes its individual character. It follows from this that, since each of these substances exactly represents the whole universe in its own way and from a certain point of view, and since the perceptions or expressions of external things reach the soul at the proper time by virtue of its own laws and, as it were, in a world apart, as if nothing else existed but only God and itself... there will be a perfect agreement between all these substances, producing the same effect as would occur if these communicated with one another by means of a transmission of species or qualities, as the common run of philosophers maintain. Furthermore, the organized mass, within which is the point of view of the soul, is itself more nearly expressed by it, and finds itself in its turn ready to act of itself according to the laws of the corporeal machine whenever the soul desires, without either disturbing the laws of the other, the animal spirits and the blood having precisely at the given moment the motions necessary to make them respond to the passions and perceptions of the soul; and it is this mutual relation, regulated in advance in every substance in the universe, which produces what we call their *communication*, and which alone constitutes *the union of the soul and the body*. And this makes it possible to understand how the soul has its seat in the body by an immediate presence, which could not be closer than it is, since it is present in the way in which the unity is present in that resultant of unities which is a plurality.

This hypothesis is very possible. For why should not God be able in the first instance to give to substance a nature or internal force capable of producing for it in an orderly way (as if it were an *automaton, spiritual and formal, but free* in the case of a substance which has a share of reason) everything that is going to happen to it,

---

[1] The 'deus ex machina' was the god often lowered onto the stage at the end of Greek tragedies to sort out all the outstanding problems in the drama.

that is to say all the appearances and expressions it is going to have, and that without the assistance of any created thing? This is rendered all the more probable by the fact that the nature of substance necessarily requires and essentially involves a progress or change, without which it would have no force to act. And since it is the very nature of the soul to be representative of the universe in a very exact way (although with varying distinctness), the sequence of representations which the soul produces for itself will naturally correspond to the sequence of changes in the universe itself: while on the other hand the body has also been adjusted to the soul, in regard to the experiences in which the latter is conceived as acting outside itself. This is all the more reasonable in that bodies are only made for those minds which are capable of entering into society with God, and of celebrating His glory. Thus once we recognize the possibility of this *hypothesis of agreements*, we recognize also that it is the most reasonable one, and that it gives a wonderful idea of the harmony of the universe and of the perfection of the works of God.

There is in it this great advantage also, that instead of saying that we are free only in appearance and in a manner adequate for practice, as several ingenious men have held, we must rather say that we are determined in appearance only; and that in strict metaphysical language we are perfectly independent as regards the influence of all other created things. This again shows up in a marvellously clear light the immortality of our soul, and the ever uniform conservation of our individual self, which is perfectly well regulated of its own nature, and is beyond the reach of all accidents from outside, whatever the appearances to the contrary. No system has ever so clearly exhibited our exalted position. Since each mind is as it were a world apart, sufficient unto itself, independent of all other created things, including the infinite, expressing the universe, it is as lasting, as subsistent, and as absolute as the very universe of created things itself. We must therefore conclude that it must always play its part in the way most suited to contribute to the perfection of that society of all minds which constitutes their moral union in the City of God. Here, too, is a new and wonderfully clear proof of the existence of God. For this perfect agreement of all these substances, which have absolutely no communication with one another, could only come from the one common cause...

These considerations, metaphysical though they may appear, are yet wonderfully useful in physics, for establishing the laws of motion...For the truth is that in the shock of impact each body suffers only from its own elasticity, caused by the motion which is already in it...It is reasonable to attribute to bodies true motions, in accordance with the supposition which explains phenomena in the most intelligible way; and this way of speaking is in conformity with the notion of *activity* which we have just established.

6 Nothing Outside the Mind: George Berkeley, *Principles of Human Knowledge**

The debates in the early modern period over the ultimate nature of reality led in many different directions. Descartes, as we have seen (extract 3, above) regarded matter as inert, passive extension; and both he and Locke considered that our ideas of sensible properties (such as colours, tastes, smells) did not really inhere in, or belong to the physical world, but rather were effects produced in the mind alone. Reflection on these issues led the Irish philosopher George Berkeley to the radical conclusion that *nothing at all* could be said to exist outside the mind. In the following extract from the *Principles of Human Knowledge* (1710), he attacks the Lockean distinction between primary and secondary qualities (see above, extract 4), and insists that all the arguments applying to sensible properties (like colour) apply equally to the supposed primary qualities (such as extension and shape): 'where the other sensible qualities are, there must these be also, to wit in the mind, and nowhere else'.

Berkeley's immaterialism has often been regarded as an affront to common sense (Dr Johnson famously 'refuted' it by simply kicking a stone). But Berkeley (as is clear from our extract) refers quite happily to 'houses, mountains and rivers', and to 'all those bodies which compose the mighty frame of the world'. He does not deny the reality of such things, but asserts that their *existence* consists in their *being perceived* (or, as Berkeley puts it in Latin, their *esse* is *percipi*). So does the table in my study continue to exist when there is no one in the room? Berkeley suggests at one point that to say it does means that *if* I *were* in my study I *would* perceive it (a view sometimes called 'phenomenalism' – the analysing of physical objects as 'permanent possibilities of sensation'). But Berkeley's more characteristic line is to say that tables, chairs, mountains, rivers and all natural phenomena do indeed have a being independent of the *human* perceiver. They subsist as ideas 'in the mind of some Eternal Spirit'; the uniformity and regularity of things, which we know is not dependent on us, 'testifies the wisdom and benevolence' of that governing spirit whose will generates those regular successions of ideas which we call the 'laws of nature'. Berkeley's metaphysical immaterialism is thus linked to his theology: in place of what he regarded as the godless materialism of those who conceived of the physical world as an alien reality, existing 'out there' independent of the mind, Berkeley offers a picture of reality as something essentially mind-dependent, and grounded in the divine consciousness. His labours will have been useless, he went on to observe in the closing paragraph of the *Principles*, unless he can 'inspire his readers with a pious sense of the Presence of God'.

It is evident to anyone who takes a survey of the objects of human knowledge that they are either ideas actually imprinted on the senses; or else such as are perceived by attending to the passions and operations of the mind; or lastly ideas formed by help of memory and imagination, either compounding, dividing, or barely representing those originally perceived in the aforesaid ways. By sight I have the ideas of light and colours with their several degrees and variations. By touch I perceive, for example, hard and soft, heat and cold, motion and resistance; and of all these more and less either as to quantity or degree. Smelling furnishes me with odours, the palate with tastes, and hearing conveys sounds to the mind in all their variety of tone and composition. And

* George Berkeley, *Treatise Concerning the Principles of Human Knowledge* [1710; 2nd edn 1734], Part I, paras 1–10, 14, 19, 23–6, 28–30; with omissions, and some changes of spelling and punctuation. There are many available editions of the *Principles*, including one with a full introduction for students, ed. J. Dancy (Oxford: Oxford University Press, 1998). See also the handy collection, *Berkeley: Philosophical Works*, ed. M. Ayers (London: Dent, 1975).

as several of these are observed to accompany each other, they come to be marked by one name, and so to be reputed as one thing. Thus, for example, a certain colour, taste, smell, figure and consistency having been observed to go together, are accounted one distinct thing, signified by the name *apple*. Other collections of ideas constitute a stone, a tree, a book, and the like sensible things; which, as they are pleasing or disagreeable, excite the passions of love, hatred, joy, grief, and so forth.

But besides all that endless variety of ideas or objects of knowledge, there is likewise something which knows or perceives them; and exercises divers[1] operations, as willing, imagining, remembering, about them. This perceiving, active being is what I call *mind, spirit, soul* or *myself.* By which words I do not denote any one of my ideas, but a thing entirely distinct from them, wherein they exist, or, which is the same thing, whereby they are perceived; for the existence of an idea consists in being perceived.

That neither our thoughts, nor passions, nor ideas formed by the imagination, exist without the mind,[2] is what everybody will allow. And it seems no less evident that the various sensations or ideas imprinted on the sense, however blended or combined together (that is, whatever objects they compose) cannot exist otherwise than in a mind perceiving them. I think an intuitive knowledge may be obtained of this by anyone that shall attend to what is meant by the term *exist* when applied to sensible things. The table I write on I say exists; that is, I see and feel it; and if I were out of my study I should say it existed, meaning thereby that if I was in my study I might perceive it, or that some other spirit actually does perceive it. There was an odour, that is, it was smelled; there was a sound, that is, it was heard; a colour or figure, and it was perceived by sight or touch. This is all that I can understand by these and the like expressions. For as to what is said of the absolute existence of unthinking things without any relation to their being perceived, that seems perfectly unintelligible. Their *esse* is *percipi*, nor is it possible they should have any existence, out of the minds or thinking things which perceive them.

It is indeed an opinion strangely prevailing amongst men that houses, mountains, rivers, and in a word all sensible objects, have an existence natural or real, distinct from their being perceived by the understanding. But with how great an assurance and acquiescence soever this principle may be entertained in the world, yet whoever shall find in his heart to call it in question, may, if I mistake not, perceive it to involve a manifest contradiction. For what are the forementioned objects but the things we perceive by sense? and what do we perceive besides our own ideas or sensations? and is it not plainly repugnant that any one of these or any combination of them should exist unperceived?

If we thoroughly examine this tenet, it will, perhaps, be found at bottom to depend on the doctrine of *abstract ideas*. For can there be a nicer strain of abstraction than to distinguish the existence of sensible objects from their being perceived, so as to conceive them existing unperceived? Light and colours, heat and cold, extension and figures, in a word the things we see and feel – what are they but so many sensations, notions, ideas or impressions on the sense? and is it possible to separate, even in thought, any of these from perception? For my part I might easily divide a thing from itself. I may indeed divide in my thoughts or conceive apart from each

[1] Various.
[2] 'Without', as often in eighteenth-century English, here means 'outside'.

other those things which, perhaps, I never perceived by sense so divided. Thus, I imagine the trunk of a human body without the limbs, or conceive the smell of a rose without thinking on the rose itself. So far I will not deny I can abstract, if that may properly be called *abstraction*, which extends only to the conceiving separately such objects, as it is possible may really exist or be actually perceived asunder. But my conceiving or imagining power does not extend beyond the possibility of real exist-ence or perception. Hence as it is impossible for me to see or feel anything without an actual sensation of that thing, so is it impossible for me to conceive in my thoughts any sensible thing or object distinct from the sensation or perception of it.

Some truths there are so near and obvious to the mind that a man need only open his eyes to see them. Such I take this important one to be, to wit, that all the choir of heaven and furniture of the earth, in a word all those bodies which compose the mighty frame of the world, have not any subsistence without a mind; that their being is to be perceived or known; that consequently so long as they are not actually perceived by me, or do not exist in my mind or that of any other created spirit, they must either have no existence at all, or else subsist in the mind of some Eternal Spirit: it being perfectly unintelligible, and involving all the absurdity of abstraction, to attribute to any single part of them an existence independent of a spirit. To be convinced of which, the reader need only reflect and try to separate in his own thoughts the being of a sensible thing from its being perceived.

From what has been said it follows there is not any other substance than *spirit*, or that which perceives. But for the fuller proof of this point, let it be considered, the sensible qualities are colour, figure, motion, smell, taste, and such like, that is, the ideas perceived by sense. Now for an idea to exist in an unperceiving thing is a manifest contradiction; for to have an idea is the same as to perceive; that therefore wherein colour, figure, and the like qualities, exist, must perceive them; hence it is clear there can be no unthinking substance or *substratum* of those ideas.

But, say you, though the ideas themselves do not exist without the mind, yet there may be things like them whereof they are copies or resemblances, which things exist without the mind, in an unthinking substance. I answer, an idea can be like nothing but an idea; a colour or figure can be like nothing but another colour or figure. If we look but ever so little into our thoughts, we shall find it impossible for us to conceive a likeness except only between our ideas. Again, I ask whether these supposed originals or external things, of which our ideas are the pictures or representations, be themselves perceivable or no? If they are, then they are ideas, and we have gained our point; but if you say they are not, I appeal to anyone whether it be sense, to assert a colour is like something which is invisible; hard or soft, like something which is intangible; and so of the rest.

Some there are who make a distinction betwixt *primary* and *secondary* qualities. By the former, they mean extension, figure, motion, rest, solidity or impenetrability and number; by the latter they denote all other sensible qualities, as colours, sounds, tastes, and so forth. The ideas we have of these they acknowledge not to be the resemblances of anything existing without the mind or unperceived; but they will have our ideas of the primary qualities to be patterns or images of things which exist without the mind, in an unthinking substance which they call *matter*. By matter therefore we are to understand an inert, senseless substance, in which extension, figure, and motion do actually subsist. But it is evident from what we have already shown, that extension, figure, and motion are only ideas existing in the mind, and that an idea can be like nothing but another idea, and that consequently neither they nor their archetypes can exist in an unperceiving substance. Hence it is plain that the very notion of what is called *matter* or *corporeal substance* involves a contradiction in it.

They who assert that figure, motion, and the rest of the primary or original qualities, do exist without the mind, in unthinking substances, do at the same time acknowledge that colours, sounds, heat, cold, and suchlike secondary qualities, do not – which they tell us are sensations existing in the mind alone, that depend on and are occasioned by the different size, texture and motion of the minute particles of matter. This they take for an undoubted truth, which they can demonstrate beyond all exception. Now if it be certain that those original qualities are inseparably united with the other sensible qualities, and not, even in thought, capable of being abstracted from them, it plainly follows that they exist only in the mind. But I desire anyone to reflect, and try whether he can, by any abstraction of thought, conceive the extension and motion of a body without all other sensible qualities. For my own part, I see evidently that it is not in my power to frame an idea of a body extended and moved, but I must withal give it some colour or other sensible quality which is acknowledged to exist only in the mind. In short, extension, figure, and motion, abstracted from all other qualities, are inconceivable. Where therefore the other sensible qualities are, there must these be also, to wit, in the mind and nowhere else...

I shall farther add, that after the same manner as modern philosophers prove certain sensible qualities to have no existence in matter, or without the mind, the same thing may be likewise proved of all other sensible qualities whatsoever. Thus, for instance, it is said that heat and cold are affections only of the mind, and not at all patterns of real beings, existing in the corporeal substances which excite them; for... the same body which appears cold to one hand, seems warm to another. Now why may we not as well argue that figure and extension are not patterns or resemblances of qualities existing in matter, because to the same eye at different stations, or eyes of a different texture at the same station, they appear various, and cannot therefore be the images of anything settled and determinate without the mind? Again, it is proved that sweetness is not really in the sapid thing, because the thing remaining unaltered the sweetness is changed into bitter, as in case of a fever or otherwise vitiated palate. Is it not as reasonable to say that motion is not without the mind, since if the succession of ideas in the mind become swifter, the motion, it is acknowledged, shall appear slower without any alteration in any external object?...

But though we might possibly have all our sensations without them, yet perhaps it may be thought easier to conceive and explain the manner of their production by supposing external bodies in their likeness rather than otherwise; and so it might be at least probable there are such things as bodies that excite their ideas in our minds. But neither can this be said. For though we give the materialists their external bodies, they by their own confession are never the nearer knowing how our ideas are produced, since they own themselves unable to comprehend in what manner body can act upon spirit, or how it is possible it should imprint any idea in the mind. Hence it is evident [that] the production of ideas or sensations in our minds can be no reason why we should suppose matter or corporeal substances, since that is acknowledged to remain equally inexplicable, with or without this supposition. If therefore it were possible for bodies to exist without the mind, yet to hold they do so must needs be a very precarious opinion; since it is to suppose, without any reason at all, that God has created innumerable beings that are entirely useless, and serve... no manner of purpose...

But, say you, surely there is nothing easier than to imagine trees, for instance, in a park, or books existing in a closet, and nobody by to perceive them. I answer, you may so, there is no difficulty in it; but what is all this, I beseech you, more than framing in your mind certain ideas which you call *books* and *trees*, and at the same time omitting to frame the idea of anyone that may perceive them? But do not you yourself perceive or think of them all the while? This therefore is nothing to the purpose. It only shows you have the power of imagining or forming ideas in your mind; but it does not show that you can conceive it possible [that] the objects of your thought may exist without the mind. To make out this, it is necessary that you conceive them existing uncon-ceived or unthought of – which is a manifest repugnancy.[1] When we do our utmost to conceive the existence of external bodies, we are all the while only contemplating our own ideas. But the mind, taking no notice of itself, is deluded to think it can and does conceive bodies existing unthought of or without the mind; though at the same time they are apprehended by, or exist in, itself. A little attention will discover to anyone the truth and evidence of what is here said, and make it unnecessary to insist on any other proofs against the existence of material substance.

It is very obvious, upon the least inquiry into our own thoughts, to know whether it be possible for us to understand what is meant by the *absolute existence of sensible objects in themselves, or without the mind.* To me it is evident those words mark out either a direct contradiction, or else nothing at all. And to convince others of this, I know no readier or fairer way, than to entreat they would calmly attend to their own thoughts, and if by this attention the emptiness or repugnancy of those expressions does appear, surely nothing more is requisite for their conviction. It is on this therefore that I insist, to wit, that the *absolute existence of unthinking things* are words without a meaning, or which include a contradiction. This is what I repeat and inculcate, and earnestly recommend to the attentive thoughts of the reader.

All our ideas, sensations, or the things which we perceive, by whatsoever names they may be distinguished, are visibly inactive: there is nothing of power or agency included in them. So that one idea or object of thought cannot produce, or make any alteration in, another. To be satisfied of the truth of this, there is nothing else requisite but a bare observation of our ideas. For since they and every part of them exist only in the mind, it follows that there is nothing in them but what is perceived. But whoever shall attend to his ideas, whether of sense or reflection, will not perceive in them any power or activity; there is therefore no such thing contained in them. A little attention will discover to us that the very being of an idea implies passiveness and inertness in it, insomuch that it is impossible for an idea to do anything, or, strictly speaking, to be the cause of anything... Whence it plainly follows that extension, figure, and motion cannot be the cause of our sensations. To say, therefore, that these are the effects of powers resulting from the configuration, number, motion, and size of corpuscles, must certainly be false.

We perceive a continual succession of ideas; some are anew excited, others are changed or totally disappear. There is therefore some cause of these ideas whereon

---

[1] Repugnancy: contradiction.

they depend, and which produces and changes them. That this cause cannot be any quality or idea, or combination of ideas, is clear from the preceding section. It must therefore be a substance; but it has been shown that there is no corporeal or material substance; it remains therefore that the cause of ideas is an incorporeal active substance or spirit...

I find I can excite ideas in my mind at pleasure, and vary and shift the scene as oft as I think fit. It is no more than willing, and straightway this or that idea arises in my fancy; and by the same power it is obliterated, and makes way for another... But whatever power I may have over my own thoughts, I find the ideas actually perceived by sense have not a like dependence on my will. When in broad daylight I open my eyes, it is not in my power to choose whether I shall see or no, or to determine what particular objects shall present themselves to my view; and so likewise as to the hearing and other senses, the ideas imprinted on them are not creatures of my will. There is therefore some other will or spirit that produces them.

The ideas of sense are more strong, lively, and distinct than those of the imagination; they have likewise a steadiness, order, and coherence, and are not excited at random, as those which are the effects of human wills often are, but in a regular train or series – the admirable connection whereof sufficiently testifies the wisdom and benevolence of its Author. Now the set rules or established methods, wherein the mind we depend on excites in us the ideas of sense, are called the *Laws of Nature*; and these we learn by experience, which teaches us that such and such ideas are attended with such and such other ideas, in the ordinary course of things.

7   The Limits of Metaphysical Speculation: David Hume, *Enquiry concerning Human Understanding* *

A bewildering array of metaphysical theories of reality was on offer by the mid-eighteenth century. We have already looked at three: Locke's world of objects characterized by real primary qualities inhering in an unknown material substrate; Leibniz's theory of individual substances as active centres of energy; Berkeley's total denial of material substance, or indeed anything outside the perceptions of a mind or Spirit. In his *Treatise of Human Nature* (1739–40), the Scottish philosopher David Hume asserted that the notion which Locke had referred to, of an unknown 'something' supposed to 'support' qualities was an 'unintelligible chimera'.[1] Our knowledge cannot go beyond our experience (see Part I, extract 7, above), and 'our ideas of bodies are nothing but collections formed by the mind of the ideas of the several distinct sensible qualities of which objects are composed'.[2]

In the following extracts from *An Enquiry concerning Human Understanding* (1748), Hume divides all the objects of legitimate human

---

* David Hume, *An Enquiry concerning Human Understanding* [1748]. Extracts from Section IV, part 1, and Section XII, part 3; with some changes of spelling and punctuation. There are many editions, including that by Tom L. Beauchamp (Oxford: Oxford University Press, 1999), which contains a useful introduction for students.
[1] *Treatise*, Bk I, part iv, section 3, para. 7.
[2] Ibid., para. 2.

inquiry into two classes, which he terms *Relations of Ideas* and *Matters of Fact*. The former, typified by the truths of mathematics, are established *a priori* (independently of experience), 'by the mere operation of thought'. But they form a closed system, arising merely from how our ideas or concepts are defined: they do not give us any information about what really exists in the world. Matters of fact, by contrast, concern what really exists, but no propositions of this kind can be conclusively demonstrated: there is no contradiction in denying them (that the sun will not rise tomorrow 'is no less intelligible and implies no more contradiction than that it will rise'). Instead, such truths are based entirely on experience; but all that experience reveals is what has actually been observed to happen up till now.[1] Hume goes on to underline our inability to predict, in advance of experience, how even the most familiar objects will behave: for all we know *a priori*, when one billiard ball hits another, both balls 'may remain absolutely at rest'. Moreover, though the scientist may aim to reduce all observed phenomena to a set of simple laws or principles, any attempt to speculate further

about the ultimate reality responsible for these general truths is in vain: the most perfect natural science only 'staves off our ignorance', since 'the ultimate springs and principles' of reality are 'totally shut up from human curiosity and enquiry'.[2] Finally, in our concluding passage (from the last part of the *Enquiry*) Hume summarizes his position on the two classes of truths we can know, and issues a firm warning about the futility of metaphysical inquiry going beyond these limits. Relations between ideas may be investigated by the 'abstract reasoning' of mathematics; this aside, all claims to further our knowledge about what exists must be based on experience – yet this can tell us only about actually observed phenomena, and is 'entirely silent' about any supposed ultimate reality underlying them. The closed, *a priori* reasonings of mathematics, on the one hand, and the limited results of actual observation on the other, exhaust the proper sphere of human inquiry. Any metaphysical speculation which tries to go beyond these boundaries should be committed 'to the flames: for it can contain nothing but sophistry and illusion'.

All the objects of human reason or enquiry may naturally be divided into two kinds, to wit, *Relations of Ideas*, and *Matters of Fact*. Of the first kind are the sciences of Geometry, Algebra, and Arithmetic; and in short, every affirmation which is either intuitively or demonstratively certain. *That the square of the hypotenuse is equal to the sum of the squares of the other sides* is a proposition which expresses a relation between these figures. *That three times five is equal to the half of thirty* expresses a relation between these numbers. Propositions of this kind are discoverable by the mere operation of thought, without dependence on what is anywhere existent in the universe. Though there never were a circle or triangle in nature, the truths demonstrated by Euclid would for ever retain their certainty and evidence.

Matters of fact, which are the second objects of human reason, are not ascertained in the same manner; nor is our evidence of their truth, however great, of a like nature with the foregoing. The contrary of every matter of fact is still possible; because it can never imply a contradiction, and is conceived by the mind with the same facility and distinctness, as if ever so conformable to reality. *That the sun will not rise tomorrow* is no less intelligible a proposition, and implies no more contradiction, than the affirmation *that it will rise*. We should in vain, therefore, attempt to demonstrate its falsehood. Were it demonstratively false, it would imply a contradiction, and could never be distinctly conceived by the mind.

---

[1] Hume argues elsewhere that our tendency to generalize on the basis of limited experience is based more on custom and habit than on any sound reasoning: see below, Part VII, extract 5 and extract 6.

[2] For more on why Hume maintains this, see Part VII, extract 6.

It may, therefore, be a subject worthy of curiosity, to enquire what is the nature of that evidence which assures us of any real existence and matter of fact, beyond the present testimony of our senses, or the records of our memory. This part of philosophy, it is observable, has been little cultivated, either by the ancients or moderns; and therefore our doubts and errors, in the prosecution of so important an enquiry, may be the more excusable, while we march through such difficult paths without any guide or direction. They may even prove useful, by exciting curiosity, and destroying that implicit faith and security, which is the bane of all reasoning and free enquiry. The discovery of defects in the common philosophy, if any such there be, will not, I presume, be a discouragement, but rather an incitement, as is usual, to attempt something more full and satisfactory than has yet been proposed to the public.

All reasonings concerning matter of fact seem to be founded on the relation of *Cause and Effect*. By means of that relation alone we can go beyond the evidence of our memory and senses. If you were to ask a man, why he believes any matter of fact which is absent – for instance, that his friend is in the country or in France – he would give you a reason; and this reason would be some other fact; as a letter received from him, or the knowledge of his former resolutions and promises. A man finding a watch or any other machine in a desert island would conclude that there had once been men in that island. All our reasonings concerning fact are of the same nature. And here it is constantly supposed that there is a connection between the present fact and that which is inferred from it. Were there nothing to bind them together, the inference would be entirely precarious. The hearing of an articulate voice and rational discourse in the dark assures us of the presence of some person. Why? because these are the effects of the human make and fabric, and closely connected with it. If we anatomize all the other reasonings of this nature, we shall find that they are founded on the relation of cause and effect, and that this relation is either near or remote, direct or collateral. Heat and light are collateral effects of fire, and the one effect may justly be inferred from the other.

If we would satisfy ourselves, therefore, concerning the nature of that evidence, which assures us of matters of fact, we must enquire how we arrive at the knowledge of cause and effect.

I shall venture to affirm, as a general proposition, which admits of no exception, that the knowledge of this relation is not, in any instance, attained by reasonings *a priori*, but arises entirely from experience, when we find that any particular objects are constantly conjoined with each other. Let an object be presented to a man of ever so strong natural reason and abilities, if that object be entirely new to him, he will not be able, by the most accurate examination of its sensible qualities, to discover any of its causes or effects. Adam, though his rational faculties be supposed, at the very first, entirely perfect, could not have inferred from the fluidity and transparency of water that it would suffocate him, or from the light and warmth of fire that it would consume him. No object ever discovers, by the qualities which appear to the senses, either the causes which produced it, or the effects which will arise from it; nor can our reason, unassisted by experience, ever draw any inference concerning real existence and matter of fact.

This proposition, *that causes and effects are discoverable, not by reason but by experience*, will readily be admitted with regard to such objects as we remember to have once been altogether unknown to us; since we must be conscious of the utter inability, which we then lay under, of foretelling what would arise from them. Present two smooth pieces of marble to a man who has no tincture of natural philosophy; he will never discover that they will adhere together in such a manner as to require great force to separate them in a direct line, while they make so small a resistance to a lateral pressure. Such events as bear little analogy to the common course of nature are also readily confessed to be known only by experience; nor does any man imagine that the explosion of gunpowder, or the attraction of a loadstone, could ever be discovered by arguments *a priori*. In like manner, when an effect is supposed to depend upon an intricate machinery or secret structure of parts, we make no difficulty in attributing all our knowledge of it to experience. Who will assert that he can give the ultimate reason why milk or bread is proper nourishment for a man, not for a lion or a tiger?

But the same truth may not appear, at first sight, to have the same evidence with regard to events which have become familiar to us from our first appearance in the world, which bear a close analogy to the whole course of nature, and which are supposed to depend on the simple qualities of objects, without any secret structure of parts. We are apt to imagine that we could discover these effects by the mere operation of our reason, without experience. We fancy, that were we brought on a sudden into this world, we could at first have inferred that one billiard ball would communicate motion to another upon impulse; and that we needed not to have waited for the event, in order to pronounce with certainty concerning it. Such is the influence of custom that, where it is strongest, it not only covers our natural ignorance, but even conceals itself, and seems not to take place, merely because it is found in the highest degree.

But to convince us that all the laws of nature, and all the operations of bodies without exception, are known only by experience, the following reflections may, perhaps, suffice. Were any object presented to us, and were we required to pronounce concerning the effect which will result from it, without consulting past observation, after what manner, I beseech you, must the mind proceed in this operation? It must invent or imagine some event which it ascribes to the object as its effect; and it is plain that this invention must be entirely arbitrary. The mind can never possibly find the effect in the supposed cause, by the most accurate scrutiny and examination. For the effect is totally different from the cause, and consequently can never be discovered in it. Motion in the second billiard ball is a quite distinct event from motion in the first; nor is there anything in the one to suggest the smallest hint of the other. A stone or piece of metal raised into the air, and left without any support, immediately falls; but to consider the matter *a priori*, is there anything we discover in this situation which can beget the idea of a downward, rather than an upward, or any other motion, in the stone or metal?

And as the first imagination or invention of a particular effect, in all natural operations, is arbitrary, where we consult not experience, so must we also esteem the supposed tie or connection between the cause and effect, which binds them together, and renders it impossible that any other effect could result from the operation of that cause. When I see, for instance, a billiard ball moving in a straight line towards another; even suppose motion in the second ball should by accident be suggested to me as the result of their contact or impulse, may I not conceive that a hundred different events might as well follow from that cause? May not both these balls remain at absolute rest? May not the first ball return in a straight line, or leap off from the second in any line or direction? All these suppositions are consistent and conceivable. Why then should we give the preference to one, which is no more consistent or conceivable than the rest? All our reasonings *a priori* will never be able to show us any foundation for this preference.

In a word, then, every effect is a distinct event from its cause. It could not, therefore, be discovered in the cause, and the first invention or conception of it, *a priori*, must be entirely arbitrary. And even after it is suggested, the conjunction of it with the cause must appear equally arbitrary; since there are always many other effects, which, to reason, must seem fully as consistent and natural. In vain, therefore, should we pretend to determine any single event, or infer any cause or effect, without the assistance of observation and experience.

Hence we may discover the reason why no philosopher, who is rational and modest, has ever pretended to assign the ultimate cause of any natural operation, or to show distinctly the action of that power which produces any single effect in the universe. It is confessed that the utmost effort of human reason is to reduce the principles, productive of natural phenomena, to a greater simplicity, and to resolve the many particular effects into a few general causes, by means of reasonings from analogy, experience, and observation. But as to the causes of these general causes, we should in vain attempt their discovery; nor shall we ever be able to satisfy ourselves, by any particular explication of them. These ultimate springs and principles are totally shut up from human curiosity and enquiry. Elasticity, gravity, cohesion of parts, communication of motion by impulse; these are probably the ultimate causes and principles which we shall ever discover in nature; and we may esteem ourselves sufficiently happy, if, by accurate enquiry and reasoning, we can trace up the particular phenomena to, or near to, these general principles. The most perfect philosophy of the natural kind only staves off our ignorance a little longer; as perhaps the most perfect philosophy of the moral or metaphysical kind serves only to discover larger portions of it. Thus the observation of human blindness and weakness is the result of all philosophy, and meets us at every turn, in spite of our endeavours to elude or avoid it ...

It seems to me that the only objects of the abstract sciences or of demonstration are quantity and number, and that all attempts to extend this more perfect species of knowledge beyond these bounds are mere sophistry and illusion. As the component parts of quantity and number are entirely similar, their relations become intricate and involved; and nothing can be more curious, as well as useful, than to trace, by a variety of mediums, their equality or inequality, through their different appearances. But as all other ideas are clearly distinct and different from each other, we can never advance farther, by our utmost scrutiny, than to observe this diversity, and, by an obvious reflection, pronounce one thing not to be another. Or if there be any difficulty in these decisions, it proceeds entirely from the undeterminate meaning of words, which is corrected by juster definitions. That *the square of the hypotenuse is equal to the squares of the other two sides* cannot be known, let the terms be ever so exactly defined, without a train of reasoning and enquiry. But to convince us of this proposition, *that where there is no property, there can be no injustice*, it is only necessary to define the terms, and explain injustice to be a violation of property. This proposition is, indeed, nothing but a more imperfect definition. It is the same case with all those pretended syllogistical reasonings, which may be found in every other branch of learning, except the sciences of quantity and number; and these may safely, I think, be pronounced the only proper objects of knowledge and demonstration.

All other enquiries of men regard only matter of fact and existence; and these are evidently incapable of demonstration. Whatever *is* may *not be*. No negation of a fact can involve a contradiction. The non-existence of any being, without exception, is as clear and distinct an idea as its existence. The proposition which affirms it not to be, however false, is no less conceivable and intelligible, than that which affirms it to be. The case is different with the sciences, properly so called.[1] Every proposition which is not true, is there confused and unintelligible. That the cube root of 64 is equal to the half of 10 is a false proposition, and can never be distinctly conceived. But that Caesar, or the angel Gabriel, or any being never existed, may be a false proposition, but still is perfectly conceivable, and implies no contradiction.

The existence, therefore, of any being can only be proved by arguments from its cause or its effect; and these arguments are founded entirely on experience. If we reason *a priori*, anything may appear able to produce anything. The falling of a pebble may, for aught we know, extinguish the sun; or the wish of a man control the planets in their orbits. It is only experience which teaches us the nature and bounds of cause and effect, and enables us to infer the existence of one object from that of another. Such is the foundation of moral reasoning, which forms the greater part of human knowledge, and is the source of all human action and behaviour.

Moral reasonings are either concerning particular or general facts. All deliberations in life regard the former; as also all disquisitions in history, chronology, geography, and astronomy.

The sciences which treat of general facts, are politics, natural philosophy, physic, chemistry, &c. where the qualities, causes and effects of a whole species of objects are enquired into.

Divinity or Theology, as it proves the existence of a Deity, and the immortality of souls, is composed partly of reasonings concerning particular, partly concerning general facts. It has a foundation in *reason*, so far as it is supported by experience. But its best and most solid foundation is *faith* and divine revelation.

Morals and criticism are not so properly objects of the understanding as of taste and sentiment. Beauty, whether moral or natural, is felt, more properly than perceived. Or if we reason concerning it, and endeavour to fix its standard, we regard a new fact, to wit, the general tastes of mankind, or some such fact, which may be the object of reasoning and enquiry.

When we run over libraries, persuaded of these principles, what havoc must we make? If we take in our hand any volume; of divinity or school metaphysics, for instance; let us ask, *Does it contain any abstract reasoning concerning quantity or number?* No. *Does it contain any experimental reasoning concerning matters of fact and existence?* No. Commit it then to the flames: for it can contain nothing but sophistry and illusion.

---

[1] Hume means the abstract mathematical sciences whose truths are capable of rigorous demonstration.

8   Metaphysics, Old and New: Immanuel Kant, *Prolegomena**

Hume's challenge to speculative metaphysics exerted a strong influence on subsequent philosophy, and was taken up in a systematic way by the famous German philosopher Immanuel Kant, first in his mammoth and highly complex *Critique of Pure Reason* (1781), and then in the *Prolegomena* (1783), which was intended as a more popular abstract of that work. The full title of the 'Prolegomena' ('Preamble' or 'Preliminary Remarks') is *Prolegomena to any future metaphysics which will be able to present itself as a science (Prolegomena zu einer jeden künftigen Metaphysik die als Wissenschaft wird auftreten können)*; the question Kant addresses is 'whether such a thing as metaphysics is even possible at all'.

Hume had convinced Kant that previous attempts to ascend beyond the empirical world and describe the supposed ultimate nature of reality (for example the theory of substance proposed by Leibniz (see above, extract 5)) were doomed to failure. Kant condemned such vain aspirations in a famous metaphor: 'the light dove, cleaving the air in her free flight, might imagine [absurdly] that flight would be easier still in empty space'.[1] There is, for Kant, no possible description of the world which can free itself from some reference to experience. But Kant argues that in experiencing the world, the mind is already armed with certain fundamental categories of understanding; these are *a priori*, but not in the traditional sense of being wholly abstract and independent of experience; rather they constitute the *preconditions* for all possible experience (see above, Part I, extract 8).

In the following set of extracts Kant argues that we do already possess knowledge that is both *a priori* and also genuinely informative or *synthetic*.[2] To begin with, he argues that *a priori* mathematical judgements (for example that $7 + 5 = 12$) are synthetic, since we cannot arrive at the concept of twelve merely by reflection on the notions of seven and five.[3] Second, and more important, he takes up Hume's challenge with respect to scientific knowledge (Hume had argued, extract 7 above, that we can never know any causal connections *a priori*). For Kant, the principle that every event has a cause is synthetic; yet it is *a priori* in the sense of being presupposed by experience (Kant argues elsewhere that we could not even begin to classify sets of perceptions as constituting genuine events unless the mind had the power to interpret the world in terms of causal frameworks).[4]

So there is, after all, room for a genuine metaphysics – not one which fruitlessly attempts to speculate about what lies beyond experience, but one which instead analyses and systematically lays out all the *a priori* concepts of the understanding which the mind necessarily employs in processing and interpreting the data of experience (see penultimate paragraph of extracts below). Though Kant does from time to time talk of a hidden world beyond experience, a

---

* Immanuel Kant, *Prolegomena* [1783], excerpts from §§ 1, 5, 11, 12, 18, 29, 30, 32, 33 and 'Solution of the General Problem of the Prolegomena'. English version trans. E. Belfort, in *Kant's Prolegomena* (London: Bell, 1891), pp. 12–15, 22–3, 30–1, 44, 59–60, 60–1, 62–3, 115–16; with minor modifications.

[1] *Critique of Pure Reason*, A5; B8.

[2] 'Coal burns', or 'bread nourishes', are *synthetic* propositions, since their truth cannot be established merely by analysing the meaning of the subject terms ('coal', 'bread'). Contrast this with ultimately uninformative tautological or *analytic* propositions, such as 'bachelors are unmarried', where the predicate (unmarried) is contained within the subject (contained within the concept of bachelorhood). Kant's position should be compared with that of Hume, who argues that no genuinely informative propositions can be known *a priori* (see introduction to extract 7, above).

[3] His argument here seems questionable, since the relevant proposition is clearly analytic if we define 'analytic' (as Kant himself sometimes does) as that which cannot be denied without contradiction.

[4] This argument is developed in the *Critique of Pure Reason*; see below, Part VII, extract 7.

world of what he calls *noumena* or 'Things in Themselves', he makes it clear that there can be no valid philosophical speculation about what such an independent reality might be like; human reason, when it operates properly, is necessarily confined to *phenomena* – to the world as experienced. The confusions and pretensions of traditional metaphysics arose from its attempt to describe the supposed nature of reality 'in itself'; the new 'critical' metaphysics, mapping out the necessary preconditions for human experience, can hope to provide instead 'definite and perfect knowledge'. It has, Kant concludes, the kind of validity and authority which modern astronomy has when compared to the pretensions of fortune-telling or astrology.

The distinction between analytic and synthetic judgements.

Metaphysical knowledge must contain simply judgements *a priori*; so much is demanded by the speciality of its sources. But judgements, let them have what origin they may, or let them even as regards logical form be constituted as they may, possess a distinction according to their content, by virtue of which they are either simply *explanatory* and contribute nothing to the content of a cognition, or they are *extensive*, and enlarge the given cognition; the first may be termed *analytic*, and the second *synthetic* judgements.

Analytic judgements say nothing in the predicate, but what was already thought in the conception of the subject, though perhaps not so clearly, or with the same degree of consciousness. When I say, all bodies are extended, I do not thereby enlarge my conception of a body in the least, but simply analyse it, inasmuch as extension, although not expressly stated, was already thought in that conception; the judgement is, in other words, analytic. On the other hand, the proposition 'some bodies are heavy' contains something in the predicate which was not already thought in the general conception of a body; it enlarges, that is to say, my knowledge, in so far as it adds something to my conception; and must therefore be termed a synthetic judgement.

The common principle of all analytic judgements is the principle of contradiction.

All analytic judgements are based entirely on the principle of contradiction, and are by their nature cognitions *a priori*, whether the conceptions serving as their matter be empirical or not. For inasmuch as the predicate of an affirmative analytic judgement is previously thought in the conception of the subject, it cannot without contradiction be denied of it; in the same way, its contrary, in a negative analytic judgement, must necessarily be denied of the subject, likewise in accordance with the principle of contradiction. It is thus with the propositions 'every body is extended'; 'no body is unextended'. For this reason all analytic propositions are judgements *a priori*, although their conceptions may be empirical. Let us take as an instance the proposition 'gold is a yellow metal'. Now, to know this, I require no further experience beyond my conception of gold, which contains the propositions that this body is yellow and a metal, for this constitutes precisely my conception, and therefore I have only to dissect it, without needing to look around for anything elsewhere.

Synthetic judgements demand a principle other than that of contradiction.

There are synthetic judgements *a posteriori* whose origin is empirical; but there are also others of an *a priori* certainty that spring from the Understanding and the Reason. But both are alike in this, that they can never have their source solely in the axiom of analysis, viz., the principle of contradiction; they require an altogether different principle, notwithstanding that whatever principle they may be deduced from, they must always *conform to the principle of contradiction*, for nothing can be opposed to this principle, although not everything can be deduced from it. I will first of all bring synthetic judgements under certain classes.

(1) *Judgements of experience* are always synthetic. It would be absurd to found an analytic judgement on experience, as it is unnecessary to go beyond my own conception in order to construct the judgement, and therefore the confirmation of experience is unnecessary to it. That a body is extended is a proposition possessing *a priori* certainty, and no judgement of experience. For before I go to experience I have all the conditions of my judgement already present in the conception, out of which I simply draw the predicate in accordance with the principle of contradiction, and thereby at the same time the necessity of the judgement may be known, a point which experience could never teach me.

(2) *Mathematical judgements* are in their entirety synthetic. This truth seems hitherto to have altogether escaped the analysts of human Reason; indeed, to be directly opposed to all their suppositions, although it is indisputably certain and very important in its consequences. For, because it was found that the conclusions of mathematicians all proceed according to the principle of contradiction (which the nature of every demonstrative certainty demands), it was concluded that the axioms were also known through the principle of contradiction, which was a great error; for though a synthetic proposition can be viewed in the light of the above principle, it can only be so by presupposing another synthetic proposition from which it is derived, but never by itself.

It must be first of all remarked that essentially mathematical propositions are always *a priori*, and never empirical, because they involve necessity, which cannot be inferred from experience. Should anyone be unwilling to admit this, I will limit my assertion to *pure mathematics*, the very conception of which itself brings with it the fact that it contains nothing empirical, but simply pure knowledge *a priori*.

At first sight, one might be disposed to think the proposition $7 + 5 = 12$ merely analytic, resulting from the conception of a sum of seven and five, according to the principle of contradiction. But more closely considered it will be found that the conception of the sum of 7 and 5 comprises nothing beyond the union of two numbers in a single one, and that therein nothing whatever is thought as to what the single number is that combines both the others. The conception of twelve is by no means already thought, when I think merely of the union of seven and five, and I may dissect my conception of such a possible sum as long as I please, without discovering therein the number twelve. One must leave these conceptions, and call to one's aid an intuition corresponding to one or other of them, as for instance one's five fingers... and so gradually add the units of the five given in intuition to the conception of the seven. One's conception is therefore really enlarged by the proposition $7 + 5 = 12$; to the first a new one being added, that was in no way thought in the former; in other words, arithmetical propositions are always synthetic, a truth which is more apparent when we take rather larger numbers, for we must then be clearly convinced, that turn and twist our conceptions as we may, without calling intuition to our aid, we shall never find the sum required, by the mere dissection of them ...

How is knowledge possible from pure reason?

We have already seen the important distinction between analytic and synthetic judgements. The possibility of analytic propositions can be very easily conceived, for they are based simply on the principle of contradiction. The possibility of synthetic propositions *a posteriori*, i.e., of such as are derived from experience, requires no particular explanation, for experience is nothing more than a continual adding together (synthesis) of perceptions. There remains, then, only synthetic propositions *a priori*, the possibility of which has yet to be sought for, or examined, because it must rest on other principles than that of contradiction.

But we do not require to search out the possibility of such propositions, that is, to ask whether they are possible, for there are enough of them, actually given, and with unquestionable certainty; and as the method we are here following is analytic, we shall assume at the outset that such synthetic but pure knowledge from Reason, is real; but thereupon we must investigate the ground of this possibility and proceed to ask – how is this knowledge possible? in order that, from the principles of its possibility, we may be in a position to determine the conditions, the scope, and limits of its use. The proper problem, on which everything turns, when expressed with scholastic precision, will accordingly stand thus: HOW ARE SYNTHETIC PROPOSITIONS *A PRIORI* POSSIBLE?

... Upon the solution of this problem, the standing or falling of metaphysics, in other words, its very existence, entirely depends. Let any one lay down assertions, however plausible, with regard to it, pile up conclusions upon conclusions to the point of overwhelming, if he has not been able first to answer satisfactorily the above question, I have a right to say: It is all vain, baseless philosophy, and false wisdom. You speak through pure Reason, and claim to create *a priori* cognitions, inasmuch as you pretend not merely to dissect given conceptions but new connections which do not rest on the principle of contradiction, and which you think you conceive quite independently of all experience. How do you arrive at them, and how will you justify yourself in such pretensions? ...

How is pure mathematics possible?

Pure mathematics is only possible as synthetic knowledge *a priori* in so far as it refers simply to objects of sense, whose empirical intuition has for its foundation a pure intuition *a priori* (that of time and space). Such intuition is able to serve as a foundation because it is nothing more than the pure form of sensibility itself, that precedes the real appearance of objects, in that it makes them in the first place possible. This faculty of intuiting *a priori* does not concern the *matter* of the phenomenon ... for that constitutes the empirical element therein, but only its *form*, space and time ...

To contribute something to the explanation and confirmation of the above, we have only to consider the ordinary and necessary procedure of geometricians. All the proofs of complete likeness between two figures turn finally on the fact of their covering each other – in other words the possibility of substituting one, in every point, for the other; and this is obviously nothing else but a synthetic proposition, resting on immediate intuition. Now this intuition must be given pure and *a priori*, for otherwise the proposition in question could not count as demonstratively certain, but would possess only empirical certainty (in the latter case, we would only be able to say that it has always been so observed, or it is valid only in so far as our perception has hitherto extended) . . .

How is pure natural science possible?

Although all the judgements of experience are empirical (i.e. have their ground in the immediate perception of sense), on the other hand all empirical judgements are not judgements of experience. Beyond the empirical, and beyond the given sense-intuition generally, special conceptions must be added, which have their origin entirely *a priori* in the pure understanding. Every perception is primarily subsumed under these conceptions, and it is only by means of them that it can be transformed into experience . . .

Let us now attempt a solution of Hume's problematical conception . . . namely the conception of Cause. First, there is given me *a priori*, by means of logic, the form of a conditioned judgement generally (one cognition as antecedent, the other as consequent). But it is possible that in the perception, a rule of the relation may be met with which will say that on the occurrence of a given phenomenon another always follows (though not conversely). This would be a case of making use of the hypothetical judgement – to say, for instance, if a body is illuminated long enough by the sun it will become warm. There is certainly no necessity of connection here, in other words, no conception of cause. But to continue: if the above proposition, which is merely a subjective connection of perception, is to be a proposition of experience, it must be regarded as necessary and universally valid. Such a proposition would run: sun is, through its light, the cause of heat. The above empirical rule is now looked upon as law, and indeed not just as valid of phenomena, but valid of them in relation to a possible experience – which requires thoroughly, and therefore necessarily, valid rules. I perfectly understand, then, the conception of cause as a conception necessarily belonging to the mere *form* of experience, and its possibility as a synthetic union of perceptions, in a consciousness in general. But the possibility of a thing in general as a cause I do not understand, because the conception of cause does not refer at all to things, but only indicates the condition attaching to experience: that this can only be an objectively valid knowledge of phenomena, and their sequence in time, in so far as their antecedent can be united to the consequent according to the rule of hypothetical judgements.

Hence, the pure conceptions of the understanding have no meaning whatever, when they quit the objects of experience and refer to things in themselves (*noumena*). They serve, as it were, to spell out phenomena, that these may be able to be read as experience. The axioms arising from their relation to the world of sense, only serve our understanding for use in experience. Beyond this, are only arbitrary combinations, destitute of objective reality, and the possibility of which can neither be known *a priori*, nor their reference to objects be confirmed, or even made intelligible by an example, because all examples are borrowed from some possible experience, and consequently the objects of those conceptions are nothing but what may be met with in a possible experience.

This complete solution of Hume's problem, although it turns out to be contrary to the opinion of its originator, preserves for the pure conceptions of the understanding their origin *a priori*, and for the universal laws of Nature their validity as laws of the understanding, but in such a manner that their use is limited to experience, because their possibility has its basis, solely, in the reference of the understanding to experience; not because they are derived from experience, but because experience is derived from them, which completely reversed mode of connection never occurred to Hume.

The following result of all previous researches follows from the above investigations: 'All synthetic axioms *a priori* are nothing more than principles of possible experience', and can never be referred to things in themselves, but only to phenomena as objects of experience. Hence pure mathematics no less than pure natural science can never refer to anything more than mere phenomena, and only present that which either makes experience in general possible, or which, inasmuch as it is derived from these principles, must always be able to be presented in some possible experience . . .

From the earliest ages of philosophy, investigators of pure reason have postulated, beyond the sensible essences (*phenomena*) which constitute the world of sense, special essences of the understanding (*noumena*) which are supposed to constitute a world of understanding; and since they regarded appearance and illusion as the same thing, which in an undeveloped epoch is to be excused, ascribed reality to the intelligible essence alone.

In fact, when we regard the objects of sense, as is correct, as mere appearances, we thereby at the same time confess that a thing in itself lies at their foundation although we do not know it as it is constituted in itself, but only its appearance, that is, the manner in which our senses are affected by this unknown something. The understanding then, by accepting appearances, admits also the existence of things in themselves, and we may even say that the presentation of such essences as lie at the basis of appearances, in short, mere essences of the understanding, is not only admissible, but unavoidable.

Our critical deduction does not by any means exclude such things (*noumena*), but rather limits the principles of aesthetic,[1] in such a way that these should not be extended to all things (which would change everything into mere appearance) but should only be valid of objects of a possible experience. Essences of the understanding are hereby admitted only by the emphasizing of this rule, which admits of no exception, that we know nothing definite whatever of these pure essences of the understanding, neither can we know anything of them, because our pure conceptions of the understanding, no less than our pure intuitions, concern nothing but objects of a possible experience, in short, mere essences of sense; and as soon as we leave these, the above conceptions have not the least significance remaining.

There is indeed something seductive about our pure conceptions of the understanding, namely a temptation to a transcendent use; for so I name that which transcends all

---

[1] 'Aesthetic' (from the Greek word for sensory awareness) is the term used by Kant in the *Critique of Pure Reason* to refer to the temporal and spatial intuitions in terms of which we experience the world.

possible experience. Not only do our conceptions of substance, force, action, reality, &c., which are entirely independent of experience containing no phenomenon of sense, really seem to concern things in themselves (*noumena*); but what strengthens this supposition is, that they contain a necessity of determination in themselves, to which experience can never approach. The conception of cause contains a rule, according to which from one state another follows in a necessary manner; but experience only teaches us that often, or at most usually, one state of a thing follows upon another, and can therefore acquire neither strict universality nor necessity.

Hence these conceptions of the understanding seem to have far too much significance and content for mere use in experience to exhaust their entire determination, and the understanding builds in consequence, unobserved, by the side of the house of experience, a much more imposing wing, which it fills with sheer essences of thought, without even noticing that it has overstepped the legitimate bounds of its otherwise correct conceptions...

Solution of the general problem of the Prolegomena: How is metaphysics as a science possible?

Metaphysics, as a natural disposition of Reason is real, but it is also, in itself, dialectical and deceptive... Hence to attempt to draw our principles from it, and in their employment to follow this natural but none the less fallacious illusion can never produce science, but only an empty dialectical art, in which one school may indeed outdo the other, but none can ever attain a justifiable and lasting success. In order that, as science, it may lay claim not merely to deceptive persuasion, but to insight and conviction, a Critique of Reason must exhibit in a complete system the whole stock of conceptions *a priori*, arranged according to their different sources – the Sensibility, the Understanding, and the Reason; it must present a complete table of these conceptions, together with their analysis and all that can be deduced from them, but more especially the possibility of synthetic knowledge *a priori* by means of their deduction, the principles of its use, and finally, its boundaries. Thus criticism contains, and it alone contains, the whole plan well tested and approved, indeed all the means whereby metaphysics may be perfected as a science – by other ways and means this is impossible. The question now is not, however, how this business is possible, but only how we are to set about it; how good heads are to be turned from their previous mistaken and fruitless path to a non-deceptive treatment, and how such a combination may be best directed towards the common end.

This much is certain: he who has once tried criticism will be sickened for ever of all the dogmatic trash he was compelled to content himself with before, because his Reason, requiring something, could find nothing better for its occupation. Criticism stands to the ordinary school-metaphysics exactly in the same relation as *chemistry* to *alchemy,* or as *astronomy* to fortune-telling *astrology.* I guarantee that no one who has comprehended and thought out the conclusions of criticism, even in these Prolegomena, will ever return to the old sophistical pseudo-science. He will rather look forward with a kind of pleasure to a metaphysics, certainly now within his power, which requires no more preparatory discoveries, and which alone can procure for reason permanent satisfaction.

9   Being and Involvement: Martin Heidegger, *Being and Time**

Kant's critique of traditional metaphysics aimed finally to lay to rest the claims of philosophers to describe the ultimate nature of reality as it is in itself. Many of those who followed him continued to practise metaphysics, and still sought to provide a general philosophical overview of the world and our place in it, but the characteristic orientation of these inquiries now tended to allow a central role to human consciousness (compare, for example, Hegel's account of knowledge as a gradual historical progression towards full self-consciousness: see Part I, extract 9, above). In the early twentieth century the German philosopher Martin Heidegger reintroduced the fundamental question of 'Being' as the chief topic of philosophy. In his monumental work *Being and Time* (*Sein und Zeit*, 1927), Heidegger insisted that the question of being must be prior to all other philosophical inquiries. In this he was partly harking back to Aristotle's notion of a general metaphysics of being *qua* being, a general 'ontology' mapping out the fundamental categories of being, over and above the detailed descriptions of the particular sciences (see introduction to Part II, above). 'Ontological inquiry,' as Heidegger put it, 'is indeed more primordial, as over against the ontical inquiry of the positive sciences.'

But Heidegger's metaphysics focuses on a special kind of being, that characteristic of the *human subject*. His approach to philosophy forms part of what has come to be known as *existentialism* – an approach which starts not from the objective definitions or essences of things, but from the immediate predicament of the existing human being as he or she confronts the world (on this conception, as the famous slogan has it, 'existence is prior to essence'[1]). Heidegger's ontology thus gives pride of place to our own understanding of ourselves as existing beings in the world, 'the understanding of oneself which we call *existentiell*'. Heidegger's special (and untranslatable) name for the existing human subject is *Dasein* (literally 'There-being').

We are, prior to all neat objective classifications and comfortable explanations, simply *there*; we find ourselves thrown into the world (*Geworfenheit* or 'thrownness' is, as Heidegger puts it, the 'characteristic of Dasein's being').

This characterization of the human predicament is far from a comfortable one. In common with other existentialist philosophers, Heidegger traces the vulnerability and alienation, a kind of vertigo,[2] that arises from the awareness of our raw existence in the world. But he also offers an account of our relationship to the world that is in a certain sense less alienating than seeing the world around us in terms of the abstract mathematical category of 'extended substance' (see above, extract 3). For Heidegger, the world is encountered in fundamentally human terms. In our dealings with the world we come across 'gear' or 'tackle' (*Zeug*): 'equipment for writing, sewing, transport, measurement...' We encounter a room 'not as something between four walls (in the geometrical, spatial, sense) but as equipment for residing'. The being of objects is thus a function of what Heidegger calls their 'readiness-to-hand' (for example, a hammer exists not as an object with abstract physical properties, but in the context of its use and function, in terms of our human concerns). This practical slant to Heidegger's ontology makes it importantly different from those rather austere earlier metaphysical systems which had aimed to delineate the objective essences of things in abstraction from the human perspective (compare extracts 3 and 4 above). To exist as a human being is, for Heidegger, already to be involved in specific projects and concerns; Heideggerian metaphysics thus turns out in the end to be not an abstract study of being, but rather an enterprise where understanding and valuing are inextricably intertwined. In coming to terms with the world we are drawn into a practical community of other involved agents, and thus into 'solicitous concern for others' – what Heidegger calls *Sorge*, or 'Caring'.

---

* Martin Heidegger, *Being and Time* [*Sein und Zeit*, 1927], excerpts from §§ 1, 2, 3, 4, 15, 26, 29. Trans. J. Macquarrie and E. Robinson (New York: Harper & Row, 1962), pp. 21, 25, 31, 32–5, 95–8, 160–1, 172–4.
[1] Cf. Jean-Paul Sartre, *Existentialism and Humanism* [*L'existentialisme est un humanisme*, 1946].
[2] Heidegger's term is 'falling': *Being and Time*, § 38.

The question of Being has today been forgotten. Even though in our time we deem it progressive to give our approval to 'metaphysics' again, it is here that we have been exempted from the exertions of a newly rekindled 'battle of the giants concerning being'. Yet the question we are touching upon is not just *any* question. It is one which provided a stimulus for the researches of Plato and Aristotle, only to subside from then on as a theme for actual investigation...

Inquiry, as a kind of seeking, must be guided beforehand by what is sought. So the meaning of Being must already be available to us in some way... We always conduct our activities in an understanding of being. Out of this understanding arise both the explicit question of the meaning of Being, and the tendency that leads us towards its conception. We do not *know* what being means. But even if we ask 'What *is* "Being"?', we keep within an understanding of the 'is', though we are unable to fix conceptually what that 'is' signifies. We do not even know the horizon in terms of which that meaning is to be grasped and fixed. *But this vague average understanding of Being is still a fact...*

...The positive outcome of Kant's *Critique of Pure Reason* lies in what it has contributed towards the working out of what belongs to any Nature whatsoever, not in a 'theory' of knowledge. His transcendental logic is an *a priori* logic for the subject-matter of that area of Being called 'Nature'.

But such an inquiry itself – ontology taken in the widest sense without favouring any particular ontological directions or tendencies – requires a further clue. Ontological inquiry is indeed more primordial, as over against the ontical inquiry of the positive sciences. But it remains itself naïve and opaque if in its researches into the Being of entities it fails to discuss the different possible ways of Being in general. And the ontological task of the genealogy of the different possible ways of Being (which is not to be constructed deductively) is precisely of such a sort as to require that we first come to an understanding of 'what we mean by this expression "Being"'.

The question of Being aims, therefore, at ascertaining the *a priori* conditions not only for the possibility of the sciences which examine entities as entities of such and such a type, and in so doing already operate with an understanding of Being, but also for the possibility of those ontologies themselves which are prior to the ontical sciences, and which provide their foundations. *Basically, all ontology, no matter how rich and firmly compacted a system of categories it has at its disposal, remains blind and perverted from its utmost aim if it has not first adequately clarified the meaning of Being, and conceived this clarification as its fundamental task...*

Science in general may be defined as the totality established through an interconnection of true propositions. This definition is not complete, nor does it reach the meaning of science. As ways in which man behaves, sciences have the manner of Being which this entity – man himself – possesses. This entity we denote by the term *Dasein*. Scientific research is not the only manner of Being which this entity can have, nor is it the one which lies closest. Moreover, Dasein itself has a special distinctiveness as compared with other entities, and it is worth our while to bring this to view in a provisional way...

Dasein is an entity which does not just occur among other entities. Rather it is ontically distinguished by the fact that, in its very Being, that Being is an *issue* for it. But in that case, this is a constitutive state of Dasein's Being, and this implies that Dasein, in its Being, has a relationship towards that Being – a relationship which itself is one of Being. And this means further that there is some way in which Dasein understands itself in its Being, and that to some degree it does so explicitly. It is peculiar to this entity that with it and through its Being, this Being is disclosed to it. *Understanding of Being is itself a definite characteristic of Dasein's Being.* Dasein is ontically distinctive in that it is ontological...

That kind of Being towards which Dasein can comport itself in one way or another, and always does comport itself somehow, we call *existence.* And because we cannot define Dasein's essence by citing a 'what' of the kind that pertains to a subject-matter, and because its essence lies rather in the fact that in each case it has its Being to be, and has it as its own, we have chosen to designate this entity as 'Dasein', a term which is purely an expression of its Being.

Dasein always understands itself in terms of its existence – in terms of a possibility of itself: to be itself or not itself. Dasein has either chosen these possibilities itself, or got itself into them, or grown up in them already. Only the particular Dasein decides its existence, whether it does so by taking hold or by neglecting. The question of existence never gets straightened out except through existing itself. The understanding of oneself which leads along this way we call *existentiell.* The question of existence is one of Dasein's ontical 'affairs'...

Sciences are ways of Being in which Dasein comports itself towards entities which it need not be itself. But to Dasein, Being in the world is something that belongs essentially. Thus Dasein's understanding of Being pertains with equal primordiality both to an understanding of something like a 'world' and to the understanding of the Being of those entities which become accessible within the world. So whenever an ontology takes for its theme entities whose character of Being is other than that of Dasein, it has its own foundation and motivation in Dasein's own ontical structure, in which a pre-ontological understanding of Being is comprised as a definite characteristic.

Therefore *fundamental ontology,* from which alone all other ontologies can take their rise, must be sought in the *existential analytic of Dasein...*

The Being of those entities which we encounter as closest to us can be exhibited phenomenologically if we take as our clue our everyday Being-in-the-world, which we also call our '*dealings*' in the world and *with* entities within-the-world. Such dealings have already dispersed themselves into manifold ways of concern. The kind of dealing which is closest to us is...not a bare perceptual cognition, but rather that kind of concern which manipulates things and puts them to use; and this has its own kind of 'knowledge'. The phenomenological question applies in the first instance to the Being of those entities which we encounter in such concern. To assure the kind of seeing which is here required, we must first make a remark about method.

In the disclosure and explication of Being, entities are in every case our preliminary and our accompanying theme; but our real theme is Being. In the domain of the present analysis, the entities we shall take as our preliminary theme are those which show themselves in our concern with the environment. Such entities are not thereby objects for knowing the 'world' theoretically; they are simply what gets used, what gets produced, and so forth. As entities so encountered, they become the preliminary theme of the purview of a 'knowing' which, as phenomenological, looks primarily towards Being, and which, in thus taking Being as its theme, takes these entities as its accompanying theme. This phenomenological interpretation is accordingly not a way of knowing those characteristics of entities which themselves *are*; it is rather a determination of the structure of the Being which entities possess. But as an investigation of Being, it brings to completion, autonomously and explicitly, that understanding of Being which belongs already to Dasein and which comes alive in any of its dealings with entities. Those entities which serve phenomenologically as our preliminary theme, in this case those which are used, or which are to be found in the course of production, become accessible when we put ourselves into the position of concerning ourselves with them in some such way. Taken strictly, this talk about 'putting ourselves into such a position' is misleading; for the kind of Being which belongs to such concernful dealings is not one into which we need to put ourselves first. This is the way in which everyday Dasein always *is*: when I open the door, for example, I use the latch. The achieving of phenomenological access to the entities which we encounter consists rather in thrusting aside our interpretative tendencies, which keep thrusting themselves upon us and running along with us, and which conceal not only the phenomenon of such concern, but even more those entities themselves *as* encountered of their own accord *in* our concern with them. These entangling errors become plain if in the course of our investigation we now ask which entities shall be taken as our preliminary theme and established as the pre-phenomenal basis for our study.

One may answer: 'Things'. But with this obvious answer we have perhaps already missed the pre-phenomenal basis we are seeking. For in addressing these entities as 'Things' (*res*) we have tacitly anticipated their ontological character. When analysis starts with such entities and goes on to inquire about Being, what it meets is Thinghood and Reality. Ontological explication discovers, as it proceeds, such characteristics of Being as substantiality, materiality, extendedness, side-by-sideness and so forth. But even pre-ontologically, in such Being as this, the entities which we encounter in concern are proximally hidden. When one designates Things as the entities that are 'proximally given', one goes ontologically astray, even though ontically one has something else in mind. What one really has in mind remains undetermined. But suppose one characterizes these 'Things' as Things 'invested with value'? What does 'value' mean ontologically? How are we to categorize this 'investing' and Being invested? Disregarding the obscurity of this structure of investiture with value, have we thus met that phenomenal characteristic of Being which belongs to what we encounter in our concernful dealings?

The Greeks had an appropriate term for 'Things' – *pragmata* – that is to say, that which one has to do with in one's concernful dealings (*praxis*). But ontically, the specifically pragmatic character of the *pragmata* is just what the Greeks left in obscurity; they thought of these 'proximally' as 'mere Things'. We shall call those entities which we encounter in concern *equipment* (*das Zeug*). In our dealings we come across equipment for writing, sewing, working, transportation, measurement. The kind of Being which equipment possesses must be exhibited. The clue for doing this lies in our first defining what makes an item of equipment – namely its equipmentality.

Taken strictly, then, there is no such thing as *an* equipment. To the Being of any equipment there always belongs a totality of equipment, in which it can be this equipment that it is. Equipment is essentially 'something-in-order-to...' A totality of equipment is constituted by various ways of the 'in-order-to', such as serviceability, conduciveness, usability, manipulability.

In the 'in-order-to' as a structure there lies an *assignment* or *reference* of something to something . . . Equipment, in accordance with its equipmentality, always is *in terms of* its belonging to other equipment: ink-stand, pen, ink, paper, blotting pad, table, lamp, furniture, windows, doors, room. These 'Things' never show themselves proximally as they are for themselves, so as to add up to a sum of *realia* and fill up a room. What we encounter as closest to us (though not as something taken as a theme) is the room; and we encounter it not as something 'between four walls' in a geometrical sense, but as equipment for residing. Out of this the 'arrangement' emerges, and it is in this that any individual item of equipment shows itself. Before it does so, a totality of equipment has already been discovered.

Equipment can genuinely show itself only in dealings cut to its own measure – hammering with a hammer for example. But in such dealings an entity of this kind is not grasped thematically as an occurring Thing, nor is the equipment-structure known as such even in the using. The hammering does not simply have knowledge about the hammer's character as equipment, but it has appropriated this equipment in a way which could not possibly be more suitable. In dealings such as this, where something is put to use, our concern subordinates itself to the 'in-order-to' which is constitutive for the equipment we are employing at the time; the less we just stare at the hammer-Thing, and the more we seize hold of it and use it, the more primordial does our relationship to it become, and the more unveiledly is it encountered as that which it is – as equipment. The hammering itself uncovers the specific 'manipulability' (*Handlichkeit*), of the hammer. The kind of Being which equipment possesses, in which it manifests itself in its own right, we call readiness-to-hand [*Zuhandenheit*] . . .

Being with Others belongs to the Being of Dasein, which is an issue for Dasein in its very Being. Thus as Being-with, Dasein 'is' essentially for the sake of Others. This must be understood as an existential statement as to its essence. Even if the particular factical Dasein does *not* turn to Others, and supposes that it has no need of them or manages to get along with them, it *is* in the way of Being-with. In Being with, as the existential 'for the sake of' of Others, these have already been disclosed in their Dasein. With the Being-with, their disclosedness has been constituted beforehand; accordingly this disclosedness also goes to make up significance, that is to say, worldhood. And, significance, as worldhood, is tied up with the existential 'for the sake of which'. Since the worldhood of that world in which every Dasein essentially is already, is thus constituted, it accordingly lets us encounter what is environmentally ready-to-hand as something with which we are circumspectively concerned, and it does so in such a way that together with it we encounter the Dasein-with of Others. The structure of the world's worldhood is such that Others are not proximally present-at-hand as free-floating subjects along with other Things, but show themselves in the world in their special environmental Being, and do so in terms of what is ready-to-hand in that world.

Being-with is such that the disclosedness of the Dasein-with of Others belongs to it; this means that because Dasein's Being is Being-with, its understanding of Being already implies the understanding of Others. This understanding, like any understanding, is not an acquaintance derived from knowledge about them, but a primordially existential kind of Being, which, more that anything else, makes such knowledge and acquaintance possible. Knowing oneself is grounded in Being-with, which understands primordially. It operates proximately in accordance with the kind of Being which is closest to us – Being in the world as Being-with; and it does so by an acquaintance with that which Dasein, along with Others, comes across in its environmental circumspection and concerns itself with – an acquaintance in which Dasein understands. Solicitous concern is understood in terms of what we are concerned with, and along with our understanding of it. Thus, in concernful solicitude the Other is proximally disclosed . . .

What we indicate ontologically by the term 'state of mind' is ontically the most familiar and everyday sort of thing; our mood, our Being-attuned. Prior to all psychology of moods . . . it is necessary to see this phenomenon as a fundamental *existentiale*, and to outline its structure . . .

In having a mood, Dasein is always disclosed moodwise as that entity to which it has been delivered over in its Being; and in this way it has been delivered over to the Being which, in existing, it has to be. 'To be disclosed' does not mean 'to be known as this sort of thing'. And even in the most indifferent and inoffensive everydayness, the Being of Dasein can burst forth as a naked '*that it is and has to be*'. The pure 'that is' shows itself, but the 'whence' and the 'whither' remain in darkness. The fact that it is just as everyday a matter for Dasein not to 'give in' to such moods, in other words not to follow up their disclosure and allow itself to be brought before that which is disclosed, is no evidence *against* the phenomenal facts of the case, in which the Being of the 'there' is disclosed moodwise in its 'that it is'; it is rather evidence for it. In an *ontico*-existentiell sense, Dasein for the most part evades the Being which is disclosed in the mood. In an *ontologico*-existential sense this means that even in that to which such a mood pays no attention, Dasein is unveiled in its Being-delivered-over to the 'there'. In the evasion of itself, the 'there' is something disclosed.

This characteristic of Dasein's being – this 'that it is' – is veiled in its 'whence' and 'whither', yet disclosed in itself all the more unveiledly. We call this the *throwness* of this entity into its 'there'; indeed, it is thrown in such a way that, as Being-in-the-world, it is the 'there' . . . An entity of the character of Dasein is its 'there' in such a way that, whether explicitly or not, it finds itself in its thrownness. In a state-of-mind, Dasein is always brought before itself, and has always found itself, not in the sense of coming across itself by perceiving itself, but in the sense of finding itself in the mood that it has.

10   The End of Metaphysics? Rudolf Carnap, *The Elimination of Metaphysics**

The whole enterprise of metaphysics came under heavy attack in the 1920s and '30s from a group of philosophers (originally based in Vienna) who came to be known as 'logical positivists'. Prominent among these was Rudolph Carnap, who taught at Vienna and Prague, and later (after emigrating to the United States in 1936) at Chicago and Los Angeles. One of the slogans of the positivists (to be found in the extract that follows) was 'the meaning of a statement lies in the method of its verification'. David Hume, as we have seen (extract 7, above), insisted that all our knowledge concerning matters of fact must be based on experience; Immanuel Kant (extract 8) had denied the viability of metaphysics that attempted to free itself from all reference to sensory experience. Carnap's position is that the traditional claims of metaphysicians are, in the strict sense, meaningless: they are 'pseudo-statements' that fail to assert anything at all.

Carnap argues first, that many of the individual words used by metaphysicians are no more than 'empty shells', since those who use them do not provide any empirical criterion for their use. In order to be meaningful a given word 'F' must be supported by rules which enable us to verify, in a concrete case, whether something is F or not. For a word (such as 'arthropod') to mean something, it must be possible to specify the truth-conditions for the basic sentences in

which that word occurs (these basic sentences are ones whose content can be fixed through some kind of observation or sensory experience). So for Carnap the only meaningful sentences are *either* those which (like those of logic and mathematics) are true simply in virtue of their form, *or* those which 'fall within the domain of empirical science'. 'Any statement one desires to construct which does not fall within these categories is automatically meaningless.'

Using this framework, Carnap argues that it is over-generous to dismiss traditional metaphysics as merely a collection of 'speculations' or 'fairy tales'. For assertions in these latter categories, though we may dismiss them, are at least *capable* of being true or false; metaphysical claims, by contrast, fail to make any intelligible assertions whatever. At best they can be thought of as expressions of some kind of 'attitude towards life' – something that could better be done in poetry or music.

Despite the vigorous and in some ways salutary challenge it offered, the programme of the positivists for the 'elimination of metaphysics' had ground to a halt by the 1960s. There turned out to be serious problems in formulating the verification principle in a way which was stringent enough to exclude traditional metaphysics, yet liberal enough to accommodate the complex theoretical statements of natural science.

There have been many *opponents of metaphysics* from the Greek sceptics to the empiricists of the nineteenth century. Criticisms of very diverse kinds have been set forth. Many have declared that the doctrine of metaphysics is *false*, since it contradicts our empirical knowledge. Others have believed it to be *uncertain*, on the ground that its problems transcend the limits of human knowledge. Many anti-metaphysicians have declared that occupation with metaphysical questions is *sterile*. Whether or not these questions can be answered, it is at any rate unnecessary to worry about them; let us devote ourselves entirely to the practical tasks which confront active men every day of their lives!

* Rudolf Carnap, 'The Elimination of Metaphysics through Logical Analysis of Language' [*Überwindung der Metaphysik durch Logische Analyse der Sprache*, 1932]. First published in *Erkenntnis*, vol. II. Trans. Arthur Pap, in A. J. Ayer (ed.), *Logical Positivism* (New York: Free Press, 1959), pp. 60–80; abridged.

The development of *modern logic* has made it possible to give a new and sharper answer to the question of the validity and justification of metaphysics. The researches of applied logic or the theory of knowledge, which aim at clarifying the cognitive content of scientific statements and thereby the meanings of the terms that occur in the statements, by means of logical analysis, lead to a positive and to a negative result. The positive result is worked out in the domain of empirical science; the various concepts of the various branches of science are clarified; their formal, logical and epistemological connections are made explicit. In the domain of *metaphysics*, including all philosophy of value and normative theory, logical analysis yields the negative result *that the alleged statements in this domain are entirely meaningless.* Therewith a radical elimination of metaphysics is attained, which was not yet possible from the earlier anti-metaphysical standpoints...

In saying that the so-called statements of metaphysics are *meaningless*, we intend this word in its strictest sense. In a loose sense of the word a statement or a question is at times called meaningless if it is entirely sterile to assert or ask it. We might say this for instance about the question 'what is the average weight of those inhabitants of Vienna whose telephone number ends with "3"?' or about a statement which is quite obviously false like 'in 1910 Vienna had 6 inhabitants' or about a statement which is not just empirically, but logically false, a contradictory statement such as 'persons A and B are each a year older than the other'. Such sentences are really meaningful, though they are pointless or false; for it is only meaningful sentences that are even divisible into (theoretically) fruitful and sterile, true and false. In the strict sense, however, a sequence of words is *meaningless* if it does not, within a specified language, constitute a statement. It may happen that such a sequence of words looks like a statement at first glance; in that case we call it a *pseudo-statement*. Our thesis, now, is that logical analysis reveals the alleged statements of metaphysics to be pseudo-statements...

A word which (within a definite language) has a meaning, is usually also said to designate a concept; if it only seems to have a meaning while it really does not, we speak of a 'pseudo-concept'. How is the origin of a pseudo-concept to be explained? Has not every word been introduced into the language for no other purpose than to express something or other, so that it had a definite meaning from the very beginning of its use? How, then, can a traditional language contain meaningless words? To be sure, originally every word (excepting rare cases which we shall illustrate later) had a meaning. In the course of historical development a word frequently changes its meaning. And it also happens at times that a word loses its old sense without acquiring a new one. It is thus that a pseudo-concept arises.

What, now, is *the meaning of a word*? What stipulations concerning a word must be made in order for it to be significant? (It does not matter for our investigation whether these stipulations are explicitly laid down, as in the case of some words and symbols of modern science, or whether they have been tacitly agreed upon, as is the case for most words of traditional language.) First, the *syntax* of the word must be fixed, i.e. the mode of its occurrence in the simplest sentence form in which it is capable of occurring; we call this sentence form its *elementary sentence*. The elementary sentence form for the word 'stone' e.g. is '*x* is a stone'; in sentences of this form some designation from the category of things occupies the place of '*x*', e.g. 'this diamond', 'this apple'. Secondly, for an elementary sentence S containing the word, an answer must be given to the following question, which can be formulated in various ways:

(1) What sentences is S *deducible* from, and what sentences are deducible from S?
(2) Under what conditions is S supposed to be true, and under what conditions false?
(3) How is S to be *verified*?
(4) What is the *meaning* of S?

. . . In the case of many words, specifically in the case of the overwhelming majority of scientific words, it is possible to specify their meaning by reduction to other words . . . e.g. '"arthropods" are animals with segmented bodies and jointed legs'. Thereby the above-mentioned question for the elementary sentence form of the word 'arthropod', that is for the sentence form 'the thing *x* is an arthropod', is answered: it has been stipulated that a sentence of this form is deducible from premises of the form '*x* is an animal', '*x* has a segmented body', '*x* has jointed legs', and that conversely each of these sentences is deducible from the former sentence. By means of these stipulations about deducibility (in other words: about the truth-condition, about the method of verification, about the meaning) of the elementary sentence about 'arthropod', the meaning of the word 'arthropod' is fixed. In this way every word of the language is reduced to other words and finally to the words which occur in the so-called 'observation sentences' or 'protocol sentences'. It is through this reduction that the word acquires its meaning.

For our purposes we may ignore entirely the question concerning the content and form of the primary sentences (protocol sentences) which has not yet been definitely settled. In the theory of knowledge it is customary to say that the primary sentences refer to 'the given'; but there is no unanimity on the question what it is that is given. At times the position is taken that sentences about the given speak of the simplest qualities of sense and feeling (e.g. 'warm', 'blue', 'joy' and so forth); others incline to the view that basic sentences refer to total experiences and similarities between them; a still different view has it that even the basic sentences speak of things. Regardless of this diversity of opinion it is certain that a sequence of words has a meaning only if its relations of deducibility to the protocol sentences are fixed, whatever the character-istics of the protocol sentences may be; and similarly, that a word is significant only if the sentences in which it may occur are reducible to protocol sentences.

Since the meaning of a word is determined by its criterion of application (in other words by the relations of deducibility entered into by its elementary sentence-form, by its truth-conditions, by the method of its verification), the stipulation of the criterion takes away one's freedom to decide what one wishes to 'mean' by the word. If the word is to receive an exact meaning, nothing less than the criterion of application must be given; but one cannot, on the other hand, give more than the criterion of application, for the latter is a sufficient determination of meaning. The meaning is implicitly contained in the criterion; all that remains to be done is to make the meaning explicit.

Let us suppose, by way of illustration, that someone invented the new word 'teavy' and maintained that there are things which are teavy and things which are not teavy. In order to learn the meaning of this word, we ask him about its criterion of application: how is one to ascertain in a concrete case whether a given thing is teavy or not? Let us suppose to begin with that we get no answer from him: there are no empirical signs of teavyness, he says. In that case we would deny the legitimacy of using this word. If the person who uses the word says that all the same there are things which are teavy and there are things which are not teavy, only it remains for the weak, finite intellect of man an eternal secret which things are teavy and which are not, we shall regard this as empty verbiage. But perhaps he will assure us that he means, after all, something by the word 'teavy'. But from this we only learn the psychological fact that he associates some kind of images and feelings with the word. The word does not acquire a meaning through such associations. If no criterion of application for the word is stipulated, then nothing is asserted by the sentences in which it occurs; they are but pseudo-statements.

Secondly, take the case when we are given a criterion of application for a new word, say 'toovy'; in particular, let the sentence 'this thing is toovy' be true if and only if the thing is quadrangular. (It is irrelevant in this context whether the criterion is explicitly stated or whether we derive it by observing the affirmative and the negative uses of the word.) Then we will say: the word 'toovy' is synonymous with the word 'quadrangular'. And we will not allow its users to tell us that nevertheless they 'intended' something else by it than 'quadrangular'; that though every quadrangular thing is also toovy and conversely, this is only because quadrangularity is the visible manifestation of toovyness, but that the latter itself is a hidden, not itself observable property. We would reply that after the criterion of application has been fixed, the synonymy of 'toovy' and 'quadrangular' is likewise fixed, and that we are no further at liberty to 'intend' this or that by the word.

Let us briefly summarize the result of our analysis. Let 'a' be any word and 'S(a)' the elementary sentence in which it occurs. Then the sufficient and necessary condition for 'a' being meaningful may be given by each of the following formulations, which ultimately say the same thing:

1 The *empirical criteria* for 'a' are known.
2 It has been stipulated from what protocol sentences 'S(a)' *is deducible*.
3 The *truth-conditions* for 'S(a)' are fixed.
4 The method of *verification* of 'S(a)' is known.

Many words of metaphysics, now, can be shown not to fulfil the above requirement, and therefore to be devoid of meaning... [An] example is the word 'God'. Here we must, apart from the variations of its usage within each domain, distinguish the linguistic usage in three different contexts or historical epochs, which, however, overlap temporally. In its mythological use the word has a clear meaning. It, or parallel words in other languages, is sometimes used to denote physical beings which are enthroned on Mount Olympus, in Heaven or in Hades, and which are endowed with power, wisdom, goodness and happiness to a greater or lesser extent. Sometimes the word also refers to spiritual beings which, indeed, do not have manlike bodies, yet manifest themselves nevertheless somehow in the things or processes of the visible world and are therefore empirically verifiable. In its metaphysical use on the other hand, the word 'God' refers to something beyond experience. The word is deliberately divested of its reference to a physical being or to a spiritual being that is immanent in the physical. And as it is not given a new meaning, it becomes meaningless. To be sure, it often looks as though the word 'God' had a meaning even in metaphysics. But the definitions which are set up prove on closer inspection to be pseudo-definitions. They lead either to logically illegitimate combinations of words, or to other metaphysical words (e.g. 'primordial basis', 'the absolute', 'the unconditioned', 'the autonomous', 'the self-dependent' and so forth), but in no case to the truth conditions of its elementary sentences ...

Just like ... 'God', most of the other specifically metaphysical terms are devoid of meaning, e.g. 'the Idea', 'the Absolute', 'the Unconditioned', 'the Infinite', 'the being of being', 'non-being', 'thing in itself', 'absolute spirit', 'objective spirit', 'essence', 'being in itself', 'being-for-itself', 'emanation', 'manifestation' ... etc. These expressions are in the same boat as our previously fabricated example 'teavy'. The metaphysician tells us that empirical truth-conditions cannot be specified; if he asserts that nevertheless he 'means' something, we show that this is merely an allusion to associated images and feelings which, however, do not bestow a meaning on the word. The alleged statements of metaphysics which contain such words have no sense, assert nothing, are mere pseudo-statements ...

Having found that many metaphysical statements are meaningless, we confront the question whether there is not perhaps a core of meaningful statements in metaphysics which would remain after elimination of all the meaningless ones.

Indeed, the results we have obtained so far might give rise to the view that there are many dangers of falling into nonsense in metaphysics, and that one must accordingly endeavour to avoid these traps with great care if one wants to do metaphysics. But actually the situation is that meaningful metaphysical statements are impossible. This follows from the task which metaphysics sets itself: to discover and formulate a kind of knowledge which is not accessible to empirical science.

We have seen earlier that the meaning of a statement lies in the method of its verification. A statement asserts only so much as is verifiable with respect to it. Therefore a sentence can be used only to assert an empirical proposition, if indeed it is used to assert anything at all. If something were to lie, in principle, beyond possible experience, it could be neither said nor thought nor asked.

(Meaningful) statements are divided into the following kinds. First there are statements which are true solely by virtue of their form ('tautologies' according to Wittgenstein; they correspond approximately to Kant's 'analytic judgements'). They say nothing about reality. The formulae of logic and mathematics are of this kind. They are not themselves factual statements, but serve for the transformation of such statements. Secondly there are the negations of such statements ('*contradictions*'). They are self-contradictory, hence false by virtue of their form. With respect to all other statements the decision about truth or falsehood lies in the protocol sentences. They are therefore (true or false) *empirical statements* and belong to the domain of empirical science. Any statement one desires to construct which does not fall within these categories becomes automatically meaningless. Since metaphysics does not want to assert analytic propositions, nor to fall within the domain of empirical science, it is compelled to employ words for which no criteria of application are specified and which are therefore devoid of sense, or else to combine meaningful words in such a way that neither an analytic (or contradictory) statement nor an empirical statement is produced. In either case pseudostatements are the inevitable product ...

Our claim that the statements of metaphysics are entirely meaningless, that they do not assert anything, will leave even those who agree intellectually with our results with a painful feeling of strangeness: how could it be explained that so many men in all ages and nations, among them eminent minds, spent so much energy, nay veritable fervour, on metaphysics if the latter consisted of nothing but mere words, nonsensically juxtaposed? And how could one account for the fact that metaphysical books have exerted such a strong influence on readers up to the present day, if they contained not even errors, but nothing at all? These doubts are justified since metaphysics does indeed have a content; only it is not theoretical content. The (pseudo)statements of metaphysics do not serve for the *description of states of affairs,* neither existing ones (in that case they would be true statements) nor non-existing ones (in that case they would be at least false statements). They serve for the *expression of the general attitude of a person towards life.*

...The metaphysician believes that he travels in territory in which truth and falsehood are at stake. In reality, however, he has not asserted anything, but only expressed something, like an artist. That the metaphysician is thus deluding himself cannot be inferred from the fact that he selects language as the medium of expression and declarative sentences as the form of expression; for lyrical poets do the same without succumbing to self-delusion. But the metaphysician supports his statements by arguments, he claims assent to their content, he polemicizes against metaphysicians of divergent persuasion by attempting to refute their assertions in his treatise. Lyrical poets, on the other hand, do not try to refute in their poem the statements in a poem by some other lyrical poet; for they know they are in the domain of art and not in the domain of theory.

Perhaps music is the purest means of expression of the basic attitude because it is entirely free from any reference to objects. The harmonious feeling or attitude, which the metaphysician tries to express in a moralistic system, is more clearly expressed in the music of Mozart. And when a metaphysician gives verbal expression to his dualistic-heroic attitude towards life in a dualistic system, is it not perhaps because he lacks the ability of a Beethoven to express this attitude in an adequate medium? Metaphysicians are musicians without musical ability. Instead they have a strong inclination to work within the medium of the theoretical, to connect concepts and thoughts. Now, instead of activating, on the one hand, this inclination in the domain of science, and satisfying, on the other hand, the need for expression in art, the metaphysician confuses the two and produces a structure which achieves nothing for knowledge and something inadequate for the expression of attitude.

11   The Problem of Ontology: W. V. O. Quine, *On What There Is**

Our penultimate extract, by the American thinker Willard Van Orman Quine, one of the most distinguished analytic philosophers of the twentieth century, takes a robustly down-to-earth approach to philosophical questions about ontology or being. Quine begins by addressing the 'Platonic riddle' of non-being: how can we talk coherently about non-existent entities (like Father Christmas, or the mythical winged horse, Pegasus)? Talking about these beings is surely not the same as talking about *nothing*, so must we not concede that they have some sort of being?

In responding to this puzzle, Quine avows a 'taste for desert landscapes'. To avoid cluttering up our ontology with all sorts of dubious entities, like non-existent beings, and merely possible (as opposed to actual) beings, like the 'possible fat man in the doorway', Quine follows the lead of Bertrand Russell (see Part III, extract 9, below) and proposes to analyse statements referring to such putative entities by using 'quantificational words' or 'bound variables' – expressions such as 'there is something such that …'. So the statement 'the round square cupola on Berkeley College is wooden', instead of being taken to refer to some weird non-existent entity, would simply come out as the false assertion 'there is something such that it is round and it is square and it is atop Berkeley College and it is wooden'.

One great advantage of this approach is that it avoids our being misled by what look like *names* into supposing that some entity must be being referred to: 'names are … altogether immaterial to the ontological issue, for [they] can be converted into descriptions'; and by the use of bound variables, 'descriptions can be eliminated'. Quine's manoeuvre here exemplifies a characteristic feature of the analytic school of philosophy in the mid to late twentieth century – the tendency to 'defuse' portentous metaphysical issues by the use of careful logical and linguistic analysis.

Another significant and influential aspect of Quine's approach, which emerges towards the end of our extract, is the respect it accords to science as a model for philosophy. Our acceptance of an ontology, Quine argues, is similar to our acceptance of a scientific theory, such as a system of physics: 'we adopt … the simplest conceptual scheme into which the disordered fragments of raw experiences can be fitted and arranged.' There are no absolute rules here: what will be the most convenient ontology will depend on our 'various interests and purposes'. But with simplicity as the watchword, and making sense of 'raw experiences' as the basic test, many of the grand metaphysical schemes of earlier philosophers seem likely, in the Quinean scheme of things, to lose much of their appeal.

A curious thing about the ontological problem is its simplicity. It can be put in three Anglo-Saxon monosyllables: 'What is there?' It can be answered, moreover, in a word – 'Everything' – and everyone will accept this answer as true. However, this is merely to say that there is what there is. There remains room for disagreement over cases; and so the issue has stayed alive down the centuries.

Suppose now that two philosophers, McX and I, differ over ontology. Suppose McX maintains there is something which I maintain there is not. McX can, quite consistently with his own point of view, describe our difference of opinion by saying that

* First published as an article in the *Review of Metaphysics* (1948), repr. in W. V. O. Quine, *From a Logical Point of View* (New York: Harper & Row, 1953; 2nd edn 1961); excerpts from pp. 1–2, 4, 5, 6, 7, 12, 13, 16, 17, 18, 19.

I refuse to recognize certain entities. I should protest, of course, that he is wrong in his formulation of our disagreement, for I maintain that there are no entities, of the kind which he alleges, for me to recognize; but my finding him wrong in his formulation of our disagreement is unimportant, for I am committed to considering him wrong in his ontology anyway.

When *I* try to formulate our difference of opinion, on the other hand, I seem to be in a predicament. I cannot admit that there are some things which McX countenances and I do not, for in admitting that there are such things I should be contradicting my own rejection of them.

It would appear, if this reasoning were sound, that in any ontological dispute the proponent of the negative side suffers the disadvantage of not being able to admit that his opponent disagrees with him.

This is the old Platonic riddle of nonbeing. Nonbeing must in some sense be, otherwise what is it that there is not? This tangled doctrine might be nicknamed *Plato's beard*; historically it has proved tough, frequently dulling the edge of Ockham's Razor.[1]

It is some such line of thought that leads philosophers like McX to impute being where they might otherwise be quite content to recognize that there is nothing. Thus, take Pegasus. If Pegasus *were* not, McX argues, we should not be talking about anything when we use the word; therefore it would be nonsense to say even that Pegasus is not. Thinking to show thus that the denial of Pegasus cannot be coherently maintained, he concludes that Pegasus is...

[An] overpopulated universe is in many ways unlovely. It offends the aesthetic sense of us who have a taste for desert landscapes, but this is not the worst of it. [A] slum of possibles is a breeding ground for disorderly elements. Take, for instance, the possible fat man in that doorway; and, again, the possible bald man in that doorway. Are they the same possible man, or two possible men? How do we decide? How many possible men are there in that doorway? Are there more possible thin ones than fat ones? How many of them are alike? Or would their being alike make them one? Are no *two* possible things alike? Is this the same as saying that it is impossible for two things to be alike? Or, finally, is the concept of identity simply inapplicable to unactualized possibles? But what sense can be found in talking of entities which cannot meaning-fully be said to be identical with themselves and distinct from one another? These elements are well nigh incorrigible...I feel we'd do better simply to clear [the] slum and be done with it...

Russell, in his theory of so-called singular descriptions,[2] showed clearly how we might meaningfully use seeming names without supposing that there be the entities allegedly named. The names to which Russell's theory directly applies are complex descriptive names such as 'the author of *Waverley*', 'the present King of France', 'the round square cupola on Berkeley College'. Russell analyzes such phrases systematically as fragments of the whole sentences in which they occur. The sentence 'The author of *Waverley* was a poet', for example, is explained as a whole as meaning 'Someone (better: something) wrote *Waverley* and was a poet, and nothing else wrote *Waverley*'. (The point of this added clause is to affirm the uniqueness which is implicit in the

---

[1] See introduction to Part III, extract 3, below.
[2] See Part III, extract 9, below.

word 'the', in '*the* author of *Waverley*'.) The sentence 'The round square cupola on Berkeley College is pink' is explained as 'Something is round and square and is a cupola on Berkeley College and is pink, and nothing else is round and square and a cupola on Berkeley College.' ...

The unanalyzed statement 'The author of *Waverley* was a poet' contains a part, 'the author of *Waverley*', which is wrongly supposed by McX ... to demand objective reference in order to be meaningful at all. But in Russell's translation, 'Something wrote *Waverley* and was a poet and nothing else wrote *Waverley*', the burden of objective reference which had been put upon the descriptive phrase is now taken over by words of the kind that logicians call bound variables, variables of quantification, namely, words like 'something', 'nothing', 'everything'. These words, far from purporting to be names specifically of the author of *Waverley*, do not purport to be names at all; they refer to entities generally, with a kind of studied ambiguity peculiar to themselves. These quantificational words or bound variables are, of course, a basic part of language, and their meaningfulness, at least in context, is not to be challenged. But their meaningfulness in no way presupposes there being either the author of *Waverley* or the round square cupola on Berkeley College or any other specifically preassigned objects.

Where descriptions are concerned, there is no longer any difficulty in affirming or denying being. 'There *is* the author of *Waverley*' is explained by Russell as meaning 'Someone (or, more strictly, something) wrote *Waverley* and nothing else wrote *Waverley*'. 'The author of *Waverley* is not' is explained, correspondingly, as the alternation 'Either each thing failed to write *Waverley* or two or more things wrote *Waverley*'. This alternation is false, but meaningful; and it contains no expression purporting to name the author of *Waverley*. The statement 'The round square cupola on Berkeley College is not' is analyzed in similar fashion. So the old notion that statements of nonbeing defeat themselves goes by the board. When a statement of being or nonbeing is analyzed by Russell's theory of descriptions, it ceases to contain any expression which even purports to name the alleged entity whose being is in question, so that the meaningfulness of the statement no longer can be thought to presuppose that there be such an entity.

Now what of 'Pegasus'? This being a word rather than a descriptive phrase, Russell's argument does not immediately apply to it. However, it can easily be made to apply. We have only to rephrase 'Pegasus' as a description, in any way that seems adequately to single out our idea; say, 'the winged horse that was captured by Bellerophon'. Substituting such a phrase for 'Pegasus', we can then proceed to analyze the statement 'Pegasus is', or 'Pegasus is not', precisely on the analogy of Russell's analysis of 'The author of *Waverley* is' and 'The author of *Waverley* is not.' ...

We commit ourselves to an ontology containing numbers when we say there are prime numbers larger than a million; we commit ourselves to an ontology containing centaurs when we say there are centaurs; and we commit ourselves to an ontology containing Pegasus when we say Pegasus is. But we do not commit ourselves to an ontology containing Pegasus or the author of *Waverley* or the round square cupola on Berkeley College when we say that Pegasus or the author of *Waverley* or the cupola in question is *not*. We need no longer labour under the delusion that the meaningfulness of a statement containing a singular term presupposes an entity named by the term. A singular term need not name to be significant ...

We can very easily involve ourselves in ontological commitments by saying, for example, that *there is something* (bound variable) which red houses and sunsets have in common; or that *there is something* which is a prime number larger than a million. But this is, essentially, the *only* way we can involve ourselves in ontological commitments: by our use of bound variables. The use of alleged names is no criterion, for we can repudiate their namehood at the drop of a hat unless the assumption of a corresponding entity can be spotted in the things we affirm in terms of bound variables. Names are, in fact, altogether immaterial to the ontological issue, for... names can be converted to descriptions, and Russell has shown that descriptions can be eliminated. Whatever we say with the help of names can be said in a language which shuns names altogether. To be assumed as an entity is, purely and simply, to be reckoned as the value of a variable. In terms of the categories of traditional grammar, this amounts roughly to saying that to be is to be in the range of reference of a pronoun. Pronouns are the basic media of reference; nouns might better have been named propronouns. The variables of quantification, 'something', 'nothing', 'everything', range over our whole ontology, whatever it may be; and we are convicted of a particular ontological presupposition if, and only if, the alleged presuppositum has to be reckoned among the entities over which our variables range in order to render one of our affirmations true.

We may say, for example, that some dogs are white and not thereby commit ourselves to recognizing either doghood or whiteness as entities. 'Some dogs are white' says that some things that are dogs are white; and, in order that this statement be true, the things over which the bound variable 'something' ranges must include some white dogs, but need not include doghood or whiteness. On the other hand, when we say that some zoological species are cross-fertile we are committing ourselves to recognizing as entities the several species themselves, abstract though they are. We remain so committed at least until we devise some way of so paraphrasing the statement as to show that the seeming reference to species on the part of our bound variable was an avoidable manner of speaking...

Our acceptance of an ontology is, I think, similar in principle to our acceptance of a scientific theory, say a system of physics: we adopt, at least insofar as we are reasonable, the simplest conceptual scheme into which the disordered fragments of raw experiences can be fitted and arranged. Our ontology is determined once we have fixed upon the over-all conceptual scheme which is to accommodate science in the broadest sense; and the considerations which determine a reasonable construction of any part of that conceptual scheme, for example, the biological or the physical part, are not different in kind from the considerations which determine a reasonable construction of the whole. To whatever extent the adoption of any system of scientific theory may be said to be a matter of language, the same – but no more – may be said of the adoption of an ontology.

But simplicity, as a guiding principle in constructing conceptual schemes, is not a clear and unambiguous idea; and it is quite capable of presenting a double or multiple standard. Imagine, for example, that we have devised the most economical set of concepts adequate to the play-by-play reporting of immediate experience. The entities under this scheme – the values of bound variables – are, let us suppose, individual subjective events of sensation or reflection. We should still find, no doubt, that a physicalistic conceptual scheme, purporting to talk about external objects, offers great advantages in simplifying our over-all reports. By bringing together scattered sense events and treating them as perceptions of one object, we reduce the complexity of our stream of experience to a manageable conceptual simplicity. The rule of simplicity is indeed our guiding maxim in assigning sense data to objects: we associate an earlier and a later round sensum with the same so-called penny, or with two different so-called pennies, in obedience to the demands of maximum simplicity in our total world-picture.

Here we have two competing conceptual schemes, a phenomenalistic one and a physicalistic one. Which should prevail? Each has its advantages; each has its special simplicity in its own way. Each, I suggest, deserves to be developed. Each may be said, indeed, to be the more fundamental, though in different senses: the one is epistemologically, the other physically, fundamental.

The physical conceptual scheme simplifies our account of experience because of the way myriad scattered sense events come to be associated with single so-called objects; still there is no likelihood that each sentence about physical objects can actually be translated, however deviously and complexly, into the phenomenalistic language. Physical objects are postulated entities which round out and simplify our account of the flux of experience, just as the introduction of irrational numbers simplifies laws of arithmetic. From the point of view of the conceptual scheme of the elementary arithmetic of rational numbers alone, the broader arithmetic of rational and irrational numbers would have the status of a convenient myth, simpler than the literal truth (namely, the arithmetic of rationals) and yet containing that literal truth as a scattered part. Similarly, from a phenomenalistic point of view, the conceptual scheme of physical objects is a convenient myth, simpler than the literal truth and yet containing that literal truth as a scattered part.

Now what of classes or attributes of physical objects, in turn? A platonistic ontology of this sort is, from the point of view of a strictly physicalistic conceptual scheme, as much a myth as that physicalistic conceptual scheme itself is for phenomenalism. This higher myth is a good and useful one, in turn, insofar as it simplifies our account of physics. Since mathematics is an integral part of this higher myth, the utility of this myth for physical science is evident enough. In speaking of it nevertheless as a myth, I echo that philosophy of mathematics to which I alluded earlier under the name of formalism. But an attitude of formalism may with equal justice be adopted toward the physical conceptual scheme, in turn, by the pure aesthete or phenomenalist...

But the question what ontology actually to adopt still stands open, and the obvious counsel is tolerance and an experimental spirit. Let us by all means see how much of the physicalistic conceptual scheme can be reduced to a phenomenalistic one; still, physics also naturally demands pursuing, irreducible *in toto* though it be. Let us see how, or to what degree, natural science may be rendered independent of platonistic mathematics; but let us also pursue mathematics and delve into its platonistic foundations.

From among the various conceptual schemes best suited to these various pursuits, one – the phenomenalistic – claims epistemological priority. Viewed from within the phenomenalistic conceptual scheme, the ontologies of physical objects and mathematical objects are myths. The quality of myth, however, is relative; relative, in this case, to the epistemological point of view. This point of view is one among various, corresponding to one among our various interests and purposes.

12   Why is There Anything?
Derek Parfit, *The Puzzle of Reality**

Although much ontology and metaphysics as practised by modern professional philosophers is often concerned with rather dry conceptual and logical matters, there remains an interest in what is perhaps the oldest and most mysterious metaphysical question: *Why is there anything at all?* The Oxford philosopher Derek Parfit tackles this puzzle in our final extract, and starts by observing that it could not possibly be answered in terms of a causal explanation. Going back to our introduction at the start of this Part of the volume, we might say that it thus qualifies as a truly 'metaphysical' question – one that takes us *beyond (meta)* the descriptions and explanations of the natural world that are the domain of physics. Nevertheless, that does not prevent some physicists, along with some philosophers, from speculating on such 'cosmological' matters.

In the first part of his paper, Parfit raises the much debated question of why the initial conditions of our universe were 'fine-tuned', in such a way as to allow stars, planets and life to exist. Some say this was 'just a coincidence', some that God designed it so; some (favouring the 'many worlds hypothesis') that ours is merely one of countless universes, only a few of which are fine-tuned. But this does not touch the 'Why anything?' question. Antecedently, there seem to be a number of 'global' possibilities: that every conceivable world exists, that only some possible worlds exist, and that nothing exists. Perhaps the last (the 'null hypothesis') would leave nothing to be explained? Parfit maintains that even such an empty scenario (or non-scenario) would still require explanation; though he does suggest that it might be the *easiest* possibility to explain, because the simplest. But whether simple or not, it does not get us much further forward, since it is not the possibility that actually obtains: here we all are, so there is, in fact, a universe.

In the second part of the extract, Parfit asks whether there could be a theory about the existence of the universe that leaves nothing to be explained. The belief in God is often supposed to provide such a complete explanation (compare Part VI, extracts 1 and 2, below); but Parfit considers instead a slightly different position which he calls the 'Axiarchic View' – that the universe exists because its existence is good. This view he rejects (just as, implicitly, he rejects the theistic view) on account of the notorious problem of evil: 'our world appears to be flawed' (compare Part VI, extract 5, below).

The answer Parfit eventually leaves us with is that it may be just a 'brute fact' that the universe exists: on this view, not only would the universe have no cause, it would have 'no explanation of any kind'. So we should not look for any 'selector' – any feature (like being best, or most simple, or including God) which accounts for why there is a universe (or many, or none). The mind may revolt at such apparent arbitrariness or randomness, but our extract ends with the thought that since there necessarily has to be one possibility that obtains (one universe, or many, or none), mere logic ensures that a selection is made: 'there is no need for hidden machinery'.

It is clear that in such cosmological speculations the human mind is working at the very limits of its capacity. Critics of Parfit's argument may wonder whether the timeless overarching framework of logic, which he takes to support the plausibility of the Brute Fact View, does not itself presuppose that reality is not, in the end, random and arbitrary. However that may be, such 'ultimate' metaphysical inquiries about the universe and its origins seem sure to remain a part of philosophical inquiry as long as human beings confront the mystery of existence.

---

* Derek Parfit, 'The Puzzle of Reality: Why Does the Universe Exist?', *Times Literary Supplement* (3 July 1992), 3–5; abridged.

It might have been true that nothing ever existed: no minds, no atoms, no space, no time. When we imagine this possibility, it can seem astonishing that anything exists. Why is there a universe? And things might have been, in countless ways, different. So why is the Universe as it is?

These facts cannot be causally explained. No law of nature could explain why there are any laws of nature, or why these laws are as they are. And, if God created the world, there cannot be a causal explanation of why God exists.

Since our questions cannot have causal answers, we may wonder whether they make sense. But there may be other kinds of answer.

Consider, first, a more particular question. Many physicists believe that, for stars, planets and life to be able to exist, the initial conditions in the Big Bang had to be precisely as they were. Why were these conditions so precisely right? Some say: 'If they had not been right, we couldn't even ask this question.' But that is no answer. It could be baffling how we survived some crash even though, if we hadn't, we could not be baffled.

Others say: 'There had to be some initial conditions, and those conditions were as likely as any others. So there is nothing to be explained.' To see what is wrong with this reply, we must distinguish two kinds of case. Suppose that, of a million people facing death, only one can be rescued. If there is a lottery to pick this one survivor, and I win, I would be very lucky. But there would be nothing to be explained. Someone had to win, and why not me? Consider next a second lottery. Unless my gaoler picks the longest of a million straws, I shall be beheaded. If I win this lottery, there *would* be something to be explained. It would not be enough to say, 'That result was as likely as any other.' In the first lottery, nothing special happened: whatever the result, someone's life would be saved. In this second lottery, the result *was* special. Of the million possible results, only one would save a life. Why was *this* what happened? Though this might be a coincidence, the chance of that is only one in a million. I could be almost certain that this lottery was rigged.

The Big Bang, it seems, was like the second lottery. For life to be possible, the initial conditions had to be selected with the kind of accuracy that would be needed to hit a bull's-eye in a distant galaxy. Since it is not arrogant to think life special, this appearance of fine-tuning needs to be explained. Of the countless possible initial conditions, why were the ones that allowed for life *also* the ones that actually obtained?

On one view, this was a mere coincidence. That is conceivable, but most unlikely. On some estimates, the chance is below one in a billion billion. Others say: 'The Big Bang *was* fine-tuned. It is not surprising that God chose to make life possible.' We may be tempted to dismiss this answer, thinking it improbable that God exists. But should we put the chance as low as one in a billion billion? If not, this is a better explanation.

There is, however, a rival explanation. Our Universe may not be the whole of reality. Some physicists suggest that there are many other Universes – or, to avoid confusion, *worlds*. These worlds have the same laws of nature as our own world, and they emerged from similar Big Bangs, but each had slightly different initial conditions. On this *many-worlds hypothesis*, there would be no need for fine-tuning. If there were enough Big Bangs, it would be no surprise that, in a few of these, conditions were just right for life. And it would be no surprise that our Big Bang was one of these few.

On most versions of this theory, these many worlds are not causally related, and each has its own space and time. Some object that, since our world could not be affected by such other worlds, we have no reason to believe in them. But we do have such a reason, since their existence would explain an otherwise puzzling feature of our world: the appearance of fine-tuning.

How should we choose between these explanations? The many-worlds hypothesis is more cautious, since it merely claims that there is more of the kind of reality we know. But God's existence has been claimed to be intrinsically more plausible. By 'God' we mean a being who is omnipotent, omniscient and wholly good. The existence of such a being has been claimed to be both simpler, and less arbitrary, than the existence of many complicated and specific worlds.

If such a God exists, however, why is the Universe as it is? It may not be surprising that God chose to make life possible. But the laws of nature could have been different, so there are many possible worlds that would have contained life. It is hard to understand why, with all these possibilities, God chose to create *our* world. The greatest difficulty here is the problem of evil. There appears to be suffering which any good person, knowing the truth, would have prevented if he could. If there is such suffering, there cannot be a God who is omnipotent, omniscient and wholly good.

One response to this problem is to revise our view of God. Some suggest that God is not omnipotent. But, with that revision, the hypothesis that God exists becomes less plausible. How could there be a being who, though able to create our world, cannot prevent such suffering? Others believe in a god who, whatever he is called, is not good. Though that view more easily explains the character of life on Earth, it may seem in other ways less credible.

As we shall see, there may be other answers to this problem. But we have larger questions to consider. I began by asking why things are as they are. We must also ask *how* things are. There is much about our world that we have not discovered. And, just as there may be other worlds like ours, there may be worlds that are very different.

It will help to distinguish two kinds of possibility. For each particular kind of possible world, there is the *local* possibility that such a world exists. If there is such a world, that leaves it open whether there are also other worlds. *Global* possibilities, in contrast, cover the whole Universe, or everything that ever exists. One global possibility is that *every* conceivable world exists. That is claimed by the *all-worlds hypothesis*. Another possibility, which might have obtained, is that nothing ever exists. This we can call the *Null Possibility*. In each of the remaining possibilities, the number of possible worlds that exist is between none and all. There are countless of these possibilities, since there are countless combinations of particular possible worlds.

Of these different global possibilities, one must obtain, and only one can obtain. So we have two questions. Which obtains, and why? These questions are connected. If some possibility would be less puzzling, or easier to explain, we have more reason to think that it obtains. That is why, rather than believing that the Big Bang merely happened to be right for life, we should believe either in God or in many worlds.

Is there some global possibility whose obtaining would be in no way puzzling? That might be claimed of the Null Possibility. It might be said that, if no one had ever existed, no one would have been puzzled. But that misunderstands our question. Suppose that, in a mindless and finite Universe, an object looking like the *Times*

Literary Supplement spontaneously formed. Even with no one to be puzzled, that would be, in the sense I mean, puzzling. It may next be said that, if there had never been anything, there wouldn't have been anything to be explained. But that is not so. When we imagine that nothing ever existed, what we imagine away are such things as minds and atoms, space and time. There would still have been truths. It would have been true that nothing existed, and that things might have existed. And there would have been other truths, such as the truth that 27 is divisible by 3. We can ask why these things would have been true.

These questions may have answers. We can explain why, even if nothing had ever existed, 27 would have been divisible by 3. There is no conceivable alternative. And we can explain the non-existence of such things as two-horned unicorns, or spherical cubes. Such things are logically impossible. But why would *nothing* have existed? Why would there have been no stars or atoms, no minds or bluebell woods? How could *that* be explained?

We should not claim that, if nothing had existed, there would have been nothing to be explained. But we might claim something less. Perhaps, of all the global possibilities, this would have needed the least explanation. It is much the simplest. And it seems the easiest to understand. When we imagine there never being anything, that does not seem, as our own existence can, astonishing.

Here, for example, is one natural line of thought. It may seem that, for any particular thing to exist, its existence must have been caused by other things. If that is so, what could have caused them *all* to exist? If there were an infinite series of things, the existence of each might be caused by other members of that series. But that could not explain why there was this whole series, rather than some other series, or no series. In contrast, the Null Possibility raises no such problem. If nothing had ever existed, that state of affairs would not have needed to be caused.

Even if this possibility would have been the easiest to explain, it does not obtain. Reality does not take its simplest and least puzzling form.

Consider next the all-worlds hypothesis. That may seem the next least puzzling possibility. For one thing, it avoids arbitrary distinctions. If only one world exists, we have the question: 'Out of all the possible worlds, why is *this* the one that exists?' On the many-worlds hypothesis, we have the question: 'Why are *these* the ones?' But, if *all* possible worlds exist, there is no such question. Though the all-worlds hypothesis avoids that question, it is not as simple as it seems. Is there a sharp distinction between those worlds that are and are not possible? Must all worlds be governed by natural laws? Does each kind of world exist only once? And there are further complications.

Whichever global possibility obtains, we can ask why it obtains. All that I have claimed so far is that, with some possibilities, this question would be less puzzling. We should now ask: Could this question have an answer? Is there a theory that leaves nothing unexplained?

On one kind of view, it is logically necessary that God, or the whole Universe, exists. Though it may seem conceivable that there might never have been anything, that is not really logically possible. Some people even claim that there is only one coherent global possibility. If such a view were true, everything would be explained. But the standard objections to such views, which I shall not repeat, seem to me convincing.

Others claim that the Universe exists because its existence is good. This is the Platonic, or Axiarchic View. Even if we think this view absurd, it is worth asking whether it makes sense. That may suggest other possibilities... The main objection to this view is the problem of evil. Our world appears to be flawed...

If we reject the Axiarchic View, what conclusion should we draw? Is the existence of our world a mere brute fact, with no explanation? That does not follow. If we abstract from the optimism of this view, its claims are these. One global possibility has a special feature, this is the possibility that obtains, and it obtains because it has this feature. Other views can make such claims.

Suppose that our world were part of the worst possible Universe. Its bright days may only make its tragedies worse. If reality were as bad as it could be, could we not suspect that this was no coincidence?

Suppose next, more plausibly, that all possible worlds exist. That would also be grim, since the evil of the worst worlds could hardly be outweighed. But that would be incidental. If every conceivable world exists, reality has a different distinctive feature. It is *maximal*: as full and varied as it could possibly be. If this is true, is it a coincidence? Does it merely happen to be true that, of all the countless global possibilities, the one that obtains is at this extreme? As always, that is conceivable. Coincidences can occur. But it seems hard to believe. We can reasonably assume that, if all possible worlds exist, that is *because* that makes reality as full as it could be.

Similar remarks apply to the Null Possibility. If there had never been anything, would that have been a coincidence? Would it have merely happened that, of all the possibilities, what obtained was the *only* possibility in which nothing exists? That is also hard to believe. Rather, if this possibility had obtained, that would have been because it had that feature.

Here is another special feature. Perhaps reality is as it is because that makes its fundamental laws as mathematically beautiful as they could be. That is what many physicists believe.

If some possibility obtains because it has some feature, that feature selects what reality is like. Let us call it the *Selector*. A feature is a *plausible* Selector if we can reasonably believe that, were reality to have that feature, that would not merely happen to be true.

There are countless features which are not plausible Selectors. Suppose that fifty-eight worlds exist. Like all numbers, 58 has some special features. For example, it is the smallest number that is the sum of seven primes. But that could hardly be *why* that number of worlds exist.

I have mentioned certain plausible Selectors. A possibility might obtain because it is the best, or the simplest, or the least arbitrary, or because it makes reality as full as it could be, or because its fundamental laws are as elegant as they could be. There are, I assume, other such features, some of which we have yet to discover.

For each of these features, there is the *explanatory* possibility that this feature *is* the Selector. That feature then explains why reality is as it is. There is one other, special explanatory possibility: that there is *no* Selector. This is like the global possibility that nothing exists. If there is no Selector, it is random that reality is as it is. Events may be in one sense random, even though they are causally inevitable. That is how it is random whether a meteorite strikes the land or the sea. Events are random in a stronger sense if they have no cause. That is what most physicists believe about some facts at the quantum level, such as how some particles move. If it is random what reality is like, the Universe would not only have no cause. It would have no explanation of any kind. This we can call the *Brute Fact View*.

On this view, we should not expect reality to have very special features, such as being maximal, or best, or having very simple laws, or including God. In much the largest range of the global possibilities, there would exist an arbitrary set of messily complicated worlds. That is what, with a random selection, we should expect. It is unclear whether ours is one such world.

The Brute Fact View may seem hard to understand. It may seem baffling how reality could be even randomly selected. What kind of *process* could select whether time had no beginning, or whether anything ever exists? But this is not a real problem. It is logically necessary that one global possibility obtains. There is no conceivable alternative. Since it is necessary that one possibility obtains, it is necessary that it be settled which obtains. Even without any kind of process, logic ensures that a selection is made. There is no need for hidden machinery.

If reality were randomly selected, it would not be mysterious *how* the selection is made. It would be in one sense inexplicable why the Universe is as it is. But this would be no more puzzling than the random movement of a particle. If a particle can simply happen to move as it does, it could simply happen that reality is as it is. Randomness may even be *less* puzzling at the level of the whole Universe, since we know that facts at this level could not have been caused.[1]

Specimen Questions

1 Why does Plato compare ordinary human existence to that of chained prisoners in a cave?

2 What does Aristotle mean by 'substance'? How do his views on reality differ from Plato's?

3 Explain Descartes's theory of matter as 'extended substance'. Why was it suited to the 'new' quantitative approach to science?

4 Why does Locke maintain some of our ideas 'resemble' qualities actually in objects, while others do not? Can his distinction be defended?

5 Explain why Leibniz thought a purely mathematical account of nature was inadequate. What special features of reality does his theory of substance try to explain?

6 Examine Berkeley's argument that 'houses, mountains and rivers' do not have an existence apart from being perceived. Explain the role of God in his conception of reality.

7 Explain Hume's distinction between 'relations of ideas' and 'matters of fact'. Why did he think much traditional metaphysics should be 'committed to the flames'?

---

[1] For a longer, later discussion of these questions, see Parfit, 'Why Anything? Why This?', *London Review of Books*, 20: 2 (22 Jan. 1998), 24–7; 20: 3 (5 Feb. 1998), 22–5.

8   Examine Kant's answer to the question: how is metaphysics as a science possible?

9   What did Heidegger mean by saying that '*Dasein* always understands itself in terms of its existence'? What did he mean by saying that we understand the being of an object like a hammer in terms of its 'readiness-to-hand'?

10   Why did Carnap maintain that much traditional metaphysics was not just false but meaningless? Is his view defensible?

11   How does Quine propose to solve the 'riddle of non-being'?

12   Does Parfit succeed in dealing with, or at least reducing, the puzzle of existence?

Suggestions for Further Reading

A useful reference work containing articles on most of the philosophers included in this Part is J. Kim and E. Sosa (eds), *A Companion to Metaphysics* (Oxford: Blackwell, 1995).

Plato
Plato, *Republic.* For editions and other relevant materials see reading list at the end of Part I, above. For Plato's theory of Forms, see J. Annas, *An Introduction to Plato's Republic* (Oxford: Oxford University Press, 1981).

See also G. Vlastos, 'Degrees of Reality in Plato', in R. Bambrough (ed.), *New Essays on Plato and Aristotle* (London: Routledge, 1965); N. P. White, *Plato on Knowledge and Reality* (Indianapolis: Hackett, 1976); R. Kraut (ed.), *The Cambridge Companion to Plato* (Cambridge: Cambridge University Press, 1991).

Aristotle
Aristotle, *Categories and De Interpretatione*, trans. and ed. J. Ackrill (Oxford: Clarendon, 1963). For general introductory materials on Aristotle, see readings at the end of Part I. An excellent discussion of Aristotle's metaphysical views may be found in chapter 3 of J. Barnes (ed.), *The Cambridge Companion to Aristotle* (Cambridge: Cambridge University Press, 1995).

For a more detailed study of Aristotle's metaphysics, see T. H. Irwin, *Aristotle's First Principles* (Oxford: Clarendon, 1988).

See also the collection of articles in J. Barnes, M. Schofield, and R. Sorabji (eds), *Articles on Aristotle*, vol. III: *Metaphysics* (London: Duckworth, 1979).

Descartes
See readings on Descartes at the end of Part I.

For a stimulating discussion of the Cartesian revolution in physics and metaphysics, see D. Garber, *Descartes' Metaphysical Physics* (Chicago: University of Chicago Press, 1992).

Locke
See readings on Locke at the end of Part I.

For a clear account of the Lockean distinction between primary and secondary qualities, see P. Alexander, *Ideas, Qualities and Corpuscles* (Cambridge: Cambridge University Press, 1985).

Leibniz
Leibniz, *New System* [1695], in *Philosophical Writings*, ed. G. H. R. Parkinson (rev. edn, London: Dent, 1973).

For other texts and commentaries on Leibniz, see readings at the end of Part I.

A detailed study of the metaphysical aspects of Leibniz's philosophy is R. M. Adams, *Leibniz: Determinist, Theist, Idealist* (New York: Oxford University Press, 1994).

Berkeley
Berkeley, G., *Principles of Human Knowledge* [1710]. See also *Three Dialogues* [1713] in *Philosophical Works*, ed. M. Ayers (London: Dent, 1975).

Useful introductions to Berkeley's thought are J. Dancy, *Berkeley: An Introduction* (Oxford: Blackwell, 1987); J. O. Urmson, *Berkeley* (Oxford: Oxford University Press, 1982); G. Warnock, *Berkeley* (3rd edn, Oxford: Blackwell, 1982).

More detailed studies are: A. Grayling, *Berkeley: The Central Arguments* (London: Duckworth, 1986); I. C. Tipton, *Berkeley: The Philosophy of Immaterialism* (London: Methuen, 1974); K. P. Winkler, *Berkeley: An Interpretation* (Oxford: Clarendon, 1989); R. Fogelin, *Berkeley and the Principles of Knowledge* (London: Routledge, 2001).

Hume

See readings on Hume at the end of Part I. See also ch. 3 of D. F. Norton (ed.), *The Cambridge Companion to Hume* (Cambridge: Cambridge University Press, 1994).

Kant

Kant, I., *Prolegomena* [1783], ed. G. Zöller (Oxford: Oxford University Press, 2004); contains an introduction and analysis of the arguments.

For other texts and commentaries on Kant, see readings at the end of Part I.

See also H. E. Allinson, *Kant's Transcendental Idealism* (New Haven, Conn.: Yale University Press, 1983) and P. Guyer (ed.), *The Cambridge Companion to Kant* (Cambridge: Cambridge University Press, 1992), esp. introduction and ch. 4.

Heidegger

Heidegger, M., *Being and Time* [*Sein und Zeit*, 1927], trans. J. Macquarrie and E. Robinson (New York: Harper & Row, 1962).

For a clear and accessible introduction to Heidegger's thought, see G. Steiner, *Heidegger* (2nd edn, London: Harper Collins, 1992), and for a more detailed commentary, H. L. Dreyfus, *Being in the World: A Commentary on Heidegger's 'Being and Time', Division I* (Cambridge, Mass.: MIT Press, 1991).

For a useful collection of essays on all aspects of Heidegger's philosophy, see C. B. Guignon (ed.), *The Cambridge Companion to Heidegger* (Cambridge: Cambridge University Press, 1993).

Carnap

Carnap, R., 'The Elimination of Metaphysics through Logical Analysis of Language' [*Überwindung der Metaphysik durch Logische Analyse der Sprache*, 1932]. English version in the following useful collection with a valuable introduction by the editor: A. J. Ayer (ed.), *Logical Positivism* (New York: Free Press, 1959).

See also O. Hanfling (ed.), *Essential Readings in Logical Positivism* (Oxford: Blackwell, 1987); A. J. Ayer (ed.), *Language, Truth and Logic* (2nd edn, London: Gollancz, 1946); P. Schlipp, *The Philosophy of Rudolph Carnap* (La Salle, Ill.: Open Court, 1963).

Quine

Several of Quine's most important philosophical papers are contained in his *From A Logical Point of View* (Cambridge, Mass.: Harvard University Press, 1953; rev. edn 1961).

For an excellent study of Quine's philosophy, see Christopher Hookway's *Quine: Language, Experience and Reality* (Stanford, Calif.: Stanford University Press, 1988).

A useful collection of critical essays is R. Barrett and R. Gibson (eds), *Perspectives on Quine* (Oxford: Blackwell, 1990).

Parfit

Recent discussions on the puzzle of existence (noted by Parfit as having influenced him) include John Leslie, *Value and Existence* (Oxford: Blackwell, 1979) and *Universes* (London: Routledge, 1989), and Robert Nozick, *Philosophical Explanations* (Oxford: Clarendon, 1981), ch. 3.

There is a response to Parfit's article by Richard Swinburne in P. van Inwagen and M. Zimmerman (eds), *Metaphysics: The Big Questions* (Oxford: Blackwell, 1998).

A careful analytic discussion of some of the issues is Bede Rundle, *Why There is Something Rather than Nothing* (Oxford: Clarendon, 2004).

PART III

Language and Meaning

Language and Meaning
Introduction

Philosophy has always been concerned with language and meaning; indeed, some would say that this is its true and distinctive subject-area. Such was the view of the Oxford philosopher Michael Dummett, writing in the 1970s, at the height of the so-called 'linguistic movement' in philosophy. In the past, he argued, philosophers had taken themselves to be investigating the most general properties of the universe, or the workings of the human mind, or the justifications for our knowledge claims. But only with the rise of the modern logical and analytic style of philosophizing 'was the proper object of philosophy finally established, namely... the analysis of the structure of *thought*, [for which] the only proper method [is] the analysis of *language*'.[1]

The 'analytic' movement Dummett refers to here was inaugurated by the German philosopher Gottlob Frege, and, in England, Bertrand Russell; extracts from both authors are included below. But, as we often find in this volume, modern developments did not spring from nowhere. Classical, medieval and early-modern thinkers had uncovered crucial issues about the nature of language and its relation on the one hand to our thought, and on the other hand to the world around us; and the questions raised, and the answers offered, shaped much subsequent philosophical inquiry. The extent to which the analysis of language is the key to philosophy remains a matter for debate. It is undeniable that many of the puzzles of philosophy arise from conceptual and linguistic confusions; hence the great twentieth-century philosopher Ludwig Wittgenstein maintained that the job of philosophy was to free us from the 'bewitchment of our intellect by means of language' (*Philosophical Investigations* [1953], §109). Although it seems doubtful that all philosophical problems could be solved through conceptual clarification, getting clear about the logical structure of our language is certainly of vital importance for all areas of philosophical inquiry.

---

[1] Michael Dummett, 'Can Analytic Philosophy Be Systematic?' [1975], in *Truth and Other Enigmas* (London: Duckworth, 1978), p. 458.

1   The Meanings of Words: Plato, *Cratylus**

Philosophical inquiry often begins when we start to ask awkward questions about what is normally taken for granted. In our opening extract, from the start of Plato's dialogue *Cratylus*, we are plunged into a discussion about how words get their meaning. Hermogenes begins by stating the view of Cratylus that everything has a right name of its own, which is somehow determined by nature, not merely by convention. Hermogenes is inclined to disagree. After all, the names of children are given to them at birth by their parents, and it seems that they can be changed at will (for 'we frequently change the names of our slaves, and the new name is as correct as the old'). So perhaps there is nothing more to meaning than the decision to use a word in a certain way.

But whatever might be true of names, or proper nouns, Socrates is quick to point out that in the case of common nouns (such as 'horse') the meaning cannot be a matter of arbitrary decision – as if I could just decide to use the word 'horse' to refer to a cow. For names, Socrates explains, are the smallest units that figure in propositions (for example, the noun *horse* figures in the proposition, or assertion, that this horse is white); and so they play a role in the *truth* of those propositions. This already suggests that their meanings cannot simply depend on the arbitrary choice of the speaker.

Socrates then proceeds to mount a frontal attack on the kind of relativism associated with his contemporary, the sophist Protagoras, who famously declared that 'man is the measure of all things'. Such radical relativism, Socrates argues, contradicts our strong intuition that there are genuine objective differences in people and their actions: 'things must be supposed to have their own proper and permanent essence; they are not in relation to us, or influenced by us, fluctuating according to our fancy'. The argument then proceeds to draw an analogy with various arts and crafts, like weaving or drilling,

where the instruments appropriate in each case do not depend on the arbitrary wishes of the user, but are determined by the nature of the activity in question. So just as there are right and wrong ways of using instruments (like the weaver's shuttle), so there are right and wrong ways of using words. And just as in manufacture we look to the expert craftsman, so when it comes to the meanings of words, we should look to the expert 'legislator', who 'ought to know how to put the true natural name of each thing into sounds and syllables'.

The idea of a 'linguistic legislator' who has knowledge of the 'true natural name of each thing' might seem very odd – especially when we remember that there are many different languages in the world, each with its own vocabulary. But Socrates allows that 'different legislators will not use the same syllables' any more than 'every metalworker makes instruments of the same iron': 'the instrument may be equally good, of whatever iron it is made, whether in Greece or in a foreign country.'

But what determines the 'correctness' of a name or word? Developing his idea that naming demands technical knowledge, Socrates goes on (after the passage excerpted below) to give many examples of names or words that are formed by derivation or composition from other words. So meaning, again, is not an arbitrary matter, but is tied to etymology – the science of how words are derived. Later on in the dialogue, Socrates discusses the notion that words represent things, either by having some natural likeness to the things they represent, or simply by association; this latter alternative suggests there may be some truth in Hermogenes' original suggestion: custom and convention do after all play a role in determining meaning. No final conclusions are reached, but Plato has succeeded in raising some central philosophical questions about the nature of language and its relation to the world.

* Plato, *Cratylus* [*c*.375 BC], 383a–391b. Trans. B. Jowett, in *The Dialogues of Plato* (Oxford: Clarendon, 1892); with minor modifications.

HERMOGENES: I should explain to you, Socrates, that our friend Cratylus has been arguing about names; he says that they are natural and not conventional; not a portion of the human voice which men agree to use; but that there is a truth or correctness in them, which is the same for Greeks as for foreigners. Whereupon I ask him, whether his own name of Cratylus is a true name or not, and he answers 'Yes.' And Socrates? 'Yes.' Then every man's name, as I tell him, is that which he is called. To this he replies – 'If all the world were to call you Hermogenes, that would not be your name.' And when I am anxious to have a further explanation he is ironical and mysterious, and seems to imply that he has a notion of his own about the matter, if he would only tell, and could entirely convince me, if he chose to be intelligible. Tell me, Socrates, what this oracle means; or rather tell me, if you will be so good, what is your own view of the truth or correctness of names, which I would far sooner hear.

SOCRATES: Son of Hipponicus, there is an ancient saying, that 'hard is the knowledge of the good'. And the knowledge of names is a great part of knowledge. If I had not been poor, I might have heard the fifty-drachma course of the great Prodicus, which is a complete education in grammar and language – these are his own words – and then I should have been at once able to answer your question about the correctness of names. But, indeed, I have only heard the single-drachma course, and therefore, I do not know the truth about such matters; I will, however, gladly assist you and Cratylus in the investigation of them. When he declares that your name is not really Hermogenes, I suspect that he is only making fun of you; – he means to say that you are no true son of Hermes, because you are always looking after a fortune and never in luck. But, as I was saying, there is a good deal of difficulty in this sort of knowledge, and therefore we had better leave the question open until we have heard both sides.

HERMOGENES: I have often talked over this matter, both with Cratylus and others, and cannot convince myself that there is any principle of correctness in names other than convention and agreement; any name which you give, in my opinion, is the right one, and if you change that and give another, the new name is as correct as the old – we frequently change the names of our slaves, and the newly-imposed name is as good as the old: for there is no name given to anything by nature; all is convention and habit of the users; – such is my view. But if I am mistaken I shall be happy to hear and learn of Cratylus, or of any one else.

SOCRATES: I dare say that you may be right, Hermogenes: let us see; – Your meaning is, that the name of each thing is merely that which anybody agrees to call it?

HERMOGENES: That is my notion.

SOCRATES: Whether the giver of the name be an individual or a city?

HERMOGENES: Yes.

SOCRATES: Well, now, let me take an instance. Suppose that I call a man a horse or a horse a man, you mean to say that a man will be rightly called a horse by me individually, and rightly called a man by the rest of the world; and a horse again would be rightly called a man by me and a horse by the world – that is your meaning?

HERMOGENES: That is my opinion.

SOCRATES: But how about truth, then? You would acknowledge that there is in words a true and a false?

HERMOGENES: Certainly.

SOCRATES: And there are true and false propositions?

HERMOGENES: To be sure.

SOCRATES: And a true proposition says that which is, and a false proposition says that which is not?

HERMOGENES: Yes; what other answer is possible?

SOCRATES: Then in a proposition there is a true and false?

HERMOGENES: Certainly.

SOCRATES: But is a proposition true as a whole only, and are the parts untrue?

HERMOGENES: No; the parts are true as well as the whole.

SOCRATES: Would you say the large parts and not the smaller ones, or every part?

HERMOGENES: I should say that every part is true.

SOCRATES: Is a proposition resolvable into any part smaller than a name?

HERMOGENES: No; that is the smallest.

SOCRATES: Then the name is a part of the true proposition?

HERMOGENES: Yes.

SOCRATES: Yes, and a true part, as you say.

HERMOGENES: Yes.

SOCRATES: And is not the part of a falsehood also a falsehood?

HERMOGENES: Yes.

SOCRATES: Then, if propositions may be true and false, names may be true and false?

HERMOGENES: So we must infer.

SOCRATES: And the name of anything is that which any one affirms to be the name?

HERMOGENES: Yes.

SOCRATES: And will there be so many names of each thing as everybody says that there are? And will they be true names at the time of uttering them?

HERMOGENES: Yes, Socrates, I can conceive no correctness of names other than this. You give one name, and I another. And in different cities and countries there are different names for the same things; Hellenes differ from foreigners in their use of names, and the several Hellenic tribes from one another.

SOCRATES: But would you say, Hermogenes, that the things differ as the names differ? Are they relative to individuals, as Protagoras tells us? For he says that man is the measure of all things, and that things are to me as they appear to me, and that they are to you as they appear to you. Do you agree with him, or would you say that things have a permanent essence of their own?

HERMOGENES: There have been times, Socrates, when I have been driven in my perplexity to take refuge with Protagoras; not that I agree with him at all.

SOCRATES: What! Have you ever been driven to admit that there was no such thing as a bad man?

HERMOGENES: No, indeed; but I have often had reason to think that there are very bad men, and a good many of them.

SOCRATES: Well, and have you ever found any very good ones?

HERMOGENES: Not many.

SOCRATES: Still you have found them?

HERMOGENES: Yes.

SOCRATES: And would you hold that the very good were the very wise, and the very evil very foolish? Would that be your view?

HERMOGENES: It would.

SOCRATES: But if Protagoras is right, and the truth is that things are as they appear to any one, how can some of us be wise and some of us foolish?

HERMOGENES: Impossible.

SOCRATES: And if, on the other hand, wisdom and folly are really distinguishable, you will allow, I think, that the assertion of Protagoras can hardly be correct. For if what appears to each man is true to him, one man cannot in reality be wiser than another.

HERMOGENES: He cannot.

SOCRATES: Nor will you be disposed to say with Euthydemus, that all things equally belong to all men at the same moment and always; for neither on his view can there be some good and others bad, if virtue and vice are always equally to be attributed to all.

HERMOGENES: There cannot.

SOCRATES: But if neither is right, and things are not relative to individuals, and all things do not equally belong to all at the same moment and always, they must be supposed to have their own proper and permanent essence: they are not in relation to us, or influenced by us, fluctuating according to our fancy, but they are independent, and maintain to their own essence the relation prescribed by nature.

HERMOGENES: I think, Socrates, that you have said the truth.

SOCRATES: Does what I am saying apply only to the things themselves, or equally to the actions which proceed from them? Are not actions also a class of being?

HERMOGENES: Yes, the actions are real as well as the things.

SOCRATES: Then the actions also are done according to their proper nature, and not according to our opinion of them? In cutting, for example, we do not cut as we please, and with any chance instrument; but we cut with the proper instrument only, and according to the natural process of cutting; and the natural process is right and will succeed, but any other will fail and be of no use at all.

HERMOGENES: I should say that the natural way is the right way.

SOCRATES: Again, in burning, not every way is the right way; but the right way is the natural way, and the right instrument the natural instrument.

HERMOGENES: True.

SOCRATES: And this holds good of all actions?

HERMOGENES: Yes.

SOCRATES: And speech is a kind of action?

HERMOGENES: True.

SOCRATES: And will a man speak correctly who speaks as he pleases? Will not the successful speaker rather be he who speaks in the natural way of speaking, and as things ought to be spoken, and with the natural instrument? Any other mode of speaking will result in error and failure.

HERMOGENES: I quite agree with you.

SOCRATES: And is not naming a part of speaking? For in giving names men speak.

HERMOGENES: That is true.

SOCRATES: And if speaking is a sort of action and has a relation to acts, is not naming also a sort of action?

HERMOGENES: True.

SOCRATES: And we saw that actions were not relative to ourselves, but had a special nature of their own?

HERMOGENES: Precisely.

SOCRATES: Then the argument would lead us to infer that names ought to be given according to a natural process, and with a proper instrument, and not at our pleasure: in this and no other way shall we name with success.

HERMOGENES: I agree.

SOCRATES: But again, that which has to be cut has to be cut with something?

HERMOGENES: Yes.

SOCRATES: And that which has to be woven or pierced has to be woven or pierced with something?

HERMOGENES: Certainly.

SOCRATES: And that which has to be named has to be named with something?

HERMOGENES: True.

SOCRATES: What is that with which we pierce?

HERMOGENES: A drill.

SOCRATES: And with which we weave?

HERMOGENES: A shuttle.

SOCRATES: And with which we name?

HERMOGENES: A name.

SOCRATES: Very good: then a name is an instrument?

HERMOGENES: Certainly.

SOCRATES: Suppose that I ask, 'What sort of instrument is a shuttle?' And you answer, 'A weaving instrument.'

HERMOGENES: Well.

SOCRATES: And I ask again, 'What do we do when we weave?' The answer is, that we separate or disengage the warp from the woof.

HERMOGENES: Very true.

SOCRATES: And may not a similar description be given of a drill, and of instruments in general?

HERMOGENES: To be sure.

SOCRATES: And now suppose that I ask a similar question about names: will you answer me? Regarding the name as an instrument, what do we do when we name?

HERMOGENES: I cannot say.

SOCRATES: Do we not give information to one another, and distinguish things according to their natures?

HERMOGENES: Certainly we do.

SOCRATES: Then a name is an instrument of teaching and of distinguishing natures, as the shuttle is of distinguishing the threads of the web.

HERMOGENES: Yes.

SOCRATES: And the shuttle is the instrument of the weaver?

HERMOGENES: Assuredly.

SOCRATES: Then the weaver will use the shuttle well – and 'well' means like a weaver? And the teacher will use the name well – and 'well' means like a teacher?

HERMOGENES: Yes.

SOCRATES: And when the weaver uses the shuttle, whose work will he be using well?

HERMOGENES: That of the carpenter.

SOCRATES: And is every man a carpenter, or the skilled only?

HERMOGENES: Only the skilled.

SOCRATES: And when the piercer uses the drill, whose work will he be using well?

HERMOGENES: That of the metal worker.

SOCRATES: And is every man a metal worker, or only the skilled?

HERMOGENES: The skilled only.

SOCRATES: And when the teacher uses the name, whose work will he be using?

HERMOGENES: There again I am puzzled.

SOCRATES: Cannot you at least say who gives us the names which we use?

HERMOGENES: Indeed I cannot.

SOCRATES: Does not the law seem to you to give us them?

HERMOGENES: Yes, I suppose so.

SOCRATES: Then the teacher, when he gives us a name, uses the work of the legislator?

HERMOGENES: I agree.

SOCRATES: And is every man a legislator, or the skilled only?

HERMOGENES: The skilled only.

SOCRATES: Then, Hermogenes, not every man is able to give a name, but only a maker of names; and this is the legislator, who of all skilled artisans in the world is the rarest.

HERMOGENES: True.

SOCRATES: And how does the legislator make names? To what does he look? Consider this in the light of the previous instances: to what does the carpenter look in making the shuttle? Does he not look to that which is naturally fitted to act as a shuttle?

HERMOGENES: Certainly.

SOCRATES: And suppose the shuttle to be broken: will he make another, looking to the broken one? Or will he look to the form according to which he made the other?

HERMOGENES: To the latter, I should imagine.

SOCRATES: Might not that be justly called the true or ideal shuttle?

HERMOGENES: I think so.

SOCRATES: And whatever shuttles are wanted – for the manufacture of garments, thin or thick, of flaxen, woollen, or other material – ought all of them to have the true form of the shuttle? And whatever is the shuttle best adapted to each kind of work, that ought to be the form which the maker produces in each case?

HERMOGENES: Yes.

SOCRATES: And the same holds of other instruments: when a man has discovered the instrument which is naturally adapted to each work, he must express this natural form, and not others which he fancies, in the material which he employs, whatever it may be. For example, he ought to know how to put into iron the forms of drills adapted by nature to their several uses?

HERMOGENES: Certainly.

SOCRATES: And how to put into wood forms of shuttles adapted by nature to their uses?

HERMOGENES: True.

SOCRATES: For the several forms of shuttles naturally answer to the several kinds of weaving; and this is true of instruments in general.

HERMOGENES: Yes.

SOCRATES: Then, as to names: ought not our legislator also to know how to put the true natural name of each thing into sounds and syllables, and to make and give all names with a view to the ideal name, if he is to be a namer in any true sense? And we must remember that different legislators will not use the same syllables. For neither does every metalworker, although he may be making the same instrument for the same purpose, make them all of the same iron. The form must be the same, but the material may vary, and still the instrument may be equally good, of whatever iron it is made, whether in Greece or in a foreign country – there is no difference.

HERMOGENES: Very true.

SOCRATES: And the legislator, whether he be Greek or barbarian, is not therefore to be deemed by you a worse legislator, provided he gives the true and proper form of the name in whatever syllables; this or that country makes no matter.

HERMOGENES: Quite true.

SOCRATES: But who then is to determine whether the proper form is given to the shuttle, whatever sort of wood may be used? The carpenter who makes, or the weaver who is to use them?

HERMOGENES: I should say, he who is to use them, Socrates.

SOCRATES: And who uses the work of the lyre-maker? Will not he be the man who knows how to direct what is being done, and who will know also whether the work is being well done or not?

HERMOGENES: Certainly.

SOCRATES: And who is he?

HERMOGENES: The player of the lyre.

SOCRATES: And who will direct the shipwright?

HERMOGENES: The pilot.

SOCRATES: And who will be best able to direct the legislator in his work, and will know whether the work is well done, in this or any other country? Will not the user be the man?

HERMOGENES: Yes.

SOCRATES: And this is the person who knows how to ask questions?

HERMOGENES: Yes.

SOCRATES: And how to answer them?

HERMOGENES: Yes.

SOCRATES: And the person who knows how to ask and answer you would call a dialectician?

HERMOGENES: Yes; that would be his name.

SOCRATES: Then the work of the carpenter is to make a rudder, and the pilot has to direct him, if the rudder is to be well made.

HERMOGENES: True.

SOCRATES: And the work of the legislator is to give names, and the dialectician must be his director if the names are to be rightly given?

HERMOGENES: That is true.

SOCRATES: Then, Hermogenes, I should say that this giving of names can be no such light matter as you fancy, or the work of light or chance persons; and Cratylus is right in saying that things have names by nature, and that not every man is a maker of names, but only the person who looks to the name which each thing by nature has, and is able to express the true forms of things in letters and syllables.

HERMOGENES: I cannot answer you, Socrates; but I find a difficulty in changing my opinion all in a moment, and I think that I should be more readily persuaded if you would show me what this is which you term the 'natural fitness' of names.

SOCRATES: My good Hermogenes, I have none to show. Was I not telling you just now (but you have forgotten), that I knew nothing, and proposing to share the enquiry with you? But now that you and I have talked over the matter, a step has been gained; for we have discovered that names have by nature a truth, and that not every man knows how to give a thing a name.

2   Language and its Acquisition: Augustine, *Confessions**

Plato's discussion above invites us to consider on what basis names are assigned to things. But each of us is born into and brought up in a pre-existing linguistic community, where the assignments of meaning are, so to speak, already in place. How do we as children manage at a very young age to become relatively competent users of our native language? The following short extract, from one of the world's great spiritual and philosophical classics, the *Confessions* of Augustine, presents a vivid and initially quite plausible picture of how we learn the meanings of words: we hear our elders use certain sounds to refer to certain things, and so we work out that a given word has a given meaning.

On reflection, however, there appears to be something radically wrong with this picture, persuasive though it may seem at first sight. For it cannot surely be that the child thinks to itself something like 'they are using that sound, d–o–g, to refer to that four-footed barking creature over there, so "dog" must be the word for such things'. This would imply that the infant is already capable of advanced conceptual thought, and merely has to fit certain names, or sounds, to the thoughts it already has. Words,

on this picture, are a kind of optional extra to the pre-existing concepts inside the mind. But can we really suppose infants are endowed with such a pre-linguistic conceptual apparatus? Is it not rather that the baby, as it gradually learns to talk, is thereby gradually acquiring concepts – in other words it is thereby *learning to think*?

It may seem hard to settle this matter, since although we have all been through the infantile stage described by Augustine, we have (as he underlines) no recollection of it – it is as 'darkly hidden in forgetfulness' as the time we spent in the womb. Yet one might think the utter blankness of our memory of this pre-linguistic period is at least some evidence that it was not as full of thinking as Augustine's model suggests. In a celebrated critique of the Augustinian picture, the twentieth-century philosopher Ludwig Wittgenstein observed that 'Augustine describes the learning of human language as if the child came into a strange country, and did not understand the language of the country; that is, as if it already had a language, only not this one. Or again, as if the child could already *think*, only not yet speak. And "think" would here mean something like "talk to

---

* Augustine of Hippo, *Confessions* [*c*.397], Bk I, excerpts from chs 7 and 8. Translation by John Cottingham.

itself"' (*Philosophical Investigations* [1953], I, 32). The absurdity, Wittgenstein suggests, lies in supposing an infant who has not yet learned to understand or speak a language could nevertheless formulate thoughts to itself. Part of what is at stake here, philosophically, is whether we should think of language as merely the external clothing for inner feelings and thoughts – outward signs whereby we 'express what is felt in the heart', as Augustine puts it – or whether the connection between language and thought is altogether more intimate and integral.

The very early period of my infancy, O Lord, I cannot remember. My beliefs about it depend on what others have told me, and I reliably suppose from the existence of other infants that I went through this phase. But I find it disturbing to count it as part of the life that I lead in this world, since it is as darkly hidden in forgetfulness as the time I lived inside my mother's womb. If I was indeed 'conceived in iniquity', and 'in sin did my mother nourish me in the womb',[1] where, my God, where, I beseech you O Lord, was I ever your servant, or when was I ever innocent? But let me pass over that early time: what have I to do with it, seeing there is not a single trace of it that I can recall?

So from infancy I grew to childhood. Or perhaps I should say that the period of infancy was supplanted, and I was overtaken by childhood. Not that infancy departed – for where did it go? – but nevertheless it was now over. I was no longer an infant, incapable of speech,[2] but I was a child: I could talk. This is something I can remember, and I have later come to realize how I learned to speak. The grown-ups did not teach me by introducing me to words in a set order of lessons, as they did soon afterwards with reading and writing. Rather it was I, with the mind you gave me, O God, who myself struggled to express what I felt in my heart by means of cries and various sounds and movements of my limbs, aimed at getting me what I wanted – even though I was unable to convey everything I wished for, or make all the signs I would like. But when the grown-ups named something, and turned towards it as they uttered the word, I noticed this, and gathered that the thing in question was called by the sound they made when they wanted to point it out. All this I pondered in my memory. The fact that they meant this or that thing was clear from their bodily movements, the natural words, as it were, of people all over the world, expressed by their facial expressions and glances and physical gestures and tones of voice, indicating their state of mind regarding what they wanted to get or keep or reject or avoid. So in this way, from constantly hearing the words as they occurred in their proper place in various sentences, I slowly started to gather what they stood for. And once I had succeeded in training my mouth to pronounce these signs, I thereby conveyed my wishes, and by this means managed to communicate to those around me the appropriate signs for the expression of what was wanted. Thus did I launch myself deeper into the stormy society of human life, though dependent on the authority of my parents and the approval of those older than myself.

---

[1] Psalm 51 (or 50, in the numbering of the Vulgate (Latin) text).
[2] 'Infant' (Latin *infans*) means literally 'not-speaking'.

3   Thought, Language and its Components: William of Ockham, *Writings on Logic**

Medieval philosophy saw a great wave of interest in the philosophy of logic and language. Our next set of extracts is taken from one of the most important thinkers of the 'high middle ages' (the thirteenth and fourteenth centuries), the philosopher and theologian William of Ockham. Ockham is famous for his maxim now known as 'Ockham's razor' – that 'entities should not be multiplied beyond what is necessary', and some of his views on thought and language illustrate this cautious desire not to complicate our explanations by introducing more than we strictly need. Ockham was a 'nominalist': that is, he denied the reality of universals (see Part II, introductions to extracts 1 and 2, above), and held that all linguistic signs simply represent individual things. General terms, he argues in the opening passage below, are able to stand for any number of individual things as a result of the mind's ability to abstract from particulars, thereby creating a kind of artificial mental construct. In the passage in the second paragraph (which represents Ockham's more developed thought on these matters), he trims things down still further: there is no need to postulate inner objects in the mind, but only particular thoughts, or states of mind, whereby the intellect is able to conceive of objects in the world.

In the final excerpt, focusing on the fundamental structure of a proposition or statement (such as 'snow is white'), Ockham explains its basic elements, or *terms* – the subject ('snow') and the predicate ('white'). In a broad sense, we may say

that terms include any of the components making up a sentence, like an adverb (e.g. 'often'), or a connecting term (such as the copula 'is'); but Ockham goes on to suggest that the subject and the predicate are the most important elements. Two particular points of interest emerge from this discussion of the fundamental nature of language. First, Ockham argues (partly influenced by Augustine: see previous extract) that in addition to the external language of written and spoken words there is a conceptual or mental language which 'remains in the mind alone': the written and spoken words we use are 'signs' which should be regarded as 'subordinate' to mental concepts. This is a very influential idea which we shall see surfacing later on (for example in Locke's theory of 'ideas': see below, extract 5); but it is questionable how much explanatory power it really has. Secondly, Ockham divides the elements of a proposition into 'categorematic' and 'syncategorematic' terms: the former are the basic signifying units (the subject and the predicate), while the latter are what modern logicians call quantifiers (such as 'all' and 'some'), plus other logical operators (such as 'except'). Ockham here shows what was for his time a powerful insight into the way language is built up out of various components, some of which straightforwardly refer to or describe objects in the world ('tree', 'tall'), while others serve as logical operators ('*all* trees are tall'), indicating the scope of the terms, and thereby setting the conditions for the truth or falsity of what is asserted.

 I maintain that a universal is not something real that has existence as a subject, either in the mind or outside the mind, but that it merely has being as an object of thought, in the mind... When the intellect sees something outside the mind, it constructs a similar thing in the mind... For just as an architect, when he sees a house or some

---

* The first excerpt (comprising the opening paragraph) comes from the *Commentary on the Sentences of Lombard* [*In libros Sententiarum*, 1318], D 2, Qu. 8; the second excerpt (paras 2 and 3) comes from the *Exposition of Aristotle's 'On Interpretation'* [*Expositio in librum Perihermenias Aristotelis*, 1321–4]; and the remaining material comes from the *Compendium of Logic* [*Summa logicae*, c.1323], Bk I, chs 1, 2 and 4. All material translated by John Cottingham. The Latin text may be found in *Ockham: Philosophical Writings*, sel. and trans. P. Boehner (London: Nelson, 1957), ch. 2, items 7 and 8, and ch. 3, items 1, 2 and 3.

building, constructs in his mind a similar building, and later on produces a similar house in reality, which is only numerically distinct from the first one, so in this case the construct in the mind derived from seeing something outside would be a pattern. For just as the mentally constructed house is a pattern for the architect, should he be able to build one in reality, in the same way this mental construct would function as a pattern. It may be called a *universal*, because it is a pattern, and relates indifferently to all singular things outside the mind. Because of the similarity between a mental object and the things that resemble it outside the mind, it can stand for such things. And so in this way a universal does not come about by generation, but merely by abstraction, which is simply a kind of mental construct . . .

An alternative view, which now seems to me more probable, is this . . . The intellect, apprehending a singular thing, comes up with a conception[1] which is merely of this singular thing – a conception that we call a state of mind – which is capable by its very nature of standing for this singular thing. By convention the word 'Socrates' stands for the thing which it signifies, so that someone hearing the phrase 'Socrates is running' does not thereby conceive that the *word* 'Socrates', which he hears, is running, but that the real person signified by the word is running. In the same way, someone who knows or understands that something is asserted regarding this conception of a singular thing would not conceive that the *conception* was such and such, but would conceive that the corresponding real thing is such and such. So just as the word by convention stands for the thing, so the conception by its nature, without any convention, stands for the corresponding thing.

In addition to this conception of a singular thing, the intellect also forms other conceptions, which are not of any one particular thing as opposed to another. Thus just as the word 'man' does not signify Socrates any more than Plato, and hence does not stand for Socrates any more than Plato, so the conception in question does not relate to Socrates any more that Plato, or any other man. Similarly, one could have a conception whereby *this* animal is not meant any more that *that one*, and so with other conceptions. So in brief, these conceptions of the mind are called states of mind, and by nature they stand for the external things themselves . . . just as words stand for things by convention . . .

All those who write about logic aim to establish that arguments consist of propositions and propositions of terms. So a *term* is nothing but a component of a proposition. Aristotle, in his definition of a term in the *Prior Analytics*, Book One, says 'I call a term that into which a proposition is resolved, namely a predicate, or what the predicate is applied to, when it is asserted or denied that something *is* or *is not* something.'

Although every term is or can be a part of a proposition, not all terms are of the same nature. Hence, if we want to have perfect knowledge of them, we must first be aware of some distinctions between terms. Following Boethius, in his *De Interpretatione*, Book One, we need to realize that language has a threefold nature – written, spoken and conceptual, with the last existing merely in the intellect; and correspondingly there are three kinds of term, written, spoken and conceptual. A written term is

---

[1] Latin *cognitio*, literally, 'cognition': in this context, a conception, notion or idea.

part of a proposition written on some physical material, which is seen or can be seen with the bodily eye. A spoken term is part of a vocalized proposition, designed to be heard by the bodily ear. A conceptual term is a mental content or impression of the mind which naturally signifies something...and is meant to be a part of a mental proposition, and to stand for the thing in question. These conceptual terms, and the propositions formed with them, are those mental words which St Augustine says, in *De Trinitate*, Book 15, belong to no language, since they remain in the mind alone and cannot be produced in the external world; the words which are signs subordinated to them can however be pronounced externally.

I say that pronounced words are signs subordinated to mental concepts or contents. But if this word 'sign' is taken in its strict sense, these words should not be taken to be properly or primarily signs of mental concepts; rather, the words are applied to signify the same things which are signified by mental concepts. Hence in the first place the concept naturally signifies something, and in the second place the word signifies the same thing...Accordingly, Aristotle says that words are the signs of impressions that are in the soul...

The noun 'term' has three senses. In one sense, a term is anything that can be the copula, or one of the two other elements in a categorical proposition, namely the subject and the predicate (or some qualification of either, or of the verb). Thus even a proposition can be a term, since it can be part of a proposition. In the true statement '"Man is an animal" is a true proposition', the whole proposition 'Man is an animal' is the subject, and 'true proposition' is the predicate. But in another sense, the noun 'term' is used in contrast to a sentence, so that all non-complex components are called terms...In a third sense, 'term' taken strictly means that which in its signifying function can be either a subject or a predicate of a proposition. So a verb or conjunction or adverb or preposition or interjection would not qualify as a term in this sense...

Some terms are categorematic, while others are syncategorematic. Categorematic terms have a definite and fixed signification, as the term 'man' signifies all men, and the word 'animal' all animals, and the word 'whiteness' all cases of whiteness. But syncategorematic terms, like 'all', 'none', 'something', 'whole', 'except', 'only' 'in so far as' and so on, do not have a fixed and definite signification, and do not signify things distinct from the things signified by the categorematic terms. Instead, just as, in arithmetic, zero on its own signifies nothing, but imparts meaning when added to another number, so a syncategorematic term strictly speaking signifies nothing, but when added to another term makes it signify something, or makes it stand for something or other in a definite way, or exercises some other function with respect to a categorematic term. Thus the syncategorematic term 'every' does not have a fixed signification, but when it is added to 'man' it makes it stand for all men, in an indefinite and distributive way, and when added to 'stone' it makes it stand for all stones, and when added to 'whiteness' it makes it stand for all cases of whiteness. What applies to 'all' applies to the other syncategorematics, though each of the syncategorematic terms has different functions.

If someone should object that the term 'all' is significant and hence must signify something, I reply that it is called significant not in virtue of signifying something in a determinate way, but in virtue of making something else signify or stand for something, as explained above...

4   Language, Reason and Animal Utterance: René Descartes, *Discourse on the Method**

The idea of words as 'signs', found in the previous extract, might perhaps seem to encourage the thought that language is not a specifically human phenomenon; for do not animals produce noises that are signs of their desires and emotions, showing they are afraid, for example, or hungry? In the following extract, by the great seventeenth-century philosopher René Descartes, a radical distinction is drawn between animal utterance and genuine speech. Descartes in his scientific inquiries was very interested in the physiological basis of animal and human behaviour, and held that much of it could be explained in purely mechanical terms – rather as the workings of a clock can be explained by examining its cogs and wheels. Shocking many of his contemporaries, he suggested that there was nothing in the repertoire of a dog or cat that could not in principle be replicated by an artificial machine; indeed, in our passage he goes so far as to propose that the body is really no more than a machine (albeit a very complex one, 'made by the hand of God'). Yet he goes on to argue that although a mechanical dog might be possible, one could never have a mechanical human being.

It is language that is the key indicator of this non-mechanical aspect of our humanity, and Descartes points to two features of genuine human language that set it apart from animal utterance. First, language has a complex synthetic structure (compare Ockham's discussion in the previous extract): that is, its components are put together in intricate patterns to make up meaningful propositions, and it is 'not conceivable that...a machine should produce different arrangements of words so as to give an appropriately meaningful answer to whatever is said in its presence'. Admittedly, a dog might be trained in a circus to produce a certain number of barks on a specific command, or a bird might naturally emit certain sounds in particular circumstances (for example, a warning signal); but Descartes argues in effect that this will always be a patterned response to a given stimulus, whereas genuine language is stimulus-free. Descartes links this creative aspect of language, whereby we are able to talk about each new contingency that arises in life, to our use of the 'universal instrument of reason': in other words, language is intimately related to thought and understanding.

In the light of our knowledge of how much in common we have with the higher animals, it may seem difficult to accept the Cartesian thesis that our linguistic capacity puts a great gulf between them and us. Descartes's arguments, however, are not easy to counter, and have appealed to many later thinkers, including the twentieth-century linguistic theorist Noam Chomsky, who follows the same kind of reasoning proposed by Descartes in our passage, arguing that genuine linguistic output is potentially infinite in its versatility and scope, thus differing radically from the finite outputs of animals, that are always closely correlated to the stimulus of a specific input.

[In my earlier work][1] I showed what structure the nerves and muscles of the human body must have in order to make the animal spirits[2] inside them strong enough to move its limbs – as when we see severed heads continue to move about and bite the earth although they are no longer alive. I also indicated what changes must occur in

---

* René Descartes, *Discourse on the Method* [*Discours de la méthode*, 1637], extract from Part V. Trans. J. Cottingham, R. Stoothoff and D. Murdoch, in *The Philosophical Writings of Descartes*, vol. I (Cambridge: Cambridge University Press, 1985), pp. 139–40.

[1] Descartes refers to his *Treatise on Man* [*Traité de l'homme*], written in the 1630s.

[2] A fine gas or vapour supposed in Descartes's time to be the medium whereby neural impulses are transmitted.

the brain in order to cause waking, sleep and dreams; how light, sounds, smells, tastes, heat and the other qualities of external objects can imprint various ideas on the brain through the mediation of the senses; and how hunger, thirst and the other internal passions can also send their ideas there. And I explained which part of the brain must be taken to be the 'common' sense,[1] where these ideas are received; the memory which perceives them, the corporeal imagination, which can change them in various ways, form them into new ideas, and by distributing the animal spirits to the muscles, make the parts of this body move in as many different ways as the parts of our bodies can move without being guided by the will, and in a manner which is just as appropriate to the objects of the senses and the internal passions. This will not seem at all strange to those who know how many kinds of automatons, or moving machines, the skill of man can construct with the use of very few parts, in comparison with the great multitude of bones, muscles, nerves, arteries, veins and all the other parts that are in the body of an animal. For they will regard this body as a machine which having been made by the hand of God, is incomparably better ordered than any machine that can be devised by man, and contains in itself movements more wonderful than those in any such machine.

I made special efforts to show that if any such machines had the organs and outward shape of a monkey or of some other animal that lacks reason, we should have no means of knowing that they did not possess entirely the same nature as these animals; whereas if any such machine bore a resemblance to our bodies and imitated our actions as closely as possible for all practical purposes, we should still have two very certain means of recognizing that they were not real men. The first is that they could never use words, or put together other signs, as we do in order to declare our thoughts to others. For we can certainly conceive of a machine so constructed that it utters words, and even utters words which correspond to bodily action causing a change in its organs (e.g. if you touch it in one spot it asks what you want of it, if you touch it in another it cries out that you are hurting it, and so on). But it is not conceivable that such a machine should produce different arrangements of words so as to give an appropriately meaningful answer to whatever is said in its presence, as the dullest of men can do. Secondly, even though such machines might do some things as well as we do them, or perhaps even better, they would inevitably fail in others, which would reveal that they were acting not through understanding but only from the disposition of their organs. For whereas reason is a universal instrument which can be used in all kinds of situations, these organs need some particular disposition for each particular action; hence it is for all practical purposes impossible for a machine to have enough different organs to make it act in all the contingencies of life in the way which our reason makes us act.

Now in just these two ways we can also know the difference between man and beast. For it is quite remarkable that there are no men so dull-witted or stupid – and this includes even madmen – that they are incapable of arranging various words together and forming an utterance from them in order to make their thoughts understood; whereas there is no other animal, however perfect and well endowed it may be, that can do the like. This does not happen because they lack the necessary organs; for we

---

[1] The internal sense traditionally supposed to receive and co-ordinate impressions from the five external senses.

see that magpies and parrots can utter words as we do, and yet they cannot speak as we do: that is, they cannot show that they are thinking what they are saying. On the other hand, men born deaf and dumb, and thus deprived of speech-organs as much as the beasts, or even more so, normally invent their own signs to make themselves understood by those who are regularly in their company and have the time to learn their language. This shows not merely that the beasts have less reason than humans but that they have no reason at all. For it patently requires very little reason to be able to speak; and since as much inequality can be observed among the animals of a given species as among human beings, and some animals are more easily trained than others, it would be incredible that a superior specimen of the monkey or parrot species should not be able to speak as well as the stupidest child – or at least as well as a child with a defective brain – if their souls were not completely different in nature from ours.

And we must not confuse speech with the natural movements which express passions and which can be imitated by machines as well as by animals. Nor should we think, like some of the ancients, that the beasts speak, although we do not understand their language. For if that were true, then since they have many organs that correspond to ours, they could make themselves understood by us as well as by their fellows. It is also a very remarkable fact that although many animals show more skill than we do in some of their actions, yet the same animals show none at all in many others; so what they do better does not prove that they have any intelligence, for if it did then they would have more intelligence than any of us and would excel us in everything. It proves rather that they have no intelligence at all, and that it is nature which acts in them according to the disposition of their organs. In the same way a clock, consisting only of wheels and springs, can count the hours and measure time more accurately than we can with all our wisdom.

5   Abstract General Ideas: John Locke, *Essay concerning Human Understanding**

At the end of the seventeenth century, the English philosopher John Locke put forward his empiricist theory of knowledge: all our ideas are originally derived from sensory inputs (see above, Part I, extract 5). In the following passage, he describes the transition to full-blown linguistic awareness. The mind has the power of composition, whereby it puts together the simple ideas received from sensation and reflection so as to form more complex ideas. Words are then developed as signs, or, in Locke's phrase, the 'outward marks of our internal ideas' (compare Augustine's conception of language in extract 2, above).

But what exactly is the nature of the 'ideas' formed in the mind, and how are they related to the things we encounter via our senses? We encounter particular objects, says Locke, but if each idea, and its corresponding word or sign, were to map one-to-one onto these particular objects, then 'names would be endless'. Locke proposes

---

* John Locke, *An Essay concerning Human Understanding* [1690], extracts (with omissions) from Bk II, ch. 11, §§ 6 –10, and Bk III, ch. 3, §§ 1, 2, 6, 7, 8, 9; with revised spelling and punctuation and some minor revisions of phrasing. There are many available editions of the *Essay*, of which the most definitive is the critical edition of P. H. Nidditch (Oxford: Clarendon, 1975).

that to avoid this the mind must have a faculty of *abstracting*, whereby 'ideas taken from particular beings become general representatives of all of the same kind'; the corresponding words are thus 'general names, applicable to whatever exists conformable to such abstract ideas'. Locke goes on to insist (in this respect, at least, agreeing with Descartes: see above, extract 4) that this implies a radical difference in kind between humans and other animals: the latter have no faculty of abstraction, and hence 'no use of words, or any other general signs'.

In the latter part of our excerpt, Locke describes in more detail the process whereby, according to his view, the mind forms these 'abstract general ideas'. His theory focuses on a crucial aspect of language – the ability of a general term such as 'cat' to apply indifferently to any one of an indefinite range of individuals. Nevertheless, his view is not without its problems. In the first place, instead of a simple investigation of words and how they work, Locke seems to introduce a kind of internal duplication, where everything that is true of a word is replicated in the inner world of the mind and its ideas. If we are setting out to understand how language relates to the world, does the introduction of these 'ideas' really add anything of explanatory power? Secondly, the alleged process of abstraction itself raises certain logical and psychological problems, as Locke's successor Berkeley was quick to point out (see extract 6, below).

 The next operation we may observe in the mind about its ideas is *composition*, whereby it puts together several of those simple [ideas] it has received from sensation and reflection, and combines them into complex ones. Under this [operation] of composition may be reckoned also that of *enlarging*, wherein though the composition does not so much appear as in more complex ones, yet it is nevertheless a putting several ideas together, though of the same kind. Thus by adding several units together we make the idea of a dozen, and putting together the repeated ideas of several perches, we frame that of [a] furlong.[1]

In this also, I suppose, brutes come far short of men. For though they take in and retain together several combinations of simple ideas, as possibly the shape, smell and voice of his master make up the complex idea a dog has of him – or rather are so many distinct marks whereby he knows him – yet I do not think they do of themselves ever compound them and make complex ideas. And perhaps even where we think they have complex ideas, it is only one simple one that directs them in the knowledge of several things, which possibly they distinguish less by their sight than we imagine. For I have been credibly informed that a bitch will nurse, play with and be fond of young foxes, as much as and in place of her puppies, if you can but get them once to suck her so long that her milk may go through them. And those animals which have a numerous brood of young ones at once, appear not to have any knowledge of their number; for though they are mightily concerned for any of their young that are taken from them whilst they are in sight or hearing, yet if one or two of them be stolen from them in their absence, or without notice, they appear not to miss them, or to have any sense that their number is lessened.

When children have, by repeated sensation, got *ideas* fixed in their memories, they begin, by degrees, to learn the use of *signs*. And when they have got the skill to apply the organs of speech to their framing of articulate sounds, they begin to make use of *words*, to signify their ideas to others. These verbal signs they sometimes borrow from others and sometimes make themselves, as one may observe among the new and unusual names children often give to things in their first use of language.

[1]   Old English measures of distance: forty perches make up one furlong (an eighth of a mile).

The use of words, then, being to stand as outward marks of our internal ideas, and those ideas being taken from particular things, if every particular idea that we take in should have a distinct name, names must be endless. To prevent this, the mind makes the particular ideas, received from particular objects, become general. This is done by considering them as they are in the mind ... separate from all other existences, and the circumstances of real existence, as time, place, or any other concomitant ideas. This is called *abstraction*, whereby ideas taken from particular beings become general representatives of all of the same kind, and their names general names, applicable to whatever exists conformable to such abstract ideas. Such precise, naked appearances in the mind, without considering how, whence, or with what others they came here, the understanding lays up (with names commonly annexed to them) as the standard to rank real existences into sorts, as they agree with these patterns, and to denominate them accordingly. Thus the same colour being observed today in chalk or snow, which the mind yesterday received from milk, it considers that appearance alone, [and] makes it a representative of all of that kind; and having given it the name *whiteness*, it by that sound signifies the same quality, wheresoever it be imagined or met with; and thus universals, whether ideas or terms, are made.

If it be may be doubted whether beasts compound and enlarge their ideas that way, to any degree, this I think I may be positive in: that the power of abstracting is not in them, and that the having of general ideas is that which puts a perfect distinction between man and brutes, and is an excellence which the faculties of brutes do by no means attain to. For it is evident that we observe no foot-steps in them of making use of general signs for universal ideas; from which we have reason to imagine that they have not the faculty of abstracting, or making general ideas, since they have no use of words, or any other general signs...

All things that exist being particulars, it may perhaps be thought reasonable that words, which ought to be conformed to things, should be so too, I mean in their signification. But yet we find quite the contrary. The far greatest part of words that make all languages are *general terms*: which has not been the effect of neglect, or chances, but of reason, and necessity.

First, it is impossible that every particular thing should have a distinct peculiar name ... It is beyond the power of human capacity to frame and retain distinct ideas of all the particular things we meet with: every bird and beast men saw, every tree and plant that affected the senses, could not find a place in the most capacious understanding...

The next thing to be considered is how *general words* come to be made. For since all things that exist are only particulars, how come we by general terms, or where find we those general natures they are supposed to stand for? Words become general by being made the signs of general ideas; and ideas become general by separating from them the circumstances of time and place, and any other ideas that may determine them to this or that particular existence. By this way of abstraction they are made capable of representing more individuals than one; each of which, having in it a conformity to that abstract idea, is (as we call it) of that sort.

But to deduce this a little more distinctly, it will not perhaps be amiss to trace out our notions and names from their beginning, and observe by what degrees we proceed, and by what steps we enlarge our ideas from our first infancy. There is nothing more evident than that the ideas of the persons children converse with ... are like the persons themselves, only particular. The ideas of the nurse, and the mother, are well framed in their minds; and, like pictures of them there, represent only those individuals. The names they first give to them are confined to these individuals; and the names of *Nurse* and *Mamma* the child uses determine themselves to those persons. Afterwards, when time and a larger acquaintance has made them observe that there are a great many other things in the world, that in some common agreements of shape and several other qualities resemble their father and mother and those persons they have been used to, they frame an idea which they find those many particulars partake in; and to that they give, with others, the name *man*, for example. And thus they come to have a *general name*, and a *general idea*. Wherein they make nothing new, but only leave out of the complex idea they had of Peter and James, Mary and Jane, that which is peculiar to each, and retain only what is common to all.

By the same way that they come by the general name and idea of man, they easily advance to more general names and notions. For observing that several things that differ from their idea of man, and cannot therefore be comprehended under that name, have yet certain qualities wherein they agree with man, by retaining only those qualities, and uniting them into one idea, they have again another and a more general idea; to which having given a name, they make a term of a more comprehensive extension. Which new idea is made, not by any new addition, but only, as before, by leaving out the shape, and some other properties, signified by the name *man*, and retaining only a body, with life, sense and spontaneous motion, comprehended under the name *animal*.

That this is the way whereby men first formed general ideas and general names to them, I think is so evident that there need no other proof of it but the considering of a man's self, or others, and the ordinary proceedings of their minds in knowledge. And he that thinks general natures or notions are anything else but such abstract and partial ideas of more complex ones, taken at first from particular instances, will, I fear, be at a loss where to find them. For let anyone reflect, and then tell me, wherein does his idea of *man* differ from that of *Peter* and *Paul*; or his idea of *horse* from that of *Bucephalus*, but in the leaving out something that is peculiar to each individual, and retaining so much of those particular complex ideas, of several particular existences, as they are found to agree in? Of the complex ideas signified by the names *man* and *horse*, leaving out but those particulars wherein they differ, and retaining only those wherein they agree, and to those making a new distinct complex idea, and giving the name *animal* to it, one has a more general term, that comprehends, with man, several other creatures. Leave out the idea of animal, sense and spontaneous motion, and the remaining complex idea, made up of the remaining simple ones of body, life and nourishment, becomes a more general one, under the more comprehensive term *vivens* [living]. And not to dwell longer upon this particular, so evident in itself, by the same way the mind proceeds to *body, substance*, and at last to *being, thing*, and such universal terms, which stand for any of our ideas whatsoever. To conclude, this whole mystery of *genera* and *species*, which make such a noise in the Schools, and are, with justice, so little regarded out of them, is nothing else but abstract ideas, more or less comprehensive, with names annexed to them.

6   Particular Ideas and General Meaning: George Berkeley, *Principles of Human Knowledge**

George Berkeley, writing at the start of the eighteenth century, was strongly influenced by, but was also a strong critic of, the views of his predecessor John Locke. Locke's account of language (see previous extract) starts with our encountering particular objects in sensory experience, and then supposes that we have the power of *abstracting* from these particulars, so as to form general ideas, with their associated 'general names'. Thus, having seen John and Peter, a child eventually 'advances', by abstraction, to frame the general idea of *man*. In the following extract, from his *Principles of Human Knowledge*, Berkeley expresses serious doubts about this alleged process. The mind, he argues, just cannot work this way; for if we think about how we form ideas or images in our minds, they are always *particular*: 'whatever hand or eye I imagine, it must have some particular shape and colour. Likewise the idea of man that I frame to myself, must be either of a white, or a black, or a tawny, a straight, or a crooked, a tall, or a low, or a middle-sized man.'

One might want to ask here whether having an idea of something necessarily involves a mental picturing or imagining of something (and yet if it does not, then what exactly is an 'idea'?). Such problems are perhaps inherent in the picture of an inner realm of 'ideas' alongside the public linguistic realm of words and signs (compare Augustine and Ockham, extracts 2 and 3, above). But leaving that aside, how does Berkeley, if he rejects abstract ideas, explain how

we have general words (like 'cat') which can pick out not just Felix or Ginger, but any feline creature? Berkeley's answer is, in a way, to deny any problem. For 'a word becomes general' he tells us, 'by being made the sign, not of an abstract general idea but of several particular ideas, any one of which it indifferently suggests to the mind'. Just as a geometrician working on triangles is able to demonstrate his results (for example, that its angles equal 180°) by taking his particular diagram to refer generally to any triangle, so the mind can take particular ideas as proxies for a whole class of objects, without having to construct some supposed 'abstract general' object; such an object (Berkeley suggests) would in any case be some monstrous contradictory amalgam, like a diagram of a triangle that was somehow isosceles and right-angled at the same time.

An interesting moral that Berkeley draws from his discussion is that we should not assume that one word ('triangle', 'cat') must, in order to be meaningful, refer to one single object. To look for a single 'abstract idea' that such words relate to is to suppose a strict one–one correspondence between a sign and what it signifies – as if all words were like name-tags; whereas the whole point of general words is that they refer ('indifferently', as Berkeley puts it) to any number of objects of a given type. Berkeley's insights here are part of a long struggle by philosophers to rid themselves of misleading pictures of how language relates to reality.

We are told that the mind, being able to consider each quality singly, or abstracted from those other qualities with which it is united, does by that means frame to itself abstract ideas. For example, there is perceived by sight an object extended, coloured, and moved: this mixed or compound idea the mind resolves into its simple, constituent parts, and

* George Berkeley, *Principles of Human Knowledge* [1710; 2nd edn 1734], Introduction, §§ 7, 8, 9, 10, 11, 12, 14, 15, 16, 18, 19; with omissions, and some minor changes of phrasing and punctuation. There are many available editions of the *Principles*, including that edited by J. Dancy in the Oxford Philosophical Texts series (Oxford: Oxford University Press, 1998), which contains an introduction for students and explanatory notes.

viewing each by itself, exclusive of the rest, frames the abstract ideas of extension, colour, and motion. Not that it is possible for colour or motion to exist without extension: but only that the mind can frame to itself by abstraction the idea of colour exclusive of extension, and of motion exclusive of both colour and extension.

Again [we are told], the mind having observed that in the particular extensions perceived by sense there is something common and alike in all, and some other things peculiar, as this or that figure or magnitude, which distinguish them one from another, it considers apart or singles out by itself that which is common, making thereof a most *abstract idea of extension*, which is neither line, surface, nor solid, nor has any figure or magnitude but is an idea entirely prescinded from all these. So likewise the mind by leaving out of the particular colours perceived by sense, that which distinguishes them one from another, and retaining that only which is common to all, makes an idea of *colour in abstract* which is neither red, nor blue, nor white, nor any other determinate colour. And in like manner by considering motion abstractedly not only from the body moved, but likewise from the figure it describes, and all particular directions and velocities, the abstract idea of motion is framed; which equally corresponds to all particular motions whatsoever that may be perceived by sense.

And as the mind frames to itself abstract ideas of qualities or modes, so [we are told] does it, by the same precision or mental separation, attain abstract ideas of the more compounded beings, which include several coexistent qualities. For example, the mind having observed that Peter, James and John resemble each other in certain common agreements of shape and other qualities, leaves out of the complex or compounded idea it has of Peter, James and any other particular man that which is peculiar to each, retaining only what is common to all; and so makes an abstract idea wherein all the particulars equally partake, abstracting entirely from and cutting off all those circumstances and differences, which might determine it to any particular existence. And in this manner, it is said, we come by the abstract idea of *man* or, if you please, *humanity* or *human nature*; wherein it is true there is included colour, because there is no man but has some colour, but then it can be neither white, nor black, nor any particular colour; because there is no one particular colour wherein all men partake. So likewise there is included stature, but then it is neither tall stature nor low stature, nor yet middle stature, but something abstracted from all these. And so of the rest. Moreover, there being a great variety of other creatures that partake in some parts, but not all, of the complex idea of man, the mind leaving out those parts which are peculiar to men, and retaining those only which are common to all the living creatures, frames the idea of *animal*, which abstracts not only from all particular men, but also all birds, beasts, fishes and insects. The constituent parts of the abstract idea of animal are body, life, sense, and spontaneous motion. By *body* is meant, body without any particular shape or figure, there being no one shape or figure common to all animals, without covering, either of hair or feathers, or scales, etc. nor yet naked; hair, feathers, scales, and nakedness being the distinguishing properties of particular animals, and for that reason left out of the abstract idea. Upon the same account the spontaneous motion must be neither walking, nor flying, nor creeping: it is nevertheless a motion, but what that motion is, it is not easy to conceive.

Whether others have this wonderful faculty of *abstracting their ideas*, they best can tell. For myself, I find indeed I have a faculty of imagining, or representing to myself the ideas of those particular things I have perceived and of variously compounding and dividing them. I can imagine a man with two heads or the upper parts of a man joined to the body of a horse. I can consider the hand, the eye, the nose, each by itself abstracted or separated from the rest of the body. But then whatever hand or eye I imagine, it must have some particular shape and colour. Likewise the idea of man that I frame to myself, must be either of a white, or a black, or a tawny, a straight, or a crooked, a tall, or a low, or a middle-sized man. I cannot by any effort of thought conceive the abstract idea above described. And it is equally impossible for me to form the abstract idea of motion distinct from the body moving, and which is neither swift nor slow, curvilinear nor rectilinear; and the like may be said of all other abstract general ideas whatsoever. To be plain, I admit myself able to abstract in one sense, as when I consider some particular parts or qualities separated from others, with which though they are united in some object, yet it is possible they may really exist without them. But I deny that I can abstract one from another, or conceive separately, those qualities which it is impossible should exist so separated; or that I can frame a general notion by abstracting from particulars in the manner aforesaid...

It seems that a word becomes general by being made the sign, not of an abstract general idea but of several particular ideas, any one of which it indifferently suggests to the mind. For example, when it is said 'the change of motion is proportional to the impressed force', or that 'whatever has extension is divisible'; these propositions are to be understood of motion and extension in general, and nevertheless it will not follow that they suggest to my thoughts an idea of motion without a body moved, or any determinate direction and velocity, or that I must conceive an abstract general idea of extension, which is neither line, surface nor solid, neither great nor small, black, white, nor red, nor of any other determinate colour...

By observing how ideas become general, we may the better judge how words are made so. And here it is to be noted that I do not deny absolutely there are general ideas, but only that there are any *abstract general ideas*: for in the passages above quoted, wherein there is mention of general ideas, it is always supposed, that they are formed by *abstraction*... Now if we will annex a meaning to our words, and speak only of what we can conceive, I believe we shall acknowledge that an idea, which considered in itself is particular, becomes general, by being made to represent or stand for all other particular ideas of the same sort. To make this plain by an example, suppose a geometrician is demonstrating the method of cutting a line in two equal parts. He draws, for instance, a black line of an inch in length: this, which in itself is a particular line, is nevertheless with regard to its signification general, since (as it is there used) it represents all particular lines whatsoever; so that what is demonstrated of it is demonstrated of all lines, or, in other words, of a line in general. And as that particular line becomes general, by being made a sign, so the name *line*, which taken absolutely is particular, by being a sign is made general. And as the former owes its generality not to its being the sign of an abstract or general line but of all particular right lines that may possibly exist, so the latter must be thought to derive its generality from the same cause, namely, the various particular lines which it indifferently denotes...

Much is here said of the difficulty that abstract ideas carry with them, and the pains and skill requisite to the forming them. And it is on all hands agreed that there is need of great toil and labour of the mind, to emancipate our thoughts from particular objects, and raise them to those sublime speculations that are conversant about abstract ideas. From all which the natural consequence should seem to be that so difficult a thing as the forming [of] abstract ideas was not necessary for communication, which is so easy and familiar to all sorts of men. But we are told that if they seem obvious and easy to grown men it is only because by constant and familiar use they are made so. Now I would gladly know at what time it is that men are employed in surmounting that difficulty, and furnishing themselves with those necessary helps for discourse. It cannot be when they are grown up, for then it seems they are not conscious of any such pains-taking; it remains therefore to be the business of their childhood. And surely the great and multiplied labour of framing abstract notions will be found a hard task for that tender age. Is it not a hard thing to imagine, that a couple of children cannot prate together of their sugar-plums and rattles and the rest of their little trinkets, till they have first tacked together numberless inconsistencies, and so framed in their minds abstract general ideas, and annexed them to every common name they make use of?

Nor do I think them any more needful for the enlargement of knowledge than for communication. It is I know a point much insisted on that all knowledge and demonstration are about universal notions, to which I fully agree: but then it does not appear to me that those notions are formed by abstraction in the manner premised; universality, so far as I can comprehend, not consisting in the absolute, positive nature or conception of anything, but in the relation it bears to the particulars signified or represented by it: by virtue whereof it is that things, names, or notions, being in their own nature particular, are rendered universal. Thus when I demonstrate any proposition concerning triangles, it is to be supposed that I have in view the universal idea of a triangle; which ought not to be understood as if I could frame an idea or a triangle which was neither equilateral nor scalenon nor equicrural. But only that the particular triangle I consider, whether of this or that sort it matters not, does equally stand for and represent all rectilinear triangles whatsoever, and is in that sense universal. All which seems very plain and not to include any difficulty in it.

But here it will be demanded, how we can know any proposition to be true of all particular triangles, unless we have first seen it demonstrated of the abstract idea of a triangle which equally agrees to all? . . . To which I answer that though the idea I have in view whilst I make the demonstration be, for instance, that of an isosceles rectangular triangle, whose sides are of a determinate length, I may nevertheless be certain it extends to all other rectilinear triangles, of whatever sort or bigness. And that because neither the right angle, nor the equality, nor determinate length of the sides, are at all concerned in the demonstration . . . And here it must be acknowledged that a man may consider a figure merely as triangular, without attending to the particular qualities of the angles, or relations of the sides. So far he may abstract: but this will never prove that he can frame an abstract general inconsistent idea of a triangle. In like manner we may consider Peter so far forth as man, or so far forth as animal, without framing the aforementioned abstract idea, either of man or of animal, inasmuch as all that is perceived is not considered . . .

I come now to consider the source of this prevailing notion, and, that seems to me to be language . . . Let us therefore examine the manner wherein words have contributed to the origin of that mistake. First then, it is thought that every name has, or ought to have, one only precise and settled signification, which inclines men to think there are certain abstract, determinate ideas, which constitute the true and only immediate signification of each general name. And that it is by the mediation of these abstract ideas that a general name comes to signify any particular thing. Whereas, in truth, there is no such thing as one precise and definite signification annexed to any general name, they all signifying indifferently a great number of particular ideas. All which does evidently follow from what has been already said and will clearly appear to anyone by a little reflection. To this it will be objected that every name that has a definition is thereby restrained to one certain signification. For example, a triangle is defined to be a plain surface comprehended by three right lines; by which that name is limited to denote one certain idea and no other. To which I answer that in the definition it is not said whether the surface be great or small, black or white, nor whether the sides are long or short, equal or unequal, nor with what angles they are inclined to each other; in all which there may be great variety, and consequently there is no one settled idea which limits the signification of the word 'triangle'. It is one thing to keep a name constantly to the same definition, and another to make it stand everywhere for the same idea: the one is necessary, the other useless and impracticable.

But to give a further account how words came to produce the doctrine of abstract ideas, it must be observed that it is a received opinion that language has no other end but the communicating [of] our ideas, and that every significant name stands for an idea. This being so, and it being [also] certain that names, which yet are not thought altogether insignificant, do not always mark out particular conceivable ideas, it is straightway concluded that they stand for abstract notions. That there are many names in use amongst speculative men, which do not always suggest to others determinate particular ideas, is what nobody will deny. And a little attention will discover that it is not necessary (even in the strictest reasonings) that significant names which stand for ideas should, every time they are used, excite in the under-standing the ideas they are made to stand for. In reading and discoursing, names are for the most part used as letters are in algebra: though a particular quantity is marked by each letter, yet to proceed correctly it is not requisite that in every step each letter should suggest to your thoughts that particular quantity it was appointed to stand for.

7 Denotation versus Connotation: John Stuart Mill, *A System of Logic**

The nineteenth century saw considerable advances in systematic philosophical thinking about language, and one of the most important contributors to this was J. S. Mill, who opened his formidable *System of Logic* by observing that language is 'one of the principal instruments of thought', and hence that 'inquiry into language

[should be the] earliest subject of the logician's consideration'.

In the following extracts, Mill begins by correcting a common source of confusion (one we have seen causing trouble in the work of Locke and Berkeley – extracts 5 and 6, above), namely the notion that words stand for ideas in the

* John Stuart Mill, *A System of Logic* (1843; 8th edn 1872), Bk I, ch. 2, § 1, 5; with omissions.

mind: it is better and simpler, Mill observes, to follow common usage and insist that the word 'sun' stands for the sun, not for my idea of the sun. Mill then proceeds to make a crucial distinction, between the *denotation* and the *connotation* of a word. The denotation is what a word refers to or picks out – thus the word 'white' picks out snow, wool, icing sugar and a host of other things. But in addition to referring or pointing to many different objects in this way, the word 'white' also has a connotation – it signifies or conveys the attribute (namely whiteness) that all these objects have in common.

Are there words which connote but do not denote? An example would be 'ghost', which connotes or signifies a cluster of attributes (flitting around at night, haunting old buildings), but – assuming there are no such things as ghosts – lacks a denotation: the word fails to pick out any actual entities. Conversely, there are words which denote but do not connote: a proper name, for example like 'Tony Blair', refers to a certain individual, but does not of itself seem to imply any descriptive or other attributes. Thus, if we call a dog 'Caesar' (to take Mill's

example), this name simply functions as a kind of mark, enabling us to know what we are talking about, without signifying any features or characteristics: it is rather like a chalk squiggle drawn on a house wall, which serves to identify a particular building for future reference, without itself having any intrinsic meaning.

An interesting feature of Mill's discussion is how he proceeds to apply this terminology to what have later come to be known as 'definite descriptions', for example 'the father of Socrates' or 'the present prime minister of Britain'. The very wording of such phrases (through the use of the definite article 'the') implies uniqueness of reference – there can be only one individual who is picked out. Moreover, although such phrases may contain words like 'prime minister' which obviously have a connotation, they nevertheless typically function more like names – picking out an individual for discussion, rather than conveying further information about that individual. Mill's reflections on these and other aspects of naming and describing provide much food for thought, and were to stimulate important later developments in the philosophy of language (see extracts 8 and 9 below).

 'A name,' says Hobbes, 'is a word taken at pleasure to serve for a mark which may raise in our mind a thought like to some thought we had before, and which, being pronounced to others, may be to them a sign of what thought the speaker had before in his mind.' ... Are names more properly said to be the names of things or of our ideas of things? The first is the expression in common use; the last is that of some metaphysicians who conceived that, in adopting it, they were introducing a highly important distinction. The eminent thinker just quoted seems to countenance the latter opinion. 'But seeing,' he continues, 'names ordered in speech (as is defined) are signs of our conceptions, it is manifest they are not signs of the things themselves; for that the sound of this word *stone* should be the sign of a stone cannot be understood in any sense but this, that he that hears it collects that he that pronounces it thinks of a stone.'

If it be merely meant that the conception alone, and not the thing itself, is recalled by the name or imparted to the hearer, this of course cannot be denied. Nevertheless there seems good reason for adhering to the common usage, and calling (as indeed Hobbes himself does in other places) the word *sun* the name of the sun and not the name of our idea of the sun. For names are not intended only to make the hearer conceive what we conceive, but also to inform him what we believe. Now, when I use a name for the purpose of expressing a belief, it is a belief concerning the thing itself, not concerning my idea of it. When I say, 'the sun is the cause of day,' I do not mean that my idea of the sun causes or excites in me the idea of day, or, in other words, that thinking of the sun makes me think of day. I mean that a certain physical fact, which is called the sun's presence (and which, in the ultimate analysis, resolves itself into sensations, not ideas), causes another physical fact, which is called day. It seems proper to consider a word as the *name* of that which we intend to be understood by it when we use it; of that which any fact that we assert of it is to be understood of; that, in short, concerning which, when we employ the word, we intend to give information. Names, therefore, shall always be spoken of in this work as the names of things themselves and not merely of our ideas of things...

[The] division of names, into *connotative* and *non-connotative*...is one of the most important distinctions which we shall have occasion to point out and one of those which go deepest into the nature of language.

A non-connotative term is one which signifies a subject only, or an attribute only. A connotative term is one which denotes a subject and implies an attribute. By a subject is here meant anything which possesses attributes. Thus John, or London, or England are names which signify a subject only. Whiteness, length, virtue, signify an attribute only. None of these names, therefore, are connotative. But *white, long, virtuous,* are connotative. The word *white* denotes all white things, as snow, paper, the foam of the sea, etc., and implies, or in the language of the schoolmen, *connotes*, the attribute *whiteness.* The word *white* is not predicated of the attribute, but of the subjects, snow, etc.; but when we predicate it of them, we convey the meaning that the attribute whiteness belongs to them. The same may be said of the other words above cited. Virtuous, for example, is the name of a class which includes Socrates, Howard, the Man of Ross, and an undefinable number of other individuals, past, present, and to come. These individuals, collectively and severally, can alone be said with propriety to be denoted by the word; of them alone can it properly be said to be a name. But it is a name applied to all of them in consequence of an attribute which they are supposed to possess in common, the attribute which has received the name of virtue. It is applied to all beings that are considered to possess this attribute, and to none which are not so considered.

All concrete general names are connotative. The word *man*, for example, denotes Peter, Jane, John, and an indefinite number of other individuals of whom, taken as a class, it is the name...In regard to those concrete names which are not general but individual, a distinction must be made.

Proper names are not connotative; they denote the individuals who are called by them, but they do not indicate or imply any attributes as belonging to those individuals. When we name a child by the name Paul or a dog by the name Caesar, these names are simply marks used to enable those individuals to be made subjects of discourse. It may be said, indeed, that we must have had some reason for giving them those names rather than any others, and this is true, but the name, once given, is independent of the reason. A man may have been named John because that was the name of his father; a town may have been named Dartmouth because it is situated at the mouth of the Dart. But it is no part of the signification of the word John that the father of the person so called bore the same name, nor even of the word Dartmouth to be situated at the mouth of the Dart. If sand should choke up the mouth of the river or an earthquake change its course and remove it to a distance from the town, the name of the town would not necessarily be changed. That fact, therefore, can form no part of the signification of the word; for otherwise, when the fact confessedly ceased to be true, no one would any longer think of applying the name. Proper names are attached to the objects themselves and are not dependent on the continuance of any attribute of the object.[1]

But there is another kind of names, which, although they are individual names – that is, predicable only of one object – are really connotative. For, though we may give to an individual a name utterly unmeaningful which we call a proper name – a word which answers the purpose of showing what thing it is we are talking about, but not of telling anything about it – yet a name peculiar to an individual is not necessarily of this description. It may be significant of some attribute or some union of attributes which, being possessed by no object but one, determines the name exclusively to that individual. 'The sun' is a name of this description; 'God', when used by a monotheist, is another. These, however, are scarcely examples of what we are now attempting to illustrate, being, in strictness of language, general, not individual names, for, however they may be *in fact* predicable only of one object, there is nothing in the meaning of the words themselves which implies this; and, accordingly, when we are imagining and not affirming, we may speak of many suns; and the majority of mankind have believed, and still believe, that there are many gods. But it is easy to produce words which are real instances of connotative individual names. It may be part of the meaning of the connotative name itself, that there can exist but one individual possessing the attribute which it connotes, as, for instance, 'the *only* son of John Stiles'; 'the *first* emperor of Rome'. Or the attribute connoted may be a connection with some determinate event, and the connection maybe of such a kind as only one individual could have, or may, at least, be such as only one individual actually had, and this may be implied in the form of the expression. 'The father of Socrates' is an example of the one kind (since Socrates could not have had two fathers), 'the author of the Iliad', 'the murderer of Henri Quatre', of the second. For, though it is conceivable that more persons than one might have participated in the authorship of the Iliad or in the murder of Henri Quatre, the employment of the article *the* implies that, in fact, this was not the case. What is here done by the word *the* is done in other cases by the context; thus, 'Caesar's army' is an individual name if it appears from the context that the army meant is that which Caesar commanded in a particular battle. The still more general expressions, 'the Roman army', or 'the Christian army', may be individualized in a similar manner. Another case of frequent occurrence has already been noticed; it is the following: The name, being a many-worded one, may consist, in the first place, of a *general* name, capable therefore, in itself, of being affirmed of more things than one, but which is, in the second place, so limited by other words joined with it that the entire expression can only be predicated of one object, consistently with the meaning of the general term. This is exemplified in such an instance as the following: 'the present prime minister of England'. 'Prime Minister of England' is a general name; the attributes which it connotes may be possessed by an indefinite number of persons, in succession, however, not simultaneously, since the meaning of the name itself imports (among other things) that there can be only one such person at a time. This being the case, and the application of the name being afterward limited, by the article and the word *present*, to such individuals as possess the

---

[1] For some later criticism of this argument by Saul Kripke, see the first two paragraphs of extract 12, below.

attributes at one indivisible point of time, it becomes applicable only to one individual. And, as this appears from the meaning of the name without any extrinsic proof, it is strictly an individual name.

From the preceding observations it will easily be collected that whenever the names given to objects convey any information, that is, whenever they have properly any meaning, the meaning resides not in what they *denote* but in what they *connote*. The only names of objects which connote nothing are *proper* names, and these have, strictly speaking, no signification.

If, like the robber in the Arabian Nights, we make a mark with chalk on a house to enable us to know it again, the mark has a purpose, but it has not properly any meaning. The chalk does not declare anything about the house; it does not mean, 'This is such a person's house,' or 'This is a house which contains booty.' The object of making the mark is merely distinction. I say to myself, 'All these houses are so nearly alike that if I lose sight of them I shall not again be able to distinguish that which I am now looking at from any of the others; 1 must therefore contrive to make the appearance of this one house unlike that of the others, that I may hereafter know when I see the mark – not, indeed, any attribute of the house – but simply that it is the same house which I am now looking at.' Morgiana chalked all the other houses in a similar manner and defeated the scheme. How? Simply by obliterating the difference of appearance between that house and the others. The chalk was still there, but it no longer served the purpose of a distinctive mark.

When we impose a proper name, we perform an operation in some degree analogous to what the robber intended in chalking the house. We put a mark, not, indeed, upon the object itself but, so to speak, upon the idea of the object. A proper name is but an unmeaning mark which we connect in our minds with the idea of the object, in order that, whenever the mark meets our eyes or occurs to our thoughts, we may think of that individual object. Not being attached to the thing itself, it does not, like the chalk, enable us to distinguish the object when we see it, but it enables us to distinguish it when it is spoken of, either in the records of our own experience or in the discourse of others; to know that what we find asserted in any proposition of which it is the subject is asserted of the individual thing with which we were previously acquainted.

When we predicate of anything its proper name, when we say, pointing to a man, 'This is Brown or Smith,' or pointing to a city, 'It is York,' we do not, merely by so doing, convey to the reader any information about them except that those are their names. By enabling him to identify the individuals, we may connect them with information previously possessed by him; by saying, 'This is York,' we may tell him that it contains the Minster. But this is in virtue of what he has previously heard concerning York, not by anything implied in the name. It is otherwise when objects are spoken of by connotative names. When we say, 'The town is built of marble,' we give the hearer what may be entirely new information, and this merely by the signification of the many-worded connotative name, 'built of marble'. Such names are not signs of the mere objects, invented because we have occasion to think and speak of those objects individually, but signs which accompany an attribute, a kind of livery in which the attribute clothes all objects which are recognized as possessing it. They are not mere marks but more, that is to say, significant marks, and the connotation is what constitutes their significance.

8   Names and their Meaning: Gottlob Frege: *Sense and Reference**

The work of the German philosopher Gottlob Frege was relatively unknown in his lifetime, but has since come to be acknowledged as laying the foundations for modern analytic philosophy. In the extract below, from an article published in 1892, Frege makes a crucial distinction between the *sense* and the *reference* of a term (which may be compared with Mill's distinction between 'connotation' and 'denotation': see previous extract). Frege begins with a puzzle: is a statement of equality or identity (for example, 'The morning star is [the same as] the evening star') about objects or about names? The latter seems wrong, since if the *names* were identical in meaning, our statement would amount to saying 'The morning star is the morning star'; yet this last assertion is a mere tautology, known *a priori* (independently of experience), whereas the fact that the morning star is the same as the evening star is an important astronomical discovery. So we should say instead that the two names *designate* or *refer to* the same object (the planet Venus), while their *sense* (or 'mode of presentation' – the *manner* in which a word designates something) is different.

Frege goes on to observe that there are terms or expressions (like 'the least rapidly convergent series', or 'the largest prime number') which have a sense, but no reference. An elementary, but very important, convention is then introduced. Philosophers need to flag up those cases where they are talking about words, rather than the objects those words refer to; and inverted commas are used for this purpose. Thus, 'Socrates' (in inverted commas) stands for the *word* or *name*, whereas if the name is used without the inverted commas it is understood as standing for the actual person (*Socrates was a philosopher*; but

'Socrates' *has eight letters*). Similar considerations apply to 'indirect speech', when we are not using words to refer directly, but merely quoting someone else's words. The general rule is: 'A word standing between quotation marks must not be taken as having its ordinary reference.' (This has come to be known as the *use/mention* distinction: outside inverted commas you are actually *using* words, but within inverted commas you are only *mentioning* them.)

In the remainder of the extract, Frege draws our attention to one of his most characteristic themes – the distinction between the psychological and the logical domains. Your *idea* of something, for instance of Bucephalus (Alexander the Great's horse), may have all sorts of psychological overtones for you, depending for example on whether you are a painter, a horseman or a zoologist; yet these various private associations are not part of the *sense* of the term, which is something much more fixed and public. Logic deals with the public domains of sense and reference, not with the ideas that may be going on inside an individual's mind. A suggestive three-part analogy is used to sum up Frege's position. (1) When I look at the Moon through a telescope, the *reference* of the term 'Moon' is the actual celestial body orbiting the Earth. (2) The *sense* – what the word 'Moon' normally expresses or signifies (the bright night-time object with regular phases, etc.) – is analogous to the image projected on the telescope's object glass: a 'mode of presentation', but still something public and objective. (3) Finally the *idea* you have of the Moon (perhaps as frightening, or romantic, or reminding you of the Apollo programme) is something more individual and private, related to one's own mind.

---

* From the article 'Sense and Reference' [*Sinn und Bedeutung*, 1892]; excerpts from the English version in *Translations from the Philosophical Writings of Gottlob Frege*, ed. Peter Geach and Max Black (Oxford: Blackwell, 1952), pp. 56–62.

Equality[1] gives rise to challenging questions which are not altogether easy to answer. Is it a relation? A relation between objects, or between names or signs of objects? ... The reasons which seem to favour [the latter] are the following: $a = a$ and $a = b$ are obviously statements of differing cognitive value; $a = a$ holds *a priori* and, according to Kant, is to be labelled analytic, while statements of the form $a = b$ often contain very valuable extensions of our knowledge and cannot always be established *a priori*. The discovery that the rising sun is not new every morning, but always the same, was one of the most fertile astronomical discoveries. Even today the identification of a small planet or a comet is not always a matter of course. Now if we were to regard equality as a relation between that which the names 'a' and 'b' designate, it would seem that $a = b$ could not differ from $a = a$ (i.e. provided $a = b$ is true). A relation would thereby be expressed of a thing to itself, and indeed one in which each thing stands to itself but to no other thing. What is intended to be said by $a = b$ seems to be that the signs or names 'a' and 'b' designate the same thing, so that those signs themselves would be under discussion; a relation between them would be asserted. But this relation would hold between the names or signs only in so far as they named or designated something. It would be mediated by the connexion of each of the two signs with the same designated thing. But this is arbitrary. Nobody can be forbidden to use any arbitrarily producible event or object as a sign for something. In that case the sentence $a = b$ would no longer refer to the subject matter, but only to its mode of designation; we would express no proper knowledge by its means. But in many cases this is just what we want to do. If the sign 'a' is distinguished from the sign 'b' only as object (here, by means of its shape), not as sign (i.e. not by the manner in which it designates something), the cognitive value of $a = a$ becomes essentially equal to that of $a = b$, provided $a = b$ is true. A difference can arise only if the difference between the signs corresponds to a difference in the mode of presentation of that which is designated. Let a, b, c be the lines connecting the vertices of a triangle with the midpoints of the opposite sides. The point of intersection of a and b is then the same as the point of intersection of b and c. So we have different designations for the same point, and these names ('point of intersection of a and b', 'point of intersection of b and c') likewise indicate the mode of presentation; and hence the statement contains actual knowledge.

It is natural, now, to think of there being connected with a sign (name, combination of words, letter), besides that to which the sign refers, which may be called the *reference* of the sign, also what I should like to call the *sense* of the sign, wherein the mode of presentation is contained. In our example, accordingly, the reference of the expressions 'the point of intersection of a and b' and 'the point of intersection of b and c' would be the same, but not their senses. The reference of 'evening star' would be the same as that of 'morning star', but not the sense.

It is clear from the context that by 'sign' and 'name' I have here understood any designation representing a proper name, which thus has as its reference a definite object (this word taken in the widest range), but not a concept or a relation ... The designation of a single object can also consist of several words or other signs. For brevity, let every such designation be called a proper name.

---

[1] *I use this word strictly and understand '$a = b$' to have the sense of 'a is the same as b' or 'a and b coincide'.

The sense of a proper name is grasped by everybody who is sufficiently familiar with the language or totality of designations to which it belongs;[1] but this serves to illuminate only a single aspect of the reference, supposing it to have one. Comprehensive knowledge of the reference would require us to be able to say immediately whether any given sense belongs to it. To such knowledge we never attain.

The regular connexion between a sign, its sense, and its reference is of such a kind that to the sign there corresponds a definite sense and to that in turn a definite reference, while to a given reference (an object) there does not belong only a single sign. The same sense has different expressions in different languages or even in the same language. To be sure, exceptions to this regular behaviour occur. To every expression belonging to a complete totality of signs, there should certainly correspond a definite sense; but natural languages often do not satisfy this condition, and one must be content if the same word has the same sense in the same context. It may perhaps be granted that every grammatically well-formed expression representing a proper name always has a sense. But this is not to say that to the sense there also corresponds a reference. The words 'the celestial body most distant from the Earth' have a sense, but it is very doubtful if they also have a reference. The expression 'the least rapidly convergent series' has a sense; but it is known to have no reference, since for every given convergent series, another convergent, but less rapidly convergent, series can be found. In grasping a sense, one is not certainly assured of a reference.

If words are used in the ordinary way, what one intends to speak of is their reference. It can also happen, however, that one wishes to talk about the words themselves or their sense. This happens, for instance, when the words of another are quoted. One's own words then first designate words of the other speaker, and only the latter have their usual reference. We then have signs of signs. In writing, the words are in this case enclosed in quotation marks. Accordingly, a word standing between quotation marks must not be taken as having its ordinary reference.

In order to speak of the sense of an expression 'A' one may simply use the phrase 'the sense of the expression "A"'. In reported speech one talks about the sense, e.g., of another person's remarks. It is quite clear that in this way of speaking words do not have their customary reference but designate what is usually their sense. In order to have a short expression, we will say: In reported speech, words are used *indirectly* or have their *indirect* reference. We distinguish accordingly the *customary* from the *indirect* reference of a word; and its *customary* sense from its *indirect* sense. The indirect reference of a word is accordingly its customary sense. Such exceptions must always be borne in mind if the mode of connexion between sign, sense, and reference in particular cases is to be correctly understood.

The reference and sense of a sign are to be distinguished from the associated idea. If the reference of a sign is an object perceivable by the senses, my idea of it is an internal image, arising from memories of sense impressions which I have had and acts, both

---

[1] *In the case of an actual proper name such as 'Aristotle' opinions as to the sense may differ. It might, for instance, be taken to be the following: the pupil of Plato and teacher of Alexander the Great. Anybody who does this will attach another sense to the sentence 'Aristotle was born in Stagira' than will a man who takes as the sense of the name: the teacher of Alexander the Great who was born in Stagira. So long as the reference remains the same, such variations of sense may be tolerated, although they are to be avoided in the theoretical structure of a demonstrative science and ought not to occur in a perfect language.

internal and external, which I have performed. Such an idea is often saturated with feeling; the clarity of its separate parts varies and oscillates. The same sense is not always connected, even in the same man, with the same idea. The idea is subjective: one man's idea is not that of another. There result, as a matter of course, a variety of differences in the ideas associated with the same sense. A painter, a horseman, and a zoologist will probably connect different ideas with the name 'Bucephalus'. This constitutes an essential distinction between the idea and the sign's sense, which may be the common property of many and therefore is not a part of a mode of the individual mind. For one can hardly deny that mankind has a common store of thoughts which is transmitted from one generation to another.

In the light of this, one need have no scruples in speaking simply of *the* sense, whereas in the case of an idea one must, strictly speaking, add to whom it belongs and at what time. It might perhaps be said: Just as one man connects this idea, and another that idea, with the same word, so also one man can associate this sense and another that sense. But there still remains a difference in the mode of connexion. They are not prevented from grasping the same sense; but they cannot have the same idea . . . If two persons picture the same thing, each still has his own idea. It is indeed sometimes possible to establish differences in the ideas, or even in the sensations, of different men; but an exact comparison is not possible, because we cannot have both ideas together in the same consciousness.

The reference of a proper name is the object itself which we designate by its means; the idea, which we have in that case, is wholly subjective; in between lies the sense, which is indeed no longer subjective like the idea, but is yet not the object itself. The following analogy will perhaps clarify these relationships. Somebody observes the Moon through a telescope. I compare the Moon itself to the reference; it is the object of the observation, mediated by the real image projected by the object glass in the interior of the telescope, and by the retinal image of the observer. The former I compare to the sense, the latter is like the idea or experience. The optical image in the telescope is indeed one-sided and dependent upon the standpoint of observation; but it is still objective, inasmuch as it can be used by several observers. At any rate it could be arranged for several to use it simultaneously. But each one would have his own retinal image. On account of the diverse shapes of the observers' eyes, even a geometrical congruence could hardly be achieved, and an actual coincidence would be out of the question. This analogy might be developed still further, by assuming A's retinal image made visible to B; or A might also see his own retinal image in a mirror. In this way we might perhaps show how an idea can itself be taken as an object, but as such is not for the observer what it directly is for the person having the idea. But to pursue this would take us too far afield.

We can now recognize three levels of difference between words, expressions, or whole sentences. The difference may concern at most the ideas, or the sense but not the reference, or, finally, the reference as well. With respect to the first level, it is to be noted that, on account of the uncertain connexion of ideas with words, a difference may hold for one person, which another does not find. The difference between a translation and the original text should properly not overstep the first level. To the possible differences here belong also the colouring and shading which poetic elo-quence seeks to give to the sense. Such colouring and shading are not objective, and must be evoked by each hearer or reader according to the hints of the poet or the speaker. Without some affinity in human ideas art would certainly be impossible; but it can never be exactly determined how far the intentions of the poet are realized.

In what follows there will be no further discussion of ideas and experiences; they have been mentioned here only to ensure that the idea aroused in the hearer by a word shall not be confused with its sense or its reference.

To make short and exact expressions possible, let the following phraseology be established:

A proper name (word, sign, sign combination, expression) *expresses* its sense, *stands for* or *designates* its reference. By means of a sign we express its sense and designate its reference.

Idealists or sceptics will perhaps long since have objected: 'You talk, without further ado, of the Moon as an object; but how do you know that the name "the Moon" has any reference? How do you know that anything whatsoever has a reference?' I reply that when we say 'the Moon', we do not intend to speak of our idea of the Moon, nor are we satisfied with the sense alone, but we presuppose a reference. To assume that in the sentence 'The Moon is smaller than the Earth' the idea of the Moon is in question, would be flatly to misunderstand the sense. If this is what the speaker wanted, he would use the phrase 'my idea of the Moon'. Now we can of course be mistaken in the presupposition, and such mistakes have indeed occurred. But the question whether the presupposition is perhaps always mistaken need not be answered here; in order to justify mention of the reference of a sign it is enough, at first, to point out our intention in speaking or thinking. (We must then add the reservation: provided such reference exists.)

9 Definite and Indefinite Descriptions: Bertrand Russell, *Introduction to Mathematical Philosophy**

The rise of analytic philosophy from around the start of the twentieth century saw a steady growth of interest in the structure of language; but the concerns of philosophers in this area are importantly different from those of the grammarian or student of linguistics. In our next extract, the famous British philosopher Bertrand Russell points out that *grammatical* form may often be misleading as a guide to the correct analysis of the *logical* form of an expression; the surface grammar does not always exactly match the underlying meaning. The sentences 'I met Jones' and 'I met a man' are grammatically very similar; but logically, Russell argues, they are quite different. The first names an actual entity – the person Jones – while in the second case I am using an *indefinite* description, which does not name an actual person (for if I were to call all the people in the world by name, there would not be, alongside all these individuals, an additional person called 'a man').

Russell, like his predecessor Frege (see previous extract) did a great deal of work on the logic of mathematics, and his analysis of language reflects this. To explain the logical form of expressions like 'I met a man', he introduces the

---

* Bertrand Russell, *Introduction to Mathematical Philosophy* (London: Allen & Unwin, 1919), extracts from ch. 16.

idea of a *propositional function*, which is rather like an algebraic function involving unknown quantities. So 'I met a man' does not name an individual whom I met, but is an instance of the function 'I met *x* and *x* is male and adult and human'. When this function is turned into an assertion by introducing an existential operator ('*There is* an *x* such that I met *x*, and *x* is male etc . . .), the conditions for its truth or falsity can be clearly seen. This simple but important device enables us, according to Russell, to avoid puzzles about non-existent entities like unicorns: instead of supposing that sentences containing 'unicorn' actually refer to some sort of entity, we can simply analyse them via propositional functions. (So 'A unicorn came into my house' can be spelt out as 'There is an *x* such that *x* is one-horned, and like a horse, and *x* came into my house'.) In this analysis, 'unicorn' no longer appears as the subject of the sentence, tempting us to allow it some kind of shadowy existence. As Russell puts it, 'logic should no more admit a unicorn than zoology', for 'a robust sense of reality' is necessary for correct logical analysis of propositions (compare Quine, Part II, extract 11, above).

In the remainder of the extract, Russell develops these techniques to deal with *definite* descriptions (expressions using the definite article 'the', such as 'the present king of France'). Because uniqueness of reference is implied here, we may be tempted to suppose that something must be being named or designated. But with Russell's device of propositional functions, and some further logical apparatus to convey uniqueness, the apparent singular referring expression can be analysed away. The puzzle about identity statements that had worried Frege (see preceding extract) is also neatly dealt with. If we were to treat 'the author of *Waverley*' as a name, then when we say 'Scott was the author of *Waverley*' we would seem to be asserting no more than the tautology that 'Scott is Scott'. But by construing 'the author of *Waverley*' via the use of propositional functions, Russell is able to show how 'Scott is the author of *Waverley*' can be a genuinely informative statement. The extract ends with Russell offering a detailed example of how his techniques can be used to exhibit the true logical structure of propositions containing definite descriptions.

Russell's account of propositions in which definite descriptions occur has been highly influential. Although there has been much subsequent debate over the exact details of his analysis, his work is acknowledged to have opened a new chapter in the quest for a better understanding of logic and language.

A 'description' may be of two sorts, definite and indefinite (or ambiguous). An indefinite description is a phrase of the form 'a so-and-so', and a definite description is a phrase of the form 'the so-and-so' (in the singular). Let us begin with the former.

'Who did you meet?' 'I met a man.' 'That is a very indefinite description.' We are therefore not departing from usage in our terminology. Our question is: What do I really assert when I assert 'I met a man'? Let us assume, for the moment, that my assertion is true, and that in fact I met Jones. It is clear that what I assert is *not* 'I met Jones'. I may say 'I met a man, but it was not Jones'; in that case, though I lie, I do not contradict myself, as I should do if when I say I met a man I really mean that I met Jones. It is clear also that the person to whom I am speaking can understand what I say, even if he is a foreigner and has never heard of Jones.

But we may go further: not only Jones, but no actual man, enters into my statement. This becomes obvious when the statement is false, since then there is no more reason why Jones should be supposed to enter into the proposition than why anyone else should. Indeed the statement would remain significant, though it could not possibly be true, even if there were no man at all. 'I met a unicorn' or 'I met a sea-serpent' is a perfectly significant assertion, if we know what it would be to be a unicorn or a sea-serpent, i.e. what is the definition of these fabulous monsters. Thus it is only what we may call the *concept* that enters into the proposition. In the case of 'unicorn', for example, there is only the concept: there is not also, somewhere among the shades, something unreal which may be called 'a unicorn'. Therefore, since it is significant (though false) to say 'I met a unicorn', it is clear that this proposition, rightly analysed, does not contain a constituent 'a unicorn', though it does contain the concept 'unicorn'.

The question of 'unreality', which confronts us at this point, is a very important one. Misled by grammar, the great majority of those logicians who have dealt with this question have dealt with it on mistaken lines. They have regarded grammatical form as a surer guide in analysis than, in fact, it is. And they have not known what differences in grammatical form are important. 'I met Jones' and 'I met a man' would count traditionally as propositions of the same form, but in actual fact they are of quite different forms: the first names an actual person, Jones; while the second involves a *propositional function*, and becomes, when made explicit: 'The function "I met x and x is human" is sometimes true.' (It will be remembered that we adopted the convention of using 'sometimes' as not implying more than once.) This proposition is obviously not of the form 'I met x', which accounts for the existence of the proposition 'I met a unicorn' in spite of the fact that there is no such thing as 'a unicorn'.

For want of the apparatus of propositional functions, many logicians have been driven to the conclusion that there are unreal objects. It is argued, e.g. by Meinong,[1] that we can speak about 'the golden mountain', 'the round square', and so on; we can make true propositions of which these are the subjects; hence they must have some kind of logical being, since otherwise the propositions in which they occur would be meaningless. In such theories, it seems to me, there is a failure of that feeling for reality which ought to be preserved even in the most abstract studies. Logic, I should maintain, must no more admit a unicorn than zoology can; for logic is concerned with the real world just as truly as zoology, though with its more abstract and general features. To say that unicorns have an existence in heraldry, or in literature, or in imagination, is a most pitiful and paltry evasion. What exists in heraldry is not an animal, made of flesh and blood, moving and breathing of its own initiative. What exists is a picture, or a description in words. Similarly, to maintain that Hamlet, for example, exists in his own world, namely, in the world of Shakespeare's imagination, just as truly as (say) Napoleon existed in the ordinary world, is to say something deliberately confusing, or else confused to a degree which is scarcely credible. There is only one world, the 'real' world: Shakespeare's imagination is part of it, and the thoughts that he had in writing Hamlet are real. So are the thoughts that we have in reading the play. But it is of the very essence of fiction that only the thoughts, feelings, etc., in Shakespeare and his readers are real, and that there is not, in addition to them, an objective Hamlet. When you have taken account of all the feelings roused by Napoleon in writers and readers of history, you have not touched the actual man; but in the case of Hamlet you have come to the end of him. If no one thought about Hamlet, there would be nothing left to him; if no one had thought about Napoleon,

---

[1] Russell refers to Alexius Meinong, *Inquiries into the Theory of Objects and Psychology* [*Untersuchungen zur Gegenstandstheorie und Psychologie*, 1904], which he had reviewed in 1904 in the journal *Mind*.

he would have soon seen to it that someone did. The sense of reality is vital in logic, and whoever juggles with it by pretending that Hamlet has another kind of reality is doing a disservice to thought. A robust sense of reality is very necessary in framing a correct analysis of propositions about unicorns, golden mountains, round squares, and other such pseudo-objects.

In obedience to the feeling of reality, we shall insist that, in the analysis of propositions, nothing 'unreal' is to be admitted. But, after all, if there *is* nothing unreal, how, it may be asked, *could* we admit anything unreal? The reply is that, in dealing with propositions, we are dealing in the first instance with symbols, and if we attribute significance to groups of symbols which have no significance, we shall fall into the error of admitting unrealities, in the only sense in which this is possible, namely, as objects described. In the proposition 'I met a unicorn', the whole four words together make a significant proposition, and the word 'unicorn' by itself is significant, in just the same sense as the word 'man'. But the *two* words 'a unicorn' do not form a subordinate group having a meaning of its own. Thus if we falsely attribute meaning to these two words, we find ourselves saddled with 'a unicorn', and with the problem how there can be such a thing in a world where there are no unicorns. 'A unicorn' is an indefinite description which describes nothing. It is not an indefinite description which describes something unreal. Such a proposition as 'x is unreal' only has meaning when 'x' is a description, definite or indefinite; in that case the proposition will be true if 'x' is a description which describes nothing. But whether the description 'x' describes something or describes nothing, it is in any case not a constituent of the proposition in which it occurs; like 'a unicorn' just now, it is not a subordinate group having a meaning of its own. All this results from the fact that, when 'x' is a description, 'x is unreal' or 'x does not exist' is not nonsense, but is always significant and sometimes true...

We come now to the main subject of the present chapter, namely, the definition of the word *the* (in the singular). One very important point about the definition of 'a so-and-so' applies equally to 'the so-and-so'; the definition to be sought is a definition of propositions in which this phrase occurs, not a definition of the phrase itself in isolation. In the case of 'a so-and-so', this is fairly obvious: no one could suppose that 'a man' was a definite object, which could be defined by itself. Socrates is a man, Plato is a man, Aristotle is a man, but we cannot infer that 'a man' means the same as 'Socrates' means and also the same as 'Plato' means and also the same as 'Aristotle' means, since these three names have different meanings. Nevertheless, when we have enumerated all the men in the world, there is nothing left of which we can say, 'This is a man, and not only so, but it is *the* "a man", the quintessential entity that is just an indefinite man without being anybody in particular.' It is of course quite clear that whatever there is in the world is definite: if it is a man it is one definite man and not any other. Thus there cannot be such an entity as 'a man' to be found in the world, as opposed to specific men. And accordingly it is natural that we do not define 'a man' itself, but only the propositions in which it occurs.

In the case of 'the so-and-so' this is equally true, though at first sight less obvious. We may demonstrate that this must be the case, by a consideration of the difference between a *name* and a *definite description*. Take the proposition, 'Scott is the author of *Waverley*.' We have here a name, 'Scott', and a description, 'the author of *Waverley*', which are asserted to apply to the same person. The distinction between a name and all other symbols may be explained as follows:

A name is a simple symbol whose meaning is something that can only occur as subject, i.e. something of the kind ... defined as an 'individual' or a 'particular'. And a 'simple' symbol is one which has no parts that are symbols. Thus 'Scott' is a simple symbol, because, though it has parts (namely, separate letters), these parts are not symbols. On the other hand, 'the author of *Waverley*' is not a simple symbol, because the separate words that compose the phrase are parts which are symbols ...

We have, then, two things to compare: (1) a *name*, which is a simple symbol, directly designating an individual which is its meaning, and having this meaning in its own right, independently of the meanings of all other words; (2) a *description*, which consists of several words, whose meanings are already fixed, and from which results whatever is to be taken as the 'meaning' of the description.

A proposition containing a description is not identical with what that proposition becomes when a name is substituted, even if the name names the same object as the description describes. 'Scott is the author of *Waverley*' is obviously a different proposition from 'Scott is Scott': the first is a fact in literary history, the second a trivial truism. And if we put anyone other than Scott in place of 'the author of *Waverley*', our proposition would become false, and would therefore certainly no longer be the same proposition. But, it may be said, our proposition is essentially of the same form as (say) 'Scott is Sir Walter', in which two names are said to apply to the same person. The reply is that, if 'Scott is Sir Walter' really means 'the person named "Scott" is the person named "Sir Walter"', then the names are being used as descriptions: i.e. the individual, instead of being named, is being described as the person having that name. This is a way in which names are frequently used in practice, and there will, as a rule, be nothing in the phraseology to show whether they are being used in this way or *as* names. When a name is used directly, merely to indicate what we are speaking about, it is no part of the *fact* asserted, or of the falsehood if our assertion happens to be false: it is merely part of the symbolism by which we express our thought. What we want to express is something which might (for example) be translated into a foreign language; it is something for which the actual words are a vehicle, but of which they are no part. On the other hand, when we make a proposition about 'the person called "Scott"', the actual name 'Scott' enters into what we are asserting, and not merely into the language used in making the assertion. Our proposition will now be a different one if we substitute 'the person called "Sir Walter"'. But so long as we are using names *as* names, whether we say 'Scott' or whether we say 'Sir Walter' is as irrelevant to what we are asserting as whether we speak English or French. Thus so long as names are used *as* names, 'Scott is Sir Walter' is the same trivial proposition as 'Scott is Scott'. This completes the proof that 'Scott is the author of *Waverley*' is not the same proposition as results from substituting a name for 'the author of *Waverley*', no matter what name may be substituted.

When we use a variable, and speak of a propositional function, ϕx say, the process of applying general statements about x to particular cases will consist in substituting a name for the letter 'x', assuming that ϕ is a function which has individuals for its arguments. Suppose, for example, that ϕx is 'always true'; let it be, say, the 'law of identity', $x = x$. Then we may substitute for 'x' any name we choose, and we shall obtain a true proposition. Assuming for the moment that 'Socrates', 'Plato', and 'Aristotle' are names (a very rash assumption), we can infer from the law of identity that Socrates is Socrates, Plato is Plato, and Aristotle is Aristotle. But we shall commit a fallacy if we attempt to infer, without further premisses, that the author of *Waverley* is the author of *Waverley*. This results from what we have just proved, that, if we substitute a name for 'the author of *Waverley*' in a proposition, the proposition we obtain is a different one. That is to say, applying the result to our present case: If 'x' is a name, '$x = x$' is not the same proposition as 'the author of *Waverley* is the author of *Waverley*', no matter what name 'x' may be. Thus from the fact that all propositions of the form '$x = x$' are true we cannot infer, without more ado, that the author of *Waverley* is the author of *Waverley*. In fact, propositions of the form 'the so-and-so is the so-and-so' are not always true: it is necessary that the so-and-so should *exist*... It is false that the present King of France is the present King of France, or that the round square is the round square. When we substitute a description for a name, propositional functions which are 'always true' may become false, if the description describes nothing. There is no mystery in this as soon as we realize (what was proved in the preceding paragraph) that when we substitute a description the result is not a value of the propositional function in question.

We are now in a position to define propositions in which a definite description occurs. The only thing that distinguishes 'the so-and-so' from 'a so-and-so' is the implication of uniqueness. We cannot speak of '*the* inhabitant of London', because inhabiting London is an attribute which is not unique. We cannot speak about 'the present King of France', because there is none; but we can speak [in 1919] about 'the present King of England'. Thus propositions about 'the so-and-so' always imply the corresponding propositions about 'a so-and-so', with the addendum that there is not more than one so-and-so. Such a proposition as 'Scott is the author of *Waverley*' could not be true if *Waverley* had never been written, or if several people had written it; and no more could any other proposition resulting from a propositional function x by the substitution of 'the author of *Waverley*' for 'x'. We may say that 'the author of *Waverley*' means 'the value of x for which "x wrote *Waverley*" is true'. Thus the proposition 'the author of *Waverley* was Scotch', for example, involves:

(1) 'x wrote *Waverley*' is not always false;
(2) 'if x and y wrote *Waverley*, x and y are identical' is always true;
(3) 'if x wrote *Waverley*, x was Scotch' is always true.

These three propositions, translated into ordinary language, state:

(1) at least one person wrote *Waverley*;
(2) at most one person wrote *Waverley*;
(3) whoever wrote *Waverley* was Scotch.

All these three are implied by 'the author of *Waverley* was Scotch'. Conversely, the three together (but no two of them) imply that the author of *Waverley* was Scotch. Hence the three together may be taken as defining what is meant by the proposition 'the author of *Waverley* was Scotch'.

10   Non-descriptive Uses of Language: J. L. Austin, *Performative Utterances**

By the middle of the twentieth century, the philosophical study of language had reached full flood. Much of this work was (and is) increasingly formal and technical, developing the tradition of logical analysis inaugurated by Frege and Russell (see previous two extracts). But alongside this, there arose the so-called 'ordinary language' movement in philosophy, which aimed to make progress through the careful piecemeal study of language as actually used in ordinary life. Prominent in this movement was the Oxford philosopher J. L. Austin, author of our next extract.

Austin begins by noting that much previous philosophical work on language had focused on its basic function of making statements about the world – assertions capable of truth or falsity. Ludwig Wittgenstein, for example, in his *Tractatus* [1921], had compared propositions to pictures, whose function was to map directly the states of affairs they described. Later on, however, by the time he came to write the *Investigations* [1953], Wittgenstein had come to realize that language has a multiplicity of different functions in addition to this simple descriptive one. Taking his cue from this, Austin implicitly condemns the 'descriptive fallacy' (that language's sole function is to report or describe facts or states of affairs), and observes that there are a 'great many uses of language'; he then proceeds to highlight one important example – 'performative' discourse, whose function is not to make an assertion (whether true or false), but to *do* something.

Saying 'I promise', as Austin goes on to explain, is one classic example of a performative utterance. By saying the words in the appropriate circumstances, you are not asserting anything true or false (indeed, it makes no sense to ask whether what you said was true or false); instead, you are, by the very utterance of the words, thereby committing yourself, or pledging your word. Austin draws an interesting analogy here with legal enactments, where certain words ('I hereby bequeath my watch to my brother') are, by being appropriately uttered, taken to be *operative*. Lawyers, of course, are often interested in the intention of the agent; but Austin warns us against supposing that when we use performatives, the uttered phrase is merely the outward sign of some inner or private mental act. Rather, the utterance of the phrase itself constitutes the act. Of course, the act may 'misfire' in various ways, but that will not depend on some interior event, or lack of it, but on the conventions, linguistic and social, that are in force when the utterance is made.

As well as drawing attention to the multiplicity and diversity of our linguistic behaviour, Austin's work also illustrates how the philosophy of language can develop in a direction quite different from the formalistic models inspired by science and mathematics, cultivating instead a meticulous sensitivity to the actual workings of human speech and discourse.

 You are more than entitled not to know what the word 'performative' means. It is a new word and an ugly word, and perhaps it does not mean anything very much. But at any rate there is one thing in its favour, it is not a profound word. I remember once when I had been talking on this subject that somebody afterwards said: 'You know, I haven't the least idea what he means, unless it could be that he simply means what he says.' Well, that is what I should like to mean.

---

* J. L. Austin, 'Performative Utterances', originally published in *Proceedings of the Aristotelian Society*, supplementary vol. 32 (1957–8); repr. in J. L. Austin, *Philosophical Papers*, ed. J. O. Urmson and G. J. Warnock (3rd edn, Oxford: Clarendon, 1979), pp. 233–52, extract from section I.

Let us consider first how this affair arises. We have not got to go very far back in the history of philosophy to find philosophers assuming more or less as a matter of course that the sole business, the sole interesting business, of any utterance – that is, of anything we say – is to be true or at least false. Of course they had always known that there are other kinds of things which we say – things like imperatives, the expressions of wishes, and exclamations – some of which had even been classified by grammarians, though it wasn't perhaps too easy to tell always which was which. But still philosophers have assumed that the only things that they are interested in are utterances which report facts or which describe situations truly or falsely. In recent times this kind of approach has been questioned – in two stages, I think. First of all people began to say: 'Well, if these things are true or false it ought to be possible to decide which they are, and if we can't decide which they are they aren't any good but are, in short, nonsense.' And this new approach did a great deal of good; a great many things which probably are nonsense were found to be such. It is not the case, I think, that all kinds of nonsense have been adequately classified yet, and perhaps some things have been dismissed as nonsense which really are not; but still this movement, the verification movement, was, in its way, excellent.[1]

However, we then come to the second stage. After all, we set some limits to the amount of nonsense that we talk, or at least the amount of nonsense that we are prepared to admit we talk; and so people began to ask whether after all some of those things which, treated as statements, were in danger of being dismissed as nonsense did after all really set out to be statements at all. Mightn't they perhaps be intended not to report facts but to influence people in this way or that, or to let off steam in this way or that? Or perhaps at any rate some elements in these utterances performed such functions, or, for example, drew attention in some way (without actually reporting it) to some important feature of the circumstances in which the utterance was being made. On these lines people have now adopted a new slogan, the slogan of the 'different uses of language'. The old approach, the old statemental approach, is sometimes called even a fallacy, the descriptive fallacy.

Certainly there are a great many uses of language. It's rather a pity that people are apt to invoke a new use of language whenever they feel so inclined, to help them out of this, that, or the other well-known philosophical tangle; we need more of a framework in which to discuss these uses of language; and also I think we should not despair too easily and talk, as people are apt to do, about the *infinite* uses of language. Philosophers will do this when they have listed as many, let us say, as seventeen; but even if there were something like ten thousand uses of language, surely we could list them all in time. This, after all, is no larger than the number of species of beetle that entomologists have taken the pains to list. But whatever the defects of either of these movements – the 'verification' movement or the 'use of language' movement – at any rate they have effected, nobody could deny, a great revolution in philosophy and, many would say, the most salutary in its history. (Not, if you come to think of it, a very immodest claim.)

Now it is one such sort of use of language that I want to examine here. I want to discuss a kind of utterance which looks like a statement and grammatically,

---

[1] For the movement Austin refers to here, see introduction to Part II, extract 10, above.

I suppose, would be classed as a statement, which is not nonsensical, and yet is not true or false. These are not going to be utterances which contain curious verbs like 'could' or 'might', or curious words like 'good', which many philosophers regard nowadays simply as danger signals. They will be perfectly straightforward utterances, with ordinary verbs in the first person singular present indicative active, and yet we shall see at once that they couldn't possibly be true or false. Furthermore, if a person makes an utterance of this sort we should say that he is *doing* something rather than merely *saying* something. This may sound a little odd, but the examples I shall give will in fact not be odd at all, and may even seem decidedly dull. Here are three or four. Suppose, for example, that in the course of a marriage ceremony I say, as people will, 'I do' – (sc. take this woman to be my lawful wedded wife). Or again, suppose that I tread on your toe, and say 'I apologize'. Or again, suppose that I have the bottle of champagne in my hand and say 'I name this ship the *Queen Elizabeth*'. Or suppose I say 'I bet you sixpence it will rain tomorrow'. In all these cases it would be absurd to regard the thing that I say as a report of the performance of the action which is undoubtedly done – the action of betting, or christening, or apologizing. We should say rather that, in saying what I do, I actually perform that action. When I say 'I name this ship the *Queen Elizabeth*' I do not describe the christening ceremony, I actually perform the christening; and when I say 'I do' (sc. take this woman to be my lawful wedded wife), I am not reporting on a marriage, I am indulging in it.

Now these kinds of utterance are the ones that we call *performative* utterances. This is rather an ugly word, and a new word, but there seems to be no word already in existence to do the job. The nearest approach that I can think of is the word 'operative', as used by lawyers. Lawyers when talking about legal instruments will distinguish between the preamble, which recites the circumstances in which a transaction is effected, and on the other hand the operative part – the part of it which actually performs the legal act which it is the purpose of the instrument to perform. So the word 'operative' is very near to what we want. 'I give and bequeath my watch to my brother' would be an operative clause and is a performative utterance. However, the word 'operative' has other uses, and it seems preferable to have a word specially designed for the use we want.

Now at this point one might protest, perhaps even with some alarm, that I seem to be suggesting that marrying is simply saying a few words, that just saying a few words *is* marrying. Well, that certainly is not the case. The words have to be said in the appropriate circumstances, and this is a matter that will come up again later. But the one thing we must not suppose is that what is needed in addition to the saying of the words in such cases is the performance of some internal spiritual act, of which the words then are to be the report. It's very easy to slip into this view at least in difficult, portentous cases, though perhaps not so easy in simple cases like apologizing. In the case of promising – for example, 'I promise to be there tomorrow' – it's very easy to think that the utterance is simply the outward and visible (that is, verbal) sign of the performance of some inward spiritual act of promising, and this view has certainly been expressed in many classic places. There is the case of Euripides' Hippolytus, who said 'My tongue swore to, but my heart did not' – perhaps it should be 'mind' or 'spirit' rather than 'heart', but at any rate some kind of backstage artiste. Now it is clear from this sort of example that, if we slip into thinking that such utterances are reports, true or false, of the performance of inward and spiritual acts, we open a loophole to perjurers and welshers and bigamists and so on, so that there are disadvantages in being excessively solemn in this way. It is better, perhaps, to stick to the old saying that our word is our bond.

However, although these utterances do not themselves report facts and are not themselves true or false, saying these things does very often *imply* that certain things are true and not false, in some sense at least of that rather woolly word 'imply'. For example, when I say 'I do take this woman to be my lawful wedded wife', or some other formula in the marriage ceremony, I do imply that I'm not already married, with wife living, sane, undivorced, and the rest of it. But still it is very important to realize that to imply that something or other is true, is not at all the same as saying something which is true itself.

These performative utterances are not true or false, then. But they do suffer from certain disabilities of their own. They can fail to come off in special ways, and that is what I want to consider next. The various ways in which a performative utterance may be unsatisfactory we call, for the sake of a name, the infelicities; and an infelicity arises – that is to say, the utterance is unhappy – if certain rules, transparently simple rules, are broken. I will mention some of these rules and then give examples of some infringements.

First of all, it is obvious that the conventional procedure which by our utterance we are purporting to use must actually exist. In the examples given here this procedure will be a verbal one, a verbal procedure for marrying or giving or whatever it may be; but it should be borne in mind that there are many non-verbal procedures by which we can perform exactly the same acts as we perform by these verbal means. It's worth remembering too that a great many of the things we do are at least in part of this conventional kind. Philosophers at least are too apt to assume that an action is always in the last resort the making of a physical movement, whereas it's usually, at least in part, a matter of convention.

The first rule is, then, that the convention invoked must exist and be accepted. And the second rule, also a very obvious one, is that the circumstances in which we purport to invoke this procedure must be appropriate for its invocation. If this is not observed, then the act that we purport to perform would not come off – it will be, one might say, a misfire. This will also be the case if, for example, we do not carry through the procedure – whatever it may be – correctly and completely, without a flaw and without a hitch. If any of these rules are not observed, we say that the act which we purported to perform is void, without effect. If, for example, the purported act was an act of marrying, then we should say that we 'went through a form' of marriage, but we did not actually succeed in marrying.

Here are some examples of this kind of misfire. Suppose that, living in a country like our own, we wish to divorce our wife. We may try standing her in front of us squarely in the room and saying, in a voice loud enough for all to hear, 'I divorce you'. Now this procedure is not accepted. We shall not thereby have succeeded in divorcing our wife, at least in this country and others like it. This is a case where the convention, we should say, does not exist or is not accepted. Again, suppose that, picking sides at a children's party, I say 'I pick George'. But George turns red in the face and says

'Not playing'. In that case I plainly, for some reason or another, have not picked George – whether because there is no convention that you can pick people who aren't playing, or because George in the circumstances is an inappropriate object for the procedure of picking. Or consider the case in which I say 'I appoint you Consul', and it turns out that you have been appointed already – or perhaps it may even transpire that you are a horse; here again, we have the infelicity of inappropriate circumstances, inappropriate objects, or what not. Examples of flaws and hitches are perhaps scarcely necessary – one party in the marriage ceremony says 'I will', the other says 'I won't'; I say 'I bet sixpence', but nobody says 'Done': nobody takes up the offer. In all these and other such cases, the act which we purport to perform, or set out to perform, is not achieved.

But there is another and a rather different way in which this kind of utterance may go wrong. A good many of these verbal procedures are designed for use by people who hold certain beliefs or have certain feelings or intentions. And if you use one of these formulae when you do not have the requisite thoughts or feelings or intentions then there is an abuse of the procedure, there is insincerity. Take, for example, the expression, 'I congratulate you'. This is designed for use by people who are glad that the person addressed has achieved a certain feat, believe that he was personally responsible for the success, and so on. If I say 'I congratulate you' when I'm not pleased or when I don't believe that the credit was yours, then there is insincerity. Likewise if I say I promise to do something, without having the least intention of doing it or without believing it feasible. In these cases there is something wrong certainly, but it is not like a misfire. We should not say that I didn't in fact promise, but rather that I did promise but promised insincerely; I did congratulate you but the congratulations were hollow. And there may be an infelicity of a somewhat similar kind when the performative utterance commits the speaker to future conduct of a certain description and then in the future he does not in fact behave in the expected way. This is very obvious, of course, if I promise to do something and then break my promise, but there are many kinds of commitment of a rather less tangible form than that in the case of promising. For instance, I may say 'I welcome you', bidding you welcome to my home or wherever it may be, but then I proceed to treat you as though you were exceedingly unwelcome. In this case the procedure of saying 'I welcome you' has been abused in a way rather different from that of simple insincerity.

Now we might ask whether this list of infelicities is complete, whether the kinds of infelicity are mutually exclusive, and so forth. Well, it is not complete, and they are not mutually exclusive; they never are... [W]e could be issuing any of these utterances, as we can issue an utterance of any kind whatsoever, in the course, for example, of acting a play or making a joke or writing a poem in which case of course it would not be seriously meant and we shall not be able to say that we seriously performed the act concerned. If the poet says 'Go and catch a falling star' or whatever it may be, he doesn't seriously issue an order. Considerations of this kind apply to any utterance at all, not merely to performatives.

That, then, is perhaps enough to be going on with. We have discussed the performative utterance and its infelicities. That equips us, we may suppose, with two shining new tools to crack the crib of reality maybe. It also equips us – it always does – with two shining new skids under our metaphysical feet. . . .

11   Language, Meaning and Context: Paul Grice, *Logic and Conversation**

A near contemporary of Austin (see previous extract) was the British philosopher Paul Grice, who also taught at Oxford, and later on at Berkeley. Like Austin, he reacted against the attempt to codify meaning through formalized accounts of the structure of propositions and their logical relations, and in the following excerpt (from a lecture given at Harvard in the late 1960s), he begins by discussing the relationship between the formal symbols of logicians and their counterparts in natural language. Taking his cue from Austin, he focuses on the conditions and conventions governing ordinary conversations, and their importance in determining exactly what meaning is conveyed.

The main idea to emerge from the subsequent discussion is that of *conversational implicature*. Suppose, writing a philosophy reference for a pupil, I simply say 'he is always polite and conscientious, and invariably punctual in handing in his work'. Although there is nothing in what I have said that logically implies the applicant is not much good at philosophy, in the context of replying to a request for an account of his philosophical ability, such a terse letter would be pretty damning. My remarks 'implicate' that he is no good, even though that is not explicitly stated, or strictly entailed, by what I have said.

Grice's point, once made, may seem an obvious one, but it has important implications for our understanding of the nature of language and meaning. The initial assumption of many logicians is likely to be that linguistic meaning is something fairly fixed and determinate – a function of the definitions of words, and the logical and grammatical operators used to connect those words together to form a sentence. What Grice's argument suggests is that the formal meaning of an utterance may be only the tip of the iceberg: what is conveyed may depend on a complex network of conventions governing how people expect each other to behave, and how much information they expect them to convey for a given purpose. Although Grice in the course of his article suggests that there may be various 'maxims and submaxims' governing what we expect of each other in our linguistic encounters, subsequent philosophers have debated how far these could be codified, given the indefinite variety of circumstances and assumptions applying in any given case. However that may be, it is important to note that Gricean 'implicature' is parasitic on there being a rule-governed core of fixed meaning in the first place: what we are able to 'conversationally implicate' by our words in a particular context must depend on those words already having a basic meaning, independent of context.

It is a commonplace of philosophical logic that there are, or appear to be, divergences in meaning between, on the one hand, at least some of what I shall call the formal devices [the symbols used by logicians] and, on the other, what are taken to be their analogues or counterparts in natural language – such expressions as *not*, *and*, *or*, *if*, *all*, *some* (*or at least one*), *the*...

Those who concede that such divergences exist adhere, in the main, to one or the other of two rival groups, which I shall call the formalist and the informalist groups. An outline of a not uncharacteristic formalist position may be given as follows: Insofar as logicians are concerned with the formulation of very general patterns of valid inference, the formal devices possess a decisive advantage over their natural

* Originally delivered as part of the William James Lectures at Harvard University in 1967; first published as part I, ch. 2 of P. Grice, *Studies in the Way of Words* (Cambridge, Mass.: Harvard University Press, 1989), pp. 22–40; excerpted.

counterparts... [F]rom a philosophical point of view, the possession by the natural counterparts of those elements in their meaning, which they do not share with the corresponding formal devices, is to be regarded as an imperfection of natural languages; the elements in question are undesirable excrescences. For... the indefiniteness of these concepts not only is objectionable in itself but also leaves open the way to metaphysics – we cannot be certain that none of these natural language expressions is metaphysically 'loaded'... The proper course is to conceive and begin to construct an ideal language, incorporating the formal devices, the sentences of which will be clear, determinate in truth value, and certifiably free from metaphysical implications; the foundations of science will now be philosophically secure, since the statements of the scientist will be expressible... within this ideal language...

To this, an informalist might reply in the following vein. The philosophical demand for an ideal language rests on certain assumptions that should not be conceded; these are, that the primary yardstick by which to judge the adequacy of a language is its ability to serve the needs of science, that an expression cannot be guaranteed as fully intelligible unless an explication or analysis of its meaning has been provided... Language serves many important purposes besides those of scientific inquiry... Moreover... there are very many inferences and arguments, expressed in natural language and not in terms of these devices, which are nevertheless recognizably valid. So there must be a place for an unsimplified, and so more or less unsystematic, logic of the natural counterparts of these devices; this logic may be aided and guided by the simplified logic of the formal devices but cannot be supplanted by it. Indeed, not only do the two logics differ, but sometimes they come into conflict...

On the general question of the place in philosophy of the reformation of natural language, I shall... have nothing to say. I shall confine myself to the dispute in its relation to the alleged divergences. I have, moreover, no intention of entering the fray on behalf of either contestant. I wish, rather, to maintain that the common assumption [of divergences between formal and informal logic is] a common mistake, and that the mistake arises from inadequate attention to the nature and importance of the conditions governing conversation. I shall, therefore, inquire into the general conditions that, in one way or another, apply to conversation as such, irrespective of its subject matter. I begin with a characterization of the notion of 'implicature'.

Implicature

Suppose that A and B are talking about a mutual friend, C, who is now working in a bank. A asks B how C is getting on in his job, and B replies, *Oh quite well, I think; he likes his colleagues, and he hasn't been to prison yet.* At this point, A might well inquire what B was implying, what he was suggesting, or even what he meant by saying that C had not yet been to prison. The answer might be any one of such things as that C is the sort of person likely to yield to the temptation provided by his occupation, that C's colleagues are really very unpleasant and treacherous people, and so forth. It might, of course, be quite unnecessary for A to make such an inquiry of B, the answer to it being, in the context, clear in advance. It is clear that whatever B implied, suggested, meant in this example, is distinct from what B said, which was simply that C had not been to prison yet. I wish to introduce, as terms of art, the verb *implicate* and the related nouns *implicature* (compare *implying*) and *implicatum* (compare *what is implied*) . . .

In the sense in which I am using the word *say*, I intend what someone has said to be closely related to the conventional meaning of the words (the sentence) he has uttered. Suppose someone to have uttered the sentence *He is in the grip of a vice.* Given a knowledge of the English language, but no knowledge of the circumstances of the utterance, one would know something about what the speaker had said, on the assumption that he was speaking standard English, and speaking literally. One would know that he had said, about some particular male person or animal x, that at the time of the utterance (whatever that was), either (1) x was unable to rid himself of a certain kind of bad character trait or (2) some part of x's person was caught in a certain kind of tool or instrument (approximate account, of course). But for a full identification of what the speaker had said, one would need to know (*a*) the identity of x, (*b*) the time of utterance, and (*c*) the meaning, on the particular occasion of utterance, of the phrase *in the grip of a vice* [a decision between (1) and (2)] . . .

I wish to represent a certain subclass of nonconventional implicatures, which I shall call *conversational* implicatures, as being essentially connected with certain general features of discourse; so my next step is to try to say what these features are. The following may provide a first approximation to a general principle. Our talk exchanges do not normally consist of a succession of disconnected remarks, and would not be rational if they did. They are characteristically, to some degree at least, cooperative efforts; and each participant recognizes in them, to some extent, a common purpose or set of purposes, or at least a mutually accepted direction. This purpose or direction may be fixed from the start (e.g., by an initial proposal of a question for discussion), or it may evolve during the exchange; it may be fairly definite, or it may be so indefinite as to leave very considerable latitude to the participants (as in a casual conversation). But at each stage, *some* possible conversational moves would be excluded as conversationally unsuitable. We might then formulate a rough general principle which participants will be expected (ceteris paribus) to observe, namely: Make your conversational contribution such as is required, at the stage at which it occurs, by the accepted purpose or direction of the talk exchange in which you are engaged. One might label this the *Cooperative Principle.*

. . . [O]ne may perhaps distinguish four categories under one or another of which will fall certain more specific maxims and submaxims, the following of which will, in general, yield results in accordance with the Cooperative Principle, [namely] Quantity, Quality, Relation, and Manner. The category of *Quantity* relates to the quantity of information to be provided, and under it fall the following maxims:

1. Make your contribution as informative as is required (for the current purposes of the exchange).
2. Do not make your contribution more informative than is required.

. . . Under the category of *Quality* falls a supermaxim – 'Try to make your contribution one that is true' – and two more specific maxims:

1. Do not say what you believe to be false.
2. Do not say that for which you lack adequate evidence.

Under the category of *Relation* I place a single maxim, namely, 'Be relevant'. Though the maxim itself is terse, its formulation conceals a number of problems that exercise me a good deal: questions about what different kinds and focuses of relevance there may be, how these shift in the course of a talk exchange, how to allow for the fact that subjects of conversation are legitimately changed, and so on. I find the treatment of such questions exceedingly difficult, and I hope to revert to them in a later work.

Finally, under the category of *Manner*, which I understand as relating not (like the previous categories) to what is said but, rather, to *how* what is said is to be said, I include the supermaxim – 'Be perspicuous' – and various maxims such as:

1. Avoid obscurity of expression.
2. Avoid ambiguity.
3. Be brief (avoid unnecessary prolixity).
4. Be orderly.

And one might need others...

There are, of course, all sorts of other maxims (aesthetic, social, or moral in character), such as 'Be polite', that are also normally observed by participants in talk exchanges, and these may also generate nonconventional implicatures. The conversational maxims, however, and the conversational implicatures connected with them, are specially connected (I hope) with the particular purposes that talk (and so, talk exchange) is adapted to serve and is primarily employed to serve. I have stated my maxims as if this purpose were a maximally effective exchange of information; this specification is, of course, too narrow, and the scheme needs to be generalized to allow for such general purposes as influencing or directing the actions of others...

Examples of conversational implicature

...A is writing a testimonial about a pupil who is a candidate for a philosophy job, and his letter reads as follow: 'Dear Sir, Mr X's command of English is excellent, and his attendance at tutorials has been regular. Yours etc.' (Gloss: A cannot be opting out, since if he wished to be uncooperative, why write at all? He cannot be unable, through ignorance, to say more, since the man is his pupil; moreover, he knows that more information than this is wanted. He is, therefore, wishing to impart information that he is reluctant to write down. This supposition is tenable only if he thinks Mr X is no good at philosophy. This, then, is what he is implicating.)...

...[As an example of failure to be brief], compare the remarks:

(*a*) Miss X sang 'Home Sweet Home'.
(*b*) Miss X produced a series of sounds that corresponded closely with the score of 'Home Sweet Home'.

Suppose that a reviewer has chosen to utter (*b*) rather than (*a*). (Gloss: Why has he selected that rigmarole in place of the concise and nearly synonymous *sang*?

Presumably, to indicate some striking difference between Miss X's performance and those to which the word singing is usually applied. The most obvious supposition is that Miss X's performance suffered from some hideous defect. The reviewer knows that this supposition is what is likely to spring to mind, so that is what he is implicating.)

Generalized conversational implicature

I have so far considered only cases of what I might call 'particularized conversational implicature' – that is to say, cases in which an implicature is carried by saying that *p* on a particular occasion in virtue of special features of the context, cases in which there is no room for the idea that an implicature of this sort is normally carried by saying that *p*. But there are cases of generalized conversational implicature. Sometimes one can say that the use of a certain form of words in an utterance would normally (in the absence of special circumstances) carry such-and-such an implicature or type of implicature. Noncontroversial examples are perhaps hard to find, since it is all too easy to treat a generalized conversational implicature as if it were a conventional implicature. I offer an example that I hope may be fairly noncontroversial.

Anyone who uses a sentence of the form *X is meeting a woman this evening* would normally implicate that the person to be met was someone other than X's wife, mother, sister, or perhaps even close platonic friend. Similarly, if I were to say *X went into a house yesterday and found a tortoise inside the front door*, my hearer would normally be surprised if some time later I revealed that the house was X's own. I could produce similar linguistic phenomena involving the expressions *a garden, a car, a college*, and so on. Sometimes, however, there would normally be no such implicature ('I have been sitting in a car all morning'), and sometimes a reverse implicature ('I broke a finger yesterday'). I am inclined to think that one would not lend a sympathetic ear to a philosopher who suggested that [such cases involve different *senses* of the form of expression *an X*] ... Would we not much prefer an account on the following lines ... When someone, by using the form of expression an X, implicates that the X does not belong to or is not otherwise closely connected with some identifiable person, the implicature is present because the speaker has failed to be specific in a way in which he might have been expected to be specific, with the consequence that it is likely to be assumed that he is not in a position to be specific. This is a familiar implicature situation and is classifiable as a failure, for one reason or another, to fulfil the first maxim of Quantity. The only difficult question is why it should, in certain cases, be presumed, independently of information about particular contexts of utterance, that specification of the closeness or remoteness of the connection between a particular person or object and a further person who is mentioned or indicated by the utterance should be likely to be of interest. The answer must lie in the following region: Transactions between a person and other persons or things closely connected with him are liable to be very different as regards their concomitants and results from the same sort of transactions involving only remotely connected persons or things; the concomitants and results, for instance, of my finding a hole in my roof are likely to be very different from the concomitants and results of my finding a hole in someone else's roof. Information, like money, is often given without the giver's knowing to just what use the recipient will want to put it. If someone to whom a transaction is mentioned gives it further consideration, he is likely to find himself wanting the answers to further questions that the speaker may not be able to identify in advance; if the appropriate specification will be likely to enable the hearer to answer a considerable variety of such questions for himself, then there is a presumption that the speaker should include it in his remark; if not, then there is no such presumption.

Finally, we can now show that, conversational implicature being what it is, it must possess certain features:

1. Since, to assume the presence of a conversational implicature, we have to assume that at least the Cooperative Principle is being observed, and since it is possible to opt out of the observation of this principle, it follows that a generalized conversational implicature can be cancelled in a particular case. It may be explicitly cancelled, by the addition of a clause that states or implies that the speaker has opted out, or it may be contextually cancelled, if the form of utterance that usually carries it is used in a context that makes it clear that the speaker is opting out.

2. Insofar as the calculation that a particular conversational implicature is present requires, besides contextual and background information, only a knowledge of what has been said (or of the conventional commitment of the utterance), and insofar as the manner of expression plays no role in the calculation, it will not be possible to find another way of saying the same thing, which simply lacks the implicature in question, except where some special feature of the substituted version is itself relevant to the determination of an implicature (in virtue of one of the maxims of Manner). If we call this feature nondetachability, one may expect a generalized conversational implicature that is carried by a familiar, nonspecial locution to have a high degree of nondetachability.

3. To speak approximately, since the calculation of the presence of a conversational implicature presupposes an initial knowledge of the conventional force of the expression the utterance of which carries the implicature, a conversational implicatum will be a condition that is not included in the original specification of the expression's conventional force. Though it may not be impossible for what starts life, so to speak, as a conversational implicature to become conventionalized, to suppose that this is so in a given case would require special justification. So, initially at least, conversational implicata are not part of the meaning of the expressions to the employment of which they attach.

4. Since the truth of a conversational implicatum is not required by the truth of what is said (what is said may be true – what is implicated may be false), the implicature is not carried by what is said, but only by the saying of what is said, or by 'putting it that way'.

5. Since, to calculate a conversational implicature is to calculate what has to be supposed in order to preserve the supposition that the Cooperative Principle is being observed, and since there may be various possible specific explanations, a list of which may be open, the conversational implicatum in such cases will be [a] disjunction of such specific explanations; and if the list of these is open, the implicatum will have just the kind of indeterminacy that many actual implicata do in fact seem to possess.

12   How the Reference of Terms is Fixed: Saul Kripke, *Naming and Necessity**

Our final extract in this Part of the volume, from the contemporary American philosopher Saul Kripke, connects up with issues about naming and describing that have already surfaced in the work of Mill, Frege and Russell (extracts 7, 8 and 9, above). Is a name like 'Napoleon' a pure referring 'mark' (as Mill had proposed), or, following a suggestion of Frege, is it short for a description (e.g. 'the French Emperor defeated at Waterloo')? Kripke allows that in cases where the subject is no longer around to be pointed at, we may need a description to be clear whom we are talking about. But although the description may sometimes be needed to help fix the reference of the name, nevertheless the name, for Kripke, remains essentially a tag or marker (going back, as it were, to the original baptism): its meaning is directly linked to the actual object or person it designates.

Kripke now proceeds to break with previous tradition by proposing that such an account can be applied not just to proper names, but also to *common names* – terms for ordinary natural kinds, such as 'cow' and 'gold'. Instead of (as Mill proposed) connoting a cluster of attributes – such as (for 'cow') *horned, four-footed,* etc., or (for 'gold') *yellow, ductile,* etc. – Kripke argues that these terms actually name or designate their respective natural kinds: 'cow' is, so to speak, like a fixed chalk mark, tagging or denoting this particular type of animal: 'natural kinds are much closer to proper names than is ordinarily supposed.'

So the term 'water' names a particular kind of stuff – the stuff scientists have now discovered to consist of H_2O. No doubt we initially fixed the reference of 'water' by describing a cluster of ordinary attributes ('the stuff that falls from the sky and is good to drink'); but once the reference is fixed, the description drops out of the picture, as it were, and the meaning of the term 'water' is wholly determined by the natural kind which it tags – namely (as science has now discovered) H_2O. The term 'water', in Kripke's terminology,

is a 'rigid' designator – it names or designates this particular substance in all possible worlds. Thus, even if we imagine a parallel 'science fiction' universe where human sense-organs are quite different (so that, for example, water tastes vile), that doesn't affect the meaning of the label 'water': it still picks out the same stuff, namely H_2O. For, as Kripke puts it, 'that's what the phenomenon *is*'.

This thesis has important consequences for the meaning of 'water is H_2O', and the countless other identity statements established by science: on Kripke's view, these turn out to be *necessary* truths. Many of the ordinary descriptive properties we use to identify natural kinds (e.g., in the case of water, being palatable to drink) turn out to be contingent (since we can imagine their being otherwise); but for Kripke the essential composition of the natural kinds denoted by terms like 'water' or 'gold' holds good in all possible worlds.

One interesting result of this (alluded to in the final paragraph of our extract) concerns the widely accepted view of David Hume that all truths known by empirical investigation must be merely contingent (see Part II, extract 7, above). If Kripke's account is right (which some philosophers would dispute) there are some necessary truths – truths about the essential composition of natural kinds – that are necessary, even though they require empirical scientific investigation to establish. Kripke's reflections about 'counter-factual' or parallel universes (e.g. where no one can feel heat) may seem strangely speculative to some tastes, but they are closely connected with his basic account of how the meaning of terms is fixed. At all events, our final extract, like many of the preceding ones, shows how often questions about language and meaning are integrally related to other central areas of philosophical inquiry. In whatever direction philosophy develops in the future, that is likely to remain the case.

---

* Saul Kripke, *Naming and Necessity* [1972] (rev. 2nd edn, Oxford: Blackwell, 1980), excerpts (pp. 26, 27–8, 48–9, 57, 96, 127–33, 138).

Now, what is the relation between names and descriptions? There is a well known doctrine of John Stuart Mill, in his book *A System of Logic*, that names have denotation but not connotation. To use one of his examples,[1] when we use the name 'Dartmouth' to describe a certain locality in England, it may be so called because it lies at the mouth of the Dart. But even, he says, had the Dart (that's a river) changed its course so that Dartmouth no longer lay at the mouth of the Dart, we could still with propriety call this place 'Dartmouth', even though the name may suggest that it lies at the mouth of the Dart. Changing Mill's terminology, perhaps we should say that a name such as 'Dartmouth' *does* have a 'connotation' to some people, namely, it *does* connote (not to me – I never thought of this) that any place called 'Dartmouth' lies at the mouth of the Dart. But then in some way it doesn't have a 'sense'. At least, it is not part of the *meaning* of the name 'Dartmouth' that the town so named lies at the mouth of the Dart. Someone who said that Dartmouth did not lie at the Dart's mouth would not contradict himself...

The basic problem for any view such as Mill's is how we can determine what the referent of a name, as used by a given speaker, is. According to the description view [of Frege and Russell], the answer is clear. If 'Joe Doakes' is just short for 'the man who corrupted Hadleyburg', then whoever corrupted Hadleyburg uniquely is the referent of the name 'Joe Doakes'. However, if there is *not* such a descriptive content to the name, then how do people ever use names to refer to things at all? Well, they may be in a position to point to some things and thus determine the references of certain names ostensively. This was Russell's doctrine of acquaintance, which he thought the so-called genuine or proper names satisfied. But of course ordinary names refer to all sorts of people, like Walter Scott, to whom we can't possibly point. And our reference here seems to be determined by our knowledge of them. Whatever we know about them determines the referent of the name as the unique thing satisfying those properties. For example, if I use the name 'Napoleon' and someone asks, 'To whom are you referring?', I will answer something like, Napoleon was emperor of the French in the early part of the nineteenth century; he was eventually defeated at Waterloo, thus giving a uniquely identifying description to determine the referent of the name. Frege and Russell, then, appear to give the natural account of how reference is determined here; Mill appears to give none...

Let's use some terms quasi-technically. Let's call something a *rigid designator* if in every possible world it designates the same object, a *nonrigid* or *accidental designator* if that is not the case. Of course we don't require that the objects exist in all possible worlds. Certainly Nixon might not have existed if his parents had not gotten married, in the normal course of things. When we think of a property as essential to an object we usually mean that it is true of that object in any case where it would have existed...

One of the intuitive theses I will maintain in these talks is that *names* are rigid designators. Certainly they seem to satisfy the intuitive test mentioned above: although someone other than the U.S. President in 1970 might have been the U.S. President in 1970 (e.g., Humphrey might have), no one other than Nixon might have been Nixon. In the same way, a designator rigidly designates a certain object if it

---

[1] See extract 7, above.

designates that object wherever the object exists; if, in addition, the object is a necessary existent, the designator can be called *strongly* rigid. For example, 'the President of the U.S. in 1970' designates a certain man, Nixon; but someone else (e.g., Humphrey) might have been the President in 1970, and Nixon might not have; so this designator is not rigid...

In the case of names, one might make this distinction too. Suppose the reference of a name is given by a description or a cluster of descriptions. If the name *means the same* as that description or cluster of descriptions, it will not be a rigid designator. It will not necessarily designate the same object in all possible worlds, since other objects might have had the given properties in other possible worlds, unless (of course) we happened to use essential properties in our description. So suppose we say, 'Aristotle is the greatest man who studied with Plato'. If we used that as a *definition*, the name 'Aristotle' is to mean 'the greatest man who studied with Plato'. Then of course in some other possible world that man might not have studied with Plato and some other man would have been Aristotle. If, on the other hand, we merely use the description *to fix the referent* then that man will be the referent of 'Aristotle' in all possible worlds. The only use of the description will have been to pick out to which man we mean to refer. But then, when we say counterfactually 'suppose Aristotle had never gone into philosophy at all', we need not mean 'suppose a man who studied with Plato, and taught Alexander the Great, and wrote this and that, and so on, had never gone into philosophy at all', which might seem like a contradiction. We need only mean, 'suppose that *that man* had never gone into philosophy at all'...

A rough statement of a theory might be the following: An initial 'baptism' takes place. Here the object may be named by ostension, or the reference of the name may be fixed by a description. When the name is 'passed from link to link', the receiver of the name must, I think, intend when he learns it to use it with the same reference as the man from whom he heard it. If I hear the name 'Napoleon' and decide it would be a nice name for my pet aardvark, I don't satisfy this condition...

According to the view I advocate, terms for natural kinds are much closer to proper names than is ordinarily supposed. The old term 'common name' is thus quite appropriate for predicates marking out species or natural kinds, such as 'cow' or 'tiger'. My considerations apply also, however, to certain mass terms for natural kinds, such as 'gold', 'water', and the like. It is interesting to compare my views to those of Mill. Mill counts both predicates like 'cow', definite descriptions, and proper names as names. He says of 'singular' names that they are connotative if they are definite descriptions but non-connotative if they are proper names. On the other hand, Mill says that *all* 'general' names are connotative; such a predicate as 'human being' is defined as the conjunction of certain properties which give necessary and sufficient conditions for humanity–rationality, animality, and certain physical features. The modern logical tradition, as represented by Frege and Russell, seems to hold that Mill was wrong about singular names, but right about general names. More recent philosophy has followed suit, except that, in the case of both proper names and natural kind terms, it often replaces the notion of defining properties by that of a cluster of properties, only some of which need to be satisfied in each particular case. My own view, on the other hand, regards Mill as more-or-less right about 'singular' names, but wrong about 'general' names. *Perhaps* some 'general' names ('foolish', 'fat', 'yellow') express properties. In a significant sense, such general names as 'cow' and 'tiger' do not, unless *being* a *cow* counts trivially as a property. Certainly 'cow' and 'tiger' are *not* short for the conjunction of properties a dictionary would take to define them, as Mill thought. Whether science *can* discover empirically that certain properties are *necessary* of cows, or of tigers, is another question, which I answer affirmatively.

Let's consider how this applies to the types of identity statements expressing scientific discoveries... – say, that water is H_2O. It certainly represents a discovery that water is H_2O. We identified water originally by its characteristic feel, appearance, and perhaps taste (though the taste may usually be due to the impurities). If there were a substance, even actually, which had a completely different atomic structure from that of water, but resembled water in these respects, would we say that some water wasn't H_2O? I think not. We would say instead that just as there is a fool's gold there could be a fool's water; a substance which, though having the properties by which we originally identified water, would not in fact be water. And this, I think, applies not only to the actual world but even when we talk about counterfactual situations. If there had been a substance, which was a fool's water, it would then be fool's water and not water. On the other hand if this substance can take another form – such as the polywater allegedly discovered in the Soviet Union, with very different identifying marks from that of what we now call water – it is a form of water because it is the same substance, even though it doesn't have the appearances by which we originally identified water.

Let's consider the statement 'Light is a stream of photons' or 'Heat is the motion of molecules'. By referring to light, of course, I mean something which we have some of in this room. When I refer to heat, I refer not to an internal sensation that someone may have, but to an external phenomenon which we perceive through the sense of feeling; it produces a characteristic sensation which we call the sensation of heat. Heat *is* the motion of molecules. We have also discovered that increasing heat corresponds to increasing motion of molecules, or, strictly speaking, increasing average kinetic energy of molecules. So temperature is identified with mean molecular kinetic energy. However I won't talk about temperature because there is the question of how the actual scale is to be set. It might just be set in terms of the mean molecular kinetic energy. But what represents an interesting phenomenological discovery is that when it's hotter the molecules are moving faster. We have also discovered about light that light is a stream of photons; alternatively it is a form of electromagnetic radiation. Originally we identified light by the characteristic internal visual impressions it can produce in us, that make us able to see. Heat, on the other hand, we originally identified by the characteristic effect on one aspect of our nerve endings or our sense of touch.

Imagine a situation in which human beings were blind or their eyes didn't work. They were unaffected by light. Would that have been a situation in which light did not exist? It seems to me that it would not. It would have been a situation in which our eyes were not sensitive to light. Some creatures may have eyes not sensitive to light. Among such creatures are unfortunately some people, of course; they are called 'blind'. Even if all people had had awful vestigial growths and just couldn't see a thing, the light might have been around; but it would not have been able to affect people's eyes in the proper way. So it seems to me that such a situation would be a situation in which there was light, but people could not see it. So, though we may identify light by the characteristic visual impressions it produces in us, this seems to be a good example of fixing a reference. We fix what light is by the fact that it is whatever, out in the world, affects our eyes in a certain way. But now, talking about counterfactual situations in which, let's say, people were blind, we would not then say that since, in such situations, nothing could affect their eyes, light would not exist; rather we would say that that would be a situation in which light – the thing we have identified as that which in fact enables us to see – existed but did not manage to help us see due to some defect in us.

Perhaps we can imagine that, by some miracle, sound waves somehow enabled some creature to see. I mean, they gave him visual impressions just as we have, maybe exactly the same colour sense. We can also imagine the same creature to be completely *insensitive* to light (photons). Who knows what subtle undreamt of possibilities there may be? Would we say that in such a possible world, it was sound which was light, that these wave motions in the air were light? It seems to me that, given our concept of light, we should describe the situation differently. It would be a situation in which certain creatures, maybe even those who were called 'people' and inhabited this planet, were sensitive not to light but to sound waves, sensitive to them in exactly the same way that we are sensitive to light. If this is so, once we have found out what light is when we talk about other possible worlds we are talking about *this* phenomenon in the world, and not using 'light' as a phrase *synonymous* with 'whatever gives us the visual impression – whatever helps us to see'; for there might have been light and it not have helped us to see; and even something else might have helped us to see. The way we identified light *fixed a reference.*

And similarly for other such phrases, such as 'heat'. Here heat is something which we have identified (and fixed the reference of its name) by its giving a certain sensation, which we call 'the sensation of heat'. We don't have a special name for this sensation other than as a sensation of heat. It's interesting that the language is this way. Whereas you might suppose it, from what I am saying, to have been the other way. At any rate, we identify heat and are able to sense it by the fact that it produces in us a sensation of heat. It might here be so important to the concept that its reference is fixed in this way, that if someone else detects heat by some sort of instrument, but is unable to feel it, we might want to say, if we like, that the concept of heat is not the same even though the referent is the same.

Nevertheless, the term 'heat' doesn't *mean* 'whatever gives people these sensations'. For first, people might not have been sensitive to heat, and yet the heat still have existed in the external world. Secondly, let us suppose that somehow light rays, because of some difference in their nerve endings, *did* give them these sensations. It would not then be heat but light which gave people the sensation which we call the sensation of heat.

Can we then imagine a possible world in which heat was not molecular motion? We can imagine, of course, having discovered that it was not. It seems to me that any case which someone will think of, which he thinks at first is a case in which heat – contrary to what is actually the case – would have been something other than molecular motion, would actually be a case in which some creatures with different nerve endings from ours inhabit this planet (maybe even we, if it's a contingent fact about us that we have this particular neural structure), and in which these creatures were sensitive to that something else, say light, in such a way that they felt the same thing that we feel when we feel heat. But this is not a situation in which, say, light would have been heat, or even in which a stream of photons would have been heat, but a situation in which a stream of photons would have produced the characteristic sensations which *we* call 'sensations of heat'.

Similarly for many other such identifications, say, that lightning is electricity. Flashes of lightning are flashes of electricity. Lightning is an electrical discharge. We can imagine, of course, I suppose, other ways in which the sky might be illuminated at night with the same sort of flash without any electrical discharge being present. Here too, I am inclined to say, when we imagine this, we imagine something with all the visual appearances of lightning but which is not, in fact, lightning. One could be told: this appeared to be lightning but it was not. I suppose this might even happen now. Someone might, by a clever sort of apparatus, produce some phenomenon in the sky which would fool people into thinking that there was lightning even though in fact no lightning was present. And you wouldn't say that that phenomenon, because it looks like lightning, was in fact lightning. It was a different phenomenon from lightning, which is the phenomenon of an electrical discharge; and this is not lightning but just something that deceives us into thinking that there is lightning.

What characteristically goes on in these cases of, let's say, 'heat is molecular motion'? There is a certain referent which we have fixed, for the real world and for all possible worlds, by a contingent property of it, namely the property that it's able to produce such and such sensations in us. Let's say it's a contingent property of heat that it produces such and such sensations in people. It's after all contingent that there should ever have been people on this planet at all. So one doesn't know *a priori* what physical phenomenon, described in other terms – in basic terms of physical theory – is the phenomenon which produces these sensations. We don't know this, and we've discovered eventually that this phenomenon is in fact molecular motion. When we have discovered this, we've discovered an identification which gives us an essential property of this phenomenon. We have discovered a phenomenon which in all possible worlds will be molecular motion, which could not have failed to be molecular motion, because that's what the phenomenon *is*. On the other hand, the property by which we identify it originally, that of producing such and such a sensation in us, is not a necessary property but a contingent one. This very phenomenon could have existed, but due to differences in our neural structures and so on, have failed to be felt as heat...

[S]uch theoretical identifications as 'heat is molecular motion' are *necessary*, though not *a priori*. The type of property identity used in science seems to be associated with *necessity*, not with apriority or analyticity: for all bodies x and y, x is hotter than y if and only if x has higher mean molecular kinetic energy than y. Here the coextensiveness of the predicates is *necessary* but not *a priori*...[1]

---

[1] For the notions of *a priori* knowledge and *analyticity*, see the introductions to Part I, extract 8 and Part II, extract 8.

Specimen Questions

1 Examine Socrates' arguments against the view that 'the name of each thing is merely that which anybody agrees to call it'.

2 Critically discuss Augustine's view of how infants learn to speak.

3 Explain what is meant by a *term* and a *proposition*. Evaluate Ockham's suggestion that there are mental propositions in addition to spoken and written ones.

4 Do you agree with Descartes that human speech is radically different from animal utterance? Explain your reasons for agreeing or disagreeing.

5 'Since all things that exist are only particulars, how come we by general terms, or where find we those general natures they are supposed to stand for?' What is Locke's answer to this question, and is it satisfactory?

6 Critically evaluate Berkeley's criticisms of Locke's theory of abstract general ideas.

7 Expound and evaluate Mill's distinction between denotation and connotation.

8 'The Morning Star is the Evening Star.' Do Frege's accounts of *sense* and of *reference* show how asserting this is not the same as asserting 'The Morning Star is the Morning Star'?

9 Set out Russell's account of definite and indefinite descriptions. What are the advantages of his analysis?

10 Indicate what Austin means by 'performatives', and explain why they do not fit the 'descriptive' model of language.

11 What does Grice mean by 'conversational implicature', and why is context so important for this dimension of meaning?

12 What, according to Kripke, is going on when we identify heat with molecular motion? Is he right in saying that such identity statements are *necessary truths*, discovered by experience?

Suggestions for Further Reading

General

A very useful survey of some of the key issues in this Part of the volume is the chapter on 'Philosophy of Language' by Martin Davies, in N. Bunnin and E. P. Tsui-James (eds), *The Blackwell Companion to Philosophy* (2nd edn, Oxford: Blackwell, 2003).

The second edition of K. Brown (ed.), *Encyclopedia of Language and Linguistics* (St Louis, Mo.: Elsevier, 2005) has a whole volume on philosophy of language, with many good introductory entries on key issues.

A valuable introduction to the subject is W. Lycan, *The Philosophy of Language* (London: Routledge, 1999).

See also Mark Sainsbury's introduction to philosophical logic in A. Grayling (ed.), *Philosophy: A Guide through the Subject* (Oxford: Oxford University Press, 1995), ch. 2.

Plato

Some interesting discussions of the arguments in the *Cratylus* may be found in Stephen Everson's Introduction to his edited collection

Language, in the Companions to Ancient Thought series (Cambridge: Cambridge University Press, 1994). The same volume also contains useful essays by David Boston ('Plato on Understanding Language') and Bernard Williams ('*Cratylus*' Theory of Names and its Refutation').

Plato's views on language and meaning may be compared with those of Aristotle in his *De Interpretatione* (which takes up some of the themes of the *Cratylus*); see J. L. Ackrill's commentary, *Aristotle's Categories and 'De Interpretatione'* (Oxford: Clarendon, 1963), and the essay by David Charles in Everson (ed.), *Language*.

Augustine

For Augustine's views on language, see Gareth Matthews, *Augustine* (Oxford: Blackwell, 2005), ch. 4, and Anthony Kenny, *A New History of Western Philosophy*, vol. II: *Medieval Philosophy* (Oxford: Clarendon, 2005), ch. 3.

A more detailed discussion may be found in C. Kirwan, 'Augustine on the Nature of Speech', in Everson (ed.), *Language*.

Augustine's conception of language acquisition is extensively criticized from the start of Ludwig Wittgenstein's *Philosophical Investigations* (Oxford: Blackwell, 1958).

There is an excellent essay on Augustine's views and Wittgenstein's critique by Miles Burnyeat, in G. Matthews (ed.), *The Augustinian Tradition* (Berkeley: University of California Press, 1999), ch. 16.

Ockham

There is a good discussion of Ockham's views on logic and language in A. Kenny, *Medieval Philosophy* (Oxford: Clarendon, 2005); see also F. Copleston, *A History of Philosophy* (New York: Doubleday, 1963), vol. 3, chs 3 and 4.

The distinction between written, spoken and mental language is discussed in essays by C. Panaccio and D. Chalmers in P. V. Spade (ed.), *The Cambridge Companion to Ockham* (Cambridge: Cambridge University Press, 1999); for Ockham's nominalism, see Spade's essay in the same volume.

Descartes

For Descartes's views on the relation between thought and language, see J. Cottingham, ' "The only sure sign…": Descartes on Thought and Language', in J. M. Preston (ed.), *Thought and Language* (Cambridge: Cambridge University Press, 1998), pp. 29–50. The views of several other philosophers on this topic are discussed in the same volume.

For the idea of language as 'stimulus-free', see N. Chomsky, *Language and Mind* (New York: Harcourt, Brace & World, 1968).

For Descartes's general conception of the capacities of non-human animals, see J. Cottingham, 'Descartes' Treatment of Animals', in Cottingham (ed.), *Descartes*, Oxford Readings in Philosophy (Oxford: Oxford University Press, 1998).

Locke

For a good general introduction to Locke's philosophy, see N. Jolley, *Locke* (Oxford: Oxford University Press, 1999), esp. ch. 3.

Locke's account of abstract general ideas is discussed in the essay by V. Chappell in Chappell (ed.), *The Cambridge Companion to Locke* (Cambridge: Cambridge University Press, 1994).

For a detailed scholarly discussion, see M. Ayers, *Locke* (London: Routledge, 1991), vol. I, parts 1 and 4.

Berkeley

A good exposition of Berkeley's arguments is A. C. Grayling, *Berkeley* (London: Duckworth, 1986); see also J. Dancy, *Berkeley* (Oxford: Blackwell, 1987), and the Introduction to his edition of Berkeley's *Principles of Human Knowledge* (Oxford: Oxford University Press, 1998), § 8.

For Berkeley's criticisms of Locke on abstract general ideas, see the works by Jolley and Ayers cited under Locke, above.

Mill

A full and clear account of Mill's views on denotation and connotation may be found in J. Skorupski, *John Stuart Mill* (London: Routledge, 1989), ch. 2.

There are some good papers relating to issues arising in the work of Mill, and also of Frege and Russell (below), in A. Moore (ed.), *Meaning and Reference* (Oxford: Oxford University Press, 1993).

Frege

An excellent introduction is *Frege* by Anthony Kenny (London: Penguin, 1995); see esp. ch. 7.

An advanced but first-rate study of Frege's arguments is Michael Dummett's *Frege: Philosophy of Language* (London: Duckworth, 1973, 2nd edn 1992).

See also the essay by Sainsbury, mentioned under Russell, below.

A useful collection of Frege texts is M. Beaney (ed.), *The Frege Reader* (Oxford: Blackwell, 1997).

Russell

A short and readable introduction to Russell's philosophy is A. C. Grayling, *Russell* (Oxford: Oxford University Press, 1996).

An interesting discussion of the respective approaches to meaning and reference in Mill, Russell and Frege may be found in R. M. Sainsbury, *Reference without Referents* (Oxford: Oxford University Press, 2005).

There is a famous critique of Russell's theory of descriptions by P. F. Strawson, 'On Referring' (*Mind*, 1950), reprinted in A. G. N. Flew (ed.), *Essays in Conceptual Analysis* (London: Macmillan, 1956). See also Strawson, *Subject and Predicate in Logic and Grammar* (London: Methuen, 1972), ch. 2.

Austin

Some of the views of Austin, and of Grice (below), are discussed in the chapter 'Intention and Convention' by Anita Avramides, in B. Hale and C. Wright (eds), *A Companion to the Philosophy of Language* (Oxford: Blackwell, 1997).

A good study of Austin's work is G. J. Warnock, *J. L. Austin* (London: Routledge, 1989).

For detailed criticism of his approach, see K. Graham, *J. L. Austin: A Critique of Ordinary Language Philosophy* (London: Prometheus, 1978).

For a more general collection of essays, see Isaiah Berlin (ed.), *Essays on J. L. Austin* (Oxford: Oxford University Press, 1973).

Grice

There is a useful summary of Grice's position by Martin Davis in Bunnin and Tsui-James (eds), *The Blackwell Companion to Philosophy*.

A detailed discussion of philosophical issues arising from Grice's work may be found in D. Sperber and D. Wilson, *Relevance, Communication and Cognition* (Oxford: Blackwell, 1995).

An important philosopher of language influenced by but sometimes critical of Grice is John Searle; see his *Speech Acts* (Cambridge: Cambridge University Press, 1969), and *Expression and Meaning* (Cambridge: Cambridge University Press, 1979).

See also S. Blackburn, *Spreading the Word* (Oxford: Oxford University Press, 1984).

The relation between formal systems and natural language is discussed in E. Borg and E. Lepore, 'Natural Language and Symbolic Logic', in D. Jacquette (ed.), *The Blackwell Companion to Symbolic Logic* (Oxford: Blackwell, 2002).

Kripke

Kripke's position is discussed in the course of a very useful survey article by Mark Sainsbury, 'Philosophical Logic', in A. C. Grayling (ed.), *Philosophy* (Oxford: Oxford University Press, 1995), ch. 2.

A thorough essay covering many aspects of Kripke's views is R. Stalnaker, 'Reference and Necessity', in B. Hale and C. Wright (eds), *A Companion to the Philosophy of Language* (Oxford: Blackwell, 1997).

PART IV
Mind and Body

Mind and Body
Introduction

Of all the things in the universe, only some are alive; of living things, only some have sensation; and of creatures with sensation, only some think and reason. From early times, philosophers have struggled to account for the mental capacities that set human beings apart, and to explain how (if at all) these are related to our bodily nature. The Greek term *psyche* (generally translated 'soul') is connected with the verb for 'to breathe', and originally meant 'the breath of life' – what distinguishes a living body from a corpse. So there is a basic contrast in Greek between *psyche* and *soma*, soul and body. But what exactly *is* the soul? And, more particularly, what is the *human* soul (since in addition to what they share with other living things, humans have higher faculties of thought and perception and self-awareness)? Among the ancient Greek philosophers, some took a materialist line; Democritus, for example (born in 460 BC), maintained that our consciousness is entirely explicable in physical terms, and the soul is simply an arrangement of atoms (and hence is perishable, like the rest of the body). Others, notably Plato, took what has come to be known as a 'dualist' line, maintaining that the soul is utterly separate from the body, and of an altogether different nature from anything material. In the history of Western ideas, Plato's views came to take on a peculiarly favourable resonance for many subsequent thinkers, since they seemed to harmonize with later Christian doctrine on the immortality of the soul. Even from its earliest formulations, however, the dualist position was perceived as by no means free of philosophical difficulties. Part IV of our volume, devoted to that branch of philosophy known as the Philosophy of Mind, explores the long philosophical struggle to understand the nature of mental phenomena and their relationship to bodily processes and events. It begins with one of Plato's celebrated discussions of the immateriality and immortality of the soul.

1   The Immortal Soul: Plato, *Phaedo**

The setting of the *Phaedo* is the condemned cell. Socrates has been sentenced to death by the Athenian court, and his friends are gathered round him for the few hours of life that remain to him.[1] The discussion turns to the immortality of the soul. Socrates maintains that the true philosopher spends his life 'in the practice of dying' – aiming for wisdom and rational understanding, for release from the confining pressures of the body and its appetites; saying goodbye to the body entirely will enable the soul to become truly itself. Challenged to justify his faith in the soul's immortality, Socrates draws a distinction between the changing perishable world of the senses, and the unchanging objects of knowledge and understanding (see above, Part I, extract 2); since the soul is concerned with the latter, it has a natural affinity with what is eternal and immortal. At this point, Simmias, one of the participants in the dialogue,

raises the objection that the soul might depend on the organization of the materials of the body; he compares the harmony which comes from a tuned instrument – something 'all-beautiful and divine and bodiless', no doubt, but none the less dependent on the strings of the lute, and unable to survive their destruction. Socrates mounts a series of objections to this analogy, pointing out in particular that the soul often sings a tune wholly opposed to the appetites and urges of the body, which would be impossible if it was merely a 'harmony' arising from the body's workings. At the end of the dialogue (after the passages reproduced below) Socrates goes on to describe the blessed life awaiting the virtuous who have 'purified themselves enough by philosophy to live without bodies altogether'; the work closes with a moving account of Socrates' calm and dignified death, as he drains the cup of hemlock brought by the state executioner.

And now, O my judges, said Socrates, I desire to prove to you that the real philoso- pher has reason to be of good cheer when he is about to die, and that after death he may hope to obtain the greatest good in the other world. And how this may be, Simmias and Cebes, I will endeavour to explain. For I deem that the true votary of philosophy is likely to be misunderstood by other men; they do not perceive that he is always pursuing death and dying; and if this be so, and he has had the desire of death all his life long, why when his time comes should he repine at that which he has been always pursuing and desiring?

Simmias said laughingly: Though not in a laughing humour, you have made me laugh, Socrates; for I cannot help thinking that the many when they hear your words will say how truly you have described philosophers, and our people at home will likewise say that the life which philosophers desire is in reality death, and that they have found them out to be deserving of the death which they desire.

And they are right, Simmias, in thinking so, with the exception of the words 'they have found them out'; for they have not found out either what is the nature of that death which the true philosopher deserves, or how he deserves or desires death. But enough of them: – let us discuss the matter among ourselves. Do we believe that there is such a thing as death?

To be sure, replied Simmias.

---

* Plato, *Phaedo* [*Phaidon*, c.380 BC], 63e–65c; 67e; 70a–c; 78c–81b; 93a–95a. Trans. B. Jowett, in *The Dialogues of Plato* (Oxford: Clarendon, 1892), pp. 202–4, 207, 209–10, 221–4, 237–40.
[1] The actual date of Socrates' execution was 399 BC, but Plato wrote the *Phaedo* many years later.

Is it not the separation of soul and body? And to be dead is the completion of this; when the soul exists herself, and is released from the body and the body is released from the soul, what is this but death?

Just so, he replied.

There is another question, which will probably throw light on our present enquiry if you and I can agree about it. Ought the philosopher to care about the pleasures – if they are to be called pleasures – of eating and drinking?

Certainly not, answered Simmias.

And what about the pleasures of love – should he care for them?

By no means.

And will he think much of the other ways of indulging the body, for example, the acquisition of costly raiment, or sandals, or other adornments of the body? Instead of caring about them, does he not rather despise anything more than nature needs? What do you say?

I should say that the true philosopher would despise them.

Would you not say that he is entirely concerned with the soul and not with the body? He would like, as far as he can, to get away from the body and to turn to the soul.

Quite true.

In matters of this sort philosophers, above all other men, may be observed in every sort of way to dissever the soul from the communion of the body.

Very true.

Whereas, Simmias, the rest of the world are of the opinion that to him who has no sense of pleasure and no part in bodily pleasure, life is not worth having; and that he who is indifferent about them is as good as dead.

That is also true.

What again shall we say of the actual acquirement of knowledge? Is the body, if invited to share in the enquiry, a hinderer or a helper? I mean to say, have sight and hearing any truth in them? Are they not, as the poets are always telling us, inaccurate witnesses? And yet, if even they are inaccurate and indistinct, what is to be said of the other senses? – for you will allow that they are the best of them?

Certainly, he replied.

Then when does the soul attain truth? – for in attempting to consider anything in company with the body she is obviously deceived.

True.

Then must not true existence be revealed to her in thought, if at all?

Yes.

And thought is best when the mind is gathered into herself and none of these things trouble her – neither sounds nor sights nor pain nor any pleasure, – when she takes leave of the body, and has as little as possible to do with it, when she has no bodily sense or desire, but is aspiring after true being?

Certainly.

And in this the philosopher dishonours the body; his soul runs away from his body and desires to be alone and by herself?

That is true...

And the true philosophers, Simmias, are always occupied in the practice of dying, wherefore to them least of all men is death terrible. Look at the matter thus. If they have been in every way the enemies of the body, and are wanting to be alone with the soul, when this desire of theirs is granted, how inconsistent would they be if they trembled and repined, instead of rejoicing at their departure to that place where, when they arrive, they hope to gain that which in life they desired – and this was wisdom – and at the same time to be rid of the company of their enemy...

Cebes answered: I agree, Socrates, in the greater part of what you say. But in what concerns the soul, men are apt to be incredulous; they fear that when she has left the body her place may be nowhere, and that on the very day of death she may perish and come to an end – immediately on her release from the body, issuing forth dispersed like smoke or air and in her flight vanishing away into nothingness. If she could only be collected into herself after she has obtained release from the evils of which you were speaking, there would be good reason to hope, Socrates, that what you say is true. But surely it requires a great deal of argument and many proofs to show that when the man is dead his soul yet exists, and has any force or intelligence.

True, Cebes, said Socrates; and shall I suggest that we converse a little of the probabilities of these things?

I am sure, said Cebes, that I should greatly like to know your opinion about them.

I reckon, said Socrates, that no one who heard me now, not even if he were one of my old enemies, the Comic poets, could accuse me of idle talking about matters in which I have no concern. If you please, then, we will proceed with the enquiry...

[Socrates proceeds to argue, amongst other things, that the soul must have existed before the birth of the body.[1] He then turns to the soul's future existence.]

Is that idea or essence, which in the dialectical process we define as essence or true existence – whether essence of equality, beauty, or anything else – are these essences, I say, liable at times to some degree of change? Or are they each of them always what they are, having the same simple self-existent and unchanging forms, not admitting of variation at all, or in any way, or at any time?[2]

They must be always the same, Socrates, replied Cebes.

And what would you say of the many beautiful – whether men or horses or garments or any other things which are named by the same names and may be called equal or beautiful, – are they all unchanging and the same always, or quite the reverse? May they not rather be described as almost always changing and hardly ever the same, either with themselves or with one another?

The latter, replied Cebes; they are always in a state of change.

And these you can touch and see and perceive with the senses, but the unchanging things you can only perceive with the mind – they are invisible and are not seen?

That is very true, he said.

Well then, added Socrates, let us suppose that there are two sorts of existences – one seen, the other unseen.

Let us suppose them.

The seen is the changing, and the unseen is the unchanging?

---

[1] Because we know, untaught, ideas 'recollected' from a previous state; for this argument see Part I, extract 1, above.
[2] See Part II, extract 1, above.

That may be also supposed.

And, further, is not one part of us body, another part soul?

To be sure.

And to which class is the body more alike and akin?

Clearly to the seen – no one can doubt that.

And is the soul seen or not seen?

Not by man, Socrates.

And what we mean by 'seen' and 'not seen' is that which is or is not visible to the eye of man?

Yes, to the eye of man.

And is the soul seen or not seen?

Not seen.

Unseen then?

Yes.

Then the soul is more like to the unseen, and the body to the seen?

That follows necessarily, Socrates.

And were we not saying long ago that the soul when using the body as an instrument of perception, that is to say, when using the sense of sight or hearing or some other sense (for the meaning of perceiving through the body is perceiving through the senses) – were we not saying that the soul too is then dragged by the body into the region of the changeable, and wanders and is confused; the world spins round her, and she is like a drunkard, when she touches change?

Very true.

But when returning into herself she reflects, then she passes into the other world, the region of purity, and eternity, and immortality, and unchangeableness, which are her kindred, and with them she ever lives, when she is by herself and is not let or hindered; then she ceases from her erring ways, and being in communion with the unchanging is unchanging. And this state of the soul is called wisdom?

That is well and truly said, Socrates, he replied.

And to which class is the soul more nearly alike and akin, as far as may be inferred from this argument...?

I think, Socrates, that, in the opinion of every one who follows the argument, the soul will be infinitely more like the unchangeable – even the most stupid person will not deny that.

And the body is more like the changing?

Yes.

Yet once more consider the matter in another light: When the soul and the body are united, then nature orders the soul to rule and govern, and the body to obey and serve. Now which of these two functions is akin to the divine? and which to the mortal? Does not the divine appear to you to be that which naturally orders and rules, and the mortal to be that which is subject and servant?

True.

And which does the soul resemble?

The soul resembles the divine, and the body the mortal – there can be no doubt of that, Socrates.

Then reflect, Cebes: of all which has been said is not this the conclusion? – that the soul is in the very likeness of the divine, and immortal, and intellectual, and uniform, and indissoluble, and unchangeable; and that the body is in the very likeness of the human, and mortal, and unintellectual, and multiform, and dissoluble, and change-able. Can this, my dear Cebes, be denied?

It cannot.

But if it be true, then is not the body liable to speedy dissolution? and is not the soul almost or altogether indissoluble?

Certainly.

And do you further observe, that after a man is dead, the body, or visible part of him, which is in the visible world, and is called a corpse, and would naturally be dissolved and decomposed and dissipated, is not dissolved or decomposed at once, but may remain for some time, nay even for a long time, if the constitution be sound at the time of death, and the season of the year favourable? For the body when shrunk and embalmed, as the manner is in Egypt, may remain almost entire through infinite ages; and even in decay, there are still some portions, such as the bones and ligaments, which are practically indestructible: – Do you agree?

Yes.

And is it likely that the soul, which is invisible, in passing to the place of the true Hades, which like her is invisible, and pure, and noble, and on her way to the good and wise God, whither, if God will, my soul is also soon to go, – that the soul, I repeat, if this be her nature and origin, will be blown away and destroyed immediately on quitting the body, as the many say? That can never be, my dear Simmias and Cebes. The truth rather is, that the soul which is pure at departing and draws after her no bodily taint, having never voluntarily during life had connection with the body, which she is ever avoiding, herself gathered into herself; – and making such abstraction her perpetual study – which means that she has been a true disciple of philosophy; and therefore has in fact been always engaged in the practice of dying? For is not philosophy the study of death? –

Certainly –

That soul, I say, herself invisible, departs to the invisible world – to the divine and immortal and rational: thither arriving, she is secure of bliss and is released from the error and folly of men, their fears and wild passions and all other human ills, and for ever dwells, as they say of the initiated, in company with the gods. Is not this true, Cebes?

Yes, said Cebes, beyond a doubt...

[Simmias objects that the soul might be like a harmony from a tuned harp or lyre, 'invisible and bodiless and all-beautiful and divine', yet nevertheless bound to perish when someone breaks the lyre or cuts or bursts the strings.]

Let me put the matter, Simmias, he said, in another point of view: Do you imagine that a harmony or any other composition can be in a state other than that of the elements, out of which it is compounded?

Certainly not.

Or do or suffer anything other than they do or suffer?

He agreed.

Then a harmony does not, properly speaking, lead the parts or elements which make up the harmony, but only follows them.

He assented.

For harmony cannot possibly have any motion, or sound, or other quality which is opposed to its parts.

That would be impossible, he replied.

And does not the nature of every harmony depend upon the manner in which the elements are harmonized?

I do not understand you, he said.

I mean to say that a harmony admits of degrees, and is more of a harmony, and more completely a harmony, when more truly and fully harmonized, to any extent which is possible; and less of a harmony, and less completely a harmony, when less truly and fully harmonized.

True.

But does the soul admit of degrees? or is one soul in the very least degree more or less, or more or less completely, a soul than another?

Not in the least.

Yet surely of two souls, one is said to have intelligence and virtue, and to be good, and the other to have folly and vice, and to be an evil soul: and this is said truly?

Yes, truly.

But what will those who maintain the soul to be a harmony say of this presence of virtue and vice in the soul? Will they say that here is another harmony, and another discord, and that the virtuous soul is harmonized, and herself being a harmony has another harmony within her, and that the vicious soul is inharmonical and has no harmony within her?

I cannot tell, replied Simmias; but I suppose that something of the sort would be asserted by those who say that the soul is a harmony.

And we have already admitted that no soul is more a soul than another; which is equivalent to admitting that harmony is not more or less harmony, or more or less completely a harmony?

Quite true.

And that which is not more or less a harmony is not more or less harmonized?

True.

And that which is not more or less harmonized cannot have more or less of harmony, but only an equal harmony?

Yes, an equal harmony.

Then one soul not being more or less absolutely a soul than another, is not more or less harmonized?

Exactly.

And therefore has neither more nor less of discord, nor yet of harmony?

She has not.

And having neither more nor less of harmony or of discord, one soul has no more vice or virtue than another, if vice be discord and virtue harmony?

Not at all more.

Or speaking more correctly, Simmias, the soul, if she is a harmony, will never have any vice; because a harmony, being absolutely a harmony, has no part in the inharmonical.

No.

And therefore a soul which is absolutely a soul has no vice?

How can she have, if the previous argument holds?

Then, if all souls are equally by their nature souls, all souls of all living creatures will be equally good?

I agree with you, Socrates, he said.

And can all this be true, think you? he said; for these are the consequences which seem to follow from the assumption that the soul is a harmony?

It cannot be true.

Once more, he said, what ruler is there of the elements of human nature other than the soul, and especially the wise soul? Do you know of any?

Indeed, I do not.

And is the soul in agreement with the affections of the body? or is she at variance with them? For example, when the body is hot and thirsty, does not the soul incline us against drinking? and when the body is hungry, against eating? And this is only one instance out of ten thousand of the opposition of the soul to the things of the body.

Very true.

But we have already acknowledged that the soul, being a harmony, can never utter a note at variance with the tensions and relaxations and vibrations and other affections of the strings out of which she is composed; she can only follow, she cannot lead them?

It must be so, he replied.

And yet do we not now discover the soul to be doing the exact opposite – leading the elements of which she is believed to be composed; almost always opposing and coercing them in all sorts of ways throughout life, sometimes more violently with the pains of medicine and gymnastic; then again more gently; now threatening, now admonishing the desires, passions, fears, as if talking to a thing which is not herself, as Homer in the Odyssey represents Odysseus doing in the words: –

> He beat his breast, and thus reproached his heart:
> Endure, my heart; far worse hast thou endured!

Do you think that Homer wrote this under the idea that the soul is a harmony capable of being led by the affections of the body, and not rather of a nature which should lead and master them – herself a far diviner thing than any harmony?

Yes, Socrates, I quite think so.

Then, my friend, we can never be right in saying that the soul is a harmony, for we should contradict the divine Homer, and contradict ourselves.

True, he said.

2   Soul and Body, Form and Matter: Aristotle, *De Anima**

As our previous account makes clear, Plato takes the soul to be some kind of separate entity, capable of surviving apart from the body. Aristotle, in his treatise *De Anima* ('Concerning the Soul')[1] challenges this framework. Though he himself had been a pupil of Plato, he presents a crucially different account of the nature of the soul. For Aristotle, all living things are 'ensouled' (*empsychos*), but this does not have to imply that they are made up of two distinct and separable types of entity, soul and body. Rather, the matter of which they are composed has a certain form or organizational principle, and the 'soul' is simply the *form* of a natural (biological) body. To simplify somewhat, the form or recipe is what enables a given set of materials to perform their functions (for example the way the iron is shaped and placed on its handle enables a tool to function as an axe); but we should not suppose the form could exist 'on its own', apart from matter (any more than shape can exist in isolation from a shaped object). Soul, for Aristotle, stands to body in the same way as form stands to matter.

In Aristotle's jargon, to say of a creature that it is ensouled is to say that the potentialities of the body are *actualized*; to use an analogy, if we consider the eye as a set of material structures (muscle, jelly and so on), then the form is that in virtue of which the potentialities for vision are actualized, so that the organ actually has the power to see. 'If the eye were an animal,' as Aristotle puts in his typically compressed fashion, 'sight would be its soul.' Aristotle's 'materioformal' account of the body–soul relation has come to be known as 'hylemorphism' (from the

Greek words for matter (*hyle*) and form (*morphe*), and has proved durable and influential. It has seemed to many philosophers in our own day to offer a credible middle way between radical materialism on the one hand (the attempt to reduce all mental descriptions to purely physical language), and dualism (the introduction of a Platonic-style 'pure' incorporeal soul) on the other. In the Aristotelian model, there is a sense in which the 'formal' and the material ('soul' language and physical language) simply describe two aspects of one and the same single, individual biological creature. Just as, to understand a house, we need to know about not just its material aspects (the bricks and mortar), but also its 'formal' aspects (its role as a permanent shelter from the elements), so to understand anger we need to know about not just the material (physiological) causes but also its role in our lives and behaviour (e.g. its connection with aggression and revenge). Though many details of Aristotle's account are expressed in rather cryptic, summary form (the text is based on lecture notes), it is clear that he proposes to treat complex human faculties like perception as part of a hierarchy which includes other biological functions such as growth and nutrition. As the concluding sentence of the extract indicates, Aristotle hesitates over the special case of intellect, which he allows may be separable from the body. But in general he strongly resists treating the soul as a special immaterial entity, and instead opens the way for integrating an account of human psychology into the rest of our understanding of the natural and biological world.

 Knowledge we regard as a fine and worthwhile thing, and one kind as more so than another, either in virtue of its accuracy or in virtue of its being concerned with superior and more remarkable things. On both these grounds we should with reason place the study of the soul in the first rank. It would seem also that an acquaintance

---

* Aristotle, *De Anima* [c.325 BC], extracts from Bk I, chs 1 and 4; Bk II, chs 1–3. Trans. D. W. Hamlyn, in *Aristotle's De Anima* (Oxford: Clarendon, 1968), pp. 1–16; with modifications.
[1] In Greek, *Peri psyches*. Since the Middle Ages, when Aristotle's works were widely studied in the universities in Latin translations, it has become customary to refer to many of Aristotle's works by their Latin titles.

with it makes a great contribution to truth as a whole, and especially to the study of nature; for the soul is as it were the *first principle of animal life*. We seek to inquire into and ascertain both its nature and its essence, and after that all the attributes belonging to it; of these, some are thought to be properties peculiar to the soul, while others are thought to belong because of it to animals also.

...First surely we must determine how to classify the soul, and what it is; I mean whether it is a particular thing and substance or quality or quantity or some other of the categories which have been distinguished. And second we must determine whether it is one of those things which are in *potentiality*, or whether it is rather a kind of *actuality*; for this makes no small difference...

For as things are, people who speak and inquire about the soul seem to study the human soul only. But we must take care not to overlook the question whether there is one definition of the soul, as of animal, or whether there is a different one for each animal, as of horse, dog, man and god...

There is also the problem whether the properties of the soul are all common to that which has it, or whether they are peculiar to the soul itself. We need to deal with this, though it is not easy. It appears that in most cases the soul is not affected nor does it act apart from the body – for example in being angry, being confident, wanting and perceiving in general. Thinking, however, looks most special to the soul; but if this too is a form of imagination, or does not exist apart from imagination, it would not be possible for it to exist apart from the body...

It seems that all the affections[1] of the soul involve the body – passion, gentleness, fear, pity, confidence, and also joy and both loving and hating. For at the same time as these occur, the body is affected in a certain way. This is shown by the fact that sometimes when severe and manifest sufferings befall us we are not provoked to exasperation or fear, while at other times we are moved by small and imperceptible sufferings when the body is aroused, and is in a similar state to when it is angry. This is confirmed by the fact that people may come to have the affection of fear, even though nothing frightening is taking place.

If this is so, it is clear that the affections of the soul are *principles involving matter*. Hence their definitions are such as 'Being angry is a particular movement of a body of such and such a kind (or a part or potentiality of it), as a result of so and so, and for the sake of such and such.' Hence an inquiry concerning the soul (either every soul or this kind of soul) is the province of the natural scientist.

But the natural scientist and the conceptual inquirer would define each of these differently (e.g. what anger is). For the latter would define it as a desire for retaliation, or something of that sort, while the former would define it as the boiling of the blood and hot material round the heart. Of these, the one gives the *matter*, the other the *form and principle*. But the principle of the thing must be *in* matter of such and such a kind if it is to exist. Thus, the principle of a house is, say, that it is a covering to prevent destruction by winds, rain and heat; but someone else will say that a house is stones, bricks and timber, and another again that it is the form in them for the sake of these other things...

---

[1] 'Affections': the states of a thing, or the ways in which it is affected.

Let us return to the point from which our account began. We were saying that the affections of the soul are (at any rate in so far as they are such as passion and fear) inseparable from the natural matter of the animals in which they occur...

...There will be greater reason for raising the question of whether the soul is moved, on consideration of the following. We say that the soul is grieved, rejoices, is confident and afraid, and again is angry, perceives and thinks. And all these seem to be movements. One might conclude from this that the soul itself is moved; but this is not necessary.

Suppose it is indeed the case that being grieved, rejoicing and thinking are movements, that each of them consists in being moved, and that the movement is due to the soul (e.g. that being angry and being afraid consists in the heart's being moved in a particular way and that thinking is a movement either of this perhaps or of some other part, and that some of these happen because of spatial movements in place and others because of movement constituting alteration). Even granting this, to say that the *soul* is angry would be like saying the soul weaves or builds. It is surely better not to say that the soul pities, learns or thinks, but that the human being does this by means of soul. This is not because the movement takes place in it, but because sometimes it reaches as far as it, or at other times it comes from it (e.g. perception starts from particular things, while recollection starts from the soul itself and extends to the movements or persistent states in the sense organs).

The intellect seems to be born in us as a kind of substance, and it seems not to be destroyed. For it would be destroyed if at all by the feebleness of old age, while in fact what happens is similar to what happens in the case of the sense-organs. For if an old man acquired an eye of a certain kind he could see as well as even a young man. Hence old age is not due to the soul's being affected in a certain way, but to something's happening to that which the soul is *in*, as in the case of drunkenness and disease.

Thus thought and contemplation decay because something else within is destroyed, while thought is in itself unaffected. But thinking or loving or hating are not affections of that, but of the individual thing that has it, in so far as it does. Hence when this too is destroyed, we neither remember, nor love, for these did not belong to that, but to the composite thing which has perished. But the intellect is surely something more divine and is unaffected...

Let us start again as it were from the beginning and try to determine what the soul is and what would be its most comprehensive definition.

We speak of one of the kinds of things that there are as *substance*, and under this heading we speak of one aspect as *matter* (which in itself is not a particular), and another as *shape and form* (in virtue of which it is then spoken of as a particular), and a third as the product of the two. And matter is potentiality, while form is actuality – and the latter in two senses, first in the way knowledge is and second in the way contemplation is.[1]

---

[1] A lump of bronze has the potentiality to be a ball; when it takes on a spherical form, the potential is actualized. By talking of 'actuality', however, one might mean to refer to a *disposition* (such as knowledge, which need not be functioning all the time) or to an actual *activity* (such as contemplating). Aristotle is about to define 'soul' in terms of actuality in the first sense.

It is bodies especially which are thought to be substances, and of these especially natural bodies; for these are sources of the rest. Of natural bodies, some have life and some do not; and it is self-nourishment and growth and decay that we speak of as life. Hence, every natural body which partakes of life will be a substance, and substance of a composite kind.

Since substance is indeed a body of such a kind (for it is one having life), the soul will not be body. For the body is not something predicated of a subject, but exists rather as subject and matter. The soul must then be substance as *form* of a natural body which has life potentially. Substance is actuality. The soul therefore will be the actuality of a body of this kind.

But actuality is spoken of in two ways, first as knowledge is and second as contemplation is. It is clear that the soul is actuality as knowledge is, for both sleep and waking depend on the existence of soul, and waking is analogous to contemplation, and sleep to the possession but not the exercise of knowledge. (In the same individual knowledge is in origin prior.) Hence the soul is the *first actuality* of a *natural body* which *has life potentially*.

Whatever has organs will be a body of this kind. Even the parts of the plants are organs, although extremely simple ones – for example the leaf is a cover for the pod, and the pod for the fruit, while roots are analogous to the mouth, for both take in food.

If we are to speak of something common to every soul, it will be the *first actuality of a natural body which has organs*. Hence we should not ask whether the soul and the body are one, any more than whether the wax and the impression are one, or in general whether the matter of each thing, and that of which it is the matter are one ...

It has been stated in general what the soul is: it is substance corresponding to the principle of a thing. And this is 'what it is to be' for a body of the relevant kind. Compare the following: if an instrument, for example an axe, were a natural body, then its substance would be what it is to be an axe, and this would be a soul (if this were removed, it would no longer be an axe in the strict sense). But as it is, it is an axe. The soul is 'what it is to be', or the principle – though not of a body like an axe, but of a certain kind of natural body having within itself a source of movement and rest.

We must consider this in relation to the parts of the body also. If the eye were an animal, sight would be its soul. For this is an eye's substance, that corresponding to its principle. The eye is matter for sight, and if this fails it is no longer an eye in the strict sense, but more like an eye in stone, or a painted eye. We must now apply to the whole living body that which applies to the part ...

It is not that which has lost its soul which is potentially such as to live, but that which possesses it. Seeds and fruit are bodies of this kind only in potentiality. As cutting or seeing is actuality, so is being awake; the soul is like sight and the potentiality of an instrument; the body is like the thing merely in potentiality. But just as the pupil and sight make up an eye, so the soul and body make up a living animal.

So it is clear that the soul, or certain parts of it, if it is divisible, cannot be separated from the body; for in some cases it is the actuality of the parts themselves. Not that anything prevents at any rate some parts from being separable, because these are actualities of nothing bodily. Furthermore, it is not clear whether the soul is the actuality of the body in the way the sailor is of the ship. Let this suffice as a rough definition and sketch about the soul ...

What has soul is distinguished from what has not by *life*. But life is spoken of in many ways, for we say that a thing lives if one of the following is present: intellect, perception, movement and rest with respect to place, and also the movement involved in nutrition and both decay and growth.

For this reason, all plants too are regarded as alive. For they evidently have in them such a potentiality and first principle, through which they come to grow and decay in opposite directions. For they do not grow upwards without growing downwards, but they grow in both directions alike and in every direction – this being so of every plant that is constantly nourished and continues to live, as long as it is able to receive nourishment. This form of life – nutrition – can exist apart from the others, but the others cannot exist apart from it in mortal creatures. This is obvious in the case of plants, for they have no other potentiality of soul.

It is because of this first principle that living things have life. But it is primarily because of sense perception in that they will be *animal* (for even things which do not move or change their place, but which do have sense-perception are spoken of as animals, not merely as living)...

For the present, let it suffice to say that the soul is the source of the things mentioned above, and is defined by them – by the faculties of nutrition, perception, thought, and by movement. Whether each of these is a soul, or a part of a soul (and if a part, whether such as to occupy a distinct place, or merely distinct in definition) are questions which it is not hard to answer in some cases, though others present difficulty... Concerning the intellect and the potentiality for contemplation, the situation is not so far clear, but it seems to be a different kind of soul, and this alone can exist separately, as the everlasting can from the perishable. But the remaining parts of the soul are not separable...

3   The Human Soul: Thomas Aquinas, *Summa Theologiae**

Aristotle was greatly revered in the early Middle Ages, when after the period of chaos known as the 'dark ages', his ideas were gradually reintroduced to Western Europe, initially via the writings of the great Islamic philosophers and scholars of the tenth and eleventh centuries. The general thrust of Aristotle's 'hylemorphism' (see previous extract) is *away* from the notion of a soul as a separate entity distinct from the body; and this left some problems for the Christian philosopher-theologians of the Middle Ages, notably Thomas Aquinas, who set themselves the task of reconciling the principles of Aristotle's philosophy with the doctrines of the Church. In the following extract from Aquinas's monumental *Summa Theologiae*, we see many Aristotelian elements – for example the description of the soul as 'the act of a body'. But Aristotle had hesitated over whether the intellect, at least, might be distinct from the body, and Aquinas, eagerly taking his cue from this, argues that the intellectual soul of human beings is something 'subsistent' – capable of existing in its own right – and also incorruptible. The result is a somewhat uneasy compromise between a broadly Aristotelian account of our human faculties as 'principles involving matter'

---

* Thomas Aquinas, *Summa Theologiae* [1266–73], Part I, question 75, articles 1–6. Dominican translation (London: Washbourne, 1912), pp. 2–16; with minor omissions and changes.

(see extract 2), and a more 'separatist' or Platonic conception (see extract 1) – perhaps better suited to the Christian doctrine of a future state in which the soul will continue after the body's death, awaiting final reunion with the body at the resurrection. Notice that Aquinas does not treat all the aspects of the soul in the same way. What he calls the 'sensitive' and 'nutritive' parts of the soul (those responsible for sensation and nutrition, and shared with animals) belong to the human being as 'composite' of soul and body; but the higher faculties of intellect and will (which set us apart from other animals) 'belong to the soul alone', and hence 'such powers must remain in the soul after the destruction of the body'. The special treatment of intellect and will paves the way for the radical mind/body dualism of Descartes developed many centuries later (see below, extract 4). The austere and unadorned style adopted by Aquinas in the excerpts that follow is influenced by Aristotle, but is more formalized. Each article opens with a 'question', and then lists a series of 'objections' to the answer which Aquinas himself wishes eventually to propose. Various authorities are then cited, after which, in his 'replies' to the objections, Aquinas makes his own philosophical position clear.

Concerning Man, who is composed of a spiritual and a corporeal substance. First, what belongs to the essence of the soul.

Is the soul a body?

Objection 1. It seems that the soul is a body. For the soul is the moving principle of the body. Nor does it move unless moved: firstly, because it seems that nothing can move unless it is itself moved, since nothing gives what it has not, as, for instance, what is not hot does not give heat: secondly, if there be anything that moves and is not moved, it must be the cause of eternal, unchanging movement, as we find proved (Aristotle, *Physics*, Book viii); and this does not appear to be the case in the movement of an animal, which is caused by the soul. Therefore the soul is a mover moved. But every mover moved is a body; therefore the soul is a body...

On the contrary, are the words of Augustine (*De Trinitate*, vi), who says that the soul is 'more simple than the body, inasmuch as it does not occupy space by its bulk'.

I answer as follows. To seek the nature of the soul, we must premise that the soul is defined as the first principle of life in those things which live; for we call living things animate (souled), and those things which have no life, inanimate (soulless). Now life is shown principally by two actions, knowledge and movement. The philosophers of old, not being able to rise above their imagination, supposed that the principle of these actions was something corporeal; for they asserted that only bodies were real things; and that what is not corporeal is nothing: hence they maintained that the soul is something corporeal. This opinion can be proved to be false in many ways; but we shall only make use of one proof, based on universal and certain principles, which shows clearly that the soul is not a body.

It is manifest that not every principle of vital action is a soul, for then the eye would be a soul, as it is a principle of vision; and the same might be applied to the other instruments of the soul; but it is the *first* principle of life which we call the soul. Now, though a body may be a principle of life, as the heart is a principle of life in an animal, yet nothing corporeal can be the first principle of life. For it is clear that to be a principle of life, or to be a living thing, does not belong to a body as such; since, if that were the case, everything corporeal would be a living thing, or a principle of life.

Therefore a body is a living thing or even a principle of life, only in so far as it is a body of a certain kind. Now the fact that it is actually such a body is due to some principle which is called its act. Therefore the soul, which is the first principle of life, is not a body, but the act of a body (just as heat, which is the principle of calefaction, is not a body, but an act of a body).

Reply to Objection 1. As everything which is in motion must be moved by something else, a process which cannot be prolonged indefinitely, we must allow that not every mover is moved. For, since to be moved is to pass from potentiality to actuality, the mover gives what it has to the thing moved, inasmuch as it causes it to be in act. But, as is shown in *Physics* viii, there is a mover which is altogether immovable, and not moved either essentially, or accidentally; and such a mover can cause an invariable movement. There is, however, another kind of mover, which, though not moved essentially, is moved accidentally; and for this reason it does not cause an invariable movement; such a mover is the soul. There is, again, another mover, which is moved essentially – namely, the body. And because the philosophers of old believed that nothing existed but bodies, they maintained that every mover is moved; and that the soul is moved directly, and is a body.

Is the human soul something subsistent?

Objection 1. It seems that the human soul is not something subsistent. For that which subsists is said to be *this particular* thing. Now *this particular* thing is said not of the soul, but of that which is composed of soul and body; therefore the soul is not something subsistent.

Objection 2. Further, everything subsistent operates. But the soul does not operate; for, as the Philosopher says (*De Anima* i), 'to say that the soul feels or understands is like saying that the soul weaves or builds'.[1] Therefore the soul is not subsistent.

Objection 3. Further, if the soul were subsistent, it would have some operation apart from the body. But it has no operation apart from the body, not even that of understanding: for the act of understanding does not take place without a phantasm,[2] which cannot exist apart from the body. Therefore the human soul is not something subsistent.

On the contrary, we may cite the words of Augustine (*De Trinitate* x): 'Whoever understands that the nature of the soul is that of a substance and not that of a body, will see that those who maintain the corporeal nature of the soul are led astray through associating with the soul those things without which they are unable to think of any nature – i.e., imaginary pictures of corporeal things.' Therefore the nature of the human intellect is not only incorporeal, but it is also a substance that is, something subsistent.

I answer as follows. It must necessarily be allowed that the principle of intellectual operation which we call the soul is a principle both incorporeal and subsistent. For it is clear that by means of the intellect man can have knowledge of all corporeal things. Now whatever knows certain things cannot have any of them in its own nature

---

[1] 'The Philosopher' is Aristotle. For the remark quoted, see extract 2, above.
[2] An image.

because that which is in it naturally would impede the knowledge of other things. Thus we observe that a sick man's tongue being vitiated by a feverish and bitter humour, is insensible to anything sweet, and everything seems bitter to it. Therefore, if the intellectual principle had something corporeal in its nature, it would be unable to know all bodies. Now every body has its own determinate nature. Therefore it is impossible for the intellectual principle to be a body. It is likewise impossible for it to understand by means of a bodily organ; since the determinate nature of that organ would impede knowledge of all bodies – as when a certain determinate colour is not only in the pupil of the eye, but also in a glass vase, the liquid in the vase seems to be of that same colour. Therefore the intellectual principle which we call the mind or the intellect has an operation of its own apart from the body. Now only a self-subsisting thing can have an operation of its own, for nothing can operate but what is actual. Hence a thing operates according as it exists; for which reason we do not say that heat imparts heat, but that what is hot gives heat. We must conclude, therefore, that the human soul, which is called the intellect or the mind, is something incorporeal and subsistent.

Reply to Objection 1. This particular thing can be taken in two senses. Firstly, for anything subsistent; secondly, for that which subsists, and is complete in a specific nature. The former sense excludes the inherence of an accident or of a material form; the latter excludes also the imperfection of the part, so that a hand can be called *this particular thing* in the first sense, but not in the second. Therefore, as the human soul is a part of human nature, it can indeed be called *this particular thing*, in the first sense, as being something subsistent; but not in the second, for in this sense, what is composed of body and soul is said to be *this particular thing*.

Reply to Objection 2. ... To operate of itself belongs to what exists of itself. But for a thing to exist of itself, it suffices sometimes that it be not inherent, as an accident or a material form; even though it be part of something. Nevertheless, that is rightly said to subsist of itself, which is neither inherent in the above sense, nor part of anything else. In this sense, the eye or the hand cannot be said to subsist of itself; nor can it for that reason be said to operate of itself. Hence the operation of the parts is through each part attributed to the whole. For we say that man sees with the eye, and feels with the hand, and not in the same sense as when we say that what is hot gives heat by its heat; for heat, strictly speaking, does not give heat. We may therefore say that the soul understands, as the eye sees; but it is more correct to say that man understands through the soul.

Reply to Objection 3. The body is necessary for the action of the intellect, not as its organ of action, but on the part of the object; for the phantasm is to the intellect what colour is to the sight. Neither does such a dependence on the body prove the intellect to be non-subsistent; otherwise it would follow that an animal is non-subsistent, since it requires external objects of the senses in order to perform its act of perception.

Are the souls of brute animals subsistent?

Objection 1. It seems that the souls of brute animals are subsistent. For man is of the same *genus* as other animals; and, as we have just shown, the soul of man is subsistent. Therefore the souls of other animals are subsistent.

Objection 2. Further, the relation of the sensitive faculty to sensible objects is like the relation of the intellectual faculty to intelligible objects. But the intellect, apart from the body, apprehends intelligible objects. Therefore the sensitive faculty, apart from the body, perceives sensible objects. Therefore, since the souls of brute animals are sensitive, it follows that they are subsistent; just as the human intellectual soul is subsistent.

Objection 3. Further, the soul of brute animals moves the body. But the body is more moved than mover. Therefore the soul of brute animals has an operation apart from the body.

On the contrary, is what is written in the Book of Ecclesiastical Dogma: 'Man alone we believe to have a subsistent soul: whereas the souls of animals are not subsistent.'

I answer as follows. The ancient philosophers made no distinction between sense and intellect, and referred both to a corporeal principle. Plato, however, drew a distinction between intellect and sense yet he referred both to an incorporeal principle, maintaining that feeling, just as understanding belongs to the soul as such. From this it follows that even the souls of brute animals are subsistent. But the Philosopher [Aristotle] held that of the operations of the soul, understanding alone is performed without a corporeal organ. On the other hand, feeling and the consequent operations of the sensitive soul are evidently accompanied with change in the body; as in the act of vision, the pupil of the eye is affected by a reflection of colour: and so with the other senses. So it is clear that the sensitive soul has no operation absolutely proper and belonging to itself alone; but every operation of the sensitive soul is an operation of the composite (soul plus body). Whence we conclude that as the soul of brute animals does not exercise its operations of itself, it is not subsistent. For the operation of anything follows the mode of its existence.

Reply to Objection 1. Although man is of the same *genus* as other animals, he is of a different *species.* Specific difference is derived from the difference of form; nor does every difference of form necessarily imply a diversity of *genus.*

Reply to Objection 2. The relation of the sensitive faculty to the sensible object is to a certain extent the same as that of the intellectual faculty to the intelligible object; each being in potentiality to its object. But there is a difference in their relations, inasmuch as the impression of the object on the sense is accompanied with change in the body; so that excessive strength of the sensible corrupts sense; a thing that never occurs in the case of the intellect. For an intellect that understands the highest of intelligible objects has greater facility in understanding those that are lower. If, however, in the process of intellectual operation the body is weary, this result is accidental, inasmuch as the intellect requires the operation of the sensitive powers in the production of the phantasms.

Reply to Objection 3. Motive power is of two kinds. One, the appetitive power, commands motion; the operation of this power in the sensitive soul is not apart from the body; for anger, joy, and passions of a like nature are accompanied by a change in the body. The other motive power is that which executes motion in adapting the members for obeying the appetite; and the act of this power does not consist in moving, but in being moved. Whence it is clear that to move is not an act of the sensitive soul without the body.

Is the soul man?

Objection 1. It seems that the soul is man. For it is written: 'Though our outward man is corrupted, yet the inward man is renewed day by day' (2 Corinthians 4: 16). But that which is within man is the soul. Therefore the soul is the inward man...

On the contrary, Augustine (*De Civitate Dei* xix) commends Varro as holding that 'man is not a mere soul, nor a mere body, but both soul and body'.

I answer that, The assertion, *the soul is man* can be taken in two senses. Firstly, that man is a soul; though this particular man, Socrates, for instance, is not a soul, but composed of soul and body. I say this, since some held that the form alone belongs to the species while matter is part of the individual, and not of the species. This is not true; for to the nature of the species belongs what the definition signifies; and in natural things the definition does not signify the form only, but the form and the matter. Hence in natural things the matter is part of the species... For as it belongs to the notion of this particular man to be composed of this soul, of this flesh, and these bones, it belongs to the notion of man to be composed of soul, flesh, and bones; for whatever belongs in common to the substance of all the individuals contained under a given species, must belong also to the substance of the species.

It may also be understood in this sense, that this soul *is* this man; and this could be held if it were supposed that the operation of the sensitive soul were proper to it, apart from the body; because in that case all the operations which are attributed to man would belong to the soul only; and whatever performs the operations proper to a thing, is that thing; wherefore that which performs the operations of a man is man. But it has been shown above that to feel is not the operation of the soul only. Since, then, to feel is an operation of man, but not proper to him, it is clear that man is not a soul only, but something composed of soul and body. Plato, supposing that feeling was proper to the soul, maintained man to be a soul making use of the body.

Reply to Objection 1. According to the Philosopher (*Ethics* ix), a thing seems to be chiefly what is principal in it; thus what the king does, the kingdom is said to do. In this way sometimes what is principal in man is said to be man; sometimes, indeed, the intellectual part which, in accordance with truth, is called the *inward* man; and sometimes the sensitive part with the body is called man in the opinion of those whose observation does not go beyond the senses. And this is called the *outward* man.

Is the soul composed of matter and form?

[*Reply*] The soul has no matter. We may consider this question in two ways. Firstly, from the notion of a soul in general; for it belongs to the notion of a soul to be the form of a body. Now, either it is a form by virtue of itself, in its entirety, or by virtue of some part of itself. If by virtue of itself in its entirety, then it is impossible that any part of it should be matter, if by matter we understand something purely potential; for a form, as such, is an act; and that which is purely potential cannot be part of an act, since potentiality is repugnant to actuality, as being opposite thereto. If, however, it be a form by virtue of a part of itself, then we call that part the soul: and that matter, which it actualizes first, we call the 'primary animated thing'.

Secondly, we may proceed from the specific notion of the human soul, inasmuch as it is intellectual. For it is clear that whatever is received into something is received according to the condition of the recipient. Now a thing is known in as far as its form is in the knower. But the intellectual soul knows a thing in its nature absolutely; for instance, it knows a stone absolutely as a stone; and therefore the form of a stone absolutely, as to its proper formal idea, is in the intellectual soul. Therefore the intellectual soul itself is an absolute form, and not something composed of matter and form. For if the intellectual soul were composed of matter and form, the forms of things would be received into it as individuals, and so it would only know the individual; just as it happens with the sensitive powers which receive forms in a corporeal organ; since matter is the principle by which forms are individualized. It follows, therefore, that the intellectual soul, and every intellectual substance which has knowledge of forms absolutely, is exempt from composition of matter and form.

Whether the human soul is corruptible.

Objection 1. It seems that the human soul is corruptible. For those things that have a like beginning and mode of acting seemingly have a like end. But the beginning by generation of men is like that of animals, for they are made from the earth. And the process of life is alike in both; because 'all things breathe alike: and man hath nothing more than the beast', as it is written (Ecclesiastes 3: 19). Therefore, as the same inspired writer concludes: 'The death of man and beast is one, and the condition of both is equal.' But the souls of brute animals are corruptible. Therefore also, the human soul is corruptible...

On the contrary, Dionysius says (*Divina Nomina* iv) that human souls owe to Divine goodness that they are *intellectual,* and that they have *an incorruptible substantial life.*

I answer that, We must assert that the intellectual principle which we call the human soul is incorruptible. For a thing may be corrupted in two ways – of itself and accidentally. Now it is impossible for any substance to be generated or corrupted accidentally, that is, by the generation or corruption of something else. For generation and corruption belong to a thing, just as existence belongs to it, which is acquired by generation and lost by corruption. Therefore, whatever has existence of itself cannot be generated or corrupted except of itself; while things which do not subsist, such as accidents and material forms, acquire existence or lose it through the generation or corruption of composite things. Now it was shown above that the souls of brutes are not subsistent, whereas the human soul is; so that the souls of brutes are corrupted, when their bodies are corrupted; while the human soul could not be corrupted unless it were corrupted of itself. This, indeed, is impossible, not only as regards the human soul, but also as regards anything subsistent that is a form alone. For it is clear that what belongs to a thing by virtue of itself is inseparable from it; but existence belongs to a form, which is an act, by virtue of itself. Hence matter acquires actual existence as it acquires the form; while it is corrupted so far as the form is separated from it. But it is impossible for a form to be separated from itself; and therefore it is impossible for a subsistent form to cease to exist.

Even granting that the soul is composed of matter and form, as some propose, we should nevertheless have to maintain that it is incorruptible. For corruption is found only where there is contrariety; since generation and corruption are from contraries and into contraries. Wherefore the heavenly bodies, since they have no matter subject to contrariety, are incorruptible. Now there can be no contrariety in the intellectual soul; for it receives according to the manner of its existence, and those things which it receives are without contrariety; for the notions even of contraries are not themselves contrary, since contraries belong to the same knowledge. Therefore it is impossible for the intellectual soul to be corruptible. Moreover we may take a sign of this from the fact that everything naturally aspires to existence after its own manner. Now, in things that have knowledge, desire ensues upon knowledge. The senses indeed do not know existence, except under the conditions of *here* and *now*, whereas the intellect apprehends existence absolutely, and for all time; so that everything that has an intellect naturally desires always to exist. But a natural desire cannot be in vain. Therefore every intellectual substance is incorruptible...

4   The Incorporeal Mind: René Descartes, *Meditations**

What has come to be known to philosophers as 'the mind–body problem' first crystallized in the seventeenth century with the ideas of René Descartes. Descartes aimed to provide a comprehensive scientific account of the universe based on mechanical principles and simple mathematical laws (see above, Part II, extract 3), but he argued that the human capacity for thought and language could not be explained in this way. The 'rational soul', he wrote in the *Discourse on the Method* (1637), 'cannot be derived in any way from the potentiality of matter, but must be specially created'.

Not only did Descartes believe a non-material soul was needed to explain what physical science could not account for, but he also produced a series of independent arguments to show that the soul, or thinking self, must be entirely distinct from anything material. In the *Discourse*, he reasons that since it is possible to doubt the existence of the body, but not his own existence as a conscious, thinking being, it must follow

that the soul is entirely distinct from the body and could exist without it. (The argument seems dubious: suppose (being ignorant of chemistry) it is possible for me to doubt the existence of carbohydrates, but I cannot doubt that this potato in front of me exists; does it follow that the potato could exist entirely independently of carbohydrates?) In the first of the extracts below, from the *Meditations* (1641), Descartes recapitulates, in a more elaborate form, the argument of the *Discourse*: the application of the systematic method of doubt[1] shows that 'thought alone is inseparable from me' (Second Meditation). In the second extract, from the Sixth Meditation, he argues that the mind or soul (he does not distinguish the two terms) is not just distinct from the body, but entirely opposite in nature: the body is extended and divisible, the mind is unextended and indivisible. But Descartes goes on to acknowledge that our *sensations*, such as those of hunger and thirst, testify to the fact that our relationship to the body is a peculiarly close

---

* René Descartes, *Meditations on First Philosophy* [*Meditationes de Prima Philosophia*, 1641]. Trans. J. Cottingham (Cambridge: Cambridge University Press, 1986, rev. edn 1996), pp. 17–19 and 51–9; with omissions.
[1] See Part I, extract 4, above.

and intimate one, amounting to a 'union'. And this gave rise to a serious philosophical difficulty with which Descartes's successors wrestled: how, if their natures are so distinct, can mind and body interact so closely, as we know they do (for example, dryness in the throat will cause a mental change – a wish to drink, while a mental event, e.g. a wish to vote, can cause a physical change – the arm goes up)? In later writings, Descartes was obliged to admit that he had left the nature of mind–body union somewhat obscure: our reason tells us that mind and body are distinct, but our daily experience tells us they are united.

 I do not yet have a sufficient understanding of what this 'I' is, that now necessarily exists. So I must be on my guard against carelessly taking something else to be this 'I', and so making a mistake in the very item of knowledge that I maintain is the most certain and evident of all. I will therefore go back and meditate on what I originally believed myself to be, before I embarked on this present train of thought. I will then subtract anything capable of being weakened, even minimally, by the arguments now introduced, so that what is left at the end may be exactly and only what is certain and unshakeable.

What then did I formerly think I was? A man. But what is a man? Shall I say 'a rational animal'? No; for then I should have to inquire what an animal is, what rationality is, and in this way one question would lead me down the slope to other harder ones, and I do not now have the time to waste on subtleties of this kind. Instead I propose to concentrate on what came into my thoughts spontaneously and quite naturally whenever I used to consider what I was. Well, the first thought to come to mind was that I had a face, hands, arms and the whole mechanical structure of limbs which can be seen in a corpse, and which I called the body. The next thought was that I was nourished, that I moved about, and that I engaged in sense-perception and thinking; and these actions I attributed to the soul. But as to the nature of this soul, either I did not think about this or else I imagined it to be something tenuous, like a wind or fire or ether, which permeated my more solid parts. As to the body, however, I had no doubts about it, but thought I knew its nature distinctly. If I had tried to describe the mental conception I had of it, I would have expressed it as follows: by a body I understand whatever has a determinable shape and a definable location and can occupy a space in such a way as to exclude any other body; it can be perceived by touch, sight, hearing, taste or smell, and can be moved in various ways, not by itself but by whatever else comes into contact with it. For, according to my judgement, the power of self-movement, like the power of sensation or of thought, was quite foreign to the nature of a body; indeed, it was a source of wonder to me that certain bodies were found to contain faculties of this kind.

But what shall I now say that I am, when I am supposing that there is some supremely powerful and, if it is permissible to say so, malicious deceiver, who is deliberately trying to trick me in every way he can?[1] Can I now assert that I possess even the most insignificant of all the attributes which I have just said belong to the nature of a body? I scrutinize them, think about them, go over them again, but nothing suggests itself; it is tiresome and pointless to go through the list once more. But what about the attributes I assigned to the soul? Nutrition or movement? Since now I do not have a body, these are mere fabrications. Sense-perception? This surely does not occur without a body, and besides, when asleep I have appeared to perceive

---

[1] See Part I, extract 4, above.

through the senses many things which I afterwards realized I did not perceive through the senses at all. Thinking? At last I have discovered it – thought; this alone is inseparable from me. I am, I exist – that is certain. But for how long? For as long as I am thinking. For it could be that were I totally to cease from thinking, I should totally cease to exist. At present I am not admitting anything except what is necessarily true. I am, then, in the strict sense only a thing that thinks; that is, I am a mind, or intelligence, or intellect, or reason – words whose meaning I have been ignorant of until now. But for all that I am a thing which is real and which truly exists. But what kind of a thing? As I have just said – a thinking thing.

What else am I? I will use my imagination. I am not that structure of limbs which is called a human body. I am not even some thin vapour which permeates the limbs – a wind, fire, air, breath, or whatever I depict in my imagination; for these are things which I have supposed to be nothing. Let this supposition stand; for all that I am still something. And yet may it not perhaps be the case that these very things which I am supposing to be nothing, because they are unknown to me, are in reality identical with the 'I' of which I am aware? I do not know, and for the moment I shall not argue the point, since I can make judgements only about things which are known to me. I know that I exist; the question is, what is this 'I' that I know? If the 'I' is understood strictly as we have been taking it, then it is quite certain that knowledge of it does not depend on things of whose existence I am as yet unaware; so it cannot depend on any of the things which I invent in my imagination. And this very word 'invent' shows me my mistake. It would indeed be a case of fictitious invention if I used my imagination to establish that I was something or other; for imagining is simply contemplating the shape or image of a corporeal thing. Yet now I know for certain both that I exist and at the same time that all such images and, in general, everything relating to the nature of body, could be mere dreams. Once this point has been grasped, to say 'I will use my imagination to get to know more distinctly what I am' would seem to be as silly as saying 'I am now awake, and see some truth; but since my vision is not yet clear enough, I will deliberately fall asleep so that my dreams may provide a truer and clearer representation. I thus realize that none of the things that the imagination enables me to grasp is at all relevant to this knowledge of myself which I possess, and that the mind must therefore be most carefully diverted from such things if it is to perceive its own nature as distinctly as possible.

But what then am I? A thing that thinks. What is that? A thing that doubts, understands, affirms, denies, is willing, is unwilling, and also imagines and has sensory perceptions...

To begin with, I will go back over all the things which I previously took to be perceived by the senses, and reckoned to be true; and I will go over my reasons for thinking this. Next, I will set out my reasons for subsequently calling these things into doubt. And finally I will consider what I should now believe about them.

First of all then, I perceived by my senses that I had a head, hands, feet and other limbs making up the body which I regarded as part of myself, and perhaps even as my whole self. I also perceived by my senses that this body was situated among many other bodies which could affect it in various favourable or unfavourable ways; and I gauged the favourable effects by a sensation of pleasure, and the unfavourable ones by a sensation of pain. In addition to pain and pleasure, I also had sensations within me of hunger, thirst, and other such appetites, and also of physical propensities towards cheerfulness, sadness, anger and similar emotions. And outside me, besides the extension, shapes and movements of bodies, I also had sensations of their hardness and heat, and of the other tactile qualities. In addition, I had sensations of light, colours, smells, tastes and sounds, the variety of which enabled me to distinguish the sky, the earth, the seas, and all other bodies, one from another. Considering the ideas of these qualities which presented themselves to my thought, although the ideas were, strictly speaking, the only immediate objects of my sensory awareness, it was not unreasonable for me to think that the items which I was perceiving through the senses were things quite distinct from my thought, namely bodies which produced the ideas. For my experience was that these ideas came to me quite without my consent, so that I could not have sensory awareness of any object, even if I wanted to, unless it was present to my sense organs; and I could not avoid having sensory awareness of it when it was present. And since the ideas perceived by the senses were much more lively and vivid and even, in their own way, more distinct than any of those which I deliberately formed through meditating, or which I found impressed on my memory, it seemed impossible that they should have come from within me; so the only alternative was that they came from other things. Since the sole source of my knowledge of these things was the ideas themselves, the supposition that the things resembled the ideas was bound to occur to me . . . As for the body which by some special right I called 'mine', my belief that this body, more than any other, belonged to me had some justification. For I could never be separated from it, as I could from other bodies; and I felt all my appetites and emotions in, and on account of, this body; and finally, I was aware of pain and pleasurable ticklings in parts of this body, but not in other bodies external to it. But why should that curious sensation of pain give rise to a particular distress of mind; or why should a certain kind of delight follow on a tickling sensation? Again, why should that curious tugging in the stomach which I call hunger tell me that I should eat, or a dryness of the throat tell me to drink, and so on? I was not able to give any explanation of all this, except that nature taught me so. For there is absolutely no connection (at least that I can understand) between the tugging sensation and the decision to take food, or between the sensation of something causing pain and the mental apprehension of distress that arises from that sensation. These and other judgements that I made concerning sensory objects, I was apparently taught to make by nature; for I had already made up my mind that this was how things were, before working out any arguments to prove it.

Later on, however, I had many experiences which gradually undermined all the faith I had had in the senses. Sometimes towers which had looked round from a distance appeared square from close up; and enormous statues standing on their pediments did not seem large when observed from the ground. In these and countless other such cases, I found that the judgements of the external senses were mistaken. And this applied not just to the external senses but to the internal senses as well. For what can be more internal than pain? And yet I had heard that those who had had a leg or an arm amputated sometimes still seemed to feel pain intermittently in the missing part of the body. So even in my own case it was apparently not quite certain that a particular limb was hurting, even if I felt pain in it. To these reasons for doubting, I recently added two very general ones. The first was that every sensory experience I have ever thought I was having while awake I can also think of myself as sometimes having while asleep; and since I do not believe that what I seem to perceive in sleep comes from things located outside me, I did not see why I should be any more inclined to believe this of what I think I perceive while awake. The second reason for doubt was that since I did not know the author of my being (or at least was pretending not to), I saw nothing to rule out the possibility that my natural constitution made me prone to error even in matters which seemed to me most true. As for the reasons for my previous confident belief in the truth of the things perceived by the senses, I had no trouble in refuting them. For since I apparently had natural impulses towards many things which reason told me to avoid, I reckoned that a great deal of confidence should not be placed in what I was taught by nature. And despite the fact that the perceptions of the senses were not dependent on my will, I did not think that I should on that account infer that they proceeded from things distinct from myself, since I might perhaps have a faculty not yet known to me which produced them.

But now, when I am beginning to achieve a better knowledge of myself and the author of my being, although I do not think I should heedlessly accept everything I seem to have acquired from the senses, neither do I think that everything should be called into doubt.

First, I know that everything which I clearly and distinctly understand is capable of being created by God so as to correspond exactly with my understanding of it. Hence the fact that I can clearly and distinctly understand one thing apart from another is enough to make me certain that the two things are distinct, since they are capable of being separated, at least by God. The question of what kind of power is required to bring about such a separation does not affect the judgement that the two things are distinct. Thus, simply by knowing that I exist and seeing at the same time that absolutely nothing else belongs to my nature or essence except that I am a thinking thing, I can infer correctly that my essence consists solely in the fact that I am a thinking thing. It is true that I may have (or, to anticipate, that I certainly have) a body that is very closely joined to me. But nevertheless, on the one hand I have a clear and distinct idea of myself, in so far as I am simply a thinking, non-extended thing; and on the other hand I have a distinct idea of body, in so far as this is simply an extended, non-thinking thing. And accordingly, it is certain that I am really distinct from my body, and can exist without it.

Besides this, I find in myself faculties for certain special modes of thinking, namely imagination and sensory perception. Now I can clearly and distinctly understand myself as a whole without these faculties; but I cannot, conversely, understand these faculties without me, that is, without an intellectual substance to inhere in. This is because there is an intellectual act included in their essential definition; and hence I perceive that the distinction between them and myself corresponds to the distinction between the modes of a thing and the thing itself. Of course I also recognize that there are other faculties (like those of changing position, of taking on various shapes, and so on) which, like sensory perception and imagination, cannot be understood apart from some substance for them to inhere in, and hence cannot exist without it. But it is clear that these other faculties, if they exist, must be in a corporeal or extended substance and not an intellectual one; for the clear and distinct conception of them includes extension, but does not include any intellectual act whatsoever. Now there is in me a passive faculty of sensory perception, that is, a faculty for receiving and recognizing the ideas of sensible objects; but I could not make use of it unless there was also an active faculty, either in me or in something else, which produced or brought about these ideas. But this faculty cannot be in me, since clearly it presupposes an intellectual act on my part, and the ideas in question are produced without my cooperation and often even against my will...I do not see how God could be understood to be anything but a deceiver if the ideas were transmitted from a source other than corporeal things. It follows that corporeal things exist. They may not all exist in a way that exactly corresponds with my sensory grasp of them, for in many cases the grasp of the senses is very obscure and confused. But at least they possess all the properties which I clearly and distinctly understand, that is, all those which, in general terms, are comprised within the subject matter of pure mathematics.

What of the other aspects of corporeal things which are particular (for example, that the sun is of such and such a size or shape) or less clearly understood, such as light or sound or pain, and so on? Despite the high degree of doubt and uncertainty involved here, the very fact that God is not a deceiver, and the consequent impossibility of there being any falsity in my opinions which cannot be corrected by some faculty supplied by God, offers me a sure hope that I can attain the truth even in these matters. Indeed, there is no doubt that everything that I am taught by nature contains some truth. For if nature is considered in its general aspect, then I understand by the term nothing other than God himself, or the ordered system of created things established by God. And by my own nature in particular I understand nothing other than the totality of things bestowed on me by God.

There is nothing that my own nature teaches me more vividly than that I have a body, and that when I feel pain there is something wrong with the body, and that when I am hungry or thirsty the body needs food and drink, and so on. So I should not doubt that there is some truth in this.

Nature also teaches me, by these sensations of pain, hunger, thirst and so on, that I am not merely present in my body as a sailor is present in a ship, but that I am very closely joined and, as it were, intermingled with it, so that I and the body form a unit. If this were not so, I, who am nothing but a thinking thing, would not feel pain when the body was hurt, but would perceive the damage purely by the intellect, just as a sailor perceives by sight if anything in his ship is broken. Similarly, when the body needed food or drink, I should have an explicit understanding of the fact, instead of having confused sensations of hunger and thirst. For these sensations of hunger, thirst, pain and so on are nothing but confused modes of thinking which arise from the union and, as it were, intermingling of the mind with the body.

I am also taught by nature that various other bodies exist in the vicinity of my body, and that some of these are to be sought out and others avoided. And from the fact that I perceive by my senses a great variety of colours, sounds, smells and tastes, as well as differences in heat, hardness and the like, I am correct in inferring that the bodies which are the source of these various sensory perceptions possess differences corresponding to them, though perhaps not resembling them. Also, the fact that some of the perceptions are agreeable to me while others are disagreeable makes it quite certain that my body, or rather my whole self, in so far as I am a combination of body and mind, can be affected by the various beneficial or harmful bodies which surround it...

There is a great difference between the mind and the body, inasmuch as the body is by its very nature always divisible, while the mind is utterly indivisible. For when I consider the mind, or myself in so far as I am merely a thinking thing, I am unable to distinguish any parts within myself; I understand myself to be something quite single and complete. Although the whole mind seems to be united to the whole body, I recognize that if a foot or arm or any other part of the body is cut off, nothing has thereby been taken away from the mind. As for the faculties of willing, of understanding, of sensory perception and so on, these cannot be termed parts of the mind, since it is one and the same mind that wills, and understands and has sensory perceptions. By contrast, there is no corporeal or extended thing that I can think of which in my thought I cannot easily divide into parts; and this very fact makes me understand that it is divisible. This one argument would be enough to show me that the mind is completely different from the body, even if I did not already know as much from other considerations.

5   The Identity of Mind and Body: Benedict Spinoza, *Ethics**

In different ways, the extracts presented above from Plato, Aquinas and Descartes all indicate a belief that there is something about the mind or soul that is not dependent on the body. Many thinkers in the twentieth century have taken a more robustly materialist line, maintaining that mental functions are nothing more than complex physical processes. Though this is often thought of as a 'modern' view, it has a long philosophical history. Some of the ancient Greek philosophers regarded the 'soul' as simply a set of bodily structures (see the Introduction to Part IV, above); and in the seventeenth century Thomas Hobbes advocated a radically materialist outlook. In his *Leviathan* (1651), Hobbes proposed a 'reductionist' scheme of explanation, invoking only material structures: by taking something apart, and looking at how the moving parts operate, we can understand the workings of a complex structure like a watch, and the same, for Hobbes, is in principle true of human beings. All the mental faculties and activities of human beings (such as sensing and thinking) are to be accounted for purely in terms of moving particles in the nervous system.

A rather more subtle line was taken later in the seventeenth century by Benedict Spinoza, in his *Ethics* (written *c.*1665). Like Hobbes, Spinoza attacks the notion of an immaterial soul, and wholly rejects the idea of a separate spiritual realm existing in its own right. But he avoids reducing everything to physical language. According to Spinoza, to explain human actions and decisions we need to use mental language (the language of 'thought'), just as we need to use physical language (the language of 'extension') to describe the workings of the body and nervous system. It is wrong to cross these levels of explanation, as if the body could 'determine the mind to thinking', or mind 'determine the body to motion'. Nevertheless, despite the two levels of explanation, there is only one set of events going on: 'soul and body are one and the same thing, conceived now under the attribute of thought and now under the attribute of extension'. Those who think a separate soul is needed to account for the complexities of human behaviour are on weak ground, according to Spinoza, since the body is an enormously complicated system, and we just do not know what it is or is not capable of doing on its own. As for the objection that our ability to act freely requires the existence of a soul, Spinoza replies that our belief in a 'free' soul, wholly independent of the body, is due merely to our ignorance of the physical determinants of action.

---

* Benedict Spinoza, *Ethics* [*Ethica ordine geometrico demonstrata, c.*1665], extracts from Part III, prop. 2. Translation by John Cottingham. A complete English version of the *Ethics* may be found in *The Collected Works of Spinoza*, vol. I, ed. E. Curley (Princeton: Princeton University Press, 1985).

The body cannot determine the mind to thinking, nor can the mind determine the body to motion, or rest or anything else (if there is anything else).

...The motion and rest of a body must arise from another body, which in its turn has been determined to motion and rest by another body...Mind and body are one and the same thing, which is conceived now under the attribute of thought, now under that of extension. Hence it comes about that the order or connection of things is one and the same, whether its nature is conceived under the former or the latter attribute. And consequently the order of the actions and passions of our body is the same as the order of the actions and passions of the mind...

But although all these matters are such as to leave no reason for doubt, I can hardly believe people will be induced to give them fair consideration unless I provide some confirmation based on experience. For they are firmly convinced that it is by the command of the mind alone that the body moves at one time and is at rest at another, and that it does a great many things which depend entirely on the will of the mind and its power of thinking.

No one, however, has yet settled what the body is capable of. No one, that is to say, has shown by experiment what the body is capable of doing solely from the laws of nature, that is, considered simply as something corporeal, or what it is incapable of doing without being determined by the mind. For no one has yet achieved such an accurate knowledge of the structure of the body as to be able to explain all its functions – and here I pass over the many things observed in the lower animals, which far exceed human ingenuity, and the things sleepwalkers do which they would not dare to perform while awake. This is quite enough to show that the body alone, merely from the laws of its nature, is capable of many things that astonish the mind.

Moreover, no one yet knows in what way and by what means the mind moves the body, or how many degrees of motion it can give to it, nor with what speed it can move it. It follows that when men say that this or that action has its origins in the mind which has control over the body, they really do not know what they are talking about, and are only dressing up in fancy language their admission that, apart from being amazed at the action, they are ignorant of its true cause.

But they may say that irrespective of whether they do or do not know the means whereby the mind moves the body, they still know by experience that unless the human mind was capable of thinking, the body would be inert. And they may add that experience also teaches them that it lies solely in the power of the mind to speak or to be silent, and to do many other things; and consequently they believe such things must depend entirely on the decision of the mind.

But as regards the first point, I ask them whether experience does not also teach, in the converse case, that if the body is inert, the mind is unable to think? For when the body lies resting in sleep, during this time the mind remains inactive along with it, and does not have the power of thinking which it has when awake. Further, I believe everyone must have discovered by his own experience that the mind is not always equally capable of thinking of the same object, but that the more readily the image of this or that object can be produced within the body, the greater will be the mind's aptitude for contemplating the relevant object.

Now they may say that the laws of nature alone, considered solely as something corporeal, cannot provide the basis for deducing the causes of buildings, pictures and things of this kind which come about by human art alone; and that the human body, unless it was determined and led by the mind, would be incapable of constructing a temple. But I have already shown that they do not know what the body is capable of, or what can be deduced from the consideration of its nature alone. They themselves must have had experience of many things happening solely by the laws of nature, which they would never have believed possible unless done under the direction of the mind – such as the actions of sleepwalkers, which the subjects themselves are amazed by when they are awake. Let me add that the structure of the human body itself vastly exceeds in its intricacy anything made by human skill ...

As regards the second point, human affairs would certainly be in a far happier state if people had as much ability to keep silent as they have to speak out. But experience provides more than ample evidence that the tongue is the organ people have least control over, and that moderating their appetites is the thing they are least able to do. Hence most believe that it is only when we have a slight inclination to do something that we do it freely, since in such cases our desire can easily be curtailed by recalling some other desire which is frequently in our mind; whereas we are scarcely free at all when we pursue something with a great passion that cannot be suppressed by thinking of something else. They would even be ready to believe that all our actions were free, did they not know by experience that we do many things we are afterwards sorry for, and that often, when we are agitated by conflicting passions, we see the better course yet choose the worse. Thus the infant may believe that it freely desires the milk, the angry child that he freely wants revenge, the timid person that he freely chooses to run away. Or again the drunkard may believe it is by a free decision of the mind that he says the things that later, once he has sobered up, he wishes he had not said. It is the same with those who are ranting and raving, or eagerly chattering away, or with young children, and many others: they may all believe it is a free decision of the mind that leads them to speak, when in fact they cannot restrain their impulse to talk.

Thus experience, no less clearly than reason, amply shows that the only reason people believe themselves free is that they are conscious of their actions, while being unaware of the causes that determine them. The decisions of the mind are nothing but its appetites, which vary depending on the various states of the body. Our own emotions are the basis for all the decisions we take; those of us who are afflicted by contrary emotions do not know what we want, while if no emotion is present, it takes but a slight impulse to drive us in one direction or another.

All this clearly shows that a decision of the mind on the one hand, and an appetite and determination of the body on the other, are by nature simultaneous; or rather they are one and the same thing, which when considered under the attribute of *thought*, and explained by it, we call a 'decision', and when considered under the attribute of *extension*, and deduced from the laws of motion and rest, we call a 'determination'.

6   Mind–Body Correlations: Nicolas Malebranche, *Dialogues on Metaphysics**

One of the problems faced by a materialist account of the mind, such as that of Hobbes (see introduction to previous extract), is that the language of physical science does not seem to capture what might be called the 'qualitative' dimension of our human experience – the peculiar character of our feelings, sensations and emotions as they are experienced by the conscious subject. Can a description of molecular events in the brain or nervous system explain what it is like to smell a rose, or to feel a toothache? As the preceding extract makes clear, one of Spinoza's main conclusions was that a purely physiological account is incomplete from an explanatory point of view – hence his insistence on the need for the language of consciousness as well as the language of bodily events. Nevertheless, the relationship between the two languages was something he left rather obscure, beyond the bald assertion that mental and physical descriptions refer to 'one and the same thing'. As for the dualist approach of Descartes (see extract 4, above), this faced even more of a problem in explaining sensations and emotions. Descartes had contented himself with saying sensations 'arise' in the soul as a result of its union with the body, but had left it unclear how a bodily change (say an empty stomach) could cause the 'curious tugging sensation' we call hunger.

In the later seventeenth century, Nicolas Malebranche, who was broadly speaking a supporter of Descartes, subjected his predecessor's concept of the mind–body 'union' to close critical attention. In his *Dialogues on Metaphysics*, Malebranche accepts Descartes's distinction between the extended material world and the immaterial mind or soul. But he argues first (contrary to

Descartes) that we have no clear idea of the nature of the mind. Descartes (see extract 4, above) had maintained we know the nature of mind more clearly than that of matter; for Malebranche, while our idea of matter is clear, our conception of our own nature, the nature of the mind or soul, is highly obscure: 'I am not a light unto myself.' Second, with regard to sensory experience, and other psycho-physical transactions, Malebranche maintains that it makes no sense to say that bodily events *cause* mental changes, or vice versa. The Cartesian concept of the 'union' of mind and body solves nothing, for however thoroughly we investigate the mechanisms of our bodies, what causes the tongue to move when we want to say something, or what makes us feel hungry when our stomach is empty, is something that remains utterly unexplained. Malebranche's own solution, known as *occasionalism*, is that God is the sole cause of the relevant events – for example, he brings it about that I feel toothache on the 'occasion' of my tooth's being decayed. 'He willed that I have certain sensations when there are certain traces in my brain; he willed and wills unceasingly, that the modalities of mind and body be reciprocal.' The invoking of God has seemed to many of Malebranche's critics to be more of a confession of ignorance than a solution. But Malebranche's work succeeded in making subsequent philosophers think long and hard about the precise relationship between brain events and conscious sensations, and whether it makes sense to speak of one *causing* the other.[1] In the passages that follow, as throughout his book, the arguments are presented in dialogue form; the words of 'Theodore' express Malebranche's own philosophical position.

---

* Nicolas Malebranche, *Dialogues on Metaphysics* [*Entretiens sur la métaphysique*, 1688], extracts from Dialogues III and VII. Translation by John Cottingham.

[1] More generally, Malebranche's replacement of causal interaction with divinely decreed correlations can be said to have paved the way for Hume's reduction of causation to constant conjunction; see Part VII, extract 6, below.

THEODORE: I know the parts of extension clearly, because I can see quite evidently the relations that apply to them. I see clearly that similar triangles have proportional sides, that there is no plane triangle whose three angles are not equal to two right angles. I see these truths or these relations clearly, in the idea or archetype of extension. For this idea is so luminous that it is by contemplating it that people become geometers and good physicists; the idea is so productive of truths that it can never be exhausted, even by all minds working together.

It is not at all the same with respect to my own being. I have no idea of it whatever: I do not see its archetype at all. I am unable to discover the relations that apply to those of its modifications which affect my mind; I am unable, when I turn to myself, to recognize any of my faculties or my capacities. The inner sensation which I have of myself informs me that I am, that I think, that I will, that I have sensory awareness, that I suffer, and so on; but it provides me with no knowledge whatever of *what* I am – of the nature of my thought, my will, my sensations, my passions, or my pain – or of the mutual relations which obtain between all these things. For...I have no idea whatever of my soul, and do not see its archetype in the divine Word; hence I cannot contemplate it to discover what it is, or what modalities it is capable of, or the relations which obtain between its modalities. I have a lively sensory awareness of these relations without knowing them, whereas God has clear knowledge of them without having sensory awareness of them. All this is true, my dear Aristes, because, as I have already told you, I am not my own light to myself: my substance and my modalities are but darkness to me, and God has not deemed it appropriate, for many reasons, to reveal to me the idea or archetype which represents the nature of spiritual beings. For suppose my substance were intelligible through itself or in itself – suppose it were luminous, and it could enlighten me: in that case, since I am not separated from myself, I should certainly be able to see, merely by contemplating myself, that I am capable of being affected by such and such sensations, even though I have never experienced them and may never be acquainted with them. I should not have needed a concert to know what the sweetness of harmony is; and I should, without ever having tasted such and such a fruit, have been able to have evident knowledge (I do not say sensory awareness) of the nature of the sensation it arouses in me. But we can have knowledge of the nature of beings only in Reason, which contains them in an intelligible manner; so although I have sensory awareness of myself only within myself, it is only in Reason that I can discover what I am, and the modalities applicable to my nature. There are even stronger reasons for maintaining that it is only in Reason that I can discover the first principles of the sciences and all the truths capable of enlightening the mind...

ARISTES: It seems to me, Theodore, that there is nothing to which I am more closely united than I am to my own body. For it cannot be touched without causing some disturbance to myself. As soon as it is hurt, I feel I am being injured or discomposed. Nothing is smaller than the proboscis of those tiresome fellow-creatures who attack us on our evening walks; yet when my skin receives the slightest prick from the imperceptible point of that poisonous organ, I feel a pricking sensation in my soul. The mere noise they make round my ears makes me alarmed – a sure sign that I am more closely united to my body than to anything else. Yes, Theodore, this is so true that even our union with all the objects in the environment comes about only by means of our body. If the sun produced no disturbance in my eyes, it would be invisible to my gaze; and if I were unlucky enough to become deaf, I would no longer experience such delight in being with my friends. My body even provides the means whereby I hold to my religion, for it is through my ears and eyes that faith entered my mind and heart. To conclude, I am related to everything else by means of my body. I am therefore united to my body more closely than I am to anything else.

THEODORE: Have you meditated for a long time, my dear Aristes, in order to arrive at this great discovery? . . .

ARISTES: I see I have made a very bad beginning.

THEODORE: Very bad indeed. I was not expecting this, for I did not think you would have forgotten today what you learnt yesterday. But prejudices always return to the attack and drive us off the territory we have gained, unless we dig in and hold our ground vigilantly. Now look: I tell you that so far from being more closely joined to the body than to anything else, we are in no way united to it. I am putting this rather over-emphatically so my words have an impact on you, and you won't forget them a second time. No, Aristes; if we put the matter exactly and strictly, your mind is not and cannot be united to your body. For it can be united only to what can act on it. Now do you think that your body can act on your mind? Do you think that it is by means of the body that you are rational, happy or unhappy, and the like? Is it your body that unites you to God, to reason, which enlightens us? Or is it God who unites you to your body, and by way of your body, to everything else around you?

ARISTES: Certainly, Theodore, it is God who has united my mind to my body. But could we not say . . .

THEODORE: What? That it is now your mind which acts on your body and your body on your mind? I understand you. God originally made this union of mind and body, but after that, there your body is – the means whereby all objects can act on your mind. And once the union has been set up, there is your mind too – capable of acting on the body, and thereby on everything around you. Is that perhaps what might be said?

ARISTES: There is something here that I do not understand too well. How does all this come about? I speak to you as if I had forgotten most of what you told me, for lack of having thought about it.

THEODORE: I thought so. You want me to provide a more exact and detailed proof of the principles which I have so far talked to you about. I must try to satisfy you. But I beg you to pay attention and answer these questions . . .

Do you think, Aristes, that matter, which you may well judge incapable of moving itself, or giving itself any modality, can ever modify a mind – make it happy or unhappy, represent ideas to it, give it different sensations? Give me your considered answer.

ARISTES: That would not seem to me to be possible.

THEODORE: Consider the matter further. Consult the idea of extension, and judge by that idea (which represents bodies, if anything does) whether bodies can have any property beyond the passive faculty of receiving various shapes and motions. Is it not absolutely evident that the properties of extension can consist only in relations of distance?

ARISTES: That is clear, and I have already agreed.

THEODORE: So it is not possible that bodies should act on minds?

ARISTES: Not by themselves, by their own force. But why should they not be capable of this through a power that results from their union with minds?

THEODORE: What are you saying? 'By a power that results from their union?' I understand nothing by these general terms. Remember, Aristes, the principle of clear ideas. If you abandon it, you are immediately lost in the dark, and at the first step you take you will fall into a precipice...I do not understand how bodies in themselves can take on a power enabling them to act on the mind. What would this power be – a substance or a modality? If it is a substance, then it would not be the bodies that are acting, but this substance present in the bodies. If the power is a modality, then there will be a modality in bodies which turns out to be neither motion nor shape; and in that case extension will be able to have modalities other than relations of distance. But why am I hesitating here? The onus is on you, Aristes, to give me some idea of this power which you conceive of as resulting from the union of soul and body.

ARISTES: We do not know what this power is – that is what may be said. But what inference can you draw from our confession of ignorance?

THEODORE: That it is better to be silent than not to know what one is saying.

ARISTES: I agree. But in proposing that bodies act on minds, we are asserting only what we know. For nothing is more certain: experience allows no doubts on that score.

THEODORE: Yet I still have serious doubts, or rather I do not believe a word of it. Experience teaches me that I feel pain, for example when a thorn pricks me. That is certain. But this is where we must stop. For experience in no way teaches us that the thorn acts on our mind or that it possesses some power. We should not believe any of *that*, if you will take my advice.

ARISTES: Well, Theodore, I do not believe that a thorn can act on my mind. But it may well be said that it can act on my body, and by way of my body, on my mind, in virtue of their union. For I admit that matter cannot act immediately on a mind – provided you note the qualification *immediately*.

THEODORE: But is your body not matter?

ARISTES: Yes, undoubtedly.

THEODORE: So your body cannot act *immediately* on your mind. Hence, although your finger was pricked by a thorn, and although your brain was stimulated by its action, neither finger nor brain was able to act on your soul and make it feel pain. Neither finger nor brain can act immediately on your mind, since your brain and your finger are merely matter.

ARISTES: But it is certainly not my soul that produces in itself this sensation of pain that troubles it; for it feels the pain in spite of itself. I am well aware that the pain comes to me from some extraneous cause. Your argument thus proves too much. I can see you are about to tell me that it is God who causes my pain in me, and I agree. But he causes it only in consequence of the general laws of the union of soul and body...

THEODORE: You want to maintain that your soul is united to your body more closely than to anything else. Very well, I will agree for the moment, but only on condition that for a day or two you accept my rule of not trying to explain things by a principle of which neither you nor I have any knowledge at all. Is this not reasonable?

ARISTES: But what do you mean?

THEODORE: This. There is between your mind and body that closest union in the world: how, you ask, can we doubt that? But you would be quite unable to say what precisely this union is. So we must not take this 'union' as a principle of explanation for the effects whose cause we are inquiring after.

ARISTES: But if these effects necessarily depend on it?

THEODORE: If they do depend on it, we shall of course be obliged to return to it. But let us not assume that they do. If I were to ask you, Aristes, how it comes about that when you pull the arm of this chair the rest of the chair follows, would you reckon you had provided an adequate explanation of the effect if you were to reply that it comes about because the arm of the chair is 'united' with the other parts of which it is composed... We allow children to give answers of this kind, but not philosophers, except when they are not claiming to philosophize. To satisfy [a philosopher] on this question we should have to go back to the physical cause of the union of the parts of which hard bodies are composed; we should have to demonstrate that the hardness of bodies can come only from their being compressed by the invisible matter which surrounds them. The word 'union' explains nothing; it is itself in need of explanation. So, Aristes, though you may take vague and general words for rational explanations, if you so wish, please do not pretend that this is anything but counterfeit coin...

[There follows a discussion of supposed causal interaction between bodies. The participants agree that bodies have, in themselves, no active power to impart motion, but that they 'can only be moved by the continual action of the Creator'. An encounter between two bodies is the 'occasion' for God, the only true cause, to exercise his power.]

THEODORE: So, Aristes, you are unable, by yourself, to move your arm, change your place, situation or posture, treat other people well or badly, or produce the smallest change in the universe. There you are in the world, without any power, as immobile as a rock, as stupid as a block of wood, as it were. Let your soul be united to your body as closely as you like; let it be in contact, via the body, with everything around you: what advantage will you get from this imaginary union? What will you do to move even your fingertip, or to utter a single syllable? If, poor man, God does not come to your assistance, all your efforts will be futile; you will form only impotent desires. Give the matter a little reflection: do you really know what has to be done in order to utter the name of your best friend? Think of the finger you use most every day: do you know what has to be done to bend or straighten it? Let us even suppose that you know what all ordinary people are quite ignorant of, and what even the scientists do not agree on: that our arms can be moved only by means of animal spirits[1] which flow through the nerves to the muscles, tighten the muscles, and pull on the bones to which they are attached. Let us suppose you know about anatomy and the operation of your bodily machine as precisely as a clockmaker knows his own products. Yet you must still remember the principle that it is only the Creator

---

[1] 'Animal spirits': the fine vapour or gas which the followers of Descartes supposed to be the vehicle for the transmission of motion through the nerves.

of bodies who can be their mover. This principle is sufficient to threaten – why do I say threaten? – to *annihilate* all your alleged faculties. For in the end, animal spirits, however small they may be, are bodies; they are simply the tiniest and fastest moving portion of the blood and the bodily fluids. God alone can move these small bodies. He alone has the power and the knowledge to make them flow from the brain into the nerves, from the nerves to the muscles . . . all of which is necessary for the movement of our limbs.

Hence, despite the union of soul and body which you like to imagine, you remain quite motionless and dead, unless God is willing to harmonize his volitions with yours – his volitions, which are always efficacious, to your desires, which are always powerless. This, my dear Aristes, is how the great mystery is resolved. Creatures are united to God alone, by an immediate union. It is on him alone, essentially and directly, that they depend. As they are all equally powerless, they certainly do not have any mutual dependence on each another. People may describe them as 'united' among themselves and even say that they are 'inter-dependent'. I accept this, provided we do not understand such dependence according to our ordinary ideas, and provided we agree that it comes about only as a result of the immutable and always efficacious decrees of the Creator, only in consequence of general laws which God has established, and by which he regulates the ordinary course of his Providence.

God willed that my arm should move, at the very instant at which I willed it myself (I am taking all the necessary conditions as satisfied). His will is efficacious; it is immutable. This is the source from which I derive my power and my faculties. He willed that I should have certain sensations and emotions, whenever certain traces, and certain movements of animal spirits, occur in my brain. In a word, he has willed, and he wills unceasingly, that the modalities of mind and body should be reciprocal. Here you have the 'union' and the natural dependence of the two parts of which we are composed. It is merely the mutual reciprocity of our modalities, based on the unshakeable foundation of the divine decrees. These decrees, by their efficacy, impart to me the power I have over my own body, and, through it, over some other bodies; by their immutability they unite me to my body and, through it, to my friends, to my possessions, to everything around me. I get nothing from my nature, and nothing from the imaginary nature invoked by the philosophers. Everything is from God, and from his decrees. God has linked all his works together, though without producing linking entities in them. He has subordinated some of his works to others, though without bestowing efficacious qualities on them. The latter are empty pretensions of human pride, fantastical products of the ignorance of philosophers. The source of the error is that people's senses are stimulated in the presence of bodies, and they are internally affected by the sensation of their own efforts; but when this happens, they have completely failed to recognize the invisible operation of the Creator, the uniformity of his action, the richness of his laws, the ever-actualized efficacy of his decrees, and the infinite wisdom of his ordinary providence. So stop saying, I beg you, my dear Aristes, that your soul is united to your body more closely than to anything else. It is united immediately to God alone. His divine decrees are the indissoluble links that bind all the parts of the universe; they are the wonderful chain of subordination that encompasses all causes.

7   Body and Mind as Manifestations of Will: Arthur Schopenhauer, *The World as Will and Idea**

Many of the above readings indicate a conception of the mental and the physical realms as somehow opposed, or in tension. Some philosophers attempted to overcome the tension by reducing the mental to the physical.[1] The opposite route from such materialism is followed by those philosophers known as *idealists*, who aim to reduce the physical to the mental; an idealist conception is clearly central to the philosophy of Berkeley (see above, Part II, extract 6). In the early nineteenth century, the German philosopher Arthur Schopenhauer developed a philosophy which he himself saw as in a direct line of succession to that of Berkeley. For Schopenhauer, it makes no sense to talk of a world 'out there' independently of the 'representations' of the mind; the phenomenal world, the world we experience, is world as 'idea' or 'representation' (*Vorstellung*). But Schopenhauer proceeds to ground this idealist framework in a highly distinctive theory of his own: all phenomena – whether those which we observe in the world around us, or those which we are aware of in our own mental operations – are merely manifestations of the underlying reality that is *will*. The philosophy of Immanuel Kant, which strongly influenced Schopenhauer, had stressed the role of the mind in interpreting phenomena, but had left the nature of the ultimate reality behind those phenomena (the 'thing in itself') unknown and unknowable (see above, Part II, extract 8). Schopenhauer argues, by contrast, that each of us, in the conscious awareness we have of what is going on inside us, is directly in touch with the ultimate basis – Will – on which all phenomena, or 'representations' are founded.

Although Schopenhauer is no materialist, the label 'idealism' can also be misleading if it is taken to imply the view that everything is pure 'spirit'. For Schopenhauer, a correct account of the phenomenal world will include reference to my body and its workings (and indeed bodies in general): as is made clear in the following extract, Schopenhauer firmly rejects the notion that we are incorporeal entities (like a 'winged cherub without a body'). So what is the relationship between these physical workings and the activities of the will? Here Schopenhauer wholly abandons the earlier dualism of Descartes (see extract 4 above), and attempts to bypass the problems of mind–body interaction which had so exercised Malebranche (see extract 6). Instead, Schopenhauer proposes an account of the relationship between body and mind that is strongly influenced by Spinoza: 'the act of the will and the movement of the body are not two things, but one thing' (compare Spinoza, extract 6, above). For Schopenhauer, we are directly and introspectively aware of the activity or force of our will, and that selfsame event is represented in physiological terms (for example as a series of occurrences in the nervous system). The notion that there is a single event here, but, in Schopenhauer's words 'given in two entirely different ways' is an extremely suggestive one. Schopenhauer's direct influence on contemporary philosophy of mind has, however, been slight, perhaps because few have been prepared to accept his metaphysical conception of will as the key to *all* the phenomena in the universe.

 We can never arrive at the real nature of things from without. However much we investigate, we can never reach anything but images and names. We are like a man who goes round a castle seeking in vain for an entrance, and sometimes sketching all the facades. And yet this is the method that has been followed by all philosophers before me.

---

* Arthur Schopenhauer, *The World as Will and Idea* [*Die Welt als Wille und Vorstellung*, 1819]. Trans. R. B. Haldane and J. Kemp (London: Routledge, 1883), extracts from Vol. I, Bk 2, §§ 17, 18, 20, 21, 22, 23.
[1]   An example is Thomas Hobbes; see introduction to extract 5, above.

In fact, the meaning for which we seek of that world which is present to us only as our idea, for the transition from the world as mere idea of the knowing subject to whatever it may be besides this, would never be found if the investigator himself were nothing more than the pure knowing subject (a winged cherub without a body). But he is himself rooted in that world; he finds himself in it as an *individual,* that is to say his knowledge, which is the necessary supporter of the whole world as idea, is none the less always given through the medium of a body, whose affections are the starting-point for the understanding in its perception of that world. His body is for the pure knowing subject an idea like every other idea, an object among objects. Its movements and actions are so far known to him in precisely the same way as the changes of all other perceived objects, and would be just as strange and incomprehensible to him if their meaning were not explained for him in an entirely different way. Otherwise he would see his actions follow upon given motives with the constancy of a law of nature, just as the changes of other objects follow upon causes, stimuli or motives. But he would not understand the influence of the motives, any more than the connection between every other effect which he sees and its cause. He would then call the inner nature of these manifestations and actions of his body which he did not understand a force, a quality or a character as he pleased, but he would have no further insight into it. But all this is not the case; indeed, the answer to the riddle is given to the subject of knowledge who appears as an individual, and the answer is *will.* This and this alone gives him the key to his own existence, reveals to him the significance, shows him the inner mechanism of his being, of his action, his movements.

The body is given in two entirely different ways to the subject of knowledge, who becomes an individual only through his identity with it. It is given as an idea in the perception of the understanding, as an object among objects and subject to the laws of objects. And it is also given in quite a different way as that which is immediately known to everyone, and is signified by the word *will.* Every true act of his will is also at once and without exception a movement of his body. The act of will and the movement of the body are not two different things objectively known, which the bond of causality unites; they do not stand in the relation of cause and effect; they are one and the same but they are given in entirely different ways – on the one hand immediately, and on the other in perception for the understanding. The action of the body is nothing but the act of the will objectified, i.e. passed into perception. It will appear that this is true of every movement of the body, not merely those which follow upon motives, but also involuntary movements which follow upon mere stimuli, and indeed that the whole body is nothing but objectified will, i.e. will become idea. All this will be proved and become clear in the course of this work...

If every action of my body is the manifestation of an act of will in which my will itself in general, and as a whole, thus my character, expresses itself under given motives, manifestation of the will must be the inevitable condition and presupposition of every action. For the fact of its manifestation cannot depend upon something which does not exist directly and only through it, which consequently is for it merely accidental, and through which its manifestation itself would be merely accidental. Now that condition is just the whole body itself. Thus the body itself must be manifestation of the will, and it must be related to my will as a whole, that is to my intelligible character, as the particular action of the body is related to the particular action of the will. The whole body then must be simply my will become visible, must be my will itself, so far as this is object of perception...

Whoever has gained from all these expositions a knowledge in the abstract, and therefore clear and certain, of what everyone knows directly and in the concrete, i.e. as feeling, a knowledge that his will is the real inner nature of his phenomenal being, which manifests itself to him as an idea...will find that of itself it affords him the key to the knowledge of the inmost being of the whole of nature. For he now transfers it to all those phenomena which are not given to him, like his own phenomenal existence, both in direct and indirect knowledge, but only in the latter, thus entirely one-sidedly, as idea alone. He will recognize this will of which we are speaking not only in those phenomenal existences which exactly resemble his own, in men and animals as their inmost nature, but the course of reflecting will lead him to recognize the force which germinates and vegetates in the plant, and indeed the force through which the crystal is formed, that by which the magnet turns to the north pole, the force whose shock he experienced from the contact of two different kinds of metal, the force which appears in the elective affinities of matter as repulsion and attraction, decomposition and combination, and lastly even gravitation, which acts so powerfully throughout matter, draws the stone to the earth and the earth to the sun – all these, I say, he will recognize as different only in their phenomenal existence, but in their nature as identical, as that which is directly known to him so intimately and so much better than anything else, and which in its most distinct manifestation is called *will*...

Hitherto it was not recognized that every kind of active and operating force in nature is essentially identical with will, and therefore the multifarious kinds of phenomena were not seen to be merely different species of the same genus, but were treated as heterogeneous. Consequently there could be no word to denote the concept of this genus. I therefore name the genus after its most important species, the direct knowledge of which lies nearer to us and guides us to the indirect knowledge of all other species. But whoever is incapable of carrying out the required extension of the concept will remain involved in a permanent misunderstanding. For by the word 'will' he understands only that species of it which has hitherto been exclusively denoted by it, the will which is guided by knowledge, and whose manifestation follows only upon motives, and indeed merely abstract motives, and thus takes place under the guidance of reason. This, we have seen, is only the most prominent example of the manifestation of will. We must now distinctly separate in thought the inmost essence of this manifestation which is known to us directly, and then transfer it to all the weaker, less distinct manifestations of the same nature, and thus we shall accomplish the desired extension of the concept of will. From another point of view, I should be equally misunderstood by anyone who thought that it is all the same in the end whether we denote this inner nature of all phenomena by the word *will* or by any other. This would be the case if the 'thing in itself' were something whose existence we merely *inferred*, and thus know indirectly and only in the abstract. Then indeed we might call it what we pleased; the name would stand merely as the symbol of an unknown quantity. But the word *will*, which like a magic spell discloses to us the inmost being of everything in nature, is by no means an unknown quantity, something arrived at only by inference, but is fully and immediately comprehended, and is so familiar to us that we can know and understand what will is far better than anything else whatever. The concept of will has hitherto commonly been subordinated to that of force, but I reverse the matter entirely, and desire that every force in nature should be thought as will. It must not be supposed that this is mere verbal quibbling of no consequence; rather it is of the greatest significance and importance. For at the foundation of the concept of force, as of all other concepts, there ultimately lies the knowledge in sense-perception of the objective world, that is to say, the phenomenon, the idea; and the concept is constructed out of this. It is an abstraction from the province in which cause and effect reign, i.e. from ideas of perception, and means just the causal nature of causes at the point at which this causal nature is not further causally explicable, but is the necessary presupposition of all causal explanation. The concept of the will, on the other hand, is of all possible concepts the only one which has its source not in the phenomenal, not in the mere idea of perception, but comes from within, and proceeds from the most immediate consciousness of each of us, in which each of us knows his own individuality, according to its nature, immediately, apart from all form, even that of subject and object, and which at the same time is this individuality; for here the subject and the object of knowledge are one. If, therefore, we refer the concept of *force* to that of *will*, we have in fact referred the less known to what is infinitely better known – indeed to the one thing that is really immediately and fully known to us – and have very greatly extended our knowledge. If, on the contrary, we subsume the concept of will under that of force, as has hitherto always been done, we renounce the only immediate knowledge which we have of the inner nature of the world, for we allow it to disappear in a concept which is abstracted from the phenomenal and with which we can therefore never go beyond the phenomenal . . .

If we observe the strong and unceasing impulse with which the waters hurry to the ocean, the persistency with which the magnet turns ever to the north pole, the readiness with which iron flies to the magnet, the eagerness with which the electric poles seek to be reunited, and which, just like human desire, is increased by obstacles; if we see the crystal quickly and suddenly take form with such wonderful regularity of construction, which is clearly only a perfectly definite and accurately determined impulse in different directions, seized and retained by crystallization; if we observe the choice with which bodies repel and attract each other, combine and separate, when they are set free in a fluid state, and emancipated from the bounds of rigidness; lastly, if we feel directly how a burden which hampers our body by its gravitation towards the earth unceasingly presses and strains upon it in pursuit of its one tendency; if we observe all this, I say, it will require no great effort of the imagination to recognize, even at so great a distance, our own nature. That which in us pursues its ends by the light of knowledge, but here in the weakest of its manifestations only strives dumbly and blindly in a onesided and unchangeable manner, must yet in both cases come under the name of will. For it is everywhere one and the same, just as the first dim light of dawn must share the name of sunlight with the rays of the full midday. The name *will* denotes that which is the inner nature of everything in the world, and the kernel of every phenomenon.

8   The Problem of Other Minds: John Stuart Mill, *An Examination of Sir William Hamilton's Philosophy**

In his celebrated investigation into the nature of the mind and its relation to the body, René Descartes (see extract 4, above) worked with an assumption that has continued to dominate much subsequent philosophy of mind, namely that each individual is directly and indubitably aware of what is going on in the mind. While every judgement I make about the 'external' world is open to doubt, the contents of my consciousness are present to my mind in a way that leaves no room for error. But this picture gives rise to a special problem: it appears to entail that while I can be certain of my own mental states (for example that I am happy, or in pain), I can at best only conjecture, with more or less probability, about the mental states of others.

In the following extract, the British philosopher John Stuart Mill explicitly addresses the question 'How do I know that the walking and speaking figures I see and hear have sensations and thoughts, in other words possess Minds?' Mill wholly accepts the Cartesian view that I have direct acquaintance with my own mental states (though unlike Descartes, he maintains the 'I' is not a soul or substance, but can be reduced to a 'series of feelings' or a 'thread of consciousness'; compare Hume, Part V, extract 3, below). But the mental states of *others*, Mill argues, are known to me only via a generalizing inference from my own case: I conclude that others have

feelings like me because 'they exhibit the acts and other outward signs which in my own case I know to be caused by feelings'. This 'argument from analogy' as it has come to be known, has been subjected to searching criticism in the twentieth century by Ludwig Wittgenstein. Wittgenstein scathingly attacked the suggestion that belief in other minds was comparable to any other scientific inference from observed data: if it is only in my own case that I can establish a link between sensations and bodily events, how can it be rational for me to generalize so irresponsibly from a single instance? Wittgenstein went on to argue that in order to have meaning in our language, terms for mental states must be employed on the basis of public *criteria*, or rules for their correct application; and if this is so, then it cannot be right that expressions such as 'I am in pain' get their meaning from referring to a private event accessible only to the subject.[1] What this criticism suggests is that the whole model of the mind, which Mill inherited from Descartes, may embody serious philosophical confusions. To suppose that my knowledge of the mind starts from my own private awareness, and that I subsequently project this outwards to others, is to ignore the fact that our understanding of mental phenomena is inescapably rooted in a public, inter-personal framework of social and linguistic practice.

 We have no conception of Mind itself, as distinguished from its conscious manifestations. We neither know nor can imagine it, except as represented by the succession of manifold feelings which metaphysicians call by the name of states or modifications of Mind. It is nevertheless true that our notion of Mind, as well as of Matter, is the notion of a permanent something, contrasted with the perpetual flux of the sensations and other feelings or mental states which we refer to it; a something which we figure as remaining the same, while the particular feelings through which it reveals its existence, change. This attribute of permanence, supposing that there were nothing

---

* John Stuart Mill, *An Examination of Sir William Hamilton's Philosophy* [1865] (6th edn, London: Longmans, 1889), ch. 12; abridged.

[1] Compare Ludwig Wittgenstein, *Philosophical Investigations* (Oxford: Blackwell, 1953), §§ 246, 293, 303.

else to be considered, would admit of the same explanation when predicated of Mind, as of Matter. The belief I entertain that my mind exists when it is not feeling, nor thinking, nor conscious of its own existence, resolves itself into the belief of a Permanent Possibility of these states. If I think of myself as in dreamless sleep, or in the sleep of death, and believe that I, or in other words my mind, is or will be existing through these states, though not in conscious feeling, the most scrupulous examination of my belief will not detect in it any fact actually believed, except that my capability of feeling is not, in that interval, permanently destroyed, and is suspended only because it does not meet with the combination of conditions which would call it into action: the moment it did meet with that combination it would revive, and remains, therefore, a Permanent Possibility. Thus far, there seems no hindrance to our regarding Mind as nothing but the series of our sensations (to which must now be added our internal feelings), as they actually occur, with the addition of infinite possibilities of feeling requiring for their actual realization conditions which may or may not take place, but which as possibilities are always in existence, and many of them present.

In order to [ensure] the further understanding of the bearings of this theory of the Ego, it is advisable to consider it in its relation to three questions, which may very naturally be asked with reference to it, and which often have been asked, and sometimes answered very erroneously. If the theory is correct, and my mind is but a series of feelings, or, as it has been called, a thread of consciousness, however supplemented by believed Possibilities of consciousness which are not, though they might be, realized; if this is all that Mind, or Myself, amounts to, what evidence have I (it is asked) of the existence of my fellow creatures? What evidence of a hyperphysical world, or, in one word, of God? and, lastly, what evidence of immortality?

Dr Reid unhesitatingly answers, None. If the doctrine is true, I am alone in the universe.[1]

I hold this to be one of Reid's most palpable mistakes. Whatever evidence to each of the three points there is on the ordinary theory, exactly that same evidence is there on this.

In the first place, as to my fellow creatures. Reid seems to have imagined that if I myself am only a series of feelings, the proposition that I have any fellow creatures, or that there are any Selves except mine, is but words without a meaning. But this is a misapprehension. All that I am compelled to admit, if I receive this theory, is that other people's Selves also are but series of feelings, like my own. Though my Mind, as I am capable of conceiving it, be nothing but the succession of my feelings, and though Mind itself may be merely a possibility of feelings, there is nothing in that doctrine to prevent my conceiving, and believing, that there are other successions of feelings besides those of which I am conscious, and that these are as real as my own. The belief is completely consistent with the metaphysical theory. Let us now see whether the theory takes away the grounds of it.

What are those grounds? By what evidence do I know, or by what considerations am I led to believe, that there exist other sentient creatures; that the walking and speaking figures which I see and hear, have sensations and thoughts, or in other

---

[1] Mill refers to the Scottish philosopher Thomas Reid, author of *Inquiry into the Human Mind on the Principles of Common Sense* [1764].

words, possess Minds? The most strenuous Intuitionist does not include this among the things that I know by direct intuition. I conclude it from certain things, which my experience of my own states of feeling proves to me to be marks of it. These marks are of two kinds, antecedent and subsequent; the previous conditions requisite for feeling, and the effects or consequences of it. I conclude that other human beings have feelings like me, because, first, they have bodies like me, which I know, in my own case, to be the antecedent condition of feelings; and because, secondly, they exhibit the acts, and other outward signs, which in my own case I know by experience to be caused by feelings. I am conscious in myself of a series of facts connected by a uniform sequence, of which the beginning is modifications of my body, the middle is feelings, the end is outward demeanour. In the case of other human beings I have the evidence of my senses for the first and last links of the series, but not for the intermediate link. I find, however, that the sequence between the first and last is as regular and constant in those other cases as it is in mine. In my own case I know that the first link produces the last through the intermediate link, and could not produce it without. Experience, therefore, obliges me to conclude that there must be an intermediate link; which must either be the same in others as in myself, or a different one: I must either believe them to be alive, or to be automatons: and by believing them to be alive, that is, by supposing the link to be of the same nature as in the case of which I have experience, and which is in all other respects similar, I bring other human beings, as phenomena, under the same generalizations which I know by experience to be the true theory of my own existence. And in doing so I conform to the legitimate rules of experimental enquiry. The process is exactly parallel to that by which Newton proved that the force which keeps the planets in their orbits is identical with that by which an apple falls to the ground. It was not incumbent on Newton to prove the impossibility of its being any other force; he was thought to have made out his point when he had simply shown that no other force need be supposed. We know the existence of other beings by generalization from the knowledge of our own: the generalization merely postulates that what experience shows to be a mark of the existence of something within the sphere of our consciousness may be concluded to be a mark of the same thing beyond that sphere.

This logical process loses none of its legitimacy on the supposition that neither Mind nor Matter is anything but a permanent possibility of feeling. Whatever sensation I have, I at once refer it to one of the permanent groups of possibilities of sensation which I call material objects. But among these groups I find there is one (my own body) which is not only composed, like the rest, of a mixed multitude of sensations and possibilities of sensation, but is also connected, in a peculiar manner, with all my sensations. Not only is this special group always present as an antecedent condition of every sensation I have, but the other groups are only enabled to convert their respective possibilities of sensation into actual sensations, by means of some previous change in that particular one. I look about me, and though there is only one group (or body) which is connected with all my sensations in this peculiar manner, I observe that there is a great multitude of other bodies, closely resembling in their sensible properties (in the sensations composing them as groups) this particular one, but whose modifications do not call up, as those of my own body do, a world of sensations in my consciousness. Since they do not do so in my consciousness, I infer that they do it out of my consciousness, and that to each of them belongs a world of consciousness of its own, to which it stands in the same relation in which what I call my own body stands to mine. And having made this generalization, I find that all other facts within my reach accord with it. Each of these bodies exhibits to my senses a set of phenomena (composed of acts and other manifestations) such as I know, in my own case, to be effects of consciousness, and such as might be looked for if each of the bodies has really in connection with it a world of consciousness. All this is as good and genuine an inductive process on the theory we are discussing, as it is on the common theory. Any objection to it in the one case would be an equal objection in the other. I have stated the postulate required by the one theory: the common theory is in need of the same. If I could not, from my personal knowledge of one succession of feelings, infer the existence of other successions of feelings, when manifested by the same outward signs, I could just as little, from my personal knowledge of a single spiritual substance, infer by generalization, when I find the same outward indications, the existence of other spiritual substances.

As the theory leaves the evidence of the existence of my fellow creatures exactly as it was before, so does it also with that of the existence of God. Supposing me to believe that the divine Mind is simply the series of the Divine thoughts and feelings prolonged through eternity, that would be, at any rate, believing God's existence to be as real as my own. And as for evidence, the argument of Paley's Natural Theology, or, for that matter, of his Evidences of Christianity would stand exactly where it does. The Design argument is drawn from the analogy of human experience.[1] From the relation which human works bear to human thoughts and feelings, it infers a corresponding relation between works, more or less similar but superhuman, and superhuman thoughts and feelings. If it proves these, nobody but a metaphysician needs care whether or not it proves a mysterious substratum for them. Again, the arguments for Revelation undertake to prove by testimony, that within the sphere of human experience works were done requiring a greater than human power, and words said requiring a greater than human wisdom. These positions, and the evidences of them, neither lose nor gain anything by our supposing that the wisdom only means wise thoughts and volitions, and that the power means thoughts and volitions followed by imposing phenomena.

As to immortality, it is precisely as easy to conceive that a succession of feelings, a thread of consciousness, may be prolonged to eternity, as that a spiritual substance for ever continues to exist: and any evidence which would prove the one, will prove the other. Metaphysical theologians may lose the *a priori* argument by which they have sometimes flattered themselves with having proved that a spiritual substance, by the essential constitution of its nature, *cannot* perish. But they had better drop this argument in any case. To do them justice, they seldom insist on it now...

The theory, therefore, which resolves Mind into a series of feelings, with a background of possibilities of feeling, can effectually withstand the most invidious of the arguments directed against it. But, groundless as are the extrinsic objections, the theory has intrinsic difficulties which we have not yet set forth, and which it seems to be beyond the power of metaphysical analysis to remove. Besides present feelings, and possibilities of present feeling, there is another class of phenomena to be included in an enumeration of the elements making up our conception of Mind. The thread of

---

[1] See below, Part VI, extract 6.

consciousness which composes the mind's phenomenal life, consists not only of present sensations, but likewise, in part, of memories and expectations. Now what are these? In themselves, they are present feelings, states of present consciousness, and in that respect not distinguished from sensations. They all, moreover, resemble some given sensations or feelings, of which we have previously had experience. But they are attended with the peculiarity, that each of them involves a belief in more than its own present existence. A sensation involves only this: but a remembrance of sensation, even if not referred to any particular date, involves the suggestion and belief that a sensation, of which it is a copy or representation, actually existed in the past: and an expectation involves the belief, more or less positive, that a sensation or other feeling to which it directly refers, will exist in the future. Nor can the phenomena involved in these two states of consciousness be adequately expressed, without saying that the belief they include is, that I myself formerly had, or that I myself, and no other, shall hereafter have, the sensations remembered or expected. The fact believed is that the sensations did actually form, or will hereafter form, part of the selfsame series of states, or thread of consciousness, of which the remembrance or expectation of those sensations is the part now present. If, therefore, we speak of the mind as a series of feelings, we are obliged to complete the statement by calling it a series of feelings which is aware of itself as past and future; and we are reduced to the alternative of believing that the Mind, or Ego, is something different from any series of feelings, or possibilities of them, or of accepting the paradox that something which *ex hypothesi* is but a series of feelings, can be aware of itself as a series.

The truth is that we are here face to face with that final inexplicability at which ... we inevitably arrive when we reach ultimate facts ... The real stumbling block is perhaps not in any theory of the fact, but in the fact itself. The true incomprehensibility perhaps is, that something which has ceased or is not yet in existence, can still be, in a manner, present: that a series of feelings, the infinitely greater part of which is past or future, can be gathered up, as it were, into a single present conception, accompanied by a belief of reality. I think by far the wisest thing we can do is to accept the inexplicable fact without any theory of how it takes place: and when we are obliged to speak of it in terms which assume a theory, to use them with a reservation as to their meaning.

9   The Hallmarks of Mental Phenomena: Franz Brentano, *Psychology from an Empirical Standpoint**

Despite attempts to evade or eliminate it, the Cartesian distinction between the mental and the physical realms continued to dominate the philosophy of mind for most of the eighteenth and nineteenth centuries. Although there were widely differing views on the 'ultimate reality' underlying the phenomena of our experience (see, for example, extract 7, above), it was largely taken for granted that, as the opening sentence of our next extract has it, 'the data of our

* Franz Brentano, *Psychology from an Empirical Standpoint* [*Psychologie vom empirischen Standpunkt*, 1874], extracts from Bk II, ch. 1. English trans. ed. Linda L. McAlister (London: Routledge, 1974).

consciousness make up a world which falls into two great classes, the class of mental and the class of physical phenomena'. Having articulated this standard distinction, the nineteenth-century German philosopher-psychologist Franz Brentano set himself the task of finding a clear criterion which would mark out that class of phenomena which we intuitively classify as 'mental'. Descartes (extract 4, above) had proposed that whatever is physical is spatial and extended, and whatever mental non-spatial and unextended; but Brentano is not satisfied with this, since he notes (without committing himself as to his own views) that various thinkers have suggested that some physical phenomena can manifest themselves without extension,[1] and conversely that some psychological phenomena can appear as having a definite location. Another criterion Brentano discusses, this time with approval, is that mental phenomena are objects of 'inner perception', or perceived in a way that is 'immediately evident'. This (though Brentano does not explicitly acknowledge it) is a conception that springs very much from Descartes's way of looking at the mind: the mind, in Descartes's definition, is a 'thinking thing', and a thought is defined as that 'which is in me in such a way that I am immediately aware of it'. Hence it is a criterion of a mental state, for Brentano, that it is a state of which there is direct inner awareness; each individual has an 'indubitable', 'infallible' or 'self-evident' grasp of the contents of his or her mind (for difficulties with this, see introduction to extract 10, below).

But the most interesting feature which Brentano isolates as marking out the class of the mental is 'Intentionality'. This has nothing specially to do with intending; rather, the term comes from the Latin *intendere*, to 'point to', and indicates the fact that mental states such as beliefs or desires *point to* or are *about* certain objects ('Intentionality' might more transparently be labelled 'Aboutness'). If I desire to go up the Eiffel Tower, or believe the Eiffel Tower is made of iron, then there is something which my belief and desire is *about*; my mental states have, one might say, a representational content. Notice, incidentally, that one can apparently have beliefs or desires even about non-existent objects – for example a desire to see the Abominable Snowman; hence Brentano suggests in the passage below that a mental or Intentional object does not have to be identified with 'a reality'. But the key point is that when we have beliefs or desires or make judgements, something is always presented as an *object* of those beliefs, desires and judgements – that which they are about; and, Brentano declares, 'no physical phenomenon manifests anything similar'. A physical system might reflect or mirror something outside itself (for example the surface of a lake might reflect the image of a tree or a mountain), but we could not say this reflection was 'about' the tree or the mountain; only minds have the unique property of being directed on intentional objects in this way. The consequences of this apparently simple point have seemed to many modern philosophers of mind to be far-reaching: Brentano has apparently succeeded in isolating a feature which is not only characteristic of the mental,[2] but which also seems resistant to explanation in purely physical terms.

All the data of our consciousness are divided into two great classes, the class of *physical* and the class of *mental* phenomena ... Every idea or presentation which we acquire either through sense perception or imagination is an example of a mental phenomenon. By 'presentation' I do not mean that which is presented, but rather the act of presentation. Thus, hearing a sound, seeing a coloured object, feeling warmth or cold, as well as similar states of imagination, are examples of what I mean by this term. I also mean by it the thinking of a general concept, provided such a thing does

---

[1] The examples Brentano refers to are (as he himself notes) not particularly clear or convincing; but the modern physicist could certainly instance phenomena at the micro level (such as electrons) which are clearly regarded as physical, even though the notion of spatial extension is not applicable to them.

[2] Though it is not entirely clear that *all* mental states have intentionality; might not a pain, for example, be identified merely by its 'phenomenal quality' (the way it feels), without being 'about' anything?

actually occur. Furthermore, every judgement, every recollection, every expectation, every inference, every conviction or opinion, every doubt, is a mental phenomenon. Also to be included under this term is every emotion: joy, sorrow, fear, hope, courage, despair, anger, love, hate, desire, act of will, intention, astonishment, admiration, contempt, etc.

Examples of physical phenomena, on the other hand, are a colour, a figure, a landscape which I see; a chord, which I hear; warmth, cold, odour, which I sense; as well as similar images, which appear to me in my imagination.

These examples may suffice to illustrate the differences between the two classes of phenomena.

Yet we still want to try to find a different and a more unified way of explaining mental phenomena. For this purpose we make use of a definition we used earlier, when we said that the term, 'mental phenomena' applies to presentations, as well as all the phenomena which are based on presentations. It is hardly necessary to mention again that by 'presentation' we do not mean that which is presented, but rather the presenting of it. This act of presentation forms the foundation not merely of the act of judging, but also of desiring and of every other mental act. Nothing can be judged, desired, hoped or feared unless one has a presentation of that thing. Thus the definition given includes all the examples of mental phenomena which we listed above, and in general all the phenomena belonging to this domain...

Yet it may still be the case that with respect to some kinds of sensory pleasure and pain feelings, someone may really be of the opinion that there are not presentations involved, even of sense. At least we cannot deny that there is a certain temptation to do this. This is true, for example, with regard to feelings which are present when one is cut or burned. When someone is cut he has no perception of touch, and someone who is burned has no feeling of warmth, but in both cases there is only the feeling of pain.

Nevertheless there is no doubt that even here the feeling is based upon a presentation. In cases such as this we always have a presentation of a definite spatial location, which we usually characterize in relation to some visible and touchable parts of our body. We say that our foot or our hand hurts, or that this or that part of the body is in pain. Those who consider such a spatial presentation something originally given by the neural stimulation itself cannot deny that a presentation is the basis of this feeling. But others cannot avoid this assumption either. For there is in us not only the idea of a definite spatial location, but also of a particular sensory quality, analogous to colour, sound, and other so-called sensory qualities, which is a physical phenomenon and which must be clearly distinguished from the accompanying feeling. If we hear a pleasing and mild sound or a shrill one, a harmonious chord or dissonance, it would not occur to anyone to identify the sound with the accompanying feeling of pleasure or pain. But then in cases where a feeling of pain or pleasure is aroused by a cut, a burn, or a tickle, we must distinguish in the same way between a physical phenomenon, which appears as the object of external perception, and the mental phenomenon of feeling, which accompanies its appearance, even though in this case the superficial observer is rather inclined to confuse them.

The principal basis for this misconception is probably the following. It is well known that our perceptions are mediated by the so-called afferent nerves. In the past people thought that certain nerves served as conductors of each kind of sensory qualities, such as colour, sound, etc. Recently, however, physiologists have been more and more inclined to take the opposite point of view. And they teach almost universally that the nerves for tactile sensations, if stimulated in a certain way, produce sensations of warmth and cold in us, and if stimulated in another way, produce in us so-called pleasure and pain. In reality, however, something similar is true for all the nerves, in so far as a sensory phenomenon of the kind just mentioned can be produced in us by every nerve. In the presence of very strong stimuli, all nerves produce painful phenomena, which cannot be distinguished from one another. When a nerve transmits different kinds of sensations, it often happens that it transmits several at the same time. Looking into an electric light, for example, produces simultaneously a 'beautiful', i.e. pleasant, colour phenomenon and a phenomenon of another sort which is painful. The nerves of the tactile sense often simultaneously transmit a so-called sensation of pain or pleasure. Now we notice that when several sensory phenomena appear at the same time, they are not infrequently regarded as *one*. This has been demonstrated in a striking manner in regard to the sensations of smell and taste. It is well established that almost all the differences usually considered differences in taste are, in fact, only differences in concomitant olfactory phenomena. Something similar occurs when we eat food cold or warm; we often think it tastes different while in reality only the temperature sensations differ. It is not surprising, then, if we do not always distinguish precisely between a phenomenon which is a temperature sensation and another which is a tactile sensation. Perhaps we would not even distinguish them at all if they did not ordinarily appear independently of one another. If we now look at the sensations of feeling, we find on the contrary that their phenomena are usually linked with another sort of sensation, and when the excitation is very strong these other sensations sink into insignificance beside them. Thus the fact that a given individual has been mistaken about the appearance of a particular class of sensory qualities, and has believed that he has had one single sensation instead of two, is very easily explained. Since the intervening presentation was accompanied by a relatively very strong feeling, incomparably stronger than the one which followed upon the first kind of quality, the person considered this mental phenomenon as the only new thing he has experienced. In addition, if the first kind of quality disappeared completely, then he would believe that he possessed only a feeling, without any underlying presentation of a physical phenomenon.

A further basis for this illusion is the fact that the quality which precedes the feeling, and the feeling itself, do not have two distinct names. The physical phenomenon which appears along with the feeling of pain is also called pain. Indeed, we do not say that we sense this or that phenomenon in the foot with pain; we say that we feel pain in the foot. This is an equivocation such as, indeed, we often find when different things are closely related to one another. We call the body healthy, and in reference to it, we say that the air, the food, the colour of the face, etc., are healthy, but obviously in another sense. In our case, a physical phenomenon itself is called pleasure or pain, after the feeling of pleasure or pain which accompanies the appearance of the physical phenomenon, and there, too, in a modified sense of the words. It is as if we would say of a harmonious chord that it is a pleasure because we experience pleasure when we hear it, or, too, that the loss of a friend is a great sorrow to us. Experience shows that equivocation is one of the main obstacles to recognizing distinctions. And it must necessarily be the largest obstacle here, where there is an inherent danger of confusion, and perhaps the extension of the term was itself the result of this confusion. Thus many psychologists were deceived by this equivocation, and this error fostered further errors. Some came to the false conclusion that the sensing subject must be present at the spot in the injured limb in which a painful phenomenon is located in perception. Then, since they identified the phenomenon with the accompanying pain sensation, they regarded this phenomenon as a mental, rather than a physical, phenomenon. It is precisely for this reason that they thought that its perception in the limb was an inner, and consequently evident and infallible perception. Their view is contradicted by the fact that the same phenomena often appear the same way after the amputation of the limb. For this reason others argued, in a rather sceptical manner, against the self-evidence of inner perception. The difficulty disappears if we distinguish between pain in the sense in which the term describes the apparent condition of a part of our body, and the feeling of pain which is connected with the concomitant sensation. Keeping this in mind, we shall no longer be inclined to assert that there is no presentation at the basis of the feeling of sensory pain which is experienced when one is injured.

Accordingly, we may consider the following definition of mental phenomena as indubitably correct: they are either presentations or they are based on presentations in the sense described above. Such a definition offers a second, more simple definition of this concept. This explanation, of course, is not completely unified, because it separates mental phenomena into two groups.

People have tried to formulate a completely unified definition which distinguishes all mental phenomena from physical phenomena by means of negation. All physical phenomena, it is said, have extension and spatial location, whether they are phenomena of vision or of some other sense, or products of the imagination, which presents similar objects to us. The opposite, however, is true of mental phenomena; thinking, willing, and so on appear without extension and without spatial location.

According to this view, it would be possible for us to characterize physical phenomena easily and exactly in contrast to mental phenomena by saying that they are those which appear extended and localized in space. Mental phenomena would then be definable with equal exactness as those phenomena which do not have extension or spatial location. Descartes and Spinoza could be cited in support of such a distinction...

But even on this point there is no unanimity among the psychologists, and we hear it denied that extension and the lack of extension are characteristics which distinguish physical and mental phenomena.

Many declare that the definition is false because not only mental phenomena, but also many physical phenomena, appear to be without extension. A large number of not unimportant psychologists, for example, teach that the phenomena of some, or even of all of our senses, originally appear apart from all extension and spatial location. In particular, this view is quite generally held with respect to sounds and olfactory phenomena... Indeed, it seems that the phenomena revealed by the external senses, especially sight and the sense of touch, are all spatially extended. The reason for this, it is said, is that we connect them with spatial presentations that are gradually developed on the basis of earlier experiences. They are originally without spatial location, and we subsequently localize them. If this were the only way in which physical phenomena attain spatial location, we could obviously no longer separate the two areas by reference to this property. In fact, mental phenomena are also localized by us in this way, as, for example, when we locate a phenomenon of anger in the irritated lion, and our own thoughts in the space we occupy.

This is one way in which the above definition has been criticized...Others will reject the definition for contrary reasons. It is not so much the assertion that all physical phenomena appear extended that provokes them, but rather the assertion that all mental phenomena lack extension. According to them, certain mental phenomena also appear to be extended. Aristotle seems to have been of this opinion when, in the first chapter of his treatise on sensation and the object of sense [*De Sensu*] he considers it immediately evident, without any prior proof, that sense perception is the act of a bodily organ. Modern psychologists and physiologists sometimes express themselves in the same way regarding certain affects. They speak of feelings of pleasure and pain which appear in external organs, sometimes even after the amputation of the limb; and yet feeling, like perception, is a mental phenomenon. Some authors even maintain that sensory appetites appear localized. This view is shared by the poet when he speaks, not, to be sure, of thought, but of rapture and longing which suffuse the heart and all parts of the body.

Thus we see that the distinction under discussion is disputed from the point of view of both physical and mental phenomena. Perhaps both of these objections are equally unjustified. At any rate, another definition common to all mental phenomena is still desirable. Whether certain mental and physical phenomena appear extended or not, the controversy proves that the criterion given for a clear separation is not adequate. Furthermore, this criterion gives us only a negative definition of mental phenomena.

What positive criterion shall we now be able to advance? Or is there, perhaps, no positive definition at all which holds true of all mental phenomena generally?... Psychologists in earlier times have already directed attention to a particular affinity and analogy which exists among all mental phenomena, and which physical phenomena do not share in.

Every mental phenomenon is characterized by what the scholastics of the Middle Ages called the intentional (or mental) *in-existence*[1] of an object and what we might call, though not wholly unambiguously, the reference to a content, a *direction towards an object* (which is not to be understood here as meaning a thing), or an immanent objectivity. Each mental phenomenon includes something as object within itself, although they do not all do so in the same way. In presentation something is presented, in judgement something is affirmed or denied, in love loved, in hate hated, in desire desired, and so on.

This intentional in-existence is characteristic exclusively of mental phenomena. No physical phenomenon exhibits anything like it. We can, therefore, define mental phenomena by saying that they are those phenomena which contain an object intentionally within themselves...

Another characteristic which all mental phenomena have in common is the fact that they are perceived only in inner consciousness, while in the case of physical phenomena only outer external perception is possible...

---

[1] That is to say, existence-as-an-object-of-thought.

It could be argued that such a definition is not very meaningful. In fact, it seems much more natural to define the act according to the object, and therefore to state that inner perception, in contrast to every other kind, is the perception of mental phenomena. However, despite the fact that it has a special object, inner perception possesses another distinguishing characteristic: its immediate, infallible self-evidence. Of all the types of knowledge of the objects of experience, inner perception alone possesses this characteristic. Consequently, when we say that mental phenomena are those which are apprehended by means of inner perception, we say that their perception is immediately evident.

Moreover, inner perception is not merely the only kind of perception which is immediately evident; it is really the only perception in the strict sense of the word... The phenomena of so-called external perception cannot be proved true and real, even by means of indirect demonstration. For this reason, anyone who in good faith has taken them for what they seem to be is being misled by the manner in which the phenomena are connected. Therefore, strictly speaking, so-called external perception is not perception. Mental phenomena, therefore, may be described as the only phenomena of which perception in the strict sense of the word is possible.

This definition, too, is an adequate characterization of mental phenomena. That is not to say that all mental phenomena are internally perceivable by all men, and so all those which someone cannot perceive are to be included by him among physical phenomena. On the contrary... it is obvious that no mental phenomenon is perceived by more than one individual. At the same time, however... every type of mental phenomenon is present in every fully developed mental life. For this reason, the reference to the phenomena which constitute the realm of inner perception serves our purpose satisfactorily...

Let us, in conclusion, summarize the results of the discussion about the difference between physical and mental phenomena. First of all, we illustrated the specific nature of the two classes by means of *example*. We then defined mental phenomena as *presentations* or as phenomena which are *based upon presentation*; all the other phenomena being physical phenomena. Next we spoke of *extension*, which psychologists have asserted to be the specific characteristic of all physical phenomena; all mental phenomena are supposed to be unextended. This assertion ran into contradictions, however, which can only be clarified by later investigations. All that can be determined now is that all mental phenomena really appear to be unextended. Further we found that the *intentional in-existence*, the reference to something as an object, is a distinguishing characteristic of all mental phenomena. No physical phenomenon exhibits anything similar. We went on to define mental phenomena as the exclusive *object of inner perception*; they alone, therefore, are perceived with immediate evidence. Indeed, in the strict sense of the word, they alone are perceived...

10 The Myth of the 'Ghost in the Machine': Gilbert Ryle, *The Concept of Mind**

One of the features which Brentano, following Descartes, identifies as characteristic of the mental realm is that we have immediate indubitable access to it (see previous extract). In our next extract, from the twentieth-century British philosopher Gilbert Ryle, this assumption, along with many other elements in the Cartesian framework, is systematically challenged. Ryle attacks the whole notion of a split between the public, observable world of matter, and the 'private' inner theatre of the mind. Further, he argues that talking of the mind as a separate realm existing alongside the bodily realm is a confusion – what he calls a 'category-mistake'. Mental events and properties are not separate events over and above bodily events and properties, any more than a university is a separate item existing alongside the libraries, laboratories, administration, students, and so on, that make it up. To say that someone is in a mental state is, for Ryle, to say how he is disposed to behave and react in certain circumstances, not a statement about private, inaccessible occurrences going on in the subjective theatre of the mind.

Though Ryle was a little wary of the label, his approach to the mind may be called a kind of 'behaviourism', since it holds that mental language can be analysed in terms of dispositions to behave in various ways. It is not clear, however, that this approach can cope successfully with what is happening when, for example, someone sits in an armchair for half an hour, just *thinking* intensely about a problem. None the less, the anti-Cartesian thrust of Ryle's work has met with wide support; moreover the influential work of Ludwig Wittgenstein has shown that beliefs, desires, and mental terms in general must be applied on the basis of public rules of language, and hence that the mind cannot be construed as an entirely private arena accessible only to the subject (see introduction to extract 8, above).

The official doctrine

There is a doctrine about the nature and place of minds which is so prevalent among theorists and even among laymen that it deserves to be described as the official theory. Most philosophers, psychologists and religious teachers subscribe, with minor reservations, to its main articles and, although they admit certain theoretical difficulties in it, they tend to assume that these can be overcome without serious modifications being made to the architecture of the theory. It will be argued here that the central principles of the doctrine are unsound and conflict with the whole body of what we know about minds when we are not speculating about them.

The official doctrine, which hails chiefly from Descartes, is something like this. With the doubtful exceptions of idiots and infants in arms every human being has both a body and a mind. Some would prefer to say that every human being is both a body and a mind. His body and his mind are ordinarily harnessed together, but after the death of the body his mind may continue to exist and function.

Human bodies are in space and are subject to the mechanical laws which govern all other bodies in space. Bodily processes and states can be inspected by external observers. So a man's bodily life is as much a public affair as are the lives of animals and reptiles and even as the careers of trees, crystals and planets.

* Gilbert Ryle, *The Concept of Mind* (London: Hutchinson, 1949), extracts from chs 1 and 7.

But minds are not in space, nor are their operations subject to mechanical laws. The workings of one mind are not witnessable by other observers; its career is private. Only I can take direct cognizance of the states and processes of my own mind. A person therefore lives through two collateral histories, one consisting of what happens in and to his body, the other consisting of what happens in and to his mind. The first is public, the second private. The events in the first history are events in the physical world, those in the second are events in the mental world.

It has been disputed whether a person does or can directly monitor all or only some of the episodes of his own private history; but, according to the official doctrine, of at least some of these episodes he has direct and unchallengeable cognizance. In consciousness, self-consciousness and introspection he is directly and authentically apprised of the present states and operations of his mind. He may have great or small uncertainties about concurrent and adjacent episodes in the physical world, but he can have none about at least part of what is momentarily occupying his mind.

It is customary to express the bifurcation of his two lives and of his two worlds by saying that the things and events which belong to the physical world, including his own body, are external, while the workings of his own mind are internal. This antithesis of outer and inner is of course meant to be construed as a metaphor, since minds, not being in space, could not be described as being spatially inside anything else, or as having things going on spatially inside themselves. But relapses from this good intention are common and theorists are found speculating how stimuli, the physical sources of which are yards or miles outside a person's skin, can generate mental responses inside his skull, or how decisions framed inside his cranium can set going movements of his extremities.

Even when 'inner' and 'outer' are construed as metaphors, the problem how a person's mind and body influence one another is notoriously charged with theoretical difficulties. What the mind wills, the legs, arms and the tongue execute; what affects the ear and the eye has something to do with what the mind perceives; grimaces and smiles betray the mind's moods and bodily castigations lead, it is hoped, to moral improvement. But the actual transactions between the episodes of the private history and those of the public history remain mysterious, since by definition they can belong to neither series. They could not be reported among the happenings described in a person's autobiography of his inner life, but nor could they be reported among those described in someone else's biography of that person's overt career. They can be inspected neither by introspection nor by laboratory experiment. They are theoretical shuttlecocks which are forever being bandied from the physiologist back to the psychologist and from the psychologist back to the physiologist.

Underlying this partly metaphorical representation of the bifurcation of a person's two lives there is a seemingly more profound and philosophical assumption. It is assumed that there are two different kinds of existence or status. What exists or happens may have the status of physical existence or it may have the status of mental existence. Somewhat as the faces of coins are either heads or tails, or somewhat as living creatures are either male or female, so, it is supposed, some existing is physical existing, other existing is mental existing. It is a necessary feature of what has physical existence that it is in space and time; its is a necessary feature of what has mental existence that it is in time but not in space. What has physical existence is composed of matter, or else is a function of matter; what has mental existence consists of consciousness, or else is a function of consciousness.

There is thus a polar opposition between mind and matter, an opposition which is often brought out as follows. Material objects are situated in a common field, known as 'space', and what happens to one body in one part of space is mechanically connected with what happens to other bodies in other parts of space. But mental happenings occur in insulated fields, known as 'minds', and there is, apart maybe from telepathy, no direct causal connection between what happens in one mind and what happens in another. Only through the medium of the public, physical world can the mind of one person make a difference to the mind of another. The mind is its own place and in his inner life each of us lives the life of a ghostly Robinson Crusoe. People can see, hear, and jolt one another's bodies, but they are irremediably blind and deaf to the workings of one another's minds and inoperative upon them...

The absurdity of the official doctrine

Such in outline is the official theory. I shall often speak of it, with deliberate abusiveness, as 'the dogma of the Ghost in the Machine'. I hope to prove that it is entirely false, and false not in detail but in principle. It is not merely an assemblage of particular mistakes. It is one big mistake and a mistake of a special kind. It is, namely, a category-mistake. It represents the facts of mental life as if they belonged to one logical type or category (or range of types or categories), when they actually belong to another. The dogma is therefore a philosopher's myth. In attempting to explode the myth I shall probably be taken to be denying well-known facts about the mental life of human beings, and my plea that I aim at doing nothing more than rectify the logic of mental-conduct concepts will probably be disallowed as mere subterfuge.

I must first indicate what is meant by the phrase 'category-mistake'. This I do in a series of illustrations.

A foreigner visiting Oxford or Cambridge for the first time is shown a number of colleges, libraries, playing fields, museums, scientific departments and administrative offices. He then asks 'But where is the University? I have seen where the members of the Colleges live, where the Registrar works, where the scientists experiment and the rest. But I have not yet seen the University in which reside and work the members of your University.' It has then to be explained to him that the University is not another collateral institution, some ulterior counterpart to the colleges, laboratories and offices which he has seen. The University is just the way in which all that he has already seen is organized. When they are seen and when their coordination is understood, the University has been seen. His mistake lay in his innocent assumption that it was correct to speak of Christ Church, the Bodleian Library, the Ashmolean Museum *and* the University, to speak, that is, as if 'the University' stood for an extra member of the class of which these other units are members. He was mistakenly allocating the University to the same category as that to which the other institutions belong.

The same mistake would be made by a child witnessing the march-past of a division who, having had pointed out to him such and such battalions, batteries, squadrons, etc., asked when the division was going to appear. He would be supposing that a division was a counterpart to the units already seen, partly similar to them and partly unlike them. He would be shown his mistake by being told that in watching the battalions, batteries and squadrons marching past he had been watching the division marching past. The march-past was not a parade of battalions, batteries, squadrons *and* a division; it was a parade of the battalions, batteries and squadrons *of* a division...

My destructive purpose is to show that a family of radical category mistakes is the source of the double-life theory. The representation of a person as a ghost mysteriously ensconced in a machine derives from this argument. Because, as is true, a person's thinking, feeling and purposive doing cannot be described solely in the idioms of physics, chemistry and physiology, therefore they must be described in counterpart idioms. As the human body is a complex organized unit, so the human mind must be another complex organized unit, though one made of a different sort of stuff and with a different sort of structure. Or, again, as the human body, like any other parcel of matter, is a field of causes and effects, so the mind must be another field of causes and effects, though not (Heaven be praised) mechanical causes and effects.

Origin of the category-mistake

One of the chief intellectual origins of what I have yet to prove to be the Cartesian category-mistake seems to be this. When Galileo showed that his methods of scientific discovery were competent to prove a mechanical theory which should cover every occupant of space, Descartes found in himself two conflicting motives. As a man of scientific genius he could not but endorse the claims of mechanics, yet as a religious and moral man he could not accept, as Hobbes accepted, the discouraging rider to those aims, namely that human nature differs only in degree of complexity from clockwork. The mental could not be just a variety of the mechanical.

He and subsequent philosophers naturally but erroneously availed themselves of the following escape route. Since mental-conduct words are not to be construed as signifying the occurrence of mechanical processes, they must be construed as signifying the occurrence of non-mechanical processes; since mechanical laws explain movements in space as the effects of other movements in space, other laws must explain some of the non-spatial workings of minds as the effects of other non-spatial workings of minds. The difference between the human behaviours which we describe as intelligent and those which we describe as unintelligent must be a difference in their causation; so, while some movements of human tongues and limbs are the effects of mechanical causes, others must be the effects of mental causes, i.e. some issue from movements of particles of matter, others from workings of the mind. The differences between the physical and the mental were thus represented as differences inside the common framework of the categories of 'thing', 'stuff', 'attribute', 'state', 'process', 'change', 'cause' and 'effect'. Minds are things, but different sorts of causes and effects from bodily movements. And so on. Somewhat as the foreigner expected the University to be an extra edifice, rather like a college but also considerably different, so the repudiators of mechanism represented minds as extra centres of causal processes, rather like machines but also considerably different from them. Their theory was a para-mechanical hypothesis.

That this assumption was at the heart of the doctrine is shown by the fact that there was from the beginning felt to be a major theoretical difficulty in explaining how minds can influence and be influenced by bodies. How can a mental process, such as willing, cause spatial movements like the movements of the tongue? How can a physical change in the optic nerve have among its effects a mind's perception of a flash of light? ...

When two terms belong to the same category, it is proper to construct conjunctive propositions embodying them. Thus a purchaser may say that he bought a left-hand glove and a right-hand glove, but not that he bought a left-hand glove, a right-hand glove and a pair of gloves. 'She came home in a flood of tears and a sedan chair' is a well-known joke based on the absurdity of conjoining terms of different types. It would have been equally ridiculous to construct the disjunction 'She came home either in a flood of tears or else in a sedan chair'. Now the dogma of the Ghost in the Machine does just this. It maintains that there exist both bodies and minds; that there occur physical processes and mental processes; that there are mechanical causes of corporeal movements and mental causes of corporeal movements. I shall argue that these and other analogous conjunctions are absurd; but it must be noticed, the argument will not show that either of the illegitimately conjoined propositions is absurd in itself. I am not, for example, denying that there occur mental processes. Doing long division is a mental process and so is making a joke. But I am saying that the phrase 'there occur mental processes' does not mean the same sort of thing as 'there occur physical processes', and, therefore, that it makes no sense to conjoin or disjoin the two.

If my argument is successful, there will follow some interesting consequences. First, the hallowed contrast between Mind and Matter will be dissipated, but dissipated not by either the equally hallowed absorptions of Mind by Matter, or of Matter by Mind, but in quite a different way. For the seeming contrast of the two will be shown to be as illegitimate as would be the contrast of 'she came home in a flood of tears' and 'she came home in a sedan chair'. The belief that there is a polar opposition between Mind and Matter is the belief that they are terms of the same logical type.

It will also follow that both Idealism and Materialism are answers to an improper question. The 'reduction' of the material world to mental states and processes, as well as the 'reduction' of mental states and processes to physical states and processes, presuppose the legitimacy of the disjunction 'Either there exist minds or there exist bodies (but not both)'. It would be like saying, 'Either she bought a left-hand and a right-hand glove or she bought a pair of gloves (but not both)'.

It is perfectly proper to say, in one logical tone of voice, that there exist minds and to say, in another logical tone of voice, that there exist bodies. But these expressions do not indicate two different species of existence, for 'existence' is not a generic word like 'coloured' or 'sexed'. They indicate two different senses of 'exist', somewhat as 'rising' has different senses in 'the tide is rising', 'hopes are rising', and 'the average age of death is rising'. A man would be thought to be making a poor joke who said that three things are now rising, namely the tide, hopes and the average age of death. It would be just as good or bad a joke to say that there exist prime numbers and Wednesdays and public opinions and navies, or that there exist both minds and bodies ...

One of the central motives of this book is to show that 'mental' does not denote a status, such that a person can sensibly ask of a given thing or event whether it is mental or physical, 'in the mind' or 'in the outside world'. To talk of a person's mind is not to talk of a repository which is permitted to house objects that something called 'the physical world' is forbidden to house; it is to talk of the person's abilities, liabilities and inclinations to do and undergo certain sorts of things, and of the doing and undergoing of these things in the ordinary world...

11   Mental States as Functional States: Hilary Putnam, *Psychological Predicates**

In the aftermath of Ryle and Wittgenstein (see introduction to preceding extract), many philosophers emphasized the importance of outward and observable behaviour in understanding the meaning of mental terms. Others, wishing to retain the idea of mental events as internal causes of outward behaviour, but at the same time attracted by the explanatory success of modern physical science, proposed a radically materialist solution: mental states were simply physical states (for example electrical or chemical states) of the brain or of the nervous system.

In our penultimate extract, the American philosopher Hilary Putnam begins by noting that many common criticisms of such 'mind–brain identity theories' are ineffective. For example, critics had objected that I can know I am in pain without knowing anything about my brain states, which would be impossible if the two concepts (pain state and brain state) were the same. But Putnam replies that those who propose mental states are identical with brain states are not proposing a conceptual identity – they are not saying that being in pain is *synonymous* with being in a certain brain state; rather, the proposed identity is an 'empirical reduction',

rather like the identification of heat with mean molecular kinetic energy.[1]

Nevertheless, Putnam goes on (in section 3) to raise a devastating criticism of mind–brain identity theories: it is very 'ambitious' – in other words very implausible – to suppose that a given mental state such as pain always has the selfsame neuro-physical realization across different species, whose physical structure and biology may be very different. Why should pain in an octopus, or in an alien from another galaxy, have exactly the same electrochemistry as human pain?

Instead of a physicalist account of mental states, Putnam therefore proposes a *functionalist* account. In section 2, this is developed rather technically, using the idea of a machine, or 'Probabilistic Automaton', whose states are specified by a 'Machine Table'. But the basic idea is simple: the functional states are *organizational states*, identified by their causal links to one another and to sensory inputs and behavioural outputs. Keeping things at this formal, organizational level,[2] and abstracting from the physical details, enables Putnam to define states like pain in a way that allows they may be realized in many

---

* Hilary Putnam, 'Psychological Predicates', in W. H. Capitan and D. D. Merrill (eds), *Art, Mind, and Religion* (Pittsburgh: University of Pittsburgh Press, 1967); repr. as 'The Nature of Mental States', in Putnam's *Mind, Language and Reality: Philosophical Papers*, vol. ii (Cambridge: Cambridge University Press, 1975); with omissions.

[1] For a different but related view of identity statements of this kind, see the extract from Kripke, in Part III, extract 12, above.

[2] The focus on the *formal*, in contrast to the *material*, aspects of the mental is in certain ways reminiscent of the much earlier approach of Aristotle, albeit Aristotle's 'hylomorphism' lays equal stress on both components (compare extract 2, above).

different biological structures,[1] provided those structures play the appropriate causal role. For example, when the sensory inputs signal damage to the body, the 'inputs... have a high disvalue in the Machine's preference function'; in other words the 'Machine' (which may be a human, or an animal) is organized in such a way that it attaches great importance to avoiding the noxious stimulus.

One advantage of such functionalism over simple behaviourism, mentioned by Putnam in section 4, is that behaviourists had found it very difficult to specify the required bodily disposition in terms of which mental states are supposedly defined. Is pain, for example, simply a disposition to groan? Clearly not, since groaning is but one of an indefinite range of possible pain manifestations; and in taking account of this the behaviourist risks ending up with something circular – X's pain is 'a disposition of X to behave as if X were in pain'! The functionalist, by contrast, *can* (argues Putnam) specify the relevant

functional state in a non-circular way, without using the notion of pain: it is 'the state of receiving sensory inputs which play a certain role in the... organization of the organism'. This role, Putnam goes on to explain, can be explicated via the fact that the input organs have the function of detecting damage, and 'represent a condition that the organism assigns a high disvalue to'.

Putnam ends our extract by arguing that his functionalism promises to be both a scientifically and a conceptually fruitful approach to mental phenomena; and it has certainly been very influential among both scientific researchers and philosophers. Nevertheless, critics have suggested that his theory does not fully capture the essence of conscious mental experience: could not an organism exhibit all the organizational or functional properties mentioned by Putnam, yet without having the distinctive subjective experience of pain? We shall see this crucial objection developed later on, in our final extract for this Part of the volume.

The typical concerns of the Philosopher of Mind might be represented by three questions: (1) How do we know that other people have pains? (2) Are pains brain states? (3) What is the analysis of the concept *pain*? I do not wish to discuss questions (1) and (3) in this paper. I shall say something about question (2).

1 Identity questions

...Many philosophers believe that the statement 'pain is a brain state' violates some rules or norms of English. But the arguments offered are hardly convincing. For example, if the fact that I can know that I am in pain without knowing that I am in brain state S shows that pain cannot be brain state S, then, by exactly the same argument, the fact that I can know that the stove is hot without knowing that the mean molecular kinetic energy is high (or even that molecules exist) shows that it is *false* that temperature is mean molecular kinetic energy, physics to the contrary. In fact, all that immediately follows from the fact that I can know that I am in pain without knowing that I am in brain state S is that the concept of pain is not the same concept as the concept of being in brain state S. But either pain, or the state of being in pain, or some pain, or some pain state, might still be brain state S. After all, the

---

[1] Or perhaps purely mechanical structures, or indeed any other suitably organized system. Indeed, so neutral is Putnam about how a system might be realized that his theory does not rule out the possibility that a mental state might be realized by 'a system consisting of a body and a "soul", if such things there be'. Functionalism (though clearly inspired by modern computer science) is thus not technically incompatible with dualism (see extract 4, above).

concept of temperature is not the same concept as the concept of mean molecular kinetic energy. But temperature is mean molecular kinetic energy.

Some philosophers maintain that both 'pain is a brain state' and 'pain states are brain states' are unintelligible. The answer is to explain to these philosophers, as well as we can, given the vagueness of all scientific methodology, what sorts of considerations lead one to make an empirical reduction (i.e., to say such things as 'water is H_2O', 'light is electro-magnetic radiation', 'temperature is mean molecular kinetic energy'). If, without giving reasons, he still maintains in the face of such examples that one cannot imagine parallel circumstances for the use of 'pains are brain states' (or, perhaps, 'pain states are brain states') one has grounds to regard him as perverse...

... [I]f we regard the 'change of meaning' issue as a pseudo-issue in this case, then how are we to discuss the question with which we started? 'Is pain a brain state?' The answer is to allow statements of the form 'pain is A' where 'pain' and 'A' are in no sense synonyms, and to see whether any such statement can be found which might be acceptable on empirical and methodological grounds. This is what we shall now proceed to do.

2 Is pain a brain state?

... Since I am discussing not what the concept of pain comes to, but what pain is, in a sense of 'is' which requires empirical theory-construction (or, at least, empirical speculation), I shall not apologize for advancing an empirical hypothesis. Indeed, my strategy will be to argue that pain is *not* a brain state, not on *a priori* grounds, but on the grounds that another hypothesis is more plausible. The detailed development and verification of my hypothesis would be just as Utopian a task as the detailed development and verification of the brain-state hypothesis. But the putting-forward, not of detailed and scientifically 'finished' hypotheses, but of schemata for hypotheses, has long been a function of philosophy. I shall, in short, argue that pain is not a brain state, in the sense of a physical-chemical state of the brain (or even the whole nervous system), but another *kind* of state entirely. I propose the hypothesis that pain, or the state of being in pain, is a functional state of a whole organism.

To explain this it is necessary to introduce some technical notions. In previous papers I have explained the notion of a *Turing Machine* and discussed the use of this notion as a model for an organism. The notion of a *Probabilistic Automaton* is defined similarly to a Turing Machine, except that the transitions between 'states' are allowed to be with various probabilities rather than being 'deterministic'. (Of course, a Turing Machine is simply a special kind of Probabilistic Automaton, one with transition probabilities 0, 1.) I shall assume the notion of a Probabilistic Automaton has been generalized to allow for 'sensory inputs' and 'motor outputs' – that is, the Machine Table specifies, for every possible combination of a 'state' and a complete set of 'sensory inputs', an 'instruction' which determines the probability of the next 'state', and also the probabilities of the 'motor outputs'...I shall also assume that the physical realization of the sense organs responsible for the various inputs, and of the motor organs, is specified, but that the 'states' and the 'inputs' themselves are, as usual, specified only 'implicitly' – i.e., by the set of transition probabilities given by the Machine Table.

Since an empirically given system can simultaneously be a 'physical realization' of many different Probabilistic Automata, I introduce the notion of a *Description* of a system. A Description of S where S is a system, is any true statement to the effect that S possesses distinct states $S_1, S_2, \ldots, S_n$ which are related to one another and to the motor outputs and sensory inputs by the transition probabilities given in such-and-such a Machine Table. The Machine Table mentioned in the Description will then be called the Functional Organization of S relative to that Description, and the S_i such that S is in state S_i at a given time will be called the Total State of S (at that time) relative to that Description. It should be noted that knowing the Total State of a system relative to a Description involves knowing a good deal about how the system is likely to 'behave', given various combinations of sensory inputs, but does *not* involve knowing the physical realization of the S_i as, e.g., physical-chemical states of the brain. The S_i, to repeat, are specified only *implicitly* by the Description – i.e., specified *only* by the set of transition probabilities given in the Machine Table.

The hypothesis that 'being in pain is a functional state of the organism' may now be spelled out more exactly as follows:

(1) All organisms capable of feeling pain are Probabilistic Automata.
(2) Every organism capable of feeling pain possesses at least one Description of a certain kind (i.e., being capable of feeling pain *is* possessing an appropriate kind of Functional Organization).
(3) No organism capable of feeling pain possesses a decomposition into parts which separately possess Descriptions of the kind referred to in (2).
(4) For every Description of the kind referred to in (2), there exists a subset of the sensory inputs such that an organism with that Description is in pain when and only when some of its sensory inputs are in that subset.

This hypothesis is admittedly vague, though surely no vaguer than the brain-state hypothesis in its present form. For example, one would like to know more about the kind of Functional Organization that an organism must have to be capable of feeling pain, and more about the marks that distinguish the subset of the sensory inputs referred to in (4). With respect to the first question, one can probably say that the Functional Organization must include something that resembles a 'preference function', or at least a preference partial ordering, and something that resembles an 'inductive logic' (i.e., the Machine must be able to 'learn from experience')...In addition, it seems natural to require that the Machine possess 'pain sensors', i.e., sensory organs which normally signal damage to the Machine's body, or dangerous temperatures, pressures, etc., which transmit a special subset of the inputs, the subset referred to in (4). Finally, and with respect to the second question, we would want to require at least that the inputs in the distinguished subset have a high disvalue on the Machine's preference function or ordering...The purpose of condition (3) is to rule out such 'organisms' (if they can count as such) as swarms of bees as single pain-feelers. The condition (1) is, obviously, redundant, and is only introduced for expository reasons. (It is, in fact, empty, since everything is a Probabilistic Automaton under *some* Description.)

I contend, in passing, that this hypothesis, in spite of its admitted vagueness, is far *less* vague than the 'physical-chemical state' hypothesis is today, and far more susceptible to investigation of both a mathematical and an empirical kind. Indeed, to investigate this hypothesis is just to attempt to produce 'mechanical' models of organisms – and isn't this, in a sense, just what psychology is about? The difficult step, of course, will be to pass from models of *specific* organisms to a *normal form* for the psychological description of organisms – for this is what is required to make (2) and (4) precise. But this too seems to be an inevitable part of the program of psychology.

I shall now compare the hypothesis just advanced with (*a*) the hypothesis that pain is a brain state, and (*b*) the hypothesis that pain is a behaviour disposition.

3 Functional state versus brain state

It may, perhaps, be asked if I am not somewhat unfair in taking the brain-state theorist to be talking about *physical-chemical* states of the brain. But (*a*) these are the only sorts of states ever mentioned by brain-state theorists. (*b*) The brain-state theorist usually mentions (with a certain pride, slightly reminiscent of the Village Atheist) the incompatibility of his hypothesis with all forms of dualism and mentalism. This is natural if physical-chemical states of the brain are what is at issue. However, functional states of whole systems are something quite different. In particular, the functional-state hypothesis is *not* incompatible with dualism! Although it goes without saying that the hypothesis is 'mechanistic' in its inspiration, it is a slightly remarkable fact that a system consisting of a body and a 'soul', if such things there be, can perfectly well be a Probabilistic Automaton...

Taking the brain-state hypothesis in this way, then, what reasons are there to prefer the functional-state hypothesis over the brain-state hypothesis? Consider what the brain-state theorist has to do to make good his claims. He has to specify a physical-chemical state such that *any* organism (not just a mammal) is in pain if and only if (*a*) it possesses a brain of a suitable physical-chemical structure; and (*b*) its brain is in that physical-chemical state. This means that the physical-chemical state in question must be a possible state of a mammalian brain, a reptilian brain, a mollusc's brain (octopuses are mollusca, and certainly feel pain), etc. At the same time, it must *not* be a possible (physically possible) state of the brain of any physically possible creature that cannot feel pain. Even if such a state can be found, it must be nomologically certain that it will also be a state of the brain of any extraterrestrial life that may be found that will be capable of feeling pain before we can even entertain the supposition that it may *be* pain.

It is not altogether impossible that such a state will be found. Even though octopus and mammal are examples of parallel (rather than sequential) evolution, for example, virtually identical structures (physically speaking) have evolved in the eye of the octopus and in the eye of the mammal, notwithstanding the fact that this organ has evolved from different kinds of cells in the two cases. Thus it is at least possible that parallel evolution, all over the universe, might *always* lead to *one and the same* physical 'correlate' of pain. But this is certainly an ambitious hypothesis.

Finally, the hypothesis becomes still more ambitious when we realize that the brain-state theorist is not just saying that *pain* is a brain state; he is, of course, concerned to maintain that *every* psychological state is a brain state. Thus if we can find even one psychological predicate which can clearly be applied to both a mammal and an octopus (say 'hungry'), but whose physical-chemical 'correlate' is different in the two cases, the brain-state theory has collapsed. It seems to me overwhelmingly probable that we can do this. Granted, in such a case the brain-state theorist can save himself by *ad hoc* assumptions (e.g., defining the disjunction of two states to be a single 'physical-chemical state'), but this does not have to be taken seriously.

Turning now to the considerations *for* the functional-state theory, let us begin with the fact that we identify organisms as in pain, or hungry, or angry, or in heat, etc., on the basis of their *behaviour*. But it is a truism that similarities in the behaviour of two systems are at least a reason to suspect similarities in the functional organization of the two systems, and a much *weaker* reason to suspect similarities in the actual physical details. Moreover, we expect the various psychological states – at least the basic ones, such as hunger, thirst, aggression, etc. – to have more or less similar 'transition probabilities' (within wide and ill-defined limits, to be sure) with each other and with behaviour in the case of different species, because this is an artefact of the way in which we identify these states. Thus, we would not count an animal as *thirsty* if its 'unsatiated' behaviour did not seem to be directed toward drinking and was not followed by 'satiation' for liquid. Thus any animal that we count as capable of these various states will at least *seem* to have a certain rough kind of functional organization. And, as already remarked, if the program of finding psychological laws that are not species-specific – i.e., of finding a normal form for psychological theories of different species – ever succeeds, then it will bring in its wake a delineation of the kind of functional organization that is necessary and sufficient for a given psycho-logical state, as well as a precise definition of the notion 'psychological state'. In contrast, the brain-state theorist has to hope for the eventual development of neuro-physiological laws that are species-independent, which seems much less reasonable than the hope that psychological laws (of a sufficiently general kind) may be species-independent, or, still weaker, that a species-independent *form* can be found in which psychological laws can be written.

4 Functional state versus behaviour-disposition

The theory that being in pain is neither a brain state nor a functional state but a behaviour disposition has one apparent advantage: it appears to agree with the way in which we verify that organisms are in pain. We do not in practice know anything about the brain state of an animal when we say that it is in pain; and we possess little if any knowledge of its functional organization, except in a crude intuitive way. In fact, however, this 'advantage' is no advantage at all: for, although statements about how we verify that *x* is *A* may have a good deal to do with what the concept of being *A* comes to, they have precious little to do with what the property *A is*. To argue on the ground just mentioned that pain is neither a brain state nor a functional state is like arguing that heat is not mean molecular kinetic energy from the fact that ordinary people do not (they think) ascertain the mean molecular kinetic energy of something when they verify that it is hot or cold. It is not necessary that they should; what is necessary is that the marks that they take as indications of heat should in fact be explained by the mean molecular kinetic energy. And, similarly, it is necessary to our hypothesis that the marks that are taken as behavioural indications of pain should be explained by the fact that the organism is in a functional state of the appropriate kind, but not that speakers should *know* that this is so.

The difficulties with 'behaviour disposition' accounts are so well known that I shall do little more than recall them here. The difficulty – it appears to be more than 'difficulty', in fact – of specifying the required behaviour disposition except as 'the disposition of X to behave as if X were in *pain*', is the chief one, of course. In contrast, we *can* specify the functional state with which we propose to identify pain, at least roughly, without using the notion of pain. Namely, the functional state we have in mind is the state of receiving sensory inputs which play a certain role in the Functional Organization of the organism. This role is characterized, at least partially, by the fact that the sense organs responsible for the inputs in question are organs whose function is to detect damage to the body, or dangerous extremes of temperature, pressure, etc., and by the fact that the 'inputs' themselves, whatever their physical realization, represent a condition that the organism assigns a high disvalue to...

5 Methodological considerations

So far we have considered only what might be called the 'empirical' reasons for saying that being in pain is a functional state, rather than a brain state or a behaviour disposition; viz., that it seems more likely that the functional state we described is invariantly 'correlated' with pain, species-independently, than that there is either a physical-chemical state of the brain (must an organism have a *brain* to feel pain? perhaps some ganglia will do) or a behaviour disposition so correlated. If this is correct, then it follows that the identification we proposed is at least a candidate for consideration. What of methodological considerations?

The methodological considerations are roughly similar in all cases of reduction, so no surprises need be expected here. First, identification of psychological states with functional states means that the laws of psychology can be derived from statements of the form, 'such-and-such organisms have such-and-such Descriptions' together with the identification statements ('being in pain is such-and-such a functional state', etc.). Secondly, the presence of the functional state (i.e., of inputs which play the role we have described in the Functional Organization of the organism) is not merely 'correlated with' but actually explains the pain behaviour on the part of the organism. Thirdly, the identification serves to exclude questions which (if a naturalistic view is correct) represent an altogether wrong way of looking at the matter, e.g., 'What *is* pain if it isn't either the brain state or the functional state?' and 'What causes the pain to be always accompanied by this sort of functional state?' In short, the identification is to be tentatively accepted as a theory which leads to both fruitful predictions and to fruitful *questions*, and which serves to discourage fruitless and empirically senseless questions, where by 'empirically senseless' I mean 'senseless' not merely from the standpoint of verification, but from the standpoint of what there in fact *is*.

12   The Subjective Dimension of Consciousness: Thomas Nagel, *What is it Like to be a Bat?* *

By the close of the twentieth century, problems about the nature of *consciousness* had begun to dominate the philosophy of mind. Despite considerable scientific progress in understanding the nature and workings of the mind, many came to feel that there are certain aspects of conscious experience that have not yet (and perhaps never could be) fully explained by any of the leading philosophical and scientific accounts of mental phenomena, whether behaviourist, physicalist or functionalist (see introduction to previous extract). A remarkable article by the American philosopher Thomas Nagel, from which our final extract is taken, has been enormously influential in setting the stage for this continuing debate.

Nagel starts from the idea that for an organism to have a conscious experience means that there is something it is like to *be* that organism. For example, there is something it is like for a normal human being to smell a rose, or to taste a cup of coffee.[1] Such experiences have a distinctive, qualitative 'feel' to them – they have a particular 'subjective character' (as Nagel puts it), which may sometimes be hard to put into words, but which nevertheless you and I are vividly aware of, when we lift the rose to our nostrils, or take a sip from the coffee mug. This subjective aspect, Nagel argues, is not 'captured' by any of the standard analyses of the mental, such as functionalism (compare extract 11, above). For a 'robot' might be functionally identical to you (all its inputs and outputs impeccably wired up, and all its information-processing perfect, so that it correctly identifies the English rose and the Colombian coffee in front of it), yet it has no subjective mental life – it 'experiences nothing'. It follows, according to Nagel, that genuine mental states cannot be exhaustively reduced to functional states – or indeed to neurophysiological states, or any states

suitable for inclusion in objective scientific theories, as we now understand them; for the irreducible element of subjective experience will always, it seems, be left out.

The bat of Nagel's title provides a particularly vivid example of this problem. Bats typically find their way around not by vision but by 'echolocation' (emitting high-pitched squeaks whose reflected sound, as it bounces off the objects in their environment, enables them to navigate efficiently). Since we possess no such sense, it is virtually impossible for us to imagine 'what it is like for a bat to be a bat'; yet (assuming there is indeed something it is like), 'these experience have . . . a specific subjective character, which it is beyond our ability to conceive'. We may of course achieve complete scientific understanding of the bat's brain and nervous system, but, claims Nagel, 'if the facts of experience – facts about what it is like *for* the experiencing organism – are accessible only from one point of view, then it is a mystery how the true character of experience could be revealed in the physical operation of that organism'.

Does this argument permanently undermine the attempts of modern physical science to explain mental phenomena? As the conclusion of our extract makes clear, Nagel does not draw the conclusion that physicalism is false, but rather that we are not remotely in a position to understand how it might be true. If Nagel is right, there are certain experiential facts that are accessible only from a particular point of view – namely the subjective point of view – and we do not yet have any clear handle on how science, which is committed to observing and analysing phenomena from the objective point of view, could account for, or incorporate, this subjective dimension.

Vast discussion has been generated by this article. Some philosophers have questioned

---

* Thomas Nagel, 'What is it Like to be a Bat?', *Philosophical Review*, 83 (1974); repr. in Nagel's *Mortal Questions* (Cambridge: Cambridge University Press, 1979), ch. 12; abridged.

[1] The examples are not Nagel's. For earlier discussions of the problem of subjective sensory awareness, see introduction to extract 6, above.

whether Nagel is justified in claiming that there are genuine *facts* involved in the phenomena he discusses: according to this objection, what distinguishes bats from us is merely that they have certain special abilities that we lack, not that there are special facts accessible only from their point of view. Others have objected that his conception of 'robots' may be question-begging: for although the popular connotations of the label 'robot' invite us to accept Nagel's stipulation that such creatures 'experience nothing', does it really make coherent sense to maintain this, on the supposed assumption that all their behaviour, responsiveness, language, physiology and causal organization matches our own, point for point, in every single respect? However that may be, Nagel's seminal article has undoubtedly succeeded in raising crucial questions about the relation between the subjective and objective domains – questions that lie at the heart of so much difficulty in the long philosophical history of the mind–body problem.

 . . . Conscious experience is a widespread phenomenon. It occurs at many levels of animal life, though we cannot be sure of its presence in the simpler organisms, and it is very difficult to say in general what provides evidence of it. (Some extremists have been prepared to deny it even of mammals other than man.) No doubt it occurs in countless forms totally unimaginable to us, on other planets in other solar systems throughout the universe. But no matter how the form may vary, the fact that an organism has conscious experience *at all* means, basically, that there is something it is like to *be* that organism. There may be further implications about the form of the experience; there may even (though I doubt it) be implications about the behaviour of the organism. But fundamentally an organism has conscious mental states if and only if there is something that it is like to *be* that organism – something it is like *for* the organism.

We may call this the subjective character of experience. It is not captured by any of the familiar, recently devised reductive analyses of the mental, for all of them are logically compatible with its absence. It is not analysable in terms of any explanatory system of functional states, or intentional states, since these could be ascribed to robots or automata that behaved like people though they experienced nothing.[1] It is not analysable in terms of the causal role of experiences in relation to typical human behaviour – for similar reasons. I do not deny that conscious mental states and events cause behaviour, nor that they may be given functional characterizations. I deny only that this kind of thing exhausts their analysis. Any reductionist program has to be based on an analysis of what is to be reduced. If the analysis leaves something out, the problem will be falsely posed. It is useless to base the defence of materialism on any analysis of mental phenomena that fails to deal explicitly with their subjective character. For there is no reason to suppose that a reduction which seems plausible when no attempt is made to account for consciousness can be extended to include consciousness. Without some idea, therefore, of what the subjective character of experience is, we cannot know what is required of a physical theory.

While an account of the physical basis of mind must explain many things, this appears to be the most difficult. It is impossible to exclude the phenomenological features of experience from a reduction in the same way that one excludes the

---

[1] *Perhaps there could not actually be such robots. Perhaps anything complex enough to behave like a person would have experiences. But that, if true, is a fact which cannot be discovered merely by analysing the concept of experience.

phenomenal features of an ordinary substance from a physical or chemical reduction of it – namely, by explaining them as effects on the minds of human observers. If physicalism is to be defended, the phenomenological features must themselves be given a physical account. But when we examine their subjective character it seems that such a result is impossible. The reason is that every subjective phenomenon is essentially connected with a single point of view, and it seems inevitable that an objective, physical theory will abandon that point of view.

Let me first try to state the issue somewhat more fully than by referring to the relation between the subjective and the objective . . . This is far from easy. Facts about what it is like to be an X are very peculiar, so peculiar that some may be inclined to doubt their reality, or the significance of claims about them. To illustrate the connection between subjectivity and a point of view, and to make evident the importance of subjective features, it will help to explore the matter in relation to an example that brings out clearly the divergence between the two types of conception, subjective and objective.

I assume we all believe that bats have experience. After all, they are mammals, and there is no more doubt that they have experience than that mice or pigeons or whales have experience. I have chosen bats instead of wasps or flounders because if one travels too far down the phylogenetic tree, people gradually shed their faith that there is experience there at all. Bats, although more closely related to us than those other species, nevertheless present a range of activity and a sensory apparatus so different from ours that the problem I want to pose is exceptionally vivid (though it certainly could be raised with other species). Even without the benefit of philosophical reflection, anyone who has spent some time in an enclosed space with an excited bat knows what it is to encounter a fundamentally alien form of life.

I have said that the essence of the belief that bats have experience is that there is something that it is like to be a bat. Now we know that most bats (the microchiroptera, to be precise) perceive the external world primarily by sonar, or echolocation, detecting the reflections, from objects within range, of their own rapid, subtly modulated, high-frequency shrieks. Their brains are designed to correlate the outgoing impulses with the subsequent echoes, and the information thus acquired enables bats to make precise discriminations of distance, size, shape, motion, and texture comparable to those we make by vision. But bat sonar, though clearly a form of perception, is not similar in its operation to any sense that we possess, and there is no reason to suppose that it is subjectively like anything we can experience or imagine. This appears to create difficulties for the notion of what it is like to be a bat. We must consider whether any method will permit us to extrapolate to the inner life of the bat from our own case,[1] and if not, what alternative methods there may be for understanding the notion.

Our own experience provides the basic material for our imagination, whose range is therefore limited. It will not help to try to imagine that one has webbing on one's arms, which enables one to fly around at dusk and dawn catching insects in one's mouth; that one has very poor vision, and perceives the surrounding world by a system of reflected high-frequency sound signals; and that one spends the day hanging upside down by one's feet in an attic. In so far as I can imagine this (which is not very

---

[1] *By 'our own case' I do not mean just 'my own case', but rather the mentalistic ideas that we apply unproblematically to ourselves and other human beings.

far), it tells me only what it would be like for *me* to behave as a bat behaves. But that is not the question. I want to know what it is like for a *bat* to be a bat. Yet if I try to imagine this, I am restricted to the resources of my own mind, and those resources are inadequate to the task. I cannot perform it either by imagining additions to my present experience, or by imagining segments gradually subtracted from it, or by imagining some combination of additions, subtractions, and modifications...

So if extrapolation from our own case is involved in the idea of what it is like to be a bat, the extrapolation must be incompletable. We cannot form more than a schematic conception of what it *is* like. For example, we may ascribe general *types* of experience on the basis of the animal's structure and behaviour. Thus we describe bat sonar as a form of three-dimensional forward perception; we believe that bats feel some versions of pain, fear, hunger, and lust, and that they have other, more familiar types of perception besides sonar. But we believe that these experiences also have in each case a specific subjective character, which it is beyond our ability to conceive. And if there is conscious life elsewhere in the universe, it is likely that some of it will not be describable even in the most general experiential terms available to us.[1] (The problem is not confined to exotic cases, however, for it exists between one person and another. The subjective character of the experience of a person deaf and blind from birth is not accessible to me, for example, nor presumably is mine to him. This does not prevent us each from believing that the other's experience has such a subjective character.)...

If anyone is inclined to deny that we can believe in the existence of facts like this whose exact nature we cannot possibly conceive, he should reflect that in contemplating the bats we are in much the same position that intelligent bats or Martians[2] would occupy if they tried to form a conception of what it was like to be us. The structure of their own minds might make it impossible for them to succeed, but we know they would be wrong to conclude that there is not anything precise that it is like to be us: that only certain general types of mental state could be ascribed to us (perhaps perception and appetite would be concepts common to us both; perhaps not). We know they would be wrong to draw such a sceptical conclusion because we know what it is like to be us. And we know that while it includes an enormous amount of variation and complexity, and while we do not possess the vocabulary to describe it adequately, its subjective character is highly specific, and in some respects describable in terms that can be understood only by creatures like us. The fact that we cannot expect ever to accommodate in our language a detailed description of Martian or bat phenomenology should not lead us to dismiss as meaningless the claim that bats and Martians have experiences fully comparable in richness of detail to our own. It would be fine if someone were to develop concepts and a theory that enabled us to think about those things; but such an understanding may be permanently denied to us by the limits of our nature. And to deny the reality or logical significance of what we can never describe or understand is the crudest form of cognitive dissonance.

This brings us to the edge of a topic that requires much more discussion than I can give it here: namely, the relation between facts on the one hand and conceptual schemes or systems of representation on the other. My realism about the subjective

---

[1] Therefore the analogical form of the English expression 'what it is *like*' is misleading: it does not mean 'what (in our experience) it *resembles*', but rather 'how it is for the subject himself'.

[2] Any intelligent extraterrestrial beings totally different from us.

domain in all its forms implies a belief in the existence of facts beyond the reach of human concepts. Certainly it is possible for a human being to believe that there are facts which humans never will possess the requisite concepts to represent or comprehend. Indeed, it would be foolish to doubt this, given the finiteness of humanity's expectations. After all, there would have been transfinite numbers even if everyone had been wiped out by the Black Death before Cantor discovered them. But one might also believe that there are facts which *could* not ever be represented or comprehended by human beings, even if the species lasted forever – simply because our structure does not permit us to operate with concepts of the requisite type. This impossibility might even be observed by other beings, but it is not clear that the existence of such beings, or the possibility of their existence, is a precondition of the significance of the hypothesis that there are humanly inaccessible facts. (After all, the nature of beings with access to humanly inaccessible facts is presumably itself a humanly inaccessible fact.) Reflection on what it is like to be a bat seems to lead us, therefore, to the conclusion that there are facts that do not consist in the truth of propositions expressible in a human language. We can be compelled to recognize the existence of such facts without being able to state or comprehend them.

I shall not pursue this subject, however. Its bearing on the topic before us (namely, the mind–body problem) is that it enables us to make a general observation about the subjective character of experience. Whatever may be the status of facts about what it is like to be a human being, or a bat, or a Martian, these appear to be facts that embody a particular point of view.

I am not adverting here to the alleged privacy of experience to its possessor. The point of view in question is not one accessible only to a single individual. Rather it is a *type*. It is often possible to take up a point of view other than one's own, so the comprehension of such facts is not limited to one's own case. There is a sense in which phenomenological facts are perfectly objective: one person can know or say of another what the quality of the other's experience is. They are subjective, however, in the sense that even this objective ascription of experience is possible only for someone sufficiently similar to the object of ascription to be able to adopt his point of view – to understand the ascription in the first person as well as in the third, so to speak. The more different from oneself the other experiencer is, the less success one can expect with this enterprise. In our own case we occupy the relevant point of view, but we will have as much difficulty understanding our own experience properly if we approach it from another point of view as we would if we tried to understand the experience of another species without taking up *its* point of view.

This bears directly on the mind–body problem. For if the facts of experience – facts about what it is like *for* the experiencing organism – are accessible only from one point of view, then it is a mystery how the true character of experiences could be revealed in the physical operation of that organism. The latter is a domain of objective facts *par excellence* – the kind that can be observed and understood from many points of view and by individuals with differing perceptual systems. There are no comparable imaginative obstacles to the acquisition of knowledge about bat neurophysiology by human scientists, and intelligent bats or Martians might learn more about the human brain than we ever will.

This is not by itself an argument against reduction. A Martian scientist with no understanding of visual perception could understand the rainbow, or lightning, or clouds as physical phenomena, though he would never be able to understand the human concepts of rainbow, lightning, or cloud, or the place these things occupy in our phenomenal world. The objective nature of the things picked out by these concepts could be apprehended by him because, although the concepts themselves are connected with a particular point of view and a particular visual phenomenology, the things apprehended from that point of view are not: they are observable from the point of view but external to it; hence they can be comprehended from other points of view also, either by the same organisms or by others. Lightning has an objective character that is not exhausted by its visual appearance, and this can be investigated by a Martian without vision. To be precise, it has a *more* objective character than is revealed in its visual appearance. In speaking of the move from subjective to objective characterization, I wish to remain noncommittal about the existence of an end point, the completely objective intrinsic nature of the thing, which one might or might not be able to reach. It may be more accurate to think of objectivity as a direction in which the understanding can travel. And in understanding a phenomenon like lightning, it is legitimate to go as far away as one can from a strictly human viewpoint.

In the case of experience, on the other hand, the connection with a particular point of view seems much closer. It is difficult to understand what could be meant by the *objective* character of an experience, apart from the particular point of view from which its subject apprehends it. After all, what would be left of what it was like to be a bat if one removed the viewpoint of the bat? But if experience does not have, in addition to its subjective character, an objective nature that can be apprehended from many different points of view, then how can it be supposed that a Martian investigating my brain might be observing physical processes which were my mental processes (as he might observe physical processes which were bolts of lightning), only from a different point of view? How, for that matter, could a human physiologist observe them from another point of view?[1] ...

What moral should be drawn from these reflections, and what should be done next? It would be a mistake to conclude that physicalism must be false. Nothing is proved by the inadequacy of physicalist hypotheses that assume a faulty objective analysis of mind. It would be truer to say that physicalism is a position we cannot understand because we do not at present have any conception of how it might be true...

Specimen Questions

1 Does Plato convincingly show that the soul must be more than a mere 'harmony' arising from bodily elements?
2 Explain what Aristotle means by saying the soul is the 'form' of a natural body. Does his account rule out the soul's existing in separation from the body?

---

[1] The problem is not just that when I look at the *Mona Lisa*, my visual experience has a certain quality, no trace of which is to be found by someone looking into my brain. For even if he did observe there a tiny image of the *Mona Lisa*, he would have no reason to identify it with the experience.

3 Why does Aquinas maintain that the 'sensitive' soul (of both humans and animals) depends on the body, and is destroyed with it, while the 'intellectual soul' is immaterial and incorruptible? Can this view be defended?

4 How does Descartes try to prove that the mind or soul is, in its essential nature, entirely distinct from the body? Is he successful?

5 'The order or connection of things is one and the same, whether its nature is conceived under the attribute of thought or the attribute of extension' (Spinoza). Explain and discuss.

6 What are Malebranche's objections to Descartes's doctrine of the 'union' of soul and body? Does he have anything better to put in its place?

7 Explain what Schopenhauer means by saying that an act of will and a movement of the body are one and the same thing 'given in entirely different ways'.

8 What is Mill's 'argument from analogy' for the existence of other minds? Does it correspond to the way we really know about the mental states of others?

9 What features does Brentano claim to be characteristic of mental as opposed to physical phenomena? Is he right?

10 Why does Ryle reject the notion of the mind as a private arena directly accessible only to the conscious subject? Do you find his arguments convincing?

11 Explain Putnam's hypothesis that conscious states such as pain are 'functional states'. Why does he think this is better than identifying conscious states with brain states, and is he right?

12 Critically examine Nagel's claim that it is a 'mystery' how the facts concerning the subjective character of experience could be revealed by examining a creature's behaviour or physiology.

Suggestions for Further Reading

Plato

Plato, *Phaedo*. Various editions are available, including W. H. D. Rouse (New York: Mentor, 1956).

For introductions to Plato, see readings at the end of Part I, above.

See also ch. 7 of R. Kraut (ed.), *The Cambridge Companion to Plato* (Cambridge: Cambridge University Press, 1991).

For a modern discussion of the problem of existence after death, see T. Penelhum, *Survival and Disembodied Existence* (New York: Humanities Press, 1970).

Aristotle

Aristotle, *De Anima*, Books II and III, ed. and trans. D. W. Hamlyn (Oxford: Clarendon, 1968). The complete text, with a useful introduction, is to be found in Aristotle, *De Anima*, trans. H. Lawson-Tancred (Penguin: Harmondsworth, 1986).

For general introductory materials on Aristotle, see readings at the end of Part I, above. For a useful discussion of Aristotle's theory of the mind, see the essay by S. Everson in J. Barnes (ed.), *The Cambridge Companion to Aristotle* (Cambridge: Cambridge University Press, 1995).

Two valuable collections of papers are M. Nussbaum and A. O. Rorty (eds), *Essays on Aristotle's 'De Anima'* (Oxford: Clarendon, 1995), and J. Barnes, M. Schofield, and R. Sorabji (eds), *Articles on Aristotle* (London: Duckworth, 1975–9), vol. I.

Aquinas

Kenny, A., *Aquinas* (Harmondsworth: Penguin, 1979). For an excellent account of Aquinas's philosophy of mind, see the chapter by Kretzman in N. Kretzman and E. Stump (eds), *The Cambridge Companion to Aquinas* (Cambridge: Cambridge University Press, 1993).

On the independence of the intellect from the body, see G. McCabe, 'The Immortality of the Soul', in A. Kenny (ed.), *Aquinas: A Collection of Critical Essays* (Garden City, NY: Doubleday, 1969). See also E. Anscombe and P. T. Geach, *Three Philosophers* (Oxford: Blackwell, 1961).

Descartes

Descartes, René, *Principles of Philosophy* [1644], in *The Philosophical Writings of Descartes*, trans. J. Cottingham, R. Stoothoff and D. Murdoch (Cambridge: Cambridge University Press, 1985), vol. I.

For general commentaries on Descartes, see readings at the end of Part I, above. For an account of various aspects of Descartes's dualism, see ch. 8 of J. Cottingham (ed.), *The Cambridge Companion to Descartes* (Cambridge: Cambridge University Press, 1993).

See also the entries on 'Mind and Body' and 'Human Being', in J. Cottingham, *A Descartes Dictionary* (Oxford: Blackwell, 1993).

Spinoza

Spinoza, Benedict, *Ethics* [*c*.1665], trans. G. H. R. Parkinson (Oxford: Oxford University Press, 2000).

For a survey of Spinoza's philosophy and its relation to his views on the mind, see J. Cottingham, *The Rationalists* (Oxford: Oxford University Press, 1988).

A good general introduction to Spinoza is S. Hampshire, *Spinoza* (Harmondsworth: Penguin, 1951). See also H. Allinson, *Benedict de Spinoza: An Introduction* (New Haven: Yale University Press, 1987).

Good critical discussions of Spinoza's views may be found in J. Bennett, *A Study of Spinoza's Ethics* (Cambridge: Cambridge University Press, 1984); R. J. Delahunty, *Spinoza* (London: Routledge, 1985); A. Donagan, *Spinoza* (London: Harvester, 1988); and S. Nadler, *Spinoza's Ethics* (Cambridge: Cambridge University Press, 2006).

For a clear introduction to the structure of the *Ethics*, see E. Curley, *Behind the Geometrical Method* (Princeton: Princeton University Press, 1988).

Spinoza's views on mind and body may be contrasted with the reductionistic materialism of Hobbes. For the latter, see Thomas Hobbes, *Leviathan* [1651], ed. C. B. Macpherson (Harmondsworth: Penguin, 1968); and, for an analysis of his arguments, T. Sorell, *Hobbes* (London: Routledge, 1986).

Malebranche

Malebranche, Nicolas, *Dialogues on Metaphysics* [*Entretiens sur la métaphysique*, 1688], trans. W. Doney (New York: Abaris, 1980).

See also N. Malebranche, *The Search after Truth* [*La recherche de la vérité*, 1674], trans. T. Lennon and P. Olscamp (Columbus: Ohio State University Press, 1980).

A stimulating study which 'rehabilitates' some of Malebranche's ideas is N. Jolley, *The Light of the Soul* (Oxford: Clarendon, 1990).

Also of great value are S. Nadler, *Malebranche and Ideas* (New York: Oxford University Press, 1992), and D. Radner, *Malebranche: A Study of a Cartesian System* (Amsterdam: Van Gorcum, 1978).

Schopenhauer

Schopenhauer, Arthur, *The World as Will and Idea* [*Die Welt als Wille und Vorstellung*, 1819], trans. R. B. Haldane and J. Kemp (London: Routledge, 1883).

An excellent survey of Schopenhauer's thought is C. Janaway, *Schopenhauer* (Oxford: Oxford University Press, 1994), with a fuller treatment in C. Janaway, *Self and World in Schopenhauer's Philosophy* (Oxford: Clarendon, 1989).

See also P. Gardiner, *Schopenhauer* (Harmondsworth: Penguin, 1963); D. W. Hamlyn, *Schopenhauer* (London: Routledge, 1980);

B. Magee, *The Philosophy of Schopenhauer* (Oxford: Clarendon, 1983).

Mill

Mill, J. S., *An Examination of Sir William Hamilton's Philosophy* [1865] (3rd edn, London: Longmans, 1867).

An excellent study of all aspects of Mill's philosophy is J. Skorupski, *Mill* (London: Routledge, 1989).

For Wittgenstein's celebrated objections to the argument from analogy, see L. Wittgenstein, *Philosophical Investigations* (Oxford: Blackwell, 1953), esp. part I, § 293.

See also N. Malcolm, 'Knowledge of Other Minds', in *Knowledge and Certainty* (Englewood Cliffs, NJ: Prentice-Hall, 1963).

Brentano

Brentano, Franz, *Psychology from an Empirical Standpoint* [*Psychologie vom Empirischen Standpunkt*, 1874], trans. L. McAlister (London: Routledge, 1973).

See also R. M. Chisholm, *Brentano and Meinong Studies* (Amsterdam: Rodopi, 1982); B. Smith, *Austrian Philosophy: The Legacy of Franz Brentano* (La Salle, Ill.: Open Court, 1994).

For the general problem of Intentionality in philosophy of mind, see J. Searle, *Intentionality* (Cambridge: Cambridge University Press, 1983).

Ryle

Ryle, G., *The Concept of Mind* (London: Hutchinson, 1949).

See also G. Ryle, *Dilemmas* (Cambridge: Cambridge University Press, 1966).

For an uncompromising behaviourist approach to mind, see B. F. Skinner, *Beyond Freedom and Dignity* (Harmondsworth: Penguin, 1973).

For a good discussion of issues related to behaviourism, see J. Hornsby, 'Physicalist Thinking and Conceptions of Behaviour', in P. Pettit and J. McDowell (eds), *Subject, Thought and Content* (Oxford: Oxford University Press, 1986).

Putnam, Nagel and recent work in the philosophy of mind

Valuable general reference volumes on the philosophy of mind, covering much recent work, include S. Guttenplan (ed.), *A Companion to the Philosophy of Mind* (Oxford: Blackwell, 1994), and J. Heil (ed.), *Philosophy of Mind: A Guide and Anthology* (Oxford: Oxford University Press, 2004).

A useful collection of essays is W. G. Lycan (ed.), *Mind and Cognition* (Oxford: Blackwell, 1990).

For more radically physicalist approaches, see the essays by P. Churchland and U. Place in Lycan (ed.), *Mind and Cognition*.

For a detailed survey of functionalist accounts, including Putnam's, see N. Block, 'Introduction: What is Functionalism?', in N. Block (ed.), *Readings in Philosophy of Psychology* (Cambridge, Mass.: Harvard University Press, 1980).

For broader philosophical implications of Nagel's account of the explanatory gap between the subjective and objective domains, see Nagel's *The View from Nowhere* (Oxford: Oxford University Press, 1986).

For the issue of the qualitative dimension of subjective experience, see Frank Jackson, 'Epiphenomenal qualia' (1982), in Lycan (ed.), *Mind and Cognition*. See also David Lewis, 'Mad Pain and Martian Pain', in *Philosophical Papers*, vol. I (Oxford: Oxford University Press, 1983).

See D. Papineau, *Thinking about Consciousness* (Oxford: Clarendon, 2002), for an interesting account of how materialist accounts of the mind may be able to deal with the problem of 'phenomenal consciousness' (our awareness of colours, tastes and so on).

See also D. C. Dennett, 'Epiphenomenal qualia?', in his *Consciousness Explained* (Harmondsworth: Penguin, 1992), pp. 398–406.

For a detailed discussion of 'robots', or 'zombies', from a functionalist perspective, see R. Kirk, *Zombies and Consciousness* (Oxford: Clarendon, 2005).

Also of interest are D. Rosenthal (ed.), *The Nature of Mind* (Oxford: Oxford University Press, 1991), and M. Lockwood, *Mind, Brain and the Quantum* (Oxford: Blackwell, 1989).

PART V

The Self and Freedom

The Self and Freedom
Introduction

One crucial feature that sets human beings apart from other living creatures is that we are, or believe we are, responsible for our actions. The concept of responsibility presupposes at least two things. First, almost all the judgements we pass on our own past actions and those of others seem to require the notion of selfhood, of a single enduring subject who continues through time. For Smith to be answerable for a crime committed last year, he must be the *selfsame person* who did it. Secondly, responsibility seems to imply freedom – that human beings, unlike other animals, have a certain power to make choices, to implement decisions and to control at least some aspects of their lives. Selfhood and freedom are thus basic ingredients in our conception of what it is to be a human agent. The extracts that follow, in sections (a) and (b) respectively, deal with various philosophical attempts to understand these two notions, both of which may initially seem straightforward, but which turn out to be highly problematic. Although the issues involved here are sufficiently distinctive to merit special treatment, the materials to be found below connect closely with topics covered in other Parts of the volume, notably with accounts of the mind and its relation to the body (Part IV), questions in the philosophy of religion (Part VI) and many issues in moral philosophy (Parts VIII and IX).

(a) The Self

1 The Self and Consciousness: John Locke, *Essay concerning Human Understanding**

Although we undergo many changes in life, it seems necessary for us to have a sense of selfhood, of personal identity, if we are to understand our lives and make sense of ourselves as beings who somehow endure despite all the changes. But what are the criteria or conditions for personal identity – for saying, for example, that the individual I see across the street in London is the same person I met in Los Angeles last year? One of the most influential philosophical writers on personal identity was the seventeenth-century English philosopher John Locke. In the extract that follows, Locke identifies the self with a *conscious thinking thing*. Although he sometimes uses the language of 'dualism' – the conception of an immaterial mind or soul as a substance in its own right (see above, Part IV, extract 4) – he makes it clear that it does not really matter what kind of 'substance' the self is ('whether spiritual or material, simple or compounded, it matters not'). The important thing is the *consciousness*

we have of ourselves as enduring subjects, a consciousness that depends on the memories that link who we now are with who we were in the past.

Notice that Locke's 'memory criterion' yields a test for personal identity that does not have to coincide with the conditions for physical or bodily identity. In Locke's famous example of an imaginary 'body-swap', if a prince took over the body of a cobbler, then, provided he still had all the conscious memories of the prince when he woke up in the cobbler's body, we would have to say that he was still the same *person* (though because of the change of body we could not say he was the same *man*, the same physical human being). Locke's account of personal identity thus rejects 'external' (physiological or biological) tests in favour of that inner awareness each individual has of itself as a conscious being enduring through time, as a centre of self-concern (in Locke's words, 'concerned for itself as far as that consciousness extends').

To find wherein *personal identity* consists, we must consider what *person* stands for; which, I think, is a thinking intelligent being that has reason and reflection and can consider itself as itself, the same thinking thing in different times and places; which it does only by that consciousness which is inseparable from thinking and, as it seems to me, essential for it – it being impossible for anyone to perceive without perceiving that he does perceive. When we see, hear, smell, taste, feel, meditate, or will anything, we know that we do so. Thus it is always as to our present sensations and perceptions; and by this everyone is to himself that which he calls *self*, it not being considered in this case whether the same *self* be continued in the same or different substances. For since consciousness always accompanies thinking, and it is that which makes everyone to be what he calls *self*, and thereby distinguishes himself from all other thinking things, in this alone consists *personal identity*, i.e. the sameness of a rational being. And as far as this consciousness can be extended backwards to any past action or thought, so far reaches the identity of that *person*. It is the same *self* now it was

---

* John Locke, *An Essay concerning Human Understanding* [1690], Bk II, ch. 27, §§ 9–19, 22–3; with omissions, modernized spelling and punctuation and some minor modifications of phrasing. Several editions of the *Essay* are available; the original formatting is reproduced in the standard critical edition of P. H. Nidditch (Oxford: Clarendon, 1975).

then, and it is by the same *self* as this present one that now reflects on it, that that action was done.

But it is further inquired whether it be the same identical substance. This, few would think they had reason to doubt of, if these perceptions, with their consciousness, always remained present in the mind whereby the same thinking thing would be always consciously present and ... evidently the same to itself. But that which seems to make the difficulty is this: that this consciousness is interrupted always by forgetfulness, there being no moment of our lives wherein we have the whole train of all our past actions before our eyes in one view, but even the best memories lose the sight of one part whilst they are viewing another; and we sometimes – and that the greatest part of our lives – do not reflect on our past selves, being intent on our present thoughts, and in sound sleep have no thoughts at all, or at least none with that consciousness which remarks our waking thoughts. I say, in all these cases, our consciousness being interrupted, and we losing the sight of our past *selves*, doubts are raised whether we are the same thinking thing, i.e. the same substance, or no. Which, however reasonable or unreasonable, concerns not *personal identity* at all: the question being what makes the same *person*, and not whether it be the same identical substance, which always thinks in the same person; which, in this case, matters not at all ... For, it being the same consciousness that makes a man be himself to himself, *personal identity* depends on that only, [irrespective of] whether it be annexed solely to one individual substance, or can be continued in a succession of several substances. For as far as any intelligent being can repeat the idea of any past action with the same consciousness it had of it at first, and with the same consciousness it has of any present action, so far it is the same *personal self*. For it is by the consciousness it has of its present thoughts and actions that it is *self* to *itself* now, and so will be the same *self* as far as the same consciousness can extend to actions past or to come; and [it] would be by distance of time or change of substance no more two *persons* than a man be two men by wearing other clothes today than he did yesterday, with a long or a short sleep between. The same consciousness unites those distant actions into the same *person*, whatever substances contributed to their production.

That this is so, we have some kind of evidence in our very bodies, all whose particles, whilst vitally united to this same thinking conscious self (so that we feel when they are touched and are affected by and conscious of good or harm that happens to them) are a part of our *selves*, i.e. of our thinking conscious *self*. Thus, the limbs of his body are to everyone a part of *himself*; he sympathizes and is concerned for them. Cut off a hand, and thereby separate it from that consciousness he had of its heat, cold, and other affections, and it is then no longer a part of that which is *himself*, any more than the remotest part of matter. Thus, we see the *substance* whereof *personal self* consisted at one time may be varied at another, without the change of personal *identity*, there being no question about the same person, though the limbs, which but now were a part of it, be cut off.

But the question is whether, if the same substance, which thinks, be changed, it can be the same person, or, remaining the same, it can be different persons. And to this I answer, first, this can be no question at all to those who place thought in a purely material animal constitution, void of an immaterial substance. For, whether their supposition be true or no, it is plain they conceive personal identity preserved in something else than identity of substance, as animal identity is preserved in identity of life and not of substance. And therefore those who place thinking in an immaterial substance only, before they can come to deal with these men, must show why personal identity cannot be preserved in the change of immaterial substances, or variety of particular immaterial substances, as well as animal identity is preserved in the change of material substances, or variety of particular bodies. Unless they will say it is one immaterial spirit that makes the same life in brutes, as it is one immaterial spirit that makes the same person in men; which the Cartesians at least will not admit, for fear of making brutes thinking things too.[1]

But next, as to the first part of the question, whether, if the same thinking substance (supposing immaterial substances only to think) be changed, it can be the same person, I answer this. It can only be resolved by those who know what kind of substances they are that think, and whether the consciousness of past actions can be transferred from one thinking substance to another... It must be allowed that, if the same consciousness (which, as has been shown, is quite a different thing from the same numerical figure or motion in body) can be transferred from one thinking substance to another, it will be possible that two thinking substances may make but one person. For the same consciousness being preserved, whether in the same or different substances, the personal identity is preserved.

As to the second part of the question, whether, the same immaterial substance remaining, there may be two distinct persons, the question seems to me to be built on this: whether the same immaterial being, being conscious of the actions of its past duration, may be wholly stripped of all the consciousness of its past existence and lose it beyond the power of ever retrieving again; and so, as it were beginning a new account from a new period, have a consciousness that cannot reach beyond this new state... Let anyone reflect upon himself and conclude that he has in himself an immaterial spirit, which is that which thinks in him and in the constant change of his body keeps him the same, and is that which he calls himself; let him also suppose it to be the same soul that was in Nestor or Thersites at the siege of Troy (for souls being, as far as we know anything of them, in their nature indifferent to any parcel of matter, the supposition has no apparent absurdity in it)... But if he now has no consciousness of any of the actions either of Nestor or Thersites, does or can he conceive himself the same person with either of them? Can he be concerned in either of their actions, attribute them to himself, or think them his own, more than the actions of any other men that ever existed? So that, this consciousness not reaching to any of the actions of either of those men, he is no more one *self* with either of them than if the soul or immaterial spirit that now informs him had been created and began to exist when it began to inform his present body, though it were ever so true that the same spirit that informed Nestor's or Thersites' body were numerically the same that now informs his. For this would no more make him the same person as Nestor than if some of the particles of matter that were once a part of Nestor were now a part of this man. The same immaterial substance, without the same consciousness, no more makes the same person by being united to any body than the same particle of matter, without consciousness, united to any body, makes the same person. But let him once find himself conscious of any of the actions of Nestor, he then finds himself the same person as Nestor.

---

[1] Descartes's followers regarded animals as mechanical automata devoid of consciousness.

And thus we may be able, without any difficulty, to conceive the same person at the resurrection, though in a body not exactly in make or parts the same which he had here, the same consciousness going along with the soul that inhabits it. But yet the soul alone, in the change of bodies, would scarcely to anyone...be enough to make the same *man*. For should the soul of a prince, carrying with it the consciousness of the prince's past life, enter and inform the body of a cobbler as soon as deserted by his own soul, everyone sees he would be the same *person* as the prince, accountable only for the prince's actions; but who would say it was the same *man*? The body too goes to the making the man and would, I guess, to everybody, determine the man in this case: for the soul, with all its princely thoughts about it, would not make another man; but he would be the same cobbler to everyone besides himself. I know that in the ordinary way of speaking 'the same person' and 'the same man' stand for one and the same thing. And indeed, everyone will always have a liberty to speak as he pleases and to apply what articulate sounds to what ideas he thinks fit, and change them as often as he pleases. But yet when we will inquire what makes the same *spirit, man, or person*, we must fix the ideas of *spirit, man, or person* in our minds; and having resolved with ourselves what we mean by them, it will not be hard to determine...when it is the *same* and when not.

But though the same immaterial substance or soul does not alone, wherever it be, and in whatsoever state, make the same man: yet, it is plain, consciousness, as far as ever it can be extended, even to ages past, unites existences and actions very remote in time into the same person, as well as it does the existences and actions of the immediately preceding moment. So whatever has the consciousness of present and past actions is the same person to whom they both belong. Had I the same consciousness that I saw the ark and Noah's flood as that I saw an overflowing of the Thames last winter, or as that I write now, I could no more doubt that I that write this now, that saw the Thames overflowed last winter, and that viewed the flood at the general deluge, was the same *self* (place that *self* in what substance you please) than that I that write this am the same *myself* now whilst I write (whether I consist of all the same substance, material or immaterial, or no) that I was yesterday. For as to this point of being the same *self*, it matters not whether this present *self* be made up of the same or other substances, I being as much concerned and as justly accountable for any action that was done a thousand years since, appropriated to me now by this self-consciousness, as I am for what I did the last moment.

Self is that conscious thinking thing (whatever substance made up of, whether spiritual or material, simple or compounded, it matters not) which is sensible or conscious of pleasure and pain, capable of happiness or misery, and so is concerned for itself, as far as that consciousness extends. Thus everyone finds that, whilst comprehended under that consciousness, the little finger is as much a part of *itself* as what is most so. Upon separation of this little finger, should this consciousness go along with the little finger and leave the rest of the body, it is evident the little finger would be the *person*, the *same person*, and self then would have nothing to do with the rest of the body. As in this case it is the consciousness that goes along with the substance, when one part is separate from another, which makes the same *person* and constitutes this inseparable *self*, so it is in reference to substances remote in time. That with which the *consciousness* of this present thinking thing can join itself makes the same *person* and is one *self* with it, and with nothing else, and so attributes to *itself* and owns all the actions of that thing as its own, as far as that consciousness reaches, and no further; as everyone who reflects will perceive.

In this *personal identity* is founded all the right and justice of reward and punishment, happiness and misery being that for which everyone is concerned for *himself*, and not mattering what becomes of any substance not joined to or affected with that consciousness. For, as it is evident in the instance I gave but now, if the consciousness went along with the little finger when it was cut off, that would be the same *self* which was concerned for the whole body yesterday, as making part of *itself*, whose actions then it cannot but admit as its own now. Though, if the same body should still live and immediately from the separation of the little finger have its own peculiar consciousness, whereof the little finger knew nothing, it would not at all be concerned for it as a part of *itself*, nor could it own any of its actions, or have any of them imputed to him.

This may show us wherein *personal identity* consists: not in the identity of substance but, as I have said, in the identity of *consciousness*, wherein, if Socrates and the present mayor of Quinborough agree, they are the same person. If the same Socrates waking and sleeping do not partake of the same *consciousness*, Socrates waking and sleeping is not the same person. And to punish Socrates waking for what sleeping Socrates thought, and waking Socrates was never conscious of, would be no more right than to punish one twin for what his brother-twin did, whereof he knew nothing, because their outsides were so like that they could not be distinguished (for such twins have been seen).

But yet possibly it will still be objected, suppose I wholly lose the memory of some parts of my life beyond a possibility of retrieving them, so that perhaps I shall never be conscious of them again: yet am I not the same person that did those actions, had those thoughts that I once was conscious of, though I have now forgot them? To which I answer that we must here take notice what the word *I* is applied to, which, in this case, is the man only. And the same man being presumed to be the same person, *I* is easily here supposed to stand also for the same person. But if it be possible for the same man to have distinct incommunicable consciousness at different times, it is past doubt the same man would at different times make different persons; which, we see, is the sense of mankind in the solemnest declaration of their opinions, human laws not punishing the mad man for the sober man's actions, nor the sober man for what the mad man did, thereby making them two persons. This is somewhat explained by our way of speaking in English when we say such a one *is not himself*, or is *beside himself*; in which phrases it is insinuated, as if those who now, or at least first used them, thought that *self* was changed, the *selfsame* person was no longer in that man…

But is not a man drunk and sober the same person – why else is he punished for the fact he commits when drunk, though he be never afterwards conscious of it? Just as much the same person as a man that walks and does other things in his sleep is the same person and is answerable for any mischief he shall do in it. Human laws punish both, with a justice suitable to their way of knowledge, because, in these cases, they cannot distinguish certainly what is real, what counterfeit; and so the ignorance in drunkenness or sleep is not admitted as a plea. For, though punishment be annexed to personality, and personality to consciousness, and the drunkard perhaps be not conscious of what he did, yet human judicatures justly punish him, because the fact is proved against him, but lack of consciousness cannot be proved for him. But in the

Great Day, wherein the secrets of all hearts shall be laid open, it may be reasonable to think no one shall be made to answer for what he knows nothing of, but shall receive his final judgement, his conscience accusing or excusing him ...

Could we suppose two distinct incommunicable consciousnesses acting the same body, the one constantly by day, the other by night; and, on the other side, the same consciousness acting by intervals, two distinct bodies: I ask, in the first case, whether the *day-* and the *night-man* would not be two as distinct persons as *Socrates* and *Plato*? And whether, in the second case, there would not be one person in two distinct bodies, as much as one man is the same in two distinct clothings? Nor is it at all material to say that this same and this distinct *consciousness*, in the cases above mentioned, is owing to the same and distinct immaterial substances, bringing it with them to those bodies. This, whether true or no, alters not the case, since it is evident the *personal identity* would equally be determined by the consciousness, whether that consciousness were annexed to some individual immaterial substance or no. For, granting that the thinking substance in man must be necessarily supposed immaterial, it is evident that immaterial thinking thing may sometimes part with its past consciousness and be restored to it again, as appears in the forgetfulness men often have of their past actions; and the mind many times recovers the memory of a past consciousness, which it had lost for twenty years together. Make these intervals of memory and forgetfulness to take their turns regularly by day and night, and you have two persons with the same immaterial spirit, as much as in the former instance two persons with the same body. So that *self* is not determined by identity or diversity of substance, which it cannot be sure of, but only by identity of consciousness ...

2   The Self as Primitive Concept: Joseph Butler, *Of Personal Identity**

It is clear on reflection that Locke's memory criterion of personal identity presents serious problems. It may be true that without memory we would not be able to have a sense of self, but that is not to say that *S*'s being able to remember doing *x* is what it *means* to say he is the same person who did *x*. Clearly it is often possible vividly to remember something one did ten years ago, yet forget what one did last week. Moreover, since I can genuinely *remember* doing something only if I am indeed the same person who did it, it seems that the concept of memory cannot be used to define personal identity, since it presupposes it in the first place. This is the most telling criticism which Joseph Butler makes of Locke in the short essay (published in 1736) which now follows. For Butler, our personal identity is a basic notion, or primitive concept, like that of equality: all attempts to define it would merely 'perplex it'. Butler does, however, get into some confusions when discussing the identity of plants: if after ten years, every component molecule of a given tree is changed, can we say it is the same tree? Butler thinks we can say so only in a 'loose', as opposed to the strict philosophical sense. Yet in the case of

* Joseph Butler, *The Analogy of Religion* [1736], appendix 1; with modifications of spelling and punctuation. The full text is reproduced in J. Butler, *Works*, ed. W. E. Gladstone (Oxford: Oxford University Press, 1896).

persons Butler simply asserts that despite all the changes we go through, we are the 'same' in the strict sense, and moreover that we have an irresistible awareness of our own identity. Against this, Butler's contemporary Hume (see extract 3, below) maintained that there is no enduring entity called the 'self', and that the notion of personal identity is a kind of fiction. For Butler such a view would contradict the 'certain conviction which necessarily and every moment arises within us when we turn our thoughts upon ourselves'.

Whether we are to live in a future state, as it is the most important question which can possibly be asked, so it is the most intelligible one which can be expressed in language. Yet strange perplexities have been raised about the meaning of that identity or sameness of person which is implied in the notion of our living now and hereafter, or in any two successive moments. And the solution of these difficulties has been stranger than the difficulties themselves. For personal identity has been explained by some in such a way as to render the inquiry concerning a future life of no consequence at all to us the persons who are making it. And though few men can be misled by such subtleties, yet it may be proper a little to consider them.

Now when it is asked wherein personal identity consists, the answer should be the same as if it were asked wherein consists similitude, or equality: that all attempts to define would but perplex it. Yet there is no difficulty at all in ascertaining the idea. For just as, upon two triangles being compared or viewed together, there arises to the mind the idea of similitude, or upon twice two and four the idea of equality, so likewise, upon comparing the consciousnesses of one's self, or one's own existence, in any two moments, there immediately arises to the mind the idea of personal identity. And as the two former comparisons not only give us the ideas of similitude and equality, but also show us that two triangles are alike and twice two and four are equal, so the latter comparison shows us the identity of ourselves in those two moments – the present (suppose) and that immediately past, or the present and that a month, a year, or twenty years past. Or in other words, by reflection upon that which is my self now, and that which was my self twenty years ago, I discern that they are not two, but one and the same self.

But though consciousness of what is past does thus ascertain our personal identity to ourselves, yet to say that it *makes* personal identity, or is necessary to our being the same persons, is to say that a person has not existed a single moment, nor done one action, but what he can remember – indeed none but what he reflects on. And one should really think it self-evident that consciousness of personal identity presupposes, and therefore cannot constitute, personal identity, any more than knowledge, in any other case, can constitute truth, which it presupposes.

This wonderful mistake may possibly have arisen from hence: that to be endued with consciousness is inseparable from the idea of a person, or intelligent being. For this might be expressed inaccurately thus: that consciousness makes personality. And from hence it might be concluded to make personal identity. But though present consciousness of what we at present do and feel is necessary to our being the persons we now are, yet present consciousness of past actions or feelings is not necessary to our being the same persons who performed those actions or had those feelings.

The inquiry, what makes vegetables the same in the common acceptation of the word, does not appear to have any relation to this of personal identity, because the word *same* when applied to them and to persons is not only applied to different subjects but it is also used in different senses. For when a man swears to the same tree, as having stood fifty years in the same place, he means only the same as to all the purposes and properties of common life, and not that the tree has been all that time the same. For he does not know whether any one particle of the present tree be the same with any one particle of the tree which stood in the same place fifty years ago. And if they have not one common particle of matter, they cannot be the same tree in the proper philosophic sense of the word *same*, it being evidently a contradiction in terms to say they are, when no particle of their substance and no one of their properties is the same (no part of their substance, by the supposition [that not one particle of the original tree remains]; no one of their properties, because it is allowed that the same property cannot be transferred from one substance to another). And therefore when we say the identity or sameness of a plant consists in a continuation of the same life, communicated under the same organization to a number of particles of matter, whether the same or not, the word *same* when applied to life and to organization cannot possibly be understood to signify what it signifies in this very sentence, when applied to matter. In a loose and popular sense, then, the life and the organization and the plant are justly said to be the same, notwithstanding the perpetual change of the parts. But in a strict and philosophical manner of speech, no man, no being, no mode of being, no anything, can be the same with that with which it has indeed nothing the same. Now sameness is used in the latter sense, when applied to persons. The identity of these therefore cannot subsist with diversity of substance.

The thing here considered, and demonstratively, as I think, determined, is proposed by Mr Locke in these words: 'whether it, [i.e. the same self or person] be the same identical substance?' And he has suggested what is a much better answer to the question than that which he gives it in form. For he defines *person* 'a thinking intelligent being', and *personal identity* 'the sameness of a rational being'. The question then is whether the same rational being is the same substance, which needs no answer, because Being and Substance in this place stand for the same idea. The ground of the doubt, whether the same person be the same substance, is said to be this: that the consciousness of our own existence in youth and in old age, or in any two joint successive moments, is not the *same individual action*, i.e. not the same consciousness, but different successive consciousnesses. Now it is strange that this should have occasioned such perplexities. For it is surely conceivable that a person may have a capacity of knowing some object or other to be the same now which it was when he contemplated it formerly. Yet in this case, where, by the supposition, the object is perceived to be the same, the perception of it in any two moments cannot be one and the same perception. And thus, though the successive consciousnesses which we have of our own existence are not the same, yet are they consciousnesses of one and the same thing or object, of the same person, self, or living agent. The person of whose existence the consciousness is felt now, and was felt an hour or a year ago, is discerned to be not two persons but one and the same person, and therefore is one and the same.

Mr Locke's observations upon this subject appear hasty, and he seems to profess himself dissatisfied with suppositions which he has made relating to it. But some of those hasty observations have been carried to a strange length by others, whose notion, when traced and examined to the bottom, amounts I think to this: 'That personality is not a permanent, but a transient thing; that it lives and dies, begins and ends, continually; that no one can any more remain one and the same person two moments together than two successive moments can be one and the same moment; that our substance is indeed continually changing, but whether this be so or not is, it seems, nothing to the purpose, since it is not substance but consciousness alone which constitutes personality, which consciousness, being successive, cannot be the same in any two moments, nor consequently the personality constituted by it.' And from hence it must follow that it is a fallacy upon ourselves to charge our present selves with anything we did, or to imagine our present selves interested in anything which befell us yesterday, or that our present self will be interested in what will befall us tomorrow; since our present self is not, in reality, the same with the self of yesterday, but another like self or person coming in its room, and mistaken for it, to which another self will succeed tomorrow. This, I say, must follow. For if the self or person of today and that of tomorrow are not the same, but only like persons, the person of today is really no more interested in what will befall the person of tomorrow than in what will befall any other person. It may be thought, perhaps, that this is not a just representation of the opinion we are speaking of, because those who maintain it allow that a person is the same as far back as his remembrance reaches. And indeed they do use the *words* 'identity' and 'same person'. Nor will language permit these words to be laid aside, since if they were, there must be I know not what ridiculous periphrasis substituted in the room of them. But they cannot, consistently with themselves, mean that the person is really the same. For it is self-evident that the personality cannot be really the same, if, as they expressly assert, that in which it consists is not the same. And as, consistently with themselves, they cannot, so I think it appears, they do not, mean that the person is *really* the same, but only that he is so in a fictitious sense – in such a sense only as they assert (for this they do assert) that any number of persons whatever may be the same person. The bare unfolding of the notion, and laying it thus naked and open, seems the best confutation of it. However, since great stress is said to be put upon it, I add the following things.

First, this notion is absolutely contradictory to that certain conviction which necessarily and every moment arises within us when we turn our thoughts upon ourselves, when we reflect upon what is past, and look forward upon what is to come. All imagination of a daily change of that living agent which each man calls himself, for another, or of any such change throughout our whole present life, is entirely borne down by our natural sense of things. Nor is it possible for a person in his wits to alter his conduct, with regard to his health or affairs, from a suspicion that, though he should live tomorrow, he should not however be the same person he is today. And yet, if it be reasonable to act with respect to a future life on this notion, that personality is transient, it is reasonable to act upon it with respect to the present.

Here then is a notion equally applicable to religion and to our temporal concerns, and everyone sees and feels the inexpressible absurdity of it in the latter case. If therefore any can take up with it in the former, this cannot proceed from the reason of the thing, but must be owing to an inward unfairness and secret corruption of heart.

Secondly, it is not an idea, or abstract notion, or quality, but a *being* only which is capable of life and action, of happiness and misery. Now all beings confessedly continue the same during the whole time of their existence. Consider then a living being now existing, and which has existed for any time alive: this living being must have done and suffered and enjoyed what it has done and suffered and enjoyed formerly (this living being, I say, and not another), as really as it does and suffers and enjoys what it does and suffers and enjoys this instant. All these successive actions, enjoyments and sufferings are actions, enjoyments and sufferings of the same living being. And they are so prior to all consideration of its remembering and forgetting, since remembering or forgetting can make no alteration in the truth of past matter of fact. And suppose this being endued with limited powers of knowledge and memory, there is no more difficulty in conceiving it to have a power of knowing itself to be the same living being which it was some time ago, of remembering some of its actions, sufferings and enjoyments, and forgetting others, than in conceiving it to know or remember or forget anything else.

Thirdly, every person is conscious that he is now the same person or self he was as far back as his remembrance reaches, since when anyone reflects upon a past action of his own, he is just as certain of the person who did that action, namely himself – the person who now reflects on it – as he is certain that the action was at all done. Nay very often a person's assurance of an action having been done, of which he is absolutely assured, arises wholly from the consciousness that he himself did it. And this he, person, or self, must either be a substance, or the property of some substance. If he, if person, be a substance, then consciousness that he is the same person is consciousness that he is the same substance. If the person, or he, be the property of a substance, still consciousness that he is the same property is as certain a proof that his substance remains the same as consciousness that he remains the same substance would be (since the same property cannot be transferred from one substance to another).

But though we are thus certain that we are the same agents, living beings, or substances now which we were as far back as our remembrance reaches, yet it is asked whether we may not possibly be deceived in it. And this question may be asked at the end of any demonstration whatever, because it is a question concerning the truth of perception by memory. And he who can doubt whether perception by memory can in this case be depended upon, may doubt also whether perception by deduction and reasoning, which also include memory, or indeed wither intuitive perception can. Here then we can go no further. For it is ridiculous to attempt to prove the truth of those perceptions whose truth we can no otherwise prove than by other perceptions of exactly the same kind with them, and which there is just the same ground to suspect; or to attempt to prove the truth of our faculties, which can no otherwise be proved than by the use or means of those very suspected faculties themselves.

3   The Self as Bundle:
David Hume, *A Treatise of Human Nature**

Just as Butler's views on personal identity were a reaction against those of Locke, so the famous Scottish philosopher David Hume reacted against Butler to produce a disturbingly radical attack on the whole concept of personal identity. In his *Treatise of Human Nature* (1739–40) Hume points out, first of all, that the idea of the 'self' is not based on any experience or internal impression. When I 'enter most intimately' into what I call myself, all I encounter is 'some particular perception' (e.g. a sensation of heat or cold, or a feeling like love or hatred): I am never aware of any entity or object that is 'the self'. And he goes on to argue that the self is indeed a kind of fiction or illusion: we are 'nothing but a bundle of perceptions which succeed each other with an inconceivable rapidity'. Hume had taken a similarly radical line earlier in the *Treatise* with regard to the identity of external objects. Each time I open my eyes and look at a

table in my room, all I am in fact aware of on each occasion is a distinct and fresh impression; so when the mind ascribes identity to what is in fact a constant flux of diverse data, this is due to its 'propensity to feign' that there is some single continuing object.[1] In the case of the self, Hume maintains that we make a similar kind of systematic mistake: we have a propensity to be confused, by the smooth and uninterrupted flow of distinct impressions, into running them together, and ascribing to the mind an identity which is in reality 'only a fictitious one'. Though Hume's psychological explanation of this 'confusion' may strike some readers as bizarre, his general view that the sense of an enduring self is an illusion is one with which many writers (for example those in the Buddhist tradition) would concur, and it has found an echo in 'reductionist' accounts of personhood proposed by some recent philosophers (see below, extract 5).

There are some philosophers who imagine we are every moment intimately conscious of what we call our SELF; that we feel its existence and its continuance in existence; and are certain, beyond the evidence of a demonstration, both of its perfect identity and simplicity. The strongest sensation, the most violent passion, say they, instead of distracting us from this view, only fix it the more intensely, and make us consider their influence on *self* either by their pain or pleasure. To attempt a farther proof of this were to weaken its evidence; since no proof can be derived from any fact, of which we are so intimately conscious; nor is there anything of which we can be certain, if we doubt of this.

Unluckily all these positive assertions are contrary to that very experience which is pleaded for them, nor have we any idea of *self*, after the manner it is here explained. For from what impression could this idea be derived? This question it is impossible to answer without a manifest contradiction and absurdity; and yet it is a question which must necessarily be answered, if we would have the idea of self pass for clear and intelligible. It must be some one impression that gives rise to every real idea. But self or person is not any one impression, but that to which our several impressions and ideas are supposed to have a reference. If any impression gives rise to the idea of self,

---

* David Hume, *A Treatise of Human Nature* [1739–40], extracts from Bk I, part iv, section 6; with some modifications of spelling and punctuation. There are many editions of the *Treatise*, including that by D. F. and M. J. Norton (Oxford: Oxford University Press, 2000).

[1] *Treatise*, Bk I, part iv, section 2.

that impression must continue invariably the same, through the whole course of our lives, since self is supposed to exist after that manner. But there is no impression constant and invariable. Pain and pleasure, grief and joy, passions and sensations succeed each other, and never all exist at the same time. It cannot, therefore, be from any of these impressions, or from any other, that the idea of self is derived; and consequently there is no such idea.

But farther, what must become of all our particular perceptions upon this hypothesis? All these are different, and distinguishable, and separate from each other, and may be separately considered, and may exist separately, and have no need of any thing to support their existence. After what manner, therefore, do they belong to self; and how are they connected with it? For my part, when I enter most intimately into what I call *myself*, I always stumble on some particular perception or other, of heat or cold, light or shade, love or hatred, pain or pleasure. I never can catch *myself* at any time without a perception, and never can observe anything but the perception. When my perceptions are removed for any time, as by sound sleep, so long am I insensible of *myself*, and may truly be said not to exist. And were all my perceptions removed by death, and could I neither think, nor feel, nor see, nor love, nor hate after the dissolution of my body, I should be entirely annihilated, nor do I conceive what is farther requisite to make me a perfect non-entity. If any one upon serious and unprejudiced reflection thinks he has a different notion of *himself*, I must confess I can reason no longer with him. All I can allow him is that he may be in the right as well as I, and that we are essentially different in this particular. He may, perhaps, perceive something simple and continued, which he calls *himself*, though I am certain there is no such principle in me.

But setting aside some metaphysicians of this kind, I may venture to affirm, of the rest of mankind, that they are nothing but a bundle or collection of different perceptions, which succeed each other with an inconceivable rapidity, and are in a perpetual flux and movement. Our eyes cannot turn in their sockets without varying our perceptions. Our thought is still more variable than our sight; and all our other senses and faculties contribute to this change; nor is there any single power of the soul, which remains unalterably the same, perhaps for one moment. The mind is a kind of theatre, where several perceptions successively make their appearance, pass, re-pass, glide away, and mingle in an infinite variety of postures and situations. There is properly no *simplicity* in it at one time, nor *identity* in different [times], whatever natural propensity we may have to imagine that simplicity and identity. The comparison of the theatre must not mislead us. [It is merely] the successive perceptions...that constitute the mind; nor have we the most distant notion of the place where these scenes are represented, or of the materials of which it is composed.

What then gives us so great a propensity to ascribe an identity to these successive perceptions, and to suppose ourselves possessed of an invariable and uninterrupted existence through the whole course of our lives? In order to answer this question, we must distinguish betwixt personal identity, as it regards our thought or imagination, and as it regards our passions or the concern we take in ourselves. The first is our present subject; and to explain it perfectly we must take the matter pretty deep, and account for that identity which we attribute to plants and animals, there being a great analogy betwixt it, and the identity of a self or person.

We have a distinct idea of an object that remains invariable and uninterrupted through a supposed variation of time; and this idea we call that of *identity* or *sameness.* We have also a distinct idea of several different objects existing in succession, and connected together by a close relation; and this to an accurate view affords as perfect a notion of *diversity* as if there was no manner of relation among the objects. But though these two ideas of identity, and a succession of related objects, be in themselves perfectly distinct, and even contrary, yet it is certain that in our common way of thinking they are generally confounded with each other. That action of the imagination by which we consider the uninterrupted and invariable object, and that by which we reflect on the succession of related objects, are almost the same to the feeling, nor is there much more effort of thought required in the latter case than in the former. The relation facilitates the transition of the mind from one subject to another, and renders its passage as smooth as if it contemplated one continued object. This resemblance is the cause of the confusion and mistake, and makes us substitute the notion of identity, instead of that of related objects. However at one instant we may consider the related succession as variable or interrupted, we are sure the next to ascribe to it a perfect identity, and regard it as invariable and uninterrupted. Our propensity to this mistake is so great, from the resemblance above-mentioned, that we fall into it before we are aware; and though we incessantly correct ourselves by reflection, and return to a more accurate method of thinking, yet we cannot long sustain our philosophy, or take off this bias from the imagination. Our last resource is to yield to it, and boldly assert that these different related objects are in effect the same, however interrupted and variable. In order to justify to ourselves this absurdity, we often feign some new and unintelligible principle, that connects the objects together, and prevents their interruption or variation. Thus we feign the continued existence of the perceptions of our senses, to remove the interruption, and run into the notion of a *soul*, and *self*, and *substance*, to disguise the variation. But we may farther observe that where we do not give rise to such a fiction, our propensity to confound identity with relation is so great that we are apt to imagine something unknown and mysterious, connecting the parts, beside their relation; and this I take to be the case with regard to the identity we ascribe to plants and vegetables. And even when this does not take place, we still feel a propensity to confound these ideas, though we are not able fully to satisfy ourselves in that particular, nor find any thing invariable and uninterrupted to justify our notion of identity.

Thus the controversy concerning identity is not merely a dispute of words. For when we attribute identity, in an improper sense, to variable or interrupted objects, our mistake is not confined to the expression, but is commonly attended with a fiction, either of something invariable and uninterrupted, or of something mysterious and inexplicable, or at least with a propensity to such fictions. What will suffice to prove this hypothesis to the satisfaction of every fair enquirer is to show, from daily experience and observation, that the objects which are variable or interrupted, and yet are supposed to continue the same, are such only as consist of a succession of parts, connected together by resemblance, contiguity, or causation. For as such a succession answers evidently to our notion of diversity, it can only be by mistake we ascribe to it an identity; and as the relation of parts, which leads us into this mistake, is really nothing but a quality which produces an association of ideas, and an easy transition of the imagination from one to another, it can only be from the resemblance, which this act of the mind bears to that by which we contemplate one continued object, that the error arises. Our chief business, then, must be to prove that all objects to which we ascribe identity, without observing their invariableness and uninterruptedness, are such as consist of a succession of related objects.

In order to do this, suppose any mass of matter, of which the parts are contiguous and connected, to be placed before us; it is plain we must attribute a perfect identity to this mass, provided all the parts continue uninterruptedly and invariably the same, whatever motion or change of place we may observe either in the whole or in any of the parts. But suppose some very *small* or *inconsiderable* part to be added to the mass, or subtracted from it: though this absolutely destroys the identity of the whole, strictly speaking, yet as we seldom think so accurately, we scruple not to pronounce a mass of matter the same, where we find so trivial an alteration. The passage of the thought from the object before the change to the object after it is so smooth and easy that we scarce perceive the transition, and are apt to imagine that it is nothing but a continued survey of the same object.

There is a very remarkable circumstance that attends this experiment: though the change of any considerable part in a mass of matter destroys the identity of the whole, yet we must measure the greatness of the part not absolutely, but by its *proportion* to the whole. The addition or diminution of a mountain would not be sufficient to produce a diversity in a planet, though the change of a very few inches would be able to destroy the identity of some bodies. It will be impossible to account for this but by reflecting that objects operate upon the mind, and break or interrupt the continuity of its actions, not according to their real greatness, but according to their proportion to each other. And therefore, since this interruption makes an object cease to appear the same, it must be the uninterrupted progress of the thought which constitutes the imperfect identity.

This may be confirmed by another phenomenon. A change in any considerable part of a body destroys its identity; but it is remarkable that where the change is produced *gradually* and *insensibly* we are less apt to ascribe to it the same effect. The reason can plainly be no other than that the mind, in following the successive changes of the body, feels an easy passage from the surveying [of] its condition in one moment to the viewing of it in another, and at no particular time perceives any interruption in its actions. From which continued perception it ascribes a continued existence and identity to the object.

But whatever precaution we may use in introducing the changes gradually, and making them proportionable to the whole, it is certain that where the changes are at last observed to become considerable, we make a scruple of ascribing identity to such different objects. There is, however, another artifice by which we may induce the imagination to advance a step farther, and that is by producing a reference of the parts to each other, and a combination to some *common end* or purpose. A ship, of which a considerable part has been changed by frequent reparations, is still considered as the same; nor does the difference of the materials hinder us from ascribing an identity to it. The common end, in which the parts conspire, is the same under all their variations, and affords an easy transition of the imagination from one situation of the body to another.

But this is still more remarkable when we add a *sympathy* of parts for their *common end*, and suppose that they bear to each other the reciprocal relation of cause and effect in all their actions and operations. This is the case with all animals and vegetables, where not only the several parts have a reference to some general purpose, but also a mutual dependence on, and connection with, each other. The effect of so strong a relation is, that though every one must allow that in a very few years both vegetables and animals endure a *total* change, yet we still attribute identity to them, while their form, size, and substance are entirely altered. An oak, that grows from a small plant to a large tree, is still the same oak, though there be not one particle of matter, or figure of its parts the same. An infant becomes a man, and is sometimes fat, sometimes lean, without any change in his identity.

We may also consider the two following phenomena, which are remarkable in their kind. The first is, that though we commonly are able to distinguish pretty exactly betwixt numerical and specific identity, yet it sometimes happens that we confound them, and in our thinking and reasoning employ the one for the other. Thus a man who hears a noise that is frequently interrupted and renewed says it is still the same noise; though it is evident that sounds have only a specific identity or resemblance, and there is nothing numerically the same but the cause which produced them. In like manner it may be said, without breach of the propriety of language, that such a church, which was formerly of brick, fell to ruin, and that the parish rebuilt the same church of free-stone, and according to modern architecture. Here neither the form nor materials are the same, nor is there any thing common to the two objects but their relation to the inhabitants of the parish, and yet this alone is sufficient to make us denominate them the same. But we must observe that in these cases the first object is in a manner annihilated before the second comes into existence; by which means we are never presented in any one point of time with the idea of difference and multiplicity; and for that reason are less scrupulous in calling them the same.

Secondly, we may remark that though in a succession of related objects it be in a manner requisite that the change of parts be not sudden nor entire, in order to preserve the identity, yet where the objects are in their nature changeable and inconstant, we admit of a more sudden transition than would otherwise be consistent with that relation. Thus as the nature of a river consists in the motion and change of parts, though in less than four and twenty hours these be totally altered, this hinders not the river from continuing the same during several ages. What is natural and essential to any thing is, in a manner, expected, and appears of less moment than what is unusual and extraordinary. A considerable change of the former kind seems really less to the imagination than the most trivial alteration of the latter; and by breaking less the continuity of the thought, has less influence in destroying the identity.

We now proceed to explain the nature of *personal identity*, which has become so great a question in philosophy, especially of late years in England, where all the abstruser sciences are studied with a peculiar ardour and application. And here it is evident the same method of reasoning must be continued which has so successfully explained the identity of plants, and animals, and ships, and houses, and of all the compounded and changeable productions either of art or nature. The identity which we ascribe to the mind of man is only a fictitious one, and of a like kind with that which we ascribe to vegetables and animal bodies. It cannot, therefore, have a different origin, but must proceed from a like operation of the imagination upon like objects...

As memory alone acquaints us with the continuance and extent of this succession of perceptions, it is to be considered, upon that account chiefly, as the source of personal identity. Had we no memory, we never should have any notion of causation, nor consequently of that chain of causes and effects which constitute our self or person. But having once acquired this notion of causation from the memory, we can extend the same chain of causes, and consequently the identity of our persons, beyond our memory, and can comprehend times and circumstances and actions which we have entirely forgot, but suppose in general to have existed. For how few of our past actions are there of which we have any memory? Who can tell me, for instance, what were his thoughts and actions on the first of January 1715, the 11th of March 1719, and the 3rd of August 1733? Or will he affirm, because he has entirely forgot the incidents of these days, that the present self is not the same person as the self of that time, and by that means overturn all the most established notions of personal identity? In this view, therefore, memory does not so much *produce* as *discover* personal identity, by showing us the relation of cause and effect among our different perceptions. It will be incumbent on those who affirm that memory produces entirely our personal identity to give a reason why we can thus extend our identity beyond our memory.

The whole of this doctrine leads us to a conclusion, which is of great importance in the present affair, viz. that all the nice and subtle questions concerning personal identity can never possibly be decided, and are to be regarded rather as grammatical than as philosophical difficulties. Identity depends on the relations of ideas; and these relations produce identity, by means of that easy transition they occasion. But as the relations, and the easiness of the transition, may diminish by insensible degrees, we have no just standard by which we can decide any dispute concerning the time when they acquire or lose a title to the name of identity. All the disputes concerning the identity of connected objects are merely verbal, except so far as the relation of parts gives rise to some fiction or imaginary principle of union...

4   The Partly Hidden Self: Sigmund Freud, *Introductory Lectures on Psychoanalysis**

As we have seen, Locke explains the self in terms of the continuities of memory and consciousness; Butler takes the sense of self as a primitive 'given'; and Hume reduces the idea of self to a mere constant succession of impressions. But all these philosophers appear to take it for granted that each of us does possess a transparent awareness of the mental contents that constitute our personal lives. At the start of the twentieth century, however, the Austrian physician and founder of psychoanalysis Sigmund Freud propounded a revolutionary account of the mind which challenged the long-standing identification of the self with the conscious thinking subject (a conception with its roots in the philosophy of Descartes: see Part IV, extract 4). Freud argued that a large part of what makes up my mind is often hidden from me as a conscious subject. The notion of a 'divided self' was nothing very new; Plato, for example, had referred to 'conflicts' in the soul produced by different faculties (reason, spirit and desire);[1] but

* Sigmund Freud, *Introductory Lectures on Psychoanalysis* [*Vorlesungen zur Einführung in die Psychoanalyse*, 1916–17]. Trans. J. Riviere (London: Allen & Unwin, 1922), extracts from chs 17 and 18.
[1] See Plato, *Republic*, 441–5.

for Plato these conflicts were all, as it were, 'out in the open'. What Freud advances is the striking proposition that the desires, attitudes and actions that make up our conscious selves are strongly influenced by *unconscious* mental processes – wishes, beliefs, fears and anxieties of which we are typically unaware. Anyone who accepts Locke's account of the self as constituted by *consciousness*, by immediate or transparently remembered impressions, will find Freud's views bordering on the incomprehensible (and his ideas did, and still do, arouse strong opposition for violating established definitions of the mind). But Freud's claim that there are hidden contents which are none the less genuinely attributable to the subject's mind is made plausible by his account of how the subject can come to acknowledge those contents via the therapeutic process of guided self-discovery. In the course of psychoanalysis, those parts of the self which were before concealed from the thinking 'ego' now make their influence felt as beliefs, wishes, fears or anxieties that we recognize were, in a certain sense, there 'all along'. Although many of the details of Freud's theories have given rise to intense critical discussion, his ideas have irreversibly changed our ways of thinking about the self and the mind, and the full implications of those changes are still in process of being assimilated. The following extract is translated from lectures Freud originally delivered in Vienna in 1915–17.

A lady of nearly thirty years of age suffered from very severe obsessional symptoms. In the course of a day she would run out of her room into the adjoining one, there take up a certain position at the table in the centre of the room, ring for her maid, give her a trivial order or send her away, and then run back... Every time I asked the patient 'What is the meaning of it?' or 'Why do you do it?' she had answered 'I don't know'. But one day, after I had succeeded in overcoming a great hesitation on her part, she suddenly did know, for she related the history of the obsessive act. More than ten years previously she had married a man very much older than herself, who had proved impotent on the wedding night. Innumerable times on that night he had run out of his room into hers in order to make the attempt, but had failed every time. In the morning he had said angrily, 'It's enough to disgrace one in the eyes of the maid who does the beds', and seizing a bottle of red ink which happened to be at hand, he poured it on the sheet, but not exactly in the place where such a mark might have been. At first I did not understand what this recollection could have to do with the obsessive act in question; for I could see no similarity between the two situations, except perhaps the appearance of the servant upon the scene. The patient then led me to the table in the adjoining room, where I found a great mark on the table cover. She explained further that she stood by the table in such a way that when the maid came in she could not miss seeing this mark. After this, there could no longer be any doubt about the connection between the current obsessive act and the scene of the wedding night, although there was still a great deal to learn about it...

We have heard of the senseless obsessive act she performed and of the intimate memories she recalled in connection with it; we also considered the relation between the two, and deduced the purpose of the obsessive act from its connection with the memory. But there is one factor which we have entirely neglected, and yet it is one which deserves our fullest attention. As long as the patient continued this performance she did not know that it was in any way connected with the previous experience; the connection between the two things was hidden; she could quite truly answer that she did not know what impulse led her to do it. Then it happened suddenly that, under the influence of the treatment, she found this connection and was able to tell it. But even then she knew nothing of the purpose she had in performing the action, the purpose that was to correct a painful event of the past and to raise the husband she loved in her own estimation. It took a long time and much effort for her to grasp, and admit to me, that such a motive as this alone could have been the driving force behind the obsessive act.

The connection with the scene on the morning after the unhappy bridal night, and the patient's own tender feeling for her husband, together, make up what we have called the 'meaning' of the obsessive act. But both sides of this meaning were hidden from her: she understood neither the *whence* nor the *whither* of her act, as long as she carried it on. Mental processes had been at work in her, therefore, of which the obsessive act was the effect; she was aware in a normal manner of their effect, but nothing of the mental antecedents of this effect had come to the knowledge of her consciousness. She was behaving exactly like a subject under hypnotism who had been ordered by the hypnotist to open an umbrella in the ward five minutes after he awoke, but who had no idea why he was doing it. This is the kind of occurrence we have in mind when we speak of the existence of *unconscious mental processes*; we may challenge anyone in the world to give a more correctly scientific explanation of this matter, and will then gladly withdraw our inference that unconscious mental processes exist. Until they do, however, we will adhere to this inference and, when anyone objects that in a scientific sense the Unconscious has no reality, that it is a mere makeshift, *une façon de parler*, we must resign ourselves with a shrug to rejecting his statement as incomprehensible. Something unreal which can nevertheless produce something so real and palpable as an obsessive action!

...Consider now, in addition, that the facts established in these cases are confirmed in every symptom of every neurotic disease; that always and everywhere the meaning of the symptoms is unknown to the sufferer; that analysis invariably shows that these symptoms are derived from unconscious mental processes which can, however, under various favourable conditions, become conscious. You will then understand that we cannot dispense with the unconscious part of the mind in psycho-analysis, and that we are accustomed to deal with it as with something actual and tangible. Perhaps you will also be able to realize how unfitted all those who only know the Unconscious as a phrase, who have never analysed, never interpreted dreams, or translated neurotic symptoms into their meaning and intention, are to form an opinion on this matter. I will repeat the substance of it again in order to impress it upon you. The fact that it is possible to find meaning in neurotic symptoms by means of analytic interpretation is an irrefutable proof of the existence – or, if you prefer it, of the necessity for assuming the existence – of unconscious mental processes.

But that is not all. Thanks to a discovery of Breuer's,[1] for which he alone deserves credit and which seems to me even more far-reaching in its significance, more still has been learnt about the relation between the Unconscious and the symptoms of neurotics. Not merely is the meaning of the symptom invariably unconscious; there exists also a connection of a substitutive nature between the two; the existence of the symptom is only possible by reason of this unconscious activity. You will soon understand what I mean. With Breuer, I maintain the following: Every time we meet with a symptom we may conclude that definite unconscious activities which

---

[1] Dr Joseph Breuer, an early colleague of Freud's.

contain the meaning of the symptom are present in the patient's mind. Conversely, this meaning must be unconscious before a symptom can arise from it. Symptoms are not produced by conscious processes; as soon as the unconscious processes involved are made conscious the symptom must vanish. You will perceive at once that here is an opening for therapy, a way by which symptoms can be made to disappear. It was by this means that Breuer actually achieved the recovery of his patient, that is, freed her from her symptoms; he found a method of bringing into her consciousness the unconscious processes which contained the meaning of her symptoms, and the symptoms vanished.

This discovery of Breuer's was not the result of any speculation but of a fortunate observation made possible by the cooperation of the patient. Now you must not rack your brains to try and understand this by seeking to compare it with something similar that is already familiar to you; but you must recognize in it a fundamentally new fact, by means of which much else becomes explicable. Allow me therefore to express it again to you in other words.

The symptom is formed as a substitute for something else which remains submerged. Certain mental processes would, under normal conditions, develop until the person became aware of them consciously. This has not happened; and, instead, the symptom has arisen out of these processes which have been interrupted and interfered with in some way and have had to remain unconscious. Thus something in the nature of an exchange has occurred; if we can succeed in reversing this process by our therapy we shall have performed our task of dispersing the symptom.

Breuer's discovery still remains the foundation of psychoanalytic therapy. The proposition that symptoms vanish when their unconscious antecedents have been made conscious has been borne out by all subsequent research; although the most extraordinary and unexpected complications are met with in attempting to carry this proposition out in practice. Our therapy does its work by transforming something unconscious into something conscious, and only succeeds in its work in so far as it is able to effect this transformation.

Now for a rapid digression, lest you should run the risk of imagining that this therapeutic effect is achieved too easily. According to the conclusions we have reached so far, neurosis would be the result of a kind of ignorance, a not-knowing of mental processes which should be known. This would approach very closely to the well-known Socratic doctrine according to which even vice is the result of ignorance. Now it happens in analysis that an experienced practitioner can usually surmise very easily what those feelings are which have remained unconscious in each individual patient. It should not therefore be a matter of great difficulty to cure the patient by imparting this knowledge to him and so relieving his ignorance. At least, one side of the unconscious meaning of the symptom would be easily dealt with in this way, although it is true that the other side of it, the connection between the symptom and the previous experiences in the patient's life, can hardly be divined thus; for the analyst does not know what the experiences have been, he has to wait till the patient remembers them and tells him. But one might find a substitute even for this in many cases. One might ask for information about his past life from the friends and relations; they are often in a position to know what events have been of a traumatic nature, perhaps they can even relate some of which the patient is ignorant because they took place at some very early period of childhood. By a combination of these two means it would seem that the pathogenic ignorance of the patients might be overcome in a short time without much trouble.

If only it were so! But we have made discoveries that we were quite unprepared for at first. There is knowing and knowing; they are not always the same thing. There are various kinds of knowing which psychologically are not by any means of equal value. *Il y a fagots et fagots*, as Molière says. Knowing on the part of the physician is not the same thing as knowing on the part of the patient and does not have the same effect. When the physician conveys his knowledge to the patient by telling him what he knows, it has no effect. No, it would be incorrect to say that. It does not have the effect of dispersing the symptoms; but it has a different one, it sets the analysis in motion, and the first result of this is often an energetic denial. The patient has learned something that he did not know before – the meaning of his symptom – and yet he knows it as little as ever. Thus we discover that there is more than one kind of ignorance. It requires a considerable degree of insight and understanding of psychological matters in order to see in what the difference consists. But the proposition that symptoms vanish with the acquisition of knowledge of their meaning remains true, nevertheless. The necessary condition is that the knowledge must be founded upon an inner change in the patient which can only come about by a mental operation directed to that end. We are here confronted by problems which to us will soon develop into the *dynamics* of symptom-formation.

Now I must really stop and ask you whether all that I have been saying is not too obscure and complicated? Am I confusing you by so often qualifying and restricting, spinning out trains of thought and then letting them drop? I should be sorry if it were so. But I have a strong dislike of simplification at the expense of truth. I am not averse from giving you a full impression of the many-sidedness and intricacy of the subject, and also I believe that it does no harm to tell you more about each point than you can assimilate at the moment. I know that every listener and every reader arranges what is offered him as suits him in his own mind, shortens it, simplifies it, and extracts from it what he will retain. Within certain limits it is true that the more we begin with the more we shall have at the end. So let me hope that, in spite of the elaboration, you will have grasped the essential substance of my remarks concerning the meaning of symptoms, the Unconscious, and the connection between the two. You have probably understood also that our further efforts will proceed in two directions: first, towards discovering how people become ill, how they come to take up the characteristic neurotic attitude towards life, which is a clinical problem; and secondly, how they develop the morbid symptoms out of the conditions of a neurosis, which remains a problem of mental dynamics. The two problems must somewhere have a point of contact.

I shall not go further into this today; but as our time is not yet up I propose to draw your attention to another characteristic of our two analyses; namely, *the memory gaps or amnesias*, again a point which only later will appear in its full significance. You have heard that the task of the psycho-analytic treatment can be summed up in this formula: everything pathogenic in the Unconscious must be transferred into consciousness. Now you will be perhaps astonished to hear that another formula may be substituted for that one: all gaps in the patient's memory must be filled in, his amnesias removed. It amounts to the same thing; which means that an important connection is to be recognized between the development of the symptoms and the amnesias. If you consider the case of the first patient analysed you will, however, not find this view of amnesia justified; the patient had not forgotten the scene from which the obsessive act is derived; on the contrary, it was vivid in her memory, nor is there any other forgotten factor involved in the formation of her symptom...What is remarkable about it is that the patient, although she had carried out her obsessive act such a countless number of times, had not *once* been reminded of its similarity to the scene after the wedding night, nor did this recollection ever occur to her when she was directly asked to search for the origin of her obsessive act...This was not really an amnesia, a lapse of memory; but a connection, which should have existed intact and have led to the reproduction, the recollection, of the memory, had been broken. This kind of disturbance of memory suffices for the obsessional neurosis; in hysteria it is different. This latter neurosis is usually characterized by amnesias on a grand scale. As a rule the analysis of each single hysterical symptom leads to a whole chain of former impressions, which upon their return may be literally described as having been hitherto forgotten. This chain reaches, on the one hand, back to the earliest years of childhood, so that the hysterical amnesia is seen to be a direct continuation of the infantile amnesia which hides the earliest impressions of our mental life from all of us. On the other hand, we are astonished to find that the most recent experiences of the patient are liable to be forgotten also, and that in particular the provocations which induced the outbreak of the disease or aggravated it are at least partially obliterated, if not entirely wiped out, by amnesia. From the complete picture of any such recent recollection important details have invariably disappeared or been replaced by falsifications. It happens again and again, almost invariably, that not until shortly before the completion of an analysis do certain recollections of recent experiences come to the surface, which had managed to be withheld throughout it and had left noticeable gaps in the context.

These derangements in the capacity to recall memories are, as I have said, characteristic of hysteria, in which disease it also happens even that states occur as symptoms (the hysterical attacks) without necessarily leaving a trace of recollection behind them. Since it is otherwise in the obsessional neurosis, you may infer that these amnesias are part of the psychological character of the hysterical change and are not a universal trait of neurosis in general. The importance of this difference will be diminished by the following consideration. Two things are combined to constitute the meaning of a symptom; its *whence* and its *whither or why*; that is, the impressions and experiences from which it sprang, and the purpose which it serves. The *whence* of a symptom is resolved into impressions which have been received from without, which were necessarily at one time conscious, and which may have become unconscious by being forgotten since that time. The *why* of the symptom, its tendency, is however always an endo-psychic process, which may possibly have been conscious at first, but just as possibly may never have been conscious and may have remained in the Unconscious from its inception. Therefore it is not very important whether the amnesia has also infringed upon the *whence*, the impressions upon which the symptom is supported, as happens in hysteria; the *whither*, the tendency of the symptom, which may have been unconscious from the beginning, is what maintains the symptom's dependence upon the Unconscious, in the obsessional neurosis no less strictly than in hysteria.

By thus emphasizing the unconscious in mental life we have called forth all the malevolence in humanity in opposition to psycho-analysis. Do not be astonished at this and do not suppose that this opposition relates to the obvious difficulty of conceiving the Unconscious or to the relative inaccessibility of the evidence which supports its existence. I believe it has a deeper source. Humanity has in the course of time had to endure from the hands of science two great outrages upon its naïve self-love. The first was when it realized that our earth was not the centre of the universe, but only a tiny speck in a world-system of a magnitude hardly conceivable; this is associated in our minds with the name of Copernicus, although Alexandrian doctrines taught something very similar. The second was when biological research robbed man of his peculiar privilege of having been specially created, and relegated him to a descent from the animal world, implying an ineradicable animal nature in him: this transvaluation has been accomplished in our own time upon the instigation of Charles Darwin, Wallace, and their predecessors, and not without the most violent opposition from their contemporaries. But man's craving for grandiosity is now suffering the third and most bitter blow from present-day psychological research which is endeavouring to prove to the 'ego' of each one of us that he is not even master in his own house, but that he must remain content with the veriest scraps of information about what is going on unconsciously in his own mind. We psycho-analysts were neither the first nor the only ones to propose to mankind that they should look inward; but it appears to be our lot to advocate it most insistently and to support it by empirical evidence which touches every man closely.

5   Liberation from the Self: Derek Parfit, *Reasons and Persons*＊

The psychoanalytic process aims to recover parts of the self which can become buried as a result of past psychological disturbances (see previous extract); but even without invoking the Freudian unconscious, the notion that what is past can be integrated into present consciousness is an important part of our concept of the enduring self. But the self also projects itself forward in its hopes and fears for the future (indeed, the topic of a supposed future existence in the next world was the framework for many early discussions of personal identity). When we think of our future (either here on earth or in the next world), what exactly is it that is important for our survival? Is there some enduring entity called the 'self' which supports our continuous identity, or is our future survival just a matter of bodily constraints, or (as Locke suggested, extract

1 above) of psychological links supplied by memory?

In our next extract, the contemporary British philosopher Derek Parfit argues first of all that beyond physical and psychological continuity there is no 'deep' further fact about the survival of the 'self'. He discusses the imaginary case of 'teletransportation': a machine scans my body, destroying it in the process, but the information is recorded electronically and transmitted by radio to Mars, and an exact replica body created there, based on the transmitted information. Once we have freed ourselves from the idea that there is some special, deeply important thing called 'personal identity' which we want to preserve, then, Parfit argues, there is nothing to fear in 'travelling' in this unorthodox way. For in teletransportation, all the relations of psychological

＊ Derek Parfit, *Reasons and Persons* (Oxford: Oxford University Press, 1984; repr. 1987), extracts from sections 95 and 96 (pp. 279–87).

continuity are preserved, and on Parfit's 'reductionist' view these are all there really is to the notion of future survival, even in the ordinary everyday sense. All that matters is certain kinds of continuity, which are in any case matters of degree; and Parfit goes on to suggest that my special attachment to this particular body or brain is without any rational basis. Parfit's views, like those of Hume (see above, extract 3) pose a challenge to our ordinary ways of thinking; but whereas Hume supposed that philosophical perplexities about identity are best forgotten in the context of our ordinary day-to-day lives, Parfit argues that his results can and should make an important difference to how we live: giving up the idea of an identical 'self' is a source of enlightenment which can reduce our anxiety about our future lives and eventual inevitable deaths.

Why our identity is not what matters

...On the Reductionist View, my continued existence just involves physical and psychological continuity. On the Non-Reductionist view, it involves a further fact. It is natural to believe in this further fact, and to believe that, compared with the continuities, it is a *deep* fact, and is the fact that really matters. When I fear that, in Teletransportation, *I* shall not get to Mars, my fear is that the abnormal cause may fail to produce this further fact. As I have argued, there is no such fact. What I fear will not happen, *never* happens. I want the person on Mars to be me in a specially intimate way in which no future person will ever be me. My continued existence never involves this deep further fact. What I fear will be missing is *always* missing. Even a spaceship journey would not produce the further fact in which I am inclined to believe.

When I come to see that my continued existence does not involve this further fact, I lose my reason for preferring a spaceship journey. But, judged from the standpoint of my earlier belief, this is not because Teletransportation is *about as good as* ordinary survival. It is because ordinary survival is *about as bad as*, or little better than, Teletransportation. *Ordinary survival is about as bad as being destroyed and replicated.*

By rehearsing arguments like these, I might do enough to reduce my fear. I might be able to bring myself to press the green button. But I expect that I would never completely lose my intuitive belief in the Non-Reductionist View. It is hard to be serenely confident in my Reductionist conclusions. It is hard to believe that personal identity is not what matters. If tomorrow someone will be in agony, it is hard to believe that it could be an empty question whether this agony will be felt by *me*. And it is hard to believe that, if I am about to lose consciousness, there might be no answer to the question 'Am I about to die?'

Nagel once claimed that it is psychologically impossible to believe the Reductionist View.[1] Buddha claimed that, though this is very hard, it is possible. I find Buddha's claim to be true. After reviewing my arguments, I find that, at the reflective or intellectual level, though it is very hard to believe the Reductionist View, this is possible. My remaining doubts or fears seem to me irrational. Since I can believe this view, I assume that others can do so too. We can believe the truth about ourselves.

---

[1] See Suggestions for Further Reading at the end of this Part.

Liberation from the self

The truth is very different from what we are inclined to believe. Even if we are not aware of this, most of us are Non-Reductionists. If we considered my imagined cases, we would be strongly inclined to believe that our continued existence is a deep further fact, distinct from physical and psychological continuity, and a fact that must be all-or-nothing. This is not true.

Is the truth depressing? Some may find it so. But I find it liberating, and consoling. When I believed that my existence was such a further fact, I seemed imprisoned in myself. My life seemed like a glass tunnel, through which I was moving faster every year, and at the end of which there was darkness. When I changed my view, the walls of my glass tunnel disappeared. I now live in the open air. There is still a difference between my life and the lives of other people. But the difference is less. Other people are closer. I am less concerned about the rest of my own life, and more concerned about the lives of others.

When I believed the Non-Reductionist View, I also cared more about my inevitable death. After my death, there will no one living who will be me. I can now redescribe this fact. Though there will later be many experiences, none of these experiences will be connected to my present experiences by chains of such direct connections as those involved in experience-memory, or in the carrying out of an earlier intention. Some of these future experiences may be related to my present experiences in less direct ways. There will later be some memories about my life. And there may later be thoughts that are influenced by mine, or things done as the result of my advice. My death will break the more direct relations between my present experiences and future experiences, but it will not break various other relations. This is all there is to the fact that there will be no one living who will be me. Now that I have seen this, my death seems to me less bad.

Instead of saying, 'I shall be dead', I should say, 'There will be no future experiences that will be related, in certain ways, to these present experiences.' Because it reminds me what this fact involves, this redescription makes this fact less depressing. Suppose next that I must undergo some ordeal. Instead of saying, 'The person suffering will be me', I should say, 'There will be suffering that will be related, in certain ways, to these present experiences.' Once again, the redescribed fact seems to me less bad.

I can increase these effects by vividly imagining that I am about to undergo one of the operations I have described. I imagine that I am in a central case in the Combined Spectrum,[1] where it is an empty question whether I am about to die. It is very hard to believe that this question could be empty. When I review the arguments for this belief, and reconvince myself, this for a while stuns my natural concern for my future. When my actual future will be grim – as it would be if I shall be tortured, or shall face a firing squad at dawn – it will be good that I have this way of briefly stunning my concern.

[1] The Combined Spectrum: Parfit refers here to his discussion, earlier in the book, of a range of possible cases involving variations in the degrees of physical and psychological connectedness. For example, at the 'near' end of the spectrum, scientists replace a few of my brain cells, thereby altering just a few of my memories and other psychological characteristics. In cases further along the spectrum, a much larger percentage of cells is changed, leading to more radical changes in psychological connectedness. In the case at the far end, the resulting person would have none of my cells, and be in no way psychologically connected with me.

After Hume thought hard about his arguments, he was thrown into 'the most deplorable condition imaginable, environed with the deepest darkness'.[1] The cure was to dine and play backgammon with his friends. Hume's arguments supported total scepticism. This is why they brought darkness and utter loneliness. The arguments for Reductionism have on me the opposite effect. Thinking hard about these arguments removes the glass wall between me and others. And, as I have said, I care less about my death. This is merely the fact that, after a certain time, none of the experiences that will occur will be related, in certain ways, to my present experiences. Can this matter all that much?

The continuity of the body

Because it affects my emotions in these ways, I am glad that the Reductionist View is true. This is simply a report of psychological effects. The effects on others may be different.

... [P]ersonal identity is not what matters. It is merely true that, in most cases, personal identity coincides with what matters. What does matter in *the way in which* personal identity is, mistakenly, thought to matter? What is it rational to care about, in our concern about our own future?

This question can be restated. Assume, for simplicity, that it could be rational to be concerned only about one's own self-interest. Suppose that I am an Egoist, and that I could be related in one of several ways to some resulting person. What is the relation that would justify egoistic concern about this resulting person? If the rest of this person's life will be well worth living, in what way should I want to be related to this person? If the rest of his life will be much worse than nothing, in what way should I want *not* to be related to this person? In short, what is the relation that, for an Egoist, should fundamentally matter? This relation will also be what, for all of us, should fundamentally matter, in our concern for our own future. But since we may be concerned about the fate of the resulting person, *whatever* his relation is to us, it is clearest to ask what, for an Egoist, should matter.

Here are the simplest answers:

(1) Physical continuity,
(2) Relation *R* with its normal cause,
(3) *R* with any reliable cause,
(4) *R* with any cause.

R is psychological connectedness and/or continuity, with the right kind of cause. If we decide that *R* is what matters, we must then consider the relative importance of connectedness and continuity. It might be suggested that what matters is *both* R *and* physical continuity. But this is the same as answer (2), since physical continuity is part of *R*'s normal cause.

Can we defend (1), the claim that only physical continuity matters? Can we claim that, if I shall be physically continuous with some resulting person, this is what matters, even if I shall not be *R*-related to this person?

---

[1] *Treatise of Human Nature* [1739–40], Bk I, part iv, section 7, para 8.

Reconsider Williams's example,[1] where the surgeon totally destroys any distinctive kind of psychological continuity. Suppose that this surgeon is about to operate on me, in a painless way, and that the resulting person will have a life that is much worse than nothing. If I was an Egoist, I might regard this prospect as being no worse than a painless death, since I do not care what will happen to the resulting person. I might instead regard this prospect as much worse than death, because I am egoistically concerned about this person's appalling future. Which should my attitude be? . . . I must ask whether, *in itself*, physical continuity justifies egoistic concern.

I believe that the answer must be No. As I argued, those who believe in the Physical Criterion cannot plausibly require the continuity of the whole body. It cannot matter whether I receive some transplanted organ, if this organ functions just as well. All that could be claimed to matter is that enough of my brain continues to exist.

Why should the brain be singled out in this way? The answer must be 'Because the brain is the carrier of psychological continuity, or Relation R'. If this is why the brain is singled out, the continuity of the brain would not matter when it was *not* the carrier of Relation R. The continuity of the brain would here be no more important than the continuity of any other part of the body. And the continuity of these other parts does not matter at all. It would not matter if these other parts were replaced with sufficiently similar duplicates. We should claim the same about the brain. The continuity of the brain matters if it is the cause of the holding of Relation R. If R will *not* hold, the continuity of the brain would have no significance for the person whose brain it originally was. It would not justify egoistic concern.

Reductionists cannot plausibly claim that only physical continuity matters. They can at most claim that this continuity is part of what matters. They can at most defend (2), the claim that Relation R would not matter if it did not have its normal cause, part of which is physical continuity.

I believe that (2) is also indefensible.[2] . . .

On my view, my relation to my Replica contains what fundamentally matters. This relation is about as good as ordinary survival. Judged from the standpoint of the Non-Reductionist View, ordinary survival is, on my view, little better than – or about as bad as – being destroyed and Replicated. It would therefore be irrational to pay much more for a conventional spaceship journey.

Many people would be afraid of Teletransportation. I admit that, at some level, I might be afraid. But, as I have argued, such fear cannot be rational. Since I know exactly what will happen, I cannot fear that the worse of two outcomes will be what happens.

My relation to my Replica is R without its normal cause. The abnormality of the cause seems to me trivial. Reconsider the artificial eyes which would restore sight to those who have gone blind. Suppose that these eyes would give to these people visual sensations just like those involved in normal sight, and that these sensations would provide true beliefs about what can be seen. This would surely be as good as normal sight. It would not be plausible to reject these eyes because they were not the normal cause of human sight. There would be some grounds for disliking artificial eyes since they would make one's appearance disturbing to others. But there is no analogue to

---

[1] See Suggestions for Further Reading, below.

[2] A portion of the original text has been omitted here at the request of the author.

this in Teletransportation. My Replica, though he is artificially produced, will be just like me in every way. He will have a normal brain and body...

My attitude to this outcome should not be affected by our decision whether to call my Replica me. I know the full facts even if we have not yet made this decision. If we do decide not to call my Replica me, the fact

(*a*) that my Replica will not be me

would just consist in the fact

(*b*) that there will not be physical continuity,

and

(*c*) that, because this is so, R will not have its normal cause.

Since (*a*) would just consist in (*b*) and (*c*), I should ignore (*a*). My attitude should depend on the importance of facts (*b*) and (*c*). These facts are all there is to my Replica's not being me.

When we see that this last claim is true, we cannot rationally, I believe, claim that (*c*) matters much. It cannot matter much that the cause is abnormal. It is the *effect* which matters. And this effect, the holding of Relation *R*, is in itself the same. It is true that, if this effect has the abnormal cause, we can describe the effect in a different way. We can say that, though my Replica is psychologically continuous with me, he will not be me. But this is not a further difference in what happens, beyond the difference in the cause. If I decide not to press the button, and to pay much more for a conventional spaceship journey, I must admit that this is merely because I do not like the thought of an abnormal method of causation. It cannot be rational to care much about the abnormality of this cause.

Similar remarks apply to the continued existence of one's present brain and body. It may be rational to want the body of my Replica to be like my present body. But this is a desire for a certain kind of body, not a desire for the same particular body. Why should I want it to be true that *this* brain and body gets to Mars? Once again, the natural fear is that only this ensures that I shall get to Mars. But this again assumes that whether or not I get to Mars is, here, a real question. And we have been forced to conclude that it is an empty question. Even if this question has a best answer, we could know exactly what will happen before deciding what this answer is. Since this is so, can I rationally care a great deal whether or not this person's brain and body will be my present brain and body? I believe that, while it may not be irrational to care a little, to care a great deal would be irrational.

Why would it not be irrational to care a little? This could be like one's wish to keep the same wedding ring, rather than a new ring that is exactly similar. We understand the sentimental wish to keep the very ring that was involved in the wedding ceremony. In the same way, it may not be irrational to have a mild preference that the person on Mars have my present brain and body.

There remains one question. If there will be some person who will be *R*-related to me, would it matter if this relation did not have a reliable cause?

There is an obvious reason for preferring, in advance, that the cause will be reliable. Suppose that Teletransportation worked perfectly in a few cases, but in most cases was a complete failure. In a few cases, the person on Mars would be a perfect Replica of me. But in most cases he would be totally unlike me. If these were the facts, it would clearly be rational to pay the larger fare of a spaceship journey. But this is irrelevant. We should ask, 'In the few cases, where my Replica will be fully *R*-related to me, would it matter that *R* did not have a reliable cause?'

I believe that the answer must again be No. Suppose that there is an unreliable treatment for some disease. In most cases the treatment achieves nothing. But in a few cases it completely cures this disease. In these few cases, only the effect matters. The effect is just as good, even though its cause was unreliable. We should claim the same about Relation *R*. I conclude that, of the answers I described, we should accept (4). In our concern about our own future, *what fundamentally matters is relation* R, *with any cause*.

6   Selfhood and Narrative Understanding: Charles Taylor, *Sources of the Self**

In our last extract for this first half of Part V, the Canadian philosopher Charles Taylor advances a radically different view of the self from that put forward by Derek Parfit in the preceding passage. Approaching the problems of selfhood from an ethical perspective, Taylor begins by arguing that to make sense of our lives, and indeed to have an identity at all, 'we need an orientation to the good'; we need to have some sense of our lives as moving towards moral growth and maturity. It follows from this that our lives have a *narrative* shape: as I develop, and learn from my failings and mistakes, there is always a story to be told about how I have become what I now am, and where my current journey towards improvement will take me. Just as my sense of where I am in physical space depends on how I got here and where I am going next, so it is, Taylor argues, with 'my orientation in moral space'.

As Taylor goes on to explain, this idea takes us far away from Parfit's view (see preceding extract) that there are no 'deep' facts about the identity of the self, and indeed that selfhood itself is reducible to certain relations of psycho-logical continuity across time, which are merely matters of degree. For Taylor, this is a 'neutral' and 'bleached' conception of personhood, which tries to abstract from the framework of moral significance which gives shape to my life as a whole. '[A]s a being who grows and becomes I can only know myself through the history of my maturations and regressions, overcomings and defeats. My self-understanding necessarily has temporal depth and incorporates narrative.'

If Taylor is right, there is something misguided about the approach to the self (discernible in several of the preceding extracts) that attempts to treat it simply as a topic for analysis in the philosophy of mind, as if it could be understood merely in terms of certain purely descriptive psychological or biological properties. Taylor's conception, by contrast, sees the self as an in-escapably normative notion – it is a concept that is defined in terms of values, goals and moral standards. Human persons exist only, as Taylor puts it, 'in a certain space of questions' – questions about the meaning and purpose of my life as a whole. Many will find this a highly

* Charles Taylor, *Sources of the Self: The Making of Modern Identity* (Cambridge: Cambridge University Press, 1989), pp. 46–52.

attractive picture, though it implicitly presupposes a commitment (which some may want to
question) to the idea of an independent and
objective good towards which I can 'orient'
myself, and which serves to give 'shape' and
meaning to a human life.[1]

The issue of our condition can never be exhausted for us by what we are, because we
are always also changing and *becoming*. It is only slowly that we grow through infancy
and childhood to be autonomous agents who have something like our own place
relative to the good at all. And even then, that place is constantly challenged by the
new events of our lives, as well as constantly under potential revision, as we experience
more and mature. So the issue for us has to be not only where we are, but where we're
going; and though the first may be a matter of more or less, the latter is a question of
towards or away from, an issue of yes or no. That is why an absolute question always
frames our relative ones. Since we cannot do without an orientation to the good, and
since we cannot be indifferent to our place relative to this good, and since this place is
something that must always change and become, the issue of the direction of our lives
must arise for us.

Here we connect up with another inescapable feature of human life. I have been
arguing that in order to make minimal sense of our lives, in order to have an identity,
we need an orientation to the good, which means some sense of qualitative discrimination, of the incomparably higher. Now we see that this sense of the good has to be
woven into my understanding of my life as an unfolding story. But this is to state
another basic condition of making sense of ourselves, that we grasp our lives in a
narrative. This has been much discussed recently, and very insightfully. It has often
been remarked[2] that making sense of one's life as a story is also, like orientation to the
good, not an optional extra; that our lives exist also in this space of questions, which
only a coherent narrative can answer. In order to have a sense of who we are, we have
to have a notion of how we have become, and of where we are going.

Heidegger, in *Being and Time*,[3] described the inescapable temporal structure of
being in the world: that from a sense of what we have become, among a range of
present possibilities, we project our future being. This is the structure of any situated
action, of course, however trivial. From my sense of being at the drugstore, among the
possible other destinations, I project to walk home. But it applies also to this crucial
issue of my place relative to the good. From my sense of where I am relative to it, and
among the different possibilities, I project the direction of my life in relation to it. My
life always has this degree of narrative understanding, that I understand my present
action in the form of an 'and then': there was A (what I am), and then I do B (what
I project to become).

But narrative must play a bigger role than merely structuring my present. What
I am has to be understood as what I have become. This is normally so even for such
everyday matters as knowing where I am. I usually know this partly through my sense
of how I have come there. But it is inescapably so for the issue of where I am in moral
space. I can't know in a flash that I have attained perfection, or am halfway there.

---

[1] For more on the meaning of human life, see Part XII, below.

[2] *For instance in Alasdair MacIntyre, *After Virtue* (London: Duckworth, 1981; 2nd edn 1985). [Compare
Part VIII, extract 11, below.]

[3] *Martin Heidegger, *Being and Time* [*Sein und Zeit*, 1927], Div. II, chs 3 and 4.

Of course, there are experiences in which we are carried away in rapture and may believe ourselves spoken to by angels; or less exaltedly, in which we sense for a minute the incredible fullness and intense meaning of life; or in which we feel a great surge of power and mastery over the difficulties that usually drag us down. But there is always an issue of what to make of these instants, how much illusion or mere 'tripping' is involved in them, how genuinely they reflect real growth or goodness. We can only answer this kind of question by seeing how they fit into our surrounding life, that is, what part they play in a narrative of this life. We have to move forward and back to make a real assessment.

To the extent that we move back, we determine what we are by what we have become, by the story of how we got there. Orientation in moral space turns out again to be similar to orientation in physical space. We know where we are through a mixture of recognition of landmarks before us and a sense of how we have travelled to get here, as I indicated above. If I leave the local drugstore, and turn the corner to find the Taj Mahal staring me in the face, I am more likely to conclude that the movie industry is once again earning its tax write-offs in Montreal than to believe myself suddenly by the Jumna. This is analogous to my distrust of sudden rapture. Part of my sense of its genuineness will turn on how I got there. And our entire understanding beforehand of states of greater perfection, however defined, is strongly shaped by our striving to attain them. We come to understand in part what really characterizes the moral states we seek through the very effort of trying, and at first failing, to achieve them.

Of course, the immediate experience could be strong and convincing enough on its own. If it really were all there, Taj, Jumna, the city of Agra, bullocks, sky, everything, I would have to accept my new location, however mysterious my translation. Something analogous may exist spiritually. But even here, your past striving and moral experience would alone enable you to understand and identify this rapturous state. You would recognize it only through having striven in a certain direction, and that means again that you know what you are through what you have become. Thus making sense of my present action, when we are not dealing with such trivial questions as where I shall go in the next five minutes but with the issue of my place relative to the good, requires a narrative understanding of my life, a sense of what I have become which can only be given in a story. And as I project my life forward and endorse the existing direction or give it a new one, I project a future story, not just a state of the momentary future but a bent for my whole life to come. This sense of my life as having a direction towards what I am not yet is what Alasdair MacIntyre captures in his notion quoted above that life is seen as a 'quest'.[1]

This of course connects with an important philosophical issue about the unity of a life, which has once more been brought to the fore by Derek Parfit's interesting book, *Reasons and Persons*.[2] Parfit defends some version of the view that a human life is not an a priori unity or that personal identity doesn't have to be defined in terms of a whole life. It is perfectly defensible for me to consider (what I would conventionally call) my earlier, say, preadolescent self as another person and, similarly, to consider what 'I' (as we normally put it) shall be several decades in the future as still another person.

---

[1] *After Virtue*, pp. 203–4.
[2] *Reasons and Persons* (Oxford: Oxford University Press, 1984). [See preceding extract.]

This whole position draws on the Lockean (further developed in the Humean) understanding of personal identity.[1] Parfit's arguments draw on examples which are of a kind inaugurated by Locke, where because of the unusual and perplexing relation of mind to body our usual intuitions about the unity of a person are disturbed.[2] From my point of view, this whole conception suffers from a fatal flaw. Personal identity is the identity of the self, and the self is understood as an object to be known. It is not on all fours with other objects, true. For Locke it has this peculiarity that it essentially appears to itself. Its being is inseparable from self-awareness.[3] Personal identity is then a matter of self-consciousness.[4] But it is not at all what I have been calling the self, something which can exist only in a space of moral issues. Self-perception is the crucial defining characteristic of the person for Locke.[5] . . . All that remains of the insight that the self is crucially an object of significance to itself is this requirement of self-consciousness. But what has been left out is precisely the mattering. The self is defined in neutral terms, outside of any essential framework of questions. In fact, of course, Locke recognizes that we are not indifferent to ourselves; but he has no inkling of the self as a being which essentially is constituted by a certain mode of self-concern – in contrast to the concern we cannot but have about the quality of our experiences as pleasurable or painful . . . [This] neutral and 'bleached' sense of the person corresponds to Locke's aspiration to a disengaged subject of rational control. We have here a paradigm example of . . . how the assertion of the modern individual has spawned an erroneous understanding of the self.

This is what I want to call the 'punctual' or 'neutral' self – 'punctual' because the self is defined in abstraction from any constitutive concerns and hence from any identity in the sense in which I have been using the term . . . Its only constitutive property is self-awareness. This is the self that Hume set out to find and, predictably, failed to find. And it is basically the same notion of the self that Parfit is working with, one whose 'identity over time just involves . . . psychological connectedness and/or psychological continuity, with the right kind of cause'.[6]

If we think of the self as neutral, then it does perhaps make sense to hold that it is an ultimately an arbitrary question how we count selves. Our picking out of enumerable objects in the world can be thought to depend ultimately on the interests and concerns we bring to them. My car to me is a single thing. To a skilled garage

---

[1] *John Locke, *Essay concerning Human Understanding* [1690] [see extract 1, above]; David Hume, *A Treatise of Human Nature* [1739–40], Bk I, pt iv, § 6 [see extract 3, above].

[2] *Parfit, *Reasons and Persons*, chs 10–13. Locke relies on the case of minds 'switching bodies'; Parfit puts particular weight on division of a person into two.

[3] *Essay concerning Human Understanding*, Bk II, ch 27, § 9.

[4] *'For, it being the same consciousness that makes a man be himself to himself, *personal identity* depends on that only, whether it be annexed solely to one individual substance, or can be continued in a succession of several substances' (Locke, *Essay concerning Human Understanding*, Bk II, ch 27, § 9). [See extract 1, above.] Parfit wants to sidetrack the old issue of personal identity, but what takes its place is a kind of psychological connectedness or continuity, which is a descendant of Locke's criterion [see extract 5, above].

[5] 'To find wherein *personal identity* consists, we must consider what *person* stands for; which, I think, is a thinking intelligent being that has reason and reflection and can consider itself as itself, the same thinking thing in different times and places' (*Essay concerning Human Understanding*, Bk II, ch 27, § 9). [See extract 1, above.]

[6] Compare preceding extract, p. 299, above.

mechanic, it may be an assemblage of discrete functioning units. There is no sense to the question what it 'really' is, *an sich* [in itself], as it were.

But if my position here is right, then we can't think of human persons, of selves in the sense that we are selves, in this light at all. They are not neutral, punctual objects; they exist only in a certain space of questions, through certain constitutive concerns. The questions or concerns touch on the nature of the good that I orient myself by and on the way I am placed in relation to it. But then what counts as a unit will be defined by the scope of the concern, by just what is in question. And what is in question is, generally and characteristically, the shape of my life as a whole. It is not something up for arbitrary determination.

. . . I don't have a sense of where/what I am . . . without some understanding of how I have got there or become so. My sense of myself is of a being who is growing and becoming. In the very nature of things this cannot be instantaneous. It is not only that I need time and many incidents to sort out what is relatively fixed and stable in my character, temperament and desires from what is variable and changing, though that is true. It is also that as a being who grows and becomes I can only know myself through the history of my maturations and regressions, overcomings and defeats. My self-understanding necessarily has temporal depth and incorporates narrative.

But does that mean that I have to consider my whole past life as that of a single person? Isn't there room for decision here? After all, even what happened before I was born might on one reading be seen as part of the process of my becoming. Isn't birth itself an arbitrary point? There is perhaps an easy answer to this last question. There clearly is a kind of continuity running through my lifetime that doesn't extend before it. But the objector seems to have some point here: don't we often want to speak of what we were as children or adolescents in terms like this: 'I was a different person then'?

But it is clear that this image doesn't have the import of a real counter-example to the thesis I'm defending. And this becomes obvious when we look at another aspect of our essential concern here. We want our lives to have meaning, or weight, or substance, or to grow towards some fullness, or however the concern is formulated that we have been discussing in this section. But this means our whole lives. If necessary, we want the future to 'redeem' the past, to make it part of a life story which has sense or purpose, to take it up in a meaningful unity. A famous, perhaps for us moderns a paradigm, example of what this can mean is recounted by Proust in his *À la recherche du temps perdu*. In the scene in the Guermantes's library, the narrator recovers the full meaning of his past and thus restores the time which was 'lost' in the two senses I mentioned above. The formerly irretrievable past is recovered in its unity with the life yet to live, and all the 'wasted' time now has a meaning, as the time of preparation for the work of the writer who will give shape to this unity.[1]

To repudiate my childhood as unredeemable in this sense is to accept a kind of mutilation as a person; it is to fail to meet the full challenge involved in making sense of my life. This is the sense in which it is not up for arbitrary determination what the temporal limits of my personhood are.

---

[1]   In *Le temps retrouvé* [*Time Regained*], the final volume of Marcel Proust's eight-part novel *À la recherche du temps perdu* [1913–27], translated into English as *Remembrance of Things Past*.

If we look towards the future, the case is even clearer. On the basis of what I am I project my future. On what basis could I consider that only, say, the next ten years were 'my' future, and that my old age would be that of another person? Here too we note that a future project will often go beyond my death. I plan the future for my family, my country, my cause. But there is a different sense in which I am responsible for myself (at least in our culture). How could I justify considering myself in my sixties, say, as another person for this purpose? And how would *his* life get its meaning?

It seems clear from all this that there is something like an a priori unity of a human life through its whole extent. Not quite, because one can imagine cultures in which it might be split. Perhaps at some age, say forty, people go through a horrendous ritual passage, in which they go into ecstasy and then emerge as, say, the reincarnated ancestor. That is how they describe things and live them. In that culture there is a sense to treating this whole life cycle as containing two persons. But in the absence of such a cultural understanding, e.g., in our world, the supposition that I could be two temporally succeeding selves is either an overdramatized image, or quite false. It runs against the structural features of a self as a being who exists in a space of concerns.

In the previous section we saw that our being selves is essentially linked to our sense of the good, and that we achieve selfhood among other selves. Here I have been arguing that the issue of how we are placed in relation to this good is of crucial and inescapable concern for us, that we cannot but strive to give our lives meaning or substance, and that this means that we understand ourselves inescapably in narrative.

My underlying thesis is that there is a close connection between the different conditions of identity, or of one's life making sense, that I have been discussing. One could put it this way: because we cannot but orient ourselves to the good, and thus determine our place relative to it and hence determine the direction of our lives, we must inescapably understand our lives in narrative form, as a 'quest'. But one could perhaps start from another point: because we have to determine our place in relation to the good, therefore we cannot be without an orientation to it, and hence must see our life in story. From whichever direction, I see these conditions as connected facets of the same reality, inescapable structural requirements of human agency.

(b) Freedom

7   Human Freedom and Divine Providence: Augustine, *The City of God**

We think of ourselves as having freedom to make decisions and to control, at least to some extent, the course of our lives. But we can also see that we are part of a universe that appears to operate in ways that are pretty much fixed and unalterable from the human point of view. In the ancient world, it was widely believed that the doings of mortals (and even the Gods) were subject to

---

* Augustine of Hippo, *The City of God* [*De Civitate Dei*, 413–26], Bk V, chs 9–11. Trans. in *The Works of Aurelius Augustine*, ed. M. Dods (Edinburgh: T. & T. Clark, 1872), pp. 190–8; with modifications.

something called Fate; as the leading Stoic philosopher Chrysippus (3rd century BC) defined it, 'Fate is a certain natural everlasting ordering of the whole: one set of things follows on and succeeds another, and the interconnection is inviolable.'[1] Many later scientific writers regarded the universe as a closed deterministic system, where every event necessarily follows as a result of fixed causal laws.[2] And this gives rise to what philosophers call the problem of free will and determinism: how can we humans be truly free in a world where everything is in a sense determined beforehand?

In our first extract, from the early Christian writer St Augustine of Hippo (354–430), the problem is discussed within a theological setting: given the existence of an all-powerful, all-knowing God, who 'knows unchangeably all things which shall be', is the freedom of our will threatened? Augustine gives a firmly negative answer: 'it does not follow that because there is for God a

certain order of all causes, there must therefore be nothing depending on the free exercise of our wills; for our wills themselves are included in that order of causes which is certain to God and embraced by his foreknowledge'. Augustine's position has come to be known as a 'compatibilist' view of freedom and determinism: a universal causality is compatible with (does not rule out) human freedom, since (as Augustine puts it) 'our wills still exist *as wills*'. If everything is unalterably determined (or subject to the 'laws of divine providence' in Augustine's words), this may seem to entail the idea of necessity, that we *have to* act in such and such a way. But Augustine aptly points out that necessity is only worrying if it implies that we have to do something whether we want to or not; in those cases where we do something because *we will* to do it, then 'we should have no dread of that necessity taking away the freedom of our will'.

 ## The foreknowledge of God, and the free will of man (in opposition to the opinion of Cicero)

The manner in which Cicero addresses himself to the task of refuting the Stoics shows that he did not think he could effect anything against them in argument unless he had first demolished divination.[3] And this he attempts to accomplish by denying that there is any knowledge of future things, and maintains with all his might that there is no such knowledge either in God or man, and that there is no prediction of events. Thus he both denies the foreknowledge of God, and attempts by pointless arguments, and by attacking certain oracles that are very easily refuted, to overthrow all prophecy, even such as is clearer than the light . . . Nevertheless, those who assert the fatal influence of the stars are far more acceptable than they who deny the foreknowledge of future events. For to confess that God exists, and at the same time to deny that He has foreknowledge of future things, is the most manifest folly. This Cicero himself saw, and therefore attempted to assert the doctrine embodied in the words of Scripture, 'The fool hath said in his heart, There is no God.' . . . However, in his book on divination, he in his own person most openly opposes the doctrine of the prescience of future things. But all this he seems to do in order that he may not grant the doctrine of fate, and by so doing destroy free will. For he thinks that, the knowledge of future things being once conceded, fate follows as so necessary a consequence that it cannot be denied.

[1] *On Providence*, Bk 4. Included in A. A. Long and D. N. Sedley (eds), *The Hellenistic Philosophers* (Cambridge: Cambridge University Press, 1987), p. 336.

[2] Compare extract 9, below.

[3] Marcus Tullius Cicero (106–43 BC), Roman orator, statesman and philosopher. In his *De Divinatione* ('On Divination'), to which Augustine refers here, he attacked the Stoic doctrine of unalterable fate governing every detail of the world cycle.

But, let these perplexing debatings and disputations of the philosophers go on as they may, we, in order that we may confess the most high and true God Himself, do confess His will, supreme power, and prescience. Neither let us be afraid lest, after all, we do not do by will that which we do by will because He, whose foreknowledge is infallible, foreknew that we would do it. It was this which Cicero was afraid of, and therefore opposed foreknowledge. The Stoics also maintained that all things do not come to pass by necessity, although they contended that all things happen according to destiny. What is it, then, that Cicero feared in the prescience of future things? Doubtless it was this – that if all future things have been foreknown, they will happen in the order in which they have been foreknown; and if they come to pass in this order, there is a certain order of things foreknown by God; and if a certain order of things, then a certain order of causes, for nothing can happen which is not preceded by some efficient cause. But if there is a certain order of causes according to which everything happens which does happen, then by fate, says he, all things happen which do happen. But if this be so, then is there nothing in our own power, and there is no such thing as freedom of will; and if we grant that, says he, the whole organization of human life is subverted. In vain are laws enacted. In vain are reproaches, praises, chidings, exhortations had recourse to; and there is no justice whatever in the appointment of rewards for the good, and punishments for the wicked. In order that consequences so disgraceful, and absurd, and pernicious to humanity may not follow, Cicero chooses to reject the foreknowledge of future things, and shuts up the religious mind to this alternative, to make choice between two things, either that something is in our own power, or that there is foreknowledge – both of which cannot be true; but if the one is affirmed, the other is thereby denied. He therefore, like a truly great and wise man, and one who consulted very much and very skilfully for the good of humanity, of those two chose the freedom of the will, to confirm which he denied the foreknowledge of future things; and thus, wishing to make men free, he makes them sacrilegious. But the religious mind chooses both, confesses both, and maintains both by the faith of piety. But how so says Cicero; for the knowledge of future things being granted, there follows a chain of consequences which ends in this, that there can be nothing depending on our own free wills. And further, if there is anything depending on our wills, we must go backwards by the same steps of reasoning till we arrive at the conclusion that there is no foreknowledge of future things. For we go backwards through all the steps in the following order: – If there is free will, all things do not happen according to fate; if all things do not happen according to fate, there is not a certain order of causes; and if there is not a certain order of causes, neither is there a certain order of things foreknown by God – for things cannot come to pass unless they are preceded by efficient causes – but, if there is no fixed and certain order of causes foreknown by God, all things cannot be said to happen according as He foreknew that they would happen. And further, if it is not true that all things happen just as they have been foreknown by Him, there is not, says he, in God any foreknowledge of future events.

Now, against the sacrilegious and impious darings of reason, we assert both that God knows all things before they come to pass, and that we do by our free will whatsoever we know and feel to be done by us only because we will it. But that all things come to pass by fate, we do not say; indeed we affirm that nothing comes to pass by fate; for we demonstrate that the term 'fate', as it is generally used by those who speak of fate, meaning thereby the position of the stars at the time of each one's conception or birth, is a meaningless word, for astrology itself is a delusion. But an order of causes in which the highest efficiency is attributed to the will of God, we neither deny nor do we designate it by the name of fate, unless, perhaps, we may understand fate to mean that which is spoken, deriving it from *fari*, to speak; for we cannot deny that it is written in the sacred Scriptures, 'God hath spoken once; these two things have I heard, that power belongeth unto God. Also unto Thee, O God, belongeth mercy: for Thou wilt render unto very man according to his works' (Psalm 62). Now the expression, 'Once hath He spoken,' is to be understood as meaning '*immovably*, that is, unchangeably hath He spoken', inasmuch as He knows unchangeably all things which shall be, and all things which He will do. We might, then, use the word 'fate' in the sense it bears when derived from *fari* to speak, had it not already come to be understood in another sense, into which I am unwilling that the hearts of men should unconsciously slide. But it does not follow that, though there is for God a certain order of all causes, there must therefore be nothing depending on the free exercise of our own wills, for our wills themselves are included in that order of causes which is certain to God, and is embraced by his foreknowledge, for human wills are also causes of human actions; and he who foreknew all the causes of things would certainly among those causes not have been ignorant of our wills...

How, then, does an order of causes which is certain to the foreknowledge of God necessitate that there should be nothing which is dependent on our wills, when our wills themselves have a very important place in the order of causes? Cicero contends with those who call this order of causes fatal, or rather designate this order itself by the name of fate: to which we have an abhorrence, especially on account of the word, which men have become accustomed to understand as meaning what is not true. But, whereas he denies that the order of all causes is most certain, and perfectly clear to the prescience of God, we detest his opinion more than the Stoics do. For he either denies that God exists – which, indeed, in an assumed personage, he has laboured to do, in his book *De Natura Deorum* – or if he confesses that He exists, but denies that He is prescient of future things, what is that but just 'the fool saying in his heart there is no God'? For one who is not prescient of all future things is not God. Wherefore our wills also have just so much power as God willed and foreknew that they should have, and therefore whatever power they have, they have it within most certain limits; and whatever they are to do, they are most assuredly to do; for He whose foreknowledge is infallible foreknew that they would have the power to do it, and would do it. Wherefore, if I should choose to apply the name of fate to anything at all, I should rather say that fate belongs to the weaker of two parties, will to the stronger, who has the other in his power, than that the freedom of our will is excluded by that order of causes which, by an unusual application of the word peculiar to themselves, the Stoics call *Fate*.

Are our wills ruled by necessity?

It follows that there is also nothing to fear in that necessity, for dread of which the Stoics laboured to make such distinctions among the causes of things as should enable them to rescue certain things from the dominion of necessity and to subject others to it. Among those things which they wished not to be subject to necessity they placed our wills, knowing that they would not be free if subjected to necessity. For if that is to be called *our necessity* which is not in our power, but even though we be unwilling effects what it can effect – as, for instance, the necessity of death – it is manifest that our wills by which we live uprightly or wickedly are not under such a necessity; for we do many things which, if we were not willing, we should certainly not do. This is primarily true of the act of willing itself – for if we will, it *is*; if we will not, it *is not* – for we should not will if we were unwilling. But if we define necessity to be that according to which we say that it is necessary that anything be of such or such a nature, or be done in such and such a manner, I know not why we should have any dread of that necessity taking away the freedom of our will. For we do not put the life of God or the foreknowledge of God under necessity if we should say that it is necessary that God should live forever, and foreknow all things; as neither is His power diminished when we say that He cannot die or fall into error – for this is in such a way impossible to Him, that if it were possible for Him, He would be of less power. But assuredly He is rightly called omnipotent, though He can neither die nor fall into error. For He is called omnipotent on account of His doing what He wills, not on account of His suffering what He wills not; for if that should befall Him, He would by no means be omnipotent. Wherefore He cannot do some things for the very reason that He is omnipotent. So also, when we say that it is necessary that, when we will, we will by free choice, in so saying we both affirm what is true beyond doubt, and do not still subject our wills thereby to a necessity which destroys liberty.

Our wills, therefore, *exist as wills*, and do themselves whatever we do by willing, and which would not be done if we were unwilling. But when any one suffers anything being unwilling, by the will of another, even in that case will retains its essential validity – we do not mean the will of the party who inflicts the suffering, for we resolve it into the power of God. For if a will should simply exist, but not be able to do what it wills, it would be overborne by a more powerful will. Nor would this be the case unless there had existed will, and that not the will of the other party, but the will of him who willed, but was not able to accomplish what he willed. Therefore, whatsoever a man suffers contrary to his own will, he ought not to attribute to the will of men, or of angels, or of any created spirit, but rather to His will who gives power to wills. It is not the case, therefore, that because God foreknew what would be in the power of our wills, there is for that reason nothing in the power of our wills. For He who foreknew this did not foreknow nothing. Moreover, if He who foreknew what would be in the power of our wills did not foreknow nothing, but something, assuredly, then even though He did foreknow, there is something in the power of our wills. Therefore we are by no means compelled, either, retaining the prescience of God, to take away the freedom of the will, or, retaining the freedom of the will, to deny that He is prescient of future things, which is impious. But we embrace both. We faithfully and sincerely confess both. The former, that we may believe well; the latter, that we may live well. For he lives ill who does not believe well concerning God. Wherefore, be it far from us, in order to maintain our freedom, to deny the prescience of Him by whose help we are or shall be free. Consequently, it is not in vain that laws are enacted, and that reproaches, exhortations, praises, and vituperations are had recourse to; for these also He foreknew, and they are of great avail, even as great as He foreknew that they would be of. Prayers, also, are of avail to procure those things which He foreknew that He would grant to those who offered them; and with justice have rewards been appointed for good deeds, and punishments for sins. For a man does not therefore sin because God foreknew that he would sin. Nay, it cannot be doubted but that it is the man himself who sins when he does sin, because He, whose foreknowledge is infallible, foreknew not that fate, or fortune, or something else would sin, but that the man himself would sin, who, if he wills not, sins not. But if he shall not will to sin, even this did God foreknow.

The universal providence of God, in the laws of which all things are included

Therefore God is supreme and true, with His Word and Holy Spirit (which three are one), one God omnipotent, creator and maker of every soul and of every body; by whose gift all are happy who are happy through verity and not through vanity; who made man a rational animal consisting of soul and body; who, when he sinned, neither permitted him to go unpunished, nor left him without mercy; who has given to the good and to the evil, being in common with stones, vegetable life in common with trees, sensuous life in common with brutes, intellectual life in common with angels alone; from whom is every mode, every species, every order; from whom are measure, number, weight; from whom is everything which has an existence in nature, of whatever kind it be, and of whatever value; from whom are the seeds of forms and the forms of seeds, and the motion of seeds and of forms; who gave also to flesh its origin, beauty, health, reproductive fecundity, disposition of members, and the salutary concord of its parts; who also to the irrational soul has given memory, sense, appetite, but to the rational soul, in addition to these, has given intelligence and will; who has not left, not to speak of heaven and earth, angels and men, but not even the entrails of the smallest and most contemptible animal, or the feather of a bird, or the little flower of a plant, or the leaf of a tree, without a harmony, and, as it were, a mutual peace among all its parts; – that God can never be believed to have left the kingdoms of men, their dominations and servitudes, outside of the laws of His providence.

8   Freedom to Do What We Want: Thomas Hobbes, *Liberty, Necessity and Chance**

The question of whether there is a clash between causal necessity and human freedom was taken up by many writers in the early modern period. Among the most influential proponents of a 'compatibilist' position (see introduction to extract 7, above) was the seventeenth-century English philosopher Thomas Hobbes. In a celebrated debate with Dr John Bramhall, Bishop of Derry ('J.D.' in the extracts that follow), Hobbes ('T.H.') argues that I am free to do something when I can do it if I so will. And this kind of freedom we indisputably have, whether or not

* Adapted and abridged (with some modernizing and rearrangement of the text) from *The Questions concerning Liberty and Necessity and Chance* [1654]. Original version repr. in *The English Works of Thomas Hobbes*, ed. W. Molesworth (London: Bohn, 1841), vol. V.

there is some chain of prior causes that necessitates our willing as we do. Bramhall, by contrast, argues that true freedom cannot coexist with necessity; to be truly free, our actions must proceed from a genuinely independent 'elective power of the rational will'. Unless our wills are *themselves* free and independent, the acts which proceed from our will are 'no more free than a staff in a man's hand'.

The broad lines of the debate between Hobbes and Bramhall have been followed in much subsequent discussion of these issues. For those who support Hobbes, it is enough that we have what is sometimes called 'liberty of spontaneity' – the ability to do *x*, without hindrance, interference or obstruction, when we want *x*. For the supporters of Bramhall's position, this is not enough: to be free we must have 'liberty of indifference' – an absolute contra-causal or two-way power to choose *x* or *not-x* ('the power to do or forbear', as Bramhall puts it). And while the first type of freedom can, it seems, be reconciled with belief in a chain of unalterable causes which necessitate my willing as I do, the second, it appears, cannot. Notice, finally, the connection which both writers make between their views on freedom and the institutions of praise, blame and responsibility. Bramhall fears that if it is accepted that we are causally determined to will as we do, then all responsibility for action will be undermined ('no one blames a fire for burning a city, yet if the will of man be not in his own disposition, he is no more a free agent than the fire'). Hobbes replies that blame is still appropriate in the human case, since it is an expression of disapproval which may be effective in modifying people's attitudes (for example by 'making people ask forgiveness when they hurt us'). The issues raised here show that the philosophical problem of free will and determinism is not just an 'academic' one, but has important implications for human conduct and its evaluation.

J.D.: Either I am free to write this discourse for liberty against necessity, or I am not free. If I be free, I have proved my point, and ought not to suffer for the truth. If I be not free, yet I ought not to be blamed, since I do it not out of any voluntary choice, but out of an inevitable necessity.

T.H.: The preface is a handsome one, but it appears even in that, that he has mistaken the question; for whereas he says 'if I be free to write this discourse, I have proved my point,' I deny that to be true. If he will prove his point, he must prove that, before he wrote it, it was not necessary he should write it afterwards. It may be he thinks it all one to say 'I was free to write it' and 'it was not necessary I should write it'. But I think otherwise; for he is free to do a thing who may do it if he have the will to do it, and may forbear if he have the will to forbear. And yet if there be a necessity that he shall have the will to do it, the action is necessarily to follow; and if there be a necessity that he shall have the will to forbear, the forbearing also will be necessary. The question, therefore, is not whether a man be a free agent, that is to say, whether he can write or forbear, speak or be silent, according to his will; but whether the will to write, and the will to forbear, come upon him according to his will, or according to any thing else in his own power. I acknowledge this liberty, that *I can do if I will*; but to say, I can *will* if I will, I take to be an absurd speech. Wherefore I cannot grant him the point upon this preface.

J.D.: That is no true necessity, which he calls necessity; nor that liberty, which he calls liberty. To clarify this, it behoves us to know the difference between these three, *necessity, spontaneity*, and *liberty*. Necessity and spontaneity may sometimes meet together; so may spontaneity and liberty; but real necessity and true liberty can never meet together. Some things are necessary and not voluntary or spontaneous; some things are both necessary and voluntary; some things are voluntary and not free; some things are both voluntary and free; but those things which are truly necessary can never be free, and those things which are truly free can never be necessary. Necessity consists in an antecedent determination; spontaneity consists in a conformity of the appetite, either intellectual or sensitive, to the object; true liberty consists in the elective power of the rational will. That which is determined without my concurrence may nevertheless agree well enough with my fancy or desires, and obtain my subsequent consent; but that which is determined without my concurrence or consent cannot be the object of my choice. I may like that which is inevitably imposed upon me by another, but if it be inevitably imposed upon me by extrinsical causes, it is both folly for me to deliberate, and impossible for me to choose, whether I shall undergo it or not. Reason is the root, the fountain, the origin of true liberty, which judges and represents to the will, whether this or that be convenient, whether this or that be more convenient. Judge then what a pretty kind of liberty it is which is maintained by T.H., such a liberty as is in little children before they have the use of reason, before they can consult or deliberate of any thing. Is not this a childish liberty; and such a liberty as is in brute beasts, as bees and spiders, which do not learn their faculties as we do our trades, by experience and consideration? This is a brutish liberty, such a liberty as a bird has to fly when her wings are clipped, or such a liberty as a lame man, who has lost the use of his limbs, has to walk. Is not this a ridiculous liberty? Lastly (which is worse than all these), such a liberty as a river has to descend down the channel. What! will he ascribe liberty to inanimate creatures also, which have neither reason, nor spontaneity, nor so much as sensitive appetite? Such is T.H.'s liberty.

T.H.:   I did expect that for the knowing of the difference between *necessity, spontaneity*, and *liberty*, he would have set down their definitions. For without these, their difference cannot possibly appear. For how can a man know how things differ, unless he first know what they are? He tells us that *necessity* and *spontaneity* may meet together, and *spontaneity* and *liberty*; but *necessity* and *liberty* never. I note only this, that *spontaneity* is a word not used in common English; and they that understand Latin, know it means no more than *appetite*, or *will*, and is not found but in living creatures. And seeing, he says, that *necessity* and *spontaneity* may stand together, I may say also, that *necessity* and *will* may stand together, and then is not the will free, as he would have it, from necessitation? I do not understand how reason can be the root of true liberty, if the Bishop, as he says in the beginning, had the liberty to write this discourse. I understand how objects, and the conveniences and the inconveniences of them may be represented to a man, by the help of his senses; but how reason represents anything to the will, I understand no more than the Bishop understands how there may be liberty in children, in beasts, and inanimate creatures. For he seems to wonder how children may be left at liberty; how beasts in prison may be set at liberty; and how a river may have a free course; and says, 'What! will he ascribe liberty to inanimate creatures, also'. And thus he thinks he has made it clear how *necessity, spontaneity*, and *liberty* differ from one another. If the reader find it so, I am contented.

J.D.:   His necessity is a necessity upon supposition, arising from the concourse of all the causes, including the last dictate of the understanding in reasonable creatures. The adequate cause and the effect are together in time, and when all the concurrent causes are determined, the effect is determined also, and is become so necessary that it is actually in being; but there is a great difference between determining, and being determined. If all the collateral causes concurring to the production of an effect were antecedently determined [as to] what they must of necessity produce, and when they must produce it, then there is no doubt but the effect is necessary.

T.H.:   The Bishop might easily have seen that the necessity I hold is the same necessity that he denies; namely, a necessity of things future, that is, an antecedent necessity derived from the very beginning of time; and that I put necessity for an impossibility of not being, and that impossibility as well as possibility are never truly said but of the future. I know as well as he that the cause, when it is adequate, as he calls it, or entire, as I call it, is together in time with the effect. But for all that, the necessity may be and is before the effect, as much as any necessity can be. And though he call it a necessity of supposition, it is no more so than all other necessity is. The fire burns necessarily; but not without supposition that there is fuel put to it. And it burns the fuel, when it is put to it, necessarily; but it is by supposition, that the ordinary course of nature is not hindered.

J.D.:   That which T.H. makes the question, is not the question. 'The question is not,' says he, 'whether a man may write if he will and forbear if he will, but whether the will to write or the will to forbear come upon him according to his will, or according to anything else in his own power.' Here is a distinction without a difference. If his will do not come upon him according to his will, then he is not a free, nor yet so much as a voluntary agent, which is T.H.'s liberty. Certainly all the freedom of the agent is from the freedom of the will. If the will have no power over itself, the agent is no more free than a staff in a man's hand. Secondly, he makes but an empty show of power in the will, either to write or not to write.

T.H.:   He has very little reason to say this. He requested me to tell him my opinion in writing concerning free will. Which I did, and did let him know a man was free, in those things that were in his power, to follow his will; but that he was not free to will, that is, that his will did not follow his will. Which I expressed in these words: 'The question is, whether the will to write, or the will to forbear, come upon a man according to his will, or according to any thing else in his own power.' He that cannot understand the difference between *free to do if he will*, and *free to will*, is not fit, as I have said in the stating of the question, to hear this controversy disputed, much less to be a writer in it. His consequence, 'if a man be not free to will, he is not free nor a voluntary agent', and his saying, 'the freedom of the agent is from the freedom of the will', is put here without proof. For why? He never before had heard, I believe, of any distinction between free to do and free to will; which makes him also say, 'if the will have not power over itself, the agent is no more free, than a staff in a man's hand'. As if it were not freedom enough for a man to do what he will, unless his will also have power over his will, and that his will be not the power itself, but must have another power within it to do all voluntary acts.

J.D.:   If it be precisely and inevitably determined in all occurrences whatsoever, what a man shall will, and what he shall not will, what he shall write, and what he shall not write, to what purpose is this power? God and nature never made any thing in vain; but vain and empty is that power which never was and never shall be led into action.

Either the agent is determined before he acts, what he shall will, and what he shall not will, what he shall act, and what he shall not act, and then he is no more free to act than he is to will; or else he is not determined, and then there is no necessity. No effect can exceed the virtue of its cause; if the action be free to write or to forbear, the power or faculty to will or not must of necessity be more free. If the will be determined, the writing or not writing is likewise determined, and then he should not say, 'he may write or he may forbear,' but he *must* write or he *must* forbear. Thirdly, this answer contradicts the sense of all the world, that the will of man is determined without his will, or without any thing in his power. Why do we ask men whether they will do such a thing or not? Why do we represent reasons to them? Why do we pray them? Why do we entreat them? Why do we blame them, if their will come not upon them according to their will? How easily might they answer, according to T.H.'s doctrine, 'Alas! blame not us; our wills are not in our own power or disposition; if they were, we would thankfully embrace so great a favour.'

T.H.:   'To what purpose is this power?', he asks. It is to this purpose, that all those things may be brought to pass, which God has from eternity predetermined. It is therefore to no purpose here to say that God and nature have made nothing in vain. But see what weak arguments he brings next, which, though answered in that which is gone before, yet, if I answer not again, he will say they are too hot for my fingers. One is: 'If the agent be determined what he shall will, and what he shall act, then he is no more free to act than he is to will'; as if the will being necessitated, the doing of what we will were not liberty. Another is: 'If a man be free to act, he is much more free to will because no effect can exceed the virtue of its cause'; as if he should say, 'if I make him angry, then I am more angry'. The third is: 'If the will be determined, then the writing is determined, and he ought not to say he *may* write, but he *must* write.' It is true, it follows that he must write, but it does not follow I ought to say he must write, unless he would have me say more than I know, as himself does often in this reply. After his arguments come his difficult question, 'If the will of man be determined without his will or without any thing in his power, why do we ask men whether they will do such a thing or not?' I answer, because we desire to know, and cannot know but by their telling, nor then neither, for the most part. 'Why do we represent reasons to them? Why do we pray them? Why do we entreat them?' I answer, because thereby we think to make them have the will they have not. 'Why do we blame them?' I answer, because they please us not. I might ask him, whether blaming be any thing else but saying the thing blamed is ill or imperfect? May we not say a horse is lame, though his lameness came from necessity? or that a man is a fool or a knave, if he be so, though he could not help it? 'How easily might they answer, according to T.H.'s doctrine, Alas! blame not us, our wills are not in our own power?' I answer, they are to be blamed though their wills be not in their own power. Is not good good, and evil evil, though they be not in our power? And shall not I call them so, and is not that praise and blame? But it seems the Bishop takes blame, not for the dispraise of a thing, but for a pretext and colour of malice and revenge against him he blames. And where he says our wills are in our power, he sees not that he speaks absurdly; for he ought to say, the will is the power.

J.D.:   This is the belief of all mankind, which we have not learned from our tutors, but is imprinted in our hearts by nature; we need not turn over any obscure books to find out this truth. The poets chant it in the theatres, the shepherds in the mountains, the pastors teach it in their churches, the doctors in the universities, the common people in the markets, and all mankind in the whole world do assent unto it, except an handful of men who have poisoned their intellects with paradoxical principles. This necessity which T.H. has devised, which is grounded upon the necessitation of a man's will without his will, is the worst of all others, and is so far from lessening those difficulties and absurdities which flow from the fatal destiny of the Stoics, that it increases them, and renders them unanswerable.

T.H.:   It is true, very few have learned from tutors that a man is not free to will; nor do they find it much in books. That they find in books, that which the poets chant in their theatres and the shepherds in the mountains, that which the pastors teach in the churches and the doctors in the universities, and that which the common people in the markets, and all mankind in the whole world do assent unto, is the same that I assent unto, namely, that a man has freedom to do if he will; but whether he has freedom to will, is a question which it seems neither the Bishop nor they ever thought on.

J.D.:   No man blames fire for burning whole cities; no man taxes poison for destroying men; but those persons who apply them to such wicked ends. If the will of man be not in his own disposition, he is no more a free agent than the fire or the poison. Three things are required to make an act or omission culpable. First, that it be in our power to perform it or forbear it; secondly, that we be obliged to perform it, or forbear it, respectively; thirdly, that we omit that which we ought to have done, or do that which we ought to have omitted.

T.H.:   Here again he is upon his arguments from blame which I have answered before; and we do as much blame them as we do men. For we say fire hath done hurt, and the poison hath killed a man as well as we say the man hath done unjustly; but we do not seek to be revenged of the fire and of poison, because we cannot make them ask forgiveness, as we would make men to do when they hurt us. So that the blaming of the one and the other, that is, the declaring of the hurt or evil action done by them, is the same in both; but the malice of man is only against man.

J.D.:   So my preface remains yet unanswered. Either I was extrinsically and inevitably predetermined to write this discourse, without any concurrence of mine in the determination, and without any power in me to change or oppose it, or I was not so predetermined. If I was, then I ought not to be blamed, for no man is justly blamed for doing that which never was in his power to shun. If I was not so predetermined, then mine actions and my will to act, are neither compelled nor necessitated by any extrinsical causes, but I elect and choose, either to write or to forbear according to mine own will and mine own power. And when I have resolved and elected, it is but a necessity of supposition, which may and does consist with true liberty, not a real antecedent necessity. The two horns of this dilemma are so straight, that no mean can be given, nor room to pass between them. And the two consequences are so evident, that instead of answering he is forced to decline them.

T.H.:   That which he says in the preface is, 'that if he be not free to write this discourse, he ought not to be blamed; but if he be free, he hath obtained the cause'. The first consequence I should have granted him, if he had written it rationally and civilly; the latter I deny, and have shown that he ought to have proved that a man is free to will. For that which he says, any thing else whatsoever would think, if it knew it were moved, and did not know what moved it. A wooden top that is lashed by the boys, and runs about sometimes to one wall, sometimes to another, sometimes spinning, sometimes hitting men on the shins, if it were sensible of its own motion, would think it proceeded from its own will, unless it felt what lashed it. And is a man any wiser, when he runs to one place for a benefice, to another for a bargain, and troubles the world with writing errors and requiring answers, because he thinks he does it without other cause than his own will, and sees not what are the lashings that cause his will?

9   Absolute Determinism: Pierre Simon de Laplace, *Philosophical Essay on Probability* *

With the advance of the physical sciences during the age of the enlightenment, typified by Isaac Newton's spectacular success in establishing the law of universal gravitation, it became common to regard the universe as a rigidly determined system. In the following extract from his *Philosophical Essay on Probability* (1819), the French mathematician and philosopher Laplace argues that all events are connected with previous ones by the 'tie' of universal causation. There are two important observations that he then proceeds to make. First, since the universe is a complete and all-encompassing system, any belief that things come about independently, or by chance, is simply due to our ignorance of the causes. He cites the appearance of comets, formerly supposed to be supernatural portents, but now (through the work of mathematical physicists like Halley) shown to be regular and predictable, part of the deterministic system of the universe. Second, Laplace insists that human actions too are all part of the deterministic system. Any belief in freedom of 'indifference' (a supposed contra-causal power to choose between two options in an utterly undetermined way) is an illusion (compare the views of Hobbes's opponent in extract 8, above). For Laplace, it is absurd to suppose that when we choose x rather than y there are really no motivating factors inclining us in one way rather than another; if that was really the case, our behaviour would be like 'blind chance of the Epicureans' – a kind of mysterious 'swerve' in the otherwise determined universe. When people think they have 'freedom of indifference' to select one of two options, this is due to their ignorance of the hidden causes which are in fact moving them to select one rather than the other. The very idea of contingency, of a genuinely open future, is thus due to ignorance; nothing can avoid the universally necessary chains of causality.

It is quite often pointed out that twentieth-century science has abandoned Laplace's rigid clockwork universe in favour of something more fluid; at the micro level, in particular, quantum theory tells us it is impossible in principle to predict the behaviour of individual

---

* Pierre Simon, Marquis de Laplace, *Essai philosophique sur les probabilités* [1819]. Translated by John Cottingham from *Oeuvres de Laplace* (Paris, 1847), vol. VII, pp. vi–viii. (The *Essay* first appeared as an introduction to the third edition of Laplace's *Théorie Analytique des Probabilités*, which was originally published in 1812.) There is an English version of the complete essay by F. W. Truscott and F. L. Emory (New York: Dover, 1951).

particles. It is doubtful, however, that this gives much comfort to those who are worried by Laplace's deterministic view of human action, since indeterminism at the micro level does not appear to 'carry over' to the macro level (quantum effects at the level of subatomic particles are not reflected in the behaviour of the larger entities composed of those particles, such as planets or tables or cats, which apparently continue to behave in a deterministic way). In broad terms, the Laplacean challenge, asking how we can both be parts of the universal system and yet not subject to its laws, retains much of its interest.

All events, even those which because of their small scale do not appear to keep to the great laws of nature, are just as necessary a result of those laws as are the revolutions of the sun. In ignorance of the ties which bind these events to the entire system of the universe, people have made them depend on final causes,[1] or upon chance, depending on whether they happen and recur with regularity, on the one hand, or in an apparently disorderly way, on the other. But these imaginary causes have been gradually pushed out of the way as the boundaries of our knowledge have increased, and they would completely vanish in the face of sound philosophy, which sees in them only the expression of our present ignorance of the true causes.

Present events have a connection with previous ones that is based on the self-evident principle that a thing cannot come into existence without a cause that produces it. This axiom, known under the name of the *principle of sufficient reason*, extends even to actions which people regard as indifferent.[2] The freest will is unable to give birth to them without a determinate motive. Take two situations characterized by exactly similar circumstances: if the will were to act in the first case and refrain from acting in the second, its choice would be an effect without a cause – so it would be, as Leibniz puts it, a case of the 'blind chance' which the Epicureans talk of. Believing in such uncaused events is an illusion of the mind, which loses sight of the elusive reasons underlying the will's choice in 'indifferent' situations, and convinces itself that the will is self-determined and motiveless.

We must therefore regard the present state of the universe as the effect of its preceding state and as the cause of the one which is to follow. An intelligence which in a single instant could know all the forces which animate the natural world, and the respective situations of all the beings that made it up, could, provided it was vast enough to make an analysis of all the data so supplied, be able to produce a single formula which specified all the movements in the universe from those of the largest bodies in the universe to those of the lightest atom. For such an intelligence, nothing would be 'uncertain', and the future, like the past, would be present before its eyes. The human mind, in the perfection which it has been able to give to astronomy, presents a feeble shadow of this intelligence. Its discoveries in mechanics and geometry, added to that of universal gravity, have brought it within reach of including within the same analytical formulae all the past and future states of the world system. By applying the same method to various other objects of its knowledge, it has managed to reduce the observed phenomena to general laws, and to predict the results which must be

---

[1] Explanations referring to the end state or goal towards which a process or action is apparently directed.

[2] That is, actions where I seem to have an entirely 'open' choice between two options. In traditional terminology, someone was said to possess 'liberty of indifference' when entirely free and undetermined as to which of two courses of action to select (see also the introduction to extract 8, above).

generated by any given set of circumstances. All the efforts of the human mind in its search for truth tend to bring it continually closer to that vast intelligence we have just imagined; though it will always remain infinitely far removed from it. This onward tendency, peculiar to the human race, is what makes us superior to the animals; it is progress in this area which distinguishes nations and epochs and is their true glory.

Let us recall that in former times, still not so very far away, a heavy rainfall or prolonged drought, a comet trailing a very long tail, eclipses, the aurora borealis, and in general all out of the ordinary phenomena, were regarded as so many signs of celestial anger. Heaven was invoked in order to avert their dire influence. No one prayed to heaven to stop the courses of the planets and the sun; observation had soon made people see the futility of such prayers. But because these unusual phenomena, appearing and disappearing at long intervals, seemed to contravene the order of nature, men supposed that heaven created and altered them at will to punish crimes done on earth. Thus the comet of 1456, with its long tail, spread terror throughout Europe, already appalled by the rapid successes of the Turks, who had just overthrown the Lower Empire. But for us, now that four successive revolutions of the body in question have elapsed, it has aroused a very different interest. The knowledge of the laws of the world-system acquired during the interval had dissipated the fears produced by ignorance of the true relationship of man to the universe; and Halley, having recognized that the appearances of 1531, 1607 and 1682 all related to the same comet, predicted its next return for the end of 1758 or the start of 1759. The learned world impatiently awaited this return, which was destined to confirm one of the greatest discoveries ever made in the sciences, and fulfil the prediction of Seneca when he said, speaking of the revolution of those stars which come from an enormous distance: 'The day will come when studies pursued over many centuries will reveal in all clarity things that are now hidden, and posterity will be astonished that we had failed to grasp such clear truths.' Clairaut then undertook to analyse the perturbations which the comet had undergone as a result of the action of the two great planets, Jupiter and Saturn; after vast calculations he fixed its next passage at perihelion towards the beginning of April 1759 – which was quickly confirmed by observation. There is no doubt that this regularity which has been demonstrated by astronomy in the movement of the comets also obtains in all other phenomena. The curve described by a simple molecule of air or vapour is determined in just as certain a manner as that of the planetary orbits; there are no differences between the two cases, except those which are a function of our own ignorance.

10   Condemned to be Free: Jean-Paul Sartre, *Being and Nothingness**

The Laplacean vision is of a wholly determined universe in which the 'great laws of nature' extend to every domain, including that of human action (see previous extract). Against this, the French existentialist philosopher Jean-Paul Sartre made a fundamental distinction between ordinary objects or 'being-in-themselves' and human agents. A human agent is a 'being-for-itself',

---

* Jean-Paul Sartre, *L'Etre et le Néant* [1943], extracts from Part IV, ch. 1, sections i and iii. Trans. H. E. Barnes (London: Methuen, 1957), pp. 433–7, 440–1, 553–6; abridged.

a being with conscious plans, purposes and intentions, who is always able to 'project forward' from a given situation to a future possibility not yet realized. In the following extracts from his magnum opus, *Being and Nothingness* (1943), Sartre argues that for human beings the stage is never unalterably set. If I say I am 'constrained' by external circumstances, this often conceals my *decision* to interpret them in a certain way. And as far as my own motives are concerned, again, these do not and cannot constrain me in the way some determinists suggest. Psychologically, we often 'try to take the causes and motives as *things*'. Yet this, says Sartre, is an evasion: 'we attempt to hide from ourselves that their nature and their weight depend each moment on the meaning which I give to them'.

The idea that we often try to evade our responsibility for our actions (what he elsewhere calls 'bad faith') is a recurring theme in Sartre's philosophy. Appeals to determinism are but one form of bad faith, of our attempt to deny our inescapable human capacity for interpreting our lives and deciding how they should be lived. Of course there is, as Sartre puts it, a certain 'facticity' in our existence: we did not ask to be born, we are causally linked to an alien world that we did not create.[1] But even here, Sartre argues, the sense of 'abandonment' we feel derives precisely from the fact that every moment of our lives we are responsible for who we are and what we decide to be. 'I am *abandoned* in the world, not in the sense that I might remain abandoned and passive in a hostile universe like a board floating on the water, but rather in the sense that I find myself suddenly alone and without help, engaged in a world for which I bear the whole responsibility without being able to tear myself away from this responsibility for an instant.' Sartre thus firmly rejects the deterministic challenge to human freedom – and yet the conception of freedom he defends is far from a comfortable or comforting one; as human beings we are, in his famous phrase, 'condemned to be free'.

It is strange that philosophers have been able to argue endlessly about determinism and free-will, to cite examples in favour of one or the other thesis without ever attempting first to make explicit the structures contained in the very idea of *action*. We should observe first that an action is on principle *intentional*. The careless smoker who has through negligence caused the explosion of a powder magazine has not *acted*. On the other hand the worker who is charged with dynamiting a quarry, and who obeys the given orders, has acted when he has produced the expected explosion; he knew what he was doing or, if you prefer, he intentionally realized a conscious project.

This does not mean, of course, that one must foresee all the consequences of his act. The emperor Constantine when he established himself at Byzantium, did not foresee that he would create a centre of Greek culture and language, the appearance of which would ultimately provoke a schism in the Christian Church and which would contribute to weakening the Roman Empire. Yet he performed an act just in so far as he realized his project of creating a new residence for emperors in the Orient. Equating the result with the intention is here sufficient for us to be able to speak of action. But if this is the case, we establish that the action necessarily implies as its condition the recognition of a 'desideratum'; that is, of an objective lack or *négatité*.[2] The *intention* of providing a rival for Rome can come to Constantine only through the apprehension of an objective lack: Rome lacks a counterweight; to this still profoundly pagan city ought to be opposed a Christian city which at the moment is *missing*. Creating Constantinople is understood as an act only if first the conception

---

[1] Compare Heidegger, Part II, extract 9, above.

[2] Sartre's term for human experiences and actions (e.g. of feeling a lack, of desire to change) which essentially involve an idea of non-being or negation.

of a new city has preceded the action itself or at least if this conception serves as an organizing theme for all later steps. But this conception cannot be the pure representation of the city as *possible*. It apprehends the city in its essential characteristic, which is to be a *desirable* and not yet realized possible.

This means that from the moment of the first conception of the act, consciousness has been able to withdraw itself from the full world of which it is consciousness and to leave the level of being in order frankly to approach that of non-being. Consciousness in so far as it is considered exclusively in its being, is perpetually referred from being to being and cannot find in being any motive for revealing non-being...

Two important consequences result. (1) No factual state whatever it may be (the political and economic structure of society, the psychological 'state', etc.) is capable by itself of motivating any act whatsoever. For an act is a projection of the for-itself toward what is not, and what is can in no way determine by itself what is not. (2) No factual state can determine consciousness to apprehend it as a *négatité* or as a lack...

Thus at the outset we can see what is lacking in those tedious discussions between determinists and the proponents of free will. The latter are concerned to find cases of decision for which there exists no prior cause, or deliberations concerning two opposed acts which are equally possible and possess causes (and motives) of exactly the same weight. To which the determinists may easily reply that there is no action without a *cause* and that the most insignificant gesture (raising the right hand rather than the left hand, etc.) refers to causes and motives which confer its meaning upon it. Indeed the case could not be otherwise since every action must be *intentional*; each action must, in fact, have an end, and the end in turn is referred to a cause. The end or temporalization of my future implies a cause (or motive); that is, it points toward my past, and the present is the upsurge of the act. To speak of an act without a cause is to speak of an act which would lack the intentional structure of every act; and the proponents of free will by searching for it on the level of the act which is in the process of being performed can only end up by rendering the act absurd. But the determinists in turn are weighting the scale by stopping their investigation with the mere designation of the cause and motive. The essential question lies beyond the complex organization 'cause–intention-act-end'; indeed we ought to ask how a cause (or motive) can be constituted as such.

Now if there is no act without a cause, this is not in the sense that we can say that there is no phenomenon without a cause. In order to be a *cause*, the *cause* must be *experienced* as such. Of course this does not mean that it is to be thematically conceived and made explicit as in the case of deliberation. But at the very least it means that the *for-itself* must confer on it its value as cause or motive. And this constitution of the cause as such can not refer to another real and positive existence, that is, to a prior cause. For otherwise the very nature of the act as engaged intentionally in non-being would disappear. The motive is understood only by the end; that is, by the nonexistent. It is therefore in itself a *négatité*. If I accept a niggardly salary it is doubtless because of fear; and fear is a motive. But it is *fear of dying from starvation*; that is, this fear has meaning only outside itself in an end ideally posited, which is the preservation of a life which I apprehend as 'in danger'. And this fear is understood in turn only in relation to the *value* which I implicitly give to this life; that is, it is referred to that hierarchal system of ideal objects which are values. Thus the motive makes itself understood as what it is by means of the ensemble of beings which 'are not', by ideal existences, and by the future. Just as the future turns back upon the present and the past in order to elucidate them, so it is the ensemble of my projects which turns back in order to confer upon the motive its structure as a motive...

The ultimate meaning of determinism is to establish within us an unbroken continuity of existence in itself. The motive conceived as a psychic fact – i.e., as a full and given reality – is, in the deterministic view, articulated without any break with the decision and the act, both of which are equally conceived as psychic givens. The in-itself has got hold of all these 'data'; the motive provokes the act as the physical cause its effect; everything is real, everything is full. Thus the refusal of freedom can be conceived only as an attempt to apprehend oneself as being-in-itself; it amounts to the same thing. Human reality may be defined as a being such that in its being its freedom is at stake because human reality perpetually tries to refuse to recognize its freedom. Psychologically in each one of us this amounts to trying to take the causes and motives as *things*. We try to confer permanence upon them. We attempt to hide from ourselves that their nature and their weight depend each moment on the meaning which I give to them; we take them for constants. This amounts to considering the meaning which I gave to them just now or yesterday – which is irremediable because it *is past* – and extrapolating from it a character fixed still in the present...

Cause, act, and end constitute a *continuum*, a *plenum*. These abortive attempts to stifle freedom under the weight of being (they collapse with the sudden upsurge of anguish before freedom) show sufficiently that freedom in its foundation coincides with the nothingness which is at the heart of man. Human-reality is free because it *is not enough*. It is free because it is perpetually wrenched away from itself and because it has been separated by a nothingness from what it is and from what it will be. It is free, finally, because its present being is itself a nothingness in the form of the 'reflection-reflecting'. Man is free because he is not himself but presence to himself. The being which is what it is cannot be free. Freedom is precisely the nothingness which *is made-to-be* at the heart of man and which forces human-reality to *make itself* instead of to *be*. As we have seen, for human reality, to be is to *choose oneself*; nothing comes to it either from the outside or from within which it can receive or accept. Without any help whatsoever, it is entirely abandoned to the intolerable necessity of making itself be – down to the slightest detail. Thus freedom is not a being; it is *the being* of man – i.e., his nothingness of being. If we start by conceiving of man as a plenum, it is absurd to try to find in him afterwards moments or psychic regions in which he would be free. As well look for emptiness in a container which one has filled beforehand up to the brim. Man cannot be sometimes slave and sometimes free; he is wholly and forever free or he is not free at all...

Man being condemned to be free carries the weight of the whole world on his shoulders; he is responsible for the world and for himself as a way of being. We are taking the word 'responsibility' in its ordinary sense as 'consciousness (of) being the incontestable author of an event or of an object'. In this sense the responsibility of the for-itself is overwhelming since he is the one by whom it happens that *there is* a world; since he is also the one who makes himself be, then whatever may be the situation in which he finds himself, the for-itself must wholly assume this situation with its peculiar coefficient of adversity, even though it be insupportable. He must assume the situation with the proud consciousness of being the author of it, for the very worst disadvantages or the worst threats which can endanger my person have meaning only in and through my project; and it is on the ground of the engagement which I am that they appear. It is therefore senseless to think of complaining, since nothing foreign has decided what we feel, what we live, or what we are.

Furthermore this absolute responsibility is not resignation; it is simply the logical requirement of the consequences of our freedom. What happens to me happens through me, and I can neither affect myself with it nor revolt against it nor resign myself to it. Moreover everything which happens to me is *mine*. By this we must understand first of all that I am always equal to what happens to me *qua* man, for what happens to a man through other men and through himself can be only human. The most terrible situations of war, the worst tortures do not create a non-human state of things; there is no non-human situation. It is only through fear, flight, and recourse to magical types of conduct that I shall decide on the non-human, but this decision is human, and I shall carry the entire responsibility for it. But in addition the situation is mine because it is the image of my free choice of myself, and everything which it presents to me is *mine* in that this represents me and symbolizes me. Is it not I who decide the coefficient of adversity in things and even their unpredictability by deciding myself?

Thus there are no *accidents* in a life; a community event which suddenly burst forth and involves me in it does not come from the outside. If I am mobilized in a war, this war is my war; it is in my image and I deserve it. I deserve it first because I could always get out of it by suicide or by desertion; these ultimate possibles are those which must always be present for us when there is a question of envisaging a situation. For lack of getting out of it, I have *chosen* it. This can be due to inertia, to cowardice in the face of public opinion, or because I prefer certain other values to the value of the refusal to join in the war (the good opinion of any relatives, the honour of my family, etc.). Any way you look at it, it is a matter of a choice. This choice will be repeated later on again and again without a break until the end of the war. So we must agree with the statement 'In war there are no innocent victims.' If therefore I have preferred war to death or to dishonour, everything takes place as if I bore the entire responsibility for this war. Of course others have declared it, and one might be tempted perhaps to consider me as a simple accomplice. But this notion of complicity has only a juridical sense, and it does not hold here. For it depended on me that for me and by me this war should not exist, and I have decided that it does exist. There was no compulsion here, for the compulsion could have got no hold on a freedom. I did not have any excuse; for as we have said repeatedly in this book, the peculiar character of human-reality is that it is without excuse. Therefore it remains for me only to lay claim to this war.

But in addition the war is *mine* because by the sole fact that it arises in a situation which I cause to be, and that I can discover it there only by engaging myself for or against it, I can no longer distinguish at present the choice which I make of myself from the choice which I make of the war. To live this war is to choose myself through it and to choose it through my choice of myself. There can be no question of considering it as 'four years of vacation' or as a 'reprieve', as a 'recess', the essential part of my responsibilities being elsewhere in my married, family or professional life. In this war which I have chosen I choose myself from day to day, and

I make it mine by making myself. If it is going to be four empty years, then it is I who bear the responsibility for this.

Finally, as we pointed out earlier, each person is an absolute choice of self from the standpoint of a world of knowledges and of techniques which this choice both assumes and illumines; each person is an absolute upsurge at an absolute date and is perfectly unthinkable at another date. It is therefore a waste of time to ask what I should have been if this war had not broken out, for I have chosen myself as one of the possible meanings of the epoch which imperceptibly led to war. I am not distinct from this same epoch; I could not be transported to another epoch without contradiction. Thus I *am* this war which restricts and limits and makes comprehensible the period which preceded it. In this sense we may define more precisely the responsibility of the for-itself, if to the earlier quoted statement, 'There are no innocent victims', we add the words, 'We have the war we deserve.' Thus, totally free, undistinguishable from the period for which I have chosen to be the meaning, as profoundly responsible for the war as if I had myself declared it, unable to live without integrating it in *my* situation, engaging myself in it wholly and stamping it with my seal, I must be without remorse or regrets as I am without excuse; for from the instant of my upsurge into being, I carry the weight of the world by myself alone without anything or any person being able to lighten it.

Yet this responsibility is of a very particular type. Someone will say, 'I did not ask to be born.' This is a naïve way of throwing greater emphasis on our facticity. I am responsible for everything, in fact, except for my very responsibility, for I am not the foundation of my being. Therefore everything takes place as if I were compelled to be responsible. I am *abandoned* in the world, not in the sense that I might remain abandoned and passive in a hostile universe like a board floating on the water, but rather in the sense that I find myself suddenly alone and without help, engaged in a world for which I bear the whole responsibility without being able, whatever I do, to tear myself away from this responsibility for an instant. For I am responsible for my very desire of fleeing responsibilities. To make myself passive in the world, to refuse to act upon things and upon Others is still to choose myself, and suicide is one mode among others of being-in-the-world. Yet I find an absolute responsibility for the fact that my facticity (here the fact of my birth) is directly inapprehensible and even inconceivable, for this fact of my birth never appears as a brute fact but always across a projective reconstruction of my for-itself. I am ashamed of being born or I am astonished at it or I rejoice over it, or in attempting to get rid of my life I affirm that I live and I assume this life as bad. Thus in a certain sense I *choose* being born. This choice itself is integrally affected with facticity since I am not able not to choose, but this facticity in turn will appear only in so far as I surpass it toward my ends. Thus facticity is everywhere but inapprehensible; I never encounter anything except my responsibility. That is why I cannot ask, '*Why* was I born?' or curse the day of my birth or declare that I did not ask to be born, for these various attitudes toward my birth – i.e., toward the *fact* that I realize a presence in the world – are absolutely nothing else but ways of assuming this birth in full responsibility and of making it *mine*. Here again I encounter only myself and my projects so that finally my abandonment – i.e., my facticity – consists simply in the fact that I am condemned to be wholly responsible for myself...

11   Determinism and our Attitudes to Others: Peter Strawson, *Freedom and Resentment**

The debate over freedom and determinism has important implications for our beliefs about responsibility for action (compare the end of the introduction to extract 8 above). Suppose universal determinism is true: would this mean that everything we do is traceable to causes ultimately beyond our control, and hence that moral condemnation and approval have no justified application? Would it follow that it is as irrational to blame people for antisocial behaviour as it would be to blame them for the colour of their eyes? Over the years many different and conflicting answers have been given to these questions, and it is probably fair to say that among contemporary philosophers opinions are still strongly divided. But in the following extract, from a highly influential essay by the Oxford philosopher P. F. Strawson, a fresh light is thrown on the issue.

Strawson focuses on 'what it is actually like to be involved in ordinary interpersonal relationships'; and he argues that (except when dealing with cases of radical psychological abnormality) there is a whole range of responses, such as resentment, gratitude, forgiveness, anger, antagonism, and reciprocal love, in terms of which we typically react to the conduct of our fellow humans. Now what effect would the truth of universal determinism have on such 'participant reactive attitudes' as Strawson calls them? Strawson argues that for all practical purposes it is inconceivable that we could abandon these patterns of response: 'human commitment to participation in ordinary interpersonal relationships is too thoroughgoing and deeply rooted'. One of the implications of this approach is that the correct solution to the issue of determinism is not something that can be decided on a purely intellectual plane – indeed, later in the essay Strawson attacks the philosopher's wish to 'over-intellectualize' such notions as moral responsibility, guilt and blame. Understanding how the notion of responsibility works will involve more than an intellectual analysis of such concepts as those of freedom and determinism; we also need to recognize the importance of deeply ingrained patterns of emotional commitment and response which structure our lives. Our reactions to those around us make sense within a context of commitment to ordinary interpersonal attitudes which, as Strawson puts it, 'are part of the general framework of human life, not something that can come up for review as particular cases can come up for review within this framework'.

 What I have to say consists largely of commonplaces. So my language, like that of commonplaces generally, will be quite unscientific and imprecise. The central commonplace that I want to insist on is the very great importance that we attach to the attitudes and intentions towards us of other human beings, and the great extent to which our personal feelings and reactions depend upon, or involve, our beliefs about these attitudes and intentions. I can give no simple description of the field of phenomena at the centre of which stands this commonplace truth; for the field is too complex. Much imaginative literature is devoted to exploring its complexities; and we have a large vocabulary for the purpose. There are simplifying styles of handling it in a general way. Thus we may, like La Rochefoucauld, put self-love or self-esteem or vanity at the centre of the picture and point out how it may be caressed by the esteem, or wounded by the indifference or contempt, of others. We might speak, in another jargon, of the need for love, and the loss of security which results

* Extract from P. F. Strawson, 'Freedom and Resentment' [1962], in *Freedom and Resentment and Other Essays* (London: Methuen, 1974), pp. 5–13.

from its withdrawal; or, in another, of human self-respect and its connection with the recognition of the individual's dignity. These simplifications are of use to me only if they help to emphasize how much we actually mind, how much it matters to us, whether the actions of other people – and particularly of *some* other people – reflect attitudes towards us of goodwill, affection or esteem on the one hand or contempt, indifference or malevolence on the other. If someone treads on my hand accidentally, while trying to help me, the pain may be no less acute than if he treads on it in contemptuous disregard of my existence or with a malevolent wish to injure me. But I shall generally feel in the second case a kind and degree of resentment that I shall not feel in the first. If someone's actions help me to some benefit I desire, then I am benefited in any case; but if he intended them so to benefit me because of his general goodwill towards me, I shall reasonably feel a gratitude which I should not feel at all if the benefit was an incidental consequence unintended or even regretted by him, of some plan of action with a different aim.

These examples are of actions which confer benefits or inflict injuries over and above any conferred or inflicted by the mere manifestation of attitude and intention themselves. We should consider also in how much of our behaviour the benefit or injury resides mainly or entirely in the manifestation of attitude itself. So with good manners, and much of what we call kindness, on the one hand; with deliberate rudeness, studied indifference or insult on the other.

Besides resentment and gratitude, I mentioned just now forgiveness. This is a rather unfashionable subject in moral philosophy at present; but to be forgiven is something we sometimes ask, and forgiving is something we sometimes say we do. To ask to be forgiven is in part to acknowledge that the attitude displayed in our actions was such as might properly be resented and in part to repudiate that attitude for the future (or at least for the immediate future); and to forgive is to accept the repudiation and to forswear the resentment.

We should think of the many different kinds of relationship which we can have with other people – as sharers of a common interest; as members of the same family; as colleagues; as friends; as lovers; as chance parties to an enormous range of transactions and encounters. Then we should think, in each of these connections in turn, and in others, of the kind of importance we attach to the attitudes and intentions towards us of those who stand in these relationships to us, and of the kinds of *reactive* attitudes and feelings to which we ourselves are prone. In general, we demand some degree of goodwill or regard on the part of those who stand in these relationships to us, though the forms we require it to take vary widely in different connections. The range and intensity of our *reactive* attitudes towards goodwill, its absence or its opposite vary no less widely. I have mentioned, specifically, resentment and gratitude; and they are a usefully opposed pair. But, of course, there is a whole continuum of reactive attitude and feeling stretching on both sides of these and – the most comfortable area – in between them.

The object of these commonplaces is to try to keep before our minds something it is easy to forget when we are engaged in philosophy, especially in our cool, contemporary style, viz. what it is actually like to be involved in ordinary interpersonal relationships, ranging from the most intimate to the most casual.

It is one thing to ask about the general causes of these reactive attitudes I have alluded to; it is another to ask about the variations to which they are subject, the particular conditions in which they do or do not seem natural or reasonable or appropriate; and it is a third thing to ask what it would be like, what it is like, not to suffer them. I am not much concerned with the first question; but I am with the second; and perhaps even more with the third.

Let us consider, then, occasions for resentment: situations in which one person is offended or injured by the action of another and in which – in the absence of special considerations – the offended person might naturally or normally be expected to feel resentment. Then let us consider what sorts of special considerations might be expected to modify or mollify this feeling or remove it altogether. It needs no saying now how multifarious these considerations are. But, for my purpose, I think they can be roughly divided into two kinds. To the first group belong all those which might give occasion for the employment of such expressions as 'He didn't mean to', 'He hadn't realized', 'He didn't know'; and also all those which might give occasion for the use of the phrase 'He couldn't help it', when this is supported by such phrases as 'He was pushed', 'He had to do it', 'It was the only way', 'They left him no alternative', etc. Obviously these various pleas, and the kinds of situations in which they would be appropriate, differ from each other in striking and important ways. But for my present purpose they have something still more important in common. None of them invites us to suspend towards the agent, either at the time of his action or in general, our ordinary reactive attitudes. They do not invite us to view the *agent* as one in respect of whom these attitudes are in any way inappropriate. They invite us to view the *injury* as one in respect of which a particular one of these attitudes is inappropriate. They do not invite us to see the *agent* as other than a fully responsible agent. They invite us to see the *injury* as one for which he was not fully, or at all, responsible. They do not suggest that the agent is in any way an inappropriate object of that kind of demand for goodwill or regard which is reflected in our ordinary reactive attitudes. They suggest instead that the fact of injury was not in this case incompatible with that demand's being fulfilled, that the fact of injury was quite consistent with that demand's being fulfilled, that the fact of injury was quite consistent with the agent's attitude and intentions being just what we demand they should be. The agent was just ignorant of the injury he was causing, or had lost his balance through being pushed or had reluctantly to cause the injury for reasons which acceptably override his reluctance. The offering of such pleas by the agent and their acceptance by the sufferer is something in no way opposed to, or outside the context of, ordinary interpersonal relationships and the manifestation of ordinary reactive attitudes. Since things go wrong and situations are complicated, it is an essential and integral element in the transactions which are the life of these relationships.

The second group of considerations is very different. I shall take them in two subgroups of which the first is far less important than the second. In connection with the first subgroup we may think of such statements as 'He wasn't himself', 'He has been under very great strain recently', 'He was acting under post-hypnotic suggestion'; in connection with the second, we may think of 'He's only a child', 'He's a hopeless schizophrenic', 'His mind has been systematically perverted', 'That's purely compulsive behaviour on his part'. Such pleas as these do, as pleas of my first general group do not, invite us to suspend our ordinary reactive attitudes towards the agent, either at the time of his action or all the time. They do not invite us to see the agent's action in a way consistent with the full retention of ordinary interpersonal attitudes and merely inconsistent with one particular attitude. They invite us to view the agent himself in a different light from the light in which we should normally view one who has acted as he has acted. I shall not linger over the first subgroup of cases. Though they perhaps raise, in the short term, questions akin to those raised, in the long term, by the second subgroup, we may dismiss them without considering those questions by taking that admirably suggestive phrase, 'He wasn't himself', with the seriousness that – for all its being logically comic – it deserves. We shall not feel resentment against the man he is for the action done by the man he is not; or at least we shall feel less. We normally have to deal with him under normal stresses; so we shall not feel towards him, when he acts as he does under abnormal stresses, as we should have felt towards him had he acted as he did under normal stresses.

The second and more important subgroup of cases allows that the circumstances were normal, but presents the agent as psychologically abnormal – or as morally undeveloped. The agent was himself; but he is warped or deranged, neurotic or just a child. When we see someone in such a light as this, all our reactive attitudes tend to be profoundly modified. I must deal here in crude dichotomies and ignore the ever-interesting and ever-illuminating varieties of case. What I want to contrast is the attitude (or range of attitudes) of involvement or participation in a human relationship, on the one hand, and what might be called the objective attitude (or range of attitudes) to another human being, on the other. Even in the same situation, I must add, they are not altogether *exclusive* of each other; but they are, profoundly, *opposed* to each other. To adopt the objective attitude to another human being is to see him, perhaps, as an object of social policy; as a subject for what, in a wide range of sense, might be called treatment; as something certainly to be taken account, perhaps precautionary account, of; to be managed or handled or cured or trained; perhaps simply to be avoided, though *this* gerundive is not peculiar to cases of objectivity of attitude. The objective attitude may be emotionally toned in many ways, but not in all ways: it may include repulsion or fear, it may include pity or even love, though not all kinds of love. But it cannot include the range of reactive feelings and attitudes which belong to involvement or participation with others in interpersonal human relationships; it cannot include resentment, gratitude, forgiveness, anger, or the sort of love which two adults can sometimes be said to feel reciprocally, for each other. If your attitude towards someone is wholly objective, then though you may fight him, you cannot quarrel with him, and though you may talk to him, even negotiate with him, you cannot reason with him. You can at most pretend to quarrel, or to reason, with him.

Seeing someone, then, as warped or deranged or compulsive in behaviour or peculiarly unfortunate in his formative circumstances – seeing someone so tends, at least to some extent, to set him apart from normal participant reactive attitudes on the part of one who so sees him, tends to promote, at least in the civilized, objective attitudes. But there is something curious to add to this. The objective attitude is not only something we naturally tend to fall into in cases like these, where participant attitudes are partially or wholly inhibited by abnormalities or by immaturity. It is also something which is available as a resource in other cases too. We look with an objective eye on the compulsive behaviour of the neurotic or the tiresome behaviour of a very young child, thinking in terms of treatment or training. But we *can* sometimes look with something like the same eye on the behaviour of the normal and the mature. We *have* this resource and can sometimes use it: as a refuge, say, from the strains of involvement; or as an aid to policy; or simply out of intellectual curiosity. Being human, we cannot, in the normal case, do this for long, or altogether. If the strains of involvement, say, continue to be too great, then we have to do something else – like severing a relationship. But what is above all interesting is the tension there is, in us, between the participant attitude and the objective attitude. One is tempted to say: between our humanity and our intelligence. But to say this would be to distort both notions.

What I have called the participant reactive attitudes are essentially natural human reactions to the good or ill will or indifference of others towards us, as displayed in *their* attitudes and actions. The question we have to ask is: What effect would, or should, the acceptance of the truth of a general thesis of determinism have upon these reactive attitudes? More specifically, would, or should, the acceptance of the truth of the thesis lead to the decay or the repudiation of all such attitudes? Would, or should, it mean the end of gratitude, resentment and forgiveness; of all reciprocated adult loves; of all the essentially *personal* antagonisms?

But how can I answer, or even pose, this question without knowing *exactly* what the thesis of determinism is? Well, there is one thing we do know: that if there is a coherent thesis of determinism, then there must be a sense of 'determined' such that, if that thesis is true, then all behaviour whatever is determined in that sense. Remembering this, we can consider at least what possibilities lie formally open; and then perhaps we shall see that the question can be answered *without* knowing exactly what the thesis of determinism is. We can consider what possibilities lie open because we have already before us an account of the ways in which particular reactive attitudes, or reactive attitudes in general, may be, and, sometimes, we judge, should be, inhibited. Thus I considered earlier a group of considerations which tend to inhibit, and, we judge, should inhibit, resentment, in particular cases of an agent causing an injury, without inhibiting reactive attitudes in general towards that agent. Obviously this group of considerations cannot strictly bear upon our question; for that question concerns reactive attitudes in general. But resentment has a particular interest; so it is worth adding that it has never been claimed as a consequence of the truth of determinism that one or another of *these* considerations was operative in every case of an injury being caused by an agent; that it would follow from the truth of determinism that anyone who caused an injury *either* was quite simply ignorant of causing it *or* had acceptably overriding reasons for acquiescing reluctantly in causing it *or...*, etc. The prevalence of this happy state of affairs would not be a consequence of the reign of universal determinism, but of the reign of universal goodwill. We cannot, then, find here the possibility of an affirmative answer to our question, even for the particular case of resentment.

Next, I remarked that the participant attitude, and the personal reactive attitudes in general, tend to give place, and it is judged by the civilized should give place, to objective attitudes, just in so far as the agent is seen as excluded from ordinary adult human relationships by deep-rooted psychological abnormality – or simply by being a child. But it cannot be a consequence of any thesis which is not itself self-contradictory that abnormality is the universal condition.

Now this dismissal might seem altogether too facile; and so, in a sense, it is. But whatever is too quickly dismissed in this dismissal is allowed for in the only possible form of affirmative answer that remains. We can sometimes, and in part, I have remarked, look on the normal (those we rate as 'normal') in the objective way in which we have learned to look on certain classified cases of abnormality. And our question reduces to this: could, or should, the acceptance of the determinist thesis lead us always to look on everyone exclusively in this way? For this is the only condition worth considering under which the acceptance of determinism could lead to the decay or repudiation of participant reactive attitudes.

It does not seem to be self-contradictory to suppose that this might happen. So I suppose we must say that it is not absolutely inconceivable that it should happen. But I am strongly inclined to think that it is, for us as we are, practically inconceivable. The human commitment to participation in ordinary interpersonal relationships is, I think, too thoroughgoing and deeply rooted for us to take seriously the thought that a general theoretical conviction might so change our world that, in it, there were no longer any such things as interpersonal relationships as we normally understand them; and being involved in interpersonal relationships as we normally understand them precisely is being exposed to the range of reactive attitudes and feelings that is in question.

This, then, is a part of the reply to our question. A sustained objectivity of interpersonal attitude, and the human isolation which that would entail, does not seem to be something of which human beings would be capable, even if some general truth were a theoretical ground for it. But this is not all. There is a further point, implicit in the foregoing, which must be made explicit. Exceptionally, I have said, we can have direct dealings with human beings without any degree of personal involvement, treating them simply as creatures to be handled in our own interests, or our side's, or society's – or even theirs. In the extreme case of the mentally deranged, it is easy to see the connection between the possibility of a wholly objective attitude and the impossibility of what we understand by ordinary interpersonal relationships. Given this latter impossibility, no other civilized attitude is available than that of viewing the deranged person simply as something to be understood and controlled in the most desirable fashion. To view him as outside the reach of personal relationships is already, for the civilized, to view him in this way. For reasons of policy or self-protection we may have occasion, perhaps temporary, to adopt a fundamentally similar attitude to a 'normal' human being; to concentrate, that is, on understanding 'how he works', with a view to determining our policy accordingly or to finding in that very understanding a relief from the strains of involvement. Now it is certainly true that in the case of the abnormal, though not in the case of the normal, our adoption of the objective attitude is a consequence of our viewing the agent as *incapacitated* in some or all respects for ordinary interpersonal relationships. He is thus incapacitated, perhaps, by the fact that his picture of reality is pure fantasy, that he does not, in a sense, live in the real world at all; or by the fact that his behaviour is, in part, an unrealistic acting out of unconscious purposes; or by the fact that he is an idiot, or a moral idiot. But there is something else which, *because* this is true, is equally certainly *not* true. And that is that there is a sense of 'determined' such that (1) if determinism is true, all behaviour is determined in this sense, and (2) determinism might be true, i.e. it is not inconsistent with the facts as we know them to suppose that all behaviour might be determined in this sense, and (3) our adoption of the objective attitude towards the abnormal is the result of a prior embracing of the belief that the behaviour, or the relevant stretch of behaviour, of the human being in question is determined in this sense. Neither in the case of the normal, then, nor in the case of the abnormal is it true that, when we adopt an objective attitude, we do so *because* we hold such a belief. So my answer has two parts. The first is that we cannot, as we are, seriously envisage ourselves adopting a thoroughgoing objectivity of attitude to others as a result of theoretical conviction of the truth of determinism; and the second is that when we do in fact adopt such an attitude in a particular case, our doing so is not the consequence of a theoretical conviction which might be expressed as 'Determinism in this case', but is a consequence of our abandoning, for different reasons in different cases, the ordinary interpersonal attitudes.

It might be said that all this leaves the real question unanswered, and that we cannot hope to answer it without knowing exactly what the thesis of determinism is. For the real question is not a question about what we actually do, or why we do it. It is not even a question about what we would *in fact* do if a certain theoretical conviction gained general acceptance. It is a question about what it would be *rational* to do if determinism were true, a question about the rational justification of ordinary interpersonal attitudes in general. To this I shall reply, first, that such a question could seem real only to one who had utterly failed to grasp the purport of the preceding answer, the fact of our natural human commitment to ordinary interpersonal attitudes. This commitment is part of the general framework of human life, not something that can come up for review as particular cases can come up for review within this general framework. And I shall reply, second, that if we could imagine what we cannot have, viz. a choice in this matter, then we could choose rationally only in the light of an assessment of the gains and losses to human life, its enrichment or impoverishment; and the truth or falsity of a general thesis of determinism would not bear on the rationality of *this* choice.

12   Freedom, Responsibility and the Ability to do Otherwise: Harry G. Frankfurt, *Alternate Possibilities and Moral Responsibility**

There is an obvious and strong link between freedom and responsibility: we generally hold someone answerable for an action only when they were free to do it or not to do it – in other words, when there were genuine alternative options open to them. This suggests a principle many people find intuitively clear – that a person is morally responsible for what he has done only if he *could have done otherwise*. In the last of our extracts on freedom, the American philosopher Harry Frankfurt offers an ingenious argument that calls this principle ('the principle of alternative possibilities') into question.

Frankfurt first considers cases of coercion – when someone ('Jones') is threatened with a terrible sanction unless he does X (for example,

* Harry G. Frankfurt, 'Alternate Possibilities and Moral Responsibility', *Journal of Philosophy*, 66 (1969), 829–39; abridged.

someone threatens to kill him unless he leaves town).[1] One might suppose that if he goes ahead and leaves town he is therefore to be excused on the grounds that he could not have done otherwise. But Frankfurt points out that Jones might have already taken a rational decision to leave town, prior to the threat. If he now goes ahead and leaves town on the basis of his original reasons, and not because of the threat, then surely he is responsible; for in this case the threat had no effect on what he actually did. In this kind of case, Jones's scope for staying in town seems nil: had he not already decided to leave town, then the threat would have been quite enough to make him leave. Yet even though he could not have done otherwise than leave, we surely still want to hold him responsible for leaving, since he would have left even without the threat.

The case of coercion raises complications, however, since someone might object that alternatives *are* open for the threatened person – it is always possible to resist the threat. (Consider, for example the case when someone threatens to kill you unless you set off an atomic bomb: despite your appalling predicament, it seems that you both can, and should, resist.) To meet such an objection, Frankfurt alters the example from one of threat to a more complex manipulation. Suppose the manipulator ('Black') can read Jones's mind: if Jones decides to leave town, Black need do nothing; but if Jones decides to stay, Black can hypnotise him and implant in his mind an irresistible compulsion to leave. Frankfurt has thus managed to set the case up so that Jones has in fact no alternative possibility but to leave; yet in the case where he leaves because of his original decision (and Black's hypnotism does not need to be activated), he surely remains responsible. Hence, Frankfurt argues, the principle of alternative possibilities is false. And our extract concludes with some suggestions as to how the principle might be reformulated.

One implication of Frankfurt's interesting argument is that freedom and responsibility depend not so much on whether we have alternative options open to us, as on the kinds of circumstances that lead us to act: our freedom is undermined by external manipulations, but not by our own rational decisions – even in cases where no alternative option actually obtains. The argument thus may be seen as providing support for the 'compatibilist' position that has surfaced in several earlier extracts – the view that determinism does not after all rule out moral responsibility.

A dominant role in nearly all recent inquiries into the free-will problem has been played by a principle which I shall call 'the principle of alternate possibilities'. This principle states that a person is morally responsible for what he has done only if he could have done otherwise...But the principle of alternate possibilities is false. A person may well be morally responsible for what he has done even though he could not have done otherwise. The principle's plausibility is an illusion, which can be made to vanish by bringing the relevant moral phenomena into sharper focus.

I

In seeking illustrations of the principle of alternate possibilities, it is most natural to think of situations in which the same circumstances both bring it about that a person does something and make it impossible for him to avoid doing it. These include, for example, situations in which a person is coerced into doing something, or in which he is impelled to act by a hypnotic suggestion, or in which some inner compulsion drives him to do what he does. In situations of these kinds there are circumstances that make

---

[1] The particular example of leaving town is not Frankfurt's, but is supplied for illustration.

it impossible for the person to do otherwise, and these very circumstances also serve to bring it about that he does whatever it is that he does.

However ... [a] person may do something in circumstances that leave him no alternative to doing it, without these circumstances actually moving him or leading him to do it – without them playing any role, indeed, in bringing it about that he does what he does ... I propose to develop some examples of this kind in the context of a discussion of coercion and to suggest that our moral intuitions concerning these examples tend to disconfirm the principle of alternate possibilities. Then I will discuss the principle in more general terms, explain what I think is wrong with it, and describe briefly and without argument how it might appropriately be revised.

II

It is generally agreed that a person who has been coerced to do something did not do it freely and is not morally responsible for having done it ... It is natural enough to say of a person who has been coerced to do something that he could not have done otherwise. And it may easily seem that being coerced deprives a person of freedom and of moral responsibility simply because it is a special case of being unable to do otherwise. The principle of alternate possibilities may in this way derive some credibility from its association with the very plausible proposition that moral responsibility is excluded by coercion.

It is not right, however, that it should do so ... Let us suppose that someone is threatened convincingly with a penalty he finds unacceptable and that he then does what is required of him by the issuer of the threat. We can imagine details that would make it reasonable for us to think that the person was coerced to perform the action in question, that he could not have done otherwise, and that he bears no moral responsibility for having done what he did. But just what is it about situations of this kind that warrants the judgment that the threatened person is not morally responsible for his act?

This question may be approached by considering situations of the following kind. Jones decides for reasons of his own to do something, then someone threatens him with a very harsh penalty (so harsh that any reasonable person would submit to the threat) unless he does precisely that, and Jones does it. Will we hold Jones morally responsible for what he has done? I think this will depend on the roles we think were played, in leading him to act, by his original decision and by the threat.

One possibility is that $Jones_1$ is not a reasonable man: he is, rather, a man who does what he has once decided to do no matter what happens next and no matter what the cost. In that case, the threat actually exerted no effective force upon him. He acted without any regard to it, very much as if he were not aware that it had been made ... It seems evident that in these circumstances the fact that $Jones_1$ was threatened in no way reduces the moral responsibility he would otherwise bear for his act. This example, however, is not a counterexample either to the doctrine that coercion excuses or to the principle of alternate possibilities. For we have supposed that $Jones_1$ is a man upon whom the threat had no coercive effect and, hence, that it did not actually deprive him of alternatives to doing what he did.

Another possibility is that Jones$_2$ was stampeded by the threat. Given that threat, he would have performed that action regardless of what decision he had already made. The threat upset him so profoundly, moreover, that he completely forgot his own earlier decision and did what was demanded of him entirely because he was terrified of the penalty with which he was threatened. In this case ... he can hardly be said to be morally responsible for his action. For he performed the action simply as a result of the coercion to which he was subjected. His earlier decision played no role in bringing it about that he did what he did, and it would therefore be gratuitous to assign it a role in the moral evaluation of his action.

Now consider a third possibility. Jones$_3$ was neither stampeded by the threat nor indifferent to it. The threat impressed him, as it would impress any reasonable man, and he would have submitted to it wholeheartedly if he had not already made a decision that coincided with the one demanded of him. In fact, however, he performed the action in question on the basis of the decision he had made before the threat was issued. When he acted, he was not actually motivated by the threat but solely by the considerations that had originally commended the action to him. It was not the threat that led him to act, though it would have done so if he had not already provided himself with a sufficient motive for performing the action in question.

... Then I think we would be justified in regarding his moral responsibility for what he did as unaffected by the threat even though, since he would in any case have submitted to the threat, he could not have avoided doing what he did. It would be entirely reasonable for us to make the same judgment concerning his moral responsibility that we would have made if we had not known of the threat. For the threat did not in fact influence his performance of the action. He did what he did just as if the threat had not been made at all.

III

The case of Jones$_3$ may appear at first glance to combine coercion and moral responsibility, and thus to provide a counterexample to the doctrine that coercion excuses. It is not really so certain that it does so, however, because it is unclear whether the example constitutes a genuine instance of coercion. Can we say of Jones$_3$ that he was coerced to do something, when he had already decided on his own to do it and when he did it entirely on the basis of that decision? Or would it be more correct to say that Jones$_3$ was not coerced to do what he did, even though he himself recognized that there was an irresistible force at work in virtue of which he had to do it? My own linguistic intuitions lead me toward the second alternative, but they are somewhat equivocal. Perhaps we can say either of these things, or perhaps we must add a qualifying explanation to whichever of them we say.

This murkiness, however, does not interfere with our drawing an important moral from an examination of the example. Suppose we decide to say that Jones$_3$ was *not* coerced. Our basis for saying this will clearly be that it is incorrect to regard a man as being coerced to do something unless he does it *because of* the coercive force exerted against him. The fact that an irresistible threat is made will not, then, entail that the person who receives it is coerced to do what he does. It will also be necessary that the threat is what actually accounts for his doing it. On the other hand, suppose we decide to say that Jones$_3$ *was* coerced. Then we will be bound to admit that being coerced does not exclude being morally responsible. And we will also surely be led to the view that coercion affects the judgment of a person's moral responsibility only when the person acts as he does because he is coerced to do so – i.e., when the fact that he is coerced is what accounts for his action.

Whichever we decide to say, then, we will recognize that the doctrine that coercion excludes moral responsibility is not a particularized version of the principle of alternate possibilities. Situations in which a person who does something cannot do otherwise because he is subject to coercive power are either not instances of coercion at all, or they are situations in which the person may still be morally responsible for what he does if it is not because of the coercion that he does it. When we excuse a person who has been coerced, we do not excuse him because he was unable to do otherwise. Even though a person is subject to a coercive force that precludes his performing any action but one, he may nonetheless bear full moral responsibility for performing that action.

IV

To the extent that the principle of alternate possibilities derives its plausibility from association with the doctrine that coercion excludes moral responsibility, a clear understanding of the latter diminishes the appeal of the former. Indeed the case of Jones$_3$ may appear to do more than illuminate the relationship between the two doctrines. It may well seem to provide a decisive counterexample to the principle of alternate possibilities and thus to show that this principle is false. For the irresistibility of the threat to which Jones$_3$ is subjected might well be taken to mean that he cannot but perform the action he performs. And yet the threat, since Jones$_3$ performs the action without regard to it, does not reduce his moral responsibility for what he does.

The following objection will doubtless be raised against the suggestion that the case of Jones$_3$ is a counterexample to the principle of alternate possibilities ... His knowledge that he stands to suffer an intolerably harsh penalty does not mean that Jones$_3$, strictly speaking, *cannot* perform any action but the one he does perform. After all it is still open to him, and this is crucial, to defy the threat if he wishes to do so and to accept the penalty his action would bring down upon him. In the sense in which the principle of alternate possibilities employs the concept of 'could have done otherwise', Jones$_3$'s inability to resist the threat does not mean that he cannot do otherwise than perform the action he performs. Hence the case of Jones$_3$ does not constitute an instance contrary to the principle.

... I believe that whatever force this objection may be thought to have can be deflected by altering the example in the following way. Suppose someone – Black, let us say – wants Jones$_4$ to perform a certain action. Black is prepared to go to considerable lengths to get his way, but he prefers to avoid showing his hand unnecessarily. So he waits until Jones$_4$ is about to make up his mind what to do, and he does nothing unless it is clear to him (Black is an excellent judge of such things) that Jones$_4$ is going to decide to do something *other* than what he wants him to do. If it does become clear that Jones$_4$ is going to decide to do something else, Black takes effective steps to ensure that Jones$_4$ decides to do, and that he does do, what he wants him to do.[1] Whatever Jones$_4$'s initial preferences and inclinations, then, Black will have his way.

What steps will Black take, if he believes he must take steps, in order to ensure that Jones$_4$ decides and acts as he wishes? Anyone with a theory concerning what 'could have done otherwise' means may answer this question for himself by describing whatever measures he would regard as sufficient to guarantee that, in the relevant sense, Jones$_4$ cannot do otherwise. Let Black pronounce a terrible threat, and in this way both force Jones$_4$ to perform the desired action and prevent him from performing a forbidden one. Let Black give Jones$_4$ a potion, or put him under hypnosis, and in some such way as these generate in Jones$_4$ an irresistible inner compulsion to perform the act Black wants performed and to avoid others. Or let Black manipulate the minute processes of Jones$_4$'s brain and nervous system in some more direct way, so that causal forces running in and out of his synapses and along the poor man's nerves determine that he chooses to act and that he does act in the one way and not in any other. Given any conditions under which it will be maintained that Jones$_4$ cannot do otherwise, in other words, let Black bring it about that those conditions prevail. The structure of the example is flexible enough, I think, to find a way around any charge of irrelevance by accommodating the doctrine on which the charge is based.[2]

Now suppose that Black never has to show his hand because Jones$_4$, for reasons of his own, decides to perform and does perform the very action Black wants him to perform. In that case, it seems clear, Jones$_4$ will bear precisely the same moral responsibility for what he does as he would have borne if Black had not been ready to take steps to ensure that he do it. It would be quite unreasonable to excuse Jones for his action, or to withhold the praise to which it would normally entitle him, on the basis of the fact that he could not have done otherwise. This fact played no role at all in leading him to act as he did. He would have acted the same even if it had not been a fact. Indeed, everything happened just as it would have happened without Black's presence in the situation and without his readiness to intrude into it.

In this example there are sufficient conditions for Jones$_4$'s performing the action in question. What action he performs is not up to him. Of course it is in a way up to him whether he acts on his own or as a result of Black's intervention. That depends upon what action he himself is inclined to perform. But whether he finally acts on his own or as a result of Black's intervention, he performs the same action. He has no

---

[1] *The assumption that Black can predict what Jones$_4$ will decide to do does not beg the question of determinism. We can imagine that Jones$_4$ has often confronted the alternatives – A and B – that he now confronts, and that his face has invariably twitched when he was about to decide to do A and never when he was about to decide to do B. Knowing this, and observing the twitch, Black would have a basis for prediction. This does, to be sure, suppose that there is some sort of causal relation between Jones$_4$'s state at the time of the twitch and his subsequent states. But any plausible view of decision or of action will allow that reaching a decision and performing an action both involve earlier and later phases, with causal relations between them, and such that the earlier phases are not themselves part of the decision or of the action. The example does not require that these earlier phases be deterministically related to still earlier events.

[2] *The example is also flexible enough to allow for the elimination of Black altogether. Anyone who thinks that the effectiveness of the example is undermined by its reliance on a human manipulator, who imposes his will on Jones$_4$, can substitute for Black a machine programmed to do what Black does. If this is still not good enough, forget both Black and the machine and suppose that their role is played by natural forces involving no will or design at all.

alternative but to do what Black wants him to do. If he does it on his own, however, his moral responsibility for doing it is not affected by the fact that Black was lurking in the background with sinister intent, since this intent never comes into play.

V

The fact that a person could not have avoided doing something is a sufficient condition of his having done it. But, as some of my examples show, this fact may play no role whatever in the explanation of why he did it. It may not figure at all among the circumstances that actually brought it about that he did what he did, so that his action is to be accounted for on another basis entirely. Even though the person was unable to do otherwise, that is to say, it may not be the case that he acted as he did *because* he could not have done otherwise. Now if someone had no alternative to performing a certain action but did not perform it because he was unable to do otherwise, then he would have performed exactly the same action even if he *could* have done otherwise. The circumstances that made it impossible for him to do otherwise could have been subtracted from the situation without affecting what happened or why it happened in any way. Whatever it was that actually led the person to do what he did, or that made him do it, would have led him to do it or made him do it even if it had been possible for him to do something else instead.

Thus it would have made no difference, so far as concerns his action or how he came to perform it, if the circumstances that made it impossible for him to avoid performing it had not prevailed. The fact that he could not have done otherwise clearly provides no basis for supposing that he *might* have done otherwise if he had been able to do so. When a fact is in this way irrelevant to the problem of accounting for a person's action it seems quite gratuitous to assign it any weight in the assessment of his moral responsibility. Why should the fact be considered in reaching a moral judgment concerning the person when it does not help in any way to understand either what made him act as he did or what, in other circumstances, he might have done?

This, then, is why the principle of alternate possibilities is mistaken. It asserts that a person bears no moral responsibility – that is, he is to be excused – for having performed an action if there were circumstances that made it impossible for him to avoid performing it. But there may be circumstances that make it impossible for a person to avoid performing some action without those circumstances in any way bringing it about that he performs that action. It would surely be no good for the person to refer to circumstances of this sort in an effort to absolve himself of moral responsibility for performing the action in question. For those circumstances, by hypothesis, actually had nothing to do with his having done what he did. He would have done precisely the same thing, and he would have been led or made in precisely the same way to do it, even if they had not prevailed.

We often do, to be sure, excuse people for what they have done when they tell us (and we believe them) that they could not have done otherwise. But this is because we assume that what they tell us serves to explain why they did what they did. We take it for granted that they are not being disingenuous, as a person would be who cited as an excuse the fact that he could not have avoided doing what he did but who knew full well that it was not at all because of this that he did it.

What I have said may suggest that the principle of alternate possibilities should be revised so as to assert that a person is not morally responsible for what he has done if he did it *because* he could not have done otherwise ... I do not believe, however, that this revision of the principle is acceptable.

Suppose a person tells us that he did what he did because he was unable to do otherwise; or suppose he makes the similar statement that he did what he did because he had to do it. We do often accept statements like these (if we believe them) as valid excuses, and such statements may well seem at first glance to invoke the revised principle of alternate possibilities. But I think that when we accept such statements as valid excuses it is because we assume that we are being told more than the statements strictly and literally convey. We understand the person who offers the excuse to mean that he did what he did *only because* he was unable to do otherwise, or *only because* he had to do it. And we understand him to mean, more particularly, that when he did what he did it was not because that was what he really wanted to do. The principle of alternate possibilities should thus be replaced, in my opinion, by the following principle: a person is not morally responsible for what he has done if he did it *only* because he could not have done otherwise. This principle does not appear to conflict with the view that moral responsibility is compatible with determinism.

The following may all be true: there were circumstances that made it impossible for a person to avoid doing something; these circumstances actually played a role in bringing it about that he did it, so that it is correct to say that he did it because he could not have done otherwise; the person really wanted to do what he did; he did it because it was what he really wanted to do, so that it is not correct to say that he did what he did only because he could not have done otherwise. Under these conditions, the person may well be morally responsible for what he has done. On the other hand, he will not be morally responsible for what he has done if he did it only because he could not have done otherwise, even if what he did was something he really wanted to do.

Specimen Questions

1 Critically examine Locke's claim that the concept 'same person' is to be understood in terms of *continuity of consciousness*.
2 'Consciousness of personal identity presupposes, and therefore cannot constitute, personal identity, any more than knowledge, in any other case, can constitute truth, which it presupposes' (Butler). Explain and discuss.
3 Does Hume have sound arguments to show that we are 'nothing but a bundle or collection of different perceptions'?
4 Does Freud provide a convincing case for the existence of 'unconscious mental processes'? Does this notion, if accepted, show that earlier views of the self were oversimplified?
5 If you were about to be 'teletransported', would you agree with Parfit that your relation to your future replica is 'about as good as ordinary survival'?
6 Explain and evaluate Charles Taylor's claim that 'my self-understanding necessarily has temporal depth and incorporates narrative'.

7 'We are by no means compelled, either, retaining the prescience of God, to take away the freedom of the will, or, retaining the freedom of the will, to deny that He is prescient of future things, which is impious. But we embrace both' (Augustine). Explain and critically discuss.

8 Explain what Hobbes means by calling an action free, and why he maintains our freedom is not threatened by causal necessity. Do the concepts of praise, blame and responsibility pose a problem for Hobbes's views?

9 Do you accept Laplace's claim that, given all the antecedent causes leading up to a given event or action, the notion that there could be two possible alternative outcomes is 'an illusion of the mind due to ignorance'?

10 Why does Sartre say we are 'condemned to be free'? Do you think he answers the challenge to human freedom posed by determinism?

11 Strawson argues that it is 'practically inconceivable' that the acceptance of determinism could lead to the decay or repudiation of participant reactive attitudes (such as resentment, anger, gratitude and forgiveness). Do you agree?

12 Examine the claim that someone is responsible for their actions only when he or she could have done otherwise. Are Frankfurt's counter-examples to this claim convincing?

Suggestions for Further Reading

Personal identity and the self

A useful general introduction is J. Glover, *The Philosophy and Psychology of Personal Identity* (Harmondsworth: Penguin, 1988).

For a valuable collection of classic and contemporary readings, see J. Perry (ed.), *Personal Identity* (Berkeley, Calif.: University of California Press, 1985).

A stimulating debate on psychological versus physical approaches to personal identity is S. Shoemaker and R. Swinburne, *Personal Identity* (Oxford: Blackwell, 1984). See also T. Penelhum, *Survival and Disembodied Existence* (London: Routledge, 1970).

More advanced studies are P. F. Strawson, *Individuals* (London: Methuen, 1959); D. Wiggins, *Identity and Spatio-temporal Continuity* (Oxford: Blackwell, 1967); B. Williams, *Problems of the Self* (Cambridge: Cambridge University Press, 1973).

For detailed discussions of Freud's views, a valuable source is J. Neu (ed.), *The Cambridge Companion to Freud* (Cambridge: Cambridge University Press, 1992).

For criticism of Parfit's views (extract 5), see T. Nagel, *The View from Nowhere* (Oxford: Oxford University Press, 1986), ch. 3.

For discussion of Taylor, see J. Tully (ed.), *Philosophy in an Age of Pluralism: The Philosophy of Charles Taylor* (Cambridge: Cambridge University Press, 1994).

Freedom and determinism

For an introductory survey of some of the standard positions, see D. J. O'Connor, *Free Will* (Garden City, NY: Doubleday, 1971).

An engaging and readable discussion of free will from a compatibilist standpoint is D. Dennett, *Elbow Room* (Oxford: Oxford University Press, 1984).

For a very clear discussion of the concept of responsibility with special reference to the law, see A. Kenny, *Freewill and Responsibility* (London: Routledge, 1978).

The following are useful collections of papers on the various issues: S. Hook (ed.), *Determinism and Freedom in the Age of Modern Science* (New York: Macmillan, 1961); T. Honderich (ed.), *Essays on Freedom of Action* (London: Routledge, 1973); G. Watson (ed.), *Free Will* (Oxford: Oxford University Press, 1982).

The views of Sartre on freedom are discussed in several of the essays in C. Howells (ed.), *The Cambridge Companion to Sartre* (Cambridge: Cambridge University Press, 1992).

More advanced studies are M. Klein, *Determinism, Blameworthiness and Deprivation* (Oxford: Clarendon, 1990); P. Van Inwagen, *An Essay on Free Will* (Oxford: Clarendon, 1983).

Useful surveys of some of the issues raised by Frankfurt may be found in the articles on 'Free Will', 'Freedom and Determinism' and 'Responsibility' in L. C. Becker and C. Becker (eds), *Encyclopedia of Ethics* (2nd edn, London and New York: Routledge, 2001).

PART VI

God and Religion

God and Religion
Introduction

In the past, philosophy and religion were often not clearly separated, both being concerned with understanding the nature of the universe and the place of mankind within it. As some of readings in Part II (above) make clear, several of the great metaphysical system-builders of earlier ages developed theories of reality in which God occupied an absolutely central place. But it is equally true that the practice of religion does not always require complex theoretical speculation. A long-standing tradition in religious thought allows that simple faith can be as sound a route to awareness of God as that afforded by intellectual debate: 'the road to heaven', as Descartes observed, invoking an ancient theme, 'is just as open to the ignorant as to the learned'.[1] Nevertheless, with the revival of philosophical thought in Western Europe after the Dark Ages, many scholars and theologians became increasingly preoccupied with showing that the Christian religion did not depend on revelation alone, but could be defended with all the rigour of philosophical argument. In this climate, it became a central task of philosophical theology to be able to provide clear and compelling proofs of the existence of the one true God of the Bible, the omnipotent and perfect creator of the world. This Part of the volume begins with a number of classic contributions to this project of 'natural theology', the attempt to demonstrate the existence of God by rational argument. The story then moves on to the vexed debates of the early modern period over such critical issues as the problem of evil, the possibility of divine revelation (through miracles), and the status of appeals to the order found in the natural world as supposed evidence of the world's divine authorship. Finally, as we move closer to the present, the claims of traditional religion come under increasing pressure; and our concluding extracts examine the struggle of nineteenth- and twentieth-century philosophers to achieve new kinds of understanding of the nature of religious belief and the meaning of religious language.

---

[1] *Discourse on the Method* [1637], part i.

1 The Existence of God: Anselm of Canterbury, *Proslogion**

Perhaps the shortest and most elegant proof of God's existence ever devised is what has since come to be called the 'ontological argument'. Originally formulated in the eleventh century by St Anselm of Canterbury in his *Proslogion* ('Discourse'), the argument works entirely *a priori* – that is to say, it does not require any premise drawn from experience or observation of the world. Instead it focuses simply on the concept or definition of God as the utterly supreme being – or as Anselm puts it, 'that than which nothing greater can be thought'. So far, of course, nothing is assumed about whether such a being actually exists, since that would beg the question. But Anselm now proceeds to consider two possibilities: either such a being truly exists in reality, or else he exists only in the mind of the believer. Yet to exist in reality is surely greater than to exist only in someone's mind. So if God exists only in the mind, then something greater *can* be thought, which contradicts the original definition. Hence it follows, Anselm argues, that God, defined as 'that than which nothing greater can be thought', must necessarily exist not merely in the understanding but in actual reality.

The argument has fascinated and exasperated critics ever since. A contemporary of Anselm, the monk Gaunilo, objected that if we grant Anselm's premise that it is more excellent to exist in reality than to exist merely in the mind, then we would be able (absurdly) to prove that the mythical lost island of Oceanea, supposed to be superior in abundance of riches to all other lands, must indeed exist. Anselm replied that the logic of his argument applied not to such relatively perfect things but *only* to the utterly supreme reality, 'that than which a greater cannot be thought'. His general line of argument was later revived by René Descartes, who started from the definition of God as the sum of all perfections, and maintained that existence could no more be separated from such a being than the property of having its angles equal to 180 degrees could be separated from the essence of a triangle. But why should perfection or greatness imply existence? A good deal of later discussion of the argument has centred on this point; indeed, following an objection raised by Immanuel Kant, many have questioned whether existence should rightly be thought of as a predicate at all (is there not something odd in treating real existence as something that belongs to an object, alongside the other properties it has?).[1] The most serious worry for defenders of the argument seems to be this: even if we grant that Anselm has shown that whatever qualifies for the title *greatest thinkable being* must exist, is it not still an open question whether there is anything which does qualify for this title in the first place?

The mind stirred up to the contemplation of God

Come now, wretched man, escape for a moment from your preoccupations and draw back a little while from your seething thoughts. Lay aside for now your burdensome worries and put off your wearisome tasks. Empty yourself to God for a little while, and rest a short time in him. Enter the private chamber of your mind, shut out everything except God and whatever may help you to search for him; lock the door and seek him out. Speak now, my whole heart, and say to God 'I seek thy face; thy face Lord will I seek'.[2]

---

* Anselm of Canterbury, *Proslogion* [1077–8], ch. 1 (excerpts), chs 2–5. Translation from the Latin by John Cottingham.
[1] For the reference to Descartes and Kant, see Suggestions for Further Reading at the end of this Part.
[2] Psalm 27: 8 (26: 8 in the Vulgate (Latin) version).

...I acknowledge and give thanks, Lord, that you have created me in this your image, so that I may be mindful of you, and think of you and love you. But the image is so scraped and worn away by my vices, so darkened by the smoke of my sins, that it cannot do what it was created to do unless you renew and reform it. I will not attempt, Lord, to reach your height, for my understanding falls so far short of it. But I desire to understand your truth just a little, the truth that my heart believes and loves. I do not seek to understand in order that I may believe, but I believe in order that I may understand. For this also I believe: unless I believe, I shall not understand.

God truly exists

So, Lord, you who give understanding to those who have faith, grant me to understand, so far as you judge it fit, that you indeed exist as we believe, and that you are what we believe you to be. Now we believe that you are *something than which nothing greater can be thought.* Is there then no such being, since 'the fool hath said in his heart: there is no God'?[1] Yet surely this same fool, when he hears the very words I now speak – 'something than which nothing greater can be thought' – understands what he hears; and what he understands exists in his understanding, even if he does not understand that it actually exists. For it is one thing for an object to exist in the understanding, and another to understand that the object exists. When an artist thinks in advance of what he is about to paint, he has it in his understanding, but does not yet understand it to exist, since he has not yet painted it. But when he has painted it, then he both has it in his understanding and also understands that it exists, since he has painted it. Hence even the fool must agree that there exists, in the understanding at least, something than which nothing greater can be thought; for when he hears this expression he understands it, and whatever is understood exists in the understanding. Yet surely *that than which a greater cannot be thought* cannot exist in the understanding alone. For once granted that it exists, if only in the understanding, it can be thought of as existing in reality, and this is greater. Hence if *that than which a greater cannot be thought* exists solely in the understanding, it would follow that the very thing than which a greater *cannot* be thought turns out to be that than which a greater *can* be thought; but this is clearly impossible. Hence something than which a greater cannot be thought undoubtedly exists both in the understanding and in reality.

God cannot be thought not to exist

And certainly this entity so truly exists that it cannot be thought not to exist. For it is possible to think of a being which cannot be thought of as not existing; and this is greater than that something which can be thought of as not existing. So if *that than which a greater cannot be thought* can be thought not to exist, it would follow that the very same thing than which a greater cannot be thought is *not* that than which a

---

[1] Psalm 14: 1 (13: 1 in the Vulgate).

greater cannot be thought; and this is inconsistent. Hence something than which a greater cannot be thought exists so truly that it cannot even be thought not to exist.

And this being is you, O Lord our God. So truly do you exist, O Lord my God, that you cannot even be thought not to exist. And how appropriate this is. For if some mind could think of something better than you, then a created being would rise above its creator and judge its creator, which is utterly absurd. Moreover, everything there is, apart from you alone, can be thought not to exist. You alone of all things possess existence in the truest sense and to the highest degree; for whatever else there is does not exist as truly, and so possesses existence to a lesser degree. Why then is it that 'the fool hath said in his heart there is no God', since it is so obvious to the rational mind that you exist to the greatest degree of all? Why, except that he is indeed dull and foolish!

How the fool said in his heart what cannot be thought

But how did he come to say in his heart what he could not think; or how was it impossible for him to think what he said in his heart, given that saying in one's heart and thinking are one and the same? Did he really both think it, since he said it in his heart, and also not say it in his heart, because he could not think it? If this is so, indeed since it is so, then there is more than one sense in which something is 'said in one's heart' or 'thought': a thing is thought in one sense when we think of the word signifying it, but in another sense when we understand what the thing itself is. In the former sense, then, God can be thought not to exist, but not at all in the latter sense. For no one who understands what God is can think that God does not exist, even though he may say the words in his heart without any sense, or in some strange sense. For God is *that than which a greater cannot be thought.* And if someone understands this clearly, he understands that this being exists in such a way that he cannot not exist, even in thought. Hence he who understands that God exists in this way cannot think that he does not exist.

I give you thanks, good Lord, that what I formerly believed through your gift of faith, I now understand through the light which you bestow; so much so that the truth of your existence, even if I were unwilling to believe it, is now something I cannot fail to understand.

God is whatever is better to be than not to be; he alone, existing through himself, makes all other things from nothing

What are you then, lord God, you than whom nothing greater can be thought? What are you but the supreme being, the only being who exists through itself, and the one who has made all other things from nothing? For whatever falls short of this is *less* than what can be thought, and this cannot be thought true of you. So can any good thing be lacking in the supreme good, the source of every good that exists? You are therefore just, truthful, blessed and whatever is better to be than not to be; for it is better to be just than unjust, and better to be blessed than not.

2   The Five Proofs of God: Thomas Aquinas, *Summa Theologiae**

By common consent, the greatest philosopher-theologian of the Middle Ages was St Thomas Aquinas (see introduction to Part IV, extract 3). In the following extract from his monumental *Summa Theologiae* Aquinas sets out no less than five proofs of the existence of God, based on Aristotelian principles. The ontological argument (see previous extract) is not among them, since Aquinas regarded its validity as suspect; instead of proceeding purely *a priori*, all the five 'ways' deployed by Aquinas depend partly on what are taken to be empirical facts about the world.[1]

In the *first* proof, Aquinas argues that since some things move, and whatever moves is caused to move by something other than itself, then either the chain of movers goes back infinitely far (which is impossible) or else there is a first, unmoved, mover, an original source of motion – and this is God. This compressed summary is perhaps easier to understand than Aquinas's own more elaborate formulation, which relies on a considerable amount of Aristotelian jargon. For example, he follows Aristotle in using 'motion' in a very broad sense, including any qualitative change which a body may undergo, and also in construing motion as the bringing of something from 'potentiality' to 'actuality'. Thus, when a piece of wood is heated, it is brought from a state of merely being potentially hot to a state of being actually hot, as a result of the action of

something like fire, which is 'actually hot'. In such cases there is always a transition from potentiality to actuality: something cannot be both in actuality and potentiality in the same respect at the same time, as Aquinas puts it. It follows that something cannot both be mover (the cause of change) and moved (undergoing change) in the same respect at the same time; so 'whatever is in motion is moved by something else'. Aquinas then argues that this sequence cannot continue back *ad infinitum*, and 'hence it is necessary to arrive at a *first mover which is moved by nothing else*' – and this everyone thinks of as God. Whatever we make of the individual steps of the argument, it is doubtful that the argument succeeds in establishing that there must be a *single* prime mover; nor is it clear that there is anything impossible in the idea of a chain of movers stretching back *ad infinitum*. Similar difficulties beset the *second* way, which is very like the first in structure, but takes the fact that some things are *caused* as its premise, and reasons to the conclusion that to account for this (since the chain of causes cannot stretch back for ever)[2] we must ultimately arrive at a first (uncaused) cause, which is God.

The *third* proof (sometimes called the proof 'from the contingency of the world') starts from the fact that some things come into being and pass away, and are hence contingent (they can either be, or not be) as opposed to necessary. But if

---

* From *Summa Theologiae* [1266–73], Part I, question 2, article 3. Translation by John Cottingham.

[1] Arguments for God which start from a feature of the world as it is are often called 'cosmological arguments', but the use of this term in the philosophical literature is not fully consistent. Sometimes the label is reserved for the kind of proof which starts from the fact that anything exists at all (asking 'why is there something rather than nothing?'), and argues that the explanation must be sought in the existence of a being who contains the reason for existence within himself; for an example of this type of proof, see opening paragraph of extract 5, below.

[2] To support this, Aquinas reasons that 'if any one cause is taken away, the effect will also be absent. Hence if there was not a first item in the series, there will be no intermediate items.' This seems unfair as it stands, since the defender of an infinite backward chain is not, as it were, 'taking away' a first item, but simply denying that if we trace the chain backwards it would ever terminate. Elsewhere, however, Aquinas concedes that we cannot prove that the world ever had a beginning, so it seems he has no logical objection to an infinite backward chain as such. So his point here may hinge on the kind of *dependence* each effect has on its cause: for causation to operate at all, such a chain of dependent items requires an independent (uncaused) cause.

everything were like this, Aquinas argues, then at some time in the past nothing whatever would have existed (the logic of this is obscure: why should there not always be a time when at least some contingent things exist, even though each of them is capable of ceasing to be?). At all events, Aquinas proceeds to reason that to explain why there is anything at all we must eventually posit a necessary being in the strong sense of something which 'is necessary in its own right' or 'necessary of itself' (*per se necessarium*); and this is God.

The *fourth* proof starts from the degrees of perfection found in the world; in order for things to be more or less good, or have more or less being, than others, there must ultimately be a supreme entity which is the source of all being and goodness, and this is God. One might object that degrees of goodness imply only that there is something relatively or comparatively pre-eminent, not that there is a wholly supreme divine source of goodness. Here Aquinas seems to rely on a framework inherited from Plato, according to which ordinary objects which are good, or beautiful, or whatever, owe their (limited) possession of these properties to the existence of a pure form which they participate in, or reflect – a form which is itself perfectly good or beautiful

(compare Part I, extract 2, and Part II, extract 1). Finally, in the *fifth* proof (often known as the 'teleological argument', from the Greek *telos*, meaning 'end' or 'goal'), Aquinas starts from the fact that even non-conscious objects often operate for the sake of some end, or tend towards some goal; such teleological behaviour could not be manifested by things which lack awareness unless they were directed by an intelligent being – 'and this we call God'. This last argument has some close similarities with the 'argument from design' which became popular in the eighteenth century, and was devastatingly criticized by Hume (see extract 6, below). Aquinas here gives no examples of the kinds of teleological action he has in mind, but elsewhere (in his other magnum opus, the *Summa Contra Gentiles*), he mentions the way the leaves in plants are shaped to protect their fruit, and how the structure of animals' teeth is suited to the functions of biting and chewing. Modern evolutionary science, of course, aims to account for such goal-adapted phenomena on purely mechanical principles;[1] supporters of Aquinas's position would argue that the *ultimate* explanation for the phenomena in question must be sought in the directive intelligence of God.

The existence of God can be proved in five ways

The first and quite obvious way is taken from a consideration of motion. It is certain and agreed on the basis of what our senses tell us that some things in this world are in motion. But whatever is in motion is moved by something else; for nothing undergoes motion except in so far as it is in a state of *potentiality* in respect of that towards which it is moved. A thing moves in the active sense, on the other hand, in so far as it is in *actuality*. For moving in this sense is simply bringing something from potentiality to actuality; but nothing can be brought into actuality except by something which is itself in actuality. For example, something which is actually hot, like fire, makes wood, which is hot in potentiality, hot in actuality, thereby moving and altering it. Now it is not possible for the same thing to be, at the same time and in the same respect, both in actuality and in potentiality (for what is actually hot cannot be at the same time potentially hot, though it may be potentially cold). So it is impossible that (in the same respect and in the same way) something should be both mover and moved, or that it should move itself. Hence whatever is in motion is moved by something else. And if this something else is itself moved, it must in turn be moved by something

[1] It is worth noting that Aquinas himself seems at one point to allow for the possibility of some kind of evolution; see *Summa Theologiae*, Ia, qu. 118, art. 2.

else, and so on. But the sequence cannot continue *ad infinitum*, since in this case there would not be any first mover, and hence nothing would move anything else, since subsequent moving things do not move unless moved by an original mover (just as a stick does not move unless moved by a hand). Hence it is necessary to arrive at a first mover which is moved by nothing else; and this everyone understands to be God.

The second way is taken from the notion of an efficient cause. In the world that we perceive around us we find an order of efficient causes, but we never find, nor is it possible that there should be, something that is the efficient cause of itself; for if there were, it would have to be prior to itself, which is impossible. But it is not possible for the series of efficient causes to go on *ad infinitum*. For in each ordered series of efficient causes, the first item is the cause of the next item, and this in turn is the cause of the final item (though there may be more than one intermediate step); and if any one cause is taken away, the effect will also be absent. Hence if there was not a first item in the series of efficient causes, there will be no intermediate or final items. But if the series of efficient causes stretches back *ad infinitum*, there will be no first efficient cause, which will mean that there will be no final effect, and no intermediate efficient causes, which is patently not the case. Hence it is necessary to posit some first efficient cause; and this everyone calls 'God'.

The third way is taken from possibility and necessity, and goes as follows. We come across some things which are merely *possibles* – they can both be and not be; for example we find some things coming into being and passing away, and hence having the possibility of being and not being. But it is impossible for everything there is to be of this sort, since if something has the possibility of not being, then at some time or other it lacks being. So if all things have the possibility of not being, at some time there was nothing at all. But if this were the case, then there would still be nothing now, since what lacks being does not begin to be except through something which is. So if nothing was in being, it was impossible for anything to begin to be, and so there would still be nothing, which is patently not the case. Hence not all beings are possibles, but there must be something in the world which is necessary. Now everything which is necessary either has the cause of its necessity from elsewhere, or it does not. But it is not possible that a sequence of necessary beings having the cause of their necessity elsewhere should continue *ad infinitum* (as was proved in the case of efficient causes). So it is necessary to posit something which is necessary in its own right, and does not have the cause of its necessity from elsewhere but is itself the cause of necessity in other things; and this everyone calls 'God'.

The fourth way is taken from the gradations to be found in things. We come across some things which are more or less good, or true or noble than others, and so on. But 'more' and 'less' are terms used of different things by reference to how close they are to what is greatest of its kind (for example, something is 'hotter' if it is closer to what is hottest). Hence there is something which is truest and best and noblest, and consequently greatest in being; for things which are truest are greatest in being, as Aristotle says in Book II of his *Metaphysics*. Now what we call the greatest in any kind is the cause of everything of that kind, just as fire, which has the greatest heat, is the cause of everything hot (as Aristotle says in the same book). Hence there is something which is the cause of being and goodness and every other perfection in things; and this we call 'God'.

The fifth way is taken from the manner in which things are directed or guided. We see some things that lack knowledge, namely natural bodies, working for the sake of a goal or end. This is clear from the fact that they always or often act in the same way to pursue what is best; and this shows that they reach their goal not by chance but from directedness. But things which do not have knowledge do not tend towards a goal unless they are guided by something with knowledge and intelligence, as an arrow is by the archer. Hence there is some intelligent being by whom all natural things are directed to their goal or end; and this we call 'God'.

3   God and the Idea of Perfection: René Descartes, *Meditations**

Although philosophy is often said to have made a 'new start' in the seventeenth century, many of the great thinkers of the early modern period continued to place God at the heart of the new philosophical and scientific systems they developed. This is certainly true of Descartes, who argues in his metaphysical masterpiece the *Meditations* [1641] that without a sure demonstration of the existence of God, no reliable system of knowledge is possible (for the role of God in the resulting metaphysical system, see Part II, extract 3 above). The *Meditations* contains two purported proofs of God: in the Fifth Meditation Descartes puts forward a version of the ontological argument first developed by Anselm (see extract 1 above), while in the Third Meditation we find a different argument, reproduced below, which has come to be known as the 'Trademark argument'.

Since Descartes's 'meditator' in his search for truth has suspended his belief in all external things, applying universal doubt to the point where he is certain only of his own existence (see Part I, extract 4), he is unable to draw on evidence from the world around him in order to prove God (contrast Aquinas, extract 2, above). Instead he reflects on the *idea* of God which he finds within him. Now ideas are rather like pictures – they represent things, or as Descartes puts it, they have a certain 'objective' or representational reality (the term 'objective' in Descartes has nothing to do with whether the objects represented by our ideas actually exist: at this stage we are talking only of their representational *content*). The content of most of my

ideas, reasons the meditator, is such that I could easily have thought them up myself; but the content of one idea, that of a supremely perfect, infinite being, is so great that it cannot have been produced from the resources of my own (imperfect and finite) mind, but must have been implanted in me by God, like the 'mark which a craftsman stamps on his work'.

But why cannot an imperfect being produce an idea of perfection? Descartes here relies on the causal principle that what is more perfect cannot arise from what is less perfect – a notion that many subsequent critics have questioned, especially when it is applied not to real things but to mere ideas. Descartes later clarified his argument using a comparison with a very perfect machine, the idea of which is in the mind of some engineer: 'just as the complexity belonging to the idea must have some cause, namely the knowledge of the engineer, or of someone who passed this idea on to him, so the idea of God which is in us must have God for its cause'.[1] The end of the Third Meditation sees the meditator lost in contemplation of the 'immense light' of the divine nature which almost blinds the eye of his own 'darkened intellect': the intellectual mode of rational argument here gives way to the more passionate mode of submission and adoration. Throughout Descartes's trademark argument we can discern a common tension or paradox in philosophical theology – how may the finite human mind articulate the notion of an infinite being whose greatness far exceeds the mind's power to comprehend it?

---

* René Descartes, *Meditations on First Philosophy* [*Meditationes de Prima Philosophia*, 1641], extract from the Third Meditation. Trans. J. Cottingham (Cambridge: Cambridge University Press, 1986).
[1] From the *Synopsis* published as part of the preliminary matter to the *Meditations*.

But now it occurs to me that there is another way of investigating whether some of the things of which I possess ideas exist outside me. In so far as the ideas are considered simply as modes of thought, there is no recognizable inequality among them: they all appear to come from within me in the same fashion. But in so far as different ideas are considered as images which represent different things, it is clear that they differ widely. Undoubtedly, the ideas which represent substances to me amount to something more and, so to speak, contain within themselves more *objective reality* than the ideas which merely represent modes or accidents. Again, the idea that gives me my understanding of a supreme God, eternal, infinite, immutable, omniscient, omnipotent and the creator of all things that exist apart from him, certainly has in it more objective reality than the ideas that represent finite substances.

Now it is manifest by the natural light that there must be at least as much reality in the efficient and total cause as in the effect of that cause. For where, I ask, could the effect get its reality from, if not from the cause? And how could the cause give it to the effect unless it possessed it? It follows from this both that something cannot arise from nothing, and also that what is more perfect – that is, contains in itself more reality – cannot arise from what is less perfect. And this is transparently true not only in the case of effects which possess what the philosophers call actual or formal reality, but also in the case of ideas, where one is considering only what they call objective reality. A stone, for example, which previously did not exist, cannot begin to exist unless it is produced by something which contains, either formally or eminently everything to be found in the stone; similarly, heat cannot be produced in an object which was not previously hot, except by something of at least the same order of perfection as heat, and so on. But it is also true that the *idea* of heat, or of a stone, cannot exist in me unless it is put there by some cause which contains at least as much reality as I conceive to be in the heat or in the stone. For although this cause does not transfer any of its actual or formal reality to my idea, it should not on that account be supposed that it must be less real. The nature of an idea is such that of itself it requires no formal reality except what it derives from my thought, of which it is a mode. But in order for a given idea to contain such and such objective reality, it must surely derive it from some cause which contains at least as much formal reality as there is objective reality in the idea. For if we suppose that an idea contains something which was not in its cause, it must have got this from nothing; yet the mode of being by which a thing exists objectively or representatively in the intellect by way of an idea, imperfect though it may be, is certainly not nothing, and so it cannot come from nothing.

And although the reality which I am considering in my ideas is merely objective reality, I must not on that account suppose that the same reality need not exist formally in the causes of my ideas, but that it is enough for it to be present in them objectively. For just as the objective mode of being belongs to ideas by their very nature, so the formal mode of being belongs to the causes of ideas – or at least the first and most important ones – by *their* very nature. And although one idea may perhaps originate from another, there cannot be an infinite regress here; eventually one must reach a primary idea, the cause of which will be like an archetype which contains formally and in fact all the reality or perfection which is present only objectively or representatively in the idea. So it is clear to me, by the natural light, that the ideas in me are like pictures, or images which can easily fall short of the perfection of the things from which they are taken, but which cannot contain anything greater or more perfect.

The longer and more carefully I examine all these points, the more clearly and distinctly I recognize their truth. But what is my conclusion to be? If the objective reality of any of my ideas turns out to be so great that I am sure the same reality does not reside in me, either formally or eminently, and hence that I myself cannot be its cause, it will necessarily follow that I am not alone in the world, but that some other thing which is the cause of this idea also exists. But if no such idea is to be found in me, I shall have no argument to convince me of the existence of anything apart from myself. For despite a most careful and comprehensive survey, this is the only argument I have so far been able to find.

Among my ideas, apart from the idea which gives me a representation of myself, which cannot present any difficulty in this context, there are ideas which variously represent God, corporeal and inanimate things, angels, animals and finally other men like myself.

As far as concerns the ideas which represent other men, or animals, or angels, I have no difficulty in understanding that they could be put together from the ideas I have of myself, of corporeal things and of God, even if the world contained no men besides me, no animals and no angels.

As to my ideas of corporeal things, I can see nothing in them which is so great or excellent as to make it seem impossible that it originated in myself. For if I scrutinize them thoroughly and examine them one by one, in the way in which I examined the idea of the wax yesterday, I notice that the things which I perceive clearly and distinctly in them are very few in number. The list comprises size, or extension in length, breadth and depth; shape, which is a function of the boundaries of this extension; position, which is a relation between various items possessing shape; and motion, or change in position; to these may be added substance, duration and number. But as for all the rest, including light and colours, sounds, smells, tastes, heat and cold and the other tactile qualities, I think of these only in a very confused and obscure way, to the extent that I do not even know whether they are true or false, that is, whether the ideas I have of them are ideas of real things or of non-things. For although, as I have noted before, falsity in the strict sense, or formal falsity, can occur only in judgements, there is another kind of falsity, material falsity, which occurs in ideas, when they represent non-things as things. For example, the ideas which I have of heat and cold contain so little clarity and distinctness that they do not enable me to tell whether cold is merely the absence of heat or vice versa, or whether both of them are real qualities, or neither is. And since there can be no ideas which are not as it were of things, if it is true that cold is nothing but the absence of heat, the idea which represents it to me as something real and positive deserves to be called false; and the same goes for other ideas of this kind.

Such ideas obviously do not require me to posit a source distinct from myself. For on the one hand, if they are false, that is, represent non-things, I know by the natural light that they arise from nothing, that is, they are in me only because of a deficiency and lack of perfection in my nature. If on the other hand they are true, then since the reality which they represent is so extremely slight that I cannot even distinguish it from a non-thing, I do not see why they cannot originate from myself.

With regard to the clear and distinct elements in my ideas of corporeal things, it appears that I could have borrowed some of these from my idea of myself, namely substance, duration, number and anything else of this kind. For example, I think that a stone is a substance, or is a thing capable of existing independently, and I also think that I am a substance. Admittedly I conceive of myself as a thing that thinks and is not extended, whereas I conceive of the stone as a thing that is extended and does not think, so that the two conceptions differ enormously;[1] but they seem to agree with respect to the classification 'substance'. Again, I perceive that I now exist, and remember that I have existed for some time; moreover, I have various thoughts which I can count; it is in these ways that I acquire the ideas of duration and number which I can then transfer to other things. As for all the other elements which make up the ideas of corporeal things, namely extension, shape, position and movement, these are not formally contained in me, since I am nothing but a thinking thing; but since they are merely modes of a substance, and I am a substance, it seems possible that they are contained in me eminently [in a higher form].

So there remains only the idea of God; and I must consider whether there is anything in the idea which could not have originated in myself. By the word 'God' I understand a substance that is infinite, eternal, immutable, independent, supremely intelligent, supremely powerful, and which created both myself and everything else (if anything else there be) that exists. All these attributes are such that, the more carefully I concentrate on them, the less possible it seems that they could have originated from me alone. So from what has been said it must be concluded that God necessarily exists.

It is true that I have the idea of substance in me in virtue of the fact that I am a substance; but this would not account for my having the idea of an infinite substance, when I am finite, unless this idea proceeded from some substance which really was infinite.

And I must not think that, just as my conceptions of rest and darkness are arrived at by negating movement and light, so my perception of the infinite is arrived at not by means of a true idea but merely by negating the finite. On the contrary, I clearly understand that there is more reality in an infinite substance than in a finite one, and hence that my perception of the infinite, that is God, is in some way prior to my perception of the finite, that is myself. For how could I understand that I doubted or desired – that is, lacked something – and that I was not wholly perfect, unless there were in me some idea of a more perfect being which enabled me to recognize my own defects by comparison?

Nor can it be said that this idea of God is perhaps materially false and so could have come from nothing – which is what I observed just a moment ago in the case of the ideas of heat and cold, and so on. On the contrary it is utterly clear and distinct, and contains in itself more objective reality than any other idea; hence there is no idea which is in itself truer or less liable to be suspected of falsehood. This idea of a supremely perfect and infinite being is, I say, true in the highest degree; for although perhaps one may imagine that such a being does not exist, it cannot be supposed that the idea of such a being represents something unreal, as I said with regard to the idea of cold. The idea is, moreover, utterly clear and distinct; for whatever I clearly and distinctly perceive as being real and true, and implying any perfection, is wholly contained in it. It does not matter that I do not grasp the infinite, or that there are

---

[1] See above, Part IV, extract 4.

countless additional attributes of God which I cannot in any way grasp, and perhaps cannot even reach in my thought; for it is in the nature of the infinite not to be grasped by a finite being like myself. It is enough that I understand the infinite, and that I judge that all the attributes which I clearly perceive and know to imply some perfection – and perhaps countless others of which I am ignorant – are present in God either formally or eminently. This is enough to make the idea that I have of God the truest and most clear and distinct of all my ideas.

But perhaps I am something greater than I myself understand, and all the perfections which I attribute to God are somehow in me potentially, though not yet emerging or actualized. For I am now experiencing a gradual increase in my knowledge, and I see nothing to prevent its increasing more and more to infinity. Further, I see no reason why I should not be able to use this increased knowledge to acquire all the other perfections of God. And finally, if the potentiality for these perfections is already within me, why should not this be enough to generate the idea of such perfections?

But all this is impossible. First, though it is true that there is a gradual increase in my knowledge, and that I have many potentialities which are not yet actual, this is all quite irrelevant to the idea of God, which contains absolutely nothing that is potential; indeed, this gradual increase in knowledge is itself the surest sign of imperfection. What is more, even if my knowledge always increases more and more, I recognize that it will never actually be infinite, since it will never reach the point where it is not capable of a further increase; God, on the other hand, I take to be actually infinite, so that nothing can be added to his perfection. And finally, I perceive that the objective being of an idea cannot be produced merely by potential being, which strictly speaking is nothing, but only by actual or formal being...

It only remains for me to examine how I received this idea from God. For I did not acquire it from the senses; it has never come to me unexpectedly, as usually happens with the ideas of things that are perceivable by the senses, when these things present themselves to the external sense organs – or seem to do so. And it was not invented by me either; for I am plainly unable either to take away anything from it or to add anything to it. The only remaining alternative is that it is innate in me, just as the idea of myself is innate in me.

And indeed it is no surprise that God, in creating me, should have placed this idea in me to be, as it were, the mark of the craftsman stamped on his work – not that the mark need be anything distinct from the work itself. But the mere fact that God created me is a very strong basis for believing that I am somehow made in his image and likeness and that I perceive that likeness, which includes the idea of God, by the same faculty which enables me to perceive myself. That is, when I turn my mind's eye upon myself, I understand that I am a thing which is incomplete and dependent on another and which aspires without limit to ever greater and better things; but I also understand at the same time that he on whom I depend has within him all those greater things, not just indefinitely and potentially but actually and infinitely, and hence that he is God. The whole force of the argument lies in this: I recognize that it would be impossible for me to exist with the kind of nature I have – that is having within me the idea of God – were it not the case that God really existed. By 'God' I mean the very being the idea of whom is within me that is, the possessor of all the perfections which I cannot grasp, but can somehow reach in my thought, who is subject to no defects whatsoever. It is clear enough from this that he cannot be a deceiver, since it is manifest by the natural light that all fraud and deception depend on some defect.

But before examining this point more carefully and investigating other truths which may be derived from it, I should like to pause here and spend some time in the contemplation of God; to reflect on his attributes and to gaze with wonder and adoration on the beauty of this immense light, so far as the eye of my darkened intellect can bear it. For just as we believe through faith that the supreme happiness of the next life consists solely in the contemplation of the divine majesty, so experience tells us that this same contemplation, albeit much less perfect, enables us to know the greatest joy of which we are capable in this life.

4   The Wager: Blaise Pascal, *Pensées**

The theme (found in the previous extract) of the contemplation by the finite human mind of the infinite being that is God, recurs in our next passage, from the *Pensées* ('Thoughts', published posthumously in 1670) by Descartes's distinguished contemporary Blaise Pascal. But Pascal differed profoundly from Descartes on the role of reason in religious belief. He came to think that intellectual reasoning alone could not support religion: the key was passionate commitment and faith. Towards the end of the extract we find the recommendation that we need to 'tame' (*abêtir*) the human mind by devotion and repeated religious practice, such as attending Mass; the verb *abêtir* (literally 'make dull like the beasts') suggests that salvation lies in the kind of automatic and unthinking response characteristic of the animals who lack reason altogether. But though reason alone cannot lead us to God, Pascal sets out an ingenious argument that it is rational, on prudential grounds, to behave as if God exists. Given the lack of conclusive rational grounds for belief, we are in the position of having to wager or bet on his existence. If God exists, the consequence of accepting the bet, and committing oneself to a life of piety, will be an eternal life of happiness; if he does not exist, then one will have lost nothing by accepting.

A possible criticism of this argument is one raised by Pascal himself in the mouth of an imaginary objector: 'perhaps I am betting too much'; in other words, there is a price to be paid in accepting the bet, namely forgoing the unbeliever's life of 'luxury and glory' for the sake of an afterlife that may never be realized, if death is indeed the final end. Pascal's reply here is that it would be irrational to pass up the chance of an infinite gain (eternal life of happiness) to avoid a finite loss. But he has perhaps slanted the argument by assuming that the rewards of the unbeliever's life of self-indulgence are 'tainted'. If, as the libertine might maintain, the (admittedly finite) rewards of vice are concrete and substantial, would it necessarily be irrational to forgo them in exchange for a slim chance of an infinite gain?[1]

 Our soul is thrown into the body, where it finds number, time and dimensions; it then reasons about this and calls it 'nature' or 'necessity', and can believe nothing else.

Unity when joined to the infinite does not increase it at all, any more than a foot when added to an infinite length. The finite annihilates itself in the presence of the

---

* Blaise Pascal, *Pensées* ('Thoughts') [1670]. Translation by John Cottingham. The French text may be found in the edition of L. Lafuma (Paris: Seuil, 1962), no. 418. An English version of the *Pensées* is available by A. J. Krailsheimer (Harmondsworth: Penguin, 1966).

[1] Compare Plato's discussion of the rewards of vice and virtue: Part VIII, extract 1, below.

infinite, and becomes a pure nothing. So does our mind when confronted with God, so does our justice before divine justice. Yet the disproportion between our justice and God's is not as great as that between unity and infinity.

The justice of God must be as enormous as his mercy. The justice he shows to the damned is less enormous and should shock us less than the mercy he shows to the elect.

We know that there is an infinite, and we are ignorant of its nature. Similarly, we know it is false that the series of numbers is finite, and it is therefore true that there is an infinite number, but we do not know what it is. It is false that it is even; it is false that it is odd; for by adding a unit the infinite does not change its nature. Yet it is a number, and every number is even or odd – this may be truly understood of every finite number.

Thus we can perfectly well recognize that there is a God, without knowing what he is.

Is there not a substantial truth, seeing there are so many true things which are not truth itself?

We know the existence and the nature of the finite, since we, like it, are finite and extended.

We know the existence of the infinite and we are ignorant of its nature, since it has extension like us, but does not have limits as we do.

But we do not know either the existence or the nature of God, because he has neither extension nor limits.

But by faith we know his existence, and in glory we shall come to know his nature.

Now I have already shown that one may quite well know the existence of a thing without knowing its nature.

Let us now speak according to our natural lights.

If there is a God, he is infinitely beyond our comprehension, since having neither parts nor limits he bears no relation to us. We are thus incapable of knowing either what he is or if he is. This being so, who will dare undertake to resolve this question? Surely not we, who bear no relation to him.

Who then will blame Christians for not being able to provide reasons for their belief, since they profess a religion for which they cannot provide a rational basis? In proclaiming it to the world they declare that it is 'folly', and will you then complain that they do not prove it? If they were to prove it, they would not be keeping their word. This very lack of proof shows they do not lack sense. 'Yes; but even if this excuses those who offer their religion in this way and takes away any blame for their putting it forward without reason, it does not excuse those who *accept* it without reason.' Let us then examine this point. Let us say: either God is, or he is not. But which side shall we incline towards? Reason cannot settle anything here. There is an infinite chaos which separates us. A game is being played at the far end of this infinite distance: the coin will come down heads or tails. How will you bet? Reason will not enable you to decide either way, or rule out either alternative.

So do not blame those who have made a choice, or say they have chosen a false path, for you know nothing of the matter. 'No, but I will blame them for having made not *this* choice but *a* choice; for though the player who chooses heads is no more at fault than the other one, both of them are still at fault. The correct option is not to bet at all.'

Yes, but you must bet. It is not voluntary; you are already involved. Which will you choose then? Look: since you must choose, let us see which is the less profitable option. You have two things to lose, the true and the good, and two things to stake, your reason and your will, your knowledge and your happiness. Your nature has two things to avoid, error and wretchedness. Since a choice must necessarily be made, your reason is no more offended by choosing one rather than the other. There is one point settled. But your happiness? Let us weigh up the gain and the loss in choosing heads, that God exists. Let us figure out the two results: if you win, you win everything, and if you lose, you lose nothing. So bet that he exists, without any hesitation. 'This is splendid: yes, I must bet, but maybe I am betting too much.' Let us see. Since there is an equal chance of gain and loss, if you stood merely to gain merely two lives for one, you could still bet. But suppose you had three lives to gain?

You would have to play (since you must necessarily play), and you would be foolish, since you are forced to play, not to risk your life to gain three lives in a game where there is equal chance of losing and winning. But there is an eternity of life and happiness. This being so, in a game where there were an infinity of chances and only one in your favour, you would still be right to wager one life in order to gain two; and you would be making the wrong choice, given that you were obliged to play, if you refused to bet one life against three in a game where there were an infinity of chances and only one in your favour, if the prize were an infinity of infinitely happy life. But the prize here *is* an infinity of infinitely happy life, one chance of winning against a finite number of chances of losing, and what you are staking is finite. This leaves only one choice open, in any game that involves infinity, where there is not an infinite number of chances of losing to set against the chance of winning. There is nothing to ponder – you must stake everything. When you are forced to play, you would have to be renouncing reason if you were to hang on to life rather than risk it for an infinite gain which is just as likely to come about as a loss which is a loss of nothing.

It is no use saying that it is uncertain whether you will win and certain that you are taking a chance; or that the infinite distance between the certainty of what you are risking and the uncertainty of what you stand to gain makes the finite good which you are certainly risking as great as the infinite gain that is uncertain. This is not how things stand. Every player takes a certain risk in exchange for an uncertain gain; but it is no sin against reason for him to take a certain and finite risk for an uncertain finite gain. It is just not true that there is an infinite distance between the certainty of what is risked and the uncertainty of the gain. There is, in truth, an infinite distance between the certainty of winning and the certainty of losing; but the proportion between the uncertainty of winning and the certainty of what is being risked corresponds to the proportion between the chances of winning and losing. From this it follows that if there are as many chances on one side as on the other, the game is being played for even odds. And hence the certainty of what you are risking is equal to the uncertainty of the possible gain, so far from being infinitely distant from it. There is thus infinite force in the position I am taking, when the stakes are finite in a game where the chances of winning and losing are equal and the prize is infinite.

This result has demonstrative force, and if human beings are capable of any truth, this is it.

'I confess it, I admit it, but is there not any way at all of seeing what lies behind the game?' Yes, Holy Scripture and the rest. 'Yes, but my hands are tied and my mouth is gagged; I am being forced to wager and I am not at liberty. I cannot get free and my constitution is such that I am incapable of believing. So what do you want me to do?' What you say is true, but you must at least realize that your inability to believe comes from your passions. Since reason moves you to believe, and nevertheless you cannot, your task is not to convince yourself by adding on more proofs of God, but by reducing your passions. Your desired destination is faith, but you do not know the road. You want to cure yourself of unbelief, and you ask for remedies: learn from those who were tied like you and who now wager all they possess. These are people who know the road you would like to follow; they are cured of the malady for which you seek a cure; so follow them and begin as they did – by acting as if they believed, by taking holy water, by having masses said, and so on. In the natural course of events this in itself will make you believe, this will tame you. 'But that is just what I fear.' Why? What have you to lose? If you want to know why this is the right way, the answer is that it reduces the passions, which are the great obstacles to your progress . . .

Now what harm will come to you if you make this choice? You will be faithful, honest, humble, grateful, a doer of good works, a good friend, sincere and true. Admittedly you will not dwell amid tainted pleasures, in glory and luxury, but will you not have others?

I tell you that you will be the gainer in this life, and that on every step you take on this path you will see such certainty of gain, and such emptiness of what you hazard, that you will finally know that what you have wagered for is something certain and infinite, and what you have given in exchange is nothing.

'This discussion moves me and delights me.' If you like my discussion and find it powerful, you should know that the author is a man who knelt down before and afterwards to beg this infinite and indivisible being, to whom he submits his own entire being, to bring your being too into submission, for your own good and for his glory, praying that strength and humbleness might thus be brought together.

5 The Problem of Evil: Gottfried Leibniz, *Theodicy**

One of the greatest obstacles to belief in a supreme and perfect deity has always been what philosophers have come to call the 'problem of evil' – a problem neatly formulated by the ancient Greek philosopher Epicurus (341–271 BC): 'if God is willing to prevent evil but not able, then he is not omnipotent; if he is able but not willing, he is not benevolent; if he is both able and willing, whence comes evil?' In the following extract from the *Theodicy* ('A vindication of God's justice') published in 1710 by the German philosopher G. W. Leibniz, we find a systematic attempt to resolve the issue. Leibniz begins by introducing the concept of God as the supreme

* G. W. Leibniz, *Theodicy: Essays on the Goodness of God, the Liberty of Man and the Origin of Evil* [*Essais de théodicée sur la bonté de Dieu, la liberté de l'homme et l'origine du mal*, 1710], Part I, §§ 7–15, 19–26; with omissions. Trans. E. M. Huggard (London: Routledge, 1951).

and perfect necessary being who is the cause of all contingent things, and contains within himself the reason for his existence (compare the third of Aquinas's 'five ways', extract 2, above). He then argues that the universe we live in must be the best of all possible worlds: of all the worlds capable of existence, the infinitely good and wise creator must have chosen the best, or else there would be something to correct in his actions. The background to this argument is that only certain combinations of things can exist together (or are 'compossible' as Leibniz puts it elsewhere); so there are logical constraints on what even the most benevolent creator can bring into existence. To suppose that one could simply eliminate undesirable elements from creation ignores that 'the universe is all of a piece, so that if the smallest evil that comes to pass were missing, it would no longer be this world'.

One may object that this does not explain why there should be any evil in the first place. Here Leibniz makes a useful distinction between three kinds of evil, metaphysical, physical and moral. Metaphysical evil consists in 'mere imperfection': some imperfection must exist if there is to be a created universe at all, since if there was nothing but complete perfection, only God would exist. Physical evil (for example disease and natural disasters) Leibniz explains, perhaps somewhat glibly, as 'often a penalty owing to guilt, and often as a means to an end, to prevent greater evils or to obtain greater good'. Finally, in the case of moral evil (the evil wrought by human beings), Leibniz deploys a common line among religious apologists known as the 'free will defence': if men are to be free agents rather than puppets, they must be able to act badly. Since God is all-powerful, we must admit that he could prevent such evil, and hence that he *permits* it; but Leibniz argues that he wills it not *antecedently* but only *consequently*; that is, he wills it not in itself, but only as a necessary consequence of producing the best possible world (containing free human agents). This last line of reasoning involves complexities which are still the subject of debate among philosophers of religion; roughly, the issue is whether the existence of human freedom is on balance a sufficient good to make the world that contains it better than any other possible world.

 God is the first reason of things: for such things as are bounded (as all that which we see and experience), are contingent and have nothing in them to render their existence necessary, it being plain that time, space and matter, united and uniform in themselves and indifferent to everything, might have received entirely other motions and shapes, and in another order. Therefore one must seek the reason for the existence of the world, which is the whole assemblage of *contingent* things, and seek it in the substance which carries with it the reason for its existence, and which in consequence is *necessary* and eternal. Moreover, this cause must be intelligent: for this existing world being contingent and an infinity of other worlds being equally possible, and holding, so to say, equal claim to existence with it, the cause of the world must needs have had regard or reference to all these possible worlds in order to fix upon one of them. This regard or relation of an existent substance to simple possibilities can be nothing other than the *understanding* which has the ideas of them, while to fix upon one of them can be nothing other than the act of the *will* which chooses. It is the *power* of this substance that renders its will efficacious. Power relates to being, wisdom or understanding to *truth*, and will to *good*. And this intelligent cause ought to be infinite in all ways, and absolutely perfect in *power*, in *wisdom* and in *goodness*, since it relates to all that which is possible. Furthermore, since all is connected together, there is no ground for admitting more than *one*. Its understanding is the source of *essences*, and its will is the origin of *existences*. There in few words is the proof of one only God with his perfections, and through him of the origin of things.

Now this supreme wisdom, united to a goodness that is no less infinite, cannot but have chosen the best. For as a lesser evil is a kind of good, even so a lesser good is a kind of evil if it stands in the way of a greater good; and there would be something to correct in the actions of God if it were possible to do better. As in mathematics, when there is no maximum nor minimum, in short nothing distinguished, everything is done equally, or when that is not possible nothing at all is done: so it may be said likewise in respect of perfect wisdom, which is no less orderly than mathematics, that if there were not the best (*optimum*) among all possible worlds, God would not have produced any. I call 'World' the whole succession and the whole agglomeration of all existent things, lest it be said that several worlds could have existed in different times and different places. For they must needs be reckoned all together as one world or, if you will, as one universe. And even though one should fill all times and all places, it still remains true that one might have filled them in innumerable ways, and that there is an infinitude of possible worlds among which God must needs have chosen the best, since he does nothing without acting in accordance with supreme reason.

Some adversary not being able to answer this argument will perchance answer the conclusion by a counter-argument, saying that the world could have been without sin and without sufferings; but I deny that then it would have been *better*. For it must be known that all things are *connected* in each one of the possible worlds: the universe, whatever it may be, is all of one piece, like an ocean: the least movement extends its effect there to any distance whatsoever, even though this effect become less perceptible in proportion to the distance. Therein God has ordered all things beforehand once for all, having foreseen prayers, good and bad actions, and all the rest; and each thing *as an idea* has contributed before its existence to the resolution that has been made upon the existence of all things; so that nothing can be changed in the universe (any more than in a number) save its essence, or, if you will, save its numerical individuality. Thus if the smallest evil that comes to pass in the world were missing in it, it would no longer be this world; which, with nothing omitted and all allowance made, was found the best by the creator who chose it.

It is true that one may imagine possible worlds without sin and without unhappiness, and one could make some such Utopian... romances; but these same worlds again would be very inferior to ours in goodness. I cannot show you this in detail. For can I know and can I present infinities to you and compare them together? But you must judge with me from the effects, since God has chosen this world as it is. We know, moreover, that often an evil brings forth a good whereto one would not have attained without that evil... A general sometimes makes a fortunate mistake which brings about the winning of a great battle; and do they not sing on the Eve of Easter in the churches of the Roman rite:

> O certe necessarium Adae peccatum, quod Christi morte deletum est.
> O felix culpa, quae talem ac tantum meruit habere Redemptorem![1]

...A little acid, sharpness or bitterness is often more pleasing than sugar; shadows enhance colours; and even a dissonance in the right place gives relief to harmony. We

[1] O surely needful was the sin of Adam, which took the death of Christ to wipe it out! O blessed was that guilt which did require so strong and mighty a Redeemer's power!

wish to be terrified by rope-dancers on the point of falling and we wish that tragedies shall well-nigh cause us to weep. Do men relish health enough, or thank God enough for it, without having ever been sick? And is it not most often necessary that a little evil render the good more discernible, that is to say, greater?

But it will be said that evils are great and many in number in comparison with the good: that is erroneous. It is only want of attention that diminishes our good, and this attention must be given to us through some admixture of evils. If we were usually sick and seldom in good health, we should be wonderfully sensible of that great good and we should be less sensible of our evils. But is it not better, notwithstanding, that health should be usual and sickness the exception? Let us then by our reflection supply what is lacking in our perception, in order to make the good of health more discernible. Even if we did not have knowledge of the life to come, I believe there would be few persons who, being at the point of death, would not be content to take up life again, on condition of passing through the same amount of good and evil, provided always that it were not the same kind; one would be content with variety, without requiring a better condition than that wherein one had been...

The ancients had puny ideas on the works of God, and St Augustine, for want of knowing modern discoveries, was at a loss when there was question of explaining the prevalence of evil. It seemed to the ancients that there was only one earth inhabited, and even of that men held the antipodes in dread; the remainder of the world was, according to them, a few shining globes and a few crystalline spheres. Today, whatever bounds are given or not given to the universe, it must be acknowledged that there is an infinite number of globes, as great as and greater than ours, which have as much right as it to hold rational inhabitants, though it follows not at all that they are human. It is only one planet, that is to say one of the six principal satellites of our sun; and as all fixed stars are suns also, we see how small a thing our earth is in relation to visible things, since it is only an appendix of one amongst them. It may be that all suns are peopled only by blessed creatures... and the immense space encircling all this region may in any case be filled with happiness and glory. It can be imagined as like the Ocean, whither flow the rivers of all blessed creatures, when they shall have reached their perfection in the system of the stars. What will become of the consideration of our globe and its inhabitants? Will it not be something incomparably less than a physical point, since our earth is as a point in comparison with the distance of some fixed stars? Thus since the proportion of that part of the universe which we know is almost lost in nothingness compared with that which is unknown, and which we have yet to have cause to assume, and since all the evils that may be raised in objection before us are in this near nothingness, haply it may be that all evils are almost nothingness in comparison with the good things which are in the universe.

But it is necessary also to meet the more speculative and metaphysical difficulties which have been mentioned, and which concern the cause of evil. The question is asked first of all, whence does evil come? *If there be a God, whence cometh evil; if there be not, whence cometh good?* The ancients attributed the cause of evil to matter, which they believed uncreated and independent of God; but we, who derive all being from God, where shall we find the source of evil? The answer is that it must be sought in the ideal nature of the creature, in so far as this nature is contained in the eternal truths which are in the understanding of God, independently of his will. For we must consider that there is an *original imperfection in the creature* before sin, because the creature is limited in its essence; whence it follows that it cannot know all, and that it can deceive itself and commit other errors. Plato said in *Timaeus* that the world originated in Understanding united to Necessity. Others have united God and Nature. This can be given a reasonable meaning. God will be the Understanding; and the Necessity, that is, the essential nature of things, will be the object of the understanding, in so far as this object consists in the eternal truths. But this object is inward and abides in the divine understanding. And therein is found not only the primitive form of good, but also the origin of evil: the Region of the Eternal Truths must be substituted for matter when we are concerned with seeking out the source of things.

This region is the ideal cause of evil (as it were) as well as of good: but, properly speaking, the formal character of evil has no *efficient* cause, for it consists in privation, as we shall see, namely, in that which the efficient cause does not bring about. That is why the Schoolmen are wont to call the cause of evil *deficient.*

Evil may be taken metaphysically, physically and morally. *Metaphysical evil* consists in mere imperfection, *physical evil* in suffering, and *moral evil* in sin. Now although physical evil and moral evil be not necessary, it is enough that by virtue of the eternal verities they be possible. And as this vast Region of Truths contains all possibilities, it is necessary that there be an infinitude of possible worlds, that evil enter into some of them, and that even the best of all contain a measure thereof. Thus has God been induced to permit evil.

But someone will say to me: why do you speak to us of 'permitting'? Is it not God that does the evil and that wills it? Here it will be necessary to explain what 'permission' is, so that it may be seen how this term is not employed without reason. But before that one must explain the nature of will, which has its own degrees. Taking it in the general sense, one may say that *will* consists in the inclination to do something in proportion to the good it contains. This will is called *antecedent* when it is detached and considers each good separately in the capacity of a good. In this sense it may be said that God tends to all good, as good . . . and this by an antecedent will. He is earnestly disposed to sanctify and to save all men, to exclude sin, and to prevent damnation. It may even be said that this will is efficacious *of itself* (*per se*), that is, in such a way that the effect would ensue if there were not some stronger reason to prevent it: for this will does not pass into final exercise, else it would never fail to produce its full effect, God being the master of all things. Success entire and infallible belongs only to the *consequent will,* as it is called. This it is which is complete; and in regard to it this rule obtains, that one never fails to do what one wills, when one has the power. Now this consequent will, final and decisive, results from the conflict of all the antecedent wills, of those which tend towards good, as well as of those which repel evil; and from the concurrence of all these particular wills comes the total will. So in mechanics compound movement results from all the tendencies that concur in one and the same moving body, and satisfies each one equally, in so far as it is possible to do all at one time. It is as if the moving body took equal account of these tendencies . . . In this sense also it may be said that the antecedent will is efficacious in a sense and even effective with success.

Thence it follows that God wills *antecedently* the good and *consequently* the best. And as for evil, God wills moral evil not at all, and physical evil or suffering he does not will absolutely... One may say of physical evil, that God wills it often as a penalty owing to guilt, and often also as a means to an end, that is, to prevent greater evils or to obtain greater good. The penalty serves also for amendment and example. Evil often serves to make us savour good the more; sometimes too it contributes to a greater perfection in him who suffers it, as the seed that one sows is subject to a kind of corruption before it can germinate; this is a beautiful similitude, which Jesus Christ himself used.

Concerning sin or moral evil, although it happens very often that it may serve as a means of obtaining good or of preventing another evil, it is not this that renders it a sufficient object of the divine will or a legitimate object of a created will. It must only be admitted or *permitted* in so far as it is considered to be a certain consequence of an indispensable duty: as for instance if a man who was determined not to permit another's sin were to fail of his own duty, or as if an officer on guard at an important post were to leave it especially in time of danger, in order to prevent a quarrel in the town between two soldiers of the garrison who wanted to kill each other.

The rule which states that *evil may not be done that good may come about*, and which even forbids the permission of a moral evil with the end of obtaining a physical good, far from being violated, is here proved, and its source and its reason are demonstrated. One will not approve the action of a queen who, under the pretext of saving the state, commits or even permits a crime. The crime is certain and the evil for the state is open to question. Moreover, this manner of giving sanction to crimes, if it were accepted, would be worse than a disruption of some one country, which is liable enough to happen in any case, and would perchance happen all the more by reason of such means chosen to prevent it. But in relation to God nothing is open to question, nothing can be opposed to *the rule of the best*, which allows neither exception nor dispensation. It is in this sense that God permits sin: for he would fail in what he owes to himself, in what he owes to his wisdom, his goodness, his perfection, if he did not follow the grand result of all his tendencies to good, and if he did not choose that which is absolutely the best, notwithstanding the evil of guilt, which is involved therein by the supreme necessity of the eternal truths. Hence the conclusion that God wills all good *in himself antecedently*, that he wills the best *consequently* as an *end*; that he wills what is indifferent, and physical evil, sometimes as a *means*, but that he will only permit moral evil as the *sine quo non* or as a hypothetical necessity which connects it with the best. Therefore the *consequent will* of God, which has sin for its object, is only *permissive*.

It is again well to consider that moral evil is an evil so great only because it is a source of physical evils, a source existing in one of the most powerful of creatures, who is also most capable of causing those evils. For an evil will is in its department what the evil principle of the Manichaeans would be in the universe; and reason, which is an image of the Divinity, provides for evil souls great means of causing much evil. One single Caligula, one Nero, has caused more evil than an earthquake. An evil man takes pleasure in causing suffering and destruction, and for that there are only too many opportunities. But God being inclined to produce as much good as possible, and having all the knowledge and all the power necessary for that, it is impossible that in him there be fault, or guilt, or sin; and when he permits sin, it is wisdom, it is virtue.

6   The Argument from Design: David Hume, *Dialogues concerning Natural Religion**

One of the most enduring and popular arguments for the existence of God is the 'argument from design'. A version of it is found in the fifth of Aquinas's 'five ways' (see extract 2, above), but it reached its heyday in the late eighteenth and early nineteenth century, finding its most famous expression in the comparison of the universe to a watch made by Archdeacon William Paley:

Every indication of contrivance, every manifestation of design...in the watch, exists in the works of nature; with the difference, on the side of nature, of being greater and more, and that in a degree which exceeds all computation. I mean that the contrivances of nature surpass the contrivances of art in the complexity, subtlety, and curiosity of the mechanism; and still more, if possible, do they go beyond them in number and variety; yet, in a multitude of cases, are not less evidently mechanical, not less evidently contrivances, not less evidently accommodated to their end, or suited to their office, than are the most perfect productions of human ingenuity.[1]

Some thirty years earlier, the great Scottish philosopher David Hume had produced a telling critique of theism in his *Dialogues concerning Natural Religion*, first published in 1777, the year following his death. In the passage printed below (from Part II of the *Dialogues*) Hume presents a version of the argument from design in the mouth of 'Cleanthes', and then offers his own objections to it in the person of 'Philo'.

Hume objects, first, that arguments based on analogy, as this argument is, are at best only of limited use; and in any case the analogy offered by the theist is singularly weak, since the similarity between the universe and a product of human design such as a house is very thin. Second he notes that the apparent directedness of natural phenomena (the 'order, arrangement or adjustment of final causes') is not in itself any proof of design: matter itself, for all we know, may contain the source or spring of order within itself. Why fasten on rational design as the only possible cause of the order we find: 'what peculiar privilege has this little agitation of the brain which we call *thought* that we must make it the model of the whole universe?' And finally he points out that all reasoning concerning cause and effect must be based on past instances, yet in the case of the universe we are by definition dealing with something unique – 'singular, individual, without parallel or specific resemblance'. In the century following Hume, Charles Darwin in his *The Origin of Species* (1859) was to offer a purely naturalistic explanation for goal-adaptive phenomena, namely random mutation plus 'natural selection' in the struggle for survival; these were entirely 'blind' mechanisms not requiring any guiding intelligence. If Hume's arguments are correct, however, the argument from design is in any case inconclusive, irrespective of whether an alternative explanation is available for the 'adaptation of means to ends' which we find in the natural world.

Not to lose any time in circumlocutions, said Cleanthes,...I shall briefly explain how I conceive this matter. Look round the world, contemplate the whole and every part of it: you will find it to be nothing but one great machine, subdivided into an infinite number of lesser machines, which again admit of subdivisions to a degree beyond what human senses and faculties can trace and explain. All these various machines, and even their most minute parts, are adjusted to each other with an accuracy which

---

* David Hume, *Dialogues concerning Natural Religion* [published posthumously, 1777], Part II; abridged and with modified punctuation. The full text may be found in *The Philosophical Works of David Hume* (Edinburgh: Black & Tait, 1876), vol. II; many other editions available.
[1] From W. Paley, *Natural Theology* [1802].

ravishes into admiration all men who have ever contemplated them. The curious adapting of means to ends, throughout all nature, resembles exactly though it much exceeds the productions of human contrivance, of human designing, thought, wisdom and intelligence. Since therefore the effects resemble each other, we are led to infer by all the rules of analogy, that the causes also resemble, and that the Author of Nature is somewhat similar to the mind of man, though possessed of much larger faculties, proportioned to the grandeur of the work which he has executed. By this argument *a posteriori*, and by this alone, do we prove at once the existence of a Deity and his similarity to human mind and intelligence...

[Philo] That a stone will fall, that fire will burn, that the earth has solidity, we have observed a thousand and a thousand times; and when any new instance of this nature is presented, we draw without hesitation the accustomed inference. The exact similarity of the cases gives us a perfect assurance of a similar event and a stronger evidence is never desired nor sought after. But wherever you depart, in the least, from the similarity of the cases, you diminish proportionately the evidence and may at last bring it to a very *weak analogy* which is confessedly liable to error and uncertainty. After having observed the circulation of the blood in human creatures, we make no doubt that it takes place in Titius and Maevius; but from its circulation in frogs and fishes it is only a presumption, though a strong one, from analogy that it takes place in men and other animals. The analogical reasoning is much weaker when we infer the circulation of the sap in vegetables from our experience that the blood circulates in animals; and those who hastily followed that imperfect analogy are found, by more accurate experiments, to have been mistaken.

If we see a house, Cleanthes, we conclude, with the greatest certainty, that it had an architect or builder; because this is precisely that species of effect which we have experienced to proceed from that species of cause. But surely you will not affirm that the universe bears such a resemblance to a house, that we can with the same certainty infer a similar cause, or that the analogy is here entire and perfect. The dissimilitude is so striking, that the utmost you can here pretend to is a guess, a conjecture, a presumption concerning a similar cause; and how that pretension will be received in the world, I leave you to consider.

It would surely be very ill received, replied Cleanthes, and I should be deservedly blamed and detested, did I allow that the proofs of a Deity amounted to no more than a guess or conjecture. But is the whole adjustment of means to ends in a house and in the universe so slight a resemblance? The economy of final causes? The order, proportion and arrangement of every part? Steps of a stair are plainly contrived that human legs may use them in mounting; and this inference is certain and infallible. Human legs are also contrived for walking and mounting, and this inference, I allow is not altogether so certain, because of the similarity which you remark, but does it therefore deserve the name only of presumption or conjecture?...

[Philo] Were a man to abstract from everything which he knows or has seen, he would be altogether incapable, merely from his own ideas, to determine what kind of scene the universe must be, or to give the preference to one state or situation of things above another. For as nothing which he clearly conceives could be esteemed impossible or implying a contradiction, every chimera of his fancy would be upon an equal footing; nor could he assign any just reason why he adheres to one idea or system, and rejects the others which are equally possible.

Again; after he opens his eyes, and contemplates the world as it really is, it would be impossible for him at first to assign the cause of any one event, much less of the whole of things, or of the universe. He might set his fancy a rambling; and she might bring him in an infinite variety of reports and representations. These would all be possible; but being all equally possible, he would never of himself give a satisfactory account for his preferring one of them to the rest. Experience alone can point out to him the true cause of any phenomenon.

Now, according to this method of reasoning ... it follows that order, arrangement, or the adjustment of final causes, is not of itself any proof of design; but only so far as it has been experienced to proceed from that principle. For aught we can know *a priori*, matter may contain the source or spring of order originally within itself, as well as mind does; and there is no more difficulty in conceiving that the several elements, from an internal unknown cause, may fall into the most exquisite arrangement, than to conceive that their ideas, in the great universal mind, from a like internal unknown cause, fall into that arrangement. The equal possibility of both these suppositions is allowed. But, by experience, we find (according to Cleanthes) that there is a difference between them. Throw several pieces of steel together, without shape or form; they will never arrange themselves so as to compose a watch. Stone, and mortar, and wood, without an architect, never erect a house. But the ideas in a human mind, we see, by an unknown, inexplicable economy, arrange themselves so as to form the plan of a watch or house. Experience, therefore, proves that there is an original principle of order in mind, not in matter. From similar effects we infer similar causes. The adjustment of means to ends is alike in the universe, as in a machine of human contrivance. The causes, therefore, must be resembling ...

That all inferences, Cleanthes, concerning fact, are founded on experience, and that all experimental reasonings are founded on the supposition that similar causes prove similar effects, and similar effects similar causes, I shall not at present much dispute with you. But observe, I entreat you, with what extreme caution all just reasoners proceed in the transferring of experiments to similar cases. Unless the cases be exactly similar, they repose no perfect confidence in applying their past observation to any particular phenomenon. Every alteration of circumstances occasions a doubt concerning the event; and it requires new experiments to prove certainly that the new circumstances are of no moment or importance. A change in bulk, situation, arrangement, age, disposition of the air, or surrounding bodies – any of these particulars may be attended with the most unexpected consequences. And unless the objects be quite familiar to us, it is the highest temerity to expect with assurance, after any of these changes, an event similar to that which before fell under our observation. The slow and deliberate steps of philosophers here, if anywhere, are distinguished from the precipitate march of the vulgar, who, hurried on by the smallest similitude, are incapable of all discernment or consideration.

But can you think, Cleanthes, that your usual phlegm and philosophy have been preserved in so wide a step as you have taken, when you compared to the universe houses, ships, furniture, machines, and, from their similarity in some circumstances, inferred a similarity in their causes? Thought, design, intelligence, such as we discover in men and other animals, is no more than one of the springs and principles of the universe, as well as heat or cold, attraction or repulsion, and a hundred others, which fall under daily observation. It is an active cause, by which some particular parts of nature, we find, produce alterations on other parts. But can a conclusion, with any propriety, be transferred from parts to the whole? Does not the great disproportion bar all comparison and inference? From observing the growth of a hair, can we learn anything concerning the generation of a man? Would the manner of a leaf's blowing, even though perfectly known, afford us any instruction concerning the vegetation of a tree?

But, allowing that we were to take the operations of one part of nature upon another for the foundation of our judgement concerning the *origin* of the whole (which never can be admitted), yet why select so minute, so weak, so bounded a principle, as the reason and design of animals is found to be upon this planet? What peculiar privilege has this little agitation of the brain which we call *thought*, that we must thus make it the model of the whole universe? Our partiality in our own favour does indeed present it on all occasions; but sound philosophy ought carefully to guard against so natural an illusion.

So far from admitting, continued Philo, that the operations of a part can afford us any just conclusion concerning the origin of the whole, I will not allow any one part to form a rule for another part, if the latter be very remote from the former. Is there any reasonable ground to conclude that the inhabitants of other planets possess thought, intelligence, reason, or anything similar to these faculties in men? When nature has so extremely diversified her manner of operation in this small globe, can we imagine that she incessantly copies herself throughout so immense a universe? And if thought, as we may well suppose, be confined merely to this narrow corner, and has even there so limited a sphere of action, with what propriety can we assign it for the original cause of all things? The narrow views of a peasant, who makes his domestic economy the rule for the government of kingdoms, is in comparison a pardonable sophism.

But were we ever so much assured that a thought and reason, resembling the human, were to be found throughout the whole universe, and were its activity elsewhere vastly greater and more commanding than it appears in this globe; yet I cannot see why the operations of a world constituted, arranged, adjusted, can with any propriety be extended to a world which is in its embryo-state, and is advancing towards that constitution and arrangement. By observation, we know somewhat of the economy, action and nourishment of a finished animal; but we must transfer with great caution that observation to the growth of a foetus in the womb, and still more to the formation of an animalcule in the loins of its male parent. Nature, we find, even from our limited experience, possesses an infinite number of springs and principles, which incessantly discover themselves on every change of her position and situation. And what new and unknown principles would actuate her in so new and unknown a situation as that of the formation of a universe, we cannot, without the utmost temerity, pretend to determine.

A very small part of this great system, during a very short time, is very imperfectly discovered to us; and do we thence pronounce decisively concerning the origin of the whole?

Admirable conclusion! Stone, wood, brick, iron, brass, have not, at this time, in this minute globe of earth, an order or arrangement without human art and contrivance; therefore the universe could not originally attain its order and arrangement without something similar to human art! But is a part of nature a rule for another part very wide of the former? Is it a rule for the whole? Is a very small part a rule for the universe? Is nature in one situation a certain rule for nature in another situation vastly different from the former?

And can you blame me, Cleanthes, if I here imitate the prudent reserve of Simonides, who, according to the noted story, being asked by Hero, *What God was?* desired a day to think of it, and then two days more; and after that manner continually prolonged the term, without ever bringing in his definition or description? Could you ever blame me, if I had answered at first, *that I did not know*, and was sensible that this subject lay vastly beyond the reach of my faculties? You might cry out sceptic and rallier,[1] as much as you pleased; but having found, in so many other subjects much more familiar, the imperfections and even contradictions of human reason, I never should expect any success from its feeble conjectures, in a subject so sublime, and so remote from the sphere of our observation. When two *species* of objects have always been observed to be conjoined together, I can *infer*, by custom, the existence of one wherever I *see* the existence of the other; and this I call an argument from experience. But how this argument can have place, where the objects, as in the present case, are single, individual, without parallel, or specific resemblance, may be difficult to explain. And will any man tell me with a serious countenance, that an orderly universe must arise from some thought and art like the human, because we have experience of it? To ascertain this reasoning, it were requisite that we had experience of the origin of worlds; and it is not sufficient, surely, that we have seen ships and cities arise from human art and contrivance.

Philo was proceeding in this vehement manner, somewhat between jest and earnest, as it appeared to me, when he observed some signs of impatience in Cleanthes, and then immediately stopped short. What I had to suggest, said Cleanthes, is only that you would not abuse terms, or make use of popular expressions to subvert philosophical reasonings. You know that the vulgar often distinguish reason from experience, even where the question relates only to matter of fact and existence; though it is found, where that *reason* is properly analysed, that it is nothing but a species of experience. To prove by experience the origin of the universe from mind is not more contrary to common speech than to prove the motion of the earth from the same principle. And a caviller might raise all the same objections to the Copernican system, which you have urged against my reasonings. Have you other earths, might he say, which you have seen to move? Have...

Yes! cried Philo, interrupting him, we have other earths. Is not the moon another earth, which we see to turn round its centre? Is not Venus another earth, where we observe the same phenomenon? Are not the revolutions of the sun also a confirmation, from analogy, of the same theory? All the planets, are they not earths, which revolve about the sun? Are not the satellites moons, which move round Jupiter and Saturn, and along with these primary planets round the sun? These analogies and resemblances, with others which I have not mentioned, are the sole proofs of the Copernican system; and to you it belongs to consider whether you have any analogies of the same kind to support your theory.

In reality, Cleanthes, continued he, the modern system of astronomy is now so much received by all inquirers, and has become so essential a part even of our earliest education, that we are not commonly very scrupulous in examining the reasons upon

---

[1] To rally: to joke or banter.

which it is founded. It is now become a matter of mere curiosity to study the first writers on that subject, who had the full force of prejudice to encounter, and were obliged to turn their arguments on every side in order to render them popular and convincing. But if we peruse Galileo's famous dialogues concerning the system of the world, we shall find that that great genius, one of the sublimest that ever existed, first bent all his endeavours to prove that there was no foundation for the distinction commonly made between elementary and celestial substances. The Schools, proceeding from the illusions of sense, had carried this distinction very far; and had established the latter substances to be ingenerable, incorruptible, inalterable, impassible; and had assigned all the opposite qualities to the former. But Galileo, beginning with the moon, proved its similarity in every particular to the earth; its convex figure, its natural darkness when not illuminated, its density, its distinction into solid and liquid, the variations of its phases, the mutual illuminations of the earth and moon, their mutual eclipses, the inequalities of the lunar surface, &c. After many instances of this kind, with regard to all the planets, men plainly saw that these bodies became proper objects of experience; and that the similarity of their nature enabled us to extend the same arguments and phenomena from one to the other.

In this cautious proceeding of the astronomers, you may read your own condemnation, Cleanthes; or rather may see, that the subject in which you are engaged exceeds all human reason and inquiry. Can you pretend to show any such similarity between the fabric of a house, and the generation of a universe? Have you ever seen nature in any such situation as resembles the first arrangement of the elements? Have worlds ever been formed under your eye; and have you had leisure to observe the whole progress of the phenomenon, from the first appearance of order to its final consummation? If you have, then cite your experience, and deliver your theory.

7 Against Miracles: David Hume, *Enquiry concerning Human Understanding**

Though philosophy of religion has traditionally been most concerned with attempts to establish the existence of God by rational means (several examples of which occur in the extracts provided so far), many theists would say that the principal source of their belief is not *reason* but *revelation* – the way God has manifested himself to humanity through the Scriptures and through miraculous supernatural interventions of one kind or another; the Christian doctrines of the incarnation and the resurrection purport to provide prime examples of this. David Hume, who in his

Dialogues concerning Natural Religion (see previous extract) attacked the alleged rational basis for theism, also mounted a strong attack on belief in miracles in his *Enquiry concerning Human Understanding* (1748), from which our next extract is taken.

Though Hume readily concedes that evidence derived from eye-witnesses and spectators is most 'useful and even necessary to human life', he points out that the value of such testimony diminishes in force as the alleged fact is more unusual. And since a miracle is a violation of the

---

* David Hume, *An Enquiry concerning Human Understanding* [1748], section X; with omissions and modifications of punctuation and spelling. A useful edition, with introduction and notes, is that by T. L. Beauchamp (Oxford: Oxford University Press, 1999).

usual pattern of events established by normal observation, in so far as uniform experience amounts to a proof 'there is here a direct and full *proof*, from the nature of the fact, against the existence of any miracle'. His powerful and elegantly phrased conclusion is that 'no testimony is sufficient to establish a miracle unless the testimony be of such a kind that its falsehood would be more miraculous than the fact which it endeavours to establish'. Hume goes on to supplement his argument by observing certain facts about human nature – the gullibility of mankind, its tendency to swallow eagerly whatever is most 'extraordinary and marvellous'. He adds that reports of miracles tend to be accepted most among 'ignorant and barbarous nations', and finally that a host of incompatible religions, with incompatible views of the deity, all claim to support their faith by miraculous evidence. In closing this section of the *Enquiry* (a few paragraphs after the extract printed below), he presents the reader with a heavily ironic and challenging conclusion: 'that the Christian religion not only was at first attended with miracles, but even at this day cannot be believed by any reasonable person without one'.

Though experience be our only guide in reasoning concerning matters of fact, it must be acknowledged that this guide is not altogether infallible, but in some cases is apt to lead us into errors. One who in our climate should expect better weather in any week of June than in one of December would reason justly, and conformably to experience; but it is certain that he may happen, in the event, to find himself mistaken. However, we may observe, that, in such a case, he would have no cause to complain of experience; because it commonly informs us beforehand of the uncertainty, by that contrariety of events which we may learn from a diligent observation. All effects follow not with like certainty from their supposed causes. Some events are found, in all countries and all ages, to have been constantly conjoined together; others are found to have been more variable, and sometimes to disappoint our expectations; so that, in our reasonings concerning matter of fact, there are all imaginable degrees of assurance, from the highest certainty to the lowest species of moral evidence.

A wise man, therefore, proportions his belief to the evidence. In such conclusions as are founded on an infallible experience, he expects the event with the last degree of assurance, and regards his past experience as a full *proof* of the future existence of that event. In other cases, he proceeds with more caution. He weighs the opposite experiments. He considers which side is supported by the greater number of experiments. To that side he inclines, with doubt and hesitation; and when at last he fixes his judgement, the evidence exceeds not what we properly call *probability*. All probability, then, supposes an opposition of experiments and observations, where the one side is found to overbalance the other, and to produce a degree of evidence proportioned to the superiority. A hundred instances or experiments on one side, and fifty on another, afford a doubtful expectation of any event; though a hundred uniform experiments, with only one that is contradictory, reasonably beget a pretty strong degree of assurance. In all cases, we must balance the opposite experiments, where they are opposite, and deduct the smaller number from the greater, in order to know the exact force of the superior evidence.

To apply these principles to a particular instance, we may observe that there is no species of reasoning more common, more useful, and even necessary to human life, than that which is derived from the testimony of men, and the reports of eye-witnesses and spectators. This species of reasoning, perhaps, one may deny to be founded on the relation of cause and effect. I shall not dispute about a word. It will be sufficient to observe that our assurance in any argument of this kind is derived from no other principle than our observation of the veracity of human testimony, and of the usual conformity of facts to the reports of witnesses. It being a general maxim that no objects have any discoverable connection together, and that all the inferences which we can draw from one to another are founded merely on our experience of their constant and regular conjunction, it is evident that we ought not to make an exception to this maxim in favour of human testimony, whose connection with any event seems, in itself, as little necessary as any other. Were not the memory tenacious to a certain degree; had not men commonly an inclination to truth and a principle of probity; were they not sensible to shame when detected in a falsehood – were not these, I say, discovered by *experience* to be qualities inherent in human nature, we should never repose the least confidence in human testimony. A man delirious, or noted for falsehood and villainy, has no manner of authority with us.

And as the evidence derived from witnesses and human testimony is founded on past experience, so it varies with the experience, and is regarded either as a *proof* or a *probability*, according as the conjunction between any particular kind of report and any kind of object has been found to be constant or variable. There are a number of circumstances to be taken into consideration in all judgements of this kind; and the ultimate standard, by which we determine all disputes that may arise concerning them, is always derived from experience and observation. Where this experience is not entirely uniform on any side, it is attended with an unavoidable contrariety in our judgements, and with the same opposition and mutual destruction of argument as in every other kind of evidence. We frequently hesitate concerning the reports of others. We balance the opposite circumstances, which cause any doubt or uncertainty; and when we discover a superiority on any side, we incline to it; but still with a diminution of assurance, in proportion to the force of its antagonist.

This contrariety of evidence, in the present case, may be derived from several different causes; from the opposition of contrary testimony; from the character or number of the witnesses; from the manner of their delivering their testimony, or from the union of all these circumstances. We entertain a suspicion concerning any matter of fact, when the witnesses contradict each other; when they are but few, or of a doubtful character; when they have an interest in what they affirm; when they deliver their testimony with hesitation, or on the contrary, with too violent asseverations. There are many other particulars of the same kind, which may diminish or destroy the force of any argument derived from human testimony.

Suppose, for instance, that the fact, which the testimony endeavours to establish, partakes of the extraordinary and the marvellous; in that case, the evidence resulting from the testimony admits of a diminution, greater or less in proportion as the fact is more or less unusual. The reason why we place any credit in witnesses and historians is not derived from any connection which we perceive *a priori* between testimony and reality, but because we are accustomed to find a conformity between them. But when the fact attested is such a one as has seldom fallen under our observation, here is a contest of two opposite experiences; of which the one destroys the other, as far as its force goes, and the superior can only operate on the mind by the force which remains. The very same principle of experience, which gives us a certain degree of assurance in the testimony of witnesses, gives us also, in this case, another degree of assurance against the fact which they endeavour to establish;

from which contradiction there necessarily arises a counterpoise, and mutual destruction of belief and authority...

But in order to increase the probability against the testimony of witnesses, let us suppose that the fact which they affirm, instead of being only marvellous, is really miraculous; and suppose also that the testimony, considered apart and in itself, amounts to an entire proof; in that case, there is proof against proof, of which the strongest must prevail, but still with a diminution of its force, in proportion to that of its antagonist.

A miracle is a violation of the laws of nature; and as a firm and unalterable experience has established these laws, the proof against a miracle, from the very nature of the fact, is as entire as any argument from experience can possibly be imagined. Why is it more than probable that all men must die; that lead cannot, of itself, remain suspended in the air; that fire consumes wood, and is extinguished by water; unless it be that these events are found agreeable to the laws of nature, and there is required a violation of these laws, or in other words a miracle, to prevent them? Nothing is esteemed a miracle if it ever happen in the common course of nature. It is no miracle that a man, seemingly in good health, should die on a sudden; because such a kind of death, thought more unusual than any other, has yet been frequently observed to happen. But it is a miracle that a dead man should come to life; because that has never been observed, in any age or country. There must, therefore, be a uniform experience against every miraculous event, otherwise the event would not merit that appellation. And as an uniform experience amounts to a proof, there is here a direct and full *proof*, from the nature of the fact, against the existence of any miracle; nor can such a proof be destroyed, or the miracle rendered credible, but by an opposite proof, which is superior.

The plain consequence is (and it is a general maxim worthy of our attention) 'That no testimony is sufficient to establish a miracle, unless the testimony be of such a kind that its falsehood would be more miraculous than the fact which it endeavours to establish. And even in that case there is a mutual destruction of arguments, and the superior only gives us an assurance suitable to that degree of force which remains, after deducting the inferior.' When anyone tells me that he saw a dead man restored to life, I immediately consider with myself whether it be more probable that this person should either deceive or be deceived, or that the fact, which he relates, should really have happened. I weigh the one miracle against the other; and according to the superiority which I discover, I pronounce my decision, and always reject the greater miracle. If the falsehood of his testimony would be more miraculous than the event which he relates, then, and not till then, can he pretend to command my belief or opinion.

In the foregoing reasoning we have supposed that the testimony upon which a miracle is founded may possibly amount to an entire proof, and that the falsehood of that testimony would be a real prodigy. But it is easy to see that we have been a great deal too liberal in our concession, and that there never was a miraculous event established on so full an evidence.

For *first*, there is not to be found, in all history, any miracle attested by a sufficient number of men, of such unquestioned good-sense, education and learning as to secure us against all delusion in themselves; of such undoubted integrity as to place them beyond all suspicion of any design to deceive others; of such credit and reputation in the eyes of mankind as to have a great deal to lose in case of their being detected in any falsehood; and at the same time, attesting facts, performed in such a public manner, and in so celebrated a part of the world, as to render the detection unavoidable. All which circumstances are requisite to give us a full assurance in the testimony of men.

Secondly. We may observe in human nature a principle which, if strictly examined, will be found to diminish extremely the assurance which we might, from human testimony, have in any kind of prodigy. The maxim by which we commonly conduct ourselves in our reasonings is that the objects of which we have no experience resemble those of which we have; that what we have found to be most usual is always most probable; and that where there is an opposition of arguments, we ought to give the preference to such as are founded on the greatest number of past observations. But though, in proceeding by this rule, we readily reject any fact which is unusual and incredible in an ordinary degree, yet in advancing farther, the mind observes not always the same rule; but when anything is affirmed utterly absurd and miraculous, it rather the more readily admits of such a fact, upon account of that very circumstance, which ought to destroy all its authority. The passion of *surprise* and *wonder,* arising from miracles, being an agreeable emotion, gives a sensible tendency towards the belief of those events from which it is derived. And this goes so far, that even those who cannot enjoy this pleasure immediately, nor can believe those miraculous events of which they are informed, yet love to partake of the satisfaction at second-hand or by rebound, and place a pride and delight in exciting the admiration of others.

With what greediness are the miraculous accounts of travellers received, their descriptions of sea and land monsters, their relations of wonderful adventures, strange men, and uncouth manners? But if the spirit of religion join itself to the love of wonder, there is an end of common sense; and human testimony, in these circumstances, loses all pretensions to authority. A religionist may be an enthusiast, and imagine he sees what has no reality. He may know his narrative to be false, and yet persevere in it, with the best intentions in the world, for the sake of promoting so holy a cause. Or even where this delusion has not place, vanity, excited by so strong a temptation, operates on him more powerfully than on the rest of mankind in any other circumstances; and self-interest with equal force. His auditors may not have, and commonly have not, sufficient *judgement* to canvass his evidence. What judgement they have, they renounce by principle, in these sublime and mysterious subjects. Or if they were ever so willing to employ it, passion and a heated imagination disturb the regularity of its operations. Their credulity increases his impudence: and his impudence overpowers their credulity... The many instances of forged miracles, and prophesies of supernatural events, which in all ages have either been detected by contrary evidence, or which detect themselves by their absurdity, prove sufficiently the strong propensity of mankind to the extraordinary and the marvellous, and ought reasonably to beget a suspicion against all relations of this kind...

Thirdly. It forms a strong presumption against all supernatural and miraculous relations that they are observed chiefly to abound among ignorant and barbarous nations; or if a civilized people has ever given admission to any of them, that people will be found to have received them from ignorant and barbarous ancestors, who transmitted them with that inviolable sanction and authority which always attend received opinions. When we peruse the first histories of all nations, we are apt to imagine ourselves transported into some new world; where the whole frame of nature is disjointed, and every element performs its operations in a different manner from what it does at present. Battles, revolutions, pestilence, famine and death, are never the effect of those natural causes which we experience. Prodigies, omens, oracles, judgements, quite obscure the few natural events that are intermingled with them. But as the former grow thinner every page, in proportion as we advance nearer the enlightened ages, we soon learn that there is nothing mysterious or supernatural in the case, but that all proceeds from the usual propensity of mankind towards the marvellous, and that, though this inclination may at intervals receive a check from sense and learning, it can never be thoroughly extirpated from human nature...

I may add as a *fourth* reason, which diminishes the authority of prodigies, that there is no testimony for any, even those which have not been expressly detected, that is not opposed by an infinite number of witnesses; so that not only the miracle destroys the credit of testimony, but the testimony destroys itself. To make this the better understood, let us consider that, in matters of religion, whatever is different is contrary; and that it is impossible the religions of ancient Rome, of Turkey, of Siam, and of China should, all of them, be established on any solid foundation. Every miracle, therefore, pretended to have been wrought in any of these religions (and all of them abound in miracles), as its direct scope is to establish the particular system to which it is attributed, so has it the same force, though more indirectly, to overthrow every other system. In destroying a rival system, it likewise destroys the credit of those miracles on which that system was established; so that all the prodigies of different religions are to be regarded as contrary facts, and the evidences of these prodigies, whether weak or strong, as opposite to each other. According to this method of reasoning, when we believe any miracle of Mahomet or his successors, we have for our warrant the testimony of a few barbarous Arabians. And on the other hand, we are to regard the authority of Titus Livius, Plutarch, Tacitus and, in short, of all the authors and witnesses, Grecian, Chinese and Roman Catholic, who have related any miracle in their particular religion; I say, we are to regard their testimony in the same light as if they had mentioned that Mahometan miracle, and had in express terms contradicted it, with the same certainty as they have for the miracle they relate. This argument may appear over subtle and refined; but is not in reality different from the reasoning of a judge, who supposes that the credit of two witnesses, maintaining a crime against any one, is destroyed by the testimony of two others, who affirm him to have been two hundred leagues distant, at the same instant when the crime is said to have been committed...

Upon the whole, then, it appears that no testimony for any kind of miracle has ever amounted to a probability, much less to a proof; and that, even supposing it amounted to a proof, it would be opposed by another proof, derived from the very nature of the fact which it would endeavour to establish. It is experience only which gives authority to human testimony; and it is the same experience, which assures us of the laws of nature. When, therefore, these two kinds of experience are contrary, we have nothing to do but subtract the one from the other, and embrace an opinion, either on one side or the other, with that assurance which arises from the remainder. But according to the principle here explained, this subtraction, with regard to all popular religions, amounts to an entire annihilation; and therefore we may establish it as a maxim that no human testimony can have such force as to prove a miracle, and make it a just foundation for any such system of religion.

8   Faith and Subjectivity: Søren Kierkegaard, *Concluding Unscientific Postscript**

Challenges to established religion of the kind mounted by Hume (see the two previous extracts) led some philosophical supporters of theism in the nineteenth century to seek radically new ways of defending their beliefs. Our next extract is by the Danish philosopher Søren Kierkegaard, often regarded as one of the founders of the movement known as existentialism (see Part II, extract 9, and Part V, extract 10). Kierkegaard rejects the whole idea of scientific objectivity as a guide to how we should believe and act in matters that concern our personal lives. In a famous slogan he declares that 'Truth is subjectivity'. Even if the most thoroughgoing scientific evidence for the truth of the Scriptures were forthcoming, Kierkegaard maintains, this would not alter the human predicament one wit, any more than it would if the results of scholarly and scientific research were to point conclusively in the opposite direction. For 'all essential decisiveness is rooted in subjectivity'. What matters is not a set of scientific results, or a body of objective doctrine, but the deep personal commitment of an individual who takes the leap of faith. This stress on the primacy of faith corresponds to a long-standing tradition in religious thought: Anselm (see extract 1 above) had coined the slogan 'I believe in order to understand', and Pascal too (see extract 4) had exalted faith and devotion above rational proof. But Kierkegaard adds to this a striking paradox, namely that it is precisely the lack of objective certainty that generates the 'risk' which is the essential precondition for true faith: 'if I am capable of grasping God objectively I do not believe; but precisely because I cannot do this, I must believe'.

 Let us assume that the critics have succeeded in proving about the Bible everything that any learned theologian in his happiest moments has ever wished to prove about the Bible. These books and no other belong to the canon; they are authentic; they are integral; their authors are trustworthy – one could say that it is as if every letter were inspired... Well, everything being assumed to be in order with respect to the Scriptures, what follows? Has anyone who previously did not have faith been brought a step nearer to its acquisition? No, not a single step. Faith does not result simply from a scientific inquiry; it does not come directly at all. On the contrary, in this objectivity one tends to lose the infinite personal interestedness in passion which is the condition of faith, the 'everywhere and nowhere' in which faith can come into being. Has anyone who previously had faith gained anything with respect to its strength and power? No, not in the least. Rather is it the case that in this voluminous knowledge, this certainty that lurks at the door of faith and threatens to devour it, he is in so dangerous a situation that he will need to put forth much effort in great fear and trembling, lest he fall victim to the temptation to confuse knowledge with faith. While faith has hitherto had a profitable schoolmaster in the existing uncertainty, it would have in the new certainty its most dangerous enemy. For if passion is eliminated, faith no longer exists, and certainty and passion do not go together. Whoever believes that there is a God, and an over-ruling providence, finds it easier to preserve his faith, easier to acquire something that definitely is faith and not an illusion, in an imperfect world where

---

* S. Kierkegaard, *Afsluttende Uvidenskabelig Efterskrift* [1846]. Trans. D. F. Swenson (Princeton: Princeton University Press, 1941), extracts from pp. 26–35 and 177–82; with minor modifications.

passion is kept alive, than in an absolutely perfect world. In such a world faith is in fact unthinkable. Hence also the teaching that faith is abolished in eternity.

How fortunate then that this wishful hypothesis, this beautiful dream of critical theology, is an impossibility, because even the most perfect realization would still remain an approximation. And again how fortunate for the critics that the fault is by no means in them! If all the angels in heaven were to put their heads together, they could still bring to pass only an approximation, because an approximation is the only certainty attainable for historical knowledge – but also an inadequate basis for an eternal happiness.

I assume now the opposite, that the opponents have succeeded in proving what they desire about the Scriptures, with a certainty transcending the most ardent wish of the most passionate hostility – what then? Have the opponents thereby abolished Christianity? By no means. Has the believer been harmed? By no means, not in the least. Has the opponent made good a right to be relieved of responsibility for not being a believer? By no means. Because these books are not written by these authors, are not authentic, are not in an integral condition, are not inspired (though this cannot be disproved since it is an object of faith), it does not follow that these authors have not existed; and above all it does not follow that Christ has not existed. As far as all this goes the believer is equally free to assume it – equally free (let us note this well) since if he had assumed it by virtue of any proof he would have been on the verge of giving up his faith. If matters ever come to this pass, the believer will have some share of guilt, in so far as he has himself invited this procedure, and begun to play into the hands of unbelief by proposing to provide a proof.

Here is the crux of the matter, and I come back to the case of learned theology. For whose sake is it that the proof is sought? Faith does not need it; indeed, it must even regard the proof as its enemy. But when faith begins to feel embarrassed and ashamed like a young woman for whom her love is no longer sufficient, but secretly feels ashamed of her lover and must therefore have it established that there is something remarkable about him – when faith thus begins to lose its passion, when faith begins to cease to be faith, then a proof becomes necessary so as to command respect from the side of unbelief...

When the question is treated in an objective manner it becomes impossible for the subject to face the decision with passion, least of all with an infinitely interested passion if at all. It is a self-contradiction, and therefore comical, to be infinitely interested in that which in its maximum still always remains an approximation. If, in spite of this, passion is nevertheless imported, we get fanaticism. For an infinitely interested passion every iota will be of infinite value. The fault is not in the infinitely interested passion, but in the fact that its object has become an approximation-object.

The objective mode of approach to the problem persists from generation to generation precisely because the individuals, the contemplative individuals, become more and more objective, less and less possessed by an infinite passionate interest. Supposing that we continue in this manner to prove and seek the proof of Christianity, the remarkable phenomenon would finally emerge that just when the proof for its truth had become completely realized, it would have ceased to exist as a present fact. It would then have become so completely an historical phenomenon as to be something entirely past, whose truth, i.e. whose historical truth, had finally been brought to a satisfactory determination. In this way perhaps the anxious prophecy of Luke 18: 8 might be fulfilled: 'Nevertheless, when the Son of Man cometh, shall he find faith on the earth?'

The more objective the contemplative enquirer, the less he bases an eternal happiness, i.e. his eternal happiness, upon his relationship to the enquiry; for there can be no question of an eternal happiness except for the passionately and infinitely interested subject. Objectively, the contemplative enquirer, whether learned scholar or dilettante member of the laity, understands himself in the following farewell words as he faces the final end: 'When I was a young man, such and such books were in doubt; now their genuineness has been demonstrated, but then again a doubt has recently been raised about certain books which have never before been under suspicion. But there will doubtless soon arise a scholar who will...' and so forth.

The accommodating and objective subject holds himself aloof, displaying an applauded heroism. He is completely at your service, and ready to accept the truth as soon as it is brought to light. But the goal toward which he strives is far distant – undeniably so since an approximation can continue indefinitely; and while the grass grows under his feet the enquirer dies, his mind at rest, for he was objective. It is not without reason that you have been praised, O wonderful Objectivity, for you can do all things; not even the firmest believer was ever so certain of his eternal happiness and above all of not losing it, as the objective subject! Unless this objective and accommodating temper should perhaps be in the wrong place, so that it is possibly unchristian; in that case, it would naturally be a little dubious to have arrived at the truth of Christianity in this manner. Christianity is spirit, spirit is inwardness, inwardness is subjectivity, subjectivity is essential passion, and in its maximum an infinite, personal, passionate interest in one's eternal happiness.

As soon as subjectivity is eliminated, and passion eliminated from subjectivity, and the infinite interest eliminated from passion, there is in general no decision at all, either in this problem or in any other. All decisiveness, all essential decisiveness, is rooted in subjectivity. A contemplative spirit, and this is what the objective subject is, feels nowhere any infinite need of a decision, and sees no decision anywhere. This is the falsity that is inherent in all objectivity; and this is the significance of mediation as the mode of transition in the continuous process where nothing is fixed and nothing is infinitely decided. For the movement turns back upon itself and again turns back, so that the movement is chimerical, and the philosopher is wise only after the event. But there is no decisive result anywhere. This is quite as it should be, since decisiveness adheres in subjectivity alone, essentially in its passion, and maximally in the personal passion which is infinitely interested in an eternal happiness...

In an attempt to make clear the difference of way that exists between an objective and subjective reflection, I shall now proceed to show how a subjective reflection makes its way inwardly in inwardness. Inwardness in an existing subject culminates in passion; corresponding to passion in the subject, the truth becomes a paradox; and the fact that the truth becomes a paradox is rooted precisely in its having a relationship to an existing subject. Thus the one corresponds to the other. By forgetting that one is an existing subject, passion goes by the board, and the truth is no longer a paradox; the knowing subject becomes a fantastic entity rather than a human being, and the truth becomes a fantastic object for the knowledge of this fantastic entity.

When the question of truth is raised in an objective manner, reflection is directed objectively to the truth, as an object to which the knower is related. Reflection is not focused upon the relationship, however, but upon the question of whether it is the truth to which the knower is related. If only the object to which he is related is the truth, the subject is accounted to be in the truth. When the question of the truth is raised subjectively, reflection is directed subjectively to the nature of the individual's relationship: if only the mode of this relationship is in the truth, the individual is in the truth, even if he should happen to be thus related to what is not true. Let us take as an example the knowledge of God. Objectively, reflection is directed to the problem of whether this object is the true God; subjectively, reflection is directed to the question whether the individual is related to a something *in such a manner* that his relation is in truth a Godrelationship. On which side is the truth now to be found? May we not here resort to a mediation, and say 'it is on neither side, but in the mediation of both'? Excellently well said, provided we could have it explained how an existing individual manages to be in a state of mediation. For to be in a state of mediation is to be finished, while to exist is to become. Nor can an existing individual be in two places at the same time – he cannot be an identity of subject and object. When he is nearest to being in two places at the same time, he is in passion; but passion is momentary, and passion is also the highest expression of subjectivity.

The existing individual who chooses to pursue the objective way enters upon the entire approximation-process by which it is proposed to bring God to light objectively. But this is in all eternity impossible, because God is a subject, and therefore exists only for subjectivity in inwardness. The existing individual who chooses the subjective way apprehends instantly the entire dialectical difficulty involved in having to use some time, perhaps a long time, in finding God objectively; and he feels this dialectical difficulty, in all its painfulness, because every moment is wasted in which he does not have God. That very instant he has God, not by virtue of any objective deliberation, but by virtue of the infinite passion of inwardness. The objective inquirer, on the other hand, is not embarrassed by such dialectical difficulties as are involved in devoting an entire period of investigation to finding God, since it is possible that the inquirer may die tomorrow; and if he lives he can scarcely regard God as something to be taken along if convenient, since God is precisely that which one takes *à tout prix*,[1] which in the understanding of passion constitutes the true inward relationship to God.

It is at this point, so difficult dialectically, that the way swings off for everyone who knows what it means to think and to think existentially; this is something very different from sitting at a desk and writing about what one has never done, something very different from writing *de omnibus dubitandum*,[2] and at the same time being as credulous existentially as the most sensuous of men. Here is where the way swings off, and the change is marked by the fact that while objective knowledge rambles comfortably on by way of the long road of approximation without being impelled by the urge of passion, subjective knowledge counts every delay a deadly peril, and the decision so infinitely important and so instantly pressing that it is as if the opportunity has already passed.

---

[1] 'At any price'.
[2] 'One should doubt everything'.

Now when the problem is to reckon up on which side there is most truth, whether on the side of one who seeks the true God objectively, and pursues the approximate truth of the God-idea, or on the side of one who, driven by the infinite passion of his need of God, feels an infinite concern for his own relationship to God in truth . . . the answer cannot be in doubt for anyone who has not been demoralized with the aid of science. If one who lives in the midst of Christendom goes up to the house of God, the house of the true God, with the true conception of God in his knowledge, and prays, but prays in a false spirit; and if he who lives in an idolatrous community prays with the passion of the infinite, although his eyes rest upon the image of an idol: where is the most truth? The one prays in truth to God though he worships an idol; the other prays falsely to the true God, and hence worships in fact an idol.

When one man investigates objectively the problem of immortality, and another embraces an uncertainty with the passion of the infinite, where is there most truth and who has the greater certainty? The one has entered upon a never-ending approximation, for the certainty of immortality lies precisely in the subjectivity of the individual; the other is immortal, and fights for this immortality by struggling with the uncertainty. Let us consider Socrates. Nowadays everyone dabbles in a few proofs; some have several such proofs, others fewer. But Socrates! He puts the question objectively in a problematic manner: *if* there is immortality. Must he therefore be accounted a doubter in comparison with one of our modern thinkers with their 'three proofs'? By no means. On this 'if' he risks his entire life; he has the courage to meet death; and he has with the passion of the infinite so determined the pattern of his life that it must be found acceptable – *if* there is immortality. Is any better proof capable of being given for the immortality of the soul? But those who have the three proofs do not at all determine their lives in conformity with them; if there is immortality it must feel disgust over the manner of their lives. Can any better refutation be given of the three proofs? The fact that Socrates had a bit of uncertainty helped him because he himself contributed the passion of the infinite; the three proofs that the others had do not profit them at all, because they are dead to spirit and enthusiasm. And their three proofs, instead of proving anything else, prove just this. A young girl may enjoy all the sweetness of love on the basis of what is merely a weak hope that she is beloved, because she rests everything on this weak hope. But many a wedded matron, more than once subjected to the strongest expressions of love, has to this extent indeed had proofs, but strangely enough has not enjoyed *quod erat demonstrandum*.[1] The Socratic ignorance, which Socrates held fast with the entire passion of his inwardness, was thus an expression of the principle that eternal truth is related to an existing individual and that this truth must therefore be a paradox for him as long as he exists; and yet it is possible that there was more truth in the Socratic ignorance, as it was in him, than in the entire objective truth of the System, which flirts with what the times demand, and accommodates itself to the university lecturers.

The objective accent falls on WHAT is said, the subjective accent on HOW it is said. This distinction holds even in the aesthetic realm, and receives definite expression in the principle that what is in itself true may in the mouth of such and such a person become untrue. In these times this distinction is particularly worthy of notice, for if we wish to

---

[1] '[that] which was to be demonstrated' (the phrase is used in Euclid's geometry after each theorem has been proved).

express in a single sentence the difference between ancient times and our own, we should doubtless have to say: 'In ancient times only an individual here and there knew the truth; now all know it, except that the inwardness of its appropriation stands in an inverse relationship to the extent of its dissemination.' Aesthetically, the contradiction that truth becomes untruth, in this or that person's mouth, is best construed comically: in the ethico-religious sphere, the accent is again on the 'how'. But this is not to be understood as referring to demeanour, expression or the like; rather it refers to the relationship sustained by the existing individual, in his own existence, to the content of his utterance. Objectively, the interest is focused merely on the thought-content, subjectively on the inwardness. At its maximum, this inward 'how' is the passion of the infinite, and the passion of the infinite is the truth. But the passion of the infinite is precisely subjectivity, and thus subjectivity becomes the truth. Objectively, there is no infinite decisiveness, and hence it is objectively appropriate to annul the difference between good and evil, together with the principle of contradiction and therewith also the infinite difference between the true and the false. Only in subjectivity is there decisiveness; to seek objectivity is to be in error. It is the passion of the infinite that is the decisive factor, and not its content, for its content is precisely itself. In this manner, subjectivity and the subjective 'how' constitute the truth.

But the 'how' which is thus subjectively accentuated precisely because the subject is an existing individual, is also subject to a dialectic with respect to time. In the passionate movement of decision, where the road swings away from objective know-ledge, it seems as if the infinite decision were thereby realized. But in the same moment, the existing individual finds himself in the temporal order, and the subject-ive 'how' is transformed into a striving, a striving which receives indeed its impulse and repeated renewal from the decisive passion of the infinite, but is nevertheless a striving.

When subjectivity is the truth, the conceptual determination of the truth must include an expression for the antithesis to objectivity, a memento of a fork in the road where the way swings off; this expression will at the same time serve as an indication of the subjective inwardness. Here is such a definition of truth: *an objective uncertainty held fast in an appropriation-process of the most passionate inwardness is the truth* – the highest truth attainable for an *existing* individual. At the point where the way swings off (and where this is cannot be specified objectively, since it is a matter of subject-ivity) there objective knowledge is placed in abeyance. Thus the subject merely has, objectively, the uncertainty; but it is this which precisely increases the tension of that infinite passion which constitutes his inwardness. The truth is precisely the venture which chooses an objective uncertainty with the passion of the infinite. I contemplate the order of nature in the hope of finding God, and I see omnipotence and wisdom; but I also see much else that disturbs my mind and excites anxiety. The sum of all this is an objective uncertainty. But it is for this very reason that the inwardness becomes as intense as it is, for it embraces this objective uncertainty with the entire passion of the infinite. In the case of a mathematical proposition, the objectivity is given, but for this reason the truth of such a proposition is also an indifferent truth.

But the above definition of truth is an equivalent expression for faith. Without risk there is no faith. Faith is precisely the contradiction between the infinite passion of the individual's inwardness and the objective uncertainty. If I am capable of grasping God objectively, I do not believe; but precisely because I cannot do this, I must believe.

If I wish to preserve myself in faith, I must constantly be intent on holding fast the objective uncertainty, so as to remain out upon the deep, over seventy thousand fathoms of water, still preserving my faith.

9   Reason, Passion and the Religious Hypothesis: William James, *The Will to Believe**

In the course of assessing the value of supposed miracles as support for religious belief, David Hume had enunciated a principle which many philosophers would find self-evidently sound and sensible: 'a wise man proportions his belief to the strength of the evidence' (see extract 7, above). This implies it is foolish to believe a proposition for which the evidence is weak or inconclusive; one could go further and say that belief in such cases is irresponsible and wrong. In the following extract from an address given to the Philosophical Clubs of Yale and Brown Universities at the end of the nineteenth century, the celebrated American philosopher William James strongly rejects this argument. There are, he concedes, many cases where our belief is determined by the facts: we cannot just *decide* whether or not to believe, for example, that Abraham Lincoln existed. But where we are faced with a genuine option that cannot be decided on intellectual grounds, James argues that our 'passional nature not only lawfully may but must decide'. Both moral and religious questions provide examples of questions where our will need not, and indeed should not wait on the evidence. The sceptic may claim to remain aloof and suspend judgement, but James argues that this is just as much a matter of passion, of

exalting our fear of being in error above our hope that the religious hypothesis may be true.

James goes on to argue that an act of will or faith may itself bring benefits that cannot be achieved any other way; friendship, for example, would be impossible if everything were assessed by the standards of 'snarling logicality' and 'pure intellectualism'. The extolling of passionate commitment over austere rational objectivity seems in some respects reminiscent of Kierkegaard (see preceding extract). But James adds a dimension drawn from his pragmatist theory of belief, according to which the content of a belief is intimately bound up with the difference it makes to the way we behave: 'belief', as he puts it in the penultimate footnote of the extract, 'is measured by action'. He ends with a resounding quotation comparing the human predicament with that of a traveller on a mountain pass in the midst of whirling snow and blinding mist; if we stand still, we shall be frozen to death. Accepting the religious hypothesis, for James, enables us to act with courage and integrity. That is indeed a signal benefit; the question his critics may be inclined to press is why such benefits should be beyond the reach of the resolute and sincere atheist or the agnostic.

 In the recently published Life by Leslie Stephen of his brother, Fitz-James, there is an account of a school to which the latter went when he was a boy. The teacher, a certain Mr Guest, used to converse with his pupils in this wise: 'Gurney, what is the difference between justification and sanctification?'; 'Stephen, prove the omnipotence of God!' etc. In this midst of our Harvard freethinking and indifference we are prone to

* William James, *The Will to Believe and Other Essays in Popular Philosophy* (New York: Longmans Green, 1897), ch. 1; abridged.

imagine that here at your good old orthodox College conversation continues to be somewhat upon this order; and to show you that we at Harvard have not lost all interest in these vital subjects, I have brought with me tonight something like a sermon on justification by faith to read to you, – I mean an essay in justification *of* faith, a defence of our right to adopt a believing attitude in religious matters, in spite of the fact that our merely logical intellect may not have been coerced. 'The Will to Believe', accordingly, is the title of my paper...

...The thesis I defend is, briefly stated, this: *Our passional nature not only lawfully may, but must, decide an option between propositions, whenever it is a genuine option that cannot by its nature be decided on intellectual grounds; for to say, under such circumstances, 'Do not decide, but leave the question open', is itself a passional decision – just like deciding yes or no, and is attended with the same risk of losing the truth...*

...'Le cœur a ses raisons', as Pascal says, 'que la raison ne connaît pas';[1] and however indifferent to all but the bare rules of the game the umpire, the abstract intellect, may be, the concrete players who furnish him the materials to judge of are usually each one of them, in love with some pet 'live hypothesis' of his own. Let us agree, however, that wherever there is no forced option, the dispassionately judicial intellect with no pet hypothesis, saving us, as it does from dupery at any rate, ought to be our ideal.

The question next arises: Are there not somewhere forced options in our specula-tive questions, and can we (as men who may be interested at least as much in positively gaining truth as in merely escaping dupery) always wait with impunity till the coercive evidence shall have arrived? It seems *a priori* improbable that the truth should be so nicely adjusted to our needs and powers as that. In the great boarding-house of nature, the cakes and the butter and syrup seldom come out so even and leave the plates so clean. Indeed, we should view them with scientific suspicion if they did.

Moral questions immediately present themselves as questions whose solution can-not wait for sensible proof. A moral question is a question not of what sensibly exists, but of what is good, or would be good if it did exist. Science can tell us what exists; but to compare the *worths*, both of what exists and what does not exist, we must consult not science, but what Pascal calls our heart...

Turn now from these wide questions of good to a certain class of questions of fact, questions concerning personal relations, states of mind between one man and an-other. *Do you like me or not?* – for example. Whether you do or not depends, in countless instances, of whether I meet you half way, am willing to assume that you must like me, and show you trust and expectation. The previous faith on my part in your liking's existence is in such cases what makes your liking come. But if I stand aloof, and refuse to budge an inch until I have objective evidence, until you shall have done something apt, as the absolutists say, *ad extorquendum assensum meum* [to compel my assent], ten to one your liking never comes. How many women's hearts are vanquished by the mere sanguine insistence of some man that they must love him! He will not consent to the hypothesis that they cannot. The desire for a certain kind of truth here brings about that special truth's existence; and so it is in innumerable cases

[1] 'The heart has its reasons, of which reason is unaware.'

of other sorts. Who gains promotions, boons, appointments, but the man in whose life they are seen to play the part of live hypotheses, who discounts them, sacrifices other things for their sake before they have come, and takes risks for them in advance? His faith acts on the powers above him as a claim, and creates its own verification.

A social organism of any sort whatever, large or small, is what it is because each member proceeds to his own duty with a trust that the other members will simultaneously do theirs. Wherever a desired result is achieved by the cooperation of many independent persons, its existence as a fact is a pure consequence of the precursive faith of one another of those immediately concerned. A government, an army, a commercial system, a ship, a college, an athletic team, all exist on this condition, without which not only is nothing achieved, but nothing is even attempted. A whole train of passengers (individually brave enough) will be looted by a few highwaymen, simply because the latter can count on one another, while each passenger fears that if he makes a movement of resistance, he will be shot before any one else backs him up. If we believed that the whole car-full would rise at once with us, we should each severally rise, and train-robbing would never even be attempted. There are, then, cases where a fact cannot come at all unless a preliminary faith exists in its coming. *And where faith in a fact can help create the fact*, that would be an insane logic, which should say that faith running ahead of scientific evidence is the 'lowest kind of immorality' onto which a thinking being can fall. Yet such is the logic by which our scientific absolutists pretend to run their lives!

In truths dependent on our personal action, then, faith based on desire is certainly a lawful and possibly an indispensable thing.

But now, it will be said, these are all childish human cases, and have nothing to do with great cosmical matters, like the question of religious faith. Let us then pass on to that. Religions differ so much in their accidents that in discussing the religious question we must make it very generic and broad. What then do we now mean by the religious hypothesis? Science says things are; morality says some things are better than other things; and religion says essentially two things.

First, she says that the best things are the more eternal things, the overlapping things, the things in the universe that throw the last stone, so to speak, and say the last word. 'Perfection is eternal,' – this phrase of Charles Secrétan seems a good way of putting this first affirmation of religion, an affirmation which obviously cannot yet be verified scientifically at all.

The second affirmation of religion is that we are better off even now if we believe her first affirmation to be true.

Now let us consider what the logical elements of this situation are *in case the religious hypothesis in both its branches be really true.* (Of course, we must admit that possibility at the outset. If we are to discuss the question at all, it must involve a living option. If for any of you religion be a hypothesis that cannot by any living possibility be true, then you need go no farther. I speak to the 'saving remnant' alone.) So proceeding, we see, first, that religion offers itself as a *momentous* option. We are supposed to gain, even now, by our belief, and to lose by our nonbelief, a certain vital good. Secondly, religion is a *forced* option, so far as that good goes. We cannot escape the issue by remaining sceptical and waiting for more light, because, although we do avoid error in that way *if religion be untrue*, we lose the good, *if it be true*, just as certainly as if we positively choose to disbelieve. It is as if a man should hesitate indefinitely to ask a certain woman to marry him because he was not perfectly sure that she would prove an angel after he brought her home. Would he not cut himself off from that particular angel-possibility as decisively as if he went and married someone else? Scepticism, then, is not avoidance of option; it is option of a certain particular kind of risk. *Better risk loss of truth than chance of error,* – that is your faith-vetoer's exact position. He is actively playing his stake as much as the believer is; he is backing the field against the religious hypothesis, just as the believer is backing the religious hypothesis against the field. To preach scepticism to us as a duty until 'sufficient evidence' for religion be found, is tantamount therefore to telling us, when in presence of the religious hypothesis, that to yield to our fear of its being error is wiser and better than to yield to our hope that it may be true. It is not intellect against all passions, then; it is only intellect with one passion laying down its law. And by what, forsooth, is the supreme wisdom of this passion warranted? Dupery for dupery, what proof is there that dupery through hope is so much worse than dupery through fear? I, for one, can see no proof; and I simply refuse obedience to the scientist's command to imitate his kind of option, in a case where my own stake is important enough to give me the right to choose my own form of risk. If religion be true and the evidence for it be still insufficient, I do not wish, by putting your extinguisher upon my nature (which feels to me as if it had after all some business in this matter) to forfeit my sole chance in life of getting on the winning side, – that chance depending, of course, on my willingness to run the risk of acting as if my passional need of taking the world religiously might be prophetic and right.

All this is on the supposition that it really may be prophetic and right, and that, even to us who are discussing the matter, religion is a live hypothesis which may be true. Now to most of us religion comes in a still further way that makes a veto on our active faith even more illogical. The more perfect and more eternal aspect of the universe is represented in our religions as having personal form. The universe is no longer a mere *It* to us, but a *Thou*, if we are religious; and any relation that may be possible from person to person might be possible here. For instance, although in one sense we are passive portions of the universe, in another we show a curious autonomy, as if we were small active centres on our own account. We feel, too, as if the appeal of religion to us were made to our own active goodwill, as if evidence might be forever withheld from us unless we met the hypothesis half way. To take a trivial illustration: just as a man who in a company of gentlemen made no advances, asked a warrant for every concession, and believed no one's word without proof, would cut himself off by such churlishness from all the social rewards that a more trusting spirit would earn, so here, one who should shut himself up in snarling logicality and try to make the gods extort his recognition willy-nilly, or not get it at all, might cut himself off forever from his only opportunity of making the gods' acquaintance. This feeling, forced on us we know not whence, that by obstinately believing that there are gods (although not to do so would be so easy both for our logic and our life) we are doing the universe the deepest service we can, seems part of the living essence of the religious hypothesis. If the hypothesis *were* true in all its parts, including this one, then pure intellectualism, with its veto on our making willing advances, would be an absurdity; and some participation of our sympathetic nature would be logically required. I, therefore, for one, cannot see my way to accepting the agnostic rules for truth-seeking, or wilfully agree to keep my willing nature out of the game. I cannot do so for this plain reason, that *a rule of thinking which would absolutely prevent me from acknowledging certain kinds of truth if those kinds of truth were really there, would be an irrational rule.* That for me is the long and short of the formal logic of the situation, no matter what the kinds of truth might materially be.

I confess I do not see how this logic could be escaped. But sad experience makes me fear that some of you may still shrink from radically saying with me, *in abstracto*, that we have the right to believe at our own risk any hypothesis that is live enough to tempt our will. I suspect, however, that if this is so, it is because you have got away from the abstract logical point of view altogether, and are thinking (perhaps without realizing it) of some particular religious hypothesis which for you is dead. The freedom to 'believe what we will' you apply to the case of some patent superstition; and the faith you think of is the faith defined by the schoolboy when he said 'Faith is when you believe something that you know ain't true.' I can only repeat that this is misapprehension. *In concreto*, the freedom to believe can only cover living options which the intellect of the individual cannot by itself resolve; and living options never seem absurdities to him who has them to consider. When I look at the religious question as it really puts itself to concrete men, and when I think of all the possibilities which both practically and theoretically it involves, then this command that we shall put a stopper on our heart, instincts, and courage, and wait – acting of course meanwhile more or less as if religion were *not* true[1] – till doomsday, or till such time as our intellect and senses working together may have taken in evidence enough, – this command, I say, seems to me the queerest idol ever manufactured in the philosophical cave. Were we scholastic absolutists, there might be more excuse. If we had an infallible intellect with its objective certitudes, we might feel ourselves disloyal to such a perfect organ of knowledge in not trusting to it exclusively, in not waiting for its releasing word. But if we are empiricists, if we believe that no bell in us tolls to let us know for certain when truth is in our grasp, then it seems a piece of idle fantasticality to preach so solemnly our duty of waiting for the bell. Indeed we *may* wait if we will, – I hope you do not think that I am denying that, – but if we do so, we do so at our peril as much as if we believed. In either case we *act*, taking our life in our hands. No one of us ought to issue vetoes to the other, nor should we bandy words of abuse. We ought, on the contrary, delicately and profoundly to respect one another's mental freedom: then only shall we bring about the intellectual republic; then only shall we have that spirit of inner tolerance without which all our outer tolerance is soulless, and which is empiricism's glory; then only shall we live and let live, in speculative as well as practical things.

I began by a reference to Fitz-James Stephen; let me end by a quotation from him. 'What do you think of yourself? What do you think of the world?...These are questions with which all must deal as it seems good to them. They are riddles of

---

[1] *Since belief is measured by action, he who forbids us to believe religion to be true, necessarily also forbids us to act as we should if we did believe it to be true. The whole defence of religious faith hinges upon action. If the action required or inspired by the religious hypothesis is in no way different from that dictated by the naturalistic hypothesis, then religious faith is a pure superfluity, better pruned away, and controversy about its legitimacy is a piece of idle trifling, unworthy of serious minds. I myself believe, of course, that the religious hypothesis gives to the words an expression which specifically determines our reactions, and makes them in a large part unlike what they might be on a purely naturalistic scheme of belief.

the Sphinx and in some way or other we must deal with them...In all important transactions of life we have to take a leap in the dark...If we decide to leave the riddles unanswered, that is a choice; if we waver in our answer, that, too, is a choice but whatever choice we make, we make it at our peril. If a man chooses to turn his back altogether on God and the future, no one can prevent him; no one can show beyond reasonable doubt that he is mistaken. If a man thinks otherwise and acts as he thinks, I do not see that anyone can prove that *he* is mistaken. Each must act as he thinks best; and if he is wrong, so much the worse for him. We stand on a mountain pass in the midst of whirling snow, and blinding mist, through which we get glimpses now and then of paths which may be deceptive. If we stand still we shall be frozen to death. If we take the wrong road we shall be dashed to pieces. We do not certainly know whether there is any right one. What must we do? "Be strong and of a good courage." Act for the best, hope for the best, and take what comes...If death ends all, we cannot meet death better.'[1]

10   The Meaning of Religious Language: John Wisdom, *Gods**

A study of our previous extracts shows there are two very different ways of approaching the claims of religion: logical analysis and the scrutiny of evidence on the one hand, and, on the other, an emphasis on faith, passion and the will to believe. Philosophy of religion in the twentieth century has further explored these two paths, with, on the one hand, debates on the verifiability of religious doctrines and the rational justification for belief in God, and, on the other hand, attempts to understand religious theory and practice as an entirely different enterprise from what is done in the objective world of scientific theory. Particularly influential in connection with the latter route has been the work of Ludwig Wittgenstein which emphasizes the importance of religion not as a set of quasi-scientific doctrines, but as a *form of life*. The following extract, from the Cambridge philosopher John Wisdom, takes a similar line in arguing that religious claims should not be construed as referring to experimental issues, but should be assessed in terms of the differences they make to the life of the believer.

Wisdom likens religious disputes to the conflicts that arise in aesthetic appreciation, when two people differ as to the beauty of a work of art. In another comparison (much discussed since) he describes two people returning to a long-neglected garden: one expresses his appreciation for the beauty and order found there by talking of an invisible gardener who tends it, while the other rejects such talk. Although nothing experimental can settle the issue, 'with [the] difference in what they say about the gardener goes a difference in how they feel towards the garden, in spite of the fact that neither expects anything of it which the other does not expect'. Towards the end of the paper Wisdom refers to Freudian theory, with its suggestion that religious talk is merely a projection of internal feelings and infantile fantasies. But the issue ultimately hinges on more than merely subjective feelings. Ancient talk of gods, of mysterious presences outside us, may have been ways of expressing truths about the good that can inform and enrich our lives. The great artists, says Wisdom, do not speak to us only of 'fairylands'

[1] *Liberty, Equality, Fraternity* (2nd edn, London, 1874), p. 353.
* John Wisdom, 'Gods', *Proceedings of the Aristotelian Society*, 45 [1944–5], 185–206; considerably abridged.

but of how it is possible to achieve 'exhilaration without anxiety, peace without boredom'. This is not only a different approach to religious language from that taken in the intellectual debates featured in many of our previous readings; it is also striking that the tone of the discussion itself, the way of philosophizing about religion, has undergone a marked shift. The aim is to engage the reader by poetic and persuasive language, by literary allusion, by direct appeal to a cultural tradition which continues to influence our lives, even though we can no longer construe it as making verifiable claims about the world.

To its opponents, there appears a risk that this kind of approach involves abandoning that linguistic and logical precision that is the essence of sound philosophy. To its supporters, the appeal to the manifold richness and complexity of our ways of describing the human predicament need not necessarily imply an abandonment of rational debate; as Wisdom himself puts it, 'if we say... that...a difference as to the existence of a God is not...experimental and therefore not as to the facts, we must not forthwith assume that there is no right and wrong about it, no rationality or irrationality, no appropriateness or inappropriateness, no procedure which tends to settle it.'

 The existence of God is not an experimental issue in the way it was. An atheist or agnostic might say to a theist 'You still think there are spirits in the trees, nymphs in the streams, a God of the world.' He might say this because he noticed the theist in time of drought pray for rain and make a sacrifice and in the morning look for rain. But disagreement about whether there are gods is now less of this experimental or betting sort than it used to be. This is due in part, if not wholly, to our better knowledge of why things happen as they do.

It is true that even in these days it is seldom that one who believes in God has no hopes or fears which an atheist has not. Few believers now expect prayer to still the waves, but some think it makes a difference to people and not merely in ways the atheist would admit. Of course with people, as opposed to waves and machines, one never knows what they won't do next, so that expecting prayer to make a difference to them is not so definite a thing as believing in its mechanical efficacy. Still, just as primitive people pray in a business-like way for rain, so some people still pray for others with a real feeling of doing something to help. However, in spite of this persistence of an experimental element in some theistic belief, it remains true that Elijah's method on Mount Carmel of settling the matter of what god or gods exist would be far less appropriate today than it was then.

Belief in gods is not merely a matter of expectation of a world to come. Someone may say 'The fact that a theist no more than an atheist expects prayer to bring down fire from heaven or cure the sick does not mean that there is no difference between them as to the facts; it does not mean that the theist has no expectations different from the atheist. For very often those who believe in God believe in another world and believe that God is there and that we shall go to that world when we die.'

This is true, but I do not want to consider here expectations as to what one will see and feel after death nor what sort of reasons these logically unique expectations could have. So I want to consider those theists who do not believe in a future life, or rather, I want to consider the differences between atheists and theists in so far as these differences are not a matter of belief in a future life.

What are these differences? And is it that theists are superstitious or that atheists are blind? A child may wish to sit a while with his father and he may, when he has done what his father dislikes, fear punishment and feel distress at causing vexation, and while his father is alive he may feel sure of help when danger threatens and feel that there is sympathy for him when disaster has come. When his father is dead he will no longer expect punishment or help. Maybe for a moment an old fear will come or a cry for help escape him, but he will at once remember that this is no good now. He may feel that his father is no more until perhaps someone says to him that his father is still alive though he lives now in another world and one so far away that there is no hope of seeing him or hearing his voice again. The child may be told that nevertheless his father can see him and hear all he says. When he has been told this the child will still fear no punishment nor expect any sign of his father, but now, even more than he did when his father was alive, he will feel that his father sees him all the time and will dread distressing him and when he has done something wrong he will feel separated from his father until he has felt sorry for what he has done. Maybe when he himself comes to die he will be like a man who expects to find a friend in the strange country where he is going, but even when this is so, it is by no means all of what makes the difference between a child who believes that his father lives still in another world and one who does not.

Likewise one who believes in God may face death differently from one who does not, but there is another difference between them besides this. This other difference may still be described as belief in another world, only this belief is not a matter of expecting one thing rather than another here or hereafter, it is not a matter of a world to come but of a world that now is thought beyond our senses.

We are at once reminded of those other unseen worlds which some philosophers 'believe in' and others 'deny', while non-philosophers unconsciously 'accept' them by using them as models with which to 'get the hang of' the patterns in the flux of experience. We recall the timeless entities whose changeless connections we seek to represent in symbols, and the values which stand firm amidst our flickering satisfaction and remorse, and the physical things which, though not beyond the corruption of moth and rust, are yet more permanent than the shadows they throw upon the screen before our minds. We recall, too, our talk of souls and of what lies in their depths and is manifested to us partially and intermittently in our own feelings and the behaviour of others. The hypothesis of mind, of other human minds and of animal minds, is reasonable because it explains for each of us why certain things behave so cunningly all by themselves unlike even the most ingenious machines. Is the hypothesis of minds in flowers and trees reasonable for like reasons? Is the hypothesis of a world mind reasonable for like reasons – someone who adjusts the blossom to the bees, someone whose presence may at times be felt – in a garden in high summer, in the hills when clouds are gathering, but not, perhaps, in a cholera epidemic? . . .

Let us now approach these same points by a different road. How it is that an explanatory hypothesis, such as the existence of God, may start by being experimental and gradually become something quite different can be seen from the following story:

Two people return to their long-neglected garden and find among the weeds a few of the old plants surprisingly vigorous. One says to the other 'It must be that a gardener has been coming and doing something about these plants.' Upon inquiry they find that no neighbour has ever seen anyone at work in their garden. The first man says to the other 'He must have worked while people slept.' The other says 'No, someone would have heard him and besides, anybody who cared about the plants would have kept down these weeds.' The first man says 'Look at the way these are arranged. There is purpose and a feeling for beauty here. I believe that someone comes, someone invisible to mortal eyes. I believe that the more carefully we look the more we shall find confirmation of this.' They examine the garden ever so carefully and sometimes they come on new things suggesting that a gardener comes and sometimes they come on new things suggesting the contrary and even that a malicious person has been at work. Besides examining the garden carefully they also study what happens to gardens left without attention. Each learns all the other learns about this and about the garden. Consequently, when after all this, one says 'I still believe a gardener comes' while the other says 'I don't', their different words now reflect no difference as to what they have found in the garden, no difference as to what they would find in the garden if they looked further and no difference about how fast untended gardens fall into disorder. At this stage, in this context, the gardener hypothesis has ceased to be experimental, the difference between one who accepts and one who rejects it is now not a matter of the one expecting something the other does not expect. What is the difference between them? The one says 'A gardener comes unseen and unheard. He is manifested only in his works with which we are all familiar', the other says 'There is no gardener', and with this difference in what they say about the gardener goes a difference in how they feel towards the garden, in spite of the fact that neither expects anything of it which the other does not expect.

But is this the whole difference between them – that the one calls the garden by one name and feels one way towards it, while the other calls it by another name and feels in another way towards it? And if this is what the difference has become then is it any longer appropriate to ask 'Which is right?' or 'Which is reasonable?'

And yet surely such questions *are* appropriate when one person says to another 'You still think the world's a garden and not a wilderness, and that the gardener has not forsaken it' or 'You still think there are nymphs of the streams, a presence in the hills, a spirit of the world.' Perhaps when a man sings 'God's in His heaven' we need not take this as more than an expression of how he feels. But when Bishop Gore or Dr Joad write about belief in God and young men read them in order to settle their religious doubts the impression is not simply that of persons choosing exclamations with which to face nature and the 'changes and chances of this mortal life'. The disputants speak as if they are concerned with a matter of scientific fact, or of trans-sensual, trans-scientific and metaphysical fact, but still of fact and still a matter about which reasons for and against may be offered, although no scientific reasons in the sense of field surveys for fossils or experiments on delinquents are to the point...

Suppose two people are looking at a picture or natural scene. One says 'Excellent' or 'Beautiful' or 'Divine', the other says 'I don't see it'. He means he doesn't see the beauty. And this reminds us of how we felt the theist accuse the atheist of blindness and the atheist accuse the theist of seeing what isn't there. And yet surely each sees what the other sees. It isn't that one can see part of the picture which the other can't see. So the difference is in a sense not one as to the facts. And so it cannot be removed by the one disputant discovering to the other what so far he hasn't seen. It isn't that the one sees the picture in a different light and so, as we might say, sees a different picture. Consequently the difference between them cannot be resolved by putting the picture in a different light. And yet surely this is just what can be done in such a case – not by moving the picture but by talk perhaps. To settle a dispute as to whether a piece of music is good or better than another we listen again, with a picture we look again. Someone perhaps points to emphasize certain features and we see it in a different light. Shall we call this 'field work' and 'the last of observation' or shall we call it 'reviewing the premises' and 'the beginning of deduction . . .'?

And if we say as we did at the beginning that when a difference as to the existence of a God is not one as to future happenings then it is not experimental and therefore not as to the facts, we must not forthwith assume that there is no right and wrong about it, no rationality or irrationality, no appropriateness or inappropriateness, no procedure which tends to settle it, *nor even that this procedure is in no sense a discovery of new facts.* After all even in science this is not so. Our two gardeners even when they had reached the stage when neither expected any experimental result which the other did not, might yet have continued the dispute, each presenting and representing the features of the garden favouring his hypothesis, that is, fitting his model for describing the accepted fact; each emphasizing the pattern he wishes to emphasize. True, in science, there is seldom or never a pure instance of this sort of dispute, for nearly always with difference of hypothesis goes some difference of expectation as to the facts. But scientists argue about rival hypotheses with a vigour which is not exactly proportioned to difference in expectations of experimental results.

The difference as to whether a God exists involves our feelings more than most scientific disputes and in this respect is more like a difference as to whether there is beauty in a thing.

The Connecting Technique. Let us consider again the technique used in revealing or proving beauty, in removing a blindness, in inducing an attitude which is lacking, in reducing a reaction that is inappropriate . . . Imagine that a man picks up some flowers that lie half withered on a table and gently puts them in water. Another man says to him 'You believe flowers feel'. He says this although he knows that the man who helps the flowers doesn't expect anything of them which he himself doesn't expect; for he himself expects the flowers to be 'refreshed' and to be easily hurt, injured, I mean, by rough handling, while the man who puts them in water does not expect them to whisper 'Thank you'. The Sceptic says 'You believe flowers feel' because something about the way the other man lifts the flowers and puts them in water suggests an attitude to the flowers which he feels inappropriate although perhaps he would not feel it inappropriate to butterflies. He feels that this attitude to flowers is somewhat crazy *just as it is sometimes felt that a lover's attitude is somewhat crazy even when this is not a matter of his having false hopes about how the person he is in love with will act.* It is often said in such cases that reasoning is useless. But the very person who says this feels that the lover's attitude is crazy, is inappropriate like some dreads and hatreds, such as some horrors of enclosed places. And often one who says 'It is useless to reason' proceeds at once to reason with the lover, nor is this reasoning always quite without effect. We may draw the lover's attention to certain things done by her he is in love with and trace for him a path to these from things done by others at other times which have disgusted and infuriated him. And by this means we may weaken his admiration and confidence, make him feel it unjustified and arouse his suspicion and contempt and make him feel our suspicion and contempt reasonable. It is possible, of course, that he has already noticed the analogies, the connections, we point out and that he has accepted them – that is, he has not denied them nor passed them off. He has recognized them and they have altered his attitude, altered his love, but he still loves. We then feel that perhaps it is we who are blind and cannot see what he can see.

What happens, what should happen, when we inquire in this way into the reasonableness, the propriety of belief in the Gods?... What are the stories of the gods? What are our feelings when we believe in God? They are feelings of awe before power, dread of the thunderbolts of Zeus, confidence in the everlasting arms, unease beneath the all-seeing eye. They are feelings of guilt and inescapable vengeance, of smothered hate and of a security we can hardly do without. We have only to remind ourselves of these feelings and the stories of the gods and goddesses and heroes in which these feelings find expression, to be reminded of how we felt as children to our parents and the big people of our childhood. Writing of a first telephone call from his grandmother, Proust says: '... it was rather that this isolation of the voice was like a symbol, a presentation, a direct consequence of another isolation, that of my grandmother, separated for the first time in my life, from myself. The orders or prohibitions which she addressed to me at every moment in the ordinary course of my life, the tedium of obedience or the fire of rebellion which neutralized the affection that I felt for her were at this moment eliminated... "Granny!" I cried to her... but I had beside me only that voice, a phantom, as unpalpable as that which would come to revisit me when my grandmother was dead. "Speak to me!" but then it happened that, left more solitary still, I ceased to catch the sound of her voice. My grandmother could no longer hear me... I continued to call her, sounding the empty night, in which I felt that her appeals also must be straying. I was shaken by the same anguish which, in the distant past, I had felt once before, one day when, a little child, in a crowd, I had lost her.'...

When a man's father fails him by death or weakness, how much he needs another father, one in the heavens with whom is 'no variableness nor shadow of turning'... Freud says: 'The ordinary man cannot imagine this Providence in any other form but that of a greatly exalted father, for only such a one could understand the needs of the sons of men, or be softened by their prayers and be placated by the signs of their remorse. The whole thing is so patently infantile, so incongruous with reality...' 'So incongruous with reality'! It cannot be denied.

But here a new aspect of the matter may strike us. For the very facts which make us feel that now we can recognize systems of superhuman, subhuman, elusive, beings for what they are – the persistent projections of infantile phantasies – include facts which make these systems less fantastic. What are these facts? They are patterns in human reactions which are well described by saying that we are as if there were hidden within us powers, persons, not ourselves and stronger than ourselves. That this is so may perhaps be said to have been common knowledge yielded by ordinary observation of people, but we did not know the degree in which this is so until recent study of extraordinary cases in extraordinary conditions had revealed it. I refer, of course, to the study of multiple personalities and the wider studies of psycho-analysts. Even when the results of this work are reported to us, that is not the same as tracing the patterns in the details of the cases on which the results are based; and even that is not the same as taking part in the studies oneself. One thing not sufficiently realized is that some of the things shut within us are not bad but good.

Now the gods, good and evil and mixed, have always been mysterious powers outside us rather than within. But they have also been within. It is not a modern theory but an old saying that in each of us a devil sleeps. Eve said: 'The serpent beguiled me.' Helen says to Menelaus:

> ...And yet how strange it is!
> I ask not thee; I ask my own sad thought,
> What was there in my heart, that I forgot
> My home and land and all I loved, to fly
> With a strange man? Surely it was not I,
> But Cypris there![1]

Elijah found that God was not in the wind, nor in the thunder, but in a still small voice. The kingdom of Heaven is within us, Christ insisted, though usually about the size of a grain of mustard seed, and he prayed that we should become one with the Father in Heaven.

New knowledge made it necessary either to give up saying 'The sun is sinking' or to give the words a new meaning. In many contexts we preferred to stick to the old words and give them a new meaning which was not entirely new, but, on the contrary, *practically* the same as the old. The Greeks did not speak of the dangers of repressing instincts, but they did speak of the dangers of thwarting Dionysos, of neglecting Cypris for Diana, of forgetting Poseidon for Athena. We have eaten of the fruit of a garden we cannot forget, though we were never there, a garden we still look for though we can never find it...

The artists who do most for us don't tell us only of fairylands. Proust, Manet, Breugel, even Botticelli and Vermeer, show us reality. And yet they give us for a moment exhilaration without anxiety, peace without boredom. And those who, like Freud, work in a different way against that which too often comes over us and forces us into deadness or despair,[2] also deserve critical, patient and courageous attention. For they too work to release us from human bondage into human freedom.

Many have tried to find ways of salvation. The reports they bring back are always incomplete and apt to mislead even when they are not in words but in music or paint. But they are by no means useless; and not the worst of them are those which speak of oneness with God. But in so far as we become one with Him He becomes one with us. St John says he is in us as we love one another.

This love, I suppose, is not benevolence but something that comes of the oneness with one another of which Christ spoke.[3] Sometimes it momentarily gains strength.[4] Hate and the Devil do too. And what is oneness without otherness?

[1] *Euripides, *The Trojan Women*, trans. Gilbert Murray.
[2] Matthew Arnold, *Summer Night*.
[3] *St John 16: 21.
[4] *'The Harvesters', in Kenneth Grahame, *The Golden Age*.

11   God's Commands as the Foundation for Morality: Robert M. Adams, *Moral Arguments for Theistic Belief* *

Our next extract, by the distinguished American metaphysician and philosopher of religion Robert Adams, takes the form of an argument for God's existence based on the nature of right and wrong. Adams's first premise is that there are certain truths about moral rightness and wrongness that we accept without hesitation – for example that wanton cruelty is wrong. Second, such truths are *objective* facts (they are not just a function of personal preference or inclination);[1] and, third, they are *non-natural* facts (that is, they are not reducible to empirical truths of the kind that could be established by physics, or biology or psychology).[2] The best explanation for the existence of facts of this kind, Adams argues, is the existence of God – or more specifically, the theory that 'moral rightness and wrongness consist in agreement and disagreement, respectively, with the will or commands of a loving God.'

Adams then discusses three prominent objections to such a theory.

(1) In the first place, surely people can use terms like 'right' and 'wrong' without believing in God? Adams agrees, but points out that his theory is not meant to be an account of the *meaning* of the words 'right' and 'wrong'; rather, the theory is supposed to explain the true nature of rightness and wrongness – in somewhat similar fashion to how a scientific theory explains the true nature of heat, for example, in terms of molecular motion. It is no objection to such a scientific theory that people use the word 'hot' without having any idea of molecular motion. Similarly, Adams's divine command account is an explanatory theory of rightness and wrong-

ness, not an analysis of the way these terms are used in ordinary speech.

(2) The second objection discussed by Adams relates to an ancient problem known to philosophers as the 'Euthyphro' dilemma (named after a dialogue of Plato where the issue was first raised). The dilemma asks: is something right just because God commands it; or is it the other way round – does God command it because it is right? The first alternative seems to make morality arbitrary (could pointless or cruel acts, for example, become right merely in virtue of a divine order to perform them?). But the second alternative appears to make rightness something that is prior to, or independent of, God's commands. Either way, the divine command theory seems unsatisfactory. Adams focuses on the first horn of the dilemma, and points out that his theory identifies rightness with agreement with, and wrongness with being contrary to, the commands of a *loving* God. A loving God would not command wanton cruelty, so it would not be wrong to disobey a supposed 'divine commandment' to be wantonly cruel. Yet what if God does not exist – is not cruelty still wrong? This, Adams argues, is no problem for his position: if God does not exist, then the divine command theory is false, but in that case one may fall back on one of the other rival theories that aim to explain the wrongness of cruelty. (Although such theories are less satisfactory on Adams's view, they are still more plausible than denying cruelty is wrong).

(3) Finally, Adams considers the objection that the benefits of the divine command theory

---

* Robert M. Adams, 'Moral Arguments for Theistic Belief', section I. Originally published in C. F. Delaney (ed.), *Rationality and Religious Belief* (Notre Dame, Ind.: University of Notre Dame Press, 1979), and repr. in R. M. Adams, *The Virtue of Faith* (Oxford: Oxford University Press, 1987), ch. 10.

[1] This premise, though it has strong support nowadays among both theistic and non-theistic philosophers, is not universally accepted: compare for example David Hume's view that morality is based ultimately on feelings or sentiments (see introduction to Part VIII, extract 4).

[2] This premise too is not universally accepted; compare John Stuart Mill's theory that rightness can be explained in empirical and psychological terms as the property of promoting happiness (see Part VIII, extract 6, below).

can be secured without positing God, by modifying it as follows: an action is right if it *would* agree with the demands of a loving God, if one existed. This would be rather like identifying the moral point of view with the perspective of an 'ideal observer' (whether or not such an observer actually exists). Adams's objection to this modification is that it is not easy to determine what a loving God *would* command, were he to exist. The question, Adams argues, could only be settled either conceptually or causally. But we cannot appeal to causal laws if we are dealing with a 'counterfactual' (i.e. non-existent) entity. And on the conceptual side, many ethical controversies (for example about whether we may sacrifice some people to increase the happiness of others)

surely cannot be settled by simply analysing the concept of love, or of deity.

Like much contemporary philosophy of religion, Adams's paper can seem intricate and technical in its detail, but the details repay careful study, since (as with most good philosophy) the main building blocks of the argument correspond to simple and clear intuitions which are widely shared. In linking the existence of God to central questions about the nature of morality, the paper shows that religious belief is not something to be placed in an isolated compartment, but can profitably be scrutinized with respect to its explanatory power, and how well it coheres (or fails to cohere) with one's wider philosophical outlook.

Let us begin with one of the most obvious, though perhaps never the most fashionable, arguments: an Argument from the Nature of Right and Wrong. We believe quite firmly that certain things are morally right and others are morally wrong (for example, that it is wrong to torture another person to death just for fun). Questions may be raised about the nature of that which is believed in these beliefs: what does the rightness or wrongness of an act consist in? I believe that the most adequate answer is provided by a theory that entails the existence of God – specifically, by the theory that moral rightness and wrongness consist in agreement and disagreement, respectively, with the will or commands of a loving God. One of the most generally accepted reasons for believing in the existence of anything is that its existence is implied by the theory that seems to account most adequately for some subject matter. I take it, therefore, that my metaethical views provide me with a reason of some weight for believing in the existence of God.

Perhaps some will think it disreputably 'tender-minded' to accept such a reason where the subject matter is moral. It may be suggested that the epistemological status of moral beliefs is so far inferior to that of physical beliefs, for example, that any moral belief found to entail the existence of an otherwise unknown object ought simply to be abandoned. But in spite of the general uneasiness about morality that pervades our culture, most of us do hold many moral beliefs with almost the highest degree of confidence. So long as we think it reasonable to argue at all from grounds that are not absolutely certain, there is no clear reason why such confident beliefs, in ethics as in other fields, should not be accepted as premises in arguing for the existence of anything that is required for the most satisfactory theory of their subject matter.

The divine command theory of the nature of right and wrong combines advantages not jointly possessed by any of its non-theological competitors. These advantages are sufficiently obvious that their nature can be indicated quite briefly to persons familiar with the metaethical debate, though they are also so controversial that it would take a book-length review of the contending theories to defend my claims. The first advantage of divine command metaethics is that it presents facts of moral rightness and wrongness as objective, non-natural facts – objective in the sense that whether they obtain or not does not depend on whether any human being thinks they do, and non-natural in the sense that they cannot be stated entirely in the language of physics, chemistry, biology and human or animal psychology. For it is an objective but not a natural fact that God commands, permits or forbids something. Intuitively this is an advantage. If we are tempted to say that there are only natural facts of right and wrong, or that there are no objective facts of right and wrong at all, it is chiefly because we have found so much obscurity in theories about objective, non-natural ethical facts. We seem not to be acquainted with simple, non-natural ethical properties of the intuitionists,[1] and we do not understand what a Platonic Form of the Good or the Just would be.[2] The second advantage of divine command metaethics is that it is relatively intelligible. There are certainly difficulties in the notion of a divine command, but at least it provides us more clearly with matter for thought than the intuitionist and Platonic conceptions do...

What we cannot avoid discussing, and at greater length than the advantages, are the alleged disadvantages of divine command metaethics. The advantages may be easily recognized, but the disadvantages are generally thought to be decisive. I have argued elsewhere, in some detail, that they are not decisive. Here let us concentrate on three objections that are particularly important for the present argument.

(1) In accordance with the conception of metaethics as analysis of the meanings of terms, a divine command theory is often construed as claiming that 'right' means commanded (or permitted) by God, and that 'wrong' means forbidden by God. This gives rise to the objection that people who do not believe that there exists a God to command or forbid still use the terms 'right' and 'wrong', and are said (even by theists) to believe that certain actions are right and others wrong. Surely those atheists do not mean by 'right' and 'wrong' what the divine command theory seems to say they must mean. Moreover, it may be objected that any argument for the existence of God from the premise that certain actions are right and others wrong will be viciously circular if that premise means that certain actions are commanded or permitted by God and others forbidden by God.

One might reply that it is not obviously impossible for someone to disbelieve something that is analytically implied by something else that he asserts. Nor is it impossible for the conclusion of a perfectly good, non-circular argument to be analytically implied by its premises. But issues about the nature of conceptual analysis, and of circularity in argument, can be avoided here. For in the present argument, a divine command theory need not be construed as saying that the existence of God is analytically implied by ascriptions of rightness and wrongness. It can be construed as proposing an answer to a question left open by the meaning of 'right' and 'wrong', rather than as a theory of the meaning of those terms. The ordinary meanings of many terms that signify properties, such as 'hot' and 'electrically charged', do not contain enough information to answer all questions about the nature (or even in some cases the identity) of the properties signified. Analysis of the meaning of 'wrong' might show, for example, that 'Nuclear deterrence is wrong' ascribes to nuclear deterrence a property about which the speaker may be certain of very little except that it belongs, independently of his views, to many actions that he opposes, such as torturing people just for fun. The analysis of meaning need not

[1] Compare Part VIII, extract 9, below.
[2] Compare introduction to Part II, extract 1, above.

completely determine the identity of this property, but it may still be argued that a divine command theory identifies it most adequately.

(2) The gravest objection to the more extreme forms of divine command theory is that they imply that if God commanded us, for example, to make it our chief end in life to inflict suffering on other human beings, for no other reason than that he commanded it, it would be wrong not to obey. Finding this conclusion unacceptable, I prefer a less extreme, or modified, divine command theory, which identifies the ethical property of wrongness with the property of being contrary to the commands of a loving God. Since a God who commanded us to practise cruelty for its own sake would not be a loving God, this modified divine command theory does not imply that it would be wrong to disobey such a command.

But the objector may continue his attack: 'Suppose that God did not exist, or that he existed but did not love us. Even the modified divine command theory implies that in that case it would not be wrong to be cruel to other people. But surely it would be wrong.'

The objector may have failed to distinguish sharply two claims he may want to make: that some acts *would* be wrong even if God *did* not exist, and that some acts *are* wrong even if God *does* not exist. I grant the latter. Even if divine command metaethics is the best theory of the nature of right and wrong, there are other theories which are more plausible than denying that cruelty is wrong. If God does not exist, my theory is false, but presumably the best alternative to it is true, and cruelty is still wrong.

But suppose there is in fact a God – indeed a loving God – and that the ethical property of wrongness is the property of being forbidden by a loving God. It follows that no actions would be wrong in a world in which no loving God existed, if 'wrong' designates rigidly (that is, in every possible world) the property that it actually designates.[1] For no actions would have that property in such a world. Even in a world without God, however, the best remaining alternative to divine command metaethics might be correct in the following way. In such a world there could be people very like us who would say truly, 'Kindness is right', and 'Cruelty is wrong'. They would be speaking about kindness and cruelty, but not about rightness and wrongness. That is, they would not be speaking about the properties that are rightness and wrongness, though they might be speaking about properties (perhaps natural properties) that they would be calling 'rightness' and 'wrongness'. But they would be using the words 'right' and 'wrong' with the same meaning as we actually do. For the meaning of the words, I assume, leaves open some questions about the identity of the properties they designate ...

(3) It may be objected that the advantages of the divine command theory can be obtained without an entailment of God's existence. For the rightness of an action might be said to consist in the fact that the action would agree with the commands of a loving God if one existed, or does so agree if a loving God exists. This modification transforms the divine command theory into a non-naturalistic form of the ideal observer theory of the nature of right and wrong. It has the advantage of identifying rightness and wrongness with properties that actions could have even if God does not exist. And of course it takes away the basis of my metaethical argument for theism.

The flaw in this theory is that it is difficult to see what is supposed to be the force of the counterfactual conditional that is centrally involved in it. If there is no loving God, what makes it the case if there were one, he would command this rather than that?

---

[1] For rigid designation, see Part III, extract 12, above.

Without an answer to this question, the crucial counterfactual lacks a clear sense . . . I can see only two possible answers: either that what any possible loving God would command is logically determined by the concept of a loving God, or that it is determined by a causal law. Neither answer seems likely to work without depriving the theory of some part of the advantages of divine command metaethics.

No doubt some conclusions about what he would not command follow *logically* or analytically from the concept of a loving God. He would not command us to practise cruelty for its own sake, for example. But in some cases, at least, in which we believe the act is wrong, it seems only contingent that a loving God does or would frown on increasing the happiness of other people by the painless and undetected killing of a person who wants to live but who would almost certainly not live happily. Very diverse preferences about what things are to be treated as personal rights seem compatible with love and certainly with deity. Of course, you could explicitly build all your moral principles into the definition of the kind of hypothetical divine commands that you take to make facts of right and wrong. But then the fact that your principles would be endorsed by the commands of such a God adds nothing to the principles themselves; whereas, endorsement by an actual divine command would add something, which is one of the advantages of divine command metaethics.

Nor is it plausible to suppose that there are causal laws that determine what would be commanded by a loving God, if there is no God. All causal laws, at bottom, are about actual things. There are no causal laws, though there could be legends, about the metabolism of chimeras or the susceptibility of centaurs to polio. There are physical laws about frictionless motions which never occur, but they are extrapolated from facts about actual motions. And we can hardly obtain a causal law about the commands of a possible loving God by extrapolating from causal laws governing the behaviour of monkeys, chimpanzees and human beings, as if every possible God would simply be a very superior primate. Any such extrapolation, moreover, would destroy the character of the theory of hypothetical divine commands as a theory of *non-natural* facts.

Our discussion of the Argument from the Nature of Right and Wrong may be concluded with some reflections on the nature of the God in whose existence it gives us some reason to believe. (1) The appeal of the argument lies in the provision of an explanation of moral facts of whose truth we are already confident. It must therefore be taken as an argument for the existence of a God whose commands – and presumably, whose purposes and character as well – are in accord with our most confident judgements of right and wrong. I have suggested that he must be a loving God. (2) He must be an intelligent being, so that it makes sense to speak of his having a will and issuing commands. Maximum adequacy of a divine command theory surely requires that God be supposed to have enormous knowledge and understanding of ethically relevant facts, if not absolute omnipotence. He should be a God 'unto whom all hearts are open, all desires known, and from whom no secrets are hid'. (3) The argument does not seem to imply very much about God's power, however – certainly not that he is omnipotent. Nor is it obvious that the argument supports belief in the unity or uniqueness of God. Maybe the metaethical place of divine commands could be taken by the unanimous deliverances of a senate of deities, although that conception raises troublesome questions about the nature of morality or quasi-morality that must govern the relations of gods with each other.

12   Against Evidentialism: Alvin Plantinga, *Is Belief in God Properly Basic?**

Is belief in God intellectually responsible? Those who answer 'yes' have traditionally offered arguments and evidence to support God's existence (some of these have figured in our preceding extracts), while the critics have attacked the arguments as insufficient or flawed. Both sides in the debate seem to agree on the premise that theistic belief is respectable only if there is good *evidence* for it. Yet our final extract, by the leading American philosopher of religion Alvin Plantinga, strikes a distinctive note by arguing that this premise is false.

To make his case against 'evidentialism', Plantinga uncovers a fundamental assumption of traditional 'foundationalist' epistemology, namely that I am normally justified in believing a proposition only if I rationally believe some *other* proposition, which provides support for it. Yet since this supporting process cannot go on for ever, the chain of justification must stop with some foundational beliefs that are properly regarded as *basic*. The propositions that *two plus one makes three*, or that *I now have a mild pain in my knee*, are basic in this sense – I rightly accept them, but not on the basis of deriving them from any further propositions.

The belief in God, Plantinga now argues, is itself properly basic. It is rather like the proposition that I see a tree in front of me, or that my friend who is crying out after breaking his leg is in pain, or that I remember what I had for breakfast this morning: these are all propositions I am in certain circumstances perfectly justified in believing, even though I do not derive them from other beliefs I hold.[1]

The crucial point Plantinga makes about such beliefs is that even though they are not derived from evidence in the normal sense, that does not mean they are arbitrary or gratuitous. When I am looking at the tree, my belief that there is a tree before me is entirely appropriate and responsible, given the conditions and circumstances I am in – namely that I am standing right in front of it. By the same token, Plantinga argues, there are 'many conditions and circumstances that call forth belief in God'; these include feelings of 'guilt, gratitude, danger, a sense of God's presence, a sense that he ... is speaking to me', and so on. So the belief in God is not groundless – far from it; it is just that it does not have to be *argued for*, as the conclusion of a chain of reasoning, or as an inference from other evidence. The belief is basic – and what is more it is quite properly basic, so it cannot be attacked as intellectually irresponsible.

Critics have objected that if Plantinga is allowed belief in God as basic, then others could claim similar status for all sorts of weird beliefs – for example the belief that the Great Pumpkin returns every Halloween. But Plantinga denies he is in trouble here. What is at stake in the critics' objection are the criteria or standards for basicness (or 'basicality'). Yet in the first place, Plantinga questions whether 'one must have such a criterion before one can sensibly make judgements about proper basicality' (in other words, my knowing something as basic does not depend on my being able to specify the standards for basicness). In the second place, he argues that if there are such criteria, they must be established inductively, 'from below rather than from above' – in other words, by examining relevant examples. Now religious sceptics may well agree with their opponents about some of the examples of basic belief (for example that there is a tree in front of me), but may go on to question the religious person's examples (such as his sense of God's presence in the world). But Plantinga responds

* Alvin Plantinga, 'Is Belief in God Properly Basic?', *Nous*, 15 (1981), 41–51; abridged.
[1] Cf. Part I, extract 10, above. For discussion of the foundationalist (as opposed to 'coherentist') approach to theory of knowledge, see Part I, extract 11, above. Elsewhere, Plantinga argues that his case against evidentialism can be directed against coherentists as well as foundationalists; see 'Coherentism and the Evidentialist Objection to Belief in God' in R. Audi and W. Wainwright (eds), *Rationality, Religious Belief, and Moral Commitment* (Ithaca, NY: Cornell University Press, 1986).

by asking, 'Must my criteria, or those of the Christian community, conform to their [the sceptics'] examples?' And he concludes, 'The Christian community is responsible to its set of examples, not to theirs.'

An opponent might object here that the Christian examples of basicness Plantinga cites (like sensing God's presence in the world) are far removed from the normally accepted cases of basicness: a belief is typically allowed to be basic only when it is self-evident (like 'two plus two makes four'), or incorrigible[1] (like 'I am in pain'). But Plantinga ingeniously counters that this type of criticism presupposes the rule that *being self-evident or incorrigible are necessary for basicness*; yet for the critics to insist on this rule as a basic requirement would lead them into incoherence, since the rule itself is not either self-evident or incorrigible.

Plantinga's position, which continues to generate fierce debate, seems a fitting place to bring our survey of influential texts in philosophy of religion to a close. For supporters and critics alike, it illustrates how closely the problems of religious belief are bound up with fundamental questions about the nature of human knowledge that are in one way or another central to all philosophical inquiry.

 Many philosophers have urged the evidentialist objection to theistic belief; they have argued that belief in God is irrational or unreasonable or not rationally acceptable or intellectually irresponsible or noetically substandard, because, as they say, there is insufficient evidence for it. Many other philosophers and theologians – in particular, those in the great tradition of natural theology – have claimed that belief in God is intellectually acceptable, but only because the fact is there is sufficient evidence for it. These two groups unite in holding that theistic belief is rationally acceptable only if there is sufficient evidence for it. More exactly, they hold that a person is rational or reasonable in accepting theistic belief only if she has sufficient evidence for it – only if, that is, she knows or rationally believes some other propositions which support the one in question, and believes the latter on the basis of the former... [T]he evidentialist objection is rooted in classical foundationalism, an enormously popular picture or total way of looking at faith, knowledge, justified belief, rationality and allied topics. This picture has been widely accepted ever since the days of Plato and Aristotle; its near relatives, perhaps, remain the dominant ways of thinking about these topics.

We may think of the classical foundationalist as beginning with the observation that some of one's beliefs may be based upon others; it may be that there are a pair of propositions A and B such that I believe A on the basis of B. Although this relation isn't easy to characterize in a revealing and non-trivial fashion, it is nonetheless familiar. I believe that the word 'umbrageous' is spelled u-m-b-r-a-g-e-o-u-s: this belief is based on another belief of mine: the belief that that's how the dictionary says it's spelled. I believe that $72 \times 71 = 5112$. This belief is based upon several other beliefs I hold: that $1 \times 72 = 72$; $7 \times 2 = 14$; $7 \times 7 = 49$; $49 + 1 = 50$; and others. Some of my beliefs, however, I accept but don't accept on the basis of any other beliefs. Call these beliefs basic. I believe that $2 + 1 = 3$, for example, and don't believe it on the basis of other propositions. I also believe that I am seated at my desk, and that there is a mild pain in my right knee. These too are basic to me; I don't believe them on the basis of any other propositions. According to the classical foundationalist, some propositions are properly or rightly basic for a person and some are not. Those

---

[1] Incapable of being false if sincerely uttered.

that are not are rationally accepted only on the basis of evidence, where the evidence must trace back, ultimately, to what is properly basic. The existence of God, furthermore, is not among the propositions that are properly basic; hence a person is rational in accepting theistic belief only if he has evidence for it.

Now many Reformed[1] thinkers and theologians have rejected natural theology (thought of as the attempt to provide proofs or arguments for the existence of God). They have held not merely that the proffered arguments are unsuccessful, but that the whole enterprise is in some way radically misguided ... What these Reformed thinkers really mean to hold, I think, is that belief in God need not be based on argument or evidence from other propositions at all. They mean to hold that the believer is entirely within his intellectual rights in believing as he does even if he doesn't know of any good theistic argument (deductive or inductive), even if he doesn't believe that there is any such argument and even if in fact no such argument exists. They hold that it is perfectly rational to accept belief in God without accepting it on the basis of any other beliefs or propositions at all. In a word, they hold that belief in God is properly basic. In this paper I shall try to develop and defend this position.

But first we must achieve a deeper understanding of the evidentialist objection. It is important to see that this contention is a *normative* contention. The evidentialist objector holds that one who accepts theistic belief is in some way irrational or noetically substandard. Here 'rational' and 'irrational' are to be taken as normative or evaluative terms; according to the objector, the theist fails to measure up to a standard he ought to conform to. There is a right way and a wrong way with respect to belief as with respect to actions; we have duties, responsibilities, obligations with respect to the former just as with respect to the latter. So Professor Blanshard:

everywhere and always belief has an ethical aspect. There is such a thing as a general ethics of the intellect. The main principle of that ethic I hold to be the same inside and outside religion. This principle is simple and sweeping: Equate your assent to the evidence.[2]

... The evidentialist objection therefore presupposes some view as to what sorts of propositions are correctly, or rightly, or justifiably taken as basic; it presupposes a view as to what is properly basic. And the minimally relevant claim for the evidentialist objector is that belief in God is not properly basic ... What might be the objections to the Reformed view that belief in God is properly basic?

I've heard it argued that if I have no evidence for the existence of God, then, if I accept that proposition, my belief will be groundless, or gratuitous, or arbitrary. I think this is an error; let me explain. Suppose we consider perceptual beliefs, memory beliefs and beliefs which ascribe mental states to other persons: such beliefs as

(1) I see a tree,
(2) I had breakfast this morning,
(3) That person is angry.

---

[1] The reference is to the tradition going back to the Reformation, especially John Calvin (1509–64).

[2] *Brand Blanshard, *Reason and Belief* (London: Allen & Unwin, 1974), p. 401. [Compare the introduction to extract 9, above.]

Although beliefs of this sort are typically and properly taken as basic, it would be a mistake to describe them as groundless. Upon having experience of a certain sort, I believe that I am perceiving a tree. In the typical case I do not hold this belief on the basis of other beliefs; it is nonetheless not groundless. My having that characteristic sort of experience...plays a crucial role in the formation and justification of that belief. We might say this experience, together, perhaps, with other circumstances, is what justifies me in holding it; this is the ground of my justification, and, by extension, the ground of the belief itself.

If I see someone displaying typical pain behaviour, I take it that he or she is in pain. Again, I don't take the displayed behaviour as evidence for that belief; I don't infer that belief from others I hold; I don't accept it on the basis of other beliefs. Still, my perceiving the pain behaviour plays a unique role in the formation and justification of that belief; as in the previous case, it forms the ground of my justification for the belief in question. The same holds for memory beliefs. I seem to remember having breakfast this morning; that is, I have an inclination to believe the proposition that I had breakfast, along with a certain past-tinged experience that is familiar to all but hard to describe...In this case as in the others, however, there is a justifying circumstance present, a condition that forms the ground of my justification for accepting the memory belief in question.

In each of these cases, a belief is taken as basic, and in each case properly taken as basic. In each case there is some circumstance or condition that confers justification; there is a circumstance that serves as the *ground* of justification. In each case there will be some true proposition of the sort

(4) In condition C, S is justified in taking p as basic.

Of course C will vary with p. For a perceptual judgement such as

(5) I see a rose-coloured wall before me,

C will include my being appeared to in a certain fashion. No doubt C will include more. If I'm appeared to in the familiar fashion but know that I'm wearing rose-coloured glasses, or that I am suffering from a disease that causes me to be thus appeared to, no matter what the colour of the nearby objects, then I'm not justified in taking (5) as basic. Similarly for memory. Suppose I know that my memory is unreliable; it often plays me tricks. In particular, when I seem to remember having breakfast, then, more often than not, I haven't had breakfast. Under these conditions I am not justified in taking it as basic that I had breakfast, even though I seem to remember that I did.

So being appropriately appeared to, in the perceptual case, is not sufficient for justification; some further condition – a condition hard to state in detail – is clearly necessary. The central point, here, however, is that a belief is properly basic only in certain conditions; these conditions are, we might say, the ground of its justification and, by extension, the ground of the belief itself. In this sense, basic beliefs are not, or are not necessarily, groundless beliefs. Now similar things may be said about belief in God. When the Reformers claim that this belief is properly basic, they do not mean to say, of course, that there are no justifying circumstances for it, or that it is in that sense groundless or gratuitous. Quite the contrary. Calvin holds that God 'reveals and daily discloses himself to the whole workmanship of the universe', and the divine 'reveals itself in the innumerable and yet distinct and well-ordered variety of the heavenly host'. God has so created us that we have a tendency or disposition to see his hand in the world about us. More precisely, there is in us a disposition to believe propositions of the sort *this flower was created by God* or *this vast and intricate universe was created by God* when we contemplate the flower or behold the starry heavens or think about the vast reaches of the universe.

Calvin recognizes, at least implicitly, that other sorts of conditions may trigger this disposition. Upon reading the Bible, one may be impressed with a deep sense that God is speaking to him. Upon having done what I know is cheap, or wrong, or wicked I may feel guilty in God's sight and form the belief God disapproves of what I've done. Upon confession and repentance, I may feel forgiven, forming the belief God forgives me for what I've done. A person in grave danger may turn to God, asking for his protection and help; and of course he or she then forms the belief that God is indeed able to hear and help if he sees fit. When life is sweet and satisfying, a spontaneous sense of gratitude may well up within the soul; someone in this condition may thank and praise the Lord for his goodness, and will of course form the accompanying belief that indeed the Lord is to be thanked and praised.

There are therefore many conditions and circumstances that call forth belief in God: guilt, gratitude, danger, a sense of God's presence, a sense that he speaks, perception of various parts of the universe. A complete job would explore the phenomenology of all these conditions and of more besides. This is a large and important topic; but here I can only point to the existence of these conditions. Of course none of the beliefs I mentioned a moment ago is the simple belief that God exists. What we have instead are such beliefs as

(6)   God is speaking to me,
(7)   God has created all this,
(8)   God disapproves of what I have done,
(9)   God forgives me, and
(10) God is to be thanked and praised.

These propositions are properly basic in the right circumstances. But it is quite consistent with this to suppose that the proposition there is such a person as God is neither properly basic nor taken as basic by those who believe in God. Perhaps what they take as basic are such propositions as (6)–(10), believing in the existence of God on the basis of propositions such as those. From this point of view, it isn't exactly right to say that it is belief in God that is properly basic; more exactly, what are properly basic are such propositions as (6)–(10), each of which self-evidently entails that God exists. It isn't the relatively high level and general proposition *God exists* that is properly basic, but instead propositions detailing some of his attributes or actions.

Suppose we return to the analogy between belief in God and belief in the existence of perceptual objects, other persons and the past. Here too it is relatively specific and concrete propositions rather than their more general and abstract colleagues that are properly basic. Perhaps such items as

(11) There are trees,
(12) There are other persons,

and

(13) The world has existed for more than 5 minutes,

are not in fact properly basic; it is instead such propositions as

(14) I see a tree,
(15) That person is pleased,

and

(16) I had breakfast more than an hour ago,

that deserve that accolade. Of course propositions of the latter sort immediately and self-evidently entail propositions of the former sort; and perhaps there is thus no harm in speaking of the former as properly basic, even though so to speak is to speak a bit loosely.

The same must be said about belief in God. We may say, speaking loosely, that belief in God is properly basic; strictly speaking, however, it is probably not that proposition but such propositions as (6)–(10) that enjoy that status. But the main point, here, is that belief in God, or (6)–(10), are properly basic; to say so, however, is not to deny that there are justifying conditions for these beliefs, or conditions that confer justification on one who accepts them as basic. They are therefore not groundless or gratuitous.

A second objection I've often heard: if belief in God is properly basic, why can't just any belief be properly basic? Couldn't we say the same for any bizarre aberration we can think of? What about voodoo or astrology? What about the belief that the Great Pumpkin returns every Halloween? Could I properly take that as basic? And if I can't, why can I properly take belief in God as basic? Suppose I believe that if I flap my arms with sufficient vigour I can take off and fly about the room; could I defend myself against the charge of irrationality by claiming this belief is basic? If we say that belief in God is properly basic, won't we be committed to holding that just anything, or nearly anything, can properly be taken as basic, thus throwing wide the gates to irrationalism and superstition? Certainly not. What might lead one to think the Reformed epistemologist is in this kind of trouble? The fact that he rejects the criteria for proper basicality purveyed by classical foundationalism? But why should that be thought to commit him to such tolerance of irrationality? . . .

But what then is the problem? Is it that the Reformed epistemologist not only rejects those criteria for proper basicality, but also seems in no hurry to produce what he takes to be a better substitute? If he has no such criterion, how can he fairly reject belief in the Great Pumpkin as properly basic?

This objection betrays an important misconception. How do we rightly arrive at or develop criteria for . . . justified belief, or proper basicality? Where do they come from? Must one have such a criterion before one can sensibly make any judgements – positive or negative – about proper basicality? Surely not. Suppose I don't know of a satisfactory substitute for the criteria proposed by classical foundationalism; I am nevertheless entirely within my rights in holding that certain propositions are not properly basic in certain conditions. Some propositions seem self-evident when in fact they are not ... Nevertheless it would be irrational to take as basic the denial of a proposition that seems self-evident to you. Similarly, suppose it seems to you that you see a tree; you would then be irrational in taking as basic the proposition that you don't see a tree, or that there aren't any trees ...

And this raises an important question ... What is the status of criteria for know-ledge, or proper basicality, or justified belief? Typically, these are universal statements. The modern foundationalist's criterion for proper basicality, for example, is doubly universal:

(18) For any proposition A and person S, A is properly basic for S if and only if A is incorrigible for S or self-evident to S.

But how could one know a thing like that? What are its credentials? Clearly enough, (18) isn't self-evident or just obviously true. But if it isn't, how does one arrive at it? What sorts of arguments would be appropriate? Of course a foundationalist might find (18) so appealing, he simply takes it to be true, neither offering argument for it, nor accepting it on the basis of other things he believes. If he does so, however, his noetic structure will be self-referentially incoherent. (18) itself is neither self-evident nor incorrigible; hence in accepting (18) as basic, the modern foundationalist violates the condition of proper basicality he himself lays down in accepting it. On the other hand, perhaps the foundationalist will try to produce some argument for it from premises that are self-evident or incorrigible: it is exceedingly hard to see, however, what such an argument might be like. And until he has produced such argument what shall the rest of us do – we who do not find (18) at all obvious or compelling? How could he use (18) to show us that belief in God, for example, is not properly basic? Why should we believe (18), or pay it any attention?

The fact is, I think, that neither (18) nor any other revealing necessary and sufficient condition for proper basicality follows from clearly self-evident premises by clearly acceptable arguments. And hence the proper way to arrive at such a criterion is, broadly speaking, inductive. We must assemble examples of beliefs and conditions such that the former are obviously properly basic in the latter, and examples of beliefs and conditions such that the former are obviously *not* properly basic in the latter. We must then frame hypotheses as to the necessary and sufficient conditions of proper basicality and test those hypotheses by reference to those examples. Under the right conditions, example, it is clearly rational to believe that you see a human person before you: a being who has thoughts and feelings, who knows and believes things, who makes decisions and acts. It is clear, furthermore, that you are under no obligation to reason to this belief from others you hold; under those conditions that belief is properly basic for you. But then (18) must be mistaken; the belief in question, under those circumstances, is properly basic, though neither self-evident nor incorrigible for you. Similarly, you may seem to remember that you had breakfast this morning, and perhaps you know of no reason to suppose your memory is playing you tricks. If so, you are entirely justified in taking that belief as basic.

Of course it isn't properly basic on the criterion offered by classical foundationalists; but that fact counts not against you but against those criteria.

Accordingly, criteria for proper basicality must be reached from below rather than above; they should not be presented as *ex Cathedra*, but argued to and tested by a relevant set of examples. But there is no reason to assume, in advance, that everyone will agree on the examples. The Christian will of course suppose that belief in God is entirely proper and rational; if he doesn't accept this belief on the basis of other propositions, he will conclude that it is basic for him and quite properly so. Followers of Bertrand Russell and Madelyn Murray O'Hare may disagree, but how is that relevant? Must my criteria, or those of the Christian community, conform to their examples? Surely not. The Christian community is responsible to its set of examples, not to theirs.

Accordingly, the Reformed epistemologist can properly hold that belief in the Great Pumpkin is not properly basic, even though he holds that belief in God is properly basic and even if he has no full-fledged criterion of proper basicality. Of course he is committed to supposing that there is a relevant difference between belief in God and belief in the Great Pumpkin, if he holds that the former but not the latter is properly basic. But this should prove no great embarrassment; there are plenty of candidates. These candidates are to be found in the neighbourhood of the conditions I mentioned in the last section that justify and ground belief in God. Thus, for example, the Reformed epistemologist may concur with Calvin in holding that God has implanted in us a natural tendency to see his hand in the world around us; the same cannot be said for the Great Pumpkin, there being no Great Pumpkin and no natural tendency to accept beliefs about the Great Pumpkin.

By way of conclusion...then: being self-evident, or incorrigible or evident to the senses is not a necessary condition of proper basicality. Furthermore, one who holds that belief in God is properly basic is not thereby committed to the idea that belief in God is groundless or gratuitous or without justifying circumstances. And even if he lacks a general criterion of proper basicality, he is not obliged to suppose that just any or nearly any belief – belief in the Great Pumpkin, for example – is properly basic. Like everyone should, he begins with examples; and he may take belief in the Great Pumpkin as a paradigm of irrational basic belief.

Specimen Questions

1   Explain Anselm's argument for God's existence, showing how it depends on the premise that to exist in reality is greater than to exist in the mind alone. Is the premise acceptable?

2   Expound and critically assess any one of Aquinas's five proofs of the existence of God.

3   Evaluate Descartes's argument that since I am imperfect I could not have within me the idea of a perfect being unless it were placed in my mind by God.

4   What is Pascal's wager? Do you agree that betting on the existence of God is the most prudent option?

5 Critically discuss Leibniz's attempts to show the presence of evil in the world is compatible with the existence of a wholly good and wise creator.

6 Are Hume's criticisms of the argument from design decisive?

7 Evaluate Hume's claim that there could never be sound evidence for belief in miracles.

8 What does Kierkegaard mean by saying that 'truth is subjectivity'? Is his approach to the meaning and truth of religious claims persuasive?

9 Critically discuss James's thesis that 'our passional nature not only lawfully may, but must, decide an option between propositions, whenever it is a genuine option that cannot by its nature be decided on intellectual grounds'.

10 Can the answers to religious questions be determined in the way scientific or experimental issues are? If the answer, as Wisdom suggests, is no, in what sense can it be proper or reasonable to have religious beliefs?

11 Does Adams succeed in showing that rightness and wrongness can be identified with agreement or disagreement with the commands of a loving God?

12 Can we hold any belief, including a religious belief, without evidence? Discuss with reference to Plantinga's conception of 'properly basic beliefs'.

Suggestions for Further Reading

Note: the readings below are divided into sections for the reader's convenience, but there is considerable overlap; many of the general books listed contain discussions of several of the topics included in this Part of the volume.

Anselm and the ontological argument

Anselm, *Proslogion*, trans. M. J. Charlesworth (Oxford: Clarendon, 1965). Contains the original Latin text and translation, and a detailed philosophical commentary.

For an excellent survey of the arguments of Anselm and other philosophers and theologians of the period, see F. Copleston, *A History of Philosophy* (Garden City, NY: Doubleday, 1962), vol. II.

For Descartes's version of the argument, see R. Descartes, *Meditations on First Philosophy* [*Meditationes de Prima Philosophia*, 1641], trans. J. Cottingham (Cambridge: Cambridge University Press, 1986), Meditation V.

For Kant's criticisms of the argument, see I. Kant, *Critique of Pure Reason* [*Kritik der reinen Vernunft*, 1781; 2nd edn 1787], trans. N. Kemp Smith (London: Macmillan, 1964), A592 ff.; B620 ff.

Two useful anthologies of papers dealing with the argument (including modern versions of it) are A. Plantinga (ed.), *The Ontological Argument* (Garden City, NY: Doubleday, 1965), and J. Hick and A. C. McGill (eds), *The Manyfaced Argument* (New York: Macmillan, 1967).

Aquinas and the five ways

For the Latin text, translation and very thorough analysis and criticism of all five arguments, see A. Kenny, *The Five Ways* (London: Routledge, 1969).

A clear general summary is given in Copleston (see under Anselm above). A lucid and readable introduction to Aquinas's thought, including the five ways, is B. Davies, *Aquinas* (London: Continuum, 2002). See also R. Pasnau and C. Shields, *The Philosophy of Aquinas* (Boulder, Colo.: Westview, 2003).

For a detailed study of the metaphysical framework of Aquinas's thought, see the essay by

J. Wippel in N. Kretzman and E. Stump, *The Cambridge Companion to Aquinas* (Cambridge: Cambridge University Press, 1993).

For the argument from contingency, see the debate between Bertrand Russell and Frederick Copleston, reprinted in B. Brody (ed.), *Readings in the Philosophy of Religion* (Englewood Cliffs, NJ: Prentice-Hall, 1974).

The arguments of Aquinas are also discussed in A. G. N. Flew, *God and Philosophy* (London: Hutchinson, 1966); E. Gilson, *Elements of Christian Philosophy* (Garden City, NY: Doubleday, 1960).

Descartes

See readings on Descartes at end of Part I, above. The books by Cottingham, Kenny, Williams and Wilson listed all contain discussions of the trademark argument; see also J.-M. Beyssade, 'The Idea of God and the Proofs of His Existence', in Cottingham (ed.), *The Cambridge Companion to Descartes* (Cambridge: Cambridge University Press, 1993).

Pascal and the wager

Pascal, B., *Pensées* ['Thoughts', 1670], ed. L. Lafuma (Paris: Seuil, 1962). For an English version with introduction, see B. Pascal, *Pensées* trans. A. J. Krailsheimer (Harmondsworth: Penguin, 1966).

For philosophical analysis of the wager argument, see Antony Flew, 'Is Pascal's Wager a Safe Bet?', in A. G. N. Flew (ed.), *God, Freedom and Immortality* (Buffalo, NY: Prometheus, 1984); see also W. Lycan and G. Schlesinger, 'You Bet Your Life: Pascal's Wager Defended', in J. Feinberg (ed.), *Reason and Responsibility* (7th edn, Belmont, Calif.: Wadsworth, 1989).

Leibniz and the problem of evil

Leibniz, G. W., *Theodicy* [1710], trans. D. Allen (New York: Bobbs-Merrill, 1966).

For some general books on Leibniz, see the readings listed at the end of Part I.

For an overview of the argument of the *Theodicy*, see ch. 5 of J. Cottingham, *The Rationalists* (Oxford: Oxford University Press, 1988).

Detailed philosophical discussion of the problem of evil may be found in A. Plantinga, *God, Freedom and Evil* (New York: Harper & Row, 1974); A. Flew and A. C. MacIntyre (eds), *New*

Essays in Philosophical Theology (New York: Macmillan, 1955); J. Mackie, *The Miracle of Theism* (Oxford: Clarendon, 1982), ch. 9; E. Stump and M. Murray (eds), *Philosophy of Religion* (Oxford: Blackwell, 1999), Part 3.

The argument from design

Hume, D., *Dialogues concerning Natural Religion* [published posthumously, 1777], in *The Philosophical Works of David Hume* (Edinburgh: Black & Tait, 1876), vol. II. A paperback edition is available with introduction by D. Aitken (New York: Haffner, 1958).

Paley, W., *Natural Theology* [1802]. The famous passage comparing the universe to a watch is reproduced in W. L. Rowe and W. J. Wainwright (eds), *The Philosophy of Religion* (New York: Harcourt Brace Jovanovich, 1973).

For philosophical criticism of the argument from design, see the books by Mackie, Flew and Plantinga listed under Leibniz, above; see also J. Hick, *The Existence of God* (New York: Macmillan, 1964).

Hume on miracles

Hume, D., *An Enquiry concerning Human Understanding* [1748], section X. The full text may be found in the edition of L. A. Selby-Bigge, 3rd edn, rev. P. H. Nidditch (Oxford: Clarendon, 1975).

For other important texts on miracles, see R. Swinburne (ed.), *Miracles* (London: Macmillan, 1989).

For some useful essays on the topic of revelation, see S. Hook (ed.), *Religious Experience and Truth* (New York: New York University Press, 1961).

See also B. Mitchell (ed.), *Faith and Logic* (London: Allen & Unwin, 1957); C. S. Lewis, *Miracles* (London: Macmillan, 1963).

Kierkegaard, existentialism and truth as subjectivity

Kierkegaard, S., *Concluding Unscientific Postscript* [*Afsluttende Uvidenskabelig Efterskrift*, 1846], trans. D. F. Swenson (Princeton: Princeton University Press, 1941).

An engaging introduction to Kierkegaard and other existentialist thinkers is W. Barrett, *Irrational Man* (London: Heinemann, 1961). For detailed analysis and discussion of

Kierkegaard's position, see R. M. Adams, 'Kierkegaard's Arguments against Objective Reasoning in Religion', *Monist*, 60 (1977), 213–28.

James and the will to believe

James, W., *The Will to Believe and Other Essays in Popular Philosophy* (New York: Longmans Green, 1897), ch. 1. In direct opposition to James, see W. K. Clifford, *The Ethics of Belief* (London: Macmillan, 1901).

For critical discussion of James's views on belief, see P. Naknikian, *An Introduction to Philosophy* (New York: Knopf, 1967).

For a useful introduction to the pragmatist approach to belief and truth, see J. E. Smith, *Purpose and Thought: The Meaning of Pragmatism* (London: Hutchinson, 1978).

Wisdom and the meaning of religious language

Wisdom, J., 'Gods' [1944–5], repr. in *Philosophy and Psychoanalysis* (Oxford: Blackwell, 1953).

A critical discussion of Wisdom's gardener parable may be found in A. Flew, 'Theology and Falsification', in B. Mitchell (ed.), *The Philosophy of Religion* (London: Methuen, 1971).

For Wittgenstein's views on language, see L. Wittgenstein, *Philosophical Investigations* (Oxford: Blackwell, 1968). For their application to religious language, see C. Barrett, *Wittgenstein on Ethics and Religious Belief* (Oxford: Blackwell, 1991).

For a good introduction to the topic of the nature of religious language, see B. Davies, *An Introduction to the Philosophy of Religion* (Oxford: Oxford University Press, 1982), ch. 2.

See also D. Z. Phillips, *Religion without Explanation* (Oxford: Blackwell, 1976); C. F. Delaney (ed.), *Rationality and Religious Belief* (London and Notre Dame, Ind.: University of Notre Dame Press, 1979).

Adams and divine command theory

There is a vast literature on the relation between God and morality in general and divine command theory in particular. A valuable survey is C. Taliaferro (ed.), *Contemporary Philosophy of Religion* (Oxford: Blackwell, 1998), ch. 7.

Some influential papers are included in E. Stump and M. Murray (eds), *Philosophy of Religion: The Big Questions* (Oxford: Blackwell, 1999), Part 6; and in B. Davies (ed.), *Philosophy of Religion* (Oxford: Oxford: Oxford University Press, 2000), Part VI.

See also P. Helm (ed.), *Divine Commands and Morality* (Oxford: Oxford University Press, 1981), and J. Cottingham, *The Spiritual Dimension* (Cambridge: Cambridge University Press, 2005), ch. 3.

For a more detailed presentation of Adams's own view, see his *Finite and Infinite Goods* (Oxford: Oxford University Press, 1999).

Plantinga and basic beliefs

For an introduction to some of the issues raised by Plantinga's position, see C. Taliaferro (ed.), *Contemporary Philosophy of Religion* (Oxford: Blackwell, 1998), ch. 8.

See also K. Meeker, 'Religious Epistemology: Introduction', in W. L. Craig (ed.), *Philosophy of Religion* (Edinburgh: Edinburgh University Press, 2002), and the collection of essays (including Plantinga's own further development of his argument) in A. Plantinga and N. Wolterstorff (eds), *Faith and Rationality* (Notre Dame, Ind.: University of Notre Dame Press, 1988).

See also M. Peterson et al., *Philosophy of Religion: Selected Readings*, Part VI, and Plantinga's major study, *Warranted Christian Belief* (Oxford: Oxford University Press, 2000).

Also useful are C. F. Delaney (ed.), *Rationality and Religious Belief* (Notre Dame, Ind.: University of Notre Dame Press, 1978), and D. Hoitenga, *An Introduction to Reformed Epistemology* (Albany, NY: SUNY Press, 1983).

Other interesting work that relates the 'reformed' approach to epistemology includes N. Wolterstorff, *Reason within the Bounds of Religion* (Grand Rapids, Mich.: Eerdemans, 1984), and W. Alston, *Perceiving God* (Ithaca, NY: Cornell University Press, 1991).

For a rather different perspective see D. Z. Phillips, *Faith after Foundationalism* (London: Routledge, 1988).

PART VII

Science and Method

Science and Method
Introduction

Are the enterprises of the philosopher and the scientist distinct? In the past they were often closely intertwined, both being concerned with what there is in the world and how we are to understand it (compare introduction to Part II, above). Aristotle, one of the co-founders (with Plato) of Western philosophy, was also what we should now call a natural scientist – what used to be called a 'natural philosopher'. But although philosophy and science are closely related, they differ in focus. The philosopher of science is less occupied with the truth or falsity of particular theories than with a general investigation into the nature and justification of scientific activity itself. What is the relation between a scientific theory and the data which are supposed to confirm it? Can theories be conclusively proved (or disproved)? Can we justify the universal generalizations scientists make on the basis of necessarily limited data? What is meant by a cause, or a causal explanation? What are the respective roles of mathematical theory and empirical observation in science? Is science a 'purely rational' activity, to be assessed in terms of timeless standards of truth and validity, or can the theories of scientists only be understood within a particular historical and social context? These are some of the questions with which the philosopher of science is concerned; the extracts that follow trace some key landmarks in the quest for determining what is meant by a systematic scientific understanding of the world.

1 Four Types of Explanation: Aristotle, *Physics**

The achievements of Aristotle, both in science and in the philosophy of science, were formidably impressive and wide ranging; so much so that his ideas remained dominant throughout the Middle Ages and right up to the seventeenth century. In his *Posterior Analytics*, he laid down a model of scientific knowledge which strongly influenced subsequent thinking (see Part I, extract 3). But one of his most significant contributions, found both in his *Metaphysics* and in his *Physics* (from which our first extract is taken) was his account of what it is to *explain* something. The fourfold structure he produced is often misleadingly called Aristotle's doctrine of 'the four causes'; in fact, a better name might be 'the four "becauses"', since the account maps out four ways in which we use the term 'because', or four ways in which we answer the question 'why?'

(1) 'Why is the bridge strong?' 'Because it is made of steel and concrete.' This type of answer gives what Aristotelians call the 'material cause' – an explanation in terms of the component parts or constituent ingredients. (2) 'Why is this stuff correctly classified as salt?' 'Because it is a compound of sodium and chloride.' This gives the Aristotelian 'formal cause' – an explanation in terms of the form, definition or essential properties of something. (3) 'Why did this baseball move?' 'Because someone struck it with a bat.' This gives the 'efficient cause' – an explanation in terms of what initiated or produced the relevant movement or change. (This is the sense in which the term 'cause' is most often used nowadays.) Finally, (4) 'Why does a row of sunflowers face east in the morning and gradually turn westward during the day?' 'To maximize the exposure to sunlight.' This last answer gives the 'final cause' (from the Latin *finis*, meaning 'end' or 'goal'); the explanation specifies, as Aristotle puts it, 'that for the sake of which' something is done. Notice that Aristotle lays great stress on this last type of cause, and he views much of the natural world as operating in terms of final causes, or (to use the more common expression nowadays) 'teleologically' (from the Greek *telos*, 'end' or 'goal'). As we shall see later on, the revolution which led to the emergence of modern science saw a systematic attack on the value and importance of this type of explanation in the sciences.

In one sense ['material cause'], that out of which a thing comes to be and which persists is called a 'cause', e.g. the bronze and the silver (and the kinds of things of which they are species) are the causes of a statue and a bowl respectively.

In another sense ['formal cause'], the form or original pattern is a cause – the account of what it is to be such and such (and the kind to which it belongs); for example, the ratio of two to one (and more generally, number) is the cause of an octave.

In another sense ['efficient cause'], the primary source of something's changing (or remaining as it is) is a cause. For example, the man who has deliberated is the cause (of his actions), the father is the cause of the child, and in general what makes something is the cause of what is made, and what produces change is the cause of what is changed.

In another sense ['final cause'], the end, or 'that for the sake of which' something is done is a cause. For example, health is the cause of a walk ('Why is he taking a walk?' Answer: 'In order to be healthy' – in saying this, we think we have given the cause.)

---

* Aristotle, *Physics* [*c.*325 BC], Bk II, chs 3 and 8 (extracts). Translation taken (with adaptations) from Aristotle, *Physica*, trans. R. P. Hardie and R. K. Gaye (Oxford: Clarendon, 1930).

The same applies to all the intermediate steps which are brought about by the action of something else as a means towards the end; thus slimming, purging, drugs and surgical instruments are means towards health. All these things are 'for the sake of' the ends, though they differ from one another in that some are activities and others are instruments.

This then perhaps exhausts the number of ways in which the term 'cause' is used. As the word has several senses, it follows that one and the same thing can have several different causes (and not just incidentally). For example, both the art of the sculptor and the bronze are causes of the statue. These are causes of it not in so far as it is anything else, but causes of it *as a statue*; but they are not causes in the same way, since one is the material cause, and the other the efficient cause which is the source of the change. Some things can cause each other reciprocally; for example hard work is the cause of fitness and vice versa, but again not in the same way, since one is the cause as an end, and the other as a source of change…

But why should not nature work not *for the sake of* something, nor because it is *better* so, but just as the sky rains – not in order to make the corn grow, but out of necessity? What is drawn up must cool, and what has been cooled must become water and descend, the result of this being that the corn grows. Similarly if a man's crop is spoiled on the threshing floor, the rain did not fall 'for the sake of' this – in order that the crop might be spoiled, but the result just followed. Why then should it not be the same with the parts in nature, for example that our teeth should come up of necessity – the front teeth sharp, fitted for tearing, the molars broad and useful for grinding – not that they arose for this end, but it was merely a coincident result; and so with all the parts in which we suppose there is a purpose? Wherever all the parts came about just as they would have done if they had come to be for an end, such things survived, being organized spontaneously in a fitting way, whereas those which grew otherwise perished and continued to perish, as Empedocles says his 'man-faced ox-progeny' did.

Such are the arguments (and others of this kind) which may cause difficulty on this point. Yet it is impossible that this should be the true view. For teeth and all other natural things either invariably or normally come about in a given way; but this is not true of any of the results of chance or spontaneity. We do not ascribe to chance or mere coincidence the frequency of rain in winter, but we do just this in the case of frequent rain in summer; nor heat in the dog-days, but only if we have it in winter. If then it is agreed that things are either the result of coincidence or for an end, and these cannot be the result of coincidence of spontaneity, it follows that they must be for an end; and that such things are all due to nature even the champions of the theory under discussion would agree. Therefore action *for an end* is present in things which come to be, and are, by nature.

Further, where a series has a completion, all the previous steps are done for the sake of that. Now surely as in intelligent action, so in nature; and as in nature, so it is in each action, if nothing interferes. Now intelligent action is for the sake of an end; therefore the nature of things also is so. Thus if a house had been a thing made by nature, it would have been made in the same way as it is now by art; and if things made by nature were made also by art, they would come to be in the same way as by nature. So each step in the series is for the sake of the next; and generally art partly completes what nature cannot bring to a finish, and partly imitates her. If, therefore, artificial products are for the sake of an end, so clearly also are natural products. The relation of the latter to the earlier terms of the series is the same in both.

This is most obvious in animals other than man: they make things neither by art nor after inquiry or deliberation. Hence people discuss whether it is by intelligence or by some other faculty that these creatures work – spiders, ants and the like. By gradual advance in this direction we come to see clearly that in plants too something is produced which is conducive to the end – for example leaves grow to produce shade for the fruit. If then it is both by nature and for an end that the swallow makes its nest and the spider its web, and plants grow leaves for the sake of the fruit and send their roots down (not up) for the sake of nourishment, it is plain that this kind of cause is operative in things which come to be and are by nature. And since 'nature' means two things, the matter and the form, of which the latter is the end, the form must be the cause in the sense of 'that for the sake of which'.

Now mistakes come to pass even in the operations of art: the grammarian makes a mistake in writing and the doctor pours out the wrong dose. Hence clearly mistakes are possible in the operations of nature also. If then in art there are cases in which what is rightly produced serves a purpose, and if where mistakes occur there was a purpose in what was attempted, only it was not attained, so must it be also in natural products, and monstrosities will be failures in the purposive effort. Thus when things were originally put together, the 'ox-progeny', if they failed to reach a determinate end, must have arisen through the corruption of some principle corresponding to what is now the seed . . .

It is absurd to suppose that the purpose is not present because we do not observe the agent deliberate. Art does not deliberate. If the shipbuilding art were present in the wood, it would produce the same results by nature. Hence if purpose is present in art, it is present in nature also. The best illustration is a doctor doctoring himself: nature is like that. It is plain then, that nature is a cause, a cause that operates for a purpose.

2   Experimental Methods and True Causes: Francis Bacon, *Novum Organum**

The 'revolution' which inaugurated the modern scientific age was in fact a long and sometimes tortuous process of change in the way human beings came to understand the natural world and how it should be interpreted. One of the heralds of that revolution was the English philosopher Francis Bacon, whose *Novum Organum* (the 'New Instrument' or 'New Method') was published in Latin in 1620. The 'Organum' (or 'Organon' in Greek) was the conventional term used to refer to Aristotle's logical works, in particular his theory of the syllogism (see introduction to Part I, extract 3, above). Bacon came to believe that the traditional process of deducing results from supposedly self-evident axioms had led to little, if any, new scientific knowledge; it either merely unravelled what we already knew, or else led us astray by giving a spurious

---

* Francis Bacon, *Novum Organum* [1620], Bk I, §§ 1–3, 11–31, 36, 38–44, 46; Bk II, §§ 1–3, 11–13, 15–16. From *The Philosophical Works of Francis Bacon*, ed. J. M. Robertson, repr. from the translation of Ellis and Spedding (London: Routledge, 1905), pp. 259–66, 302–3, 307–9, 315, 320; with omissions and minor modifications.

'stability' to often confused or false assumptions. The 'understanding left to itself' is powerless to increase our knowledge; what is needed is an empirical method (based on observation) for the systematic understanding and control of nature.

Bacon sets out four *idols* or obstacles to true knowledge (the Greek term originally meant 'illusions' or 'false appearances'). The 'idols of the tribe' are the illusions stemming from human nature – our tendency to mistake the surface appearances provided by the senses (including sensory qualities like bitterness or heaviness) for the true underlying nature of things. The 'idols of the cave' reflect the private obsessions and preoccupations of individuals which may throw them off track in the search for truth. The 'idols of the market-place' are the illusions due to the use of language – our tendency to rely on specious technical terms and conventional labels which often mask the truth. And lastly the 'idols of the theatre' are the false systems of traditional philosophy to which we give undue authority.

The Aristotelian approach to science is one of Bacon's chief targets here, and he vigorously attacks the value of explanations based on 'final causes' (see previous extract). Instead Bacon proposes a thorough interrogation of nature, based on the methods of *induction*: the Table of Presence, the Table of Absence and the Table of Comparison. These are systematic and rigorous methods for precisely determining all the empirical circumstances in which a given phenomenon obtains, or is absent, or is found in different degrees. Of particular importance is the Table of Absence: humans are apt to be impressed by positive correlations, and this may lead them to generalize uncritically; hence, as Bacon acutely observes, it is 'the negative instance that has greater force'. Bacon's methods are the cornerstone for what we now think of as the scientific investigation of the natural world by careful observation and experiment. But though Bacon is often (and appropriately) called an 'empiricist', he certainly does not believe good science is merely a matter of collecting data: the results of induction are significant, for him, because they lead us towards the underlying 'Forms' of things – the 'hidden schematisms', or micro processes and configurations of matter, which are responsible for the behaviour of all observed physical phenomena.

 Man, being the servant and interpreter of Nature, can do and understand so much and so much only as he has observed in fact or in thought of the course of nature; beyond this he neither knows anything nor can do anything.

Neither the naked hand nor the understanding left to itself can effect much. It is by instruments and helps that the work is done, which are as much wanted for the understanding as for the hand. And as the instruments of hand either give motion or guide it, so the instruments of the mind supply either suggestions for the mind or cautions.

Human knowledge and human power meet in one; for where the cause is not known, the effect cannot be produced. Nature to be commanded must be obeyed...

As all the sciences we now have do not help us in finding out new works, so neither does the logic we now have help us in finding out new sciences.

The logic now in use serves rather to fix and give stability to the errors which have their foundation in commonly received notions than to help the search for truth. So it does more harm than good.

The syllogism consists of propositions, propositions consist of words, words are symbols of notions. Therefore, if the notions themselves (which is the root of the matter) are confused and over-hastily abstracted from the facts, there can be no firmness in the superstructure. Our only hope therefore lies in a true induction.

There is no soundness in our notions whether logical or physical. Substance, Quality, Passion, Essence itself, are not sound notions; much less are Heavy, Light, Dense, Rare, Moist, Dry, Generation, Corruption, Attraction, Repulsion, Element, Matter, Form, and the like. All are but fantastical and ill defined.

Our notions of less general species, as Man, Dog, Dove, and of the intermediate perceptions of the sense, as Hot, Cold, Black, White, do not materially mislead us; yet even these are sometimes confused by the flux and alteration of matter and the mixing of one thing with another. All the others which men have hitherto adopted are but wanderings, not being abstracted and formed from things by proper methods.

Nor is there less wilfulness and wandering in the construction of axioms than in the formation of notions; not excepting even those very principles which are obtained by common induction; but much more in the axioms and lower propositions educed by the syllogism.

The discoveries which have hitherto been made in the sciences are such as lie close to vulgar notions, scarcely beneath the surface. In order to penetrate into the inner and further recesses of nature, it is necessary that both notions and axioms be derived from things by a more sure and guarded way; and that a method of intellectual operation be introduced altogether better and more certain.

There are and can be only two ways of searching into and discovering truth. The one flies from the senses and particulars to the most general axioms, and from these principles, the truth of which it takes for settled and immovable, proceeds to judgement and to the discovery of middle axioms. And this way is now in fashion. The other derives axioms from the senses and particulars, rising by a gradual and unbroken ascent, so that it arrives at the most general axioms last of all. This is the true way, but as yet untried.

The understanding left to itself takes the same course (namely the former) which it takes in accordance with logical order. For the mind longs to spring up to positions of higher generality, that it may find rest there; and so after a little while wearies of experiment. But this evil is increased by logic, because of the order and solemnity of its disputations.

The understanding left to itself, in a sober, patient and grave mind, especially if it be not hindered by received doctrines, tries a little that other way, which is the right one, but with little progress; for the understanding, unless directed and assisted, is a thing unequal, and quite unfit to contend with the obscurity of things.

Both ways set out from the senses and particulars, and rest in the lightest generalities; but the difference between them is infinite. For the one just glances at experiment and particulars in passing, the other dwells duly and orderly among them. The one, again, begins at once by establishing certain abstract and useless generalities, the other rises by gradual steps to that which is prior and better known in the order of nature.

There is a great difference between the idols of the human mind and the ideas of the divine. That is to say, between certain empty dogmas, and the true signatures and marks set upon the worlds of creation as they are found in nature.

It cannot be that axioms established by argumentation should avail for the discovery of new works; for the subtlety of nature is greater many times over than the subtlety of argument. But axioms duly and orderly formed from particulars easily discover the way to new particulars, and thus render sciences active.

The axioms now in use, having been suggested by a scanty and manipular experience and a few particulars of most general occurrence, are made for the most part just large enough to fit and take these in; and therefore it is no wonder if they do not lead to new particulars. And if some opposite instance, not observed or not known before, chances to come in the way, the axiom is rescued and preserved by some frivolous distinction; whereas the truer course would be to correct the axiom itself.

The conclusions of human reasoning as ordinarily applied in matter of nature, I call for the sake of distinction *anticipations of nature* (as something rash or premature). That reason which is elicited from facts by a just and methodical process, I call *interpretation of nature.*

Anticipations are a sufficiently firm ground for consent; for even if men went mad all after the same fashion, they might agree with one another well enough.

For the winning of assent, indeed, anticipations are far more powerful than interpretations; for being collected from a few instances, and those for the most part of familiar occurrence, they straightway touch the understanding and fill the imagination; whereas interpretations on the other hand, being gathered here and there from very various and widely dispersed facts, cannot suddenly strike the understanding; and therefore they must needs, in respect of the opinions of the time, seem harsh and out of tune, much as the mysteries of faith do.

In sciences founded on opinions and dogmas, the use of anticipations and logic is good; for in them the object is to command assent to the propositions, not to master the thing.

Though all the wits of all the ages should meet together and combine and transmit their labours, yet will not great progress ever be made in science by means of anticipations; for radical errors in the first concoction of the mind are not to be cured by the excellence of subsequent functions and remedies.

It is idle to expect any great advancement in science from the superinducing and engrafting of new things upon old. We must begin anew from the very foundations, unless we would revolve for ever in a circle with mean and contemptible progress...

One method of discovery alone remains to us, which is simply this. We must lead men to the particulars themselves, and their series and order; while men on their side must force themselves for a while to lay their notions by and begin to familiarize themselves with facts...

The idols and false notions which are now in possession of the human understanding, and have taken deep root therein, not only so beset men's minds that truth can hardly find entrance, but even after entrance is obtained, they will again, in the very instauration of the sciences, meet and trouble us, unless men being forewarned of the danger fortify themselves as far as may be against their assaults.

There are four classes of idols that beset men's minds. To these for distinction's sake I have assigned names, calling the first class *Idols of the Tribe*; the second *Idols of the Cave*; the third, *Idols of the Market Place*; the fourth, *Idols of the Theatre.*

The formation of ideas and axioms by induction is without doubt the proper remedy to be applied for the keeping off and clearing away of idols. To point them out, however, is of great use; for the doctrine of idols is to the interpretation of nature what the doctrine of the refutation of sophisms is to common logic.

The *Idols of the Tribe* have their foundation in human nature itself, and in the tribe or race of men. For it is a false assertion that the sense of man is the measure of things.[1] On the contrary, all perceptions both of the sense and of the mind are according to the measure of the individual, and not according to the measure of the universe. And the human understanding is like a false mirror, which, receiving rays irregularly, distorts and discolours the nature of things by mingling its own nature with it.

The *Idols of the Cave* are the idols of the individual man. For every one (besides the errors common to human nature in general) has a cave or den of his own, which refracts and discolours the light of nature, owing either to his own proper and peculiar nature; or to his education and conversation with others; or to the reading of books and the authority of those whom he esteems and admires; or to the differences of impressions, accordingly as they take place in a mind preoccupied and predisposed or in a mind indifferent and settled; and the like. So that the spirit of man (according as it is meted out to different individuals) is in fact a thing variable and full of perturbation, and governed as it were by chance. Whence it was well observed by Heraclitus that men look for sciences in their own lesser worlds, and not in the greater or common world.

There are also idols formed by the intercourse and association of men with each other, which I call *Idols of the Market Place*, on account of the commerce and consort of men there. For it is by discourse that men associate; and words are imposed according to the apprehension of the vulgar. And therefore the ill and unfit choice of words wonderfully obstructs the understanding. Nor do the definitions or explanations, wherewith in some things learned men are wont to guard and defend themselves, by any means set the matter right. But words plainly force and overrule the understanding, and throw all into confusion, and lead men away into numberless empty controversies and idle fancies.

Last, there are idols which have immigrated into men's minds from the various dogmas of philosophies, and also from wrong laws of demonstration. These I call *Idols of the Theatre*, because in my judgement all the received systems are but so many stage-plays, representing worlds of their own creation after an unreal and scenic fashion. Nor is it only of the systems now in vogue or only of the ancient sects and philosophies that I speak; for many more plays of the same kind may yet be composed and in like artificial manner set forth, seeing that the most widely different errors have causes which are for the most part alike. Neither again do I mean this only of entire systems, but also of many principles and axioms in science which by tradition, credulity and negligence have come to be received...

The human understanding when it has once adopted an opinion (either as being the received opinion or as being agreeable to itself) draws all other things to support and agree with it. And though there be a greater number and weight of instances to be found on the other side, yet these it either neglects and despises, or else by some distinction sets aside and rejects, in order that by this great and pernicious predetermination the authority of its former conclusions may remain inviolate. And therefore it was a good answer that was made by one who, when they showed him hanging in a temple a picture of those who had paid their vows as having escaped shipwreck, and would have him say whether he did not now acknowledge the power of the

---

[1] 'Man is the measure of all things': slogan attributed to the ancient Greek sophist Protagoras (quoted by Plato in *Theaetetus*, 160d); See introduction to Part III, extract 1, above.

gods, – 'Yes', he asked again, 'but where are the pictures of those who were drowned after their vows?' And such is the way of all superstition, whether in astrology, dreams, omens, divine judgements, or the like: men, having a delight in such vanities, notice the events where they are fulfilled, but where they fail, though this happens much more often, neglect and pass them by. But this mischief insinuates itself with much more subtlety into philosophy and the sciences: here the first conclusion colours and brings into conformity with itself all that come after, though the latter may be far sounder and better. Besides, independently of that delight and vanity which I have described, it is the peculiar and perpetual error of the human intellect to be more moved and excited by affirmatives than by negatives, whereas it ought properly to hold itself indifferently disposed towards both alike. Indeed, in the establishment of any true axiom, it is the negative instance which has the greater force ...

On a given body to generate and superinduce a new nature, or new natures, is the work and aim of human power. Of a given nature to discover the form, or true specific difference, or nature-engendering nature, or source of emanation (for these are the terms which come nearest the description of the thing) is the work and aim of human knowledge. Subordinate to these primary tasks are two others that are secondary and of inferior mark: to the former, the transformation of concrete bodies, so far as this is possible; to the latter, the discovery, in every case of generation and motion, of the *latent process* carried on from the manifest efficient and the manifest material to the form which is engendered; and in like manner the discovery of the *latent configuration* of bodies at rest and not in motion.

In what an ill condition human knowledge is at the present time is apparent even from the commonly received axioms. It is a correct position that 'true knowledge is knowledge by causes'. And causes again are not improperly distributed into four kinds: the material, the formal, the efficient and the final. But of these the final cause rather corrupts than advances the sciences, except such as have to do with human action. The discovery of the formal is despaired of. The efficient and the material (as they are investigated and received, that is, as remote causes, without reference to the latent process leading to the form) are but slight and superficial, and contribute little, if anything, to true and active science...

If a man be acquainted with the cause of any nature (as whiteness or heat) in certain subjects only, his knowledge is imperfect; and if he be able to superinduce an effect on certain substances only (of those susceptible of such an effect), his power is in like manner imperfect. Now if a man's knowledge be confined to the efficient and material causes (which are unstable causes and merely vehicles, or causes which convey the form in certain cases) he may arrive at new discoveries in reference to substances in some degree similar to one another, and selected beforehand; but he does not touch the deeper boundaries of things. But whosoever is acquainted with Forms embraces the unity of nature in substances that are very dissimilar; and is able therefore to detect and bring to light things never yet done, and such as neither the vicissitudes of nature, nor industry in experimenting, nor accident itself, would ever have actualized, and which would never have occurred to the thought of man. From the discovery of the Forms, therefore, results truth in speculation and freedom in operation...

The investigation of Forms proceeds as follows. A nature being given, we must first of all have a muster or presentation before the understanding of all known instances which agree in the same nature, though they may occur in substances which are quite dissimilar. And such collection must be made in the manner of a history, without premature speculation or any great amount of subtlety... This table I call the *Table of Essence and Presence*.

Secondly, we must make a presentation to the understanding of instances in which the given nature is wanting; for the Form, as stated above, ought no less to be absent when the nature is absent than present when it is present. The negatives should therefore be subjoined to the affirmatives, and the absence of the given nature inquired of in those subjects only that are most akin to the others in which it is present and forthcoming. This I call the *Table of Deviation, or of Absence in Proximity*...

Thirdly, we must make a presentation to the understanding of instances in which the nature under inquiry is found in different degrees, more or less; which must be done by making a comparison either of its increase and decrease in the same subject, or of its amount in different subjects, as compared one with another. For since the Form of a thing is the very thing itself, and the thing differs from the form no otherwise than as the apparent differs from the real, or the external from the internal, or the thing in reference to man from the thing in reference to the universe, it necessarily follows that no nature can be taken as the true form, unless it always decreases when the nature in question decreases, and in like manner always increases when the nature in question increases. This table, therefore, I call the *Table of Degrees*, or the *Table of Comparison*...

The work and office of these three tables, I call the Presentation of Instances to the Understanding. Which presentation having been made, Induction itself must be set at work; for the problem is, upon a review of the instances, all and each, to find such a nature as is always present or absent with the given nature, and always increases and decreases with it... Now if the mind attempt this affirmatively from the first, as when left to itself it is always wont to do, the result will be fancies and guesses and notions ill defined, and axioms that must be mended every day... To God truly, the Giver and Architect of Forms, and maybe to the angels and higher intelligences, it belongs to have an affirmative knowledge of Forms immediately and from the first contemplation. But this assuredly is more than man can do, to whom it is granted only to proceed at first by negatives, and at last to end in affirmatives, after exclusion has been exhausted.

We must therefore make a complete solution and separation of nature, not indeed by fire, but by the mind, which is a kind of divine fire. The first work therefore of true induction (as far as regards the discovery of Forms) is the rejection or exclusion of the several natures which are not found in some instance where the given nature is present, or are found in some instance where the given nature is absent, or are found to increase in some instance when the given nature decreases, or to decrease when the given nature increases. Then indeed, after the rejection and exclusion has been truly made, there will remain at the bottom, all lightweight opinions vanishing into smoke, an affirmative Form, solid and true and well defined.

3   Mathematical Science and the Control of Nature: René Descartes, *Discourse on the Method**

If Bacon (see preceding extract) was one of the heralds of the modern scientific age, the role of René Descartes was even more decisive, particularly in his insistence on the importance of mathematics for physics – something Bacon had failed to see. In the following passages from Descartes's *Discourse on the Method* (published in 1637) we find a kind of manifesto for a comprehensive new science of nature based on mathematical principles. To explain the source of these principles, Descartes invokes metaphysics: the laws of nature, ordained by God, are truths of which we have innate knowledge (God has implanted 'notions' of them in our hearts). But once the mathematical principles are established, Descartes claims to be able to use them to construct a complete account of everything that occurs in nature – the workings of the entire universe, the stars and planets, and all phenomena on earth, including animal life; mathematical physics becomes the master discipline that can in principle explain everything.[1] Notice that though God is invoked as the ultimate author of the laws of nature, He is not described as intervening in the workings of the natural world.

Even if the universe began as a pure chaos, asserts Descartes, the basic laws of physics are sufficient to explain all subsequent evolutionary developments.

Two important further points emerge from what Descartes goes on to say. First, the point of the new science is not just to impart knowledge, but to give us technological control: understanding the environment and our own bodies will enable us to become 'masters and possessors of nature'. Second, there is a crucial role in science for systematic *observations* or *experiments* (Descartes's term *expériences* has the same root as the Latin verb for 'to test'). Though we can deduce certain general principles from the innate truths implanted in us by God, this only gives us a very general mathematical structure; to decide between competing hypotheses, we have to put them to the test and compare them with actually observed results. Much of this may now seem common sense; but it was Descartes's achievement to articulate clearly the requirements for progress in science, and to glimpse the enormous power which it would put into the hands of mankind.

 I would gladly go on and reveal the whole chain of other truths that I deduced from these first ones.[2] But in order to do this I would have to discuss many questions that are being debated among the learned, and I do not wish to quarrel with them. So it will be better, I think, for me not to do this, and merely to say in general what these questions are, so as to let those who are wiser decide whether it would be useful for the public to be informed more specifically about them. I have always remained firm in the resolution I had taken to assume no principle other than the one I have just used to demonstrate the existence of God and of the soul, and to

---

* René Descartes, *Discourse on the Method* [*Discourse de la Méthode*, 1637], extracts from parts v and vi. Translation from *The Philosophical Writings of Descartes*, ed. J. Cottingham, R. Stoothoff and D. Murdoch (Cambridge: Cambridge University Press, 1985), pp. 131–4, 142–4.

[1]   With the notable exception of consciousness: see Part IV, extract 4. Compare also Part II, extract 3.

[2]   Descartes refers back to his argument establishing the certainty of his own existence as a thinking being, and the existence of God. Compare the extracts above in Part I, extract 4; Part II, extract 3; Part IV, extract 4; and Part VI, extract 3.

accept nothing as true which did not seem to me clearer and more certain than the demonstrations of the geometers had hitherto seemed. And yet I venture to say that I have found a way to satisfy myself within a short time about all the principal difficulties usually discussed in philosophy. What is more, I have noticed certain laws which God has so established in nature, and of which he has implanted such notions in our minds, that after adequate reflection we cannot doubt that they are exactly observed in everything which exists or occurs in the world. Moreover, by considering what follows from these laws it seems to me that I have discovered many truths more useful and important than anything I had previously learned or even hoped to learn.

I endeavoured to explain the most important of these truths in a treatise which certain considerations prevent me from publishing, and I know of no better way to make them known than by summarizing its contents.[1] My aim was to include in it everything I thought I knew about the nature of material things before I began to write it. Now a painter cannot represent all the different sides of a solid body equally well on his flat canvas, and so he chooses one of the principal ones, sets it facing the light, and shades the others so as to make them stand out only when viewed from the perspective of the chosen side. In just the same way, fearing that I could not put everything I had in mind into my discourse, I undertook merely to expound quite fully what I understood about light. Then, as the occasion arose, I added something about the sun and fixed stars, because almost all light comes from them; about the heavens, because they transmit light; about planets, comets and the earth, because they reflect light; about terrestrial bodies in particular, because they are either coloured or transparent or luminous; and finally about man, because he observes these bodies. But I did not want to bring these matters too much into the open, for I wished to be free to say what I thought about them without having either to follow or to refute the accepted opinions of the learned. So I decided to leave our world wholly for them to argue about, and to speak solely of what would happen in a new world. I therefore supposed that God now created, somewhere in imaginary spaces, enough matter to compose such a world; that he variously and randomly agitated the different parts of this matter so as to form a chaos as confused as any the poets could invent; and that he then did nothing but lend his regular concurrence to nature, leaving it to act according to the laws he established. First of all, then, I described this matter, trying to represent it so that there is absolutely nothing, I think, which is clearer and more intelligible, with the exception of what has just been said about God and the soul. In fact I expressly supposed that this matter lacked all those forms or qualities about which they dispute in the Schools, and in general that it had only those features the knowledge of which was so natural to our souls that we could not even pretend not to know them. Further, I showed what the laws of nature were, and without basing my arguments on any principle other than the infinite perfections of God, I tried to demonstrate all those laws about which we could have any doubt, and to show that they are such that, even if God created many worlds, there could not be any in which they failed to be observed. After this, I showed how, in consequence of these laws, the greater part of the matter of this chaos had to become disposed and

---

[1] Descartes refers to his treatise on physics, *Le Monde* [1633], which he cautiously suppressed following the condemnation of Galileo.

arranged in a certain way, which made it resemble our heavens; and how, at the same time, some of its parts had to form an earth, some planets and comets, and others a sun and fixed stars. Here I dwelt upon the subject of light, explaining at some length the nature of the light that had to be present in the sun and the stars, how from there it travelled instantaneously across the immense distances of the heavens, and how it was reflected from the planets and comets to the earth. To this I added many points about the substance, position, motions and all the various qualities of these heavens and stars; and I thought I had thereby said enough to show that for anything observed in the heavens and stars of our world, something wholly similar had to appear, or at least could appear, in those of the world I was describing. From that I went on to speak of the earth in particular: how, although I had expressly supposed that God had put no gravity into the matter of which it was formed, still all its parts tended exactly towards its centre; how, there being water and air on its surface, the disposition of the heavens and heavenly bodies (chiefly the moon), had to cause an ebb and flow similar in all respects to that observed in our seas, as well as a current of both water and air from east to west like the one we observe between the tropics; how mountains, seas, springs and rivers could be formed naturally there, and how metals could appear in mines, plants grow in fields, and generally how all the bodies we call 'mixed' or 'composite' could come into being there. Among other things, I took pains to make everything belonging to the nature of fire very clearly understandable, because I know nothing else in the world, apart from the heavenly bodies, that produces light. Thus I made clear how it is formed and fuelled, how sometimes it possesses only heat without light, and sometimes light without heat; how it can produce different colours and various other qualities in different bodies; how it melts some bodies and hardens others; how it can consume almost all bodies, or turn them into ashes and smoke; and finally how it can, by the mere force of its action, form glass from these ashes – something I took particular pleasure in describing since it seems to me as wonderful a transmutation as any that takes place in nature.

Yet I did not wish to infer from all this that our world was created in the way I proposed, for it is much more likely that from the beginning God made it just as it had to be. But it is certain, and it is an opinion commonly accepted among theologians, that the act by which God now preserves it is just the same as that by which he created it. So, even if in the beginning God had given the world only the form of a chaos, provided that he established the laws of nature and then lent his concurrence to enable nature to operate as it normally does, we may believe without impugning the miracle of creation that by this means alone all purely material things could in the course of time have come to be just as we now see them. And their nature is much easier to conceive if we see them develop gradually in this way than if we consider them only in their completed form.

From the description of inanimate bodies and plants I went on to describe animals, and in particular men. But I did not yet have sufficient knowledge to speak of them in the same manner as I did of the other things – that is, by demonstrating effects from causes and showing from what seeds and in what manner nature must produce them. So I contented myself with supposing that God formed the body of a man exactly like our own both in the outward shape of its limbs and in the internal arrangement of its organs, using for its composition nothing but the matter that I had described. I supposed, too, that in the beginning God did not place in this body any rational soul or any other thing to serve as a vegetative or sensitive soul, but rather that he kindled in its heart one of those fires without light which I had already explained, and whose nature I understood to be no different from that of the fire which heats hay when it has been stored before it is dry, or which causes new wine to seethe when it is left to ferment from the crushed grapes. And when I looked to see what functions would occur in such a body I found precisely those which may occur in us without our thinking of them, and hence without any contribution from our soul (that is, from that part of us, distinct from the body, whose nature, as I have said previously, is simply to think). These functions are just the ones in which animals without reason may be said to resemble us. But I could find none of the functions which, depending on thought, are the only ones that belong to us as men; though I found all these later on, once I had supposed that God created a rational soul and joined it to this body in a particular way which I described ...

I have never made much of the products of my own mind; and so long as the only fruits I gathered from the method I use were my own satisfaction regarding certain difficulties in the speculative sciences, or else my attempts to govern my own conduct by the principles I learned from it, I did not think I was obliged to write anything about it. For as regards conduct, everyone is so full of his own wisdom that we might find as many reformers as heads if permission to institute change in these matters were granted to anyone other than those whom God has set up as sovereigns over his people or those on whom he has bestowed sufficient grace and zeal to be prophets. As regards my speculations, although they pleased me very much, I realized that other people had their own which perhaps pleased them more. But as soon as I had acquired some general notions in physics and had noticed, as I began to test them in various particular problems, where they could lead and how much they differ from the principles used up to now, I believed that I could not keep them secret without sinning gravely against the law which obliges us to do all in our power to secure the general welfare of mankind. For they opened my eyes to the possibility of gaining knowledge which would be very useful in life, and of discovering a practical philosophy which might replace the speculative philosophy taught in the schools. Through this philosophy we could know the power and action of fire, water, air, the stars, the heavens and all the other bodies in our environment as distinctly as we know the various crafts of our artisans; and we could use this knowledge – as the artisans use theirs – for all the purposes for which it is appropriate, and thus make ourselves, as it were, the lords and masters of nature. This is desirable not only for the invention of innumerable devices which would facilitate our enjoyment of the fruits of the earth and all the goods we find there, but also, and most importantly, for the maintenance of health, which is undoubtedly the chief good and the foundation of all the other goods in this life. For even the mind depends so much on the temperament and disposition of the bodily organs that if it is possible to find some means of making men in general wiser and more skilful than they have been up till now, I believe we must look for it in medicine. It is true that medicine as currently practised does not contain much of any significant use; but without intending to disparage it, I am sure there is no one, even among its practitioners, who would not admit that all we know in medicine is almost nothing in comparison with what remains to be known, and that we might free ourselves from innumerable diseases, both of the body and of the mind, and perhaps even from the infirmity of old age, if we had sufficient knowledge of their causes and of all the remedies that nature has provided. Intending as I did to devote my life to the pursuit of such indispensable knowledge, I discovered a path which would, I thought, inevitably lead one to it, unless prevented by the brevity of life or the lack of observations. And I judged that the best remedy against these two obstacles was to communicate faithfully to the public what little I had discovered, and to urge the best minds to try and make further progress by helping with the necessary observations, each according to his inclination and ability, and by communicating to the public everything they learn. Thus, by building upon the work of our predecessors and combining the lives and labours of many, we might make much greater progress working together than anyone could make on his own.

I also noticed, regarding observations, that the further we advance in our knowledge, the more necessary they become. At the beginning, rather than seeking those which are more unusual and highly contrived, it is better to resort only to those which, presenting themselves spontaneously to our senses, cannot be unknown to us if we reflect even a little. The reason for this is that the more unusual observations are apt to mislead us when we do not yet know the causes of the more common ones, and the factors on which they depend are almost always so special and so minute that it is very difficult to discern them. But the order I have adopted in this regard is the following. First I tried to discover in general the principles or first causes of everything that exists or can exist in the world. To this end I considered nothing but God alone, who created the world; and I derived these principles only from certain seeds of truth which are naturally in our souls. Next I examined the first and most ordinary effects deducible from these causes. In this way, it seems to me, I discovered the heavens, the stars, and an earth; and, on the earth, water, air, fire, minerals, and other such things which, being the most common of all and the simplest, are consequently the easiest to know. Then, when I sought to descend to more particular things, I encountered such a variety that I did not think the human mind could possibly distinguish the forms or species of bodies that are on the earth from an infinity of others that might be there if it had been God's will to put them there. Consequently I thought the only way of making these bodies useful to us was to progress to the causes by way of the effects and to make use of many special observations. And now, reviewing in my mind all the objects that have ever been present to my senses, I venture to say that I have never noticed anything in them which I could not explain quite easily by the principles I had discovered. But I must also admit that the power of nature is so ample and so vast, and these principles so simple and so general, that I notice hardly any particular effect of which I do not know at once that it can be deduced from the principles in many different ways; and my greatest difficulty is usually to discover in which of these ways it depends on them. I know no other means to discover this than by seeking further observations whose outcomes vary according to which of these ways provides the correct explanation. Moreover, I have now reached a point where I think I can see quite clearly what line we should follow in making most of the observations which serve this purpose; but I see also that they are of such a kind and so numerous that neither my dexterity nor my income (were it even a thousand times greater than it is) could suffice for all of them. And so the advances I make in the knowledge of nature will depend henceforth on the opportunities I get to make more or fewer of these observations. I resolved to make this known in the treatise I had written, and to show clearly how the public could benefit from such knowledge. This would oblige all who desire the general well-being of mankind – that is, all who are really virtuous, not virtuous only in appearance or merely in repute – both to communicate to me the observations they have already made and to assist me in seeking those which remain to be made.

4   The Limits of Scientific Explanation: George Berkeley, *On Motion**

Despite Descartes's influential vision of a complete mathematical physics (see previous extract), the actual laws of motion which he formulated were defective, and were destined to be swept away by the towering achievement of Isaac Newton, whose *Principia* ('Mathematical Principles of Natural Philosophy', 1687) laid down the famous inverse square law of universal gravitation. But although Newton articulated the principles of celestial and terrestrial mechanics in mathematical terms, many philosophers and scientists (including Newton himself) considered that mathematics alone could not explain the nature of the *force* of gravity. 'The cause of gravity,' observed Newton, 'I do not pretend to know.' In the following extract from the *De*

Motu ('On Motion'), published in 1721, the celebrated Irish philosopher George Berkeley makes a clear distinction between the province of mathematics and mechanics on the one hand, and that of metaphysics on the other. The former is a matter of formulating universal abstract laws from which we may deduce the observed motions of bodies – 'this is the sole mark at which the physicist must aim'. All too often, however, scientists invoke such notions as 'conatus', 'effort' and 'force'. Yet we can grasp such metaphysical notions, Berkeley argues, only when they are applied to animate beings; but if we attribute such powers to material things we are invoking a mysterious 'occult' property which cannot properly be understood in physical terms.

In the pursuit of truth we must beware of being misled by terms which we do not rightly understand. That is the chief point. Almost all philosophers utter the caution; few observe it. Yet it is not so difficult to observe, where sense, experience and geometrical reasoning obtain, as is especially the case in physics. Laying aside, then, as far as possible, all prejudice, whether rooted in linguistic usage or in philosophical authority, let us fix our gaze on the very nature of things. For no one's authority ought to rank so high as to set a value on his words and terms unless they are based on clear and certain fact.

The consideration of motion greatly troubled the minds of the ancient philosophers, giving rise to various exceedingly difficult opinions (not to say absurd) which have almost entirely gone out of fashion, and not being worth a detailed discussion need not delay us long. In works on motion by the more recent and

* George Berkeley, *On Motion* [*De Motu*, 1721], §§ 1–5, 11, 17–18, 26–8, 35–41, 52–3, 58, 67, 71–2. Translation by A. A. Luce, in *The Works of George Berkeley*, ed. A. A. Luce and T. E. Jessop (London: Nelson, 1948–51).

sober thinkers of our age, not a few terms of somewhat abstract and obscure signification are used, such as *solicitation of gravity, urge, dead forces,* etc., terms which darken writings in other respects very learned, and beget opinions at variance with truth and the common sense of men. These terms must be examined with great care, not from a desire to prove other people wrong, but in the interest of truth.

Solicitation and *effort* or *conation* belong properly to animate beings alone. When they are attributed to other things, they must be taken in a metaphorical sense; but a philosopher should abstain from metaphor. Besides, anyone who has seriously considered the matter will agree that those terms have no clear and distinct meaning apart from all affection of the mind and motion of the body.

While we support heavy bodies we feel in ourselves effort, fatigue and discomfort. We perceive also in heavy bodies falling an accelerated motion towards the centre of the earth; and that all the senses tell us. By reason, however, we infer that there is some cause or principle of these phenomena, and that is popularly called *gravity.* But since the cause of the fall of heavy bodies is unseen and unknown, gravity in that usage cannot properly be styled a sensible quality. It is, therefore, an occult quality. But what an occult quality is, or how any quality can act or do anything, we can scarcely conceive – indeed we cannot conceive. And so men would do better to let the occult quality go, and attend only to the sensible effects. Abstract terms (however useful they may be in argument) should be discarded in meditation, and the mind should be fixed on the particular and the concrete, that is, on the things themselves.

Force likewise is attributed to bodies; and that word is used as if it meant a known quality, and one distinct from motion, figure, and every other sensible thing and also from every affection of the living thing. But examine the matter more carefully and you will agree that such force is nothing but an occult quality. Animal effort and corporeal motion are commonly regarded as symptoms and measures of this occult quality.

Obviously then it is idle to lay down gravity or force as the principle of motion; for how could that principle be known more clearly by being styled an occult quality? What is itself occult explains nothing. And I need not say that an unknown acting cause could be more correctly styled substance than quality. Again, *force, gravity* and terms of that sort are more often used in the concrete (and rightly so) so as to connote the body in motion, the effort of resisting, etc. But when they are used by philosophers to signify certain natures carved out and abstracted from all these things, natures which are not objects of sense, nor can be grasped by any force of intellect, nor pictured by the imagination, then indeed they breed errors and confusion...

The force of gravitation is not to be separated from momentum; but there is no momentum without velocity, since it is mass multiplied by velocity; again, velocity cannot be understood without motion, and the same holds therefore of the force of gravitation. Then no force makes itself known except through action, and through action it is measured; but we are not able to separate the action of a body from its motion; therefore as long as a heavy body changes the shape of a piece of lead put under it, or of a cord, so long is it moved; but when it is at rest, it does nothing, or (which is the same thing) it is prevented from acting. In brief, those terms *dead force* and *gravitation* by the aid of metaphysical abstraction are supposed to mean something different from moving, moved, motion and rest, but, in point of fact, the supposed difference in meaning amounts to nothing at all...

Force, gravity, attraction and terms of this sort are useful for reasonings and reckonings about motion and bodies in motion, but not for understanding the simple nature of motion itself or for indicating so many distinct qualities. As for attraction, it was clearly introduced by Newton, not as a true, physical quality, but only as a mathematical hypothesis. Indeed Leibniz, when distinguishing elementary effort or solicitation from impetus, admits that those entities are not really found in nature, but have to be formed by abstraction.

A similar account must be given of the composition and resolution of any direct forces into any oblique ones by means of the diagonal and sides of the parallelogram. They serve the purpose of mechanical science and reckoning; but to be of service to reckoning and mathematical demonstrations is one thing, to set forth the nature of things is another...

Heavy bodies are borne downwards, although they are not affected by any apparent impulse; but we must not think on that account that the principle of motion is contained in them. Aristotle gives this account of the matter, 'Heavy and light things are not moved by themselves; for that would be a characteristic of life, and they would be able to stop themselves.' All heavy things by one and the same settled and constant law seek the centre of the earth, and we do not observe in them a principle or any faculty of halting that motion, of diminishing it or increasing it except in fixed proportion, or finally of altering it in any way. They behave quite passively. Again, in strict and accurate speech, the same must be said of percussive bodies. Those bodies as long as they are being moved, as also in the very moment of percussion, behave passively, exactly as when they are at rest. Inert body so acts as body moved acts, if the truth be told. Newton recognizes that fact when he says that the force of inertia is the same as impetus. But body, inert and at rest, does nothing; therefore body moved does nothing.

Body in fact persists equally in either state, whether of motion or of rest. Its existence is not called its action; nor should its persistence be called its action. Persistence is only continuance in the same way of existing which cannot properly be called action. Resistance which we experience in stopping a body in motion we falsely imagine to be its action, deluded by empty appearance. For that resistance which we feel is in fact passion in ourselves, and does not prove that the body acts, but that we are affected; it is quite certain that we should be affected in the same way, whether that body were to be moved by itself, or impelled by another principle.

Action and reaction are said to be in bodies, and that way of speaking suits the purposes of mechanical demonstrations; but we must not on that account suppose that there is some real virtue in them which is the cause or principle of motion. For those terms are to be understood in the same way as the term *attraction*; and just as attraction is only a mathematical hypothesis, and not a physical quality, the same must be understood also about action and reaction, and for the same reason. For in mechanical philosophy the truth and the use of theorems about the mutual attraction of bodies remain firm, as founded solely in the motion of bodies, whether that motion be supposed to be caused by the action of bodies mutually attracting each other, or by the action of some agent different from the bodies, impelling and controlling them. Similarly the traditional formulations of rules and laws of motions, along with the theorems thence deduced, remain unshaken, provided that sensible effects and the reasonings grounded in them are granted, whether we suppose the action itself or the force that causes these effects to be in the body or in an incorporeal agent...

The imperfect understanding of this situation has caused some to make the mistake of rejecting the mathematical principles of physics on the ground that they do not assign the efficient causes of things.[1] It is not, however, in fact the business of physics or mechanics to establish efficient causes, but only the rules of impulsions or attractions, and, in a word, the laws of motions, and from the established laws to assign the solution, not the efficient cause, of particular phenomena.

It will be of great importance to consider what properly a principle is, and how that term is to be understood by philosophers. The true, efficient and conserving cause of all things by supreme right is called their fount and principle. But the principles of experimental philosophy are properly to be called foundations and springs, not of their existence, but of our knowledge of corporeal things, both knowledge by sense and knowledge by experience, foundations on which that knowledge rests, and springs from which it flows. Similarly in mechanical philosophy those are to be called principles in which the whole discipline is grounded and contained, those primary laws of motions which have been proved by experiments, elaborated by reason and rendered universal. These laws of motion are conveniently called principles, since from them are derived both general mechanical theorems and particular explanations of the phenomena.

A thing can be said to be explained mechanically then indeed when it is reduced to those most simple and universal principles, and shown by accurate reasoning to be in agreement and connection with them. For once the laws of nature have been found out, then it is the philosopher's task to show that each phenomenon is in constant conformity with those laws, that is, necessarily follows from those principles. In that consist the explanation and solution of phenomena and the assigning their cause, i.e. the reason why they take place.

The human mind delights in extending and expanding its knowledge; and for this purpose general notions and propositions have to be formed in which particular propositions and cognitions are in some way comprised, which then, and not till then, are believed to be understood. Geometers know this well. In mechanics also notions are premised, i.e. definitions and first and general statements about motion from which afterwards by mathematical method conclusions more remote and less general are deduced. And just as, by the application of geometrical theorems, the sizes of particular bodies are measured, so also by the application of the universal theorems of mechanics, the movements of any parts of the mundane system, and the phenomena thereon depending, become known and are determined. And that is the sole mark at which the physicist must aim.

And just as geometers for the sake of their art make use of many devices which they themselves cannot describe nor find in the nature of things, even so the mechanician makes use of certain abstract and general terms, imagining in bodies force, action, attraction, solicitation, etc., which are of first utility for theories and formulations, as also for computations about motion, even if in the truth of things, and in bodies actually existing, they would be looked for in vain, just like the geometers' fictions made by mathematical abstraction.

---

[1] For efficient causes, see the introduction to extract 1 above.

We actually perceive by the aid of the senses nothing except the effects or sensible qualities and corporeal things entirely passive, whether in motion or at rest; and reason and experience advise us that there is nothing active except mind or soul. Whatever else is imagined must be considered to be of a kind with other hypotheses and mathematical abstractions. This ought to be laid to heart; otherwise we are in danger of sliding back into the obscure subtlety of the Schoolmen, which for so many ages like some dread plague, has corrupted philosophy.[1]

Mechanical principles and universal laws of motions or of nature, happy discoveries of the last century, treated and applied by aid of geometry, have thrown a remarkable light upon philosophy. But metaphysical principles and real efficient causes of the motion and existence of bodies or of corporeal attributes in no way belong to mechanics or experiment, nor throw light on them, except in so far as by being known beforehand they may serve to define the limits of physics, and in that way to remove imported difficulties and problems...

The Peripatetics[2] used to distinguish various kinds of motion corresponding to the variety of changes which a thing could undergo. Today those who discuss motion understand by the term only local motion. But local motion cannot be understood without understanding the meaning of the *locus* [place]. Now *place* is defined by moderns as 'the part of space which a body occupies', whence it is divided into relative and absolute corresponding to space. For they distinguish between absolute or true space and relative or apparent space. That is, they postulate space on all sides – measureless, immovable, insensible, permeating and containing all bodies, which they call absolute space. But space comprehended or defined by bodies, and therefore an object of sense, is called relative, apparent, vulgar space.

And so let us suppose that all bodies were destroyed and brought to nothing. What is left they call absolute space, all relation arising from the situation and distances of bodies being removed together with the bodies. Again, that space is infinite, immovable, indivisible, insensible, without relation and without distinction. That is, all its attributes are privative or negative. It seems therefore to be mere nothing. The only slight difficulty arising is that it is extended, and extension is a positive quality. But what sort of extension, I ask, is that which cannot be divided or measured, no part of which can be perceived by sense or pictured by the imagination? For nothing enters the imagination which from the nature of the things cannot be perceived by sense, since indeed the imagination is nothing else than the faculty which represents sensible things either actually existing or at least possible. Pure intellect, too, knows nothing of absolute space. That faculty is concerned only with spiritual and inextended things, such as our minds, their states, passions, virtues and such like. From absolute space then let us take away now the words of the name, and nothing will remain in sense, imagination or intellect. Nothing else then is denoted by those words than pure privation or negation, i.e. mere nothing...

[1] Schoolmen: adherents of the scholastic philosophy, based on Aristotle, which dominated universities throughout the Middle Ages. Compare introduction to extract 2, above.
[2] The followers of Aristotle.

From the foregoing it is clear that the following rules will be of great service in determining the true nature of motion: (1) to distinguish mathematical hypotheses from the natures of things; (2) to beware of abstractions; (3) to consider motion as something sensible, or at least imaginable; and to be content with relative measures. If we do so, all the famous theorems of the mechanical philosophy by which the secrets of nature are unlocked, and by which the system of the world is reduced to human calculation, will remain untouched; and the study of motion will be freed from a thousand minutiae, subtleties and abstract ideas. And let these words suffice about the nature of motion ...

It remains to discuss the cause of the communication of motions. Most people think that the force impressed on the movable body is the cause of motion in it ... It is clear ... that *force* is not something settled and determinate, from the fact that great men advance very different opinions, even contrary opinions, about it, and yet in their results attain the truth. For Newton says that impressed force consists in action alone, and is the action exerted on the body to change its state, and does not remain after the action. Torricelli contends that a certain heap or aggregate of forces impressed by percussion is received into the mobile body, and there remains and constitutes impetus. Borelli and others say much the same. But although Newton and Torricelli seem to be disagreeing with one another, they each advance consistent views, and the thing is sufficiently well explained by both. For all forces attributed to bodies are mathematical hypotheses just as are attractive forces in planets and sun. But mathematical entities have no stable essence in the nature of things; and they depend on the notion of the definer. Whence the same thing can be explained in different ways ...

In physics, sense and experience, which reach only to apparent effects, hold sway; in mechanics the abstract notions of mathematicians are admitted. In first philosophy or metaphysics we are concerned with incorporeal things, with causes, truth and the existence of things. The physicist studies the series or successions of sensible things, noting by what laws they are connected, and in what order, what precedes as cause, and what follows as effect. And on this method we say that the body in motion is the cause of motion in the other, and impresses motion on it, draws it also or impels it. In this sense second corporeal causes ought to be understood, no account being taken of the actual seat of the forces or of the active powers or of the real cause in which they are. Further, besides body, figure and motion, even the primary axioms of mechanical science can be called causes or mechanical principles, being regarded as the causes of the consequences.

Only by meditation and reasoning can truly active causes be rescued from the surrounding darkness and be to some extent known. To deal with them is the business of first philosophy or metaphysics. Allot to each science its own province; assign its bounds; accurately distinguish the principles and objects belonging to each. Thus it will be possible to treat them with greater ease and clarity.

5   The Problem of Induction: David Hume, *Enquiry concerning Human Understanding**

In the aftermath of Newton, at the very time when science was beginning to score spectacular successes in the explanation and prediction of natural phenomena, the sceptical philosopher David Hume profoundly disturbed the philosophical world by raising radical doubts about the very rationality of the scientific enterprise. Hume's starting-point was his distinction between *relations of ideas* and *matters of fact*.[1] The former class (comprising such truths as 'two and two make four', or 'all triangles are three-sided') provides truths which can be conclusively 'demonstrated', since they follow logically from the definitions of the terms involved; the latter class provides information about what actually happens in the world, where the relevant propositions are based not on demonstrative reasoning but on observation and experience. But Hume's devastating point is that experience can only assure us of what we are actually observing at present, or can remember having observed in the past. How can we reliably generalize beyond this necessarily very limited set of data? Since the ultimate causes of the phenomena we observe are, according to Hume, beyond the reach of human inquiry, we have no means of knowing that future instances will conform to our past experience.

Logical demonstration cannot come to our aid here, since there is no *contradiction* in supposing that the sun will not rise tomorrow, or that the bread that nourished me at lunchtime will not poison me at dinner. By using the methods of induction (see extract 2, above), scientists may formulate general principles about the behaviour of the solar system, or the nutritive properties of bread; they may, in other words, generalize from their limited experience of phenomena to universal claims about all phenomena, past, present and future. But this process, Hume argues, *assumes* that future instances will resemble the past. Our predictions may have turned out right before, but that is no conclusive argument that they will continue to do so: 'it is impossible that any arguments from experience can prove the resemblance of the past to the future, since all these arguments are founded on the supposition of that resemblance'. This is Hume's simple yet deeply challenging formulation of what has come to be known as the 'problem of induction': there is no rational, non-circular way for science to proceed from limited data to general conclusions about the behaviour of natural phenomena. Inductive expectations may be perfectly natural – the child who has burnt his hand in the flame 'will be careful not to put his hand near any candle' – but science seems to offer more than such brute expectation: it purports to offer us *rational argument* and *justification* for our general claims about the natural world. In the vividly rhetorical closing sentences of our extract, Hume defies us to indicate what this rational process could possibly be.

When it is asked, *What is the nature of all our reasonings concerning matters of fact?* the proper answer seems to be that they are founded on the relation of cause and effect. When again it is asked, *What is the foundation of all our reasonings and conclusions concerning that relation?* it may be replied, in one word, Experience. But if we still carry on our sifting humour, and ask *What is the foundation of all conclusions from*

---

* David Hume, *An Enquiry concerning Human Understanding* [1748], from Section IV, part 2; with minor changes and modified spelling and punctuation. Several editions of the complete text are available, including that by T. L. Beauchamp (Oxford: Oxford University Press, 1999), which contains an introduction and notes for students.

[1] Please refer to Part II, extract 7, above, which should be read in conjunction with the present extract.

experience? this implies a new question, which may be of more difficult solution and explication. Philosophers, that give themselves airs of superior wisdom and sufficiency, have a hard task when they encounter persons of inquisitive dispositions, who push them from every corner to which they retreat, and who are sure at last to bring them to some dangerous dilemma. The best expedient to prevent this confusion is to be modest in our pretensions; and even to discover the difficulty ourselves before it is objected to us. By this means, we may make a kind of merit of our very ignorance.

I shall content myself, in this section, with an easy task, and shall pretend only to give a negative answer to the question here proposed. I say then, that, even after we have experience of the operations of cause and effect, our conclusions from that experience are *not* founded on reasoning, or any process of the understanding. This answer we must endeavour both to explain and to defend.

It must certainly be allowed that nature has kept us at a great distance from all her secrets, and has afforded us only the knowledge of a few superficial qualities of objects; while she conceals from us those powers and principles on which the influence of those objects entirely depends. Our senses inform us of the colour, weight, and consistency of bread; but neither sense nor reason can ever inform us of those qualities which fit it for the nourishment and support of a human body. Sight or feeling conveys an idea of the actual motion of bodies; but as to that wonderful force or power, which would carry on a moving body for ever in a continued change of place, and which bodies never lose but by communicating it to others; of this we cannot form the most distant conception. But notwithstanding this ignorance of natural powers and principles, we always presume, when we see like sensible qualities, that they have like secret powers, and expect that effects, similar to those which we have experienced, will follow from them. If a body of like colour and consistency with that bread, which we have formerly eaten, be presented to us, we make no scruple of repeating the experiment, and foresee, with certainty, like nourishment and support. Now this is a process of the mind or thought of which I would willingly know the foundation. It is allowed on all hands that there is no known connection between the sensible qualities and the secret powers; and, consequently, that the mind is not led to form such a conclusion concerning their constant and regular conjunction by any-thing which it knows of their nature. As to past *experience*, it can be allowed to give *direct* and *certain* information of those precise objects only, and that precise period of time, which fell under its cognizance; but why this experience should be extended to future times, and to other objects, which for aught we know may be only in appearance similar – this is the main question on which I would insist. The bread, which I formerly ate, nourished me; that is, a body of such sensible qualities was, at that time, endued with such secret powers; but does it follow that other bread must also nourish me at another time, and that like sensible qualities must always be attended with like secret powers? The consequence seems nowise necessary. At least, it must be acknowledged that there is here a consequence drawn by the mind; that there is a certain step taken; a process of thought, and an inference, which wants to be explained. These two propositions are far from being the same, *I have found that such an object has always been attended with such an effect*, and *I foresee that other objects, which are, in appearance, similar, will be attended with similar effects.* I shall allow, if you please, that the one proposition may justly be inferred from the other; I know, in fact, that it always is inferred. But if you insist that the inference is made by a chain of reasoning, I desire you to produce that reasoning. The connection between these propositions is not intuitive. There is required a medium, which may enable the mind to draw such an inference, if indeed it be drawn by reasoning and argument. What that medium is, I must confess, passes my comprehension; and it is incumbent on those to produce it, who assert that it really exists, and is the origin of all our conclusions concerning matter of fact.

This negative argument must certainly, in process of time, become altogether convincing, if many penetrating and able philosophers shall turn their enquiries this way, and no one be ever able to discover any connecting proposition or intermediate step which supports the understanding in this conclusion. But as the question is yet new, every reader may not trust so far to his own penetration as to conclude, because an argument escapes his enquiry, that therefore it does not really exist. For this reason it may be requisite to venture upon a more difficult task; and enumerating all the branches of human knowledge, endeavour to show that none of them can afford such an argument.

All reasonings may be divided into two kinds, namely, demonstrative reasoning, or that concerning relations of ideas, and moral reasoning, or that concerning matter of fact and existence. That there are no demonstrative arguments in the case seems evident; since it implies no contradiction that the course of nature may change, and that an object, seemingly like those which we have experienced, may be attended with different or contrary effects. May I not clearly and distinctly conceive that a body, falling from the clouds, and which, in all other respects, resembles snow, has yet the taste of salt or feeling of fire? Is there any more intelligible proposition than to affirm that all the trees will flourish in December and January, and decay in May and June? Now whatever is intelligible, and can be distinctly conceived, implies no contradiction, and can never be proved false by any demonstrative argument or abstract reasoning *a priori.*

If we be, therefore, engaged by arguments to put trust in past experience, and make it the standard of our future judgement, these arguments must be probable only, or such as regard matter of fact and real existence, according to the division above mentioned. But that there is no argument of this kind, must appear, if our explication of that species of reasoning be admitted as solid and satisfactory. We have said that all arguments concerning existence are founded on the relation of cause and effect; that our knowledge of that relation is derived entirely from experience; and that all our experimental conclusions proceed upon the supposition that the future will be conformable to the past. To endeavour, therefore, the proof of this last supposition by probable arguments, or arguments regarding existence, must be evidently going in a circle, and taking that for granted which is the very point in question.

In reality, all arguments from experience are founded on the similarity which we discover among natural objects, and by which we are induced to expect effects similar to those which we have found to follow from such objects. And though none but a fool or madman will ever pretend to dispute the authority of experience, or to reject that great guide of human life, it may surely be allowed a philosopher to have so much curiosity at least as to examine the principle of human nature which gives this mighty authority to experience, and makes us draw advantage from that similarity which nature has placed among different objects. From causes which appear *similar* we expect similar effects. This is the sum of all our experimental conclusions. Now it seems evident that if this conclusion were formed by reason, it would be as perfect at first, and upon one instance, as after ever so long a course of experience. But the case is far otherwise. Nothing so like as eggs; yet no one, on account of this appearing similarity, expects the same taste and relish in all of them. It is only after a long course of uniform experiments in any kind that we attain a firm reliance and security with regard to a particular event. Now where is that process of reasoning which, from one instance, draws a conclusion so different from that which it infers from a hundred instances that are nowise different from that single one? This question I propose as much for the sake of information as with an intention of raising difficulties. I cannot find, I cannot imagine, any such reasoning. But I keep my mind still open to instruction, if any one will vouchsafe to bestow it on me.

Should it be said that, from a number of uniform experiments, we *infer* a connection between the sensible qualities and the secret powers, this, I must confess, seems the same difficulty, couched in different terms. The question still recurs, on what process of argument this *inference* is founded? Where is the medium, the interposing ideas, which join propositions so very wide of each other? It is confessed that the colour, consistency, and other sensible qualities of bread appear not, of themselves, to have any connection with the secret powers of nourishment and support. For otherwise we could infer these secret powers from the first appearance of these sensible qualities, without the aid of experience – contrary to the sentiment of all philosophers, and contrary to plain matter of fact. Here, then, is our natural state of ignorance with regard to the powers and influence of all objects. How is this remedied by experience? It only shows us a number of uniform effects, resulting from certain objects, and teaches us that those particular objects, at that particular time, were endowed with such powers and forces. When a new object, endowed with similar sensible qualities, is produced, we expect similar powers and forces, and look for a like effect. From a body of like colour and consistency with bread we expect like nourishment and support. But this surely is a step or progress of the mind which wants to be explained. When a man says *I have found, in all past instances, such sensible qualities conjoined with such secret powers,* and when he says *Similar sensible qualities will always be conjoined with similar secret powers,* he is not guilty of a tautology, nor are these propositions in any respect the same. You say that the one proposition is an inference from the other. But you must confess that the inference is not intuitive; neither is it demonstrative: Of what nature is it, then? To say it is experimental is begging the question. For all inferences from experience suppose, as their foundation, that the future will resemble the past, and that similar powers will be conjoined with similar sensible qualities. If there be any suspicion that the course of nature may change, and that the past may be no rule for the future, all experience becomes useless, and can give rise to no inference or conclusion. It is impossible, therefore, that any arguments from experience can prove this resemblance of the past to the future; since all these arguments are founded on the supposition of that resemblance. Let the course of things be allowed hitherto ever so regular; that alone, without some new argument or inference, proves not that, for the future, it will continue so. In vain do you pretend to have learned the nature of bodies from your past experience. Their secret nature, and consequently all their effects and influence, may change, without any change in their sensible qualities. This happens sometimes, and with regard to some objects: Why may it not happen always, and with regard to all objects? What logic, what process of argument secures you against this supposition? My practice, you say, refutes my doubts. But you mistake the purport of my question. As an agent, I am quite satisfied in the point; but as a philosopher, who has some share of curiosity, I will not say scepticism, I want to learn the foundation of this inference. No reading, no enquiry has yet been able to remove my difficulty, or give me satisfaction in a matter of such importance. Can I do better than propose the difficulty to the public, even though, perhaps, I have small hopes of obtaining a solution? We shall at least, by this means, be sensible of our ignorance, if we do not augment our knowledge.

I must confess that a man is guilty of unpardonable arrogance who concludes, because an argument has escaped his own investigation, that therefore it does not really exist. I must also confess that, though all the learned, for several ages, should have employed themselves in fruitless search upon any subject, it may still, perhaps, be rash to conclude positively that the subject must, therefore, pass all human comprehension. Even though we examine all the sources of our knowledge, and conclude them unfit for such a subject, there may still remain a suspicion that the enumeration is not complete, or the examination not accurate. But with regard to the present subject, there are some considerations which seem to remove all this accusation of arrogance or suspicion of mistake.

It is certain that the most ignorant and stupid peasants – nay infants, nay even brute beasts – improve by experience, and learn the qualities of natural objects, by observing the effects which result from them. When a child has felt the sensation of pain from touching the flame of a candle, he will be careful not to put his hand near any candle; but will expect a similar effect from a cause which is similar in its sensible qualities and appearance. If you assert, therefore, that the understanding of the child is led into this conclusion by any process of argument or ratiocination, I may justly require you to produce that argument; nor have you any pretence to refuse so equitable a demand. You cannot say that the argument is abstruse, and may possibly escape your enquiry, since you confess that it is obvious to the capacity of a mere infant. If you hesitate, therefore, a moment, or if, after reflection, you produce any intricate or profound argument, you, in a manner, give up the question, and confess that it is not reasoning which engages us to suppose the past resembling the future, and to expect similar effects from causes which are, to appearance, similar. This is the proposition which I intended to enforce in the present section. If I be right, I pretend not to have made any mighty discovery. And if I be wrong, I must acknowledge myself to be indeed a very backward scholar, since I cannot now discover an argument which, it seems, was perfectly familiar to me long before I was out of my cradle.

6   The Relation between Cause and Effect: David Hume, *Enquiry concerning Human Understanding**

Our next extract sees Hume taking further his critical examination of the foundations of scientific knowledge. The idea of causation is central to the scientific enterprise. Science, as commonly understood, aims to do more than produce mere statistical correlations: it purports to uncover the underlying *causes* that are responsible for the phenomena we observe. Thus, when we speak of the law of gravity, we commonly mean more than that objects have been observed behaving in certain ways; we have the notion of some *power* or *force* which *makes* a stone move towards the centre of the earth when dropped. The events studied by scientists, we believe, are typically more than series of random occurrences – they are *connected* together, so that a given cause *produces* or *necessitates* the resulting effect. In the late seventeenth and early eighteenth centuries, philosophers began a systematic inquiry into the nature of such supposed causal powers and forces (compare Berkeley's observations in extract 4, above).

In his *Enquiry concerning Human Understanding* (1748), from which the present and the preceding extract are taken, Hume set himself to examine the nature of 'power, force, energy or necessary connection'.[1] His strategy, which stems from his 'empiricist' account of knowledge, is to ask from what sensory impression this notion of necessary connection is derived.[2] His disturbing answer is that nothing we observe, either in the outside world, or from our inner awareness of how we initiate our own bodily movements, is sufficient to account for this concept. When we see one billiard ball hitting another, all we actually observe is the movement of ball A, followed by the movement of ball B: any further conception of some power or force, of some link between the first event and the second, goes beyond anything we can detect through the senses. (The same goes for the way we move our limbs – we know we do it, but the *power* or *force* involved is something entirely beyond our comprehension). 'All events,' as Hume puts it, 'seem entirely loose and separate. One event follows another; but we never can observe any tie between them.' Hume's conclusion is twofold. First, when we talk of A causing B, all we can properly mean by this is that events of type A are followed by events of type B; causation reduces to mere regularity, or 'constant conjunction'. Second, our belief in some necessary link or connection between causes and effects derives merely from our subjective expectations: 'the mind is carried by habit, upon the appearance of one event, to expect its usual attendant'. Taken together with Hume's critique of inductive generalization (see preceding extract), this constitutes a devastating attack on the rationality of science. In the first place, our tendency to generalize from limited data is not warranted by any rational process of argument or reasoning; and in the second place, our belief in real causal connections in nature is founded merely on subjective habit or expectation, not reason. If scientists think of themselves as uncovering the secret connections that will unlock the mysteries of nature, if they claim to investigate the underlying 'powers' or 'forces' in things, Hume's blunt reply is that 'we have no idea of such a connection, nor any distinct notion of what it is we desire to know'.

---

* David Hume, *An Enquiry concerning Human Understanding* [1748], extracts from Section VII, parts 1 and 2; with modified spelling and punctuation. Several editions of the complete text are available, including that edited by T. Beauchamp (Oxford: Oxford University Press, 1999), with introduction and notes for students.

[1] Note that in Hume's original text the term is spelled throughout in the old way (nowadays rarely found): 'connexion'.

[2] For the term 'empiricist', see introduction to Part I, extract 8, above. Compare also introduction to Part II, extract 7.

To be fully acquainted...with the idea of power or necessary connection, let us examine its impression; and in order to find the impression with greater certainty, let us search for it in all the sources from which it may possibly be derived.

When we look about us towards external objects, and consider the operation of causes, we are never able, in a single instance, to discover any power or necessary connection; any quality, which binds the effect to the cause and renders the one an infallible consequence of the other. We only find that the one does actually, in fact, follow the other. The impulse of one billiard-ball is attended with motion in the second. This is the whole that appears to the *outward* senses. The mind feels no sentiment or *inward* impression from this succession of objects. Consequently, there is not, in any single, particular instance of cause and effect, anything which can suggest the idea of power or necessary connection.

From the first appearance of an object, we never can conjecture what effect will result from it. But were the power or energy of any cause discoverable by the mind, we could foresee the effect, even without experience; and might, at first, pronounce with certainty concerning it, by mere dint of thought and reasoning.

In reality, there is no part of matter that does ever, by its sensible qualities, discover any power or energy, or give us ground to imagine that it could produce any thing, or be followed by any other object, which we could denominate its effect. Solidity, extension, motion; these qualities are all complete in themselves, and never point out any other event which may result from them. The scenes of the universe are continually shifting, and one object follows another in an uninterrupted succession; but the power or force, which actuates the whole machine, is entirely concealed from us, and never discovers itself in any of the sensible qualities of body. We know, that, in fact, heat is a constant attendant of flame; but what is the connection between them, we have no room so much as to conjecture or imagine. It is impossible, therefore, that the idea of power can be derived from the contemplation of bodies, in single instances of their operation; because no bodies ever discover any power, which can be the original of this idea.

Since, therefore, external objects, as they appear to the senses, give us no idea of power or necessary connection, by their operation in particular instances, let us see whether this idea be derived from reflection on the operations of our minds, and be copied from any internal impression. It may be said that we are every moment conscious of internal power; while we feel, that, by the simple command of our will, we can move the organs of our body, or direct the faculties of our mind. An act of volition produces motion in our limbs, or raises a new idea in our imagination. This influence of the will we know by consciousness. Hence we acquire the idea of power or energy; and are certain, that we ourselves and all other intelligent beings are possessed of power. This idea, then, is an idea of reflection, since it arises from reflecting on the operations of our own mind, and on the command which is exercised by will, both over the organs of the body and faculties of the soul.

We shall proceed to examine this pretension...first with regard to the influence of volition over the organs of the body. This influence, we may observe, is a fact, which, like all other natural events, can be known only by experience, and can never be foreseen from any apparent energy or power in the cause, which connects it with the effect, and renders the one an infallible consequence of the other. The motion of our body follows upon the command of our will. Of this we are every moment conscious.

But the means, by which this is effected; the energy, by which the will performs so extraordinary an operation; of this we are so far from being immediately conscious, that it must for ever escape our most diligent enquiry.

For *first*, is there any principle in all nature more mysterious than the union of soul with body; by which a supposed spiritual substance acquires such an influence over a material one, that the most refined thought is able to actuate the grossest matter? Were we empowered, by a secret wish, to remove mountains, or control the planets in their orbit, this extensive authority would not be more extraordinary, nor more beyond our comprehension. But if by consciousness we perceived any power or energy in the will, we must know this power; we must know its connection with the effect; we must know the secret union of soul and body, and the nature of both these substances; by which the one is able to operate, in so many instances, upon the other.

Secondly, we are not able to move all the organs of the body with a like authority; though we cannot assign any reason besides experience for so remarkable a difference between one and the other. Why has the will an influence over the tongue and fingers, not over the heart or liver? This question would never embarrass us, were we conscious of a power in the former case, not in the latter. We should then perceive, independent of experience, why the authority of will over the organs of the body is circumscribed within such particular limits. Being in that case fully acquainted with the power or force by which it operates, we should also know why its influence reaches precisely to such boundaries, and no farther.

A man, suddenly struck with palsy in the leg or arm, or who had newly lost those members, frequently endeavours, at first to move them, and employ them in their usual offices. Here he is as much conscious of power to command such limbs as a man in perfect health is conscious of power to actuate any member which remains in its natural state and condition. But consciousness never deceives. Consequently, neither in the one case nor in the other, are we ever conscious of any power. We learn the influence of our will from experience alone. And experience only teaches us how one event constantly follows another; without instructing us in the secret connection, which binds them together, and renders them inseparable.

Thirdly, we learn from anatomy that the immediate object of power in voluntary motion is not the member itself which is moved, but certain muscles, and nerves, and animal spirits,[1] and, perhaps, something still more minute and more unknown, through which the motion is successively propagated, ere it reach the member itself whose motion is the immediate object of volition. Can there be a more certain proof, that the power, by which this whole operation is performed, so far from being directly and fully known by an inward sentiment or consciousness, is, to the last degree mysterious and unintelligible? Here the mind wills a certain event. Immediately another event, unknown to ourselves, and totally different from the one intended, is produced. This event produces another, equally unknown. Till at last, through a long succession, the desired event is produced. But if the original power were felt, it must be known. Were it known, its effect also must be known; since all power is relative to its effect. And *vice versa*: if the effect be not known, the power cannot be known nor

---

[1] Animal spirits: a fine gas or vapour supposed to be the medium for the transmission of impulses through the nervous system.

felt. How indeed can we be conscious of a power to move our limbs, when we have no such power; but only that to move certain animal spirits, which, though they produce at last the motion of our limbs, yet operate in such a manner as is wholly beyond our comprehension?

We may, therefore, conclude from the whole, I hope, without any temerity, though with assurance, that our idea of power is not copied from any sentiment or consciousness of power within ourselves, when we give rise to animal motion, or apply our limbs to their proper use and office. That their motion follows the command of the will is a matter of common experience, like other natural events. But the power or energy by which this is effected, like that in other natural events, is unknown and inconceivable.[1]

... We have sought in vain for an idea of power or necessary connection in all the sources from which we could suppose it to be derived. It appears that, in single instances of the operation of bodies, we never can, by our utmost scrutiny, discover anything but one event following another, without being able to comprehend any force or power by which the cause operates, or any connection between it and its supposed effect. The same difficulty occurs in contemplating the operations of mind on body – where we observe the motion of the latter to follow upon the volition of the former, but are not able to observe or conceive the tie which binds together the motion and volition, or the energy by which the mind produces this effect. The authority of the will over its own faculties and ideas is not a whit more comprehensible. So that, upon the whole, there appears not, throughout all nature, any one instance of connection which is conceivable by us. All events seem entirely loose and separate. One event follows another; but we never can observe any tie between them. They seem *conjoined*, but never *connected*. And as we can have no idea of any thing which never appeared to our outward sense or inward sentiment, the necessary conclusion *seems* to be that we have no idea of connection or power at all, and that these words are absolutely without any meaning, when employed either in philosophical reasonings or common life.

But there still remains one method of avoiding this conclusion, and one source which we have not yet examined. When any natural object or event is presented, it is impossible for us, by any sagacity or penetration, to discover, or even conjecture, without experience, what event will result from it, or to carry our foresight beyond that object which is immediately present to the memory and senses. Even after one

---

[1] *It may be pretended that the resistance which we meet with in bodies, obliging us frequently to exert our force, and call up all our power, this gives us the idea of force and power. It is this *nisus*, or strong endeavour, of which we are conscious, that is the original impression from which this idea is copied. But first, we attribute power to a vast number of objects, where we never can suppose this resistance or exertion of force to take place; to the supreme Being, who never can suppose this resistance; to the mind in its command over its ideas and limbs; in common thinking and motion, where the effect follows immediately upon the will, without any exertion or summoning up of force; to inanimate matter, which is not capable of this sentiment. *Secondly,* this sentiment of an endeavour to overcome resistance has no known connection with any event. What follows it, we know by experience, but could not know it *a priori*. It must, however, be confessed that the animal *nisus* which we experience, though it can afford no accurate precise idea of power, enters very much into that vulgar, inaccurate idea which is formed of it.

instance or experiment where we have observed a particular event to follow upon another, we are not entitled to form a general rule, or foretell what will happen in like cases; it being justly esteemed an unpardonable temerity to judge of the whole course of nature from one single experiment, however accurate or certain. But when one particular species of event has always, in all instances, been conjoined with another, we make no longer any scruple of foretelling one upon the appearance of the other, and of employing that reasoning, which can alone assure us of any matter of fact or existence. We then call the one object, *Cause*; the other, *Effect*. We suppose that there is some connection between them; some power in the one, by which it infallibly produces the other, and operates with the greatest certainty and strongest necessity.

It appears, then, that this idea of a necessary connection among events arises from a number of similar instances which occur of the constant conjunction of these events; nor can that idea ever be suggested by any one of these instances, surveyed in all possible lights and positions. But there is nothing in a number of instances, different from every single instance, which is supposed to be exactly similar; except only, that after a repetition of similar instances, the mind is carried by habit, upon the appearance of one event, to expect its usual attendant, and to believe that it will exist. This connection, therefore, which we *feel* in the mind, this customary transition of the imagination from one object to its usual attendant, is the sentiment or impression from which we form the idea of power or necessary connection. Nothing farther is the case. Contemplate the subject on all sides; you will never find any other origin of that idea. This is the sole difference between one instance, from which we can never receive the idea of connection, and a number of similar instances, by which it is suggested. The first time a man saw the communication of motion by impulse, as by the shock of two billiard-balls, he could not pronounce that the one event was *connected*: but only that it was *conjoined* with the other. After he has observed several instances of this nature, he then pronounces them to be *connected*. What alteration has happened to give rise to this new idea of *connection*? Nothing but that he now *feels* these events to be *connected* in his imagination, and can readily foretell the existence of one from the appearance of the other. When we say, therefore, that one object is connected with another, we mean only that they have acquired a connection in our thought, and give rise to this inference, by which they become proofs of each other's existence – a conclusion which is somewhat extraordinary, but which seems founded on sufficient evidence. Nor will its evidence be weakened by any general diffidence of the understanding, or sceptical suspicion concerning every conclusion which is new and extraordinary. No conclusions can be more agreeable to scepticism than such as make discoveries concerning the weakness and narrow limits of human reason and capacity.

And what stronger instance can be produced of the surprising ignorance and weakness of the understanding than the present? For surely, if there be any relation among objects which it imports to us to know perfectly, it is that of cause and effect. On this are founded all our reasonings concerning matter of fact or existence. By means of it alone we attain any assurance concerning objects which are removed from the present testimony of our memory and senses. The only immediate utility of all sciences is to teach us how to control and regulate future events by their causes. Our thoughts and enquiries are, therefore, every moment, employed about this relation. Yet so imperfect are the ideas which we form concerning it, that it is impossible to give any just definition of cause, except what is drawn from something extraneous and foreign to it. Similar objects are always conjoined with similar. Of this we have experience. Suitably to this experience, therefore, we may define a cause to be *an object, followed by another, and where all the objects similar to the first are followed by objects similar to the second.* Or in other words *where, if the first object had not been, the second never had existed.* The appearance of a cause always conveys the mind, by a customary transition, to the idea of the effect. Of this also we have experience. We may, therefore, suitably to this experience, form another definition of cause, and call it *an object followed by another, and whose appearance always conveys the thought to that other.* But though both these definitions be drawn from circumstances foreign to the cause, we cannot remedy this inconvenience, or attain any more perfect definition which may point out that circumstance in the cause, which gives it a connection with its effect. We have no idea of this connection, nor even any distinct notion what it is we desire to know, when we endeavour at a conception of it. We say, for instance, that the vibration of this string is the cause of this particular sound. But what do we mean by that affirmation? We either mean *that this vibration is followed by this sound, and that all similar vibrations have been followed by similar sounds;* or *that this vibration is followed by this sound, and that upon the appearance of one the mind anticipates the senses, and forms immediately an idea of the other.* We may consider the relation of cause and effect in either of these two lights; but beyond these, we have no idea of it.

7   Causality and our Experience of Events: Immanuel Kant, *Critique of Pure Reason**

Hume's challenge to the status of scientific knowledge was taken up later in the eighteenth century by Immanuel Kant in his *Critique of Pure Reason*, published in 1781. Kant firmly rejected Hume's argument that the apparent necessity of causal judgements derives merely from the subjective expectations of the mind. The 'categories' (including causality) in terms of which we interpret reality are for Kant necessary in a much stronger sense: they are necessary preconditions for our being able to experience the world at all. (For the general structure of Kant's approach, see Part I, introduction to extract 8.) The details of his overall argument are complex and cannot be unfolded fully in a brief extract; but the passage excerpted below provides a reasonably clear idea of how he proposes to deal with our grasp of causation. His aim is to prove as a universal necessary truth that all changes 'take place in accordance with the law of cause and effect'. He then makes a fundamental distinction between the way in which we perceive an *object* (for example a house) and the way in which we perceive an *event* (e.g. a boat moving downstream). In the former case, the order of my perceptions is reversible: I can observe the basement first and then move up to the roof, but equally well I could start at the top and move downwards. With the *event*, by contrast, I can experience the various elements of what is going on only in a certain determinate order (I cannot observe the downstream position of the boat before its upstream position). So the order in this case is not subjective, or up to me – it belongs objectively to the sequence of appearances themselves.

* Immanuel Kant, *Critique of Pure Reason* [*Kritik der reinen Vernunft*, 1781; 2nd edn 1787], 'Analogies of Experience: Second Analogy', B 233–42; from *Immanuel Kant's Critique of Pure Reason*, ed. N. Kemp Smith (London: Macmillan, 1929, repr. 1965), pp. 218–24; with omissions and minor modifications.

Thus Kant argues, 'in the perception of an event there is always a rule which makes the order of the appearances necessary'. This already shows, according to Kant, that there is something wrong with the empiricist approach of Hume that challenges us to show how our ideas of causation can be derived merely from the observed data. The concept of causality, for Kant, is something we possess *a priori*, in advance of particular observations, and which has a certain kind of objective validity: unless there were a rule that makes it necessary that the order of our perceptions is thus, and not otherwise, we would not, in the first place, be able to experience certain sequences of appearances as events.

Kant thus aims to undermine Hume's sceptical worries about causation by redefining the terms of the problem: the question of how we can move from isolated data to general laws is inappropriate from the outset, since the notion of causality as a necessary and objective order of rule-governed phenomena is woven into the very framework in terms of which we experience the world. Whether all this actually disposes of the problems raised by Hume is a complex issue which defies a summary verdict. But in the case of the basic laws of physics, nothing Kant has said seems to eliminate Hume's doubts about how we are to make sense of the idea that there are real necessary connections underlying the regular sequences of events that obtain in the natural world.

All alterations take place in conformity with the law of the connection of cause and effect

I perceive that appearances follow one another, that is, that there is a state of things at one time the opposite of which was in the preceding time. Thus I am really connecting two perceptions in time. Now connection is not the work of mere sense and intuition, but is here the product of a synthetic faculty of imagination, which determines inner sense in respect of the time-relation. But imagination can connect these two states in two ways, so that either the one or the other precedes in time. For time cannot be perceived in itself, and what precedes and what follows cannot, therefore, by relation to it, be empirically determined in the object. I am conscious only that my imagination sets the one state before and the other after, not that the one state precedes the other in the object. In other words, the *objective relation* of appearances that follow upon one another is not to be determined through mere perception. In order that this relation be known as determined, the relation between the two states must be so thought that it is thereby determined as necessary which of them must be placed before, and which of them after, and that they cannot be placed in the reverse relation. But the concept which carries with it a necessity of synthetic unity can only be a pure concept that lies in the understanding, not in perception; and in this case it is the concept of the *relation of cause and effect*, the former of which determines the latter in time, as its consequence – not as in a sequence that may occur solely in the imagination (or that may not be perceived at all). Experience itself – in other words, empirical knowledge of appearances – is thus possible only in so far as we subject the succession of appearances, and therefore all alteration, to the law of causality; and, as likewise follows, the appearances, as objects of experience, are themselves possible only in conformity with the law.

The apprehension of the manifold of appearance is always successive. The representations of the parts follow upon one another. Whether they also follow one another in the object is a point which calls for further reflection, and which is not decided by the above statement. Everything, every representation even, in so far as we are conscious of it, may be entitled object. But it is a question for deeper enquiry what the word 'object' ought to signify in respect of appearances when these are viewed not in so far as they are (as representations) objects, but only in so far as they stand for an object. The appearances, in so far as they are objects of consciousness simply in virtue of being representations, are not in any way distinct from their apprehension, that is, from their reception in the synthesis of imagination; and we must therefore agree that the manifold of appearances is always generated in the mind successively. Now if appearances were things in themselves, then since we have to deal solely with our representations, we could never determine from the succession of the representations how their manifold may be connected in the object. How things may be in themselves, apart from the representations through which they affect us, is entirely outside our sphere of knowledge. In spite, however, of the fact that the appearances are not things in themselves, and yet are what alone can be given to us to know, in spite also of the fact that their representation in apprehension is always successive, I have to show what sort of a connection in time belongs to the manifold in the appearances themselves. For instance, the apprehension of the manifold in the appearance of a *house* which stands before me is successive. The question then arises, whether the manifold of the house is also in itself successive. This, however, is what no one will grant. Now immediately I unfold the transcendental meaning of my concepts of an object, I realize that the house is not a thing in itself, but only an appearance, that is, a representation, the transcendental object of which is unknown. What, then, am I to understand by the question: how may the manifold be connected in the appearance itself, which yet is nothing in itself? That which lies in the successive apprehension is here viewed as representation, while the appearance which is given to me, notwithstanding that it is nothing but the sum of these representations, is viewed as their object; and my concept, which I derive from the representations of apprehension, has to agree with it. Since truth consists in the agreement of knowledge with the object, it will at once be seen that we can here enquire only regarding the formal conditions of empirical truth, and that appearance, in contradistinction to the representations of apprehension, can be represented as an object distinct from them only if it stands under a rule which distinguishes it from every other apprehension and necessitates some one particular mode of connection of the manifold. The object is *that* in the appearance which contains the condition of this necessary rule of apprehension.

Let us now proceed to our problem. That something *happens*, i.e. that something, or some state which did not previously exist, comes to be, cannot be perceived unless it is preceded by an appearance which does not contain in itself this state. For an event which should follow upon an empty time, that is, a coming to be preceded by no state of things, is as little capable of being apprehended as empty time itself. Every apprehension of an event is therefore a perception that follows upon another perception. But since, as I have above illustrated by reference to the appearance of a house, this likewise happens in all synthesis of apprehension, the apprehension of an event is not yet thereby distinguished from other apprehensions. But, as I also note, in an appearance which contains a happening (the preceding state of the perception we may entitle A, and the succeeding B) B can be apprehended only as following upon A; the perception A cannot follow upon B but only precede it. For instance, I see *a ship move downstream*. My perception of its lower position follows upon the perception of its position higher up in the stream, and it is impossible that, in the apprehension of this appearance, the ship should first be perceived lower down in the stream and afterwards higher up. The order in which the perceptions succeed one another in apprehension is in this instance determined, and to this order apprehension is bound down. In the previous example of a *house*, my perceptions could begin with the apprehension of the roof and end with the basement or could begin from below and end above; and I could similarly apprehend the manifold of the empirical intuition either from right to left or from left to right. In the series of these perceptions there was thus no determinate order specifying at what point I must begin in order to connect the manifold empirically. But in the perception of an *event* there is always a rule that makes the order in which the perceptions (in the apprehension of this appearance) follow upon one another a *necessary* order.

In this case, therefore, we must derive the *subjective succession* of apprehension from the *objective succession* of appearances. Otherwise the order of apprehension is entirely undetermined, and does not distinguish one appearance from another. Since the subjective succession by itself is altogether arbitrary, it does not prove anything as to the manner in which the manifold is connected in the object. The objective succession will therefore consist in that order of the manifold of appearance according to which, in *conformity with a rule*, the apprehension of that which happens follows upon the apprehension of that which precedes. Thus only can I be justified in asserting, not merely of my apprehension, but of appearance itself, that a succession is to be met with in it. This is only another way of saying that I cannot arrange the apprehension otherwise than in this very succession.

In conformity with such a rule there must lie in that which precedes an event the condition of a *rule* according to which this event *invariably and necessarily follows*. I cannot reverse this order, proceeding back from the event to determine through apprehension that which precedes. For appearance never goes back from the succeeding to the preceding point of time, though it does indeed stand in relation to *some* preceding point of time. The advance, on the other hand, from a given time to the determinate time that follows is a necessary advance. Therefore, since there certainly is something that follows (i.e. that is *apprehended* as following), I must refer it necessarily to something else which precedes it and upon which it follows in conformity with a rule, that is, of necessity. The event, as the conditioned, thus affords reliable evidence of some condition, and this condition is what determines the event.

Let us suppose that there is nothing antecedent to an event, upon which it must follow according to rule. All succession of perception would then be only in the apprehension, that is, would be merely subjective, and would never enable us to determine objectively which perceptions are those that really precede and which are those that follow. We should then have only a play of representations, relating to no object; that is to say, it would not be possible through our perception to distinguish one appearance from another as regards relations of time. For the succession in our apprehension would always be one and the same, and there would be nothing in the appearance which so determines it that a certain sequence is rendered objectively necessary. I could not then assert that two states follow upon one another in the field of appearance, but only that one apprehension follows upon the other. That is something merely subjective, determining no object; and may not, therefore, be regarded as knowledge of any object, not even of an object in the field of appearance.

If, then, we experience that something happens, we in so doing always presuppose that something precedes it, on which it follows according to a rule. Otherwise I should not say of the object that it follows. For mere succession in my apprehension, if there be no rule determining the succession in relation to something that precedes, does not justify me in assuming any succession in the object. I render my subjective synthesis of apprehension objective only by reference to a rule in accordance with which the appearances in their succession, that is, as they happen, are determined by the preceding state. The experience of an event (i.e. of anything as *happening*) is itself possible only on this assumption.

This may seem to contradict all that has hitherto been taught in regard to the procedure of our understanding. The accepted view is that only through the perception and comparison of events repeatedly following in a uniform manner upon preceding appearances are we enabled to discover a rule according to which certain events always follow upon certain appearances, and that this is the way in which we are first led to construct for ourselves the concept of cause. Now the concept, if thus formed, would be merely empirical, and the rule which it supplies, that everything which happens has a cause, would be as contingent as the experience upon which it is based. Since the universality and necessity of the rule would not be grounded *a priori*, but only on induction, they would be merely fictitious and without genuinely universal validity. It is with these, as with other pure *a priori* representations – for instance, space and time. We can extract clear concepts of them from experience, only because we have put them into experience, and because experience is thus itself brought about only by their means. Certainly, the logical clearness of this representation of a rule determining the series of events is possible only after we have employed it in experience. Nevertheless, recognition of the rule, as a condition of the synthetic unity of appearances in time, has been the ground of experience itself, and has therefore preceded it *a priori*.

8   The Uniformity of Nature: John Stuart Mill, *System of Logic**

While Kant's approach to the problems of scientific knowledge (see preceding extract) exerted a powerful influence on much subsequent philosophy of science, the work of the British philosopher J. S. Mill aimed to tackle these problems without any radical departure from the earlier empiricist tradition of Bacon (see extract 2) and Hume (extracts 5 and 6). Taking up Hume's worries about inductive reasoning in science, Mill devoted a considerable portion of his lengthy *System of Logic* (1843) to trying to justify inductive procedures. All such procedures, Mill argues, are based on the assumption of the uniformity of nature. But this is not (as Hume had sometimes suggested) merely a matter of assuming that the future will resemble the past; 'fire burns' is a generalization taken to apply not just to future cases but to *all* unobserved cases, including the vast number of unobserved instances going on now, or in the past. Mill calls the

* J. S. Mill, *A System of Logic* [1843; 8th edn 1872], Bk III, ch. 3, §§ 1, 2, 3; ch. 4, §§ 1, 2, 3; with omissions and a few minor modifications. The full text is reproduced in the standard edition, *Collected Works of J. S. Mill*, ed. J. M. Robson, vol. VII (London: Routledge, 1973).

assumption of the uniformity of nature a 'first principle' or 'axiom', but in so doing he does not at all mean that it is somehow known *a priori*; on the contrary, he bites Hume's bullet and argues that it is itself based on experience. 'We have no ulterior test to which we subject experience in general; but we make experience its own test.' This may seem circular, but Mill proceeds to point out that while we have good evidence, based on past experience, to show that nature operates in a regular manner, we also have many instances of nature's variety and diversity.

It follows from this that merely to generalize blithely from a number of limited instances is the mark of ignorant and pre-scientific mind. Notoriously, the widely accepted generalization that all swans are white turned out, eventually, to be false. So how do we proceed? Again, in firmly empiricist vein, Mill appeals to experience: 'Experience must be consulted in order to learn from it under what circumstances arguments from it will be valid.' Good scientists will never be content with easy and swift inductions, but will constantly subject their generalizations to testing and modification in the light of further experience: 'The mode of correcting one

generalization by means of another, a narrower generalization by a wider, which common sense suggests and adopts in practice, is the real type of scientific Induction.' The sceptic can of course raise the old Humean objection that any given law may turn out, for all we know, to be false: a contrary instance may always be waiting round the corner. But Mill's plausible position is that this need not undermine the validity or rationality of science. The expression 'law of nature' may mislead us into thinking that we are searching for some sort of necessarily efficacious divine command regulating the natural world. Instead, taking a robustly common-sense line, Mill sees the scientific enterprise as simply one of trying to arrive at ever simpler and more comprehensive generalizations. The aim is, quite simply, to ask 'What are the fewest general propositions from which all the uniformities which exist in the universe might be deductively inferred?' If we do in fact, by the application of rigorous and carefully controlled experimental procedures, manage to arrive at such laws, then they may be taken to be certain and universal, not in some absolute sense, but 'as far as any human purpose requires certainty'.

Induction, properly so called... may be summarily defined as generalization from experience. It consists in inferring from some individual instances in which a phenomenon is observed to occur, that it occurs in all instances of a certain class; namely in all which *resemble* the former, in what are regarded as the material circumstances.

... There is a principle implied in the very statement of what Induction is; an assumption with regard to the course of nature and the order of the universe, namely that there are such things in nature as parallel cases; that what happens once will, under a sufficient degree of similarity of circumstances, happen again, and not only again, but as often as the same circumstances recur. This, I say, is an assumption involved in every case of induction. And if we consult the actual course of nature, we find that the assumption is warranted. The universe, so far as known to us, is so constituted that whatever is true in one case is true in all cases of a certain description; the only difficulty is to find what description.

This universal fact, which is our warrant from all inferences from experience, has been described by different philosophers in different forms of language: that the course of nature is uniform; that the universe is governed by general laws; and the like. One of the most usual of those modes of expression [is] also one of the most inadequate... The disposition of the human mind to generalize from experience ... they usually describe under some such name as 'our intuitive conviction that the future will resemble the past'. Now... time in its modifications of past, present and future has no concern either with the belief itself, or with the grounds of it.

We believe that fire will burn tomorrow because it burned today and yesterday; but we believe, on precisely the same grounds, that it burned before we were born, and that it burns this very day in Cochin-China. It is not from the past to the future, as past and future, that we infer, but from the known to the unknown; from facts observed to facts unobserved; from what we have perceived, or been directly conscious of, to what has not come within our experience. In this last predicament is the whole region of the future; but also the vastly greater portion of the present and of the past.

Whatever be the most proper mode of expressing it, the proposition that the course of nature is uniform is the fundamental principle, or general axiom, of Induction. It would yet be a great error to offer this large generalization as any explanation of the inductive process. On the contrary, I hold it to be itself an instance of induction, and induction by no means of the most obvious kind. Far from being the first induction we make, it is one of the last, or at all events one of those which are latest in attaining strict philosophical accuracy. As a general maxim, indeed, it has scarcely entered into the minds of any but philosophers; nor even by them...have its extent and limits been always very justly conceived. The truth is that this great generalization is itself founded on prior generalizations. The obscurer laws of nature were discovered by means of it, but the more obvious ones must have been understood and assented to as general truths before it was ever heard of. We should never have thought of affirming that all phenomena take place according to general laws if we had not first arrived, in the case of a great multitude of phenomena, at some knowledge of the laws themselves; which could be done no otherwise than by induction. In what sense, then, can a principle which is so far from being our earliest induction be regarded as our warrant for all the others? In the only sense in which...the general propositions which we place at the head of our reasonings when we throw them into syllogisms, ever really contributed to their validity...Every induction is a syllogism with the major premise suppressed; or (as I prefer expressing it) every induction may be thrown into the form of a syllogism by supplying a major premise. If this be actually done, the principle which we are now considering, that of the uniformity of the course of nature, will appear as the ultimate major premise of all inductions, and will, therefore, stand to all inductions in the relation in which...the major premise always stands to the conclusion; not contributing at all to prove it, but being a necessary condition of its being proved; for no conclusion is proved for which there cannot be found a true major premise...

Every person's consciousness assures him that he does not always expect uniformity in the course of events; he does not always believe that the unknown will be similar to the known, that the future will resemble the past. Nobody believes that the succession of rain and fine weather will be the same in every future year as in the present. Nobody expects to have the same dreams repeated every night. On the contrary, everybody mentions it as something extraordinary if the course of nature is constant, and resembles itself in those particulars. To look for constancy where constancy is not to be expected, as, for instance, that a day which has once brought good fortune will always be a fortunate day, is justly accounted superstition.

The course of nature, in truth, is not only uniform, it is also infinitely various. Some phenomena are always seen to recur in the very same combinations in which we met with them at first; others seem altogether capricious; while some, which we had been accustomed to regard as bound down exclusively to a particular set of combinations, we unexpectedly find detached from some of the elements with which we had hitherto found them conjoined, and united to others of quite a contrary disposition. To an inhabitant of Central Africa fifty years ago, no fact probably appeared to rest on more uniform experience than this, that all human beings are black. To Europeans not many years ago, the proposition, All swans are white, appeared an equally unequivocal instance of uniformity in the course of nature. Further experience has proved to both that they were mistaken; but they had to wait fifty centuries for that experience. During that long time, mankind believed in a uniformity of the course of nature where no such uniformity really existed.

According to the notion which the ancients entertained of induction, the foregoing were cases of as legitimate inference as any inductions whatever. In these two instances, in which, the conclusion being false, the ground of inference must have been insufficient, there was, nevertheless, as much ground for it as this conception of induction admitted of. The induction of the ancients had been well described by Bacon, under the name of *induction through simple enumeration, where there is not found a contradicting instance.* It consists in ascribing the character of general truths to all propositions which are true in every instance that we happen to know of. This is the kind of induction which is natural to the mind when unaccustomed to scientific methods. The tendency, which some call an instinct, and which others account for by association, to infer the future from the past, the unknown from the known, is simply a habit of expecting that what has been found true once and several times, and never yet found false, will be found true again. Whether the instances are few or many, conclusive or inconclusive, does not much affect the matter. These are considerations which occur only on reflection. The unprompted tendency of the mind is to generalize its experience, provided this points all in one direction; provided no other experience of a conflicting character comes unsought. The notion of seeking it, of experimenting for it, of *interrogating* nature (to use Bacon's expression) is of much later growth. The observation of nature by uncultivated intellects is purely passive. They accept the facts that present themselves, without taking the trouble of searching for more. It is a superior mind only which asks itself what facts are needed to enable it to come to a safe conclusion, and then looks out for these.

. . . In order to have a better understanding of the problem which the logician must solve if he would establish a scientific theory of Induction, let us compare a few cases of incorrect inductions with others that are acknowledged to be legitimate. Some, we know, which were believed for centuries to be correct, were nevertheless incorrect. That all swans are white cannot have been a good induction, since the conclusion has turned out erroneous. The experience, however, on which the conclusion rested, was genuine. From the earliest records, the testimony of the inhabitants of the known world was unanimous on the point. The uniform experience, therefore, of the inhabitants of the known world, agreeing in a common result, without one known instance of deviation from that result, is not always sufficient to establish a general conclusion.

But let us now turn to an instance apparently not very dissimilar to this. Mankind were wrong, it seems, in concluding that all swans were white; are we also wrong when we conclude that all men's heads grow above their shoulders and never below, in spite of the conflicting testimony of the naturalist Pliny? . . . Again, there are cases in which we reckon with the most unfailing confidence upon uniformity, and other cases in which we do not count upon it at all. In some we feel complete assurance that the future will resemble the past, the unknown be precisely similar to the known. In others, however variable may be the result obtained from the instances which have been observed, we draw from them no more than a very feeble presumption that the like result will hold in all other cases ... When a chemist announces the existence and properties of a newly discovered substance, if we trust in his accuracy, we feel assured that the conclusions he has arrived at will hold universally, though the induction be founded but on a single instance. We do not withhold our assent, waiting for a repetition of the experiment, or if we do, it is from a doubt whether the experiment was properly made, not whether, if properly made, it would be conclusive. Here then is a general law of nature, inferred without hesitation from a single instance; a universal proposition from a singular one. Now mark another case, and contrast it with this. Not all the instances which have been observed since the beginning of the world in support of the general proposition that all crows are black would be deemed a sufficient presumption of the truth of the proposition, to outweigh the testimony of one unexceptionable witness who should affirm that in some region of the earth not fully explored he has caught and examined a crow, and had found it to be grey.

Why is a single instance, in some cases, sufficient for a complete induction, while in others myriads of concurring instances, without a single exception known or presumed, go such a very little way towards establishing a universal proposition? Whoever can answer this question knows more of the philosophy of logic than the wisest of the ancients, and has solved the problem of Induction ...

It is the custom in science, wherever regularity of any kind can be traced, to call the general proposition which expresses the nature of that regularity a law; as when in mathematics, we speak of the law of decrease of the successive terms of a converging series. But the expression *law of nature* has generally been employed with a sort of tacit reference to the original sense of the world 'law', namely the expression of the will of a superior. When, therefore, it appeared that any of the uniformities which were observed in nature would result spontaneously from certain other uniformities, no separate act of creative will being supposed necessary for the production of the derivative uniformities, these have not usually been spoken of as laws of nature. According to one mode of expression, the question What are the laws of nature? may be stated thus: What are the fewest and simplest assumptions which, being granted, the whole existing order of nature would result? Another mode of stating it would be thus: What are the fewest general propositions from which all the uniformities which exist in the universe might be deductively inferred?

Every great advance which marks an epoch in the progress of science has consisted in a step towards the solution of this problem ... When Kepler expressed the regularity which exists in the observed motions of the heavenly bodies by the three general propositions he called laws, he in so doing pointed out three simple suppositions which, instead of a much greater number, would suffice to construct the whole scheme of the heavenly motions so far as it was known up to that time. A similar and still greater step was made when these laws, which at first did not seem to be included in any more general truths, were discovered to be cases of the three laws of motion, as obtaining among bodies which mutually tend towards one another with a certain force, and have had a certain instantaneous impulse originally impressed on them. After this great discovery, Kepler's three propositions, though still called laws, would hardly by any person accustomed to use language with precision, be termed laws of nature; that phrase would be reserved for the simpler and more general laws into which Newton is said to have resolved them.

According to this language, every well-grounded inductive generalization is either a law of nature or a result of laws of nature, capable, if those laws are known, of being predicted from them. And the problem of Inductive Logic may be summed up in two questions: how to ascertain the laws of nature; and how, after having ascertained them, to follow them into their results. On the other hand, we must not suffer ourselves to imagine that this mode of statement amounts to a real analysis, or to anything but a mere verbal transformation of the problem; for the expression Laws of Nature *means* nothing but the uniformities which exist among natural phenomena (or, in other words, the results of induction) when reduced to their simplest expression. It is, however, something to have advanced so far as to see that the study of nature is the study of laws, not *a* law; of uniformities in the plural number; that the different natural phenomena have their separate rules or modes of taking place, which, though much intermixed and entangled with one another may, to a certain extent, be studied apart; that ... the regularity which exists in nature is a web composed of distinct threads, and only to be understood by tracing each of the threads separately; for which purpose it is often necessary to unravel some portion of the web, and to exhibit some of the fibres apart. The rules of experimental inquiry are the contrivances for unravelling the web ...

Let us revert to one of our former illustrations and consider why it is that, with exactly the same amount of evidence, both negative and positive, we did not reject the assertion that there are black swans, while we should refuse credence to any testimony which asserted that there were men wearing their heads underneath their shoulders. The first assertion was more credible than the latter. But why more credible? So long as neither phenomenon had been actually witnessed, what reason was there for finding the one harder to be believed than the other? Apparently because there is less constancy in the colours of animals than in the general structure of their anatomy. But how do we know this? Doubtless from experience. It appears, then, that we need experience to inform us in what degree and in what cases, or sorts of cases, experience is to be relied on. Experience must be consulted in order to learn from it under what circumstances arguments from it will be valid. We have no ulterior test to which we subject experience in general; but we make experience its own test. Experience testifies that among the uniformities which it exhibits or seems to exhibit, some are more to be relied on than others; and uniformity, therefore, may be pursued, from any given number of instances, with a greater degree of assurance, in proportion as the case belongs to a class in which the uniformities have hitherto been found more uniform.

The mode of correcting one generalization by means of another, a narrower generalization by a wider, which common sense suggests and adopts in practice, is the real type of scientific Induction. All that art can do is but to give accuracy and precision to this process, and adapt it to all varieties of cases, without any essential alteration in its principle.

There are of course no means of applying such a test as that above described unless we already possess a general knowledge of the prevalent character of the uniformities existing throughout nature. The indispensable foundation, therefore, of a scientific formula of induction must be a survey of the inductions to which mankind have been conducted in unscientific practice, with the special purpose of ascertaining what kinds of uniformities have been found perfectly invariable, pervading all nature, and what are those which have been found to vary with difference of time, place, or other changeable circumstances...

If, then, a survey of the uniformities which have been ascertained to exist in nature should point out some which, as far as any human purpose requires certainty, may be considered quite certain and quite universal, then by means of these uniformities we may be able to raise multitudes of other inductions to the same point in the scale. For if we can show, with respect of any inductive inference, that either it must be true, or one of these certain and universal inductions must admit of an exception, the former generalization will attain the same certainty, and indefeasibleness within the bounds assigned to it, which are the attributes of the latter. It will be proved to be a law; and if not a result of other and simpler laws, it will be a law of nature.

There are such certain and universal inductions; and it is because there are such, that a Logic of Induction is possible.

9   Science and Falsifiability: Karl Popper, *Conjectures and Refutations**

According to both Bacon and Mill (extracts 2 and 8 above), the characteristic method of science is to proceed from particular observations to general laws or theories – a procedure whose validity had been thrown into serious doubt by the arguments of Hume (extract 5). A radically new perspective on this issue was provided by the Austrian-born philosopher Karl Popper, who published his ground-breaking *Logik der Forschung* [*The Logic of Scientific Discovery*] in 1935. In that work, and in a paper in his later collection *Conjectures and Refutations* (excerpted below), Popper argued that the supposed problem of induction is irrelevant to the logic of science. For in the first place scientists do not arrive at their theories by carefully collecting observational data; the instruction 'Observe!' makes no sense unless we already have some theory we wish to test. Secondly, what marks out the scientific approach is not the collection of favourable instances – since it is possible to amass a host of 'confirmatory data' for even the most bizarre and unscientific beliefs (such as those of astrologers and fortune tellers); rather, the mark of true science is its willingness to subject a theory to the possibility of *refutation*. Falsifiability, not verifiability, becomes the test which distinguishes genuine science from what Popper calls 'pseudoscience'. As for the question of how scientists arrive at their theories in the first place, according to Popper this is not a question for the philosophy of science at all. There is no standard procedure, no set of logical rules, for arriving at theories. What happens instead is that human beings constantly come up with 'conjectures' – attempts to impose some kind of intelligibility on the flux of experience. Just as (according to Darwinism) new species emerge and compete in the struggle for survival, so human beings constantly 'jump to conclusions' in their attempts to make sense of the world. Science thus forms part of a natural human activity of 'trial and error'; what gives it its rigour is not some special 'inductive method' for discovering the truth, but the determination to subject theories to the test, and to discard those which fail.

* 'Science: Conjectures and Refutations'; lecture delivered in 1953 and originally published under the title 'Philosophy of Science: A Personal Report', in C. A. Mace (ed.), *British Philosophy in Mid-Century* (1957). Repr. in K. Popper, *Conjectures and Refutations* (London: Routledge, 1963; 3rd edn 1969), ch. 1; abridged.

I [have] decided to . . . give you a report on my own work in the philosophy of science, since the autumn of 1919, when I first began to grapple with the problem '*When should a theory be ranked as scientific?*' or '*Is there a criterion for the scientific character or status of a theory?*'

The problem which troubled me at the time was neither 'When is a theory true?' nor 'When is a theory acceptable?' My problem was different. I *wished to distinguish between science and pseudo-science*, knowing very well that science often errs, and that pseudo-science may happen to stumble on the truth.

I know, of course, the most widely accepted answer to my problem: that science is distinguished from pseudo-science – or from 'metaphysics' – by its empirical *method*, which is essentially *inductive*, proceeding from observation or experiment. But this did not satisfy me. On the contrary, I often formulated my problem as one of distinguishing between a genuinely empirical method and a non-empirical or even a pseudo-empirical method – that is to say, a method which, although it appeals to observation and experiment, nevertheless does not come up to scientific standards. The latter method may be exemplified by astrology, with its stupendous mass of empirical evidence based on observation – on horoscopes and on biographies . . .

I found that those of my friends who were admirers of Marx, Freud and Adler were impressed by a number of points common to these theories, and especially by their apparent *explanatory power*. These theories appeared to be able to explain practically everything that happened within the fields to which they referred. The study of any of them seemed to have the effect of an intellectual conversion or revelation, opening your eyes to a new truth hidden from those not yet initiated. Once your eyes were thus opened you saw confirming instances everywhere: the world was full of *verification* of the theory. Whatever happened always confirmed it. Thus its truth appeared manifest; and unbelievers were clearly people who did not want to see the manifest truth; who refused to see it, either because it was against their class interest, or because of their repressions which were still 'unanalysed' and crying aloud for treatment.

The most characteristic element in this situation seemed to be the incessant stream of confirmations, of observations which 'verified' the theories in question; and this point was constantly emphasized by their adherents. A Marxist could not open a newspaper without finding on every page confirming evidence for his interpretation of history; not only in the news, but also in its presentation – which revealed the class bias of the paper – and especially of course in what the paper did *not* say. The Freudian analysts emphasized that their theories were constantly verified by their 'clinical observations'. As for Adler, I was much impressed by a personal experience. Once, in 1919, I reported to him a case which to me did not seem particularly Adlerian, but which he found no difficulty in analysing in terms of his theory of inferiority feelings, although he had not even seen the child. Slightly shocked, I asked him how he could be so sure. 'Because of my thousand-fold experience,' he replied; whereupon I could not help saying: 'And with this new case, I suppose, your experience has become thousand-and-one-fold.'

With Einstein's theory the situation was strikingly different. Take one typical instance – Einstein's prediction, just then confirmed by the findings of Eddington's expedition. Einstein's gravitational theory had led to the result that light must be attracted by heavy bodies (such as the sun), precisely as material bodies were attracted. As a consequence it could be calculated that light from a distant fixed star whose apparent position was close to the sun would reach the earth from such a direction that the star would seem to be slightly shifted away from the sun; or, in other words, that stars close to the sun would look as if they had moved a little away from the sun, and from one another. This is a thing which cannot normally be observed since such stars are rendered invisible in daytime by the sun's overwhelming brightness; but during an eclipse it is possible to take photographs of them. If the same constellation is photographed at night one can measure the distances on the two photographs, and check the predicted effect.

Now the impressive thing about this case is the *risk* involved in a prediction of this kind. If observation shows that the predicted effect is definitely absent, then the theory is simply refuted. The theory is *incompatible with certain possible results of observation* – in fact with results which everybody before Einstein would have expected. This is quite different from the situation I have previously described, when it turned out that the theories in question were compatible with the most divergent human behaviour, so that it was practically impossible to describe any human behaviour that might not be claimed to be a verification of these theories.

These considerations led me in the winter of 1919–20 to conclusions which I may now reformulate as follows.

(1) It is easy to obtain confirmations, or verifications, for nearly every theory – if we look for confirmations.

(2) Confirmations should count only if they are the result of *risky predictions*; that is to say, if, unenlightened by the theory in question, we should have expected an event which was incompatible with the theory – an event which would have refuted the theory.

(3) Every 'good' scientific theory is a prohibition: it forbids certain things to happen. The more a theory forbids, the better it is.

(4) A theory which is not refutable by any conceivable event is non-scientific. Irrefutability is not a virtue of a theory (as people often think) but a vice.

(5) Every genuine *test* of a theory is an attempt to falsify it, or to refute it. Testability is falsifiability; but there are degrees of testability: some theories are more testable, more exposed to refutation, than others; they take, as it were, greater risks.

(6) Confirming evidence should not count *except when it is the result of a genuine test of the theory*; and this means that it can be presented as a serious but unsuccessful attempt to falsify the theory. (I now speak in such cases of 'corroborating evidence'.)

(7) Some genuinely testable theories, when found to be false, are still upheld by their admirers – for example by introducing *ad hoc* some auxiliary assumption, or by reinterpreting the theory *ad hoc* in such a way that it escapes refutation. Such a procedure is always possible, but it rescues the theory from refutation only at the price of destroying, or at least lowering, its scientific status...

One can sum up all this by saying that *the criterion of the scientific status of a theory is its falsifiability, or refutability, or testability*...

I had become interested in the problem of induction in 1923. Although this problem is very closely connected with the problem of demarcation, I did not fully appreciate the connection for about five years.

I approached the problem of induction through Hume. Hume, I felt, was perfectly right in pointing out that induction cannot be logically justified. He held that there can be no valid logical arguments allowing us to establish 'that those instances, of which we have had no experience, resemble those, of which we have had experience'. Consequently 'even after the observation of the frequent or constant conjunction of objects, we have no reason to draw any inference concerning any object beyond those of which we have had experience...'[1] As a result we can say that theories can never be inferred from observation statements, or rationally justified by them.

I found Hume's refutation of inductive inference clear and conclusive. But I felt completely dissatisfied with his psychological explanation of induction in terms of custom or habit...

The central idea of Hume's theory is that of *repetition, based upon similarity* (or 'resemblance'). This idea is used in a very uncritical way. We are led to think of the water-drop that hollows the stone: of sequences of unquestionably like events slowly forcing themselves upon us, as does the tick of the clock. But we ought to realize that in a psychological theory such as Hume's, only repetition-for-us, based upon similarity-for-us, can be allowed to have any effect upon us. We must respond to situations as if they were equivalent; *take* them as similar; *interpret* them as repetitions... The kind of repetition envisaged by Hume can never be perfect; the cases he has in mind cannot be cases of perfect sameness; they can only be cases of similarity. Thus *they are repetitions only from a certain point of view*. (What has the effect upon me of a repetition may not have this effect upon a spider.) But this means that, for logical reasons, there must always be a point of view – such as a system of expectations, anticipations, assumptions or interests – before there can be any repetition; which point of view, consequently, cannot be merely the result of repetition...

Hume, I felt, had never accepted the full force of his own logical analysis. Having refuted the logical idea of induction he was faced with the following problem: how do we actually obtain our knowledge, as a matter of psychological fact, if induction is a procedure which is logically invalid and rationally unjustifiable? There are two possible answers: (1) We obtain our knowledge by a non-inductive procedure. This answer would have allowed Hume to retain a form of rationalism. (2) We obtain our knowledge by repetition and induction, and therefore by a logically invalid and rationally unjustifiable procedure, so that all apparent knowledge is merely a kind of belief – belief based on habit. This answer would imply that even scientific knowledge is irrational, so that rationalism is absurd, and must be given up.

It seems that Hume never seriously considered the first alternative. Having cast out the logical theory of induction by repetition, he struck a bargain with common sense, meekly allowing the re-entry of induction by repetition, in the guise of a psychological theory. I proposed to turn the tables upon this theory of Hume's. Instead of explaining our propensity to expect regularities as the result of repetition, I proposed to explain repetition-for-us as the result of our propensity to expect regularities and to search for them.

Thus I was led by purely logical considerations to replace the psychological theory of induction by the following view. Without waiting, passively, for repetitions to impress or impose regularities upon us, we actively try to impose regularities upon the world. We try to discover similarities in it, and to interpret it in terms of laws

---

[1] *A Treatise of Human Nature* [1739–40], Bk I, part iii, section 6. Compare extract 5, above.

invented by us. Without waiting for premises we jump to conclusions. These may have to be discarded later, should observation show that they are wrong.

This was a theory of trial and error – of *conjectures and refutations*. It made it possible to understand why our attempts to force interpretations upon the world were logically prior to the observation of similarities. Since there were logical reasons behind this procedure, I thought that it would apply in the field of science also; that scientific theories were not the digest of observations, but that they were inventions – conjectures boldly put forward for trial, to be eliminated if they clashed with observations; with observations which were rarely accidental but as a rule undertaken with the definite intention of testing a theory by obtaining, if possible, a decisive refutation.

The belief that science proceeds from observation to theory is still so widely and so firmly held that my denial of it is often met with incredulity. I have even been suspected of being insincere – of denying what nobody in his senses can doubt.

But in fact the belief that we can start with pure observations alone, without anything in the nature of a theory, is absurd; as may be illustrated by the story of the man who dedicated his life to natural science, wrote down everything he could observe, and bequeathed his priceless collection of observations to the Royal Society to be used as inductive evidence. This story should show us that though beetles may profitably be collected, observations may not.

Twenty-five years ago I tried to bring home the same point to a group of physics students in Vienna by beginning a lecture with the following instructions: 'Take pencil and paper; carefully observe, and write down what you have observed!' They asked, of course, *what* I wanted them to observe. Clearly the instruction, 'Observe!' is absurd. It is not even idiomatic, unless the object of the transitive verb can be taken as understood. Observation is always selective. It needs a chosen object, a definite task, an interest, a point of view, a problem. And its description presupposes a descriptive language, with property words; it presupposes similarity and classification, which in its turn presupposes interests, points of view, and problems...

Our propensity to look out for regularities, and to impose laws upon nature, leads to the psychological phenomenon of *dogmatic thinking* or, more generally, dogmatic behaviour: we expect regularities everywhere and attempt to find them even where there are none; events which do not yield to these attempts we are inclined to treat as a kind of 'background noise'; and we stick to our expectations even when they are inadequate and we ought to accept defeat. This dogmatism is to some extent necessary. It is demanded by a situation which can only be dealt with by forcing our conjectures upon the world. Moreover, this dogmatism allows us to approach a good theory in stages, by way of approximations: if we accept defeat too easily, we may prevent ourselves from finding that we were very nearly right.

It is clear that this *dogmatic attitude*, which makes us stick to our first impressions, is indicative of a strong belief; while a *critical attitude*, which is ready to modify its tenets, which admits doubt and demands tests, is indicative of a weaker belief. Now according to Hume's theory, and to the popular theory, the strength of a belief should be a product of repetition; thus it should always grow with experience, and always be greater in less primitive persons. But dogmatic thinking, an uncontrolled wish to impose regularities, a manifest pleasure in rites and in repetition as such, are characteristic of primitives and children; and increasing experience and maturity sometimes create an attitude of caution and criticism rather than of dogmatism...

My logical criticism of Hume's psychological theory...may seem a little removed from the field of the philosophy of science. But the distinction between dogmatic and critical thinking, or the dogmatic and the critical attitude, brings us right back to our central problem. For the dogmatic attitude is clearly related to the tendency to *verify* our laws and schemata by seeking to apply them and to confirm them, even to the point of neglecting refutations, whereas the critical attitude is one of readiness to change them – to test them; to refute them; to *falsify* them, if possible. This suggests that we may identify the critical attitude with the scientific attitude, and the dogmatic attitude with the one which we have described as pseudo-scientific.

It further suggests that genetically speaking the pseudo-scientific attitude is more primitive than, and prior to, the scientific attitude: that it is a pre-scientific attitude. And this primitivity or priority also has its logical aspect. For the critical attitude is not so much opposed to the dogmatic attitude as superimposed upon it: criticism must be directed against existing and influential beliefs in need of critical revision – in other words, dogmatic beliefs. A critical attitude needs for its raw material, as it were, theories or beliefs which are held more or less dogmatically.

Thus science must begin with myths, and with the criticism of myths; neither with the collection of observations, nor with the invention of experiments, but with the critical discussion of myths, and of magical techniques and practices. The scientific tradition is distinguished from the pre-scientific tradition in having two layers. Like the latter, it passes on its theories; but it also passes on a critical attitude towards them. The theories are passed on, not as dogmas, but rather with the challenge to discuss them and improve upon them. This tradition is Hellenic: it may be traced back to Thales, founder of the first *school* (I do not mean 'of the first *philosophical* school', but simply 'of the first school') which was not mainly concerned with the preservation of a dogma.

The critical attitude, the tradition of free discussion of theories with the aim of discovering their weak spots so that they may be improved upon, is the attitude of reasonableness, of rationality. It makes far-reaching use of both verbal argument and observation – of observation in the interest of argument, however. The Greeks' discovery of the critical method gave rise at first to the mistaken hope that it would lead to the solution of all the great old problems; that it would establish certainty; that it would help to *prove* our theories, to *justify* them. But this hope was a residue of the dogmatic way of thinking; in fact nothing can be justified or proved (outside of mathematics and logic). The demand for rational proofs in science indicates a failure to keep distinct the broad realm of rationality and the narrow realm of rational certainty: it is an untenable, an unreasonable demand.

Nevertheless, the role of logical argument, of deductive logical reasoning, remains all-important for the critical approach; not because it allows us to prove our theories, or to infer them from observation statements, but because only by purely deductive reasoning is it possible for us to discover what our theories imply, and thus to criticize them effectively. Criticism, I said, is an attempt to find the weak spots in a theory, and these, as a rule, can be found only in the more remote logical consequences which can be derived from it. It is here that purely logical reasoning plays an important part in science.

Hume was right in stressing that our theories cannot be validly inferred from what we can know to be true – neither from observations nor from anything else. He concluded from this that our belief in them was irrational. If 'belief' means here our inability to doubt our natural laws, and the constancy of natural regularities, then Hume is again right: this kind of dogmatic belief has, one might say, a physiological rather than a rational basis. If, however, the term 'belief' is taken to cover our critical acceptance of scientific theories – a *tentative* acceptance combined with an eagerness to revise the theory if we succeed in designing a test which it cannot pass – then Hume was wrong. In such an acceptance of theories there is nothing irrational. There is not even anything irrational in relying for practical purposes upon well-tested theories, for no more rational course of action is open to us.

Assume that we have deliberately made it our task to live in this unknown world of ours; to adjust ourselves to it as well as we can; to take advantage of the opportunities we can find in it; and to explain it, *if* possible (we need not assume that it is), and as far as possible, with the help of laws and explanatory theories. *If we have made this our task, then there is no more rational procedure than the method of trial and error – of conjecture and refutation*: of boldly proposing theories; of trying our best to show that these are erroneous; and of accepting them tentatively if our critical efforts are unsuccessful.

From the point of view here developed all laws, all theories, remain essentially tentative, or conjectural, or hypothetical, even when we feel unable to doubt them any longer. Before a theory has been refuted we can never know in what way it may have to be modified. That the sun will always rise and set within twenty-four hours is still proverbial as a law 'established by induction beyond reasonable doubt'. It is odd that this example is still in use, though it may have served well enough in the days of Aristotle and Pytheas of Massalia – the great traveller who for centuries was called a liar because of his tales of Thule, the land of the frozen sea and the *midnight sun.*

The method of trial and error is not, of course, simply identical with the scientific or critical approach – with the method of conjecture and refutation. The method of trial and error is applied not only by Einstein but, in a more dogmatic fashion, by the amoeba also. The difference lies not so much in the trials as in a critical and constructive attitude towards errors; errors which the scientist consciously and cautiously tries to uncover in order to refute his theories with searching arguments, including appeals to the most severe experimental tests which his theories and his ingenuity permit him to design.

The critical attitude may be described as the conscious attempt to make our theories, our conjectures, suffer in our stead in the struggle for the survival of the fittest. It gives us a chance to survive the elimination of an inadequate hypothesis – when a more dogmatic attitude would eliminate it by eliminating us. (There is a touching story of an Indian community which disappeared because of its belief in the holiness of life, including that of tigers.) We thus obtain the fittest theory within our reach by the elimination of those which are less fit. (By 'fitness' I do not mean merely 'usefulness' but truth.) I do not think that this procedure is irrational or in need of any further rational justification.

10   How Explaining Works: Carl G. Hempel, *Explanation in Science and History**

As many of the preceding extracts make clear, science aims not just to describe the natural world but to explain it; so it is a crucial task for the philosophy of science to specify exactly what such explanation consists in. In our next extract, the eminent philosopher of science Carl Hempel starts by proposing a basic model for scientific explanation, which he calls the *deductive nomological* model. 'Nomological' (from the Greek *nomos*, 'law') means that the phenomenon-to-be-explained (the 'explanandum') is accounted for as an instance of a general principle or law. The 'deductive' aspect means that the explanandum is *subsumed* under the general law, or 'brought under it': the statement of its occurrence is logically deduced from a statement of the law, together with a statement of the relevant surrounding circumstances. The total set of statements thereby invoked as the explanation are known as the *explanans* (in Latin, 'what does the explaining'). By bringing a particular event (e.g. the swelling of a soap bubble) under the scope of a general principle (e.g. a law correlating temperature with gas pressure) there is an intuitively obvious sense in which one explains that event; and Hempel's 'deductive nomological' schema provides a neat formal definition of what is involved.

Scientists often aim to show that the laws they invoke are themselves instances of still higher covering laws (for example Kepler's laws of planetary motion fall under Newton's laws of gravity, which have themselves come to be subsumed under the still more general principles of Relativity Theory). Such subsumption, as Hempel explains, increases the *scope* of our understanding (as an increasingly broad range of phenomena are covered), and also its *depth* (since often in the history of science earlier generalizations later come to be seen as valid only within certain limits, which are accounted for in the light of the higher laws subsequently discovered).

Deduction, as defined by logicians, is a rigorous and strict notion: given the premises, the conclusion cannot be denied on pain of contradiction. Yet often, Hempel goes on to observe, an explanation may be accepted even though the relevant laws are known to have plenty of exceptions. Thus, in medicine, the cure of a bacterial infection may be explained by reference to the injection of an antibiotic, even though the relevant law only predicts success in, say, 60 per cent of cases. In this type of instance, Hempel argues, the explanation is still nomological, since a general law is invoked; but the law in question is statistical rather than universal: we cannot deduce that the particular result will follow inevitably, but only with a certain degree of inductive probability.

Often an explanation, though still following the basic nomological pattern, is *elliptical*: the explainer leaves out things that are taken for granted. (Thus we say that striking the match explains the explosion, omitting to mention the presence of oxygen and other circumstances that are strictly also necessary in order for the result to follow.) Other explanations are *partial*, predicting a general type of event, but not the exact form it actually took (thus, the presence of the wolf does not explain why the sheep ran exactly 53.4 metres to the left, but only that it would flee).[1]

In explaining human behaviour, we are often content with referring to general tendencies (to avoid danger, to seek profit and so on), but Hempel argues that such explanations are still broadly nomological: there are 'psychological generalizations as to the manner in which an intelligent individual will act...to attain a certain objective'. This leads Hempel on to a crucial question: when we explain someone's conduct by reference to his *motivating reason*, is this a special and distinctive (or 'sui-generis') type of explanation, quite different from the scientific

---

*   Carl G. Hempel, 'Explanation in Science and in History', in R. G. Colodny (ed.), *Frontiers of Science and Philosophy* (London and Pittsburgh: Allen & Unwin/University of Pittsburgh Press, 1962), pp. 7–33; abridged.
[1]   This is not Hempel's example; the more complex case he cites is taken from Freud (see below).

explanations previously discussed? Many philosophers have supposed that rational explanation is indeed radically different from normal scientific explanation, since my reasons for action are 'normative' (specifying what I have good reason to do), as opposed to causal factors impelling me to behave in a certain way. Thus Smith's toothache, which is a reason for him to go to the dentist, provides a reason why he *ought* to seek treatment, but is not in itself sufficient to cause him actually to go (since he might, for example, be lazy, or frightened). Hempel argues, however, that if our explanandum is *why A did in fact do X* (e.g. why Smith in fact went to the dentist), then the correct explanation will be (i) that Smith was in a situation which made it rational for him to do so; and further (ii) that Smith was disposed to act rationally; and (iii) that there is a high probability that any rational person in such a situation will do the act in question.

Critics may object that Hempel has simply strait-jacketed the case to force it into his preferred nomological pattern; but defenders may reply that this is quite reasonable, since an appeal to reasons is frequently used to *explain* someone's actual conduct, and if actions are to be explained at all, how else is one to explain them except by applying the kind of law-like schema Hempel has suggested? Some may be worried that Hempel's stress on covering laws even in the case of human action threatens our status as free agents; but Hempel insists that to apply his nomological schema (whether deductive or probabilistic) to the human case 'does not in any way imply a mechanistic view of man'. There are complex and still fiercely debated issues at stake here, but if Hempel is right, then a single pattern of explanation can be seen to operate in a wide variety of domains, including that of human action, thus exhibiting the 'methodological unity of all empirical science'.

Two basic types of scientific explanation

(1) Deductive-nomological explanation

In his book, *How We Think*, John Dewey[1] describes an observation he made one day when, washing dishes, he took some glass tumblers out of the hot soap suds and put them upside down on a plate: he noticed that soap bubbles emerged from under the tumblers' rims, grew for a while, came to a standstill, and finally receded inside the tumblers. Why did this happen? The explanation Dewey outlines comes to this: In transferring a tumbler to the plate, cool air is caught in it; this air is gradually warmed by the glass, which initially has the temperature of the hot suds. The warming of the air is accompanied by an increase in its pressure, which in turn produces an expansion of the soap film between the plate and the rim. Gradually, the glass cools off, and so does the air inside, with the result that the soap bubbles recede.

This explanatory account may be regarded as an argument to the effect that the event to be explained (let me call it the explanandum-event) was to be expected by reason of certain explanatory facts. These may be divided into two groups: (i) particular facts and (ii) uniformities expressed by general laws. The first group includes facts such as these: the tumblers had been immersed, for some time, in soap suds of a temperature considerably higher than that of the surrounding air; they were put on a plate on which a puddle of soapy water had formed ... etc. The second group of items presupposed in the argument includes the gas laws and various other laws that have not been explicitly suggested concerning the exchange of heat between

---

[1] John Dewey (1859–1952), celebrated American philosopher and educational theorist; his *How We Think* was published in 1910.

bodies of different temperature, the elastic behaviour of soap bubbles, etc. If we imagine these various presuppositions explicitly spelled out, the idea suggests itself of construing the explanation as a deductive argument of this form:

(D)
$$\frac{\begin{array}{c} C_1, C_2, \ldots, C_k \\ L_1, L_2, \ldots, L_r \end{array}}{E}$$

Here, $C_1, C_2, \ldots, C_k$ are statements describing the particular facts invoked; $L_1, L_2, \ldots,$ L_r are general laws: jointly, these statements will be said to form the explanans. The conclusion E is a statement describing the explanandum-event; let me call it the explanandum-statement, and let me use the word 'explanandum' to refer to either E or to the event described by it.

The kind of explanation thus characterized I will call *deductive nomological explanation*; for it amounts to a deductive subsumption of the explanandum under principles which have the character of general laws: it answers the question '*Why* did the explanandum event occur?' by showing that the event resulted from the particular circumstances specified in $C_1, C_2, \ldots, C_k$ in accordance with the laws $L_1, L_2, \ldots, L_r$. This conception of explanation, as exhibited in schema (D), has therefore been referred to as the covering law model, or as the deductive model, of explanation.

A good many scientific explanations can be regarded as deductive-nomological in character. Consider for example, images, of rainbows, or of the appearance that a spoon handle is bent at the point where it emerges from a glass of water: in all these cases, the explanandum is deductively subsumed under the laws of reflection and refraction. Similarly, certain aspects of free fall and of planetary motion can be accounted for by deductive subsumption under Galileo's or Kepler's laws.

In the illustrations given so far the explanatory laws had, by and large, the character of empirical generalizations connecting different observable aspects of the phenomena under scrutiny: angle of incidence with angle of reflection or refraction, distance covered with falling time, etc. But science raises the question 'Why?' also with respect to the uniformities expressed by such laws, and often answers it in basically the same manner, namely, by subsuming the uniformities under more inclusive laws, and eventually under comprehensive theories. For example, the question, 'Why do Galileo's and Kepler's laws hold?' is answered by showing that these laws are but special consequences of the Newtonian laws of motion and of gravitation; and these, in turn, may be explained by subsumption under the more comprehensive general theory of relativity. Such subsumption under broader laws or theories usually increases both the breadth and the depth of our scientific understanding. There is an increase in *breadth*, or scope, because the new explanatory principles cover a broader range of phenomena; for example, Newton's principles govern free fall on the earth and on other celestial bodies, as well as the motions of planets, comets and artificial satellites, the movements of pendulums, tidal changes, and various other phenomena. And the increase thus effected in the *depth* of our understanding is strikingly reflected in the fact that, in the light of more advanced explanatory principles, the original empirical laws are usually seen to hold only approximately, or within certain limits. For example, Newton's theory implies that... since every planet undergoes gravitational attraction not only from the sun, but also from the other planets, the planetary orbits are not strictly ellipses, as stated in Kepler's laws...

One further point deserves brief mention here. An explanation of a particular event is often conceived as specifying its *cause*, or causes. Thus, the account outlined in our first illustration might be held to explain the growth and the recession of the soap bubbles by showing that the phenomenon was *caused* by a rise and a subsequent drop of the temperature of the air trapped in the tumblers. Clearly, however, these temperature changes provide the requisite explanation only in conjunction with certain other conditions, such as the presence of a soap film, practically constant pressure of the air surrounding the glasses, etc. Accordingly, in the context of explanation, a cause must be allowed to consist in a more or less complex set of particular circumstances... And, as suggested by the principle 'Same cause, same effect', the assertion that those circumstances jointly caused a given event... implies that whenever and wherever circumstances of the kind in question occur, an event of the kind to be explained comes about. Hence, the given causal explanation implicitly claims that there are general laws – such as $L_1, L_2, \ldots, L_r$, in schema (D) – by virtue of which the occurrence of the causal antecedents... is a sufficient condition for the occurrence of the event to be explained. Thus, the relation between causal factors and effect is reflected in schema (D): causal explanation is deductive-nomological in character...

(2) Probabilistic explanation

In deductive-nomological explanation as schematized in (D), the laws and theoretical principles involved are of *strictly universal form*: they assert that in *all* cases in which certain specified conditions are realized an occurrence of such and such a kind will result; the law that any metal, when heated under constant pressure, will increase in volume, is a typical example; Galileo's, Kepler's, Newton's, Boyle's and Snell's laws, and many others, are of the same character.

Now let me turn next to a second basic type of scientific explanation. This kind of explanation, too, is nomological, i.e. it accounts for a given phenomenon by reference to general laws or theoretical principles; but some or all of these are of *probabilistic-statistical form*, i.e. they are, generally speaking, assertions to the effect that if certain specified conditions are realized, then an occurrence of such-and-such a kind will come about with such-and-such a statistical probability.

For example, the subsiding of a violent attack of hay fever in a given case might well be attributed to, and thus explained by reference to, the administration of 8 milligrams of chlor-trimeton. But if we wish to connect this antecedent event with the explanandum, and thus to establish its explanatory significance for the latter, we cannot invoke a universal law to the effect that the administration of 8 milligrams of that antihistamine will invariably terminate a hay fever attack: this simply is not so. What can be asserted is only a generalization to the effect that administration of the drug will be followed by relief with high statistical probability, i.e., roughly speaking, with a high relative frequency in the long run. The resulting explanans will thus be of the following type:

John Doe had a hay fever attack and took 8 milligrams of chlor-trimeton.
The probability for subsidence of a hay fever attack upon administration of 8 milligrams of chlor-trimeton is high.

Clearly, this explanans does not deductively imply the explanandum, 'John Doe's hay fever attack subsided'; the truth of the explanans makes the truth of the explanandum not certain (as it does in a deductive-nomological explanation) but only more or less likely or, perhaps 'practically' certain. Reduced to its simplest essentials, a probabilistic explanation thus takes the following form:

$$Fi$$

(P) $\underline{p(O, F) \text{ is very high}}$ makes very likely

$$Oi$$

The explanandum, expressed by the statement 'Oi', consists in the fact that in the particular instance under consideration, here called i (e.g. John Doe's allergic attack), an outcome of kind O (subsidence) occurred. This is explained by means of two explanans-statements. The first of these, 'Fi', corresponds to C_1, $C_2, \ldots, C_k$ in (D); it states that in case i, the factors F (which may be more or less complex) were realized. The second expresses a law of probabilistic form, to the effect that the statistical probability for outcome O to occur in cases where F is realized is very high (close to 1). The double line separating explanandum from explanans is to indicate that, in contrast to the case of deductive-nomological explanation, the explanans does not logically imply the explanandum, but only confers a high likelihood upon it ...

Thus, probabilistic explanation, just like explanation in the manner of schema (D), is nomological in that it presupposes general laws; but because these laws are of statistical rather than of strictly universal form, the resulting explanatory arguments are inductive rather than deductive in character. An inductive argument of this kind *explains* a given phenomenon by showing that, in view of certain particular events and certain statistical laws, its occurrence was to be expected with high logical, or inductive, probability ...

Elliptical and partial explanations: explanation sketches

... When a mathematician proves a theorem, he will often omit mention of certain propositions which he presupposes in his argument and which he is in fact entitled to presuppose because, for example, they follow readily from the postulates of his system or from previously established theorems or perhaps from the hypothesis of his theorem, if the latter is in hypothetical form; he then simply assumes that his readers or listeners will be able to supply the missing items if they so desire. If judged by ideal standards, the given formulation of the proof is elliptic or incomplete; but the departure from the ideal is harmless: the gaps can readily be filled in. Similarly, explanations put forward in everyday discourse and also in scientific contexts are often *elliptically formulated*. When we explain, for example, that a lump of butter melted because it was put into a hot frying pan ... we may be said to offer elliptic formulations of deductive-nomological explanations; an account of this kind omits mention of certain laws or particular facts which it tacitly takes for granted, and whose explicit citation would yield a complete deductive-nomological argument.

In addition to elliptic formulation, there is another, quite important, respect in which many explanatory arguments deviate from the theoretical model. It often happens that the statement actually included in the explanans, together with those which may reasonably be assumed to have been taken for granted in the context at hand, explain the given explanandum only *partially*...In his *Psychopathology of Everyday Life* [1901], Freud offers the following explanation of a slip of the pen that occurred to him: 'On a sheet of paper containing principally short daily notes of business interest, I found, to my surprise, the incorrect date, "Thursday, October 20th", bracketed under the correct date of the month of September. It was not difficult to explain this anticipation as the expression of a wish. A few days before I had returned fresh from my vacation and felt ready for any amount of professional work, but as yet there were few patients. On my arrival I had found a letter from a patient announcing her arrival on the 20th of October. As I wrote the same date in September I may certainly have thought "X ought to be here already; what a pity about that whole month!", and with this thought I pushed the current date a month ahead.'

Clearly, the formulation of the intended explanation is *at least incomplete* in the sense considered a moment ago. In particular, it fails to mention any laws or theoretical principles in virtue of which the subconscious wish, and the other antecedent circumstances referred to, could be held to explain Freud's slip of the pen. However, the general theoretical considerations Freud presents here and elsewhere in his writings suggests strongly that his explanatory account relies on a hypothesis to the effect that when a person has a strong, though perhaps unconscious, desire, then if he commits a slip of pen, tongue, memory, or the like, the slip will take a form in which it expresses, and perhaps symbolically fulfils, the given desire.

...Even then, the resulting explanans permits us to deduce only that the slip made by Freud would, *in some way or other*, express and perhaps symbolically fulfil Freud's subconscious wish. But clearly, such expression and fulfilment might have been achieved by many other kinds of slip of the pen than the one actually committed. In other words, the explanans does not imply, and thus fully explain, that the particular slip, say *s*, which Freud committed on this occasion, would fall within the narrow class, say *W*, of acts which consist in writing the words 'Thursday, October 20th'; rather, the explanans implies only that *s* would fall into a wider class, say *F*, which includes *W* as a proper subclass, and which consists of all acts which would express and symbolically fulfil Freud's subconscious wish in *some way or other*.

The argument under consideration might be called a *partial explanation*: it provides complete, or conclusive, grounds for expecting *s* to be a member of *F*, and since *W* is a subclass of *F*, it thus shows that the explanandum, i.e. *s* falling within *W*, accords with, or bears out, what is to be expected in consideration of the explanans. By contrast, a deductive-nomological explanation of the form (D) might then be called *complete* since the explanans here does imply the explanandum...

Nomological explanation in history

...[S]ome historical explanations are surely nomological in character: they aim to show that the explanandum phenomenon resulted from certain antecedent, and perhaps, concomitant, conditions; and in arguing these, they rely more or less explicitly on relevant generalizations. These may concern, for example, psychological or sociological tendencies and may best be conceived as broadly probabilistic in character. [Hempel quotes the example of 'Parkinson's Law', viz. that 'as the activities of the government are enlarged, more people develop a vested interest in the continuation and expansion of governmental functions', 'people who have jobs do not like to lose them', etc.] The psychological generalizations here explicitly adduced will reasonably have to be understood as expressing, not strict uniformities, but strong *tendencies*, which might be formulated by means of rough probability statements; so that the explanation here suggested is probabilistic in character.

As a rule, however, the generalizations underlying a proposed historical explanation are largely left unspecified; and most concrete explanatory accounts have to be qualified as partial explanations or as explanation sketches. Consider, for example, F. J. Turner's essay 'The Significance of the Frontier in American History' [1893] ... 'Why was it', Turner asks, 'that the Indian trader passed so rapidly across the continent?'; and he answers,

The explanation of the rapidity of this advance is bound up with the effects of the trader on the Indian. The trading post left the unarmed tribes at the mercy of those that had purchased firearms – a truth which the Iroquois Indians wrote in blood, and so the remote and unvisited tribes gave eager welcome to the trader...

There is no explicit mention here of any laws, but it is clear that this sketch of an explanation presupposes, first of all, various particular facts, such as that the remote and unvisited tribes had heard of the efficacy and availability of firearms; and that there were no culture patterns or institutions precluding their use by those tribes; but in addition, the account clearly rests also on certain assumptions as to how human beings will tend to behave in situations presenting the kinds of danger and of opportunity that Turner refers to...

But if this be granted there still remains another question, to which we must now turn, namely, whether, in addition to explanations of a broadly nomological character, the historian also employs certain other distinctly historical ways of explaining and understanding whose import cannot be adequately characterized by means of our two models...

Genetic explanation in history

In order to make the occurrence of a historical phenomenon intelligible, a historian will frequently offer a 'genetic explanation' aimed at exhibiting the principal stages in a sequence of events which led up to the given phenomenon. [Hempel goes on to quote from historical accounts of the fourteenth-century practice of selling of indulgences, which trace the practice back to the papal need to raise funds for the crusades, going right back to the ninth century.]

... Undeniably, a genetic account of this kind can enhance our understanding of a historical phenomenon. But its explanatory role, far from being *sui generis*, seems to me basically nomological in character. For the successive stages singled out for consideration surely must be qualified for their function by more than the fact that they form a temporal sequence and that they all precede the final stage, which is to be explained: the mere enumeration in a yearbook of 'the year's important events' in the order of their occurrence clearly is not a genetic explanation of the final event or of anything else. In a genetic explanation each stage must be shown to 'lead to' the next, and thus to be linked to its successor by virtue of some general principle which makes the occurrence of the latter at least reasonably probable, given the former...Thus, schematically speaking, a genetic explanation will begin with a pure description of an initial stage; thence, it will proceed to an account of a second stage, part of which is nomologically linked to, and explained by, the characteristic features of the initial stage...and so forth.

In our illustration the connecting laws are hinted at in the mention made of motivating factors: the explanatory claims made for the interest of the popes in securing a fighting force and in amassing ever larger funds clearly presuppose suitable psychological generalizations as to the manner in which an intelligent individual will act, in the light of his factual beliefs, when he seeks to attain a certain objective...

Explanation by motivating reasons

Let us now turn to another kind of historical explanation that is often considered as *sui generis*, namely, the explanation of an action in terms of the underlying rationale, which will include, in particular, the ends the agent sought to attain, and the alternative courses of action he believed to be open to him...

The kind of explanation achieved by specifying the rationale underlying a given action is widely held to be fundamentally different from nomological explanation as found in the natural sciences...According to W. Dray[1]...a rational explanation answers a question of the form 'Why did agent A do X?' by offering an explanans of the following type...

(R)   A was in a situation of type C
      In a situation of type C, the appropriate thing to do is X

But can an explanans of this type possibly serve to explain A's having in fact done X? It seems to me beyond dispute that in any adequate explanation of an empirical phenomenon the explanans must provide good grounds for believing or asserting that the explanandum phenomenon did in fact occur. Yet this requirement, which is necessary though not sufficient for an adequate explanation, is not met by a rational explanation as conceived by Dray. For the two statements included in the contemplated explanans (R) provide good reasons for believing that the appropriate thing for A to do was X, but not for believing that A did in fact do X. Thus, a rational explanation in the sense in which Dray appears to understand it does not explain what it is meant to explain.

---

[1] W. Dray, *Laws and Explanations in History* (Oxford: Oxford University Press, 1957).

Indeed, the expression 'the thing to do', in the standard formulation of a principle of action, 'functions as a value term', as Dray himself points out: but then, it is unclear, on purely logical grounds, how the valuational principle expressed by the second sentence in (R), in conjunction with the plainly empirical, non-valuational first sentence, should permit any inferences concerning empirical matters such as A's action, which could not be drawn from the first sentence alone.

To explain, in the general vein here under discussion, why A did in fact do X, we have to refer to the underlying rationale not by means of a normative principle of action, but by descriptive statements to the effect that, at the time in question A was a rational agent, or had the disposition to act rationally; and that a rational agent, when in circumstances of kind C, will always (or: with high probability) do X. Thus construed, the explanans takes on the following form:

(R')   1. A was in a situation of type C
       2. A was disposed to act rationally
       3. Any person who is disposed to act rationally will, when in a situation of type C, invariably (with high probability) do X

But by this explanans, A's having done X is accounted for in the manner of a deductive or of a probabilistic nomological explanation. Thus, in so far as reference to the rationale of an agent does explain his action, the explanation conforms to one of our nomological models...

Concluding remarks

We have surveyed some of the most prominent candidates for the role of characteristically historical mode of explanation; and we have found that they conform essentially to one or the other of our two basic types of scientific explanation. This result and the arguments that led to it do not in any way imply a mechanistic view of man, of society and of historical processes; nor, of course, do they deny the importance of ideas and ideals for human decision and action. What the preceding considerations do suggest is, rather, that the nature of understanding, in the sense in which explanation is meant to give us an understanding of empirical phenomena, is basically the same in all areas of scientific inquiry; and that the deductive and the probabilistic models of nomological explanation accommodate vastly more than just the explanatory arguments of, say, classical mechanics: in particular, they accord well also with the character of explanations that deal with the influence of rational deliberation, of conscious and subconscious motives, and of ideas and ideals on the shaping of historical events. In so doing, our schemata exhibit, I think, one important aspect of the methodological unity of all empirical science.

11   Scientific Realism versus Instrumentalism: Grover Maxwell, *The Ontological Status of Theoretical Entities**

Empirical investigation is a vital and indispensable part of scientific inquiry (compare extract 2, above), and because of this it is perhaps not surprising that the philosophy of empiricism has had an important influence on the philosophy of science. John Locke in the early-modern period asserted that all our knowledge about the world stems from sensory impressions,[1] a position shared by his arch-empiricist successor David Hume, who argued that it places severe limits on the scope of scientific knowledge (see extract 5, above). Following in this tradition, several nineteenth- and twentieth-century philosophers advanced the radical thesis that science could properly deal only with the directly observable – either with ordinary everyday objects, or perhaps only the 'sense-contents' or 'sense-data' with which we are directly acquainted in experience.[2]

Yet clearly a great deal of science goes beyond such basic data – it includes reference to such entities as, for example, electrons and X-rays, not to mention the even stranger world of quarks and their properties. How are we to understand such things? According to *instrumentalism*, which is rooted in the empiricist tradition, we should adopt a resolutely non-realist view of such things: theoretical entities of this kind should be construed not as real objects, but merely as place-holders for mathematical calculations, or simply as convenient devices enabling us to move from a given set of observations to a predicted set of results.

In our penultimate extract, Grover Maxwell subjects such instrumentalism to vigorous attack. He tells a deliberately amusing story (loosely based on the real history of medicine)

about a scientist who, before the days of microscopes, posits unseen entities called 'crobes' to explain the spread of disease. Noting that such entities cannot be observed, the philosophers of the time jump in and insist that 'crobes' are not genuine entities, but merely convenient theoretical fictions, enabling us to 'predict successfully and otherwise organize data in a convenient fashion'. Maxwell's way of telling the story makes clear his scorn for such manoeuvres; for him, there is no reason why we should not adopt a robustly realist attitude to 'crobes' (microbes), or indeed any of the other entities posited by theoretical scientists. It is true that there are difficulties in 'directly observing' many such entities, but this, Maxwell argues, is a matter of degree: 'there is a continuous transition from the observable to the unobservable (theoretical)'. For Maxwell, the line between the observable and the unobservable is 'diffuse', and as science advances, and better instruments are developed, it is constantly shifting.

Maxwell makes two telling points in the concluding part of his paper. First, the emphasis that many radically empiricist philosophers of science have placed on sense-impressions is misguided: 'the referents of most . . . of the statements of the linguistic framework used in everyday life and in science are not sense contents but, rather, physical objects and other publicly observable entities.' Second, even in the case of highly theoretical entities, we can train ourselves to 'observe directly' the relevant items: after sitting on a hard bench listening to a boring speech 'we begin to become poignantly aware of the presence of a . . . strong gravitational field'. One might object that Maxwell is glossing over some

---

* First published in Herbert Feigl and Grover Maxwell (eds), *Scientific Explanation, Space, and Time*, Minnesota Studies in the Philosophy of Science, vol. 3 (Minneapolis: University of Minnesota Press, 1962), pp. 3–15; with omissions.

[1] See Part I, extract 5, above.

[2] Compare Carnap on the importance of 'observation sentences' or 'protocol sentences' (Part II, extract 10, above).

difficulties here: could we really ever 'train our-selves' to have this kind of observational know-ledge of the various sub-atomic particles posited by modern physics, such as neutrinos? Even granting Maxwell's idea of a continuous spec-trum between the observable and the unobserv-able, there remain serious epistemological and ontological questions about the status of such highly theoretical entities. Despite Maxwell's challenging conclusion that the drawing of the observational/theoretical line at any given point has 'no ontological significance whatever', fascin-ating questions remain to be answered about what the 'truth' of the highly abstract theories of modern physics amounts to, and about the 'reality' of entities that are, perhaps neces-sarily, beyond the reach of any normal human perception.

That anyone today should seriously contend that the entities referred to by scientific theories are only convenient fictions, or that talk about such entities is translatable without remainder into talk about sense contents or everyday physical objects, or that such talk should be regarded as belonging to a mere calculating device and, thus, without cognitive content – such contentions strike me as so incongruous with the scientific and rational attitude and practice that I feel this paper *should* turn out to be a demolition of straw men. But the instrumentalist views of outstanding physicists such as Bohr and Heisenberg are too well known to be cited ... I shall limit myself to a small number of constructive arguments (for a radically realistic interpretation of theories) and to a critical examination of some of the more crucial assumptions (sometimes tacit, sometimes explicit) that seem to have generated most of the problems in this area.

The problem

Although this essay is not comprehensive, it aspires to be fairly self-contained. Let me, therefore, give a pseudo-historical introduction to the problem with a piece of science fiction (or fictional science).

In the days before the advent of microscopes, there lived a Pasteur-like scientist whom, following the usual custom, I shall call Jones. Reflecting on the fact that certain diseases seemed to be transmitted from one person to another by means of bodily contact or by contact with articles handled previously by an afflicted person, Jones began to speculate about the mechanism of the transmission. As a 'heuristic crutch', he recalled that there is an obvious *observable* mechanism for transmission of certain afflictions (such as body lice), and he postulated that all, or most, infectious diseases were spread in a similar manner but that in most cases the corresponding 'bugs' were too small to be seen and, possibly, that some of them lived inside the bodies of their hosts. Jones proceeded to develop his theory and to examine its testable consequences. Some of these seemed to be of great importance for preventing the spread of disease.

After years of struggle with incredulous recalcitrance, Jones managed to get some of his preventative measures adopted. Contact with or proximity to diseased persons was avoided when possible, and articles which they handled were 'disinfected' (a word coined by Jones) either by means of high temperatures or by treating them with certain toxic preparations which Jones termed 'disinfectants'. The results were spec-tacular: within ten years the death rate had declined 40 per cent. Jones and his theory received their well-deserved recognition.

However, the 'crobes' (the theoretical term coined by Jones to refer to the disease-producing organisms) aroused considerable anxiety among many of the philosophers and philosophically inclined scientists of the day. The expression of this anxiety usually began something like this: 'In order to account for the facts, Jones must assume that his crobes are too small to be seen. Thus the very postulates of his theory preclude their being observed; they are *unobservable in principle*.' (Recall that no one had envisaged such a thing as a microscope.) This common prefatory remark was then followed by a number of different 'analyses' and 'interpretations' of Jones's theory. According to one of these, the tiny organisms were merely convenient fictions – *façons de parler* – extremely useful as heuristic devices for facilitating (in the 'context of discovery') the thinking of scientists but not to be taken seriously in the sphere of cognitive knowledge (in the 'context of justification'). A closely related view was that Jones's theory was merely an instrument, useful for organizing observation statements and (thus) for producing desired results, and that, therefore, it made no more sense to ask what was the nature of the entities to which it referred than it did to ask what was the nature of the entities to which a hammer or any other tool referred. 'Yes,' a philosopher might have said, 'Jones's theoretical expressions are just meaningless sounds or marks on paper which, when correlated with observation sentences by appropriate syntactical rules, enable us to predict successfully and otherwise organize data in a convenient fashion.' These philosophers called themselves 'instrumentalists.'

According to another view (which, however, soon became unfashionable), although expressions containing Jones's theoretical terms were genuine sentences, they were translatable without remainder into a set (perhaps infinite) of observation sentences. For example, 'There are crobes of disease X on this article' was said to translate into something like this: 'If a person handles this article without taking certain precautions, he will (probably) contract disease X; and if this article is first raised to a high temperature, then if a person handles it at any time afterward, before it comes into contact with another person with disease X, he will (probably) not contract disease X; and ...'

...Now Jones had the good fortune to live to see the invention of the compound microscope. His crobes were 'observed' in great detail, and it became possible to identify the specific kind of *microbe* (for so they began to be called) which was responsible for each different disease. Some philosophers freely admitted error and were converted to realist positions concerning theories. Others resorted to subjective idealism or to a thoroughgoing phenomenalism, of which there were two principal varieties. According to one, the one 'legitimate' observation language had for its descriptive terms only those which referred to sense data. The other maintained the stronger thesis that *all* 'factual' statements were *translatable* without remainder into the sense-datum language. In either case, any two non-sense data (e.g., a theoretical entity and what would ordinarily be called an 'observable physical object') had virtually the same status. Others contrived means of modifying their views much less drastically. One group maintained that Jones's crobes actually never had been unobservable in principle, for, they said, the theory did not imply the impossibility of finding a means (e.g., the microscope) of observing them. A more radical contention was that the crobes were not observed at all; it was argued that what was seen by means of the microscope was just a shadow or an image rather than a corporeal organism.

The observational–theoretical dichotomy

Let us turn from these fictional philosophical positions and consider some of the actual ones to which they roughly correspond. Taking the last one first, it is interesting to note the following passage from Bergmann: 'But it is only fair to point out that if this...methodological and terminological analysis [for the thesis that there are no atoms]...is strictly adhered to, even stars and microscopic objects are not physical things in a literal sense, but merely by courtesy of language and pictorial imagination. This might seem awkward. But when I look through a microscope, all I see is a patch of colour which creeps through the field like a shadow over a wall. And a shadow, though real, is certainly not a physical thing.'[1]

I should like to point out that it is also the case that if this analysis is strictly adhered to, we cannot observe physical things through opera glasses, or even through ordinary spectacles, and one begins to wonder about the status of what we see through an ordinary windowpane. And what about distortions due to temperature gradients – however small and, thus, always present – in the ambient air? It really does 'seem awkward' to say that when people who wear glasses describe what they see they are talking about shadows, while those who employ unaided vision talk about physical things – or that when we look through a windowpane, we can only *infer* that it is raining, while if we raise the window, we may 'observe directly' that it is. The point I am making is that there is, in principle, a continuous series beginning with looking through a vacuum and containing these as members: looking through a windowpane, looking through glasses, looking through binoculars, looking through a low-power microscope, looking through a high-power microscope, etc., in the order given. The important consequence is that, so far, we are left without criteria which would enable us to draw a non-arbitrary line between 'observation' and 'theory.'...

However, it might be argued that things seen through spectacles and binoculars look like ordinary physical objects, while those seen through microscopes and tele-scopes look like shadows and patches of light. I can only reply that this does not seem to me to be the case, particularly when looking at the moon, or even Saturn, through a telescope or when looking at a small, though 'directly observable', physical object through a low-power microscope. Thus, again, a continuity appears...

Another argument for the continuous transition from the observable to the unob-servable (theoretical) may be adduced from theoretical considerations themselves. For example, contemporary valency theory tells us that there is a virtually continuous transition from very small molecules (such as those of hydrogen) through 'medium-sized' ones (such as those of the fatty acids, polypeptides, proteins and viruses) to extremely large ones (such as crystals of the salts, diamonds and lumps of polymeric plastic). The molecules in the last-mentioned group are macro, 'directly observable' physical objects but are, nevertheless, genuine, single molecules; on the other hand, those in the first-mentioned group have the same perplexing properties as sub-atomic particles (de Broglie waves, Heisenberg indeterminacy, etc.). Are we to say that a large protein molecule (e.g., a virus) which can be 'seen' only with an electron microscope

[1] *G. Bergmann, 'Outline of an Empiricist Philosophy of Physics', *American Journal of Physics* (1943), repr. in H. Feigl and M. Brodbeck (eds), *Readings in the Philosophy of Science* (New York: Appleton, 1953).

is a little less real or exists to somewhat less an extent than does a molecule of a polymer which can be seen with an optical microscope? And does a hydrogen molecule partake of only an infinitesimal portion of existence or reality? Although there certainly *is* a continuous transition from observability to unobservability, any talk of such a continuity from full-blown existence to non-existence is, clearly, nonsense.

Let us now consider the next to last modified position which was adopted by our fictional philosophers. According to them, it is only those entities which are *in principle* impossible to observe that present special problems...I shall begin by putting my head on the block and argue that the present-day status of, say, electrons is in many ways similar to that of Jones's crobes before microscopes were invented. I am well aware of the numerous theoretical arguments for the impossibility of observing electrons. But suppose new entities are discovered which interact with electrons in such a mild manner that if an electron is, say, in an eigenstate of position, then, in certain circumstances, the interaction does not disturb it. Suppose also that a drug is discovered which vastly alters the human perceptual apparatus – perhaps even activates latent capacities so that a new sense modality emerges. Finally, suppose that in our altered state we are able to perceive (not necessarily visually) by means of these new entities in a manner roughly analogous to that by which we now *see* by means of photons...

Consider a somewhat less fantastic example, and one which does not involve any change in physical theory. Suppose a human mutant is born who is able to 'observe' ultraviolet radiation, or even X-rays, in the same way we 'observe' visible light.

Now I think that it is extremely improbable that we will ever observe electrons directly (i.e., that it will ever be reasonable to assert that we have so observed them). But this is neither here nor there; it is not the purpose of this essay to predict the future development of scientific theories, and, hence, it is not its business to decide what actually is observable or what will become observable (in the more or less intuitive sense of 'observable' with which we are now working). After all, we are operating, here, under the assumption that it is theory, and thus science itself, which tells us what is or is not, in this sense, observable (the 'in principle' seems to have become superfluous). And this is the heart of the matter; for it follows that, at least for this sense of 'observable', there are no a priori or philosophical criteria for separating the observable from the unobservable. By trying to show that we can talk about the *possibility* of observing electrons without committing logical or conceptual blunders, I have been trying to support the thesis that any (non-logical) term is a *possible* candidate for an observation term.

...Although I have contended that the line between the observable and the unobservable is diffuse, that it shifts from one scientific problem to another, and that it is constantly being pushed toward the 'unobservable' end of the spectrum as we develop better means of observation – better instruments – it would, nevertheless, be fatuous to minimize the importance of the observation base, for it is absolutely necessary as a confirmation base for statements which do refer to entities which are unobservable at a given time. But we should take as its basis and its unit not the 'observational term' but, rather, the quickly decidable sentence...A quickly decidable sentence (in the technical sense employed here) may be defined as a singular, non-analytic sentence such that a reliable, reasonably sophisticated language user can very quickly decide whether to assert it or deny it when he is reporting on an occurrent situation. 'Observation term' may now be defined as a 'descriptive (non-logical) term which may occur in a quickly decidable sentence', and 'observation sentence' as a 'sentence whose only descriptive terms are observation terms'.

. . . Let me emphasize that I am not among those philosophers who hold that there are no such things as sense contents (even sense data), nor do I believe that they play no important role in our perception of 'reality'. But the fact remains that the referents of most (not all) of the statements of the linguistic framework used in everyday life and in science are *not* sense contents but, rather, physical objects and other publicly observable entities. Except for pains, odours, 'inner states', etc., *we do not usually observe sense contents*; and although there is good reason to believe that they play an indispensable role in observation, *we are usually not aware of them when we* (visually or tactilely) *observe physical objects*. For example, when I observe a distorted, obliquely reflected image in a mirror, I may seem to be seeing a baby elephant standing on its head; later I discover it is an image of Uncle Charles taking a nap with his mouth open and his hand in a peculiar position. Or, passing my neighbour's home at a high rate of speed, I observe that he is washing a car. If asked to report these observations I could quickly and easily report a baby elephant and a washing of a car; I probably would not, without subsequent observations, be able to report what colours, shapes, etc. (i.e., what sense data) were involved.

Two questions naturally arise at this point. How is it that we can (sometimes) quickly decide the truth or falsity of a pertinent observation sentence? and, What role do sense contents play in the appropriate tokening of such sentences? The heart of the matter is that these are primarily scientific-theoretical questions rather than 'purely logical', 'purely conceptual', or 'purely epistemological'. If theoretical physics, psychology, neurophysiology, etc., were sufficiently advanced, we could give satisfactory answers to these questions, using, in all likelihood, the physical-thing language as our observation language and *treating sensations, sense contents, sense data, and 'inner states' as theoretical* (yes, theoretical!) *entities*.

It is interesting and important to note that, even before we give completely satisfactory answers to the two questions considered above, we can, with due effort and reflection, train ourselves to 'observe directly' what were once theoretical entities – the sense contents (colour sensations, etc.) involved in our perception of physical things. As has been pointed out before, we can also come to observe other kinds of entities which were once theoretical. Those which most readily come to mind involve the use of instruments as aids to observation. Indeed, using our painfully acquired theoretical knowledge of the world, we come to see that we 'directly observe' many kinds of so-called theoretical things. After listening to a dull speech while sitting on a hard bench, we begin to become poignantly aware of the presence of a considerably strong gravitational field, and . . . if we were carrying a heavy suitcase in a changing gravitational field, we could observe the changes of the $G\mu\nu$ of the metric tensor.

I conclude that our drawing of the observational–theoretical line at any given point is an accident and a function of our physiological makeup, our current state of knowledge, and the instruments we happen to have available and, therefore, that it has no ontological significance whatever.

12   Change and Crisis in Science: Thomas Kuhn, *The Structure of Scientific Revolutions**

People sometimes speak of 'science' and 'scientific knowledge' as if these terms referred to some fixed and timelessly valid set of methods and procedures. But it should be clear from some of our earlier extracts that this cannot be right. Part of what Bacon and Descartes were doing in the seventeenth century (extracts 2 and 3, above) was laying down new conditions and criteria for scientific knowledge – perhaps even shaping the very concept of 'science' as we have come to understand the term. But even within the domain of 'modern science', it may be a mistake to suppose that there is a steady and orderly growth of knowledge in accordance with fixed rules. According to Thomas Kuhn, in his highly influential *The Structure of Scientific Revolutions*, a scrutiny of the way science actually develops from age to age shows a considerable variation. Taking issue with Popper (see extract 9, above), Kuhn argues that during periods of 'normal science', theories are seldom discarded, even in the face of seemingly striking anomalies in the observational data. This is because normal science, on Kuhn's view, operates within the terms of reference determined by a 'paradigm' – his term for the ruling assumptions and standards of inquiry associated with dominant scientific theory; only when the ruling paradigm runs into crisis, and only when some alternative paradigm is available, will there be the possibility of a 'scientific revolution' in which the dominant theory is overthrown.

Kuhn's choice of the term 'revolution', with its historical and political connotations, is quite deliberate. Political revolutions take place when existing institutions break down, or fail to cope with crisis; they take place, moreover, outside the rules of the existing institutions, creating (if they are successful) their own new standards and institutional structures. Revolutionary scientific change is, for Kuhn, very similar, and it follows that the justification for the shift from one paradigm to its successor cannot be provided within the terms of the older model. A paradigm shift involves a radical hiatus, a sudden Gestalt-switch, or change in our ways of seeing the world: 'the choice is not and cannot be determined merely by the evaluative procedures characteristic of normal science, for those depend in part upon a particular paradigm, and that paradigm is at issue'. Kuhn's views have led to a continuing debate among philosophers of science concerning the extent to which science has to be understood as a human institution like any other, shaped in part by the same kinds of historical and social forces. And this in turn leads to scrutiny of the whole idea of 'progress' in science – the notion of science as a series of objectively demonstrable 'improvements' in our journey towards a deeper and more accurate knowledge of the world. Descartes, as we saw earlier (extract 3), believed that the fundamental framework for physics was implanted in the human mind by God. While few nowadays would claim that kind of objectivity for science, many none the less believe that the story of science is a story of genuine advance in our understanding of nature; a continuing task for the philosophy of science will be to examine in what sense, if any, that view can be justified.

In this essay, 'normal science' means research firmly based upon one or more past scientific achievements, achievements that some particular scientific community acknowledges for a time as supplying the foundation for its further practice. Today, such achievements are recounted, though seldom in their original form, by science

* Thomas S. Kuhn, *The Structure of Scientific Revolutions* [1962] (2nd edn, Chicago: University of Chicago Press, 1970), extracts from chs 2, 6, 7, 8, 9 and 10 (pp. 10–11, 64–5, 76–7, 81–3, 93–5, 112, 117–18).

textbooks, elementary and advanced. These textbooks expound the body of accepted theory, illustrate many or all of its successful applications, and compare these applications with exemplary observations and experiments. Before such books became popular early in the nineteenth century (and until even more recently in the newly matured sciences) many of the famous classics of sciences fulfilled a similar function... They served for a time implicitly to define the legitimate problems and methods of a research field for succeeding generations of practitioners. They were able to do so because they shared two essential characteristics. Their achievement was sufficiently unprecedented to attract an enduring group of adherents away from competing modes of scientific activity. Simultaneously, it was sufficiently open-ended to leave all sorts of problems for the redefined group of practitioners to resolve.

Achievements that share these two characteristics I shall henceforth refer to as 'paradigms', a term that relates closely to 'normal science'. By choosing it, I mean to suggest that some accepted examples of actual scientific practice – examples which include law, theory, application and instrumentation together – provide models from which spring particular coherent traditions of scientific research. These are the traditions which the historian describes under such rubrics as 'Ptolemaic astronomy' (or 'Copernican'), 'Aristotelian dynamics' (or 'Newtonian'), 'corpuscular optics' (or 'wave optics'), and so on. The study of paradigms, including many that are far more specialized than those named illustratively above, is what mainly prepares the student for membership in the particular scientific community with which he will later practice. Because he there joins men who learned the bases of their belief from the same concrete models, his subsequent practice will seldom evoke overt disagreement over fundamentals. Men whose research is based on shared paradigms are committed to the same rules and standards for scientific practice. That commitment and the apparent consensus it produces are prerequisites for normal science, i.e., for the genesis and continuation of a particular research tradition...

In the development of any science, the first received paradigm is usually felt to account quite successfully for most of the observations and experiments easily accessible to that science's practitioners. Further development, therefore, ordinarily calls for the construction of elaborate equipment, the development of an esoteric vocabulary and skills, and a refinement of concepts that increasingly lessens their resemblance to their usual common-sense prototypes. That professionalization leads, on the one hand, to an immense restriction of the scientist's vision and to a considerable resistance to paradigm change. The scientist has become increasingly rigid. On the other hand, within those areas to which the paradigm directs the attention of the group, normal science leads to a detail of information and to a precision of the observation-theory match that could be achieved in no other way. Furthermore, that detail and precision-of-match have a value that transcends their not always very high intrinsic interest. Without the special apparatus that is constructed mainly for anticipated functions, the results that lead ultimately to novelty could not occur. And even when the apparatus exists, novelty ordinarily emerges only for the man who, knowing *with precision* what he should expect, is able to recognize that something has gone wrong. Anomaly appears only against the background provided by the paradigm. The more precise and far-reaching that paradigm is, the more sensitive an indicator it provides of anomaly and hence of an occasion for paradigm change. In the normal mode of discovery, even resistance to change has a use ... Resistance to change guarantees that scientists will not be lightly distracted and that the anomalies that lead to paradigm change will penetrate existing knowledge to the core. The very fact that a significant scientific novelty so often emerges simultaneously from several laboratories is an index both to the strongly traditional nature of normal science and to the completeness with which that traditional pursuit prepares the way for its own change ...

Philosophers of science have repeatedly demonstrated that more than one theoretical construction can always be placed upon a given collection of data. History of science indicates that, particularly in the early developmental stages of a new paradigm, it is not even very difficult to invent such alternates. But that invention of alternates is just what scientists seldom undertake ... So long as the tools a paradigm provides continue to prove capable of solving the problems it defines, science moves fastest and penetrates most deeply through confident employment of those tools. The reason is clear. As in manufacture so in science – retooling is an extravagance to be reserved for the occasion that demands it. The significance of crises is the indication they provide that an occasion for retooling has arrived.

Let us then assume that crises are a necessary precondition for the emergence of novel theories and ask next how scientists respond to their existence. Part of the answer, as obvious as it is important, can be discovered by noting first what scientists never do when confronted by even severe and prolonged anomalies. Though they may begin to lose faith and then to consider alternatives, they do not renounce the paradigm that has led them into crisis. They do not, that is, treat anomalies as counter-instances, though in the vocabulary of philosophy of science that is what they are ... Once it has achieved the status of a paradigm, a scientific theory is declared invalid only if an alternate candidate is available to take its place. No process yet disclosed by the historical study of scientific development at all resembles the methodological stereotype of falsification by direct comparison with nature. That remark does not mean that scientists do not reject scientific theories, or that experience and experiment are not essential to the process in which they do so. But it does mean ... that the act of judgement that leads scientists to reject a previously accepted theory is always based upon more that a comparison of that theory with the world. The decision to reject one paradigm is always simultaneously the decision to accept another, and the judgement leading to that decision involves the comparison of both paradigms with nature *and* each other ...

How, then, ... do scientists respond to the awareness of an anomaly in the fit between theory and nature? ... Even a discrepancy unaccountably larger than that experienced in other applications of the theory need not draw any very profound response. There are always some discrepancies. Even the most stubborn ones usually respond at last to normal practice. Very often scientists are willing to wait, particularly if there are many problems available in other parts of the field ... During the sixty years after Newton's original computation, the predicted motion of the moon's perigee remained only half of that observed. As Europe's best mathematical physicists continued to wrestle unsuccessfully with the well-known discrepancy, there were occasional proposals for a modification of Newton's inverse square law. But no one took these proposals very seriously, and in practice this patience with a major anomaly proved justified. Clairaut in 1750 was able to show that only the mathematics of the application had been wrong and that Newtonian theory could stand as before. Even in cases where no mere mistake seems quite possible (perhaps because the mathematics involved is simpler or of a familiar and elsewhere successful sort), persistent and recognized anomaly does not always induce crisis. No one seriously questioned Newtonian theory because of the long-recognized discrepancies between predictions from that theory and both the speed of sound and the motion of Mercury. The first discrepancy was ultimately and quite unexpectedly resolved by experiments on heat undertaken for a very different purpose; the second vanished with the general theory of relativity after a crisis that it had no role in creating. Apparently neither had seemed sufficiently fundamental to evoke the malaise that goes with crisis. They could be recognized as counter-instances and still be set aside for later work.

It follows that if an anomaly is to evoke crisis, it must usually be more than just an anomaly. There are always difficulties somewhere in the paradigm-nature fit; most of them are set right sooner or later, often by processes that could not have been foreseen. The scientist who pauses to examine every anomaly he notes will seldom get significant work done. We therefore have to ask what it is that makes an anomaly seem worth concerted scrutiny, and to that question there is probably no fully general answer...Sometimes an anomaly will clearly call into question explicit and fundamental generalizations of the paradigm, as the problem of ether drag did for those who accepted [James] Maxwell's theory [of electromagnetism]. Or, as in the Copernican revolution, an anomaly without apparent fundamental import may evoke crisis if the applications that it inhibits have a particular practical importance, in this case for calendar design and astrology. Or, as in eighteenth-century chemistry, the development of normal science may transform an anomaly that had previously been only a vexation into a source of crisis: the problem of weight relations had a very different status after the evolution of pneumatic-chemical techniques. Presumably there are still other circumstances that can make an anomaly particularly pressing, and ordinarily several of these can combine. We have already noted, for example, that one source of the crisis that confronted Copernicus was the mere length of time during which astronomers had wrestled unsuccessfully with the reduction of the discrepancies in Ptolemy's system.

When, for these reasons or others like them, an anomaly comes to seem more than just another puzzle of normal science, the transition to crisis and to extraordinary science has begun. The anomaly itself now comes to be more generally recognized as such by the profession. More and more attention is devoted to it by more and more of the field's most eminent men. If it still continues to resist, as it usually does not, many of them may come to view its resolution as *the* subject matter of their discipline. For them the field will no longer look the same as it had earlier. Part of its different appearance results simply from the new fixation point of scientific scrutiny. An even more important source of change is the divergent nature of the numerous partial solutions that concerted attention to the problem has made available. The early attacks on the resistant problem will have followed the paradigm rules quite closely. But with continuing resistance, more and more of the attacks upon it will have involved some minor or not so minor articulation of the paradigm, no two of them quite alike, each partially successful, but none sufficiently so to be accepted as a paradigm by the group. Though this proliferation of divergent articulations (more and more frequently they will come to be described as *ad hoc* adjustments), the rules of normal science become increasingly blurred. Though there is still a paradigm, few practitioners prove to be entirely agreed about what it is. Even formerly standard solutions of solved problems are called in question...

What are scientific revolutions and what is their function in scientific development?...Scientific revolutions are here taken to be those non-cumulative developmental episodes in which an older paradigm is replaced in whole or in part by an incompatible new one. There is more to be said, however, and an essential part of it can be introduced by asking one further question. Why should a change of paradigm be called a revolution? In the face of the vast and essential differences between political and scientific development, what parallelism can justify the metaphor that finds revolutions in both?

One aspect of the parallelism must already be apparent. Political revolutions are inaugurated by a growing sense, often restricted to a segment of the political community, that existing institutions have ceased adequately to meet the problems posed by an environment that they have in part created. In much the same way, scientific revolutions are inaugurated by a growing sense, again often restricted to a narrow subdivision of the scientific community, that an existing paradigm has ceased to function adequately in the exploration of an aspect of nature to which that paradigm itself had previously led the way. In both political and scientific development the sense of malfunction that can lead to crisis is prerequisite to revolution. Furthermore, though it admittedly strains the metaphor, that parallelism holds not only for the major paradigm changes, like those attributable to Copernicus and Lavoisier, but also for the far smaller ones associated with the assimilation of a new sort of phenomenon, like oxygen or X-rays. Scientific revolutions...need seem revolutionary only to those whose paradigms are affected by them. To outsiders they may, like the Balkan revolutions of the early twentieth century, seem normal parts of the developmental process. Astronomers, for example, could accept X-rays as a mere addition to knowledge, for their paradigms were unaffected by the existence of the new radiation. But for men like Kelvin, Crookes and Röntgen, whose research dealt with radiation theory or with cathode ray tubes, the emergence of X-rays necessarily violated one paradigm as it created another. That is why these rays could be discovered only through something's first going wrong with normal research.

This genetic aspect of the parallel between political and scientific development should no longer be open to doubt. The parallel has, however, a second and more profound aspect upon which the significance of the first depends. Political revolutions aim to change political institutions in ways that those institutions themselves prohibit. Their success therefore necessitates the partial relinquishment of one set of institutions in favour of another, and in the interim, society is not fully governed by institutions at all. Initially it is crisis alone that attenuates the role of political institutions as we have already seen it attenuate the role of paradigms. In increasing numbers individuals become increasingly estranged from political life and behave more and more eccentrically within it. Then, as the crisis deepens, many of these individuals commit themselves to some concrete proposal for the reconstruction of society in a new institutional framework. At that point the society is divided into competing camps or parties, one seeking to defend the old institutional constellation, the other seeking to institute some new one. And once that polarization has occurred, *political recourse fails.* Because they differ about the institutional matrix within which political change is to be achieved and evaluated, because they acknowledge no supra-institutional framework for the adjudication of revolutionary difference, the parties to a revolutionary conflict must finally resort to the techniques of mass persuasion, often including force. Though revolutions have had a vital role in the evolution of political institutions, that role depends upon their being partially extra-political or extra-institutional events.

. . . The historical study of paradigm change reveals very similar characteristics in the evolution of the sciences. Like the choice between competing political institutions, that between competing paradigms proves to be a choice between incompatible modes of community life. Because it has that character, the choice is not and cannot be determined merely by the evaluative procedures characteristic of normal science, for those depend in part upon a particular paradigm, and that paradigm is at issue. When paradigms enter, as they must, into a debate about paradigm choice, their role is necessarily circular. Each group uses its own paradigm to argue in that paradigm's defence . . .

Examining the record of past research from the vantage of contemporary historiography, the historian of science may be tempted to exclaim that when paradigms change, the world itself changes with them. Led by a new paradigm, scientists adopt new instruments and look in new places. Even more important, during revolutions scientists see new and different things when looking with familiar instruments in places they have looked before. It is rather as if the professional community had been suddenly transported to another planet where familiar objects are seen in a different light, and are joined by unfamiliar ones as well. Of course, nothing of quite that sort does occur: there is no geographical transplantation; outside the laboratory everyday affairs usually continue as before. Nevertheless, paradigm changes do cause scientists to see the world of their research-engagement differently. In so far as their only recourse to that world is through what they see and do, we may want to say that after a revolution scientists are responding to a different world . . .

Let us return to the data and ask what sorts of transformation in the scientist's world the historian who believes in such changes can discover. Sir William Herschel's discovery of Uranus provides a first example . . . A celestial body that had been observed on and off for almost a century was seen differently after 1781 because, like an anomalous playing card, it could no longer be fitted to the perceptual categories (star or comet) that had previously prevailed. The shift of vision that enabled astronomers to see Uranus the planet does not . . . seem to have affected only the perception of that previously observed object. Probably, though the evidence is equivocal, the minor paradigm change forced by Herschel helped to prepared astronomers for the rapid discovery, after 1801, of the numerous minor planets or asteroids. Nevertheless, astronomers prepared to find additional planets were able, with standard instruments, to identify twenty of them in the first fifty years of the nineteenth century. The history of astronomy provides many other examples of paradigm-induced changes in scientific perception . . . Can it be an accident, for example, that Western astronomers first saw change in the previously immutable heavens during the half-century after Copernicus's new paradigm was first proposed? The Chinese, whose cosmological beliefs did not preclude celestial change, had recorded the appearance of many new stars in the heavens at a much earlier date. Also, even without the aid of a telescope, the Chinese had systematically recorded the appearance of sunspots centuries before these were seen by Galileo and his contemporaries. Nor were sunspots and a new star the only examples of celestial change to emerge in the heavens of Western astronomy immediately after Copernicus. Using traditional instruments, some as simple as a piece of thread, late sixteenth-century astronomers repeatedly discovered that comets wandered at will through the space previously reserved for the immutable planets and stars. The very ease and rapidity with which astronomers saw new things when looking at old objects with old instruments may make us wish to say that, after Copernicus, astronomers lived in a different world. In any case, their research responded as if this were the case.

Specimen Questions

1 Expound Aristotle's account of the 'Four Causes'. Is he right in his belief in the importance of 'final causes' for the understanding of the natural world?

2 Explain the importance of the ideas of Francis Bacon for the development of modern scientific thinking.

3 Given that Descartes holds we have *a priori* knowledge of the basic laws of physics, why does he insist on the need for observation and experiment?

4 Why does Berkeley maintain that the explanation of *force* is beyond the scope of mathematical physics?

5 What is the 'problem of induction', and why, according to Hume, does it represent an insuperable obstacle to the rationality of science?

6 'In single instances of the operation of bodies, we never can, by our utmost scrutiny, discover anything but one event following another, without being able to comprehend any force or power by which the cause operates, or any connection between it and its supposed effect' (Hume). Explain and discuss.

7 Hume asked how we could arrive at the idea of causation on the basis of repeated observations. Explain why Kant thought this approach to our idea of causation was fundamentally mistaken.

8 'We make experience its own test' (J. S. Mill). Critically expound Mill's views on the uniformity of nature and the correct methods of scientific inquiry.

9 'The criterion of the scientific status of a theory is its falsifiability' (Karl Popper). Explain and discuss.

10 Explain what Hempel means by a 'deductive nomological' explanation. Is this type of explanation appropriate for explaining human actions?

11 Are the theoretical entities of modern physics best understood in realist or in instrumentalist terms? Discuss with reference to Maxwell's critique of instrumentalism.

12 What does Kuhn mean by a 'paradigm', and why does he maintain the choice between paradigms cannot be settled from within the framework of 'normal' science?

Suggestions for Further Reading

A useful collection of contemporary readings covering many issues arising in this Part of the volume is M. Lange (ed.), *Philosophy of Science* (Oxford: Blackwell, 2007).

Aristotle
For general works on Aristotle, see the books listed at the end of Part I.
For Aristotle's conception of science, see the essay by R. Hankinson in J. Barnes (ed.), *The Cambridge Companion to Aristotle* (Cambridge: Cambridge University Press, 1995).
For Aristotle's views on teleology, see the discussion by W. Wieland in J. Barnes et al., *Articles on Aristotle*, vol. I (London: Duckworth, 1975), ch. 7; See also R. Sorabji, *Necessity, Cause and Blame* (London: Duckworth, 1980).
See also A. Woodfield, *Teleology* (Oxford: Clarendon, 1982).

Bacon
Bacon, Francis, *Novum Organum* [1620], in J. M. Robertson (ed.), *The Philosophical Works of Francis Bacon*, reprinted from the translation of Ellis and Spedding (London: Routledge, 1905).
See also Francis Bacon, *The Advancement of Learning* [1605], in the edition cited, and also G. W. Kitchin's edition (London: Dent, 1915).
For a good survey of Bacon's thought, see A. Quinton, *Francis Bacon* (Oxford: Oxford University Press, 1980).
See also A. Pérez-Ramos, *Francis Bacon's Idea of Science and the Maker's Knowledge Tradition* (Oxford: Oxford University Press, 1988); P. Rossi, *Francis Bacon: From Magic to Science* (London: Routledge, 1968).

Descartes
See the books listed at the end of Part I.
For Descartes's conception of science, see D. Clarke, *Descartes' Philosophy of Science* (Manchester: Manchester University Press, 1982); S. Voss (ed.), *Essays on the Philosophy and Science of René Descartes* (Oxford: Oxford University Press, 1993); D. Garber, *Descartes' Metaphysical Physics* (Chicago: University of Chicago Press, 1992).

Berkeley
See the books listed at the end of Part II.
See also Margaret Wilson, 'Berkeley and the Essences of the Corpuscularians', and W. Newton Smith, 'Berkeley's Philosophy of Science', in J. Foster and H. Robinson (eds), *Essays on Berkeley* (Oxford: Clarendon, 1985).

Hume and Kant on induction and causation
For general introductions to Hume and Kant, which include discussion of their views on these topics, see the books listed at end of Parts I and II.
See also, for Hume, D. C. Stove, *Probability and Hume's Inductive Scepticism* (Oxford: Oxford University Press, 1973); and, for Kant, M. Friedman, 'Causal Laws and the Foundations of Natural Science', in P. Guyer (ed.), *The Cambridge Companion to Kant* (Cambridge: Cambridge University Press, 1992).
For more recent discussions of the problem of induction, see B. van Fraassen, *Laws and Symmetry* (Oxford: Oxford University Press, 1989); N. Goodman, *Fact, Fiction and Forecast* (2nd edn, Indianapolis: Bobbs-Merrill, 1965); C. G. Hempel, *Aspects of Scientific Explanation* (New York: Free Press, 1965).

Mill
See the books listed at the end of Part III, especially Skorupski, *John Stuart Mill*.
See also J. L. Mackie, *The Cement of the Universe* (Oxford: Oxford University Press, 1973), ch. 6.

Popper and falsifiability
Popper, K., *The Logic of Scientific Discovery* [*Logik der Forschung*, 1935] (London: Hutchinson, 1959).
Popper, K., *Conjectures and Refutations* (London: Routledge, 1963).
See also Popper's own excellent introduction to his views: K. Popper, *Unended Quest* (London: Fontana, 1976).
An insightful study of Popper's ideas is A. O'Hear, *Karl Popper* (London: Routledge, 1980).
Several of Popper's arguments are implicitly criticized in Kuhn's *Structure of Scientific Revolutions* (see below).

Hempel and scientific explanation

For a solid introduction to the deductive-nomological concept of explanation, with frequent
reference to Hempel, see J. Woodward, 'Explanation', in P. Machamer and M. Silberstein
(eds), *The Blackwell Guide to the Philosophy of
Science* (Oxford: Blackwell, 2002).

A stimulating collection of essays is W. Salmon
and P. Kitcher (eds), *Scientific Explanation,
Minnesota Studies in the Philosophy of Science*, vol. 13 (Minneapolis: University of Minnesota Press, 1989).

See also Y. Balashov and A. Rosenberg (eds),
Philosophy of Science: Contemporary Readings
(London: Routledge, 2002), Part II ('Explan-
ation, Causation and Laws').

*Maxwell and scientific realism versus
instrumentalism*

Apart from Maxwell, a classic statement of the
realist position is W. Sellars, *Perception and
Reality* (New York: Humanities, 1963).

A good introduction to the debate, and several
useful articles, may be found in Balashov and
Rosenberg (eds), *Philosophy of Science: Contemporary Readings*, Part IV ('Scientific Realism'); see esp. the papers by Gutting and
McMullin.

Also valuable is the introduction in D. Papineau
(ed.), *The Philosophy of Science* (Oxford:
Oxford University Press, 1996), and, for

an empiricist approach, the paper by B. van
Fraassen in the same collection.

See also van Fraassen's *The Scientific Image*
(Oxford: Clarendon, 1980).

Kuhn

Kuhn's major work, which implicitly criticizes
some of Popper's ideas, is T. Kuhn, *The Structure of Scientific Revolutions* (Chicago: University of Chicago Press, 1970).

See also his later writings in T. Kuhn, *The Essential Tension: Selected Studies in Scientific Tradition and Change* (Chicago: University of
Chicago Press, 1977).

For an excellent introduction to Kuhn's work see
A. Bird, *Thomas Kuhn* (Chesham: Acumen,
2000).

Compare also the essay by P. Feyerabend, 'Explan-
ation, Reduction, and Empiricism', in H. Feigl
and G. Maxwell (eds), *Scientific Explanation,
Space and Time*, Minnesota Studies in the
Philosophy of Science, vol. 3 (Minneapolis:
University of Minnesota Press, 1962).

Useful critical discussion of some of the issues
raised by Popper's and Kuhn's work may be
found in I. Lakatos and A. Musgrave (eds),
Criticism and the Growth of Knowledge (Cambridge: Cambridge University Press, 1970).

See also D. C. Stove, *Popper and After* (Oxford:
Pergamon, 1982); J. W. N. Watkins, *Science
and Scepticism* (London: Hutchinson, 1984).

PART VIII

Morality and the Good Life

Morality and the Good Life
Introduction

Although philosophy is sometimes represented as a purely theoretical subject, concerned with abstract contemplation, philosophers have from earliest times seen it as part of their task to discover how human beings can live fulfilled and worthwhile lives. All of us acquire directly from parents and teachers, and more indirectly from the general social ethos in which we grow up, certain guidelines on how to live; the term 'morality' comes from the Latin *mores*, meaning a network of social customs and institutions. But, true to its characteristically critical function, philosophy never rests content with an acceptance of prevailing norms: it seeks to scrutinize those norms, to examine whether they are consistent and coherent, and so see how far they can be rationally justified. What is the ultimate source of our ideas of good and evil, right and wrong? Are there objective, rationally defensible standards of right action? What is the relationship between the ethical principles we are encouraged to adopt and individual self-interest? What connection is there, if any, between how we ought to behave, and how we can achieve happy and contented lives? These are some of the fundamental issues with which moral philosophers have been concerned; the materials presented in this part of the volume uncover some of the principal landmarks in the long tradition of Western moral philosophy.

1   Morality and Happiness: Plato, *Republic**

As with so many branches of philosophy, it is the writings of Plato that set the direction of much subsequent inquiry in the Western philosophical tradition. Plato, and his mentor Socrates, saw philosophy (the 'love of wisdom') as the key to understanding how human beings should live. In his monumental work, the *Republic*, Plato sets out a vision of justice in the state and the individual. The dominant element in that vision is a conception of life lived in accordance with reason, where goodness and virtue flow from an intellectual understanding of reality, and where the enlightened philosopher-rulers devote their lives to the contemplation of truth and the service of the state. But Plato is well aware that these austere and high-minded ideals are at odds with what many people see as the more immediate and tangible rewards of self-interest. In our first extract, Plato raises the issue of whether goodness and virtue are really worthwhile for the individual. The story of Gyges' ring (which makes the wearer become invisible at will)

graphically poses the question of how we would act if we could be sure of getting away with immoral conduct. Life is not, of course, like this: the offender often risks getting caught (and most religious teaching promises the wrongdoer punishment in the next world, if not in this). But though it may be prudent to act morally for this kind of reason ('honesty is the best policy'), this does not show that the virtuous life is intrinsically good – valuable for its own sake. The dialogue (from Book II of the *Republic*) is opened by Glaucon, who challenges Socrates to defend the life of virtue. Socrates (speaking in the first person) responds, for once, more as a listener than a leader of the discussion; later on Glaucon's brother, Adeimantus, supports Glaucon's argument. Putting the case for immorality in its strongest and most troubling form, Glaucon and Adeimantus demand an answer to what has become one of the defining questions of moral philosophy: why should I be moral?

Let me ask you now. How would you arrange goods – are there not some which we welcome for their own sakes, and independently of their consequences, as, for example, harmless pleasures and enjoyments, which delight us at the time, though nothing follows from them?

I agree in thinking there is such a class, I replied.

Is there not also a second class of good, such as knowledge, sight, health, which are desirable not only in themselves, but also for their results?

Certainly, I said.

And would you not recognize a third class, such as gymnastics, and the care of the sick, and the physician's art; also the various ways of money-making – these do us good but we regard them as disagreeable; and no one would choose them for their own sakes, but only for the sake of some reward or result which flows from them?

There is, I said, this third class also. But why do you ask?

Because I want to know in which of the three classes you would place justice.

In the highest class, I replied – among those goods which he who would be happy desires both for their own sake and for the sake of their results.

Then the majority are of another mind; they think that justice is to be reckoned in the troublesome class, among goods which are to be pursued for the sake of rewards and of reputation, but in themselves are disagreeable and rather to be avoided.

* Plato, *Republic* [*Politeia*, *c*.380 BC], Bk II (357b2–367c5). Trans. B. Jowett, in *The Dialogues of Plato* (Oxford: Clarendon, 1892), vol. II, pp. 36–47; with omissions.

I know, I said, that this is their manner of thinking... But I am too stupid to be convinced...

I wish, he said, that you would hear me... To my mind the nature of justice and injustice have not yet been made clear. Setting aside their rewards and results, I want to know what they are in themselves, and how they inwardly work in the soul. If you please then... I will speak first... of the nature and origin of justice, according to the common view of them. Secondly, I will show that all men who practise justice do so against their will, of necessity but not as a good. And thirdly, I will argue that there is reason in this view, for the life of the unjust is after all better far than the life of the just – if what they say is true, Socrates, since I myself am not of their opinion... Will you say whether you approve of my proposal?

Indeed I do; nor can I imagine any theme about which a man of sense would oftener wish to converse.

I am delighted, he replied, to hear you say so, and shall begin by speaking, as I proposed, of the nature and origin of justice.

They say that to do injustice is, by nature, good; to suffer injustice, evil; but that the evil is greater than the good. And so when men have both done and suffered injustice and have had experience of both, not being able to avoid the one and obtain the other, they think that they had better agree among themselves to have neither; hence there arise laws and mutual covenants; and that which is ordained by law is termed by them lawful and just. This they affirm to be the origin and nature of justice; – it is a mean or compromise, between the best of all, which is to do injustice and not be punished, and the worst of all, which is to suffer injustice without the power of retaliation; and justice, being at a middle point between the two, is tolerated not as a good, but as the lesser evil, and honoured by reason of the inability of men to do injustice. For no man who is worthy to be called a man would ever submit to such an agreement if he were able to resist; he would be mad if he did. Such is the received account, Socrates, of the nature and origin of justice.

Now that those who practise justice do so involuntarily, and because they have not the power to be unjust, will best appear if we imagine something of this kind: having given both to the just and the unjust power to do what they will, let us watch and see where desire will lead them; then we shall discover in the very act the just and unjust man to be proceeding along the same road, following their interest... and only diverted into the path of justice by the force of law.

The liberty which we are supposing may be most completely given to them in the form of such a power as is said to have been possessed by Gyges, the ancestor of Croesus the Lydian. According to the tradition, Gyges was a shepherd in the service of the king of Lydia; there was a great storm, and an earthquake made an opening in the earth at the place where he was feeding his flock. Amazed at the sight, he descended into the opening, where, among other marvels, he beheld a hollow brazen horse, having doors, at which stooping and looking in he saw a dead body of stature, as appeared to him, more than human, and having nothing on but a gold ring; this he took from the finger of the dead and re-ascended. Now the shepherds met together, according to custom, that they might send their monthly report about the flocks to the king; into their assembly he came having the ring on his finger, and as he was sitting among them he chanced to turn the bezel of the ring inside his hand, when instantly he became invisible to the rest of the company and they began to speak of him as if he were no longer present.

He was astonished at this, and again touching the ring he turned the bezel outwards and reappeared; he made several trials of the ring, and always with the same result – when he turned the bezel inwards he became invisible, when outwards he reappeared. Whereupon he contrived to be chosen one of the messengers who were sent to the court; where as soon as he arrived he seduced the queen, and with her help conspired against the king and slew him, and took the kingdom.

Suppose now that there were two such magic rings, and the just put on one of them and the unjust the other; no man can be imagined to be of such an iron nature that he would stand fast in justice. No man would keep his hands off what was not his own when he could safely take what he liked out of the market, or go into houses and lie with any one at his pleasure, or kill or release from prison whom he would, and in all respects be like a God among men. Then the actions of the just would be as the actions of the unjust; they would both come at last to the same point. And this we may truly affirm to be a great proof that a man is just, not willingly or because he thinks that justice is any good to him individually, but of necessity, for wherever any one thinks that he can safely be unjust, there he is unjust. For all men believe in their hearts that injustice is far more profitable to the individual than justice, and he who argues as I have been supposing, will say that they are right. If you could imagine any one obtaining this power of becoming invisible and never doing any wrong or touching what was another's, he would be thought by the lookers-on to be a most wretched idiot, although they would praise him to one another's faces, and keep up appearances with one another from a fear that they too might suffer injustice. Enough of this.

Now, if we are to form a real judgement of the life of the just and unjust, we must isolate them... Therefore I say that in the perfectly unjust man we must assume the most perfect injustice; there is to be no deduction, but we must allow him, while doing the most unjust acts, to have acquired the greatest reputation for justice. If he has taken a false step he must be able to recover himself; he must be one who can speak with effect, if any of his deeds come to light, and who can force his way where force is required by his courage and strength, and command of money and friends.

And at his side let us place the just man in his nobleness and simplicity, wishing, as Aeschylus says, to be and not to seem good. There must be no seeming, for if he seems to be just he will be honoured and rewarded, and then we shall not know whether he is just for the sake of justice or for the sake of honours and rewards; therefore, let him be clothed in justice only, and have no other covering; and he must be imagined in a state of life the opposite of the former. Let him be the best of men, and let him be thought the worst; then he will have been put to the proof; and we shall see whether he will be affected by the fear of infamy and its consequences. And let him continue thus to the hour of death; being just and seeming to be unjust.... The just man who is thought unjust will be scourged, racked, bound – will have his eyes burnt out; and, at last, after suffering every kind of evil, he will be impaled. Then he will understand that he ought to seem only, and not to be, just; the words of Aeschylus may be more truly spoken of the unjust than of the just. For the unjust is pursuing a reality; he does not live with a view to appearances – he wants to be really unjust and not to seem only: –

> His mind has a soil deep and fertile
> Out of which spring his prudent counsels

In the first place, he is thought just, and therefore bears rule in the city; he can marry whom he will, and give in marriage to whom he will; also he can trade and deal where he likes, and always to his own advantage, because he has no misgivings about injustice; and at every contest, whether in public or private, he gets the better of his antagonists, and gains at their expense, and is rich, and out of his gains he can benefit his friends, and harm his enemies; moreover, he can offer sacrifices, and dedicate gifts to the gods abundantly and magnificently, and can honour the gods or any man whom he wants to honour in a far better style than the just, and therefore he is likely to be dearer than they are to the gods. And thus, Socrates, gods and men are said to unite in making the life of the unjust better than the life of the just.

I was going to say something in answer to Glaucon, when Adeimantus, his brother, interposed: Socrates, he said, you do not suppose that there is nothing more to be urged?

Why, what else is there? I answered.

The strongest point of all has not been even mentioned, he replied.

Well, then, according to the proverb, 'Let brother help brother' – if he fails in any part do you assist him; although I must confess that Glaucon has already said quite enough to lay me in the dust, and take from me the power of helping justice.

Nonsense, he replied. But let me add something more. There is another side to Glaucon's argument about the praise and censure of justice and injustice, which is equally required in order to bring out what I believe to be his meaning. Parents and tutors are always telling their sons and their wards that they are to be just; but why? not for the sake of justice, but for the sake of character and reputation; in the hope of obtaining for him who is reputed just some of those offices, marriages and the like which Glaucon has enumerated among the advantages accruing to the unjust from the reputation of justice. More, however, is made of appearances by this class of persons than by the others; for they throw in the good opinion of the gods, and will tell you of a shower of benefits which the heavens, as they say, rain upon the pious...They take them down into the world below, where they have the saints lying on couches at a feast, everlastingly drunk, crowned with garlands; their idea seems to be that an immortality of drunkenness is the highest reward of virtue. Some extend their rewards yet further; the posterity, as they say, of the faithful and just shall survive to the third and fourth generation. This is the style in which they praise justice. But about the wicked there is another strain; they bury them in a slough in Hades, and make them carry water in a sieve; also while they are yet living they bring them to infamy, and inflict upon them the punishments which Glaucon described as the portion of the just who are reputed to be unjust; nothing else does their invention supply. Such is their manner of praising the one and censuring the other.

Once more, Socrates, I will ask you to consider another way of speaking about justice and injustice, which is not confined to the poets, but is found in prose writers. The universal voice of mankind is always declaring that justice and virtue are honourable, but grievous and toilsome; and that the pleasures of vice and injustice are easy of attainment, and are only censured by law and opinion. They say also that honesty is for the most part less profitable than dishonesty; and they are quite ready to call wicked men happy, and to honour them both in public and private when they are rich or in any other way influential, while they despise and overlook those who may be weak and poor, even though acknowledging them to be better than the others.... And the poets are the authorities to whom they appeal, now smoothing the path of vice with the words of Hesiod: –

> Vice may be had in abundance without trouble;
> the way is smooth and her dwelling-place is near.
> But before virtue the gods have set toil,

and a tedious and uphill road... And now when the young hear all this said about virtue and vice, and the way in which gods and men regard them, how are their minds likely to be affected, my dear Socrates, – those of them, I mean, who are quick-witted and, like bees on the wing, light on every flower, and from all that they hear are prone to draw conclusions as to what manner of persons they should be and in what way they should walk if they would make the best of life? Probably the youth will say to himself in the words of Pindar –

> Can I by justice or by crooked ways of deceit
> ascend a loftier tower
> which may be a fortress to me all my days?

For what men say is that, if I am really just and am not also thought just, profit there is none, but the pain and loss on the other hand are unmistakable. But if, though unjust I acquire the reputation of justice, a heavenly life is promised to me. Since then, as philosophers prove, appearance tyrannizes over truth and is lord of happiness, to appearance I must devote myself. I will describe around me a picture and shadow of virtue to be the vestibule and exterior of my house; behind I will trail the subtle and crafty fox, as Archilochus, greatest of sages, recommends. But I hear someone exclaiming that the concealment of wickedness is often difficult; to which I answer, Nothing great is easy. Nevertheless, the argument indicates this, if we would be happy, to be the path along which we should proceed. With a view to concealment we will establish secret brotherhoods and political clubs. And there are professors of rhetoric who teach the art of persuading courts and assemblies; and so, partly by persuasion and partly by force, I shall make unlawful gains and not be punished. Still I hear a voice saying that the gods cannot be deceived, neither can they be compelled. But what if there are no gods? or, suppose them to have no care of human things – why in either case should we mind about concealment? And even if there are gods, and they do care about us, yet we know of them only from tradition and the genealogies of the poets; and these are the very persons who say that they may be influenced and turned by 'sacrifices and soothing entreaties and by offerings'. Let us be consistent then, and believe both or neither. If the poets speak truly, why then we had better be unjust, and offer of the fruits of injustice; for if we are just, although we may escape the vengeance of heaven, we shall lose the gains of injustice; but, if we are unjust, we shall keep the gains, and by our sinning and praying, and praying and sinning, the gods will be propitiated, and we shall not be punished...

Now as you have admitted that justice is one of that highest class of goods which are desired indeed for their results, but in a far greater degree for their own sakes – like sight or hearing or knowledge or health, or any other real and natural and not merely conventional good – I would ask you in your praise of justice to regard one point only: I mean the essential good and evil which justice and injustice work in the possessors of them. Let others praise justice and censure injustice, magnifying the rewards and honours of the one and abusing the other; that is a manner of arguing which, coming from them, I am ready to tolerate, but from you who have spent your whole life in the consideration of this question, I expect something better. And therefore, I say, not only prove to us that justice is better than injustice, but show what they either of them do to the possessor of them, which makes the one to be a good and the other an evil, whether seen or unseen by gods and men.

2   Ethical Virtue: Aristotle, *Nicomachean Ethics**

The relationship between virtue and happiness, which had much exercised Plato, was also a central issue in the ethical writings of his pupil Aristotle. Aristotle was in no doubt that the life of virtue, informed by reason, constituted the good for mankind; he argued consistently that living in accordance with virtue was the key to achieving *eudaimonia*, happiness or fulfilment. But what if selfish desires are in conflict with the demands of virtue – suppose we ought to be courageous and help defend our fellow citizens against foreign attack, but selfishness makes us want to run away? Aristotle's crucial insight here is that ethical virtue is not merely something intellectual (a rational grasp of how one should act), but involves ingrained dispositions of character, habits of feeling and action (he connects the very word 'ethical' with the Greek noun *ethos*, 'custom' or 'habit'). Ethical excellence, Aristotle argues, is in this respect like musical excellence: you become good by constant practice. It is therefore a mistake to think that we can be good just by weighing up calculations, or balancing the costs and benefits of various courses of action.[1] The virtuous individual will have been trained from an early age to have the right kinds of desires, and to behave in the right kind of way, at the appropriate time. So

the presence (for example) of an excessive desire to run away, in the face of reasonable odds, is already an indication that the ethical character has not been developed as it should have been. Here Aristotle introduces his famous doctrine of the *mean*: courage is a disposition (to act and react in certain ways) that lies in between two extremes – the vice of excess (foolhardiness), and the vice of deficiency (cowardice). And so with the other virtues (generosity, for instance, lies on a mean between being a spendthrift and being stingy).

Aristotle's doctrine of the mean does not, and is not meant to, provide a decision procedure or criterion for determining what should be done on any given occasion. Indeed, part of the point of Aristotle's approach is that ethical virtue is not a matter of isolated acts, but involves an ingrained pattern of action and desire that is manifested over a whole lifetime – hence the importance of his account of virtue as a *disposition* of character. The dispositions of the virtuous agent, however, are not a matter of mindless habituation: the patterns of virtue which we aim to acquire, and instil into our children, are those which reason can recognize as making for a maximally worthwhile human life, a life where we can develop our human potentialities to the full.

---

* Aristotle, *Nicomachean Ethics* [*Ethika Nikomacheia*, c.325 BC], extracts from Bk I, ch. 7, and Bk II, chs 1, 5 and 6 (1097b21–1098a18; 1103a16–b25; 1105b19–1107a8). Translation by John Cottingham.

[1] Contrast the utilitarian approach: see extract 6, below.

To say that happiness is the supreme good perhaps seems something that is generally agreed, and we need a clearer account of what it is. This might be available if we find the function of a human being...What might this be? Living seems common to plants, but we are looking for something special to humans, so we should set aside the life of nutrition and growth. Next would come some sort of sentient life, but this is common to horses, oxen and every animal. There remains some sort of active life of the rational part of the soul...Suppose, then, that the function of a human being is an activity of the soul in accordance with, or involving, reason. Now the function of an X and a good X are of the same kind (for example of a harpist and a good harpist); this is true in all cases, when we add to the function the outstanding accomplishment that corresponds to the virtue (the harpist's function is to play, that of the good harpist to play well). So if we take the function of a human being to be a certain life, namely an activity of the soul and actions expressing reason, then the excellent man's function will be to do this well and in a fine way (each function being discharged well when performed in accordance with its special virtue). So it follows that the good for humankind is an activity of the soul in accordance with virtue (or if there are several virtues, in accordance with the best and most complete virtue). And we must add, in a complete life. For one swallow does not make a summer, nor does one day; and similarly neither one day, nor a short time, is enough to make someone blessed and happy...

Virtue is of two kinds, intellectual and ethical. Intellectual virtue owes its origins and its growth more to teaching, and so needs experience and time; but ethical virtue comes about from habit – hence even its name derives (by a slight modification) from the word 'ethos', custom or habit. It is clear from this that none of the ethical virtues arises in us by nature; for none of the things that exist by nature can be radically altered by habituation. For instance, a stone, which by nature moves downwards, cannot be habituated to move upwards no matter how many thousand times you try to train it by throwing it upwards; and you cannot get fire to move downwards, or train anything that naturally behaves in one way to behave in another. Hence the ethical virtues do not come about by nature – but neither do they come about contrary to nature: we are naturally constituted so as to acquire them, but it is by habit that they are fully developed.

Now whenever we come to have something by nature, we are first provided with the relevant capacities, and subsequently come to exercise the activities. (This is clear in the case of the senses: it was not from frequent seeing or hearing that we acquired these senses, but the other way around – we had the senses and then used them, rather than acquiring them as a result of using them). But in the case of the virtues, we acquire them by previously exercising them, as happens with the other arts. Whatever we have to learn to do, we learn by doing it: people become builders by building, and lutanists by playing the lute. Thus it is by doing just things that we become just, and by acting temperately that we become temperate, and by doing brave things that we become brave. This is confirmed by what happens in city-states: legislators make the citizens good by instilling good habits (this is the intention of every legislator, and those who do not achieve it fail in their aims – this is how a good constitution differs from a poor one).

The causes and means whereby every virtue is cultivated or destroyed are the same, just as in the case of all the arts. It is by playing the lute that people become good or bad lute players, and the same holds for builders and all the rest. By building well people get to be good builders, and they become bad builders from building badly. If this was not the case, there would be no need for teachers, and everyone would be born good or bad. It is just like this with the virtues. By behaving in a certain way in our dealings with human beings some of us become just and others unjust; by what we do in the face of danger, and by acquiring habits of timidity or boldness, we become brave or cowardly. And the same holds good with respect to desires and feelings of anger: some people become temperate and patient, while others become self-indulgent and bad-tempered, depending on the way they behave in the relevant situations. In a word, activities of a certain kind produce corresponding dispositions. This is why the activities we perform must be of a certain kind; for as these differ, so the dispositions that follow from them will differ. Thus the kinds of habits we form from early childhood are of no small importance; they matter a great deal – indeed, they make all the difference...

We must now examine what virtue is. Since there are three conditions arising in the soul – feelings, capacities and dispositions, virtue must be one of these. By *feelings* I mean anger, fear, boldness, envy, joy, love, hatred, longing, jealousy pity and in general whatever is accompanied by pleasure or pain. By *capacities* I mean what makes us capable of the relevant feelings – in virtue of which we are said to be capable of being angry or sorrowful, or feeling pity. *Dispositions* are what make us in a good or bad way in respect to the feelings; for example, in the case of being angry, we are in a bad way if our feeling is too vehement or too feeble, and so in other cases.

Neither the virtues nor the vices are feelings, for we are not called worthy or worthless on account of our feelings, but on account of our virtues and vices. Moreover, we are not praised or blamed on account of our feelings. For a person is not praised for being frightened or angry; it is not simply for being angry that someone is blamed, but for being angry in a particular way. But we are praised or blamed on account of our virtues and vices. Then again, we feel angry or frightened without choosing to, whereas virtues are choices of some kind, or involve choice. In addition, we are said to be moved with respect to our feelings, but in the case of the virtues and vices it is not a matter of being moved but of being in a certain condition. By the same token, the virtues are not capacities either. For we are not said to be good or bad, or praised or blamed, simply in virtue of being capable of feeling. And again, we have capacities by nature, but we are not good or bad by nature, as noted above. So if the virtues are neither feelings nor capacities, it remains that they are dispositions. This then is our account of the kind of thing virtue is.

But to say, as we have, that virtue is a disposition is not enough – we need to specify what kind of disposition. Whenever something has a virtue, the virtue is what ensures it is in a good state and makes it perform its function well. Thus the virtue of the eye makes the eye and its function good – it is the virtue of the eye that makes us see well. Similarly, the virtue of a horse makes it an excellent one – good at galloping and carrying its rider and withstanding the enemy. If this applies to all cases, then the virtue of a human being will be the disposition that makes a human being good, and makes him perform his function well...

In everything continuous and divisible, one can have a larger or smaller or equal quantity, either with respect to the object or relative to us; and the equal amount is a mean between excess and deficiency. I call the mean with respect to the object that which is equidistant from the two extremes, and this is one and the same for everyone; but the mean in relation to us is what is neither excessive nor deficient, and this is not one and the same for all. Thus ten is many and two is few, we take six as the mean with respect to the object, for it is equidistant between the larger and the smaller numbers. This is the mean as an arithmetical ratio. But the mean in relation to us cannot be taken in this way. If ten pounds is a lot to eat and two pounds a little, it does not follow that the trainer will prescribe six, since this may be a lot or a little for the person who is to take it (for Milo the athlete it may be too little, but for someone starting to train too much; and similarly for running or wrestling). So everyone who understands what they are doing avoids excess and deficiency and seeks out and chooses the mean – but not the mean with respect to the object, but relative to us.

Let us take it then that every science performs its function well when it looks to the mean and guides its products towards it. Hence people say of products that are in a good state that one cannot take away or add anything, any excess or deficiency being enough to destroy the good state, while the mean preserves it; and good craftsmen, as we have said, look to the mean when they work. If this is so, then since virtue, like nature, is more accurate and efficient than any craft, it too will aim at the mean. I am speaking here of ethical virtue, or virtue of character; for this is concerned with feelings and actions, and here we find excess, deficiency and the mean. For one may feel fear and confidence and desire and anger and pity, and pleasure and pain generally, too much or too little; and neither of these is good. But to have these feelings at the right time, on the right grounds, towards the right people, for the right purpose and in the right way – this is the intermediate and best condition, and the characteristic of true virtue.

In the case of actions too, there is, in the same way, excess, deficiency and the mean. Virtue is concerned with feelings and actions, in which excess and deficiency go astray, while the mean is praised and on the right path, both of which are marks of virtue. So virtue is a mean, and it aims at what is intermediate.

Now it is possible to go astray in many ways, but there is only one correct path (for evil, as the Pythagorean model has it, belongs to the Unlimited, while good belongs to the limited). Hence the former is easy and the latter difficult, and it is easy to miss the target and hard to hit it. This again shows that excess and deficiency relate to vice, and the mean to virtue: 'Many the paths of vice; of goodness only one.'

Virtue then is a disposition concerned with choice, lying on a mean that is relative to us, determined by reason, in the way a prudent man would determine it. It is a mean between two vices, one of excess and the other of deficiency. And while some vices fall short and others exceed the right amount, in both feelings and actions, virtue discovers the mean and chooses it. So as far as its nature and essential definition goes, virtue is a mean; but in respect of what is best and right, it is an extreme.

3   Virtue, Reason and the Passions: Benedict Spinoza, *Ethics**

Aristotle's vision of the good life, as we have seen, was one informed by reason and characterized by moderate patterns of desire, neither excessive nor deficient. But to the Stoic thinkers who immediately followed Aristotle, it seemed clear that the life of reason was in constant danger of being blown off course by the turbulence of our human emotions. Accordingly, in place of the Aristotelian ideal of *metriopatheia*, moderate desire, they advocated a life of *apatheia* – a life in which the potentially harmful passions were entirely suppressed. Many centuries later, Benedict Spinoza made the conquest of the passions the central theme of his *Ethics* (*c*.1665). Following the Stoics, Spinoza equates the life of virtue with a life lived in accordance with our rational nature: when we are pursuing what reason perceives as genuinely beneficial to us, we are acting freely and virtuously. But when we are in the grip of the passions we are like slaves, acting at the behest of some external power (compare the case of someone who has genuinely decided that avoiding fatty foods is best for his health, but who is 'driven' by his lust for chocolate to finish the entire box). Spinoza's remedy against the passions is essentially a cognitive one: the use of reason will enable us to understand the inevitable causes of all things (Spinoza is a strict determinist),[1] and the knowledge so gained will reduce and ultimately eliminate our longing for what cannot be. As Spinoza puts it, 'the more this knowledge [that things are necessary] is applied to individual cases, which we imagine more vividly and distinctly, the greater is the power of the mind over the passions'.

The good life, for Spinoza, is essentially a tranquil and harmonious one, and this links up with the chief reason why the passions should be overcome – they are responsible for disharmony and discord, both in relations with one's fellow human beings and within oneself. With respect to internal disharmony, one of Spinoza's central points is that when we are acting in accordance with our rational nature, and with maximal knowledge and understanding, we can be said to be truly autonomous agents – in charge of our own lives; in Spinoza's words, we can be said to *act*, rather than being *acted on*. But when we are driven by desires we imperfectly understand, towards goals which often, on reflection, we see to be unworthy, then we are not 'in charge': we are 'acted on', rather than acting. In Spinozan ethics there thus turns out to be a very intimate connection between philosophical understanding and the good life. Without such understanding, buffeted by alien forces we do not understand, we live from moment to moment, existing only in so far as things are happening *to us*; but the person who is possessed of philosophical wisdom will 'be aware of himself and of God and of all things by a kind of eternal necessity' and hence 'possesses true peace of mind'.

 The lack of power human beings have in moderating and restraining the passions I call slavery. For someone who is beholden to the passions is not independent, but under the control of fortune. He is so much in fortune's power that often, though he can see what is better for him, he is none the less compelled to take the worser course...

---

* Benedict Spinoza, *Ethics* [*Ethica ordine geometrico demonstrata*, *c*.1665], extracts from Part IV ('Human Slavery'), Preface; Props. 5D, 17S, 18D, 18S, 20, 20S, 22C, 24, 26, 26D, 27, 28D, 31, 31C, 32, 33, 34, 35, 35D, 35C2, 35S; Part V ('Human Freedom'), Props. 6, 6D, 6S, 10, 10D, 10S, 20S, 42S; heavily abridged. Translation by John Cottingham. It should be noted that in the original text Spinoza supports his propositions by complex geometrical-style demonstrations from axioms and definitions.

[1] Compare introduction to Part V, extract 8, above.

The essence of a passion cannot be explained through our nature alone. For the power of a passion cannot be defined in terms of the power by which we strive to preserve our existence, but must be defined by the power of some external cause when compared with our own...

It is necessary to get to know both the power and the lack of power our nature has, so that we can determine what reason is capable or incapable of in moderating the emotions...

The very essence of a human being is desire, that is, a striving by which a man tries to preserve his existence...

Since reason demands nothing contrary to nature, it demands that everyone should love himself and seek his own benefit – what is really advantageous to him, and whatever really leads a man to greater perfection. And in an absolute sense, it demands of each human being that he should strive to preserve his being, in so far as he can.

Next, since virtue is nothing else but acting from the laws of our own nature, and no one strives to preserve his being except from the laws of his own nature, it follows, first, that the foundation of virtue is this very striving for self-preservation, and that happiness consists in man's ability to preserve his existence. Second, it follows that we should seek virtue for its own sake, and not for any ulterior purpose, since there is nothing that is more important or more beneficial for us...

The more each person seeks what is beneficial to him, that is, strives to preserve his existence, and the greater power he has to do this, the more he is endowed with virtue. Conversely, in so far as anyone neglects what is beneficial to him, namely preserving his existence, the less power he has...

No one, then, unless he is overcome by external causes which are contrary to his nature, neglects to seek what is beneficial to him, or preserve his existence. No one avoids food, or takes his own life, from the necessity of his own nature, but only when compelled by external causes. This can happen in many ways. Someone holding a sword in his hand may be forced to kill himself by someone else who twists his hand and makes him direct the sword at his own heart. Or he may be compelled to open his veins on the orders of a tyrant, as Seneca was – a case of choosing a lesser evil to avoid a greater. Or finally, hidden external causes may so influence his imagination, and affect his body, that he takes on a completely different nature...But it is no more possible that someone should strive not to exist, or to change into another form, from the necessity of his own nature, than it is for something to come from nothing...

The striving to preserve oneself is the first and only foundation of virtue. No other principle or virtue can be conceived prior to this, or apart from it...

For us to act out of virtue in the absolute sense is nothing else but acting and living and preserving our existence (these three mean the same) by the guidance of reason, on the basis of seeking what is beneficial to ourselves...

Whatever we strive for from reason is nothing but understanding. The mind, in so far as it employs reason, judges nothing to be beneficial to itself but what conduces to understanding...

This striving by which the mind, in so far as it reasons, endeavours to preserve its existence, is nothing else but understanding; and hence this striving to understand is the first and only foundation of virtue. We do not strive to understand things for the sake of some further goal; on the contrary, the mind, in so far as it reasons, is unable to conceive of anything that is good for it apart from what conduces to understanding.

There is nothing we know for certain to be good except what really conduces to understanding, and nothing we know for certain to be bad except what can hinder us from understanding...

The greatest thing the mind can understand is God, that is, a being that is absolutely infinite and without which nothing can exist or be conceived. Hence what is supremely beneficial or good for the mind is the knowledge of God. Now only in so far as it understands does the mind *act*; and only in so far as it understands can it be said to act from virtue in the absolute sense. But the greatest thing the mind can understand is God. Hence the supreme virtue of the mind is to understand, or know, God...

In so far as a thing agrees with our nature, it is necessarily good... From this it follows that the more something agrees with our nature, the more advantageous or good it is; and conversely, the more advantageous for us something is, the more it agrees with our nature...

In so far as people are subject to the passions, they cannot be said to be in harmony in their nature...

People can be in discord in their nature in so far as they are afflicted with passions. In this respect one and the same person can be changeable and inconstant...

In so far as human beings are afflicted by the passions, they can be in conflict with one another...

Only in so far as human beings live under the guidance of reason are they necessarily always in harmony in their nature. For in so far as humans are afflicted by the passions, they can be different in nature, and can be in conflict with one another. But human beings are said to act only in so far as they live following the guidance of reason. Hence, whatever follows from human nature, as defined by reason, must be understood through human nature alone, in so far as this is its immediate cause. But everyone, from the laws of his own nature, seeks what he judges to be good and strives to avoid what he judges to be evil; and what we judge to be good or evil when following the dictates of reason is necessarily good, and what we judge to be evil necessarily evil. Hence human beings, in so far as they live following the guidance of reason, will necessarily do what is good for human nature and consequently for each human being – that is, what is in accord with the nature of each human being. Hence human beings, in so far as they live following the guidance of reason, are necessarily always in harmony amongst themselves...

When each man most seeks what is beneficial for himself then men are most useful to one another. For the more each person seeks his own advantage and strives to preserve himself, the more he is endowed with virtue; or (which comes to the same thing) the greater power he has of acting in accordance with the laws of his own nature, that is, of living following the guidance of reason. But human beings are most in harmony in nature when they live following the guidance of reason. Hence humans will be most useful to each other when each person seeks what is advantageous to himself.

This conclusion is confirmed by daily experience; so abundant and so clear is the evidence that you will find almost everyone subscribing to the common saying 'man is a God to man'. Yet it rarely comes about that humans do live following the guidance of reason; things are organized so that they are generally envious, and troublesome to each other. None the less they are virtually incapable of living a solitary life, and hence most agree with the definition of man as a social animal. The fact is that many more benefits than burdens come from shared human society...

In so far as the mind understands all things as necessary, it has more power over the passions, and is less affected by them. The mind understands all things to be necessary, and to be determined to exist and produce their effects by an infinite chain of causes. Hence the mind can bring it about that it is less acted on by the passions arising from these causes, and less affected in respect of them.

The more this knowledge (that things are necessary) is applied to individual cases, which we imagine more vividly and distinctly, the greater is the power of the mind over the passions. This is confirmed by experience. We observe that the grief for a good man who has died diminishes as soon as the person who has suffered the loss reflects on how there could have been no way of keeping hold of the good that has been lost. Again, we see that no one pities infants for their inability to speak or talk or reason, or because they live all those early years without being aware of themselves, as it were. But if nearly everyone was born fully grown, and only one or two were born as infants, then everyone would pity infants; we would then consider infancy not as a natural and necessary thing, but as a kind of flaw or fault in nature...

For as long as we are not afflicted by the passions, which are contrary to our nature, we have the power of ordering and connecting the states of the body according to the order of the intellect. The passions which are contrary to our nature, that is, which are bad, are bad in so far as they hinder the mind from understanding. So for as long as we are not afflicted by the passions, which are contrary to our nature, the power by which the mind strives to understand things is not hindered; and hence it has the power to form clear and distinct ideas, and deduce some from others. Consequently, during this time we have the power of ordering and connecting the states of the body according to the order of the intellect. By this power of correctly ordering and connecting the states of the body we can bring it about that we are not easily affected by the evil passions...

But in order better to understand this power of the mind over the emotions, we should note first of all that when we call the emotions 'great', this is when we are comparing one man's emotion with another's and see that the first man is more afflicted with the same emotion than the second. Or alternatively it is when we are comparing different emotions in one and the same man, and notice that he is more affected or moved by one emotion than the other. Now the force of any given emotion is defined by the power of an external cause as compared with our own. But the power of the mind is defined solely by its knowledge, while lack of power, or passion, is defined solely by the privation of knowledge (i.e. that in virtue of which ideas are called 'inadequate'). From this it follows that a mind is most passive when the greatest part of it is made up of inadequate ideas, so that it is characterized more by how it is acted on than by how it acts. By contrast, a mind is most active when the greatest part of it is made up of adequate ideas; although it may have as many inadequate ideas as in the former case, it is characterized more by the ideas which belong to human virtue than by those which show our lack of power.

Notice next that maladies of the mind and misfortunes have their chief source in too much love towards something which is subject to many variations, and which we cannot ever possess. No one is worried or anxious about anything unless he loves it; and complaints and suspicions and hostility all arise from love towards things which no one can really possess.

From this we can easily conceive what can be achieved against the emotions by clear and distinct knowledge, and especially the highest kind of knowledge whose foundation is the knowledge of God. Such knowledge may not completely remove the emotions, in so far as they are passions, but at least it brings it about that they constitute the smallest part of the mind. Furthermore, it gives rise to love towards something immutable and eternal – something which we do really possess, and which therefore is not tainted by any of the vices to be found in ordinary love, but which can grow and grow till it occupies the greatest part of the mind, and spreads its influence far and wide.

... From this it is clear how much the wise man is capable of, and how he is more powerful than the ignorant person who is acted upon by lust alone. For the ignorant man, besides being buffeted in manifold ways by external causes, never acquires true peace of mind; he lives as if he has no knowledge of himself, or God or anything; and as soon as he stops being acted on, he ceases to be. The wise man, by contrast, considered as such, is scarcely subject to any disturbance of mind; being aware of himself and of God and of all things by a kind of eternal necessity, he never ceases to be, but always possesses true peace of mind.

If the way which I have shown as leading to all this seems hard, yet it is one that can be found. And indeed it must be hard, given that it is so seldom discovered. If the way to salvation were ready to hand and could be found without any great effort, how could it happen that almost everyone ignores it? Everything to be treasured is as hard to achieve as it is rare to attain.

4   Human Feeling as the Source of Ethics: David Hume, *Enquiry concerning the Principles of Morals**

The long tradition, exemplified in Spinoza, which put reason at the centre of philosophical accounts of the good life, was challenged in the mid-eighteenth century by David Hume. 'Reason,' Hume famously wrote, 'is and ought to be only the slave of the passions and can never pretend to any other office than to serve and obey them.'[1] Reason on its own, on Hume's view, is inert, and cannot provide any impulse or motivation to action. Hence, as often in Hume's philosophy, human nature has to take over where reason fails.[2] For Hume, morality is

---

* David Hume, *Enquiry concerning the Principles of Morals* [1751], Section V, parts 1 and 2; Section IX, parts 1 and 2; abridged, with minor modifications of spelling and punctuation. There are many editions available, including that by T. L. Beauchamp (Oxford: Oxford University Press, 1998), which includes an introduction for students.

[1] *A Treatise of Human Nature* [1739–40], Bk II, part iii, section 3.

[2] Compare Part I, extract 7; Part VII, extract 6.

founded ultimately on the natural feelings or sentiments we find within us. Where do such feelings come from? Against the view that virtue arises principally from education and training (compare Aristotle, extract 2, above), Hume suggests in the extract below that the social virtues have a 'natural beauty and amiableness' which 'recommends them to the esteem of uninstructed mankind and engages their affections'. Other things being equal, Hume observes in a vivid example, none of us would choose to tread on another's 'gouty toes', when we could as easily walk on the pavement. Underlying our moral impulses, then, are natural sentiments of benevolence which 'engage us to pay [regard] to the interests of mankind and society'.

Nevertheless, the potential conflict between self-interest and morality (compare Plato, extract 1, above) is never far from Hume's mind. He acknowledges that our feelings are often more vividly aroused by concern for ourselves, and those close to us, than they are by the thought of benefiting the world at large. But here evidence culled from ordinary experience enters the picture to help explain why moral virtue is desirable. In the closing part of our extract, Hume suggests, first of all, that some of the virtues (temperance, for example) are obviously beneficial to their possessor's health and well-being; others, clubbable or 'companionable' virtues like good manners and wit, evidently make our lives with our fellow men more agreeable. Finally, even the 'enlarged virtues' of humanity, generosity and beneficence are, Hume argues, clear contributors to individual happiness; while dishonest behaviour may seem to produce momentary pleasure or profit, this is of slight value compared with the rewards of virtue – 'inward peace of mind, consciousness of integrity, a satisfactory review of our own conduct'. While Hume's arguments will not, perhaps, convince the determined amoralist or the defender of ruthless self-interest, they none the less provide an engaging picture of the individual and collective advantages of living in a society where naturally based impulses of benevolence, and their associated moral virtues, have firmly taken root.

From the apparent usefulness of the social virtues, it has been readily inferred by sceptics, both ancient and modern, that all moral distinctions arise from education, and were at first invented and afterwards encouraged by the art of politicians in order to render men tractable, and subdue them for society. This principle, indeed, of precept and education, must...be owned to have a powerful influence...But that *all* moral affection or dislike arises from this origin will surely never be allowed by any judicious enquirer. Had nature made no such distinction, founded on the original constitution of the mind, the words *honourable* and *shameful, lovely* and *odious, noble* and *despicable* had never had place in any language; nor could politicians, had they invented these terms, ever have been able to render them intelligible, or make them convey any idea to the audience...

The social virtues must, therefore, be allowed to have a natural beauty and amiableness, which, at first, antecedent to all precept or education, recommends them to the esteem of uninstructed mankind, and engages their affections. And as the public utility of these virtues is the chief circumstance whence they derive their merit, it follows that the end which they have a tendency to promote must be some way agreeable to us, and take hold of some natural affection. It must please, either from considerations of self-interest, or from more generous motives and regards.

It has often been asserted that, as every man has a strong connection with society, and perceives the impossibility of his solitary subsistence, he becomes, on that account, favourable to all those habits or principles which promote order in society, and ensure to him the quiet possession of so inestimable a blessing. As much as we value our own happiness and welfare, as much must we applaud the practice of justice and humanity, by which alone the social confederacy can be maintained, and every man reap the fruits of mutual protection and assistance.

The deduction of morals from self-love, or a regard to private interest, is an obvious thought ... yet ... the voice of nature and experience seems plainly to oppose the selfish theory ... We frequently bestow praise on virtuous actions, performed in very distant ages and remote countries, where the utmost subtlety of imagination would not discover any appearance of self-interest, or find any connection of our present happiness and security with events so widely separated from us. A generous, a brave, a noble deed, performed by an adversary, commands our approbation, while in its consequences it may be acknowledged prejudicial to our particular interest ...

Compelled by these instances, we must renounce the theory which accounts for every moral sentiment by the principle of self-love. We must adopt a more public affection, and allow that the interests of society are not, even on their own account, entirely indifferent to us. Usefulness is only a tendency to a certain end; and it is a contradiction in terms that anything pleases us as means to an end, where the end in no wise affects us. If usefulness, therefore, be a source of moral sentiment, and if this usefulness be not always considered with reference to self, it follows that everything which contributes to the happiness of society recommends itself directly to our approbation and good will. Here is a principle which accounts, in great part, for the origin of morality. And what need we seek for abstruse and remote systems, when there occurs one so obvious and natural?

Have we any difficulty to comprehend the force of humanity and benevolence? Or to conceive that the very aspect of happiness, joy, prosperity, gives pleasure; that pain, suffering, sorrow, communicates uneasiness. The human countenance, says Horace, borrows smiles or tears from the human countenance. Reduce a person to solitude, and he loses all enjoyment, except either of the sensual or speculative kind; and that because the movements of his heart are not forwarded by correspondent movements in his fellow creatures. The signs of sorrow and mourning, though arbitrary, affect us with melancholy; but the natural symptoms, tears and cries and groans, never fail to infuse compassion and uneasiness. And if the effects of misery touch us in so lively a manner, can we be supposed altogether insensible or indifferent towards its causes, when a malicious or treacherous character and behaviour are presented to us?

... If any man, from a cold insensibility, or narrow selfishness of temper, is unaffected with the images of human happiness or misery, he must be equally indifferent to the images of vice and virtue; as, on the other hand, it is always found that a warm concern for the interests of our species is attended with a delicate feeling of all moral distinctions, a strong resentment of injury done to men, a lively approbation of their welfare. In this particular, though great superiority is observable of one man above another, yet none are so entirely indifferent to the interest of their fellow creatures as to perceive no distinctions of moral good and evil, in consequence of the different tendencies of actions and principles. How indeed can we suppose it possible in anyone, who wears a human heart, that if there be subjected to his censure one character or system of conduct which is beneficial, and another which is pernicious, to his species or community, he will not so much as give a cool preference to the former, or ascribe to it the smallest merit or regard? Let us suppose such a person ever so selfish; let private interest have engrossed ever so much of his attention; yet in instances where that is not concerned he must unavoidably feel *some* propensity to the good of mankind, and make it an object of choice, if everything else be equal. Would any man, who is walking along, tread as willingly on another's gouty toes, whom he has no quarrel with, as on the hard flint and pavement?...We surely take into consideration the happiness and misery of others, in weighing the several motives of action, and incline to the former, where no private regards draw us to seek our own promotion or advantage by the injury of our fellow creatures. And if the principles of humanity are capable, in many instances, of influencing our actions, they must, at all times, have *some* authority over our sentiments, and give us a general approbation of what is useful to society, and blame of what is dangerous or pernicious. The degrees of these sentiments may be the subject of controversy; but the reality of their existence, one should think, must be admitted in every theory or system...

The more we converse with mankind, and the greater social intercourse we maintain, the more shall we be familiarized to these general preferences and distinctions without which our conversation and discourse could scarcely be rendered intelligible to each other. General language, therefore, being formed for general use, must be moulded on some more general views, and must affix the epithets of praise or blame in conformity to sentiments which arise from the general interests of the community. And if these sentiments, in most men, be not so strong as those which have a reference to private good, yet still they must make some distinction, even in persons the most depraved and selfish; and must attach the notion of good to a beneficent conduct, and of evil to the contrary. Sympathy, we shall allow, is much fainter than our concern for ourselves, and sympathy with persons remote from us much fainter than that with persons near and contiguous; but for this very reason it is necessary for us, in our calm judgements and discourse concerning the characters of men, to neglect all those differences, and render our sentiments more public and social. Besides that we ourselves often change our situation in this particular, we every day meet with persons who are in a situation different from us, and who could never converse with us were we to remain constantly in that position and point of view which is peculiar to ourselves. The intercourse of sentiments, therefore, in society and conversation, makes us form some general unalterable standard by which we may approve or disapprove of characters and manners. And although the heart takes not part entirely with those general notions, nor regulates all its love and hatred by the universal abstract differences of vice and virtue, without regard to self, or the persons with whom we are more intimately connected; yet have these moral differences a considerable influence, and being sufficient, at least for discourse, serve all our purposes in company, in the pulpit, on the theatre, and in the schools.[1]

Thus, in whatever light we take this subject, the merit ascribed to the social virtues appears still uniform, and arises chiefly from that regard which the natural sentiment of benevolence engages us to pay to the interests of mankind and society. If we

---

[1] *It is wisely ordained by nature that private connections should commonly prevail over universal views and considerations; otherwise our affections and actions would be dissipated and lost, for want of a proper object. Thus a small benefit done to ourselves, or our near friends, excites more lively sentiments of love and approbation than a great benefit done to a distant commonwealth. But still we know here, as in all the senses, to correct these inequalities by reflection, and retain a general standard of vice and virtue, founded chiefly on general usefulness.

consider the principles of the human make, such as they appear to daily experience and observation, we must *a priori* conclude it impossible for such a creature as man to be totally indifferent to the well- or ill-being of his fellow creatures, and not readily, of himself, to pronounce (where nothing gives him any particular bias) that what promotes their happiness is good, what tends to their misery is evil, without any farther regard or consideration. Here then are the faint rudiments at least, or outlines, of a *general* distinction between actions...

Again, reverse these views and reasonings. Consider the matter *a posteriori*, and weighing the consequences, enquire whether the merit of social virtue be not, in a great measure, derived from the feelings of humanity with which it affects the spectators. It appears to be a matter of fact that the circumstance of *utility*, in all subjects, is a source of praise and approbation; that it is constantly appealed to in all moral decisions concerning the merit and demerit of actions; that it is the *sole* source of that high regard paid to justice, fidelity, honour, allegiance and chastity; that it is inseparable from all the other social virtues, humanity, generosity, charity, affability, lenity,[1] mercy and moderation; and in a word, that it is a foundation of the chief part of morals, which has a reference to mankind and our fellow creatures.

...It seems a happiness in the present theory that it enters not into that vulgar dispute concerning the *degrees* of benevolence or self-love which prevail in human nature – a dispute which is never likely to have any issue, both because men, who have taken part, are not easily convinced, and because the phenomena which can be produced on either side are so dispersed, so uncertain, and subject to so many interpretations that it is scarcely possible accurately to compare them, or draw from them any determinate inference or conclusion. It is sufficient for our present purpose if it be allowed, what surely without the greatest absurdity cannot be disputed, that there is some benevolence, however small, infused into our bosom; some spark of friendship for human kind; some particle of the dove kneaded into our frame, along with the elements of the wolf and the serpent. Let these generous sentiments be supposed ever so weak; let them be insufficient to move even a hand or finger of our body, they must still direct the determinations of our mind, and where everything else is equal, produce a cool preference of what is useful and serviceable to mankind above what is pernicious and dangerous. A *moral distinction*, therefore, immediately arises; a general sentiment of blame and approbation; a tendency, however faint, to the object of the one, and a proportional aversion to those of the other.

...Having explained the moral *approbation* attending merit or virtue, there remains nothing but briefly to consider our interested *obligation* to it, and to inquire whether every man who has any regard to his own happiness and welfare will not best find his account[2] in the practice of every moral duty. If this can be clearly ascertained from the foregoing theory, we shall have the satisfaction to reflect that we have advanced principles which not only, it is hoped, will stand the test of reasoning and inquiry, but may contribute to the amendment of men's lives, and their improvement in morality and social virtue...

But what philosophical truths can be more advantageous to society than those here delivered, which represent virtue in all her genuine and most engaging charms, and

---

[1] Lenity: gentleness, mildness.
[2] Find his account: discover his interest.

make us approach her with ease, familiarity and affection? The dismal dress falls off, with which many divines, and some philosophers, have covered her; and nothing appears but gentleness, humanity, beneficence, affability; nay, even at proper intervals, play, frolic and gaiety. She talks not of useless austerities and rigours, suffering and self-denial. She declares that her sole purpose is to make her votaries and all mankind, during every instant of their existence, if possible, cheerful and happy; nor does she ever willingly part with any pleasure, but in hopes of ample compensation in some other period of their lives. The sole trouble which she demands is that of just calculation, and a steady preference of the greater happiness...

That the virtues which are immediately *useful* or *agreeable*, to the person possessed of them, are desirable in a view to self-interest, it would surely be superfluous to prove. Moralists, indeed, may spare themselves all the pains which they often take in recommending these duties. To what purpose collect arguments to evince that temperance is advantageous, and the excesses of pleasure hurtful? When it appears that these excesses are only denominated such because they are hurtful; and that, if the unlimited use of strong liquors, for instance, no more impaired health, or the faculties of mind and body than the use of air or water, it would not be a whit more vicious or blameable.

It seems equally superfluous to prove that the *companionable* virtues of good manners and wit, decency and genteelness, are more desirable than the contrary qualities. Vanity alone, without any other consideration, is a sufficient motive to make us wish for the possession of these accomplishments. No man was ever willingly deficient in this particular. All our failures here proceed from bad education, want of capacity, or a perverse and unpliable disposition. Would you have your company coveted, admired, followed, rather than hated, despised, avoided? Can anyone seriously deliberate in the case? As no enjoyment is sincere, without some reference to company and society, so no society can be agreeable, or even tolerable, where a man feels his presence unwelcome, and discovers all around him symptoms of disgust and aversion.

But why in the greater society or confederacy of mankind should not the case be the same as in particular clubs and companies? Why is it more doubtful that the enlarged virtues of humanity, generosity, beneficence, are desirable with a view to happiness and self-interest, than the limited endowments of ingenuity and politeness? Are we apprehensive lest those social affections interfere, in a greater and more immediate degree than any other pursuits, with private utility, and cannot be gratified, without some important sacrifice of honour and advantage? If so, we are but ill instructed in the nature of the human passions, and are more influenced by verbal distinctions than by real differences...

Treating vice with the greatest candour, and making it all possible concessions, we must acknowledge that there is not, in any instance, the smallest pretext for giving it the preference above virtue, with a view to self-interest; except perhaps in the case of justice, where a man, taking things in a certain light, may seem to be a loser by his integrity... That *honesty is the best policy* may be a good general rule, but is liable to many exceptions; and he, it may perhaps be thought, conducts himself with most wisdom who observes the general rule and takes advantage of all the exceptions.

...But in all ingenuous natures, the antipathy to treachery and roguery is too strong to be counterbalanced by any views of profit or pecuniary advantage. Inward peace of mind, consciousness of integrity, a satisfactory review of our own conduct;

these are circumstances very requisite to happiness, and will be cherished and cultivated by any honest man who feels the importance of them.

Such a one has, besides, the frequent satisfaction of seeing knaves, with all their pretended cunning and abilities, betrayed by their own maxims; and while they purport to cheat with moderation and secrecy, a tempting incident occurs and they give into the snare; whence they can never extricate themselves without a total loss of reputation, and the forfeiture of all future trust and confidence with mankind.

But were they ever so secret and successful, the honest man, if he has any tincture of philosophy, or even common observation and reflection, will discover that they themselves are, in the end, the greatest dupes, and have sacrificed the invaluable enjoyment of a character, with themselves at least, for the acquisition of worthless toys and gewgaws. How little is requisite to supply the *necessities* of nature? And in a view to *pleasure*, what comparison between the unbought satisfaction of conversation, society, study, even health and the common beauties of nature, but above all the peaceful reflection on one's own conduct; what comparison, I say, between these and the feverish empty amusements of luxury and expense? These natural pleasures, indeed, are really without price; both because they are all below all price in their attainment, and above it in their enjoyment.

5   Duty and Reason as the Ultimate Principle: Immanuel Kant, *Groundwork of the Metaphysic of Morals**

The moral philosophy of Hume (see previous extract) gives pride of place to our natural feelings or sentiments, and links moral approval to what is useful or agreeable for human life. A view in many ways diametrically opposed to this was put forward later in the eighteenth century by Immanuel Kant. Kant's starting-point is a distinction between what is good merely as a means to an end, and what is intrinsically good, or good in itself. Health, well-being, contentment, happiness – none of these guarantee that their possessor is someone who is morally praiseworthy; only a good will has pure value in itself, 'shining like a jewel for its own sake'. Kant's position here is an uncompromising one. Suppose (in the manner suggested by Hume) we have a natural inclination to help others, and warm feelings of

human sympathy make us act benevolently. However right and amiable such action may be, says Kant, it does not merit moral esteem. Only if someone acts 'without any inclination, from the sake of duty alone, does his action for the first time have genuine moral worth'.

It is clear that the Kantian moral agent is someone who acts 'out of principle' as we nowadays say. But what *is* the guiding principle of action, given that Kant has disqualified as morally worthy anything done merely from inclination? Kant's answer is that actions are right if they conform not to any particular inclinations or desires, but to a *universal law*: 'I ought never to act except in such a way that I can also will that my maxim should become a universal law.' Deliberately breaking a promise for some

* Immanuel Kant, *Groundwork of the Metaphysic of Morals* [*Grundlegung zur Metaphysik der Sitten*, 1785], chs 1 and 2 (extracts). Trans. H. J. Paton, in *The Moral Law* (London: Hutchinson, 1948).

personal advantage is thus forbidden, since I cannot rationally will that everyone should act in such a way – if I did, the whole institution of promising would collapse. This notion has come to be known as Kant's *categorical imperative.* Most commands or recommendations ('Have a glass of wine!' 'Get down to work!' 'Take a holiday!') are hypothetical in character – they tell us to do something *if* we want a given result. But Kant's imperative is unconditionally binding.

Kant's principle appears to provide a necessary rather than sufficient condition for morality: that is, it *rules out* certain maxims (those which cannot in reason be universally adopted), rather than telling us which maxims we *should* adopt. Nevertheless, in arguing for the intrinsic value of a good will, Kant has provided a cornerstone for morality by locating the source of moral value in the autonomous will of the rational

agent. Each rational agent, exercising his or her will, is a bearer of value in him or herself, and thus deserves respect for his or her own sake. This leads to a new version of the categorical imperative (found in the last paragraph of our extract below): 'Act in such a way that you always treat humanity, whether in your own person or in that of any other, never simply as a means, but always at the same time as an end.' This principle of *respect for persons* has since come to be recognized as of enormous importance for morality. Each human being is capable of acting freely and autonomously; the Kantian moral vision is of a 'kingdom of ends' where no one is used simply as a means to the furtherance of someone else's projects, but each human being accords to all other humans the right to respect as a rational, self-determining agent.

It is impossible to conceive anything at all in the world, or even out of it, which can be taken as good without qualification, except a *good will.* Intelligence, wit, judgement, and any other *talents* of the mind we may care to name, or courage, resolution, and constancy of purpose, as qualities of *temperament,* are without doubt good and desirable in many respects; but they can also be extremely bad and hurtful when the will is not good which has to make use of these gifts of nature, and which for this reason has the term '*character*' applied to its peculiar quality. It is exactly the same with *gifts of fortune.* Power, wealth, honour, even health and that complete well-being and contentment with one's state which goes by the name of '*happiness*', produce boldness, and as a consequence often over-boldness as well, unless a good will is present by which their influence on the mind – and so too the whole principle of action – may be corrected and adjusted to universal ends...

A good will is not good because of what it effects or accomplishes – because of its fitness for attaining some proposed end: it is good through its willing alone – that is, good in itself. Considered in itself it is to be esteemed beyond comparison as far higher than anything it could ever bring about merely in order to favour some inclination or, if you like, the sum total of inclinations. Even if, by some special disfavour of destiny or by the niggardly endowment of stepmotherly nature, this will is entirely lacking in power to carry out its intentions; if by its utmost effort it still accomplishes nothing, and only good will is left (not, admittedly, as a mere wish, but as the straining of every means so far as they are in our control); even then it would still shine like a jewel for its own sake as something which has its full value in itself. Its usefulness or uselessness can neither add to, nor subtract from, this value. Its usefulness would be merely, as it were, the setting which enables us to handle it better in our ordinary dealings or to attract the attention of those not yet sufficiently expert, but not to commend it to experts or to determine its value.

... Since reason is not sufficiently serviceable for guiding the will safely as regards its objects and the satisfaction of all our needs (which it in part even multiplies) – a purpose for which an implanted natural instinct would have led us much more surely; and since none the less reason has been imparted to us as a practical power – that is, as one which is to have influence on the will; its true function must be to produce a *will* which is *good*, not as a *means* to some further end, but *in itself*; and for this function reason was absolutely necessary in a world where nature, in distributing her aptitudes, has everywhere else gone to work in a purposive manner. Such a will need not on this account be the sole and complete good, but it must be the highest good and the condition of all the rest, even of all our demands for happiness. In that case we can easily reconcile with the wisdom of nature our observation that the cultivation of reason which is required for the first and unconditioned purpose may in many ways, at least in this life, restrict the attainment of the second purpose – namely, happiness – which is always conditioned; and indeed that it can even reduce happiness to less than zero without nature proceeding contrary to its purpose; for reason, which recognizes as its highest practical function the establishment of a good will, in attaining this end is capable only of its own peculiar kind of contentment – contentment in fulfilling a purpose which in turn is determined by reason alone, even if this fulfilment should often involve interference with the purposes of inclination.

We have now to elucidate the concept of a will estimable in itself and good apart from any further end. This concept, which is already present in a sound natural understanding and requires not so much to be taught as merely to be clarified, always holds the highest place in estimating the total worth of our actions and constitutes the condition of all the rest. We will therefore take up the concept of duty, which includes that of a good will, exposed, however, to certain subjective limitations and obstacles. These, so far from hiding a good will or disguising it, rather bring it out by contrast and make it shine forth more brightly.

I will here pass over all actions already recognized as contrary to duty, however useful they may be with a view to this or that end; for about these the question does not even arise whether they could have been done for *the sake of duty* inasmuch as they are directly opposed to it. I will also set aside actions which in fact accord with duty, yet for which men have *no immediate inclination*, but perform them because impelled to do so by some other inclination. For there it is easy to decide whether the action which accords with duty has been done *from duty* or from some purpose of self-interest. This distinction is far more difficult to perceive when the action accords with duty and the subject has in addition an *immediate* inclination to the action. For example it certainly accords with duty that a grocer should not overcharge his inexperienced customer; and where there is much competition a sensible shopkeeper refrains from so doing and keeps to a fixed and general price for everybody so that a child can buy from him just as well as anyone else. Thus people are served *honestly*; but this is not nearly enough to justify us in believing that the shopkeeper has acted in this way from duty or from principles of fair dealing; his interests required him to do so. We cannot assume him to have in addition an immediate inclination towards his customers, leading him, as it were out of love, to give no man preference over another in the matter of price. Thus the action was done neither from duty nor from immediate inclination, but solely from purposes of self-interest.

On the other hand, to preserve one's life is a duty, and besides this every one has also an immediate inclination to do so. But on account of this the often anxious precautions taken by the greater part of mankind for this purpose have no inner worth, and the maxim of their action is without moral content. They do protect their lives *in conformity with duty* but not *from the motive of duty*. When on the contrary, disappointments and hopeless misery have quite taken away the taste for life; when a wretched man, strong in soul and more angered at his fate than faint-hearted or cast down, longs for death and still preserves his life without loving it – not from inclination or fear but from duty; then indeed his maxim has a moral content.

To help others where one can is a duty, and besides this there are many spirits of so sympathetic a temper that, without any further motive of vanity or self-interest, they find an inner pleasure in spreading happiness around them and can take delight in the contentment of others as their own work. Yet I maintain that in such a case an action of this kind, however right and however amiable it may be, has still no genuinely moral worth. It stands on the same footing as other inclinations – for example, the inclination for honour, which if fortunate enough to hit on something beneficial and right and consequently honourable, deserves praise and encouragement, but not esteem; for its maxim lacks moral content, namely, the performance of such actions, not from inclination, but *from duty*. Suppose then that the mind of this friend of man were overclouded by sorrows of his own which extinguished all sympathy with the fate of others, but that he still had power to help those in distress, though no longer stirred by the need of others because sufficiently occupied with his own; and suppose that, when no longer moved by any inclination, he tears himself out of this deadly insensibility and does the action without any inclination, for the sake of duty alone; then for the first time his action has its genuine moral worth . . .

To assure one's own happiness is a duty (at least indirectly); for discontent with one's state, in a press of cares and amidst unsatisfied wants, might easily become a great *temptation to the transgression of duty*. But here also, apart from regard to duty, all men have already of themselves the strongest and deepest inclination towards happiness, because precisely in this idea of happiness all inclinations are combined into a sum total . . . But . . . when the universal inclination towards happiness has failed to determine a man's will, when good health, at least for him, has not entered into his calculations as so necessary, what remains over, here as in other cases, is a law – the law of furthering his happiness, not from inclination, but from duty; and in thus for the first time his conduct has a real moral worth.

It is doubtless in this sense that we should understand too the passages from Scripture in which we are commanded to love our neighbour and even our enemy. For love out of inclination cannot be commanded; but kindness done from duty – although no inclination impels us, and even although natural and unconquerable disinclination stands in our way – is *practical*, and not *pathological*, love, residing in the will and not in the propensions of feeling, in principles of action and not of melting compassion; and it is this practical love alone which can be an object of command.

Our second proposition is this: An action done from duty has its moral worth, *not in the purpose* to be attained by it, but in the maxim in accordance with which it is decided upon; it depends therefore, not on the realization of the object of the action, but solely on the *principle* of *volition* in accordance with which, irrespective of all objects of the faculty of desire, the action has been performed . . .

Our third proposition, as an inference from the two preceding, I would express thus: *Duty is the necessity to act out of reverence for the law.* For an object as the effect of my proposed action I can have an *inclination,* but *never reverence,* precisely because it is merely the effect, and not the activity, of a will. Similarly for inclination as such, whether my own or that of another, I cannot have reverence: I can at most in the first case approve, and in the second case sometimes even love – that is, regard it as favourable to my own advantage. Only something which is conjoined with my will solely as a ground and never as an effect – something which does not serve my inclination, but outweighs it or at least leaves it entirely out of account in my choice – and therefore only bare law for its own sake, can be an object of reverence and therewith a command. Now an action done from duty has to set aside altogether the influence of inclination, and along with inclination every object of the will; so there is nothing left able to determine the will except objectively the *law* and subjectively *pure reverence* for this practical law,[1] and therefore the maxim[2] of obeying this law even to the detriment of all my inclinations ...

But what kind of law can this be the thought of which, even without regard to the results expected from it, has to determine the will if this is to be called good absolutely and without qualification? Since I have robbed the will of every inducement that might arise for it as a consequence of obeying any particular law, nothing is left but the conformity of actions to universal law as such, and this alone must serve the will as its principle. That is to say, I ought never to act except in such a way *that I can also will that my maxim should become a universal law.* Here bare conformity to universal law as such (without having as its base any law prescribing particular actions) is what serves the will as its principle, and must so serve it if duty is not to be everywhere an empty delusion and a chimerical concept. The ordinary reason of mankind also agrees with this completely in its practical judgements and always has the aforesaid principle before its eyes.

Take this question, for example. May I not, when I am hard pressed, make a promise with the intention of not keeping it? Here I readily distinguish the two senses which the question can have – Is it prudent, or is it right, to make a false promise? The first no doubt can often be the case. I do indeed see that it is not enough for me to extricate myself from present embarrassment by this subterfuge: I have to consider whether from this lie there may not subsequently accrue to me much greater

---

[1] *It might be urged against me that I have merely tried, under cover of the word '*reverence*', to take refuge in an obscure feeling instead of giving a clearly articulated answer to the question by means of a concept of reason. Yet although reverence is a feeling, it is not a feeling *received* through outside influence, but one *self-produced* by a rational concept, and therefore specifically distinct from feelings of the first kind, all of which can be reduced to inclination or fear. What I recognize immediately as law for me, I recognize with reverence, which means merely consciousness of the *subordination* of my will to a law without the mediation of external influences on my senses. Immediate determination of the will by the law and consciousness of this determination is called '*reverence*', so that reverence is regarded as the *effect* of the law on the subject and not as the cause of the law ... All reverence for a person is properly only reverence for the law (of honesty and so on) of which that person gives us an example. Because we regard the development of our talents as a duty we see too in a man of talent a sort of *example of the law* (the law of becoming like him by practice) and this is what constitutes our reverence for him. All moral *interest,* so called, consists solely in *reverence* for the law. [This note repositioned from its location in the original.]

[2] *A *maxim* is the subjective principle of a volition: an objective principle (that is, one which would also serve subjectively as a practical principle for all rational beings if reason had full control over the faculty of desire) is a practical *law.*

inconvenience than that from which I now escape, and also (since, with all my supposed *astuteness*, to foresee the consequences is not so easy that I can be sure there is no chance, once confidence in me is lost, of this proving far more disadvantageous than all the ills I now think to avoid) whether it may not be a *more prudent* action to proceed here on a general maxim and make it my habit not to give a promise except with the intention of keeping it. Yet it becomes clear to me at once that such a maxim is always founded solely on fear of consequences. To tell the truth for the sake of duty is something entirely different from doing so out of concern for inconvenient results; for in the first case the concept of the action already contains in itself a law for me, while in the second case I have first of all to look around elsewhere in order to see what effects may be bound up with it for me. When I deviate from the principle of duty, this is quite certainly bad; but if I desert my prudential maxim, this can often be greatly to my advantage, though it is admittedly safer to stick to it. Suppose I seek, however, to learn in the quickest way and yet unerringly how to solve the problem 'Does a lying promise accord with duty?' I have then to ask myself 'Should I really be content that my maxim (the maxim of getting out of a difficulty by a false promise) should hold as a universal law (one valid both for myself and others)? And could I really say to myself that every one may make a false promise if he finds himself in a difficulty from which he can extricate himself in no other way?' I then become aware at once that I can indeed will to lie, but I can by no means will a universal law of lying; for by such a law there could properly be no promises at all, since it would be futile to profess a will for future action to others who would not believe my profession or who, if they did so over-hastily, would pay me back in like coin; and consequently my maxim, as soon as it was made a universal law, would be bound to annul itself...

Now I say that man, and in general every rational being, *exists* as an end in himself, *not merely as a means* for arbitrary use by this or that will: he must in all his actions, whether they are directed to himself or to other rational beings, always be viewed *at the same time as an end*. All the objects of inclination have only a conditioned value; for if there were not these inclinations and the needs grounded on them, their object would be valueless... Thus the value of all objects that can be produced by our action is always conditioned. Beings whose existence depends, not on our will, but on nature, have none the less, if they are non-rational beings, only a relative value as means, and are consequently called *things*. Rational beings, on the other hand, are called *persons* because their nature already marks them out as ends in themselves – that is, as something which ought not to be used merely as a means – and consequently imposes to that extent a limit on all arbitrary treatment of them (and is an object of reverence). Persons, therefore, are not merely subjective ends whose existence as an object of our actions has a value *for us*; they are *objective ends* – that is, things whose existence is in itself an end, and indeed an end such that in its place we can put no other end to which they should serve *simply* as means; for unless this is so, nothing at all of *absolute* value would be found anywhere. But if all value were conditioned, – that is, contingent – then no supreme principle could be found for reason at all.

If then there is to be a supreme practical principle, and – so far as the human will is concerned – a categorical imperative, it must be such that from the idea of something which is necessarily an end for every one, because it is an *end in itself*, it forms an *objective* principle of the will, and consequently can serve as a practical law. The ground of this principle is this: *Rational nature exists as an end in itself.* This is the way in which a man necessarily conceives his own existence; it is therefore so far a principle of human actions. But it is also the way in which every other rational being conceives his existence on the same rational ground which is valid also for me; hence it is at the same time an *objective* principle, from which, as a supreme practical ground, it must be possible to derive all laws for the will. The practical imperative will therefore be as follows: *Act in such a way that you always treat humanity, whether in your own person or in the person of any other, never simply as a means, but always at the same time as an end.*

6   Happiness as the Foundation of Morality: John Stuart Mill, *Utilitarianism**

Theories of morality are nowadays often classified as either (*a*) consequentialist or (*b*) deontological, depending on whether they assess the worth of actions or classes of action (*a*) in terms of their results or consequences, or (*b*) on the basis of their conformity to some principle or principles of duty (the term 'deontological' comes from the Greek *deon*, obligatory). Kant's approach (see previous extract) is firmly deontological in character, while the extract that follows, by the celebrated nineteenth-century philosopher John Stuart Mill, belongs squarely in the consequentialist tradition. Mill argues that the rightness or wrongness of an act depends not on any intrinsic worth (contrast Kant), but on the results it produces, or tends to produce. The standard of goodness which Mill employs for assessing those results is Utility, or the Greatest Happiness Principle: actions are right in proportion as they tend to promote happiness, wrong as they tend to produce the reverse of happiness. Happiness is defined by Mill as pleasure and the absence of pain.

Mill did not invent utilitarianism. The notion that pleasure might provide a standard for evaluating action had been widely canvassed in ancient Greek philosophy (notably by Epicurus,

341–270 BC), and Mill's more immediate predecessor, Jeremy Bentham, had declared that pleasure and pain were the 'sovereign masters' determining what mankind ought to do.[1] While supporting Bentham's general approach, Mill was sensitive to the worry that such a doctrine might appear to advocate gross physical indulgence, and so be represented as a 'doctrine worthy of swine'. To counter this, he distinguishes 'higher' from 'lower' pleasures: some kinds of pleasure (those involving our more elevated intellectual faculties) are more valuable than others, and hence it is 'better to be Socrates dissatisfied than a fool satisfied'. Though Mill tries to bolster his distinction by appeal to the verdict of 'competent judges' (those who have tried both kinds of pleasure), critics have objected that it is not strictly consistent with his principles of utility: if pleasure is the only ultimate standard, then it might have been more consistent to say (as Bentham did) that 'quantity of pleasure being equal, push-pin is as good as poetry'. Among other objections to utilitarianism addressed by Mill in the following extract is the worry that a consequentialist system of ethics may lead us to break important rules of conduct: if the overall balance of pleasure is the only standard, why should I not tell lies whenever

---

*   J. S. Mill, *Utilitarianism* [1861], ch. 2; abridged, punctuation occasionally modified. Many editions available, including that by R. Crisp (Oxford: Oxford University Press, 1998), with introduction and notes.

[1]   'Nature has placed mankind under the governance of two sovereign masters, pleasure and pain. It is for them to determine what we ought to do, as well as what we shall do' (*An Introduction to the Principles of Morals and Legislation* [1789], ch. 1). See also introduction to Part IX, extract 6, below.

I can maximize pleasure by doing so? Mill replies that utilitarians will want to instil a sense of veracity in the population, since truth-telling is generally productive of happiness. Here and later on in the extract he suggests that utilitarians will not try to make each individual decision by direct reference to the greatest happiness principle, but instead will stick to rules or guidelines based on our experience of the kind of conduct that tends to maximize happiness. The resulting version of utilitarianism, now known as 'indirect' or 'rule' utilitarianism, has strongly influenced the subsequent development of moral philosophy.

The creed which accepts as the foundation of morals Utility, or the Greatest Happiness principle, holds that actions are right in proportion as they tend to promote happiness, wrong as they tend to produce the reverse of happiness. By happiness is intended pleasure, and the absence of pain; by unhappiness, pain and the privation of pleasure. To give a clear view of the moral standard set up by the theory, much more requires to be said; in particular, what things it includes in the idea of pain and pleasure; and to what extent this is left an open question. But these supplementary explanations do not affect the theory of life on which this theory of morality is grounded – namely, that pleasure, and freedom from pain, are the only things desirable as ends; and that all desirable things (which are as numerous in the utilitarian as in any other scheme) are desirable either for the pleasure inherent in themselves, or as means to the promotion of pleasure and the prevention of pain.

Now such a theory of life excites in many minds, and among them in some of the most estimable in feeling and purpose, inveterate dislike. To suppose that life has (as they express it) no higher end than pleasure – no better and nobler object of desire and pursuit – they designate as utterly mean and grovelling; as a doctrine worthy only of swine, to whom the followers of Epicurus were, at a very early period, contemptuously likened; and modern holders of the doctrine are occasionally made the subject of equally polite comparisons by its German, French and English assailants.

When thus attacked, the Epicureans have always answered that it is not they, but their accusers, who represent human nature in a degrading light; since the accusation supposes human beings to be capable of no pleasures except those of which swine are capable . . . The comparison of the Epicurean life to that of beasts is felt as degrading, precisely because a beast's pleasures do not satisfy a human being's conception of happiness. Human beings have faculties more elevated than the animal appetites, and when once made conscious of them, do not regard anything as happiness which does not include their gratification. I do not, indeed, consider the Epicureans to have been by any means faultless in drawing out their scheme of consequences from the utilitarian principle. To do this in any sufficient manner, many Stoic, as well as Christian elements require to be included. But there is no known Epicurean theory of life which does not assign to the pleasures of the intellect, of the feelings and imagination, and of the moral sentiments, a much higher value as pleasures than to those of mere sensation. It must be admitted, however, that utilitarian writers in general have placed the superiority of mental over bodily pleasures chiefly in the greater permanence, safety, uncostliness, etc., of the former – that is, in their circumstantial advantages rather than in their intrinsic nature. And on all these points utilitarians have fully proved their case; but they might have taken the other, and, as it may be called, higher ground, with entire consistency. It is quite compatible with the principle of utility to recognize the fact that some *kinds* of pleasure are more desirable and more valuable than others. It would be absurd that while, in estimating all others things, quality is considered as well as quantity, the estimation of pleasures should be supposed to depend on quantity alone.

If I am asked what I mean by difference of quality in pleasures, or what makes one pleasure more valuable than another, merely as a pleasure, except its being greater in amount, there is but one possible answer. Of two pleasures, if there be one to which all or almost all who have experience of both give a decided preference, irrespective of any feeling of moral obligation to prefer it, that is the more desirable pleasure. If one of the two is, by those who are competently acquainted with both, placed so far above the other that they prefer it, even though knowing it to be attended with a greater amount of discontent, and would not resign it for any quantity of the other pleasure which their nature is capable of, we are justified in ascribing to the preferred enjoyment a superiority in quality, so far out-weighing quantity as to render it, in comparison, of small account.

Now it is an unquestionable fact that those who are equally acquainted with, and equally capable of appreciating and enjoying, both, do give a most marked preference to the manner of existence which employs their higher faculties ... A being of higher faculties requires more to make him happy, is capable probably of more acute suffering, and certainly accessible to it at more points, than one of an inferior type; but in spite of these liabilities, he can never really wish to sink into what he feels to be a lower grade of existence ... Whoever supposes that this preference takes place at a sacrifice of happiness – that the superior being, in anything like equal circumstances, is not happier than the inferior – confounds the two very different ideas, of happiness, and content. It is indisputable that the being whose capacities of enjoyment are low has the greatest chance of having them fully satisfied; and a highly endowed being will always feel that any happiness which he can look for, as the world is constituted, is imperfect. But he can learn to bear its imperfections, if they are at all bearable; and they will not make him envy the being who is indeed unconscious of the imperfections, but only because he feels not at all the good which those imperfections qualify. It is better to be a human being dissatisfied than a pig satisfied; better to be Socrates dissatisfied than a fool satisfied. And if the fool, or the pig, are of a different opinion, it is because they only know their own side of the question. The other party to the comparison knows both sides ...

From this verdict of the competent judges, I apprehend there can be no appeal. On a question which is the best worth having of two pleasures, or which of two modes of existence is the most grateful to the feelings, apart from its moral attributes and from its consequences, the judgement of those who are qualified by knowledge of both, or, if they differ, that of the majority among them, must be admitted as final. And there needs be the less hesitation to accept this judgement respecting the quality of pleasures, since there is no other tribunal to be referred to even on the question of quantity. What means are there of determining which is the acutest of two pains, or the intensest of two pleasurable sensations, except the general suffrage of those who are familiar with both? Neither pains nor pleasures are homogenous, and pain is always heterogeneous with pleasure. What is there to decide whether a particular pleasure is worth purchasing at the cost of a particular pain, except the feelings and judgement of the experienced? When, therefore, those feelings and judgement declare the pleasures derived from the higher faculties to be preferable *in kind*, apart from the question of intensity, to those of which the animal nature, disjoined from the higher faculties, is susceptible, they are entitled on this subject to the same regard...

According to the Greatest Happiness Principle, as above explained, the ultimate end, with reference to and for the sake of which all other things are desirable (whether we are considering our own good or that of other people), is an existence exempt as far as possible from pain, and as rich as possible in enjoyments, both in point of quantity and quality... This being, according to the utilitarian opinion, the end of human action, is necessarily also the standard of morality; which may accordingly be defined [as] the rules and precepts for human conduct by the observance of which an existence such as has been described might be, to the greatest extent possible, secured to all mankind; and not to them only, but, so far as the nature of things admits, to the whole sentient creation...

I must again repeat what the assailants of utilitarianism seldom have the justice to acknowledge, that the happiness which forms the utilitarian standard of what is right in conduct is not the agent's own happiness, but that of all concerned. As between his own happiness and that of others, utilitarianism requires him to be as strictly impartial as a disinterested and benevolent spectator. In the golden rule of Jesus of Nazareth we read the complete spirit of the ethics of utility. To do as you would be done by, and to love your neighbour as yourself, constitute the ideal perfection of utilitarian morality. As the means of making the nearest approach to this ideal, utility would enjoin, first, that laws and social arrangements should place the happiness, or (as speaking practically it may be called) the interest, of every individual as nearly as possible in harmony with the interest of the whole; and secondly, that education and opinion, which have so vast a power over human character, should so use that power as to establish in the mind of every individual an indissoluble association between his own happiness and the good of the whole...

The objectors to utilitarianism cannot always be charged with representing it in a discreditable light. On the contrary, those among them who entertain anything like a just idea of its disinterested character sometimes find fault with its standard as being too high for humanity. They say it is exacting too much to require that people shall always act from the inducement of promoting the general interests of society. But this is to mistake the very meaning of a standard of morals, and confound the rule of actions with the motive of it. It is the business of ethics to tell us what are our duties, or by what test we may know them, but no system of ethics requires that the motive of all we do shall be a feeling of duty; on the contrary, ninety-nine hundredths of all our actions are done from other motives, and rightly so done, if the rule of duty does not condemn them... He who saves a fellow creature from drowning does what is morally right, whether his motive be duty, or the hope of being paid for his trouble... But to speak only of actions done from the motive of duty, and in direct obedience to principle: it is a misapprehension of the utilitarian mode of thought to conceive it as implying that people should fix their minds upon so wide a generality as the world, or society at large. The great majority of good actions are directed not for the benefit of the world, but for that of the individual, of which the good of the world is made up; and the thoughts of the most virtuous man need not on these occasions travel beyond the particular persons concerned, except as far as is necessary to assure himself that in benefiting them he is not violating the rights, that is, the legitimate and authorized expectations, of anyone else. The multiplication of happiness is, according to the utilitarian ethics, the object of virtue: the occasions on which any person (except one in a thousand) has it in his power to do this on an extended scale, in other words to be a public benefactor, are but exceptional; and on these occasions alone is he called on to consider public utility; in every other case, private utility, the interest or happiness of some few persons, is all he has to attend to. Those alone, the influence of whose actions extends to society in general, need concern themselves habitually about so large an object. In the case of abstinences indeed – of things which people forbear to do from moral considerations, though the consequences in the particular case might be beneficial – it would be unworthy of an intelligent agent not be consciously aware that the action is of a class which, if practised generally, would be generally injurious, and that this is the ground of the obligation to abstain from it. The amount of regard for the public interest implied in this recognition is not greater than is demanded by every system of morals, for they all enjoin to abstain from whatever is manifestly pernicious to society...

Again, Utility is often summarily stigmatized as an immoral doctrine, by giving it the name of Expediency, and taking advantage of the popular use of that term to contrast it with Principle. But the Expedient, in the sense in which it is opposed to the Right, generally means that which is expedient for the particular interest of the agent himself; as when a minister sacrifices the interest of his country to keep himself in place. When it means anything better than this, it means that which is expedient for some immediate object, some temporary purpose, but which violates a rule whose observance is expedient in a much higher degree. The Expedient, in this sense, instead of being the same thing with the useful, is a branch of the hurtful. Thus it would often be expedient, for the purpose of getting over some momentary embarrassment, or attaining some object immediately useful to ourselves or others, to tell a lie. But inasmuch as the cultivation in ourselves of a sensitive feeling on the subject of veracity is one of the most useful, and the enfeeblement of that feeling one of the most hurtful, things to which our conduct can be instrumental; and inasmuch as any, even unintentional, deviation from truth does that much towards weakening the trustworthiness of human assertion, which is not only the principal support of all present social well-being, but the insufficiency of which does more than any one thing that can be named to keep back civilization, virtue, everything on which human happiness on the largest scale depends; we feel that the violation, for a present advantage, of a rule of such transcendent expediency is not expedient, and that he who, for the sake of a convenience to himself or some other individual, does what depends on him to deprive mankind of the good, and inflict upon them the evil, involved in the greater or less reliance which they can place in each other's word, acts the part of one of their worst enemies. Yet that even this rule, sacred as it is, admits of possible exceptions, is acknowledged by all moralists; the chief of which is when the withholding of some fact (as of information from a malefactor, or of bad news from a person dangerously ill) would save an individual (especially an individual other than oneself) from great and unmerited evil, and when the withholding can only be effected by denial. But in order that the exception may not extend itself beyond the need, and may have the least possible effect in weakening reliance on veracity, it ought to be recognized, and, if possible, its limits defined; and if the principle of utility is good for anything, it must be good for weighing these conflicting utilities against one another, and marking out the regions within which one or the other preponderates.

Again, defenders of Utility often find themselves called upon to reply to such objections as this – that there is not time, previous to action, for calculating and weighing the effects of any line of conduct on the general happiness ... The answer to the objection is that there has been ample time, namely the whole past duration of the human species. During all that time, mankind have been learning by experience the tendencies of actions, on which experience all the prudence as well as all the morality of life are dependent ... [T]hat the received code of ethics is by no means of divine right; and that mankind have still much to learn as to the effects of actions on the general happiness, I admit, or rather, earnestly maintain. The corollaries from the principle of utility, like the precepts of every practical art, admit of indefinite improvement, and in a progressive state of the human mind, their improvement is perpetually going on. But to consider the rules of morality as improvable is one thing; to pass over the intermediate generalizations entirely, and endeavour to test each individual action directly by the first principle, is another. It is a strange notion that the acknowledgement of a first principle is inconsistent with the admission of secondary ones. To inform a traveller respecting the place of his ultimate destination is not to forbid the use of landmarks and direction-posts on the way. The proposition that happiness is the end and aim of morality does not mean that no road ought to be laid down to that goal, or that persons going thither should not be advised to take one direction rather than the other ... Nobody argues that the art of navigation is not founded on astronomy, because sailors cannot wait to calculate the National Almanack. Being rational creatures, they go to sea with it ready calculated; and all rational creatures go out upon the sea of life with their minds made up on the common questions of right and wrong, as well as on many of the far more difficult questions of wise and foolish. And this, as long as foresight is a human quality, it is to be presumed they will continue to do.

7   Utility and Common-sense Morality: Henry Sidgwick, *Methods of Ethics**

The ideas behind the 'indirect' version of utilitarianism propounded by J. S. Mill (see previous extract) were further examined and developed later in the nineteenth century by the Cambridge philosopher Henry Sidgwick. Though Sidgwick is often classified as a utilitarian, his discussions of utilitarianism are concerned in the main to provide a critical account of the relationship between utilitarian theory and ordinary common-sense morality. In the following extract he examines first of all the hypothesis that common

sense, based on the long experience of mankind, can be expected to be a reliable guide to those rules and practices which promote happiness. There may be all sorts of reasons, Sidgwick argues, why the prevailing code in any given society may not be an ideal maximizer of utility (such reasons include the limited sympathy and limited intelligence of the human beings involved). Given that the set of rules that has evolved over the ages is likely to be only a very imperfect guide to the general happiness,

* H. Sidgwick, *The Methods of Ethics* [1874] (7th edn, London: Macmillan, 1907), extracts from Bk IV, ch. 4, § 1; ch. 5, §§ 1–3.

Sidgwick concludes that it is the 'unavoidable duty of a systematic utilitarian to make a thorough revision of these rules'.

In the second half of our extract, however, Sidgwick provides a subtle and insightful discussion of the dangers of such revisions. What may seem an improvement may be too complicated to have any chance of being generally inculcated among the population at large. And in any case, a proposed change may itself lead to instability since 'it is practically much easier for most men to conform to a moral rule established in the society to which they belong than to one made by themselves'. Finally, Sidgwick tackles the question of whether exceptions to generally observed rules may be justified. Could I accept, for example, that truth-telling is a generally beneficial practice, to be encouraged in society, but at the same time allow myself to break the rule in order to produce a greater benefit on a given occasion? (Compare Mill's discussion of truth-telling in the previous extract.) Here Sidgwick argues that allowing such exceptions could be highly dangerous since

'however strong the actually existing sentiment against lying may be, as soon as this legitimacy [of being allowed to break the rule] is generally recognized, the sentiment must be expected to decay and vanish'. The reasoning here is complicated, and will vary from case to case. Remaining celibate, though this would be a disastrous practice if generally followed, is perfectly permissible 'on account of the general sentiments prompting to marriage'; but in the case of telling lies, there is a much greater risk of undermining valuable prevailing patterns of conduct. Sidgwick's general conclusion is that there are many rules that a conscientious utilitarian could only very rarely justify breaking. The issues he raises here concerning the status and bindingness of moral rules are still being debated by philosophers; the enduring problem for consequentialists is to show how far established ethical norms could command respect in a world dominated by consequentialist thinking, where such norms were seen as having the merely secondary status of guidelines or pointers to general good.

 [F]rom the considerations that we have just surveyed it is but a short and easy step to the conclusion that in the Morality of Common Sense we have ready to hand a body of Utilitarian doctrine; that the 'rules of morality for the multitude' are to be regarded as 'positive beliefs of mankind as to the effects of actions on their happiness',[1] so that the apparent first principles of Common Sense may be accepted as the 'middle axioms' of Utilitarian method; direct reference being only made to utilitarian considerations in order to settle points upon which the verdict of Common Sense is found to be obscure and conflicting. On this view the traditional controversy between the advocates of Virtue and the advocates of Happiness would seem to be at length harmoniously settled.

And the arguments for this view which have been already put forward certainly receive support from the hypothesis, now widely accepted, that the moral sentiments are ultimately derived, by a complex and gradual process, from experiences of pleasure and pain...But it is one thing to hold that the current morality expresses, partly consciously but to a larger extent unconsciously, the results of human experience as to the effects of actions: it is quite another thing to accept this morality *en bloc*, so far as it is clear and definite, as the best guidance we can get to the attainment of maximum general happiness. However attractive this simple reconciliation of Intuitional and Utilitarian methods may be, it is not, I think, really warranted by the evidence...For though the passions and other active impulses are doubtless themselves influenced, no less than the moral sentiments, by experiences of pleasure and

---

[1] J. S. Mill, *Utilitarianism*, ch. 2.

pain; still this influence is not sufficient to make them at all trustworthy guides to general, any more than to individual, happiness – as some of our moral sentiments themselves emphatically announce. But even if we consider our common moral sentiments as entirely due – directly or indirectly – to the accumulated and transmitted experiences of primary and sympathetic pains and pleasures; it is obvious that the degree of accuracy with which sentiments thus produced will guide us to the promotion of general happiness must largely depend upon the degree of accuracy with which the whole sum of pleasurable and painful consequences, resulting from any course of action, has been represented in the consciousness of an average member of the community. And it is seen at a glance that this representation has always been liable to errors of great magnitude... We have to allow, first, for limitation of sympathy; since in every age and country the sympathy of an average man with other sentient beings, and even his egoistic regard for their likings and aversions, has been much more limited than the influence of his actions on the feelings of others. We must allow further for limitation of intelligence: for in all ages ordinary men have had a very inadequate knowledge of natural sequences; so that such indirect consequences of conduct as have been felt have been frequently traced to wrong causes, and been met by wrong moral remedies, owing to imperfect apprehension of the relation of means to ends. Again, where the habit of obedience to authority and respect for rank has become strong, we must allow for the possibly perverting influence of a desire to win the favour or avert the anger of superiors. And similarly we must allow again for the influences of false religions; and also for the possibility that the sensibilities of religious teachers have influenced the code of duty accepted by their followers, in points where these sensibilities were not normal and representative, but exceptional and idiosyncratic.[1]

On the other hand, we must suppose that these deflecting influences have been more or less limited and counteracted by the struggle for existence in past ages among different human races and communities; since, as far as any moral habit or sentiment was unfavourable to the preservation of the social organism, it would be a disadvantage in the struggle for existence, and would therefore tend to perish with the community that adhered to it. But we have no reason to suppose that this force would be adequate to keep positive morality always in conformity with a Utilitarian ideal. For (1) imperfect morality would be only one disadvantage among many, and not, I conceive, the most important, unless the imperfection were extreme – especially in the earlier stages of social and moral development, in which the struggle for existence was most operative; and (2) a morality perfectly preservative of a human community might still be imperfectly felicific, and require considerable improvement from a Utilitarian point of view. Further, analogy would lead us to expect that however completely adapted the moral instincts of a community may be at some particular time to its conditions of existence, any rapid change of circumstances

---

[1] *No doubt this influence is confined within strict limits: no authority can permanently impose on men regulations flagrantly infelicific: and the most practically originative of religious teachers have produced their effect chiefly by giving new force and vividness to sentiments already existing (and recognized as properly authoritative) in the society upon which they acted. Still, it might have made a great difference to the human race if (e.g.) Mohammed had been fond of wine, and indifferent to women.

would tend to derange the adaptation, from survival of instincts formerly useful, which through this change become useless or pernicious...

Finally, we must not overlook the fact that the divergences which we find when we compare the moralities of different ages and countries, exist to some extent side by side in the morality of any one society at any given time. It has already been observed that whenever divergent opinions are entertained by a minority so large, that we cannot fairly regard the dogma of the majority as the plain utterance of Common Sense, an appeal is necessarily made to some higher principle, and very commonly to Utilitarianism. But a smaller minority than this, particularly if composed of persons of enlightenment and special acquaintance with the effects of the conduct judged, may reasonably inspire us with distrust of Common Sense: just as in the more technical parts of practice we prefer the judgement of a few trained experts to the instincts of the vulgar. Yet again, a contemplation of these divergent codes and their relation to the different circumstances in which men live, suggests that Common-Sense morality is really only adapted for ordinary men in ordinary circumstances – although it may still be expedient that these ordinary persons should regard it as absolutely and universally prescribed, since any other view of it may dangerously weaken its hold over their mind. So far as this is the case we must use the Utilitarian method to ascertain how far persons in special circumstances require a morality more specially adapted to them than Common Sense is willing to concede: and also how far men of peculiar physical or mental constitution ought to be exempted from ordinary rules, as has sometimes been claimed for men of genius, or men of intensely emotional nature, or men gifted with more than usual prudence and self-control...

We must conclude, then, that we cannot take the moral rules of Common Sense as expressing the *consensus* of competent judges, up to the present time, as to the kind of conduct which is likely to produce the greatest amount of happiness on the whole. It would rather seem that it is the unavoidable duty of a systematic Utilitarianism to make a thorough revision of these rules, in order to ascertain how far the causes previously enumerated (and perhaps others) have actually operated to produce a divergence between Common Sense and a perfectly Utilitarian code of morality...

If, then, we are to regard the morality of Common Sense as a machinery of rules, habits, and sentiments, roughly and generally but not precisely or completely adapted to the production of the greatest possible happiness for sentient beings generally; and if, on the other hand, we have to accept it as the actually established machinery for attaining this end, which we cannot replace at once by any other, but can only gradually modify; it remains to consider the practical effects of the complex and balanced relation in which a scientific Utilitarian thus seems to stand to the Positive Morality of his age and country.

Generally speaking, he will clearly conform to it, and endeavour to promote its development in others. For, though the imperfection that we find in all the actual conditions of human existence – we may even say in the universe at large as judged from a human point of view – is ultimately found even in Morality itself, in so far as this is contemplated as Positive; still, practically, we are much less concerned with correcting and improving than we are with realizing and enforcing it. The Utilitarian must repudiate altogether that temper of rebellion against the established morality, as something purely external and conventional, into which the reflective mind is always apt to fall when it is first convinced that the established rules are not intrinsically reasonable. He must, of course, also repudiate as superstitious that awe of it as an absolute or Divine Code which Intuitional moralists inculcate.[1] Still, he will naturally contemplate it with reverence and wonder, as a marvellous product of nature, the result of long centuries of growth, showing in many parts the same fine adaptation of means to complex exigencies as the most elaborate structures of physical organisms exhibit; he will handle it with respectful delicacy as a mechanism, constructed of the fluid element of opinions and dispositions, by the indispensable aid of which the actual *quantum* of human happiness is continually being produced; a mechanism which no 'politicians or philosophers' could create, yet without which the harder and coarser machinery of Positive Law could not be permanently maintained, and the life of man would become – as Hobbes forcibly expresses it – 'solitary, poor, nasty, brutish, and short'.[2]

Still, as this actual moral order is admittedly imperfect, it will be the Utilitarian's duty to aid in improving it; just as the most orderly, law-abiding member of a modern civilised society includes the reform of laws in his conception of political duty...

Let us suppose then that after considering the consequences of any...rule, a Utilitarian comes to the conclusion that a different rule would be more conducive to the general happiness, if similarly established in a society remaining in other respects the same as at present – or in one slightly different (in so far as our forecast of social changes can be made sufficiently clear to furnish any basis for practice)...

It is, however, of...importance to point out certain general reasons for doubting whether an apparent improvement will really have a beneficial effect on others. It is possible that the new rule, though it would be more felicific than the old one, if it could get itself equally established, may be not so likely to be adopted, or if adopted, not so likely to be obeyed, by the mass of the community in which it is proposed to innovate. It may be too subtle and refined, or too complex and elaborate; it may require a greater intellectual development, or a higher degree of self-control, than is to be found in an average member of the community, or an exceptional quality or balance of feelings. Nor can it be said in reply, that by the hypothesis the innovator's example must be good to whatever extent it operates, since *pro tanto* it tends to substitute a better rule for a worse. For experience seems to show that an example of this kind is more likely to be potent negatively than positively; that here, as elsewhere in human affairs, it is easier to pull down than to build up; easier to weaken or destroy the restraining force that a moral rule, habitually and generally obeyed, has over men's minds, than to substitute for it a new restraining habit, not similarly sustained by tradition and custom. Hence the effect of an example intrinsically good may be on the whole bad, because its destructive operation proves to be more vigorous than its constructive. And again, such destructive effect must be considered not only in respect of the particular rule violated, but of all other rules. For just as the breaking of any positive law has an inevitable tendency to encourage lawlessness generally, so

---

[1] *I do not mean that this sentiment is in my view incompatible with Utilitarianism; I mean that it must not attach itself to any subordinate rules of conduct, but only to the supreme principle of acting with impartial concern for all elements of general happiness.

[2] See Part X, extract 3.

the violation of any generally recognized moral rule seems to give a certain aid to the forces that are always tending towards moral anarchy in any society.

Nor must we neglect the reaction which any breach with customary morality will have on the agent's own mind. For the regulative habits and sentiments which each man has received by inheritance or training constitute an important force impelling his will, in the main, to conduct such as his reason would dictate; a natural auxiliary, as it were, to Reason in its conflict with seductive passions and appetites; and it may be practically dangerous to impair the strength of these auxiliaries. On the other hand, it would seem that the habit of acting rationally is the best of all habits, and that it ought to be the aim of a reasonable being to bring all his impulses and sentiments into more and more perfect harmony with Reason. And indeed when a man has earnestly accepted any moral principle, those of his pre-existing regulative habits and sentiments that are not in harmony with this principle tend naturally to decay and disappear; and it would perhaps be scarcely worthwhile to take them into account, except for the support that they derive from the sympathy of others.

But this last is a consideration of great importance. For the moral impulses of each individual commonly draw a large part of their effective force from the sympathy of other human beings. I do not merely mean that the pleasures and pains which each derives sympathetically from the moral likings and aversions of others are important as motives to felicific conduct no less than as elements of the individual's happiness; I mean further that the direct sympathetic echo in each man of the judgements and sentiments of others concerning conduct sustains his own similar judgements and sentiments. Through this twofold operation of sympathy it becomes practically much easier for most men to conform to a moral rule established in the society to which they belong than to one made by themselves. And any act by which a man weakens the effect on himself of this general moral sympathy tends *pro tanto* to make the performance of duty more difficult for him. On the other hand, we have to take into account – besides the intrinsic gain of the particular change – the general advantage of offering to mankind a striking example of consistent Utilitarianism; since, in this case as in others, a man gives a stronger proof of genuine conviction by conduct in opposition to public opinion than he can by conformity. In order, however, that this effect may be produced, it is almost necessary that the non-conformity should not promote the innovator's personal convenience; for in that case it will almost certainly be attributed to egoistic motives, however plausible the Utilitarian deduction of its rightness may seem.

The exact force of these various considerations will differ indefinitely in different cases; and it does not seem profitable to attempt any general estimate of them: but on the whole, it would seem that the general arguments which we have noticed constitute an important rational check upon such Utilitarian innovations on Common-Sense morality as are of the negative or destructive kind...

We have hitherto supposed that the innovator is endeavouring to introduce a new rule of conduct, not for himself only, but for others also, as more conducive to the general happiness than the rule recognized by Common Sense. It may perhaps be thought that this is not the issue most commonly raised between Utilitarianism and Common Sense: but rather whether exceptions should be allowed to rules which both sides accept as generally valid...

...We are supposed to see that general happiness will be enhanced (just as the excellence of a metrical composition is) by a slight admixture of irregularity along with a general observance of received rules; and hence to justify the irregular conduct of a few individuals, on the ground that the supply of regular conduct from other members of the community may reasonably be expected to be adequate.

It does not seem to me that this reasoning can be shown to be necessarily unsound, as applied to human society as at present constituted; but the cases in which it could really be thought to be applicable, by any one sincerely desirous of promoting the general happiness, must certainly be rare. For it should be observed that it makes a fundamental difference whether the sentiment in mankind generally, on which we rely to sustain sufficiently a general rule while admitting exceptions thereto, is moral or non-moral; because a moral sentiment is inseparable from the conviction that the conduct to which it prompts is objectively right – i.e. right whether or not it is thought or felt to be so – for oneself and all similar persons in similar circumstances; it cannot therefore coexist with approval of the contrary conduct in any one case, unless this case is distinguished by some material difference other than the mere non-existence in the agent of the ordinary moral sentiment against his conduct. Thus, assuming that general unveracity and general celibacy would both be evils of the worst kind, we may still all regard it as legitimate for men in general to remain celibate if they like, on account of the strength of the natural sentiments prompting to marriage, because the existence of these sentiments in ordinary human beings is not affected by the universal recognition of the legitimacy of celibacy: but we cannot similarly all regard it as legitimate for men to tell lies if they like, however strong the actually existing sentiment against lying may be, because as soon as this legitimacy is generally recognized the sentiment must be expected to decay and vanish. If therefore we were all enlightened Utilitarians, it would be impossible for any one to justify himself in making false statements while admitting it to be inexpedient for persons similarly conditioned to make them; as he would have no ground for believing that persons similarly conditioned would act differently from himself. The case, no doubt, is different in society as actually constituted; it is conceivable that the practically effective morality in such a society, resting on a basis independent of utilitarian or any other reasonings, may not be materially affected by the particular act or expressed opinion of a particular individual: but the circumstances are, I conceive, very rare, in which a really conscientious person could feel so sure of this as to conclude that by approving a particular violation of a rule, of which the *general* (though not *universal*) observance is plainly expedient, he will not probably do harm on the whole.

8   Against Conventional Morality: Friedrich Nietzsche, *Beyond Good and Evil**

The utilitarian principle of the greatest happiness of the greatest number, so earnestly discussed among the English moralists of the nineteenth century (see the two preceding extracts), was scornfully dismissed by the iconoclastic German philosopher Friedrich Nietzsche. In his *Beyond Good and Evil* (1886), Nietzsche dubs utilitarianism the morality of the herd. Setting out a 'genealogy of morals' (to use the title of one of his later books) he sees his task not in terms of the rational justification of moral systems, but rather of a historically informed critique of how various moral principles came into being. The principle of general happiness, and many other elements in traditional moral systems (for example the Christian injunction to love one's neighbour) are seen by Nietzsche as attempts by the weak masses to protect themselves against dynamic and powerful individuals – against the 'highest and strongest drives, when they break out passionately and drive the individual far above the average and the flats of the herd conscience'. Nietzsche is no less scathing of the Kantian approach to morality (see extract 5, above) – the 'morality of intentions'. In a striking anticipation of Freud,[1] Nietzsche proposes that 'the decisive value of an action lies precisely in what is unintentional in it, while everything about it that is intentional, that can been seen, known, conscious, still belongs to its surface and skin, which like every skin betrays

something but *conceals* even more'. The complexity of human existence, the darkness and power of the unconscious forces of the human psyche, is a recurring theme in Nietzsche's work. And partly because of this he derides the 'stiff seriousness, inspiring laughter', of those philosophers who have sought a rational foundation for morality (this could apply, in different ways, to both Kantians and Utilitarians alike). What, then, does Nietzsche propose in place of what he dismisses? The title 'Beyond Good and Evil' suggests a complete overcoming of conventional morality, and for Nietzsche this is essentially a task 'for the very few, a privilege for the strong'. These 'new philosophers', as they are called in the closing paragraph of our extract below, are 'spirits strong and original enough to revalue and invent eternal values'. Strength is necessary because tidily rational systems of morality will have to be discarded, and the darker, more dangerous, more passionate and mysterious aspects of human existence plumbed to the depths.[2] Perhaps because of the elusive character of the vision it offers, Nietzsche's approach to ethics has called forth very disparate reactions. Though some have seen his emphasis on the individual will to power as both sinister and arrogant, it is hard to deny the vividness and originality of his challenge to much of the Western tradition in moral philosophy.

 Every choice human being strives instinctively for a citadel and a secrecy where he is saved from the crowd, the many, the great majority – where he may forget 'men who are the rule', being their exception – excepting only the one case in which he is pushed straight to such men by a still stronger instinct, as a seeker after knowledge in the great and exceptional sense. Anyone who, in intercourse with men, does not occasionally glisten in all the colours of distress, green and grey with disgust, satiety, sympathy, gloominess and loneliness, is certainly not a man of elevated tastes; supposing, however, that he does not take all this burden and disgust upon himself voluntarily, that he persistently avoids it, and remains, as I said, quietly and proudly hidden in his

---

* Friedrich Nietzsche, *Beyond Good and Evil* [*Jenseits von Gut und Böse*, 1886], extracts from §§ 26, 29, 32, 33, 39, 186, 201, 203. Trans. W. Kaufmann (New York: Random House, 1966).
[1] See introduction to Part V, extract 4, above.
[2] Compare Nietzsche's views on the 'Dionysian' element in art: Part XI, extract 7, below.

citadel, one thing is certain: he was not made, he was not predestined, for knowledge. If he were, he would one day have to say to himself: 'The devil take my good taste! but the rule is more interesting than the exception – than myself, the exception!' And he would go *down* and above all, he would go 'inside'. The long and serious study of the *average* man, and consequently much disguise, self-overcoming, familiarity, and bad contact (all contact is bad except with one's equals) – this constitutes a necessary part of the life history of every philosopher, perhaps the most disagreeable, odious and disappointing part...

Independence is for the very few; it is a privilege of the strong. And whoever attempts it even with the best right but without inner constraint proves that he is probably not only strong, but also daring to the point of recklessness. He enters into a labyrinth, he multiplies a thousandfold the dangers which life brings with it in any case, not the least of which is that no one can see how and where he loses his way, becomes lonely, and is torn piecemeal by some minotaur of conscience. Supposing one like that comes to grief, this happens so far from the comprehension of men that they neither feel it nor sympathize. And he cannot go back any longer. Nor can he go back to the pity of men...

During the longest part of human history – so-called prehistorical times – the value or disvalue of an action was derived from its consequences. The action itself was considered as little as its origin. It was rather the way a distinction or disgrace still reaches back today from a child to its parents, in China: it was the retroactive force of success or failure that led men to think well or ill of an action. Let us call this period the *pre-moral* period of mankind: the imperative 'Know thyself!' was as yet unknown.

In the last ten thousand years, however, one has reached the point, step by step, in a few large regions on the earth, where it is no longer the consequences but the origin of an action that one allows to decide its value. On the whole this is a great event which involves a considerable refinement of vision and standards; it is the unconscious after-effect of the rule of aristocratic values and the faith in 'descent' – the sign of a period that one may call *moral* in the narrower sense. It involves the first attempt at self-knowledge. Instead of the consequences, the origin: indeed a reversal of perspective! Surely, a reversal achieved only after long struggles and vacillations. To be sure, a calamitous new superstition, an odd narrowness of interpretation, thus become dominant: the origin of an action was interpreted in the most definite sense as origin in an *intention*; one came to agree that the value of an action lay in the value of the intention. The intention as the whole origin and prehistory of an action – almost to the present day this prejudice dominated moral praise, blame, judgement, and philosophy on earth.

But today – shouldn't we have reached the necessity of once more resolving on a reversal and fundamental shift in values, owing to another self-examination of man, another growth in profundity? Don't we stand at the threshold of a period which should be designated negatively, to begin with, as *extra-moral*? After all, today at least we immoralists have the suspicion that the decisive value of an action lies precisely in what is *unintentional* in it, while everything about it that is intentional, everything about it that can be seen, known, 'conscious', still belongs to its surface and skin – which, like every skin, betrays something but *conceals* even more. In short, we believe that the intention is merely a sign and symptom that still requires interpretation – moreover, a sign that means too much and therefore, taken by itself alone, almost nothing. We believe that morality in the traditional sense, the morality of intentions, was a prejudice, precipitate and perhaps provisional – something on the order of astrology and alchemy – but in any case something that must be overcome. The overcoming of morality, in a certain sense even the self-overcoming of morality – let this be the name for that long secret work which has been saved up for the finest and most honest, also the most malicious, consciences of today, as living touchstones of the soul.

There is no other way: the feelings of devotion, self-sacrifice for one's neighbour, the whole morality of self-denial must be questioned mercilessly and taken to court – no less than the aesthetics of 'contemplation devoid of all interest' which is used today as a seductive guise for the emasculation of art, to give it a good conscience. There is too much charm and sugar in these feelings of 'for others', '*not* for myself', for us not to need to become doubly suspicious at this point and to ask: 'are these not perhaps – *seductions?*' That they *please* – those who have them and those who enjoy their fruits, and also the mere spectator – this does not yet constitute an argument in their *favour* but rather invites caution. So let us be cautious...

No one is very likely to consider a doctrine true merely because it makes people happy or virtuous – except perhaps the lovely 'idealists' who become effusive about the good, the true and the beautiful and allow all kinds of motley, clumsy, and benevolent desiderata to swim around in utter confusion in their pond. Happiness and virtue are no arguments. But people like to forget – even sober spirits – that making unhappy and evil are no counter-arguments. Something might be true while being harmful and dangerous in the highest degree. Indeed, it might be a basic characteristic of existence that those who would know it completely would perish, in which case the strength of a spirit should be measured according to how much of the 'truth' one could still barely endure – or to put it more clearly, to what degree one would *require* it to be thinned down, shrouded, sweetened, blunted, falsified.

But there is no doubt at all that the evil and unhappy are more favoured when it comes to the discovery of certain *parts* of truth, and that the probability of their success here is greater – not to speak of the evil who are happy, a species the moralists bury in silence. Perhaps hardness and cunning furnish more favourite conditions for the origin of the strong, independent spirit and philosopher than that gentle, fine, conciliatory good-naturedness and art of taking things lightly which people prize, and prize rightly, in a scholar. Assuming first of all that the concept 'philosopher' is not restricted to the philosopher who writes books – or makes books of *his* philosophy...

The moral sentiment in Europe today is as refined, old, diverse, irritable and subtle, as the 'science of morals' that accompanies it is still young, raw, clumsy and butterfingered – an attractive contrast that occasionally becomes visible and incarnate in the person of a moralist. Even the term 'science of morals' is much too arrogant considering what it designates, and offends *good* taste – which always prefers more modest terms.

One should own up in all strictness to what is still necessary here for a long time to come, to what alone is justified so far: to collect material, to conceptualize and arrange a vast realm of subtle feelings of value and differences of value which are alive, grow, beget and perish – and perhaps attempts to present vividly some of the more frequent and recurring forms of such living crystallizations – all to prepare a *typology* of morals.

To be sure, so far one has not been so modest. With a stiff seriousness that inspires laughter, all our philosophers demanded something far more exalted, presumptuous, and solemn from themselves as soon as they approached the study of morality: they wanted to supply a *rational foundation* for morality – and every philosopher so far has believed that he has provided such a foundation. Morality itself, however, was accepted as 'given'. How remote from their clumsy pride was that task which they considered insignificant and left in dust and must – the task of description – although the subtlest fingers and senses can scarcely be enough for it.

Just because our moral philosophers knew the facts of morality only very approximately in arbitrary extracts or in accidental epitomes – for example as the morality of their environment, their class, their church, the spirit of their time, their climate and part of the world – just because they were poorly informed and not even very curious about different peoples, times and past ages – they never laid eyes on the real problems of morality; for these emerge only when we compare *many* moralities. In all 'science of morals' so far one thing was *lacking*, strange as it may sound: the problem of morality itself; what was lacking was any suspicion that there was something problematic here. What the philosophers called 'a rational foundation for morality' and tried to supply was, seen in the right light, merely a scholarly variation of the common *faith* in the prevalent morality; a new means of *expression* for this faith; and thus just another fact within a particular morality; indeed, in the last analysis a kind of denial that this morality might ever be considered problematic – certainly the very opposite of an examination, analysis, questioning, and vivisection of this very faith . . .

As long as the utility reigning in moral value judgements is solely the utility of the herd, as long as one considers only the preservation of the community, and immorality is sought exactly and exclusively in what seems dangerous to the survival of the community – there can be no morality of 'neighbour-love'. Supposing that even then there was a constant little exercise of consideration, pity, fairness, mildness, reciprocity of assistance; supposing that even in that state of society all those drives are active that later receive the honorary designation of 'virtues' and eventually almost coincide with the concept of 'morality' – in that period they do not yet at all belong in the realm of moral valuations; they are still *extra-moral*. An act of pity, for example, was not considered either good or bad, moral or immoral, in the best period of the Romans; and even when it was praised, such praise was perfectly compatible with a kind of disgruntled disdain as soon as it was juxtaposed with an action that served the welfare of the whole, of the *res publica* [commonwealth].

In the last analysis, 'love of the neighbour' is always something secondary, partly conventional and arbitrary-illusory in relation to *fear of the neighbour*. After the structure of society is fixed on the whole and seems secure against external dangers, it is this fear of the neighbour that again creates new perspectives of moral valuation. Certain strong and dangerous drives, like an enterprising spirit, foolhardiness, vengefulness, craftiness, rapacity, and the lust to rule, which had so far not merely been honoured in so far as they were socially useful – under different names, to be sure, from those chosen here – but had to be trained and cultivated to make them great (because one constantly needed them in view of the dangers to the whole community, against the enemies of the community), are now experienced as doubly dangerous, since the channels to divert them are lacking, and, step upon step, they are branded as immoral and abandoned to slander.

Now the opposite drives and inclinations receive moral honours; step upon step, the herd instinct draws its conclusions. How much or how little is dangerous to the community, dangerous to equality, in an opinion, in a state or affect, in a will, in a talent – that now constitutes the moral perspective: here, too, fear is again the mother of morals.

The highest and strongest drives, when they break out passionately and drive the individual far above the average and the flats of the herd conscience, wreck the self-confidence of the community, its faith in itself, and it is as if its spine snapped. Hence just these drives are branded and slandered most. High and independent spirituality, the will to stand alone, even a powerful reason are experienced as dangers. Everything that elevates an individual above the herd and intimidates the neighbour is henceforth called *evil*; and the fair, modest, submissive, conforming mentality, the *mediocrity* of desires attains moral designations and honours. Eventually, under very peaceful conditions, the opportunity and necessity for educating one's feelings to severity and hardness is lacking more and more; and even severity, even injustice, begins to disturb the conscience; any high and hard nobility and self-reliance is almost felt to be an insult and arouses mistrust; the 'lamb', even more than the 'sheep', gains in respect.

There is a point in the history of a society when it becomes so pathologically soft and tender that among other things it sides even with those who harm it, criminals, and does this quite seriously and honestly. Punishing somehow seems unfair to it, and it is certain that imagining 'punishment' and 'being supposed to punish' hurts it, arouses fear in it. 'Is it not enough to render him *undangerous*? Why still punish? Punishing itself is terrible.' With this question, herd morality, the morality of timidity, draws its ultimate consequence. Supposing that one could altogether abolish danger, the reason for fear, this morality would thereby be abolished too: it would no longer be needed, it would no longer *consider itself* necessary.

Whoever examines the conscience of the European today will have to pull the same imperative out of a thousand moral folds and hideouts – the imperative of herd timidity: 'we want that some day there should be *nothing any more to be afraid of!*' Some day – throughout Europe, the will and way to this day is now called 'progress'...

We have a different faith; to us the democratic movement is not only a form of the decay of political organization but a form of the decay, namely the diminution, of man, making him mediocre and lowering his value. Where, then, must *we* reach with our hopes?

Toward *new philosophers*; there is no choice; toward spirits strong and original enough to provide the stimuli for opposite valuations and to revalue and invert 'eternal values'; toward forerunners, toward men of the future who in the present tie the knot and constraint that forces the will of millennia upon *new* tracks. To teach man the future of man as his *will*, as dependent on a human will, and to prepare great ventures and over-all attempts of discipline and cultivation by way of putting an end to that gruesome dominion of nonsense and accident that has so far been called 'history' – the nonsense of the 'greatest number' is merely its ultimate form: at some time new types of philosophers and commanders will be necessary for that, and whatever has existed on earth of concealed, terrible and benevolent spirits, will look pale and dwarfed by comparison. It is the image of such leaders that we envisage: may I say this out loud, you free spirits? The conditions that one would have partly to create and partly to exploit for their genesis; the probable ways and tests that would enable a soul to grow to such a height and force that it would feel the *compulsion* for such tasks; a revaluation of values under whose new pressure and hammer a conscience would be steeled, a heart turned to bronze, in order to endure the weight of such responsibility; on the other hand, the necessity of such leaders, the frightening danger that they might fail to appear or that they might turn out badly or degenerate – these are *our* real worries and gloom – do you know that, you free spirits? – these are the heavy distant thoughts and storms that pass over the sky of *our* life.

9   Duty and Intuition: W. D. Ross, *The Right and the Good**

A theory of morality interestingly different from those so far discussed was proposed in the 1930s by the English philosopher W. D. Ross, generally classified as a 'moral intuitionist'. In the following extract, Ross begins by asking 'whether there is any general character that makes acts right'. It is clear that utilitarianism (see extracts 6 and 7, above) presupposes an affirmative answer to this question: an act is right in virtue of its conducing (directly or indirectly) to pleasure or happiness. Ross notes that there are alternative consequentialist theories which allow other goods besides pleasure (for example freedom, or knowledge); but all agree in taking the test for rightness to be that the action in question produces the greatest overall amount of good. Ross now argues, against the consequentialists, that in a simple case like my obligation to keep a promise, what makes the promise-keeping action right is simply that it is my duty. This, and not the production of beneficial consequences, is the only feature that most of us reflect on when we feel obliged to keep our word. We have certain basic convictions, or intuitions of conscience, about how we ought to behave in this type of case, and Ross (as he observes in a footnote to our

extract below) assumes the correctness of many such 'moral convictions of the plain man'.

Ross's stress on duty may seem reminiscent of the views of Kant (see extract 5 above), and his approach is certainly 'deontological' rather than consequentialist (see introduction to extract 6). But Ross goes on to make it clear that he rejects the Kantian idea of categorical duties which allow of no exception. Instead he introduces the concept of *prima facie* duty, to refer to the obligatoriness which belongs to an act in virtue of its being of a certain type (e.g. an instance of promise-keeping); the term *prima facie* alerts us to the fact that the duty is only conditional, and may be outweighed by other duties which are in the circumstances more important. Ross lists six categories of *prima facie* duty – those of fidelity and of reparation, those of gratitude, those of justice, those of beneficence, those of self-improvement and those of non-maleficence (refraining from harm). He is quite prepared to concede that this is an unsystematic and possibly incomplete list, but insists it corresponds to the way we in fact think when we are considering what we ought to do, and is thus vastly superior to the appeal of a 'hastily reached simplicity'. One may object that,

---

* W. D. Ross, *The Right and the Good* (Oxford: Clarendon, 1930), ch. 2 ('What Makes Right Acts Right?'), pp. 16–24; with omissions.

since *prima facie* duties may clash, there must be some overarching principle to determine what is the correct action in cases of conflict; but Ross points out that unless the consequentialists try (implausibly) to reduce everything of value to a single good (such as pleasure), they will soon have to confront similar priority conflicts. Those who require moral theory to have a systematic architecture will find Ross's pluralistic intuitionism unappealing; but its merit is that it seems to match the way we often think and act in the moral arena, where the demands of various duties ('I promised'; 'I can't let him down'; 'I must help those in distress') often seem to defy neat reduction to a unifying schema of explanation.

 The real point at issue between hedonism and utilitarianism on the one hand and their opponents on the other is . . . whether there is any general character which makes acts right, and if so, what it is. Among the main historical attempts to state a single characteristic of all right actions which is the foundation of their rightness are those made by egoism and utilitarianism. But I do not propose to discuss these . . . because there has come to be so much agreement among moral philosophers that neither of these theories is satisfactory. A much more attractive theory has been put forward by Professor Moore: that what makes actions right is that they are productive of more *good* than could have been produced by any other action open to the agent.[1]

This theory is in fact the culmination of all the attempts to base rightness on productivity of some sort of result. The first form this attempt takes is the attempt to base rightness on conduciveness to the advantage or pleasure of the agent. This theory comes to grief over the fact, which stares us in the face, that a great part of duty consists in an observance of the rights and a furtherance of the interests of others, whatever the cost to ourselves may be. Plato and others may be right in holding that a regard for the rights of others never in the long run involves a loss of happiness of the agent, that 'the just life profits a man'. But this, even if true, is irrelevant to the rightness of the act. As soon as a man does an action *because* he thinks he will promote his own interests thereby, he is acting not from a sense of its rightness but from self-interest.

To the egoistic theory hedonistic utilitarianism[2] supplies a much-needed amendment. It points out correctly that the fact that a certain pleasure will be enjoyed by the agent is no reason why he *ought* to bring it into being rather than an equal or greater pleasure to be enjoyed by another, though, human nature being what it is, it makes it not unlikely that he *will* try to bring it into being. But hedonistic utilitarianism in its turn needs a correction. On reflection it seems clear that pleasure is not the only thing in life that we think good in itself, that for instance we think the possession of a good character, or an intelligent understanding of the world, as good or better. A great advance is made by the substitution of 'productive of the greatest good' for 'productive of the greatest pleasure'.

Not only is this theory more attractive than hedonistic utilitarianism, but its logical relation to that theory is such that the latter could not be true unless *it* were true, while it might be true though hedonistic utilitarianism were not. It is in fact one of the logical bases of hedonistic utilitarianism. For the view that what produces the maximum pleasure is right has for its bases the views (1) that what produces the

---

[1] See G. E. Moore, *Ethics* [1912] (Oxford: Oxford University Press, 1958).
[2] A theory like that of J. S. Mill; see above, extract 6.

maximum good is right, and (2) that pleasure is the only thing good in itself. If they were not assuming that what produces the maximum good is right, the utilitarians' attempt to show that pleasure is the only thing good in itself, which is in fact the point they take most pains to establish, would have been quite irrelevant to their attempt to prove that only what produces the maximum *pleasure* is right. If, therefore, it can be shown that productivity of the maximum good is not what makes all right actions right, we shall *a fortiori* have refuted hedonistic utilitarianism.

When a plain man fulfils a promise because he thinks he ought to do so, it seems clear that he does so with no thought of its total consequences, still less with any opinion that these are likely to be the best possible. He thinks in fact much more of the past than of the future. What makes him think it right to act in a certain way is the fact that he has promised to do so – that and, usually, nothing more. That his act will produce the best possible consequences is not his reason for calling it right. What lends colour to the theory we are examining, then, is not the actions (which form probably a great majority of our actions) in which some such reflection as 'I have promised' is the only reason we give ourselves for thinking a certain action right, but the exceptional cases in which the consequences of fulfilling a promise (for instance) would be so disastrous to others that we judge it right not to do so. It must of course be admitted that such cases exist. If I have promised to meet a friend at a particular time for some trivial purpose, I should certainly think myself justified in breaking my engagement if by doing so I could prevent a serious accident or bring relief to the victims of one. And the supporters of the view we are examining hold that my thinking so is due to my thinking that I shall bring more good into existence by the one action than by the other. A different account may, however, be given of the matter, an account which will, I believe, show itself to be the true one. It may be said that besides the duty of fulfilling promises I have and recognize a duty of relieving distress, and that when I think it right to do the latter at the cost of not doing the former, it is not because I think I shall produce more good thereby but because I think it the duty which is in the circumstances more of a duty. This account surely corresponds much more closely with what we really think in such a situation. If, so far as I can see, I could bring equal amounts of good into being by fulfilling my promise and by helping someone to whom I had made no promise, I should not hesitate to regard the former as my duty. Yet on the view that what is right is right because it is productive of the most good I should not so regard it.

There are two theories, each in its way simple, that offer a solution of such cases of conscience. One is the view of Kant, that there are certain duties of perfect obligation, such as those of fulfilling promises, of paying debts, of telling the truth, which admit of no exception whatever in favour of duties of imperfect obligation, such as that of relieving distress. The other is the view of, for instance, Professor Moore...that there is only the duty of producing good, and that all 'conflicts of duties' should be resolved by asking 'by which action will most good be produced?' But it is more important that our theory fit the facts than that it be simple, and the account we have given above corresponds (it seems to me) better than either of the simpler theories with what we really think, viz. that normally promise-keeping, for example, should come before benevolence, but that when and only when the good to be produced by the benevolent act is very great and the promise comparatively trivial, the act of benevolence becomes our duty.

In fact the theory of 'ideal utilitarianism', if I may for brevity refer so to the theory of Professor Moore, seems to simplify unduly our relations to our fellows. It says, in effect, that the only morally significant relation in which my neighbours stand to me is that of being possible beneficiaries by my action. They do stand in this relation to me, and this relation is morally significant. But they may also stand to me in the relation of promisee to promiser, of creditor to debtor, of wife to husband, of child to parent, of friend to friend, of fellow countryman to fellow countryman, and the like; and each of these relations is the foundation of a *prima facie* duty, which is more or less incumbent on me according to the circumstances of the case. When I am in a situation, as perhaps I always am, in which more than one of these *prima facie* duties is incumbent on me, what I have to do is to study the situation as fully as I can until I form the considered opinion (it is never more) that in the circumstances one of them is more incumbent than any other; then I am bound to think that to do this *prima facie* duty is my duty *sans phrase* in the situation.

I suggest '*prima facie* duty' or 'conditional duty' as a brief way of referring to the characteristic (quite distinct from that of being a duty proper) which an act has, in virtue of being of a certain kind (e.g. the keeping of a promise), of being an act which would be a duty proper if it were not at the same time of another kind which is morally significant. Whether an act is a duty proper or actual duty depends on *all* the morally significant kinds it is an instance of. The phrase '*prima facie* duty' must be apologized for, since (1) it suggests that what we are speaking of is a certain kind of duty, whereas it is in fact not a duty, but something related in a special way to duty. Strictly speaking, we want not a phrase in which duty is qualified by an adjective, but a separate noun. (2) '*Prima*' facie suggests that one is speaking only of an appearance which a moral situation presents at first sight, and which may turn out to be illusory; whereas what I am speaking of is an objective fact involved in the nature of the situation, or more strictly in an element of its nature, though not, as duty proper does, arising from its *whole* nature. I can, however, think of no term which fully meets the case...

There is nothing arbitrary about these *prima facie* duties. Each rests on a definite circumstance which cannot seriously be held to be without moral significance. Of *prima facie* duties I suggest, without claiming completeness or finality for it, the following division.[1]

(1) Some duties rest on previous acts of my own. These duties seem to include two kinds: (*a*) Those resting on a promise or what may fairly be called an implicit promise, such as the implicit undertaking not to tell lies which seems to be implied in the act of entering into conversation (at any rate by civilized men), or of writing

---

[1] *I should make it plain at this stage that I am *assuming* the correctness of some of our main convictions as to *prima facie* duties, or, more strictly, am claiming that we *know* them to be true. To me it seems as self-evident as anything could be, that to make a promise, for instance, is to create a moral claim on us in someone else. Many readers will perhaps say that they do not know this to be true. If so, I certainly cannot prove it to them; I can only ask them to reflect again, in the hope that they will ultimately agree that they also know it to be true. The main moral convictions of the plain man seem to me to be, not opinions which it is for philosophy to prove or disprove, but knowledge from the start; and in my own case I seem to find little difficulty in distinguishing these essential convictions from other moral convictions which I also have, which are merely fallible opinions based on an imperfect study of the working for good or evil of certain institutions or types of action.

books that purport to be history and not fiction. These may be called the duties of fidelity. (*b*) Those resting on a previous wrongful act. These may be called the duties of reparation. (2) Some rest on previous acts of other men, i.e. services done by them to me. These may be loosely described as the duties of gratitude. (3) Some rest on the fact or possibility of a distribution of pleasure or happiness (or of the means thereto) which is not in accordance with the merit of the persons concerned; in such cases there arises a duty to upset or prevent such a distribution. These are the duties of justice. (4) Some rest on the mere fact that there are other beings in the world whose condition we can make better in respect of virtue, or of intelligence, or of pleasure. These are the duties of beneficence. (5) Some rest on the fact that we can improve our own condition in respect of virtue or of intelligence. These are the duties of self-improvement. (6) I think that we should distinguish from (4) the duties that may be summed up under the title of 'not injuring others'. No doubt to injure others is incidentally to fail to do them good; but it seems to me clear that non-maleficence is apprehended as a duty distinct from that of beneficence, and as a duty of a more stringent character. It will be noticed that this alone among the types of duty has been stated in a negative way. An attempt might no doubt be made to state this duty, like the others, in a positive way. It might be said that it is really the duty to prevent ourselves from acting either from an inclination to harm others or from an inclination to seek our own pleasure, in doing which we should incidentally harm them. But on reflection it seems clear that the primary duty here is the duty not to harm others, this being a duty whether or not we have an inclination that if followed would lead to our harming them; and that when we have such an inclination the primary duty not to harm others gives rise to a consequential duty to resist the inclination. The recognition of this duty of non-maleficence is the first step on the way to the recognition of the duty of beneficence; and that accounts for the prominence of the commands 'thou shalt not kill', 'thou shalt not commit adultery', 'thou shalt not steal', 'thou shalt not bear false witness', in so early a code as the Decalogue. But even when we have come to recognize the duty of beneficence, it appears to me that the duty of non-maleficence is recognized as a distinct one, and as *prima facie* more binding. We should not in general consider it justifiable to kill one person in order to keep another alive, or to steal from one in order to give alms to another.

The essential defect of the 'ideal utilitarian' theory is that it ignores, or at least does not do full justice to, the highly personal character of duty. If the only duty is to produce the maximum of good, the question who is to have the good – whether it is myself, or my benefactor, or a person to whom I have made a promise to confer that good on him, or a mere fellow man to whom I stand in no such special relation – should make no difference to my having a duty to produce that good. But we are all in fact sure that it makes a vast difference.

... If the objection be made, that this catalogue of the main types of duty is an unsystematic one resting on no logical principle, it may be replied, first, that it makes no claim to being ultimate. It is a *prima facie* classification of the duties which reflection on our moral convictions seems actually to reveal. And if these convictions are, as I would claim that they are, of the nature of knowledge, and if I have not misstated them, the list will be a list of authentic conditional duties, correct as far as it goes though not necessarily complete. The list of *goods* put forward by the rival theory is reached by exactly the same method – the only sound one in the circumstances – viz. that of direct reflection on what we really think. Loyalty to the facts is worth more than a symmetrical architectonic or a hastily reached simplicity. If further reflection discovers a perfect logical basis for this or for a better classification, so much the better.

It may, again, be objected that our theory that there are these various and often conflicting types of *prima facie* duty leaves us with no principle upon which to discern what is our actual duty in particular circumstances. But this objection is not one which the rival theory is in a position to bring forward. For when we have to choose between the production of two heterogeneous goods, say knowledge and pleasure, the 'ideal utilitarian' theory can only fall back on an opinion, for which no logical basis can be offered, that one of the goods is the greater; and this is no better than a similar opinion that one of two duties is the more urgent. And again, when we consider the infinite variety of the effects of our actions in the way of pleasure, it must surely be admitted that the claim which *hedonism* sometimes makes, that it offers a readily applicable criterion of right conduct, is quite illusory.

I am unwilling, however, to content myself with an *argumentum ad hominem*,[1] and I would contend that in principle there is no reason to anticipate that every act that is our duty is so for one and the same reason. Why should two sets of circumstances, or one set of circumstances, *not* possess different characteristics, any one of which makes a certain act our *prima facie* duty? When I ask what it is that makes me in certain cases sure that I have a *prima facie* duty to do so and so, I find that it lies in the fact that I have made a promise; when I ask the same question in another case, I find the answer lies in the fact that I have done a wrong. And if on reflection I find (as I think I do) that neither of these reasons is reducible to the others, I must not on any *a priori* ground assume that such a reduction is possible ...

10   Rational Choice and Fairness: John Rawls, *A Theory of Justice**

Our next selection brings us down to the more recent past with an extract from the magnum opus of the influential Harvard philosopher John Rawls. Rawls's theory of justice has something in common with the Kantian approach to ethics (see extract 5, above), since it lays stress on asking what moral maxims could be rationally *chosen* or *willed* to operate in society. It also makes use of the idea of a hypothetical contract, familiar from traditional political theory (see below, Part X, extracts 3 and 4). The central idea of 'justice as fairness', as Rawls calls his theory, is that we are to imagine having to decide what principles we would choose to see adopted in society, from a hypothetical 'original position' in which each of us is ignorant of certain crucial facts about our personal characteristics and our actual situation in society. Requiring the choice of principles to be made behind this 'veil of ignorance' is a way of ensuring that we make our decisions in an impartial and fair way. For example, if I already know I am a white male, I might favour arrangements which favour whites over blacks, or men over women; but from

---

[1] An argument based merely on defects in the opponent's position.
* J. Rawls, *A Theory of Justice* (Oxford: Oxford University Press, 1972), ch. 1, sections 3 and 4; with omissions.

behind the 'veil of ignorance' I will tend to avoid such unjust systems, since I might myself turn out to be a member of the disadvantaged group.

The problem of what *is* the rational choice under conditions of uncertainty is one that has much exercised both Rawls and his critics. Some have suggested that in Rawls's original position it would be rational to vote for whatever system produces the greatest good for all – in which case the theory turns out to generate yet another version of utilitarianism (see extracts 6 and 7, above). But Rawls argues that it would be most rational for the parties to select two principles of justice: first, that there be maximum equality in the assignment of basic liberties and duties; and second, that economic inequalities be permitted only if on balance they benefit the least advantaged members of society. The second principle would no doubt require some sacrifices on the part of the better off or more fortunate; but for the supporters of Rawls it is a crucial part of the appeal of his theory that it requires us to choose the principles of justice so as to counterbalance (at least in part) those accidents of natural endowment (intelligence, gender, race, etc.) that are, as Rawls puts it, 'arbitrary from the moral point of view'.

In the final part of our extract, important questions of methodology are addressed. Rawls does not claim to arrive at his conception of the original position out of nowhere: it is partly designed to generate results that accord with our pre-reflective intuitions about morality and justice. As Rawls envisages it, however, developing a moral theory may require us on the one hand to discard some of our intuitions, where these cannot be fitted into the constraints of the theory, and on the other hand to modify the theory when it conflicts with too many of our central intuitions. Such a process of mutual adjustment continues until we reach the state of 'reflective equilibrium' – the (adjusted) theory is in balance with our (corrected) intuitions. Irrespective of the merits or otherwise of Rawls's account of justice, the notion of reflective equilibrium has stimulated considerable debate about the nature of moral theory: is it in the end just a descriptive endeavour, aimed merely at systematizing our existing intuitions, or can it aspire to lay down prescriptive rules about how human society should be regulated? The Rawlsian idea of pure rational choice under conditions of uncertainty also raises important questions about the extent to which moral theorizing can operate in abstraction from the particularities of our history and culture – a question that will be taken up in extract 11, below.

The main idea of the theory of justice

My aim is to present a conception of justice which generalizes and carries to a higher level of abstraction the familiar theory of the social contract as found, say, in Locke, Rousseau and Kant. In order to do this we are not to think of the original contract as one to enter a particular society or to set up a particular form of government. Rather, the guiding idea is that the principles of justice for the basic structure of society are the object of the original agreement. They are the principles that free and rational persons concerned to further their own interests would accept in an initial position of equality as defining the fundamental terms of their association. These principles are to regulate all further agreements; they specify the kinds of social cooperation that can be entered into and the forms of government that can be established. This way of regarding the principles of justice I shall call justice as fairness.

Thus we are to imagine that those who engage in social cooperation choose together, in one joint act, the principles which are to assign basic right and duties and to determine the division of social benefits. Men are to decide in advance how they are to regulate their claims against one another and what is to be the foundation charter of their society. Just as each person must decide by rational reflection what constitutes his good, that is, the system of ends which it is rational for him to pursue, so a group of persons must decide once and for all what is to count among them as just and unjust. The choice which rational men would make in this hypothetical situation of equal liberty, assuming for the present that this choice problem has a solution, determines the principles of justice.

In justice as fairness the original position of equality corresponds to the state of nature in the traditional theory of the social contract. This original position is not, of course, thought of as an actual historical state of affairs, much less as a primitive condition of culture. It is understood as a purely hypothetical situation characterized so as to lead to a certain conception of justice. Among the essential features of this situation is that no one knows his place in society, his class position or social status, nor does any one know his fortune in the distribution of natural assets and abilities, his intelligence, strength and the like. I shall even assume that the parties do not know their conceptions of the good or their special psychological propensities. The principles of justice are chosen behind a veil of ignorance. This ensures that no one is advantaged or disadvantaged in the choice of principles by the outcome of natural chance or the contingency of social circumstances. Since all are similarly situated and no one is able to design principles to favour his particular condition, the principles of justice are the result of a fair agreement or bargain. For given the circumstances of the original position, the symmetry of everyone's relations to each other, this initial situation is fair between individuals as moral persons, that is, as rational beings with their own ends and capable, I shall assume, of a sense of justice. The original position is, one might say, the appropriate initial status quo, and thus the fundamental agreements reached in it are fair. This explains the propriety of the name 'justice as fairness' – it conveys the idea that the principles of justice are agreed to in an initial situation that is fair. The name does not mean that the concepts of justice and fairness are the same, any more than the phrase 'poetry as metaphor' means that the concepts of poetry and metaphor are the same.

Justice as fairness begins, as I have said, with one of the most general of all choices which persons might make together, namely, with the choice of the first principles of a conception of justice which is to regulate all subsequent criticism and reform of institutions. Then, having chosen a conception of justice, we can suppose that they are to choose a constitution and a legislature to enact laws, and so on, all in accordance with the principles of justice initially agreed upon. Our social situation is just if it is such that by this sequence of hypothetical agreements we would have contracted into the general system of rules which defines it. Moreover, assuming that the original position does determine a set of principles (that is, that a particular conception of justice would be chosen), it will then be true that whenever social institutions satisfy these principles those engaged in them can say to one another that they are cooperating on terms to which they would agree if they were free and equal persons whose relations with respect to one another were fair. They could all view their arrangements as meeting the stipulations which they would acknowledge in an initial situation that embodies widely accepted and reasonable constraints on the choice of principles. The general recognition of this fact would provide the basis for a public acceptance of the corresponding principles of justice. No society can, of course, be a scheme of cooperation which men enter voluntarily in a literal sense; each person finds himself placed at birth in some particular position in some particular society, and the nature of this position materially affects his life prospects. Yet a society satisfying the principles of justice as fairness comes as close as a society can to being a voluntary scheme, for it meets the principles which free and equal persons would assent to under circumstances that are fair. In this sense its members are autonomous and the obligations they recognize self-imposed.

One feature of justice as fairness is to think of the parties in the initial situation as rational and mutually disinterested. This does not mean that the parties are egoists, that is, individuals with only certain kinds of interests, say in wealth, prestige and domination. But they are conceived as not taking an interest in one another's interests. They are to presume that even their spiritual aims may be opposed in the way that the aims of those of different religions may be opposed. Moreover, the concept of rationality must be interpreted as far as possible in the narrow sense, standard in economic theory, of taking the most effective means to given ends...

In working out the conception of justice as fairness one main task clearly is to determine which principles of justice would be chosen in the original position. To do this we must describe this situation in some detail and formulate with care the problem of choice which it presents...It may be observed, however, that once the principles of justice are thought of as arising from an original agreement in a situation of equality, it is an open question whether the principle of utility would be acknow-ledged. Offhand it hardly seems likely that persons who view themselves as equals, entitled to press their claims upon one another, would agree to a principle which may require lesser life prospects for some simply for the sake of a greater sum of advantages enjoyed by others. Since each desires to protect his interests, his capacity to advance his conception of the good, no one has a reason to acquiesce in an enduring loss for himself in order to bring about a greater net balance of satisfaction. In the absence of strong and lasting benevolent impulses, a rational man would not accept a basic structure merely because it maximized the algebraic sum of advantages irrespective of its permanent effects on his own basic rights and interests. Thus it seems that the principle of utility is incompatible with the conception of social cooperation among equals for mutual advantage. It appears to be inconsistent with the idea of reciprocity implicit in the notion of a well-ordered society. Or, at any rate, so I shall argue.

I shall maintain instead that the persons in the initial situation would choose two rather different principles: the first requires equality in the assignment of basic rights and duties, while the second holds that social and economic inequalities, for example inequalities of wealth and authority, are just only if they result in compensating benefits for everyone, and in particular for the least advantaged members of society. These principles rule out justifying institutions on the grounds that the hardships of some are offset by a greater good in the aggregate. It may be expedient but it is not just that some should have less in order that others may prosper. But there is no injustice in the greater benefits earned by a few provided that the situation of persons not so fortunate is thereby improved. The intuitive idea is that since everyone's well-being depends upon a scheme of cooperation without which no one could have a satisfac-tory life, the division of advantages should be such as to draw forth the willing cooperation of everyone taking part in it, including those less well situated. Yet this can be expected only if reasonable terms are proposed. The two principles mentioned seem to be a fair agreement on the basis of which those better endowed, or more fortunate in their social position, neither of which we can be said to deserve, could expect the willing cooperation of others when some workable scheme is a necessary condition of the welfare of all. Once we decide to look for a conception of justice that nullifies the accidents of natural endowment and the contingencies of social circumstance as counters in quest for political and economic advantage, we are led to these principles. They express the result of leaving aside those aspects of the social world that seem arbitrary from a moral point of view...

The original position and justification

I have said that the original position is the appropriate initial status quo which insures that the fundamental agreements reached in it are fair. This fact yields the name 'justice as fairness'. It is clear, then, that I want to say that one conception of justice is more reasonable than another, or justifiable with respect to it, if rational persons in the initial situation would choose its principles over those of the other for the role of justice. Conceptions of justice are to be ranked by their acceptability to persons so circumstanced. Understood in this way the question of justification is settled by working out a problem of deliberation: we have to ascertain which principles it would be rational to adopt given the contractual situation. This connects the theory of justice with the theory of rational choice.

If this view of the problem of justification is to succeed, we must, of course, describe in some detail the nature of this choice problem. A problem of rational decision has a definite answer only if we know the beliefs and interests of the parties, their relations with respect to one another, the alternatives between which they are to choose, the procedure whereby they make up their minds, and so on. As the circumstances are presented in different ways, correspondingly different principles are accepted. The concept of the original position, as I shall refer to it, is that of the most philosophically favoured interpretation of this initial choice situation for the purposes of a theory of justice.

But how are we to decide what is the most favoured interpretation? I assume, for one thing, that there is a broad measure of agreement that principles of justice should be chosen under certain conditions. To justify a particular description of the initial situation one shows that it incorporates these commonly shared presumptions. One argues from widely accepted but weak premises to more specific conclusions. Each of the presumptions should by itself be natural and plausible; some of them may seem innocuous or even trivial. The aim of the contract approach is to establish that taken together they impose significant bounds on acceptable principles of justice. The ideal outcome would be that these conditions determine a unique set of principles; but I shall be satisfied if they suffice to rank the main traditional conceptions of social justice.

One should not be misled, then, by the somewhat unusual conditions which characterize the original position. The idea here is simply to make vivid to ourselves the restrictions that it seems reasonable to impose on arguments for principles of justice, and therefore on these principles themselves. Thus it seems reasonable and generally acceptable that no one should be advantaged or disadvantaged by natural fortune or social circumstances in the choice of principles. It also seems widely agreed that it should be impossible to tailor principles to the circumstances of one's own case. We should insure further that particular inclinations and aspirations, and persons' conceptions of their good, do not affect the principles adopted. The aim is to rule out those principles that it would be rational to propose for acceptance, however little the chance of success, only if one knew certain things that are irrelevant from the standpoint of justice. For example, if a man knew that he was wealthy, he might find it rational to advance the principle that various taxes for welfare measures be counted unjust; if he knew that he was poor, he would most likely propose the contrary principle. To represent the desired restrictions one imagines a situation in which everyone is deprived of this sort of information. One excludes the knowledge of those contingencies which sets men at odds and allows them to be guided by their prejudices. In this manner the veil of ignorance is arrived at in a natural way. This concept should cause no difficulty if we keep in mind the constraints on arguments that it is meant to express. At any time we can enter the original position, so to speak, simply by following a certain procedure, namely, by arguing for principles of justice in accordance with these restrictions.

It seems reasonable to suppose that the parties in the original position are equal. That is, all have the same rights in the procedure for choosing principles; each can make proposals, submit reasons for their acceptance, and so on. Obviously the purpose of these conditions is to represent equality between human beings as moral persons, as creatures having a conception of their good and capable of a sense of justice. The basis of equality is taken to be similarity in these two respects. Systems of ends are not ranked in value; and each man is presumed to have the requisite ability to understand and to act upon whatever principles are adopted. Together with the veil of ignorance, these conditions define the principles of justice as those which rational persons concerned to advance their interests would consent to as equals when none are known to be advantaged or disadvantaged by social and natural contingencies.

There is, however, another side to justifying a particular description of the original position. This is to see if the principles which would be chosen match our considered convictions of justice or extend them in an acceptable way. We can note whether applying these principles would lead us to make the same judgements about the basic structure of society which we now make intuitively and in which we have the greatest confidence; or whether, in cases where our present judgements are in doubt and given with hesitation, these principles offer a resolution which we can affirm on reflection. There are questions which we feel sure must be answered in a certain way. For example, we are confident that religious intolerance and racial discrimination are unjust. We think that we have examined these things with care and have reached what we believe is an impartial judgement not likely to be distorted by an excessive attention to our own interests. These convictions are provisional fixed points which we presume any conception of justice must fit. But we have much less assurance as to what is the correct distribution of wealth and authority. Here we may be looking for a way to remove our doubts. We can check an interpretation of the initial situation, then, by the capacity of its principles to accommodate our firmest convictions and to provide guidance where guidance is needed.

In searching for the most favoured description of this situation we work from both ends. We begin by describing it so that it presents generally shared and preferably weak conditions. We then see if these conditions are strong enough to yield a significant set of principles. If not, we look for further premises equally reasonable. But if so, and these principles match our considered convictions of justice, then so far well and good. But presumably there will be discrepancies. In this case we have a choice. We can either modify the account of the initial situation or we can revise our existing judgements, for even the judgements we originally take as fixed are liable to revision. By going back and forth, sometimes altering the conditions of the contractual circumstances, at others withdrawing our judgements and conforming them to principle, I assume that eventually we shall find a description of the initial situation that both expresses reasonable conditions and yields principles. This state of affairs I refer to as reflective equilibrium. It is an equilibrium because at last our principles and judgements coincide; and it is reflective since we know to what principles our judgements conform and the premises of their derivation. At the moment everything is in order. But this equilibrium is not necessarily stable. It is liable to be upset by further examination of the conditions which should be imposed on the contractual situation and by particular cases which may lead us to revise our judgements. Yet for the time being we have done what we can to render coherent and to justify our convictions of social justice. We have reached a conception of the original position...

11 Ethics as Rooted in History and Culture: Alasdair MacIntyre, *After Virtue**

In the preceding extract, we found John Rawls constructing his theory of justice on a fairly 'thin' or minimal base of rational choice behind a veil of ignorance, abstracting from all the particularities of history and culture. Our next author, Alasdair MacIntyre, approaches moral theory from an almost diametrically opposed standpoint. MacIntyre would see Rawls, and indeed most contemporary moral theorists, as following a flawed model which he calls the 'Enlightenment project' – the mistaken attempt to provide an abstract justification for morality, wholly independent of social tradition, and appealing only to the rational assessments and individual preferences of supposedly independent autonomous agents.

Yet in reality, argues MacIntyre, we can have no identity as individuals except in the context of a narrative – a concrete story woven out of the history and culture that gives meaning to our lives. The idea that we could start from scratch,

acknowledging only some neutral and abstract value, such as 'happiness' (for the utilitarians), or 'rational choice' (for those influenced by Kant), is an illusion. The concept of happiness, MacIntyre suggests, has no clear content that could guide our lives (since there are so many diverse forms of human activity); and autonomous choice, cut adrift from any meaningful moral context, lacks any persuasive authority. The good life for human beings requires a sense of past and of future, and the idea of a *quest*, or search directed to some goal or purpose; in short, it presupposes what MacIntyre calls a 'living tradition'.

MacIntyre's work has been highly influential in the contemporary movement in moral philosophy known as 'virtue ethics'. In some respects, this is a revival of the Aristotelian conception (see extract 2, above), which had stressed how the virtues necessary for a fulfilled life require training and habituation within a

---

* A. MacIntyre, *After Virtue: A Study in Moral Theory* (London: Duckworth, 1981; 2nd edn 1985), extracts from ch. 6, pp. 62–8, and ch. 15, pp. 216–24.

particular moral culture. MacIntyre defines the virtues as qualities necessary to achieve the goods that are 'internal to practices'; these practices (he elsewhere explains) include arts, sciences, politics, family life and 'any coherent and complex form of socially established cooperative human activity' involving 'standards of excellence'.[1] Some crucial features of this conception are underlined by MacIntyre in our extract. First, there is a stress on cooperation and 'social identity': in place of the widespread modern turn towards individualism and personal conceptions of the good, MacIntyre's virtues are 'those required to sustain . . . households and . . . communities in which men and women can seek for the good *together*'. Second, MacIntyre's account of virtue is linked to the idea of a search that is to some extent open-ended, and always developing. It is not just a matter of perpetuating certain social practices, or pursuing a settled and already agreed objective (like digging for gold or oil); rather, we gradually come to understand our goals better, as we grow in self-knowledge and learn to 'overcome the harms . . . temptations and distractions we encounter'.

This last point offers the basis for a response to those critics of MacIntyre who have objected that his conception of the good life relies on an uncritical conservatism about inherited traditions. MacIntyre certainly insists that our moral identity is necessarily shaped by tradition: 'I find myself part of a history, and . . . whether I like it or not, whether I recognize it or not, one of the bearers of a tradition.' But he also repudiates the 'Burkean' or hyper-conservative identification of tradition with resistance to change or avoidance of critical discussion. A *living* tradition will be shaped by continuing debate about the goals and purposes of the relevant practices; it is 'an historically extended, socially embodied argument . . . in part about the goods that constitute that tradition'.

The continuing stress, throughout our extract, on the need to find our moral identity within a social and historical narrative gives rise to a possible difficulty for MacIntyre, namely that our complex modern culture seems to be an amalgam of differing and often competing worldviews: locating ourselves within a Marxist story, for example, may give a very different account of virtue and of how we should live than locating ourselves within the narrative structures of Catholic Christianity. Whether there is a viable way of adjudicating between competing traditions is a problem that MacIntyre himself has addressed in his later writings, and which has continued to generate considerable debate. Whatever the outcome of that debate, most would concede that MacIntyre's work has brought a valuable historical dimension to the enterprise of ethical theory. Against the tendency of much analytic philosophy to render the subject ever more abstract and artificial, he has contributed to making it a more humane discipline, linked to the rest of our intellectual and moral culture.

The problems of modern moral theory emerge clearly as the failure of the Enlightenment project. On the one hand the individual moral agent, freed from hierarchy and teleology, conceives of himself and is conceived of by moral philosophers as sovereign in his moral authority. On the other hand the inherited, if partially transformed, rules of morality have to be found some new status, deprived as they have been of their older teleological character and their even more ancient categorical character as expressions of a ultimately divine law. If such rules cannot be found a new status which will make appeal to them rational, appeal to them will indeed appear as a mere instrument of individual desire and will. Hence there is a pressure to vindicate them either by devising some new teleology or by finding some new categorical status for them. The first project is what lends its importance to utilitarianism; the second to all those attempts to follow Kant in representing the authority of the appeal to moral rules as grounded in the nature of practical reasons.[2] Both attempts . . . failed and fail . . .

---

[1] *After Virtue*, pp. 187–8.
[2] For utilitarian and Kantian ethics, see respectively extracts 6 and 5, above.

John Stuart Mill was right in his contention that the Benthamite conception of happiness stood in need of enlargement; in *Utilitarianism* he attempted to make a key distinction between 'higher' and 'lower' pleasures[1] and in *On Liberty* and elsewhere he connects increase in human happiness with the extension of human creative powers. But the effect of these emendations is to suggest...that the notion of human happiness is *not* a unitary, simple notion and cannot provide us with a criterion for making our key choices. If someone suggests to us, in the spirit of Bentham and Mill, that we should guide our own choices by the prospect of our own future pleasure or happiness, the appropriate retort is to enquire: 'But which pleasure, which happiness ought to guide me?' For there are too many different kinds of enjoyable activity, too many different modes in which happiness is achieved. And pleasure or happiness are not states of mind for the production of which these activities and modes are merely alternative means...

To have understood the polymorphous character of pleasure and happiness is of course to have rendered those concepts useless for utilitarian purposes: if the prospect of his or her own future pleasure or happiness cannot for the reasons I have suggested provide criteria for solving the problems of action in the case of each individual, it follows that the notion of the greatest happiness of the greatest number is a notion without any clear content at all. It is indeed a pseudo-concept available for a variety of ideological uses, but no more than that...

Both the utilitarianism of the middle and late nineteenth century and the analytical moral philosophy of the middle and late twentieth century are alike unsuccessful attempts to rescue the autonomous moral agent from the predicament in which the failure of the Enlightenment project of providing him with a secular, rational justification for his moral allegiances had left him... [T]he price paid for liberation from what appeared to be the external authority of traditional morality was the loss of any authoritative content from the would-be moral utterances of the newly autonomous agent. Each moral agent now spoke unconstrained by the externalities of divine law, natural teleology or hierarchical authority; but why would anyone else now listen to him?...

[A]n action is always an episode in a possible history... I am what I may justifiably be taken by others to be in the course of living out a story that runs from my birth to my death; I am the *subject* of a history that is my own and no one else's, that has its own peculiar meaning.[2] When someone complains – as do some of those who attempt or commit suicide – that his or her life is meaningless, he or she is often and perhaps characteristically complaining that the narrative of their life has become unintelligible to them, that it lacks any point, any movement towards a climax or a *telos*. Hence the point of doing any one thing rather than another at crucial junctures in their lives seems to such a person to have been lost...

The other aspect of narrative selfhood is correlative: I am not only accountable, I am one who can always ask others for an account, who can put others to the question. I am part of their story as they are part of mine. The narrative of any one life is part of

---

[1]   See extract 6, above.

[2]   For more on the narrative conception of selfhood, compare Charles Taylor (Part V, extract 6, above), whose outlook has much in common with MacIntyre's.

an interlocking set of narratives. Moreover this asking for and giving of accounts itself plays an important part in constituting narratives. Asking you what you did and why, saying what I did and why, pondering the differences between your account of what I did and my account of what I did, and vice versa, these are essential constituents of all but the very simplest and barest of narratives. Thus without the accountability of the self those trains of events that constitute all but the simplest and barest of narratives could not occur; and without that same accountability narratives would lack that continuity required to make both them and the actions that constitute them intelligible...

It is now possible to return to the question from which this enquiry into the nature of human action and identity started: 'In what does the unity of an individual life consist?' The answer is that its unity is the unity of a narrative embodied in a single life. To ask 'What is the good for me?' is to ask how best I might live out that unity and bring it to completion. To ask 'What is the good for man?' is to ask what all answers to the former question must have in common. But now it is important to emphasize that it is the systematic asking of these two questions and the attempt to answer them in deed as well as in word which provide the moral life with its unity. The unity of a human life is the unity of a narrative quest. Quests sometimes fail, are frustrated, abandoned or dissipated into distractions; and human lives may in all these ways also fail. But the only criteria for success or failure in a human life as a whole are the criteria of success or failure in a narrated or to-be-narrated quest. A quest for what?

Two key features of the medieval conception of a quest need to be recalled. The first is that without some at least partly determinate conception of the final *telos* there could not be any beginning to a quest. Some conception of the good for man is required. Whence is such a conception to be drawn? Precisely from those questions which led us to attempt to transcend that limited conception of the virtues which is available in and through practices. It is in looking for a conception of the good which will enable us to order other goods, for a conception of the good which will enable us to extend our understanding of the purpose and content of the virtues, for a conception of the good which will enable us to understand the place of integrity and constancy in life, that we initially define the kind of life which is a quest for the good. But secondly it is clear the medieval conception of a quest is not at all that of a search for something already adequately characterized, as miners search for gold or geologists for oil. It is in the course of the quest and only through encountering and coping with the various particular harms, dangers, temptations and distractions which provide any quest with its episodes and incidents that the goal of the quest is finally to be understood. A quest is always an education both as to the character of that which is sought and in self-knowledge.

The virtues therefore are to be understood as those dispositions which will not only sustain practices and enable us to achieve the goods internal to practices, but which will also sustain us in the relevant kind of quest for the good, by enabling us to overcome the harms, dangers, temptations and distractions which we encounter, and which will furnish us with increasing self-knowledge and increasing knowledge of the good. The catalogue of the virtues will therefore include the virtues required to sustain the kind of households and the kind of political communities in which men and women can seek for the good together and the virtues necessary for philosophical enquiry about the character of the good. We have then arrived at a provisional conclusion about the good life for man: the good life for man is the life spent in seeking for the good life for man, and the virtues necessary for the seeking are those which will enable us to understand what more and what else the good life for man is. We have also completed the second stage in our account of the virtues, by situating them in relation to the good life for man and not only in relation to practices. But our enquiry requires a third stage.

For I am never able to seek for the good or exercise the virtues only *qua* individual. This is partly because what it is to live the good life concretely varies from circumstance to circumstance even when it is one and the same conception of the good life and one and the same set of virtues which are being embodied in a human life. What the good life is for a fifth-century Athenian general will not be the same as what it was for a medieval nun or a seventeenth-century farmer. But it is not just that different individuals live in different social circumstances; it is also that we all approach our own circumstances as bearers of a particular social identity. I am someone's son or daughter, someone else's cousin or uncle; I am a citizen of this or that city, a member of this or that guild or profession; I belong to this clan, that tribe, this nation. Hence what is good for me has to be the good for one who inhabits these roles. As such, I inherit from the past of my family, my city, my tribe, my nation, a variety of debts, inheritances, rightful expectations and obligations. These constitute the given of my life, my moral starting point. This is in part what gives my life its own moral particularity.

This thought is likely to appear alien and even surprising from the standpoint of modern individualism. From the standpoint of individualism 1 am what I myself choose to be. I can always, if I wish to, put in question what are taken to be the merely contingent social features of my existence. I may biologically be my father's son; but I cannot be held responsible for what he did unless I choose implicitly or explicitly to assume such responsibility. I may legally be a citizen of a certain country; but I cannot be held responsible for what my country does or has done unless I choose implicitly or explicitly to assume such responsibility. Such individualism is expressed by those modern Americans who deny any responsibility for the effects of slavery upon black Americans, saying 'I never owned any slaves'. It is more subtly the standpoint of those other modern Americans who accept a nicely calculated responsibility for such effects measured precisely by the benefits they themselves as individuals have indirectly received from slavery. In both cases 'being an American' is not in itself taken to be part of the moral identity of the individual. And of course there is nothing peculiar to modern Americans in this attitude: the Englishman who says, 'I never did any wrong to Ireland; why bring up that old history as though it had something to do with me', or the young German who believes that being born after 1945 means that what Nazis did to Jews has no moral relevance to his relationship to his Jewish contemporaries, exhibit the same attitude, that according to which the self is detachable from its social and historical roles and statuses... The contrast with the narrative view of the self is clear. For the story of my life is always embedded in the story of those communities from which I derive my identity. I am born with a past; and to try to cut myself off from that past, in the individualist mode, is to deform my present relationships. The possession of an historical identity and the possession of a social identity coincide. Notice that rebellion against my identity is always one possible mode of expressing it.

Notice also that the fact that the self has to find its moral identity in and through its membership in communities such as those of the family, the neighbourhood, the city and the tribe does not entail that the self has to accept the moral limitations of the particularity of those forms of community. Without those moral particularities to begin from there would never be anywhere to begin; but it is in moving forward from such particularity that the search for the good, for the universal, consists. Yet particularity can never be simply left behind or obliterated. The notion of escaping from it into a realm of entirely universal maxims which belong to man as such, whether in its eighteenth-century Kantian form or in the presentation of some modern analytical moral philosophies, is an illusion and an illusion with painful consequences. When men and women identify what are in fact their partial and particular causes too easily and too completely with the cause of some universal principle, they usually behave worse than they would otherwise do. What I am, therefore, is in key part what I inherit, a specific past that is present to some degree in my present. I find myself part of a history and that is generally to say, whether I like it or not, whether I recognize it or not, one of the bearers of a tradition. It was important when I characterized the concept of a practice to notice that practices always have histories and that at any given moment what a practice is depends on a mode of understanding it which has been transmitted often through many generations. And thus, insofar as the virtues sustain the relationships required for practices, they have to sustain relationships to the past – and to the future as well as in the present. But the traditions through which particular practices are transmitted and reshaped never exist in isolation for larger social traditions. What constitutes such traditions? We are apt to be misled here by the ideological uses to which the concept of a tradition has been put by conservative political theorists. Characteristically such theorists have followed Burke[1] in contrasting tradition with reason and the stability of tradition with conflict. Both contrasts obfuscate. For all reasoning takes place within the context of some traditional mode of thought, transcending through criticism and invention the limitations of what had hitherto been reasoned in that tradition; this is as true of modern physics as of medieval logic. Moreover when a tradition is in good order it is always partially constituted by an argument about the goods the pursuit of which gives to that tradition its particular point and purpose.

So when an institution – a university, say, or a farm or a hospital – is the bearer of a tradition of practice or practices, its common life will be partly, but in a centrally important way, constituted by a continuous argument as to what a university is and ought to be or what good farming is or what good medicine is. Traditions, when vital, embody continuities of conflict. Indeed when a tradition becomes Burkean, it is always dying or dead...

A living tradition then is an historically extended, socially embodied argument, and an argument precisely in part about the goods which constitute that tradition. Within a tradition the pursuit of goods extends through generations, sometimes through many generations. Hence the individual's search for his or her good is generally and characteristically conducted within a context defined by those traditions of which the individual's life is a part, and this is true both of those goods which are internal to practices and of the goods of a single life. Once again the narrative phenomenon of

---

[1] Edmund Burke (1729–97), British statesman and influential conservative thinker.

embedding is crucial: the history of a practice in our time is generally and character-istically embedded in and made intelligible in terms of the larger and longer history of the tradition through which the practice in its present form was conveyed to us; the history of each of our own lives is generally and characteristically embedded in and made intelligible in terms of the larger and longer histories of a number of traditions. I have to say 'generally and characteristically' rather than 'always', for traditions decay, disintegrate and disappear. What then sustains and strengthens traditions? What weakens and destroys them?

The answer in key part is: the exercise or the lack of exercise of the relevant virtues. The virtues find their point and purpose not only in sustaining those relationships necessary if the variety of goods internal to practices are to be achieved and not only in sustaining the form of an individual life in which that individual may seek out his or her good as the good of his or her whole life, but also in sustaining those traditions which provide both practices and individual lives with their necessary historical context. Lack of justice, lack of truthfulness, lack of courage, lack of the relevant intellectual virtues – these corrupt traditions, just as they do those institutions and practices which derive their life from the traditions of which they are the contem-porary embodiments. To recognize this is of course also to recognize the existence of an additional virtue, one whose importance is perhaps most obvious when it is least present, the virtue of having an adequate sense of the traditions to which one belongs or which confront one. This virtue is not to be confused with any form of conserva-tive antiquarianism... It is rather the case that an adequate sense of tradition mani-fests itself in a grasp of those future possibilities which the past has made available to the present. Living traditions, just because they continue a not-yet-completed narra-tive, confront a future whose determinate and determinable character, so far as it possesses any, derives from the past.

12   Could Ethics be Objective? Bernard Williams, *Ethics and the Limits of Philosophy**

We conclude this Part of the volume with a question that occurs to many people when they start to think seriously about ethics: do our ethical judgements aspire to reflect objective truths about right and wrong – as opposed, for example, to being merely expressions of our per-sonal (or collective) preferences? In tackling this question, Bernard Williams, one of the most subtle and influential moral philosophers of the late twentieth century, claims there is a crucial difference between ethical thought and scientific thought. The latter, he argues, 'has some chance of being... [an] account of how the world really is, while ethical thought has no [such] chance'.

To elucidate this, Williams focuses on the idea of *convergence*. In science, though there may be differing theories of reality, we ideally hope for eventual convergence or agreement; this is because we suppose there must ultimately be a right answer determined by 'how things

* Bernard Williams, *Ethics and the Limits of Philosophy* (London: Collins/Fontana, 1985), excerpts from ch. 8 ('Knowledge, Science, Convergence'), pp. 135–55.

are' – shaped by the way the real world actually is. But in the area of the ethical, Williams asserts, 'there is no such coherent hope'.

Before explaining why not, Williams examines two possible objections to his initial contrast between science and ethics. The first says that the notion of science describing the world *as it really is* is untenable, since we can make no sense of 'how the world is' independently of our human descriptions of it. To this Williams replies that science may be able to abstract from the peculiarities of the human perspective, so as to arrive at an 'absolute conception' of reality – a conception that would be shared by any rational investigator, 'even if they were very different from us'. (Thus, beings from another galaxy, who had utterly different brains and sense-organs from ours, might, for example, have no colour perception as we understand it, but might agree with us on certain structural features of the cosmos, such as the inverse square law of gravity.) The second objection Williams considers against the ethics/science contrast is that convergence may be expected in ethics as well as in science. For there are agreed objective standards for the use of 'thick' ethical concepts – those which have a descriptive as well as an evaluative component, such as 'cowardly', 'generous', 'truthful', 'brutal' and so on. So will not the accepted rules for applying these concepts ensure genuinely objective ethical knowledge – for example about whether Smith is cowardly or not? Williams replies that a detached observer, while fully understanding the rules, could always disagree with such judgements; for he might see 'a whole segment of the local discourse . . . as involving a mistake'. (For example, he might refuse to accept that someone was an 'evil witch', or 'possessed by the devil', even though these terms were correctly applied within the conventions and rules of that community.)

Williams proceeds to argue that standing back from a given society's set of ethical concepts, and reflecting critically on their use, could never be expected to lead to agreement among rational observers that some of them were objectively true. In the scientific case, we can expect eventual convergence or agreement, because we suppose that the scientific theories 'track the truth' – conform to how things really are; but in the ethical case, we can make no sense of this.

Though rejecting the idea of objective ethical truth in this sense, Williams concludes by suggesting we might still seek for a weaker though still objective foundation for our ethical beliefs – a foundation based on human nature, viz. the typical needs and desires of human beings. Might convergence be possible here? Williams leaves us with the perhaps somewhat pessimistic thought that the project of basing ethics on such agreed considerations regarding human nature is 'not very likely to succeed', given the wide variety in human societies and forms of life, and the 'many and various forms of human excellence which will not fit together into a one harmonious whole'.

Williams's arguments take us very far from the idea of an objective moral order, which we find in many traditional religion-based systems of ethics. And his reminder that the detached critic can always stand back from a given socio-ethical framework – and hence that in the ethical sphere, 'reflection can destroy knowledge' – poses a tough challenge to theorists like MacIntyre (see preceding extract), who aspire to find moral value by aligning themselves with a tradition that encapsulates standards of human excellence. At all events, in his unfolding of the contrast between ethics and science, and in probing how far, if at all, moral judgement can aspire to truth and knowledge, Williams powerfully articulates fundamental questions about the nature of morality that seem likely to remain at the centre of moral philosophy for the foreseeable future.

I believe that . . . science has some chance of being more or less what it seems, a systematized theoretical account of how the world really is, while ethical thought has no chance of being everything it seems . . . The basic difference lies in . . . our reflective understanding of the best hopes we could coherently entertain for eliminating disagreement in the two areas. It is a matter of what, under the most favourable conditions, would be the best explanation of the end of disagreement: the explanation – as I shall say from now on – of convergence.

...The basic idea behind the distinction between the scientific and the ethical, expressed in terms of convergence, is very simple. In a scientific inquiry there should ideally be convergence on an answer, where the best explanation of the convergence involves the idea that the answer represents how things are; in the area of the ethical, at least at a high level of generality, there is no such coherent hope. The distinction does not turn on any difference in whether convergence will actually occur, and it is important that this is not what the argument is about. It might well turn out that there will be convergence in ethical outlook, at least among human beings. The point of the contrast is that, even if this happens, it will not be correct to think it has come about because convergence has been guided by how things actually are, whereas convergence in the sciences might be explained in that way if it does happen. This means, among other things, that we understand differently in the two cases the existence of convergence or, alternatively, its failure to come about.

I shall come back to ways in which we might understand ethical convergence. First, however, we must face certain arguments suggesting that there is really nothing at all in the distinction, expressed in those terms. There are two different directions from which this objection can come. In one version, the notion of convergence that comes about because of how things are is seen as an empty notion. According to the other, the notion of such a convergence is not empty, but it is available as much in ethical cases as in scientific...

[The first version of the objection argues that] no convergence of science, past or future, could possible be explained in any meaningful way by reference to the way the world is, because there is an insoluble difficulty with the notion of 'the world' as something that can determine belief. There is a dilemma. On the one hand, 'the world' may be characterized in terms of our current beliefs about what it contains; it is a world of stars, people, grass or tables. When 'the world' is taken in this way, we can of course say that our beliefs about the world are affected by the world, in the sense that for instance our beliefs about grass are affected by grass, but there is nothing illuminating or substantive in this – our conception of the world as the object of our beliefs can do no better than repeat the beliefs we take to represent it. If, on the other hand, we try to form some idea of a world that is prior to any description of it, the world that all systems of belief and representation are trying to represent, then we have an empty notion of something completely unspecified and unspecifiable. So either way we fail to have a notion of 'the world' that will do what is required of it.

Each side of this dilemma takes all our representations of the world together, in the one case putting them all in, and in the other leaving them out altogether. But there is a third and more helpful possibility, that we should form a conception of the world that is 'already there' in terms of some but not all of our beliefs and theories. In reflecting on the world that is there *anyway*, independent of our experience, we must concentrate not in the first instance on what our beliefs are about, but on how they represent what they are about. We can select among our beliefs and features of our world picture some that we can reasonably claim to represent the world in a way to the maximum degree independent of our perspective and its peculiarities. The resultant picture of things, if we can carry through this task, can be called the 'absolute conception' of the world. In terms of that conception, we may hope to explain the possibility of our attaining that conception itself, and also the possibility of other, perspectival, representations.

This notion of an absolute conception can serve to make effective a distinction between 'the world as it is independent of our experience', and 'the world as it seems to us'. It does this by understanding 'the world as it seems to us' as 'the world as it seems peculiarly to us'; the absolute conception will, correspondingly, be a conception of the world that might be arrived at by any investigators, even if they were very different from us...

The opposite line of objection urges that the idea of 'converging on how things are' is available, to some adequate degree, in the ethical case as well. The place where this is to be seen is above all with those substantive or thick ethical concepts I have often mentioned. Many exotic examples of these can be drawn from other cultures, but there are enough left in our own: *Coward, lie, brutality, gratitude* and so forth. They are characteristically related to ... a reason for action, though that reason need not be a decisive one, and may be outweighed by other reasons...We may say, summarily, that such concepts are 'action-guiding'.

At the same time, their application is guided by the world. A concept of this sort may be rightly or wrongly applied, and people who have acquired it can agree that it applied or fails to apply to some new situation. In many cases the agreement will be spontaneous, while in other cases there is room for judgement and comparison. Some disagreement at the margin may be irresoluble, but this does not mean that the use of the concepts is not controlled by the facts or by the users' perception of the world. (As with other concepts that are not totally precise, marginal disagreements can indeed help to show how their use *is* controlled by the facts.) We can say, then, that the application of these concepts is at the same time world-guided and action-guiding. How can it be both at once?

...An insightful observer can...come to understand and anticipate the use of [a thick] concept without actually sharing the values of the people who use it...But in imaginatively anticipating the use of the concept, the observer also has to grasp imaginatively its evaluative point. He cannot stand quite outside the evaluative interests of the community he is observing, and pick up the concept simply as a device for dividing up in a rather strange way certain neutral features of the world...

The sympathetic observer can follow the practice of the people he is observing; he can report, anticipate and even take part in discussion of the use they make of their concept. But, as with some other concepts of theirs, relating to religion, for instance, or to witchcraft, he may not be ultimately identified with the use of the concept: it may not really be his. This possibility, of the insightful but not totally identified observer, bears on an important question whether those who properly apply ethical concepts of this kind can be said to have ethical knowledge.

Let us assume, artificially, that we are dealing with a society that is maximally homogeneous and minimally given to general reflection; its members simply, all of them, use certain ethical concepts of this sort. (We may call it the 'hypertraditional' society.) What would be involved in their having ethical knowledge?

...The members of the hypertraditional society apply their thick concepts, and in doing so they make various judgements. If any of those judgements can ever properly be said to be true, then their beliefs can be said to track the truth, since they can withdraw judgements if the circumstances turn out not to be what was supposed, can make an alternative judgement if it would be more appropriate, and so on. They have, each, mastered these concepts, and they can perceive the personal and social happenings to which the concepts apply. If there is truth here, their beliefs can track it. The question left is whether any of these judgements can be true...

[An argument for saying these judgements cannot be true is] that an entire segment of the local discourse may be seen from the outside as involving a mistake. This possibility has been much discussed by theorists. Social anthropologists have asked whether ritual and magical conceptions should be seen as mistaken in our terms, or rather as operating at a different level, not commensurable with our scientific ideas...It is hard to deny that magic, at least, is a causal conception, with implications that overlap with scientific conceptions of causality. To the extent this is so, magical conceptions can be seen from the outside as false, and then no one will have known to be true any statement claiming magical influence, even though he may have correctly used all the local criteria for claiming a given piece of magical influence...If we accept the obvious truth that reflection characteristically disturbs, unseats or replaces those traditional concepts...then we reach the notably un-Socratic conclusion that in ethics, *reflection can destroy knowledge*...

[But could standing back and reflecting on the ethical concepts of a given society generate some kind of justification for those concepts, thereby providing ethical knowledge?] The reflective considerations will have to take up the job of justifying the local concepts once those have come to be questioned...If a wider objectivity were to come from all this, then the reflective ethical considerations would themselves have to be objective. This brings us back to the question whether the reflective level might generate its own ethical knowledge. If this is understood as our coming to have propositional knowledge of ethical truths, then we need some account of what 'tracking the truth' will be. The idea that our beliefs can track the truth at this level must at least imply that a range of investigators could rationally, reasonably and unconstrainedly come to converge on a determinate set of ethical conclusions. What are the hopes for such a process? I do not mean of its actually happening, but rather of our forming a coherent picture of how it might happen. If it is construed as convergence on a body of ethical truths which is brought about and explained by the fact that they are truths – this would be the strict analogy to scientific objectivity, then I see no hope for it...I cannot see any convincing theory of knowledge for the convergence of reflective ethical thought on ethical reality in even a distant analogy to the scientific case. Nor is there a convincing analogy with mathematics, a case in which the notion of an independent reality is at least problematical...

We must reject the objectivist view of ethical life as...a pursuit of ethical truth. But this does not rule out all forms of objectivism. There is still the project of trying to give an objecting grounding or foundation to ethical life. For this, we should look in the direction of...ideas about human nature...Granted that human beings need to share a social world, is there anything to be known about their needs and their basic motivations that will show us what this world would best be?

I doubt that there will turn out to be a very satisfying answer. It is probable that any such considerations will radically underdetermine the ethical options even in a given social situation...Any ethical life is going to contain restraints on such things as killing, injury and lying, but those restraints can take very different forms. Again, with respect to the virtues, which is the most natural and promising field for this kind of inquiry, we only have to compare Aristotle's catalogue of the virtues with any that might be produced now to see how pictures of an appropriate human life may differ in spirit and in the actions and institutions they call for. We also have the idea that there are many and various forms of human excellence which will not all fit together into a one harmonious whole, so any determinate ethical outlook is going to represent some kind of specialization of human possibilities...

The project of giving to ethical life an objective and determinate grounding in considerations about human nature is not, in my view, very likely to succeed. But it is at any rate a comprehensible project, and I believe it represents the only intelligible form of ethical objectivity at the reflective level...

The convergence that signalled the success of this project would be a convergence of practical reason, by which people came to lead the best kind of life and to have the desires that belong to that life; convergence in ethical belief would largely be a part and consequence of that process. One very general ethical belief [that a certain kind of life was best for human beings] would, indeed, be an object of knowledge at that level. Many particular ethical judgements, involving the favoured thick concepts, could be known to be true, but then judgements of this sort (I have argued) are very often known to be true anyway, even when they occur, as they always have, in a life that is not grounded at the objective level. The objective grounding would not bring it about that judgements using those concepts were true or could be known; this was so already. But it would enable us to recognize that certain of them were the best or most appropriate thick concepts to use. Between the two extremes of the one very general proposition and the many concrete ones, other ethical beliefs would be true only in the oblique sense that they were the beliefs that would help us to find our way around in a social world which – on this optimistic program – was shown to be the best social world for human beings.

This would be a structure very different from that of the objectivity of science. There would be a radical difference between ethics and science even if ethics were objective in the only way in which it intelligibly could be.

Specimen Questions

1 Explain the philosophical point of Plato's story of Gyges and the magic ring.
2 What is the importance of Aristotle's account of ethical virtue as a *disposition* of character?
3 Why do the passions make us 'slaves', according to Spinoza, and how can human beings achieve freedom?
4 'There is some benevolence, however small, infused into our bosom; some spark of friendship for human kind; some particle of the dove kneaded into our frame, along with the elements of the wolf and the serpent' (David Hume). Explain and discuss the importance of natural sentiments of benevolence in Hume's moral theory.
5 Critically evaluate Kant's claim that a *good will* is the only thing that is unconditionally good, or good in itself.
6 Does Mill satisfactorily counter the objection against utilitarianism that it is a 'doctrine worthy of swine'?

7   Explain why Sidgwick thinks a conscientious utilitarian could only rarely justify violating a widely accepted rule whose observance is generally beneficial. Do you find his arguments convincing?

8   Expound and evaluate Nietzsche's attack on conventional morality.

9   Explain Ross's concept of a *prima facie* duty. Is he right in resisting the attempt to reduce the idea of what is right to whatever produces the greatest amount of good?

10   Does Rawls's notion of rational choice behind a veil of ignorance provide a plausible mechanism for determining the right principles to adopt in society?

11   Explain and critically discuss the notion of a 'living tradition' in MacIntyre's account of the virtues and the good life.

12   Why does Williams maintain that 'we must reject the objectivist view of ethical life as . . . a pursuit of ethical truth', and is he right?

Suggestions for Further Reading

Plato

Plato, *Republic*. See readings at the end of Part I for texts and general introductions to Plato.

For discussion of the relation between justice and happiness in Plato, see J. Annas, *An Introduction to Plato's Republic* (Oxford: Clarendon, 1981), ch. 12.

See also T. Irwin, *Plato's Ethics* (Oxford: Oxford University Press, 1995), chs 11 and 12, and G. Vlastos (ed.), *Platonic Studies* (Princeton: Princeton University Press, 1981), ch. 5.

For a stimulating and wide-ranging study of ancient Greek approaches to ethics, see J. Annas, *The Morality of Happiness* (Oxford: Oxford University Press, 1993).

For the general question of why one should be moral, see K. Baier, *The Moral Point of View* (Ithaca, NY: Cornell University Press, 1978), and B. Williams, *Ethics and the Limits of Philosophy* (Cambridge, Mass.: Harvard University Press, 1985).

Aristotle

Aristotle, *Nicomachean Ethics*. Translations available in paperback include T. Irwin (Indianapolis: Hackett, 1985), and J. A. K. Thomson, revised translation of Tredennick (Harmondsworth: Penguin, 1976).

A very clear introduction is J. O. Urmson, *Aristotle's Ethics* (Oxford: Blackwell, 1992).

An excellent comprehensive study of Aristotle's ethics is S. Broadie, *Ethics with Aristotle* (Oxford: Oxford University Press, 1991): see esp. chs 1 and 2.

See also W. F. R. Hardie, *Aristotle's Ethical Theory* (2nd edn, Oxford: Clarendon, 1980).

A valuable collection of papers on various aspects of Aristotle's ethical theory is A. R. Rorty (ed.), *Essays on Aristotle's Ethics* (Berkeley: University of California Press, 1980).

See also the papers in J. Barnes, M. Schofield and R. Sorabji (eds), *Articles on Aristotle*, vols. 2 and 4 (London: Duckworth, 1977).

Spinoza

The complete text of the *Ethics* is translated, with an introduction for students, by G. H. R. Parkinson (Oxford: Oxford University Press, 2000).

For general introductions to Spinoza, see the readings listed at the end of Part IV, above. For discussion of some of the ethical themes in Spinoza, see esp. the books listed there by Curley, Delahunty and Donagan.

See also E. E. Harris, *Salvation from Despair: A Reappraisal of Spinoza's Philosophy* (The Hague: Nijhoff, 1973).

Hume

For general introductions to Hume, see the readings at the end of Part I, above.

More specially related to Humean ethics is J. Mackie, *Hume's Moral Theory* (London: Routledge, 1988).

See also N. Capaldi, *Hume's Place in Moral Philosophy* (New York: Lang, 1989); J. Harrison, *Hume's Moral Epistemology* (Cambridge: Cambridge University Press, 1976).

See also A. C. Baier, *Moral Prejudices* (Cambridge, Mass.: Harvard University Press, 1994), chs 4 and 5.

Kant

For general introductions to Kant, see readings at the end of Part I.

On Kantian ethics, a stimulating collection of essays is O. O'Neill, *Constructions of Reason* (Cambridge: Cambridge University Press, 1989).

See also H. Paton, *The Categorical Imperative: A Study in Kant's Moral Philosophy* (London: Hutcheson, 1947); R. O'Sullivan, *An Introduction to Kant's Ethics* (Cambridge: Cambridge University Press, 1995); B. Herman, *The Practice of Moral Judgement* (Cambridge, Mass.: Harvard University Press, 1991); T. Hill, *Autonomy and Self-Respect* (Cambridge: Cambridge University Press, 1991); R. P. Wolff, *The Autonomy of Reason* (New York: Harper & Row, 1973).

See also the essays by Onora O'Neill and J. B. Schneewind in P. Guyer (ed.), *The Cambridge Companion to Kant* (Cambridge: Cambridge University Press, 1992).

Mill

A good introduction to Mill's ethics is A. Ryan, *J. S. Mill* (London: Routledge, 1974), ch. 4.

For a stimulating discussion of Mill's utilitarianism, see J. Skorupski, *Mill* (London: Routledge, 1989), ch. 9.

A comprehensive study of Mill's moral theory is R. Berger, *Happiness, Justice and Freedom* (Berkeley: University of California Press, 1984).

For lively debate on utilitarian ethics, see J. J. C. Smart and B. Williams, *Utilitarianism: For and Against* (Cambridge: Cambridge University Press, 1973).

Nietzsche

The following critical studies may be recommended: R. J. Hollingdale, *Nietzsche: The Man and his Philosophy* (London: Routledge, 1965); W. Kaufmann, *Nietzsche: Philosopher, Psychologist, Antichrist* (Princeton: Princeton University Press, 1975); A. Nehamas, *Nietzsche: Life as Literature* (Cambridge, Mass.: Harvard University Press, 1985).

A useful collection of essays on Nietzsche's thought is B. Magnus (ed.), *The Cambridge Companion to Nietzsche* (Cambridge: Cambridge University Press, 1984).

Sidgwick

A first-rate account of Sidgwick's ideas is J. B. Schneewind, *Sidgwick's Ethics and Victorian Moral Philosophy* (Oxford: Clarendon, 1977).

See also the article by Marcus Singer in L. C. Becker (ed.), *Encyclopedia of Ethics* (New York: Garland, 1992).

Ross

An excellent survey of intuitionism may be found in the Introduction by Philip Stratton-Lake to his *Ethical Intuitionism* (Oxford: Clarendon, 2002). Several of the essays included in the volume also contains discussions of Ross.

See also the article by J. Dancy in P. Singer (ed.), *A Companion to Ethics* (Oxford: Blackwell, repr. 1993), ch. 36; J. Mackie, *Ethics* (Harmondsworth: Penguin, 1977), ch. 1; and G. J. Warnock, *Contemporary Moral Philosophy* (London: Macmillan, 1967), ch. 2.

Rawls

For critical discussion of Rawls's views, see B. Barry, *The Liberal Theory of Justice* (Oxford: Clarendon, 1973); N. Daniels (ed.), *Reading Rawls* (Oxford: Blackwell, 1975); R. Nozick, *Anarchy, State and Utopia* (Oxford: Blackwell, 1974), ch. 7. (See also Part X, extract 10, below.)

See also the article by C. Korsgaard in L. C. Becker (ed.), *Encyclopedia of Ethics* (New York: Garland, 1992).

MacIntyre

A valuable collection of essays on MacIntyre is J. Horton and S. Mendus S. (eds), *After MacIntyre* (Oxford: Polity, 1994).

Interesting general collections on virtue ethics are D. Statman (ed.), *Virtue Ethics* (Edinburgh: Edinburgh University Press, 1997), and S. Darwall (ed.), *Virtue Ethics* (Oxford: Blackwell, 2003).

A handy selection of MacIntyre's writings with a helpful introduction is K. Knight (ed.), *The MacIntyre Reader* (Oxford: Blackwell, 1998).

Williams

For some interesting discussions of Williams's work, see J. E. J. Altham and R. Harrison (eds), *World, Mind and Ethics: Essays on the Ethical Philosophy of Bernard Williams* (Cambridge: Cambridge University Press, 1995): see esp. the essays by Jardine and by Hookway on the objectivity issue and the ethics–science contrast, and Williams's own replies.

Other stimulating work by Williams, with a useful introduction by A. W. Moore, is contained in his posthumously published collection *Philosophy as a Humanistic Discipline* (Princeton: Princeton University Press, 2006).

For an informative general survey of Williams's philosophy (including bibliography), see the entry on him by T. D. J. Chappell, in the *Stanford Encyclopedia of Philosophy* <http://plato.stanford.edu/entries/williams-bernard/>

An excellent introduction to Williams's thought is M. P. Jenkins, *Bernard Williams* (Chesham: Acumen, 2006).

For a stimulating exploration of a modest kind of objectivity in ethics, which has some affinities with the picture reached at the end of Williams's argument, see D. Wiggins, *Ethics: Twelve Lectures on the Philosophy of Morality* (London: Penguin, 2006), ch. 11.

PART IX

Problems in Ethics

Problems in Ethics
Introduction

Much traditional moral philosophy is of a fairly general and abstract nature, and addresses the task of formulating fundamental principles for the guidance and evaluation of human conduct. Some of the most influential examples of this kind of moral philosophy are included in Part VIII, above. But moral philosophers have also been concerned to apply their principles to particular problems, with a view to deciding on the rightness or wrongness of specific human institutions, policies and practices. This branch of moral philosophy, often called 'Applied Ethics', forms the subject matter of the present Part of the volume. Readers will notice that it follows a rather different pattern from that found elsewhere in the book. Instead of a continuous fabric woven out of overlapping threads, what follows is more like a patchwork quilt. Some of the issues relate to social arrangements (Aristotle discussing the justification for hierarchies such as slavery; Wollstonecraft on the liberation of women; Bentham on the institution of punishment); some relate to humanity's ethical relationship with other parts of creation – the animal world (Kant), and the wider environment (Leopold); some concern our responsibility for our own lives (Hume on suicide), the welfare of those nearest to us (Godwin on partiality) and the lives of others (Thomson on abortion; Rachels on euthanasia; Kass on reproduction); and some concern the ethics of how we relate to those from different societies (Aquinas on war; Singer on our attitudes to the 'third world'). Heterogeneity, it has aptly been said, is the hallmark of Applied Ethics, and the materials included below exemplify widely differing approaches to very disparate problems. Nevertheless, the extracts, as always, are presented in chronological order, most predate the twentieth century, and all bear the stamp of the era to which they belong. All reveal something of the philosopher's continuing struggle to stand back from prevailing institutions and practices, and use the tools of reason and argument to examine what can be justified and what needs to be changed. In the terms of a famous simile, they could be said to be among the fruits that can be gathered from the outermost branches of the tree of philosophy,[1] showing how philosophical argument can be applied to practical questions about how human beings should conduct their lives.

---

[1] The image appears in the 1647 Preface to Descartes's *Principles of Philosophy*.

1   Inequality, Freedom and Slavery: Aristotle, *Politics**

The Kantian principle of respect for persons (see Part VIII, extract 5, above) implies that all rational human beings should be treated with the dignity due to free and autonomous agents. But for the overwhelming bulk of our history, human societies have been structured in terms of hierarchies involving massive distinctions of rank and esteem, where those lower in the pecking order have often been denied the most elementary personal rights. The most extreme example of such social inequality is the institution of slavery, which was an entrenched feature of the ancient Greek world. In the following extract, Aristotle resolutely defends slavery as a normal, indeed integral, feature of the ordinary household. The slave is characterized as a 'living tool', quite literally owned by the master, and used as a means to furthering his own purposes. The attempted justification Aristotle offers for such a system is threefold. First, he claims slaves are necessary for the good life – they form part of the support structure of 'necessaries' without which 'no man can live well' (though the mention of mythical self-moving tools like the 'tripods of Hephaestus' suggests that Aristotle

might have revised this part of his argument had he lived in our modern world of automated labour-saving devices). Second, Aristotle clearly believes in a 'natural' or genetically based hierarchy: there are 'slaves by nature' whose intelligence and reasoning power is such that they can recognize the authority of their superiors, but are not fitted to take decisions themselves. Finally, Aristotle invokes human conventions which seem to underpin slavery (for example the rule that those conquered in war become slaves of the victors); here, however, he resists the argument that sheer superior force justifies domination, and seems in the course of the discussion to move back to relying on supposed differences in birth. The vital questions to be asked about Aristotle's position are whether in the first place it is true that there are such radical differences of ability between human beings, and second, even if it were true, how this could even begin to justify one class being kept in servitude by the other. Aristotle's discussion is a salutary reminder of the extent to which the seemingly objective 'voice of reason' may speak in accents that betray the prevailing prejudices of a society.

Seeing then that the state is made up of households, before speaking of the state we must speak of the management of the household. The parts of household management correspond to the persons who compose the household, and a complete household consists of slaves and freemen. Now we should begin by examining everything in its fewest possible elements; and the first and fewest possible parts of a family are master and slave, husband and wife, father and children. We have therefore to consider what each of these three relations is and ought to be...

Let us first speak of master and slave, looking to the needs of practical life and also seeking to attain some better theory of their relation than exists at present. For some are of the opinion that the rule of a master is a science, and that the management of a household, and the mastership of slaves, and the political and royal rule...are all the same. Others affirm that the rule of a master over slaves is contrary to nature and that the distinction between slave and free man exists by law only, and not by nature; and being an interference with nature is therefore unjust.

* Aristotle, *Politics* [*Politika*, c.330 BC], Bk I, chs 3–7 (1253b1–1255b40). Trans. B. Jowett, in *The Works of Aristotle*, ed. W. D. Ross, vol. X (Oxford: Clarendon, 1921); with omissions.

Property is a part of the household, and the art of acquiring property is a part of the art of managing the household; for no man can live well, or indeed live at all, unless he be provided with necessaries. And as in the arts which have a definite sphere the workers must have their own proper instruments for the accomplishment of their work, so it is in the management of a household. Now instruments are of various sorts; some are living, others lifeless; in the rudder, the pilot of a ship has a lifeless instrument, in the look-out man, a living instrument; for in the arts the servant is a kind of instrument. Thus, too, a possession is an instrument for maintaining life. And so, in the arrangement of the family, a slave is a living possession, and property a number of such instruments; and the servant is himself an instrument which takes precedence over all other instruments. For if every instrument could accomplish its own work, obeying or anticipating the will of others, like the statues of Daedalus, or the tripods of Hephaestus, which, says the poet, 'of their own accord entered the assembly of the Gods';[1] if, in like manner, the shuttle would weave and the plectrum touch the lyre without a hand to guide them, chief workmen would not want servants, nor masters slaves.

Here, however, another distinction must be drawn: the instruments commonly so called are instruments of production, whilst a possession is an instrument of action. The shuttle, for example, is not only of use, but something else is made by it; whereas of a garment or of a bed there is only the use. Further, as production and action are different in kind, and both require instruments, the instruments which they employ must likewise differ in kind. But life is action and not production, and therefore the slave is the minister of action. Again, a possession is spoken of as a part is spoken of; for the part is not only a part of something else, but wholly belongs to it; and this is also true of a possession. The master is only the master of the slave; he does not belong to him, whereas the slave is not only the slave of his master but wholly belongs to him. Hence we see what is the nature and office of a slave; he who is by nature not his own but another's man, is by nature a slave; and he may be said to be another's man who, being a human being, is also a possession. And a possession may be defined as an instrument of action, separable from the possessor.

But is there any one thus intended by nature to be a slave, and for whom such a condition is expedient and right, or rather is not all slavery a violation of nature?

There is no difficulty in answering this question, on grounds both of reason and of fact. For that some should rule and others be ruled is a thing not only necessary, but expedient; from the hour of their birth, some are marked out for subjection, others for rule.

And there are many kinds both of rulers and subjects (and that rule is the better which is exercised over better subjects – for example, to rule over men is better than to rule over wild beasts; for the work is better which is executed by better workmen, and where one man rules and another is ruled, they may be said to have a work); for in all things which form a composite whole and which are made up of parts, whether continuous or discrete, a distinction between the ruling and the subject element comes to light. Such a duality exists in living creatures, but not in them only; it

---

[1] Hephaestus was the Greek God of fire and the arts of the smith (his tripods, fitted with wheels, are described in Homer, *Iliad*, XVIII, 367); Daedalus, the legendary Athenian craftsman, made statues said to be able to move themselves.

originates in the constitution of the universe; even in things which have no life there is a ruling principle, as in a musical mode. But we are wandering from the subject. We will therefore restrict ourselves to the living creature, which, in the first place, consists of soul and body: and of these two, the one is by nature the ruler, and the other the subject. But then we must look for the intentions of nature in things which retain their nature, and not in things which are corrupted. And therefore we must study the man who is in the most perfect state both of body and soul, for in him we see the true relation of the two; although in bad or corrupted natures the body will often appear to rule over the soul, because they are in an evil and unnatural condition.

At all events we may firstly observe in living creatures both a despotical and a constitutional rule; for the soul rules the body with a despotical rule, whereas the intellect rules the appetites with a constitutional and royal rule. And it is clear that the rule of the soul over the body, and of the mind and the rational element over the passionate, is natural and expedient: whereas the equality of the two or the rule of the inferior is always hurtful. The same holds good of animals in relation to men; for tame animals have a better nature than wild, and all tame animals are better off when they are ruled by man; for then they are preserved. Again, the male is by nature superior, and the female inferior; and the one rules, and the other is ruled; this principle, of necessity, extends to all mankind. Where then there is such a difference as that between soul and body, or between men and animals (as in the case of those whose business is to use their body, and who can do nothing better), the lower sort are by nature slaves, and it is better for them as for all inferiors that they should be under the rule of a master. For he who can be, and therefore is, another's, and he who participates in rational principle enough to apprehend, but not to have, such a principle, is a slave by nature. Whereas the lower animals cannot even apprehend a principle; they obey their instincts. And indeed the use made of slaves and of tame animals is not very different; for both with their bodies minister to the needs of life. Nature would like to distinguish between the bodies of freemen and slaves, making the one strong for servile labour, the other upright, and although useless for such services, useful for political life in the arts both of war and peace. But the opposite often happens – that some have the souls and others have the bodies of freemen. And doubtless if men differed from one another in the mere forms of their bodies as much as the statues of the Gods do from men, all would acknowledge that the inferior class should be slaves of the superior. And if this is true of the body, how much more just that a similar distinction should exist in the soul? But the beauty of the body is seen, whereas the beauty of the soul is not seen. It is clear, then, that some men are by nature free, and others slaves, and that for these latter slavery is both expedient and right.

But that those who take the opposite view have in a certain way right on their side, may be easily seen. For the words 'slavery' and 'slave' are used in two senses. There is a slave or slavery by law as well as by nature. The law of which I speak is a sort of convention – the law by which whatever is taken in war is supposed to belong to the victors. But this right many jurists impeach, as they would an orator who brought forward an unconstitutional measure: they detest the notion that, because one man has the power of doing violence and is superior in brute strength, another shall be his slave and subject. Even among philosophers there is a difference of opinion. The origin of the dispute, and what makes the views invade each other's territory, is as follows: in some sense virtue, when furnished with means, has actually the greatest power of exercising force: and as superior power is only found where there is superior excellence of some kind, power seems to imply virtue, and the dispute to be simply one about justice (for it is due to one party identifying justice with goodwill, while the other identifies it with the mere rule of the stronger). If these views are thus set out separately, the other views have no force or plausibility against the view that the superior in virtue ought to rule, or be master. Others, clinging, as they think, simply to a principle of justice (for law and custom are a sort of justice), assume that slavery in accordance with the custom of war is justified by law, but at the same moment they deny this. For what if the cause of the war be unjust? And again, no one would ever say that he is a slave who is unworthy to be a slave. Were this the case, men of the highest rank would be slaves and the children of slaves if they or their parents chance to have been taken captive and sold. Wherefore Hellenes do not like to call Hellenes slaves, but confine the term to barbarians. Yet in using this language, they really mean the natural slave of whom we spoke at first; for it must be admitted that some are slaves everywhere, others nowhere. The same principle applies to nobility. Hellenes regard themselves as noble everywhere, and not only in their own country, but they deem the barbarians noble only when at home, thereby implying that there are two sorts of nobility and freedom, the one absolute, the other relative. The Helen of Theodectes says: 'Who would presume to call me servant who am among both sides sprung from the stem of the Gods?' What does this mean but that they distinguish freedom and slavery, noble and humble birth, by the two principles of good and evil? They think that as men and animals beget men and animals, so from good men a good man springs. But this is what nature, though she may intend it, cannot always accomplish.

We see then that there is some foundation for this difference of opinion, and that all are not either slaves by nature or free by nature, and also that there is in some cases a marked distinction between the two classes, rendering it expedient and right for the one to be slaves and the others to be masters: the one practising obedience, the others exercising the authority and lordship which nature intended them to have. The abuse of this authority is injurious to both; for the interests of part and whole of body and soul, are the same, and the slave is a part of the master, a living but separated part of his bodily frame. Hence, where the relation of master and slave between them is natural they are friends and have a common interest, but where it rests merely on law and force the reverse is true.

The previous remarks are quite enough to show that the rule of a master is not a constitutional rule, and that all the different kinds of rule are not, as some affirm, the same as each other. For there is one rule exercised over subjects who are by nature free, another over subjects who are by nature slaves. The rule of a household is a monarchy, for every house is under one head: whereas constitutional rule is a government of freedom and equals. The master is not called a master because he has science, but because he is of a certain character, and the same remark applies to the slave and the freeman. Still there may be a science for the master and a science for the slave. The science of the slave would be such as the man of Syracuse taught, who made money by instructing slaves in their ordinary duties. And such a knowledge may be carried further, so as to include cookery and similar menial arts. For some duties are of the more necessary, others of the more honourable sort; as the proverb says, 'slave before slave, master before master'. But all such branches of knowledge are servile. There is likewise a science of the master, which teaches the use of slaves; for the master as such is concerned, not with the acquisition, but with the use of them. Yet this so-called science is not anything great or wonderful; for the master need only know how to order that which the slave must know how to execute. Hence those who are in a position which places them above toil have stewards who attend to their households while they occupy themselves with philosophy or with politics. But the art of acquiring slaves, I mean of justly acquiring them, differs both from the art of the master and the art of the slave being a species of hunting or war.

2   War and Justice: Thomas Aquinas, *Summa Theologiae**

The connection which Aristotle makes in the preceding extract between the institution of war and that of slavery is perhaps not surprising, given that the making of war and the taking of slaves both go back to the earliest recorded history of the human race. But while all forms of slavery are now universally condemned, the ethical status of warfare is less clear. The extreme pacifist position is that engaging in warfare is never ethically justifiable. Others take a more pragmatic stance, believing that war is often inevitable, and that its conduct must be determined by considerations of pure expediency and self-interest. But there is an ancient tradition which considers that the conduct of warfare, or at least certain aspects of it, can be brought within the ambit of morality, and that certain kinds of war (for example those fought in self-defence) can be morally justified. The cluster of doctrines emerging from this tradition has come to be known as the 'just war theory', and our second extract comes from its chief originator, Thomas Aquinas.

Aquinas lays down three conditions for a war to be just. First, it must be duly 'authorized by the ruler'; this corresponds to the modern notion that hostilities must be preceded by a 'declaration of war' by the government. Second, and crucially, it must be undertaken for a 'just cause': there must be wrongdoing on the part of the other side. Finally, the intention of those making war must be good. The last condition is of great importance, since it focuses attention on the moral character of the acts performed by the belligerents. If one's aim in fighting is a morally worthy one (for example protecting people from unjust aggression), and one's acts are directed towards that end, then they are justified. But if (as often happens once violence is let loose) savagery and cruelty take over, so that the intention is to gratify blood-lust, or exact a cruel revenge on the enemy, then the justification collapses. It is important to note (as Aquinas himself does) that this third requirement concerning intention operates in addition to the second one: even if the initial cause of the war was a just one, this does not absolve those fighting it from ensuring that whatever they go on to do in the war is done with a morally worthy intention.

In the second section excerpted below, Aquinas discusses the question of self-defence, and introduces a controversial idea known as the doctrine of 'double effect'. Suppose you fire at an assailant who is trying to kill you. According to the doctrine, the act may be regarded as having two effects, one (protecting your own life) directly intended, the other (killing the aggressor) foreseen, but not intended as such. The claim that the death is not directly intended may seem sophistical in cases where it is an inevitable consequence of your action (e.g. where you can only stop your

---

* Thomas Aquinas, *Summa Theologiae* [1266–73], Part II, 2, qu. 40, art. 1 and qu. 64, art. 7. Translation by John Cottingham.

attacker by firing an artillery shell straight at him); nevertheless, Aquinas's account draws attention to what has to be shown about the act – that you are doing it precisely in order to save your life – in order for it to be justified. Aquinas goes on to mention a connected proviso, that the force used must not exceed due limits; this raises an issue of enormous importance with the advent of weapons of mass destruction, where innocent civilians are killed as a result of a bombing raid intended (for example) to destroy enemy material, or to bring the war to an early end.

 ### Is making war always a sin?

In answer I declare that there are three requirements for a war to be just. First, the *authority* of the ruler by whose command the war is to be waged. For it is not appropriate for a private person to declare war, since he is able to pursue his rights by recourse to the judgement of someone of higher rank. Similarly, it is not appropriate for a private person to call the people to arms, as has to be done in wars. Looking after the state is something entrusted to rulers, and hence it belongs to them to watch over the welfare of the city or kingdom or province which is in their charge. It is within their powers to defend the state by using the sword of retribution against internal disturbers of the peace, as they do when they punish criminals, as St Paul says in his Epistle to the Romans, 13: 4, 'He beareth not the sword in vain. For he is God's minister, an avenger to execute wrath upon him that doeth evil.' And in the same way they may defend the state against external enemies by using the sword of war; this is why rulers are told in Psalm 71, 'Rescue the poor, and deliver the needy from the hand of the sinner.' And Augustine says in the *Contra Faustum* (Book 23, ch. 73): 'The natural order of mortals is accommodated to peace, and hence it requires that the authority and decision to undertake a war be in the power of the rulers.'

The second requirement is a *just cause*. Those who are attacked must deserve to be attacked in virtue of some culpability. Hence Augustine says in Book 83 (*super Josue*, qu. 10): 'Wars are generally defined as *just* if they avenge wrongdoing, as when a nation or a state is to be punished either for failing to make amends for some wicked act which its subjects have committed, or for failing to restore something that has been unjustly seized.'

The third requirement is that the *intention* of those making war must be good. This means that the intention must be to promote some good or avoid some evil. Thus Augustine says in his book *De verbis Domini*: 'Among true followers of God, even wars are peaceful: they are waged not in lust or cruelty, but out of a desire for peace, and with the purpose of restraining the wicked and helping the good.' It can happen that even if the authority of those who declare war is legitimate, and the cause is a just one, the war is still made impermissible because of the evil intention. For Augustine says in *Contra Faustum*, chapter 74: 'the desire to hurt, the cruel wish for revenge, anger that is harsh and implacable, savagery in conquest, lust for domination, and anything of this kind, are all justly condemned in war'.

Is it permissible to kill a human being in self-defence?

One and the same act can have two effects, only one of which is intended, while the other is outside the intention. Now moral acts are categorized in accordance with what is intended, not what happens outside the intention, since this is incidental ... The act of defending oneself may have two effects – saving one's own life and killing the aggressor. This kind of act, since the intention is to save one's own life, is not impermissible, since it is natural for everything to maintain itself in existence, as far as it can.

Yet even if it proceeds from a good intention, an act can become impermissible if it is out of proportion to the end at which it aims. Hence it is impermissible to use more than necessary force to defend one's own life. But if one uses moderation in resisting violence, this is permissible self-defence, for according to the papal decrees 'It is lawful to resist force with force, provided it is an act of innocent self-defence and does not exceed due limits.' Now it is not necessary for salvation that a person should forbear to perform an act of moderate self-defence so as to avoid killing another person, since we are obliged to take more care of our own lives than those of others. But ... it is not allowed for someone to intend to kill another when acting in self-defence, except where this is a justified act of self-defence done in virtue of public authority by reference to the public good. This latter type of case includes the case of a soldier fighting the enemy or a law-enforcement officer struggling with robbers; even in these cases, however, the agents would be committing a sin if they were motivated by private animosity.

3   Taking One's Own Life: David Hume, *On Suicide**

While the killing of one human being by another (see previous extract) is evidently something problematic from the moral point of view, one might initially suppose that the ethical status of someone's deciding to end their own life was more straightforward: if my life is 'my own', is it not simply up to me to decide when to end it? In fact, however, the issue of suicide has always called forth widely differing responses from moral philosophers. Some ancient Greek thinkers considered suicide to be rarely, if ever, justified; but by the time of the Roman empire there was widespread acceptance of the Stoic viewpoint which regarded suicide, in certain circumstances, as a defensible and even noble act. The prevailing Christian attitude, however, at

any rate from the time of Aquinas onwards, was strongly condemnatory of suicide.

The following extract, from a celebrated essay by the eighteenth-century philosopher David Hume, begins by extolling the value of philosophy as an antidote to 'superstition and false religion'. A leading thinker of the so-called 'Enlightenment', Hume aimed to provide a non-religious basis for deciding moral issues.[1] – The early part of his essay is concerned to undermine some traditional religious arguments against suicide. These traditional arguments (stemming from Aquinas) had laid great stress on suicide's being 'unnatural' – a violation of the divinely implanted instinct for the preservation of life. Hume replies that our situation in the

---

* D. Hume, 'On Suicide'; typeset in 1757, but withdrawn; published posthumously in *Essays Moral, Political and Literary* [1777]; abridged, with modified spelling and punctuation. The complete text is reprinted in *Essays Moral, Political and Literary by David Hume*, ed. T. H. Green and T. H. Grose (London: Longmans Green, 1875), vol. II, pp. 406ff.

[1] Hume's general attitude to theism was strongly negative, though he often expressed himself in a cautious and even seemingly ambivalent way. Cf. Part VI, extracts 6 and 7.

natural world is such that each person has the power freely to dispose of his own life: 'may he not lawfully employ that power with which nature has endowed him?' If anything which disturbs the 'natural order' is to be condemned, then it would presumably be wrong to 'build houses, cultivate the ground, or sail upon the ocean'. Turning to non-religious arguments, Hume then suggests that suicide cannot be a violation of any duty I owe to my fellow men: 'I am not obliged to do a small good to society at the expense of a real harm to myself: why then should I prolong a miserable existence, because of some frivolous advantage which the public may perhaps receive from me?' Finally, as far as

duty to self is concerned, 'both prudence and courage should engage us to rid ourselves at once of existence when it becomes a burden'.

Hume's writing here, as often, is an engaging mixture of careful philosophical arguments and rhetorical flourishes. But many of the issues he raises remain important, particularly in the light of renewed current debate on the moral defensibility or otherwise of euthanasia and 'assisted suicide' for the terminally ill (compare extract 11, below). If Hume is correct, then there are situations where the voluntary decision to end life is justified by considerations both of individual autonomy and also of utility (the overall balance of happiness for all concerned).

 One considerable advantage that arises from Philosophy consists in the sovereign antidote which it affords to superstition and false religion...It will here be superfluous to magnify the merits of Philosophy by displaying the pernicious tendency of that vice of which it cures the human mind. The superstitious man, says Cicero, is miserable in every scene, in every incident of life. Even sleep itself, which banishes all other cares of unhappy mortals, affords to him matter of new terror, while he examines his dreams, and finds in those visions of the night prognostications of future calamities. I may add, that though death alone can put a full period to his misery, he dares not fly to this refuge, but still prolongs a miserable existence, from a vain fear lest he offend his maker, by using the power with which that beneficent being has endowed him. The presents of God and Nature are ravished from us by this cruel enemy; and notwithstanding that one step would remove us from the regions of pain and sorrow, her menaces still chain us down to a hated being, which she herself chiefly contributes to render miserable.

It is observed by such as have been reduced by the calamities of life to the necessity of employing this fatal remedy, that if the unseasonable care of their friends deprive them of that species of death which they proposed to themselves, they seldom venture upon any other, or can summon up so much resolution a second time, as to execute their purpose. So great is our horror of death, that when it presents itself under any form besides that to which a man has endeavoured to reconcile his imagination, it acquires new terrors, and overcomes his feeble courage; but when the menaces of superstition are joined to this natural timidity, no wonder it quite deprives men of all power over their lives, since even many pleasures and enjoyments, to which we are carried by a strong propensity, are torn from us by this inhuman tyrant. Let us here endeavour to restore men to their native liberty, by examining all the common arguments against suicide, and showing that that action may be free from every imputation of guilt or blame, according to the sentiments of all the ancient philosophers.

If suicide be criminal, it must be a transgression of our duty either to God, our neighbour, or ourselves.

To prove that suicide is no transgression of our duty to God, the following considerations may perhaps suffice...The providence of the deity appears not

immediately in any operation, but governs every thing by those general and immutable laws which have been established from the beginning of time. All events, in one
sense, may be pronounced the action of the almighty; they all proceed from those
powers with which he has endowed his creatures. A house which falls by its own
weight is not brought to ruin by his providence, more than one destroyed by the
hands of men; nor are the human faculties less his workmanship than the laws of
motion and gravitation. When the passions play, when the judgement dictates, when
the limbs obey – this is all the operation of God; and upon these animate principles, as
well as upon the inanimate, has he established the government of the universe.

Every event is alike important in the eyes of that infinite Being, who takes in at one
glance the most distant regions of space, and remotest periods of time. There is no
event, however important to us, which he has exempted from the general laws that
govern the universe, or which he has peculiarly reserved for his own immediate action
and operation. The revolution of states and empires depends upon the smallest
caprice or passion of single men; and the lives of men are shortened or extended by
the smallest accident of air or diet, sunshine or tempest. Nature still continues her
progress and operation; and if general laws be ever broke by particular volitions of the
deity, it is after a manner which entirely escapes human observation.[1] As, on the one
hand, the elements and other inanimate parts of the creation carry on their action
without regard to the particular interest and situation of men; so men are entrusted to
their own judgement and discretion in the various shocks of matter, and may employ
every faculty with which they are endowed, in order to provide for their ease,
happiness or preservation.

What is the meaning then of that principle, that a man, who, tired of life, and
hunted by pain and misery, bravely overcomes all the natural terrors of death,
and makes his escape from this cruel scene; that such a man, I say, has incurred the
indignation of his creator, by encroaching on the office of divine providence, and
disturbing the order of the universe? Shall we assert that the Almighty has reserved to
himself, in any peculiar manner, the disposal of the lives of men, and has not
submitted that event, in common with others, to the general laws by which the
universe is governed? This is plainly false: the lives of men depend upon the same
laws as the lives of all other animals; and these are subjected to the general laws of
matter and motion. The fall off a tower, or the infusion of a poison, will destroy a man
equally with the meanest creature; an inundation sweeps away every thing without
distinction that comes within the reach of its fury. Since therefore the lives of men are
for ever dependent on the general laws of matter and motion, is a man's disposing of
his life criminal, because in every case it is criminal to encroach upon these laws, or
disturb their operation? But this seems absurd: all animals are entrusted to their own
prudence and skill for their conduct in the world; and have full authority, as far as
their power extends, to alter all the operations of nature. Without the exercise of this
authority, they could not subsist a moment; every action, every motion of a man,
innovates on the order of some parts of matter, and diverts from their ordinary course
the general laws of motion. Putting together therefore these conclusions, we find that
human life depends upon the general laws of matter and motion, and that it is
no encroachment on the office of providence to disturb or alter these general laws.

---

[1] For Hume's view of miracles, see Part VI, extract 7, above.

Has not every one of consequence the free disposal of his own life? And may he not lawfully employ that power with which nature has endowed him?

In order to destroy the evidence of this conclusion, we must show a reason why this particular case is excepted. Is it because human life is of such great importance, that it is a presumption for human prudence to dispose of it? But the life of a man is of no greater importance to the universe than that of an oyster; and were it of ever so great importance, the order of human nature has actually submitted it to human prudence, and reduced us to a necessity, in every incident, of determining concerning it.

Were the disposal of human life so much reserved as the peculiar province of the Almighty that it were an encroachment on his right for men to dispose of their own lives, it would be equally criminal to act for the preservation of life as for its destruction. If I turn aside a stone which is falling upon my head, I disturb the course of nature; and I invade the peculiar province of the Almighty, by lengthening out my life beyond the period which, by the general laws of matter and motion, he has assigned it.

A hair, a fly, an insect, is able to destroy this mighty being whose life is of such importance. Is it an absurdity to suppose that human prudence may lawfully dispose of what depends on such insignificant causes?

It would be no crime in me to divert the Nile or Danube from its course, were I able to effect such purposes. Where then is the crime of turning a few ounces of blood from their natural channels!

Do you imagine that I repine at Providence, or curse my creation, because I go out of life, and put a period to a being which, were it to continue, would render me miserable? Far be such sentiments from me. I am only convinced of a matter of fact which you yourself acknowledge possible, that human life may be unhappy; and that my existence, if further prolonged, would become ineligible: but I thank providence, both for the good which I have already enjoyed, and for the power with which I am endowed of escaping the ills that threaten me. To you it belongs to repine at providence, who foolishly imagine that you have no such power; and who must still prolong a hated life, though loaded with pain and sickness, with shame and poverty.

Do not you teach that when any ill befalls me, though by the malice of my enemies, I ought to be resigned to providence; and that the actions of men are the operations of the Almighty, as much as the actions of inanimate beings? When I fall upon my own sword, therefore, I receive my death equally from the hands of the deity as if it had proceeded from a lion, a precipice, or a fever.

The submission which you require to providence, in every calamity that befalls me, excludes not human skill and industry, if possibly by their means I can avoid or escape the calamity. And why may I not employ one remedy as well as another?

If my life be not my own, it were criminal for me to put it in danger, as well as to dispose of it; nor could one man deserve the appellation of *hero*, whom glory or friendship transports into the greatest dangers; and another merit the reproach of *wretch* or *miscreant*, who puts a period to his life from the same or like motives.

There is no being which possesses any power or faculty that it receives not from its creator; nor is there any one, which, by ever so irregular an action, can encroach upon the plan of his providence, or disorder the universe. Its operations are his works equally with that chain of events which it invades; and whichever principle prevails, we may for that very reason conclude it to be most favoured by him. Be it animate or inanimate; rational or irrational, it is all the same case: its power is still derived from the supreme creator, and is alike comprehended in the order of his providence. When the horror of pain prevails over the love of life; when a voluntary action anticipates the effects of blind causes; it is only in consequence of those powers and principles which he has implanted in his creatures. Divine providence is still inviolate, and placed far beyond the reach of human injuries.

It is impious, says the old Roman superstition, to divert rivers from their course, or invade the prerogatives of nature. It is impious, says the French superstition, to inoculate for the smallpox, or usurp the business of providence by voluntarily producing distempers and maladies. It is impious, says the modern European super-stition, to put a period to our own life, and thereby rebel against our creator: and why not impious, say I, to build houses, cultivate the ground, or sail upon the ocean? In all these actions we employ our powers of mind and body to produce some innovation in the course of nature; and in none of them do we any more. They are all of them therefore equally innocent, or equally criminal.

But you are placed by providence, like a sentinel, in a particular station; and when you desert it without being recalled, you are equally guilty of rebellion against your Almighty Sovereign, and have incurred his displeasure. I ask, Why do you conclude that Provi-dence has placed me in this station? For my part, I find that I owe my birth to a long chain of causes, of which many depended upon voluntary actions of men. *But Providence guided all these causes, and nothing happens in the universe without its consent and cooperation.* If so, then neither does my death, however voluntary, happen without its consent; and whenever pain or sorrow so far overcome my patience as to make me tired of life, I may conclude that I am recalled from my station in the clearest and most express terms.

It is providence surely that has placed me at this present moment in this chamber; but may I not leave it when I think proper, without being liable to the imputation of having deserted my post or station? When I shall be dead, the principles of which I am composed will still perform their part in the universe, and will be equally useful in the grand fabric, as when they composed this individual creature. The difference to the whole will be no greater than betwixt my being in a chamber and in the open air. The one change is of more importance to me than the other; but not more so to the universe.

It is a kind of blasphemy to imagine that any created being can disturb the order of the world, or invade the business of providence! It supposes, that that being possesses powers and faculties which it received not from its creator, and which are not subordinate to his government and authority. A man may disturb society, no doubt, and thereby incur the displeasure of the Almighty: but the government of the world is placed far beyond his reach and violence. And how does it appear that the Almighty is displeased with those actions that disturb society? By the principles which he has implanted in human nature, and which inspire us with a sentiment of remorse if we ourselves have been guilty of such actions, and with that of blame and disapprobation, if we ever observe them in others. Let us now examine, according to the method proposed, whether Suicide be of this kind of actions, and be a breach of our duty to our *neighbour* and to society.

A man who retires from life does no harm to society: he only ceases to do good; which, if it is an injury, is of the lowest kind.

All our obligations to do good to society seem to imply something reciprocal. I receive the benefits of society, and therefore ought to promote its interests; but when I withdraw myself altogether from society, can I be bound any longer?

But allowing that our obligations to do good were perpetual, they have certainly some bounds; I am not obliged to do a small good to society at the expense of a real harm to myself: why then should I prolong a miserable existence, because of some frivolous advantage which the public may perhaps receive from me? If upon account of age and infirmities, I may lawfully resign any office, and employ my time altogether in fencing against these calamities, and alleviating as much as possible the miseries of my future life, why may I not cut short these miseries at once by an action which is no more prejudicial to society?

But suppose that it is no longer in my power to promote the interest of the public; suppose that I am a burden to it; suppose that my life hinders some person from being much more useful to the public: in such cases, my resignation of life must not only be innocent, but laudable. And most people who lie under any temptation to abandon existence are in some such situation; those who have health, or power, or authority, have commonly better reason to be in humour with the world.

A man is engaged in a conspiracy for the public interest; is seized upon suspicion; is threatened with the rack; and knows from his own weakness that the secret will be extorted from him: could such a one consult the public interest better than by putting a quick period to a miserable life? This was the case of the famous and brave Strozzi of Florence.

Again, suppose a malefactor is justly condemned to a shameful death; can any reason be imagined why he may not anticipate his punishment, and save himself all the anguish of thinking on its dreadful approaches? He invades the business of Providence no more than the magistrate did who ordered his execution; and his voluntary death is equally advantageous to society, by ridding it of a pernicious member.

That suicide may often be consistent with interest and with our duty to *ourselves*, no one can question, who allows that age, sickness or misfortune, may render life a burden and make it worse even than annihilation. I believe that no man ever threw away life while it was worth keeping. For such is our natural horror of death, that small motives will never be able to reconcile us to it; and though perhaps the situation of a man's health or fortune did not seem to require this remedy, we may at least be assured, that anyone who, without apparent reason, has had recourse to it, was cursed with such an incurable depravity or gloominess of temper as must poison all enjoyment, and render him equally miserable as if he had been loaded with the most grievous misfortune.

If suicide be supposed a crime, it is only cowardice can impel us to it. If it be no crime, both prudence and courage should engage us to rid ourselves at once of existence when it becomes a burden. It is the only way that we can then be useful to society, by setting an example, which, if imitated, would preserve to every one his chance for happiness in life, and would effectually free him from all danger or misery.

4   Gender, Liberty and Equality: Mary Wollstonecraft, *A Vindication of the Rights of Women**

The institution of slavery, defended by Aristotle in our first extract, was still widespread in the eighteenth century, though increasingly under attack as inhuman and degrading. But towards the end of that century, Mary Wollstonecraft, aptly regarded as a herald of what was to become the feminist movement, mounted a courageous attack on another kind of subordination – that created by the prevailing social ethos which denied to women basic educational and other rights needed for equality of status. In the following extract Wollstonecraft speaks in uncompromising terms of the 'tyranny of men', and calls for nothing less than a 'revolution' in social attitudes. Some of her arguments are prudently deferential to masculine interests; thus, she appears to plead that women be allowed to be educated not so much for their own sakes but in order to become fitter and more elevated companions for their husbands. But she goes on to warn of the limitations of merely educational measures, and to raise more fundamental questions about what we now call 'sexual politics'. Attitudes and habits of feeling which encourage women to appeal to the protective instinct of men, by 'feigning a sickly delicacy', she condemns as ultimately insulting: 'fondness', she acidly observes, 'is a poor substitute for friendship'. And she voices the 'wild wish' for a society

to evolve in which 'the distinctions of sex are confounded' – that is to say, in which they are mixed up, or in other words ignored. Prefigured here is the ideal, now widely accepted in aspiration, if not always in practice, of a society which treats its citizens on their individual merits, and is 'blind' to their gender (as indeed to their class, race, religion and all similar features unfairly used in the past as a basis for discrimination).

Towards the end of our extract, Wollstonecraft raises even subtler and more profound issues about sexual psychology and its social determinants. She comments acutely on the separation of sexuality from love (as much a feature of today's society as it was in hers, as the success of our modern mass pornography industry clearly shows); the 'libertine', who pursues women purely as sexual objects, generally turns out to have the 'meanest' opinion of them as people. As long as our sexuality is cultivated in a way which encourages 'selfish gratification', which men 'learn to separate from esteem and affection', there can be no true friendship between the sexes. Many complex ethical issues arise here and elsewhere in Wollstonecraft's groundbreaking essay, some of which have still to be resolved in current philosophical debates on the nature and direction of feminist ethics.

Contending for the rights of woman, my main argument is built on this simple principle, that if she be not prepared by education to become the companion of man, she will stop the progress of knowledge and virtue; for truth must be common to all, or it will be inefficacious with respect to its influence on general practice. And how can woman be expected to cooperate unless she know why she ought to be virtuous? Unless freedom strengthen her reason till she comprehend her duty, and see in what manner it is connected with her real good? If children are to be educated to understand the true principle of patriotism, their mother must be a patriot; and the love of mankind, from which an orderly train of virtues spring, can only be produced

---

* M. Wollstonecraft, *A Vindication of the Rights of Women* [1792], extracts from Introduction, and chs 2, 4 and 13, section vi; with minor changes in spelling and punctuation.

by considering the moral and civil interest of mankind; but the education and situation of woman, at present, shuts her out from such investigations...

To account for and excuse the tyranny of man, many ingenious arguments have been brought forward to prove that the two sexes, in the acquirement of virtue, ought to aim at attaining a very different character; or, to speak explicitly, women are not allowed to have sufficient strength of mind to acquire what really deserves the name of virtue. Yet it should seem, allowing them to have souls, that there is but one way appointed by Providence to lead mankind to either virtue or happiness.

If then women are not a swarm of ephemeron triflers, why should they be kept in ignorance under the specious name of innocence? Men complain, and with reason, of the follies and caprices of our sex, when they do not keenly satirize our headstrong passions and grovelling vices. Behold, I should answer, the natural effect of ignorance! The mind will ever be unstable that has only prejudices to rest on, and the current will run with destructive fury when there are no barriers to break its force. Women are told from their infancy, and taught by the example of their mothers, that a little knowledge of human weakness, justly termed cunning, softness of temper, *outward* obedience, and a scrupulous attention to a puerile kind of propriety, will obtain for them the protection of man; and should they be beautiful, everything else is needless, for, at least, twenty years of their lives.

Thus Milton describes our first frail mother; though when he tells us that women are formed for softness and sweet attractive grace,[1] I cannot comprehend his meaning, unless, in the true Mahometan strain, he meant to deprive us of our souls, and insinuate that we were beings only designed by sweet attractive grace, and docile blind obedience, to gratify the senses of man when he can no longer soar on the wings of contemplation.

How grossly do they insult us who thus advise us only to render ourselves gentle, domestic brutes! For instance, the winning softness so warmly, and frequently, recommended, that governs by obeying. What childish expression, and how insignificant is the being – can it be an immortal one? – who will condescend to govern by such sinister methods. Certainly, says Lord Bacon, 'man is of kin to the beasts by his body; and if he be not of kin to God by his spirit, he is a base and ignoble creature!'[2] Men indeed appear to me to act in a very unphilosophical manner when they try to secure the good conduct of women by attempting to keep them always in a state of childhood. Rousseau was more consistent when he wished to stop the progress of reason in both sexes, for if men eat of the tree of knowledge, women will come in for a taste; but from the imperfect cultivation which their understanding now receives, they only attain a knowledge of evil.

Children, I grant, should be innocent; but when the epithet is applied to men, or women, it is but a civil term for weakness. For if it be allowed that women were destined by Providence to acquire human virtues, and, by the exercise of their understandings, that stability of character which is the firmest ground to rest our future hopes upon, they must be permitted to turn to the fountain of light, and not

---

[1] From John Milton's description of Adam and Eve: 'For contemplation he and valour formed / For softness she and sweet attractive grace, / He for God only, she for God in him' (*Paradise Lost* [1667], IV, 279ff.).

[2] From Francis Bacon, 'Of Atheism', in *Essays or Counsels Civil and Moral* [1625].

forced to shape their course by the twinkling of a mere satellite. Milton, I grant, was of a very different opinion; for he only bends to the indefeasible right of beauty, though it would be difficult to render two passages which I now mean to contrast, consistent. But into similar inconsistencies are great men often led by their senses.

> To whom thus Eve, with *perfect beauty* adornd.
> My Author and Disposer, what thou bidst
> *Unargu'd* I obey; so God ordains,
> God is *thy Law, thou mine*: to know no more
> Is Woman's *happiest* knowledge and her *praise*.[1]

These are exactly the arguments that I have used to children; but I have added, your reason is now gaining strength, and, till it arrives at some degree of maturity, you must look up to me for advice – then you ought to *think*, and only rely on God.

Yet in the following lines Milton seems to coincide with me, when he makes Adam thus expostulate with his Maker:

> Hast thou not made me here thy substitute,
> And these inferior far beneath me set?
> Among *unequals* what society
> Can sort, what harmony or true delight?
> Which must be mutual, in proportion due
> Giv'n and receiv'd; but in *disparity*
> The one intense, the other still remiss,
> Cannot well suit with either, but soon prove
> Tedious alike: of *fellowship* I speak
> Such as I see, fit to participate
> All rational delight...[2]

In treating, therefore, of the manners of women, let us, disregarding sensual arguments, trace what we should endeavour to make them in order to cooperate, if the expression be not too bold, with the supreme Being.

By individual education, I mean, for the sense of the word is not precisely defined, such an attention to the child as will slowly sharpen the senses, form the temper, regulate the passions as they begin to ferment, and set the understanding to work before the body arrives at maturity; so that the man may only have to proceed, not to begin, the important task of learning to think and reason.

To prevent any misconstruction, I must add that I do not believe that a private education can work the wonders which some sanguine writers have attributed to it. Men and women must be educated, in a great degree, by the opinions and manners of the society they live in. In every age there has been a stream of popular opinion that has carried all before it, and given a family character, as it were, to the century. It may then fairly be inferred that, till society be differently constituted, much cannot be expected from education...

---

[1] *Paradise Lost*, IV, 634–8; italics are Wollstonecraft's.
[2] *Paradise Lost*, VIII, 389–91; italics are Wollstonecraft's.

Women ought to endeavour to purify their heart; but can they do so when their uncultivated understanding makes them entirely dependent on their senses for employment and amusement, when no noble pursuit sets them above the little vanities of the day, or enables them to curb the wild emotions that agitate a reed over which every passing breeze has power? To gain the affections of a virtuous man, is affectation necessary? Nature has given woman a weaker frame than man; but to ensure her husband's affections, must a wife, who by the exercise of her mind and body whilst she was discharging the duties of a daughter, wife and mother, has allowed her constitution to retain its natural strength, and her nerves a healthy tone – is she, I say, to condescend to use art and feign a sickly delicacy in order to secure her husband's affection? Weakness may excite tenderness, and gratify the arrogant pride of man; but the lordly caresses of a protector will not gratify a noble mind that pants for, and deserves to be respected. Fondness is a poor substitute for friendship...

I lament that women are systematically degraded by receiving the trivial attentions which men think it manly to pay to the sex, when in fact they are insultingly supporting their own superiority. It is not condescension to bow to an inferior. So ludicrous, in fact, do these ceremonies appear to me that I scarcely am able to govern my muscles when I see a man start with eager and serious solicitude to lift a handkerchief, or shut a door, when the *lady* could have done it herself, had she only moved a pace or two.

A wild wish has just flown from my heart to my head, and I will not stifle it though it may excite a horse-laugh. I do earnestly wish to see the distinction of sex confounded in society, unless where love animates the behaviour. For this distinction is, I am firmly persuaded, the foundation of the weakness of character ascribed to women; is the cause why the understanding is neglected, whilst accomplishments are acquired with sedulous care; and the same cause accounts for their preferring the graceful before the heroic virtues...

Moralists have unanimously agreed that unless virtue be nursed by liberty, it will never attain due strength – and what they say of man I extend to mankind, insisting that in all cases morals must be fixed on immutable principles; and that the being cannot be termed rational or virtuous who obeys any authority but that of reason.

To render women truly useful members of society, I argue that they should be led, by having their understandings cultivated on a large scale, to acquire a rational affection for their country, founded on knowledge, because it is obvious that we are little interested in what we do not understand. And to render this general knowledge of due importance, I have endeavoured to show that private duties are never properly fulfilled unless the understanding enlarges the heart; and the public virtue is only an aggregate of the private. But the distinctions established in society undermine both, by beating out the solid gold of virtue, till it becomes only the tinsel-covering of vice. For whilst wealth renders a man more respectable than virtue, wealth will be sought before virtue; and whilst women's persons are caressed, when a childish simper shows an absence of mind, the mind will lie fallow. Yet true voluptuousness must proceed from the mind – for what can equal the sensations produced by mutual affection, supported by mutual respect? What are the cold or feverish caresses of appetite but sin embracing death, compared with the modes overflowing of a pure heart and exalted imagination? Yes, let me tell the libertine of fancy, when he despises understanding in woman, that the mind, which he disregards, gives life to the enthusiastic affection from which rapture, short-lived as it is, alone can flow! And that, without virtue, a sexual attachment must expire, like a tallow candle in the socket, creating intolerable disgust. To prove this, I need only observe that men who have wasted a great part of their lives with women, and with whom they have sought for pleasure with eager thirst, entertain the meanest opinion of the sex. Virtue, true refiner of joy! If foolish men were to fright thee from earth, in order to give loose to all their appetites without a check, some sensual wight of taste would scale the heavens to invite thee back, to give a zest to pleasure!

That women at present are by ignorance rendered foolish or vicious is, I think, not to be disputed; and that the most salutary effects tending to improve mankind might be expected from a REVOLUTION in female manners, appears, at least with a face of probability, to rise out of the observation. For as marriage has been termed the parent of those endearing charities which draw man from the brutal herd, the corrupting intercourse that wealth, idleness and folly produce between the sexes is more universally injurious to morality than all the other vices of mankind collectively considered. To adulterous lust the most sacred duties are sacrificed, because before marriage men, by a promiscuous intimacy with women, learned to consider love as a selfish gratification – learned to separate it not only from esteem, but from the affection merely built on habit, which mixes a little humanity with it. Justice and friendship are also set at defiance, and that purity of taste is vitiated which would naturally lead a man to relish an artless display of affection rather than affected airs. But that noble simplicity of affection, which dares to appear unadorned, has few attractions for the libertine, though it be the charm, which by cementing the matrimonial tie, secures to the pledges of a warmer passion the necessary parental attention; for children will never be properly educated till friendship subsists between parents. Virtue flies from a house divided against itself – and a whole legion of devils take up their residence there.

The affection of husbands and wives cannot be pure when they have so few sentiments in common, and when so little confidence is established at home, as must be the case when their pursuits are so different. That intimacy from which tenderness should flow will not, cannot, subsist between the vicious.

Contending therefore that the sexual distinction which men have so warmly insisted upon is arbitrary, I have dwelt on an observation that several sensible men with whom I have conversed on the subject allowed to be well-founded; and it is simply this, that the little chastity to be found amongst men, and consequent disregard of modesty, tend to degrade both sexes; and further, that the modesty of women, characterized as such, will often be only the artful veil of wantonness, instead of being the natural reflection of purity, till modesty be universally respected.

From the tyranny of man, I firmly believe, the greater number of female follies proceed; and the cunning, which I allow makes at present a part of their character, I likewise have repeatedly endeavoured to prove, is produced by oppression...

Asserting the rights which women in common with men ought to contend for, I have not attempted to extenuate their faults; but to prove them to be the natural consequence of their education and station in society. If so, it is reasonable to suppose that they will change their character, and correct their vices and follies, when they are allowed to be free in a physical, moral and civil sense.

5   Partiality and Favouritism: William Godwin, *Enquiry concerning Political Justice**

In the preceding extract, we can observe Wollstonecraft's interest both in wider social questions of rights and fairness (in the treatment of women) and also in more intimate aspects of individual relationships (the nature of love and sexuality within a marriage). This contrast connects up with an important distinction between on the one hand universal ethical demands like those of justice and philanthropy, and on the other hand the particular ties of love, friendship and personal commitment. Most of us on reflection would probably acknowledge the ethical pull of both types of concern in our lives, and this accords with much mainstream moral philosophy (Aristotle, for instance, finds space in his ethics for both the impartial virtue of justice and the more partialistic virtue of love or affection). Our next extract, by the prolific eighteenth-century philosopher William Godwin, is remarkable for its attempt to exclude from ethical consideration all feelings arising from the ties of personal commitment. Partialism, any favoured treatment for oneself or those to whom one is specially related, is for Godwin ethically improper. Godwin produces what has become a famous example to illustrate his point: if two people (a philanthropic archbishop and a chambermaid) are trapped in a burning building, and I can rescue only one, then I should rescue the one who can do most good for mankind as a whole. Given that this is the archbishop, then it is he who should be rescued; I should resolutely set aside the fact that the chambermaid happens to be my mother, for 'What magic is in the pronoun "my" to overturn the decisions of everlasting truth?'

Few of us would be capable of living in this impartialistic way; but can our preferential attitudes to those we are close to be justified from the moral point of view? One possible justification is that by looking after our own we do our bit to promote the general good. In the last paragraph of our extract Godwin considers the argument that a system of mutual ties of affection – a 'mutual commerce of benefits' – itself increases general happiness, and so can be justified from an impersonal standpoint. He firmly rejects this line, however, in favour of a more radical stance which recommends revising our existing commitments and ways of thinking: each case should be examined on its merits, and in strictly impartial terms, irrespective of any personal ties of affection or gratitude. Godwin's work has the merit of highlighting fundamental questions about the ethical status of partiality and self-preference, and the issues he raises are the subject of continuing debate among moral philosophers today.

 By justice I understand that impartial treatment of every man in matters that relate to his happiness, which is measured solely by a consideration of the properties of the receiver, and the capacity of him that bestows. Its principle, therefore is, according to a well-known phrase, to be 'no respecter of persons'.

Considerable light will probably be thrown upon our investigation if, quitting for the present the political view, we examine justice merely as it exists among individuals. Justice is a rule of conduct originating in the connection of one percipient being with another. A comprehensive maxim which has been laid down upon the subject is 'that we should love our neighbour as ourselves'. But this maxim, though possessing considerable merit as a popular principle, is not modelled with the strictness of philosophical accuracy.

---

* W. Godwin, *An Inquiry concerning Political Justice* [1793], from Bk II, ch. 2; with minor modifications, and some additions from the 2nd edn of 1796.

In a loose and general view I and my neighbour are both of us men, and of consequence entitled to equal attention. But in reality it is probable that one of us is a being of more worth and importance than the other. A man is of more worth than a beast, because, being possessed of higher faculties, he is capable of a more refined and genuine happiness. In the same manner the illustrious archbishop of Cambrai[1] was of more worth than his chambermaid, and there are few of us that would hesitate to pronounce, if his palace were in flames and the life of only one of them could be preserved, which of the two ought to be preferred.

But there is another ground of preference beside the private consideration of one of them being farther removed from the state of a mere animal. We are not connected with one or two percipient beings, but with a society, a nation, and in some sense with the whole family of mankind. Of consequence, that life ought to be preferred which will be most conducive to the general good. In saving the life of Fénelon, suppose at the moment when he conceived the project of his immortal *Telemachus*, I should be promoting the benefit of thousands who have been cured by the perusal of it of some error, vice and consequent unhappiness. Nay, my benefit would extend farther than this, for every individual thus cured has become a better member of society and has contributed in his turn to the happiness, the information and improvement of others.

Supposing I had been myself the chambermaid, I ought to have chosen to die rather than that Fénelon should have died. The life of Fénelon was really preferable to that of the chambermaid. But understanding is the faculty that perceives the truth of this and similar propositions; and justice is the principle that regulates my conduct accordingly. It would have been just in the chambermaid to have preferred the archbishop to herself. To have done otherwise would have been a breach of justice.

Suppose the chambermaid had been my wife, my mother or my benefactor.[2] This would not alter the truth of the proposition. The life of Fénelon would still be more valuable than that of the chambermaid; and justice – pure, unadulterated justice – would still have preferred that which was most valuable. Justice would have taught me to save the life of Fénelon at the expense of the other. What magic is there in the pronoun 'my' to overturn the decisions of everlasting truth? My wife or my mother may be a fool or a prostitute, malicious, lying or dishonest. If they be, of what consequence is it that they are mine?

'But my mother endured for me the pains of child bearing, and nourished me in the helplessness of infancy.' When she first subjected herself to the necessity of these cares, she was probably influenced by no particular motives of benevolence to her future offspring. Every voluntary benefit however entitles the bestower to some kindness and retribution. But why so? Because a voluntary benefit is an evidence of benevolent intention; that is, of virtue. It is the disposition of the mind, not the external action, that entitles to respect. But the merit of this disposition is equal whether the benefit was conferred upon me or upon another. I and another man cannot both be right in preferring our own individual benefactor, for no man can be at the same time both better and worse than his neighbour. My benefactor ought to

---

[1] 'Fénelon' (François de la Motte), author of *Telemachus* [1699], a biting satire on the reign of Louis XIV. Godwin takes him to be a paradigm of someone who has benefited mankind.

[2] In the 1796 edition, the example of the chambermaid is replaced with that of a valet who might be my brother or my father.

be esteemed, not because he bestowed a benefit upon me, but because he bestowed it upon a human being. His desert will be in exact proportion to the degree in which that human being was worthy of the distinction conferred.

Thus every view of the subject brings us back to the consideration of my neighbour's moral worth and his importance to the general weal as the only standard to determine the treatment to which he is entitled. Gratitude therefore, a principle which has so often been the theme of the moralist and the poet, is no part either of justice or virtue.

It may be objected 'that my relation, my companion, or my benefactor, will of course in many instances obtain an uncommon portion of my regard; for not being universally capable of discriminating the comparative worth of different men, I shall inevitably judge most favourably of him of whose virtues I have received the most unquestionable proofs; and thus shall be compelled to prefer the man of moral worth whom I know to another who may possess, unknown to me, an essential superiority.' This compulsion, however, is founded only in the imperfection of human nature. It may serve as an apology for my error, but can never change error into truth. It will always remain contrary to the strict and universal decisions of justice...

It may in the second place be objected that a mutual commerce of benefits tends to increase the mass of benevolent action, and that to increase the mass of benevolent action is to contribute to the general good. Indeed! Is the general good promoted by falsehood, by treating a man of one degree of worth as if he had ten times that worth? or as if he were in any degree different from what he really is? Would not the most beneficial consequences result from a different plan: from my constantly and carefully enquiring into the deserts of all those with whom I am connected, and from their being sure, after a certain allowance for the fallibility of human judgement, of being treated by me exactly as they deserved? Who can describe the benefits that would result from such a plan of conduct, if universally adopted? ... The soundest criterion of virtue is to put ourselves in the place of an impartial spectator, of an angelic nature, suppose, beholding us from an elevated station, and uninfluenced by our prejudices, conceiving what would be his estimate of the intrinsic circumstances of our neighbour, and acting accordingly.

6 The Status of Non-human Animals: Immanuel Kant, *Lectures on Ethics**

Most applied ethics concerns how human beings should treat each other. But the radical reforming philosopher Jeremy Bentham (author of extract 7, below), taking the greatest happiness principle as the foundation of ethics,[1] argued that there was no good reason for excluding the pleasures and pains of animals from the ethical calculus. What matters, he famously declared, is

---

* Immanuel Kant, *Einer Vorlesung über Ethik* [1775–80], ed. G. Gerhardt (Frankfurt: Fischer, 1990), Part B, section IX. Translation by John Cottingham. The German text is a compilation from notes of Kant's lectures taken by T. F. Brauer, G. Kutzner and C. Mongrovius. The complete work is available in English as *Lectures on Ethics*, trans. L. Infield (London: Methuen, 1930).

[1] For the principle of utility, or the greatest happiness of the greatest number, see above, Part VIII, extract 6.

not whether they can reason or talk, but whether they can suffer.[1] A very different line was taken by the great German philosopher Immanuel Kant, writing about the same time as Bentham. Basing his ethics on the principle of 'respect for persons', Kant argued that only rational and autonomous agents could be bearers of moral worth – only they had the status of 'ends in themselves' (see Part VIII, extract 5, above). In the following extract, Kant applies this principle to the question of whether we have duties to non-human animals. Since animals are not self-conscious, Kant suggests, they cannot qualify as self-determining agents, and hence cannot be 'ends in themselves'. So while it is utterly impermissible to use a human being merely as a means to an end, this is precisely what we may do when dealing with animals: 'they are there only as a means to an end'.

Kant goes on to argue that such duties as we have to animals are 'indirect': since animals are 'analogues' of human beings, our dealings with them provide a kind of shadowy image of our (morally significant) dealings with our fellow humans. Thus a man who acts with cruelty towards animals 'thereby becomes hardened even in his dealings with human beings'. Kant illustrates his point by referring to an old story concerning the 'bell of ingratitude'. The details (which Kant does not supply) are as follows. Those complaining of some act of ingratitude could ring the bell to summon a court of inquiry. A weak old ass, turned out by its owner, strayed into the bell tower and began nibbling some

leaves twined round the bell-rope, thus ringing the bell. Kant's stressing that the bell was rung 'by accident' is important. The ass does not feel a sense of injustice (it is not a self-conscious being) nor, according to Kant, does the owner have a direct duty towards it (since it is a mere 'means' not an 'end in itself'). But the accidental ringing of the bell serves to remind us of the 'analogy' between ingratitude towards animals and ingratitude towards fellow humans (towards whom we do have direct duties).

Critics of Kant's position have asked why the fact that animals are not autonomous agents should mean they are not entitled to moral consideration and even respect. Defenders of Kant can point out that his concept of 'indirect duty' does put considerable constraints on what we may do to animals; wanton cruelty (that inflicted for sport, for example) is firmly condemned in the passage below. The regarding of animals purely as a means does, however, permit vivisection for scientific purposes, and would presumably allow many of the practices associated with modern farming which are strongly condemned by animal liberationists. Yet not all problems are solved by following Bentham, and allowing animal pains and pleasure into the ethical calculus, since a sufficient amount of human pleasure could, presumably, be held to counterbalance widespread animal suffering. Hence some modern ethicists have argued that our thinking in these matters needs to be supplemented by introducing the idea of animal *rights* – itself a highly complex and problematic concept. The debate continues.

Baumgarten[2] speaks of duties towards beings which are below us and those which are above us. Yet animals are there only as a means to an end, since they are not conscious of themselves; a human being, by contrast, is an end. So I cannot ask 'Why is man there?', in the way I can in the case of the animals. Hence we have no immediate duties towards animals; our duties towards animals are merely indirect duties towards humanity.

Animals are an analogue of humanity, and so we observe duties towards humanity when we observe the corresponding duties towards the analogues; in so doing we further our duties towards humanity. For example, when a dog has served its master faithfully for a long time, this is an analogue of merit, and accordingly I must give the

---

[1] J. Bentham, *Principles of Morals and Legislation* [1789], ch. xvii, section 1.
[2] Kant refers to the *Ethica philosophica* (1740) of Alexander Baumgarten (1714–1762).

appropriate reward, and look after the dog, when he is incapable of serving me any longer, till he ends his days. In so doing I further my duty toward humanity, where the corresponding action is something I am obliged to do.

So when the behaviour of animals arises from the same principle from which the behaviour of human beings arises, and is the animal analogue of the corresponding human behaviour, we have duties towards animals in so far as we thereby promote our duties to humanity. Thus when someone has his dog shot, because it can no longer earn its keep, he certainly does not contravene his duty towards the dog, since the dog is incapable of passing judgement; yet he does damage the kindness and humanity in himself – that humanity which he ought to exercise in observing the duties relating to mankind.

If a human being is not to destroy this kindness and humanity in himself, he must be kind-hearted to the animals; for a man who acts with cruelty towards animals thereby becomes hardened even in his dealings with human beings. It is easy to judge the heart of a man from how he treats animals. Hogarth shows this in his engravings: the 'beginning of cruelty' is portrayed in children's behaviour towards animals, e.g. when they pinch the dog's or cat's tail; next comes the 'progress in cruelty', as the adult runs over a child; and finally the 'end of cruelty', depicted in a murder, where the final requital for cruelty appears in all its terrible colours.[1] This is a good lesson for children.

The more involved we are in observing animals and their behaviour, the more we love them, seeing how much they care for their young. Then it becomes impossible to entertain cruel thoughts even towards a wolf. Leibniz, after observing a little worm, put it back with its leaf on the tree, so it should come to no harm through any fault of his. A human being finds it distressing to destroy such a creature for no reason. And tender feelings of this kind flow over into our dealings with mankind.

In England no butcher or surgeon or doctor may serve as one of the twelve jurors in a law court, since their frequent contact with death has hardened them.

When anatomists use living animals for their experiments, it is certainly cruel, even though it is done for a good purpose. Since animals are regarded as instruments of human beings, it is acceptable, but this is certainly not the case when it is done for sport. When a master turns out his donkey or his dog because it cannot earn its keep any more, such an action is always a sign of extreme small-mindedness on the part of the master. The Greeks had a noble attitude in such matters, as is shown in the fable of the ass, who pulled the bell of ingratitude by accident.[2]

Our duties towards animals, then, are indirect duties towards mankind.

[1] William Hogarth (1697–1764), English painter and engraver; his 'The Stages of Cruelty' appeared in 1751.
[2] For details of the story, see introduction to this extract. The story appears to be of southern Italian rather than Greek origin.

7   The Purpose of Punishment: Jeremy Bentham, *Principles of Morals and Legislation**

One of the most important applications of moral philosophy to practical issues has to do with the way society deals, or ought to deal, with those who do not conform to its rules. There is, first of all, the question of how much of the prevailing moral code may legitimately be enforced – an issue which concerns the proper limits of the law and belongs in the domain of political theory (see below, Part X, extract 9). But aside from this, there is the more immediate issue of how we treat offenders, and what morally justifiable aims (if any) we are pursuing through the operation of the penal system. Our next extract, by the utilitarian philosopher Jeremy Bentham,[1] begins by setting out the fundamental object of the law as that of augmenting 'the total happiness of the community'. But if the production of general happiness is the fundamental test in ethics, then it is immediately clear that punishment, at least as far as the offender is concerned, hardly increases happiness; and this leads Bentham to take as his initial premise the proposition that 'all punishment in itself is evil'. Punishment thus calls (on Bentham's view) for justification in terms of some counterbalancing good it produces. The main justification he famously produces is *deterrence* – offering the potential offender an inducement not to offend. The institution of punishment is designed to 'prevent, in as far as is possible and worthwhile, all sorts of offences whatsoever'.

Bentham aims to derive from his general utilitarian stance several principles governing the operation of punishment. Since the aim is to maximize welfare, the system should be as 'cheap' to operate as possible – that is, it should

buy the greatest amount of happiness in exchange for the smallest amount of pain. 'A lot of punishment is a lot of pain', but 'the profit of an offence is a lot of pleasure'. So we need to give as much (but no more) punishment as is necessary to counteract the advantage a criminal would get from offending. But since the chances of being caught may vary, and the threat of possible punishment is in any case a long way off when the offender is contemplating the crime, the penalty may need to be further increased 'in proportion to that whereby it falls short in *certainty* or *proximity*'.

The Benthamite approach to punishment has been heavily criticized by those philosophers who see punishment as designed to exact moral *retribution* for wrongdoing. Punishment, on this alternative view, is something the offender *deserves* to suffer, and therefore retributivists would take issue with Bentham's basic premise that punishment is in itself inherently evil. Furthermore, the *amount* of punishment which seems fitting on retributivist grounds will depend on the moral gravity of the offence, and this may not at all correspond with the amount determined by Bentham's utilitarian cost – benefit calculation (consider, for example, illegal parking, which is not regarded as morally wicked, but is an enormous nuisance which might be effectively reduced by savage penalties). There is also the question of *whom* we should punish; here Bentham's rationale for excluding from punishment classes of offender such as the insane differs radically from what a retributivist would say (Bentham's arguments turn on *efficaciousness*, not *desert*). Finally, at the end of our

* Jeremy Bentham, *An Introduction to the Principles of Morals and Legislation* [printed in 1780 and first published 1789; rev. edn 1823]. Extracts from chs 13 ('Cases Unmeet for Punishment'), 14 ('The Proportion between Punishments and Offences') and 15 ('Properties to be given to a Lot of Punishment'); some modifications of punctuation and layout. The complete text may be found in *A Fragment on Government and Introduction to the Principles of Morals and Legislation* by Jeremy Bentham, ed. W. Harrison (Oxford: Blackwell, 1948; repr. 1967).
[1] For utilitarianism, compare Part VIII, extract 6, above.

extract, Bentham rules out capital punishment on the ground that judicial mistakes could not be compensated for after execution. But suppose (though this is a disputed matter) that capital punishment can be shown to be a strongly effective deterrent: would worries about com-pensating possible injustices really be decisive on Bentham's cost/benefit principles? Though it is far from free of problems, Bentham's account of the justification, distribution and appropriate amount of punishment has been a benchmark for much subsequent philosophical discussion.

 The immediate principal end of punishment is to control action. This action is either that of the offender, or of others. That of the offender it controls by its influence, either on his will, in which case it is said to operate in the way of *reformation*; or on his physical power, in which case it is said to operate in the way of *disablement*. That of others it can influence no otherwise than by its influence over their wills; in which case it is said to operate in the way of *example*. A kind of collateral end, which it has a natural tendency to answer, is that of affording a pleasure or satisfaction to the party injured, where there is one, and in general, to parties whose ill-will, whether on a self-regarding account, or on the account of sympathy or antipathy, has been excited by the offence. This purpose, as far as it can be answered *gratis*, is a beneficial one. But no punishment ought to be alloted merely to this purpose, because (setting aside its effects in the way of control) no such pleasure is ever produced by punishment as can be equivalent to the pain...

The general object which all laws have, or ought to have, in common, is to augment the total happiness of the community; and therefore, in the first place, to exclude, as far as may be, everything that tends to subtract from that happiness: in other words, to exclude mischief.

But all punishment is mischief: all punishment in itself is evil. Upon the principle of utility, if it ought at all to be admitted, it ought only to be admitted in as far as it promises to exclude some greater evil.

It is plain, therefore, that in the following cases punishment ought not to be inflicted.

1. Where it is *groundless*. Where there is no mischief for it to prevent; the act not being mischievous upon the whole.

2. Where it must be *inefficacious*. Where it cannot act so as to prevent the mischief... Where the penal provision, though it were conveyed to a man's notice, *could produce no effect on him*, with respect to the preventing him from engaging in any act of the *sort* in question. Such is the case (1) in extreme *infancy*; where a man has not yet attained that state or disposition of mind in which the prospect of evils so distant as those which are held forth by the law has the effect of influencing his conduct. (2) In *insanity*; where the person, if he has attained to that disposition, has since been deprived of it through the influence of some permanent though unseen cause. (3) In *intoxication*; where he has been deprived of it by the transient influence of a visible cause, such as the use of wine, or opium, or other drugs, that act in this manner on the nervous system; which condition is indeed neither more nor less than a temporary insanity produced by an assignable cause.

3. Where it is *unprofitable*, or too *expensive*: where the mischief it would produce would be greater than what it prevented.

4. Where it is *needless*: where the mischief may be prevented, or cease of itself, without it: that is, at a cheaper rate...

We have seen that the general object of all law is to prevent mischief; that is to say, when it is worthwhile; but that, where there are no other means of doing this than punishment, there are four cases in which it is *not* worthwhile.

When it is worthwhile, there are four subordinate designs or objects, which, in the course of his endeavours to compass, as far as may be, that one general object, a legislator, whose views are governed by the principle of utility, comes naturally to propose to himself.

His first, most extensive, and most eligible object, is to prevent, in as far as it is possible, and worthwhile, all sorts of offences whatsoever; in other words, so to manage, that no offence whatsoever may be committed.

But if a man must needs commit an offence of some kind or other, the next object is to induce him to commit an offence *less* mischievous, *rather* than one *more* mischievous: in other words, to choose always the *least* mischievous, of two offences that will either of them suit his purpose.

When a man has resolved upon a particular offence, the next object is to dispose him to do *no more* mischief than is *necessary* to his purpose: in other words, to do as little mischief as is consistent with the benefit he has in view.

The last object is, whatever the mischief be, which it is proposed to prevent, to prevent it at as *cheap* a rate as possible.

Subservient to these four objects, or purposes, must be the rules or canons by which the proportion of punishments to offences is to be governed.

Rule 1. The first object, it has been seen, is to prevent, in as far as it is worthwhile, all sorts of offences; therefore, *The value of the punishment must not be less in any case than what is sufficient to outweigh that of the profit of the offence.* If...the offence (unless some other considerations, independent of the punishment, should intervene...) will be sure to be committed notwithstanding: the whole lot of punishment will be thrown away: it will be altogether *inefficacious.*

The above rule has been often objected to, on account of its seeming harshness: but this can only have happened for want of its being properly understood. The strength of the temptation, *ceteris paribus*,[1] is as the profit of the offence: the quantum of the punishment must rise with the profit of the offence; *ceteris paribus*, it must therefore rise with the strength of the temptation. This there is no disputing. True it is that the stronger the temptation, the less conclusive is the indication which the act of delinquency affords of the depravity of the offender's disposition. So far then as the absence of any aggravation, arising from extraordinary depravity of disposition, may operate (or at the utmost, so far as the presence of a ground of extenuation, resulting from the innocence or beneficence of the offender's disposition, can operate), the strength of the temptation may operate in abatement of the demand for punishment. But it can never operate so far as to indicate the propriety of making the punishment ineffectual, which it is sure to be when brought below the level of the apparent profit of the offence.

The partial benevolence which should prevail for the reduction of it below this level, would counteract those purposes which such a motive would actually have in view, as well as those more extensive purposes which extensive benevolence ought to

---

[1] *Ceteris paribus*: other things being equal.

have in view; it would be cruelty not only to the public, but to the very persons in whose behalf it pleads – in its effects, I mean, however opposite in its intention. Cruelty to the public, that is cruelty to the innocent, by suffering them, for want of an adequate protection, to lie exposed to the mischief of the offence; cruelty even to the offender himself, by punishing him to no purpose, and without the chance of compassing that beneficial end, by which alone the introduction of the evil of punishment is to be justified.

Rule 2. But whether a given offence shall be prevented in a given degree, by a given quantity of punishment, is never anything better than a chance; for the purchasing of which, whatever punishment is employed, is so much expended in advance. However, for the sake of giving it the better chance of outweighing the profit of the offence, *The greater the mischief of the offence, the greater is the expense, which it may be worthwhile to be at, in the way of punishment.*

Rule 3. The next object is, to induce a man to choose always the least mischievous of two offences; therefore, *Where two offences come in competition, the punishment for the greater offence must be sufficient to induce a man to prefer the less.*

Rule 4. When a man has resolved upon a particular offence, the next object is to induce him to do no more mischief than what is necessary for his purpose: therefore, *The punishment should be adjusted in such manner to each particular offence, that for every part of the mischief there may be a motive to restrain the offender from giving birth to it.*

Rule 5. The last object is, whatever mischief is guarded against, to guard against it at as cheap a rate as possible: therefore *The punishment ought in no case to be more than what is necessary to bring it into conformity with the rules here given.*

Rule 6. It is further to be observed, that owing to the different manners and degrees in which persons under different circumstances are affected by the same exciting cause, a punishment which is the same in name will not always either really produce, or even so much as appear to others to produce, in two different persons the same degree of pain: therefore, *That the quantity actually inflicted on each individual offender may correspond to the quantity intended for similar offenders in general, the several circumstances influencing sensibility ought always to be taken into account.*

Of the above rules of proportion, the four first, we may perceive, serve to mark out the limits on the side of diminution; the limits *below* which a punishment ought not to be *diminished*: the fifth, the limits on the side of increase; the limits *above* which it ought not to be *increased*. The five first are calculated to serve as guides to the legislator: the sixth is calculated, in some measure, indeed, for the same purpose; but principally for guiding the judge in his endeavours to conform, on both sides, to the intentions of the legislator.

Let us look back a little. The first rule, in order to render it more conveniently applicable to practice, may need perhaps to be a little more particularly unfolded. It is to be observed, then, that for the sake of accuracy, it was necessary, instead of the word *quantity* to make use of the less perspicuous term *value*. For the word *quantity* will not properly include the circumstances either of certainty or proximity: circumstances which, in estimating the value of a lot of pain or pleasure, must always be taken into the account. Now, on the one hand, a lot of punishment is a lot of pain; on the other hand, the profit of an offence is a lot of pleasure, or what is equivalent to it. But the profit of the offence is commonly more *certain* than the punishment, or, what comes to the same thing, *appears* so at least to the offender. It is at any rate commonly more *immediate*. It follows, therefore, that, in order to maintain its superiority over the profit of the offence, the punishment must have its value made up in some other way, in proportion to that whereby it falls short in the two points of *certainty* and *proximity*. Now there is no other way in which it can receive any addition to its *value*, but by receiving an addition in point of *magnitude*. Wherever then the value of the punishment falls short, either in point of *certainty*, or of *proximity*, of that of the profit of the offence, it must receive a proportionable addition in point of *magnitude*.[1]

Yet farther. To make sure of giving the value of the punishment the superiority over that of the offence, it may be necessary, in some cases, to take into the account the profit not only of the *individual* offence to which the punishment is to be annexed, but also of such *other* offences of the *same sort* as the offender is likely to have already committed without detection. This random mode of calculation, severe as it is, it will be impossible to avoid having recourse to, in certain cases: in such, to wit, in which the profit is pecuniary, the chance of detection very small, and the obnoxious act of such a nature as indicates a habit: for example, in the case of frauds against the coin. If it be *not* recurred to, the practice of committing the offence will be sure to be, upon the balance of the account, a gainful practice. That being the case, the legislator will be absolutely sure of *not* being able to suppress it, and the whole punishment that is bestowed upon it will be thrown away. In a word (to keep to the same expressions we set out with) that whole quantity of punishment will be *inefficacious*.

These things being considered, the three following rules may be laid down by way of supplement and explanation to Rule 1.

Rule 7. *To enable the value of the punishment to outweigh that of the profit of the offence, it must be increased, in point of magnitude, in proportion as it falls short in point of certainty.*

Rule 8. *Punishment must be further increased in point of magnitude, in proportion as it falls short in point of proximity.*

Rule 9. *Where the act is conclusively indicative of a habit, such an increase must be given to the punishment as may enable it to outweigh the profit not only of the individual offence, but of such other like offences as are likely to have been committed with impunity by the same offender.*

There may be a few other circumstances or considerations which may influence, in some small degree, the demand for punishment: but as the propriety of these is either not so demonstrable, or not so constant, or the application of them not so determinate, as that of the foregoing, it may be doubted whether they be worth putting on a level with the others.

Rule 10. *When a punishment, which in point of quality is particularly well calculated to answer its intention, cannot exist in less than a certain quantity, it may sometimes be of use, for the sake of employing it, to stretch a little beyond that quantity which, on other accounts, would be strictly necessary.*

---

[1] *It is for this reason, for example, that simple compensation is never looked on as sufficient punishment for theft or robbery.

Rule 11. *In particular, this may sometimes be the case, where the punishment proposed is of such a nature as to be particularly well calculated to answer the purpose of a moral lesson.*

Rule 12. The tendency of the above considerations is to dictate an augmentation in the punishment: the following rule operates in the way of diminution. There are certain cases (it has been seen) in which, by the influence of accidental circumstances, punishment may be rendered unprofitable in the whole: in the same cases it may chance to be rendered unprofitable as to a part only. Accordingly, *In adjusting the quantum of punishment, the circumstances, by which all punishment may be rendered unprofitable, ought to be attended to.*

Rule 13. It is to be observed, that the more various and minute any set of provisions are, the greater the chance is that any given article in them will not be borne in mind, without which no benefit can ensure from it. Distinctions which are more complex than what the conception of those whose conduct it is designed to influence can take in, will even be worse than useless. The whole system will present a confused appearance, and thus the effect, not only of the proportions established by the articles in question, but of whatever is connected with them, will be destroyed. To draw a precise line of direction in such cases seems impossible. However, by way of memento, it may be of some use to subjoin the following rule: *Among provisions designed to perfect the proportion between punishments and offences, if any occur which by their own particular good effect would not make up for the harm they would do by adding to the intricacy of the Code, they should be omitted* . . .

[Bentham proceeds to list a number of properties which punishment should have; one of these is that it should be capable of being *remitted*.]

It may happen that punishment shall have been inflicted where, according to the intention of the law itself, it ought not to have been inflicted; that is, where the sufferer is innocent of the offence. At the time of the sentence passed he appeared guilty; but since then, accident has brought his innocence to light. This being the case, so much of the destined punishment as he has suffered already, there is no help for. The business is then to free him from as much as is yet to come. But *is* there any yet to come? There is very little chance of there being any, unless it be so much as consists of *chronical* punishment, such as imprisonment, banishment, penal labour and the like. So much consists of *acute* punishment, to whit where the penal process itself is over presently, however permanent the punishment may be in its effects, may be considered as *irremissible*. That is the case, for example, with whipping, branding, mutilation and capital punishment. The most perfectly irremissible of any is capital punishment. For though other punishments cannot, when they are over, be remitted, they may be compensated for; and although the unfortunate victim cannot be put into the same condition, yet possibly means may be found of putting him to as good a condition as he would have been if he had never suffered . . .

8   Our Relationship to the Environment: Aldo Leopold, *The Land Ethic**

We have already drawn attention to the philosophical debate over whether the sphere of ethics should be extended beyond the human domain to include the interests of non-rational animals (see introduction to extract 6, above). In the following extract, Aldo Leopold, often called the prophet of the conservation movement, argues for a still wider extension, to cover the entire ecosystem: 'the land ethic enlarges the boundaries of the community to include soils, water, plants, animals, or collectively: the land'. Though Leopold's was a relatively lone voice when 'The Land Ethic' appeared (in the 1940s), we have all now become familiar with the idea of our responsibility to conserve the environment. But what is the ethical basis of such responsibility? In the passage that follows, Leopold sometimes appears to argue that conserving the ecosystem is important because of our human dependence on it, which might suggest the relevant obligations are ultimately derivative from human interests. But a deeper reading of the text reveals that Leopold is proposing a fundamental shift in our ethical outlook. Instead of considering everything in terms of human use and human values, we should aim at a more *harmonious* relationship with our environment: the land ethic 'changes the role of *homo sapiens* from conqueror of the land-community to plain member and citizen of it'.

Man, then, is but one member of the 'biotic community', and Leopold proceeds to give a general criterion of rightness which makes explicit reference to this: 'a thing is right when it tends to preserve the integrity, stability and beauty of the biotic community; it is wrong when it tends otherwise'. As some academic critics have been eager to point out, there is something very simplistic about this proposal, and it would no doubt need very careful qualification before it could be used as an ultimate test for right action. Other critics have raised doubts about whether something like an ecosystem (a non-rational, and not even sentient, entity) can be a bearer of ethical value in itself; can there be an ethical relationship with something which is not aware, has no plans or projects, and cannot even feel pleasure or pain? For defenders of 'ecological ethics', however, this criticism is based on a narrowly anthropocentric conception of value – the idea that only human beings, and by extension perhaps the 'higher' animals, matter from the moral point of view. Certainly the language Leopold uses is that of a genuine *relationship* with the environment – a relationship which he says cannot exist without 'love, respect and admiration' for the land. This is a resonant and moving idea; part of the task of philosophers working in the rapidly growing discipline of environmental ethics is to examine whether it can be made coherent; if so, what are its implications; and if not, whether there are any better ways of evaluating our conduct with respect to the environment.

When god-like Odysseus returned from the wars in Troy, he hanged all on one rope a dozen slave-girls of his household whom he suspected of misbehaviour during his absence.

This hanging involved no question of propriety. The girls were property. The disposal of property was then, as now, a matter of expediency, not of right and wrong.

Concepts of right and wrong were not lacking from Odysseus's Greece: witness the fidelity of his wife through the long years before at last his black-prowed galleys clove the wine-dark seas for home. The ethical structure of that day covered wives, but had

* From Aldo Leopold, *A Sand County Almanac: And Sketches Here and There* (Oxford: Oxford University Press, 1949; repr. 1977), pp. 201–26; abridged. The full essay is reprinted in M. Zimmerman (ed.), *Environmental Philosophy* (Englewood Cliffs, NJ: Prentice-Hall, 1993).

not yet been extended to human chattels. During the three thousand years which have since elapsed, ethical criteria have been extended to many fields of conduct, with corresponding shrinkages in those judged by expediency only...

This extension of ethics, so far studied only by philosophers, is actually a process in ecological evolution. Its sequences may be described in ecological as well as philosophical terms. An ethic, ecologically, is a limitation on freedom of action in the struggle for existence. An ethic, philosophically, is a differentiation of social from anti-social conduct. These are two definitions of one thing. The thing has its origin in the tendency of interdependent individuals or groups to evolve modes of cooperation. The ecologist calls these symbioses. Politics and economics are advanced symbioses in which the original free-for-all competition has been replaced, in part, by cooperative mechanisms with an ethical content.

The complexity of cooperative mechanisms has increased with population density, and with the efficiency of tools. It was simpler, for example, to define the anti-social uses of sticks and stones in the days of the mastodons than of bullets and billboards in the age of motors.

The first ethics dealt with the relation between individuals; the Mosaic Decalogue is an example. Later accretions dealt with the relation between the individual and society. The Golden Rule tries to integrate the individual to society; democracy to integrate social organization to the individual.

There is as yet no ethic dealing with man's relation to land and the animals and plants which grow upon it. Land, like Odysseus's slave-girls, is still property. The land-relation is still strictly economic, entailing privileges but not obligations.

The extension of ethics to this third element in human environment is, if I read the evidence correctly, an evolutionary possibility and an ecological necessity. It is the third step in a sequence. The first we have already taken. Individual thinkers since the days of Ezekiel and Isaiah have asserted that the despoliation of land is not only inexpedient but wrong. Society, however, has not yet affirmed their belief. I regard the present conservation movement as the embryo of such an affirmation.

An ethic may be regarded as a mode of guidance for meeting ecological situations so new or intricate, or involving such deferred reactions, that the path of social expediency is not discernible to the average individual. Animal instincts are modes of guidance for the individual in meeting such situations. Ethics are possibly a kind of community instinct in-the-making...

All ethics so far evolved rest upon a single premise: that the individual is a member of a community of interdependent parts. His instincts prompt him to compete for his place in that community, but his ethics prompt him also to cooperate (perhaps in order that there may be a place to compete for).

The land ethic simply enlarges the boundaries of the community to include soils, waters, plants, and animals, or collectively: the land.

This sounds simple: do we not already sing our love for and obligation to the land of the free and the home of the brave? Yes, but just what and whom do we love? Certainly not the soil, which we are sending helter-skelter downriver. Certainly not the waters, which we assume have no function except to turn turbines, float barges and carry off sewage. Certainly not the plants, of which we exterminate whole communities without batting an eye. Certainly not the animals, of which we have already extirpated many of the largest and most beautiful species. A land ethic of course cannot prevent the alteration, management and use of these 'resources', but it does affirm their right to continued existence in a natural state.

In short, a land ethic changes the role of *Homo sapiens* from conqueror of the land-community to plain member and citizen of it. It implies respect for his fellow members, and also respect for the community as such.

In human history we have learned (I hope) that the conqueror role is eventually self-defeating. Why? Because it is implicit in such a role that the conqueror knows, *ex cathedra*, just what makes the community clock tick, and just what and who is valuable, and what and who is worthless, in community life. It always turns out that he knows neither, and this is why his conquests eventually defeat themselves.

In the biotic community, a parallel situation exists. Abraham knew exactly what the land was for: it was to drip milk and honey into Abraham's mouth. At the present moment, the assurance with which we regard this assumption is inverse to the degree of our education.

The ordinary citizen today assumes that science knows what makes the community clock tick; the scientist is equally sure that he does not. He knows that the biotic mechanism is so complex that its working may never be fully understood.

That man is, in fact, only a member of a biotic team is shown by an ecological interpretation of history. Many historical events, hitherto explained solely in terms of human enterprise, were actually biotic interactions between people and land. The characteristic of the land determined the facts quite as potently as the characteristics of the men who lived on it.

Consider for example the settlement of the Mississippi valley. In the years following the Revolution, three groups were contending for its control: the native Indian, the French and English traders, and the American settlers. Historians wonder what would have happened if the English at Detroit had thrown a little more weight into the Indian side of those tipsy scales which decided the outcome of the colonial migration into the cane-lands of Kentucky. It is time now to ponder the fact that the cane-lands, when subjected to the particular mixture of forces represented by the cow, plough, fire and axe of the pioneer, became bluegrass. What if the plant succession inherent in this dark and bloody ground had, under the impact of these forces, given us some worthless sedge, shrub or weed? Would Boone and Kenton have held out? Would there have been any overflow into Ohio, Indiana, Illinois and Missouri? Any Louisiana Purchase? Any transcontinental union of new states? Any civil war? ...

In short, the plant succession steered the course of history; the pioneer simply demonstrated, for good or ill, what successions entered in the land. Is history taught in this spirit? It will be, once the concept of land as a community really penetrates our intellectual life ...

Conservation is a state of harmony between men and land. Despite nearly a century of propaganda, conservation still proceeds at a snail's pace; progress still consists largely of letterhead pieties and convention oratory. On the back forty we still slip two steps backward for each forward stride ...

When the private landowner is asked to perform some unprofitable act for the good of the community, he today assents only with outstretched palm. If the act costs him cash this is fair and proper, but when it costs only forethought, open-mindedness or time, the issue is at least debatable. The overwhelming growth of land-use subsidies in recent years must be ascribed, in large part, to the government's own agencies of conservation education: the land bureaus, the agricultural colleges and the extension services. As far as I can detect, no ethical obligation toward land is taught in these institutions...

To sum up: a system of conservation based solely on economic self-interest is hopelessly lopsided. It tends to ignore, and thus eventually to eliminate, many elements in the land community that lack commercial value, but that are (as far as we know) essential to its healthy functioning. It assumes, falsely, I think, that the economic parts of the biotic clock will function without the uneconomic parts. It tends to relegate to government many functions eventually too large, too complex or too widely dispersed to be performed by government.

An ethical obligation on the part of the private owner is the only visible remedy for these situations...

An ethic to supplement and guide the economic relation to land presupposes the existence of some mental image of land as a biotic mechanism. We can be ethical only in relation to something we can see, feel, understand, love, or otherwise have faith in.

The image commonly employed in conservation education is 'the balance of nature'. For reasons too lengthy to detail here, this figure of speech fails to describe accurately what little we know about the land mechanism. A much truer image is the one employed in ecology: the biotic pyramid...

In the beginning, the pyramid of life was low and squat; the food chains short and simple. Evolution has added layer after layer, link after link. Man is one of thousands of accretions to the height and complexity of the pyramid. Science has given us many doubts, but it has given us at least one certainty: the trend of evolution is to elaborate and diversify the biota.

Land, then, is not merely soil; it is a fountain of energy flowing through a circuit of soils, plants and animals. Food chains are the living channels which conduct energy upwards; death and decay return it to the soil. The circuit is not closed; some energy is dissipated in decay, some is added by absorption from the air, some is stored in soils, peats and long-lived forests; but it is a sustained circuit, like a slowly augmented revolving fund of life. There is always a net loss by downhill wash, but this is normally small and offset by the decay of rocks. It is deposited in the ocean, and, in the course of geological time, raised to form new lands and new pyramids...

When a change occurs in one part of the circuit, many other parts must adjust themselves to it. Change does not necessarily obstruct or divert the flow of energy; evolution is a long series of self-induced changes, the net result of which has been to elaborate the flow mechanism and to lengthen the circuit. Evolutionary changes, however, are usually slow and local. Man's invention of tools has enabled him to make changes of unprecedented violence, rapidity and scope...

The combined evidence of history and ecology seems to support one general deduction: the less violent the man-made changes, the greater the probability of successful readjustment to the pyramid...

A land ethic, then, reflects the existence of an ecological conscience, and this in turn reflects a conviction of individual responsibility for the health of the land. Health is the capacity of the land for self-renewal. Conservation is our effort to understand and preserve this capacity.

Conservationists are notorious for their dissensions. Superficially these seem to add up to mere confusion, but a more careful scrutiny reveals a single plane of cleavage common to many specialized fields. In each field, one group (A) regards the land as soil, and its function as commodity-production; another group (B) regards the land as a biota, and its function as something broader. How much broader is admittedly in a state of doubt and confusion . . .

In all these cleavages we see repeated the same basic paradoxes: man the conqueror *versus* man the biotic citizen; science the sharpener of his sword *versus* science the search-light on his universe; land the slave and servant *versus* land the collective organism. Robinson's injunction to Tristram may well be applied at this juncture to *Homo sapiens* as a species in geological time:

> Whether you will or not
> You are King, Tristram, for you are one
> Of the time-tested few that leave the world,
> When they are gone, not the same place it was.
> Mark what you leave.

It is inconceivable to me that an ethical relation to land can exist without love, respect and admiration for land, and a high regard for its value. By value, I of course mean something far broader than mere economic value. I mean value in the philosophical sense.

Perhaps the most serious obstacle impeding the evolution of a land ethic is the fact that our educational and economic system is headed away from, rather than towards, an intense consciousness of land. Your true modern is separated from the land by many middlemen, and by innumerable physical gadgets. He has no vital reaction to it; to him it is the space between cities on which crops grow. Turn him loose for a day on the land, and if the spot does not happen to be a golf links or a 'scenic' area, he is bored stiff. If crops could be raised by hydroponics instead of farming, it would suit him very well. Synthetic substitutes for wood, leather, wool and other natural land products suit him better than the originals. In short, land is something he has outgrown.

Almost equally serious as an obstacle to a land ethic is the attitude of the farmer for whom the land is still an adversary, or a taskmaster that keeps him in slavery. Theoretically, the mechanization of farming ought to cut the farmer's chains, but whether it really does is debatable.

One of the prerequisites for an ecological comprehension of land is an understanding of ecology, and this is by no means coextensive with ecological concepts. An understanding of ecology does not necessarily originate in courses bearing ecological labels; it is quite as likely to be labelled geography, botany, agronomy, history or economics. This is as it should be, but whatever the label, ecological training is scarce.

The case for a land ethic would appear hopeless but for the minority which is in obvious revolt against these 'modern' trends.

The 'key-log' which must be moved to release the evolutionary process for an ethic is simply this: quit thinking about decent land use as solely an economic problem.

Examine each question in terms of what is ethically and aesthetically right, as well as what is economically expedient. A thing is right when it tends to preserve the integrity, stability and beauty of the biotic community. It is wrong when it tends otherwise.

It of course goes without saying that economic feasibility limits the tether of what can or cannot be done for land. It always has and it always will. The fallacy the economic determinists have tied around our collective neck, and which we now need to cast off, is the belief that economics determines *all* land use. This is simply not true. An innumerable host of actions and attitudes, comprising perhaps the bulk of all land relations, is determined by the land-user's tastes and predilections, rather than by his purse. The bulk of all land relations hinges on investments of time, forethought, skill and faith rather than on investments of cash. As a land-user thinketh, so is he.

I have purposely presented the land ethic as a product of social evolution because nothing so important as an ethic is ever 'written'. Only the most superficial students of history suppose that Moses 'wrote' the Decalogue: it evolved in the minds of a thinking community, and Moses wrote a tentative summary of it for a 'seminar'. I say tentative because evolution never stops.

The evolution of a land ethic is an intellectual as well as emotional process. Conservation is paved with good intentions which prove to be futile or even danger-ous, because they are devoid of critical understanding either of the land, or of economic land use. I think it is a truism that as the ethical frontier advances from the individual to the community, its intellectual content increases.

The mechanism of operation is the same for any ethic: social approbation for right actions, social disapproval for wrong actions.

By and large, our present problem is one of attitudes and implements. We are remodelling the Alhambra with a steam-shovel, and we are proud of our yardage. We shall hardly relinquish the shovel, which after all has many good points, but we are in need of gentler and more objective criteria for its successful use.

9   Abortion and Rights: Judith Jarvis Thomson, *A Defense of Abortion**

The Kantian principle of *respect for persons* requires us not to infringe the rights of free and autonomous agents (see above, extract 6, and Part VIII, extract 5). But how does this affect the ethical status of the unborn? One may argue that a foetus is not a person in Kant's sense, since it is not yet a rational, self-determining being. On the other hand, just like an already born infant, it will, in the natural course of events *become* a full person, and for this reason many people feel strongly that it has a right to life.

Modern medical science, however, possesses the technology to enable a woman safely to end her pregnancy, should she choose to do so, thus ending the life of the foetus. This has given rise to an intense debate over the morality of abor-tion, which pits the 'right to choice' of the preg-nant woman against the 'right to life' of the unborn child, foetus or embryo.

The extract that follows, by the contemporary American philosopher Judith Jarvis Thomson, represents an unusual contribution to the

* Judith Jarvis Thomson, 'A Defense of Abortion', *Philosophy and Public Affairs* (Fall 1971); abridged.

debate, precisely because it sidesteps the question of whether or not the foetus has a right to life. Thomson's defence of abortion begins by conceding, for the sake of argument, that the foetus is 'a person from the moment of conception' and that it therefore has the right to life. She then proceeds to deploy what has become a celebrated analogy – that of a famous violinist hooked up to your circulatory system against your will, whose survival depends on your granting permission for him to remain so hooked up for a specified period. Thomson argues that *even though* the violinist has a right to life, you are within your rights to unplug him from your circulatory system. For his right to life does not entail a right to live at your expense.

Thomson's example is vividly and clearly presented, and needs no further expounding here. Philosophical debate over the implications of her argument has centred around three main issues. First, can the analogy, which seems best to fit the case of involuntary pregnancy due to rape, be extended to other cases? Thomson, as the extract makes clear, aims to make just this extension, by modifying the analogy in various ways. Second, can the claim that you are 'within your rights' to unplug be extended to the case where the being who is dependent on you is entirely innocent of wrongdoing? Here Thomson argues that the issue turns on whether, and if so how, that innocent being can be said to have acquired a right to the use of the mother's body. Finally, the questions arise of whether the mother *ought* to allow the foetus continued use of her body, irrespective of the issue of what rights it has, and if so, whether the law ought to enforce that obligation (by prohibiting abortion). Here Thomson points out that the law does not normally require people to be 'good Samaritans' – to make great personal sacrifices to help others, or to save their lives. The issues here are complex enough to defy a summary verdict, but both philosophical critics and opponents of Thomson have agreed that her thought-provoking analogy throws much light on what is one of the most difficult problems in applied ethics.

Most opposition to abortion relies on the premise that the foetus is a human being, a person, from the moment of conception . . . I think that the premise is false . . . A newly fertilized ovum, a newly implanted clump of cells, is no more a person than an acorn is an oak tree. But I shall not discuss any of this. For it seems to me to be of great interest to ask what happens if, for the sake of argument, we allow the premise . . . I propose, then, that we grant that the foetus is a person from the moment of conception. How does the argument go from here? Something like this, I take it. Every person has a right to life. So the foetus has a right to life. No doubt the mother has a right to decide what shall happen in and to her body; everyone would grant that. But surely a person's right to life is stronger and more stringent than the mother's right to decide what happens in and to her body, and so outweighs it. So the foetus may not be killed; an abortion may not be performed.

It sounds plausible. But now let me ask you to imagine this. You wake up in the morning and find yourself back to back in bed with an unconscious violinist. A famous unconscious violinist. He has been found to have a fatal kidney ailment, and the Society of Music Lovers has canvassed all the available medical records and found that you alone have the right blood type to help. They have therefore kidnapped you, and last night the violinist's circulatory system was plugged into yours, so that your kidneys can be used to extract poisons from his blood as well as your own. The director of the hospital now tells you, 'Look, we're sorry the Society of Music Lovers did this to you – we would never have permitted it if we had known. But still, they did it, and the violinist now is plugged into you. To unplug you would be to kill him. But never mind, it's only for nine months. By then he will have recovered from his ailment, and can safely be unplugged from you.' Is it morally incumbent on you to accede to this situation? No doubt it would be very nice of you if you did, a great kindness. But do you *have* to accede to it? What if it were not nine months, but nine years? Or longer still? What if the director of the hospital says, 'Tough luck, I agree, but you've now got to stay in bed, with the violinist plugged into you, for the rest of your life. Because remember this. All persons have a right to life, and violinists are persons. Granted you have a right to decide what happens in and to your body, but a person's right to life outweighs your right to decide what happens in and to your body. So you cannot ever be unplugged from him.' I imagine you would regard this as outrageous, which suggests that something really is wrong with that plausible-sounding argument I mentioned a moment ago.

In this case, of course, you were kidnapped; you didn't volunteer for the operation that plugged the violinist into your kidneys. Can those who oppose abortion on the ground I mentioned make an exception for a pregnancy due to rape? Certainly. They can say that persons have a right to life only if they didn't come into existence because of rape; or they can say that all persons have a right to life, but that some have less of a right to life than others, in particular, that those who came into existence because of rape have less. But these statements have a rather unpleasant sound. Surely the question of whether you have a right to life at all, or how much of it you have, shouldn't turn on the question of whether or not you are the product of a rape. And in fact the people who oppose abortion on the ground I mentioned do not make this distinction, and hence do not make an exception in case of rape.

Nor do they make an exception for a case in which the mother has to spend the nine months of her pregnancy in bed. They would agree that would be a great pity, and hard on the mother, but all the same, all persons have a right to life, the foetus is a person, and so on. I suspect, in fact, that they would not make an exception for a case in which, miraculously enough, the pregnancy went on for nine years, or even the rest of the mother's life.

Some won't even make an exception for a case in which continuation of the pregnancy is likely to shorten the mother's life; they regard abortion as impermissible even to save the mother's life. Such cases are nowadays very rare, and many opponents of abortion do not accept this extreme view. All the same, it is a good place to begin: a number of points of interest come out in respect to it.

Let us call the view that abortion is impermissible even to save the mother's life 'the extreme view'. I want to suggest first that it does not issue from the argument I mentioned earlier without the addition of some fairly powerful premises. Suppose a woman has become pregnant, and now learns that she has a cardiac condition such that she will die if she carries the baby to term. What may be done for her? The foetus, being a person, has a right to life, but as the mother is a person too, so has she a right to life. Presumably they have an equal right to life. How is it supposed to come out that an abortion may not be performed? If mother and child have an equal right to life, shouldn't we perhaps flip a coin? Or should we add to the mother's right to life her right to decide what happens in and to her body, which everybody seems to be ready to grant – the sum of her rights now outweighing the foetus's right to life?

... If directly killing an innocent person is murder, and thus impermissible, then the mother's directly killing the innocent person inside her is murder, and thus is impermissible. But it cannot seriously be thought to be murder if the mother performs an abortion on herself to save her life. It cannot seriously be said that she *must* refrain, that she *must* sit passively by and wait for her death. Let us look again at the case of you and the violinist. There you are, in bed with the violinist, and the director of the hospital says to you, 'It's all most distressing, and I deeply sympathize, but you see this is putting an additional strain on your kidneys, and you'll be dead within the month. But you *have* to stay where you are all the same. Because unplugging you would be directly killing an innocent violinist, and that's murder, and that's impermissible.' If anything in the world is true, it is that you do not commit murder, you do not do what is impermissible, if you reach around to your back and unplug yourself from that violinist to save your life . . .

I should perhaps stop to say explicitly that I am not claiming that people have a right to do anything whatever to save their lives. I think, rather, that there are drastic limits to the right of self-defence. If someone threatens you with death unless you torture someone else to death, I think you have not the right, even to save your life, to do so. But the case under consideration here is very different. In our case there are only two people involved, one whose life is threatened, and one who threatens it. Both are innocent: the one who is threatened is not threatened because of any fault, the one who threatens does not threaten because of any fault. For this reason we may feel that we bystanders cannot intervene. But the person threatened can.

In sum, a woman surely can defend her life against the threat to it posed by the unborn child, even if doing so involves its death . . .

Where the mother's life is not at stake, the argument I mentioned at the outset seems to have a much stronger pull. 'Everyone has a right to life, so the unborn person has a right to life.' And isn't the child's right to life weightier than anything other than the mother's own right to life, which she might put forward as ground for an abortion?

This argument treats the right to life as if it were unproblematic. It is not, and this seems to me to be precisely the source of the mistake.

For we should now . . . ask what it comes to, to have a right to life. In some views having a right to life includes having a right to be given at least the bare minimum one needs for continued life. But suppose that what in fact is the bare minimum a man needs for continued life is something he has no right at all to be given? If I am sick unto death, and the only thing that will save my life is the touch of Henry Fonda's cool hand on my fevered brow, then all the same, I have no right to be given the touch of Henry Fonda's cool hand on my fevered brow. It would be frightfully nice of him to fly in from the West Coast to provide it. It would be less nice, though no doubt well meant, if my friends flew out to the West Coast and carried Henry Fonda back with them. But I have no right at all against anybody that he should do this for me. Or again, to return to the story I told earlier, the fact that for continued life that violinist needs the continued use of your kidneys does not establish that he has a right to be given the continued use of your kidneys. He certainly has no right against you that you should give him continued use of your kidneys. For nobody has any right to use your kidneys unless you give him such a right; and nobody has the right against you that you shall give him this right – if you do allow him to go on using your kidneys, this is a kindness on your part, and not something he can claim from you as his due. Nor has he any right against anybody else that *they* should give him continued use of your kidneys. Certainly he had no right against the Society of Music Lovers that they should plug him into you in the first place. And if you now start to unplug yourself, having learned that you will otherwise have to spend nine years in bed with him, there is nobody in the world who must try to prevent you, in order to see to it that he is given something he has a right to be given...

I suppose we may take it as a datum that in a case of pregnancy due to rape the mother has not given the unborn person a right to the use of her body for food and shelter. Indeed, in what pregnancy could it be supposed that the mother has given the unborn person such a right? It is not as if there were unborn persons drifting about the world, to whom a woman who wants a child says 'I invite you in.'

But it might be argued that there are other ways one can have acquired a right to the use of another person's body than by having been invited to use it by that person. Suppose a woman voluntarily indulges in intercourse, knowing of the chance it will issue in pregnancy, and then she does become pregnant; is she not in part responsible for the presence, in fact the very existence, of the unborn person inside her? No doubt she did not invite it in. But doesn't her partial responsibility for its being there itself give it a right to the use of her body?...

And then, too, it might be asked whether or not she can kill it even to save her own life: If she voluntarily called it into existence, how can she now kill it, even in self-defence?

...This argument would give the unborn person a right to its mother's body only if her pregnancy resulted from a voluntary act, undertaken in full knowledge of the chance a pregnancy might result from it. It would leave out entirely the unborn person whose existence is due to rape. Pending the availability of some further argument, then, we would be left with the conclusion that unborn persons whose existence is due to rape have no right to the use of their mothers' bodies, and thus that aborting them is not depriving them of anything they have a right to and hence is not unjust killing.

...It is not at all plain that this argument really does go even as far as it purports to. For there are cases and cases, and the details make a difference. If the room is stuffy, and I therefore open a window to air it, and a burglar climbs in, it would be absurd to say, 'Ah, now he can stay, she's given him a right to the use of her house – for she is partially responsible for his presence there, having voluntarily done what enabled him to get in, in full knowledge that there are such things as burglars, and that burglars burgle.' It would be still more absurd to say this if I had had bars installed outside my windows, precisely to prevent burglars from getting in, and a burglar got in only because of a defect in the bars. It remains equally absurd if we imagine it is not a burglar who climbs in, but an innocent person who blunders or falls in. Again, suppose it were like this: people-seeds drift about in the air like pollen, and if you open your windows, one may drift in and take root in your carpets or upholstery. You don't want children, so you fix up your windows with fine mesh screens, the very best you can buy. As can happen, however, and on very, very rare occasions does happen, one of the screens is defective; and a seed drifts in and takes root. Does the person-plant who now develops have a right to the use of your house? Surely not – despite the fact that you voluntarily opened your windows, you knowingly kept carpets and upholstered furniture, and you knew that screens were sometimes defective. Someone may argue that you are responsible for its rooting, that it does have a right to your house, because after all you *could* have lived out your life with bare floors and furniture, or with sealed windows and doors. But this won't do – for by the same token anyone can avoid a pregnancy due to rape by having a hysterectomy, or anyway by never leaving home without a (reliable!) army.

It seems to me that the argument we are looking at can establish at most that there are *some* cases in which the unborn person has a right to the use of its mother's body, and therefore *some* cases in which abortion is unjust killing. There is room for much discussion and argument as to precisely which, if any. But I think we should sidestep this issue and leave it open, for at any rate the argument certainly does not establish that all abortion is unjust killing.

There is room for yet another argument here, however. We surely must all grant that there may be cases in which it would be morally indecent to detach a person from your body at the cost of his life. Suppose you learn that what the violinist needs is not nine years of your life, but only one hour: all you need to do to save his life is to spend one hour in that bed with him. Suppose also that letting him use your kidneys for that one hour would not affect your health in the slightest. Admittedly you were kidnapped. Admittedly you did not give anyone permission to plug him into you. Nevertheless it seems to me plain you ought to *allow* him to use your kidneys for that hour – it would be indecent to refuse...

Again, suppose pregnancy lasted only an hour, and constituted no threat to life or health. And suppose that a woman becomes pregnant as a result of rape. Admittedly she did not voluntarily do anything to bring about the existence of a child. Admittedly she did nothing at all which would give the unborn person a right to the use of her body. All the same it might well be said, as in the newly emended violinist story, that she *ought* to allow it to remain for that hour – that it would be indecent in her to refuse.

...My own view is that even though you ought to let the violinist use your kidneys for the hour he needs, we should not conclude that he has a right to do so... Similarly, that even supposing a case in which a woman pregnant due to rape ought to allow the unborn person to use her body for the hour he needs, we should not conclude that he has a right to do so; we should conclude that she is self-centred, callous, indecent, but not unjust, if she refuses. The complaints are no less grave; they are just different. However, there is no need to insist on this point. If anyone does wish to deduce 'he has a right' from 'you ought,' then all the same he must surely grant that there are cases in which it is not morally required of you that you allow that violinist to use your kidneys, and in which he does not have a right to use them, and in which you do not do him an injustice if you refuse. And so also for mother and unborn child. Except in such cases as the unborn person has a right to demand it – and we were leaving open the possibility that there may be such cases – nobody is morally *required* to make large sacrifices, of health, of all other interests and concerns, of all other duties and commitments, for nine years, or even for nine months, in order to keep another person alive.

We have in fact to distinguish between two kinds of Samaritan: the Good Samaritan and what we might call the Minimally Decent Samaritan... The Good Samaritan[1] went out of his way, at some cost to himself, to help one in need of it. [Thomson goes on to point out that most legal systems do not even require citizens to be minimally decent Samaritans; we are not legally required even to give minimal assistance, for

[1] See Luke 10: 30–5.

example to call the police when we see someone attacked]...I should think, myself, that Minimally Decent Samaritan laws would be one thing, Good Samaritan laws quite another, and in fact highly improper. But we are not here concerned with the law. What we should ask is not whether anybody should be compelled by law to be a Good Samaritan, but whether we must accede to a situation in which somebody is being compelled – by nature, perhaps – to be a Good Samaritan. We have, in other words, to look now at third-party interventions. I have been arguing that no person is morally required to make large sacrifices to sustain the life of another who has no right to demand them, and this even where the sacrifices do not include life itself; we are not morally required to be Good Samaritans or anyway Very Good Samaritans to one another. But what if a man cannot extricate himself from such a situation? What if he appeals to us to extricate him? It seems to me plain that there are cases in which we can, cases in which a Good Samaritan would extricate him. There you are, you were kidnapped, and nine years in bed with that violinist lie ahead of you. You have your own life to lead. You are sorry, but you simply cannot see giving up so much of your life to the sustaining of his. You cannot extricate yourself, and ask us to do so. I should have thought that – in light of his having no right to the use of your body – it was obvious that we do not have to accede to your being forced to give up so much. We can do what you ask. There is no injustice to the violinist in our doing so...

10   The Relief of Global Suffering: Peter Singer, *Famine, Affluence and Morality**

The argument presented by Godwin (extract 5, above) challenges us to defend the ethical credentials of our tendency to favour ourselves and our relatives over those who may be more worthy of our attention from an impartial standpoint. Our next extract effectively takes this challenge forward to the global arena, by arguing that our current attitudes and conduct in the face of the massive problem of world poverty are quite indefensible from the moral point of view. The well-known contemporary Australian philosopher Peter Singer begins his argument with an apparently straightforward principle that 'if it is in our power to prevent something bad from happening without thereby sacrificing anything of comparable moral importance, we ought morally to do it'. This seems clearly right: in the case, say, when I can save a child from drowning in a pond without suffering any

greater inconvenience than getting my shoes wet. But now Singer argues with great force first that *proximity* makes no difference to the principle (the fact that hungry people are dying thousands of miles away does not reduce my obligation from what it was in the child in pond case); and secondly that *numbers* make no difference (the fact that there are millions of others who could help the starving, while I was the only one near the pond when the child fell in, does not make a moral difference to my own obligation to help). From these premises Singer reaches the conclusion that our inaction in the face of world poverty is morally indefensible.

This is a result which many might pay lip-service to, but Singer's purpose is to show that it requires a radical shift in our moral outlook. In particular, the traditional distinction between *charity* and *duty* 'cannot be drawn, or at least

* Peter Singer, 'Famine, Affluence, and Morality', *Philosophy and Public Affairs*, 1: 3 (Spring 1972); abridged.

not in the place we normally draw it'. Each of us who fails to give substantial amounts of money to famine victims, when all we would have to sacrifice is some of our relatively trivial luxuries – each of us who acts this way is not merely failing in 'charity' but guilty of serious moral wrongdoing. Singer's paper raises fundamental questions about the degree of moral complacency in our modern affluent societies; whether we are indeed as guilty as he suggests turns in part on whether the rightness or wrongness of conduct has to be determined from an impartial and universal standpoint, or whether to give a considerable degree of priority to oneself, and those close at hand, can be morally justified. Singer's paper concludes with an apt reminder that there are many cases where philosophical argument can and should make a real difference not just to how we think, but to how we live.

As I write this, in November 1971, people are dying in East Bengal from lack of food, shelter and medical care. The suffering and death that are occurring there now are not inevitable, not unavoidable in any fatalistic sense of the term. Constant poverty, a cyclone and a civil war have turned at least nine million people into destitute refugees; nevertheless, it is not beyond the capacity of the richer nations to give enough assistance to reduce any further suffering to very small proportions. The decisions and actions of human beings can prevent this kind of suffering. Unfortunately, human beings have not made the necessary decisions. At the individual level, people have, with very few exceptions, not responded to the situation in any significant way. Generally speaking, people have not given large sums to relief funds; they have not written to their parliamentary representatives demanding increased government assistance; they have not demonstrated in the streets, held symbolic fasts, or done anything else directed toward providing the refugees with the means to satisfy their essential needs...

The Bengal emergency is just the latest and most acute of a series of major emergencies in various parts of the world, arising both from natural and from man-made causes. There are also many parts of the world in which people die from malnutrition and lack of food independent of any special emergency. I take Bengal as my example only because it is the present concern, and because the size of the problem has ensured that it has been given adequate publicity. Neither individuals nor governments can claim to be unaware of what is happening there.

What are the moral implications of a situation like this? In what follows, I shall argue that the way people in relatively affluent countries react to a situation like that in Bengal cannot be justified; indeed, the whole way we look at moral issues – our moral conceptual scheme – needs to be altered, and with it, the way of life that has come to be taken for granted in our society.

In arguing for this conclusion I will not, of course, claim to be morally neutral. I shall, however, try to argue for the moral position that I take, so that anyone who accepts certain assumptions, to be made explicit, will, I hope, accept my conclusion.

I begin with the assumption that suffering and death from lack of food, shelter and medical care are bad. I think most people will agree about this, although one may reach the same view by different routes. I shall not argue for this view. People can hold all sorts of eccentric positions, and perhaps from some of them it would not follow that death by starvation is in itself bad. It is difficult, perhaps impossible, to refute such positions, and so for brevity I will henceforth take this assumption as accepted. Those who disagree need read no further.

My next point is this: if it is in our power to prevent something bad from happening, without thereby sacrificing anything of comparable moral importance, we ought, morally, to do it. By 'without sacrificing anything of comparable moral importance' I mean without causing anything else comparably bad to happen, or doing something that is wrong in itself, or failing to promote some moral good, comparable in significance to the bad thing that we can prevent. This principle seems almost as uncontroversial as the last one. It requires us only to prevent what is bad, and not to promote what is good, and it requires this of us only when we can do it without sacrificing anything that is, from the moral point of view, comparably important. I could even, as far as the application of my argument to the Bengal emergency is concerned, qualify the point so as to make it: if it is in our power to prevent something very bad from happening, without thereby sacrificing anything morally significant, we ought, morally, to do it. An application of this principle would be as follows: if I am walking past a shallow pond and see a child drowning in it, I ought to wade in and pull the child out. This will mean getting my clothes muddy, but this is insignificant, while the death of the child would presumably be a very bad thing.

The uncontroversial appearance of the principle just stated is deceptive. If it were acted upon, even in its qualified form, our lives, our society, and our world would be fundamentally changed. For the principle takes, first, no account of proximity or distance. It makes no moral difference whether the person I can help is a neighbour's child ten yards from me or a Bengali whose name I shall never know, ten thousand miles away. Secondly, the principle makes no distinction between cases in which I am the only person who could possibly do anything and cases in which I am just one among millions in the same position.

I do not think I need to say much in defence of the refusal to take proximity and distance into account. The fact that a person is physically near to us, so that we have personal contact with him, may make it more likely that we *shall* assist him, but this does not show that we *ought* to help him rather than another who happens to be further away. If we accept any principle of impartiality, universalizability, equality, or whatever, we cannot discriminate against someone merely because he is far away from us (or we are far away from him). Admittedly, it is possible that we are in a better position to judge what needs to be done to help a person near to us than one far away, and perhaps also to provide the assistance we judge to be necessary. If this were the case, it would be a reason for helping those near to us first. This may once have been a justification for being more concerned with the poor in one's town than with famine victims in India. Unfortunately for those who like to keep their moral responsibilities limited, instant communication and swift transportation have changed the situation. From the moral point of view, the development of the world into a 'global village' has made an important, though still unrecognized, difference to our moral situation. Expert observers and supervisors, sent out by famine relief organizations or permanently stationed in famine-prone areas, can direct our aid to a refugee in Bengal almost as effectively as we could get it to someone in our own block. There would seem therefore, to be no possible justification for discriminating on geographical grounds.

There may be a greater need to defend the second implication of my principle – that the fact that there are millions of other people in the same position, in respect to the Bengali refugees, as I am, does not make the situation significantly different from a situation in which I am the only person who can prevent something very bad from occurring. Again, of course, I admit that there is a psychological difference between the cases; one feels less guilty about doing nothing if one can point to others, similarly placed, who have also done nothing. Yet this can make no real difference to our moral obligations. Should I consider that I am less obliged to pull the drowning child out of the pond if on looking around I see other people, no further away than I am, who have also noticed the child but are doing nothing? One has only to ask this question to see the absurdity of the view that numbers lessen obligation. It is a view that is an ideal excuse for inactivity; unfortunately most of the major evils – poverty, over-population, pollution – are problems in which everyone is almost equally involved.

The view that numbers do make a difference can be made plausible if stated in this way: if everyone in circumstances like mine gave £5 to the Bengal Relief Fund, there would be enough to provide food, shelter and medical care for the refugees; there is no reason why I should give more than anyone else in the same circumstances as I am; therefore I have no obligation to give more than £5. Each premise in this argument is true, and the argument looks sound. It may convince us, unless we notice that it is based on a hypothetical premise, although the conclusion is not stated hypothetically. The argument would be sound if the conclusion were: if everyone in circumstances like mine were to give £5, I would have no obligation to give more than £5. If the conclusion were so stated, however, it would be obvious that the argument has no bearing on a situation in which it is not the case that everyone else gives £5. This, of course, is the actual situation. It is more or less certain that not everyone in circumstances like mine will give £5. So there will not be enough to provide the needed food, shelter and medical care. Therefore by giving more than £5 I will prevent more suffering than I would if I gave just £5.

If my argument so far has been sound, neither our distance from a preventable evil nor the number of other people who, in respect to that evil, are in the same situation as we are, lessens our obligation to mitigate or prevent that evil. I shall therefore take as established the principle I asserted earlier. As I have already said, I need to assert it only in its qualified form: if it is in our power to prevent something very bad from happening, without thereby sacrificing anything else morally significant, we ought, morally, to do it.

The outcome of this argument is that our traditional moral categories are upset. The traditional distinction between duty and charity cannot be drawn, or at least, not in the place we normally draw it. Giving money to the Bengal Relief Fund is regarded as an act of charity in our society. The bodies which collect money are known as 'charities'. These organizations see themselves in this way – if you send them a cheque, you will be thanked for your 'generosity'. Because giving money is regarded as an act of charity, it is not thought that there is anything wrong with not giving. The charitable man may be praised, but the man who is not charitable is not condemned. People do not feel in any way ashamed or guilty about spending money on new clothes or a new car instead of giving it to famine relief. (Indeed, the alternative does not occur to them.) This way of looking at the matter cannot be justified. When we buy new clothes not to keep ourselves warm but to look 'well-dressed' we are not providing for any important need. We would not be sacrificing anything significant if we were to continue to wear our old clothes, and give the money to famine relief.

By doing so, we would be preventing another person from starving. It follows from what I have said earlier that we ought to give money away, rather than spend it on clothes which we do not need to keep us warm. To do so is not charitable, or generous. Nor is it the kind of act which philosophers and theologians have called 'supererogatory' – an act which it would be good to do, but not wrong not to do. On the contrary, we ought to give the money away, and it is wrong not to do so...

It may still be thought that my conclusions are so wildly out of line with what everyone else thinks and has always thought that there must be something wrong with the argument somewhere. In order to show that my conclusions, while certainly contrary to contemporary Western moral standards, would not have seemed so extraordinary at other times and in other places, I would like to quote a passage from a writer not normally thought of as a way-out radical, Thomas Aquinas:

> Now, according to the natural order instituted by divine providence, material goods are provided for the satisfaction of human needs. Therefore the division and appropriation of property, which proceeds from human law, must not hinder the satisfaction of man's necessity from such goods. Equally, whatever a man has in superabundance is owed, of natural right, to the poor for their sustenance. So Ambrosius says, and it is also to be found in the *Decretum Gratiani*: 'The bread which you withhold belongs to the hungry; the clothing you shut away, to the naked; and the money you bury in the earth is the redemption and freedom of the penniless.'[1]

A...point raised by the conclusion reached earlier relates to the question of just how much we all ought to be giving away. One possibility...is that we ought to give until we reach the level of marginal utility – that is, the level at which, by giving more, I would cause as much suffering to myself or my dependants as I would relieve by my gift. This would mean, of course, that one would reduce oneself to very near the material circumstances of a Bengali refuge. It will be recalled that earlier I put forward both a strong and a moderate version of the principle of preventing bad occurrences. The strong version, which required us to prevent bad things from happening unless in doing so we would be sacrificing something of comparable moral significance, does seem to require reducing ourselves to the level of marginal utility. I should also say that the strong version seems to me to be the correct one. I proposed the more moderate version – that we should prevent bad occurrences unless, to do so, we had to sacrifice something morally significant – only in order to show that even on this surely undeniable principle a great change in our way of life is required. On the more moderate principle, it may not follow that we ought to reduce ourselves to the level of marginal utility, for one might hold that to reduce oneself and one's family to this level is to cause something significantly bad to happen. Whether this is so I shall not discuss, since, as I have said, I can see no good reason for holding the moderate version of the principle rather than the strong version. Even if we accepted the principle only in its moderate form, however, it should be clear that we would have to give away enough to ensure that the consumer society, dependent as it is on people spending on trivia rather than giving to famine relief, would slow down and perhaps disappear entirely. There are several reasons why this would be desirable in itself. The value and necessity of economic growth are now being questioned not only by

---

[1] *Summa Theologiae*, II, 2, qu. 66, art. 7.

conservationists, but by economists as well. There is no doubt, too, that the consumer society has had a distorting effect on the goals and purposes of its members. Yet looking at the matter purely from the point of view of overseas aid, there must be a limit to the extent to which we should deliberately slow down our economy; for it might be the case that if we gave away, say, 40 per cent of our Gross National Product, we would slow down the economy so much that in absolute terms we would be giving less than if we gave 25 per cent of the much larger GNP that we would have if we limited our contribution to this smaller percentage. I mention this only as an indication of the sort of factor that one would have to take into account in working out an ideal. Since Western societies generally consider 1 per cent of the GNP an acceptable level for overseas aid, the matter is entirely academic. Nor does it affect the question of how much an individual should give in a society in which very few are giving substantial amounts.

It is sometimes said, though less often now than it used to be, that philosophers have no special role to play in public affairs, since most public issues depend primarily on an assessment of facts. On questions of fact, it is said, philosophers as such have no special expertise, and so it has been possible to engage in philosophy without committing oneself to any position on major public issues. No doubt there are some issues of social policy and foreign policy about which it can truly be said that a really expert assessment of the facts is required before taking sides or acting, but the issue of famine is surely not one of these. The facts about the existence of suffering are beyond dispute. Nor, I think, is it disputed that we can do something about it, either through orthodox methods of famine relief or through population control or both. This is therefore an issue on which philosophers are competent to take a position. The issue is one which faces everyone who has more money than he needs to support himself and his dependants, or who is in a position to take some sort of political action. These categories must include practically every teacher and student of philosophy in the universities of the Western world. If philosophy is to deal with matters that are relevant to both teachers and students, this is an issue that philosophers should discuss.

Discussion, though, is not enough. What is the point of relating philosophy to public (and personal) affairs if we do not take our conclusions seriously? In this instance, taking our conclusion seriously means acting upon it. The philosopher will not find it any easier than anyone else to alter his attitudes and way of life to the extent that, if I am right, is involved in doing everything that we ought to be doing. At the very least, though, one can make a start. The philosopher who does so will have to sacrifice some of the benefits of the consumer society, but he can find compensation in the satisfaction of a way of life in which theory and practice, if not yet in harmony, are at least coming together.

11   Medical Ethics and the Termination of Life: James Rachels, *Active and Passive Euthanasia**

Few problems in practical ethics raise more controversy than the issue of euthanasia, or so-called 'mercy killing', that is to say the ending of a life when doing so is taken to be in the best interests of the patient. If euthanasia is performed against someone's will, it is clearly murder; and most countries also forbid deliberate euthanasia even for patients who wish to die (e.g. because they are terminally ill and in great pain or distress), and also for those who cannot express a wish (e.g. because they are very young, or senile or in a coma) but for whom, because of their condition, it is presumed that continued life is against their interests. Yet although actively killing someone is widely[1] prohibited in all these latter cases, many jurisdictions allow what is sometimes called 'passive euthanasia' – that is, deliberately withholding treatment (and perhaps even going so far as to stop nutrition and other life-support measures) in order to 'allow' the patient to die.[2]

In our next extract, the American moral philosopher James Rachels mounts a powerful critique of the conventional doctrine that makes a moral distinction between active and passive euthanasia, forbidding the former but permitting the latter.[3] First, he argues that active euthanasia may actually be more humane than passive: if one simply withholds treatment, death may take longer, and often be slow and painful. Second, he objects that the doctrine leads to medical decisions being taken on irrelevant grounds; thus a Down's syndrome baby may be 'allowed to die' if it happens to have a stomach obstruction –

though the obstruction could in fact be cured by a relatively simple operation. Either the lives of Down's syndrome children are worth preserving or they are not, Rachels argues; but either way this should not be decided in the light of some accidental factor such as whether they happen to have a minor stomach condition. In the third place, Rachels questions whether the underlying distinction between killing and letting die has any moral importance. If someone drowns a young cousin in order to inherit his money, is that any worse than deliberately letting the cousin drown when he happens to slip and fall into the water? Rachels's fourth and final argument is that it is unsound to rely on the idea that in the passive euthanasia case 'the doctor does nothing, and the patient dies of whatever ills already afflict him'. Deliberately allowing someone to die, Rachels argues, *is* 'doing something'; and 'the decision to let a patient die is subject to moral appraisal in the same way that a decision to kill him would be subject to moral appraisal'.

One interesting result of Rachels's position is that the *moral* significance of the distinction between killing and letting die diverges radically, on his view, from its *legal* significance. For from a legal point of view, I would be clearly guilty of murder if I drown someone in a pond; while if I merely fail to rescue them from the pond when I can easily do so, I would in most cases be guilty of no legal offence whatsoever. One could argue that the law is simply misguided in making this distinction, and should be changed; but many

---

* James Rachels, 'Active and Passive Euthanasia', originally published in *New England Journal of Medicine* (1975), 78–80.

[1] Though not universally; at the time of writing, Holland and Switzerland are exceptions.

[2] See for example the legal judgments in the cases of Tony Bland (England, 1992) and Terri Schiavo (USA, 2005).

[3] This doctrine is sometimes summarized in the slogan 'Thou shalt not kill, but needst not strive / Officiously to keep alive'. However, the original poem from which these lines are taken ('The Latest Decalogue' by the nineteenth-century poet Arthur Hugh Clough) in fact bitterly satirizes the kind of morality implied by relying on such a distinction. Thus a later couplet reads: 'Thou shalt not steal; an empty feat / When it's so lucrative to cheat.'

share a powerful intuition that the law captures something important here, and that failing to rescue, even if maliciously motivated, still falls morally far short of deliberately initiating the sequence of events that causes death.

It is important to note that Rachels's arguments do not themselves settle certain fundamental underlying questions such as whether euthanasia is wrong in itself − a question that has vital importance in, for example, the Down's syndrome case, or in cases of so-called 'persistent vegetative state' comas. Those who believe it is *not* wrong may welcome his attack on the present compromise that permits only passive euthanasia, and look forward to the time when active euthanasia too will be included as permissible, thus allowing doctors to terminate such lives more quickly and easily. Those who believe deliberate killing of the innocent and vulnerable is always wrong may worry that his attack on the present legal 'halfway house' (which allows passive but not active euthanasia) may help prepare the ground for further liberalization of the law. The debate continues.

The traditional distinction between active and passive euthanasia requires critical analysis. The conventional doctrine is that there is such an important moral difference between the two that, although the latter is sometimes permissible, the former is always forbidden. This doctrine may be challenged for several reasons. First of all, active euthanasia is in many cases more humane than passive euthanasia. Secondly, the conventional doctrine leads to decisions concerning life and death on irrelevant grounds. Thirdly, the doctrine rests on a distinction between killing and letting die that itself has no moral importance. Fourthly, the most common arguments in favour of the doctrine are invalid. I therefore suggest that the American Medical Association policy statement that endorses this doctrine is unsound.

The distinction between active and passive euthanasia is thought to be crucial for medical ethics. The idea is that it is permissible, at least in some cases, to withhold treatment and allow a patient to die, but it is never permissible to take any direct action designed to kill the patient. This doctrine seems to be accepted by most doctors, and it is endorsed in a statement adopted by the House of Delegates of the American Medical Association on December 4, 1973.

> The intentional termination of the life of one human being by another − mercy killing − is contrary to that for which the medical profession stands and is contrary to the policy of the American Medical Association.
> The cessation of the employment of extraordinary means to prolong the life of the body when there is irrefutable evidence that biological death is imminent is the decision of the patient and/or his immediate family. The advice and judgment of the physician should be freely available to the patient and/or his immediate family.

However, a strong case can be made against this doctrine. In what follows I will set out some of the relevant arguments, and urge doctors to reconsider their views on this matter.

To begin with a familiar type of situation, a patient who is dying of incurable cancer of the throat is in terrible pain, which can no longer be satisfactorily alleviated. He is certain to die within a few days, even if present treatment is continued, but he does not want to go on living for those days, since the pain is unbearable. So he asks the doctor for an end to it, and his family join in the request.

Suppose the doctor agrees to withhold treatment, as the conventional doctrine says he may. The justification for his doing so is that the patient is in terrible agony, and since he is going to die anyway, it would be wrong to prolong his suffering needlessly. But now notice this. If one simply withholds treatment, it may take the patient longer to die, and so he may suffer more than he would if more direct action were taken and a lethal injection given. This fact provides strong reason for thinking that, once the initial decision not to prolong his agony has been made, active euthanasia is actually preferable to passive euthanasia, rather than the reverse. To say otherwise is to endorse the option that leads to more suffering rather than less, and is contrary to the humanitarian impulse that prompts the decision not to prolong his life in the first place.

Part of my point is that the process of being 'allowed to die' can be relatively slow and painful, whereas being given a lethal injection is relatively quick and painless. Let me give a different sort of example. In the United States about one in 600 babies is born with Down's syndrome. Most of these babies are otherwise healthy – that is, with only the usual pediatric care, they will proceed to an otherwise normal infancy. Some, however, are born with congenital defects such as intestinal obstructions that require operations if they are to live. Sometimes, the parents and the doctor will decide not to operate, and let the infant die. Anthony Shaw describes what happens then:

> When surgery is denied [the doctor] must try to keep the infant from suffering while natural forces sap the baby's life away. As a surgeon whose natural inclination is to use the scalpel to fight off death, standing by and watching a salvageable baby die is the most emotionally exhausting experience I know. It is easy at a conference, in a theoretical discussion, to decide that such infants should be allowed to die. It is altogether different to stand by in the nursery and watch as dehydration and infection wither a tiny being over hours and days. This is a terrible ordeal for me and the hospital staff – much more so than for the parents who never set foot in the nursery.[1]

I can understand why some people are opposed to all euthanasia, and insist that such infants must be allowed to live. I think I can also understand why some other people favour destroying these babies quickly and painlessly. But why should anyone favour letting 'dehydration and infection wither a tiny being over hours and days'? The doctrine that says that a baby may be allowed to dehydrate and wither, but may not be given an injection that would end its life without suffering, seems so patently cruel as to require no further refutation. The strong language is not intended to offend, but only to put the point in the clearest possible way.

My second argument is that the conventional doctrine leads to decisions concerning life and death made on irrelevant grounds.

Consider again the case of the infants with Down's syndrome who need operations for congenital defects unrelated to the syndrome to live. Sometimes there is no operation, and the baby dies, but when there is no such defect, the baby lives on. Now, an operation such as that to remove an intestinal obstruction is not prohibitively difficult. The reason why such operations are not performed in these cases is, clearly, that the child has Down's syndrome and the parents and doctor judge that because of that fact it is better for the child to die.

But notice that this situation is absurd, no matter what view one takes of the lives and potentials of such babies. If the life of such an infant is worth preserving, what does it matter if it needs a simple operation? Or, if one thinks it better that such a baby should not live on, what difference does it make that it happens to have an

---

[1] *A. Shaw, 'Doctor, Do We Have a Choice?', *New York Times Magazine* (30 January 1972), 54.

unobstructed intestinal tract? In either case, the matter of life and death is being decided on irrelevant grounds. It is the Down's syndrome, and not the intestines, that is the issue. The matter should be decided, if at all, on that basis, and not be allowed to depend on the essentially irrelevant question of whether the intestinal tract is blocked.

What makes this situation possible, of course, is the idea that when there is an intestinal blockage, one can 'let the baby die', but that when there is no such blockage there is nothing that can be done, for one must not 'kill' it. The fact that this idea leads to such results as deciding life or death on irrelevant grounds is another good reason why the doctrine should be rejected.

One reason so many people think that there is an important difference between active and passive euthanasia is that they think killing someone is morally worse than letting someone die. But is it? Is killing, in itself, worse than letting die? To investigate that issue, two cases may be considered that are exactly alike except that one involves killing whereas the other involves letting someone die. Then it can be asked whether this difference makes any difference to the moral assessments. It is important that the cases be exactly alike, except for this one difference, since otherwise one cannot be confident that it is this difference and not some other that accounts for any variation in the assessments of the two cases. So let us consider this pair of cases.

In the first, Smith stands to gain a large inheritance if anything should happen to his six-year-old cousin. One evening, while the child is taking his bath, Smith sneaks into the bathroom and drowns the child, and then arranges things so that it will look like an accident.

In the second, Jones also stands to gain if anything should happen to his six-year-old cousin. Like Smith, Jones sneaks in planning to drown the child in his bath. However, just as he enters the bathroom, Jones sees the child slip and hit his head and fall face down in the water. Jones is delighted: he stands by, ready to push the child's head back under if it is necessary, but it is not. With only a little thrashing about, the child drowns all by himself, 'accidentally', as Jones watches and does nothing.

Now Smith killed the child, whereas Jones 'merely' let the child die. That is the only difference. Did either man behave better from a moral point of view? If the difference between killing and letting die were in itself a morally important matter, one should say that Jones's behaviour was less reprehensible than Smith's. But does one really want to say that? I think not. In the first place, both men acted from the same motive, personal gain, and both had exactly the same end in view when they acted. It may be inferred from Smith's conduct that he is a bad man, although that judgement may be withdrawn or modified if certain further facts are learned about him – for example, that he is mentally deranged. But would not the very same thing be inferred about Jones from his conduct? And would not the same further considerations also be relevant to any modification of this judgement? Moreover, suppose Jones pleaded, in his own defence, 'After all, I didn't do anything except just stand there and watch the child drown. I didn't kill him: I only let him die.' Again, if letting die were in itself any less bad than killing, this defence should have at least some weight. But it does not. Such a 'defence' can only be regarded as a grotesque perversion of moral reasoning. Morally speaking, it is no defence at all.

Now, it may be pointed out, quite properly, that the cases of euthanasia with which doctors are concerned are not like this at all. They do not involve personal gain or the destruction of normal healthy children. Doctors are concerned only with cases where the patient's life is of no further use to him, or in which the patient's life has become or will soon become a terrible burden. However, the point is the same in these cases: the bare difference between killing and letting die does not, in itself, make a moral difference. If a doctor lets a patient die, for humane reasons, he is in the same moral position as if he had given the patient a lethal injection for humane reasons. If his decision was wrong – if, for example, the patient's illness was in fact curable – the decision would be equally regrettable no matter which method was used to carry it out. And if the doctor's decision was the right one, the method used is not in itself important.

The AMA policy statement isolates the crucial issue very well: the crucial issue is 'the intentional termination of the life of one human being by another'. But after identifying this issue, and forbidding 'mercy killing', the statement goes on to deny that the cessation of treatment is the intentional termination of a life. This is where the mistake comes in, for what is the cessation of treatment, in these circumstances, if it is not 'the intentional termination of the life of one human being by another'? Of course it is exactly that, and if it were not, there would be no point to it.

Many people will find this judgement hard to accept. One reason, I think, is that it is very easy to conflate the question of whether killing is, in itself, worse than letting die, with the very different question of whether most actual cases of killing are more reprehensible than most actual cases of letting die. Most actual cases of killing are clearly terrible (think, for example, of all the murders reported in the newspapers), and one hears of such cases every day. On the other hand, one hardly ever hears of a case of letting die, except for the actions of doctors who are motivated by humanitarian reasons. So one learns to think of killing in a much worse light than of letting die. But this does not mean that there is something about killing that makes it in itself worse than letting die, for it is not the bare difference between killing and letting die that makes the difference in these cases. Rather, the other factors – the murderer's motive of personal gain, for example, contrasted with the doctor's humanitarian motivation – account for different reactions to the different cases.

I have argued that killing is not in itself any worse than letting die: if my contention is right, it follows that active euthanasia is not any worse than passive euthanasia. What arguments can be given on the other side? The most common, I believe, is the following:

'The important difference between active and passive euthanasia is that, in passive euthanasia, the doctor does not do anything to bring about the patient's death. The doctor does nothing, and the patient dies of whatever ills already afflict him. In active euthanasia, however, the doctor does something to bring about the patient's death: he kills him. The doctor who gives the patient with cancer a lethal injection has himself caused his patient's death: whereas if he merely ceases treatment, the cancer is the cause of the death.'

A number of points need to be made here. The first is that it is not exactly correct to say that in passive euthanasia the doctor does nothing, for he does do one thing that is very important: he lets the patient die. 'Letting someone die' is certainly different, in some respects, from other types of action – mainly in that it is the kind of action that one may perform by way of not performing certain other actions. For example, one may let a patient die by way of not giving medication, just as one may insult someone by not shaking his hand. But for any purpose of moral assessment, it is a type of action nonetheless. The decision to let a patient die is subject to moral appraisal in the same way that a decision to kill him would be subject to moral appraisal: it may be assessed as wise or unwise, compassionate or sadistic, right or wrong. If a doctor deliberately let a patient die who was suffering from a routinely curable illness, the doctor would certainly be to blame for what he had done, just as he would be to blame if he had needlessly killed the patient. Charges against him would then be appropriate. If so, it would be no defence at all for him to insist that he didn't 'do anything'. He would have done something very serious indeed, for he let his patient die.

Fixing the cause of death may be very important from a legal point of view, for it may determine whether criminal charges are brought against the doctor. But I do not think that this notion can be used to show a moral difference between active and passive euthanasia. The reason why it is considered bad to be the cause of someone's death is that death is regarded as a great evil – and so it is. However, if it has been decided that euthanasia – even passive euthanasia – is desirable in a given case, it has also been decided that in this instance death is no greater an evil than the patient's continued existence. And if this is true, the usual reason for not wanting to be the cause of someone's death simply does not apply.

Finally, doctors may think that all of this is only of academic interest – the sort of thing that philosophers may worry about but that has no practical bearing on their own work. After all, doctors must be concerned about the legal consequences of what they do, and active euthanasia is forbidden by the law. But even so, doctors should also be concerned with the fact that the law is forcing upon them a moral doctrine that may well be indefensible, and has a considerable effect on their practices. Of course, most doctors are not now in the position of being coerced in this matter, for they do not regard themselves as merely going along with what the law requires. Rather, in statements such as the AMA policy statement that I have quoted, they are endorsing this doctrine as a central point of medical ethics. In that statement, active euthanasia is condemned not merely as illegal, but as 'contrary to that for which the medical profession stands', whereas passive euthanasia is approved. However, the preceding considerations suggest that there is really no moral difference between the two, considered in themselves (there may be important moral differences in some cases in their *consequences*, but, as I pointed out, these differences may make active euthanasia, and not passive euthanasia, the morally preferable option). So, whereas doctors may have to discriminate between active and passive euthanasia to satisfy the law, they should not do any more than that. In particular, they should not give the distinction any added authority and weight by writing it into official statements of medical ethics.

12 Cloning, Sexual Reproduction and Genetic Engineering: Leon R. Kass, *The Wisdom of Repugnance**

Our final extract deals with the problems of cloning, which are among the many ethical issues raised by humankind's rapidly increasing technological power over the natural world. The technique of producing a new living creature artificially and asexually, by manipulating a single parent cell, is already established in the case of non-human animals, and it seems only a matter of time before it will be transferred to humans. In his article, Leon Kass mounts an impassioned attack on these developing 'new technologies of human reproduction'. He begins by pointing to a natural and widespread *repugnance* that is felt about the advent of human cloning. People are 'repelled' by ideas such as the mass reproduction of human beings, the 'bizarre' prospect of a woman giving birth to and rearing a genetic copy of herself, and the 'grotesqueness' of conceiving a child as an exact replacement for another who has died, and so on.

Revulsion, Kass admits, is not an argument; but he suggests that the natural human feelings that make us 'shudder' can nonetheless be valuable pointers to aspects of cloning that are indeed morally indefensible. The drive towards human cloning gets its impetus, he argues, from three perspectives: the *technological*, which treats reproduction as a 'neutral technique with no inherent meaning of goodness'; the liberal, or *libertarian*, which puts the highest value on 'personal empowerment'; and the *meliorist*, which sees all ethical decisions as subordinate to the end of producing improvements to and for the human race.

Although these approaches can be 'fine in themselves', according to Kass they ignore the deeper *meanings* of bringing forth life. Sexual reproduction is not something established by human decision or tradition – it is a natural process. Moreover, the biological facts involved 'foretell deep truths about our identity and our human condition'. Our very individuality as humans involves our being caught up in a natural web of family relationships – the social structures, rooted in biology, that make us who we are. A critic might object here that there is no reason why our social arrangements (e.g. for producing and rearing children) have to follow the ancient lines laid down by nature and biology – since with modern science we now have the power to forge alternative, and perhaps better, systems. To this, Kass responds that the natural reproductive structures, ultimately based on sexual intercourse between two people, 'have a soul-elevating power' – in other words, a deep moral significance. Sex makes us reach out towards another being with special interest and intensity; it is mysteriously linked to our own mortality, since we reproduce ourselves in the knowledge that our offspring will take our place when we die; and it fosters love and unification, as the parents share an outgoing love for the 'third being' who is flesh of their flesh. In short, our human biology and our deepest moral destiny are inextricably linked; and hence 'the severing of procreation from sex, love and intimacy is inherently dehumanizing'.

Kass concludes by raising four specific further objections to cloning. First, by manipulating of genetic material, it involves an 'unethical experiment' on the resulting child to be.[1] Second, it 'creates serious issues of identity and individuality' (for example, a cloned baby may be the identical twin of his father). Third, cloning turns procreation into 'manufacture', moving us towards a world where all of nature is simply treated as a mechanism to further our own preconceptions of what we want and need. And

---

* From *The New Republic* (2 June 1997), 17–26; abridged.
[1] Genetic screening and prenatal diagnosis is quite different, Kass argues at the end of the extract, since 'it serves the medical goal of healing existing individuals'.

fourth, it misses the true meaning of having children. In attempting directly to control and fashion the new life, we would be forgetting the natural meaning of parenthood, which involves a certain vulnerability and letting be, as we open ourselves to the arrival of a new individual – to 'whatever this child turns out to be'. True parenting is 'open and forward-looking'; cloning, with its aim of control and manipulation, is 'inherently despotic'.

Though Kass's rich armoury of arguments is laid out with powerful emotional flourishes, they can all be subjected to scrutiny, and will no doubt be strongly criticized by those who see the technological and scientific revolution as something to be embraced, as a means of improving the human lot. Ultimately, however, the worldview that Kass implicitly advocates cannot, perhaps, be assessed by reason alone. As with much of philosophy, the intellectual analysis tells only part of the story, for it rides on the back of deep intuitions whose appeal can be made vivid, but not conclusively demonstrated.

...Cloning first came to public attention roughly thirty years ago, following the successful asexual production, in England, of a clutch of tadpole clones by the technique of nuclear transplantation... Much has happened in the intervening years. It has become harder, not easier, to discern the true meaning of human cloning. We have in some sense been softened up to the idea – through movies, cartoons, jokes and intermittent commentary in the mass media, some serious, most light-hearted. We have become accustomed to new practices in human reproduction: not just in vitro fertilization, but also embryo manipulation, embryo donation and surrogate pregnancy. Animal biotechnology has yielded transgenic animals and a burgeoning science of genetic engineering, easily and soon to be transferable to humans.

Even more important, changes in the broader culture make it now vastly more difficult to express a common and respectful understanding of sexuality, procreation, nascent life, family life, and the meaning of motherhood, fatherhood and the links between the generations. Twenty-five years ago, abortion was still largely illegal and thought to be immoral, the sexual revolution (made possible by the extramarital use of the pill) was still in its infancy, and few had yet heard about the reproductive rights of single women, homosexual men and lesbians... Then one could argue, without embarrassment, that the new technologies of human reproduction – babies without sex – and their confounding of normal kin relations – who's the mother: the egg donor, the surrogate who carries and delivers, or the one who rears? – would 'undermine the justification and support that biological parenthood gives to the monogamous marriage'. Today, defenders of stable monogamous marriage risk charges of giving offence to those adults who are living in 'new family forms' or to those children who, even without the benefit of assisted reproduction, have acquired either three or four parents or one or none at all... In a world whose once-given natural boundaries are blurred by technological changes and whose moral boundaries are seemingly up for grabs, it is much more difficult to make persuasive the still compelling case against cloning humans beings. As Raskolnikov put it,[1] 'man gets used to everything – the beast!'...

---

[1] In Dostoevsky's novel *Crime and Punishment* (1866).

The wisdom of repugnance

'Offensive.' 'Grotesque.' 'Revolting.' 'Repugnant.' 'Repulsive.' These are the words most commonly heard regarding the prospect of human cloning. Such reactions come both from the man and woman in the street and from the intellectuals, from believers and atheists, from humanists and scientists. Even Dolly's creator[1] has said he 'would find it offensive' to clone a human being.

People are repelled by many aspects of human cloning. They recoil from the prospect of mass reproduction of human beings, with large clones of look-alikes compromised in their individuality; the idea of father–son or mother–daughter twins; the bizarre prospects of a woman giving birth to and rearing a genetic copy of herself, her spouse or even her deceased father or mother; the grotesqueness of conceiving a child as an exact replacement for another who has died; the utilitarian replacement of embryonic genetic duplicates of oneself, to be frozen away or created when necessary, in case of need for homologous tissues or organs for transplantation; the narcissism of those who would clone themselves and the arrogance of others who think they know who deserves to be cloned or which genotype any child-to-be should be thrilled to receive; the Frankensteinian hubris to create human life and increasingly to control its destiny; man playing God. Almost no one finds any of the suggested reasons for human cloning compelling; almost everyone anticipates its possible misuses and abuses. Moreover, many people feel oppressed by the sense that there is probably nothing we can do to prevent it from happening. This makes the prospect of it all the more revolting.

Revulsion is not an argument; and some of yesterday's repugnances are today calmly accepted – though, one must add, not always for the better. In crucial cases, however, repugnance is the emotional expression of deep wisdom, beyond reason's power fully to articulate it. Can anyone really give an argument fully adequate to the horror which is father–daughter incest (even with consent), or having sex with animals, or mutilating a corpse, or eating human flesh, or even (just!) raping or murdering another human being? Would anybody's failure to give full rational justification for his or her revulsion at these practices make that revulsion ethically suspect? Not at all. On the contrary, we are suspicious of those who think that they can rationalize away our horror, say by trying to explain the enormity of incest with arguments only about the genetic risks of inbreeding.

The repugnance of cloning belongs in this category. We are repelled by the prospect of cloning human beings not because of the strangeness or novelty of the undertaking, but because we intuit and feel, immediately and without argument, the violation of things that we rightfully hold dear. Repugnance, here as elsewhere, revolts against the excesses of human wilfulness, warning us not to transgress what is unspeakably profound. Indeed, in this age in which everything is held to be permissible so long as it is freely done, in which our given human nature no longer commands respect, in which our bodies are regarded as mere instruments of our autonomous rational wills, repugnance may be the only voice left that speaks up to defend the central core of our humanity. Shallow are the souls that have forgotten how to shudder.

---

[1] Dolly the sheep, born in Edinburgh in 1997, was the first mammal to be cloned from an adult cell. She died, of progressive lung disease, in 2003.

The goods protected by our repugnance are generally overlooked by our customary ways of approaching all new biomedical technologies. The way we evaluate cloning ethically will in fact be shaped by how we characterize it descriptively, by the context into which we place it, and by the perspective from which we view it. The first task for ethics is proper description. And here is where our failure begins.

Typically, cloning is discussed in one or more of three familiar contexts, which one might call the technological, the liberal and the meliorist. Under the first, cloning will be seen as an extension of existing techniques for assisting reproduction and determining the genetic makeup of children. Like them cloning is to be regarded as a neutral technique, with no inherent meaning of goodness, but subject to multiple uses, some good, some bad. The morality of cloning thus depends absolutely on the goodness or badness of the motives and intentions of the cloners: as one bioethicist puts it, 'the ethics must be judged only by the way the parents nurture and rear their resulting child and whether they bestow the same love and affection on a child brought into existence by a technique of assisted reproduction as they would on a child born in the usual way.'

The liberal (or libertarian or liberationist) perspective sets cloning in the context of rights, freedoms and personal empowerment. Cloning is just a new option for exercising an individual's right to reproduce or to have the kind of child that he or she wants. Alternatively, cloning enhances our liberation (especially women's liberation) from the confines of nature, the vagaries of chance, or the necessity for sexual mating... For those who hold this outlook, the only moral restraints on cloning are adequately informed consent and the avoidance of bodily harm...

The meliorist[1] perspective embraces valetudinarians and also eugenicists... These people see in cloning a new prospect for improving human beings – minimally, by ensuring the perpetuation of healthy individuals by avoiding the risks of genetic disease inherent in the lottery of sex, and maximally, by producing 'optimum babies', preserving outstanding genetic material and (with the help of soon-to-come techniques for precise genetic engineering) enhancing inborn human capacities on many fronts. Here the morality of cloning as a means is justified solely by the excellence of the end, that is, by the outstanding traits of the individuals cloned – beauty or brawn or brains...

These three approaches... all perfectly fine in their places, are sorely wanting as approaches to human procreation... The technical, liberal and meliorist approaches all ignore the deeper anthropological, social and indeed ontological meanings of bringing forth new life. To this more fitting and more profound point of view, cloning shows itself to be a major alteration, indeed a major violation, of our given nature as embodied, gendered and engendering beings – and of the social relations built on this natural ground. Once this perspective is recognized, the ethical judgement on cloning can no longer be reduced to a matter of motives and intentions, rights and freedoms, benefits and harms, or even means and ends. It must be regarded primarily as a matter of meaning: Is cloning a fulfilment of human begetting and belonging? Or is cloning rather, as I contend, their pollution and perversion? To pollution and perversion, the fitting response can only be horror and revulsion; and conversely, generalized horror and revulsion are prima facie evidence of foulness and violation. The burden of moral

---

[1] Aimed at improvement; from the Latin word *melior* (better).

argument must fall entirely on those who want to declare the widespread repugnances of mankind to be merely timidity or superstition.

Yet repugnance need not stand naked before the bar of reason. The wisdom of our horror at human cloning can be partially articulated, even if this is finally one of those instances about which the heart has its reason that reason cannot entirely know.[1]

The profundity of sex

To see cloning in its proper context, we must begin, not as I did before, with laboratory technique, but with the anthropology – natural and social – of sexual reproduction.

Sexual reproduction, by which I mean the generation of new life from (exactly) two complementary elements, one female, one male (usually), through coitus – is established (if that is the right term) not by human decision, culture or tradition, but by nature; it is the natural way of all mammalian reproduction. By nature, each child has two complementary biological progenitors. Each child thus stems from and unites exactly two lineages. In natural generation, moreover, the precise genetic constitution of the resulting offspring is determined by a combination of nature and chance, not by human design: each human child shares the common natural human species genotype, each child is genetically equally kin to each (both) parent(s), yet each child is also genetically unique.

These biological truths about our origins foretell deep truths about our identity and about our human condition altogether. Every one of us is at once equally human, equally enmeshed in a particular familial nexus of origin, and equally individuated in our trajectory from birth to death – and, if all goes well, equally capable (despite our mortality) of participating, with a complementary other, in the very same renewal of such human possibility through procreation. Though less momentous than our common humanity, our genetic individuality is not humanly trivial. It shows itself forth in our distinctive appearance through which we are everywhere recognized: it is revealed in our 'signature' marks of fingerprints and our self-recognizing immune system: it symbolizes and foreshadows exactly the unique, never-to-be-repeated character of each human life.

Human societies virtually everywhere have structured child-rearing responsibilities and systems of identity and relationship on the bases of these deep natural facts of begetting. The mysterious yet ubiquitous 'love of one's own' is everywhere culturally exploited, to make sure that children are not just produced but well cared for and to create for everyone clear ties of meaning. But it is wrong to treat such naturally rooted social practices as mere cultural constructs (like left- or right-driving, or like burying or cremating the dead) that we can alter with little human cost. What would kinship be without its clear natural grounding? And what would identity be without kinship? We must resist those who have begun to refer to sexual reproduction as the 'traditional method of reproduction', who would have us regard as merely traditional, and by implication arbitrary, what is in truth not only natural but most certainly profound.

---

[1] 'The heart has its reasons that reason does not know' (Blaise Pascal, *Pensées* (1670)).

Asexual reproduction, which produces 'single-parent' offspring, is a radical departure from the natural human way, confounding all normal human understandings of father, mother, sibling, grandparent, etc., and all moral relations tied thereto. It becomes even more of a radical departure when the resulting offspring is a clone derived not from an embryo, but from a mature adult to whom the clone would be an identical twin: and when the process occurs not by natural accident (as in natural twinning) but by deliberate human design and manipulation: and when the child's (or children's) genetic constitution is pre-selected by the parent(s) (or scientists) ...

Let me test my claim of the profundity of the natural way by taking up a challenge recently posed by a friend. What if the given natural human way of reproduction were asexual, and we now had to deal with a new technological innovation – artificially induced sexual dimorphism and the fusing of complementary gametes – whose inventors argued that sexual reproduction promised all sorts of advantages, including hybrid vigour and the creation of greatly increased individuality? Would one then be forced to defend natural asexuality because it was natural? Could one claim that it carried deep human meaning?

The response to this challenge broaches the ontological meaning of sexual reproduction. For it is impossible, I submit, for there to have been human life – or even higher forms of animal life – in the absence of sexuality and sexual reproduction. We find asexual reproduction only in the lowest forms of life: bacteria, algae, fungi, some lower invertebrates. Sexuality brings with it a new and enriched relationship to the world. Only sexual animals can seek and find complementary others with whom to pursue a goal that transcends their own existence. For a sexual being, the world is no longer an indifferent and largely homogeneous *otherness*, in part edible, in part dangerous. It also contains some very special and related and complementary beings, of the same kind but of opposite sex, toward whom one reaches out with special interest and intensity. In higher birds and mammals, the outward gaze keeps a lookout not only for food and predators, but also for prospective mates: the beholding of the many-splendoured world is suffused with desire for union, the animal antecedent of human eros and the germ of sociality. Not by accident is the human animal both the sexiest animal – whose females do not go into heat but are receptive throughout the oestrous cycle and whose males must therefore have greater sexual appetite and energy in order to reproduce successfully – and also the most aspiring, the most social, the most open and the most intelligent animal.

The soul-elevating power of sexuality is, at bottom, rooted in its strange connection to mortality, which it simultaneously accepts and tries to overcome. Asexual reproduction may be seen as a continuation of the activity of self-preservation. When one organism buds or divides to become two, the original being is (doubly) preserved, and nothing dies. Sexuality, by contrast, means perishability and serves replacement: the two that come together to generate one soon will die. Sexual desire, in human beings as in animals, serves an end that is partly hidden from, and finally at odds with, the self-serving individual. Whether we know it or not, when we are sexually active we are voting with our genitalia for our own demise. The salmon swimming upstream to spawn and die tell the universal story: sex is bound up with death, to which it holds a partial answer in procreation.

The salmon and the other animals evince this truth blindly. Only the human being can understand what it means. As we learn so powerfully from the story of the Garden of Eden, our humanization is coincident with sexual self-consciousness, with the recognition of our sexual nakedness and all that it implies: shame at our needy incompleteness, unruly self-division and finitude; awe before the eternal; hope in the self-transcending possibilities of children and a relationship to the divine. In the sexually self-conscious animal, sexual desire can become eros, lust can become love. Sexual desire humanly regarded is thus sublimated into erotic longing for wholeness, completion and immortality, which drives us knowingly into the embrace and its generative fruit – as well as into all the higher human possibilities of deed, speech and song.

Through children, a good common to both husband and wife, male and female achieve some genuine unification (beyond the mere sexual 'union' which fails to do so). The two become one through sharing generous (not needy) love for this third being as good. Flesh of their flesh, the child is the parents' own commingled being externalized and given a separate and persisting existence. Unification is enhanced also by the commingled work of rearing. Providing an opening to the future beyond the grave, carrying not only our seed but also our names, our ways and our hopes that they will surpass us in goodness and happiness, children are a testament to the possibility of transcendence. Gender duality and sexual desire, which first draws our love upward and outside of ourselves, finally provide for the partial overcoming of the confinement and limitation of perishable embodiment altogether.

Human procreation, in sum, is not simply an activity of our rational wills. It is a more complete activity precisely because it engages us bodily, erotically and spiritually, as well as rationally. There is wisdom in the mystery of nature that has joined the pleasure of sex, the inarticulate longing for union, the communication of the loving embrace and the deep-seated and only partially articulate desire for children in the very activity by which we continue the chain of human existence and participate in the renewal of human possibility. Whether or not we know it, the severing of procreation from sex, love and intimacy is inherently dehumanizing, no matter how good the product.

We are now ready for the more specific objections to cloning.

The perversities of cloning

First, an important if formal objection: any attempt to clone a human being would constitute an unethical experiment upon the resulting child to be. As the animal experiments (frog and sheep) indicate, there are grave risks of mishaps and deformities. Moreover, because of what cloning means, one cannot presume a future cloned child's consent to be a clone, even a healthy one. Thus, ethically speaking, we cannot even get to know whether or not human cloning is feasible.

I understand, of course, the philosophical difficulty of trying to compare a life with defects against non-existence. Several bioethicists, proud of their philosophical cleverness, use this conundrum to embarrass claims that one can injure a child in its conception, precisely because it is only thanks to that complained-of conception that the child is alive to complain. But common sense tells us that we have no need to fear such philosophisms. For we surely know that people can harm and even maim children in the very act of conceiving them, say, by paternal transmission of the

AIDS virus, maternal transmission of heroin dependence ... And we believe that to do this intentionally, or even negligently, is inexcusable and clearly unethical ...

Cloning creates serious issues of identity and individuality. The cloned person may experience concerns about his distinctive identity not only because he will be in genotype and appearance identical to another human being, but in this case, because he may also be twin to the person who is his 'father' or 'mother', if one can still call them that. What would be the psychic burdens of being the 'child' or 'parent' of your twin? ...

Human cloning would also represent a giant step towards turning begetting into making, procreation into manufacture (literally, something 'handmade'), a process already begun with in vitro fertilization and genetic testing of embryos. With cloning, not only is the process in hand, but the total genetic blueprint of the cloned individual is selected and determined by the human artisans. To be sure, subsequent development will take place according to natural processes; and the resulting children will still be recognizably human. But we here would be taking a major step into making man himself simply another one of the man-made things. Human nature becomes merely the last part of nature to succumb to the technological project, which turns all of nature into raw material at human disposal, to be homogenized by our rationalized techniques according to the subjective prejudices of the day ...

Finally and perhaps most important, the practice of human cloning by nuclear transfer – like other anticipated forms of genetic engineering of the next generation – would enshrine and aggravate a profound and mischievous misunderstanding of the meaning of having children and of the parent–child relationship. When a couple now chooses to procreate, the partners are saying yes to the emergence of new life in its novelty, saying yes not only to having a child but also, tacitly, to having whatever child this child turns out to be. In accepting our finitude and opening ourselves to our replacement, we are tacitly confessing the limits of our control. In this ubiquitous way of nature, embracing the future by procreating means precisely that we are relinquishing our grip, in the very activity of taking up our own share in what we hope will be the immortality of human life and the human species. This means that our children are not *our* children: they are not our property, not our possessions. Neither are they supposed to live our lives for us, or anyone else's life but their own. To be sure, we seek to guide them on their way, imparting to them not just life but nurturing, love and a way of life; to be sure they bear our hopes that they will live fine and flourishing lives, enabling us in small measure to transcend our own limitations. Still, their genetic distinctiveness and independence are the natural foreshadowing of the deep truth that they have their own and never-before-enacted life to live. They are sprung from a past, but they take an uncharted course into the future.

Much harm is already done by parents who try to live vicariously through their children. Children are sometimes compelled to fulfil the broken dreams of unhappy parents: John Doe Jr or the III is under the burden of having to live up to his forebear's name. Still, if most parents have hopes for their children, cloning parents will have expectations. In cloning, such overbearing parents take at the start a decisive step which contradicts the entire meaning of the open and forward-looking nature of parent–child relations. The child is given a genotype that has already lived, with full expectation that this blueprint of a past life ought to be controlling of the life that is to come. Cloning is inherently despotic, for it seeks to make one's children (or someone else's children) after one's own image (or an image of one's choosing) and their future according to one's will. In some cases the despotism may be mild and benevolent. In other cases, it will be mischievous and downright tyrannical. But despotism – the control of another through one's will – it inevitably will be ...

We do indeed already practise negative eugenic selection, through genetic screening and prenatal diagnosis. Yet our practices are governed by a norm of health. We seek to prevent the birth of children who suffer from known (serious) genetic diseases. When and if gene therapy becomes possible, such diseases could then be treated in utero or even before implantation – I have no ethical objection in principle to such a practice (though I have some practical worries), precisely because it serves the medical goal of healing existing individuals. But therapy, to be therapy, implies not only an existing 'patient'. It also implies a norm of health. In this respect, even germline gene 'therapy', though practised not on a human being but on egg and sperm, is less radical than cloning, which is in no way therapeutic. But once one blurs the distinction between health promotion and genetic enhancement, between so-called negative and positive eugenics, one opens the door to all future eugenic designs ...

Specimen Questions

1 Critically assess Aristotle's justification of slavery by reference to 'natural' inequalities between human beings.

2 Explain and evaluate Aquinas's doctrine of the just war.

3 Select any two of Hume's arguments in favour of the permissibility of suicide, and explain why you find them persuasive or unpersuasive, as the case may be.

4 What do you consider to be the most interesting of Wollstonecraft's criticisms of the way in which relationships between men and women operated in her day? Are her ideas still relevant today?

5 Can preferential treatment towards friends and family be justified from the moral point of view? Discuss with reference to Godwin's example of the archbishop and the chambermaid.

6 Critically assess Bentham's general account of the purposes and justification of punishment.

7 'Our duties towards animals are merely indirect duties towards humanity' (Kant). Explain and discuss.

8 Explain what Leopold means by the need to *extend* ethics so as to cover man's relationship to the land. Does the idea of a 'land ethic' depend simply on an appeal to our emotions, or can it also be made intellectually defensible?

9 Expound and evaluate the 'violinist' analogy used by Thomson in defence of abortion.

10   Explain and critically assess Singer's argument for our obligation to relieve suffering in the third world. Why does the argument erode the traditional distinction between *duty* and *charity*?

11   Do Rachels's arguments succeed in establishing that there is no morally significant distinction between active and passive euthanasia?

12   Kass argues against cloning on the grounds that the 'severing of procreation from sex, love and intimacy is inherently dehumanizing'. Expound and critically evaluate his view.

Suggestions for Further Reading

Slavery and inequality

For a good account of the classical background, see M. I. Finley, *Ancient Slavery and Modern Ideology* (Cambridge: Cambridge University Press, 1980).

For an influential view of the ethical issues involved, see the essay 'What is Wrong with Slavery', in R. M. Hare, *Essays on Political Morality* (Oxford: Oxford University Press, 1989).

For wider discussion of the concept of equality in moral and political theory, see V. Haksar, *Equality, Liberty and Perfectionism* (Oxford: Oxford University Press, 1979).

See also Bernard Williams's famous essay 'The Idea of Equality', in P. Laslett and W. G. Runciman (eds), *Philosophy, Politics and Society* (Oxford: Blackwell, 1962).

For the question of whether a free agent should be allowed to sell himself into slavery, see J. S. Mill, *On Liberty*, ch. 5 (for details see Part X, extract 9).

War

A useful survey of just war theory may be found in R. L. Holmes, *On War and Morality* (Princeton: Princeton University Press, 1989). See also M. Walzer, *Just and Unjust Wars* (New York: Basic Books, 1977).

For a detailed discussion of Aquinas's position, see P. Ramsey, 'War and the Christian Conscience', in P. E. Sigmund (ed.), *St Thomas Aquinas on Politics and Ethics* (New York: Norton, 1988).

For a subtle discussion of the ethics of modern 'deterrent' weapons, see A. Kenny, *The Logic of Deterrence* (Chicago: University of Chicago Press, 1985).

A variety of stimulating essays on moral aspects of war may be found in R. A. Wasserstrom, *War and Morality* (Belmont, Calif.: Wadsworth, 1970).

For a critique of the doctrine of double effect, see P. Foot, *Virtues and Vices and Other Essays in Moral Philosophy* (Berkeley: University of California Press, 1978), pp. 19ff.

Taking one's own life

An excellent overview may be found in the entry on 'Suicide' in L. C. Becker (ed.), *Encyclopedia of Ethics* (New York: Garland, 1992).

A valuable collection of essays is M. P. Battin and D. J. Mayo, *Suicide: The Philosophical Issues* (New York: St Martin's, 1980). See also the essay by Battin in D. Van De Veer and T. Regan (eds), *Health Care Ethics* (Philadelphia: Temple University Press, 1987).

A famous argument against suicide, based on the 'categorical imperative' (see above, Part VIII, extract 5) is found in Immanuel Kant, *Groundwork of the Metaphysic of Morals* [1785], ch. 2, trans. H. J. Paton as *The Moral Law* (London: Hutchinson, 1948).

There is much illuminating discussion of some of the ethical issues involved in J. Glover, *Causing Death and Saving Lives* (Harmondsworth: Penguin, 1987). See also J. Rachels, *The End of Life: Euthanasia and Morality* (Oxford: Oxford University Press, 1986).

Wollstonecraft and feminist issues

Wollstonecraft, M., *A Vindication of the Rights of Women, with Strictures on Moral and Political*

Subjects [1792], ed. C. H. Poston (New York: Norton, 1988).

Wollstonecraft's ideas exerted a strong influence on a famous later work: J. S. Mill, *The Subjection of Women* [1869]. See further J. S. Mill and Harriet Taylor Mill, *Essays on Sex Equality,* ed. A. Rossi (Chicago: University of Chicago Press, 1970).

For an excellent survey of the main philosophical issues relating to feminism and the status of women, see A. M. Jaggar, 'Feminist Ethics', in L. C. Becker (ed.), *Encyclopedia of Ethics* (New York: Garland, 1992). See also C. Gilligan, *In a Different Voice: Psychological Theory and Women's Development* (Cambridge, Mass.: Harvard University Press, 1982); G. Lloyd, *The Man of Reason: 'Male' and 'Female' in Western Philosophy* (Minneapolis: University of Minnesota Press, 1984).

Partiality and favouritism

Godwin, W., *An Inquiry concerning Political Justice* [1793] (Harmondsworth: Penguin, 1976). Text based on the 3rd edn of 1798.

For the connection between morality and impartiality, see F. Hutcheson, *An Inquiry concerning Moral Good and Evil* [1725], sections I and II, in *Collected Works* (Hildesheim: Olms, 1970).

For a modern defence of impartialism, see S. Kagan, *The Limits of Morality* (Oxford: Clarendon, 1989). Compare also P. Singer, *Practical Ethics* (Cambridge: Cambridge University Press, 1979; 2nd edn 1993), chs 1 and 8.

For problems with the impartialist line, see B. Williams, *Moral Luck* (Cambridge: Cambridge University Press, 1981), ch. 1. See also L. Blum, *Friendship, Altruism and Morality* (London: Routledge, 1980).

The justification of punishment

Bentham, Jeremy, *An Introduction to the Principles of Morals and Legislation* [1789], ed. W. Harrison (Oxford: Blackwell, 1967).

For the alternative, retributivist view, see Immanuel Kant, *The Metaphysical Elements of Justice* [*Rechtslehre*, 1796], trans. J. Ladd (Indianapolis: Liberal Arts, 1979).

For a useful collection of papers representing a variety of views on punishment, see H. B. Acton (ed.), *The Philosophy of Punishment* (London: Macmillan, 1969).

For a stimulating and comprehensive treatment of the topic, see A. Duff, *Trials and Punishments* (Cambridge: Cambridge University Press, 1985). See also T. Honderich, *Punishment: The Supposed Justifications* (rev. edn, Harmondsworth: Penguin, 1984), and J. Murphy, *Retribution, Justice and Therapy* (Dordrecht: Reidel, 1979).

Our treatment of animals

An excellent collection of readings is T. Regan and P. Singer (eds), *Animal Rights and Human Obligations* (2nd edn, Englewood Cliffs, NJ: Prentice-Hall, 1989).

The ethical status of animals has aroused enormous philosophical interest in the late twentieth century. Among the many books worth reading are: S. Clark, *The Moral Status of Animals* (Oxford: Clarendon, 1977); M. Midgley, *Animals and Why They Matter* (Harmondsworth: Penguin, 1983); T. Regan, *The Case for Animal Rights* (Berkeley: University of California Press, 1982); R. G. Frey, *Interests and Rights: The Case against Animals* (Oxford: Clarendon, 1980); P. Singer, *Practical Ethics* (Cambridge: Cambridge University Press, 1979).

Environmental ethics

A stimulating collection of papers is R. Elliot (ed.), *Environmental Ethics* (Oxford: Oxford University Press, 1993).

For a handy collection covering a wide range of topics in environmental ethics, see M. E. Zimmerman (ed.), *Environmental Philosophy* (Englewood Cliffs, NJ: Prentice-Hall, 1993).

See also H. Rolston, *Environmental Ethics: Duties to and Values in the Natural World* (Philadelphia: Temple University Press, 1988); R. Attfield, *The Ethics of Environmental Concern* (New York: Columbia University Press, 1983); J. B. Callicott, *In Defense of the Land Ethic* (Albany, NY: State University of New York Press, 1988); P. W. Taylor, *Respect for Nature: A Theory of Environmental Ethics* (Princeton: Princeton University Press, 1986).

Abortion

Useful collections of articles representing various viewpoints are R. M. Baird and S. E. Rosenbaum (eds), *The Ethics of Abortion* (Buffalo,

NY: Prometheus, 1989); J. Feinberg (ed.), *The Problem of Abortion* (2nd edn, Belmont, Calif.: Wadsworth, 1984). See also J. Mohr, *Abortion in America* (Oxford: Oxford University Press, 1978).

Arguments for and against abortion respectively may be found in M. Tooley, *Abortion and Infanticide* (Oxford: Oxford University Press, 1981), and B. Brody, *Abortion and the Sanctity of Human Life* (Cambridge, Mass.: MIT Press, 1975).

Affluence, poverty and the third world

The following are valuable collections of papers: W. Aiken and H. La Follette (eds), *World Hunger and Moral Obligation* (Englewood Cliffs, NJ: Prentice-Hall, 1977); G. R. Lucas (ed.), *Lifeboat Ethics* (New York: Harper & Row, 1976).

A stimulating discussion may be found in Onora O'Neill's 'The Moral Perplexities of Famine Relief', in T. Regan (ed.), *Matters of Life and Death* (2nd edn, New York: Random House, 1985). See also O. O'Neill, *Faces of Hunger* (London: Allen & Unwin, 1986).

A useful survey of some of the issues is N. Dower's essay 'World Poverty', in P. Singer (ed.), *A Companion to Ethics* (Oxford: Blackwell, 1993). See also the readings under 'Partiality and Favouritism', above.

A clear discussion of the moral distinction between acting and omitting may be found in J. Glover, *Causing Death and Saving Lives* (Harmondsworth: Penguin, 1987).

Active and passive euthanasia

For the acting versus omitting distinction, see J. Glover, *Causing Death and Saving Lives* (see above).

A strong defence of voluntary active euthanasia may be found in D. Brock, *Life and Death: Philosophical Essays in Biomedical Ethics* (Cambridge: Cambridge University Press, 1993).

Reasons for opposing euthanasia are explored in R. Gula, *Euthanasia: Moral and Pastoral Perspectives* (New York: Paulist Press, 1994).

See also M. C. Murphy, *Natural Law and Practical Rationality* (Cambridge: Cambridge University Press, 2001).

A useful general collection on medical ethics is R. Munson (ed.), *Intervention and Reflection* (Belmont, Calif.: Wadsworth, 1988), which includes an essay on euthanasia by J. Gay-Williams.

See also J. Keown (ed.), *Euthanasia Examined* (Cambridge: Cambridge University Press, 1997), and J. McMahan, *The Ethics of Killing* (Oxford: Oxford University Press, 2002).

For some liberal arguments on euthanasia, see R. Dworkin, *Life's Dominion* (New York: Knopf, 1993).

For a useful survey of the principle of 'double effect' (which makes a distinction between directly intended and merely foreseen consequences), see the article 'Doctrine of Double Effect', in the *Stanford Encyclopedia of Philosophy* <http://plato.stanford.edu/entries/double-effect/>

Cloning

A useful study of the main issues may be found in M. Reiss and R. Straughan, *Improving Nature? The Science and Ethics of Genetic Engineering* (Cambridge: Cambridge University Press, 1996).

An accessible introduction is B. Gert et al., *Morality and the New Genetics: A Guide for Students and Health Care Providers* (Sudbury, Mass.: Jones & Bartlett, 1996).

See also R. Wachbroit, 'Genetic Encores: The Ethics of Human Cloning', *Report from the Institute for Philosophy and Public Policy*, 17, no. 21 (Fall 1997).

There are valuable survey articles in L. Becker and C. Becker (eds), *Encyclopedia of Ethics* (New York and London: Routledge; 2nd edn 2001): see index under 'cloning'.

Interesting collections of essays on the topic are C. S. Mazzoni (ed.), *Ethics and Law in Biological Research* (London: Nijhoff, 2002), and M. Nussbaum and C. Sunstein (eds), *Clones and Cones: Facts and Fantasies about Human Cloning* (New York: Norton, 1999).

PART X

Authority and the State

Authority and the State
Introduction

The human being, Aristotle famously observed, is a 'political animal'.[1] By this he meant that our nature is to live in a *polis*, or state. Our well-being as humans depends in large part on those goods which can only be achieved by association and cooperation with others: 'the state came into being as a means to secure life; it continues in existence in order to secure a good life.'[2] Our relationship to the state, however, is problematic in many respects. Though it provides many benefits, it sometimes demands sacrifices, and invariably requires some measure of conformity or obedience. So what is the basis of our obligation (if it exists) to the state? Are state institutions merely a matter of convenience – more or less efficient mechanisms for individuals to secure what they want in life? Or does the state have some higher moral status which entitles it to command our allegiance? What indeed *is* 'the state' – some kind of entity in its own right, or simply a convenient shorthand for talking about our relationships with our fellow citizens? And what are the proper limits to the authority which the state, or a majority of our fellow citizens, may exercise over each of us? These are among the central questions in political theory which have occupied the great philosophers, and the readings presented in this Part of the volume indicate some of their most influential answers.

---

[1] Aristotle, *Politics* [*c*.330 BC], Bk I, ch. 2 (1253a2).
[2] *Politics*, 1252b29.

1 Our Obligation to Respect the Laws of the State: Plato, *Crito**

When he was over 70, Socrates was accused before the Athenian assembly of impiety and corrupting the young, and was sentenced to death. In our first extract, Plato presents a dramatic scene from the condemned cell;[1] Socrates' friends urge him to escape from prison, and avoid the unjust and vindictive sentence of the court. In his reply Socrates imagines a dialogue between himself and the laws of Athens. They begin by presenting the state in the most honorific terms – 'holier far than mother or father or any ancestor' – to be revered and obeyed without question. But a calmer and more rational account of the obligation owed to the state is then offered. The laws dwell on the *benefits* the city provided for Socrates: upbringing, education and all the goods enjoyed by citizens. Second, there is the *freedom to leave* which every citizen has, if he does not like the way things are done in Athens – 'anyone may go where he likes, retaining his property'. And finally it is argued that if Socrates were to evade the law and escape, he would be breaking the implied covenant, *agreement* or contract between citizen and state. Socrates, like any other citizen, had the right to speak in opposition to the laws when they were passed, and to argue for his point of view. Having failed to carry the day for a change in the law, he is now obliged to obey, even though he may not like the result in this particular case. Plato's arguments are clear and elegant, though whether they are valid or not has been the subject of intense debate. As we shall see, many of the themes introduced here reappear in the development of subsequent political theory.

SOCRATES: Let us consider the matter together, and do you either refute me if you can, and I will be convinced; or else cease, my dear friend, from repeating to me that I ought to escape against the wishes of the Athenians: for I highly value your attempts to persuade me to do so, but I may not be persuaded against my own better judgement...Imagine that I am about to play truant (you may call the proceeding by any name which you like), and the laws and the government come and interrogate me: 'Tell us, Socrates,' they say; 'what are you about? Are you not going by an act of yours to overturn us – the laws, and the whole state, as far as in you lies? Do you imagine that a state can subsist and not be overthrown, in which the decisions of law have no power, but are set aside and trampled upon by individuals?' What will be our answer, Crito, to these and the like words? Anyone, and especially a rhetorician, will have a good deal to say on behalf of the law which requires a sentence to be carried out. He will argue that this law should not be set aside; and shall we reply, 'Yes; but the state has injured us and given an unjust sentence.' Suppose I say that?

CRITO: Very good, Socrates.

SOCRATES: 'And was that our agreement with you?' the laws would answer; 'or were you to abide by the sentence of the state?' And if I were to express my astonishment at their words, the laws would probably add 'Answer, Socrates, instead of opening your eyes – you are in the habit of asking and answering questions. Tell us, – What

* Plato, *Crito* [*Kriton*, *c*.385 BC], 50b–54e. Trans. B. Jowett, in *The Dialogues of Plato* (Oxford: Clarendon, 1892), vol. II, pp. 151–6; with omissions.

[1] The dramatic date of the dialogue is 399 BC, the same as that of the *Phaedo*; compare introduction to Part IV, extract 1.

complaint have you to make against us which justifies you in attempting to destroy us and the state? In the first place did we not bring you into existence? Your father married your mother by our aid and begat you. Say whether you have any objection to urge against those of us who regulate marriage?' None, I should reply. 'Or against those of us who after birth regulate the nurture and education of children, in which you also were trained? Were not the laws, which have the charge of education, right in commanding your father to train you in music and gymnastic?' Right, I should reply. 'Well then, since you were brought into the world and nurtured and educated by us, can you deny in the first place that you are our child and slave, as your fathers were before you? And if this is true you are not on equal terms with us; nor can you think that you have a right to do to us what we are doing to you. Would you have any right to strike or revile or do any other evil to your father or your master, if you had one, because you have been struck or reviled by him, or received some other evil at his hands? – you would not say this? And because we think right to destroy you, do you think that you have any right to destroy us in return, and your country as far as in you lies? Will you, O professor of true virtue, pretend that you are justified in this? Has a philosopher like you failed to discover that our country is more to be valued and higher and holier far than mother or father or any ancestor, and more to be regarded in the eyes of the gods and of men of understanding? also to be soothed, and gently and reverently entreated when angry, even more than a father, and either to be persuaded, or if not persuaded, to be obeyed? And when we are punished by her, whether with imprisonment or stripes, the punishment is to be endured in silence; and if she lead us to wounds or death in battle, thither we follow as is right; neither may any one yield or retreat or leave his rank, but whether in battle or in a court of law, or in any other place, he must do what his city and his country order him; or he must change their view of what is just: and if he may do no violence to his father or mother, much less may he do violence to his country.' What answer shall we make to this, Crito? Do the laws speak truly, or do they not?

CRITO: I think that they do.

SOCRATES: Then the laws will say: 'Consider, Socrates, if we are speaking truly that in your present attempt you are going to do us an injury. For, having brought you into the world, and nurtured and educated you, and given you and every other citizen a share in every good which we had to give, we further proclaim to any Athenian by the liberty which we allow him, that if he does not like us when he has become of age and has seen the ways of the city, and made our acquaintance, he may go where he pleases and take his goods with him. None of us laws will forbid him or interfere with him. Anyone who does not like us and the city, and who wants to emigrate to a colony or to any other city, may go where he likes, retaining his property. But he who has experience of the manner in which we order justice and administer the state, and still remains, has entered into an implied contract that he will do as we command him. And he who disobeys us is, as we maintain, thrice wrong; first, because in disobeying us he is disobeying his parents; secondly, because we are the authors of his education; thirdly, because he has made an agreement with us that he will duly obey our commands; and he neither obeys them nor convinces us that our commands are unjust; and we do not rudely impose them, but give him the alternative of obeying or convincing us; – that is what we offer, and he does neither.'

'These are the sort of accusations to which, as we were saying, you, Socrates, will be exposed if you accomplish your intentions; you, above all other Athenians.' Suppose now I ask, why I rather than anybody else? they will justly retort upon me that I above all other men have acknowledged the agreement. 'There is clear proof', they will say, 'Socrates, that we and the city were not displeasing to you. Of all Athenians you have been the most constant resident in the city, which, as you never leave, you may be supposed to love. For you never went out of the city either to see the games, except once when you went to the Isthmus, or to any other place unless when you were on military service; nor did you travel as other men do. Nor had you any curiosity to know other states or their laws: your affections did not go beyond us and our state; we were your special favourites, and you acquiesced in our government of you; and here in this city you begat your children, which is a proof of your satisfaction. Moreover, you might in the course of the trial, if you had liked, have fixed the penalty at banishment; the state which refuses to let you go now would have let you go then. But you pretended that you preferred death to exile and that you were not unwilling to die. And now you have forgotten these fine sentiments, and pay no respect to us the laws, of whom you are the destroyer; and are doing what only a miserable slave would do, running away and turning your back upon the compacts and agreements which you made as a citizen. And first of all answer this very question: Are we right in saying that you agreed to be governed according to us in deed, and not in word only? Is that true or not?' How shall we answer, Crito? Must we not assent?

CRITO: We cannot help it, Socrates.

SOCRATES: Then will they not say: 'You, Socrates, are breaking the covenants and agreements which you made with us at your leisure, not in any haste or under any compulsion or deception, but after you have had seventy years to think of them, during which time you were at liberty to leave the city, if we were not to your mind, or if our covenants appeared to you to be unfair. You had your choice, and might have gone either to Lacedaemon or Crete, both which states are often praised by you for their good government, or to some other Hellenic or foreign state. Whereas you, above all other Athenians, seemed to be so fond of the state, or, in other words, of us her laws (and who would care about a state which has no laws?), that you never stirred out of her; the halt, the blind, the maimed were not more stationary in her than you were. And now you run away and forsake your agreements. Not so, Socrates, if you will take our advice; do not make yourself ridiculous by escaping out of the city.'

'For just consider, if you transgress and err in this sort of way, what good will you do either to yourself or to your friends? That your friends will be driven into exile and deprived of citizenship, or will lose their property, is tolerably certain; and you yourself, if you fly to one of the neighbouring cities, as, for example, Thebes or Megara, both of which are well governed, will come to them as an enemy, Socrates, and their government will be against you, and all patriotic citizens will cast an evil eye upon you as a subverter of the laws, and you will confirm in the minds of the judges the justice of their own condemnation of you. For he who is a corrupter of the laws is more than likely to be a corrupter of the young and foolish portion of mankind. Will you then flee from well-ordered cities and virtuous men? And is existence worth having on these terms? Or will you go to them without shame, and talk to them, Socrates? And what will you say to them? What you say here about virtue and justice and institutions and laws being the best things among men? Would that be decent of you? Surely not. But if you go away from well-governed states to Crito's friends in Thessaly, where there is great disorder and licence, they will be charmed to hear the tale of your escape from prison, set off with ludicrous particulars of the manner in which you were wrapped in a goatskin or some other disguise, and metamorphosed as the manner is of runaways; but will there be no one to remind you that in your old age you were not ashamed to violate the most sacred laws from a miserable desire of a little more life? Perhaps not, if you keep them in a good temper; but if they are out of temper you will hear many degrading things; you will live, but how? – as the flatterer of all men, and the servant of all men; and doing what? – eating and drinking in Thessaly, having gone abroad in order that you may get a dinner. And where will be your fine sentiments about justice and virtue? Say that you wish to live for the sake of your children – you want to bring them up and educate them – will you take them into Thessaly and deprive them of Athenian citizenship? Is this the benefit which you will confer upon them? Or are you under the impression that they will be better cared for and educated here if you are still alive, although absent from them; for your friends will take care of them? Do you fancy that if you are an inhabitant of Thessaly they will take care of them, and if you are an inhabitant of the other world that they will not take care of them? Nay; but if they who call themselves friends are good for anything, they will – to be sure they will.'

'Listen, then, Socrates, to us who have brought you up. Think not of life and children first, and of justice afterwards, but of justice first, that you may be justified before the princes of the world below. For neither will you nor any that belong to you be happier or holier or juster in this life, or happier in another, if you do as Crito bids. Now you depart in innocence, a sufferer and not a doer of evil; a victim, not of the laws but of men. But if you go forth, returning evil for evil, and injury for injury, breaking the covenants and agreements which you have made with us, and wronging those whom you ought least of all to wrong, that is to say, yourself, your friends, your country, and us, we shall be angry with you while you live, and our brethren, the laws in the world below, will receive you as an enemy; for they will know that you have done your best to destroy us. Listen, then, to us and not to Crito.'

This, dear Crito, is the voice which I seem to hear murmuring in my ears, like the sound of the flute in the ears of the mystic; that voice, I say, is humming in my ears, and prevents me from hearing any other. And I know that anything more which you may say will be vain. Yet speak, if you have anything to say.

CRITO: I have nothing to say, Socrates.

SOCRATES: Leave me then, Crito, to fulfil the will of God, and to follow whither he leads.

2   The Just Ruler: Thomas Aquinas, *On Princely Government**

Despite notorious episodes such as the execution of Socrates, the operation of the citizens' assembly in ancient Athens prefigured many of the ideals which have become central to our modern democratic outlook. But for much of the political history of the Western world, democracy has been very much the exception. Our next extract, from the thirteenth-century theologian and philosopher Thomas Aquinas, defends the legitimacy of the monarchical form of government that was typical of medieval Europe. Aquinas begins with the Aristotelian premise that 'man is a social and political animal'; as in many other areas of his philosophy, he invokes the concept of what is *natural* in order to draw certain normative conclusions. The vulnerability of the human species, and their lack of physical defences such as horns or claws, make it natural for them to band together for security; furthermore, man's distinguishing characteristic of rationality makes 'the companionship of his fellows naturally necessary to him'.

Aquinas then proceeds to raise a crucial issue for political philosophy – the potential clash between the individual self-interest of the citizens and the common good of all. Though the city ideally provides 'a perfect community with all that is necessary for the fullness of life', the threat to unity arising from differences of individual interest is never far away. To prevent this, Aquinas advocates a single strong ruler; he goes on to support the legitimacy of monarchy by appeal to the 'natural hierarchy' found in all living things – for example, the various limbs of the body are 'ruled' by the heart; and in the mind one faculty, reason, rules over the others. This kind of hierarchy is both natural and proper, ultimately reflecting the supreme power of the one God over his creation. Though many of Aquinas's assumptions may seem questionable nowadays, it is important to see that he is not offering a blanket justification for authoritarian rule. He makes it clear that a ruler interested only in his own profit is unjust – a tyrant; only when the ruler serves the common good, in the interests of all, can he claim legitimacy and authority. Aquinas's discussion, in short, opens up the whole question of what makes the exercise of government legitimate.

Our first task must be to explain how the term 'king' is to be understood. Whenever a certain end has been decided upon, but the means for arriving there are still open to choice, someone must provide direction if that end is to be expeditiously attained. A ship, for instance, will sail first on one course and then on another, according to the winds it encounters, and it would never reach its destination but for the skill of the helmsman who steers it to port. In the same way man, who acts by intelligence, has an end toward which all his life and activities are directed; for it is clearly the nature of intelligent beings to act with some end in view. Yet the diversity of human interests and pursuits makes it equally clear that there are many courses open to men when seeking the end they desire. Man, then, needs guidance for attaining his ends. Now every man is endowed with reason, and it is by the light of reason that his actions are directed to their end. So if it befitted man to live a solitary life, after the fashion of many other animals, he would need no other guide, but each would be a king under himself, under God, the King of kings, and would have the full ordering of his own actions by the light of God-given reason.

---

* Thomas Aquinas, *De regimine principum* [1265–7], Bk I, chs 1 and 2. Trans. J. G. Dawson, in *Aquinas: Selected Political Writings*, ed. A. P. D'Entrèves (Oxford: Blackwell, 1948), pp. 3–13.

When we consider all that is necessary to human life, however, it becomes clear that man is naturally a social and political animal, destined more than all other animals to live in community. Other animals have their food provided for them by nature, and a natural coat of hair. They are also given the means of defence, be it teeth, horns, claws or at least speed in flight. Man, on the other hand, is not so provided, but having instead the power to reason must fashion such things for himself. Even so, one man alone would not be able to furnish himself with all that is necessary, for no one man's resources are adequate to the fullness of human life. For this reason, the companionship of his fellows is naturally necessary to him.

Furthermore, other animals have a natural instinct for what is useful or hurtful to them; the sheep, for instance, instinctively senses an enemy in the wolf. Some animals even appear to have an instinctive knowledge of the medicinal properties of certain herbs and of other things necessary to their existence. Man, on the other hand, has a natural knowledge of life's necessities only in a general way. Being gifted with reason, he must use it to pass from such universal principles to the knowledge of what in particular concerns his well-being. Reasoning thus, however, no one man could attain all necessary knowledge. Instead, nature has destined him to live in society, so that dividing the labour with his fellows, each may devote himself to some branch of the sciences, one following medicine, another some other science, and so forth. This is further evident from the fact that men alone have the power of speech which enables them to convey the full content of their thought to one another. Other animals show their feelings it is true, but only in a general way, as when a dog betrays its anger by barking and other animals in different ways. Man, then, is more able to communicate with his kind than any other animal, even those which appear to be the most gregarious, such as cranes, ants or bees. Solomon had this in mind when he said (Ecclesiastes 4: 9) 'It is better for two to live together than solitary, for they gain by mutual companionship.'

The fellowship of society being thus natural and necessary to man, it follows with equal necessity that there must be some principle of government within the society. For if a great number of people were to live, each intent only upon his own interests, such a community would surely disintegrate unless there were one of its number to have a care for the common good: just as the body of a man or of any other animal would disintegrate were there not in the body itself a single controlling force sustaining the general vitality of all the members. As Solomon tells us (Proverbs 11: 14): 'Where there is no ruler, the people shall be scattered.' This conclusion is quite reasonable; for the particular interest and the common good are not identical. We differ in our particular interests and it is the common good that unites the community. But matters which differ thus are the products of different causes. So in addition to the motives of interest proper to each individual, there must be some principle productive of the good of the many. For this reason, whenever there is an ordered unity arising out of a diversity of elements, there is to be found some such controlling influence. In the material universe, for example, there is a certain order of divine providence under which all bodies are controlled by the first or heavenly body. Similarly, all material bodies are controlled by rational creatures. In each man it is the soul which controls the body, and within the soul itself reason controls the faculties of passion and desire. Lastly, among the members of the body itself, one is the principal, moving all the others: some say it is the heart, but others the head. So in all multiplicity there must be some controlling principle.

When matters are thus ordered to some end it can sometimes happen that such direction takes place either aright or wrongly. So political rule is sometimes just and sometimes unjust. Now anything is directed aright when it is brought to an end which befits it, but wrongly when it is brought to an end which is not so fitting. The object of a community of free men differs, for instance, from that of a community of slaves. For a free man is one who is master of his own actions, but a slave owes all that he is to another. If a community of free men is administered by the ruler for the common good, such government will be just and fitting to free men. If, on the other hand, the community is directed in the particular interest of the ruler and not for the common good, this is a perversion of government and no longer just. Such rulers were warned by God, speaking through Ezekiel (24: 2) when he said 'Woe to those shepherds who fatten themselves (because they seek only their own comfort): is it not the duty of the shepherd to pasture his sheep?' Shepherds must care for the good of the flock and all those who are in authority for the good of those entrusted to them.

When government is unjustly exercised by one man who seeks personal profit from his position instead of the good of the community subject to him, such a ruler is called a tyrant. This word is derived from the idea of force, since a tyrant forcibly oppresses the people instead of ruling justly. The ancients were in the habit of calling all powerful chieftains tyrants. If, on the other hand, unjust government is exercised not by one man alone, but by several banded together in a clique, such a state of affairs is called an oligarchy or rule by the few. This can happen when a few rich men take advantage of their wealth to oppress the rest of the people; and such a government differs from tyranny only in the fact that the oppressors are many. Finally, unjust government can be exercised by a great number, and it is then called democracy: such is mob rule when the common folk take advantage of their number to oppress the rich. In such a case the entire community becomes a sort of tyrant.

Similarly we must distinguish the various types of just rule. If the administration is carried out by some large section of the community, it is commonly called a polity: as for instance when an army rules in a province or a city. If, however, the administration falls to a few but virtuous men it is called an aristocracy: that is rule by the best; and on account of this they are called aristocrats. Finally, if just government is exercised by one man alone, such a person is rightly called a king. So the Lord, speaking through Ezekiel (37: 24) said: 'My servant David shall be king over all; he shall be the sole shepherd of them all.' So it is quite clear that it is of the nature of kingship that there should be one to rule and that he should do so with a view to the common good without seeking private gain.

We have already seen that a communal life is proper to man because he would not be able to provide all that is necessary to life out of his own resources if he were to live like a hermit. So it follows that a communal society is the more perfect to the extent that it is sufficient in providing for life's necessities. There is indeed a certain sufficiency in the family of one household, so far as the elementary necessities of nutrition and procreation and such like are concerned. Similarly in one locality you may find all that is necessary for a particular trade or calling. In a city, however, there is a perfect community, providing all that is necessary for the fullness of life; and in a province we have an even better example, because in this case there is added the mutual assistance of allies against hostile attack. Whoever then rules a perfect community, be it a city or a province, is rightly called king. The head of a household, on the other hand, is not called king but father. Even so there is a certain similarity about the two cases, and kings are sometimes called the fathers of their people.

From what we have said, then, it is clear that a king is one who rules the people of a city or a province for their common good. So Solomon declared (Ecclesiastes 5: 8) 'The king commands over all the lands which are subject to him.'

Having introduced our question, it is now our further task to enquire whether it is better for a realm or a city to be ruled by one person or by many; and this question is best approached by considering the object of government.

The aim of any ruler should be to secure the well-being of the realm whose government he undertakes; just as it is the task of the helmsman to steer the ship through the perilous seas to a safe harbourage. But the welfare and prosperity of a community lies in the preservation of its unity; or, more simply, in peace. For without peace a communal life loses all advantage; and because of discord, becomes instead a burden. So the most important task for the ruler of any community is the establishment of peaceful unity. Nor has he the right to question whether or not he wills to promote the peace of the community, any more than a doctor has the right to question whether he will cure the sick or not. For no one ought to deliberate about the ends for which he must act, but only about the means to those ends. Thus the Apostle when stressing the unity of the faithful adds (Ephesians 4: 3) 'Be ye solicitous for the unity of the Spirit in the bond of peace.' So therefore, government is the more useful to the extent that it more effectively attains peaceful unity. For that is more fruitful which better attains its object. Now it is clear that that which is itself a unity can more easily produce unity than that which is a plurality: just as that which is itself hot is best adapted to heating things. So a government by one person is more likely to be successful than government by many.

Furthermore, it is clear that many persons will never succeed in producing unity in the community if they differ among themselves. So a plurality of individuals will already require some bond of unity before they can even begin to rule in any way whatsoever, just as the whole crew of a ship would never succeed in sailing it on any course unless they were in agreement among themselves. But many may be said to be united in so far as they approach a unity. So it is better for one to rule rather than many who must first reach agreement.

Again, that is best which most nearly approaches a natural process, since nature always works in the best way. But in nature, government is always by one. Among members of the body there is one which moves all the rest, namely the heart; in the soul there is one faculty which is pre-eminent, namely reason. The bees have one king, and in the whole universe there is one God, Creator and Lord of all. And this is quite according to reason; for all plurality derives from unity. So, since the product of art is but an imitation of the work of nature, and since the work of art is the better for being a faithful representation of its natural pattern, it follows of necessity that the best form of government in human society is that exercised by one person.

This conclusion is also borne out by experience. For cities or provinces which are not ruled by one person are torn by dissensions, and strive without peace; so that the Lord's words seem to be fulfilled when he said 'Many shepherds have destroyed my vineyard' (Jeremiah 12: 10). On the other hand, cities and provinces which are governed by one king enjoy peace, flourish in justice and are made glad by an abundance of riches. So the Lord promised his people by the Prophets that, as a great favour, he would place them under one head, and that there would be one prince over all.

3   Sovereignty and Security: Thomas Hobbes, *Leviathan**

Aquinas's picture of proper government (preceding extract) is of a just monarch ruling, under God, for the good of all. By the seventeenth century, however, searching questions were being asked about the legitimacy of monarchical government, and in England the assertion of a 'divine right' of kings to govern led to turmoil and, ultimately, civil war. One of those who fled to France during the war was the English thinker Thomas Hobbes, whose *Leviathan* was to become a landmark in political philosophy. Hobbes premises his theory of government on the need to avoid the horrors of war. But he begins by describing not any particular historical war, but a 'state of nature', prior to the setting up of any government, when men have 'no common power to keep them all in awe'. In this 'natural condition of mankind', there is an ever-present danger of violent quarrelling, chiefly due to competition for scarce resources; Hobbes goes on to give a famous and graphic description of a life where people live without any security apart from what their own strength can provide – a life of 'continual fear and danger of violent death; and the life of man, solitary, poor, nasty, brutish and short'.

The remedy for this nightmarish state of affairs is a hypothetical *contract*, a *voluntary act*
whereby individuals give up their natural freedom to do anything they want, in exchange for personal security. It is as if each person says 'I authorize and give up my right of governing myself to this man, or to this assembly of men [on condition you do likewise]'. The contract is a classic *quid pro quo*: one gives up something (absolute liberty) in exchange for something one wants (safety). The giving up of each person's individual authority into the hands of a supreme ruler or enforcement agency (the 'Leviathan' of the title) means that there will be a 'common power' to keep the peace internally, and protect against foreign invasion. Though Hobbes was himself a monarchist, he does not advocate unfettered autocracy: the monarch is entitled to govern only so long as he provides the security which is the aim of the original contract. Subject to this proviso, however, Hobbes justifies the ruler having sweeping powers in order to provide freedom from 'continual fear'. Though many have taken issue with Hobbes's argument,[1] the general structure of his contract theory as a justification for political authority was to influence subsequent thinking for a long time to come.

Of the natural condition of mankind

Nature has made men so equal, in the faculties of body and mind, that though there be found one man sometimes manifestly stronger in body or of quicker mind than another, yet when all is reckoned together, the difference between man and man is not so considerable that one man can thereupon claim to himself any benefit to which another may not pretend as well as he...

From this equality of ability arises equality of hope in the attaining of our ends. And therefore if any two men desire the same thing, which nevertheless they cannot

---

* Thomas Hobbes, *Leviathan* [1651], extracts from chs XIII, XIV and XVII; with modernized spelling and punctuation and a few minor changes of phrasing. There are several editions of the *Leviathan*, including those by M. Oakshott (Oxford: Blackwell, 1946), and by C. B. Macpherson (Harmondsworth: Penguin, 1968), which reproduces Hobbes's original text.

[1] Compare Hume's strictures, extract 5, below.

both enjoy, they become enemies; and in the way to their end (which is principally their own conservation, and sometimes their delectation only) endeavour to destroy or subdue one another. And from hence it comes to pass that where an invader has no more to fear than another man's single power, if one plant, sow, build, or possess a convenient seat, others may probably be expected to come prepared with forces united to dispossess, and deprive him, not only of the fruit of his labour, but also of his life, or liberty. And the invader again is in the like danger of another.

And from this diffidence[1] of one another, there is no more reasonable way for any man to secure himself than anticipation; that is, by force, or wiles, to master the persons of all men he can, until he sees no other power great enough to endanger him. And this is no more than his own conservation requires, and is generally allowed. Also, because there are some who take pleasure in contemplating their own power in the acts of conquest (which they pursue farther than their security requires), if others, that otherwise would be glad to be at ease within modest bounds, should not by invasion increase their power, they would not be able, long time, by standing only on their defence, to subsist. And by consequence, such augmentation of dominion over men, being necessary to a man's conservation, it ought to be allowed him.

Again, men have no pleasure (but on the contrary a great deal of grief) in keeping company, where there is no power able to over-awe them all. For every man looks that his companion should value him at the same rate he sets upon himself. And upon all signs of contempt, or undervaluing, naturally endeavours, as far as he dares (which amongst them that have no common power to keep them in quiet, is far enough to make them destroy each other), to extort a greater value from his contemners, by damage, and from others, by the example.

So that in the nature of man, we find three principal causes of quarrel: first, competition; secondly, diffidence; thirdly, glory.

The first, makes men invade for gain; the second, for safety; and the third, for reputation. The first use violence, to make themselves masters of other men's persons, wives, children, and cattle; the second, to defend them; the third, for trifles, as a word, a smile, a different opinion, and any other sign of undervalue, either direct in their persons, or by reflection in their kindred, their friends, their nation, their profession, or their name.

Hereby it is manifest, that during the time men live without a common power to keep them all in awe, they are in that condition which is called war; and such a war as is of every man against every man. For war consists not in battle only, or the act of fighting, but in a tract of time, wherein the will to contend by battle is sufficiently known; and therefore the notion of *time* is to be considered in the nature of war, as it is in the nature of weather. For as the nature of foul weather lies not in a shower or two of rain, but in an inclination thereto of many days together, so the nature of war consists not in actual fighting, but in the known disposition thereto, during all the time there is no assurance to the contrary. All other time is peace.

Whatsoever therefore is consequent to a time of war, where every man is enemy to every man, the same is consequent to the time wherein men live without other security than what their own strength and their own invention shall furnish them

---

[1] Diffidence: distrust.

with. In such condition, there is no place for industry, because the fruit thereof is uncertain; and consequently no culture of the earth, no navigation, nor use of the commodities that may be imported by sea; no commodious building; no instruments of moving and removing such things as require much force; no knowledge of the face of the earth; no account of time; no arts; no letters; no society; and which is worst of all, continual fear, and danger of violent death; and the life of man, solitary, poor, nasty, brutish, and short.

It may seem strange to some man, that has not well weighed these things, that nature should thus dissociate, and render men apt to invade and destroy one another; and he may therefore, not trusting to this inference, made from the passions, desire perhaps to have the same confirmed by experience. Let him therefore consider with himself, when taking a journey, he arms himself, and seeks to go well accompanied; when going to sleep, he locks his doors; when even in his house he locks his chests; and this when he knows there be laws, and public officers, armed, to revenge all injuries shall be done him: what opinion he has of his fellow subjects, when he rides armed; of his fellow citizens, when he locks his doors; and of his children, and servants, when he locks his chests. Does he not there as much accuse mankind by his actions, as I do by my words? But neither of us accuse man's nature in it. The desires, and other passions of man, are in themselves no sin. No more are the actions that proceed from those passions, till they know a law that forbids them: which till laws be made they cannot know; nor can any law be made, till they have agreed upon the person that shall make it.

It may peradventure be thought there was never such a time, nor condition of war as this; and I believe it was never generally so, over all the world; but there are many places where they live so now. For the savage people in many places of America, except the government of small families (that concord whereof depends on natural lust) have no government at all; and live at this day in that brutish manner, as I said before. Howsoever, it may be perceived what manner of life there would be, where there were no common power to fear, by the manner of life which men that have formerly lived under a peaceful government tend to degenerate into, in a civil war...

To this war of every man against every man, this also is consequent: that nothing can be unjust. The notions of right and wrong, justice and injustice, have there no place. Where there is no common power, there is no law: where no law, no injustice. Force and fraud are, in war, the two cardinal virtues. Justice and injustice are none of the faculties either of the body or mind. If they were, they might be in a man that were alone in the world, as well as his senses and passions. They are qualities that relate to men in society, not in solitude. It is consequent also to the same condition that there be no propriety, no dominion, no *Mine* and *Thine* distinct; but only that to be every man's, that he can get; and for so long as he can keep it. And thus much for the ill condition which man by mere nature is actually placed in; though with a possibility to come out of it, consisting partly in the passions, partly in his reason.

The passions that incline men to peace, are fear of death; desire of such things as are necessary to commodious living; and a hope by their industry to obtain them. And reason suggests convenient articles of peace, upon which men may be drawn to agreement. These articles are they, which otherwise are called the laws of nature...

Of the first and second natural laws, and of contracts

The *right of nature*...is the liberty each man has to use his own power, as he will himself, for the preservation of his own nature, that is to say, of his own life; and consequently, of doing anything, which in his own judgement and reasons, he shall conceive to be the aptest means thereunto.

By *liberty* is understood, according to the proper signification of the word, the absence of external impediments: which impediments may oft take away part of a man's power to do what he would; but cannot hinder him from using the power left him, according as his judgement and reason shall dictate to him.

A *law of nature*...is a precept, or general rule, found out by reason, by which a man is forbidden to do that which is destructive of his life, or takes away the means of preserving the same; and to omit that by which he thinks it may be best preserved. For though they that speak of this subject tend to confound *right* and *law*, yet they ought to be distinguished; because right consists in liberty to do, or to forbear, whereas law determines, and binds to one of them. So that law and right differ as much as obligation and liberty, which in one and the same matter are inconsistent.

And because the condition of man...is a condition of war of every one against every one – in which case every one is governed by his own reason, and there is nothing he can make use of that may not be a help unto him in preserving his life against his enemies – it follows that in such a condition every man has a right to everything, even to one another's body. And therefore, as long as this natural right of every man to every thing endures, there can be no security to any man (how strong or wise soever he be) of living out the time which nature ordinarily allows men to live. And consequently it is a precept, or general rule of reason, *that every man, ought to endeavour peace, as far as he has hope of obtaining it; and when he cannot obtain it, that he may seek, and use, all helps and advantages of war*. The first branch of which rule contains the first and fundamental law of nature; which is, *to seek peace, and follow it*. The second, the sum of the right of nature; which is, *by all means we can, to defend ourselves*.

From this fundamental law of nature, by which men are commanded to endeavour peace, is derived this second law: *That a man be willing, when others are so too, as far-forth as for peace and defence of himself he shall think it necessary, to lay down this right to all things; and be contented with so much liberty against other men as he would allow other men against himself.* For as long as every man holds this right of doing anything he likes, so long are all men in the condition of war. But if other men will not lay down their right, as well as he, then there is no reason for any one to divest himself of his. For that were to expose himself to prey (which no man is bound to) rather than to dispose himself to peace. This is that law of the Gospel; *Whatsoever you require that others should do to you, that do ye to them*. And that law of all men, *Quod tibi fieri non vis, alteri ne feceris* ['Do not do to another what you do not want to be done to you.']

Whenever a man transfers his right, or renounces it, it is either in consideration of some right reciprocally transferred to himself, or for some other good he hopes for thereby. For it is a voluntary act; and of the voluntary acts of every man, the object is some *good to himself*. And therefore there be some rights which no man can be understood by any words, or other signs, to have abandoned, or transferred. As, first, a man cannot lay down the right of resisting them that assault him by force, or take away his life; because he cannot be understood to aim thereby at any good to himself... The mutual transferring of right, is that which men call *contract*.

Of the causes, generation and definition of a commonwealth

The final cause, end or design of men (who naturally love liberty, and dominion over others) in the introduction of that restraint upon themselves (in which we see them live in commonwealths) is the foresight of their own preservation, and of a more contented life thereby; that is to say, of getting themselves out from that miserable condition of war, which is necessarily consequent (as has been shown) to the natural passions of men, when there is no visible power to keep them in awe, and tie them by fear of punishment to the performance of their covenants, and observation of [the] laws of nature...

For the laws of nature (as justice, equity, modesty, mercy, and (in sum) *doing to others, as we would be done to*) of themselves, without the terror of some power to cause them to be observed, are contrary to our natural passions, that carry us to partiality, pride, revenge, and the like. And covenants, without the sword, are but words, and of no strength to secure a man at all. Therefore notwithstanding the laws of nature (which everyone has then kept, when he has the will to keep them, when he can do it safely) if there be no power erected, or not great enough for our security, every man will, and may lawfully, rely on his own strength and art, for caution against all other men...

The only way to erect such a common power, as may be able to defend them from the invasion of foreigners, and the injuries of one another, and thereby to secure them in such sort, as that by their own industry, and by the fruits of the earth, they may nourish themselves and live contentedly, is to confer all their power and strength upon one man, or upon one assembly of men, that may reduce all their wills, by plurality of voices, unto one will. Which is as much as to say, to appoint one man, or assembly of men, to bear their person; and every one to own, and acknowledge himself to be author of whatsoever he that so bears their person, shall act, or cause to be acted, in those things which concern the common peace and safety; and therein to submit their wills, every one to his will, and their judgements to his judgement. This is more than consent or concord; it is a real unity of them all, in one and the same person, made by covenant of every man with every man, in such manner, as if every man should say to every man: *I authorize and give up my right of governing myself to this man, or to this assembly of men, on this condition, that you give up your right to him, and authorize all his actions in like manner.* This done, the multitude, so united in one person, is called a commonwealth, in Latin *civitas*. This is the generation of that great Leviathan, or rather (to speak more reverently) of that *mortal God*, to which we owe, under the *immortal God*, our peace and defence. For by this authority, given him by every particular man in the commonwealth, he has the use of so much power and strength conferred on him, that by terror thereof, he is enabled to form the wills of them all, to peace at home, and mutual aid against their enemies abroad. And in him consists the essence of the commonwealth; which (to define it) is *one person, of whose acts a great multitude, by mutual covenants one with another, have made themselves every one the author, to the end he may use the strength and means of them all, as he shall think expedient, for their peace and common defence.* And he that carries this person is called *sovereign* and said to have *sovereign power*; and every one besides, his *subject.*

4 Consent and Political Obligation: John Locke, *Second Treatise of Civil Government**

Writing not long after Hobbes, the famous English philosopher John Locke adopted much of the framework devised by his predecessor for dealing with questions of political power and authority. Like Hobbes, Locke begins with an original position prior to the setting up of political society, but he is at pains to stress that the 'state of nature' is governed by a kind of natural (divinely ordained) morality. This 'law of nature' 'teaches all mankind that, being all equal and independent, no one ought to harm another in his life, health, liberty, or possessions'. The Lockean state of nature (though it may slide into war if there is unjust aggression) is one where 'men live together according to reason without a common superior on earth'; and in this state, each person has the fundamental natural right to 'property in his own person'. This means that individuals have a right not just to bodily integrity, but also to the fruits of their labour: 'as much as anyone can make use of to any advantage of life before it spoils, so much he may by his labour fix a property in'.

If this situation of free and equal entitlement is the 'natural state' of mankind, why should anyone give it up? Locke's answer (evidently influenced by Hobbes) is that our enjoyment of these natural rights is 'very uncertain and constantly exposed to the invasion of others'. Like Hobbes, Locke considers the move to civil society to be a direct voluntary act – an act whose principal purpose, according to Locke, is to allow people 'the enjoyment of their properties in peace and safety'. But is this story of a deliberate move away from the 'state of nature' supposed to be literally true? Though it does seem plausible to suggest that we all have a strong interest in the existence of a system which will ensure the mutual preservation of our bodily integrity and personal property, did we ever, in actual fact, consent to the setting up of such a system? In answer to this, Locke introduces the notion of *tacit consent*: by living within a state even for a short time, even by 'barely travelling freely on the highway', we may be said to have implicitly agreed to the authority of the government. This 'original compact', as Locke calls it, is the basis of our obligation to the state, or, more specifically, our obligation to obey the laws enacted by a majority of the citizens: 'every man, by consenting with others to make one body politic under one government, puts himself under an obligation to everyone of that society to submit to the determination of the majority'. There is much food for thought here, both in what Locke says about the nature of property rights, and in his account of our obligation to abide by the decisions of the majority. Locke's treatment of these matters takes us unmistakably into the arena of modern political theory.

* John Locke, 'The Second Treatise of Civil Government: An Essay concerning the True Original, Extent, and End of Civil Government', from *Two Treatises of Government* [1690]. Extracts from ch. II, §§ 4, 6; ch. III, § 19; ch. V, §§ 27, 31, 50; ch. VIII, §§ 95, 97, 98, 99, 119; ch. IX, §§ 123, 124; ch. XII, § 149; with minor changes, esp. of punctuation and spelling. Many editions of the full text are available, including J. W. Gough (Oxford: Blackwell, 1946), T. I. Cook (New York: Haffner, 1947) and P. Laslett (2nd edn, Cambridge: Cambridge University Press, 1967).

The state of nature

To understand political power aright, and derive it from its original, we must consider what state all men are naturally in, and that is, a state of perfect freedom to order their actions, and dispose of their possessions and persons, as they think fit, within the bounds of the law of nature, without asking leave, or depending upon the will of any other man.

A state also of equality, wherein all the power and jurisdiction is reciprocal, no one having more than another; there being nothing more evident than that creatures of the same species and rank, promiscuously born to all the same advantages of nature, and the use of the same faculties, should also be equal one amongst another, without subordination or subjection, unless the lord and master of them all should, by any manifest declaration of his will, set one above another, and confer on him, by an evident and clear appointment, an undoubted right to dominion and sovereignty...

But though this be a state of liberty, yet it is not a state of licence: though man in that state have an uncontrollable liberty to dispose of his person or possessions, yet he has not liberty to destroy himself, or so much as any creature in his possession, but where some nobler use than its bare preservation calls for it. The state of nature has a law of nature to govern it, which obliges everyone; and reason, which is that law, teaches all mankind who will but consult it, that being all equal and independent, no one ought to harm another in his life, health, liberty, or possessions. For men being all the work-manship of one omnipotent, and infinitely wise maker – all the servants of one sovereign master, sent into the world by his order, and about his business – they are his property, whose workmanship they are, made to last during his, not one another's pleasure; and being furnished with like faculties, sharing all in one community of nature, there cannot be supposed any such subordination among us, that may author-ize us to destroy one another, as if we were made for one another's uses, as the inferior ranks of creatures are for ours. Every one, as he is bound to preserve himself, and not to quit his station wilfully, so by the like reason, when his own preservation comes not in competition, ought as much as he can to preserve the rest of mankind, and not, unless it be to do justice on an offender, take away, or impair the life, or what tends to the preservation of the life, the liberty, health, limb or goods of another...

The state of war

And here we have the plain difference between the state of nature and the state of war, which however some men have confounded, are as far distant as a state of peace, good will, mutual assistance, and preservation, and a state of enmity, malice, violence, and mutual destruction are one from another. Men living together according to reason without a common superior on earth, with authority to judge between them, are properly in the state of nature. But force, or a declared design of force upon the person of another, where there is no common superior on earth to appeal to for relief, is the state of war; and it is the want of such an appeal [that] gives a man the right of war even against an aggressor, though he be in society and a fellow subject. Thus, a thief whom I cannot harm, but by appeal to the law, for having stolen all that I am worth, I may kill when he sets on me to rob me but of my horse or coat, because the law, which was made for my preservation, where it cannot interpose to secure my life from present force (which if lost is capable of no reparation) permits me my own defence and the right of war – a liberty to kill the aggressor, because the aggressor allows not time to appeal to our common judge, nor the decision of the law, for remedy in a case where the mischief may be irreparable. Want of a common judge with authority puts all men in a state of nature; force without right upon a man's person makes a state of war both where there is, and is not, a common judge...

Property

Though the earth and all inferior creatures be common to all men, yet every man has a *property* in his own *person*. This nobody has any right to but himself. The *labour* of his body and the *work* of his hands, we may say, are properly his. Whatsoever, then, he removes out of the state that nature has provided and left it in, he has mixed his labour with it, and joined to it something that is his own, and thereby makes it his property. It being by him removed from the common state nature placed it in, it has by this labour something annexed to it that excludes the common right of other men. For this labour being the unquestionable property of the labourer, no man but he can have a right to what that is once joined to, at least where there is enough, and as good, left in common for others...

It will perhaps be objected to this, that if gathering the acorns or other fruits of the earth, etc., makes a right to them, then anyone may engross as much as he will. To which I answer, Not so. The same law of nature that does by this means give us property, does also bound that property too. *God has given us all things richly* (1 Timothy 6: 12) is the voice of reason confirmed by inspiration. But how far has he given it us? To enjoy. As much as any one can make use of to any advantage of life before it spoils, so much he may by his labour fix a property in. Whatever is beyond this is more than his share, and belongs to others. Nothing was made by God for man to spoil or destroy...

But since gold and silver, being little useful to the life of man, in proportion to food, raiment, and carriage, has its value only from the consent of men, whereof labour yet makes in great part the measure, it is plain that men have agreed to disproportionate and unequal possession of the earth, they having by a tacit and voluntary consent found out a way how a man may fairly possess more land than he himself can use the product of, by receiving, in exchange for the overplus, gold and silver, which may be hoarded up without injury to anyone, these metals not spoiling or decaying in the hands of the possessor. This partage of things, in an inequality of private possessions, men have made practicable out of the bounds of society, and without compact, only by putting a value on gold and silver and tacitly agreeing in the use of money. For in governments the laws regulate the right of property, and the possession of land is determined by positive constitutions...

The beginning of political societies

Men being, as has been said, by nature all free, equal and independent, no one can be put out of this estate and subjected to the political power of another without his own consent, which is done by agreeing with other men, to join and unite into a community for their comfortable, safe and peaceable living, one amongst another, in a secure enjoyment of their properties, and a greater security against any that are not of it. This any number of men may do, because it injures not the freedom of the rest; they are left, as they were, in the liberty of the state of nature. When any number of men have so consented to make one community or government, they are thereby presently incorporated, and make one body politic, wherein the majority have a right to act and conclude the rest.

For, when any number of men have, by the consent of every individual, made a community, they have thereby made that community one body, with a power to act as one body, which is only by the will and determination of the majority. For that which acts any community being only the consent of the individuals of it, and [since] it (being one body) must move one way, it is necessary the body should move that way whither the greater force carries it, which is the consent of the majority; or else it is impossible it should act or continue one body, one community, which the consent of every individual that united into it agreed that it should; and so everyone is bound by that consent to be concluded[1] by the majority. And therefore we see that in assemblies empowered to act by positive laws, where no number is set by that positive law which empowers them, the act of the majority passes for the act of the whole, and of course determines as having, by the law of nature and reason, the power of the whole...

And thus every man, by consenting with others to make one body politic under one government, puts himself under an obligation to everyone of that society to submit to the determination of the majority, and to be concluded by it; or else this original compact, whereby he with others incorporates into one society, would signify nothing, and be no compact, if he be left free and under no other ties than he was in before in the state of nature. For what appearance would there be of any compact? What new engagement if he were no farther tied by any decrees of the society than he himself thought fit and did actually consent to? This would be still as great a liberty as he himself had before his compact, or anyone else in the state of nature has, who may submit himself and consent to any acts of it if he thinks fit.

For if the consent of the majority shall not in reason be received as the act of the whole, and conclude every individual, nothing but the consent of every individual can make anything to be the act of the whole; which, considering the infirmities of health and avocations of business, which (in a number though much less than that of a commonwealth) will necessarily keep many away from the public assembly; and the variety of opinions and contrariety of interests which unavoidably happen in all collections of men, it is next [to] impossible ever to be had...

Whosoever therefore out of a state of nature unite into a community, must be understood to give up all the power necessary to the ends for which they unite into society to the majority of the community, unless they expressly agreed in any number greater than the majority. And this is done by barely agreeing to unite into one political society, which is all the compact that is, or needs be, between the individuals that enter into or make up a commonwealth. And thus, that which begins and actually constitutes any political society is nothing but the consent of any number of freemen capable of a majority, to unite and incorporate into such a society.

---

[1] Concluded: determined, decided.

And this is that, and that only, which did or could give beginning to any lawful government in the world...

Every man being, as has been showed, naturally free, and nothing being able to put him into subjection to any earthly power, but only his own consent, it is to be considered what shall be understood to be a sufficient declaration of a man's consent to make him subject to the laws of any government. There is a common distinction of an *express* and a *tacit* consent, which will concern our present case. Nobody doubts but an express consent of any man, entering into any society, makes him a perfect member of that society, a subject of that government. The difficulty is, what ought to be looked upon as a tacit consent, and how far it binds, i.e., how far anyone shall be looked on to have consented, and thereby submitted to any government, where he has made no expressions of it at all. And to this I say, that every man that has any possession or enjoyment of any part of the dominions of any government doth thereby give his tacit consent, and is as far forth obliged to obedience to the laws of that government, during such enjoyment, as any one under it, whether this his possession be of land to him and his heirs for ever, or a lodging only for a week; or whether it be barely travelling freely on the highway; and, in effect, it reaches as far as the very being of anyone within the territories of that government...

The ends of political society and government

If man in the state of nature be so free as has been said; if he be absolute lord of his own person and possessions; equal to the greatest and subject to nobody, why will he part with his freedom? Why will he give up this empire, and subject himself to the dominion and control of any other power? To which it is obvious to answer, that though in the state of nature he has such a right, yet the enjoyment of it is very uncertain and constantly exposed to the invasion of others; for all being kings as much as he, every man his equal, and the greater part no strict observers of equity and justice, the enjoyment of the property he has in this state is very unsafe, very unsecure. This makes him willing to quit this condition which, however free, is full of fears and continual dangers; and it is not without reason that he seeks out and is willing to join in society with others who are already united, or have a mind to unite, for the mutual preservation of their lives, liberties, and estates, which I call by the general name, property...

The great end of men's entering into society being the enjoyment of their properties in peace and safety, and the great instrument and means of that being the laws established in that society, the first and fundamental positive law of all commonwealths is the establishing of the legislative power; as the first and fundamental natural law, which is to govern even the legislative itself, is the preservation of the society, and (as far as will consist with the public good) of every person in it. This legislative is not only the supreme power of the commonwealth, but sacred and unalterable in the hands where the community have once placed it; nor can any edict of anybody else, in what form soever conceived, or by what power soever backed, have the force and obligation of a law which has not its sanction from that legislative which the public has chosen and appointed; for without this the law could not have that which is absolutely necessary to its being a law, the consent of the society, over whom nobody can have a power to make laws but by their own consent and by authority received from them; and therefore all the obedience, which by the most solemn ties anyone can be obliged to pay, ultimately terminates in this supreme power, and is directed by those laws which it enacts. Nor can any oaths to any foreign power whatsoever, or any domestic subordinate power, discharge any member of the society from his obedience to the legislative, acting pursuant to their trust, nor oblige him to any obedience contrary to the laws so enacted or farther than they do allow, it being ridiculous to imagine one can be tied ultimately to obey any power in the society which is not the supreme . . .

The subordination of the powers of the commonwealth

Though in a constituted commonwealth, standing upon its own basis and acting according to its own nature, that is, acting for the preservation of the community, there can be but one supreme power, which is the legislative, to which all the rest are and must be subordinate; yet the legislative being only a fiduciary power to act for certain ends, there remains still in the people a supreme power to remove or alter the legislative when they find the legislative act contrary to the trust reposed in them. For all power given with trust for the attaining of an end being limited by that end, whenever that end is manifestly neglected or opposed, the trust must necessarily be forfeited, and the power devolve into the hands of those that gave it, who may place it anew where they shall think best for their safety and security. And thus the community perpetually retains a supreme power of saving themselves from the attempts and designs of anybody, even of their legislators, whenever they shall be so foolish or so wicked as to lay and carry on designs against the liberties and properties of the subject. For no man or society of men having a power to deliver up their preservation, or consequently the means of it, to the absolute will and arbitrary dominion of another, whenever any one shall go about to bring them into such a slavish condition, they will always have a right to preserve what they have not a power to part with, and to rid themselves of those who invade this fundamental, sacred, and unalterable law of self-preservation, for which they entered into society. And thus the community may be said in this respect to be always the supreme power, but not as considered under any form of government, because this power of the people can never take place till the government be dissolved.

5 Against Contractarianism: David Hume, *Of the Original Contract* *

The contract theory of political obligation – a theory originated by Plato (extract 1), developed by Hobbes (extract 3), and elaborated by Locke (extract 4) – was subjected to a blistering attack in the mid-eighteenth century by the famous Scottish philosopher David Hume. In the essay from which the following extract is taken Hume argues first of all that the theory has no basis in historical fact. So far from stemming from voluntary consent or mutual promise, the claims of sovereigns tend to be based on 'conquest or succession'. Contract theorists talk of the 'original' contract, but the stark reality is that 'the original establishment [of states] was formed by violence and submitted to by necessity'. Taking up Locke's suggestion that we 'tacitly' consent to the authority of the state, Hume argues that this notion only makes sense against a background of free choice – something that can hardly be attributed to the 'poor peasant or artisan' whose life's circumstances are pretty much fixed. Plato (extract 1, above) had suggested that by remaining in Athens, when he could easily have left, Socrates in effect agreed to be bound by its laws. But those who 'know no foreign languages' and live 'from day to day by [their] small wages' can scarcely be said to have a free choice to leave: 'we may as well assert that a man by remaining in a vessel, freely consents to the domination of the master, though he was carried on board while asleep, and must leap into the ocean and perish the moment he leaves her'.

The analogy is a powerful one – 'being carried on board while asleep' aptly matching the brute fact of being born into a given society. And if our entry to a society is involuntary, and we have little choice of leaving, what becomes of the much-vaunted 'contract', the essence of which must be a voluntary act? Finally, Hume questions the whole notion of trying to derive the obligation of allegiance (our duty to the state) from the prior obligation of fidelity (our duty to stick to the supposed 'contract'). 'We gain nothing from resolving the one into the other', argues Hume, since all obligations of this kind are on the same footing: they are founded on 'the general interests or necessities of society'. The suggestion is that we do not need any contract-theory or other device to *ground* our obligation to respect the state's authority, since it is simply common sense that society would collapse without such respect. This may well be right, but will not in itself explain why any given individual should feel bound to obey a particular law when it conflicts with his or her immediate self-interest – precisely the problem which the original Socratic notion of an agreement between individual and state[1] was designed to solve.

 When we consider how nearly equal all men are in their bodily force, and even in their mental powers and faculties, till cultivated by education, we must necessarily allow that nothing but their own consent could at first associate them together, and subject them to any authority. The people, if we trace government to its first origin in the woods and deserts, are the source of all power and jurisdiction, and voluntarily, for the sake of peace and order, abandoned their native liberty, and received laws from their equal and companion. The conditions upon which they were willing to submit, were either expressed, or were so clear and obvious, that it might well be esteemed

---

* David Hume, 'Of the Original Contract', first published in *Essays Moral and Political* [3rd edn 1748]; abridged, with modified spelling and punctuation. The complete text is reprinted in *Essays Moral, Political and Literary by David Hume*, ed. T. H. Green and T. H. Grose (London: Longmans Green, 1875), vol. I, pp. 443–60.

[1] See extract 1, above.

superfluous to express them. If this, then, be meant by the *original contract*, it cannot be denied that all government is, at first, founded on a contract, and that the most ancient rude combinations of mankind were formed chiefly by that principle. In vain are we asked in what records this charter of our liberties is registered. It was not written on parchment, nor yet on leaves or barks of trees. It preceded the use of writing, and all the other civilized arts of life. But we trace it plainly in the nature of man, and in the equality, or something approaching equality, which we find in all the individuals of that species. The force, which now prevails, and which is founded on fleets and armies, is plainly political, and derived from authority, the effect of established government. A man's natural force consists only in the vigour of his limbs, and the firmness of his courage; which could never subject multitudes to the command of one. Nothing but their own consent, and their sense of the advantages resulting from peace and order, could have had that influence.

Yet even this consent was long very imperfect, and could not be the basis of a regular administration. The chieftain, who had probably acquired his influence during the continuance of war, ruled more by persuasion than command; and till he could employ force to reduce the refractory and disobedient, the society could scarcely be said to have attained a state of civil government. No compact or agreement, it is evident, was expressly formed for general submission – an idea far beyond the comprehension of savages. Each exertion of authority in the chieftain must have been particular, and called forth by the present exigencies of the case. The sensible utility, resulting from his interposition, made these exertions become daily more frequent, and their frequency gradually produced an habitual, and, if you please to call it so, a voluntary, and therefore precarious, acquiescence in the people.

But philosophers who have embraced a party (if that be not a contradiction in terms) are not contented with these concessions. They assert, not only that government in its earliest infancy arose from consent, or rather the voluntary acquiescence of the people; but also that, even at present, when it has attained its full maturity, it rests on no other foundation. They affirm, that all men are still born equal, and owe allegiance to no prince or government, unless bound by the obligation and sanction of a *promise*. And as no man, without some equivalent, would forgo the advantages of his native liberty, and subject himself to the will of another, this promise is always understood to be conditional, and imposes on him no obligation, unless he meet with justice and protection from his sovereign. These advantages the sovereign promises him in return; and if he fail in the execution, he has broken, on his part, the articles of engagement, and has thereby freed his subject from all obligations to allegiance. Such, according to these philosophers, is the foundation of authority in every government, and such the right of resistance possessed by every subject.

But would these reasoners look abroad into the world, they would meet with nothing that, in the least, corresponds to their ideas, or can warrant so refined and philosophical a system. On the contrary, we find everywhere princes who claim their subjects as their property, and assert their independent right of sovereignty, from conquest or succession. We find also everywhere subjects who acknowledge this right in their prince, and suppose themselves born under obligations of obedience to a certain sovereign, as much as under the ties of reverence and duty to certain parents...Obedience or subjection becomes so familiar, that most men never make any inquiry about its origin or cause, more than about the principle of gravity, resistance, or the most universal laws of nature. Or if curiosity ever move them, as soon as they learn that they themselves and their ancestors have, for several ages, or from time immemorial, been subject to such a form of government or such a family, they immediately acquiesce, and acknowledge their obligation to allegiance. Were you to preach, in most parts of the world, that political connections are founded altogether on voluntary consent or a mutual promise, the magistrate would soon imprison you as seditious for loosening the ties of obedience, if your friends did not before shut you up as delirious, for advancing such absurdities. It is strange that an act of the mind, which every individual is supposed to have formed, and after he came to the use of reason too, otherwise it could have no authority – that this act, I say, should be so much unknown to all of them, that over the face of the whole earth there scarcely remain any traces or memory of it.

But the contract, on which government is founded, is said to be the *original contract*; and consequently may be supposed too old to fall under the knowledge of the present generation. If the agreement, by which savage men first associated and conjoined their force, be here meant, this is acknowledged to be real; but being so ancient, and being obliterated by a thousand changes of government and princes, it cannot now be supposed to retain any authority. If we would say anything to the purpose, we must assert that every particular government which is lawful, and which imposes any duty of allegiance on the subject, was, at first, founded on consent and a voluntary compact. But, besides that this supposes the consent of the fathers to bind the children, even to the most remote generations (which republican writers will never allow), besides this, I say, it is not justified by history or experience in any age or country of the world.

Almost all the governments which exist at present, or of which there remains any record in story, have been founded originally, either on usurpation or conquest, or both, without any pretence of a fair consent or voluntary subjection of the people. When an artful and bold man is placed at the head of an army or faction, it is often easy for him, by employing sometimes violence, sometimes false pretences, to estab-lish his dominion over a people a hundred times more numerous than his partisans. He allows no such open communication that his enemies can know, with certainty, their number or force. He gives them no leisure to assemble together in a body to oppose him. Even all those who are the instruments of his usurpation may wish his fall; but their ignorance of each other's intention keeps them in awe, and is the sole cause of his security. By such arts as these many governments have been established; and this is all the *original contract* which they have to boast of.

The face of the earth is continually changing, by the increase of small kingdoms into great empires, by the dissolution of great empires into smaller kingdoms, by the planting of colonies, by the migration of tribes. Is there anything discoverable in all these events but force and violence? Where is the mutual agreement or voluntary association so much talked of? . . .

It is in vain to say that all governments are, or should be at first founded on popular consent, as much as the necessity of human affairs will admit. This favours entirely my pretension. I maintain, that human affairs will never admit of this consent, seldom of the appearance of it; but that conquest or usurpation, that is, in plain terms, force, by dissolving the ancient governments, is the origin of almost all the new ones which were ever established in the world. And that in the few cases where consent may seem to have taken place, it was commonly so irregular, so confined, or so much intermixed either with fraud or violence, that it cannot have any great authority.

My intention here is not to exclude the consent of the people from being one just foundation of government. Where it has place, it is surely the best and most sacred of any. I only contend that it has very seldom had place in any degree, and never almost in its full extent; and that, therefore, some other foundation of government must also be admitted.

Were all men possessed of so inflexible a regard to justice that of themselves they would totally abstain from the properties of others, they had for ever remained in a state of absolute liberty, without subjection to any magistrate or political society; but this is a state of perfection of which human nature is justly deemed incapable. Again, were all men possessed of so perfect an understanding as always to know their own interests, no form of government had ever been submitted to but what was established on consent, and was fully canvassed by every member of the society; but this state of perfection is likewise much superior to human nature. Reason, history, and experience show us that all political societies have had an origin much less accurate and regular; and were one to choose a period of time when the people's consent was the least regarded in public transactions, it would be precisely on the establishment of a new government. In a settled constitution their inclinations are often consulted; but during the fury of revolutions, conquests, and public convulsions, military force or political craft usually decides the controversy.

When a new government is established, by whatever means, the people are commonly dissatisfied with it, and pay obedience more from fear and necessity than from any idea of allegiance or of moral obligation. The prince is watchful and jealous, and must carefully guard against every beginning or appearance of insurrection. Time, by degrees, removes all these difficulties, and accustoms the nation to regard, as their lawful or native princes, that family which at first they considered as usurpers or foreign conquerors. In order to found this opinion, they have no recourse to any notion of voluntary consent or promise, which, they know, never was, in this case, either expected or demanded. The original establishment was formed by violence, and submitted to from necessity. The subsequent administration is also supported by power, and acquiesced in by the people, not as a matter of choice, but of obligation. They imagine not that their consent gives their prince a title; but they willingly consent, because they think that, from long possession, he has acquired a title, independent of their choice or inclination.

Should it be said that, by living under the dominion of a prince which one might leave, every individual has given a *tacit* consent to his authority, and promised him obedience, it may be answered, that such an implied consent can only have place where a man imagines that the matter depends on his choice. But where he thinks (as all mankind do who are born under established governments) that, by his birth, he owes allegiance to a certain prince or certain form of government, it would be absurd to infer a consent or choice, which he expressly, in this case, renounces and disclaims.

Can we seriously say that a poor peasant or artisan has a free choice to leave his country, when he knows no foreign language or manners, and lives, from day to day, by the small wages which he acquires? We may as well assert that a man, by remaining in a vessel, freely consents to the dominion of the master; though he was carried on board while asleep, and must leap into the ocean and perish, the moment he leaves her...

The truest *tacit* consent of this kind that is ever observed, is when a foreigner settles in any country, and is beforehand acquainted with the prince, and government, and laws, to which he must submit; yet is his allegiance, though more voluntary, much less expected or depended on, than that of a natural born subject...

Did one generation of men go off the stage at once, and another succeed, as is the case with silkworms and butterflies, the new race, if they had sense enough to choose their government, which surely is never the case with men, might voluntarily, and by general consent, establish their own form of civil polity, without any regard to the laws or precedents which prevailed among their ancestors. But as human society is in perpetual flux, one man every hour going out of the world, another coming into it, it is necessary, in order to preserve stability in government, that the new brood should conform themselves to the established constitution, and nearly follow the path which their fathers, treading in the footsteps of theirs, had marked out to them. Some innovations must necessarily have place in every human institution; and it is happy where the enlightened genius of the age gives these a direction to the side of reason, liberty, and justice. But violent innovations no individual is entitled to make: they are even dangerous to be attempted by the legislature: more ill than good is ever to be expected from them: and if history affords examples to the contrary, they are not to be drawn into precedent, and are only to be regarded as proofs that the science of politics affords few rules which will not admit of some exception, and which may not sometimes be controlled by fortune and accident...

All moral duties may be divided into two kinds. The *first* are those to which men are impelled by a natural instinct or immediate propensity which operates on them, independent of all ideas of obligation, and of all views either to public or private utility. Of this nature are love of children, gratitude to benefactors, pity to the unfortunate. When we reflect on the advantage which results to society from such humane instincts, we pay them the just tribute of moral approbation and esteem; but the person actuated by them feels their power and influence antecedent to any such reflection.

The *second* kind of moral duties are such as are not supported by any original instinct of nature, but are performed entirely from a sense of obligation, when we consider the necessities of human society, and the impossibility of supporting it if these duties were neglected. It is thus *justice*, or a regard to the property of others, *fidelity*, or the observance of promises, become obligatory, and acquire an authority over mankind. For as it is evident that every man loves himself better than any other person, he is naturally impelled to extend his acquisitions as much as possible; and nothing can restrain him in this propensity but reflection and experience, by which he learns the pernicious effects of that licence, and the total dissolution of society which must ensue from it. His original inclination, therefore, or instinct, is here checked and restrained by a subsequent judgement or observation.

The case is precisely the same with the political or civil duty of *allegiance* as with the natural duties of justice and fidelity. Our preliminary instincts lead us either to indulge ourselves in unlimited freedom or to seek dominion over others; and it is reflection only which engages us to sacrifice such strong passions to the interests of peace and public order. A small degree of experience and observation suffices to teach us that society cannot possibly be maintained without the authority of magistrates, and that this authority must soon fall into contempt where exact obedience is not paid to it. The observation of these general and obvious interests is the source of the allegiance, and of that moral obligation which we attribute to it.

What necessity, therefore, is there to found the duty of *allegiance*, or obedience to magistrates, on that of *fidelity*, or a regard to promises, and to suppose that it is the consent of each individual which subjects him to government, when it appears that both allegiance and fidelity stand precisely on the same foundation, and are both submitted to by mankind on account of the apparent interests and necessities of human society? We are bound to obey our sovereign, it is said, because we have given a tacit promise to that purpose. But why are we bound to observe our promise? It must here be asserted that the commerce and intercourse of mankind, which are of such mighty advantage, can have no security where men pay no regard to their engagements. In like manner may it be said that men could not live at all in society, at least in a civilized society, without laws, and magistrates, and judges, to prevent the encroachments of the strong upon the weak, of the violent upon the just and equitable. The obligation to allegiance being of like force and authority with the obligation to fidelity, we gain nothing by resolving the one into the other. The general interests or necessities of society are sufficient to establish both...

6   Society and the Individual: Jean-Jacques Rousseau, *The Social Contract**

Despite Hume's critique of the contract theory (see preceding extract), the idea of an original contract continued to command wide support as a way of explaining the moral basis of our relationship to the state. Not long after the appearance of Hume's essay, the educational and political philosopher Jean-Jacques Rousseau published his *Social Contract*, the first chapter of which begins with the famous sentence *l'homme est né libre, et partout il est dans les fers* ('Man is born free, and is everywhere in chains'). The key idea in Rousseau's version of the contract is that 'each of us puts his person and all his power in common under the supreme direction of the general will'. The general will is conceived of by Rousseau as a 'public person formed by the union of all other persons' – a kind of abstract embodiment of the sovereign power of the state. But though it may seem risky to hand over one's individual rights to the general will, Rousseau insists that 'each man, in

giving himself to all, gives himself to nobody, and as there is no associate over whom he does not acquire the same right as he yields others over himself, he gains an equivalent of everything he loses'.

Problems remain, however, about the relationship between the general good and individual interests. Common enterprises typically require sacrifices which may from an individual standpoint appear 'gratuitous' and 'burdensome'. But we cannot, Rousseau insists, 'enjoy the rights of citizenship while refusing to fulfil the duties of a subject'; hence, anyone who refuses to obey the general will shall be compelled to do so, which 'means nothing less than that he will be forced to be free'. The phrase has an ominous ring to it, particularly when Rousseau goes on to say that the general will is infallible – it is 'always right and tends to the public advantage'. While there is a basic fairness in the idea that we should expect to shoulder

---

* Jean-Jacques Rousseau, *The Social Contract* [*Du contrat social*, 1762], extracts from Bk I, chs 6, 7, 8; Bk II, chs 1, 3, 4; Bk IV, ch. 2 (pp. 13–16, 17–19, 23–4, 26–7, 28–9, 30–1, 105–6). Trans. G. D. H. Cole (London: Dent, 1955).

our share of the burdens in exchange for the benefits of society, one may still have doubts about how society determines what is the fair distribution of such burdens; how, in short, can we be satisfied that a given policy is indeed a reflection of the true, just and infallible 'general will'? Rousseau's answer is that unanimity is needed for the social contract itself – the original setting up of society – but that thereafter 'the will of the majority always binds all the rest'. What seems to be a serious defect in the theory is the lack of adequate protection against the abuse of power by the majority claiming to act in the name of the 'general will'.[1]

 ### The social compact

The problem is to find a form of association which will defend and protect with the whole common force the person and goods of each associate, and in which each, while uniting himself with all, may still obey himself alone, and remain as free as before. This is the fundamental problem of which the Social Contract provides the solution.

The clauses of this contract are so determined by the nature of the act that the slightest modification would make them vain and ineffective; so that, although they have perhaps never been formally set forth, they are everywhere the same and everywhere tacitly admitted and recognized, until, on the violation of the social compact, each regains his original rights and resumes his natural liberty, while losing the conventional liberty in favour of which he renounced it.

These clauses, properly understood, may be reduced to one – the total alienation of each associate, together with all his rights, to the whole community. For, in the first place, as each gives himself absolutely, the conditions are the same for all; and, this being so, no one has any interest in making them burdensome to others.

Moreover, the alienation being without reserve, the union is as perfect as it can be, and no associate has anything more to demand. For, if the individuals retained certain rights, as there would be no common superior to decide between them and the public, each, being on one point his own judge, would ask to be so on all; the state of nature would thus continue, and the association would necessarily become inoperative or tyrannical.

Finally, each man, in giving himself to all, gives himself to nobody; and as there is no associate over whom he does not acquire the same right as he yields others over himself, he gains an equivalent for everything he loses, and an increase of force for the preservation of what he has.

If then we discard from the social compact what is not of its essence, we shall find that it reduces itself to the following terms: *Each of us puts his person and all his power in common under the supreme direction of the general will, and, in our corporate capacity, we receive each member as an indivisible part of the whole.*

At once, in place of the individual personality of each contracting party, this act of association creates a moral and collective body, composed of as many members as the assembly contains voters, and receiving from this act its unity, its common identity, its life, and its will. This public person, so formed by the union of all other persons, formerly took the name of *city*, and now takes that of *republic* or *body politic*; it is called by its members *state* when passive, *sovereign* when active, and *power* when

---

[1] Compare extract 9, below.

compared with others like itself. Those who are associated in it take collectively the name of *people*, and severally are called *citizens*, as sharing in the sovereign power, and *subjects*, as being under the laws of the State...

The sovereign

In fact, each individual, as a man, may have a particular will contrary or dissimilar to the general will which he has as a citizen. His particular interest may speak to him quite differently from the common interest: his absolute and naturally independent existence may make him look upon what he owes to the common cause as a gratuitous contribution, the loss of which will do less harm to others than the payment of it is burdensome to himself; and, regarding the moral person which constitutes the state as a fictitious person, because not a man, he may wish to enjoy the rights of citizenship without being ready to fulfil the duties of a subject. The continuance of such an injustice could not but prove the undoing of the body politic.

   In order then that the social compact not be an empty formula, it tacitly includes the undertaking, which alone can give force to the rest, that whoever refuses to obey the general will shall be compelled to do so by the whole body. This means nothing less than that he will be forced to be free; for this is the condition which, by giving each citizen to his country, secures him against all personal dependence. In this lies the key to the working of the political machine; this alone legitimizes civil undertakings, which, without it, would be absurd, tyrannical and liable to the most frightful abuses.

The civil state

The passage from the state of nature to the civil state produces a very remarkable change in man, by substituting justice for instinct in his conduct, and giving his actions the morality they had formerly lacked. Then only, when the voice of duty takes the place of physical impulses and right of appetite, does man, who so far had considered only himself, find that he is forced to act on different principles, and to consult his reason before listening to his inclinations. Although, in this state, he deprives himself of some advantages which he got from nature, he gains in return others so great, his faculties are so stimulated and developed, his ideas so extended, his feelings so ennobled, and his whole soul so uplifted, that, did not the abuses of this new condition often degrade him below that which he left, he would be bound to bless continually the happy moment which took him from it for ever, and, instead of a stupid and unimaginative animal, made him an intelligent being and a man.

   Let us draw up the whole account in terms easily commensurable. What man loses by the social contract is his natural liberty and an unlimited right to everything he tries to get and succeeds in getting; what he gains is civil liberty and the proprietorship of all he possesses. If we are to avoid mistake in weighing one against the other, we must clearly distinguish natural liberty, which is bounded only by the strength of the individual, from civil liberty, which is limited by the general will; and possession, which is merely the effect of force or the right of the first occupier, from property, which can be founded only on a positive title...

That sovereignty is inalienable

The first and most important deduction from the principles we have so far laid down is that the general will alone can direct the state according to the object for which it was instituted, i.e. the common good. For if the clashing of particular interests made the establishment of societies necessary, the agreement of these very interests made it possible. The common element in these different interests is what forms the social tie; and, were there no point of agreement between them all, no society could exist. It is solely on the basis of this common interest that every society should be governed.

I hold then that sovereignty, being nothing less than the exercise of the general will, can never be alienated, and that the sovereign, who is no less than a collective being, cannot be represented except by himself. The power indeed may be transmitted, but not the will.

In reality, if it is not impossible for a particular will to agree on some point with the general will, it is at least impossible for the agreement to be lasting and constant; for the particular will tends, by its very nature, to partiality, while the general will tends to equality. It is even more impossible to have any guarantee of this agreement; for even if it should always exist, it would be the effect not of art, but of chance. The sovereign may indeed say: 'I now will actually what this man wills, or at least what he says he wills'; but it cannot say: 'What he wills tomorrow, I too shall will', because it is absurd for the will to bind itself for the future, nor is it incumbent on any will to consent to anything that is not for the good of the being who wills. If then the people promises simply to obey, by that very act it dissolves itself and loses what makes it a people; the moment a master exists, there is no longer a sovereign, and from that moment the body politic has ceased to exist.

This does not mean that the commands of the rulers cannot pass for general wills, so long as the sovereign, being free to oppose them, offers no opposition. In such a case, universal silence is taken to imply the consent of the people...

Whether the general will is fallible

It follows from what has gone before that the general will is always right and tends to the public advantage; but it does not follow that the deliberations of the people are always equally correct. Our will is always for our own good, but we do not always see what that is; the people is never corrupted, but it is often deceived, and on such occasions only does it seem to will what is bad.

There is often a great deal of difference between the will of all and the general will; the latter considers only the common interest, while the former takes private interest into account, and is no more than a sum of particular wills: but take away from these same wills the pluses and minuses that cancel one another, and the general will remains as the sum of the differences.

If, when the people, being furnished with adequate information, held its deliberations, the citizens had no communication one with another, the grand total of the small differences would always give the general will, and the decision would always be good. But when factions arise, and partial associations are formed at the expense of the great association, the will of each of these associations becomes general in relation to the state: it may then be said that there are no longer as many votes as there are men, but only as many as there are associations. The differences become less numerous and give a less general result. Lastly, when one of these associations is so great as to prevail over all the rest, the result is no longer a sum of small differences, but a single difference; in this case there is no longer a general will, and the opinion which prevails is purely particular.

It is therefore essential, if the general will is to be able to express itself, that there should be no partial society within the state, and that each citizen should think only his own thoughts... But if there are partial societies, it is best to have as many as possible and to prevent them from being unequal... These precautions are the only ones that can guarantee that the general will shall be always enlightened, and that the people shall in no way deceive itself.

The limits of the sovereign power

If the state is a moral person whose life is in the union of its members, and if the most important of its cares is the care for its own preservation, it must have a universal and compelling force, in order to move and dispose each part as may be most advantageous to the whole. As nature gives each man absolute power over all his members, the social compact gives the body politic absolute power over all its members also; and it is this power which, under the direction of the general will, bears, as I have said, the name of sovereignty.

But, besides the public person, we have to consider the private persons composing it, whose life and liberty are naturally independent of it. We are bound then to distinguish clearly between the respective rights of the citizens and the sovereign, and between the duties the former have to fulfil as subjects, and the natural rights they should enjoy as men.

Each man alienates, I admit, by the social compact, only such part of his powers, goods and liberty as it is important for the community to control; but it must also be granted that the sovereign is sole judge of what is important.

Every service a citizen can render the state he ought to render as soon as the sovereign demands it; but the sovereign, for its part, cannot impose upon its subjects any fetters that are useless to the community, nor can it even wish to do so; for no more by the law of reason than by the law of nature can anything occur without a cause.

The undertakings which bind us to the social body are obligatory only because they are mutual; and their nature is such that in fulfilling them we cannot work for others without working for ourselves. Why is it that the general will is always in the right, and that all continually will the happiness of each one, unless it is because there is not a man who does not think of 'each' as meaning him, and consider himself in voting for all? This proves that equality of rights, and the idea of justice which such equality creates, originate in the preference each man gives to himself, and accordingly in the very nature of man. It proves that the general will, to be really such, must be general in its object as well as its essence; that it must both come from all and apply to all; and that it loses its natural rectitude when it is directed to some particular and determinate object, because in such a case we are judging of something foreign to us, and have no true principle of equity to guide us...

It should be seen from the foregoing that what makes the will general is less the number of voters than the common interest uniting them; for, under this system, each necessarily submits to the conditions he imposes on others: and this admirable agreement between interest and justice gives to the common deliberations an equitable character which at once vanishes when any particular question is discussed, in the absence of a common interest to unite and identify the ruling of the judge with that of the party.

From whatever side we approach our principle, we reach the same conclusion, that the social compact sets up among the citizens an equality of such a kind, that they all bind themselves to observe the same conditions and should therefore all enjoy the same rights. Thus, from the very nature of the compact, every act of sovereignty, i.e. every authentic act of the general will, binds or favours all the citizens equally; so that the sovereign recognizes only the body of the nation, and draws no distinctions between those of whom it is made up. What, then, strictly speaking, is an act of sovereignty? It is not a convention between a superior and an inferior, but a convention between the body and each of its members. It is legitimate, because based on the social contract, and equitable, because common to all; useful, because it can have no other object than the general good, and stable, because guaranteed by the public force and the supreme power. So long as the subjects have to submit only to conventions of this sort, they obey no one but their own will; and to ask how far the respective rights of the sovereign and the citizens extend, is to ask up to what point the latter can enter into undertakings with themselves, each with all, and all with each.

We can see from this that the sovereign power, absolute, sacred and inviolable as it is, does not and cannot exceed the limits of general conventions, and that every man may dispose at will of such goods and liberty as these conventions leave him; so that the sovereign never has a right to lay more charges on one subject than on another, because, in that case, the question becomes particular, and ceases to be within its competency...

Voting

There is but one law which, from its nature, needs unanimous consent. This is the social compact; for civil association is the most voluntary of all acts. Every man being born free and his own master, no one, under any pretext whatsoever, can make any man subject without his consent. To decide that the son of a slave is born a slave is to decide that he is not born a man.

If then there are opponents when the social compact is made, their opposition does not invalidate the contract, but merely prevents them from being included in it. They are foreigners among citizens. When the state is instituted, residence constitutes consent; to dwell within its territory is to submit to the sovereign.[1]

Apart from this primitive contract, the vote of the majority always binds all the rest. This follows from the contract itself. But it is asked how a man can be both free and

---

[1] *This should of course be understood as applying to a free state; for elsewhere family, goods, lack of a refuge, necessity or violence may detain a man in a country against his will; and then his dwelling there no longer by itself implies his consent to the contract or to its violation.

forced to conform to wills that are not his own. How are the opponents at once free and subject to laws they have not agreed to?

I retort that the question is wrongly put. The citizen gives his consent to all the laws, including those which are passed in spite of his opposition, and even those which punish him when he dares to break any of them. The constant will of all the members of the state is the general will; by virtue of it they are citizens and free. When in the popular assembly a law is proposed, what the people is asked is not exactly whether it approves or rejects the proposal, but whether it is in conformity with the general will, which is their will. Each man, in giving his vote, states his opinion on that point; and the general will is found by counting votes. When therefore the opinion that is contrary to my own prevails, this proves neither more nor less than that I was mistaken, and that what I thought to be the general will was not so. If my particular opinion had carried the day I should have achieved the opposite of what was my will; and it is in that case that I should not have been free.

7   The Unified State – From Individual Desire to Rational Self-determination: Georg Hegel, *The Philosophy of Right**

The ideal of freedom, which plays a central if problematic role in the thinking of Rousseau (see preceding extract), is also the main theme of the *Philosophy of Right*, a long and complex study of political theory published in 1821 by the German philosopher G. W. F. Hegel. Hegel subscribed to the basic Aristotelian premise that (as he put it) 'the rational end of man is life in the state';[1] he argued that only the state is capable of providing the conditions for the fullest human autonomy and self-determination. In the following set of extracts, Hegel presents the emergence of 'ethical life' (*Sittlichkeit*) in three phases. First comes the *family*, characterized by love and unity, where one is essentially 'not an independent person, but a member'. But this cannot serve as a fully adequate model for human existence, and must give way to *civil society*, where 'the particular person is essentially so related to other particular persons that each ... finds satisfaction by means of the others'.

This in a sense corresponds to the conception of the state to which contract theorists such as Hobbes and Locke had subscribed – an organization considered mainly as a means to providing security of person and property. But civil society risks degenerating, Hegel argues, because of the conflict between particular private interests and the universal, rationally apprehended good of all. Individuals need to have the 'singularity' of their natural condition 'raised to formal freedom and formal universality of knowing and willing'. This process gives rise to the final phase of the state as 'the actuality of concrete freedom', a 'self-dependent organism' embodied in constitutional government.

The language Hegel uses can be off-putting, but the central idea seems clear. The ultimate end of political life, for Hegel, is something which transcends the merely private interests of separate individuals: 'it is only as one of the [the state's] members that an individual has

---

* G. W. F. Hegel, *Philosophy of Right* [*Grundlinien der Philosophie des Rechts*, 1821], extracts from §§ 142, 156–9, 182–3, 185, 187–8, 257–61, 261, 273, 279, 281, 308, 316–18. Trans. T. M. Knox (Oxford: Clarendon, 1942).

[1] *Philosophy of Right*, addition to § 75; for Aristotle's view, see opening introduction to Part X, above.

objectivity, genuine individuality, and an ethical life'. But what does this come down to in practice? Hegel (elsewhere in the book) gives a detailed account of the political structure he favours, based on a constitutional monarchy – the 'single individual' (as he says below) symbolizing the 'unity' of the state. Perhaps because his style can be hard to follow, Hegel has been alternately championed and reviled by political theorists both of the right and the left. His conception of monarchy is certainly not autocratic and absolutist, but (as the concluding passage below indicates) he had an ambivalent attitude to public opinion – a 'repository of genuine needs', but at the same time easily 'infected by ignorance and perversity'. He is often characterized as having an 'organic' view of the state, though this label is misleading if it is taken to imply a conception in which all individuality is submerged; nevertheless, Hegel often seems insufficiently concerned with the practical safeguards needed to protect and foster the autonomy and individual freedom which his state is supposed to realize.

 ## Ethical life

Ethical life is the Idea of freedom in that on the one hand it is the good become alive – the good endowed in self-consciousness with knowing and willing and actualized by self-conscious action – while on the other hand self-consciousness has in the ethical realm its absolute foundation and the end which actuates its effort. This ethical life is the concept of freedom developed into the existing world and the nature of self-consciousness...

The ethical substance, as containing independent self-consciousness united with its concepts, is the actual mind of a family and a nation.

The concept of this Idea has being only as mind, as something knowing itself and actual, because it is the objectification of itself, the movement running through the form of its moments. It is therefore

(A) ethical mind in its natural or immediate phase – the *Family*. Thus substantiality loses its unity, passes over into divisions and into the phase of relation, i.e. into

(B) *Civil Society* – an association of members as self-subsistent individuals in a universality which, because of their self-subsistence, is only abstract. Their association is brought about by their needs, by the legal system – the means to security of person and property – and by an external organization for attaining their particular and common interests. The external state

(C) is brought back to and welded into unity in the *Constitution of the State* which is the end and actuality of both the substantial universal order and the public life devoted thereto.

The family

The family, as the immediate substantiality of mind, is specifically characterized by love, which is mind's feeling of its own unity. Hence in a family, one's frame of mind is to have self-consciousness of one's individuality within this unity as the absolute essence of oneself, with the result that one is in it not as an independent person, but as a member.

The right which the individual enjoys on the strength of the family unity and which is in the first place simply the individual life within this unity, takes on the *form* of right (as the abstract moment of determinate individuality) only when the family begins to dissolve. At that point those who should be family members both in their inclination and in actuality begin to be self-subsistent persons...

The family is completed in these three phases:

(a) *marriage*, the form assumed by the concept of the family in its immediate phase;
(b) *family property and capital* (the external embodiment of the concept) and attention to these;
(c) *the education of children and the dissolution of the family*...

Civil society

The concrete person, who is himself the object of his particular aims, is, as a totality of wants and a mixture of caprice and physical necessity, one principle of civil society. But the particular person is essentially so related to other particular persons that each establishes himself and finds satisfaction by means of the others, and at the same time purely and simply by means of the form of universality, the second principle here...

In the course of the actual attainment of selfish ends – an attainment conditioned in this way by universality – there is formed a system of complete interdependence, wherein the livelihood, happiness and legal status of one man is interwoven with the livelihood, happiness and rights of all. On this system, individual happiness, &c., depend, and only in this connected system are they actualized and secured. This system may be *prima facie* regarded as the external state, the state based on need, the state as the understanding envisages it...

Particularity by itself, given free rein in every direction to satisfy its needs, accidental caprices and subjective desires, destroys itself and its substantive concept in this process of gratification. At the same time, the satisfaction of need, necessary and accidental alike, is accidental because it breeds new desires without end, is in thoroughgoing dependence on caprice and external accident, and is held in check by the power of universality. In these contrasts and their complexities, civil society affords a spectacle of extravagance and want as well as of the physical and ethical degeneration common to them both...

Individuals in their capacity as burghers in this state are private persons whose end is their own interest. This end is *mediated* through the universal which thus *appears* as a *means* to its realization. Consequently, individuals can attain their ends only in so far as they themselves determine their knowing, willing and acting in a universal way and make themselves links in this chain of social connections. In these circumstances, the interest of the Idea – an interest of which these members of civil society are as such unconscious – lies in the process whereby their singularity and their natural condition are raised, as a result of the necessities imposed by nature as well as of arbitrary needs, to formal freedom and formal universality of knowing and willing – the process whereby their particularity is educated up to subjectivity...

Civil society contains three moments:

(a) The mediation of need and one man's satisfaction through his work and the satisfaction of the needs of all others – the *system of needs*.

(b) The actuality of the universal principle of freedom therein contained – the protection of property through the *administration of justice.*

(c) Provision against contingencies still lurking in systems (a) and (b), and care for particular interests as a common interest, by means of the *police* and the *corporation*...

The state

The state is the actuality of the ethical Idea. It is ethical mind *qua* the substantial will manifest and revealed to itself, knowing and thinking itself, accomplishing what it knows and in so far as it knows it. The state exists immediately in custom, mediately in individual self-consciousness, knowledge and activity, while self-consciousness, in virtue of its sentiment towards that state, finds in the state as its essence and the end and product of its activity, its substantive freedom...

The state is absolutely rational inasmuch as it is the actuality of the substantial will which it possesses in the particular self-consciousness once that consciousness has been raised to consciousness of its universality. This substantial unity is an absolute unmoved end in itself, in which freedom comes into its supreme right. On the other hand this final end has supreme right against the individual, whose supreme duty is to be a member of the state.

If the state is confused with civil society, and if its specific end is laid down as the security and protection of property and personal freedom, then the interest of the individuals as such becomes the ultimate end of their association, and it follows that membership of the state is something optional. But the state's relation to the individual is quite different from this. Since the state is mind objectified, it is only as one of its members that the individual himself has objectivity, genuine individuality and an ethical life. Unification pure and simple is the true content and aim of the individual, and the individual's destiny is the living of a universal life. His further particular satisfaction, activity and mode of conduct have this substantive and universally valid life as their starting-point and their result...

The Idea of the state

(a) has immediate actuality and is the individual state as a self-dependent organism – the *constitution* or *constitutional law*;

(b) passes over into the relation of one state to other states – *international law*;

(c) is the universal Idea as a genus and as an absolute power over individual states – the mind which gives itself its actuality in the process of *world-history.*

The state is the actuality of concrete freedom. But concrete freedom consists in this, that personal individuality and its particular interests not only achieve their complete development and gain explicit recognition for their right (as they do in the sphere of the family and civil society) but, for one thing, they also pass over of their own accord into the interest of the universal, and, for another thing, they know and will the universal; they even recognize it as their own substantive mind; they take it as their end and aim and are active in its pursuit... The essence of the modern state is that the universal be bound up with the complete freedom of its particular members and with private well-being, that thus the interests of family and civil society must concentrate themselves on the state, although the universal end cannot be advanced without the personal knowledge and will of its particular members, whose own rights must be maintained. Thus the universal must be furthered, but subjectivity on the other hand must attain its full and living development. It is only when both these moments subsist in their strength that the state can be regarded as articulated and genuinely organized...

In contrast with the spheres of private rights and private welfare (the family and civil society), the state is from one point of view an external necessity and their higher authority; its nature is such that their laws and interests are subordinate to it and dependent on it. On the other hand, however, it is the end immanent within them, and its strength lies in the unity of its own universal end and aim with the particular interest of individuals, in the fact that individuals have duties to the state in proportion as they have rights against it...

In the state[1] everything depends on the unity of universal and particular. In the states of antiquity, the subjective end simply coincided with the state's will. In modern times, however, we make claims for private judgement, private willing, and private conscience. The ancients had none of these in the modern sense; the ultimate thing with them was the will of the state. Whereas under the despots of Asia the individual had no inner life and no justification in himself, in the modern world man insists on respect being paid to his inner life. The conjunction of duty and right has a twofold aspect: what the state demands from us as a duty is *eo ipso* our right as individuals, since the state is nothing but the articulation of the concept of freedom. The determinations of the individual will are given an objective embodiment through the state, and thereby they attain their truth and their actualization for the first time. The state is the one and only prerequisite of the attainment of particular ends and welfare...

'Who is to frame the constitution?' This question seems clear but closer inspection shows at once that it is meaningless, for it presupposes that there is no constitution there, but only an agglomeration of atomic individuals. How an agglomeration of individuals could acquire a constitution, whether automatically or by someone's aid, whether as a present or by force or by thought, it would have to be allowed to settle for itself, since with an agglomeration the concept has nothing to do. But if the question presupposes an already existent constitution, then it is not about framing, but only about altering the constitution, and the very presupposition of a constitution directly implies that its alteration may come about only by constitutional means. In any case, however, it is absolutely essential that the constitution should not be regarded as something made, even though it has come into being in time. It must be treated rather as something simply existent in and by itself, as divine therefore, and constant, and so as exalted above the sphere of things that are made...

Sovereignty...comes into existence only as subjectivity sure of itself, as the will's abstract and to that extent ungrounded self-determination in which finality of decision is rooted. This is the strictly individual aspect of the state, and in virtue of which alone is the state *one*. The truth of subjectivity, however, is attained only in a

---

[1] This paragraph is from the 'Additions' (based on notes from Hegel's lectures) which Hegel's editor included in a later (1833) edition of the *Philosophy of Right*.

subject, and the truth of personality only in a person ... Hence this absolutely decisive moment of the whole is not individuality in general, but a single individual, the monarch ...

The usual sense in which men have recently begun to speak of the 'sovereignty of the people' is that it is something opposed to the sovereignty existent in the monarch. So opposed to the sovereignty of the monarch, the sovereignty of the people is one of the confused notions based on the wild idea of the 'people'. Taken without its monarch and the articulation of the whole which is the indispensable and direct concomitant of monarchy, the people is a formless mass and no longer a state. It lacks every one of those determinate characteristics – sovereignty, government, judges, magistrates, class-divisions, etc. – which are to be found only in a whole which is inwardly organized ...

An elective monarchy seems of course to be the most natural idea, i.e. the idea which superficial thinking finds handiest. Because it is the concerns and interests of his people for which a monarch has to provide, so the argument runs, it must be left to the people to entrust with its welfare whomsoever it pleases, and only with the grant of this trust does his right to rule arise. This view, like the notion of the monarch as the highest executive official in the state, or the notion of a contractual relation between him and his people, etc., etc., is grounded on the will interpreted as the whim, opinion and caprice of the many. A will of this character counts as the first thing in civil society ... or rather it tries to count as the only thing there, but it is not the guiding principle of the family, still less of the state, and in short it stands opposed to the idea of ethical life ...

To hold that every single person should share in deliberating and deciding on political matters of general concern on the ground that all individuals are members of the state, that its concerns are their concerns, and that it is their right that what is done should be done with their knowledge and volition, is tantamount to a proposal to put the democratic element without any rational form into the organism of the state, although it is only in virtue of the possession of such a form that the state is an organism at all.... The concrete state is the whole, articulated into its particular groups. The member of a state is a member of such a group, i.e. of a social class, and it is only as characterized in this objective way that he comes under consideration when we are dealing with the state. His mere character as universal implies that he is at one and the same time both a private person and also a thinking consciousness, a will which wills the universal. This consciousness and will, however, lose their emptiness and acquire a content and a living actuality only when they are filled with particularity, and particularity means determinacy as particular and a particular class status ... Hence the single person attains his actual and living destiny for universality only when he becomes a member of a corporation, a society, etc., and thereby it becomes open to him, on the strength of his skill, to enter any class for which he is qualified ...

The formal subjective freedom of individuals consists in their having and expressing their own private judgements, opinions and recommendations on affairs of state. This freedom is collectively manifested as what is called 'public opinion', in which what is absolutely universal, the substantive and the true, is linked with its opposite, the purely particular and private opinions of the many. Public opinion as it exists is thus a standing self-contradiction, knowledge as appearance, the essential just as directly present as the inessential.

Public opinion, therefore, is a repository not only of the genuine needs and correct tendencies of common life, but also, in the form of common sense (i.e. all-pervasive fundamental ethical principles disguised as prejudices), of the eternal, substantive principles of justice, the true content and result of legislation, the whole constitution, and the general position of the state. At the same time, when this inner truth emerges into consciousness and, embodied in general maxims, enters representative thinking – whether it be there on its own account or in support of concrete arguments about felt wants, public affairs, the organization of the state, and relations of parties within it – it becomes infected by all the accidents of opinion, by its ignorance and perversity, by its mistakes and falsity of judgement. Since in considering such opinion we have to do with the consciousness of an insight and conviction peculiarly one's own, the more peculiarly one's own an opinion may be the worse its content is, because the bad is that which is wholly private and personal in its content; the rational, on the other hand, is the absolutely universal... Public opinion therefore deserves to be as much respected as despised – despised for its concrete expression and for the concrete consciousness it expresses, respected for its essential basis, a basis which only glimmers more or less dimly in that concrete expression.

8   Property, Labour and Alienation: Karl Marx and Friedrich Engels, *The German Ideology**

The influence of Hegel's style (see preceding extract) is apparent in our next passage, written in the middle of the nineteenth century by the founders of Communism, Marx and Engels. Their account begins, like Hegel's, with an analysis of the family; but so far from being a form of 'ethical life', the family for Marx and Engels turns out to harbour a 'latent slavery', where the wife and children are the slaves of the husband. This slavery is linked to the 'power of disposing the labour-power of others', and the argument is then generalized to show how the whole of society is structured in ways which reflect the unequal distribution of power. The division of labour, which forces people to work exclusively at a particular task to gain their livelihood, means that 'man's own deed becomes an alien power opposed to him, which enslaves him instead of being controlled by him'. This 'alienation' brought about by the operation of the economic system is for Marx and Engels the key to the malaise of modern society. The masses are forced to work in ways which 'fix' them in a particular role, restricting their freedom, and robbing their lives of meaning. Alienation in turn generates the pressures for the revolution of the proletariat, in which the 'propertyless workers', driven to ever greater poverty by the forces of capitalist competition, will rise up and take power, and appropriate the means of production.

What happens after the revolution? Marx and Engels describe their 'communist' society in lyrical terms, as 'making it possible for me to hunt in the morning, fish in the afternoon, rear cattle in the evening, criticize after dinner... without ever becoming hunter, fisherman, cowherd or critic'. A spectacular improvement in economic and social conditions was supposed to result from the abolition of capitalist exploitation, and the substitution of common ownership for private property. The enormous influence exerted by Marx's thought in the twentieth

* K. Marx and F. Engels, *Die deutsche Ideologie* [*The German Ideology*, composed 1845–6; first published 1932], extracts from Part I, §A, §B, §D. Trans. S. Ryazanskaya (London: Lawrence & Wishart, 1965), pp. 44–8, 61, 82–7; with omissions and minor modifications.

century was partly due to the Bolshevik revolution in Russia which took his ideas as its ruling ideology. But the discrediting and eventual collapse of communist totalitarianism in Europe has shown what a wide gap there is between Marx's idealistic vision and the harsh realities of state communism. The chief philosophical importance of Marx's ideas has been the increased awareness they have generated of the inevitable links between the political and the economic domains. Though by no means all would agree with Marx's and Engels' claim that 'the ruling ideas' of any epoch are 'nothing more than the ideal expression of the dominant material relationships', their analysis invites us to consider the extent to which the structure of our political and social institutions reflects hard economic facts about the production and distribution of goods and services. Finally, the account of 'alienation' succeeds in raising serious questions about the conditions prevalent in modern systems of mass production, and the ability of the modern industrial state to offer its citizens worthwhile and satisfying work.

 With the division of labour... which in its turn is based on the natural division of labour in the family and the separation of society into individual families opposed to one another, is given simultaneously the distribution, and indeed the unequal distribution, both quantitative and qualitative, of labour and its products, hence property: the nucleus, the first form of which lies in the family, where wife and children are the slaves of the husband. This latent slavery in the family, though still very crude, is the first property, but even at this early stage it corresponds perfectly to the definition of modern economists who call it the power of disposing of the labour-power of others. Division of labour and private property are, moreover, identical expressions: in the one the same thing is affirmed with reference to activity as is affirmed in the other with reference to the product of the activity.

Further, the division of labour implies the contradiction between the interest of the separate individual or the individual family and the communal interest of all individuals who have intercourse with one another. And indeed, this communal interest does not exist merely in the imagination, as the 'general interest', but first of all in reality, as the mutual interdependence of the individuals among whom the labour is divided. And finally, the division of labour offers us the first example of how, as long as man remains in natural society, that is, as long as a cleavage exists between the particular and the common interest, as long, therefore, as activity is not voluntarily, but naturally, divided, man's own deed becomes an alien power opposed to him, which enslaves him instead of being controlled by him. For as soon as the distribution of labour comes into being, each man has a particular, exclusive sphere of activity, which is forced upon him and from which he cannot escape. He is a hunter, a fisherman, a shepherd or a critical critic, and must remain so if he does not want to lose his means of livelihood; while in communist society, where nobody has one exclusive sphere of activity but each can become accomplished in any branch he wishes, society regulates the general production and thus makes it possible for me to do one thing today and another tomorrow, to hunt in the morning, fish in the afternoon, rear cattle in the evening, criticize after dinner, just as I have a mind, without ever becoming hunter, fisherman, cowherd or critic. This fixation of social activity, this consolidation of what we ourselves produce into an objective power above us, growing out of our control, thwarting our expectations, bringing to naught our calculations, is one of the chief factors in historical development up till now.

And out of this very contradiction between the interest of the individual and that of the community the latter takes an independent form as the state, divorced from the real interests of individual and community, and at the same time as an illusory communal life, always based, however, on the real ties existing in every family and tribal conglomeration – such as flesh and blood, language, division of labour on a larger scale, and other interests – and especially... on the classes, already determined by the division of labour, which in every such mass of men separate out, and of which one dominates all the others. It follows from this that all struggles within the state, the struggle between democracy, aristocracy and monarchy, the struggle for the franchise, etc. etc. are merely the illusory forms in which the real struggles of the different classes are fought out among one another... Further, it follows that every class which is struggling for mastery, even when its domination, as is the case with the proletariat, postulates the abolition of the old form of society in its entirety and of domination itself, must first conquer for itself political power in order to represent its interest in turn as the general interest, which immediately it is forced to do. Just because individuals seek only their particular interest, which for them does not coincide with their communal interest, the latter will be imposed on them as an interest 'alien' to them, and 'independent' of them, as in its turn a particular, peculiar 'general' interest; or they themselves must remain within this discord, as in democracy. On the other hand, too, the practical struggle of these particular interests, which constantly really run counter to the communal and illusory communal interests, makes practical intervention and control necessary through the illusory 'general' interest in the form of the state.

The social power, i.e. the multiplied productive force, which arises through the cooperation of different individuals as it is determined by the division of labour, appears to these individuals, since their cooperation is not voluntary but has come about naturally, not as their own united power, but as an alien force existing outside them, of the origin and goal of which they are ignorant, which they thus cannot control, which on the contrary passes through a peculiar series of phases and stages independent of the will and the action of man, nay even being the prime governor of these...

This 'alienation' (to use a term which will be comprehensible to the philosophers) can, of course, only be abolished given two practical premises. For it to become an 'intolerable' power, i.e. a power against which men make a revolution, it must necessarily have rendered the great mass of humanity 'propertyless', and produced, at the same time, the contradiction of an existing world of wealth and culture, both of which conditions presuppose a great increase in productive power, a high degree of its development. And, on the other hand, this development of productive forces (which itself implies the actual empirical existence of men in their *world-historical* instead of local, being) is an absolutely necessary practical premise, because without it want is merely made general, and with destitution the struggle for necessities and all the old filthy business would necessarily be reproduced; and furthermore, because only with this universal development of productive forces is a universal intercourse between men established, which produces in all nations simultaneously the phenomenon of the 'propertyless' mass (universal competition), makes each nation dependent on the revolutions of the others, and finally has put world-historical, empirically universal individuals in place of local ones... Empirically communism is only possible as the act of the dominant peoples 'all at once' and simultaneously, which presupposes the universal development of productive forces and the world intercourse bound up with communism. . . .

Communism is for us not a state of affairs which is to be established, an ideal to which reality will have to adjust itself. We call communism the real movement which abolishes the present state of things. The conditions of this movement result from the premises now in existence. Moreover, the mass of propertyless workers – the utterly precarious position of labour-power on a mass scale cut off from capital or from even a limited satisfaction and, therefore, no longer merely temporarily deprived of work itself as a secure source of life – presupposes the world market through competition. The proletariat can thus only exist world-historically, just as communism, its activity, can only have a 'world-historical' existence. World-historical existence of individuals means existence of individuals which is directly linked up with world history.

The ideas of the ruling class are in every epoch the ruling ideas, i.e. the class which is the ruling material force of society is at the same time its ruling intellectual force. The class which has the means of material production at its disposal, has control at the same time over the means of mental production, so that thereby, generally speaking, the ideas of those who lack the means of mental production are subject to it. The ruling ideas are nothing more than the ideal expression of the dominant material relationships, the dominant material relationships grasped as ideas; hence of the relationships which make the one class the ruling one, therefore, the ideas of its dominance. The individuals composing the ruling class possess among other things consciousness, and therefore think. In so far, therefore, as they rule as a class and determine the extent and compass of an epoch, it is self-evident that they do this in its whole range, hence among other things rule also as thinkers, as producers of ideas, and regulate the production and distribution of the ideas of their age: thus their ideas are the ruling ideas of the epoch. For instance, in an age and in a country where royal power, aristocracy and bourgeoisie are contending for mastery and where, therefore, mastery is shared, the doctrine of the separation of powers proves to be the dominant idea and is expressed as an 'eternal law'. . .

Our investigation hitherto started from the instruments of production, and it has already shown that private property was a necessity for certain industrial stages. In raw-materials industry, private property still coincides with labour; in small industry and all agriculture up till now property is the necessary consequence of the existing instruments of production; in big industry the contradiction between the instruments of production and private property appears for the first time and is the product of big industry; moreover, big industry must be highly developed to produce this contradiction. And thus only with big industry does the abolition of private property become possible.

In big industry and competition the whole mass of conditions of existence, limitations, biases of individuals, are fused together into the two simplest forms: private property and labour. With money every form of intercourse, and intercourse itself, is considered fortuitous for the individuals. Thus money implies that all previous intercourse was only intercourse of individuals under particular conditions, not of individuals as individuals. These conditions are reduced to two: accumulated labour or private property, and actual labour. If both or one of these ceases, then intercourse comes to a standstill...On the other hand, the individuals themselves are entirely subordinated to the division of labour and hence are brought into the most complete dependence on one another. Private property, in so far as within labour itself it is opposed to labour, evolves out of the necessity of accumulation, and has still, to begin with, rather the form of the communality; but in its further development it approaches more and more the modern form of private property The division of labour implies from the outset the division of the conditions of labour, of tools and materials, and thus the splitting-up of accumulated capital among different owners, and thus, also, the division between capital and labour, and the different forms of property itself. The more the division of labour develops and accumulation grows, the sharper are the forms that this process of differentiation assumes. Labour itself can only exist on the premise of this fragmentation.

Thus two facts are here revealed. First the productive forces appear as a world for themselves, quite independent of and divorced from the individuals, alongside the individuals: the reason for this is that the individuals, whose forces they are, exist split up and in opposition to one another, while, on the other hand, these forces are only real forces in the intercourse and association of these individuals. Thus, on the one hand, we have a totality of productive forces, which have, as it were, taken on a material form and are for the individuals no longer the forces of the individuals but of private property, and hence of the individuals only in so far as they are owners of private property themselves. Never, in any earlier period, have the productive forces taken on a form so indifferent to the intercourse of individuals as individuals, because their intercourse itself was formerly a restricted one. On the other hand, standing over against these productive forces, we have the majority of the individuals from whom these forces have been wrested away, and who, robbed thus of all real life-content, have become abstract individuals, but who are, however, only by this fact put into a position to enter into relation with one another as individuals.

The only connection which still links them with the productive forces and with their own existence – labour – has lost all semblance of self-activity and only sustains their life by stunting it. While in the earlier periods self-activity and the production of material life were separated, in that they devolved on different persons, and while, on account of the narrowness of the individuals themselves, the production of material life was considered as a subordinate mode of self-activity, they now diverge to such an extent that altogether material life appears as the end, and what produces this material life, labour (which is now the only possible but, as we see, negative form of self-activity), as the means.

Thus things have now come to such a pass that the individuals must appropriate the existing totality of productive forces, not only to achieve self-activity but also merely to safeguard their very existence. This appropriation is first determined by the object to be appropriated, the productive forces, which have been developed to a totality and which only exist within a universal intercourse. From this aspect alone, therefore, this appropriation must have a universal character corresponding to the productive forces and the intercourse. The appropriation of these forces is itself nothing more than the development of the individual capacities corresponding to the material instruments of production. The appropriation of a totality of instruments of production is, for this very reason, the development of a totality of capacities in the individuals themselves.

This appropriation is further determined by the persons appropriating. Only the proletarians of the present day, who are completely shut off from all self-activity, are in a position to achieve a complete and no longer restricted self-activity, which consists in the appropriation of a totality of productive forces and in the thus postulated development of a totality of capacities. All earlier revolutionary appropriations were restricted; individuals, whose self-activity was restricted by a crude instrument of production and a limited intercourse, appropriated this crude instrument of production, and hence merely achieved a new state of limitation. Their instrument of production became their property, but they themselves remained subordinate to the division of labour and their own instrument of production. In all expropriations up to now, a mass of individuals remained subservient to a single instrument of production; in the appropriation by the proletarians, a mass of instruments of production must be made subject to each individual, and property to all. Modern universal intercourse can be controlled by individuals, therefore, only when controlled by all.

This appropriation is further determined by the manner in which it must be effected. It can only be effected through a union, which by the character of the proletariat itself can again only be a universal one, and through a revolution, in which, on the one hand, the power of the earlier mode of production and intercourse and social organization is overthrown, and, on the other hand, there develops the universal character and the energy of the proletariat, without which the revolution cannot be accomplished; and in which, further, the proletariat rids itself of everything that still clings to it from its previous position in society.

Only at this stage does self-activity coincide with material life, which corresponds to the development of individuals into complete individuals and the casting-off of all natural limitations. The transformation of labour into self-activity corresponds to the transformation of the earlier limited intercourse into the intercourse of individuals as such. With the appropriation of the total productive forces through united individuals, private property comes to an end. While previously in history a particular condition always appeared as accidental, now the isolation of individuals and the particular private gain of each man have themselves become accidental...

Finally, from the conception of history we have sketched we obtain these further conclusions: (1) In the development of productive forces there comes a stage when productive forces and means of intercourse are brought into being, which, under the existing relationships, only cause mischief, and are no longer productive but destructive forces (machinery and money); and connected with this a class is called forth, which has to bear all the burdens of society without enjoying its advantages, which, ousted from society, is forced into the most decided antagonism to all other classes; a class which forms the majority of all members of society, and from which emanates the consciousness of the necessity of a fundamental revolution, the communist consciousness, which may, of course, arise among the other classes too through the contemplation of the situation of this class. (2) The conditions under which definite productive forces can be applied are the conditions of the rule of a definite class of society, whose social power, deriving from its property, has its practical-idealistic expression in each case in the form of the state; and, therefore, every revolutionary struggle is directed against a class, which till then has been in power. (3) In all revolutions up till now the mode of activity always remained unscathed and it was only a question of a different distribution of this activity, a new distribution of labour to other persons, while the communist revolution is directed against the preceding mode of activity, does away with labour, and abolishes the rule of all classes with the classes themselves, because it is carried through by the class which no longer counts as a class in society, is not recognized as a class, and is in itself the expression of the dissolution of all classes, nationalities, etc. within present society; and (4) Both for the production on a mass scale of this communist consciousness, and for the success of the cause itself, the alteration of men on a mass scale is necessary, an alteration which can only take place in a practical movement, a revolution; this revolution is necessary, therefore, not only because the ruling class cannot be overthrown in any other way, but also because the class overthrowing it can only in a revolution succeed in ridding itself of all the muck of ages and become fitted to found society anew.

9   The Limits of Majority Rule: John Stuart Mill, *On Liberty**

A problematic feature of Rousseau's political theory (extract 6, above) is, as we have seen, the relationship between the 'general will' and the will of the majority. In the following extract, from a highly influential essay published in 1859, J. S. Mill pointedly observes that 'the will of the people practically means the will of the most numerous or most active part of the people' – the majority, or those who manage to get accepted as such. The *tyranny of the majority* is just as much a threat to individual liberty as the dictates of individual tyrants. Mill proceeds to lay down a principle which has assumed enormous importance in political philosophy, since it aims to provide a clear basis for restricting the power of the majority to interfere with the freedom of any member of society. The 'sole end' which justifies society interfering with anyone's liberty of action is *the prevention of harm to others*. What this means is that if, for example, A is attacking B, we may normally intervene (and society may pass laws prohibiting such conduct); but if A is merely harming herself, or if A is merely doing something which the majority

disapprove of, or find morally outrageous, then – provided no one else is being harmed – society has no right to intervene.

Much legislation in modern society is *paternalistic* – aimed at preventing harm to self (for example laws requiring seat belts to be worn, or preventing individuals taking dangerous drugs); many other laws are *moralistic* – enforcing the prevailing moral ethos (e.g. laws against prostitution). Mill's principle says firmly that both such types of law are outside the proper scope of the legislator. A great deal of subsequent discussion has centred around Mill's central concept of *harm*, and whether it may be clearly defined. We may want to prohibit more than physical harm (so as to curb such acts as nuisance phone calls); but widening the definition of harm to include all behaviour that people find 'offensive' could seriously erode freedom. Other critics of Mill have questioned the tenability of his implied distinction between self-regarding and other-regarding conduct: by harming myself might I not cause harm to other people? Yet Mill himself allows (at the end of our passage) that

---

* J. S. Mill, *On Liberty* [1859], extracts from chs I, II, III and IV. Many editions available, including the standard edition, *Collected Works of J. S. Mill*, ed. J. M. Robson, vol. XVIII (London: Routledge, 1977).

harm I do myself may adversely affect others; but he argues that provided I do not thereby incapacitate myself from discharging specific duties I have undertaken, 'the inconvenience is one which society can afford to bear, for the sake of the greater good of human freedom'. Mill's acute and careful discussion remains a classic text for all who are interested in investigating the proper limits of majority rule in a free society.

 The subject of this essay is...the nature and limits of the power which can be legitimately exercised by society over the individual...The struggle between liberty and authority is the most conspicuous feature in the portions of history with which we are earliest familiar, particularly in that of Greece, Rome and England. But in old times this contest was between subjects, or some classes of subjects, and the government. By liberty, was meant protection against the tyranny of the political rulers...To prevent the weaker members of the community from being preyed upon by innumerable vultures, it was needful that there should be an animal of prey stronger than the rest, commissioned to keep them down. But as the king of the vultures would be no less bent upon preying on the flock than any of the minor harpies, it was indispensable to be in a perpetual attitude of defence against his beak and claws. The aim, therefore, of patriots was to set limits to the power which the ruler should be suffered to exercise over the community; and this limitation was what they meant by liberty...

A time, however, came, in the progress of human affairs, when men ceased to think it a necessity of nature that their governors should be an independent power, opposed in interest to themselves. It appeared to them much better that the various magistrates of the state should be their tenants or delegates, revocable at their pleasure. In that way alone, it seemed, could they have complete security that the powers of government would never be abused to their disadvantage...

But, in political and philosophical theories, as well as in persons, success discloses faults and infirmities which failure might have concealed from observation...It was now perceived that such phrases as 'self-government', and 'the power of the people over themselves', do not express the true state of the case. The 'people' who exercise the power are not always the same people [as] those over whom it is exercised; and the 'self-government' spoken of is not the government of each by himself, but of each by all the rest. The will of the people, moreover, practically means the will of the most numerous or the most active *part* of the people; the majority, or those who succeed in making themselves accepted as the majority; the people, consequently *may* desire to oppress a part of their number; and precautions are as much needed against this as against any other abuse of power. The limitation, therefore, of the power of government over individuals loses none of its importance when the holders of power are regularly accountable to the community, that is, to the strongest party therein. This view of things...has had no difficulty in establishing itself; and in political speculations 'the tyranny of the majority' is now generally included among the evils against which society requires to be on its guard.

Like other tyrannies, the tyranny of the majority was at first, and is still vulgarly, held in dread, chiefly as operating through the acts of the public authorities. But reflecting persons perceived that when society is itself the tyrant – society collectively over the separate individuals who compose it – its means of tyrannizing are not restricted to the acts which it may do by the hands of its political functionaries . . . Protection, therefore, against the tyranny of the magistrate is not enough: there needs protection also against the tyranny of the prevailing opinion and feeling; against the tendency of society to impose, by other means than civil penalties, its own ideas and practices as rules of conduct on those who dissent from them; to fetter the development, and, if possible, prevent the formation, of any individuality not in harmony with its ways, and compel all characters to fashion themselves upon the model of its own. There is a limit to the legitimate interference of collective opinion with individual independence: and to find that limit, and maintain it against encroachment, is as indispensable to a good condition of human affairs, as protection against political despotism . . .

The object of this essay is to assert one very simple principle, as entitled to govern absolutely the dealings of society with the individual in the way of compulsion and control, whether the means used be physical force in the form of legal penalties, or the moral coercion of public opinion. That principle is, that the sole end for which mankind are warranted, individually or collectively, in interfering with the liberty of action of any of their number, is self-protection. That the only purpose for which power can be rightfully exercised over any member of a civilized community, against his will, is to prevent harm to others. His own good, either physical or moral, is not a sufficient warrant. He cannot rightfully be compelled to do or forbear because it will be better for him to do so, because it will make him happier, because, in the opinions of others, to do so would be wise, or even right. These are good reasons for remonstrating with him, or reasoning with him, or persuading him, or entreating him, but not for compelling him, or visiting him with any evil in case he do otherwise. To justify that, the conduct from which it is desired to deter him must be calculated to produce evil to someone else. The only part of the conduct of any one, for which he is amenable to society, is that which concerns others. In the part which merely concerns himself, his independence is, of right, absolute. Over himself, over his own body and mind, the individual is sovereign.

It is, perhaps, hardly necessary to say that this doctrine is meant to apply only to human beings in the maturity of their faculties. We are not speaking of children, or of young persons below the age which the law may fix as that of manhood or womanhood. Those who are still in a state to require being taken care of by others must be protected against their own actions as well as against external injury. For the same reason, we may leave out of consideration those backward states of society in which the race itself may be considered as in its nonage.[1] The early difficulties in the way of spontaneous progress are so great that there is seldom any choice of means for overcoming them; and a ruler full of the spirit of improvement is warranted in the use of any expedients that will attain an end, perhaps otherwise unattainable. Despotism is a legitimate mode of government in dealing with barbarians, provided the end be their improvement, and the means justified by actually effecting that end. Liberty, as a principle, has no application to any state of things anterior to the time when mankind have become capable of being improved by free and equal discussion. Until then, there is nothing for them but implicit obedience to an Akbar or a Charlemagne, if they are so fortunate as to find one. But as soon as mankind have attained the capacity of being guided to their own improvement by conviction or

---

[1] Nonage: immaturity.

persuasion (a period long since reached in all nations with whom we need here concern ourselves), compulsion, either in the direct form or in that of pains and penalties for non-compliance, is no longer admissible as a means to their own good, and justifiable only for the security of others.

It is proper to state that I forgo any advantage which could be derived to my argument from the idea of abstract right, as a thing independent of utility. I regard utility as the ultimate appeal on all ethical questions; but it must be utility in the largest sense, grounded on the permanent interests of a man as a progressive being. Those interests, I contend, authorize the subjection of individual spontaneity to external control, only in respect to those actions of each which concern the interest of other people. If anyone does an act hurtful to others, there is a *prima facie* case for punishing him, by law, or, where legal penalties are not safely applicable, by general disapprobation There are also many positive acts for the benefit of others, which he may rightfully be compelled to perform; such as to give evidence in a court of justice; to bear his fair share in the common defence, or in any other joint work necessary to the interest of the society of which he enjoys the protection; and to perform certain acts of individual beneficence, such as saving a fellow creature's life, or interposing to protect the defenceless against ill-usage, things which whenever it is obviously a man's duty to do, he may rightfully be made responsible to society for not doing. A person may cause evil to others not only by his actions but by his inaction, and in either case he is justly accountable to them for the injury. The latter case, it is true, requires a much more cautious exercise of compulsion than the former. To make any one answerable for doing evil to others is the rule; to make him answerable for not preventing evil is, comparatively speaking, the exception. Yet there are many cases clear enough and grave enough to justify that exception...

But there is a sphere of action in which society, as distinguished from the individual, has, if any, only an indirect interest; comprehending all that portion of a person's life and conduct which affects only himself, or if it also affects others, only with their free, voluntary and undeceived consent and participation...This, then, is the appropriate region of human liberty. It comprises, first, the inward domain of consciousness; demanding liberty of conscience in the most comprehensive sense; liberty of thought and feeling; absolute freedom of opinion and sentiment on all subjects, practical or speculative, scientific, moral, or theological. The liberty of expressing and publishing opinions may seem to fall under a different principle, since it belongs to that part of the conduct of an individual which concerns other people; but, being almost of as much importance as the liberty of thought itself, and resting in great part on the same reasons, is practically inseparable from it. Secondly, the principle requires liberty of tastes and pursuits; of framing the plan of our life to suit our own character; of doing as we like, subject to such consequences as may follow; without impediment from our fellow creatures, so long as what we do does not harm them, even though they should think our conduct foolish, perverse or wrong. Thirdly, from this liberty of each individual, follows the liberty, within the same limits, of combination among individuals; freedom to unite, for any purpose not involving harm to others: the persons combining being supposed to be of full age, and not forced or deceived.

No society in which these liberties are not, on the whole, respected, is free, whatever may be its form of government; and none is completely free in which they do not exist absolute and unqualified. The only freedom which deserves the name, is that of pursuing our own good in our own way, so long as we do not attempt to deprive others of theirs, or impede their efforts to obtain it. Each is the proper guardian of his own health, whether bodily, or mental and spiritual. Mankind are greater gainers by suffering each other to live as seems good to themselves, than by compelling each to live as seems good to the rest...

... Speaking generally, it is not, in constitutional countries, to be apprehended that the government ... will often attempt to control the expression of opinion, except when in doing so it makes itself the organ of the general intolerance of the public. Let us suppose, therefore, that the government is entirely at one with the people, and never thinks of exerting any power of coercion unless in agreement with what it conceives to be their voice. But I deny the right of the people to exercise such coercion, either by themselves or by their government. The power itself is illegitimate. The best government has no more title to it than the worst. It is as noxious, or more noxious, when exerted in accordance with pubic opinion than when in opposition to it. If all mankind minus one were of one opinion, and only one person were of the contrary opinion, mankind would be no more justified in silencing that one person than he, if he had the power, would be justified in silencing mankind. Were an opinion of personal possession of no value except to the owner; if to be obstructed in the enjoyment of it were simply a private injury, it would make some difference whether the injury was inflicted only on a few persons or on many. But the peculiar evil of silencing the expression of an opinion is that it is robbing the human race; posterity as well as the existing generation; those who dissent from the opinion, still more than those who hold it. If the opinion is right, they are deprived of the opportunity of exchanging error for truth; if wrong, they lose what is almost as great a benefit, the clearer perception and livelier impression of truth, produced by its collision with error...

No one pretends that actions should be as free as opinions. On the contrary, even opinions lose their immunity when the circumstances in which they are expressed are such as to constitute their expression a positive instigation to some mischievous act. An opinion that corn-dealers are starvers of the poor, or that private property is robbery, ought to be unmolested when simply circulated through the press, but may justly incur punishment when delivered orally to an excited mob assembled before the house of a corn-dealer, or when handed about among the same mob in the form of a placard. Acts, of whatever kind, which, without justifiable cause, do harm to others, may be, and in the more important cases absolutely require to be, controlled by the unfavourable sentiments, and, when needful, by the active interference of mankind. The liberty of the individual must be thus far limited; he must not make himself a nuisance to other people. But if he refrains from molesting others in what concerns them, and merely acts according to his own inclination and judgement in things which concern himself, the same reasons which show that opinion should be free, prove also that he should be allowed, without molestation, to carry his opinions into practice at his own cost...As it is useful that while mankind are imperfect there should be different opinions, so it is that there should be different experiments of living; that free scope should be given to varieties of character, short of injury to others; and that the worth of different modes of life should be proved practically, when any one thinks fit to try them. It is desirable, in short, that in things which do not primarily concern others, individuality should assert itself...

The distinction here pointed out between the part of a person's life which concerns only himself, and that which concerns others, many persons will refuse to admit. How (it may be asked) can any part of the conduct of a member of society be a matter of indifference to the other members? No person is an entirely isolated being; it is impossible for a person to do anything seriously or permanently hurtful to himself, without mischief reaching at least to his near connections, and often far beyond them. If he injures his property, he does harm to those who directly or indirectly derived support from it, and usually diminishes, by a greater or less amount, the general resources of the community. If he deteriorates his bodily or mental faculties, he not only brings evil upon all who depended on him for any portion of their happiness, but disqualifies himself for rendering the services which he owes to his fellow creatures generally; perhaps becomes a burden on their affection or benevolence; and if such conduct were very frequent, hardly any offence that is committed would detract more from the general sum of good. Finally, if by his vices or follies a person does no direct harm to others, he is nevertheless (it may be said) injurious by his example; and ought to be compelled to control himself, for the sake of those whom the sight or knowledge of his conduct might corrupt or mislead.

And even (it will be added) if the consequences of misconduct could be confined to the vicious or thoughtless individual, ought society to abandon to their own guidance those who are manifestly unfit for it? If protection against themselves is confessedly due to children and persons under age, is not society equally bound to afford it to persons of mature years who are equally incapable of self-government? If gambling, or drunkenness, or incontinence, or idleness, or uncleanliness, are as injurious to happiness, and as great a hindrance to improvement, as many or most of the acts prohibited by law, why (it may be asked) should not law, so far as is consistent with practicability and social convenience, endeavour to repress these also?...

I fully admit that the mischief which a person does to himself may seriously affect, both through their sympathies and their interests, those nearly connected with him and, in a minor degree, society at large. When, by conduct of this sort, a person is led to violate a distinct and assignable obligation to any other person or persons, the case is taken out of the self-regarding class, and becomes amenable to moral disapprobation in the proper sense of the term. If, for example, a man, through intemperance or extravagance, becomes unable to pay his debts, or, having undertaken the moral responsibility of a family, becomes from the same cause incapable of supporting or educating them, he is deservedly reprobated, and might be justly punished; but it is for the breach of duty to his family or creditors, not for the extravagance... In like manner, when a person disables himself, by conduct purely self-regarding, from the perform-ance of some definite duty incumbent on him to the public, he is guilty of a social offence. No person ought to be punished simply for being drunk; but a soldier or a policeman should be punished for being drunk on duty. Whenever, in short, there is a definite damage, or a definite risk of damage, either to an individual or to the public, the case is taken out of the province of liberty, and placed in that of morality or law.

But with regard to the merely contingent, or, as it may be called, constructive injury which a person causes to society, by conduct which neither violates any specific duty to the public, nor occasions perceptible hurt to any assignable individual except himself; the inconvenience is one which society can afford to bear, for the sake of the greater good of human freedom...

10   The Minimal State: Robert Nozick, *Anarchy, State and Utopia**

Raising the question of the proper limits of government (see previous extract) naturally leads to what should really be a prior question – perhaps indeed the very first question of political philosophy: should there be government at all? The school of thought known as *anarchism* gives a firmly negative answer to this question: people are best left to make their own voluntary and cooperative arrangements for the conduct of their lives, without any official interference or control. We have seen, however, in the ideas of Hobbes (extract 3, above) that there is at least one powerful motive – namely self-protection against violence – which would incline many to leave the 'state of nature' and set up an authority capable of keeping the peace. Yet most modern states see their role as going way beyond the minimal one of protecting citizens against force, theft, fraud and the like. The typical modern 'Western' state is committed to the provision of a vast amount of services for its citizens, in the shape of education, welfare, social security, health-care and other benefits. Can this more extensive state be justified?

In our next extract, the American philosopher Robert Nozick maintains that only the minimal state is justified, and he targets certain common conceptions of 'distributive justice' which are often used to support the more extensive state.

His argument is clear and largely self-explanatory, turning on the point that almost all accepted principles of distributive justice are 'patterned': they suggest that the ideal distribution should be made in accordance with some favoured pattern – for example in accordance with merit, or need.[1] But suppose that ideal distribution, whatever your favourite is, could be achieved. Nozick shows (by the example of a gifted basketball player whom the public will always pay to watch) that the subsequent free transactions of individuals will always upset any such ideal pattern of distribution. Provided we accept that people are entitled to the holdings they have justly acquired, and are entitled to transfer those holdings as they choose, then 'no distributional patterned principle of justice can be continuously realized without continuous interference with people's lives'. Whether this provides a conclusive argument against the more extensive state hinges in large part on how overriding a value we attach to individual liberty (for example, how important is the unfettered right of property-owners to transfer their wealth as they see fit?); and much critical discussion of Nozick's position has centred precisely on this point. Nozick's argument serves to remind us of how much scope there is for radical disagreement about what moral ends (if any) the state should embrace.

The minimal state [limited to the narrow functions of protection against force, theft, fraud, enforcement of contracts and so on] is the most extensive state that can be justified. Any state more extensive violates people's rights. Yet many persons have put forth reasons purporting to justify a more extensive state.... In this chapter we consider the claim that a more extensive state is justified, because necessary (or the best instrument) to achieve distributive justice...

The term 'distributive justice' is not a neutral one. Hearing the term 'distribution', most people presume that some thing or mechanism uses some principle or criterion to give out a supply of things. Into this process of distributing shares some error may

---

* R. Nozick, *Anarchy, State and Utopia* (Oxford: Blackwell, 1974), from ch. 7, section 1, pp. 149–63; with omissions.

[1] Marx, for example (extract 8, above), advocated distributing goods in accordance with the famous slogan 'from each according to his ability, to each according to his needs'.

have crept. So it is an open question, at least, whether *re*distribution should take place; whether we should do again what has already been done once, though poorly. However, we are not in the position of children who have been given portions of pie by someone who now makes last minute adjustments to rectify careless cutting. There is no *central* distribution, no person or group entitled to control all the resources, jointly deciding how they are to be doled out. What each person gets, he gets from others who give to him in exchange for something, or as a gift. In a free society, diverse persons control different resources, and new holdings arise out of the voluntary exchanges and actions of persons. There is no more a distributing or distribution of shares than there is a distributing of mates in a society in which persons choose whom they shall marry. The total result is the product of many individual decisions which the different individuals involved are entitled to make. Some uses of the term 'distribution', it is true, do not imply a previous distributing appropriately judged by some criterion (for example 'probability distribution'); nevertheless . . . it would be best to use a terminology that clearly is neutral. We shall speak of people's holdings; a principle of justice in holdings describes (part of) what justice tells us (requires) about holdings . . .

The entitlement theory

The subject of justice in holdings consists of three major topics. The first is the *original acquisition of holdings*, the appropriation of unowned things. This includes the issues of how unheld things may come to be held, the process, or processes, by which unheld things may come to be held, the things that may come to be held by these processes, the extent of what comes to be held by a particular process, and so on. We shall refer to the complicated truth about this topic, which we shall not reformu-late here, as the principle of justice in acquisition. The second topic concerns the *transfer of holdings* from one person to another. By what processes may a person transfer holdings to another? How may a person acquire a holding from another who holds it? Under this topic come general descriptions of voluntary exchange, and gift and (on the other hand) fraud, as well as reference to particular conventional details fixed upon a given society. The complicated truth about this subject (with placeholders for conventional details) we shall call the principle of justice in transfer. (And we shall suppose it also includes principles governing how a person may divest himself of a holding, passing it into an unheld state.)

If the world were wholly just, the following inductive definition would exhaustively cover the subject of justice in holdings.

1 A person who acquires a holding in accordance with the principle of justice in acquisition is entitled to that holding.
2 A person who acquires a holding in accordance with the principle of justice in transfer, from someone else entitled to the holding, is entitled to the holding.
3 No one is entitled to a holding except by (repeated) applications of 1 and 2.

The complete principle of distributive justice would say simply that a distribution is just if everyone is entitled to the holdings they possess under the distribution . . .

Historical principles and end-result principles

The general outlines of the entitlement theory illuminate the nature and defects of other conceptions of distributive justice. The entitlement theory of justice in distribution is *historical*; whether a distribution is just depends on how it came about. In contrast, *current time-slice principles* of justice hold that the justice of a distribution is judged by how things are distributed (who has what) as judged by some *structural* principle(s) of just distribution. A utilitarian who judges between any two distributions by seeing which has the greater sum of utility, and, if the sums tie, applies some fixed equality criterion to choose the more equal distribution, would hold a current time-slice principle of justice. As would someone who had a fixed schedule of trade-offs between the sum of happiness and equality. According to a current time-slice principle, all that needs to be looked at, in judging the justice of distribution, is who ends up with what; in comparing any two distributions one need look only at the matrix presenting the distributions. No further information need be fed into a principle of justice. It is a consequence of such principles of justice that any two structurally identical distributions are equally just. (Two distributions are structurally identical if they present the same profile, but perhaps have different persons occupying the particular slots. My having ten and your having five, and my having five and your having ten are structurally identical distributions) . . .

Most persons do not accept current time-slice principles as constituting the whole story about distributive shares. They think it relevant in assessing the justice of a situation to consider not only the distribution it embodies, but also how that distribution came about. If some persons are in prison for murder or war crimes, we do not say that to assess the justice of the distribution in the society we must look only at what this person has, and that person has, and that person has . . . at the current time. We think it relevant to ask whether someone did something so that he *deserved* to be punished, deserved to have a lower share. Most will agree to the relevance of further information with regard to punishments and penalties. Consider also desired things. One traditional socialist view is that workers are entitled to the products and full fruits of their labour; they have earned it; a distribution is unjust if it does not give the workers what they are entitled to. Such entitlements are based upon some past history. No socialist holding this view would find it comforting to be told that because the actual distribution A happens to coincide structurally with the one he desires D, A is therefore no less just than D; it differs only in that the 'parasitic' owners of capital receive under A what the workers are entitled to under D and the workers receive under A what the owners are entitled to under D, namely very little. This socialist rightly, in my view, holds onto the notions of earning, producing, entitlement, desert, and so forth, and he rejects current time-slice principles that look only to the structure of the resulting set of holdings. (The set of holdings resulting from what? Isn't it implausible that how holdings are produced and come to exist has no effect at all on who should hold what?) His mistake lies in his view of what entitlements arise out of what sorts of productive processes.

We construe the position we discuss too narrowly by speaking of *current* time-slice principles. Nothing is changed if structural principles operate upon a time sequence of current time-slice profiles and, for example, give someone more now to counter-balance the less he has had earlier. A utilitarian or an egalitarian or any mixture of the two over time will inherit the difficulties of his more myopic comrades. He is not helped by the fact that *some* of the information others consider relevant in assessing a distribution is reflected, unrecoverably, in past matrices. Henceforth, we shall refer to such unhistorical principles of distributive justice, including the current time-slice principles, as *end-result* or *end-state principles*.

In contrast to end-result principles of justice, *historical principles* of justice hold that past circumstances or actions of people can create differential entitlements or differential deserts to things. An injustice can be worked by moving from one distribution to another structurally identical one, for the second, in profile the same, may violate people's entitlements or deserts; it may not fit the actual history.

Patterning

The entitlement principles of justice in holdings that we have sketched are historical principles of justice. To better understand their precise character, we shall distinguish them from another subclass of historical principles. Consider, as an example, the principle of distribution according to moral merit. This principle requires that total distributive shares vary directly with moral merit; no person should have a greater share than anyone whose moral merit is greater... Or consider the principle that results by substituting 'usefulness to society' for 'more merit' in the previous principle. Or instead of 'distribute according to moral merit', or 'distribute according to usefulness to society', we might consider 'distribute according to the weighted sum of moral merit, usefulness to society, and need', with the weights of the different dimensions equal. Let us call a principle of distribution *patterned* if it specifies that a distribution is to vary along with some natural dimension, weighted sum of natural dimensions, or lexicographic ordering of natural dimensions. And let us say a distribution is patterned if it accords with some patterned principle... The principle of distribution in accordance with moral merit is a patterned historical principle, which specifies a patterned distribution. 'Distribute according to I.Q.' is a patterned principle that looks to information not contained in distributional matrices. It is not historical, however, in that it does not look to any past action creating differential entitlements to evaluate a distribution; it requires only distributional matrices whose columns are labelled by I.Q. scores...

Almost every suggested principle of distributive justice is patterned: to each according to his moral merit, or needs, or marginal produce, or how hard he tries, or the weighted sum of the foregoing, and so on. The principle of entitlement we have sketched is *not* patterned. There is no one natural dimension or weighted sum or combination of a small number of natural dimensions that yields the distributions generated in accordance with the principle of entitlement. The set of holdings that results when some persons receive their marginal products, others win at gambling, others receive a share of their mate's income, others receive gifts from foundations, others receive interest on loans, others receive gifts from admirers, others receive returns on investment, others make for themselves much of what they have, others find things, and so on, will not be patterned... Though the resulting set of holdings will be unpatterned, it will not be incomprehensible, for it can be seen as arising from the operation of a small number of principles. These principles specify how an initial distribution may arise (the principle of acquisition of holdings) and how distributions may be transformed into others (the principle of transfer of holdings). The process whereby the set of holdings is generated will be intelligible, though the set of holdings itself that results from those processes will be unpatterned...

To think that the task of a theory of distributive justice is to fill in the blank in 'to each according to his –' is to be predisposed to search for a pattern; and the separate treatment of 'from each according to his –' treats production and distribution as two separate and independent issues. On an entitlement view these are *not* two separate questions. Whoever makes something, having bought or contracted for all other held resources used in the process (transferring some of his holdings for these cooperating factors) is entitled to it. The situation is *not* one of something's getting made, and there being an open question of who is to get it. Things come into the world already attached to people having entitlements over them. From the point of view of the historical entitlement conception of justice in holdings, those who start afresh to complete 'to each according to his –' treat objects as if they appeared from nowhere, out of nothing...

So entrenched are maxims of the usual form that perhaps we should present the entitlement conception as a competitor. Ignoring acquisition and rectification we might say

From each according to what he chooses to do, to each according to what he makes for himself (perhaps with the contracted aid of others) and what others choose to do for him and choose to give him of what they've been given previously (under this maxim) and haven't yet expended or transferred.

This, the discerning reader will have noticed, has its defects as a slogan. So as a summary and great simplification (and not as a maxim with any independent meaning) we have

From each as they choose, to each as they are chosen.

How liberty upsets patterns

It is not clear how those holding alternative conceptions of distributive justice can reject the entitlement conception of justice in holdings. For suppose a distribution favoured by one of these non-entitlement conceptions is realized. Let us suppose it is your favourite one, and let us call this distribution D_1; perhaps everyone has an equal share, perhaps shares vary in accordance with some dimension you treasure. Now suppose Wilt Chamberlain is greatly in demand by basketball teams, being a great gate attraction. (Also suppose contracts run only for a year, with players being free agents.) He signs the following sort of contract with a team: In each home game, twenty-five cents from the price of each ticket of admission goes to him. (We ignore the question of whether he is 'gouging' the owners, letting them look out for themselves.) The season starts, and people cheerfully attend his team's games; they buy their tickets, each time dropping a separate twenty-five cents of their admission price into a special box with Chamberlain's name on it. They are excited about seeing him play; it is worth the total admission price to them. Let us suppose that in one season one million persons attend his home games, and Wilt Chamberlain winds up with $ 250,000, a much larger sum than the average income and larger even than anyone else has. Is he entitled to this income? Is this new distribution D_2 unjust? If so, why? There is *no* question about whether each of the people was entitled to the control over the resources they held in D_1; because that was the distribution (your favourite) that (for the purposes of the argument) we assumed was acceptable. Each of these persons *chose* to give twenty-five cents of their money to Chamberlain. They could have spent it on going to the movies, or on candy bars, or on copies of *Dissent* magazine, or of *Monthly Review*. But they all, at least one million of them, converged on giving it to Wilt Chamberlain in exchange for watching him play basketball. If D_1 was a just distribution, and people voluntarily moved from it to D_2 (what was it for if not to do something with?), isn't D_2 also just? If the people were entitled to dispose of the resources to which they were entitled (under D_1), didn't this include their being entitled to give it to, or exchange it with, Wilt Chamberlain? Can anyone else complain on grounds of justice? Each other person already has his legitimate share under D_1. Under D_1 there is nothing that anyone has that anyone else has a claim of justice against. After someone transfers something to Wilt Chamberlain, third parties *still* have their legitimate shares; *their* shares are not changed. By what process could such a transfer among two persons give rise to a legitimate claim of distributive justice on a portion of what was transferred, by a third party who had no claim of justice on any holding of the other *before* the transfer? To cut off objections irrelevant here, we might imagine the exchanges occurring in a socialist society, after hours. After playing whatever basketball he does in his daily work, or doing whatever other daily work he does, Wilt Chamberlain decides to put in *overtime* to earn additional money. (First his work quota is set; he works time over that.) Or imagine it is a skilled juggler people like to see, who puts on shows after hours.

Why might someone work overtime in a society in which it is assumed their needs are satisfied? Perhaps because they care about things other than needs. I like to write in books that I read, and to have easy access to books for browsing at odd hours. It would be very pleasant and convenient to have the resources of Widener Library in my back yard. No society, I assume, will provide such resources close to each person who would like them as part of his regular allotment (under D_1). Thus, persons either must do without some extra things that they want, or be allowed to do something extra to get some of these things. On what basis could the inequalities that would eventuate be forbidden? Notice also that small factories would spring up in a socialist society, unless forbidden. I melt down some of my personal possessions (under D_1) and build a machine out of the material. I offer you, and others, a philosophy lecture once a week in exchange for your cranking the handle on my machine, whose products I exchange for yet other things, and so on. (The raw materials used by the machine are given to some by others who possess them under D_1 in exchange for hearing lectures.) Each person might participate to gain things over and above their allotment under D_1. Some persons even might want to leave their job in socialist industry and work full time in this private sector...Here I wish merely to note how private property even in means of production would occur in a socialist society that did not forbid people to use as they wished some of the resources they are given under the socialist distribution D_1. The socialist society would have to forbid capitalist acts between consenting adults.

The general point illustrated by the Wilt Chamberlain example and the example of the entrepreneur in a socialist society is that no end-state principle or distributional patterned principle of justice can be continuously realized without continuous interference with people's lives. Any favoured pattern would be transformed into one unfavoured by the principle, by people choosing to act in various ways; for example by people exchanging goods and services with other people, or giving things to other people, things the transferrers are entitled to under the favoured distributional pattern. To maintain a pattern one must either continually interfere to stop people from transferring resources as they wish to, or continually (or periodically) interfere to take from some person's resources that others for some reason chose to transfer to them...

11   Social Co-operation and Rational Self-interest: David Gauthier, *Why Contractarianism?**

A recurring idea in political philosophy is that of an actual or implied *contract* as the basis of the social order. The idea was vividly presented by Hobbes, taken up and modified by Locke, and sharply criticized by Hume (see extracts 3, 4 and 5, above); and in more recent times, elements of it have resurfaced in the influential theory of justice developed by John Rawls (see Part VIII, extract 10, above). In our next extract, the North American philosopher David Gauthier presents a sophisticated defence of a contractarian approach to moral and political theory.

The basic idea Gauthier starts from is that of *rational choice*. In a complete free-for-all, when everyone tries to maximize their own advantage, people in general end up doing less well than if there were accepted limits or 'constraints' on the raw pursuit of self-interest. So each person can see that it would be rational to agree to a system of mutual restraint (and also of mutual assistance, since 'everyone would expect to do better were each to give assistance to her fellows... whenever the cost of assisting was low'). Such co-operative social arrangements, Gauthier argues, are therefore 'capable of gaining unanimous agreement among rational persons who

were choosing the terms on which they would interact with each other'.

Gauthier now considers an objection. Might it not be rational for an individual to participate in the co-operative social system, but keep his side of the bargain only when it is to his own advantage? Why should he not accept help from others but fail to return it; or break a promise whenever he stands to gain from so doing? Gauthier replies that 'real acceptance of such moral practices is possible only among those who are disposed to comply with them'. Moreover, people who are known to lack the ingrained disposition to play fair will be excluded from mutually beneficial interactions – a point illustrated by the case of the neighbouring farmers who each need help with their harvests: both will do better if they are genuinely disposed to make and keep promises.

The notion of rational agreement that informs Gauthier's account is, one might object, very hypothetical: why should we be impressed by the thought that certain social and moral constraints *would* secure agreement if people *were* choosing their terms of interaction? Gauthier makes it clear that his argument is not meant to justify all our existing moral and social

* David Gautier, 'Why Contractarianism?', in Peter Vallentyne (ed.), *Contractarianism and Rational Choice* (Cambridge: Cambridge University Press, 1981), pp. 65ff.; abridged.

arrangements; but he maintains that by applying the hypothetical test, and asking if it *would* be rational for us to agree to them, we are in effect testing how far those existing practices are rationally justified.

This idea raises the possibility of a given individual or group standing back from the existing arrangements in society, and asking if they could benefit more from some alternative set of arrangements. If enough people could so benefit, they are hardly going to accept the present system as justified: 'if there are persons whose prospects would be improved by renegotiation, then the existing order will be recognizably unstable.' Here Gauthier points to an obvious feature of many past and present political systems – namely that the arrangements that have evolved over the years, and to which people are expected to be bound, can appear quite arbitrary from the moral point of view. Gauthier's device of focusing on hypothetical rational agreement enables people to 'escape this arbitrariness [by] considering what practices they would have agreed to from an initial position not structured by existing institutions'.[1]

Gauthier concludes by suggesting that his argument is not just an abstract exercise in moral theorizing, but has a practical import. The security and stability of a society depend on the existing system being one that people are more or less happy with, not merely one that they grudgingly put up with until they have the chance to overthrow it. As Gauthier puts it, the goal of a social system is not just compliance among its members, but *stable* compliance; and 'compliance is stable if it arises from agreement among persons each of whom considers ... that the terms of agreement are sufficiently favourable ... that it is rational for her to accept them'. An interesting implication emerges here about the role of political philosophy. Of itself, no doubt, it cannot change institutions; but it can help people to realize the true character of the social relationships that structure their society, and thus lead to the 'elimination of false consciousness', and a better understanding of how far the existing moral and social order is justifiable.

 Let me sketch briefly those features of deliberative rationality that enable it to constrain maximizing choice. The key idea is that in many situations, if each person chooses what, given the choices of the others, would maximize her expected utility, then the outcome will be mutually disadvantageous in comparison with some alternative – everyone could do better. Equilibrium, which obtains when each person's action is a best response to the others' actions, is incompatible with (Pareto-)optimality, which obtains when no one could do better without someone else doing worse. Given the ubiquity of such situations, each person can see the benefit, to herself, of participating with her fellows in practices requiring each to refrain from the direct endeavour to maximize her own utility, when such mutual restraint is mutually advantageous. No one, of course, can have reason to accept any unilateral constraint on her maximizing behaviour; each benefits from, and only from, the constraint accepted by her fellows. But if one benefits more from a constraint on others than one loses by being constrained oneself, one may have reason to accept a practice requiring everyone, including oneself, to exhibit such a constraint. We may represent such a practice as capable of gaining unanimous agreement among rational persons who were choosing the terms on which they would interact with each other. And this agreement is the basis of morality.

Consider a simple example of a moral practice that would command rational agreement. Suppose each of us were to assist her fellows only when either she could

---

[1] Compare Rawls's 'veil of ignorance' (Part VIII, extract 10, above).

expect to benefit herself from giving assistance, or she took a direct interest in their well-being. Then, in many situations, persons would not give assistance to others, even though the benefit to the recipient would greatly exceed the cost to the giver, because there would be no provision for the giver to share in the benefit. Everyone would then expect to do better were each to give assistance to her fellows, regardless of her own benefit or interest, whenever the cost of assisting was low and the benefit of receiving assistance considerable. Each would thereby accept a constraint on the direct pursuit of her own concerns, not unilaterally, but given a like acceptance by others. Reflection leads us to recognize that those who belong to groups whose members adhere to such a practice of mutual assistance enjoy benefits in interaction that are denied to others. We may then represent such a practice as rationally acceptable to everyone.

This rationale for agreed constraint makes no reference to the content of anyone's preferences. The argument depends simply on the structure of interaction, on the way in which each person's endeavour to fulfil her own preferences affects the fulfilment of everyone else. Thus, each person's reason to accept a mutually constraining practice is independent of her particular desires, aims and interests, although not, of course, of the fact that she has such concerns. The idea of a purely rational agent, moved to act by reason alone, is not, I think, an intelligible one. Morality is not to be understood as a constraint arising from reason alone on the fulfilment of non-rational preferences. Rather, a rational agent is one who acts to achieve the maximal fulfilment of her preferences, and morality is a constraint on the manner in which she acts, arising from the effects of interaction with other agents.

Hobbes's Foole[1] now makes his familiar entry onto the scene, to insist that however rational it may be for a person to agree with her fellows to practices that hold out the promise of mutual advantage, yet it is rational to follow such practices only when so doing directly conduces to her maximal preference fulfilment. But then such practices impose no real constraint. The effect of agreeing to or accepting them can only be to change the expected payoffs of her possible choices, making it rational for her to choose what in the absence of the practice would not be utility maximizing. The practices would offer only true prudence, not true morality.

The Foole is guilty of a twofold error. First, he fails to understand that real acceptance of such moral practices as assisting one's fellows, or keeping one's promises, or telling the truth is possible only among those who are disposed to comply with them. If my disposition to comply extends only so far as my interests or concerns at the time of performance, then you will be the real fool if you interact with me in ways that demand a more rigorous compliance. If, for example, it is rational to keep promises only when so doing is directly utility maximizing, then among persons whose rationality is common knowledge, only promises that require such limited compliance will be made. And opportunities for mutual advantage will be thereby forgone.

Consider this example of the way in which promises facilitate mutual benefit. Jones and Smith have adjacent farms. Although neighbours, and not hostile, they are also

---

[1] 'The foole hath said in his heart there is no such thing as justice; [and that] to make, or not make, keep, or not keep, covenants was not against reason, when it conduced to one's benefit' (Hobbes, *Leviathan*, ch. 15). For more on Hobbes, see introduction to extract 3, above.

not friends, so that neither gets satisfaction from assisting the other. Nevertheless, they recognize that, if they harvest their crops together, each does better than if each harvests alone. Next week, Jones's crop will be ready for harvesting; a fortnight hence, Smith's crop will be ready. The harvest in, Jones is retiring, selling his farm and moving to Florida, where he is unlikely to encounter Smith or other members of their community. Jones would like to promise Smith that, if Smith helps him harvest next week, he will help Smith harvest in a fortnight. But Jones and Smith both know that in a fortnight, helping Smith would be a pure cost to Jones. Even if Smith helps him, he has nothing to gain by returning the assistance, since neither care for Smith nor, in the circumstances, concern for his own reputation, moves him. Hence, if Jones and Smith know that Jones acts straightforwardly to maximize the fulfilment of his preferences, they know that he will not help Smith. Smith, therefore, will not help Jones even if Jones pretends to promise assistance in return. Nevertheless, Jones would do better could he make and keep such a promise – and so would Smith.

The Foole's second error, following on his first, should be clear; he fails to recognize that in plausible circumstances, persons who are genuinely disposed to a more rigorous compliance with moral practices than would follow from their interests at the time of performance can expect to do better than those who are not so disposed. For the former, constrained maximizers as I call them, will be welcome partners in mutually advantageous co-operation, in which each relies on the voluntary adherence of the others, from which the latter, straightforward maximizers, will be excluded. Constrained maximizers may thus expect more favourable opportunities than their fellows. Although in assisting their fellows, keeping their promises and complying with other moral practices, they forgo preference fulfilment that they might obtain, yet they do better overall than those who always maximize expected utility, because of their superior opportunities.

In identifying morality with those constraints that would obtain agreement among rational persons who were choosing their terms of interaction, I am engaged in rational reconstruction. I do not suppose that we have actually agreed to existent moral practices and principles. Nor do I suppose that all existent moral practices would secure our agreement, were the question to be raised. Not all existent moral practices need be justifiable – need be ones with which we ought willingly to comply. Indeed, I do not even suppose that the practices with which we ought willingly to comply need be those that would secure our present agreement. I suppose that justifiable moral practices are those that would secure our agreement *ex ante* [in advance], in an appropriate pre-moral situation. They are those to which we should have agreed as constituting the terms of our future interaction, had we been, *per impossible*, in a position to decide those terms. Hypothetical agreement thus provides a test of the justifiability of our existent moral practices.

Many questions could be raised about this account, but here I want to consider only one. I have claimed that moral practices are rational, even though they constrain each person's attempt to maximize her own utility, insofar as they would be the objects of unanimous *ex ante* agreement. But to refute the Foole, I must defend not only the rationality of agreement, but also that of compliance, and the defence of compliance threatens to pre-empt the case for agreement, so that my title should be 'Why Constraint?' and not 'Why Contractarianism?' It is rational to dispose oneself to accept certain constraints on direct maximization in choosing and acting, if and only if so disposing oneself maximizes one's expected utility. What then is the relevance of agreement, and especially of hypothetical agreement? Why should it be rational to dispose oneself to accept only those constraints that would be the object of mutual agreement in an appropriate pre-moral situation, rather than those constraints that are found in our existent moral practices? Surely it is acceptance of the latter that makes a person welcome in interaction with his fellows. For compliance with existing morality will be what they expect, and take into account in choosing partners with whom to co-operate...

To show the relevance of agreement to the justification of constraints, let us assume an ongoing society in which individuals more or less acknowledge and comply with a given set of practices that constrain their choices in relation to what they would be did they take only their desires, aims and interests directly into account. Suppose that a disposition to conform to these existing practices is prima facie advantageous, since persons who are not so disposed may expect to be excluded from desirable opportunities by their fellows. However, the practices themselves have, or at least need have, no basis in agreement. And they need satisfy no intuitive standard of fairness or impartiality – characteristics that we may suppose relevant to the identification of the practices with those of a genuine morality. Although we may speak of the practices as constituting the morality of the society in question, we need not consider them morally justified or acceptable. They are simply practices constraining individual behaviour in a way that each finds it rational to accept.

Suppose now that our persons, as rational maximizers of individual utility, come to reflect on the practices constituting their morality. They will, of course, assess the practices in relation to their own utility, but with awareness that their fellows will be doing the same. And one question that must arise is: Why these practices? For they will recognize that the set factual moral practices is not the only possible set of constraining practices that would yield mutually advantageous, optimal outcomes. They will recognize the possibility of alternative moral orders. At this point it would not be enough to say that, as a matter of fact, each person can expect benefit from a disposition to comply with existing practices. For persons will also ask themselves: Can I benefit more, not from simply abandoning any morality, and recognizing no constraint, but from a partial rejection of existing constraints in favour of an alternative set? Once this question is asked, the situation is transformed; the existing moral order must be assessed, not only against simple non-compliance, but also against what we may call alternative compliance.

To make this assessment, each will compare her prospects under the existing practices with those she would anticipate from a set that, in the existing circumstances, she would expect to result from bargaining with her fellows. If her prospects would be improved by such negotiation, then she will have a real, although not necessarily sufficient, incentive to demand a change in the established moral order. More generally, if there are persons whose prospects would be improved by renegotiation, then the existing order will be recognizably unstable. No doubt those whose prospects would be worsened by renegotiation will have a clear incentive to resist, to appeal to the status quo. But their appeal will be a weak one, especially among persons who are not taken in by spurious ideological considerations, but focus on individual utility maximization. Thus, although in the real world, we begin with an existing set of moral practices as constraints on our maximizing behaviour, yet we are led by reflection to the idea of an amended set that would obtain the agreement of everyone, and this amended set has, and will be recognized to have, a stability lacking in existing morality.

The reflective capacity of rational agents leads them from the given to the agreed, from existing practices and principles requiring constraint to those that would receive each person's assent. The same reflective capacity, I claim, leads from those practices that would be agreed to, in existing social circumstances, to those that would receive *ex ante* agreement, pre-moral and pre-social. As the status quo proves unstable when it comes into conflict with what would be agreed to, so what would be agreed to proves unstable when it comes into conflict with what would have been agreed to in an appropriate pre-social context. For as existing practices must seem arbitrary insofar as they do not correspond to what a rational person would agree to, so what such a person would agree to in existing circumstances must seem arbitrary in relation to what she would accept in a pre-social condition.

What a rational person would agree to in existing circumstances depends in large part on her negotiating position vis-à-vis her fellows. But her negotiating position is significantly affected by the existing social institutions, and so by the currently accepted moral practices embodied in those institutions. Thus, although agreement may well yield practices differing from those embodied in existing social institutions, yet it will be influenced by those practices, which are not themselves the product of rational agreement. And this must call the rationality of the agreed practices into question. The arbitrariness of existing practices must infect any agreement whose terms are significantly affected by them. Although rational agreement is in itself a source of stability, yet this stability is undermined by the arbitrariness of the circumstances in which it takes place. To escape this arbitrariness, rational persons will revert from actual to hypothetical agreement, considering what practices they would have agreed to from an initial position not structured by existing institutions and the practices they embody.

The content of a hypothetical agreement is determined by an appeal to the equal rationality of persons. Rational persons will voluntarily accept an agreement only insofar as they perceive it to be equally advantageous to each. To be sure, each would be happy to accept an agreement more advantageous to herself than to her fellows, but since no one will accept an agreement perceived to be less advantageous, agents whose rationality is a matter of common knowledge will recognize the futility of aiming at or holding out for more, and minimize their bargaining costs by coordinating at the point of equal advantage. Now the extent of advantage is determined in a twofold way. First, there is advantage internal to an agreement. In this respect, the expectation of equal advantage is assured by procedural fairness. The step from existing moral practices to those resulting from actual agreement takes rational persons to a procedurally fair situation, in which each perceives the agreed practices to be ones that it is equally rational for all to accept, given the circumstances in which agreement is reached. But those circumstances themselves may be called into question insofar as they are perceived to be arbitrary – the result, in part, of compliance with constraining practices that do not themselves ensure the expectation of equal advantage, and so do not reflect the equal rationality of the complying parties. To neutralize this arbitrary element, moral practices to be fully acceptable must be conceived as constituting a possible outcome of a hypothetical agreement under circumstances that are unaffected by social institutions that themselves lack full acceptability. Equal rationality demands consideration of external circumstances as well as internal procedures.

But what is the practical import of this argument? It would be absurd to claim that mere acquaintance with it, or even acceptance of it, will lead to the replacement of existing moral practices by those that would secure pre-social agreement. It would be irrational for anyone to give up the benefits of the existing moral order simply because he comes to realize that it affords him more than he could expect from pure rational agreement with his fellows. And it would be irrational for anyone to accept a long-term utility loss by refusing to comply with the existing moral order, simply because she comes to realize that such compliance affords her less than she could expect from pure rational agreement. Nevertheless, these realizations do transform, or perhaps bring to the surface, the character of the relationships between persons that are maintained by the existing constraints, so that some of these relationships come to be recognized as coercive. These realizations constitute the elimination of false consciousness, and they result from a process of rational reflection...Without an argument to defend themselves in open dialogue with their fellows, those who are more than equally advantaged can hope to maintain their privileged position only if they can coerce their fellows into accepting it. And this, of course, may be possible. But coercion is not agreement, and it lacks any inherent stability. Stability plays a key role in linking compliance to agreement. Aware of the benefits to be gained from constraining practices, rational persons will seek those that invite stable compliance. Now compliance is stable if it arises from agreement among persons each of whom considers both that the terms of agreement are sufficiently favourable to herself that it is rational for her to accept them, and that they are not so favourable to others that it would be rational for them to accept terms less favourable to them and more favourable to herself. An agreement affording equally favourable terms to all thus invites, as no other can, stable compliance.

12   Liberalism, Resources and Equal Worth: Ronald Dworkin, *Why Liberals Should Care about Equality* ⃰

The outlook known as 'liberalism' broadly follows the tradition established by John Stuart Mill in his arguments for protecting individual freedom against the power of the majority (see extract 9, above). In our final extract, the distinguished American legal and social philosopher Ronald Dworkin discusses the relationship between liberalism and that other great ideal of modern democratic theory, equality.

He begins by identifying the particular species of modern liberalism he favours, namely liberalism-based-on-equality. Such liberalism treats people as equals, in the sense of respecting their sense of equal worth. This implies traditional

⃰ From Ronald Dworkin, *A Matter of Principle* (Cambridge, Mass.: Harvard University Press, 1985), ch. 9 (pp. 205–13); abridged.

liberal protections (e.g. for the freedom of minorities whose religious or sexual orientations may offend the majority); but it also has an economic dimension, namely that 'each be permitted to use ... no more than an equal share of the resources available for all'.

Dworkin is not the kind of radically redistributive egalitarian who demands complete equality of outcome; for he maintains that in working out whether someone has taken more than his share we should also take into account how much he has chosen to contribute. Hence Dworkin has a certain initial sympathy with those many liberals who are attracted by the free market as a way of allocating resources.[1] He has serious reservations, however, about the assumption often made that the less well-off 'could have had the same' as those who are richer 'if they had made the same decisions to consume, save or work that they did'. Such a notion of equality of opportunity, Dworkin argues, is 'fraudulent', since 'in the real world people do not start their lives on equal terms. For luck (e.g. of inherited genes, or of educational privilege) can play a devastating role in deciding who gets or keeps the best jobs.

Instead, therefore, Dworkin offers us a more complex kind of equality-based liberalism: he allows the market an initial role in allocating wealth as a function of how far people's choices benefit society; but he argues this market allocation should be 'corrected', so as to bring people closer to the share they would have achieved if they had initially enjoyed the same advantages.

Any such corrective mechanism will of course be messy and imperfect, and it will also be expensive. The issue of how much of its citizens' money (via taxation) the modern state should be prepared to spend to reduce economic inequality is taken up in the remainder of the paper. Dworkin considers, but attacks, the familiar argument that since welfare and other redistributive benefits produce inflation, society as a whole would be more prosperous if such benefits were reduced. Even if this latter premise is true, Dworkin argues, to ask the worst-off segment of society to accept lives of poverty and despair in the name of general economic efficiency violates the principle of treating them with equal concern and respect. Of course we do sometimes expect some citizens to sacrifice themselves for others (e.g. in warfare); but Dworkin suggests that those called on to undertake sacrifices must always 'be offered some reason why the community which benefits from that sacrifice is ... *their* community'. In order for people to feel members of a community (in a positive and active sense that goes beyond merely residing in it) they must believe they have some power to help shape society's future, and be able to hope that the brighter future envisaged as a result of their sacrifices may one day bring dividends for their own families or descendants. But if they feel themselves and their families permanently excluded from that future, they should never accept such a sacrifice, nor, Dworkin concludes, should the rest of us contemplate a future, however attractive, that requires such injustice.

Philosophical debate is sure to continue on the relationship between equality and economic prosperity, and on how these notions bear on the dignity and respect that is owed to all. The issues involved here are complex, and may not be susceptible of easy answers, but they show the importance of political philosophy as a subject that has relevance to major issues of public policy; for the arguments involved are part of the struggle to determine the future shape of the society in which we live.

 Though liberalism is often discussed as a single political theory, there are in fact two basic forms of liberalism and the distinction between them is of great importance. Both argue against the legal enforcement of private morality – both argue against the Moral Majority's views of homosexuality and abortion, for example – and both argue for greater sexual, political and economic equality. But they disagree about which of these two traditional liberal values is fundamental and which derivative. Liberalism

---

[1] Compare Nozick, extract 10, above.

based on neutrality takes as fundamental the idea that government must not take sides on moral issues, and it supports only such egalitarian measures as can be shown to be the result of that principle. Liberalism based on equality takes as fundamental that government treat its citizens equally, and insists on moral neutrality only to the degree that equality requires it.

The difference between these two versions of liberalism is crucial because both the content and appeal of liberal theory depends on which of these two values is understood to be its proper ground. Liberalism based on neutrality finds its most natural defence in some form of moral scepticism and this makes it vulnerable to the charge that liberalism is a negative theory for uncommitted people. Moreover it offers no effective argument against utilitarian and other contemporary justifications for economic inequality...Liberalism based on equality suffers from neither of these defects. It rests on a positive commitment to an egalitarian morality and provides, in that morality, a firm contrast to the economics of privilege.

In this essay I shall set out what I believe are the main principles of liberalism based on equality. This form of liberalism insists that government must treat people as equals in the following sense. It must impose no sacrifice or constraint on any citizen in virtue of an argument that the citizen could not accept without abandoning his sense of equal worth. This abstract principle requires liberals to oppose the moralism of the New Right, because no self-respecting person who believes that a particular way to live is most valuable for him can accept that this way of life is base or degrading. No self-respecting atheist can agree that a community in which religion is mandatory is for that reason finer, and no one who is homosexual that the eradication of homosexuality makes the community purer.

So liberalism as based on equality justifies the traditional liberal principle that government should not enforce private morality of this sort. But it has an economic as well as a social dimension. It insists on an economic system in which no citizen has less than an equal share of the community's resources just in order that others may have more of what he lacks. I do not mean that liberalism insists on what is often called 'equality of result', that is, that citizens must have the same wealth at every moment of their lives. A government bent on the latter ideal must constantly redistribute wealth, eliminating whatever inequalities in wealth are produced by market transactions. But this would be to devote *unequal* resources to different lives. Suppose that two people have very different bank accounts, in the middle of their careers, because one decided not to work, or not to work at the most lucrative job he could have found, while the other single-mindedly worked for gain, or because one was willing to assume especially demanding or responsible work, for example, which the other declined. Or because one took larger risks which might have been disastrous but which were in fact successful, while the other invested conservatively. The principle that people must be treated as equals provides no good reason for redistribution in these circumstances; on the contrary, it provides a good reason *against* it.

For treating people as equals requires that each be permitted to use, for the projects to which he devotes his life, no more than an equal share of the resources available for all, and we cannot compute how much any person has consumed, on balance, without taking into account the resources he has contributed as well as those he has taken from the economy. The choices people make about work and leisure and investment have an impact on the resources of the community as a whole, and this impact must be reflected in the calculation equality demands. If one person chooses work that contributes less to other people's lives than different work he might have chosen, then, although this might well have been the right choice for him, given his personal goals, he has nevertheless added less to the resources available for others, and this must be taken into account in the egalitarian calculation. If one person chooses to invest in a productive enterprise rather than spend his funds at once, and if his investment is successful because it increases the stock of goods or services other people actually want, without coercing anyone, his choice has added more to social resources than the choice of someone who did not invest, and this too must be reflected in any calculation of whether he has, on balance, taken more than his share.

This explains, I think, why liberals have in the past been drawn to the idea of a market as a method of allocating resources. An efficient market for investment, labour and goods works as a kind of auction in which the cost to someone of what he consumes, by way of goods and leisure, and the value of what he adds, through his productive labour or decisions, is fixed by the amount his use of some resources costs others, or his contributions benefit them, in each case measured by their willingness to pay for it. Indeed, if the world were very different from what it is, a liberal could accept the results of an efficient market as *defining* equal shares of community resources. If people start with equal amounts of wealth, and have roughly equal levels of raw skill, then a market allocation would ensure that no one could properly complain that he had less than others, over his whole life. He could have had the same as they if he had made the decisions to consume, save or work that they did.

But in the real world people do not start their lives on equal terms; some begin with marked advantages of family wealth or of formal and informal education. Others suffer because their race is despised. Luck plays a further and sometimes devastating part in deciding who gains or keeps jobs everyone wants. Quite apart from these plain inequities, people are not equal in raw skill or intelligence or other native capacities; on the contrary, they differ greatly, through no choice of their own, in the various capacities that the market tends to reward. So some people who are perfectly willing, even anxious, to make exactly the same choices about work and consumption and savings that other people make end up with fewer resources, and no plausible theory of equality can accept this as fair. This is the defect of the idea fraudulently called 'equality of opportunity'; fraudulent because in a market economy people do not have equal opportunity who are less able to produce what others want.

So a liberal cannot, after all, accept the market results as defining equal shares. His theory of economic justice must be complex, because he accepts two principles which are difficult to hold in the administration of a dynamic economy. The first requires that people have, at any point in their lives, different amounts of wealth insofar as the genuine choices they have made have been more or less expensive or beneficial to the community, measured by what other people want of their lives. The market seems indispensable for this principle. The second requires that people not have different amounts of wealth just because they have different inherent capacities to produce what others want, or are differently favoured by chance. This means that market allocation must be corrected in order to bring some people closer to the share of resources they would have had but for these various differences of initial advantage, luck and inherent capacity.

Obviously any practical programme claiming to respect both these principles will work imperfectly and will inevitably involve speculation, compromise and arbitrary lines in the face of ignorance. For it is impossible to discover, even in principle, exactly which aspects of any person's economic position flow from his choices and which from advantages or disadvantages that were not matters of choice; and even if we could make this determination for particular people, one by one, it would be impossible to develop a tax system for the nation as a whole that would leave the first in place and repair only the second. There is therefore no such thing as the perfectly just programme of redistribution. We must be content to choose whatever programmes we believe bring us closer to the complex and unattainable ideal of equality, all things considered, than the available alternatives, and be ready constantly to re-examine that conclusion when new evidence or new programmes are proposed.

Nevertheless, in spite of the complexity of that idea, it may sometimes be apparent that a society falls far short of any plausible interpretation of its requirements. It is, I think, apparent that the United States falls far short now. A substantial minority of Americans are chronically unemployed or earn wages below any realistic 'poverty line' or are handicapped in various ways or burdened with special needs; and most of these people would do the work necessary to earn a decent living if they had the opportunity and capacity. Equality of resources would require more rather than less redistribution than we now offer.

This does not mean, of course, that we should continue past liberal programmes, however inefficient these have proved to be, or even that we should insist on 'targeted' programmes of the sort some liberals have favoured – that is, programmes that aim to provide a particular opportunity or resource, like education or medicine, to those who need it. Perhaps a more general form of transfer, like a negative income tax, would prove on balance more efficient and fairer, in spite of the difficulties in such schemes. And whatever devices are chosen for bringing distribution closer to equality of resources, some aid undoubtedly goes to those who have avoided rather than sought jobs. This is to be regretted, because it offends one of the two principles that together make up equality of resources. But we come closer to that ideal by tolerating this inequity than by denying aid to the far greater number who would work if they could. If equality of resources were our only goal, therefore, we could hardly justify the present retreat from redistributive welfare programmes.

We must therefore consider a further and more difficult question. Must liberals insist on equality of resources no matter what the cost to the national economy as a whole? It is far from obvious that treating people as equals forbids any deviation from equality of resources for any reason whatsoever. On the contrary, people with a lively sense of their own equal worth, and pride in their own convictions, can nevertheless accept certain grounds for carrying special burdens for the sake of the community as a whole. In a defensive war, for example, we expect those who are capable of military service to assume a vastly greater share of danger than others. Nor is inequality permissible only in emergencies when the survival of the community is at stake. We might think it proper, for example, for the government to devote special resources to the training of especially talented artists or musicians, beyond what the market would pay for the services those artists produce, even though this reduces the share others have. We accept this not because we think the life of an artist is inherently more valuable than other lives, but because a community with a lively cultural tradition provides an environment within which citizens may live more imaginatively, and in which they might take pride. Liberalism need not be insensitive to these and other virtues of community. The question becomes not whether any deviation is permitted, but what reasons for deviation are consistent with equal concern and respect.

That question is now pressing for this reason. Many economists believe that reducing economic inequality through redistribution is damaging to the general economy and, in the long run, self-defeating. Welfare programmes, it is said, are inflationary, and the tax system necessary to support them depresses incentive and therefore production. The economy, it is claimed, can be re-stimulated only by reducing taxes and adopting other programmes that will, in the short run, produce high unemployment and otherwise cause special damage to those already at the bottom of the economy. But this damage will only be temporary. For a more dynamic economy will produce prosperity, and this will in the end provide more jobs and more money for the handicapped and others who are truly needy.

Each of these propositions is doubtful, and they may well all be wrong. But suppose we were to accept them. Do they make a case for ignoring those in the economic cellar now? The argument would be unanswerable, of course, if *everyone* who lost because of stringent policies now would actually be better off in the long run. But though this is often suggested in careless supply-side rhetoric, it is absurd. People laid off for several years, with no effective retraining, are very unlikely to recoup their losses later, particularly if their psychological losses are counted. Children denied adequate nutrition or any effective chance of higher education will suffer permanent loss even if the economy follows the most optimistic path of recovery. Some of those who are denied jobs and welfare now, particularly the elderly, will in any case not live long enough to share in that recovery, however general it turns out to be.

So the currently popular argument, that we must reduce benefits now in order to achieve general prosperity later, is simply a piece of utilitarianism, which attempts to justify irreversible losses to a minority in order to achieve gains for the large majority... But this denies the principle fundamental to liberalism based on equality, the principle that people must be treated with equal concern. It asks some people to accept lives of great poverty and despair, with no prospect of a useful future, just in order that the great bulk of the community may have a more ample measure of what they are forever denied. Perhaps people can be forced into this position. But they cannot accept it consistently with a full recognition of their independence, and their right to equal concern on the part of their government.

But suppose the case for the administration's policies is put differently, by calling attention to the distinct social dangers of continuing or expanding past programmes of redistribution. We might imagine two arguments of this sort. The first calls attention to the damage inflation does, not simply to the spending power, savings and prospects of the majority, as individuals, but also to the public environment in which all citizens must live and in which all might take either pride or shame. As society becomes poorer, because production falls and wealth decays, it loses a variety of features we cherish. Its culture fails, its order declines, its system of criminal and civil justice becomes less accurate and less fair; in these and other ways society steadily recedes from our conception of a good society. The decline cannot be arrested by further taxation to support these public goods, for that will only shrink production further and accelerate the decline. According to this argument, those who lose by programmes designed to halt inflation and reinvigorate the economy are called upon to a make a sacrifice, not just in order to benefit others privately, but out of a sense of loyalty to the public institutions of their own society.

The second argument is different because it calls attention to the interests of future generations. It asks us to suppose that if we are zealous for equality now, we will so depress the wealth of the community that future Americans will be even less well off than the very poor are now. Future Americans will have no more, perhaps, than the citizens of economically depressed third world countries in the present world. The second argument comes down to this: the present poor are asked to sacrifice in favour of their fellow citizens now, in order to prevent much greater injustice, to many more citizens, later.

Neither of these two arguments plainly violates the liberal's axiomatic principle of equal concern and respect. Each can be offered to people who take pride in their equal worth and in the value of their convictions. But only in certain circumstances. Both arguments, though in different ways, appeal to the idea that each citizen is a member of a community, and that he can find, in the fate of that community, a reason for special burdens he can accept with honour rather than degradation. This is appropriate when that community offers him at a minimum the opportunity to develop and lead a life he can regard as valuable both to himself and to it.

We must distinguish, that is, between passive and active membership in a community. Totalitarian regimes suppose that anyone who is present in their community, and so is amenable to its political force, is a member of the community from whom sacrifice might fairly be asked in the name of that community's greatness and future. Treating people as equals requires a more active conception of membership. If people are asked to sacrifice for their community, they must be offered some reason why the community which benefits from that sacrifice is their community; there must be some reason why, for example, the unemployed blacks of Detroit should take more interest in either the public virtue or the future generations of Michigan than they do in those of Mali.

We must ask in what circumstances someone with the proper sense of his own independence and equal worth can take pride in a community as being his community, and two conditions, at least, seem necessary to this. He can take pride in its present attractiveness – in the richness of its culture, the justice of its institutions, the imagination of its education – only if he has some power to help determine the shape of that future, and only if the promised prosperity will provide at least equal benefit to the smaller, more immediate communities for which he feels special responsibilities, for example, his family, his descendants and, if the society is one that has made this important to him, his race.

These seem minimal conditions, but they are nonetheless exigent. Together, they impose serious restraints on any policy that denies any group of citizens, however small or politically negligible, the equal resources that can provide any citizen with a life valuable in his own eyes. But these constraints set a limit to what a government that respects equality may deliberately choose when other choices are available. People must not be condemned, unless this is unavoidable, to lives in which they are effectively denied any active part in the political, economic and cultural life of the community. So if economic policy contemplates an increase in unemployment, it must also contemplate generous public provision for retraining or public employment. The children of the poor must not be stinted of education or otherwise locked into positions at the bottom of society. Otherwise their parents' loyalty to them acts not as a bridge, but as a bar to any identification with the future these parents are meant to cherish...

If our government can provide an attractive future only through present injustice – only by forcing some citizens to sacrifice in the name of a community from which they are in every sense excluded – then the rest of us should disown that future, however attractive, because we should not regard it as our future either.

Specimen Questions

1 What arguments are presented in the *Crito* for the conclusion that Socrates would be acting unjustly if he escaped from prison and evaded his sentence? Do you find them convincing?

2 'It is better for one to rule rather than many who must first reach agreement' (Aquinas). How does Aquinas reach this conclusion? Are his arguments sound?

3 'So long as every man holds this right of doing anything he likes, so long are all men in the condition of war' (Hobbes). Expound Hobbes's account of this 'condition of war' and evaluate his proposed remedy for it.

4 Summarize Locke's account of the transition from the 'state of nature' to 'the beginning of political societies'. Does he have a convincing case for suggesting this transition depends on the 'consent of each individual'?

5 Explain and evaluate Hume's criticisms of the idea of the 'original contract', with special reference to his analogy of the passenger carried on board ship while asleep.

6 'The problem is to find a form of association . . . in which each, while uniting himself with all, may still obey himself alone, and remain as free as before.' Does Rousseau have a convincing solution to the problem he poses?

7 Critically assess Hegel's claim that the state is the 'actuality of concrete freedom'.

8 Explain what Marx and Engels mean by the 'alienation' arising from the division of labour, and critically assess their proposed cure for it.

9 'The only purpose for which power can be rightfully exercised over any member of a civilized community, against his will, is to prevent harm to others' (Mill). Explain and critically discuss.

10 'There is no *central* distribution, no person or group entitled to control all the resources, jointly deciding how they are to be doled out' (Nozick). Explain and evaluate Nozick's case against 'patterned' principles of distributive justice.

11 'Those who belong to groups whose members adhere to . . . a practice of mutual assistance enjoy benefits in interaction that are denied to others. We may then represent such a practice as rationally acceptable to everyone' (Gauthier). Expound and evaluate Gauthier's contractarian test for evaluating social institutions.

12 Why, according to Dworkin, should liberals not accept the results of the free market in determining how resources are to be distributed? Are his arguments convincing?

Suggestions for Further Reading

Lucid discussions of many of the issues covered in this Part of the volume may be found in J. Wolff, *An Introduction to Political Philosophy* (Oxford: Oxford University Press, 1996).

Basic introductions to the question of our obligation to the state may be found in D. Raphael, *Problems of Political Philosophy* (London: Macmillan, 1971), ch. 4; and S. I. Benn and R. S. Peters, *Social Principles and the Democratic State* (London: Allen & Unwin, 1959), ch. 14.

See also J. G. Murphy (ed.), *Civil Disobedience and Violence* (Belmont, Calif.: Wadsworth, 1971); S. Hook (ed.), *Law and Philosophy* (New York: New York University Press, 1964), part I; and R. Dworkin, *Taking Rights Seriously* (London: Duckworth, 1977), ch. 8.

For a clear account of Aquinas's political theory, see P. E. Sigmund, 'Law and Politics', in N. Kretzman and E. Stump (eds), *The Cambridge Companion to Aquinas* (Cambridge: Cambridge University Press, 1993). See also J. Finnis, *Aquinas* (Oxford: Oxford University Press, 1998).

For an assessment of the views of Hobbes, see R. Tuck, *Hobbes* (Oxford: Oxford University Press, 1989); and M. Goldsmith, 'Hobbes: Ancient and Modern', in T. Sorell (ed.), *The Rise of Modern Philosophy* (Oxford: Clarendon, 1993).

For a clear discussion of Locke's position, see R. Ashcraft, 'Locke's Political Philosophy', in V. Chappell (ed.), *The Cambridge Companion to Locke* (Cambridge: Cambridge University Press, 1994).

A detailed account of the rise of early modern political theory may be found in Q. Skinner, *The Foundations of Modern Political Thought* (Cambridge: Cambridge University Press, 1978).

For Rousseau's ideas, see C. Bertram, *Rousseau and the Social Contract* (London: Routledge, 2003). See also H. Gildin, *Rousseau's Social Contract* (Chicago: University of Chicago Press, 1983).

A clear critical discussion of Hegel's political theory is K. Westphal, 'The Basic Context and Structure of Hegel's *Philosophy of Right*', in F. C. Beiser (ed.), *The Cambridge Companion to Hegel* (Cambridge: Cambridge University Press, 1993). For a sympathetic account of Hegel's aims, see R. L. Schacht, 'Hegel on Freedom', in A. MacIntyre (ed.), *Hegel: A Collection of Critical Essays* (Garden City, NY: Anchor Books, 1972).

A full discussion of Marx's account of alienation and his political theory generally may be found in J. Elster, *Making Sense of Marx* (Cambridge: Cambridge University Press, 1985), and in A. Wood, *Marx* (London: Routledge, 1981). See also T. Carver (ed.), *The Cambridge Companion to Marx* (Cambridge: Cambridge University Press, 1992); G. A. Cohen, *Karl Marx's Theory of History: A Defence* (Princeton: Princeton University Press, 2001); and S. Lukes, *Marxism and Morality* (Oxford: Oxford University Press, 1987).

Issues arising out of Mill's harm principle are discussed in H. Hart, *Law, Liberty and Morality* (Oxford: Oxford University Press, 1963); P. Devlin, *The Enforcement of Morals* (Oxford: Oxford University Press, 1965). See also B. Mitchell, *Law, Morality and Religion* (Oxford: Oxford University Press, 1970). A detailed account of Mill's views appears in J. N. Gray, *Mill on Liberty: A Defence* (London: Routledge, 1983).

A useful collection of critical essays on Nozick is J. Paul (ed.), *Reading Nozick* (Oxford: Blackwell, 1982). A sustained critique of Nozick appears in G. A. Cohen, *Self-ownership, Freedom and Equality* (Cambridge: Cambridge University Press, 1995).

Substantial essays on this and many other aspects of modern political theory appear in R. E. Goodin and P. Pettit, *A Companion to Contemporary Political Philosophy* (Oxford: Blackwell, 1993).

A helpful survey of contractarianism appears in the article of that name by C. Morris, in L. Becker and C. Becker (eds), *Encyclopedia of Ethics* (New York and London: Routledge, 2001). Gauthier's own views are developed at length in his *Morals by Agreement* (Oxford: Clarendon, 1986). A more recent influential development of the contractarian approach is T. Scanlon, *What We Owe to Each Other* (Cambridge Mass.: Harvard University Press, 1998), esp. ch. 5; see also the essays in P. Stratton-Lake (ed.), *On What We Owe Each Other* (Oxford: Blackwell, 2004).

A valuable collection of recent important essays on equality, including contributions by Dworkin, Nagel, Parfit, Rawls and Scanlon, is M. Clayton and A. Williams (eds), *The Ideal of Equality* (London: Palgrave, 2002). A seminal essay on equality is B. Williams, 'The Idea of Equality', in P. Laslett and W. G. Runciman (eds), *Philosophy, Politics and Society* (Oxford: Blackwell, 1962). Useful introductory articles covering issues related to Dworkin's article are J. Hampton, 'Contract and Consent', and R. Arneson, 'Equality', both in R. Goodin and P. Pettit (eds), *A Companion to Contemporary Political Philosophy* (Oxford: Blackwell, 1993).

Also of interest are the article on 'Equality' by D. Miller in G. Hunt (ed.), *Philosophy and Politics* (Cambridge: Cambridge University Press, 1990), and M. Walzer, *Spheres of Justice: An Essay on Pluralism and Equality* (New York: Basic Books, 1983). See also the chapter on 'Equality' in T. Nagel, *Mortal Questions* (Cambridge: Cambridge University Press, 1979).

PART XI
Beauty and Art

Beauty and Art
Introduction

When we look back at past cultures, we may be interested in many things – the achievements of our predecessors in science and metaphysics, their religious (or anti-religious) beliefs, their ethical and political ideas. Previous parts of this volume have been concerned with all these areas of human endeavour. But our assessment of past ages is perhaps most powerfully influenced by the works of art they have left behind; indeed, it is often the artistic achievements of an age which people tend to have principally in mind when they talk of a 'culture'. The branch of philosophy known as 'aesthetics' (the term comes originally from the Greek word for sense-perception) is concerned with our perception of beauty, whether in art or nature, and more specifically with the nature of art and our human response to it. What is it for something to be beautiful, and what is the basis of our evaluation of works of art? Are there objective standards of aesthetic taste, and if so how do they relate to the often widely differing subjective impressions people have on experiencing a work of art? How does the value of art relate to other values of central importance for human life? These are among the questions raised in this Part of the volume. As so often elsewhere, the story begins with the classical Greek era, when many of the foundations for Western philosophy were laid down.

1   Art and Imitation: Plato, *Republic**

Philosophical activity, as conceived of by the early Greek thinkers, belongs very much to the rational and intellectual part of our nature; the creation and appreciation of art, by contrast, often seems related to a wider range of faculties, involving the cultivation of emotional and perceptual sensibilities of various kinds. This contrast has given rise, rightly or wrongly, to a perceived tension between the aims of philosophy and those of art – a tension which is particularly apparent in Plato's best-known work, the *Republic*, where he lays out the conditions for his ideal state. Early on in the work, Plato had talked of the corrupting influence of art, and argued for a strict censorship of various kinds of music and poetry supposed to be unsuitable for the aspiring rulers of the state.[1] In the following extract, from towards the end of the book, he offers a more radical argument, which depends on his famous theory of Forms (see above, Part I, extract 2 and Part II, extract 1).

The Forms, according to Plato, are abstract universal objects of thought, the ideal patterns of which the ordinary objects around us are mere copies. Thus an ordinary bed is a mere instance of the abstract Form of bed (particular beds may be created or destroyed, or may perform their function more or less well, but the Form of bedhood – the essence of what it is to be a bed – endures for ever). Plato now describes the

artist as practising *imitation* (the Greek word is *mimesis*). The painter, for example, producing an image of a bed, copies or imitates the particular object. But the particular object, for Plato, is itself only a pale imitation of the eternal Form of bed. So the artist is at several removes from reality – he is 'a long way off the truth'. Plato goes on to argue that the painter is a kind of trickster, achieving various superficial effects or appearances, without having any sound knowledge of the nature of what he is depicting. Finally, referring to 'the old quarrel between philosophy and poetry', Plato condemns Homer and the tragedians for appealing to the baser part of our nature, and encouraging us to weep and give way to our feelings, when reason requires restraint and self-possession: 'poetry feeds and waters the passions instead of drying them up; she lets them rule although they ought to be controlled if mankind are ever to increase in happiness and virtue.' In defence of art on this last point, it could be argued that the release of the emotions effected by poetry could have beneficial effects, and need not lead to generally uncontrolled or irrational conduct.[2] As for the argument based on Forms, the defender of art might respond, even granting Plato his theory, that the artist, no less than the philosopher, aims to get beyond mere particular appearances to something of more universal and timeless significance.

Speaking in confidence,[3] for I should not like to have my words repeated to the tragedians and the rest of the imitative tribe – but I do not mind saying to you, that all poetical imitations are ruinous to the understanding of the hearers, and that the knowledge of their true nature is the only antidote to them.

Explain the purport of your remark.

Well, I will tell you, although I have always from my earliest youth had an awe of Homer, which even now makes the words falter on my lips, for he is the great captain and teacher of the whole of that charming tragic company; but a man is not to be reverenced more than the truth, and therefore I will speak out.

---

* Plato, *Republic* [*Politeia*, *c.*380 BC], Bk X, 595b2–608b10. Trans. B. Jowett, in *The Dialogues of Plato* (Oxford: Clarendon, 1892), vol. III, pp. 307–23; with omissions.
[1] *Republic*, Bks II and III (pp. 376–403).
[2] Compare Aristotle's notion of *catharsis* (extract 2, below).
[3] The speaker is Socrates, representing Plato's views; the respondent in the dialogue is Glaucon.

Very good, he said.

Listen to me, then, or rather answer me.

Put your question.

Can you tell me what imitation is? For I really do not know.

A likely thing, then, that I should know.

Why not? For the duller eye may often see a thing sooner than the keener.

Very true, he said. But in your presence, even if I had any faint notion, I could not muster courage to utter it. Will you enquire yourself?

Well then, shall we begin the enquiry in our usual manner: Whenever a number of individuals have a common name, we assume them to have also a corresponding idea or form: – do you understand me?

I do.

Let us take any common instance; there are beds and tables in the world – plenty of them, are there not?

Yes.

But there are only two ideas or forms of them – one the idea of a bed, the other of a table.

True.

And the maker of either of them makes a bed or he makes a table for our use, in accordance with the idea – that is our way of speaking in this and similar instances – but no artificer makes the ideas themselves: how could he?

Impossible.

And there is another artist, – I should like to know what you would say of him.

Who is he?

One who is the maker of all the works of all other workmen.

What an extraordinary man!

Wait a little, and there will be more reason for your saying so. For this is he who is able to make not only vessels of every kind, but plants and animals, himself and all other things – the earth and heaven, and the things which are in heaven or under the earth; he makes the gods also.

He must be a wizard and no mistake.

Oh! you are incredulous, are you? Do you mean that there is no such maker or creator, or that in one sense there might be a maker of all these things but in another not? Do you see that there is a way in which you could make them all yourself?

What way?

An easy way enough; or rather, there are many ways in which the feat might be quickly and easily accomplished, none quicker than that of turning a mirror round and round – you would soon enough make the sun and the heavens and the earth and yourself, and other animals and plants, and all the other things of which we were just now speaking, in the mirror.

Yes, he said; but they would be appearances only.

Very good, I said, you are coming to the point now. And the painter too is, as I conceive, just such another – a creator of appearances, is he not?

Of course.

But then I suppose you will say that what he creates is untrue. And yet there is a sense in which the painter also creates a bed?

Yes, he said, but not a real bed.

And what of the maker of the bed? Were you not saying that he too makes, not the idea which, according to our view, is the essence of the bed, but only a particular bed?

Yes, I did.

Then if he does not make that which exists he cannot make true existence, but only some semblance of existence; and if anyone were to say that the work of the maker of the bed, or of any other workman, has real existence, he could hardly be supposed to be speaking the truth.

At any rate, he replied, philosophers would say that he was not speaking the truth.

No wonder, then, that his work too is an indistinct expression of truth.

No wonder.

Suppose now that by the light of the examples just offered we enquire who this imitator is.

If you please.

Well then, here are three beds: one existing in nature, which is made by God, as I think that we may say – for no one else can be the maker?

No.

There is another which is the work of the carpenter?

Yes.

And the work of the painter is a third?

Yes.

Beds, then, are of three kinds, and there are three artists who superintend them: God, the maker of the bed, and the painter?

Yes, there are three of them.

God, whether from choice or from necessity, made one bed in nature and one only; two or more such ideal beds neither ever have been nor ever will be made by God.

Why is that?

Because even if He had made but two, a third would still appear behind them which both of them would have for their idea, and that would be the ideal bed and not the two others.

Very true, he said.

God knew this, and He desired to be the real maker of a real bed, not a particular maker of a particular bed, and therefore He created a bed which is essentially and by nature one only.

So we believe.

Shall we, then, speak of Him as the natural author or maker of the bed?

Yes, he replied; inasmuch as by the natural process of creation He is the author of this and of all other things.

And what shall we say of the carpenter – is not he also the maker of the bed?

Yes.

But would you call the painter a creator and maker?

Certainly not.

Yet if he is not the maker, what is he in relation to the bed?

I think, he said, that we may fairly designate him as the imitator of that which the others make.

Good, I said; then you call him who is third in the descent from nature an imitator?

Certainly, he said.

And the tragic poet is an imitator, and therefore, like all other imitators, he is thrice removed from the king and from the truth?

That appears to be so.

Then about the imitator we are agreed. And what about the painter? I would like to know whether he may be thought to imitate that which originally exists in nature, or only the creations of artists?

The latter.

As they are or as they appear? You have still to determine this.

What do you mean?

I mean, that you may look at a bed from different points of view, obliquely or directly or from any other point of view and the bed will appear different, but there is no difference in reality. And the same of all things.

Yes, he said, the difference is only apparent.

Now let me ask you another question: Which is the art of painting designed to be – an imitation of things as they are, or as they appear – of appearance or of reality?

Of appearance.

Then the imitator, I said, is a long way off the truth, and can do all things because he lightly touches on a small part of them, and that part an image. For example: A painter will paint a cobbler, carpenter, or any other artist, though he knows nothing of their arts; and, if he is a good artist, he may deceive children or simple persons, when he shows them his picture of a carpenter from a distance, and they will fancy that they are looking at a real carpenter.

Certainly.

And whenever any one informs us that he has found a man who knows all the arts, and all things else that anybody knows, and every single thing with a higher degree of accuracy than any other man – whoever tells us this, I think that we can only imagine him to be a simple creature who is likely to have been deceived by some wizard or actor whom he met, and whom he thought all-knowing, because he himself was unable to analyse the nature of knowledge and ignorance and imitation.

Most true.

And so, when we hear persons saying that the tragedians, and Homer, who is at their head, know all the arts and all things human, virtue as well as vice, and divine things too, for that the good poet cannot compose well unless he knows his subject, and that he who has not this knowledge can never be a poet, we ought to consider whether here also there may not be a similar illusion. Perhaps they may have come across imitators and been deceived by them; they may not have remembered when they saw their works that these were but imitations thrice removed from the truth, and could easily be made without any knowledge of the truth, because they are appearances only and not realities? Or, after all, they may be in the right, and poets do really know the things about which they seem to the many to speak so well?

The question, he said, should by all means be considered.

Now do you suppose that if a person were able to make the original as well as the image, he would seriously devote himself to the image-making branch? Would he allow imitation to be the ruling principle of his life, as if he had nothing higher in him?

I should say not.

The real artist, who knew what he was imitating, would be interested in realities and not in imitations; and would desire to leave as memorials of himself works many and fair; and, instead of being the author of encomiums, he would prefer to be the theme of them.

Yes, he said, that would be to him a source of much greater honour and profit...

Then must we not infer that all these poetical individuals, beginning with Homer, are only imitators; they copy images of virtue and the like, but the truth they never reach? The poet is like a painter who, as we have already observed, will make a likeness of a cobbler though he understands nothing of cobbling; and his picture is good enough for those who know no more than he does, and judge only by colours and figures.

Quite so...

Thus far then we are pretty well agreed that the imitator has no knowledge worth mentioning of what he imitates. Imitation is only a kind of play or sport; and the tragic poets, whether they write in iambic or in heroic verse, are imitators in the highest degree?

Very true...

And now we may fairly take [the poet] and place him by the side of the painter, for he is like him in two ways: first, inasmuch as his creations have an inferior degree of truth – in this, I say, he is like him; and he is also like him in being concerned with an inferior part of the soul; and therefore we shall be right in refusing to admit him into a well-ordered State, because he awakens and nourishes and strengthens the feelings and impairs the reason. As in a city when the evil are permitted to have authority and the good are put out of the way, so in the soul of man, as we maintain, the imitative poet implants an evil constitution, for he indulges the irrational nature which has no discernment of greater and less, but thinks the same thing at one time great and at another small – he is a manufacturer of images and is very far removed from the truth.

Exactly.

But we have not yet brought forward the heaviest count in our accusation: – the power which poetry has of harming even the good (and there are very few who are not harmed) is surely an awful thing?

Yes, certainly, if the effect is what you say.

Hear and judge: The best of us, as I conceive, when we listen to a passage of Homer, or one of the tragedians, in which he represents some pitiful hero who is drawling out his sorrows in a long oration, or weeping, and smiting his breast – the best of us, you know, delight in giving way to sympathy, and are in raptures at the excellence of the poet who stirs our feelings most.

Yes, of course I know.

But when any sorrow of our own happens to us, then you may observe that we pride ourselves on the opposite quality – we would fain be quiet and patient; this is the manly part, and the other which delighted us in the recitation is now deemed to be the part of a woman.

Very true, he said.

Now can we be right in praising and admiring another who is doing that which any one of us would abominate and be ashamed of in his own person?

No, he said, that is certainly not reasonable.

Nay, I said, quite reasonable from one point of view.

What point of view?

If you consider, I said, that when in misfortune we feel a natural hunger and desire to relieve our sorrow by weeping and lamentation, and that this feeling which is kept under control in our own calamities is satisfied and delighted by the poets; – the better nature in each of us, not having been really sufficiently trained by reason or habit, allows the sympathetic element to break loose because the sorrow is another's; and the spectator fancies that there can be no disgrace to himself in praising and pitying anyone who comes telling him what a good man he is, and making a fuss about his troubles; he thinks that the pleasure is a gain, and why should he be supercilious and lose this and the poem too? Few persons ever reflect, as I should imagine, that from the evil of other men something of evil is communicated to themselves. And so the feeling of sorrow which has gathered strength at the sight of the misfortunes of others is with difficulty repressed in our own.

How very true!

...And the same may be said of lust and anger and all the other affections, of desire and pain and pleasure, which are held to be inseparable from every action – in all of them poetry feeds and waters the passions instead of drying them up; she lets them rule, although they ought to be controlled, if mankind are ever to increase in happiness and virtue.

I cannot deny it...

And now since we have reverted to the subject of poetry, let this our defence serve to show the reasonableness of our former judgement in sending away out of our State an art having the tendencies which we have described; for reason constrained us. But that she may not impute to us any harshness or want of politeness, let us tell her that there is an ancient quarrel between philosophy and poetry...Notwithstanding this, let us assure our sweet friend and the sister arts of imitation, that if she will only prove her title to exist in a well-ordered State we shall be delighted to receive her – we are very conscious of her charms; but we may not on that account betray the truth....

If her defence fails, then, my dear friend, like other persons who are enamoured of something, but put a restraint upon themselves when they think their desires are opposed to their interests, so too must we after the manner of lovers give her up, though not without a struggle. We too are inspired by that love of poetry which the education of noble States has implanted in us, and therefore we would have her appear at her best and truest; but so long as she is unable to make good her defence, this argument of ours shall be a charm to us, which we will repeat to ourselves while we listen to her strains; that we may not fall away into the childish love of her which captivates the many. At all events we are well aware that poetry being such as we have described is not to be regarded seriously as attaining to the truth; and he who listens to her, fearing for the safety of the city which is within him, should be on his guard against her seductions and make our words his law.

Yes, he said, I quite agree with you.

Yes, I said, my dear Glaucon, for great is the issue at stake, greater than appears, whether a man is to be good or bad. And what will any one be profited if under the influence of honour or money or power, aye, or under the excitement of poetry, he neglect justice and virtue?

Yes, he said; I have been convinced by the argument as I believe that anyone else would have been.

2   The Nature and Function of Dramatic Art: Aristotle, *Poetics**

Plato's account of art as 'imitation' (see previous extract) exerted considerable influence on his pupil Aristotle, though Aristotle developed it in a very different way, reflecting his far greater sympathy with the artistic enterprise.[1] The *Poetics*, from which our second extract is taken, is largely concerned with the dramatic arts, and in particular with the tradition of tragic drama that was perhaps the highest glory of ancient Athenian culture. Aristotle defines tragedy as 'the imitation of an action', and proceeds to lay down in great detail a set of rules and requirements to which the good tragic play must conform. Its various features include fable or plot, characters, diction, thought, spectacle and melody, about all of which Aristotle has something to say. But the crucial point concerns the function and purpose of the drama. Though it operates via the 'imitation' of action by the actors, its object is to effect a *catharsis*, a purification or purging of the emotions in the spectators, by arousing pity and fear. Plato, as we have seen, was worried about art encouraging all sorts of dangerous and undesirable feelings; Aristotle gives a more subtle and nuanced account of the way in which a great dramatic spectacle produces in us a set of complex psychological events – a kind of 'cleansing' whereby our emotions are aroused and then discharged.

Aristotle also lays great stress on the moral content of a drama. It must have a certain unity, with a 'beginning, a middle and an end'; the formula, often repeated since, may sound trite, but it links up with the idea that the events unfolded in a drama must have their own internal logic. What is presented is not merely one event after another, but an unfolding of a coherent story with a significance for human life, something which relates to how 'human happiness and misery' come about. Hence the importance of development in a plot – for example the *discovery* by Oedipus of the terrible secret of his origins, and the *reversal of fortune* which this brought about. Aristotle's general approach, though it emphasizes the importance of the emotions, also indicates the way in which the dramatic arts appeal to the full range of our human responses, intellectual and moral as well as emotional.

It is clear that the general origin of poetry was due to two causes, each of them part of human nature. Imitation is natural to man from childhood, one of his advantages over the lower animals being this, that he is the most imitative creature in the world, and learns at first by imitation. And it is also natural for all to delight in works of imitation. The truth of this second point is shown by experience: though the objects themselves may be painful to see, we delight to view the most realistic representations of them in art, the forms for example of the lowest animals and of dead bodies. The explanation is to be found in a further fact: to be learning something is the greatest of pleasure not only to the philosopher, but also the rest of mankind, however small their capacity for it; the reason of the delight in seeing the picture is that one is at the same time learning – gathering the meaning of things, e.g. that the man there is so-and-so; for if one has not seen the thing before, one's pleasure will not be in the picture as an imitation of it, but will be due to the execution or colouring or some

* Aristotle, *Poetics* [*Peri Poetikes*, *c.*325 BC], extracts from chs 4, 6, 7, 8, 9, 10, 11, 25. Trans. I. Bywater, in *The Works of Aristotle*, ed. W. D. Ross (Oxford: Clarendon, 1924); with minor modifications.

[1] It should be noted, however, that Plato's own views were by no means all of a piece. In the *Symposium*, he presents a considerably more favourable account of poetry and its significance.

similar cause. Imitation, then, being natural to us – as also the sense of harmony and rhythm, the metres being obvious species of rhythms – it was through their original aptitude, and by a series of improvements for the most part gradual of their first efforts, that they created poetry out of their improvisations...

A tragedy is the imitation of an action that is serious and also, as having magnitude, complete in itself; in language with pleasurable accessories, each kind brought in separately in the part of the work; in a dramatic, not in a narrative form; with incidents arousing pity and fear, wherewith to accomplish its catharsis of such emotions. Here by 'language with pleasurable accessories' I mean that with rhythm and harmony or song superadded; and by 'the kinds separately' I mean that some portions are worked out with verse only, and others in turn with song.

As they act the stories, it follows that in the first place the spectacle (or stage-appearance of the actors) must be some part of the whole; and in the second melody and diction, these two being the means of their imitation. Here by 'diction' I mean merely the composition of the verses, and by 'melody' what is too completely under-stood to require explanations. But further: the subject represented also is an action; and the action involves agents who must necessarily have their distinctive qualities both of character and thought, since it is from these that we ascribe certain qualities to their actions. There are in the natural order of things, therefore, two causes, thought and character, of their actions, and consequently of their success or failure in their lives. Now the action (that which was done) is represented in the play by the fable or plot. The fable, in our present sense of the term, is simply this, the combination of the incidents, or things done in the story; whereas character is what makes us ascribe certain moral qualities to the agents; and thought is shown in all they say when proving a particular point or, it may be, enunciating a general truth. There are six parts consequently of every tragedy as a whole, which determine its quality, viz. a fable or plot, characters, diction, thought, spectacle and melody; two of them arising from the means, one from the manner, and three from the objects of the dramatic imitations; and there is nothing else besides these six...

The most important of the six is the combination of the incidents of the story. Tragedy is essentially an imitation not of persons but of action and life, of happiness and misery. All human happiness or misery takes the form of action; the end for which we live is a certain kind of activity, not a quality. Character gives us qualities, but it is in our actions – what we do – that we are happy or the reverse. In a play accordingly they do not act in order to portray the characters; they include the characters for the sake of the action. So it is the action in it, i.e. its fable or plot, that is the end and purpose of the tragedy; and the end is everywhere the chief thing. Besides this, a tragedy is impossible without action, but there may be one without character... One may string together a series of characteristic speeches of the utmost finish as regards diction and thought, and yet fail to produce the true tragic effect; but one will have much better success with a tragedy which, however inferior in these respects, has a plot, and combination of incidents in it. And again: the most powerful elements of attraction in tragedy, the reversals of fortune and discoveries, are parts of the plot... We maintain therefore that the first essential, the life and soul, so to speak, of tragedy is the plot, and the characters come second – compare the parallel in painting where the most beautiful colours laid on without order will not give one the same pleasure as a simple black-and-white sketch of a portrait.

We maintain that tragedy is primarily an imitation of an action, and that it is mainly for the sake of the action that it imitates the personal agents. Third comes the element of thought, i.e. the power of saying whatever can be said, or what is appropriate to the occasions. This is what, in the speeches in tragedy, falls under the arts of politics and rhetoric; for the older poets make their personages discourse like statesmen, and the moderns like rhetoricians. One must not confuse it with character. Character in a play is that which reveals the moral purpose of the agents, i.e. the sort of thing they seek to avoid, where that is not obvious – hence there is no room for character in a speech on a purely indifferent subject. Thought on the other hand is shown in all they say when proving or disproving some particular point, or enunciating some universal proposition.

Fourth among the literary elements is the diction of the personages, i.e. the expression of their thought in words, which is practically the same thing with verse as with prose. As for the two remaining parts, the melody is the greatest of the pleasurable accessories of tragedy. The spectacle, though an attraction, is the least artistic of all the parts, and has least to do with the art of poetry. The tragic effect is quite possible without a public performance and actors; and besides, the getting up of the spectacle is more a matter of the costumier than the poet.

Having thus distinguished the parts, let us now consider the proper construction of the fable or plot, as that is at once the first and the most important thing in tragedy. We have laid it down that a tragedy is an imitation of an action that is complete in itself, as whole of some magnitude; for a whole may be of no magnitude to speak of. Now a whole is that which has beginning, middle and end. A beginning is that which is not itself necessarily after anything else, and which has naturally something else after it; an end is that which is naturally after something itself, either as its necessary or usual consequent, and with nothing else after it; and a middle is that which is by nature after one thing and also has another after it. A well-constructed plot, therefore, cannot either begin or end at any point one likes; beginning and end in it must be of the forms just described. Again, to be beautiful, a living creature, and every whole made up of parts, must not only present a certain order in its arrangement of parts, but also be of a certain definite magnitude. Beauty is a matter of size and order, and therefore impossible either (1) in a very minute creature, since our perception becomes indistinct as it approaches instantaneity; or (2) in a creature of vast size – one, say, 1,000 miles long – as in that case, instead of the object being seen all at once, the unity and wholeness of it is lost to the beholder. Just in the same way, then, as a beautiful whole made up of parts, or a beautiful living creature, must be of some size, but a size to be taken in by the eye, so a story or plot must be of some length, but of a length to be taken in by the memory. As for the limit of its length, so far as that is relative to public performances and spectators, it does not fall within the theory of poetry. If they had to perform a hundred tragedies, they would be timed by water-clocks, as they are said to have been at one period. The limit, however, set by the actual nature of the thing is this: the longer the story, consistently with its being comprehensible as a whole, the finer it is by reason of its magnitude. As a rough general formula, 'a length which allows of the hero passing by a series of probable or necessary stages from misfortune to happiness, or from happiness to misfortune' may suffice as a limit for the magnitude of the story.

The unity of a plot does not consist, as some suppose, in its having one man as its subject. An infinity of things befall that one man, some of which it is impossible to reduce to unity; and in like manner there are many actions of one man which cannot be made to form one action... Homer evidently understood this point quite well, whether by art or instinct... In writing an *Odyssey*, he did not make the poem cover all that ever befell his hero – it befell him, for instance, to get wounded on Parnassus and also to feign madness at the time of the call to arms, but the two actions had no necessary or probable connection with one another – instead of doing that he took as the subject of the *Odyssey*, as also of the *Iliad*, an action with a unity of the kind we are describing. The truth is that, just as in the other imitative arts an imitation is always of one thing, so in poetry the story, as an imitation of action, must represent one action, a complete whole, with its several incidents so closely connected that the transposal or withdrawal of any one of them will disjoin and dislocate the whole. For that which makes no perceptible difference by its presence or absence is no real part of the whole.

From what we have said it will be seen that the poet's function is to describe, not the thing that has happened, but a kind of thing that might happen, i.e. what is possible as being probable or necessary. The distinction between historian and poet is not the one writing prose and the other verse – you might put the work of Herodotus into verse, and it would still be a species of history; it consists really in this, that the one describes the thing that has been, and the other a kind of thing that might be. Hence poetry is something more philosophic and of graver import than history, since its statements are of the nature rather of universals, whereas those of history are singulars. By a universal statement I mean one concerning what such or such a kind of man will probably or necessarily say or do – which is the aim of poetry, though it affixes proper names to the characters; by a singular statement, one concerning what, say, Alcibiades did or had done to him...

It is evident from the above that the poet must be more the poet of his stories or plots than of his verses, inasmuch as he is a poet by virtue of the imitative element in his work, and it is actions that he imitates. And if he should come to take a subject from actual history, he is none the less a poet for that; since some historic occurrences may very well be in the probable and possible order of things; and it is in that aspect of them that he is their poet.

Of simple plots and actions the episodic are the worst. I call a plot episodic when there is neither probability nor necessity in the sequence of its episodes. Actions of this sort bad poets construct through their own fault, and good ones on account of the players. His work being for public performance, a good poet often stretches out a plot beyond its capabilities, and is thus obliged to twist the sequence of incidents.

Tragedy however is an imitation not only of a complete action, but also of incidents arousing pity and fear. Such incidents have the very greatest effect on the mind when they occur unexpectedly and at the same time in consequence of one another; there is more of the marvellous in them then than if they had happened of themselves or by mere chance. Even matters of chance seem most marvellous if there is an appearance of design as it were in them; as for instance the statue of Mitys at Argos killed the author of Mitys' death by falling down on him when a looker-on at a public spectacle;

for incidents like that we think to be not without a meaning. A plot, therefore, of this sort is necessarily finer than others.

Plots are either simple or complex, since the actions they represent are naturally of this twofold description. The action...I call simple when the changes in the hero's fortunes takes place without reversal or discovery; and complex when it involves both. These should each of them arise out of the structure of the plot itself, so as to be consequence, necessary or probable, of the antecedents. There is a great difference between a thing happening merely *after* something and its happening *because* of it.

A reversal is a change of the kind described from one state of things within the play to its opposite, and that too in the way we are saying, in the probable or necessary sequence of events; as it is for instance in *Oedipus*. Here the opposite state of things is produced by the messenger, who, coming to gladden Oedipus and to remove his fears as to his mother, reveals the secret of his birth...A discovery is, as the very word implies, a change from ignorance to knowledge, and thus to either love or hate, in the personages marked for good or evil fortune. The finest form of discovery is one attended by reversal, like that which goes with the discovery in *Oedipus*....This will arouse either pity or fear, – actions of that nature being what tragedy is assumed to represent; and it will serve to bring about the happy or unhappy ending...

The poet being an imitator, just like the painter or other maker of likenesses, must necessarily in all instances represent things in one or other of three aspects, either as they were or are, or as they are said or thought to be or to have been, or as they ought to be. All this he does in language, with an admixture, it may be, of strange words and metaphors, as also of the various modified forms of words, since the use of these is conceded in poetry. It is to be remembered too that there is not the same kind of correctness in poetry as in politics, or indeed any other art. There is, however, within the limits of poetry itself, a possibility of two kinds of error, the one directly, the other only accidentally connected with the art. If the poet meant to describe the thing correctly, and failed through lack of power of expression, his art itself is at fault. But if it was through his having meant to describe the thing in some incorrect way (e.g. to make the horse in movement have both right legs thrown forwards) that the technical error (one in matters of, say, medicine or some other special science), or impossibilities of whatever kind they may be, have got into his description, his error in that case is not in the essentials of the poetic art.

3   The Idea of Beauty: Francis Hutcheson, *Inquiry concerning Beauty, Order, Harmony, Design**

What we expect from a work of dramatic art, and what makes us judge it good, depend on a host of complex factors, some of which are indicated in Aristotle's account of tragedy (preceding extract). But there are other cases – in some of the visual arts for example – where our appreciation seems to be a more direct and immediate response to beauty of form or line. In the eighteenth century, there was a great deal of philosophical interest in the origin of our sense of beauty, much of it stimulated by the work of the Scottish philosopher Francis (or Frances) Hutcheson. In the extract that follows, Hutcheson compares our sense of beauty with the other more ordinary senses (such as sight and hearing), and he follows John Locke's distinction between *ideas* in the mind, and the *qualities* in objects which cause those ideas (compare Part II, extract 4, above). In the case of some of our ideas, such as those of colour and taste, Locke had argued that there is no similarity between the mental 'idea' or impression we have – of sweetness or sourness, for example – and the shape and motion of the molecules in the environment which impinge on our nervous system so as to produce these ideas in us. In similar vein, Hutcheson talks of the 'idea' of beauty 'raised' in us by external objects. The external features of the world that produce or 'excite' the ideas of beauty in us, he goes on to explain, are 'those in which there is uniformity amidst variety'. But just as one may have a sensa-

tion of redness without any knowledge of the external causes which produced it, so in instances of beauty 'we may have the [pleasant] sensation without knowing [the features in the object which are] the occasion of it'.

One interesting feature of Hutcheson's position is that it allows for both an objective and a subjective element in our aesthetic appreciation. On the one hand, the sense of beauty involves a response to features ('uniformity amidst variety') which are genuinely 'out there' in the objects we call beautiful. But on the other hand, there is a direct and immediate kind of awareness when the sense of beauty is activated – something which you either have or you lack. A person may have complete mastery when it comes to distinguishing the pitches of notes, or varieties of line and shape, Hutcheson points out, 'yet perhaps they shall relish no pleasure in musical compositions [or] painting'. The characteristic 'pleasure of beauty', Hutcheson goes on to argue, is not reducible to any other judgement we may make about what may be beneficial or harmful to us: you can, by rewards or threats, encourage or discourage someone from looking at a painting, but no promises or sanctions can make any difference to whether or not they find it aesthetically pleasing. Hutcheson raises important questions here about the nature of aesthetic appreciation, several of which we shall see taken up in subsequent extracts.

 Let it be observed that in the following papers the word *beauty* is taken for the idea raised in us, and a sense of beauty for our power of receiving this idea. Harmony also denotes our pleasant ideas arising from composition of sounds, and a good ear (as it is generally taken) a power of perceiving this pleasure. In the following sections an

---

* Francis Hutcheson, 'Inquiry concerning Beauty, Order, Harmony, Design', being the first treatise of *An Inquiry into the Original of our Ideas of Beauty and Virtue* [1725], Section I, §§ 9, 10, 12–17; Section II, §§ 1, 3, 4, 5, 13, 14; with omissions, modernized spelling and punctuation, and other minor changes. A photographic facsimile of the first edition is published in volume I of *The Collected Works of Frances Hutcheson* (Hildesheim: Olms, 1971).

attempt is made to discover what is the immediate occasion of these pleasant ideas, or what real quality in the objects ordinarily excites them.

It is of no consequence whether we call these ideas of beauty and harmony perceptions of the external senses of seeing and hearing, or not. I should rather choose to call our power of perceiving these ideas an *internal sense*, were it only for the convenience of distinguishing them from other sensations of seeing and hearing, which men may have without perception of beauty and harmony. It is plain from experience that many men have, in the common meaning, the senses of seeing and hearing perfect enough; they perceive all the simple ideas separately, and have their pleasures; they distinguish them from each other, such as one colour from another, either quite different, or the stronger or fainter of the same colour; they can tell in separate notes the higher, lower, sharper or flatter, when separately sounded; in figures they discern the length, breadth, width, of each line, surface, angle, and may be as capable of hearing and seeing at great distances as any men whatsoever. And yet perhaps they shall relish no pleasure in musical compositions, in painting, architecture, natural landscape – or but a very weak one in comparison of what others enjoy from the same objects. This greater capacity of receiving such pleasant ideas we commonly call a fine genius or taste. In music we seem universally to acknowledge something like a distinct sense from the external one of hearing, and call it a good ear; and the like distinction we would probably acknowledge in other affairs, had we also got distinct names to denote these powers of perception by...

Let everyone here consider how different we must suppose the perception to be, with which a poet is transported upon the prospect of any of those objects of natural beauty which ravish us even in his description, from that cold lifeless conception which we imagine to be in a dull critic, or one of the virtuosi, without what we call a fine taste. This latter class of men may have greater perfection in that knowledge which is derived from external sensation; they can tell all the specific differences of trees, herbs, minerals, metals; they know the form of every leaf, stalk, root, flower and seed of all the species about which the poet is often very ignorant. And yet the poet shall have a vastly more delightful perception of the whole; and not only the poet, but any man of a fine taste. Our external senses may by measure teach us all the proportions of architecture to the tenth of an inch, and the situation of every muscle in the human body; and a good memory may retain these; and yet there is still something further necessary, not only to make a complete master in architecture, painting, or statuary, but even a tolerable judge in these works; or to receive the highest pleasure in contemplating them. Since then there are such different powers of perception, where what are commonly called the external senses are the same; and since the most accurate knowledge of what the external senses discover does not give the pleasure of beauty or harmony, which yet one of a good taste will enjoy at once without much knowledge, we may justly use another name for these higher and more delightful perceptions of beauty and harmony, and call the power of receiving such impressions an internal *sense*. The difference of the perceptions seems sufficient to vindicate the use of a different name.

This superior power of perception is justly called a *sense* because of its affinity to the other senses in this, that the pleasure does not arise from any knowledge of principles, proportions, causes, or of the usefulness of the object, but strikes us at first with the idea of beauty. Nor does the most accurate knowledge increase this pleasure of beauty, however it may superadd a distinct rational pleasure from prospects of advantage, or from the increase of knowledge.

And further, the ideas of beauty and harmony, like other sensible ideas, are necessarily pleasant to us, as well as immediately so; neither can any resolution of our own, nor any prospect of advantage or disadvantage, vary the beauty or deformity of an object. For as in the external sensations no view of interest will make an object grateful, nor detriment (distinct from immediate pain in the perception) make it disagreeable to the sense; so propose the whole world as a reward, or threaten the greatest evil, to make us approve a deformed object, or disapprove a beautiful one; dissimulation may be procured by rewards or threatenings, or we may in external conduct abstain from any pursuit of the beautiful, and pursue the deformed; but our sentiments of the forms, and our perceptions, would continue invariably the same.

Hence it plainly appears some objects are immediately the occasions of this pleasure of beauty, and that we have senses fitted for perceiving it; and that it is distinct from that joy which arises from self-love upon prospect of advantage. Nay, do we not often see convenience and use neglected to obtain beauty, without any other prospect of advantage in the beautiful form than the suggesting the pleasant ideas of beauty? Now this shows us that however we may pursue beautiful objects from self-love, with a view to obtain the pleasure of beauty, as in architecture, gardening and many other affairs; yet there must be a sense of beauty, antecedent to prospects of even this advantage, without which sense these objects would not be thus advantageous, nor excite in us this pleasure which constitutes them advantageous. Our sense of beauty from objects, by which they are constituted good to us, is very distinct from our desire of them when they are thus constituted. Our desire of beauty may be counterbalanced by rewards or threatenings, but never our sense of it; even as fear of death, or love of life, may make us choose and desire a bitter potion, or neglect those meats which the sense of taste would recommend as pleasant; and yet no prospect of advantage or fear of evil can make that potion agreeable to the sense, or meats disagreeable to it, that were not so antecedently to this prospect. Just in the same manner as to the sense of beauty and harmony: that the pursuit of such objects is frequently neglected from prospects of advantage, aversion to labour, or any other motive of self love, does not prove that we have no sense of beauty, but only that our desire of it may be counterbalanced by a stronger desire. So gold outweighing silver is never adduced as a proof that the latter is void of gravity.

Had we no such sense of beauty and harmony, houses, gardens, dress, equipage might have been recommended to us as convenient, fruitful, warm, easy, but never as beautiful. And in faces I see nothing that could please us but liveliness of colour, and smoothness of surface. And yet nothing is more certain than that all these objects are recommended under quite different views on many occasions. And no custom, education or example could ever give us perceptions distinct from those of the sense which we had the use of before...

Beauty is either original or comparative; or, if any like the terms better, absolute or relative. Only let it be noted that by absolute or original beauty is not understood any quality supposed to be in the object, that should of itself be beautiful without any relation to any mind which perceives it. For beauty, like other names of sensible ideas, properly denotes the perception of some mind; so cold, heat, sweet, bitter, denote the sensations in our minds to which perhaps there is no resemblance in the objects that excite these ideas in us, however we generally imagine that there is something in the object just like our perception. The ideas of beauty and harmony being excited upon our perception of some primary quality,[1] and having relation to figure and time, may indeed have a nearer resemblance to objects than these sensations that seem not so much any pictures of objects, as modifications of the perceiving mind. And yet were there no mind with a sense of beauty to contemplate objects, I see not how they could be called beautiful. We therefore by absolute beauty understand only that beauty which we perceive in objects without comparison to anything external, of which the object is supposed an imitation, or picture; such as that beauty perceived from the works of nature, artificial forms, figures, theorems. Comparative or relative beauty is that which we perceive in objects commonly considered as imitations or resemblances of something else...

Since it is certain that we have ideas of beauty and harmony, let us examine what quality in objects excites these ideas, or is the occasion of them. And let it be here observed that our inquiry is only about the qualities that are beautiful to men, or about the foundation of their sense of beauty; for, as was above hinted, beauty has always some relation to the sense of some mind; and when we afterwards show how generally the objects that occur to us are beautiful, we mean agreeable to the sense of men. For as there are not a few objects which seem no way beautiful to men, so we see a variety of other animals who seem delighted with them. They may have senses otherwise constituted than those of men, and may have the ideas of beauty excited by objects of a quite different form. We see animals fitted to every place; and what to men appears rude and shapeless or loathsome may be to them a paradise...

The figures that excite in us the ideas of beauty seem to be those in which there is *uniformity amidst variety.* There are many conceptions of objects that are agreeable upon other accounts, such as grandeur, novelty, sanctity, and some others... But what we call beautiful in objects, to speak in the mathematical style, seems to be in a compound ratio of uniformity and variety. So that where the uniformity of bodies is equal, the beauty is as the variety; and where the variety is equal, the beauty is as the uniformity...

First, the variety increases the beauty in equal uniformity. The beauty of an equilateral triangle is less than that of the square, which is less than that of a pentagon; and this again is surpassed by the hexagon. When indeed the number of sides is much increased, the proportion of them to the radius, or diameter of the figure, is so much lost to our observation that the beauty does not always increase with the number of sides; and the want of parallelism in the sides of a heptagon, and other figures of odd numbers, may also diminish their beauty. So in solids, the eicosihedron[2] surpasses the dodecahedron, and this the octahedron, which is still more beautiful than the cube; and this again surpasses the regular pyramid. The obvious ground of this is the greater variety with equal uniformity.

The greater uniformity increases the beauty amidst equal variety in these instances: an equilateral triangle, or even an isosceles, surpasses the scalene; a square surpasses the rhombus or lozenge, and this again the rhomboid, which yet is still more beautiful

---

[1] See Part II, extract 4, above.
[2] Eicosihedron: twenty-sided body.

than the trapezium or any figure with irregularly curved sides. So the regular solids vastly surpass all other solids of equal number of plain surfaces. And the same is observable not only in the five perfectly regular solids, but in all those which have any considerable uniformity, as cylinders, prisms, pyramids, obelisks; which pleasure every eye more than any rude figures, where there is no unity or resemblance among the parts...

The observations would probably hold true for the most part, and might be confirmed by the judgement of children in the simpler figures, where the variety is not too great for the comprehension. And however uncertain some of the particular aforesaid instances may seem, yet this is perpetually to be observed, that children are fond of all regular figures in their little diversions, although they be no more convenient or useful for them than the figures of our common pebbles. We see how early they discover a taste or sense of beauty, in desiring to see buildings, regular gardens, or even representations of them in pictures of any kind.

It is the same foundation which we have for our sense of beauty in the works of nature. In every part of the world which we call beautiful, there is vast uniformity amidst almost infinite variety...

Under original beauty we may include harmony, or beauty of sound, if that expression can be allowed, because harmony is not usually conceived as an imitation of anything else. Harmony often raises pleasure in those who know not what is the occasion of it. And yet the foundation of this pleasure is known to be a sort of uniformity. When the several vibrations of one note regularly coincide with the vibration of another, they make an agreeable composition; and such notes are called *chords*. Thus the vibrations of any one note coincide in time with every second vibration of its octave; and two vibrations of any note coincide with three of its fifth; and so on in the rest of the chords. Now good compositions, beside the frequency of these chords, must retain a general unity of key, a uniformity among the parts in bars, risings, fallings, closes. The necessity of this will appear by observing the dissonance which would arise from tacking parts of different tunes together as one, although both were separately agreeable. A greater uniformity is also observable among the bases, tenors, trebles, of the same tune...

But in all these instances of beauty let it be observed that the pleasure is communicated to those who never reflected on this general foundation; and that all here alleged is this, that the pleasant sensation arises only from objects in which there is *uniformity amidst variety*. We may have the sensation without knowing what is the occasion of it, as a man's taste may suggest ideas of sweets, acids, bitters, though he be ignorant of the form of the small bodies, or their motions, which excite these perceptions in him.

4   Aesthetic Appreciation: David Hume, *Of the Standard of Taste**

Some thirty years after the appearance of Hutcheson's book (see preceding extract), his renowned compatriot David Hume published what remains a classic essay on some of the central problems of aesthetics. 'There is no disputing on matters of taste' goes the old saying. But despite all the divergences in people's likes and dislikes in matters of art, can we none the less find some objective standard of appreciation? This is the question Hume sets himself; and his answer is that 'amidst all the variety and caprice of taste, there are certain general principles of approbation or blame whose influence a careful eye may trace in all the operations of the mind'. His basic premise is that we do as a matter of fact find that some people have greater powers of discrimination than others (the story he tells from *Don Quixote* of the expert wine-tasters nicely illustrates the point). And though Hume agrees with Hutcheson that beauty and deformity are not really *in* objects but 'belong entirely to the sentiment', there are none the less qualities in the objects themselves which are 'fitted' to produce the feelings of beauty or disgust in us; and some people (like the wine-tasters) have a special aptitude, fostered by constant practice, for making the relevant discriminations.

Hume's conception is a frankly elitist one: 'few are qualified to give judgement on any work of art, or establish their own sentiment as the standard of beauty'. The 'coarse daubing' or 'vulgar ballad' that would delight the 'peasant' would merely pain someone 'conversant in the highest excellence of the kind'. Though the tone here is out of tune with the more egalitarian outlook that tends to prevail nowadays, Hume is surely right in pointing out that the appreciation of music or painting is a matter of making careful comparisons which require both innate aptitude and assiduous training. Of course the 'expert' critic may turn out to be a phoney; but Hume argues convincingly that when doubts occur there are factual procedures for resolving them (compare again discrimination in wine, which can be objectively examined by wine-tasting associations). But is there not still the possibility of radical disagreement even among the 'experts'? Hume ends by acknowledging that a completely uniform set of universal standards is impossible: what appeals to us may depend on our own circumstances and dispositions ('we choose our favourite author as we do our friend'), as well as on the culture in which we grew up. His subtle and elegant discussion reaches beyond facile clichés about 'personal taste' to show just how complex the nature of aesthetic evaluation can be.

The great variety of taste, as well as of opinion, which prevails in the world, is too obvious not to have fallen under every one's observation. Men of the most refined knowledge are able to remark a difference of taste in the narrow circle of their acquaintance, even where the persons have been educated under the same government, and have early imbibed the same prejudices. But those who can enlarge their view, to contemplate distant nations and remote ages, are still more surprised at the great inconsistency and contrariety. We are apt to call *barbarous* whatever departs widely from our own taste and apprehension; but soon find the epithet of reproach retorted on us. And the highest arrogance and self-conceit is at last startled, on

---

* D. Hume, 'Of the Standard of Taste', first published in *Four Dissertations* [1757]; repr. in *Essays Moral, Political and Literary* [1777]; abridged, with modified spelling and punctuation. The complete text is reprinted in *Essays Moral, Political and Literary by David Hume*, ed. T. H. Green and T. H. Grose (London: Longmans Green, 1875), vol. I, pp. 266–84.

observing an equal assurance on all sides, and scruples, amidst such a contest of sentiment, to pronounce positively in its own favour...

It is natural for us to seek a *standard of taste*; a rule by which the various sentiments of men may be reconciled; at least a decision afforded confirming one sentiment, and condemning another.

There is a species of philosophy, which cuts off all hopes of success in such an attempt, and represents the impossibility of ever attaining any standard of taste. The difference, it is said, is very wide between judgement and sentiment. All sentiment is right; because sentiment has a reference to nothing beyond itself, and is always real, wherever a man is conscious of it. But all determinations of the understanding are not right; because they have a reference to something beyond themselves, to wit, real matter of fact; and are not always conformable to that standard. Among a thousand different opinions which different men may entertain of the same subject, there is one, and but one, that is just and true; and the only difficulty is to fix and ascertain it. On the contrary, a thousand different sentiments, excited by the same object, are all right; because no sentiment represents what is really in the object... Beauty is no quality in things themselves: it exists merely in the mind which contemplates them; and each mind perceives a different beauty. One person may even perceive deformity where another is sensible of beauty; and every individual ought to acquiesce in his own sentiment, without pretending to regulate those of others. To seek the real beauty, or real deformity, is as fruitless an inquiry, as to pretend to ascertain the real sweet or real bitter. According to the disposition of the organs, the same object may be both sweet and bitter; and the proverb has justly determined it to be fruitless to dispute concerning tastes. It is very natural, and even quite necessary, to extend this axiom to mental as well as bodily taste; and thus common sense, which is so often at variance with philosophy, especially with the sceptical kind, is found, in one instance at least, to agree in pronouncing the same decision.

But though this axiom, by passing into a proverb, seems to have attained the sanction of common sense, there is certainly a species of common sense, which opposes it, at least serves to modify and restrain it. Whoever would assert an equality of genius and elegance between Ogilby and Milton, or Bunyan and Addison, would be thought to defend no less an extravagance, than if he had maintained a mole-hill to be as high as Tenerife, or a pond as extensive as the ocean.[1] Though there may be found persons who give the preference to the former authors, no one pays attention to such a taste; and we pronounce without scruple the sentiment of these pretended critics to be absurd and ridiculous. The principle of the natural equality of tastes is then totally forgot, and while we admit it on some occasions, where the objects seem near an equality, it appears an extravagant paradox, or rather a palpable absurdity, where objects so disproportioned are compared together.

It is evident that none of the rules of composition are fixed by reasonings *a priori*, or can be esteemed abstract conclusions of the understanding, from comparing those habitudes and relations of ideas which are eternal and immutable. Their foundation is the same with that of all the practical sciences – experience; nor are they anything but

---

[1] John Ogilby published verse translations of Homer and Virgil; John Milton was England's greatest epic poet; John Bunyan was the author of *The Pilgrim's Progress*, Joseph Addison a noted essayist and playwright.

general observations, concerning what has been universally found to please in all countries and in all ages...

The same Homer who pleased at Athens and Rome two thousand years ago, is still admired at Paris and at London. All the changes of climate, government, religion, and language, have not been able to obscure his glory. Authority or prejudice may give a temporary vogue to a bad poet or orator; but his reputation will never be durable or general. When his compositions are examined by posterity or by foreigners, the enchantment is dissipated, and his faults appear in their true colours. On the contrary, a real genius, the longer his works endure, and the more wide they are spread, the more sincere is the admiration which he meets with...

It appears, then, that amidst all the variety and caprice of taste, there are certain general principles of approbation or blame, whose influence a careful eye may trace in all operations of the mind. Some particular forms or qualities, from the original structure of the internal fabric, are calculated to please, and others to displease; and if they fail of their effect in any particular instance, it is from some apparent defect or imperfection in the organ. A man in a fever would not insist on his palate as able to decide concerning flavours; nor would one affected with the jaundice pretend to give a verdict with regard to colours. In each creature there is a sound and a defective state; and the former alone can be supposed to afford us a true standard of taste and sentiment. If, in the sound state of the organ, there be an entire or a considerable uniformity of sentiment among men, we may thence derive an idea of the perfect beauty; in like manner as the appearance of objects in daylight, to the eye of a man in health, is denominated their true and real colour, even while colour is allowed to be merely a phantasm of the senses.

Many and frequent are the defects in the internal organs, which prevent or weaken the influence of those general principles on which depends our sentiment of beauty or deformity. Though some objects, by the structure of the mind, be naturally calculated to give pleasure, it is not to be expected that in every individual the pleasure will be equally felt. Particular incidents and situations occur, which either throw a false light on the objects, or hinder the true from conveying to the imagination the proper sentiment and perception.

One obvious cause why many feel not the proper sentiment of beauty, is the want of that *delicacy* of imagination which is requisite to convey a sensibility of those finer emotions. This delicacy everyone pretends to: everyone talks of it; and would reduce every kind of taste or sentiment to its standard. But as our intention in this essay is to mingle some light of the understanding with the feelings of sentiment, it will be proper to give a more accurate definition of delicacy than has hitherto been attempted. And not to draw our philosophy from too profound a source, we shall have recourse to a noted story in *Don Quixote*.

It is with good reason, says Sancho to the squire with the great nose, that I pretend to have a judgement in wine: this is a quality hereditary in our family. Two of my kinsmen were once called to give their opinion of a hogshead, which was supposed to be excellent, being old and of a good vintage. One of them tastes it, considers it; and, after mature reflection, pronounces the wine to be good, were it not for a small taste of leather which he perceived in it. The other after using the same precautions, gives also his verdict in favour of the wine; but with the reserve of a taste of iron which he could easily distinguish. You cannot imagine how much they were both ridiculed for their judgement. But who laughed in the end? On emptying the hogshead, there was found at the bottom an old key with a leathern thong tied to it.

The great resemblance between mental and bodily taste will easily teach us to apply this story. Though it be certain that beauty and deformity, more than sweet and bitter, are not qualities in objects, but belong entirely to the sentiment, internal or external, it must be allowed that there are certain qualities in objects which are fitted by nature to produce those particular feelings. Now, as these qualities may be found in a small degree, or may be mixed and confounded with each other, it often happens that the taste is not affected with such minute qualities, or is not able to distinguish all the particular flavours, amidst the disorder in which they are presented. Where the organs are so fine as to allow nothing to escape them, and at the same time so exact as to perceive every ingredient in the composition, this we call delicacy of taste, whether we employ these terms in the literal or metaphorical sense. Here then the general rules of beauty are of use, being drawn from established models and from the observation of what pleases or displeases when presented singly and in a high degree; and if the same qualities, in a continued composition, and in a smaller degree, affect not the organs with a sensible delight or uneasiness, we exclude the person from all pretensions to this delicacy. To produce these general rules or avowed patterns of composition, is like finding the key with the leathern thong, which justified the verdict of Sancho's kinsmen, and confounded those pretended judges who had condemned them...

But though there be naturally a wide difference, in point of delicacy, between one person and another, nothing tends further to increase and improve this talent than *practice* in a particular art, and the frequent survey or contemplation of a particular species of beauty. When objects of any kind are first presented to the eye or imagination, the sentiment which attends them is obscure and confused; and the mind is, in a great measure, incapable of pronouncing concerning their merits or defects... But allow him to acquire experience in those objects, his feeling becomes more exact and nice: he not only perceives the beauties and defects of each part, but marks the distinguishing species of each quality, and assigns it suitable praise or blame. A clear and distinct sentiment attends him through the whole survey of the objects; and he discerns that very degree and kind of approbation or displeasure which each part is naturally fitted to produce. The mist dissipates which seemed formerly to hang over the object; the organ acquires greater perfection in its operations, and can pronounce, without danger of mistake, concerning the merits of every performance. In a word, the same address and dexterity which practice gives to the execution of any work, is also acquired by the same means in the judging of it...

It is impossible to continue in the practice of contemplating any order of beauty, without being frequently obliged to form *comparisons* between the several species and degrees of excellence, and estimating their proportion to each other. A man who has had no opportunity of comparing the different kinds of beauty is indeed totally unqualified to pronounce an opinion with regard to any object presented to him. By comparison alone we fix the epithets of praise or blame, and learn how to assign the due degree of each. The coarsest daubing contains a certain lustre of colours and exactness of imitation, which are so far beauties, and would affect the mind of a peasant or Indian with the highest admiration. The most vulgar ballads are not entirely destitute of harmony or nature; and none but a person familiarized to superior beauties would pronounce their members harsh, or narration uninteresting.

A great inferiority of beauty gives pain to a person conversant in the highest excellence of the kind, and is for that reason pronounced a deformity; as the most finished object with which we are acquainted is naturally supposed to have reached the pinnacle of perfection and to be entitled to the highest applause. One accustomed to see, and examine, and weigh the several performances admired in different ages and nations, can alone rate the merits of a work exhibited to his view, and assign its proper rank among the productions of genius...

Thus, though the principles of taste be universal, and nearly, if not entirely, the same in all men; yet few are qualified to give judgement on any work of art, or establish their own sentiment as the standard of beauty. The organs of internal sensation are seldom so perfect as to allow the general principles their full play, and produce a feeling correspondent to those principles. They either labour under some defect, or are vitiated by some disorder; and by that means excite a sentiment, which may be pronounced erroneous. When the critic has no delicacy, he judges without any distinction, and is only affected by the grosser and more palpable qualities of the object: the finer touches pass unnoticed and disregarded. Where he is not aided by practice, his verdict is attended with confusion and hesitation. Where no comparison has been employed, the most frivolous beauties, such as rather merit the name of defects, are the object of his admiration. Where he lies under the influence of prejudice, all his natural sentiments are perverted. Where good sense is wanting, he is not qualified to discern the beauties of design and reasoning, which are the highest and most excellent. Under some or other of these imperfections the generality of men labour, and hence a true judge in the finer arts is observed, even during the most polished ages, to be so rare a character: strong sense, united to delicate sentiment, improved by practice, perfected by comparison, and cleared of all prejudice, can alone entitle critics to this valuable character; and the joint verdict of such, wherever they are to be found, is the true standard of taste and beauty.

But where are such critics to be found? By what marks are they to be known? How distinguish them from pretenders? These questions are embarrassing; and seem to throw us back into the same uncertainty from which, during the course of this essay, we have endeavoured to extricate ourselves.

But if we consider the matter aright, these are questions of fact, not of sentiment. Whether any particular person be endowed with good sense and a delicate imagination, free from prejudice, may often be the subject of dispute, and be liable to great discussion and inquiry; but that such a character is valuable and estimable, will be agreed in by all mankind. Where these doubts occur, men can do no more than in other disputable questions which are submitted to the understanding: they must produce the best arguments that their invention suggests to them; they must acknowledge a true and decisive standard to exist somewhere, to wit, real existence and matter of fact; and they must have indulgence to such as differ from them in their appeals to this standard. It is sufficient for our present purpose if we have proved that the taste of all individuals is not upon an equal footing, and that some men in general, however difficult to be particularly pitched upon, will be acknowledged by universal sentiment to have a preference above others...

But notwithstanding all our endeavours to fix a standard of taste, and reconcile the discordant apprehensions of men, there still remain two sources of variation, which are not sufficient indeed to confound all the boundaries of beauty and deformity, but will often serve to produce a difference in the degrees of our approbation or blame. The one is the different humours of particular men; the other, the particular manners and opinions of our age and country. The general principles of taste are uniform in human nature: where men vary in their judgements, some defect or perversion in the faculties may commonly be remarked; proceeding either from prejudice, from want of practice, or want of delicacy: and there is just reason for approving one taste, and condemning another. But where there is such a diversity in the internal frame or external situation as is entirely blameless on both sides, and leaves no room to give one the preference above the other; in that case a certain degree of diversity in judgement is unavoidable, and we seek in vain for a standard, by which we can reconcile the contrary sentiments.

A young man, whose passions are warm, will be more, sensibly touched with amorous and tender images, than a man more advanced in years, who takes pleasure in wise, philosophical reflections, concerning the conduct of life, and moderation of the passions. At twenty, Ovid may be the favourite author, Horace at forty, and perhaps Tacitus at fifty. Vainly would we, in such cases, endeavour to enter into the sentiments of others, and divest ourselves of those propensities which are natural to us. We choose our favourite author as we do our friend, from a conformity of humour and disposition. Mirth or passion, sentiment or reflection; whichever of these most predominates in our temper, it gives us a peculiar sympathy with the writer who resembles us . . . Such performances are innocent and unavoidable, and can never reasonably be the object of dispute, because there is no standard by which they can be decided.

For a like reason, we are more pleased, in the course of our reading, with pictures and characters that resemble objects which are found in our own age and country than with those which describe a different set of customs. It is not without some effort that we reconcile ourselves to the simplicity of ancient manners, and behold princesses carrying water from the spring, and kings and heroes dressing their own victuals. We may allow in general that the representation of such manners is no fault in the author, nor deformity in the piece; but we are not so sensibly touched with them . . .

5   The Concept of the Beautiful: Immanuel Kant, *Critique of Judgement**

Some of the questions raised in Hume's essay about the objectivity of aesthetic appreciation (see previous extract) were systematically taken up later in the eighteenth century in Immanuel Kant's *Critique of Judgement*, sometimes known as the 'Third Critique'.[1] Kant begins by stating that a judgement of taste depends on feelings of pleasure or displeasure, and therefore 'is not a cognitive judgement'; its 'determining ground', he maintains, 'cannot be other than subjective'. He then goes on to contrast the 'pure disinterested delight: which appears in the judgement of taste'

---

* Immanuel Kant, *Critique of Judgement* [*Kritik der Urteilskraft*, 1790], Part I, Bk I, §§ 1–7. Trans. J. C. Meredith (Oxford: Clarendon, 1928), pp. 41–53; with omissions.

[1] The first two were the *Critique of Pure Reason* [1781] and the *Critique of Practical Reason* [1788]. For an excerpt from the First Critique, see Part I, extract 8, above.

with the kind of delight we feel in what is *agreeable* to us (what is associated with the pursuit of personal gratification or enjoyment), and the kind of delight we feel in what is *good*. Both these latter kinds of delight are connected with some kind of interest (in the first case, our interest in sensory gratification, which we share with animals; in the second case our rational interest in what has objective worth). Only our delight in the beautiful is 'disinterested and *free* delight'; hence Kant goes on to define the beautiful as 'an object of delight apart from any interest'.

This notion of pure and free delight, whose determining ground is 'entirely subjective', might suggest that Kant was about to claim aesthetic judgement was purely a matter of private preference. But though it arises from a subjective feeling, Kant insists that our judgement of something as beautiful involves representing it as an object of *universal* delight. In the case of something which is merely agreeable or gratifying, the maxim 'each to his own taste' indeed holds good (you may find a violet shade 'soft and lovely' while I find it 'dull and faded'). But when someone calls something *beautiful* 'he judges not merely for himself but for all men, and... demands ... agreement of them'. This universality is something Kant directly connects with his definition of the beautiful as involving disinterested delight: if someone is 'conscious that his delight in an object is with him independent of interest', then he will inevitably 'look on the object as one containing a ground of delight for all men'. If Kant's theory is correct, then there is something absurd about people saying (as they often do) '*for me*, this is beautiful'. The striking feature of Kant's theory is the way it combines the demand for universality with the absence of any rational rule or cognitive procedure for settling aesthetic disagreements.

The judgement of taste is aesthetic

If we wish to discern whether anything is beautiful or not, we do not refer the representation of it to the object by means of understanding with a view to cognition, but by means of the imagination (acting perhaps in conjunction with understanding) we refer the representation to the subject and its feeling of pleasure or displeasure. The judgement of taste, therefore, is not a cognitive judgement, and so not logical, but is aesthetic – which means that it is one whose determining ground *cannot be other than subjective*. Every reference of representations is capable of being objective, even that of sensations (in which case it signifies the real in an empirical representation). The one exception to this is the feeling of pleasure or displeasure. This denotes nothing in the object, but is a feeling which the subject has of itself and of the manner in which it is affected by the representation.

To apprehend a regular and appropriate building with one's cognitive faculties, be the mode of representation clear or confused, is quite a different thing from being conscious of this representation with an accompanying sensation of delight. Here the representation is referred wholly to the subject, and what is more to its feeling of life – under the name of the feeling of pleasure or displeasure – and this forms the basis of a quite separate faculty of discriminating and estimating, that contributes nothing to knowledge. All it does is to compare the given representation in the subject with the entire faculty of representations of which the mind is conscious in the feeling of its state. Given representations in a judgement may be empirical, and so aesthetic; but the judgement which is pronounced by their means is logical, provided it refers them to the object. Conversely, be the given representations even rational, but referred in a judgement solely to the subject (to its feeling), they are always to that extent aesthetic.

The delight which determines the judgement of taste is independent of all interest

The delight which we connect with the representation of the real existence of an object is called interest. Such a delight, therefore, always involves a reference to the faculty of desire, either as its determining ground, or else as necessarily implicated with its determining ground. Now, where the question is whether something is beautiful, we do not want to know whether we, or anyone else, are, or even could be, concerned in the real existence of the thing, but rather what estimate we form of it on mere contemplation (intuition or reflection). If anyone asks me whether I consider that the palace I see before me is beautiful, I may, perhaps, reply that I do not care for things of that sort that are merely made to be gaped at. Or I may reply in the same strain as that Iroquois *sachem* who said that nothing in Paris pleased him better than the eating-houses. I may even go a step further and inveigh with the vigour of a Rousseau against the vanity of the great who spend the sweat of the people on such superfluous things. Or, in fine, I may quite easily persuade myself that if I found myself on an uninhabited island, without hope of ever again coming among men, and could conjure such a palace into existence by a mere wish, I should still not trouble to do so, so long as I had a hut there that was comfortable enough for me. All this may be admitted and approved, only it is not the point now at issue. All one wants to know is whether the mere representation of the object is to my liking, no matter how indifferent I may be to the real existence of the object of this representation. It is quite plain that in order to say that the object is *beautiful*, and to show that I have taste, everything turns on the meaning which I can give to this representation, and not on any factor which makes me dependent on the real existence of the object. Every one must allow that a judgement on the beautiful which is tinged with the slightest interest, is very partial and not a pure judgement of taste. One must not be in the least prepossessed in favour of the real existence of the thing, but must preserve complete indifference in this respect, in order to play the part of judge in matters of taste.

This proposition, which is of the utmost importance, cannot be better explained than by contrasting the pure disinterested delight which appears in the judgement of taste with that allied to an interest – especially if we can also assure ourselves that there are no other kinds of interest beyond those presently to be mentioned.

Delight in the agreeable is coupled with interest

That is *agreeable* which the senses *find pleasing in sensation*... Now, that a judgement on an object by which its agreeableness is affirmed, expresses an interest in it, is evident from the fact that through sensation it provokes a desire for similar objects, consequently the delight presupposes, not the simple judgement about it, but the bearing its real existence has upon my state so far as affected by such an object. Hence we do not merely say of the agreeable that it *pleases*, but that it *gratifies*. I do not accord it a simple approval, but inclination is aroused by it, and where agreeableness is of the liveliest type a judgement on the character of the object is so entirely out of place, that those who are always intent only on enjoyment (for that is the word used to denote intensity of gratification) would fain dispense with all judgement.

Delight in the good is coupled with interest

That is *good* which by means of reason commends itself by its mere concept. We call that *good for something* (useful) which only pleases as a means; but that which pleases on its own account we call *good in itself.* In both cases the concept of an end is implied, and consequently the relation of reason to (at least possible) willing, and thus a delight in the *existence* of an object or action, i.e. some interest or other.

To deem something good, I must always know what sort of a thing the object is intended to be, i.e. I must have a concept of it. That is not necessary to enable me to see beauty in a thing. Flowers, free patterns, lines aimlessly intertwining – technically termed foliage – have no signification, depend upon no definite concept, and yet please. Delight in the beautiful must depend upon the reflection on an object precursory to some (not definitely determined) concept. It is thus also differentiated from the agreeable, which rests entirely upon sensation.

In many cases, no doubt, the agreeable and the good seem convertible terms. Thus it is commonly said that all (especially lasting) gratification is of itself good; which is almost equivalent to saying that to be permanently agreeable and to be good are identical. But it is readily apparent that this is merely a vicious confusion of words, for the concepts appropriate to these expressions are far from interchangeable. The agreeable, which, as such, represents the object solely in relation to sense, must in the first instance be brought under principles of reason through the concept of an end, to be, as an object of will, called good. But that the reference to delight is wholly different where what gratifies is at the same time called *good* is evident from the fact that with the good the question always is whether it is mediately or immediately good, i.e. useful or good in itself; whereas with the agreeable this point can never arise, since the word always means what pleases immediately – and it is just the same with what I call beautiful.

Even in everyday parlance a distinction is drawn between the agreeable and the good. We do not scruple to say of a dish that stimulates the palate with spices and other condiments that it is agreeable – owning all the while that it is not good: because, while it immediately *satisfies* the senses, it is mediately displeasing, i.e. in the eye of reason that looks ahead to the consequences. Even in our estimate of health this same distinction may be traced. To all that possess it, it is immediately agreeable – at least negatively, i.e. as remoteness of all bodily pains. But, if we are to say that it is good, we must further apply to reason to direct it to ends, that is, we must regard it as a state that puts us in a congenial mood for all we have to do. Finally, in respect of happiness, everyone believes that the greatest aggregate of the pleasures of life, taking duration as well as number into account, merits the name of a true, nay even of the highest, good. But reason sets its face against this too. Agreeableness is enjoyment. But if this is all that we are bent on, it would be foolish to be scrupulous about the means that procure it for us – whether it be obtained passively by the bounty of nature or actively and by the work of our own hands. But that there is any intrinsic worth in the real existence of a man who merely lives for *enjoyment* (however busy he may be in this respect, even when in so doing he serves others – all equally with himself intent only on enjoyment – as an excellent means to that one end, and does so, moreover, because through sympathy he shares all their gratifications) – this is a view to which reason will never let itself be brought round. Only by what a man does heedless of enjoyment, in complete freedom and independently of what he can procure passively from the hand of nature, does he give to his existence, as the real existence of a person, an absolute worth. Happiness, with all its plethora of pleasures, is far from being an unconditioned good.[1]

But, despite all this difference between the agreeable and the good, they both agree in being invariably coupled with an interest in their object. This is true, not alone of the agreeable, and of the mediately good, i.e. the useful, which pleases as a means to some pleasure, but also of that which is good absolutely and from every point of view, namely the moral good which carries with it the highest interest. For the good is the object of will, i.e. of a rationally determined faculty of desire. But to will something, and to take a delight in its existence, i.e. to take an interest in it, are identical.

Comparison of three specifically different kinds of delight

Both the agreeable and the good involve a reference to the faculty of desire, and are thus attended, the former with a delight pathologically conditioned (by stimuli), the latter with a pure practical delight. Such delight is determined not merely by the representation of the object, but also by the represented bond of connection between the subject and the real existence of the object. It is not merely the object, but also its real existence, that pleases. On the other hand the judgement of taste is simply *contemplative*, i.e. it is a judgement which is indifferent as to the existence of an object, and only decides how its character stands with the feeling of pleasure and displeasure. But not even is this contemplation itself directed to concepts; for the judgement of taste is not a cognitive judgement (neither a theoretical one nor a practical), and hence, also, is not *grounded* on concepts, nor yet *intentionally directed* to them.

The agreeable, the beautiful and the good thus denote three different relations of representations to the feeling of pleasure and displeasure, as a feeling in respect of which we distinguish different objects or modes of representation. Also, the corresponding expressions which indicate our satisfaction in them are different. The *agreeable* is what *gratifies* a man; the *beautiful* what simply *pleases* him; the *good* what is *esteemed* (*approved*), i.e. that on which he sets an objective worth. Agreeableness is a significant factor even with irrational animals; beauty has purport and significance only for human beings, i.e. for beings at once animal and rational (but not merely for them as rational – intelligent beings – but only for them as at once animal and rational); whereas the good is good for every rational being in general. Of all these three kinds of delight, that of taste in the beautiful may be said to be the one and only disinterested and *free* delight; for, with it, no interest, whether of sense or reason, extorts approval. And so we may say that delight, in the three cases mentioned, is related to *inclination*, to *favour*, or to *respect*. For favour is the only free liking. An object of inclination, and one which a law of reason imposes upon our

---

[1] *An obligation to enjoyment is a patent absurdity. And the same, then, must also be said of a supposed obligation to actions that have merely enjoyment for their aim, no matter how spiritually this enjoyment may be refined in thought (or embellished), and even if it be a mystical, so-called heavenly, enjoyment.

desire, leaves us no freedom to turn anything into an object of pleasure. All interest presupposes a want, or calls one forth; and, being a ground determining approval, deprives the judgement on the object of its freedom.

So far as the interest of inclination in the case of the agreeable goes, everyone says hunger is the best sauce; and people with a healthy appetite relish everything, so long as it is something they can eat. Such delight, consequently, gives no indication of taste having anything to say to the choice. Only when men have got all they want can we tell who among the crowd has taste or not. Similarly there may be correct habits (conduct) without virtue, politeness without goodwill, propriety without honour, &c. For where the moral law dictates, there is, objectively, no room left for free choice as to what one has to do; and to show taste in the way one carries out these dictates, or in estimating the way others do so, is a totally different matter from displaying the moral frame of one's mind. For the latter involves a command and produces a need of something, whereas moral taste only plays with the objects of delight without devoting itself sincerely to any.

Definition of the beautiful derived from [the foregoing]

Taste is the faculty of estimating an object or a mode of representation by means of a delight or aversion *apart from any interest*. The object of such a delight is called *beautiful*.

The beautiful is that which apart from concepts is represented as the object of a UNIVERSAL delight

This definition of the beautiful is deducible from the foregoing definition of it as an object of delight apart from any interest. For where any one is conscious that his delight in an object is with him independent of interest, it is inevitable that he should look on the object as one containing a ground of delight for all men. For, since the delight is not based on any inclination of the subject (or on any other deliberate interest), but the subject feels himself completely free in respect of the liking which he accords to the object, he can find as reason for his delight no personal conditions to which his own subjective self might alone be party. Hence he must regard it as resting on what he may also presuppose in every other person; and therefore he must believe that he has reason for demanding a similar delight from everyone. Accordingly he will speak of the beautiful as if beauty were a quality of the object and the judgement logical (forming a cognition of the object by concepts of it); although it is only aesthetic, and contains merely a reference of the representation of the object to the subject; – because it still bears this resemblance to the logical judgement, that it may be presupposed to be valid for all men. But this universality cannot spring from concepts. For from concepts there is no transition to the feeling of pleasure or displeasure (save in the case of pure practical laws, which, however, carry an interest with them; and such an interest does not attach to the pure judgement of taste). The result is that the judgement of taste, with its attendant consciousness of detachment from all interest, must involve a claim to validity for all men, and must do so apart from universality attached to objects, i.e. there must be coupled with it a claim to subjective universality.

Comparison of the beautiful with the agreeable and the good by means of the above characteristic

As regards the *agreeable*, everyone concedes that his judgement, which he bases on a private feeling, and in which he declares that an object pleases him, is restricted merely to himself personally. Thus he does not take it amiss if, when he says that Canary-wine is agreeable, another corrects the expression and reminds him that he ought to say: It is agreeable *to me*. This applies not only to the taste of the tongue, the palate and the throat, but to what may with anyone be agreeable to eye or ear. A violet colour is to one soft and lovely: to another dull and faded. One man likes the tone of wind instruments, another prefers that of string instruments. To quarrel over such points with the idea of condemning another's judgement as incorrect when it differs from our own, as if the opposition between the two judgements were logical, would be folly. With the agreeable, therefore, the axiom holds good: *Every one has his own taste* (that of sense).

The beautiful stands on quite a different footing. It would, on the contrary, be ridiculous if any one who plumed himself on his taste were to think of justifying himself by saying: This object (the building we see, the dress that person has on, the concert we hear, the poem submitted to our criticism) is beautiful *for me*. For if it merely pleases him, he must not call it *beautiful*. Many things may for him possess charm and agreeableness – no one cares about that; but when he puts a thing on a pedestal and calls it beautiful, he demands the same delight from others. He judges not merely for himself, but for all men, and then speaks of beauty as if it were a property of things. Thus he says the *thing* is beautiful; and it is not as if he counted on others agreeing in his judgement of liking owing to his having found them in such agreement on a number of occasions, but he *demands* this agreement of them. He blames them if they judge differently, and denies them taste, which he still requires of them as something they ought to have; and to this extent it is not open to men to say: Every one has his own taste. This would be equivalent to saying that there is no such thing at all as taste, i.e. no aesthetic judgement capable of making a rightful claim upon the assent of all men.

Yet even in the case of the agreeable we find that the estimates men form betray a prevalent agreement among them…So of one who knows how to entertain his guests…in such a way that one and all are pleased, we say he has taste. But the universality here is only understood in a comparative sense; and the rules that apply are, like all empirical rules, *general* only, not *universal* – the latter being what the judgement of taste upon the beautiful is or claims to deal in…In respect of the good it is true that judgements also rightly assert a claim to validity for everyone; but the good is only represented as an object of universal delight by means of a concept, which is the case neither with the agreeable nor with the beautiful.

6 The Metaphysics of Beauty: Arthur Schopenhauer, *On Aesthetics**

Our next extract, from a collection of essays published in the mid-nineteenth century by the German philosopher Arthur Schopenhauer, makes an original and in some respects idiosyncratic contribution to aesthetics, which at the same time connects up with several of the ideas raised by his predecessors. Schopenhauer's metaphysics assigns primacy to the *will* as the ultimate reality underlying all the phenomena apprehended or represented by the mind; as he says below, 'the world as *will* is the first world, and the world as representation the second' (see further Part IV, extract 7, above). All our human activities (the search for knowledge, 'affairs of state', 'matters of finance or trade', and so on) reflect the will and its strivings; but 'original artistic knowledge' is exceptional, in being 'entirely separate from, and independent of, the will'. There is a kind of 'purely objective intuitive perception' which is the 'kernel and as it were soul of a genuine work of art'; in this state of will-less 'pure knowing', we can apprehend the 'objective original essence of things which constitutes their Platonic idea'.

We are partly reminded here of Kant's notion of aesthetic appreciation as pure delight detached from any interest of the subject (see previous extract). Unlike Kant, however, Schopenhauer here sees our apprehension of the beautiful very much in cognitive terms – as related to the pure Ideas or essences of things. Yet the reference to Plato in fact conceals a radical transformation

of Plato's view of art. Plato, as we saw earlier (extract 1, above) criticized artistic representation precisely for its particularity – the painting, for example, was a mere copy of an individual object, which itself was far removed from the universal Form. Schopenhauer aptly turns this around, pointing out that for the artist 'one case applies to thousands'; the artist takes 'an event, a scene from human life, and . . . with an exact presentation of the individuals concerned therein, gives us a clear and profound knowledge of the Idea of humanity itself'. This is as far removed as one could imagine from Plato's derogatory view of art as mere 'imitation'. A mere copy, like a waxwork, Schopenhauer points out, is devoid of artistic beauty; only when the individual painting or poem takes the particular as an icon of something more universal do we enter the realm of true art. In the final part of our excerpt we see a more controversial part of Schopenhauer's theory of art: his attempt to connect our sense of beauty with our response to life and energy – in short with the Will which he regards as the ultimate basis for all things. Music turns out to have a special status here, since for Schopenhauer it is, or should be, entirely non-representational, speaking 'not of things but simply of weal and woe as being *for the will* the sole realities'. Many critics have been distinctly unimpressed with Schopenhauer's claim about the special status of music, while for others it has seemed to hint at a profound truth.[1]

The real problem of the metaphysics of the beautiful may be very simply expressed by our asking how satisfaction with and pleasure in an object are possible without any reference thereof to our willing.

   Thus everyone feels that pleasure and satisfaction in a thing can really spring only from its relation to our will or, as we are fond of expressing it, to our aims, so that pleasure without a stirring of the will seems to be a contradiction. Yet the beautiful, as

---

* From Arthur Schopenhauer, *Parerga and Paralipomena* [1851], trans. E. F. J. Payne (Oxford: Clarendon, 1974), vol. II, ch. 19, §§ 205–10, 212–13, 218; with omissions and a few minor modifications.

[1] Among those strongly influenced by Schopenhauer was the composer Richard Wagner. The philosopher Nietzsche was also a great enthusiast for Schopenhauer's ideas when he wrote *The Birth of Tragedy* (see extract 7, below).

such, quite obviously gives rise to our delight and pleasure, without its having any reference to our personal aims and so to our will.

My solution has been that in the beautiful we always perceive the essential and original forms of animate and inanimate nature and thus Plato's Ideas thereof, and that this perception has as its condition their essential correlative, the *will-free subject of knowing*, in other words a pure intelligence without aims and intentions. On the occurrence of an aesthetic apprehension, the will thereby vanishes entirely from consciousness. But it alone is the source of all our sorrows and sufferings. This is the origin of that satisfaction and pleasure which accompany the apprehension of the beautiful. It therefore rests on the removal of the entire possibility of suffering. If it should be objected that the possibility of pleasure would then also be abolished, it should be remembered that, as I have often explained, happiness or satisfaction is of a *negative* nature, that is, simply the end of a suffering, whereas pain is that which is positive. And so with the disappearance of all willing from consciousness, there yet remains the state of pleasure, in other words absence of all pain, and here even absence of the possibility thereof. For the individual is transformed into a subject that merely knows and no longer wills; and yet he remains conscious of himself and of his activity precisely as such. As we know, the world as *will* is the first world, and the world as *representation*, the second. The former is the world of craving and therefore of pain and a thousand different woes. The latter, however, is in itself essentially painless; moreover, it contains a spectacle worth seeing, altogether significant, and at least entertaining. Aesthetic pleasure consists in the enjoyment thereof. To become a pure subject of knowing means to be quit of oneself; but since in most cases people cannot do this, they are, as a rule, incapable of that purely objective apprehension of things, which constitutes the gift of the artist.

However, let the individual will leave free for a while the power of representation which is assigned to it, and let it exempt this entirely from the service for which it has arisen and exists, so that, for the time being, such power relinquishes concern for the will or for one's own person, this being its only natural theme and thus its regular business; yet it does not cease to be energetically active and to apprehend clearly and with rapt attention what is intuitively perceptible. That power of representation then becomes at once perfectly *objective*, that is to say, the true mirror of objects or, more precisely, the medium of the objectification of the will that manifests itself in the objects in question. The inner nature of the will now stands out in the power of representation the more completely, the longer intuitive perception is kept up, until it has entirely exhausted that inner nature. Only thus does there arise with the pure subject the pure object, that is, the perfect manifestation of the will that appears in the intuitively perceived object, this manifestation being just the (Platonic) *Idea* thereof.

But the apprehension of such an Idea requires that, while contemplating an object, I disregard its position in time and space and thus its individuality. For it is this *position* which is always determined by the law of causality and puts that object in some relation to me as an individual. Therefore only when that position is set aside does the object become the *Idea* and do I at the same time become the pure subject of knowing. Thus through the fact that every painting for ever fixes the fleeting moment and tears it from time, it already gives us not the individual thing, but the *Idea* – that which endures and is permanent in all change. Now for that required change in the subject and object, the condition is not only that the power of knowledge is withdrawn from its original servitude and left entirely to itself, but also that it nevertheless remains active with the whole of its energy, in spite of the fact that the natural spur of its activity, the impulse of the will, is now absent. Here lies the difficulty and in this the rarity of the thing; for all our thoughts and aspirations, all our seeing and hearing, are naturally always in the direct or indirect service of our countless greater and smaller personal aims. Accordingly it is the *will* that urges the power of knowledge to carry out its function and, without such impulse, that power at once grows weary. Moreover, the knowledge thereby awakened is perfectly adequate for practical life, even for the special branches of science which are directed always only to the *relations* of things, not to the real and true inner nature thereof... Thus wherever it is a question of knowledge of cause and effect, or of other grounds and consequents, and hence in all branches of natural science and mathematics, as also of history, inventions, and so forth, the knowledge sought must be a *purpose of the will*, and the more eagerly this aspires to it, the sooner will it be attained. Similarly, in the affairs of state, war, matters of finance or trade, intrigues of every kind, and so on, the *will* through the vehemence of its craving must first compel the intellect to exert all its strength in order to discover the exact clue to all the grounds and consequents in the case in question. In fact, it is astonishing how far the spur of the will can here drive a given intellect beyond the usual degree of its powers. And so for all outstanding achievements in such things, not merely a fine or brilliant mind is required, but also an energetic will which must first urge the intellect to laborious effort and restless activity, without which such achievements cannot be effected.

Now it is quite different as regards the apprehension of the objective original essence of things which constitutes their (Platonic) Idea and must be the basis of every achievement in the fine arts. The will, which was there so necessary and indeed indispensable, must here be left wholly out of the question; for here only that is of any use which the intellect achieves entirely of itself and from its own resources and produces as a free-will offering. Here everything must go automatically; knowledge must be active without intention and so must be will-less. For only in the state of *pure knowing*, where a man's will and its aims together with his individuality are entirely removed from him, can that purely objective intuitive perception arise wherein the (Platonic) Ideas of things are apprehended. But it must always be such an apprehension which precedes the conception, i.e. the first and always intuitive knowledge. This subsequently constitutes the real material and kernel, as it were the soul, of a genuine work of art, a poem, and even a real philosophical argument. The unpremeditated, unintentional, and indeed partly unconscious and instinctive element that has at all times been observed in the works of *genius*, is just a consequence of the fact that the original artistic knowledge is one that is entirely separate from, and independent of, the will, a will-free, will-less knowledge...

Now as regards the *objective* element of such aesthetic intuitive perception, the (Platonic) Idea, this may be described as that which we should have before us if time, this formal and subjective condition of our knowledge, were withdrawn, like the glass from the kaleidoscope. For example, we see the development of the bud, blossom and fruit and are astonished at the driving force that never wearies of again going through this cycle. Such astonishment would vanish if we could know that, in spite of all that change, we have before us the one and unalterable Idea of the plant. However, we are unable intuitively to perceive this Idea as a unity of bud, blossom and fruit, but are obliged to know it by means of the form of time, whereby it is laid out for our intellect in those successive states.

If we consider that both poetry and the plastic arts take as their particular theme an *individual* in order to present this with the greatest care and accuracy in all the peculiarities of its individual nature down to the most insignificant; and if we then review the sciences that work by means of *concepts*, each of which represents countless individuals by determining and describing, once for all, the characteristic of their whole species; then on such a consideration the pursuit of art might seem to us insignificant, trifling, and almost childish. But the essence of art is that its one case applies to thousands, since what it implies through that careful and detailed presentation of the individual is the revelation of the (Platonic) *Idea* of that individual's species. For example, an event, a scene from human life, accurately and fully described and thus with an exact presentation of the individuals concerned therein, gives us a clear and profound knowledge of the Idea of humanity itself, looked at from some point of view. For just as the botanist plucks a single flower from the infinite wealth of the plant world and then dissects it in order to demonstrate the nature of the plant generally, so does the poet take from the endless maze and confusion of human life, incessantly hurrying everywhere, a single scene and often only a mood or feeling, in order then to show us what are the life and true nature of man. We therefore see that the greatest minds, Shakespeare and Goethe, Raphael and Rembrandt, do not regard it beneath their dignity to present with the greatest accuracy, earnestness and care an individual who is not even outstanding, and to give down to the smallest detail a graphic description of all his peculiarities. For only through intuitive perception is the particular and individual thing grasped; I have, therefore, defined poetry as the art of bringing the imagination into play by means of words...

The work of plastic art does not, like reality, show us that which exists only once and never again – thus the combination of *this* matter with *this* form, such combination constituting just the concrete and really particular thing – but it shows us *the form alone*, which would be the Idea itself if only it were given completely and from every point of view. Consequently, the picture at once leads us away from the individual to the mere form. This separation of the form from matter already brings it so much nearer to the Idea. But every picture is such a separation, whether it be a painting or a statue. This severance, this separation, of the form from matter belongs, therefore, to the character of the aesthetic work of art, just because the purpose thereof is to bring us to the knowledge of a (Platonic) *Idea*. It is, therefore, *essential* to the work of art to give the form alone without matter, and indeed to do this openly and avowedly. Here is to be found the real reason why wax figures make no aesthetic impression and are, therefore, not works of art (in the aesthetic sense); although, if they are well made, they produce a hundred times more illusion than can the best picture or statue. If deceptive imitation of the actual thing were the purpose of art, wax figures would necessarily occupy the front rank. Thus they appear to give not merely the form, but also the matter as well; and so they produce the illusion of our having before us the thing itself. Instead of having the true work of art that leads us away from what exists only once and never again, i.e. the individual, to what always exists an infinite number of times, in an infinite number of individuals, i.e. the mere form or Idea, we have the wax figure giving us apparently the individual himself and hence that which exists only once and never again, yet without that which lends value to such a fleeting existence, that is, without life. Therefore the wax figure causes us to shudder since its effect is like that of a stiff corpse...

The impressions we receive in our youth are so significant and in the dawn of life everything presents itself in such idealistic and radiant colours. This springs from the fact that the individual thing still makes us first acquainted with its species, which to us is still new; and thus every particular thing represents for us its species. Accordingly, we apprehend in it the (Platonic) Idea of that species to which as such beauty is essential...

Beauty and grace of the human form are in combination the clearest visibility of the will at the highest stage of its objectification and for this reason are the supreme achievement of plastic art. Yet every natural thing is certainly beautiful... and so too is every animal. If this is not obvious to us in the case of some animals, the reason is that we are not in a position to contemplate them purely objectively and thus to apprehend their Idea, but are drawn away therefrom by some unavoidable association of thoughts. In most cases, this is the result of a similarity that forces itself on us, for example, that between man and monkey. Thus we do not apprehend the Idea of this animal, but see only the caricature of a human being. The similarity between the toad and dirt and mud seems to act in just the same way. Nevertheless, this does not suffice here to explain the unbounded loathing and even dread and horror which some feel at the sight of these animals, just as do others at the sight of spiders...

In so far as inorganic nature does not consist of water, it has a very sad and even depressing effect on us when it manifests itself without anything organic. Instances of this are the districts that present us with merely bare rocks, particularly the long rocky valley without any vegetation, not far from Toulon, through which passes the road to Marseilles. The African desert is an instance on a large and much more impressive scale. The gloom of that impression of the inorganic springs primarily from the fact that the inorganic mass obeys exclusively the law of gravitation; and thus everything here tends in that direction. On the other hand, the sight of vegetation delights us directly and in a high degree, but naturally the more so, the richer, more varied, more extended it is, and also the more it is left to itself. The primary reason for this is to be found in the fact that the law of gravitation seems in vegetation to be overcome, since the plant world raises itself in a direction which is the very opposite to that of gravitation. The phenomenon of life thus immediately proclaims itself to be a new and higher order of things. We ourselves belong to this; it is akin to us and is the element of our existence; our hearts are uplifted by it. And so it is primarily that vertical direction upwards whereby the sight of the plant world directly delights us. Therefore a fine group of trees gains immensely if a couple of long, straight and pointed fir trees rise from its middle. On the other hand, a tree lopped all round no longer affects us; indeed a leaning tree has less effect than has one that has grown perfectly straight. The branches of the weeping willow which hang down and thus yield to gravity have given it this name. Water eliminates the sad and depressing effect of its inorganic nature to a large extent through its great mobility which gives it an appearance of life and through its constant play with light; moreover, it is the primary and fundamental condition of all life...

Music is the true universal language which is everywhere understood; and so it is constantly spoken in all countries and throughout the centuries most eagerly and earnestly, and a significant and suggestive melody very soon finds its way round the globe. On the other hand, a melody that is poor and says nothing soon dies away and is forgotten; which shows that the contents of a melody are very easy to understand. Nevertheless music speaks not of things, but simply of weal and woe as being for the will the sole realities. It therefore says so much to the heart, whereas to the head it has nothing direct to say; and it is an improper use if this is required of it, as happens in all *descriptive* music. Such music should therefore be rejected once for all, even though Haydn and Beethoven have been misguided into using it. Mozart and Rossini have, to my knowledge, never done this. For to express passions is one thing and to paint objects another…

7 The Two Faces of Art: Friedrich Nietzsche, *The Birth of Tragedy**

The writings of Schopenhauer (see previous extract) had a profound effect on the early development of the author of our next extract, the German poet and philosopher Friedrich Nietzsche. The general tenor of early nineteenth-century European thought is often labelled 'romanticism' – a term widely used to emphasize the importance given to the imagination, in contrast with the calmer, more rational approach to philosophy and the arts in the eighteenth-century 'enlightenment'. Though this classification is a very crude and schematic one, it does serve to indicate a broad shift of outlook in the arts that was well established in Europe by the birth of Nietzsche in 1844. As the following extract shows, the style and content of Nietzsche's writing take us worlds away from the urbane inquiries of Hutcheson and Hume (extracts 3 and 4, above), or even the carefully systematic argumentation of Kant (extract 5).

Articulating what has since become a famous contrast, Nietzsche outlines a fundamental duality in the arts, corresponding to the separate domains of the two ancient Greek art deities, Apollo and Dionysus. The gods stand respectively for the 'separate art-worlds of dreams and of intoxication'. Apollo is for Nietzsche the 'ruler over the beautiful illusion of the inner world of fantasy'. The world of our dreams is a 'creation of which every man is truly an artist'; the 'profound

delight and joyous necessity' experienced in our dreams stems from the same creative source that powers all art. But although it taps this creative source, Apollonian art nevertheless maintains a 'measured restraint', a 'freedom from the wilder emotions'. The darker, more frightening, more impersonal forces of the unconscious mind are still kept in check. Only in Dionysian art – typified in the frenzied singing and dancing of orgiastic festivals – do these wilder forces break through. Nietzsche describes the Dionysian state as one of ecstasy, in which the self is submerged, and the Apollonian 'principle of individuation' gives way to a sense of 'primordial unity' between man and man, and man and nature.

Though the Apollonian and the Dionysian are in tension, they none the less both correspond to parts of our human nature, and Nietzsche sees ancient Greek tragedy as involving a kind of synthesis of both elements, in which art is realized 'in both dreams and ecstasies'. All this may seem far removed from the meticulous survey of the elements of tragedy provided by Aristotle (extract 2, above). Nevertheless, the Aristotelian account of tragedy as a 'purging of the emotions by pity and terror' indicates an awareness of the profound and complex psychic changes which great art aims to generate. Nietzsche's fiercely original description of those changes points to

---

* Friedrich Nietzsche, *The Birth of Tragedy* [*Die Geburt der Tragödie*, 1872], sections 1 and 2. Trans. W. Kaufmann (New York: Random House, 1967).

how much of the artistic process is beyond easy reach of the analysing intellect. Many readers of *The Birth of Tragedy* have seen it as prefiguring ways of looking at the arts which have only become widespread much later, with the spread of psychoanalytic ideas. Though his powerful images defy neat interpretation, at least part of what Nietzsche suggests is that the power of great art hinges on the working out of a dynamic tension between individual self-conscious awareness, and a 'letting go' or yielding to the more mysterious forces of the unconscious mind.

We shall have gained much for the science of aesthetics, once we perceive not merely by logical inference, but with the immediate certainty of vision, that the continuous development of art is bound up with the *Apollonian* and *Dionysian* duality – just as procreation depends on the duality of the sexes, involving perpetual strife with only periodically intervening reconciliations. The terms Dionysian and Apollonian we borrow from the Greeks, who disclose to the discerning mind the profound mysteries of their view of art, not, to be sure, in concepts, but in the intensely clear figures of their gods. Through Apollo and Dionysus, the two art deities of the Greeks, we come to recognize that in the Greek world there existed a tremendous opposition, in origin and aims, between the Apollonian art of sculpture, and the non-imagistic, Dionysian art of music. These two different tendencies run parallel to each other, for the most part openly at variance; and they continually incite each other to new and more powerful births, which perpetuate an antagonism only superficially reconciled by the common term 'art'; till eventually, by a metaphysical miracle of the Hellenic 'will', they appear coupled with each other, and through this coupling ultimately generate an equally Dionysian and Apollonian form of art – Attic tragedy.

In order to grasp these two tendencies, let us first conceive of them as the separate art worlds of *dreams* and *intoxication*. These physiological phenomena present a contrast analogous to that existing between the Apollonian and the Dionysian. It was in dreams, says Lucretius, that the glorious divine figures first appeared to the souls of men; in dreams the great shaper beheld the splendid bodies of superhuman beings; and the Hellenic poet, if questioned about the mysteries of poetic inspiration, would likewise have suggested dreams, and he might have given an explanation like that of Hans Sachs in Wagner's *Meister-singer*:

> The poet's task is this, my friend,
> to read his dreams and comprehend.
> The truest human fancy seems
> to be revealed to us in dreams:
> all poems and versification
> are but true dreams' interpretation.

The beautiful illusion of the dream worlds, in the creation of which every man is truly an artist, is the prerequisite of all plastic art, and of an important part of poetry also. In our dreams we delight in the immediate understanding of figures; all forms speak to us; there is nothing unimportant or superfluous. But even when this dream reality is most intense, we still have, glimmering through it, the sensation that it is *mere appearance*: at least this is my experience, and for its frequency – indeed, normality – I could adduce many proofs, including the sayings of the poets.

Philosophical men have a presentiment that the reality in which we live and have our being is also mere appearance, and that another, quite different reality lies beneath it. Schopenhauer actually indicates as the criterion of philosophical ability the occasional ability to view men and things as mere phantoms or dream images. Thus the aesthetically sensitive man stands in the same relation to the reality of dreams as the philosopher does to the reality of existence; he is a close and willing observer, for these images afford him an interpretation of life, and by reflecting on these processes he trains himself for life.

It is not only the agreeable and friendly images that he experiences as something universally intelligible. The serious, the troubled, the sad, the gloomy, the sudden restraints, the tricks of accident, anxious expectations, in short, the whole divine comedy of life, including the inferno, also pass before him, not like mere shadows on a wall – for he lives and suffers with these scenes – and yet not without that fleeting sensation of illusion. And perhaps many will, like myself, recall how amid the dangers and terrors of dreams they have occasionally said to themselves in self-encouragement and not without success: 'It is a dream! I will dream on!' I have likewise heard of people who were able to continue one and the same dream for three and even more successive nights – facts which indicate clearly how our innermost being, our common ground, experiences dreams with profound delight and a joyous necessity.

This joyous necessity of the dream experience has been embodied by the Greeks in their Apollo: Apollo, the god of all plastic energies, is at the same time the soothsaying God. He who (as the etymology of the name indicates) is the 'shining one', the deity of light, is also ruler over the beautiful illusion of the inner world of fantasy. The higher truth, the perfection of these states in contrast to the incompletely intelligible everyday world, this deep consciousness of nature, healing and helping in sleep and dreams, is at the same time the symbolical analogue of the soothsaying faculty and of the arts generally, which make life possible and worth living. But we must also include in our image of Apollo that delicate boundary which the dream image must not overstep lest it have a pathological effect (in which case mere appearance would deceive us as if it were crude reality). We must keep in mind that measured restraint, that freedom from the wilder emotions, that calm of the sculptor god. His eye must be 'sunlike', as befits his origin; even when it is angry and distempered it is still hallowed by beautiful illusion. And so in one sense we might apply to Apollo the words of Schopenhauer when he speaks of the man wrapped in the veil of *maya*: 'just as in a stormy sea that, unbounded in all directions, raises and drops mountainous waves, howling, a sailor sits in a boat and trusts in his frail bark: so in the midst of a world of torments the individual human being sits quietly, supported by and trusting in the principle of individuation'.[1] In fact we might say of Apollo that in him the unshaken faith in this principle, and the calm repose of the man wrapped up in it, receive their most sublime expression; and we might call Apollo himself the glorious divine image of the principle of individuation, through whose gestures and eyes all the joy and wisdom of 'illusion', together with its beauty, speak to us.

In the same work Schopenhauer has depicted for us the tremendous *terror* which seizes man when he is suddenly dumbfounded by the cognitive form of phenomena

---

[1] *The World as Will and Idea* [1819]. See introduction to Part IV, extract 7, above. The veil of *maya*, in Hindu philosophy, is the veil of manifold appearance, or illusion.

because the principle of sufficient reason, in some one of its manifestations, seems to suffer an exception. If we add to this terror the blissful ecstasy that wells from the innermost depths of man, indeed of nature, at this collapse of the principle of individuation, we steal a glimpse into the nature of the *Dionysian*, which is brought home to us most intimately by the analogy of intoxication.

Either under the influence of the narcotic draught, of which the songs of all primitive men and peoples speak, or with the potent coming of spring that penetrates all nature with joy, these Dionysian emotions awake, and as they grow in intensity everything subjective vanishes into complete self-forgetfulness. In the German Middle Ages, too, singing and dancing crowds, ever increasing in number, whirled themselves from place to place under this same Dionysian impulse. In these dancers of St John and St Vitus, we rediscover the Bacchic choruses of the Greeks, with their prehistory in Asia Minor, as far back as Babylon and the orgiastic festivals. There are some who, from obtuseness or lack of experience, turn away from such phenomena as from 'folk-diseases', with contempt of pity born of the consciousness of their own 'healthy-mindedness'. But of course such poor wretches have no idea how corpselike and ghostly their so-called 'healthy-mindedness' looks when the glowing life of the Dionysian revellers roars past them.

Under the charm of the Dionysian not only is the union between man and man reaffirmed, but nature which has become alienated, hostile, or subjugated, celebrates once more her reconciliation with her lost son, man. Freely, earth proffers her gifts, and peacefully the beasts of prey of the rocks and the desert approach. The chariot of Dionysus is covered with flowers and garlands; panthers and tigers walk under its yoke. Transform Beethoven's 'Hymn to Joy' into a painting; let your imagination conceive the multitudes bowing in the dust, awestruck – then you will approach the Dionysian. Now the slave is a free man; now all the rigid, hostile barriers that necessity, caprice or impudent convention have fixed between man and man, are broken. Now, with the gospel of universal harmony, each one feels himself not only united, reconciled and fused with his neighbour, but as one with him, as if the veil of *maya* had been torn aside and were now merely fluttering in tatters before the mysterious primordial unity.

In song and in dance man expresses himself as a member of a higher community; he has forgotten how to walk and speak and is on the way toward flying into the air, dancing. His very gestures express enchantment. Just as the animals now talk, and the earth yields milk and honey, supernatural sounds emanate from him too: he feels himself a god, he himself now walks about enchanted in ecstasy, like the gods he saw walking in his dreams. He is no longer an artist, he has become a work of art: in these paroxysms of intoxication the artistic power of all nature reveals itself to the highest gratification of the primordial unity. The noblest clay, the most costly marble, man, is here kneaded and cut, and to the sound of the chisel strokes of the Dionysian world-artist rings out the cry of the Eleusinian mysteries: 'Do you prostrate yourselves, millions? Do you sense your maker, world?'[1]

Thus far we have considered the Apollonian and its opposite, the Dionysian, as artistic energies which burst forth from nature herself, *without the mediation of the human*

---

[1] From Friedrich Schiller's 'Ode to Joy' (set to music in Beethoven's 'Choral' Symphony).

artist – energies in which nature's art impulses are satisfied in the most immediate and direct way – first in the image world of dreams whose completeness is not dependent upon the intellectual attitude or the artistic culture of any single being; and then as intoxicated reality, which likewise does not heed the single unit, but even seeks to destroy the individual and redeem him by a mystic feeling of oneness. With reference to these immediate art-states of nature, every artist is an 'imitator', that is to say, either an Apollonian artist in dreams, or a Dionysian artist in ecstasies, or finally – as for example in Greek tragedy – at once artist in both dreams and ecstasies; so we may perhaps picture him sinking down in his Dionysian intoxication and mystical self-abnegation, alone and apart from the singing revellers, and we may imagine how, through Apollonian dream-inspiration, his own state, i.e. its oneness with the inmost ground of the world, is revealed to him in a *symbolical dream image*.

So much for these general premises and contrasts. Let us now approach the *Greeks* in order to learn how highly these *art impulses of nature* were developed in them. Thus we shall be in a position to understand and appreciate more deeply that relation of the Greek artist to his archetypes which is, according to the Aristotelian expression, the 'imitation of nature'. In spite of all the dream literature and the numerous dream anecdotes of the Greeks, we can speak of their *dreams* only conjecturally, though with reasonable assurance. If we consider the incredibly precise and unerring plastic power of their eyes, together with their vivid, frank delight in colours, we can hardly refrain from assuming even for their dreams (to the shame of those born later) a certain logic of line and contour, colours and groups, a certain pictorial sequence reminding us of their finest bas-reliefs, whose perfection would certainly justify us, if a comparison were possible, in designating the dreaming Greeks as Homers and Homer as a dreaming Greek – in a deeper sense than that in which modern man, speaking of his dreams, ventures to compare himself with Shakespeare.

On the other hand we need not conjecture regarding the immense gap which separates the Dionysian Greek from the Dionysian barbarian. From all quarters of the ancient world – to say nothing here of the modern – from Rome to Babylon, we can point to the existence of Dionysian festivals, types which bear, at best, the same relation to Greek festivals which the bearded satyr, who borrowed his name and attributes from the goat, bears to Dionysus himself. In nearly every case these festivals centred in extravagant sexual licentiousness, whose waves overwhelmed all family life and its venerable traditions; the most savage natural instincts were unleashed, including that horrible mixture of sensuality and cruelty which has always seemed to me the real 'witches' brew'. For some time, however, the Greeks were apparently perfectly insulated and guarded against the feverish excitements of these festivals, though knowledge of them must have come to Greece on all the routes of land and sea; for the figure of Apollo, rising full of pride, held out the Gorgon's head to this grotesquely uncouth Dionysian power – and really could not have countered any more dangerous force. It is in Doric art that this majestically rejecting attitude of Apollo is immortalized.

The opposition between Apollo and Dionysus became even more hazardous and even impossible, when similar impulses finally burst forth from the deepest roots of the Hellenic nature and made a path for themselves: the Delphic god, by a seasonably effected reconciliation, now contented himself with taking the destructive weapons from the hands of his powerful antagonist. This reconciliation is the most important moment in the history of the Greek cult: wherever we turn we note the revolutions resulting from this event. The two antagonists were reconciled; the boundary lines to be observed henceforth by each were sharply defined, and there was to be a periodic exchange of gifts of esteem. At bottom, however, the chasm was not bridged over. But if we observe how, under the pressure of this treaty of peace, the Dionysian power revealed itself, we shall now recognize in the Dionysian orgies of the Greeks, as compared with the Babylonian orgies with their reversion of man to the tiger and the ape, the significance of festivals of world redemption and days of transfiguration. It is with them that nature for the first time attains her artistic jubilee; it is with them that the destruction of the principle of individuation becomes an artistic phenomenon.

The horrible 'witches' brew' of sensuality and cruelty becomes ineffective; only the curious blending and duality in the emotions of the Dionysian revellers reminds us – as medicines remind us of deadly poisons – of the phenomenon that pain begets joy, that ecstasy may wring sounds of agony from us. At the very climax of joy there sounds a cry of horror or a yearning lamentation for an irretrievable loss. In these Greek festivals it is as if nature were heaving a sigh at her dismemberment into individuals. The song and pantomime of such dually-minded revellers was something new and unheard of in the Homeric-Greek world; and the Dionysian *music* in particular excited awe and terror. If music, as it would seem, had been known previously as an Apollonian art, it was so, strictly speaking, only as the wave-beat of rhythm, whose formative power was developed for the representation of Apollonian states. The music of Apollo was Doric architectonics in tones, but in tones that were merely suggestive, such as those of the cithara. The very element which forms the essence of Dionysian music (and hence of music in general) is carefully excluded as un-Apollonian – namely the emotional power of the tone, the uniform flow of the melody, and the utterly incomparable world of harmony. In the Dionysian dithyramb man is incited to the greatest exaltation of all his symbolic faculties; something never before experienced struggles for utterance – the annihilation of the veil of *maya*, oneness as the soul of the race and of nature itself. The essence of nature is now to be expressed symbolically; we need a new world of symbols; and the entire symbolism of the body is called into play, not the mere symbolism of the lips, face and speech, but the whole pantomime of dancing, forcing every member into rhythmic movement. Then the other symbolic powers suddenly press forward, particularly those of music, in rhythmics, dynamics and harmony. To grasp this collective release of all the symbolic powers, man must have already attained that height of self-abnegation which seeks to express itself symbolically through all these powers – and so the dithyrambic votary of Dionysus is understood only by his peers. With what astonishment must the Apollonian Greek have beheld him! With an astonishment that was all the greater the more it was mingled with the shuddering suspicion that all this was actually not so very alien to him after all, in fact, that it was only his Apollonian consciousness which, like a veil, hid this Dionysian world from his vision.

8   The Value of Art: Leo Tolstoy, *What is Art?**

The thesis of both Kant and Schopenhauer that aesthetic pleasure is detached from any personal interests or goals of the beholder (extracts 5 and 6, above) suggests that artistic appreciation is a *sui generis* phenomenon – in a class of its own, unrelated to our other moral and social concerns. And indeed some people talk of 'high art' and 'high culture' in a way which suggests that the activities in question are, as it were, self-justifying, belonging to an exalted domain which is superior to ordinary mundane values. Our next extract, from the famous nineteenth-century Russian novelist Leo Tolstoy, puts severe pressure on this conception of art.

In a highly entertaining eye-witness account of the rehearsals for an opera, Tolstoy points to the immense time, energy and expense, and above all the great personal sacrifice, that such productions demand. His analysis forces us to confront the question of the moral status of artistic activity. There are two dimensions to this. First, there is what we could call the 'internal' dimension. The case Tolstoy describes involves 'the most ordinary of operas', with an utterly banal and trivial plot (an Indian king disguises himself as a minstrel to win his bride, and everyone is delighted). Such triviality and fatuity raises the question of whether we should require of our operatic and dramatic works that they have some serious moral purpose. The issue here calls to mind Aristotle's remarks (extract 2, above) about how the plot in a drama must have a certain structure and a certain logic, connected with its role in showing the development of 'human misery and happiness'. But Aristotle was of course talking of tragic drama, and a critic of Tolstoy might object that 'pure entertainment' can be a legitimate aim of dramatic productions. Yet is pure entertainment enough: does not the concept of 'art' – let alone of 'great art', – require more than this? Secondly, there is the 'external' dimension: the human costs incurred in producing works of art. 'What is this art,' asks Tolstoy, 'that is considered so important for humanity that sacrifices of labour, of human life, and even of goodness may be made?' The kinds of 'brutal cruelty' which Tolstoy describes may no longer be seen on today's stages, but it remains true that governments expend considerable resources on the arts (albeit less than many devotees would wish) – resources which have to be provided at some sacrifice to other causes which most would consider more important from the moral point of view.[1] Tolstoy's discussion reminds us that though some philosophers tend to assign art and morality to the separate compartmentalized disciplines of 'ethics' and 'aesthetics', every human activity involves greater or lesser costs, and hence we cannot escape the question of the relative value of art in human life as a whole.

 Take up any one of our ordinary newspapers and you will find a part devoted to the theatre and music. In almost every number you will find a description of some art exhibition, or of some particular picture, and you will always find reviews of new works of art that have appeared, of volumes of poems, of short stories, or of novels.

Promptly, and in detail, as soon as it has occurred, an account is published of how such and such an actress or actor played this or that role in such and such a drama, comedy, or opera, and of the merits of the performance, as well as of the contents of the new drama, comedy or opera, with its defects and merits. With as much care and detail, or even more, we are told how such and such an artist has sung a certain piece, or has played it on the piano or violin, and what were the merits and defects of the piece and of the performance. In every large town there is sure to be at least one, if not

---

* Leo Tolstoy, *What is Art?* [*Shto Takoy Iskoostvo*, 1896], ch. 1 and part of ch. 2. Trans. Aylmer Maude (London: Brotherhood Publishing, 1898), pp. 1–10.
[1] Famine relief, for example; compare Part IX, extract 10, above.

more than one, exhibition of new pictures, the merits and defects of which are discussed in the utmost detail by critics and connoisseurs.

New novels and poems, in separate volumes or in the magazines, appear almost every day, and the newspapers consider it their duty to give their readers detailed accounts of these artistic productions.

For the support of art in Russia (where for the education of the people only a hundredth part is spent of what would be required to give everyone the opportunity of instruction), the government grants millions of roubles in subsidies to academies, conservatories and theatres. In France twenty million francs are assigned for art, and similar grants are made in Germany and England.

In every large town enormous buildings are erected for museums, academies, conservatories, dramatic schools, and for performances and concerts. Hundreds of thousands of workmen – carpenters, masons, painters, joiners, paperhangers, tailors, hairdressers, jewellers, moulders, typesetters – spend their whole lives in hard labour to satisfy the demands of art, so that hardly any other department of human activity, except the military, consumes so much energy as this.

Not only is enormous labour spent on this activity, but in it, as in war, the very lives of men are sacrificed. Hundreds of thousands of people devote their lives from childhood to learning to twirl their legs rapidly (dancers), or to touch notes and strings very rapidly (musicians), or to draw with paint and represent what they see (artists), or to turn every phrase inside out and find a rhyme to every word. And these people, often very kind and clever, and capable of all sorts of useful labour, grow savage over their specialized and stupefying occupations, and become one-sided and self-complacent specialists, dull to all the serious phenomena of life and skilful only at rapidly twisting their legs, their tongues, or their fingers.

But even this stunting of human life is not the worst. I remember being once at the rehearsal of one of the most ordinary of the new operas which are produced at all the opera houses of Europe and America.

I arrived when the first act had already begun. To reach the auditorium I had to pass through the stage entrance. By dark entrances and passages I was led through the vaults of an enormous building, past immense machines for changing the scenery and for lighting, and there in the gloom and dust I saw workmen busily engaged. One of these men, pale, haggard, in a dirty blouse, with dirty, work-worn hands and cramped fingers, evidently tired and out of humour, went past me, angrily scolding another man. Ascending by a dark stair, I came out on the boards behind the scenes. Amid various poles and rings and scattered scenery, decorations and curtains, stood and moved dozens, if not Hundreds, of painted and dressed-up men, in costumes fitting tight to their thighs and calves, and also women, as usual, as nearly nude as might be. These were all singers, or members of the chorus, or ballet dancers, waiting their turns. My guide led me across the stage and, by means of a bridge of boards across the orchestra (in which perhaps a hundred musicians of all kinds, from kettledrum to flute and harp, were seated), to the dark pit-stalls.

On an elevation, between two lamps with reflectors, and in an armchair placed before a music stand, sat the director of the musical part, baton in hand, managing the orchestra and singers, and, in general, the production of the whole opera.

The performance had already begun, and on the stage a procession of Indians who had brought home a bride was being presented. Besides men and women in costume, two other men in ordinary clothes bustled and ran about on the stage; one was the director of the dramatic part, and the other, who stepped about in soft shoes and ran from place to place with unusual agility, was the dancing master, whose salary per month exceeded what ten labourers earn in a year.

These three directors arranged the singing, the orchestra and the procession. The procession, as usual, was enacted by couples, with tinfoil halberds on their shoulders. They all came from one place and walked round and round again, and then stopped. The procession took a long time to arrange: first, the Indians with halberds came on too late; then, too soon; then, at the right time, but crowded together at the exit; then they did not crowd, but arranged themselves badly at the sides of the stage; and each time the whole performance was stopped and started again from the beginning. The procession was introduced by a recitative delivered by a man dressed up like some variety of Turk, who, opening his mouth in a curious way, sang, 'Home I bring the bri-i-ide.' He sings and waves his arm (which is of course bare) from under his mantle. The procession begins, but here the French horn, in the accompaniment of the recitative, does something wrong; and the director, with a shudder as if some catastrophe had occurred, raps with his stick on the stand. All is stopped, and the director, turning to the orchestra, attacks the French horn, scolding him in the rudest terms, as cabmen abuse each other, for taking the wrong note. And again the whole thing begins again. The Indians with their halberds again come on, treading softly in their extraordinary boots; again the singer sings, 'Home I bring the bri-i-ide.' But here the pairs get too close together. More raps with the stick, more scolding, and a recommencement. Again, 'Home I bring the bri-i-ide', again the same gesticulation with the bare arm from under the mantle, and again the couples, treading softly with halberds on their shoulders, some with sad and serious faces, some talking and smiling, arrange themselves in a circle and begin to sing. All seems to be going well, but again the stick raps, and the director, in a distressed and angry voice, begins to scold the men and women of the chorus. It appears that when singing they had omitted to raise their hands from time to time in sign of animation. 'Are you all dead, or what? Cows that you are! Are you corpses, that you can't move?' Again they start 'Home I bring the bri-i-ide', and again, with sorrowful faces, the chorus women sing, first one and then another of them raising their hands. But two chorus girls speak to each other – again a more vehement rapping with the stick. 'Have you come here to talk? Can't you gossip at home? You there in red breeches, come nearer. Look toward me! Begin!' Again, 'Home I bring the bri-i-ide.' And so it goes on for one, two, three hours. The whole of such a rehearsal lasts six hours on end. Raps with the stick, repetitions, placings, corrections of the singers, of the orchestra, of the procession, of the dancers – all seasoned with angry scolding. I heard the words 'asses', 'fools', 'idiots', 'swine', addressed to the musicians and singers at least forty times in the course of one hour. And the unhappy individual to whom the abuse is addressed – flautist, hornblower or singer – physically and mentally demoralized, does not reply and does what is demanded of him. Twenty times is repeated the one phrase, 'Home I bring the bri-i-ide', and twenty times the striding about in yellow shoes with a halberd over the shoulder. The conductor knows that these people are so demoralized that they are no longer fit for anything but to blow trumpets and walk about with halberds and in yellow shoes, and that they are also accustomed to dainty, easy living, so that they will put up with anything rather than lose their luxurious life. He therefore gives free vent to his churlishness, especially as he has seen the same thing done in Paris and Vienna, and knows that this is the way the best conductors behave, and that it is a musical tradition of great artists to be so carried away by the great business of their art that they cannot pause to consider the feelings of other artists.

It would be difficult to find a more repulsive sight. I have seen one workman abuse another for not supporting the weight piled upon him when goods were being unloaded, or, at haystacking, the village elder scold a peasant for not making the rick right, and the man submitted in silence. And, however unpleasant it was to witness the scene, the unpleasantness was lessened by the consciousness that the business in hand was needful and important, and that the fault for which the head man scolded the labourer was one which might spoil a needful undertaking.

But what was being done here? For what, and for whom? Very likely the conductor was tired out, like the workman I passed in the vaults; it was even evident that he was; but who made him tire himself? And for what was he tiring himself? The opera he was rehearsing was one of the most ordinary of operas for people who are accustomed to them, but also one of the most gigantic absurdities that could possibly be devised. An Indian king wants to marry; they bring him a bride; he disguises himself as a minstrel; the bride falls in love with the minstrel and is in despair, but afterwards discovers that the minstrel is the king, and everyone is highly delighted.

That there never were, or could be, such Indians, and that they were not only unlike Indians, but that what they were doing was unlike anything on earth except other operas, was beyond all manner of doubt; that people do not converse in such a way as recitative, and do not place themselves at fixed distances in a quartet, waving their arms to express their emotions; that nowhere, except in theatres, do people walk about in such a manner, in pairs, with tinfoil halberds and in slippers; that no one ever gets angry in such a way, or is affected in such a way, or laughs in such a way, or cries in such a way; and that no one on earth can be moved by such performances – all this is beyond the possibility of doubt.

Instinctively the question presents itself: For whom is this being done? Whom *can* it please? If there are, occasionally, good melodies in the opera to which it is pleasant to listen, they could have been sung simply, without these stupid costumes and all the processions and recitatives and handwavings.

The ballet, in which half-naked women make voluptuous movements, twisting themselves into various sensual writhings, is simply a lewd performance.

So one is quite at a loss as to whom these things are done for. The man of culture is heartily sick of them, while to a real working man they are utterly incomprehensible. If anyone can be pleased by these things (which is doubtful), it can only be some young footman or depraved artisan who has contracted the spirit of the upper classes but is not yet satiated with their amusements and wishes to show his breeding.

And all this nasty folly is prepared, not simply, nor with kindly merriment, but with anger and brutal cruelty.

It is said that it is all done for the sake of art, and that art is a very important thing. But is it true that art is so important that such sacrifices should be made for its sake? This question is especially urgent because art, for the sake of which the labour of millions, the lives of men, and, above all, love between man and man, are being sacrificed – this very art is becoming something more and more vague and uncertain to human perception.

Criticism, in which the lovers of art used to find support for their opinions, has latterly become so self-contradictory that, if we exclude from the domain of art all that to which the critics of various schools themselves deny the title, there is scarcely any art left.

The artists of various sects, like the theologians of the various sects, mutually exclude and destroy themselves. Listen to the artists of the schools of our times, and you will find, in all branches, each set of artists disowning others. In poetry the old Romanticists deny the Parnassiens and the Decadents; the Parnassiens disown the Romanticists and the Decadents; the Decadents disown all their predecessors and the Symbolists; the Symbolists disown all their predecessors and *les mages*; and *les mages* disown all, all their predecessors. Among novelists we have naturalists, psychologists, and 'nature-ists', all rejecting each other. And it is the same in dramatic art, in painting and in music. So art, which demands such tremendous labour sacrifices from the people, which stunts human lives and transgresses against human love, is not only *not* a thing clearly and firmly defined, but is understood in such contradictory ways by its own devotees that it is difficult to say what is meant by art, and especially what is good, useful art – art for the sake of which we might condone such sacrifices as are being offered at its shrine.

For the production of every ballet, circus, opera, operetta, exhibition, picture, concert or printed book, the intense and unwilling labour of thousands of people is needed at what is often harmful and humiliating work. It were well if artists made all they require for themselves, but, as it is, they all need the help of workmen, not only to produce art, but also for their own usually luxurious maintenance. And, one way or other, they get it, either through payments from rich people or through subsidies given by government (in Russia, for instance, in grants of millions of roubles to theatres, conservatories and academies). This money is collected from the people, some of whom have to sell their only cow to pay the tax and who never get those aesthetic pleasures which art gives.

It was all very well for a Greek or Roman artist, or even for a Russian artist of the first half of our century (when there were still slaves and it was considered right that there should be), with a quiet mind to make people serve him and his art; but in our day, when in all men there is at least some dim perception of the equal rights of all, it is impossible to constrain people to labour unwillingly for art without first deciding the question whether it is true that art is so good and so important an affair as to redeem this evil.

If not, we have the terrible probability to consider that while fearful sacrifices of the labour and lives of men, and of morality itself, are being made to art, that same art may be not only useless but even harmful.

And therefore it is necessary for a society in which works of art arise and are supported, to find out whether all that professes to be art is really art, whether (as is presupposed in our society) all that which is art is good, and whether it is important and worth those sacrifices which it necessitates. It is still more necessary for every conscientious artist to know this that he may be sure that all he does has a valid meaning; that it is not merely an infatuation of the small circle of people among whom he lives which excites in him the false assurance that he is doing a good work; and that what he takes from others for the support of his often very luxurious life will be compensated for by those productions at which he works. And that is why answers to the above questions are especially important in our time.

What is this art which is considered so important and necessary for humanity that for its sake these sacrifices of labour, of human life, and even of goodness may be made?

9 Imagination and Art: Jean-Paul Sartre, *The Psychology of Imagination**

The power of the imagination, which entered importantly into Nietzsche's account of art (extract 7, above), is also a central theme in an influential essay on aesthetics by the twentieth-century French existentialist philosopher Jean-Paul Sartre.[1] But whereas Nietzsche was principally concerned with the creative activities of the artist, Sartre is more exercised by the relationship of the experiencing subject to the work of art itself. The extract below begins with the formulation of a paradoxical principle: 'the work of art is an unreality'. By this, Sartre means to draw a distinction between the material object (e.g. the paint on the canvas) and the 'intentional act that apprehends it'. The notion of the 'Intentional' had been (and is) used as a technical term in the philosophy of mind to refer to what a mental state is *about* – its representational content, so to speak.[2] And it is clear that in many cases I can be thinking about something (Santa Claus, for example) that does not actually physically exist. Sartre now suggests that our experience of a work of art involves an imaginative act which brings into being the aesthetic object – something essentially unreal, or purely within the domain of the mind, distinct from the actual physical canvas (sculpture, or whatever) that is in front of us. 'What is beautiful is something which … by its very nature is out of the world.' To show the difference between the painting as aesthetic object and the painted canvas, Sartre points out that the aesthetic object cannot be *brightened*, for instance, by projecting a light on the canvas; all this would do would be to brighten the canvas, not the painting. What happens when we perceive a work of art is that 'the material thing [is] *visited* from time to time

(every time the spectator assumes the imaginative attitude) by an unreal which is precisely the painted object'.

Sartre proceeds to generalize his argument by reference to some of the other arts. In a fiction, poetry and drama, the artist 'constructs an unreal object by means of verbal analogues'. This is particularly striking in the case of a play, where the whole enterprise is to create something unreal. It is (one might say) a case of 'pretence' or 'make-believe', but as Sartre characterizes it there is a willed unreality of a subtle and profound kind: 'the transformation that occurs is like that in a dream: the actor is completely caught up, inspired by the unreal.' The tears of the actor playing Hamlet are experienced by the actor himself, and the audience, as the tears of Hamlet; the actor's tears are, as Sartre puts it, the *analogue* of unreal tears. And similarly in the case of a musical performance, Sartre argues that the work of art (Beethoven's Seventh Symphony, for instance) is an unreal object, with its own 'inner time', separate from the actual events and circumstances of a particular performance in a particular concert hall. The actual performance is simply an *analogue* of the symphony itself – an 'unreal' object apprehended in the imagination. 'Aesthetic contemplation,' Sartre declares, 'is an induced dream.' There are many fascinating implications of Sartre's approach to art, but one which he himself draws out is that there is a fundamental distinction between the aesthetic and the moral domains (contrast Tolstoy, extract 8, above). Moral values are essentially concerned with being in the world, but aesthetic value, for Sartre, belongs outside the real world, in the 'unreality' of the imagination.

---

* From *L'imaginaire: Psychologie phénoménologique de l'imagination* [1940], translated as *The Psychology of Imagination* (London: Rider, 1950), pp. 211–17.

[1] For the term 'existentialist', compare Part II, extract 9, above; see also Part V, extract 10.

[2] For more on this, compare Brentano, Part IV, extract 9, above.

It is not our intention to deal here with the problem of the work of art in its entirety. Closely related as this problem is to the question of the Imaginary, its treatment calls for a special work in itself. But it is time we drew some conclusions from the long investigations in which we used as an example a statue or the portrait of Charles VIII or a novel. The following comments will be concerned essentially with the existential type of the work of art. And we can at once formulate the law that *the work of art is an unreality.*

This appeared to us clearly from the moment we took for our example, in an entirely different connection, the portrait of Charles VIII. We understood at the very outset that this Charles VIII was an object. But this, obviously, is not the same object as is the painting, the canvas, which are the real objects of the painting. As long as we observe the canvas and the frame for themselves, the aesthetic object 'Charles VIII' will not appear. It is not that it is hidden by the picture, but because it cannot present itself to a realizing consciousness. It will appear at the moment when consciousness, undergoing a radical change in which the world is negated, will itself become imaginative. The situation here is like that of the cubes which can be seen at will to be five or six in number. It will not do to say that when they are seen as five it is because at that time the aspect of the drawing in which they are six is *concealed*. The intentional act that apprehends them as five is sufficient unto itself, it is complete and *exclusive* of the act which grasps them as six. And so it is with the apprehension of Charles VIII as an image which is depicted on the picture. This Charles VIII on the canvas is necessarily the correlative of the intentional act of an imaginative consciousness. And since this Charles VIII, who is an unreality so long as he is grasped on the canvas, is precisely the object of our aesthetic appreciations (it is he who 'moves' us, who is 'painted with intelligence, power and grace', etc.), we are led to recognize that, in a picture, the aesthetic object is something *unreal*.

This is of great enough importance once we remind ourselves of the way in which we ordinarily confuse the real and the imaginary in a work of art. We often hear it said, in fact, that the artist first has an idea in the form of an image which he then *realizes* on canvas. This mistaken notion arises from the fact that the painter can, in fact, begin with a mental image which is, as such, incommunicable, and from the fact that at the end of his labours he presents the public with an object which anyone can observe. This leads us to believe that there occurred a transition from the imaginary to the real. But this is in no way true. That which is real, we must not fail to note, are the results of the brush strokes, the stickiness of the canvas, its grain, the polish spread over the colours. But all this does not constitute the object of aesthetic appreciation. What is 'beautiful' is something which cannot be experienced as a perception and which, by its very nature, is out of the world... It cannot be *brightened* for instance, by projecting a light beam on the canvas: it is the canvas that is brightened and not the painting. The fact of the matter is that the painter did not *realize* his mental image at all: he has simply constructed a material analogue of such a kind that everyone can grasp the image provided he looks at the analogue. But the image thus provided with an external analogue remains an image. There is no realization of the imaginary, nor can we speak of its *objectification*. Each stroke of the brush was not made *for itself* nor even for the constructing of a coherent real whole (in the sense in which it can be said that a certain lever in a machine was conceived in the interest of the whole and not for itself). It was given together with an unreal synthetic whole, and the aim of the artist was to construct a whole of *real* colours which enable this unreal to manifest itself.

The painting should then be conceived as a material thing *visited* from time to time (every time that the spectator assumes the imaginative attitude) by an unreal which is precisely the *painted object*. What deceives us here is the real and sensuous pleasure which certain real colours on the canvas give us. Some reds of Matisse, for instance, produce a sensuous enjoyment in those who see them. But we must understand that this sensuous enjoyment, if thought of in isolation – for instance, if aroused by a colour in nature – has nothing of the aesthetic. It is purely and simply a pleasure of sense. But when the red of the painting is grasped, it is grasped, in spite of everything, as a part of an unreal whole and it is in this whole that it is beautiful. For instance it is the red of a rug by a table. There is, in fact, no such thing as pure colour. Even if the artist is concerned solely with the sensory relationships between forms and colours, he chooses for that very reason a rug in order to increase the sensory value of the red: tactile elements, for instance, must be intended through the red, it is a *fleecy* red, because the rug is of a fleecy material. Without this 'fleeciness' of the colour something would be lost. And surely the rug is painted there *for the red* it justifies, and not the red for the rug. If Matisse chose a rug rather than a sheet of dry and glossy paper it is because of the voluptuous mixture of the colour, the density and the tactile quality of the wool. Consequently the red can be truly enjoyed only in grasping it as the *red of the rug*, and therefore as unreal. And he would have lost his strongest contrast with the green of the wall if the green were not rigid and cold, because it is the green of a wall tapestry. It is therefore in the unreal that the relationship of colours and forms takes on its real meaning. And even when drawn objects have their usual meaning reduced to a minimum, as in the painting of the cubists, the painting is at least not flat. The forms we see are certainly not the forms of a rug, a table, nor anything else we see in the world. They nevertheless do have a density, a material, a depth, they bear a relationship of perspective towards each other. They are *things*. And it is precisely in the measure in which they are things that they are unreal.

Cubism has introduced the fashion of claiming that a painting should not *represent* or *imitate* reality but should constitute an object in itself. As an aesthetic doctrine such a programme is perfectly defensible and we owe many masterpieces to it. But it needs to be understood. To maintain that the painting, although altogether devoid of meaning, nevertheless is a *real* object, would be a grave mistake. It is certainly not an object of nature. The real object no longer functions as an analogue of a bouquet of flowers or a glade. But when I 'contemplate' it, I nevertheless am not in a realistic attitude. The painting is still an *analogue*. Only what manifests itself through it is an unreal collection of *new things*, of objects I have never seen or ever will see, but which are not less unreal because of it, objects which do not exist *in the painting*, nor anywhere in the world, but which manifest themselves by means of the canvas, and which have gotten hold of it by some sort of possession. And it is the configuration of these unreal objects that I designate as *beautiful*. The aesthetic enjoyment is real but it is not grasped for itself, as if produced by a real colour: it is but a manner of apprehending the unreal object and, far from being directed on the real painting, it serves to constitute the imaginary object through the real canvas. This is the source of the celebrated disinterestedness of aesthetic experience. This is why Kant was able to say that it does not matter whether the object of beauty, when experienced as beautiful, is or is not objectively real; why Schopenhauer was able to speak of a sort of suspension of the Will.[1] This does not come from some mysterious way of apprehending the real, which we are able to use occasionally. What happens is that the aesthetic object is constituted and apprehended by an imaginative consciousness which posits it as unreal.

What we have just shown regarding painting is readily applied to the art of fiction, poetry and drama, as well. It is self-evident that the novelist, the poet and the dramatist construct an unreal object by means of verbal analogues; it is also self-evident that the actor who plays Hamlet makes use of himself, of his whole body, as an analogue of the imaginary person . . . It is well known that certain amateurs proclaim that the actor *does not believe* in the character he portrays. Others, leaning on many witnesses, claim that the actor becomes identified in some way with the character he is enacting. To us these two views are not exclusive of each other; if by 'belief' is meant actually real, it is obvious that the actor does not actually consider himself to be Hamlet. But this does not mean that he does not 'mobilize' all his powers to make Hamlet real. He uses all his feelings, all his strength, all his gestures as analogues of the feelings and conduct of Hamlet. But by this very fact he takes the reality away from them. He *lives completely in an unreal way*. And it matters little that he is *actually* weeping in enacting the role. These tears . . . he himself experiences – and so does the audience – as the tears of Hamlet, that is as the analogue of unreal tears. The transformation that occurs here is like that . . . in the dream: the actor is completely caught up, inspired, by the unreal. It is not the character who becomes real in the actor, it is the actor who *becomes unreal* in his character.[2]

But are there not some arts whose objects seem to escape unreality by their very nature? A melody, for instance, refers to nothing but itself. Is a cathedral anything more than a mass of *real* stone which dominates the surrounding house-tops? But let us look at this matter more closely. I listen to a symphony orchestra, for instance, playing the Beethoven Seventh Symphony. Let us disregard exceptional cases – which are besides on the margin of aesthetic contemplation – as when I go mainly 'to hear Toscanini' interpret Beethoven in his own way. As a general rule what draws me to the concert is the desire 'to hear the Seventh Symphony'. Of course I have some objection to hearing an amateur orchestra, and prefer this or that well-known musical organization. But this is due to my desire to hear the symphony 'played perfectly', because the symphony will then be *perfectly itself*. The shortcomings of a poor orchestra which plays 'too fast' or 'too slow', 'in the wrong tempo', etc., seem to me to rob, to 'betray' the work it is playing. At most the orchestra effaces itself before the work it performs, and, provided I have reasons to trust the performers and their conductor, I am confronted by the symphony itself. This everyone will grant me. But now, what is the Seventh Symphony itself? Obviously it is a *thing*, that is something which is before me, which endures, which lasts. Naturally there is no need to show that that thing is a synthetic whole, which does not consist of tones but of a thematic configuration.

---

[1] For the views of Kant and Schopenhauer, see extracts 5 and 6, above.

[2] *It is in this sense that a beginner in the theatre can say that stage-fright served her to represent the timidity of Ophelia. If it did so, it is because she suddenly turned it into an unreality, that is, that she ceased to apprehend it for itself and that she grasped it as *analogue* for the timidity of Ophelia.

But is that 'thing' real or unreal? Let us first bear in mind that I am listening to the Seventh Symphony. For me that 'Seventh Symphony' does not exist in time – I do not grasp it as a dated event, as an artistic manifestation which is unrolling itself in the Chatelet auditorium on the 17 November 1938. If I hear Furtwängler tomorrow or eight days later conduct another orchestra performing the same symphony, I am in the presence of the same symphony once more. Only it is being played either better or worse.

Let us now see *how* I hear the symphony: some persons shut their eyes. In this case they detach themselves from the *visual* and dated event of this particular interpretation: they give themselves up to the pure sounds. Others watch the orchestra or the back of the conductor. But they do not see what they are looking at. This is what Revault d'Allonnes calls 'reflection with auxiliary fascination'. The auditorium, the conductor and even the orchestra have disappeared. I am therefore confronted by the Seventh Symphony, but on the express condition of understanding *nothing about it*, that I do not think of the event as an actuality and dated, and on condition that I listen to the succession of themes as an absolute succession and not as a real succession which is unfolding itself, for instance, on the occasion when Peter paid a visit to this or that friend. In the degree to which I hear the symphony it is *not here*, between these walls, at the tip of the violin bows. Nor is it 'in the past' as if I thought: this is the work that matured in the mind of Beethoven on such a date. It is completely beyond the real. It has its own time, that is, it possesses an inner time, which runs from the first tone of the allegro to the last tone of the finale, but this time is not a succession of a preceding time which it continues and which happened 'before' the beginning of the allegro; nor is it followed by a time which will come 'after' the finale. The Seventh Symphony is in no way *in time*. It is therefore in no way real. It occurs *by itself*, but as absent, as being out of reach. I cannot act upon it, change a single note of it, or slow down its movement. But it depends on the real for its appearance: that the conductor does not faint away, that a fire in the hall does not put an end to the performance. From this we cannot conclude that *the* Seventh Symphony has come to an end. No, we only think that the *performance* of the symphony has ceased. Does this not show clearly that the performance of the symphony is its *analogue*? It can manifest itself only through analogues which are dated and which unroll in our time. But to experience it in these analogues the imaginative reduction must be functioning, that is, the real sounds must be apprehended as analogues. It therefore occurs as a perpetual elsewhere, a perpetual absence. We must not picture it (as does Spandrell in *Point Counter Point* by Huxley[1] – as so many platonisms) as existing in another world, in an intelligible heaven. It is not only outside of time and space – as are essences, for instance – it is outside of the real, outside of existence. I do not hear it actually, I listen to it in the imaginary.

Here we find the explanation for the considerable difficulty we always experience in passing from the world of the theatre or of music into that of our daily affairs. There is in fact no passing from one world into the other, but only a passing from the imaginative attitude to that of reality. Aesthetic contemplation is an induced dream and the passing into the real is an actual waking up. We often speak of the 'deception' experienced on returning to reality. But this does not explain that this discomfort also

---

[1] Aldous Huxley's satirical novel *Point Counter Point* was published in 1923.

exists, for instance, after having witnessed a realistic and cruel play, in which case reality should be experienced as comforting. This discomfort is simply that of the dreamer on awakening; an entranced consciousness, engulfed in the imaginary, is suddenly freed by the sudden ending of the play, of the symphony, and comes suddenly in contact with existence. Nothing more is needed to arouse the nauseating disgust that characterizes the consciousness of reality.

From these few observations we can already conclude that the real is never beautiful. Beauty is a value applicable only to the imaginary and which means the negation of the world in its essential structure. This is why it is stupid to confuse the moral with the aesthetic. The values of the Good presume being-in-the-world, they concern action in the real and are subject from the outset to the basic absurdity of existence. To say that we 'assume' an aesthetic attitude to life is to confuse the real and the imaginary. It does happen, however, that we do assume the attitude of aesthetic contemplation towards real events or objects. But in such cases everyone of us can feel in himself a sort of recoil in relation to the object contemplated which slips into nothingness so that, from this moment on, it is no longer *perceived*; it functions as an *analogue* of itself, that is, that an unreal image of what it is appears to us through its actual presence. This image can be purely and simply the object 'itself' neutralized, annihilated, as when I contemplate a beautiful woman or death at a bull fight; it can also be the imperfect and confused appearance of *what it could be* through what it is, as when the painter grasps the harmony of two colours as being greater, more vivid, *through* the real blots he finds on a wall. The object at once appears to be *in back of* itself, becomes *untouchable*, it is beyond our reach; and hence arises a sort of sad disinterest in it. It is in this sense that we may say that great beauty in a woman kills the desire for her. In fact we cannot at the same time place ourselves both on the plane of the aesthetic, when this unreal 'herself' which we admire appears, and on the realistic plane of physical possession. To desire her we must forget she is beautiful, because desire is a plunge into the heart of existence, into what is most contingent and most absurd. Aesthetic contemplation of *real* objects is of the same structure as paramnesia, in which the real object functions as analogue of itself in the past. But in one of the cases there is a negating and in the other a placing a thing in the past. Paramnesia differs from the aesthetic attitude as memory differs from imagination.

10   What is Aesthetics? Ludwig Wittgenstein, *Lectures on Aesthetics**

A fair amount of twentieth-century philosophy has been characterized by a certain introspect-iveness about the nature and purpose of the subject, and that has been as true in aesthetics as elsewhere. In the next extract, from the post-humously published lectures of Ludwig Wittgenstein (who died in 1951), the author considers, and harshly condemns, the tendency to try to reduce aesthetics to science – to make it a branch of psychology. The idea of 'experiments'

* From 'Lectures on Aesthetics' [1938], I, §§ 17–26; II, §§ 1–12, 16–19, 35–8; IV, §§ 1–3, in L. Wittgenstein, *Lectures and Conversations on Aesthetics, Psychology and Religious Belief*, ed. C. Barrett (Oxford: Blackwell, 1978), pp. 6–8, 11–15, 17–18, 28–30.

in aesthetics Wittgenstein dismisses as absurd; aesthetic explanations are not causal explanations. Even if we imagine being able to predict accurately people's reactions to works of art, would this solve our 'aesthetic puzzlement'? No, Wittgenstein argues. To try to reduce aesthetic appreciation to the *effect* produced by a minuet would suggest, absurdly, that the minuet itself is somehow unimportant. He proceeds to illustrate the point tellingly by the example of an imaginary pill which made you draw a picture (the creation of Adam, say), and at the same time produced certain feelings inside you: which would matter more, the actual drawing, or the feelings produced?

Questions of course remain about what aesthetic appreciation is, and here again, consistently with his general approach to philosophical issues concerning the mind, Wittgenstein tries to move us away from concentration on supposed 'inner' feelings and impressions.[1] Instead, he encourages us to look outwards, to the role aesthetic judgements play in our interpersonal life, in the wider social context. We need to understand the 'language game' – the 'complicated but very definite role' expressions of aesthetic judgement play in the culture of a period. 'What belongs to a language game' as Wittgenstein puts it, 'is a whole culture'. And hence 'to describe what [aesthetic appreciation] consists in we would have to describe the whole environment'. Wittgenstein's approach certainly does not dispel the complexity of aesthetic phenomena, but it does invite us to understand that complexity within a very different context from the inner realm of 'ideas' and impressions on which earlier aestheticians had concentrated (compare extract 3, above).

In what we call the Arts, a person who has judgement develops. (A person who has judgement doesn't mean a person who says 'Marvellous!' at certain things.) If we talk of aesthetic judgements, we think, among a thousand things, of the Arts. When we make an aesthetic judgement about a thing, we do not just gape at it and say: 'Oh! How marvellous!' We distinguish between a person who knows what he is talking about and a person who doesn't. If a person is to admire English poetry, he must know English. Suppose that a Russian who doesn't know English is overwhelmed by a sonnet admitted to be good. We would say that he does not know what is in it at all. Similarly, of a person who doesn't know metres but who is overwhelmed, we would say that he doesn't know what's in it. In music this is more pronounced. Suppose there is a person who admires and enjoys what is admitted to be good but can't remember the simplest tunes, doesn't know when the bass comes in etc. We say he hasn't seen what's in it. We use the phrase 'A man is musical' not so as to call a man musical if he says 'Ah!' when a piece of music is played, any more than we call a dog musical if it wags its tail when music is played.

The word we ought to talk about is 'appreciated'. What does appreciation consist in?

If a man goes through an endless number of patterns in a tailor's and says: 'No. This is slightly too dark. This is slightly too loud', etc., he is what we call an appreciator of material. That he is an appreciator is not shown by the interjections he uses, but by the way he chooses, selects, etc. Similarly in music: 'Does this harmonize? No. The bass is not quite loud enough. Here I just want something different...' This is what we call an appreciation.

It is not only difficult to describe what appreciation consists in, but impossible. To describe what it consists in we would have to describe the whole environment.

---

[1] Compare introduction to Part IV, extract 10, above.

I know exactly what happens when a person who knows a lot about suits goes to the tailor, also I know what happens when a person who knows nothing about suits goes – what he says, how he acts, etc. There is an extraordinary number of different cases of appreciation. And, of course, what I know is nothing compared to what one could know. I would have to say what appreciation is – e.g. to explain such an enormous wart as arts and crafts, such a particular kind of disease. Also I would have to explain what our photographers do today – and why it is impossible to get a decent picture of your friend even if you pay £1,000.

You can get a picture of what you may call a very high culture, e.g. German music in the last century and the century before, and what happens when this deteriorates. A picture of what happens in Architecture when you get imitations – or when thousands of people are interested in the minutest details. A picture of what happens when a dining-room table is chosen more or less at random, when no one knows where it came from.

We talked of correctness. A good cutter won't use words except words like 'Too long', 'All right'. When we talk of a Symphony of Beethoven we don't talk of correctness. Entirely different things enter. One wouldn't talk of appreciating the *tremendous* things in Art. In certain styles in Architecture a door is correct, and the thing is you appreciate it. But in the case of a Gothic cathedral what we do is not at all to find it correct – it plays an entirely different role with us. The entire *game* is different. It is as different as to judge a human being and on the one hand to say 'He behaves well' and on the other hand 'He makes a great impression on me'.

'Correctly', 'charmingly', 'finely' etc. play an entirely different role. Cf. the famous address of Buffon – a terrific man – on style in writing; making ever so many distinctions which I only understand vaguely but which he didn't mean vaguely – all kinds of nuances like 'grand', 'charming', 'nice'.

The words we call expressions of aesthetic judgement play a very complicated role, but a very definite role, in what we call a culture of a period. To describe their use or to describe what you mean by a cultured taste, you have to describe a culture. What we now call a cultured taste perhaps didn't exist in the Middle Ages. An entirely different game is played in different ages.

What belongs to a language game is a whole culture. In describing musical taste you have to describe whether children give concerts, whether women do or whether men only give them, etc. etc. In aristocratic circles in Vienna people had such and such a taste, then it came into bourgeois circles and women joined choirs etc. This is an example of a tradition in music...

One interesting thing is the idea that people have of a kind of science of Aesthetics. I would almost like to talk of what could be meant by Aesthetics.

You might think Aesthetics is a science telling us what's beautiful – almost too ridiculous for words. I suppose it ought to include also what sort of coffee tastes well.

I see roughly this – there is a realm of utterance of delight, when you taste pleasant food or smell a pleasant smell, etc., then there is a realm of Art which is quite different, though often you may make the same face when you hear a piece of music as when you taste good food. (Though you may cry at something you like very much.)

Supposing you meet someone in the street and he tells you he has lost his greatest friend, in a voice extremely expressive of his emotion. You might say: 'It was extraordinarily beautiful, the way he expressed himself.' Supposing you then asked: 'What similarity has my admiring this person with my eating vanilla ice and liking it?' To compare them seems almost disgusting. (But you can connect them by intermediate cases.) Suppose someone says 'But this is a quite different kind of delight.' But did you learn two meanings of 'delight'? You use the same word on both occasions. There is some connection between these delights. Although in the first case the emotion of delight would in our judgement hardly count.

It is like saying: 'I classify works of Art in this way: at some I look up, and at some I look down.' This way of classifying might be interesting. We might discover all sorts of connections between looking up or down at works of Art and looking up or down at other things. If we found, perhaps, that eating vanilla ice made us look up, we might not attach great importance to looking up. There may be a realm, a small realm of experience, which may make me look up or down where I can infer a lot from the fact that I looked up or down; another realm of experience where nothing can be inferred from my looking up or down. Cf. wearing blue or green trousers may in a certain society mean a lot, but in another society it may not mean anything.

What are expressions of liking something? Is it only what we say or interjections we use or faces we make? Obviously not. It is, often, how often I read something or how often I wear a suit. Perhaps I won't even say: 'It's fine', but wear it often and look at it.

Suppose we build houses and we give doors and windows certain dimensions. Does the fact that we *like* these dimensions necessarily show in anything we say? Is what we like necessarily shown by an expression of *liking*? For instance, suppose our children draw windows and when they draw them in the wrong way we punish them. Or when someone builds a certain house we refuse to live in it or run away.

Take the case of fashions. How does a fashion come about? Say, we wear lapels broader than last year. Does this mean that the tailors like them better broader? No, not necessarily. He cuts it like this and this year he makes it broader. Perhaps this year he finds it too narrow and makes it wider. Perhaps no expression of delight is used at all.

You design a door and look at it and say: 'Higher, higher, higher...oh, all right.' (Gesture) What is this? Is it an expression of content?

Perhaps the most important thing in connection with aesthetics is what may be called aesthetic reactions, e.g. discontent, disgust, discomfort. The expression of discontent is not the same as the expression of discomfort. The expression of discontent says: 'Make it higher...too low! Do something to this.'

Is what I call an expression of discontent something like an expression of discomfort *plus* knowing the cause of the discomfort and asking for it to be removed? If I say: 'This door is too low. Make it higher', should we say I know the cause of my discomfort?

Cause is used in very many different ways, e.g. (1) 'What is the cause of unemployment?'...(2) 'What was the cause of your jumping?' 'That noise'. (3) 'What was the cause of that wheel going round?' You trace a mechanism...

To say 'I feel discomfort and know the cause' is entirely misleading because 'know the cause' normally means something quite different. How misleading it is depends on whether when you said 'know the cause', you meant it to be an explanation or not. 'I feel discomfort and know the cause', make it sound as if there were two things going on in my soul – discomfort and knowing the cause.

In these cases the word 'cause' is hardly ever used at all. You use 'why?' and 'because', but not 'cause'.

We have here a kind of discomfort which you may call 'directed', e.g. if I am afraid of you, my discomfort is directed. Saying 'I know the cause' brings in mind the case of statistics or tracing a mechanism. If I say, 'I know the cause', it looks as if I had analysed the feelings (as I analyse the feeling of hearing my own voice and, at the same time, rubbing my hands) which, of course, I haven't done. We have given, as it were, a grammatical explanation [in saying the feeling is directed].

There is a 'Why?' to aesthetic discomfort, not a 'cause' to it. The expression of discomfort takes the form of a criticism and not 'My mind is not at rest' or something. It might take the form of looking at a picture and saying 'What's wrong with it?' ...

People often say that aesthetics is a branch of psychology. The idea is that once we are more advanced, everything – all the mysteries of Art – will be understood by psychological experiments. Exceedingly stupid as the idea is, this is roughly it.

Aesthetic questions have nothing to do with psychological experiments, but are answered in an entirely different way.

'What is in my mind when I say so and so?' I write a sentence. One word isn't the word I need. I find the right word. 'What is it I want to say? Oh yes, that is what I wanted.' The answer in these cases is the one that satisfied you, e.g. someone says (as we often say in philosophy): 'I will tell you what is at the back of your mind: ...'

'Oh yes, quite so.'

The criterion for it being the one that was in your mind is that when I tell you, you agree. This is not what is called a psychological experiment. An example of a psychological experiment is: you have twelve subjects, put the same question to each and the result is that each says such and such, i.e. the result is something statistical.

You could say: 'An aesthetic explanation is not a causal explanation.' ...

Aesthetic puzzles – puzzles about the effects the arts have on us.

Paradigm of the sciences is mechanics. If people imagine a psychology, their ideal is a mechanics of the soul. If we look at what actually corresponds to that, we find there are physical experiments and there are psychological experiments. There are laws of physics and there are laws – if you wish to be polite – of psychology. But in physics there are almost too many laws; in psychology there are hardly any. So, to talk about a mechanics of the soul is slightly funny.

But we can dream of predicting the reactions of human beings, say to works of art. If we imagine the dream realized, we'd not thereby have solved what we feel to be aesthetic puzzlements, although we may be able to predict that a certain line of poetry will, on a certain person, act in such and such a way. What we really want, to solve aesthetic puzzlements, is certain comparisons – grouping together of certain cases.

There is a tendency to talk about the 'effect of a work of art' – feelings, images, etc. Then it is natural to ask: 'Why do you hear this minuet?', and there is a tendency to answer 'To get this and that effect.' And doesn't the minuet itself matter? – Hearing *this*: would another have done as well?

You could play a minuet once and get a lot out of it, and play the same minuet another time and get nothing out of it. But it doesn't follow that what you get out of it is then independent of the minuet. Cf. the mistake of thinking that the meaning or thought is just an accompaniment of the word, and the word doesn't matter. 'The sense of a proposition' is very similar to the business of 'an appreciation of art'. The idea that a sentence has a relation to an object, such that, whatever has this effect is the *sense* of the sentence. 'What about a French sentence? – There is the same accompaniment, namely the *thought*.'

A man may sing a song with expression and without expression. Then why not leave out the song – could you have the expression then?

If a Frenchman says: 'It is raining' in French and an Englishman also says it in English, it is not that something happens in both minds which is the real sense of 'It is raining'. We imagine something like *imagery*, which is the international language. Whereas in fact

(1) Thinking (or imagery) is not an accompaniment of the words as they are spoken or heard;
(2) The sense – the thought 'It's raining' – is not even the words *with* the accompaniment of some sort of imagery.

It *is* the thought 'It's raining' only within the English language.

If you ask: 'What is the peculiar effect of these words?', in a sense you make a mistake. What if they had no effect at all? Aren't they peculiar words?

'Then why do we admire this and not that?' 'I don't know.'

Suppose I give you a pill

(1) which makes you draw a picture – perhaps 'The Creation of Adam';
(2) which gives you feelings in the stomach.

Which would you call the more *peculiar* effect? Certainly – that you draw just this picture. The feelings are pretty simple.

'Look at a face – what is important is its expression – not its colour, size, etc.'

'Well give us the expression without the face.'

The expression is not an *effect* of the face – on me or anyone. You could not say that if anything else had this effect, it would have the expression on this face.

I want to make you sad. I show you a picture and you are sad. This is the effect of this face.

11   The Basis of Judgements of Taste: Frank Sibley, *Aesthetic Concepts**

Wittgenstein's comments, in the preceding passage, on the man who goes through a number of patterns at a tailor's and says, 'No. This is slightly too dark. This is slightly too loud...', raise interesting questions about the nature of aesthetic appreciation and judgements of taste generally. In the following extract, from a seminal article by the British aesthetician Frank Sibley, the author asks about the relationship between our perception of non-aesthetic properties (like 'curved', 'yellow', 'tall') and aesthetic properties (like 'graceful', 'garish' and so on). Typically, when we judge an object has a property of the latter type we do so *on the basis of* its having one of the former properties: we say it is graceful *because of* its curved lines, and so on. But is perceiving the descriptive features – the curved lines or whatever – *sufficient* for being able to judge it has the aesthetic properties? Sibley argues that it is not. Any physically normal human being can detect that an object is curved or tall; but this is not so for aesthetic concepts, since they are not 'condition-governed' in this way: 'things may be described to us in non-aesthetic terms as fully as we please, but we are not thereby put in the position of having to admit...that they are delicate or graceful ...'

Sibley goes on to make the related point that aesthetic sensitivity is, in a certain sense, a gift, since the taste and discernment needed to make good aesthetic judgements is not something that can be acquired by anyone. So someone lacking in taste who has carefully monitored the basis on which other people use aesthetic concepts would still risk making mistakes about whether an object was, for example, delicate. He would 'for himself have no more reason to choose tasteful objects... than a deaf man would to avoid noisy places'.

Important conclusions follow from this about the nature of aesthetic discourse and argument. If Sibley is right, there could be no conclusive proof that an object has a certain aesthetic property such as being 'well-balanced'; but nevertheless the ascription of such properties is not just a subjective matter, since they are intimately related to the descriptive properties. Aesthetic features are present *in virtue of* certain non-aesthetic features; and hence, by pointing to the latter, one might manage to help someone to perceive the former (though there would be no guarantee of success). Sibley's views have been vigorously discussed and criticized since their publication, and will surely continue to influence future philosophical debate on the nature of aesthetic criticism and the appreciation of works of art.

 The remarks we make about works of art are of many kinds. For the purpose of this paper, I wish to indicate two broad groups. I shall do this by examples. We say that a novel has a great number of characters and deals with life in a manufacturing town; that a painting uses pale colours, predominantly blues and greens, and has kneeling figures in the foreground; that the theme in a fugue is inverted at such a point and that there is a stretto at the close; that the action of a play takes place in the span of one day and that there is a reconciliation scene in the fifth act. Such remarks may be made by, and such features pointed out to, anyone with normal eyes, ears and intelligence. On the other hand, we also say that a poem is tightly knit or deeply moving; that a picture lacks balance, or has a certain serenity and repose, or that the grouping of the figures sets up an exciting tension; that the characters in a novel never

* 'Aesthetic Concepts', *Philosophical Review*, 68 (1959), 421–50; repr. with 'extensive minor revisions' in J. Margolis (ed.), *Philosophy Looks at the Arts: Contemporary Readings in Aesthetics* (rev. edn, Philadelphia: Temple University Press, 1978), pp. 64–87; abridged.

really come to life, or that a certain episode strikes a false note. It would be natural enough to say that the making of such judgements as these requires the exercise of taste, perceptiveness or sensitivity, of aesthetic discrimination or appreciation; one would not say this of my first group. Accordingly, when a word or expression is such that taste or perceptiveness is required in order to apply it, I shall call it an aesthetic term or expression, and I shall correspondingly speak of *aesthetic* concepts or *taste* concepts.

Aesthetic terms span a great range of types and could be grouped into various kinds of sub-species. But it is not my present purpose to attempt any such grouping; I am interested in what they all have in common. Their almost endless variety is adequately displayed in the following list: *unified, balanced, integrated, lifeless, serene, sombre, dynamic, powerful, vivid, delicate, moving, trite, sentimental, tragic.* The list of course is not limited to adjectives; expressions in artistic contexts like *telling contrast, sets up a tension, conveys a sense of* or *holds it together* are equally good illustrations. It includes terms used by both layman and critic alike, as well as some which are mainly the property of professional critics and specialists. I have gone for my examples of aesthetic expressions in the first place to critical and evaluative discourse about works of art because it is there particularly that they abound. But now I wish to widen the topic; we employ terms the use of which requires an exercise of taste not only when discussing the arts but quite liberally throughout discourse in everyday life. The examples given above are expressions which, appearing in critical contexts, most usually, if not invariably, have an aesthetic use; outside critical discourse the majority of them more frequently have some other use unconnected with taste. But many expressions do double duty even in everyday discourse, sometimes being used as aesthetic expressions and sometimes not. Other words again, whether in artistic or daily discourse, function only or predominantly as aesthetic terms; of this kind are *graceful, delicate, dainty, handsome, comely, elegant, garish.* Finally, to make the contrast with all the preceding examples, there are many words which are seldom used as aesthetic terms at all: *red, noisy, brackish, clammy, square, docile, cured, evanescent, intelligent, faithful, derelict, tardy, freakish.*

Clearly, when we employ words as aesthetic terms we are often making and using metaphors, pressing into service words which do not primarily function in this manner. Certainly also, many words *have come* to be aesthetic terms by some kind of metaphorical transference. This is so with those like 'dynamic', 'melancholy', 'balanced', 'tightly knit', which, except in artistic and critical writings, are not normally aesthetic terms. But the aesthetic vocabulary must not be thought wholly metaphorical. Many words, including the most common (*lovely, pretty, beautiful, dainty, graceful, elegant*), are certainly not being used metaphorically when employed as aesthetic terms, the very good reason being that this is their primary or only use. And though expressions like 'dynamic', 'balanced' and so forth *have come* by a metaphorical shift to be aesthetic terms, their employment in criticism can scarcely be said to be more than quasi-metaphorical. Having entered the language of art description and criticism as metaphors they are now standard vocabulary in that language.

The expressions that I am calling aesthetic terms form no small segment of our discourse. Often, it is true, people with normal intelligence and good eyesight and hearing lack, at least in some measure, the sensitivity required to apply them; a man need not be stupid or have poor eyesight to fail to see that something is graceful. Thus taste or sensitivity is somewhat more rare than certain other human capacities; people who exhibit a sensitivity both wide-ranging and refined are a minority. It is over the application of aesthetic terms too that, notoriously, disputes and differences some-times go helplessly unsettled. But almost everybody is able to exercise taste to some degree and in some matters...

In order to support our application of an aesthetic term, we often refer to features the mention of which involves other aesthetic terms: 'it has an extraordinary vitality because of its free and vigorous style of drawing', 'graceful in the smooth flow of its lines', 'dainty because of the delicacy and harmony of its colouring'. It is as normal to do this as it is to justify one mental epithet by other epithets of the same general type, *intelligent* by *ingenious, inventive, acute* and so on. But often when we apply aesthetic terms we explain why by referring to features which do *not* depend for their recog-nition upon an exercise of taste: 'delicate because of its pastel shades and curving lines', or 'it lacks balance because one group of figures is so far off to the left and is so brightly illuminated'. When no explanation of this latter kind is offered, it is legitimate to ask or search for one. Finding a satisfactory answer may sometimes be difficult, but one cannot ordinarily reject the question. When we cannot ourselves quite say what non-aesthetic features make something delicate or unbalanced or powerful or moving, the good critic often puts his finger on something which strikes us as the right explanation. In short, aesthetic terms always ultimately apply because of, and aesthetic qualities always ultimately depend on, the presence of features which, like curving or angular lines, colour contrast, placing of masses or speed of movement, are visible, audible or otherwise discernible without any exercise of taste or sensibility. Whatever kind of dependence this is, and there are various relationships between aesthetic qualities and non-aesthetic features, what I want to make clear in this paper is that there are no non-aesthetic features which serve in *any* circumstances as logically *sufficient conditions* for applying aesthetic terms. Aesthetic or taste concepts are not in this respect condition-governed at all...

Amongst [the] concepts to which attention has recently been paid are those for which no *necessary and sufficient* conditions can be provided, but for which there are a number of relevant features, A, B, C, D, E, such that the presence of some groups or combinations of these features is *sufficient* for the application of the concept. The list of the relevant features may be an open one; that is, given A, B, C, D, E, we may not wish to close off the possible relevance of other unlisted features beyond E. Examples of such concepts might be 'dilatory', 'discourteous', 'possessive', 'capricious', 'prosper-ous', 'intelligent' (but see below). If we begin a list of features relevant to 'intelligent' with, for example, ability to grasp and follow various kinds of instructions, ability to master facts and marshal evidence, ability to solve mathematical or chess problems, we might go on adding to this list almost indefinitely.

However, with concepts of this sort, although decisions may have to be made and judgement exercised, it is always possible to extract and state, from cases which have *already* clearly been decided, the sets of features or conditions which were regarded as sufficient in those cases. Those relevant features which I am calling conditions are, it should be noted, features which, though not sufficient *alone* and needing to be combined with other similar features, nevertheless carry some weight and can count only in one direction. Being a good chess player can count only *towards* and not *against* intelligence ... But what I want particularly to emphasize about features which function as conditions for a term is that *some* group or set of them *is* sufficient fully to ensure or warrant the application of that term ... There are individuals possessing a number of such features of whom one cannot deny, cannot but admit, that they are intelligent. We have left necessary-and-sufficient conditions behind, but we are still in the realm of sufficient conditions.

But aesthetic concepts are not condition-governed even in this way. There are no sufficient conditions, no non-aesthetic features such that the presence of some set or number of them will beyond question logically justify or warrant the application of an aesthetic term ... Things may be described to us in non-aesthetic terms as fully as we please, but we are not thereby put in the position of having to admit (or being unable to deny) that they are delicate or graceful or garish or exquisitely balanced ...

One way of reinforcing this is to notice how features which are characteristically associated with one aesthetic term may also be similarly associated with other and rather different aesthetic terms. 'Graceful' and 'delicate' may be on the one hand sharply contrasted with terms like 'violent', 'grand', 'fiery', 'garish' or 'massive' which have characteristic non-aesthetic features quite unlike those for 'delicate' and 'graceful'. But on the other hand 'graceful' and 'delicate' may be contrasted with aesthetic terms which stand much closer to them, like 'flaccid', 'weakly', 'washed-out', 'lanky', 'anaemic', 'wan', 'insipid'; and the range of features characteristic of *these* qualities, pale colour, slimness, lightness, lack of angularity and sharp contrast, is virtually identical with the range for 'delicate' and 'graceful'. Similarly, many of the features typically associated with 'joyous', 'fiery', 'robust' or 'dynamic' are identical with those associated with 'garish', 'strident', 'turbulent', 'gaudy' or 'chaotic'. Thus an object which is described very fully, but exclusively in terms of qualities characteristic of delicacy, may turn out on inspection to be not delicate at all, but anaemic or insipid. The failures of novices and the artistically inept prove that quite close similarity in point of line, colour or technique gives no assurance of gracefulness or delicacy. A failure and a success in the manner of Degas may be generally more alike, so far as their non-aesthetic features go, than either is like a successful Fragonard. But it is not necessary to go even this far to make my main point. A painting which has only the kind of features one would associate with vigour or energy but which even so fails to be vigorous and energetic *need* not have some other character, need not be instead, say, strident or chaotic. It may fail to have any particular character whatever. It may employ bright colours, and the like, without being particularly lively and vigorous at all, but one may feel unable to describe it as chaotic or strident or garish either. It is, rather, simply lacking in character (though of course this too is an aesthetic judgement; taste is exercised also in seeing that the painting has no character).

There are of course many features which do not in these ways characteristically count for (or against) particular aesthetic qualities. One poem has strength and power because of the regularity of its metre and rhyme; another is monotonous and lacks drive and strength because of its regular metre and rhyme. We do not feel the need to switch from 'because of' to 'in spite of'. However, I have concentrated upon features which are characteristically associated with aesthetic qualities because, if a case could be made for the view that taste concepts are in any way governed by sufficient conditions, these would seem to be the most promising candidates for governing conditions. But to say that features are associated only *characteristically* with an aesthetic term *is* to say that they can never amount to sufficient conditions; no description however full, even in terms characteristic of gracefulness, puts it beyond question that something is graceful in the way a description may put it beyond question that someone is lazy or intelligent.

It is important to observe, however, that in this paper I am not merely claiming that no sufficient conditions can be stated for taste concepts. For if this were all, taste concepts might not be after all really different from one kind of concept recently discussed. They could be accommodated perhaps with those concepts which Professor H. L. A. Hart has called 'defeasible'; it is a characteristic of defeasible concepts that we cannot state sufficient conditions for them because, for any sets we offer, there is always an (open) list of defeating conditions any of which might rule out the application of the concept.[1] The most we can say schematically for a defeasible concept is that, for example, *A*, *B* and *C* together are sufficient for the concept to apply *unless* some feature is present which overrides or voids them. But, I want to emphasize, the very fact that we *can* say this sort of thing shows that we are still to that extent in the realm of conditions. The features governing defeasible concepts can ordinarily count only one way, *either* for *or* against. To take Hart's example, 'offer' and 'acceptance' can count only towards the existence of a valid contract, and fraudulent misrepresentation, duress, and lunacy can count only against. And even with defeasible concepts, if we are told that there are no voiding features present, we can know that some set of conditions or features, *A*, *B*, *C* ..., is enough, in the absence of voiding features, to ensure, for example, that there is a contract. The very notion of a defeasible concept seems to require that some group of features *would* be sufficient *in certain circumstances*, that is, in the absence of overriding or voiding features. In a certain way, defeasible concepts lack sufficient conditions, then, but they are still, in the sense described, condition-governed. My claim about taste concepts is stronger: that they are not, except negatively,[2] governed by conditions at all. We could not conclude even in certain circumstances, e.g. if we were told of the absence of all 'voiding' or uncharacteristic features (no angularities and the like), that an object *must* certainly be graceful, no matter how fully it was described to us as possessing features characteristic of gracefulness...

The point I have argued may be reinforced in the following way. A man who failed to realize the nature of aesthetic concepts, or someone who, knowing he lacked sensitivity in aesthetic matters, did not want to reveal this lack might by assiduous application and shrewd observation provide himself with some rules and generalizations; and by inductive procedures and intelligent guessing, he might frequently say the right things. But he could have no great confidence or certainty; a slight change in an object might at any time unpredictably ruin his calculations, and he might as easily have been wrong as right. No matter how careful he has been about working out a set of consistent principles and conditions, he is only in a position to think that the object

---

[1] See H. L. A. Hart, 'The Ascription of Responsibility and Rights', in A. G. N. Flew (ed.), *Logic and Language*, 1st series (Oxford: Blackwell, 1951). For example, after the conditions for a valid contract have been specified, there is still an open-ended list of contingencies which may 'defeat' or render void the contract (though it will remain valid if no such contingencies occur).

[2] 'For instance, it may be impossible that a thing should be garish if all its colours are pale pastels, or flamboyant if all its lines are straight.' (The example is taken from an omitted portion of the paper.)

is very possibly delicate. With concepts like *lazy, intelligent* or *contract*, someone who intelligently formulated rules that led him aright appreciably often *would* thereby show the beginning of a grasp of those concepts; but the person we are considering is not even beginning to show an awareness of what delicacy is. Though he sometimes says the right thing, he has not seen, but guessed, that the object is delicate. However intelligent he might be, we could easily tell him wrongly that something was delicate and explain why without his being able to detect the deception... But if we did the same with, say, 'intelligent' he could at least often uncover some incompatibility or other which would need explaining. In a world of beings like himself he would have no use for concepts like delicacy. As it is, these concepts would play a quite different role in his life. He would, for himself, have no more reason to choose tasteful objects, pictures and so on, than a deaf man would to avoid noisy places. He could not be praised for exercising taste; at best his ingenuity and intelligence might come in for mention. In 'appraising' pictures, statuettes, poems, he would be doing something quite different from what other people do when they exercise taste...

One after another, in recent discussions, writers have insisted that aesthetic judgements are not 'mechanical': 'Critics do not formulate general standards and apply these mechanically to all, or to classes of, works of art.' 'Technical points can be settled rapidly, by the application of rules', but aesthetic questions 'cannot be settled by any mechanical method'. Instead these writers on aesthetics have emphasized that there is no 'substitute for individual judgement', with its 'spontaneity and speculation' and that 'The final standard... [is] the judgement of personal taste'.[1] What is surprising is that, though such things have been repeated again and again, no one seems to have said what is meant by 'taste' or by the word 'mechanical'. There are many judgements besides those requiring taste which demand 'spontaneity' and 'individual judgement' and are not 'mechanical'. Without a detailed comparison we cannot see in what particular way *aesthetic* judgements are not 'mechanical', or how they differ from those other judgements, nor can we begin to specify what taste is. This I have attempted. It is a characteristic and essential feature of judgements which employ an aesthetic term that they cannot be made by appealing, in the sense explained, to non-aesthetic conditions. This, I believe, is a logical feature of aesthetic or taste judgements in general, though I have argued it here only as regards the more restricted range of judgements which employ aesthetic terms. It is part of what 'taste' means.

[1] See the articles by Margaret Macdonald and J. Passmore in W. Elton (ed.), *Aesthetics and Language* (Oxford: Oxford University Press, 1954).

12   Artistic Representation and Reality: Nelson Goodman, *The Languages of Art**

Our final extract in this Part of the volume is by the distinguished American thinker Nelson Goodman, who made influential contributions not just in aesthetics but in many areas of philosophy. Here he tackles the nature of artistic *representation* – something that it is clearly vital to understand if we wish to grasp what artists are doing when they depict the world around them, and enable us to see it in new ways. Representation, Goodman begins by pointing out, cannot be a simple function of *resemblance*; for even the most favourable case, that of a portrait or landscape painting, will in many ways be more like another painting than it will be like the scene or person, or whatever, that it depicts. Works of art *refer to* or *denote* their objects, independently of any question of resemblance.[1] What this implies is that art is to be understood as operating after the fashion of linguistic and symbolic systems, rather than as a way of 'copying' reality.

In general, Goodman goes on to argue, it is a mistake to suppose that even a directly representational work of art can be understood as an *imitation* or copy of its original as it might be seen under 'normal' conditions. For there is no such thing as the innocent eye. 'The eye comes always ancient to its work', selecting, classifying, organizing, constructing: 'it does not so much mirror as take and make.' This is not to say that the artist will not often employ well-worn classifications, which may be 'serviceable even if humdrum'; but often he or she will 'force unaccustomed associations, and in some measure remake our world'. Goodman captures important

insights here into the creativity involved in art, especially in great art.

Nevertheless, we often praise paintings and novels for their realism. But in the concluding section of our extract Goodman claims that 'realism is relative, determined by the system of representation for a given culture . . . at a given time'. So what may be a straightforward and realistic way of representing something for an ancient Egyptian may not be so for us today. Of particular interest here is Goodman's notion that a 'standard system' of representation comes down to no more than a system we are used to: 'the literal or realistic or naturalistic system of representation is simply the customary one.' Hence realism, Goodman concludes, is merely a 'matter of habit'.

There are many questions to be raised about Goodman's account of how works of art represent their objects. Some critics have focused especially on what kinds of modifications to the account are needed in order to deal with the frequent case when, instead of denoting an actual object in the world, a painting is about a fictional person or thing. Part of the interest of these discussions is that they connect questions in aesthetics with wider questions in the philosophy of language and the theory of meaning. The fruitful debates over Goodman's work point to a salutary conclusion: that philosophical inquiry, in the end, can never be split up into a series of water-tight specialisms, but constantly leads us to make wider connections as we strive to understand our human activities and their relation to the world around us.

 ### Denotation

The nature of representation wants early study in any philosophical examination of the way symbols function in and out of the arts. That representation is frequent in some arts, such as painting, and infrequent in others, such as music, threatens trouble for a unified aesthetics; and confusion over how pictorial representation as a mode of

---

* From Nelson Goodman, *The Languages of Art* (Oxford: Oxford University Press, 1969), ch. 1; abridged.
[1] For the concept of denotation, see above, Part III, extracts 7 and 8.

signification is allied to and distinguished from verbal description on the one hand and, say, facial expression on the other is fatal to any general theory of symbols.

The most naive view of representation might perhaps be put somewhat like this: 'A represents B only if A appreciably resembles B.' Vestiges of this view, with assorted refinements, persist in most writings on representation. Yet more error could hardly be compressed into so short a formula.

Some of the faults are obvious enough. An object resembles itself to the maximum degree but rarely represents itself; resemblance, unlike representation, is reflexive. Again, unlike representation, resemblance is symmetric: B is as much like A as A is like B, but while a painting may represent the Duke of Wellington, the Duke doesn't represent the painting. Furthermore, in many cases neither one of a pair of very like objects represents the other: none of the automobiles off an assembly line is a picture of any of the rest; and a man is not normally a representation of another man, even his twin brother. Plainly, resemblance in any degree is no sufficient condition for representation.

Just what correction to make to the formula is not so obvious. We may attempt less, and prefix the condition 'If A is a picture … '. Of course, if we then construe 'picture' as 'representation', we resign a large part of the question: namely, what constitutes a representation. But even if we construe 'picture' broadly enough to cover all paintings, the formula is wide of the mark in other ways. A Constable painting of Marlborough Castle is more like any other picture than it is like the Castle, yet it represents the Castle and not another picture – not even the closest copy. To add the requirement that B must not be a picture would be desperate and futile; for a picture may represent another, and indeed each of the once popular paintings of art galleries represents many others.

The plain fact is that a picture, to represent an object, must be a symbol for it, stand for it, refer to it; and that no degree of resemblance is sufficient to establish the requisite relationship of reference. Nor is resemblance *necessary* for reference; almost anything may stand for almost anything else. A picture that represents – like a passage that describes – an object refers to and, more particularly, *denotes* it. Denotation is the core of representation and it is independent of resemblance.

If the relation between a picture and what it represents is thus assimilated to the relation between a predicate and what it applies to, we must examine the characteristics of representation as a special kind of denotation. What does pictorial denotation have in common with, and how does it differ from, verbal or diagrammatic denotation? One not implausible answer is that resemblance, while not sufficient for representation, is just the feature that distinguishes representation from denotation of other kinds. Is it perhaps the case that if A denotes B, then A represents B just to the extent that A resembles B? I think even this watered-down and innocuous-looking version of our initial formula betrays a grave misconception of the nature of representation.

Imitation

'To make a faithful picture, come as close as possible to copying the object as it is.' This simple-minded injunction baffles me; for the object before me is a man, a swarm of atoms, a complex of cells, a fiddler, a friend, a fool and much more. If none of these constitute the object as it is, what else might? If all are ways the object is, then none is *the* way the object is. I cannot copy all these at once; and the more nearly I succeeded, the less would the result be a realistic picture.

What I am to copy then, it seems, is one such aspect, one of the ways the object is or looks. But not, of course, any one of these at random – not, for example, the Duke of Wellington as he looks to a drunk through a raindrop. Rather, we may suppose, the way the object looks to the normal eye, at proper range, from a favourable angle, in good light, without instrumentation, unprejudiced by affections or animosities or interests, and unembellished by thought or interpretation. In short, the object is to be copied as seen under aseptic conditions by the free and innocent eye.

The catch here, as Ernest Gombrich insists, is that there is no innocent eye.[1] The eye comes always ancient to its work, obsessed by its own past and by old and new insinuations of the ear, nose, tongue, fingers, heart and brain. It functions not as an instrument self-powered and alone, but as a dutiful member of a complex and capricious organism. Not only how but what it sees is regulated by need and prejudice. It selects, rejects, organizes, discriminates, associates, classifies, analyses, constructs. It does not so much mirror as take and make; and what it takes and makes it sees not bare, as items without attributes, but as things, as food, as people, as enemies, as stars, as weapons. Nothing is seen nakedly or naked.

The myths of the innocent eye and of the absolute given are unholy accomplices. Both derive from and foster the idea of knowing as a processing of raw material received from the senses, and of this raw material as being discoverable either through purification rites or by methodical disinterpretation. But reception and interpretation are not separable operations; they are thoroughly interdependent. The Kantian dictum echoes here: the innocent eye is blind and the virgin mind empty.[2]

All the same, the artist may often do well to strive for innocence of eye. The effort sometimes rescues him from the tired patterns of everyday seeing, and results in fresh insight. The opposite effort, to give fullest rein to a personal reading, can be equally tonic – and for the same reason. But the most neutral eye and the most biased are merely sophisticated in different ways. The most ascetic vision and the most prodigal, like the sober portrait and the vitriolic caricature, differ not in how *much* but only in *how* they interpret.

The copy theory of representation, then, is stopped at the start by inability to specify what is to be copied. Not an object the way it is, nor all the ways it is, nor the way it looks to the mindless eye. Moreover, something is wrong with the very notion of copying any of the ways an object is, any aspect of it. For an aspect is not just the object-from-a-given-distance-and-angle-and-in-a-given-light; it is the object as we look upon it and conceive it, a version or construal of the object. In representing an object, we do not copy such a construal or interpretation, we *achieve* it . . .

Invention

If representing is a matter of classifying objects rather than of imitating them, of characterizing rather than of copying, it is not a matter of passive reporting. The

---

[1] *In *Art and Illusion* (New York; Pantheon, 1960), pp. 297–8 and elsewhere.
[2] Echoing Kant's dictum from the *Critique of Pure Reason*, 'thoughts without content are empty, intuitions without concepts are blind'. See above, Part I, extract 8.

object does not sit as a docile model with its attributes neatly separated and thrust out for us to admire and portray. It is one of countless objects, and may be grouped with any selection of them; and for any such grouping there is an attribute of the object. To admit all classifications on equal footing amounts to making no classification at all. Classification involves preferment; and application of a label (pictorial, verbal, etc.) as often *effects* as it records a classification. The 'natural' kinds are simply those we are in the habit of picking out for and by labelling. Moreover, the object itself is not ready-made but results from a way of taking the world. The making of a picture commonly participates in making what is to be pictured. The object and its aspects depend upon organization; and labels of all sorts are tools of organization . . .

Representation or description is apt, effective, illuminating, subtle, intriguing, to the extent that the artist or writer grasps fresh and significant relationships and devises means for making them manifest. Discourse or depiction that marks off familiar units and sorts them into standard sets under well-worn labels may some-times be serviceable even if humdrum. The marking off of new elements or classes, or of familiar ones by labels of new kinds or by new combinations of old labels, may provide new insight . . . In representation, the artist must make use of old habits when he wants to elicit novel objects and connections. If his picture is recognized as almost but not quite referring to the commonplace furniture of the everyday world, or if it calls for and yet resists assignment to a usual kind of picture, it may bring out neglected likenesses and differences, force unaccustomed associations, and in some measure remake our world. And if the point of the picture is not only successfully made but is also well-taken, if the realignments it directly and indirectly effects are interesting and important, the picture – like a crucial experiment – makes a genuine contribution to knowledge. To a complaint that his portrait of Gertrude Stein did not look like her, Picasso is said to have answered 'No matter; it will.'

In sum, effective representation and description require invention. They are cre-ative. They inform each other; and they form, relate and distinguish objects. That nature imitates art is too timid a dictum. Nature is a product of art and discourse.

Realism

This leaves unanswered the minor question what constitutes realism of representa-tion. Surely not, in view of the foregoing, any sort of resemblance to reality. Yet we do in fact compare representations with respect to their realism or naturalism or fidelity. If resemblance is not the criterion, what is?

One popular answer is that the test of fidelity is deception, that a picture is realistic just to the extent that it is a successful illusion, leading the viewer to suppose that it is, or has the characteristic of, what it represents. The proposed measure of realism, in other words, is the probability of confusing the representation with the represented. This is some improvement over the copy theory; for what counts here is not how closely the picture duplicates an object but how far the picture and object, under conditions of observation appropriate to each, give rise to the same responses and expectations . . .

Yet there are difficulties. What deceives depends upon what is observed, and what is observed varies with interests and habits. If the probability of confusion is 1, we no longer have representation – we have identity. Moreover, the probability seldom rises noticeably above zero for even the most guileful *trompe-l'oeil* painting seen under ordinary gallery conditions. For seeing a picture as a picture precludes mistaking it for anything else; and the appropriate conditions of observation (e.g. framed, against a uniform background, etc.) are calculated to defeat deception ... Deception counts less as a measure of realism than as evidence of magicianship, and is a highly atypical mishap. In looking at the most realistic picture, I seldom suppose that I can literally reach into the distance, slice the tomato or beat the drum. Rather, I recognize the images as signs for the objects and characteristics represented – signs that work instantly and unequivocally without being confused with what they denote. Of course, sometimes where deception does occur – say by a painted window in a mural – we may indeed call the picture realistic; but such cases provide no basis for the usual ordering of pictures in general as more or less realistic.

Thoughts along these lines have led to the suggestion that the most realistic picture is the one that provides the greatest amount of pertinent information. But this hypothesis can be quickly and completely refuted. Consider a realistic picture, painted in ordinary perspective and normal colour, and a second picture just like the first except that the perspective is reversed and each colour is replaced by its complementary. The second picture, appropriately interpreted, yields exactly the same information as the first. And any number of other drastic but information-preserving transformations are possible. Obviously, realistic and unrealistic pictures can be equally informative; informational yield is no test of realism ...

The alert absolutist will argue that for the second picture but not the first we need a key. Rather, the difference is that for the first the key is ready at hand. For proper reading of the second picture, we have to discover the rules of interpretation and apply them deliberately. Reading of the first is by virtually automatic habit; practice has rendered the symbols so transparent that we are not aware of any effort, of any alternatives or of making any interpretation at all. Just here, I think, lies the touchstone of realism: not in quantity of information but in how easily it issues. And this depends upon how stereotyped the mode of representation is, upon how commonplace the labels and their uses have become.

Realism is relative, determined by the system of representation standard for a given culture or person at a given time. Newer or older or alien systems are accounted artificial or unskilled. For a Fifth-Dynasty Egyptian the straightforward way of representing something is not the same as for an eighteenth-century Japanese; and neither way is the same as for an early twentieth-century Englishman. Each would to some extent have to learn how to read a picture in either of the other styles. This relativity is obscured by our tendency to omit specifying a frame of reference when it is our own. 'Realism' thus often comes to be used as the name for a particular style or system of representation. Just as on this planet we usually think of objects as fixed if they are at a constant position in relation to the earth, so in this period and place we usually think of paintings as literal or realistic if they are in a traditional European style of representation. But such egocentric ellipsis must not tempt us to infer that these objects (or any others) are absolutely fixed, or that such pictures (or any others) are absolutely realistic ... Realism is a matter not of any constant or absolute relationship between a picture and its object but of a relationship between the system of representation employed in the picture and the standard system. Most of the time, of course, the traditional system is taken as standard; and the literal or realistic or naturalistic system of representation is simply the customary one.

Realistic representation, in brief, depends not upon imitation or illusion or information but upon inculcation. Almost any picture may represent almost anything; that is, given picture and object there is usually a system of representation, a plan of correlation, under which the picture represents the object. How correct the picture is under that system depends upon how accurate is the information about the object that is obtained by reading the picture according to that system. But how literal or realistic the picture is depends upon how standard the system is. If representation is a matter of choice and correctness a matter of information, realism is a matter of habit.

Specimen Questions

1 What are Plato's reasons for disapproving of painting and poetry? Do you find them convincing?

2 'A tragedy is the imitation of an action that is serious...with incidents arousing pity and fear, wherewith to accomplish its catharsis of such emotions.' Explain and evaluate Aristotle's definition of tragedy.

3 Critically expound Hutcheson's account of the sense of beauty as an 'internal sense' whereby certain 'ideas' are 'excited' by external objects.

4 'It is natural for us to seek a *standard of taste*; a rule by which the various sentiments of men may be reconciled' (Hume). How far does Hume think such a standard may be found?

5 Explain and discuss Kant's definition of the beautiful as 'an object of delight apart from any interest'.

6 'Just as the botanist plucks a single flower from the infinite wealth of the plant world...so does the poet take from the endless maze and confusion of human life...a single scene.' Explain and evaluate Schopenhauer's account of the relationship between the particular and the universal in works of art.

7 'We shall have gained much for the science of aesthetics once we perceive not merely by logical inference but by the immediate certainty of vision, that the continuous development of art is bound up with the *Apollonian* and *Dionysian* duality' (Nietzsche). Explain and discuss.

8 Must moral values take precedence over aesthetic values? Discuss with reference to Tolstoy's challenge to the value of art.

9 'The work of art is an unreality' (Sartre). Explain and discuss.

10 Critically examine Wittgenstein's claim that aesthetics cannot be reduced to a branch of psychology.

11 'It is a characteristic and essential feature of judgements which employ an aesthetic term that they cannot be made by appealing, in the sense explained, to non-aesthetic conditions' (Sibley). Explain and critically discuss.

12 What is wrong with the view that a picture is simply a copy that resembles its object as closely as possible? Discuss with reference to Goodman's views.

Suggestions for Further Reading

A valuable reference work covering all the authors appearing in this Part is D. Cooper (ed.), *A Companion to Aesthetics* (Oxford: Blackwell, 1992).

An excellent anthology of influential modern contributions is P. Lamarque and S. H. Olsen (eds), *Aesthetics and the Philosophy of Art* (Oxford: Blackwell, 2004).

A handy collection of essays on various issues is H. Osborne (ed.), *Aesthetics* (Oxford: Oxford University Press, 1972).

For a clear discussion of Plato's attitude to the arts in the *Republic* and in other writings, see E. Asmis, 'Plato on Poetic Creativity', in R. Kraut (ed.), *The Cambridge Companion to Plato* (Cambridge: Cambridge University Press, 1992). For a stimulating assessment of Plato's challenge to the arts, see C. Janaway, *Images of Excellence: Plato's Critique of the Arts* (Oxford: Clarendon, 1995).

For Aristotle's theory of tragedy see S. Halliwell, *Aristotle's Poetics* (London: Duckworth, 1986), and A. O. Rorty (ed.), *Essays on Aristotle's Poetics* (Princeton: Princeton University Press, 1992).

A detailed account of Hutcheson's ideas will be found in P. Kivy, *The Seventh Sense: A Study of Francis Hutcheson's Aesthetics and its Influence in Eighteenth-Century Britain* (New York: Franklin, 1976).

For an interesting discussion of Hume's views (and those of several of the other philosophers featured in this Part of the volume), see M. Motherskill, *Beauty Restored* (Oxford: Clarendon, 1984). The theories of Hume and Kant are critically discussed in M. Budd, *Values of Art* (Harmondsworth: Penguin, 1995).

For discussions of Kant's theory of the beautiful, see P. Guyer, *Kant and the Claims of Taste* (Cambridge, Mass.: Harvard University Press, 1979), and M. A. McCloskey, *Kant's Aesthetic* (London: Macmillan, 1987). See also E. Shaper, 'Taste, Sublimity and Genius', in P. Guyer (ed.), *The Cambridge Companion to Kant* (Cambridge: Cambridge University Press, 1992).

Discussions of Schopenhauer's theory of art may be found in the introductions to his philosophy listed at the end of Part IV, above. See also the essay by Michael Tanner in Cooper (ed.), *A Companion to Aesthetics*.

An interesting collection of papers relating to Nietzsche's views on art is R. Sidgwick (ed.), *Nietzsche on Tragedy* (Cambridge: Cambridge University Press, 1981). A useful study is J. Young, *Nietzsche's Philosophy of Art* (Cambridge: Cambridge University Press, 1992). See also the readings on Nietzsche at the end of Part VIII above.

For a discussion of Tolstoy's essay, see T. J. Diffey, *Tolstoy's What is Art?* (London: Croom Helm, 1985). See also H. W. Garrod, *Tolstoy's Theory of Art* (Oxford: Clarendon, 1935).

For students of Sartre, an excellent collection of essays is C. Howells (ed.), *The Cambridge Companion to Sartre* (Cambridge: Cambridge University Press, 1992). See also E. F. Kaelin, *An Existentialist Aesthetic* (Madison: University of Wisconsin Press, 1966).

For a discussion of Wittgenstein's philosophy and its relation to aesthetics, see R. Wollheim, *Art and its Objects* (London: Harmondsworth, 1970).

Some useful critical discussion of Sibley's views may be found in E. Brady and J. Levinson (eds), *Aesthetic Concepts: Essays after Sibley* (Oxford: Oxford University Press, 2001). See also G. Dickie, *Evaluating Art* (Philadelphia: Temple University Press, 1988).

Goodman's ideas are discussed and criticized in K. L. Walton, 'Are Representations Symbols', in Lamarque and Olsen (eds), *Aesthetics and the Philosophy of Art*. See also the essays by Scruton, Meiland, Budd and Wollheim, in part 7 of that collection. An excellent essay for those interested in Goodman's ideas is John Hyman's 'Language and Pictorial Art', in Cooper (ed.), *A Companion to Aesthetics*.

PART XII

Human Life and its Meaning

Human Life and its Meaning
Introduction

What is the meaning of life? Some people are initially attracted to philosophy because they hope it will provide answers to this ancient riddle. If they are looking for an easy solution, they will almost certainly be disappointed, like the solemn searchers in *The Hitchhiker's Guide to the Galaxy*, who are eventually told that 'the answer to the Great Question of Life, the Universe and Everything is...Forty-two'.[1] Indeed, some philosophers would maintain that the reason the question of life's meaning seems so difficult to answer is that it is a bogus question: meaning is a property of sentences or signs, not things like human life, or the universe. Perhaps, as the great twentieth-century philosopher Ludwig Wittgenstein once remarked, the solution to the problem of the meaning of life lies in its disappearance.[2]

Nevertheless, we all seek meaning in our lives, and dread that sense of futility that can make everything seem 'weary, stale, flat and unprofitable'.[3] Being engaged on worthwhile projects and activities (building a career, raising a family and so on) may keep such negative feelings at bay, but are these individual pursuits enough, or do we need some more fundamental end that will validate our lives? Must all our human efforts seem insignificant against the backdrop of the vast and seemingly impersonal universe disclosed by modern science? Does the inescapable fact of our mortality prevent our lives from achieving any real or lasting significance? Can religion provide an ultimate answer, or must we reject its comforts as illusory, and learn to rely purely on our own resources? These are among the questions to be addressed in this final Part of the volume, and, as before, we shall start with some of the answers offered by the thinkers of the ancient world, and move gradually forwards to our own time. Since the problems involved are as old as humanity, it seems unlikely that they will ever be marked down as 'solved', in the way that can happen in science. But we can still learn much from seeing the different ways in which great philosophers have wrestled with the riddle of human existence. Their struggles are ones we can identify with, for the philosophical quest to make sense of our fleeting yet precious lives is one that we all share.

[1] Douglas Adams, *The Hitchhiker's Guide to the Galaxy* (London: Pan, 1979), p. 136.
[2] Ludwig Wittgenstein, *Tractatus Logico-Philosophicus* [1922], § 6.521.
[3] 'How weary, stale, flat and unprofitable / Seem to me all the uses of this world' (William Shakespeare, *Hamlet* [1601], Act I, scene 2, ll. 135–6).

1 How to Accept Reality and Avoid Fear: Lucretius, *On the Nature of the Universe**

Our first extract comes from the Roman poet Lucretius, who was one of the main advocates in the ancient world for the philosophy of Epicureanism. Founded by the Greek thinker Epicurus (341–271 BC), this is an uncompromisingly materialist worldview, which holds that everything has a purely natural cause, and that all phenomena, including human life, evolved from the movements of atoms in the void. In his epic poem *De Rerum Natura* ('The Nature of the Universe'), written in the first century BC, Lucretius argues that accepting this reality is the key to a worthwhile life.

Since mental functioning depends very closely on the state of the bodily organs, this shows, according to Lucretius, that the mind is entirely physical. And the conditions for a good life reflect this fact: our welfare consists fundamentally of pleasure and absence of pain. Contrary to the common caricature, however, the Epicurean goal is not excessive sensual indulgence, but a life of tranquil and balanced enjoyment. Lucretius makes it clear throughout our text that the frantic pursuit of luxury is a mistake: the pleasures

that make human life worthwhile are comparatively simple and easy to achieve, provided we take a rational view of our human limitations and, above all, of our mortality.

Towards the end of the extract, Lucretius sets out the basis for the classic Epicurean thesis that there is nothing to fear in death. All sensation and thought depends on our bodily nature as human beings, and hence the destruction of the body marks the end of all mental activity. It follows that the time after we are dead is simply the absence of awareness – something that should be no more a cause of anguish to us than the time before we were born. There is no 'ultimate' significance in life, according to this philosophy, but that does not take away the value from the enjoyment that humans can achieve during the limited time at their disposal. Whether or not such rational reflections can take away the fear of extinction, as Lucretius argues, is a matter for debate; but there is certainly something impressive about the picture he paints of how we can learn to live with a purely naturalistic view of the world and of human nature.

When the sea's mighty waters are being lashed by the wind, how sweet it is to stand on the shore and watch someone else struggling. Not that one takes pleasure at the afflictions of another – but it is pleasant to realize what troubles you are free from yourself. Or again, in wartime, when great armies are drawn up on the battlefield, how sweet it is to watch them from a distance, when you yourself have no part in the danger. Sweetest of all, though, is to dwell in the tranquil temples of the wise, fortified by sound doctrine: from here, far below you, you may see others wandering aimlessly in search of the path of life. What bitter competition about who is the brightest, what rivalry over rank and status, what furious efforts night and day to reach the summit of wealth and power! Such attitudes are truly pitiable, such feelings truly blind – that they should use up this tiny span of life in such darkness and danger! Yet all the time, could they but see it, nature is crying out for no more than this: to avoid bodily pain, to have a mind free from anxiety and fear and to enjoy the pleasures of the senses.

It is plain to see that our bodily nature needs very few things to banish pain, and to furnish us with many pleasures that are enjoyable from time to time. Nature herself

---

* Lucretius, *De Rerum Natura* [*c*.60 BC], Bk II, 1–61; Bk III, 31–40, 94–6, 161–76, 526–32, 547–55, 830–42, 1053–94. Translation by John Cottingham.

does not complain if the halls are not full of golden statues of youths holding flaming torches to light up the banquets that go on all night, or if the house is not sparkling with silver and gleaming with gold, while the music echoes round the gilded rafters. For by the riverside, stretched out on the soft grass under the shade of a tall tree, people can relax and enjoy themselves far better without all that expense, especially when the weather smiles on them and the spring scatters the green meadow with flowers. And if you have a fever, it will run its course no quicker if your coverlets are embroidered in fancy colours than if you lie on plain ordinary bedclothes.

Treasures, noble birth, regal glory – these have no beneficial effects at all on our bodies; and the next step is to see that they do not benefit our minds either. Suppose you are watching your entire private army march up and down on the parade ground practising their military manoeuvres, complete with auxiliaries and cavalry, in full equipment and full of bravado; or suppose you are watching a whole fleet of your ships sailing home on the broad sea: does such a sight drive the fearful superstitions from your mind? Does the fear of death lose its hold on your mind and leave it carefree? Or are not such lavish displays in truth ridiculous and absurd? For the reality is that our human fears, the anxieties that pursue us, are not scared off by the sound of arms and fearsome weapons. They thrive just as much in the company of kings and powerful leaders, and show no respect for the glitter of gold or the glowing splendour of richly coloured clothes.

Why doubt, then, that the power to banish fear belongs to reason alone? Our life is one long struggle in the darkness; and as children in a dark room are terrified of everything, so we in broad daylight are sometimes afraid of things that are no more to be feared than the imaginary horrors that scare children in the dark. This dread, this darkness of the mind, must be dispelled not by the rays of the sun or the bright beams of daylight, but by nature itself – by contemplating its appearance and understanding its workings...

I have explained the [material] basis of everything: how particles of various shapes fly through space of their own accord, driven on in endless motion, and how everything can be formed from these materials. In accordance with these principles, my verses must now explain the nature of the mind and spirit, and thereby banish utterly the fear of death that so deeply disturbs our human life. This fear tinges everything we do with death's blackness, leaving no pleasure clean and pure...

Firstly, I maintain that the mind, or intelligence, as we often call it, where all the planning and ordering of life resides, is simply a part of the human being, no less than hands and feet and eyes are parts of the whole organism... Reason teaches us that the nature of the mind and soul is corporeal, since we see that it moves the limbs, rouses the body from sleep, changes the expression on the face and controls the entire human being. Now all these things cannot occur without contact, and there is no contact except via bodies: so must we not concede that the mind and soul have a nature that is bodily? What is more, you can see that our mind functions along with our body and shares its sensations. If the grim force of a weapon drives deep into the bones and nerves, even if it is not fatal, it may cause a dizzy fall to the ground, and the mind becomes confused, with a feeble desire to get up again. So if bodily weapons and blows can affect it, the mind itself must have a nature that is bodily...

What is more, we often see a person pass away gradually, and lose the vital sensation in one limb after another: first the toes and toenails go white, then the feet and legs die, and slowly the cold clutches of death spread though the remaining limbs. Since the nature of the soul is divided in this way, and does not leave the body in one clean break, we must infer that it is mortal... The mind is but one part of the human being, which occupies a definite location, just like the ears and the eyes and the other senses that guide our life; and since the hands or eyes or nose cannot feel or function when they are separated from us, but soon putrefy and rot, so the soul cannot exist without the body, or without the whole human being...

So death is nothing to us, and is wholly irrelevant, once we understand that the nature of the mind is mortal. Consider the time before we were born: we felt no distress when the Carthaginians were attacking Rome on every side, and the whole world was shaken by the frightening tumult of that war – when no one knew which empire would dominate all human civilization by land and sea. And in the same way in the future, when we shall no longer exist, and the final breaking up occurs for the body and spirit from which we are now compounded into a single unit, nothing whatever will be able to happen to us, or produce any sensation – not even if the earth should collapse into the sea, or the sea explode into the sky...

People often feel a weight on their minds that bears down upon them and exhausts them. But if they could only know what are its causes – what makes such a load of evil press down on their spirits – they would not live their lives in the way we so often observe: no one knowing what he wants, everyone wanting to change his position in life, as if he could thereby lay down his burden. Look at the man who keeps leaving his vast mansion because he feels bored at home, and then suddenly decides to come back because he feels no better abroad. He drives full speed to his country retreat... and then rushes back to see the city again. Thus does everyone try to escape from themselves (yet the self we cannot escape always manages to stick to us, try as we might). We hate ourselves because we are sick, yet we cannot grasp the cause of our sickness; but if we could see it, we would abandon such frantic activity and first try to understand the nature of the universe. What is at stake is not just one hour of time, but the future eternity that stretches out after death for all of us mortals.

To conclude: it is this evil and excessive desire for life that makes us tremble with doubts and forebodings. Mortal beings have a fixed lifespan: death cannot be avoided, but awaits us all. Besides, the setting of our lives remains the same, and continuing to live will not make us able to devise any new pleasures. As long as the thing we crave is absent it seems more precious than anything, but when we get it then we immediately want something else: our mouths are always gaping open with a constant thirst for life. Yet it is uncertain what fortune the coming years will deliver, what the blows of chance will bring or what end is in store for us. And by prolonging life we do not subtract anything from the time when we shall be dead: we cannot make the time after our passing the slightest bit shorter. No matter how many generations you live through, the same eternal death is still waiting, and someone who ends his life as the sun goes down today will have just as long a period of non-existence as one who died many months and years before.

2   Life Guided by Stoic Philosophy: Seneca, *Moral Letters**

Alongside Epicureanism (see preceding extract), an equally influential creed in the classical world was Stoicism, a philosophy founded in Athens towards the end of the fourth century BC, by a contemporary of Epicurus, Zeno of Citium. More 'spiritual' in character than Epicureanism, Stoicism held that reality is not a mere collection of material particles, but is animated by an active rational principle (*logos*), and that the good life consists of a 'living in accord with nature', which implies living virtuously and in accordance with reason.

The extract is from the 'Moral Letters' of the Roman philosopher Seneca, who was strongly influenced by Stoicism, and a respected promoter of some of its key doctrines. One of these is that whatever is rationally ordained (by the active principle that we may call 'God' or 'providence') cannot be otherwise; and it is the mark of a person of wisdom to acquiesce in what cannot be altered. Living 'according to nature' is living rationally, in acceptance of the rationally ordained course of the world; the crucial point is not to agonize over what is not within our power to change. Teaching us to have this sort of acceptance emerges as the prime role for philosophy, or the 'study of wisdom'; this is the key to

that tranquillity of mind at which the Stoics aimed. To achieve this end, Seneca stresses the importance of a practical programme of meditation and mental training, which will produce a 'good frame of mind', or a 'good outlook'.

The word 'stoical', in its modern usage, has come to denote a 'stiff upper lip' outlook, which endures misfortune without showing emotion. But the extract below shows that this is something of a distortion. The Stoics made a key distinction between the external circumstances of life that cannot be changed, and the internal domain of one's own attitude, which can be modified by philosophical training. True joy, Seneca tells his friend Lucilius, comes not from worthless baubles like riches, but depends on 'the mind itself [being] happy and confident, and raised high above every external circumstance'. Critics of this idea have worried that it may lead to too passive or acquiescent an attitude to the problems of the world around us; nevertheless the core doctrine which Seneca here develops has affinities with an idea found in many spiritual traditions, that the key to finding meaning and fulfilment lies in the attainment of virtue based on interior equilibrium and detachment from the outer world.

 I know, Lucilius, that it is quite clear to you that no one can live a happy or even a tolerable life without the study of wisdom; further, that only once wisdom is perfected do we achieve a happy life, but a tolerable life is possible even when we are setting out on the road. Although this point is clear enough, it needs to be reinforced and dinned into us by daily mediation; sticking to your existing resolutions is more use than making fresh ones, however noble. You must persevere, and build up your strength by continuous study, until what were mere good intentions get transformed into a good frame of mind.

So you no longer need to send me long reports or declarations of commitment; I'm quite aware that you have made great progress. I know what is behind the things you write, and that your words are genuine and unvarnished. Let me nonetheless tell you what I think: I have great hopes of you, but I am not yet completely confident. I would like you to have a similar attitude: there's no reason for confidence to come too

* From Lucius Annaeus Seneca, *Moral Letters* [*Epistulae Morales*, c.AD 64], Letter 16 and extracts from Letter 23. Translation by John Cottingham.

quickly or easily. Test yourself by careful scrutiny and varied observation; above all make sure you are really advancing in philosophy and not just in years. Philosophy is not a device for popular consumption or public display: it consists of real achievements, not mere words. We don't practise it to round off the day with some amusement, or to rid our spare time of boredom. Philosophy shapes and constructs the soul, orders our life, governs our actions, shows us what is to be done and what avoided, sits at the helm and directs our course as we drift amid the seas of doubt. Without it no one can live with courage and free from anxiety. Every hour countless things happen that need the kind of guidance we must seek from philosophy.

Someone may object: 'What use is philosophy to me if everything is down to Fate? What use is philosophy if there is a God who rules all things? What use is it if Chance governs all? What is determined cannot be altered, and what is undetermined cannot be planned for; so either God has forestalled my plans and decided what I am to do, or else Fortune leaves no room for my deliberations.' Whichever of these views is true, Lucilius, or if they all are,[1] we must still practise philosophy. Whether the fates constrain us by an inexorable law, or God the arbiter of the universe disposes all things, or chance drives human affairs at random, it is philosophy that should watch over us. Philosophy will encourage us to obey God cheerfully, but Fortune defiantly: she will teach us to follow God and to endure Chance.

But this is not the time to enter the debate about what is under our own control, or if providence is in command, or if a chain of fated circumstances drags us along irresistibly, or if we are at the mercy of sudden and unexpected events. I want to get back to my earlier warnings that you should not allow your mental impulses to weaken or grow cold. Hold on to them, build them up, so that what are now mere impulses may become permanent dispositions of mind.

I know you well enough to know that from the start of this letter you will have been poring over it to spot what little nuggets of benefit it may bring you. Search and you will find. There is no great acumen of mine for you to admire: what I have so lavishly bestowed up till now comes only from other people. Yet why did I say 'other people'? Anything that is well said by anyone else can be my property too. And here is another saying of Epicurus: 'If you live according to nature, you will never be poor; if you live to please the opinions of others you will never be rich.' For nature has very few demands, whereas the tyranny of opinion is immense. Suppose you inherit the estates of many rich men. Fortune carries you well beyond the normal limits of a private income and covers you with gold, clothes you in the finest purple, and brings you to such an apex of luxury and wealth that you can pave your land with marble till you not merely possess riches but actually walk on them. On top of this you have statues, paintings and the ultimate adornments of luxury that any of the arts can devise. The only thing you will learn from all this will be to want still more.

The desires implanted by nature have a limit, but those born from false opinion have no way of reaching an end. The false has no limits. Someone travelling on a road

---

[1] Seneca, in the guidance he here tactfully offers to his friend Lucilius (who was attracted by Epicureanism), deliberately adopts a fairly neutral stance as to what the character of this ultimate principle may be. Elsewhere, he is more explicit: 'We are born under a kingly rule; to obey God is freedom' (*On the Happy Life* [*De vita beata*], 15).

must reach a destination, but once he leaves the track there is no end to his wanderings. So pull yourself back from empty pursuits, and if you want to know whether your ambitions stem from a natural desire or from some blind and trivial impulse, just ask whether they have a definite terminus. If, no matter how far you travel, there always seems to be some further place you need to reach, that is a sure sign that the desire is contrary to nature...

Do you think I am going to write to you about how well the winter has treated us ('How mild and short it has been!'), or what an inclement spring we are having ('So unseasonably cold!'), and other such silliness that people indulge in when they have nothing to say? I propose instead to write something that may be of some real use to both of us. And what might that be, if not to exhort you to cultivate a good mental outlook. And what, you may ask, is the basis for that? Do not take pleasure in empty things. I said this is the basis – in fact it is the final culmination. We reach the summit when we know what to enjoy and do not allow our happiness to depend on what is outside our control. The way to be anxious and unsure of oneself is to be spurred on by some hope or other, even though it may be within reach, or not hard to seek, and even if such hopes have never played us false. This above all, my dear Lucilius, you must aim for: learn the secret of true enjoyment.

You may think I am now depriving you of many pleasures by taking away all those that depend on luck, or by advising you to avoid hope, that sweetest of delights. On the contrary, I want joy to be something you are never without: I want it to be born in your house, and this can happen only if it is within you. All other pleasures do not fill our inner being; they merely change the expression on our faces, and have no lasting significance, unless you think anyone who smiles must be happy. The mind itself must be happy and confident, and raised high above every external circumstance.

True joy, believe me, is a serious matter. Do you think someone can despise death with a countenance that is carefree and 'full of fun', as our trendy commentators have it? Can he open his home to poverty, keep a curb on his pleasures or contemplate pain with endurance? The person who turns all this over in his mind is indeed in a state of great joy, but it is far from a cheery kind of joy. Yet this is precisely the joy which I want you to possess, for once you have found how to seek it, it will never leave you. The yield from shallow mines is on the surface, but the richest mines have veins hidden deep, which produce a fuller and more continuous return to the excavator. The pleasures most people pursue give enjoyment that is shallow and superficial, and such thinly coated joy has no secure basis. But the joy I am talking about, which I am trying to guide you towards, is solid, and it reveals itself more abundantly the deeper you go.

My dearest Lucilius, I beg you to do the one thing that can make you happy: throw away and trample on those outwardly splendid baubles promised by others and dependent on external sources. Keep your eyes on the true good, and take joy in what comes from inside you. What do I mean by 'from inside you'? From your very self – from the best part of you. As for the poor body, even though nothing can be accomplished without it, you must think of it as something that is necessary rather than important. The pleasures it provides are empty, short, soon to be repented and, unless they are curbed by a great deal of self-control, likely to produce their opposite. I tell you: pleasure tends swiftly to change to sorrow unless it keeps within bounds.

But it is difficult to keep within bounds when you are dealing with something you believe to be good. If something is truly good, then it is quite safe to be eager for it. What is this true good, you may ask, and where does it come from? I will tell you: from a good conscience, from honourable intentions, from right actions, from despising what depends on chance, from a serene and steady flow of life which keeps to a single course. Those who jump from one plan to another, or who do not even jump but are carried along by some chance or other – how can such unstable and capricious people lay hold of anything that is sure and lasting? . . .

Now is the time for me to pay my debts. I can wind up this letter by giving you a dictum of your friend Epicurus: 'It is a lot of bother to keep on starting one's life.' Or perhaps this puts it better: 'People do not have a good life if they are always just starting to live.' 'Why is that?' you may say – and indeed the dictum does need some explanation. It is because the life of such people is always unfinished. We cannot stand prepared for death if we are just beginning to live. We must instead make sure that we have already lived enough. And no one could think this about himself if he is for ever involved in starting to live. You should not suppose that such people are few in number: almost everyone is like this. Indeed, they begin to live only when it is time to stop. If you think this strange, I will add something which will surprise you even more: some people leave off living before they have even begun . . .

3   Meaning through Service to Others: Augustine, *Confessions**

Our sampling of early accounts of human life and its meaning would be seriously incomplete if we did not include an extract from one of the most influential early Christian philosophers. For the emerging Christian worldview, which began to spread throughout the Mediterranean world during the era of the Roman empire, influenced the development of subsequent Western thought in ways that are in many ways deeper and more pervasive than anything contributed by Hellenistic belief-systems such as Stoicism and Epicureanism (see the preceding two extracts).

In the following passages, from his celebrated *Confessions*, Augustine begins with the central premise of traditional Christianity – the existence of a supreme and unchanging God, the

'fountain of light' who is the source of all reality. But for Christians that ultimate reality is not merely an abstract idea, but is something that became incarnate and made manifest in the life of Christ. So living in accordance with that ultimate reality is living in conformity with the example of Christ. Hence Augustine makes a swift transition to the 'works of mercy', recalling Christ's injunction to feed the hungry and clothe the naked, and his command to 'do unto others as you would they would do unto you'.[1] The moral life of service to the needs of others thus gains a special significance in Augustine's picture of a meaningful existence, for it brings us closer to the very source of our life and of all reality.

As the opening paragraph of our extract makes clear, this life of ultimate value cannot,

---

*   Augustine of Hippo, *Confessions* [*c.*397], Bk XIII, excerpts from chs 16, 18 and 19. Translation by John Cottingham.

[1]   Matthew 25: 34–45; Luke 6: 31. In almost every other sentence of Augustine's writings there are explicit or implicit allusions to the Bible. Some of the most important references in our extract are indicated in footnotes below.

on Augustine's view, be achieved by our own efforts, any more than a land without water can irrigate itself. In this Christian picture there is no scope for the idea (widely held in modern times) of man as wholly 'autonomous' and self-sufficient. Augustine does not deny the need for human beings to act responsibly and exert them-selves in order to flourish and bring forth fruit (hence the Gospel image he uses of the labourers who work at sowing and harvesting); but he makes it clear that, like the farmer who depends on the sunlight and rain from above, we always need to be open to the grace that comes from a higher power than our own.

 You alone have full knowledge, O God, since you exist unchangeably and your knowledge and your will are unchangeable... A changeable thing that receives light from another can hardly have the kind of knowledge whereby unchangeable light knows itself, nor would this seem just to you. So my soul is to you like a land without water: it cannot enlighten itself, and it cannot satisfy itself. In you is the fountain of life, and we shall see the light in your light...

The souls that thirst for you and appear before you, you water with a hidden and sweet fountain, so that the earth may bring forth her fruit. She brings forth her fruit, and at the command of her God – at your command O Lord – our soul in her own way brings forth works of mercy. These consist of loving one's neighbour by providing for the needs of the body. Thus we have the seed within us, in accordance with our own likeness; for it is from our own weakness that we feel the compassion to support the needy, helping others even as we would wish to be helped if we had the same needs. Yet this applies not only to the easy cases, like a plant with seed within it, but also when the help and protection of others requires a mighty effort, like a strong tree that produces fruit: helping to rescue those who suffer injustice from the hands of the oppressor, and giving the shelter of our protection through the strong arm of just judgement.

So I pray to you, O Lord, let this fountain continue to spring forth, even as you grant us the strength and the joy to continue. Let truth spring from the earth, and righteousness drop from heaven, and let there be bright lights in the firmament. Let us break our bread for the hungry and bring the poor and homeless into our house; let us clothe the naked: and let us never neglect our own flesh and blood within our household. When these fruits spring from the earth, you behold and see that it is good;[1] and for the limited span of our time, let our own light break forth. From this lowly fruitfulness of action, let us reach the higher joys of contemplation, and hold fast to the word of life; let us appear like lights in the world, guided by the firmament of your Scriptures. It is there that you talk to us, helping us to separate the things of the intellect from those of the senses as day from night, or as we distinguish souls devoted to intelligible things from those devoted to the things of the senses. In the secret abyss of your judgement, you divided the light from the darkness, before the firmament was created; in the same way may those spiritual children of yours, set in the same firmament (though with your grace now shining through the world), give light to the earth, and divide the day from the night. May we be a sign of the times; for the old things have passed away and are made new.

---

[1] Compare Genesis 1: 10.

Our salvation is now nearer than when we believed, for the night is far spent and the day is at hand. You crown the year with your blessing, sending labourers into this harvest of yours that others have laboured to sow, and sending sowers into other fields whose harvest is to come at the end. You grant the desires of those who seek you, and you bless the years of those who are righteous; for you are always the same, and in your years, which never fail, you prepare corn for the years that are passing away. In your eternal wisdom you bestow heavenly goods on the earth in their due seasons, since to one person is given the word of wisdom through the spirit ... to another the word of knowledge[1] by the same spirit ... to another faith, to another the gift of healing, to another mighty powers, to another prophecy, to another the discerning of spirits, to another various gifts of tongues.[2] ...

But first you must wash and be clean, and put away evil from your souls. Let the sea of evil vanish from before my eyes, that the dry land may appear. Learn to do good, judge the fatherless and plead for the widow, that the earth may bring forth green herbs for food and trees for fruit. Come, let us reason together, says the Lord, that there may be lights in the firmament of the heavens to light the earth. The rich man addressed the 'good master', and asked 'what he should do to inherit eternal life'.[3] And our good master (whom the questioner thought to be no more than human, but he is 'good' because he is God) told him that if he wanted to come to life he should keep the commandments: put aside the bitterness of malice and wickedness, do not kill, do not commit adultery, do not steal, do not bear false witness. Thus the dry land may appear and the good plants germinate – honouring one's father and mother, loving one's neighbour. 'All these things have I done,' replied the rich man. But if the earth is so fruitful, where do all these thorns come from? Pull up those thick shrubs of greed, sell all you have and gain a rich harvest by giving to the poor; then you will have treasure in heaven. If you want to be perfect, follow the Lord and join those to whom he declares his wisdom. For it is he who knows what to assign to day and to night, and by following him you too may come to know this, so that there will be lights for you in the firmament of heaven. Yet this may never be unless your heart is there; and that may never be unless your treasure is there.[4] These are the very words you heard from the good teacher.

---

[1] Augustine distinguishes 'wisdom' (Lat. *sapientia*) from 'knowledge' (*scientia*), the former being the highest intellectual virtue, relating to spiritual enlightenment and awareness of God, while the latter relates to more mundane kinds of knowledge.

[2] For the various gifts of the spirit, see 1 Corinthians 12: 4–10.

[3] See Mark 10: 17–22.

[4] 'Lay not up for yourselves treasures upon earth, where moth and rust doth corrupt and where thieves break through and steal. But lay up for yourselves treasures in heaven ... For where your treasure is, there shall your heart be also' (Matthew 6: 19–21).

4   Contentment with the Human Lot: Michel de Montaigne: *On Experience**

Our next extract takes us down to the Renaissance, and to one of its most urbane and civilized writers, Michel de Montaigne. Like many intellectuals of his time, Montaigne was steeped in classical culture, and his essays abound in references to the poets and philosophers of the ancient world. But though he was thoroughly familiar with the teachings of classical antiquity – and also, of course, with the dominant Christian tradition in which he was brought up – Montaigne's philosophy is very much based on practical experience rather than theoretical doctrine, as the opening of our extract makes clear.

Montaigne relishes vivid detail rather than abstract argumentation, and his prose is larded with a wealth of anecdotes and allusions. To those accustomed to more austere forms of theorizing, his train of thought can seem rambling and haphazard, but a distinctive philosophical orientation nonetheless emerges: 'As far as philosophical opinions are concerned, I embrace most willingly those which are the most solid – that is to say those that are most human, most related to us.' The ordinary human condition, for Montaigne, is not something to be transcended, in pursuit of some exalted philosophical or religious ideal, but something that we should accept and learn to live with; our own human nature, properly understood and cultivated with humility and good humour, is the basis for a worthwhile and meaningful existence. Montaigne's humane outlook, enriched with impressive erudition but grounded in solid common sense, reminds us that the key to making sense of our human lot may be much closer to hand than many abstract theoreticians often assume. His closing quotation, from the inscription with which the ancient Athenians honoured Pompey the Great, aptly summarizes the message Montaigne offers about how human beings can achieve meaning and value in their lives: 'So far you reach the rank of deity / As you accept your own humanity.'

 There is no desire more natural than the desire for knowledge, and we sample every means that can lead us to it. When reason fails us, we use experience:

> Many are the paths, leading to art and skill,
> Experience finds: each instance shows the way.[1]

Experience is a much weaker and lowlier means than reason. But truth is something so great that we should not disdain any route that will get us there. Reason has so many forms that we do not know which to adopt, and experience has just as many. The inferences we try to draw from comparing the way events fall out are not reliable, because events are always dissimilar. When we look at things, we find no quality that is so universal as their diversity and variety. Both the Greeks and Romans, like us, used eggs as the paradigm of similarity. And yet there have been people, most famously someone at Delphi, who could spot marks of difference between eggs, so as never to mistake one for another. He had many hens, but he could always tell which one had laid a given egg. And dissimilarity always enters into our human works, so

---

* Extracts from Michel de Montaigne, 'On Experience' ('De l'experience'), in his *Essays* [*Essais*, 1580]. Translation by John Cottingham.

[1] A free verse translation of the original Latin quoted by Montaigne: 'Per varios usus artem experientia fecit / exemplo monstrante viam.' Montaigne's essays are full of classical quotations; this one is from the Roman poet Manilius (1st century AD).

that no art can achieve complete similarity. No one can clean and whiten the backs of playing cards carefully enough to prevent some of the players from telling which is which just from watching their opponents pick them up. Nature has put herself under an obligation to produce no two things that cannot be told apart...

In short, this entire mixture of scribblings that I am serving up here is simply a record of my life's experiences.[1] It provides an adequately instructive model for inner health, if only as a guide to what to avoid. But as for physical health, no one can offer more valuable experience than I can, since what I am giving the reader is pure, and quite uncorrupted or altered by art or theorizing. When it comes to medicine, experience really is at home on its own dung heap, and here reason must give way to it entirely. The Roman emperor Tiberius used to say that anyone who had reached the age of 20 ought to take responsibility for deciding what regime was beneficial or harmful for him, and should know how to look after himself without a doctor. He could have learnt from Socrates, who advised his disciples to look after their health most carefully, and make it a principal object of study – and added that a sensible person, who took care to exercise and eat and drink properly, could hardly fail to know what was good or bad for him better than any doctor...

As far as I am concerned, I love life, and cultivate it, in the form that God has been pleased to grant it to us. I do not go about wishing that we could avoid the need to eat or drink, and I would think it just as inexcusable to want these needs to be doubled. *Sapiens divitiarum naturalium quaesitor acerrimus* – 'The wise man is a keen seeker for the riches provided by nature.'[2] Nor would I wish us to be nourished simply by putting into our mouths a little of the drug that Epimenides[3] used to take away his appetite and keep himself alive; or want us to be able to beget children merely by using our fingers or our heels, even if such a process were to be as voluptuous as the normal method (if I may put it tactfully); or that the body should be without desire or titillation. Such complaints would be thankless and wicked. I accept gratefully and with a good heart all that nature has done for me, and I am pleased and proud of myself for so doing. We should be wronging the great and all-powerful Giver if we refused his gift, or nullified or disfigured it. He is wholly good, and has made all things good. *Omnia quae secundum naturam sunt, aestimatione digna sunt* – 'All things that are in accordance with nature are worthy of esteem.'[4]

As far as philosophical opinions are concerned, I embrace most willingly those which are the most solid – that is to say those that are most human, most related to us. My own philosophical discourse matches my habitual behaviour – plain and humble. Philosophy is infantile, in my opinion, when it gets on its high horse and preaches about how barbarous it is to mingle divine and earthly things, the rational with the irrational, the strict with the easy-going, the noble with the base, or tells us that pleasure is something bestial, unworthy of the sage – as if the only pleasure he can get from enjoying his beautiful young wife is that of knowing he is performing a lawful and properly regulated action, like putting on one's boots for a necessary ride ...

---

[1] In French *essais*, literally 'things tried out'.
[2] A quotation from Seneca; compare extract 2, above.
[3] Legendary Cretan poet famed for his exceptional longevity.
[4] Quotation from Cicero, *De Finibus* ('On the Ends of Good and Evil') [50 BC], Bk III, § 6.

This is not what Socrates says. He values bodily pleasure as he should, but prefers the pleasure of the mind on the grounds that it is stronger, more stable, easier to attain, more varied and more dignified. It is not the only pleasure, according to Socrates – his view is not so fantastic as that – but it is the foremost pleasure. For him, temperance is the moderator of pleasures, not its enemy.

Nature is a gentle guide, but she is as just and prudent as she is gentle. *Intrandum est in rerum naturam et penitus quid ea postulat pervidendum* – 'We must enter into the nature of things and search deeply for what she demands of us.'[1] I seek her tracks everywhere, but we have blurred them with the traces of our own artificial inventions. So the sovereign good of the Academics and the Peripatetics,[2] to live in accordance with nature, has as a result become difficult to define and explain. And the same goes for the closely related maxim of the Stoics, which is to acquiesce in the demands of nature.[3] Is it not a mistake to think that an action is less worthy in virtue of being necessary? No one will persuade me that the marriage between pleasure and necessity – which the gods always manage to engineer – is not a most appropriate match. How could we tear asunder a fabric woven of two such kindred materials? On the contrary, let us strengthen it by mutual care and attention: let the spirit arouse and enliven the heavy body, and the body hold back and restrain the light spirit. 'He who praises the nature of the soul as the highest good, and accuses the nature of the flesh as if it were evil, is surely carnal both in his pursuit of the soul and in his shunning of the body, since his attitude is based on human vanity, not divine truth.'[4] There is nothing unworthy of our care in this gift that God has bestowed on us, and we owe our body that care, down to the last hair of our heads. The duty laid upon us human beings is to conduct ourselves according to our condition, and that duty is explicit, plain and of the utmost importance, enjoined on us by a strict and grave ordinance of the Creator. Ordinary minds are impressed only by authority, and if it is in a foreign language, so much the weightier. So let us use it here: *Stultitiae proprium ... alio corpus impellere alio animum, distrahique inter diversissimos modos* – 'It is foolish to drive the body in one direction and the mind in another, and thus be torn between opposite impulses.'[5]

To verify this, ask someone one day to tell you the diverting thoughts and imaginings that so fill his head as to make him forget the good meal in front of him, or even complain of having to waste his time in order to eat. You will find that the insipid dullness of the food on your table is only exceeded by the thoughts going on in his mind ... and that his precious ideas and schemes are well below the standard of your leftover stew. And even if they were the exalted reflections of Archimedes himself, so what? I am not referring those venerable souls stirred up by devotion and religious piety to a constant and dutiful meditation on matters divine – they are quite different from the motley herd of ordinary humans like us; their minds are far above the vain desires and empty thoughts that entertain us. A lively and powerful hope makes them look forward to eternal nourishment, the final goal and resting place of

---

[1] Cicero, *De Finibus*, Bk V, § 16.
[2] The followers of Plato and of Aristotle respectively.
[3] Compare extract 2, above.
[4] Augustine, *The City of God* [*De Civitate Dei*, AD 415–25], Bk XIV, § 5.
[5] Seneca, *Letters*, 74.

all Christian longing, the sole constant and incorruptible joy. They scorn to pursue the fleeting and dubious goods we find so necessary, and are quite ready to delegate to the body the task of dealing with mere temporal and sensuous nourishment. Theirs is a pursuit for the privileged. But between ourselves, let me say that there are two things I have always observed to go hand in hand: super-celestial opinions and sub-terrestrial morals.

Aesop, that great man, saw his master pissing as he walked along. 'What!' he said, 'are we now to shit as we run?' However well we manage our time, there will always be time left over that is idle or wasted. Our mind will never accept that it has enough time to complete its tasks without having to dissociate itself from the body during the relatively small portion of time the body requires for its needs. People always try to get outside themselves and escape from their human condition. This is folly, for instead of transforming themselves into angels they end up making themselves into beasts. These desires to transcend reality frighten me, like high inaccessible mountain peaks. There is nothing in the life of Socrates that I find so tiresome to digest as his ecstasies and his demonic fits...and I find nothing so ordinary and mortal in Alexander's life as his fantasies of becoming immortal. Philotas gave him a stinging but witty retort when congratulating him on having been placed among the gods by the oracle of Jupiter Ammon: 'I am delighted for your sake, but sorry for the people who will have to live with and obey a human being who has overstepped the bounds of ordinary humanity and is no longer content with them.'...

The charming inscription with which the Athenians honoured Pompey's arrival in their city matches my own view:

> So far you reach the rank of deity
> As you accept your own humanity.

It is an absolute perfection, a perfection like that of the gods, to be able faithfully to enjoy one's own nature. We search for other conditions because we do not understand how to deal with the condition we actually have, and we go outside ourselves because we do not know what is within us. So there is really no point getting up on stilts, for even on stilts we still have to walk on our own legs. And on the most exalted throne in the world, we still have to sit upon our own bottom.

The finest lives, in my view, are those which conform to the ordinary human model, in an orderly way, without marvels and extravagances. Old age, to be sure, needs rather more tender treatment, but let us commend it to that god who is the protector of health and wisdom – but a wisdom that is happy and sociable:

> The gifts prepared for me may I enjoy
> blessed Apollo, with a mind undimmed,
> a healthy body, honourable old age,
> and the sweet music of the gentle lyre.[1]

---

[1] A free rendering of the original Latin verse quoted by Montaigne: *Frui paratis et valido mihi/ Latoe, dones, et, precor integra/ cum mente, nec turpem senectam / degere nec cithara carentem.* The lines are by the Roman poet Horace (1st century BC), from his *Odes* I, 31.

5   The Human Condition, Wretched yet Redeemable: Blaise Pascal, *Pensées**

Written less than a century after the *Essais* (see preceding extract), the *Pensées* or 'Thoughts' of another great French thinker, Blaise Pascal, are a world away from the comfortable urbanity of Montaigne's reflections. Pascal, an accomplished scientist and mathematician, was also a deeply religious philosopher, whose best-known work was written in the aftermath of a powerful conversion experience. So far from following Montaigne and accepting the human condition as it is as the basis for happiness, Pascal expounded the idea of the inherent 'wretchedness' of human nature, to be rescued only through the power of God. As he puts it elsewhere: 'the Christian faith boils down to establishing these two things: that our nature is corrupt, and that it is redeemed through Christ.'[1]

Readers may be inclined to make their acceptance or rejection of Pascal's views depend on whether or not they happen to share his Christian outlook; but it is more fruitful to look without preconceptions at what he actually argues. One of the key points made in the opening portion of our extract is that 'humanity infinitely transcends itself'. This implies that the key to a meaningful existence cannot simply consist in accepting the limits of our human nature as it stands, since human beings are irresistibly drawn to strive for something more; as Pascal puts it, 'we have an idea of happiness, yet cannot reach it'.

This gives the human predicament a fundamental seriousness: we cannot escape the quest to 'transcend ourselves', unless we dishonestly attempt to hide from ourselves the momentous character of the choices that face us. Above all, for Pascal, whether or not there is a God will make all the difference to the meaning of human life, and the possibility of ultimate human fulfil-

ment; so it ought to be our most urgent task to settle this question. But here Pascal goes on to make another crucial point: that many of those who dismiss the possibility of a religious solution do so 'without learning what it is they are attacking'. Most people assume, Pascal explains, that the evidence for God ought to be clearly available for scrutiny; but in reality, God is described in Scripture as 'hidden': his presence is 'veiled' in such a way as to be glimpsed only by those who seek him with sincerity of heart.

There is a philosophically important issue at stake here. Many philosophers and scientists are accustomed to think of truth as something established by evidence that is (in principle) universally available to anyone using the correct rational methods; what Pascal implies, by contrast, is that certain truths (including religious truths) are *not* accessible to all, but require, in order to be discerned, a certain openness or receptivity on the part of the inquirer. What is more, the emotional mindset of the inquirer can be as important as his or her intellectual outlook, as the closing part of our extract makes clear. The God of the Christians, Pascal insists, is not merely one who is rationally apprehended as 'the author of geometrical truths and the ordering of the elements', but is a 'God of love and consolation', who fills the hearts of those with 'a deep inner awareness of their own misery and his infinite mercy'.

Pascal's position is an uncompromising one, and it will certainly not convince everyone. Nevertheless few will be wholly unmoved by the passionate seriousness of his arguments, and the vividness with which he depicts the finitude of the human condition and the anguished search for an eternal source of meaning and value.

---

* Extracts from Blaise Pascal, *Pensées* [*c.*1660]. Translation by John Cottingham. The French text of the relevant passages may be found in the edition of L. Lafuma (Paris: Editions du Seuil, 1962), nos 131, 427 and 449.
[1] *Pensées*, ed. Lafuma, no. 427.

What a chimera[1] a human being is! What a novelty. What a monster, what a chaos, what a contradiction, what a prodigy! Judge of all things, imbecile worm of the earth, repository of truth, sink of uncertainty and error, the pride and refuse of the universe!

Who will unravel this tangle? It is certainly beyond dogmatism and scepticism, beyond all human philosophy. Humanity transcends itself. Let us concede to the sceptics what they have so often asserted, that truth is beyond our reach, a quarry we can never hunt down, no inhabitant of earth but a dweller in heaven, lying in the lap of God and not to be known except insofar as he is pleased to reveal it. We must learn our true nature from uncreated and incarnate truth.[2] ...

So learn, proud man, what a paradox you are to yourself. Impotent reason, be humble! Feeble nature, be silent! Realize that humanity infinitely transcends itself, and hear your true condition, which is unknown to you, from your master.

Listen to God.

Is it not as clear as day that there is a duality in our human condition? If humanity had never been corrupted we would, in our innocence, be assured of enjoying truth and felicity. And if humanity had never been anything but corrupt we would not have any idea of truth or of blessedness. But wretched as we are – more wretched than if our condition had never included any spark of greatness – we have an idea of happiness, yet cannot reach it. We perceive an image of truth, but possess only falsehood. We are equally incapable of absolute ignorance on the one hand and of certain knowledge on the other – what could make it more obvious that we were once in a degree of perfection from which we have unhappily fallen? ...[3]

These solid facts, confirmed by the inviolable authority of religion, teach us that there are two equally solid truths of faith.

One is that man in the state of creation, or in the state of grace, is elevated above all nature, made in the likeness of God and participating in his divinity. The other is that in the state of corruption and sin he has fallen from this state and become like the beasts. These two propositions are equally firm and certain ...

Before attacking a religion, people should at least learn what it is that they are attacking. If this religion of ours claimed to have a clear sight of God and to have found him unveiled and open to view, it would be a sound objection to say that we see nothing in the world that establishes his presence with this degree of self-evidence. But our religion claims, on the contrary, that human beings are in darkness and far off from God, and that he has hidden himself from their knowledge – indeed the very name he gives himself in Scripture is *deus absconditus*, 'the hidden god'.[4] Our religion labours to establish two things: that God has instituted visible signs in the Church to make himself known to those who seek him with sincerity; and that he has neverthe-less veiled these signs in such a way that he will be seen only by those who seek him

---

[1] Chimera: a freakish amalgam of different natures; in Greek mythology, a monster with a lion's head, a goat's body and a serpent's tail.

[2] Pascal's meaning here is that divine truth is revealed by God becoming 'incarnate' (i.e. taking human flesh) in Jesus Christ (who was, in the words of the Nicene Creed, 'begotten, not created').

[3] Pascal goes on to discuss the Christian doctrine of original sin – the idea that we all inherit the fallen condition of Adam.

[4] 'Truly thou art a hidden God, O God of Israel, our Saviour' (Isaiah 45: 15).

with all their heart.[1] So, given that the objectors are on their own admission not in a state of eagerness to discover this divine truth, what is the point of their complaining that they have no evidence for it? The very obscurity they find themselves in, and which they point to as an objection to the Church, merely serves to establish one of her claims, without affecting the other, and hence actually confirms the Church's position rather than undermining it.

To mount a solid objection, they would have to insist that they had made every effort to seek the truth on every side, including the religious instruction offered by the Church, but without any positive result. If this was the kind of thing they said, they would indeed have a case against one of the Church's claims. But I hope to show here that no reasonable person could talk like this, and I even venture to say that no one has ever done so. We are all quite well aware how people with this kind of attitude behave. They think they have made great efforts at self-instruction when they have spent a few hours reading a single book of Scripture, and questioned some cleric on the truths of the faith. Having done so, they then claim to have researched the matter thoroughly, both by studying the texts and by talking to members of the Church – but without any success. I should really say to such people what I have often said, namely that such a casual attitude is intolerable. In behaving this way, it is not as if we were dealing with some minor concern of someone unrelated to us; what is at stake is ourselves – our very all.

The immortality of the soul is something of such powerful importance, and which touches us so deeply, that one would have to have lost all feeling not to care about knowing whether it is a reality or not. All our actions and thoughts cannot but take a completely different course depending on whether there will be eternal joys for us to look forward to, or not. So one cannot possibly proceed sensibly or with any judgement if one does not make decisions with this matter in view; settling it should be our ultimate objective.[2]

Our primary interest and first duty, then, is to enlighten ourselves on this subject, since on it depends the entire course of our conduct. So those who are not yet convinced on this point should be separated, in my view, into two radically different camps: those who make every effort to get at the truth, and those who live without bothering about it, or even thinking about it. I can feel only compassion for those who are genuinely distressed that they are still in doubt on the question, and regard it as the worst of misfortunes, sparing no effort to resolve the issue, and making it their principal and most serious task to inquire into it.

But those who pass their whole life never thinking about this final end of life are quite different. Merely because they cannot find any enlightenment within themselves that might serve to persuade them, they do not bother to look elsewhere; they never thoroughly inquire into whether this belief is one of those that people accept through simple credulity, or one of those that, despite its inherent obscurity, nonetheless has a very solid and utterly secure basis.

---

[1] By the 'signs', Pascal means the sacraments of the Church, especially the Eucharist, where God is present but 'veiled' under the forms of bread and wine.

[2] For more on Pascal's views on the after-life, see Part VI, extract 4, above.

This casual attitude in people, when what is at stake is themselves, their eternity, their all – this excites my irritation more than my pity; I find it astonishing, appalling, quite monstrous. I do not say this out of earnest piety or spiritual devotion. I mean, on the contrary, that taking the right view on this question is simply a matter of human concern and self-interest. All we need is to see what can be seen by the least enlightened of people.

One does not require any great elevation of soul to understand that our condition affords no true or solid satisfaction, and that all our pleasures are mere vanity, while our ills are infinite. And death, which threatens us at every moment, must within a few years infallibly consign us to the horrible necessity of being for all eternity either annihilated or wretched.

Nothing is more real than this, or more terrible. We can put a brave face on it as much as we like, but that is the end that awaits the finest life in the world. If we reflect on this, we cannot but acknowledge it to be beyond doubt that there is no good in this life but the hope of another life, and that all our happiness depends on our reaching closer to it. Furthermore, just as no more ills await those who have complete assurance of eternity, so there can be no happiness for those who have no glimmering of it.

Without question it is a great evil to be in a state of doubt about this; at the very least we have an indispensable duty to try to dispel the doubt – and hence anyone who does not seek to resolve his doubts is both miserable and wrong. And if on top of this the person in question is quite calm and satisfied, and indeed openly declares as much, and is even pleased and proud of himself for feeling this way, I cannot find words to describe such an extreme attitude.

Where can such feelings come from? How could one possibly find a reason for joy in anticipating nothing but helpless misery? How could one congratulate oneself on the prospect of impenetrable darkness? How could a reasonable man entertain an argument like the following:

'I do not know who has put me in the world, or what this world is, or what I am. I am in an appalling state of ignorance about everything. I do not know what my body is, or my senses, or my soul – that part of me that thinks what I am saying, that reflects on everything and on itself, yet does not know itself any better than it knows anything else.

'I see these frightening expanses of the universe that shut me in, and I find myself stuck in one corner of this vast emptiness, without knowing why I am placed here rather than elsewhere, or why from out of the whole eternity that has gone before me and the whole eternity that will follow, this one tiny period has been given me in which to live out my life. I see only infinities on every side that shut me in like an atom, like a shadow that lasts only an instant with no prospect of return. All I know is that I must soon die; but this very death that I cannot avoid is the thing about which I know the least of all.

'Just as I do not know where I come from, so I do not know where I am going to. I only know that on leaving this world I shall fall for ever either into nothingness, or into the hands of a wrathful God, without knowing which of these two conditions must eternally be my lot. Such is my state, full of feebleness and uncertainty. And on top of all that, I conclude that I must pass all the days of my life without dreaming of inquiring into what must happen to me. Perhaps I may find some enlightenment in my doubts, but I am not willing to take the trouble, or even to take a single step to look for it...And afterwards I am willing to go, without any foresight or any fear, to face this great outcome, and let myself weakly be led towards death in a state of uncertainty as to my future condition for all eternity.'...

The God of the Christians does not consist merely of a God who is the author of geometrical truths and the ordering of the elements, as in the pagan and Epicurean outlook. He does not only consist of a God who exercises his providence on life and on human well-being, to give a long and happy life to those who worship him, as in the Jewish outlook. The God of Abraham, the God of Isaac, the God of Jacob, the God of the Christians, is a God of love and consolation – a God who fills the hearts and souls of those he makes his own. He is a God who gives them a deep inner awareness of their own misery and his infinite mercy; who unites himself to them in the depths of their soul, filling them with humility, joy, confidence and love, and makes them incapable of seeking any other end but himself.

6   Human Life as a Meaningless Struggle: Arthur Schopenhauer, *On the Vanity of Existence**

The writers so far included, though they have very different philosophical and/or religious outlooks, all suppose that the conditions for a worthwhile human life are not beyond our reach. As we move forward to the work of the German philosopher Arthur Schopenhauer, in the mid nineteenth century, we see an altogether bleaker and more pessimistic picture. Schopenhauer's general picture of reality regards the *will* as the fundamental basis of all the phenomena in the universe (see Part IV, extract 7, above); and, as shown in the following extract, he draws out the implications of this for human life. The human organism, like everything else in the world, is characterized by an elemental striving; yet because we are mortal, it is inevitable that all our strivings will in the end come to nothing: 'this most perfect manifestation of the will to live, the human organism, with the cunning and complex working of its machinery, must fall to dust and yield up itself and all its strivings to extinction.' The conclusion Schopenhauer draws is that 'the whole struggle of this will [is] in its very essence barren and unprofitable', and hence that 'human life must be some kind of mistake'.

Several questions might be raised about this. One might object to Schopenhauer's basic premise: do we have to concede that all existence, including our own, boils down to a kind of raw struggling and striving? Admittedly, it is clear that without certain basic drives (for example, to eat and to reproduce), all animal existence would soon come to an end; but cannot the life that is maintained in this way be directed towards activities and goals that are rewarding and fulfilling, and which therefore have genuine value? Schopenhauer's answer to this is that 'even when [a man's needs] are satisfied, all he obtains is a state of painlessness, where nothing remains to him but abandonment to boredom. This is direct proof that existence has no real value in itself; for what is boredom but the

---

* From Arthur Schopenhauer, *Parerga und Paralipomena* [1851], vol. II, ch. 2. Trans. T. Bailey Saunders in Schopenhauer, *Studies in Pessimism* (London: Swan Sonnenschein, 1900), ch. 2; with minor modifications.

feeling of the emptiness of life?' Here we see the seeds of the 'absurdist' philosophy developed by some later writers in the twentieth century (see for example extract 9, below, by Albert Camus): humans are condemned to an endless struggle which by its nature cannot ever achieve final success. Critics of Schopenhauer's position will no doubt want to put pressure on his claim that it is 'only distance and difficulties to be over-come [that] make our goal look as if it would satisfy us – an illusion which vanishes when we reach it'. The claim here – that the hope of genuine satisfaction is always illusory – may seem to have appeal only for an already depressive temperament; nevertheless, there is no gainsaying the power Schopenhauer's vision has to disturb us, with its stark message of unavoidable futility lurking at the heart of human existence.

This vanity finds expression in the whole way in which things exist; in the infinite nature of Time and Space, as opposed to the finite nature of the individual in both; in the ever-passing present moment as the only mode of actual existence; in the interdependence and relativity of all things; in continual Becoming without ever Being; in constant wishing and never being satisfied; in the long battle which forms the history of life, where every effort is checked by difficulties, and stopped until they are overcome. Time is that in which all things pass away; it is merely the form under which the will to live – the thing-in-itself and therefore imperishable – has revealed to it that its efforts are in vain; it is that agent by which at every moment all things in our hands become as nothing, and lose any real value they possess.

That which *has been* exists no more; it exists as little as that which has *never* been. But of everything that exists you must say, in the next moment, that it has been. Hence something of great importance now past is inferior to something of little importance now present, in that the latter is a *reality*, and related to the former as something to nothing.

A man finds himself, to his great astonishment, suddenly existing, after thousands and thousands of years of non-existence: he lives for a little while; and then, again, comes an equally long period when he must exist no more. The heart rebels against this, and feels that it cannot be true. The crudest intellect cannot speculate on such a subject without having a presentiment that Time is something ideal in its nature. This ideality of Time and Space is the key to every true system of metaphysics; because it provides for quite another order of things than is to be met with in the domain of nature. This is why Kant is so great.[1]

Of every event in our life we can say only for one moment that it *is*; for ever after, that it *was*. Every evening we are poorer by a day. It might, perhaps, make us mad to see how rapidly our short span of time ebbs away; if it were not that in the furthest depths of our being we are secretly conscious of our share in the exhaustible spring of eternity, so that we can always hope to find life in it again.

Consideration of the kind touched on above might, indeed, lead us to embrace the belief that the greatest *wisdom* is to make the enjoyment of the present the supreme object of life; because that is the only reality, all else being merely the play of thought. On the other hand, such a course might just as well be called the greatest *folly*: for that which in the next moment exists no more, and vanishes utterly, like a dream, can never be worth a serious effort.

---

[1] Compare Part II, extract 8, above.

The whole foundation on which our existence rests is the present – the ever-fleeting present. It lies, then, in the very nature of our existence to take the form of constant motion, and to offer no possibility of our ever attaining the rest for which we are always striving. We are like a man running downhill, who cannot keep on his legs unless he runs on, and will inevitably fall if he stops; or, again, like a pole balanced on the tip of one's finger; or like a planet, which would fall into its sun the moment it ceased to hurry forward on its way. Unrest is the mark of existence.

In a world where all is unstable, and nought can endure, but is swept onwards at once in the hurrying whirlpool of change; where a man, if he is to keep erect at all, must always be advancing and moving, like an acrobat on a rope – in such a world, happiness is inconceivable. How can it dwell where, as Plato says, *continual Becoming and never Being* is the sole form of existence? In the first place, a man never is happy, but spends his whole life striving after something which he thinks will make him so; he seldom attains his goal, and when he does, it is only to be disappointed; he is mostly shipwrecked in the end, and comes into harbour with masts and rigging gone. And then, it is all one whether he has been happy or miserable; for his life was never anything more than a present moment always vanishing; and now it is over.

At the same time it is a wonderful thing that, in the world of human beings as in that of animals in general, this manifold restless motion is produced and kept up by the agency of two simple impulses – hunger and the sexual instinct; aided a little, perhaps, by the influence of boredom, but by nothing else; and that, in the theatre of life, these suffice to form the *primum mobile* of how complicated a machinery, setting in motion how strange and varied a scene!

On looking a little closer, we find that inorganic matter presents a constant conflict between chemical forces, which eventually works dissolution; and on the other hand, that organic life is impossible without continual change of matter, and cannot exist if it does not receive perpetual help from without. This is the realm of *finality*; and its opposite would be *an infinite existence*, exposed to no attack from without, and needing nothing to support it; the realm of eternal peace; some timeless, changeless state, one and undiversified; the negative knowledge of which forms the dominant note of the Platonic philosophy. It is to some such state as this that the denial of the will to live opens up the way.

The scenes of our life are like pictures done in rough mosaic. Looked at close, they produce no effect. There is nothing beautiful to be found in them, unless you stand some distance off. So, to gain anything we have longed for is only to discover how vain and empty it is; and even though we are always living in expectation of better things, at the same time we often repent and long to have the past back again. We look upon the present as something to be put up with while it lasts, and serving only as the way towards our goal. Hence most people, if they glance back when they come to the end of life, will find that all along they have been living *ad interim*: they will be surprised to find that the very thing they disregarded and let slip by unenjoyed, was just the life in the expectation of which they passed all their time. Of how many a man may it not be said that hope made a fool of him until he danced into the arms of death!

Then again, how insatiable a creature is man! Every satisfaction he attains lays the seeds of some new desire, so that there is no end to the wishes of each individual will. And why is this? The real reason is simply that, taken in itself, Will is the lord of all worlds: everything belongs to it, and therefore no one single thing can ever give it satisfaction, but only the whole, which is endless. For all that, it must rouse our sympathy to think how very little the Will, this lord of the world, really gets when it takes the form of an individual; usually only just enough to keep the body together. This is why man is so very miserable.

Life presents itself chiefly as a task – the task, I mean, of subsisting at all, *gagner sa vie.*[1] If this is accomplished, life is a burden, and then there comes the second task of doing something with that which has been won – of warding off boredom, which, like a bird of prey, hovers over us, ready to swoop wherever it sees a life secure from need. The first task is to win something; the second, to banish the feeling that it has been won; otherwise it is a burden.

Human life must be some kind of mistake. The truth of this will be sufficiently obvious if we only remember that man is a compound of needs and necessities hard to satisfy; and that even when they are satisfied, all he obtains is a state of painlessness, where nothing remains to him but abandonment to boredom. This is direct proof that existence has no real value in itself; for what is boredom but the feeling of the emptiness of life? If life – the craving for which is the very essence of our being – were possessed of any positive intrinsic value, there would be no such thing as boredom at all: mere existence would satisfy us in itself, and we should want for nothing. But as it is, we take no delight in existence except when we are struggling for something; and then distance and difficulties to be overcome make our goal look as though it would satisfy us – an illusion which vanishes when we reach it; or else when we are occupied with some purely intellectual interest – when in reality we have stepped forth from life to look upon it from the outside, much after the manner of spectators at a play. And even sensual pleasure itself means nothing but a struggle and aspiration, ceasing the moment its aim is attained. Whenever we are not occupied in one of these ways, but cast upon existence itself, its vain and worthless nature is brought home to us; and this is what we mean by boredom. The hankering after what is strange and uncommon – an innate and ineradicable tendency of human nature – shows how glad we are at any interruption of that natural course of affairs which is so very tedious.

That this most perfect manifestation of the will to live, the human organism, with the cunning and complex working of its machinery, must fall to dust and yield up itself and all its strivings to extinction – this is the naive way in which Nature, who is always so true and sincere in what she says, proclaims the whole struggle of this will as in its very essence barren and unprofitable. Were it of any value in itself, anything unconditioned and absolute, it could not thus end in mere nothing.

If we turn from contemplating the world as a whole, and, in particular, the generations of men as they live their little hour of mock-existence and then are swept away in rapid succession; if we turn from this, and look at life in its small details, as presented, say, in a comedy, how ridiculous it all seems! It is like a drop of water seen through a microscope, a single drop teeming with suspended particles; or a speck of cheese full of mites invisible to the naked eye. How we laugh as they bustle about so eagerly, and struggle with one another in so tiny a space! And whether here, or in the little span of human life, this terrible activity produces a comic effect.

It is only in the microscope that our life looks so big. It is an indivisible point, drawn out and magnified by the powerful lenses of Time and Space.

---

[1] Gaining a livelihood.

7   The Death of God and the Ascendancy of the Will: Friedrich Nietzsche, *Thus Spake Zarathustra**

Schopenhauer's emphasis on the will (see preceding extract) undoubtedly influenced the thought of his famous compatriot Friedrich Nietzsche, writing later in the nineteenth century. In his strangely haunting work *Thus Spake Zarathustra*, the style of which is more like that of a myth or fable than a conventional philosophical treatise, Nietzsche brings out some of the implications of his celebrated proclamation (first made in an earlier work, *The Joyful Science*, 1882), that 'God is dead'. Our extract begins by reporting the hero Zarathustra's meeting with a saintly old man who spends his life singing hymns and praising God. Zarathustra leaves him, amazed that he has not heard the news that God is dead, and enters the nearest town where he proclaims to the crowd his new doctrine of the 'Superman' (or 'super-human being' – in the original German, *Übermensch*).

The essence of this much discussed Nietzschean doctrine is that each human being needs, by sheer determination and strength of will, to 'overcome himself', to reach a higher and more exalted state in which he can achieve true freedom and independence. In the absence of a divine source of meaning and value, what is required is a spirit 'strong and original enough to revalue and invent eternal values' (see extract from *Beyond Good and Evil*, Part VIII, extract 8, above). Value and meaning, in other words, have to be generated entirely from our own resources; or, as Zarathustra puts it in our extract below, 'the Superman *shall be* the meaning of the earth! I conjure you, my brethren, *remain true to the earth*, and do not believe those who speak unto you of super-earthly hopes!'

There then follows a kind of parable of 'three metamorphoses' – three phases through which the human spirit must pass, according to Nietzsche, in order to emerge strong and free in a godless universe. In the first phase, the human spirit becomes a camel – humbly kneeling down to receive various burdens. This seems to be an allegory for the kinds of self-abnegation advocated in some forms of traditional Christian spirituality, including 'humiliating oneself in order to mortify one's pride', and 'loving those who despise us'. Abandoning these spurious comforts, the spirit must go out into the 'loneliest wilderness' and change into a lion. This is Nietzsche's image of the courage and strength of will needed to abandon conventional values in order to 'capture freedom and lordship in its own wilderness'. Instead of the 'thou shalt...' (traditional language of the Ten Commandments), the lion proclaims 'I *will*'.

But even the lion, Zarathustra declares, cannot 'create new values'. For that, a third transformation is needed – the spirit must become a child, and embark on 'a new beginning, a game, a self-rolling wheel, a first movement...a holy *Yes* unto life'. Nietzsche seems to be arguing here that, in some kind of spontaneous, joyful and childlike way, the human spirit can free itself from all constraints and find meaning in its own willed acts of affirmation.

The exact import of this Nietzschean vision of a new kind of authentic human existence has been much debated, but in the plausible view of one interpreter, the goal is for an individual to 'dislodge what was in place as the good and the true in order to find a place for himself, for his *own* truth and goodness'.[1] Some readers may

---

* Extracts from Friedrich Nietzsche, *Thus Spake Zarathustra* [*Also Sprach Zarathustra*, 1891], Part I. English version based on the translation of Thomas Common (6th edn, London: Routledge, 1906); with modifications.

[1] Alexander Nehamas, *The Art of Living* (Berkeley: University of California Press, 1998), p. 183.

THE DEATH OF GOD: NIETZSCHE

perhaps be inspired by the courageous creativity that is envisaged here, but others may be doubtful about how value and meaning could be created merely by an act of will or affirmation. For the things we value surely cannot be valuable simply because we *decide* to choose them, but in virtue of features (being beneficial, beautiful, true and so on) that make them independently *worthy* of being chosen. The 'thou shalt' of traditional morality may seem oppressive, but to replace it simply with an 'I *will*' – the determined assertion of individual choice – may seem to risk leading humanity into moral chaos.

Zarathustra went down the mountain alone, no one meeting him. When he entered the forest, however, there suddenly stood before him an old man, who had left his holy cot to seek roots. And thus spake the old man to Zarathustra:

'No stranger to me is this wanderer: many years ago he passed by. Zarathustra he was called; but he has altered. Then you carried your ashes into the mountains: will you now carry your fire into the valleys? Fear you not the incendiary's doom?

'Yes, I recognize Zarathustra. Pure is his eye, and no loathing lurks about his mouth. Does he not go along like a dancer? Altered is Zarathustra; Zarathustra has become a child; an awakened one is Zarathustra: what will you do in the land of the sleepers? As in the sea you have lived in solitude, and it has borne you up. Alas, will you now go ashore? Alas, will you again drag your body yourself?'

Zarathustra answered: 'I love mankind.'

'Why', said the saint, 'did I go into the forest and the desert? Was it not because I loved men far too well? Now I love God: men I do not love. Man is a thing too imperfect for me. Love to man would be fatal to me.'

Zarathustra answered: 'What did I speak of love? I am bringing gifts unto men.'

'Give them nothing,' said the saint. 'Take rather part of their load, and carry it along with them – that will be most agreeable unto them: if only it be agreeable unto you! If, however, you would give something to them, give them no more than alms, and let them also beg for it!'

'No,' replied Zarathustra, 'I give no alms. I am not poor enough for that.'

The saint laughed at Zarathustra, and spake thus: 'Then see to it that they accept your treasures! They are distrustful of anchorites, and do not believe that we come with gifts. The fall of our footsteps rings too hollow through their streets. And just as at night, when they are in bed and hear a man abroad long before sunrise, so they ask themselves concerning us: "Where is the thief going?"

'Go not to men, but stay in the forest! Go rather to the animals! Why not be like me – a bear amongst bears, a bird amongst birds?'

'And what does a saint do in the forest?' asked Zarathustra.

The saint answered: 'I make hymns and sing them; and in making hymns I laugh and weep and mumble: thus do I praise God. With singing, weeping, laughing and mumbling do I praise the God who is my God. But what do you bring us as a gift?'

When Zarathustra had heard these words, he bowed to the saint and said: 'What should I have to give you! Let me rather hurry hence lest I take anything away from you!' And thus they parted from one another, the old man and Zarathustra, laughing like schoolboys.

When Zarathustra was alone, however, he said to his heart: 'Can it be possible! This old saint in the forest has not yet heard that *God is dead*!'

When Zarathustra arrived at the nearest town adjoining the forest, he found many people assembled in the market-place; for it had been announced that a rope-dancer would give a performance. And Zarathustra spake thus unto the people:

'*I teach you the superman.* Man is something that is to be surpassed. What have you done to surpass man? All beings hitherto have created something beyond themselves: and you want to be the ebb of that great tide, and would rather go back to the beast than surpass man? What is the ape to man? A laughing-stock, a thing of shame. And just the same shall man be to the Superman: a laughing-stock, a thing of shame. You have made your way from the worm to man, and much within you is still worm. Once were you apes, and even now man is more of an ape than any of the apes.

'Even the wisest among you is only a disharmony and hybrid of plant and phantom. But do I bid you become phantoms or plants? Lo, I teach you the Superman! The Superman is the meaning of the earth. Let your will say: The Superman *shall be* the meaning of the earth! I conjure you, my brethren, *remain true to the earth*, and do not believe those who speak unto you of super-earthly hopes! They are poisoners, whether they know it or not. Despisers of life are they, decaying ones and poisoned ones themselves, of whom the earth is weary: so away with them!

'Once blasphemy against God was the greatest blasphemy; but God died, and with him those blasphemers too. To blaspheme the *earth* is now the dreadfulest sin, and to rate the heart of the unknowable higher than the meaning of the earth!

'Once the soul looked contemptuously on the body, and then that contempt was the supreme thing – the soul wished the body meagre, ghastly and famished. Thus it sought to escape from the body and the earth. Oh, that soul was itself meagre, ghastly and famished; and cruelty was the delight of that soul! But you, also, my brethren, tell me: What does your body say about your soul? Is your soul not poverty and pollution and wretched self-complacency?

'Verily, man is a polluted stream. One must be a sea, to receive a polluted stream without becoming impure. Lo, I teach you the Superman: he is that sea; in him can your great contempt be submerged.

'What is the greatest thing you can experience? It is the hour of great contempt. The hour in which even your happiness becomes loathsome to you, and so also your reason and virtue.

'The hour when you say: "What good is my happiness! It is poverty and pollution and wretched self-complacency. But my happiness should justify existence itself!"

'The hour when you say: "What good is my reason! Does it long for knowledge as the lion for his food? It is poverty and pollution and wretched self-complacency!"

'The hour when you say: "What good is my virtue! As yet it has not made me passionate. How weary I am of my good and my bad! It is all poverty and pollution and wretched self-complacency!"

'The hour when you say: "What good is my justice! I do not see that I am flame and fuel. The just, however, are flame and fuel!"

'The hour when we say: "What good is my pity! Is not pity the cross on which he who loves mankind is nailed? But my pity is not a crucifixion."

'Have you ever spoken thus? Have you ever cried thus? Ah! would that I had heard you crying thus!

'It is not your sin – it is your self-satisfaction that cries unto heaven; your very sparingness in sin cries unto heaven! Where is the lightning to lick you with its tongue? Where is the frenzy with which you should be inoculated?

'Lo, I teach you the Superman: he is that lightning, he is that frenzy!'

When Zarathustra had thus spoken, one of the people called out: 'We have now heard enough of the rope-dancer; it is time now for us to see him!' And all the people laughed at Zarathustra. But the rope-dancer, who thought the words applied to him, began his performance...

The three metamorphoses

Three metamorphoses of the spirit do I show to you: how the spirit becomes a camel, the camel a lion and the lion at last a child.

Many heavy things are there for the spirit, the strong load-bearing spirit in which reverence dwells; for its strength demands the heavy and the heaviest.

What is heavy? So asks the load-bearing spirit; then it kneels down like the camel, and wants to be well laden. What is the heaviest thing, you heroes? asks the load-bearing spirit, that I may take it upon me and rejoice in my strength.

Is it not this: To humiliate oneself in order to mortify one's pride? To exhibit one's folly in order to mock at one's wisdom?

Or is it this: To desert our cause when it is celebrating its triumph? To ascend high mountains to tempt the tempter?

Or is it this: To feed on the acorns and grass of knowledge, and for the sake of truth to suffer hunger of soul?

Or is it this: To be sick and dismiss comforters, and make friends of the deaf, who never hear your requests?

Or is it this: To go into foul water when it is the water of truth, and not disclaim cold frogs and hot toads?

Or is it this: To love those who despise us, and give one's hand to the phantom when it is going to frighten us?

All these heaviest things the load-bearing spirit takes upon itself: and like the camel, which, when laden, hastens into the wilderness, so hastens the spirit into its wilderness.

But in the loneliest wilderness the second metamorphosis happens: here the spirit becomes a lion; it will capture freedom and lordship in its own wilderness. Here it seeks its last Lord. It will be hostile to him, and to its last God; and it will struggle with the great dragon.

What is the great dragon which the spirit is no longer inclined to call Lord and God? The great dragon is called *Thou Shalt*. But the spirit of the lion says, *I will! Thou-shalt* lies in its path, sparkling with gold – a scale-covered beast; and on every scale glitters the golden *Thou shalt!*

The values of a thousand years glitter on those scales, and thus speaks the mightiest of all dragons: 'All the values of things glitter on me. All values have already been created, and I represent all created values. Verily, there shall be no *I will* any more. Thus speaks the dragon.'

My brethren, wherefore is there need of the lion in the spirit? Why is not the beast of burden, which renounces and is reverent, not enough?

To create new values – that even the lion cannot yet accomplish: but to create itself freedom for new creating – that can the might of the lion do. To create itself freedom for oneself, and give a holy *No* even unto duty: for that, my brethren, there is need of the lion. To assume the right to new values – that is the most formidable assumption for a load-bearing and reverent spirit. Truly, to such a spirit it is preying, and the work of a beast of prey. At its holiest, it once loved *Thou shalt.* Now is it forced to find illusion and arbitrariness even in the holiest things, that it may capture freedom from its love: the lion is needed for this capture.

But tell me, my brethren, what the child can do, which even the lion could not do? Why has the preying lion still to become a child?

The child is innocence and forgetfulness, a new beginning, a game, a self-rolling wheel, a first movement, a holy *Yes.* For the game of creating, my brethren, there is needed a holy *Yes* unto life: The spirit now wills *its own* will; the world's outcasts wins *his own* world.

Three metamorphoses of the spirit have I shown to you: how the spirit became a camel, the camel a lion, and the lion at last a child.

Thus spake Zarathustra.

8   Idealism in a Godless Universe: Bertrand Russell, *A Free Man's Worship**

Our next extract takes us down to the start of the twentieth century. The famous English philosopher and logician Bertrand Russell was a resolute atheist, and the mythical narrative of a cruel god with which he opens his essay is both an implied critique of the religious outlook and a dramatic way of driving home what he takes to be the true nature of the universe as described by modern science. The vision initially seems as bleak as anything in Schopenhauer (see extract 6, above): all human achievement stems from 'accidental collocations of atoms', and is 'destined to extinction in the vast death of the solar system'.

The religious solution of submitting ourselves to a supposed higher being, Russell argues, is a piece of 'slavishness', and we must try to free ourselves from 'the tyranny of non-human power'. At first this looks somewhat like Nietzsche's outlook (see preceding extract); but Russell rejects what he takes to be the Nietzschean 'worship of Force', and instead suggests that our response to human mortality and the meaninglessness of the cosmos should be to learn 'that energy of faith which enables us to live constantly in the vision of the good'. Living by such a moral vision is better than the 'Promethean' strategy of indignant rebellion,[1] and an improvement on Stoic resignation.[2] Russell concedes to the Stoics that resigning to the inevitable without vain regrets is the 'gate of wisdom'; but to enter the temple of wisdom itself we need more – we need to 'worship our own ideals'.

---

* Bertrand Russell, 'A Free Man's Worship' [1903], repr. in Russell, *Collected Papers*, vol. 12 (London: Routledge, 1985).

[1] In Greek mythology, Prometheus rebelled against the Gods. Russell's rejection of this strategy yields the basis for a possible criticism of the approach later developed by Albert Camus (see next extract).

[2] Compare extract 2, above.

What exactly are these ideals that Russell believes can redeem us from futility and despair? We have 'foreshadowings' of them, he says, in 'the realm of the imagination, in music, in architecture, in the untroubled kingdom of reason', and also in poetry ('the golden sunset magic of lyrics'). The resounding purple passages that follow are perhaps a little over-written for our contemporary taste, but Russell's aim seems to be to show that exercising these human capacities (e.g. for the creative arts, and for rational inquiry) gives us goals to pursue that are every bit as exalted and inspiring as anything traditional religion has to offer.

The essay concludes with an impassioned plea for self-sacrifice and altruism, which seems, in its moral content, very close to the Christian vision of service to others.[1] Russell speaks of 'lightening the sorrows of others with the balm of sympathy', and 'instilling faith in hours of despair'. The 'free man's worship' referred to in his title turns out to be 'to abandon the struggle for private happiness, to expel all eagerness of temporary desire, to burn with passion for eternal things'. These may be noble goals, but some critics may question how far Russell, given his bleak general view of the cosmos, is logically entitled to help himself to such 'eternal' ideals.[2] The ideals, Russell is clear, are entirely our own human invention (hence he speaks in his final paragraph of mankind 'worshipping at the shrine *his own hands have built*'). Yet if the values are entirely of our own making, how can they achieve the status of 'eternal' ideals that are worthy of worship? At all events, Russell's rhetoric succeeds in broaching one of the key issues for the atheist worldview – the question of how human life can attain to genuine value and meaning in a universe that is taken to be entirely indifferent to our puny and temporary strivings.

To Dr Faustus in his study Mephistopheles told the history of the Creation, saying:

The endless praises of the choirs of angels had begun to grow wearisome; for, after all, did he not deserve their praise? Had he not given them endless joy? Would it not be more amusing to obtain undeserved praise, to be worshipped by beings whom he tortured? He smiled inwardly, and resolved that the great drama should be performed.

For countless ages the hot nebula whirled aimlessly through space. At length it began to take shape, the central mass threw off planets, the planets cooled, boiling seas and burning mountains heaved and tossed, from black masses of cloud hot sheets of rain deluged the barely solid crust. And now the first germ of life grew in the depths of the ocean, and developed rapidly in the fructifying warmth into vast forest trees, huge ferns springing from the damp mould, sea monsters breeding, fighting, devouring and passing away. And from the monsters, as the play unfolded itself, Man was born, with the power of thought, the knowledge of good and evil, and the cruel thirst for worship. And Man saw that all is passing in this mad, monstrous world, that all is struggling to snatch, at any cost, a few brief moments of life before Death's inexorable decree. And Man said: 'There is a hidden purpose, could we but fathom it, and the purpose is good; for we must reverence something, and in the visible world there is nothing worthy of reverence.' And Man stood aside from the struggle, resolving that God intended harmony to come out of chaos by human efforts. And when he followed the instincts which God had transmitted to him from his ancestry of beasts of prey, he called it Sin, and asked God to forgive him. But he doubted whether he could be justly forgiven, until he invented a divine Plan by which God's wrath was to

---

[1] Compare extract 3, above.
[2] For this kind of critique, see extract 11, below.

have been appeased. And seeing the present was bad, he made it yet worse, that thereby the future might be better. And he gave God thanks for the strength that enabled him to forgo even the joys that were possible. And God smiled; and when he saw that Man had become perfect in renunciation and worship, he sent another sun through the sky, which crashed into Man's sun; and all returned again to nebula.

'Yes,' he murmured, 'it was a good play; I will have it performed again.'

Such, in outline, but even more purposeless, more void of meaning, is the world which Science presents for our belief. Amid such a world, if anywhere, our ideals henceforward must find a home. That Man is the product of causes which had no prevision of the end they were achieving; that his origin, his growth, his hopes and fears, his loves and his beliefs, are but the outcome of accidental collocations of atoms; that no fire, no heroism, no intensity of thought and feeling, can preserve an individual life beyond the grave; that all the labours of the ages, all the devotion, all the inspiration, all the noonday brightness of human genius, are destined to extinction in the vast death of the solar system, and that the whole temple of Man's achievement must inevitably be buried beneath the debris of a universe in ruins – all these things, if not quite beyond dispute, are yet so nearly certain, that no philosophy which rejects them can hope to stand. Only within the scaffolding of these truths, only on the firm foundation of unyielding despair, can the soul's habitation henceforth be safely built.

How, in such an alien and inhuman world, can so powerless a creature as Man preserve his aspirations untarnished? A strange mystery it is that Nature, omnipotent but blind, in the revolutions of her secular hurryings through the abysses of space, has brought forth at last a child, subject still to her power, but gifted with sight, with knowledge of good and evil, with the capacity of judging all the works of his unthinking Mother. In spite of Death, the mark and seal of the parental control, Man is yet free, during his brief years, to examine, to criticize, to know, and in imagination to create. To him alone, in the world with which he is acquainted, this freedom belongs; and in this lies his superiority to the resistless forces that control his outward life.

The savage, like ourselves, feels the oppression of his impotence before the powers of Nature; but having in himself nothing that he respects more than Power, he is willing to prostrate himself before his gods, without inquiring whether they are worthy of his worship. Pathetic and very terrible is the long history of cruelty and torture, of degradation and human sacrifice, endured in the hope of placating the jealous gods: surely, the trembling believer thinks, when what is most precious has been freely given, their lust for blood must be appeased, and more will not be required. The religion of Moloch[1] – as such creeds may be generically called – is in essence the cringing submission of the slave, who dare not, even in his heart, allow the thought that his master deserves no adulation. Since the independence of ideals is not yet acknowledged, Power may be freely worshipped, and receive an unlimited respect, despite its wanton infliction of pain.

---

[1] One of the ancient tribal gods (mentioned in the Bible) whose worship involved the sacrifice of children by fire.

But gradually, as morality grows bolder, the claim of the ideal world begins to be felt; and worship, if it is not to cease, must be given to gods of another kind than those created by the savage. Some, though they feel the demands of the ideal, will still consciously reject them, still urging that naked Power is worthy of worship. Such is the attitude inculcated in God's answer to Job out of the whirlwind: the divine power and knowledge are paraded, but of the divine goodness there is no hint.[1] Such also is the attitude of those who, in our own day, base their morality upon the struggle for survival, maintaining that the survivors are necessarily the fittest. But others, not content with an answer so repugnant to the moral sense, will adopt the position which we have become accustomed to regard as specially religious, maintaining that, in some hidden manner, the world of fact is really harmonious with the world of ideals. Thus Man creates God, all-powerful and all-good, the mystic unity of what is and what should be.

But the world of fact, after all, is not good; and, in submitting our judgement to it, there is an element of slavishness from which our thoughts must be purged. For in all things it is well to exalt the dignity of Man, by freeing him as far as possible from the tyranny of non-human Power. When we have realized that Power is largely bad, that man, with his knowledge of good and evil, is but a helpless atom in a world which has no such knowledge, the choice is again presented to us: Shall we worship Force, or shall we worship Goodness? Shall our God exist and be evil, or shall he be recognized as the creation of our own conscience?

The answer to this question is very momentous, and affects profoundly our whole morality. The worship of Force, to which Carlyle[2] and Nietzsche and the creed of Militarism have accustomed us, is the result of failure to maintain our own ideals against a hostile universe: it is itself a prostrate submission to evil, a sacrifice of our best to Moloch. If strength indeed is to be respected, let us respect rather the strength of those who refuse that false 'recognition of facts' which fails to recognize that facts are often bad. Let us admit that, in the world we know, there are many things that would be better otherwise, and that the ideals to which we do and must adhere are not realized in the realm of matter. Let us preserve our respect for truth, for beauty, for the ideal of perfection which life does not permit us to attain, though none of these things meet with the approval of the unconscious universe. If Power is bad, as it seems to be, let us reject it from our hearts. In this lies Man's true freedom: in determination to worship only the God created by our own love of the good, to respect only the heaven which inspires the insight of our best moments. In action, in desire, we must submit perpetually to the tyranny of outside forces; but in thought, in aspiration, we are free, free from our fellow-men, free from the petty planet on which our bodies impotently crawl, free even, while we live, from the tyranny of death. Let us learn, then, that energy of faith which enables us to live constantly in the vision of the good; and let us descend, in action, into the world of fact, with that vision always before us.

---

[1] In the Bible story referred to here, God, in response to Job's complaints about his sufferings, denies the right of a mere creature to question his actions, asking, 'Where were you when I laid the foundations of the earth?' (Job 38: 4).

[2] Thomas Carlyle (1795–1881); his writings included essays critical of democracy and advocating rule by the strong.

When first the opposition of fact and ideal grows fully visible, a spirit of fiery revolt, of fierce hatred of the gods, seems necessary to the assertion of freedom. To defy with Promethean constancy a hostile universe, to keep its evil always in view, always actively hated, to refuse no pain that the malice of Power can invent, appears to be the duty of all who will not bow before the inevitable. But indignation is still a bondage, for it compels our thoughts to be occupied with an evil world; and in the fierceness of desire from which rebellion springs there is a kind of self-assertion which it is necessary for the wise to overcome. Indignation is a submission of our thoughts, but not of our desires; the Stoic freedom in which wisdom consists is found in the submission of our desires, but not of our thoughts. From the submission of our desires springs the virtue of resignation; from the freedom of our thoughts springs the whole world of art and philosophy, and the vision of beauty by which, at last, we half reconquer the reluctant world. But the vision of beauty is possible only to unfettered contemplation, to thoughts not weighted by the load of eager wishes; and thus Freedom comes only to those who no longer ask of life that it shall yield them any of those personal goods that are subject to the mutations of Time.

Although the necessity of renunciation is evidence of the existence of evil, yet Christianity, in preaching it, has shown a wisdom exceeding that of the Promethean philosophy of rebellion. It must be admitted that, of the things we desire, some, though they prove impossible, are yet real goods; others, however, as ardently longed for, do not form part of a fully purified ideal. The belief that what must be renounced is bad, though sometimes false, is far less often false than untamed passion supposes; and the creed of religion, by providing a reason for proving that it is never false, has been the means of purifying our hopes by the discovery of many austere truths.

But there is in resignation a further good element: even real goods, when they are unattainable, ought not to be fretfully desired. To every man comes, sooner or later, the great renunciation. For the young, there is nothing unattainable; a good thing desired with the whole force of a passionate will, and yet impossible, is to them not credible. Yet, by death, by illness, by poverty or by the voice of duty, we must learn, each one of us, that the world was not made for us, and that, however beautiful may be the things we crave, Fate may nevertheless forbid them. It is the part of courage, when misfortune comes, to bear without repining the ruin of our hopes, to turn away our thoughts from vain regrets. This degree of submission to Power is not only just and right: it is the very gate of wisdom.

But passive renunciation is not the whole of wisdom; for not by renunciation alone can we build a temple for the worship of our own ideals. Haunting foreshadowings of the temple appear in the realm of imagination, in music, in architecture, in the untroubled kingdom of reason and in the golden sunset magic of lyrics, where beauty shines and glows, remote from the touch of sorrow, remote from the fear of change, remote from the failures and disenchantments of the world of fact. In the contemplation of these things the vision of heaven will shape itself in our hearts, giving at once a touchstone to judge the world about us, and an inspiration by which to fashion to our needs whatever is not incapable of serving as a stone in the sacred temple.

Except for those rare spirits that are born without sin, there is a cavern of darkness to be traversed before that temple can be entered. The gate of the cavern is despair, and its floor is paved with the gravestones of abandoned hopes. There Self must die; there the eagerness, the greed of untamed desire must be slain, for only so can the soul be freed from the empire of Fate. But out of the cavern the Gate of Renunciation leads again to the daylight of wisdom, by whose radiance a new insight, a new joy, a new tenderness, shine forth to gladden the pilgrim's heart.

When, without the bitterness of impotent rebellion, we have learnt both to resign ourselves to the outward rules of Fate and to recognize that the non-human world is unworthy of our worship, it becomes possible at last so to transform and refashion the unconscious universe, so to transmute it in the crucible of imagination, that a new image of shining gold replaces the old idol of clay. In all the multiform facts of the world – in the visual shapes of trees and mountains and clouds, in the events of the life of man, even in the very omnipotence of Death – the insight of creative idealism can find the reflection of a beauty which its own thoughts first made. In this way mind asserts its subtle mastery over the thoughtless forces of Nature. The more evil the material with which it deals, the more thwarting to untrained desire, the greater is its achievement in inducing the reluctant rock to yield up its hidden treasures, the prouder its victory in compelling the opposing forces to swell the pageant of its triumph. Of all the arts, Tragedy is the proudest, the most triumphant; for it builds its shining citadel in the very centre of the enemy's country, on the very summit of his highest mountain; from its impregnable watchtowers, his camps and arsenals, his columns and forts, are all revealed; within its walls the free life continues, while the legions of Death and Pain and Despair, and all the servile captains of tyrant Fate, afford the burghers of that dauntless city new spectacles of beauty. Happy those sacred ramparts, thrice happy the dwellers on that all-seeing eminence. Honour to those brave warriors who, through countless ages of warfare, have preserved for us the priceless heritage of liberty, and have kept undefiled by sacrilegious invaders the home of the unsubdued.

But the beauty of Tragedy does but make visible a quality which, in more or less obvious shapes, is present always and everywhere in life. In the spectacle of Death, in the endurance of intolerable pain, and in the irrevocableness of a vanished past, there is a sacredness, an overpowering awe, a feeling of the vastness, the depth, the inexhaustible mystery of existence, in which, as by some strange marriage of pain, the sufferer is bound to the world by bonds of sorrow. In these moments of insight, we lose all eagerness of temporary desire, all struggling and striving for petty ends, all care for the little trivial things that, to a superficial view, make up the common life of day by day; we see, surrounding the narrow raft illumined by the flickering light of human comradeship, the dark ocean on whose rolling waves we toss for a brief hour; from the great night without, a chill blast breaks in upon our refuge; all the loneliness of humanity amid hostile forces is concentrated upon the individual soul, which must struggle alone, with what of courage it can command, against the whole weight of a universe that cares nothing for its hopes and fears. Victory, in this struggle with the powers of darkness, is the true baptism into the glorious company of heroes, the true initiation into the overmastering beauty of human existence. From that awful encounter of the soul with the outer world, enunciation, wisdom and charity are born; and with their birth a new life begins. To take into the inmost shrine of the soul the irresistible forces whose puppets we seem to be – Death and change, the irrevocableness of the past and the powerlessness of Man before the blind hurry of the universe from vanity to vanity – to feel these things and know them is to conquer them.

This is the reason why the Past has such magical power. The beauty of its motionless and silent pictures is like the enchanted purity of late autumn, when the leaves, though one breath would make them fall, still glow against the sky in golden glory. The Past does not change or strive; like Duncan, after life's fitful fever it sleeps well; what was eager and grasping, what was petty and transitory, has faded away, the things that were beautiful and eternal shine out of it like stars in the night. Its beauty, to a soul not worthy of it, is unendurable; but to a soul which has conquered Fate it is the key of religion.

The life of Man, viewed outwardly, is but a small thing in comparison with the forces of Nature. The slave is doomed to worship Time and Fate and Death, because they are greater than anything he finds in himself, and because all his thoughts are of things which they devour. But, great as they are, to think of them greatly, to feel their passionless splendour, is greater still. And such thought makes us free men; we no longer bow before the inevitable in Oriental subjection, but we absorb it, and make it a part of ourselves. To abandon the struggle for private happiness, to expel all eagerness of temporary desire, to burn with passion for eternal things – this is emancipation, and this is the free man's worship. And this liberation is effected by a contemplation of Fate; for Fate itself is subdued by the mind which leaves nothing to be purged by the purifying fire of Time.

United with his fellow-men by the strongest of all ties, the tie of a common doom, the free man finds that a new vision is with him always, shedding over every daily task the light of love. The life of Man is a long march through the night, surrounded by invisible foes, tortured by weariness and pain, towards a goal that few can hope to reach, and where none may tarry long. One by one, as they march, our comrades vanish from our sight, seized by the silent orders of omnipotent Death. Very brief is the time in which we can help them, in which their happiness or misery is decided. Be it ours to shed sunshine on their path, to lighten their sorrows by the balm of sympathy, to give them the pure joy of a never-tiring affection, to strengthen failing courage, to instil faith in hours of despair. Let us not weigh in grudging scales their merits and demerits, but let us think only of their need – of the sorrows, the difficulties, perhaps the blindnesses, that make the misery of their lives; let us remember that they are fellow-sufferers in the same darkness, actors in the same tragedy as ourselves. And so, when their day is over, when their good and their evil have become eternal by the immortality of the past, be it ours to feel that, where they suffered, where they failed, no deed of ours was the cause; but wherever a spark of the divine fire kindled in their hearts, we were ready with encouragement, with sympathy, with brave words in which high courage glowed.

Brief and powerless is Man's life; on him and all his race the slow, sure doom falls pitiless and dark. Blind to good and evil, reckless of destruction, omnipotent matter rolls on its relentless way; for Man, condemned today to lose his dearest, tomorrow himself to pass through the gate of darkness, it remains only to cherish, ere yet the blow falls, the lofty thoughts that ennoble his little day; disdaining the coward terrors of the slave of Fate, to worship at the shrine that his own hands have built; undismayed by the empire of chance, to preserve a mind free from the wanton tyranny that rules his outward life; proudly defiant of the irresistible forces that tolerate, for a moment, his knowledge and his condemnation, to sustain alone, a weary but unyielding Atlas, the world that his own ideals have fashioned despite the trampling march of unconscious power.

9   Futility and Defiance: Albert Camus, *The Myth of Sisyphus**

Seldom have the problems of human life and its meaning been confronted more starkly than in the work of the great French existentialist philosophers of the mid twentieth century, Jean-Paul Sartre and our next author Albert Camus. In his highly original reflections on the ancient Greek myth of Sisyphus, who was condemned by the gods to the endlessly repeated punishment of pushing a boulder up a hill only to see it roll all the way down again, Camus addresses issues we have seen troubling many of his predecessors (see for example the three preceding extracts by Schopenhauer, Nietzsche and Russell) – the plight of humankind in the face of a seemingly hostile universe, and the threat of purposelessness and futility. Camus's Sisyphus, the 'proletarian of the gods' stands for all the millions of ordinary human beings condemned to wearisome drudgery without any hope of escape. But he is above all a defiant thinker who will not abandon his fierce 'lust for life', who refuses to be docile and accepting of his plight, and who is unflinchingly conscious of the ultimate absurdity of the existence he has to endure. Sisyphus, says Camus, is 'the true hero of the absurd'.

The heroism lies partly in Sisyphus' original disobedience towards the gods that earned him his punishment; partly in his sheer physical courage (Camus powerfully depicts the desperate strain of heaving the massive boulder uphill); but especially in his snatching of those brief moments of freedom and self-awareness when he trudges back down the hill each time, to resume his gruelling task. For instead of being a time of exhaustion and depression, this time of descent, Camus insists, 'can be a time for joy'. This is no glib solution – there is no 'handbook for happiness', Camus warns. But he quotes another classical source, Sophocles' play *Oedipus at Colonus*, where the hero, despite all his sufferings, is able to declare at the close of his life that 'all is well'. As interpreted by Camus, this final joyful calmness is available once we 'banish from the world a god who had a taste for futile suffering',[1] and instead grasp that 'destiny is a human matter, a matter for human beings to arrange among themselves'. It is in the light of this that Camus is able to proclaim in his famous closing sentence that we 'must imagine Sisyphus happy'.

Camus's presentation of the Sisyphus story has undeniable power, but some may wonder whether a philosophy based on the idea of defiance can deliver the 'happiness' at which it aims. One may compare Bertrand Russell's observation that 'in the fierceness of desire from which rebellion springs there is a kind of self-assertion which it is necessary for the wise to overcome'.[2] But perhaps what makes Sisyphus 'stronger than his rock', in Camus's eyes, is the very fact of his committing himself, without illusions or false hopes, to the unending challenges of human existence: 'the struggle itself towards the heights is enough to fill a man's heart.'

The gods had condemned Sisyphus to ceaselessly rolling a rock to the top of a mountain, whence the stone would fall back of its own weight. They had thought with some reason that there is no more dreadful punishment than futile and hopeless labour.

If one believes Homer, Sisyphus was the wisest and most prudent of mortals. According to another tradition, however, he was disposed to practise the profession

---

* Albert Camus, *Le Mythe de Sisyphe* (Paris: Gallimard, 1942), final chapter. Translated by Justin O'Brien, in Camus, *The Myth of Sisyphus* (Harmondsworth: Penguin, 1975), pp. 107–11.
[1] In this bitter phrase, Camus is evidently urging us to reject what he takes to be the implications of the Christian concept of atonement through suffering.
[2] From extract 8, above. (Russell's comment, having been written several decades earlier, was of course not directed specifically at Camus's work.)

of highwayman. I see no contradiction in this. Opinions differ as to the reasons why he became the futile labourer of the underworld. To begin with, he is accused of a certain levity in regard to the gods. He stole their secrets. Aegina, the daughter of Aesopus, was carried off by Jupiter. The father was shocked by that disappearance and complained to Sisyphus. He, who knew of the abduction, offered to tell about it on condition that Aesopus would give water to the citadel of Corinth. To the celestial thunderbolts he preferred the benediction of water. He was punished for this in the underworld. Homer tells us also that Sisyphus had put Death in chains. Pluto could not endure the sight of his deserted, silent empire. He dispatched the god of war who liberated Death from the hands of her conqueror.

It is said also that Sisyphus, being near to death, rashly wanted to test his wife's love. He ordered her to cast his unburied body into the middle of the public square. Sisyphus woke up in the underworld. And there, annoyed by an obedience so contrary to human love, he obtained from Pluto permission to return to earth in order to chastise his wife. But when he had seen again the face of this world, enjoyed water and sun, warm stones and the sea, he no longer wanted to go back to the infernal darkness. Recalls, signs of anger, warnings were of no avail. Many years more, he lived facing the curve of the gulf, the sparkling sea and the smiles of earth. A decree of the gods was necessary. Mercury came and seized the impudent man by the collar and, snatching him from his joys, led him forcibly back to the underworld where his rock was ready for him.

You have already grasped that Sisyphus is the absurd hero. He *is*, as much through his passions as through his torture. His scorn of the gods, his hatred of death, and his passion for life won him that unspeakable penalty in which the whole being is exerted towards accomplishing nothing. This is the price that must be paid for the passions of this earth. Nothing is told us about Sisyphus in the underworld. Myths are made for the imagination to breathe life into them. As for this myth, one sees merely the whole effort of a body straining to raise the huge stone, to roll it and push it up a slope a hundred times over; one sees the face screwed up, the cheek tight against the stone, the shoulder bracing the clay-covered mass, the foot wedging it, the fresh start with arms outstretched, the wholly human security of two earth-clotted hands. At the very end of his long effort measured by skyless space and time without depth, the purpose is achieved. Then Sisyphus watches the stone rush down in a few moments towards that lower world whence he will have to push it up again towards the summit. He goes back down to the plain.

It is during that return, that pause, that Sisyphus interests me. A face that toils so close to stones is already stone itself! I see that man going back down with a heavy yet measured step towards the torment of which he will never know the end. That hour like a breathing-space which returns as surely as his suffering, that is the hour of consciousness. At each of those moments when he leaves the heights and gradually sinks towards the lairs of the gods, he is superior to his fate. He is stronger than his rock.

If this myth is tragic, that is because its hero is conscious. Where would his torture be, indeed, if at every step the hope of succeeding upheld him? The workman of today works every day in his life at the same tasks and this fate is no less absurd. But it is tragic only at the rare moments when it becomes conscious. Sisyphus, proletarian of the gods, powerless and rebellious, knows the whole extent of his wretched condition; it is what he thinks of during his descent. The lucidity that was to constitute his torture at the same time crowns his victory. There is no fate that cannot be surmounted by scorn.

If the descent is thus sometimes performed in sorrow, it can also take place in joy. The word is not too much. Again I fancy Sisyphus returning towards his rock, and the sorrow was in the beginning. When the images of earth cling too tightly to memory, when the call of happiness becomes too insistent, it happens that melancholy rises in man's heart: this is the rock's victory, this is the rock itself. The boundless grief is too heavy to bear. These are our nights of Gethsemane.[1] But crushing truths perish from being acknowledged. Thus Oedipus at the outset obeys fate without knowing it. But from the moment he knows, his tragedy begins. Yet at the same moment, blind and desperate, he realizes that the only bond linking him to the world is the cool hand of a girl. Then a tremendous remark rings out: 'Despite so many ordeals, my advanced age and the nobility of my soul make me conclude that all is well.'[2] Sophocles' Oedipus, like Dostoevsky's Kirilov,[3] thus gives the recipe for the absurd victory. Ancient wisdom confirms modern heroism.

One does not discover the absurd without being tempted to write a manual of happiness. 'What! by such narrow ways ...?' There is but one world, however. Happiness and the absurd are two sons of the same earth. They are inseparable. It would be a mistake to say that happiness necessarily springs from the absurd discovery. It happens as well that the feeling of the absurd springs from happiness. 'I conclude that all is well,' says Oedipus, and that remark is sacred. It echoes in the wild and limited universe of man. It teaches that all is not, has not been, exhausted. It drives out of this world a god who had come into it with dissatisfaction and a preference for futile sufferings. It makes of fate a human matter, which must be settled among men.

All Sisyphus' silent joy is contained therein. His fate belongs to him. His rock is his thing. Likewise, the absurd man, when he contemplates his torment, silences all the idols. In the universe suddenly restored to its silence, the myriad wondering little voices of the earth rise up. Unconscious, secret calls, invitations from all the faces, they are the necessary reverse and price of victory. There is no sun without shadow, and it is essential to know the night. The absurd man says yes and his effort will henceforth be unceasing. If there is a personal fate, there is no higher destiny or at least there is but one which he concludes is inevitable and despicable. For the rest, he knows himself to be the master of his days. At that subtle moment when man glances backward over his life, Sisyphus returning towards his rock, in that slight pivoting, he contemplates that series of unrelated actions which becomes his fate, created by him, combined under his memory's eye and soon sealed by his death. Thus, convinced of the wholly human origin of all that is human, a blind man eager to see who knows that the night has no end, he is still on the go. The rock is still rolling.

I leave Sisyphus at the foot of the mountain! One always finds one's burden again. But Sisyphus teaches the higher fidelity that negates the gods and raises rocks. He, too, concludes that all is well. This universe henceforth without a master seems to him neither sterile nor futile. Each atom of that stone, each mineral flake of that night-filled mountain, in itself forms a world. The struggle itself towards the heights is enough to fill a man's heart. One must imagine Sisyphus happy.

---

[1] The reference is to the anguish of Christ on the night before his crucifixion; see Matthew 26: 36–46.
[2] From *Oedipus at Colonus*, written at the end of the 5th century BC by the Greek tragedian Sophocles.
[3] Character in Dostoevsky's *The Possessed* (also translated as *The Devils*) [*Byesi*, 1872].

10   Involvement versus Detachment: Thomas Nagel, *The Absurd**

The idea of the 'absurdity' of human life (see preceding extract) is a recurring theme in much twentieth-century art and literature. In our next extract, the distinguished American philosopher Thomas Nagel begins by focusing on the *minuteness* and *brevity* of human life, and asking why these features are so often supposed to undercut its meaningfulness. It may be true (as Pascal pointed out – see extract 5, above) that our lives are the tiniest instants measured on a cosmic scale, but why should mere size or duration make what we do matter less? If our lives are absurd, asks Nagel, would they be any less absurd if we were larger or the universe were smaller? Nor is it clear why everything should be pointless just because we shall all eventually die; an activity does not have to depend on a continuing future sequence to be worthwhile (no further sequence of justifying reasons 'is needed to make it reasonable to…attend an exhibit of the work of a painter one admires').

Nevertheless, argues Nagel, concerns about our mortality and the vastness of the cosmos do point to something troubling about human life. Absurdity arises when there is a conspicuous gap between aspiration and reality. We aspire to lead worthwhile lives, and that means taking things seriously, and believing that our decisions have a certain importance. Yet it is also true that 'humans have the special capacity to step back and survey themselves and the lives to which they are committed'. And from the detached perspective – with that 'detached amazement that comes from watching an ant struggle up a heap of sand' – we can have a view of ourselves and our earnestly pursued projects that is 'at once sobering and comical'. It is the clash between two incompatible perspectives – the involved and the detached – that Nagel sees as the key to our sense of life's absurdity.

Towards the end of his essay, Nagel draws a parallel between this tension and a similar tension that arises in the philosophy of knowledge. In our ordinary day-to-day epistemic practices we accept certain types of evidence and justification as adequate; but in moments of philosophical scepticism we stand back from those practices and ask radical questions like 'how do I know I am really awake?', or 'how do I know there is a real external world outside of my sensations and thoughts?'[1] Our ability to adopt this sceptical perspective does not cause us to abandon our ordinary beliefs, says Nagel; it merely 'lends them a peculiar flavour'. We cannot but return to our normal activities and convictions, but our seriousness is now 'laced with a certain irony'. But irony, Nagel concludes, is better than despair, or the kind of 'romantic' heroic defiance that Camus recommended in the face of absurdity.

The tension between aspiration and human limitation that Nagel has here identified is clearly of great importance. It connects up with the Pascalian idea that 'man infinitely transcends himself', and will be seen by the religious believer as confirming the ancient dictum of St Augustine, that 'our heart is restless until it finds God'. For Nagel, by contrast, things are altogether more low-key: it is enough to 'approach our absurd lives with irony', and to give up trying to 'dragoon an unconvinced transcendent consciousness into the service of an immanent, limited enterprise like a human life'.

 Most people feel on occasion that life is absurd, and some feel it vividly and continually. Yet the reasons usually offered in defence of this conviction are patently inadequate: they could not really explain why life is absurd. Why then do they provide a natural expression for the sense that it is?

---

* Thomas Nagel, 'The Absurd', *Journal of Philosophy*, 63: 20 (1971); repr. in Nagel, *Mortal Questions* (Cambridge: Cambridge University Press, 1979).
[1] Compare Part I, extracts 4 and 10, above.

I

Consider some examples. It is often remarked that nothing we do now will matter in a million years. But if that is true, then by the same token, nothing that will be the case in a million years matters now. In particular, it does not matter now that in a million years nothing we do now will matter. Moreover, even if what we did now were going to matter in a million years, how could that keep our present concerns from being absurd? If their mattering now is not enough to accomplish that, how would it help if they mattered a million years from now?

Whether what we do now will matter in a million years could make the crucial difference only if its mattering in a million years depended on its mattering, period. But then to deny that whatever happens now will matter in a million years is to beg the question against its mattering, period; for in that sense one cannot know that it will not matter in a million years whether (for example) someone now is happy or miserable, without knowing that it does not matter, period. What we say to convey the absurdity of our lives often has to do with space or time: we are tiny specks in the infinite vastness of the universe; our lives are mere instants even on a geological time scale, let alone a cosmic one; we will all be dead any minute. But of course none of these evident facts can be what makes life absurd, if it is absurd. For suppose we lived forever; would not a life that is absurd if it lasts seventy years be infinitely absurd if it lasted through eternity? And if our lives are absurd given our present size, why would they be any less absurd if we filled the universe (either because we were larger or because the universe was smaller)? Reflection on our minuteness and brevity appears to be intimately connected with the sense that life is meaningless; but it is not clear what the connection is.

Another inadequate argument is that because we are going to die, all chains of justification must leave off in mid-air: one studies and works to earn money to pay for clothing, housing, entertainment, food, to sustain oneself from year to year, perhaps to support a family and pursue a career – but to what final end? All of it is an elaborate journey leading nowhere. (One will also have some effect on other people's lives, but that simply reproduces the problem, for they will die too.)

There are several replies to this argument. First, life does not consist of a sequence of activities each of which has as its purpose some later member of the sequence. Chains of justification come repeatedly to an end within life, and whether the process as a whole can be justified has no bearing on the finality of these end-points. No further justification is needed to make it reasonable to take aspirin for a headache, attend an exhibit of the work of a painter one admires or stop a child from putting his hand on a hot stove. No larger context or further purpose is needed to prevent these acts from being pointless.

Even if someone wished to supply a further justification for pursuing all the things in life that are commonly regarded as self-justifying, that justification would have to end somewhere too. If nothing can justify unless it is justified in terms of something outside itself, which is also justified, then an infinite regress results, and no chain of justification can be complete. Moreover, if a finite chain of reasons cannot justify anything, what could be accomplished by an infinite chain, each link of which must be justified by something outside itself?

Since justifications must come to an end somewhere, nothing is gained by denying that they end where they appear to, within life – or by trying to subsume the multiple, often trivial ordinary justifications of action under a single, controlling life scheme. We can be satisfied more easily than that. In fact, through its misrepresentation of the process of justification, the argument makes a vacuous demand. It insists that the reasons available within life are incomplete, but suggests thereby that all reasons that come to an end are incomplete. This makes it impossible to supply any reasons at all. The standard arguments for absurdity appear therefore to fail as arguments. Yet I believe they attempt to express something that is difficult to state, but fundamentally correct.

II

In ordinary life a situation is absurd when it includes a conspicuous discrepancy between pretension or aspiration and reality; someone gives a complicated speech in support of a motion that has already been passed; a notorious criminal is made president of a major philanthropic foundation; you declare your love over the telephone to a recorded announcement; as you are being knighted, your pants fall down.

When a person finds himself in an absurd situation, he will usually attempt to change it, by modifying his aspirations, or by trying to bring reality into better accord with them, or by removing himself from the situation entirely. We are not always willing or able to extricate ourselves from a position whose absurdity has become clear to us. Nevertheless, it is usually possible to imagine some change that would remove the absurdity – whether or not we can or will implement it. The sense that life as a whole is absurd arises when we perceive, perhaps dimly, an inflated pretension or aspiration which is inseparable from the continuation of human life and which makes its absurdity inescapable, short of escape from life itself.

Many people's lives are absurd, temporarily or permanently, for conventional reasons having to do with their particular ambitions, circumstances and personal relations. If there is a philosophical sense of absurdity, however, it must arise from the perception of something universal – some respect in which pretension and reality inevitably clash for us all. This condition is supplied, I shall argue, by the collision between the seriousness with which we take our lives and the perpetual possibility of regarding everything about which we are serious as arbitrary, or open to doubt.

We cannot live human lives without energy and attention, nor without making choices which show that we take some things more seriously than others. Yet we have always available a point of view outside the particular form of our lives, from which the seriousness appears gratuitous. These two inescapable viewpoints collide in us, and that is what makes life absurd. It is absurd because we ignore the doubts that we know cannot be settled, continuing to live with nearly undiminished seriousness in spite of them.

This analysis requires defence in two respects; first as regards the unavoidability of seriousness; second as regards the inescapability of doubt.

We take ourselves seriously whether we lead serious lives or not and whether we are concerned primarily with fame, pleasure, virtue, luxury, triumph, beauty, justice, knowledge, salvation or mere survival. If we take other people seriously and devote ourselves to them, that only multiplies the problem. Human life is full of effort, plans, calculation, success and failure; we pursue our lives, with varying degrees of sloth and energy.

It would be different if we could not step back and reflect on the process, but were merely led from impulse to impulse without self-consciousness. But human beings do not act solely on impulse. They are prudent, they reflect, they weigh consequences, they ask whether what they are doing is worthwhile. Not only are their lives full of particular choices that hang together in larger activities with temporal structure: they also decide in the broadest terms what to pursue and what to avoid, what the priorities among their various aims should be, and what kind of people they want to be or become. Some men are faced with such choices by the large decisions they make from time to time; some merely by reflection on the course their lives are taking as the product of countless small decisions. They decide whom to marry, what profession to follow, whether to join the Country Club or the Resistance; or they may just wonder why they go on being salesmen or academics or taxi drivers, and then stop thinking about it after a certain period of inconclusive reflection.

Although they may be motivated from act to act by those immediate needs with which life presents them, they allow the process to continue by adhering to the general system of habits and the form of life in which such motives have their place – or perhaps only by clinging to life itself. They spend enormous quantities of energy, risk and calculation on the details. Think of how an ordinary individual sweats over his appearance, his health, his sex life, his emotional honesty, his social utility, his self-knowledge, the quality of his ties with family, colleagues and friends, how well he does his job, whether he understands the world and what is going on in it. Leading a human life is a full-time occupation, to which everyone devotes decades of intense concern.

This fact is so obvious that it is hard to find it extraordinary and important. Each of us lives his own life – lives with himself twenty-four hours a day. What else is he supposed to do – live someone else's life? Yet humans have the special capacity to step back and survey themselves, and the lives to which they are committed, with that detached amazement which comes from watching an ant struggle up a heap of sand. Without developing the illusion that they are able to escape from their highly specific and idiosyncratic position, they can view it *sub specie aeternitatis*[1] – and the view is at once sobering and comical.

The crucial backward step is not taken by asking for still another justification in the chain, and failing to get it. The objections to that line of attack have already been stated; justifications come to an end. But this is precisely what provides universal doubt with its object. We step back to find that the whole system of justification and criticism, which controls our choices and supports our claims to rationality, rests on responses and habits that we never question, that we should not know how to defend without circularity, and to which we shall continue to adhere even after they are called into question. The things we do or want without reasons, and without requiring reasons – the things that define what is a reason for us and what is not – are the starting-points of our scepticism. We see ourselves from outside, and all the contingency and specificity of our aims and pursuits become clear. Yet when we take this view and recognize what we do as arbitrary, it does not disengage us from life, and there lies our absurdity: not in the fact that such an external view can be taken of us,

---

[1] 'Under the appearance of eternity'; cf. the outlook advocated by Spinoza, Part VIII, extract 3, above.

but in the fact that we ourselves can take it, without ceasing to be the persons whose ultimate concerns are so coolly regarded.

III

One may try to escape the position by seeking broader ultimate concerns, from which it is impossible to step back – the idea being that absurdity results because what we take seriously is something small and insignificant and individual. Those seeking to supply their lives with meaning usually envision a role or function in something larger than themselves. They therefore seek fulfilment in service to society, the state, the revolution, the progress of history, the advance of science, or religion and the glory of God.

But a role in some larger enterprise cannot confer significance unless that enterprise is itself significant. And its significance must come back to what we can understand, or it will not even appear to give us what we are seeking. If we learned that we were being raised to provide food for other creatures fond of human flesh, who planned to turn us into cutlets before we got too stringy – even if we learned that the human race had been developed by animal breeders precisely for this purpose – that would still not give our lives meaning, for two reasons. First, we would still be in the dark as to the significance of the lives of those other beings; second, although we might acknowledge that this culinary role would make our lives meaningful to them, it is not clear how it would make them meaningful to us.

Admittedly, the usual form of service to a higher being is different from this. One is supposed to behold and partake of the glory of God, for example, in a way in which chickens do not share in the glory of *coq au vin*. The same is true of service to a state, a movement or a revolution. People can come to feel when they are part of something bigger, that it is part of them too. They worry less about what is peculiar to themselves, but identify enough with the larger enterprise to find their role in it fulfilling.

However, any such larger purpose can be put in doubt in the same way that the aims of an individual life can be, and for the same reasons. It is as legitimate to find ultimate justification there as to find it earlier, among the details of individual life. But this does not alter the fact that justifications come to an end when we are content to have them end – when we do not find it necessary to look any further. If we can step back from the purposes of individual life and doubt their point, we can step back also from the progress of human history, or of science, or the success of a society, or the kingdom, power and glory of God, and put all these things into question in the same way. What seems to us to confer meaning, justification, significance, does so in virtue of the fact that we need no more reasons after a certain point.

What makes doubt inescapable with regard to the limited aims of individual life also makes it inescapable with regard to any larger purpose that encourages the sense that life is meaningful. Once the fundamental doubt has begun, it cannot be laid to rest. Camus maintains in *The Myth of Sisyphus*[1] that the absurd arises because the world fails to meet our demands for meaning. This suggests that the

---

[1] See preceding extract.

world might satisfy those demands if it were different. But now we can see that this is not the case. There does not appear to be any conceivable world (containing us) about which unsettlable doubts could not arise. Consequently the absurdity of our situation derives not from a collision between our expectations and the world, but from a collision within ourselves.

IV

It may be objected that the standpoint from which these doubts are supposed to be felt does not exist – that if we take the recommended backward step we will land on thin air, without any basis for judgement about the natural responses we are supposed to be surveying. If we retain our usual standards of what is important, then questions about the significance of what we are doing with our lives will be answerable in the usual way. But if we do not, then those questions can mean nothing to us, since there is no longer any content to the idea of what matters, and hence no content to the idea that nothing does.

But this objection misconceives the nature of the backward step. It is not supposed to give us an understanding of what is really important, so that we see by contrast that our lives are insignificant. We never, in the course of these reflections, abandon the ordinary standards that guide our lives. We merely observe them in operation, and recognize that if they are called into question we can justify them only by reference to themselves, uselessly. We adhere to them because of the way we are put together; what seems to us important or serious or valuable would not seem so if we were differently constituted.

In ordinary life, to be sure, we do not judge a situation absurd unless we have in mind some standards of seriousness, significance or harmony with which the absurd can be contrasted. This contrast is not implied by the philosophical judgement of absurdity, and that might be thought to make the concept unsuitable for the expression of such judgements. This is not so, however, for the philosophical judgement depends on another contrast which makes it a natural extension from more ordinary cases. It departs from them only in contrasting the pretensions of life with a larger context in which no standards can be discovered, rather than with a context from which alternative, overriding standards may be applied.

V

In this respect, as in others, philosophical perception of the absurd resembles epistemological scepticism. In both cases the final, philosophical doubt is not contrasted with any unchallenged certainties, though it is arrived at by extrapolation from examples of doubt within the system of evidence or justification, where a contrast with other certainties is implied. In both cases our limitedness joins with a capacity to transcend those limitations in thought (thus seeing them as limitations, and as inescapable).

Scepticism begins when we include ourselves in the world about which we claim knowledge. We notice that certain types of evidence convince us, that we are content to allow justifications of belief to come to an end at certain points, that we feel we know many things even without knowing or having grounds for believing the denial of others which, if true, would make what we claim to know false.

For example, I know that I am looking at a piece of paper, although I have no adequate grounds to claim I know that I am not dreaming; and if I am dreaming then I am not looking at a piece of paper. Here an ordinary conception of how appearance may diverge from reality is employed to show that we take our world largely for granted; the certainty that we are not dreaming cannot be justified except circularly, in terms of those very appearances which are being put in doubt. It is somewhat far-fetched to suggest I may be dreaming; but the possibility is only illustrative. It reveals that our claims to knowledge depend on our not feeling it necessary to exclude certain incompatible alternatives, and the dreaming possibility or the total-hallucination possibility are just representatives for limitless possibilities most of which we cannot even conceive.

Once we have taken the backward step to an abstract view of our whole system of beliefs, evidence and justification, and seen that it works only, despite its pretensions, by taking the world largely for granted, we are not in a position to contrast all these appearances with an alternative reality. We cannot shed our ordinary responses, and if we could it would leave us with no means of conceiving a reality of any kind.

It is the same in the practical domain. We do not step outside our lives to a new vantage point from which we see what is really, objectively significant. We continue to take life largely for granted while seeing that all our decisions and certainties are possible only because there is a great deal we do not bother to rule out.

Both epistemological scepticism and a sense of the absurd can be reached via initial doubts posed within systems of evidence and justification that we accept, and can be stated without violence to our ordinary concepts. We can ask not only why we should believe there is a floor under us, but also why we should believe the evidence of our senses at all – and at some point the framable questions will have outlasted the answers. Similarly, we can ask not only why we should take aspirin, but why we should take trouble over our own comfort at all. The fact that we shall take the aspirin without waiting for an answer to this last question does not show that it is an unreal question. We shall also continue to believe there is a floor under us without waiting for an answer to the other question. In both cases it is this unsupported natural confidence that generates sceptical doubts; so it cannot be used to settle them.

Philosophical scepticism does not cause us to abandon our ordinary beliefs,[1] but it lends them a peculiar flavour. After acknowledging that their truth is incompatible with possibilities that we have no grounds for believing do not obtain – apart from grounds in those very beliefs which we have called into question – we return to our familiar convictions with a certain irony and resignation. Unable to abandon the natural responses on which they depend, we take them back, like a spouse who has run off with someone else and then decided to return; but we regard them differently (not that the new attitude is necessarily inferior to the old, in either case). The same situation obtains after we have put in question the seriousness with which we take our lives and human life in general and have looked at ourselves without presuppositions. We then return to our lives, as we must, but our seriousness is laced with irony. Not

---

[1] Compare Hume, Part I, extract 7, above.

that irony enables us to escape the absurd. It is useless to mutter: 'Life is meaningless; life is meaningless...' as an accompaniment to everything we do. In continuing to live and work and strive, we take ourselves seriously in action no matter what we say. What sustains us, in belief as in action, is not reason or justification, but something more basic than these – for we go on in the same way even after we are convinced that the reasons have given out.[1] If we tried to rely entirely on reason, and pressed it hard, our lives and beliefs would collapse – a form of madness that may actually occur if the inertial force of taking the world and life for granted is somehow lost. If we lose our grip on that, reason will not give it back to us.

VI

In viewing ourselves from a perspective broader than we can occupy in the flesh, we become spectators of our own lives. We cannot do very much as pure spectators of our own lives, so we continue to lead them, and devote ourselves to what we are able at the same time to view as no more than a curiosity, like the ritual of an alien religion.

This explains why the sense of absurdity finds its natural expression in those bad arguments with which the discussion began. Reference to our small size and short lifespan and to the fact that all of mankind will eventually vanish without a trace are metaphors for the backward step which permits us to regard ourselves from without and to find the particular form of our lives curious and slightly surprising. By feigning a nebula's-eye view, we illustrate the capacity to see ourselves without presuppositions, as arbitrary, idiosyncratic, highly specific occupants of the world, one of countless possible forms of life.

Before turning to the question whether the absurdity of our lives is something to be regretted and if possible escaped, let me consider what would have to be given up in order to avoid it.

Why is the life of a mouse not absurd? The orbit of the moon is not absurd either, but that involves no strivings or aims at all. A mouse, however, has to work to stay alive. Yet he is not absurd, because he lacks the capacities for self-consciousness and self-transcendence that would enable him to see that he is only a mouse. If that did happen, his life would become absurd, since self-awareness would not make him cease to be a mouse and would not enable him to rise above his mousely strivings. Bringing his new-found self-consciousness with him, he would have to return to his meagre yet frantic life, full of doubts that he was unable to answer, but also full of purposes that he was unable to abandon.

Given that the transcendental step is natural to us humans, can we avoid absurdity by refusing to take that step and remaining entirely within our sublunar lives? Well, we cannot refuse consciously, for to do that we would have to be aware of the viewpoint we were refusing to adopt. The only way to avoid the relevant self-consciousness would be either never to attain it or to forget it – neither of which can be achieved by the will.

On the other hand, it is possible to expend effort on an attempt to destroy the other component of the absurd – abandoning one's earthly, individual, human life in order

---

[1] Compare Hume, Part I, extract 7, above.

to identify as completely as possible with that universal viewpoint from which human life seems arbitrary and trivial. (This appears to be the ideal of certain Oriental religions.) If one succeeds, then one will not have to drag the superior awareness through a strenuous mundane life, and absurdity will be diminished.

However, insofar as this self-etiolation is the result of effort, will power, asceticism and so forth, it requires that one take oneself seriously as an individual – that one be willing to take considerable trouble to avoid being creaturely and absurd. Thus one may undermine the aim of unworldliness by pursuing it too vigorously. Still, if someone simply allowed his individual, animal nature to drift and respond to impulse, without making the pursuit of its needs a central conscious aim, then he might, at considerable dissociative cost, achieve a life that was less absurd than most. It would not be a meaningful life either, of course; but it would not involve the engagement of a transcendent awareness in the assiduous pursuit of mundane goals. And that is the main condition of absurdity – the dragooning of an unconvinced transcendent consciousness into the service of an immanent, limited enterprise like a human life.

VII

The final escape is suicide; but before adopting any hasty solutions, it would be wise to consider carefully whether the absurdity of our existence truly presents us with a problem, to which some solution must be found – a way of dealing with prima facie disaster. That is certainly the attitude with which Camus approaches the issue, and it gains support from the fact that we are all eager to escape from absurd situations on a smaller scale.

Camus – not on uniformly good grounds – rejects suicide and the other solutions he regards as escapist. What he recommends is defiance or scorn. We can salvage our dignity, he appears to believe, by shaking a fist at the world which is deaf to our pleas, and continuing to live in spite of it. This will not make our lives un-absurd, but it will lend them a certain nobility.[1]

This seems to me romantic and slightly self-pitying. Our absurdity warrants neither that much distress nor that much defiance. At the risk of falling into romanticism by a different route, I would argue that absurdity is one of the most human things about us: a manifestation of our most advanced and interesting characteristics. Like scepticism in epistemology, it is possible only because we possess a certain kind of insight – the capacity to transcend ourselves in thought.

If a sense of the absurd is a way of perceiving our true situation (even though the situation is not absurd until the perception arises), then what reason can we have to resent or escape it? Like the capacity for epistemological scepticism, it results from the ability to understand our human limitations. It need not be a matter for agony unless we make it so. Nor need it evoke a defiant contempt of fate that allows us to feel brave or proud. Such dramatics, even if carried on in private, betray a failure to appreciate the cosmic unimportance of the situation. If *sub specie aeternitatis* there is no reason to believe that anything matters, then that doesn't matter either, and we can approach our absurd lives with irony instead of heroism or despair.

---

[1] See preceding extract.

11   Religious Belief as Necessary for Meaning: William Lane Craig, *The Absurdity of Life without God**

The human desire for transcendence, which Nagel ironically views as a source of absurdity (see preceding extract), is the starting-point for the essay by the American philosopher William Craig that forms our penultimate extract. Man is indeed the 'cosmic orphan' – burning to answer fundamental questions about his origins and destiny. But such questions can be answered, for Craig, only by reference to our creator: the typical modern expedient of trying to dispense with God simply makes our lives absurd.

Without God, Craig proceeds to argue, man and the universe are doomed. Not only is my own life 'just a momentary transition out of oblivion into oblivion', but modern science tells us that even the universe itself is 'plunging towards extinction', as its energy is inevitably used up. The consequence is that 'the life we have is without ultimate significance, value or purpose'. Craig's view here comes into diametric opposition to that of Nagel in our previous extract: for Nagel, whether something will matter a million years from now is wholly irrelevant to whether it matters now; for Craig, '[if] man ends in nothing, he is nothing'. And this means that 'our study, our jobs, our interests, our friendships, all these are in the final analysis utterly meaningless'.

Critics sometimes ask why carrying on for eternity would somehow make things more meaningful; but Craig makes it clear that immortality alone would not make things any better. 'It is not just immortality man needs if life is to be ultimately significant; he needs God and immortality.' Without God, Craig goes on to

argue, there is no ultimate value. Reason on its own gives us no basis for acting morally rather than immorally, and, what is more, without God there will be no objective standards of right and wrong, 'only our culturally and personally relative, subjective judgements'. Nor will there be any purpose to human life without God. Quoting some famous phrases from the book of Ecclesiastes, Craig insists that without God there will be no more purpose to the life of a human than to the life of a dog or an insect: 'all come from the dust and all return to the dust.'

Craig's views present an uncompromising challenge to the atheist to show how meaning and value could exist in a godless universe. We shall see in our final extract an attempt to show how life viewed as part of a purely natural process might still be seen as meaningful and worthwhile. As for Craig's claim that God is needed to underwrite 'objective standards of right and wrong', this is certainly controversial: contemporary philosophers have debated fiercely about what the supposed objectivity of morality consists in,[1] and also about whether the concept of divine commandments could logically function as the foundation for morality.[2] Whatever the outcome of these debates, Craig's position illustrates how for many people the adoption of a religious perspective is not just a matter of abstract theology, but connects vitally with one's conception of the value and significance of human life. For if Craig's arguments are valid, then (as he concludes in summarizing his position) 'if God is dead, then man is dead too'.

---

* From William Lane Craig, *Reasonable Faith, Christian Truth and Apologetics* [1984] (rev. edn, Wheaton, Ill.: Crossway, 1994), ch. 2, pp. 57–75; abridged.
[1] See Part VIII, extract 12, above.
[2] See Part VI, extract 11, above.

The necessity of God and immortality

Man, writes Loren Eiseley, is the Cosmic Orphan. He is the only creature in the universe who asks, 'Why?' Other animals have instincts to guide them, but man has learned to ask questions. 'Who am I?' man asks. 'Why am I here? Where am I going?' Since the Enlightenment when he threw off the shackles of religion, man has tried to answer these questions without reference to God. But the answers that came back were not exhilarating, but dark and terrible. 'You are the accidental by-product of nature, a result of matter plus time plus chance. There is no reason for your existence. All you face is death.'

Modern man thought that when he had gotten rid of God, he had freed himself from all that repressed and stifled him. Instead, he discovered that in killing God, he had also killed himself. For if there is no God, then man's life becomes absurd. If God does not exist, then both man and the universe are inevitably doomed to death. Man, like all biological organisms, must die. With no hope of immortality, man's life leads only to the grave. His life is but a spark in the infinite blackness, a spark that appears, flickers and dies forever. Compared to the infinite stretch of time, the span of man's life is but an infinitesimal moment; and yet this is all the life he will ever know. Therefore, everyone must come face to face with what theologian Paul Tillich has called 'the threat of non-being'. For though I know now that I exist, that I am alive, I also know that someday I will no longer exist, that I will no longer be, that I will die. This thought is staggering and threatening: to think that the person I call 'myself' will cease to exist, that I will be no more!

I remember vividly the first time my father told me that someday I would die. Somehow as a child the thought had just never occurred to me. When he told me, I was filled with fear and unbearable sadness. And though he tried repeatedly to reassure me that this was a long way off, that did not seem to matter. Whether sooner or later, the undeniable fact was that I would die and be no more, and the thought overwhelmed me. Eventually, like all of us, I grew to simply accept the fact. We all learn to live with the inevitable. But the child's insight remains true. As the French existentialist Jean-Paul Sartre observed, several hours or several years make no difference once you have lost eternity.

Whether it comes sooner or later, the prospect of death and the threat of non-being is a terrible horror. But I met a student once who did not feel this threat. He said he had been raised on the farm and was used to seeing the animals being born and dying. Death was for them simply natural – a part of life, so to speak. I was puzzled by how different our two perspectives on death were and found it difficult to understand why he did not feel the threat of non-being. Years later, I think I found my answer in reading Sartre. Sartre observed that death is not threatening so long as we view it as the death of the other, from a third-person standpoint, so to speak. It is only when we internalize it and look at it from the first-person perspective – '*my* death; I am going to die' – that the threat of non-being becomes real. As Sartre points out, many people never assume this first-person perspective in the midst of life; one can even look at one's own death from the third-person standpoint, as if it were the death of another or even of an animal, as did my friend. But the existential significance of my death can only be appreciated from the first-person perspective, as I realize that I am going to die and forever cease to exist. My life is just a momentary transition out of oblivion into oblivion.

And the universe, too, faces death. Scientists tell us that the universe is expanding, and everything in it is growing farther and farther apart. As it does so, it grows colder and colder, and its energy is used up. Eventually all the stars will burn out and all matter will collapse into dead stars and black holes. There will be no light at all; there will be no heat; there will be no life; only the corpses of dead stars and galaxies, ever expanding into the endless darkness and the cold recesses of space – a universe in ruins. The entire universe marches irreversibly toward its grave. So not only is the life of each individual person doomed; the entire human race is doomed. The universe is plunging toward inevitable extinction – death is written throughout its structure. There is no escape. There is no hope.

The absurdity of life without God and immortality

If there is no God, then man and the universe are doomed. Like prisoners condemned to death, we await our unavoidable execution. There is no God, and there is no immortality. And what is the consequence of this? It means that life itself is absurd. It means that the life we have is without ultimate significance, value or purpose. Let's look at each of these.

No ultimate meaning without immortality and God

If each individual person passes out of existence when he dies, then what ultimate meaning can be given to his life? Does it really matter whether he ever existed at all? It might be said that his life was important because it influenced others or affected the course of history. But this only shows a relative significance to his life, not an ultimate significance. His life may be important relative to certain other events, but what is the ultimate significance of any of those events? If all the events are meaningless, then what can be the ultimate meaning of influencing any of them? Ultimately it makes no difference.

Look at it from another perspective: Scientists say that the universe originated in an explosion called the 'Big Bang' about fifteen billion years ago. Suppose the Big Bang had never occurred. Suppose the universe had never existed. What ultimate difference would it make? The universe is doomed to die anyway. In the end it makes no difference whether the universe ever existed or not. Therefore, it is without ultimate significance.

The same is true of the human race. Mankind is a doomed race in a dying universe. Because the human race will eventually cease to exist, it makes no ultimate difference whether it ever did exist. Mankind is thus no more significant than a swarm of mosquitoes or a barnyard of pigs, for their end is all the same. The same blind cosmic process that coughed them up in the first place will eventually swallow them all again.

And the same is true of each individual person. The contributions of the scientist to the advance of human knowledge, the researches of the doctor to alleviate pain and suffering, the efforts of the diplomat to secure peace in the world, the sacrifices of good men everywhere to better the lot of the human race – all these come to nothing. In the end they don't make one bit of difference, not one bit. Each person's life is therefore without ultimate significance. And because our lives are ultimately meaningless, the activities we fill our lives with are also meaningless. The long hours spent in study at the university, our jobs, our interests, our friendships – all these are, in the final analysis, utterly meaningless. This is the horror of modern man: because he ends in nothing, he is nothing.

But it is important to see that it is not just immortality that man needs if life is to be meaningful. Mere duration of existence does not make that existence meaningful. If man and the universe could exist forever, but if there were no God, their existence would still have no ultimate significance. To illustrate: I once read a science-fiction story in which an astronaut was marooned on a barren chunk of rock lost in outer space. He had with him two vials: one containing poison and the other a potion that would make him live forever. Realizing his predicament, he gulped down the poison. But then to his horror, he discovered he had swallowed the wrong vial – he had drunk the potion for immortality. And that meant that he was cursed to exist forever – a meaningless, unending life. Now if God does not exist, our lives are just like that. They could go on and on and still be utterly without meaning. We could still ask of life 'So What?' So it is not just immortality man needs if life is to be ultimately significant; he needs God and immortality. And if God does not exist, then he has neither.

Twentieth-century man came to understand this. Read *Waiting for Godot* by Samuel Beckett. During the entire play two men carry on trivial conversation while waiting for a man to arrive, who never does. Our lives are like that, Beckett is saying: we just kill time waiting – for what, we don't know. In a tragic portrayal of man, Beckett wrote another play in which the curtain opens revealing a stage littered with junk. For thirty long seconds, the audience stares at that junk. Then the curtain closes. That's all.

One of the most devastating novels I've ever read was *Steppenwolf*, by Herman Hesse. At the novel's end, Harry Haller stands looking at himself in a mirror. During the course of his life he had experienced all the world offers. And now he stands looking at himself, and he mutters, 'Ah, the bitter taste of life!' He spits at himself in the looking-glass, and then he kicks it to pieces. His life has been futile and meaningless.

French existentialists Jean-Paul Sartre and Albert Camus understood this too. Sartre portrayed life in his play *No Exit* as hell – the final line of the play are the words of resignation, 'Well, let's get on with it.' Hence, Sartre writes elsewhere of the 'nausea' of existence. Camus, too, saw life as absurd. At the end of his brief novel *The Stranger*, Camus's hero discovers in a flash of insight that the universe has no meaning and there is no God to give it one. The French biochemist Jacques Monad seemed to echo those sentiments when he wrote in his work *Chance and Necessity*, 'Man finally knows he is alone in the immensity of the universe.'

Thus, if there is no God, then life itself becomes meaningless. Man and the universe are without ultimate significance.

No ultimate value without immortality and God

If life ends at the grave, then it makes no difference whether one has lived as a Stalin or as a saint. Since one's destiny is ultimately unrelated to one's behaviour, you may as well just live as you please. As Dostoevsky put it: 'If God is dead, then all things are permitted.' On this basis, a writer like Ayn Rand is absolutely correct to praise the virtues of selfishness. Live totally for self; no one holds you accountable! Indeed, it would be foolish to do anything else, for life is too short to jeopardize it by acting out of anything but pure self-interest. Sacrifice for another person would be stupid. Kai Nielsen, an atheist philosopher who attempts to defend the viability of ethics without God, in the end admits:

We have not been able to show that reason requires the moral point of view, or that all really rational persons, unhoodwinked by myth and ideology, need not be individual egoists or classical amoralists. The picture I have painted for you is not a pleasant one. Reflection on it depresses me . . . Pure practical reason, even with a good knowledge of the facts, will not take you to morality.[1]

But the problem becomes even worse. For, regardless of immortality, if there is no God, then there can be no objective standards of right and wrong. All we are confronted with is, in Jean-Paul Sartre's words, the bare, valueless fact of existence. Moral values are either just expressions of personal taste or the by-products of socio-biological evolution and conditioning. In the words of one humanist philosopher, 'The moral principles that govern our behaviour are rooted in habit and custom, feeling and fashion.'[2] In a world without God, who is to say which values are right and which are wrong? Who is to judge that the values of Adolf Hitler are inferior to those of a saint? The concept of morality loses all meaning in a universe without God. As one contemporary atheistic ethicist points out, 'to say that something is wrong because . . . it is forbidden by God, is . . . perfectly understandable to anyone who believes in a law-giving God. But to say that something is wrong, even though no God exists to forbid it, is not understandable . . . The concept of moral obligation [is] unintelligible apart from the idea of God. The words remain but their meaning is gone.'[3] In a world without God, there can be no objective right and wrong, only our culturally and personally relative, subjective judgements. This means that it is impossible to condemn war, oppression or crime as evil. Nor can one praise brotherhood, equality and love as good. For in a universe without God, good and evil do not exist – there is only the bare valueless fact of existence, and there is no one to say you are right and I am wrong.

No ultimate purpose without immortality and God

If death stands with open arms at the end of life's trail, then what is the goal of life? To what end has life been lived? Is it all for nothing? Is there no reason for life? And what of the universe? Is it utterly pointless? If its destiny is a cold grave in the recesses of outer space, the answer must be yes – it is pointless. There is no goal, no purpose, for the universe. The litter of a dead universe will just go on expanding and expanding – forever.

---

[1] Kai Nielsen, 'Why Should I Be Moral?', *American Philosophical Quarterly*, 21 (1984), 90.
[2] Paul Kurtz, *Forbidden Fruit* (Buffalo, NY: Prometheus, 1988), p. 73.
[3] Richard Taylor, *Ethics, Faith and Reason* (Englewood Cliffs, NJ: Prentice-Hall, 1985), pp. 90, 84.

And what of man? Is there no purpose at all for the human race? Or will it simply peter out some day lost in the oblivion of an indifferent universe? The English writer H. G. Wells foresaw such a prospect. In his novel *The Time Machine* Wells's time traveller journeys far into the future to discover the destiny of man. All he finds is a dead earth, save for a few lichens and moss, orbiting a gigantic red sun. The only sounds are the rush of the wind and the gentle ripple of the sea. 'Beyond these lifeless sounds', writes Wells, 'the world was silent. Silent? It would be hard to convey the stillness of it. All the sounds of man, the bleating of sheep, the cries of birds, the hum of insects, the stir that makes the background of our lives – all that was over.'[1] And so Wells's time traveller returned. But to what? – to merely an earlier point on the purposeless rush toward oblivion. When as a non-Christian I first read Wells's book, I thought, 'No, no! It can't end that way!' But if there is no God, it will end that way, like it or not. This is reality in a universe without God: there is no hope; there is no purpose. It reminds me of T. S. Eliot's haunting lines:

> This is the way the world ends
> This is the way the world ends
> This is the way the world ends
> Not with a bang but a whimper.[2]

What is true of mankind as a whole is true of each of us individually: we are here to no purpose. If there is no God, then our life is not qualitatively different from that of a dog. I know that's harsh, but it's true. As the ancient writer of Ecclesiastes put it: 'The fate of the sons of men and the fate of beasts is the same. As one dies so dies the other; indeed, they all have the same breath and there is no advantage for man over beast, for all is vanity. All go to the same place. All come from the dust and all return to the dust' (Ecclesiastes 3: 19–20). In this book, which reads more like a piece of modern existentialist literature than a book of the Bible, the writer shows the futility of pleasure, wealth, education, political fame and honour in a life doomed to end in death. His verdict? 'Vanity of vanities! All is vanity'(1: 2). If life ends at the grave, then we have no ultimate purpose for living.

But more than that: even if it did not end in death, without God life would still be without purpose. For man and the universe would then be simple accidents of chance, thrust into existence for no reason. Without God the universe is the result of a cosmic accident, a chance explosion. There is no reason for which it exists. As for man, he is a freak of nature – a blind product of matter plus time plus chance. Man is just a lump of slime that evolved into rationality. There is no more purpose in life for the human race than for a species of insect; for both are the result of the blind interaction of chance and necessity. As one philosopher has put it: 'Human life is mounted upon a subhuman pedestal and must shift for itself alone in the heart of a silent and mindless universe.'[3]

What is true of the universe and of the human race is also true of us as individuals. Insofar as we are individual human beings, we are the results of certain combinations of heredity and environment. We are victims of a kind of genetic and environmental

---

[1] H. G. Wells, *The Time Machine* [1895], ch. 11.
[2] From 'The Hollow Men' [1925].
[3] *W. E. Hocking, *Types of Philosophy* (New York: Scribner's, 1959), p. 27.

roulette. Psychologists following Sigmund Freud tell us our actions are the result of various repressed sexual tendencies. Sociologists following B. F. Skinner argue that all our choices are determined by conditioning, so that freedom is an illusion. Biologists like Francis Crick regard man as an electro-chemical machine that can be controlled by altering its genetic code. If God does not exist, then you are just a miscarriage of nature, thrust into a purposeless universe to live a purposeless life.

So if God does not exist, that means that man and the universe exist to no purpose – since the end of everything is death – and that they came to be for no purpose, since they are only blind products of chance. In short, life is utterly without reason.

Do you understand the gravity of the alternatives before us? For if God exists, then there is hope for man. But if God does not exist, then all we are left with is despair. Do you understand why the question of God's existence is so vital to man? As one writer has put it, 'If God is dead, then man is dead too.'

12   Seeing our Lives as Part of the Process: Robert Nozick, *Philosophy's Life**

The more or less systematic ideas people develop in grappling with the problems of life and its meaning are sometimes described by saying they have a 'philosophy of life'. The American philosopher Robert Nozick defines this, in our last extract, as 'having a thoughtful view of what is important, a view of... major ends and goals and of the means appropriate to reaching these'. Reflection may lead us in some cases to revise or reformulate our goals, but the final outcome of this critical process need not involve a complete general theory of living – indeed Nozick suggests that life may be too rich and multifarious to allow for any comprehensive theoretical formulation. Moreover, the aspects we may scrutinize in order to arrive at decisions and choices about how to live may (Nozick goes on to suggest) comprise only a relatively small 'discretionary' percentage of what is important. Rather than spending all our energies on the discretionary choices, our philosophy of life should always allow us time to focus on, and to appreciate, the fundamental value of being alive at all, and being human, and being at 'some reasonable threshold of functioning and competence'.

But what of 'ultimate' goals and purposes (of the kind envisaged, for instance, in the religious worldview advocated by Craig in the preceding extract)? Nozick makes the point that any supposed 'final' state (like heaven) could not plausibly be understood as a matter of mere passive contemplation, but ought to involve a desire to 'explore it, respond to it, relate within it, create... and then perhaps transform ourselves still further'. This conception of future happiness Nozick describes in terms of a continuous upward 'spiral' – in other words it cannot be static, but is an essentially active and dynamic conception. Nozick now goes on to make the crucial point that this is precisely the conception that fits the best kind of life here on earth: there is a 'holiness of the present realm', which involves 'the fullest engagement within the spiral of activities and the pursuit of reality'. So whatever may or may not be the case about any future existence, 'reality here is reality enough'.

The kind of meaning and value Nozick envisages thus arises from 'acts of responding, exploring and reacting as a celebration of reality' – in other words, the 'fullest way of exploring what it is to be alive'. Such joyful exploration has, for Nozick, an essentially moral dimension: appreciating the interplay of natural life all around us, we 'will not wantonly exploit animal or plant

* From Robert Nozick, *The Examined Life* (New York: Simon & Schuster, 1989), ch. 26, pp. 297–302.

life'; for being ourselves part of nature, we know that 'what constitutes us is had on loan'. And in the concluding paragraphs a lesson is drawn about how viewing things this way enables us to find meaning in our lives: 'we can find our significance' in being part of 'the vast (apparently) never-ending process of existence through time'.

It is perhaps fitting that this conclusion should have affinities with the Stoic and Epicurean ideals of 'living in accordance with nature', with which we began. And just as those ancient systems aimed above all at tranquillity of mind, so Nozick tells us of the 'calmness' of spirit that arises when we see ourselves as part of the immense whole. The vision has undeniable attractions, but, as always with good philosophy, there are many questions that can be raised about it. How can the universe which Nozick finds so calming be the same one that seemed to Schopenhauer a maelstrom of ceaseless and futile struggling? How can Nozick talk so optimistically of our becoming 'vehicles for truth, beauty [and] goodness', when Nietzsche spoke of the need to assert the will and create new values?

How can Nozick tell us that 'reality here' is enough, when Pascal affirmed the wretchedness of the human condition unless redeemed by hope of an eternal salvation? That such conflicting views can all be articulated with such eloquent reasoning perhaps tells us, as we come to the end of our survey of Western philosophy, that the conclusions of philosophers, however much they may wish to think so, can never be based on reason alone. Their arguments may challenge us, and stimulate us to think more carefully about the human condition and the world around us, but we will always remain creatures of passion as well as intellect, our vision of reality shaped by deep emotional responses as well as by the intricacies of argument and counter-argument. The restlessness of spirit that arises from our strange and complex nature – 'halfway between the beasts and the angels', as Augustine put it[1] – will ensure that the puzzles of our life and its meaning will never, in the present order of reality, be finally solved. Humanity's struggle to transcend itself will continue; and as long as it does so, we shall continue to philosophize.

 It is often thought that there are only two rational ways to arrive at new ends and goals that we do not already accept: first, by discovering they are effective means to existing ends of ours – deliberation is always about means, Aristotle said, never about ends – and second, by refining and recontouring some existing ends to fit better with still other existing ends that similarly get recontoured to fit – what some philosophers have called 'cospecification'. However, there is another rational way to arrive at new ends, this time at a deeper level. We can examine the diverse ends and goals we already have to discover what further ends and values might underlie and justify them or provide them with a unified grounding. In this way we can be led to quite new and unsuspected ends, surprising in their implications. We also can be led to modify or even reject some of the ends and goals we began with, including some we had been attempting to understand and ground. Compare the way adopting an explanatory scientific theory can lead one to modify or even reject some of the data or lower-level theories this theory initially was introduced to explain. (For example, it is not exactly Kepler's laws of planetary motion – but modifications instead – that Newton's laws yield and explain, although that was one place his task began.[2]) Investigating our goals and ends philosophically, then, provides a powerful tool for advancing to new ones rationally, and at a new or deeper level.

[1] *The City of God* [*De civitate Dei*, AD 413–26], ix, 13. Compare Pascal, opening of extract 5, above.
[2] See Part VII, extract 10, above.

Somebody 'has a philosophy' – we ordinarily say – when she has a thoughtful view of what is important, a view of her major ends and goals and of the means appropriate to reaching these. A coherent view of aims and goals can help to guide someone's life without being invoked explicitly. Most often, it will not be. Rather, a person will devote some of her general alertness to monitoring how her life is proceeding. Only when she is deviating significantly from what her philosophy calls for will it be brought to conscious attention. A philosophy of life need not make life over-intellectualized.

A person may feel that she and her life are richer than any theory. She might formulate a philosophy that leaves room for this feeling too, one that holds it is important sometimes to be spontaneous and not apply any maxim, including that very one. Later, a time she lives spontaneously would fall under the maxim without being an applying of it. She could then well feel she encompasses multitudes beyond any theory. This might not take the point seriously enough, however. Perhaps life itself defies formulating any general theory to cover it all. Having a philosophy of life is not the same, of course, as having a general and complete theory of what is important in life. Would such an encompassing theory be possible? Even an elaborate theory will mention at most – let us be hyperbolic here – a thousand factors, but perhaps complete accuracy will require many times that. Don't the size, scope and multifariousness of the major Russian novels, and of the body of Shakespeare's plays, show how inadequate any particular theory will have to be? Here I have been thinking of the sheer number of life's aspects and factors as thwarting a completely general theory; there also is the possibility – I do not know of reasons to accept this – that there are particular factors too complex (or too simple?) to be adequately treated by any theory...

A philosophy of life might seem insignificant before the phenomenon of life in another way, because the fact of life itself might seem more important than any particular way a life can be. If we imagine scores or points given for the components of a person's existence, where the maximum possible score is 100, being alive might bring fifty points, being human might bring thirty points, being at some reasonable threshold of competence and functioning might bring ten more points, adding up to a total of ninety points thus far. The question of how to live, according to what particular philosophy, would then concern or determine only how many of the remaining ten possible points one would achieve or gain. These remaining ten points would be the ones we could control by our actions, but whether we managed to get six or seven points would be less important than the fact that we already had ninety points, willy-nilly. (Behind these ninety, there might be still other points that are guaranteed, ones for existing or even for being a possible entity.) Any particular choices we made would pale in significance alongside the fact that we are alive and make choices. Thus, it might be important in life not to focus solely upon the discretionary ten points but always to keep in consciousness the major thresholds we and all other persons already have passed without any action on our part at all. (In a dark and cold corner of the universe, wouldn't we feel companionship with anything that was alive – provided that it didn't threaten us?) A part, then, of philosophy's advice about the discretionary part of life, the possible 10 per cent left, would be to spend some of it focusing upon and appreciating the 90 per cent that is already present. Such advice evidences a grasp of life's magnitude and helps with the remaining 10 per cent too.

We may feel a need for some further purpose, an ultimate one beyond those we have sketched thus far. It is tempting to imagine this as some further external purpose, another realm our lives are designed to reach afterward, another task we are to perform. Some traditional religious doctrines have hoped for an afterlife, a time and realm in which believers would sit at God's right hand and gaze at his face. Others have complained, with some glee and justification, that these visions, as described, are boring. If there were another realm, an afterlife, what we would want to do in it would be to explore it, respond to it, relate within it, create, utilizing whatever we had gained thereby, and then perhaps transform ourselves still further, beginning again. Any further realm would be another arena for the spiral of activities. To be sure, it might be a more conducive arena for that spiral, more richly rewarding – the perfection of that realm might consist just in its being amenable to the most intense exploring, responding, etc., alone or together – but then it is relevant to point out how far we are from having exhausted this present arena.

My reflections here have not been directed toward some further realm that comes next. But if earthly life is followed by a next realm, what we are to do there is the very same type of thing as here – encounter reality and become more real ourselves through a spiral of activities, and together enhance our-relating-to-reality – in the ways that are possible there. (If union with God were the goal, that continued existence would be a state for us to explore, respond to, etc., and within it these activities would be exceedingly real.) That further realm might allow a different level of magnitude of these activities, and display novel dimensions of reality, but it would be judged by the very same criterion: the nature of the spiral of activities there and how real we can be. (If further appropriate activities were possible there, these too would be added to the spiral.) Perhaps there is a further realm, but its purpose will not be found in a still further one, or if it is, then sooner or later there must be a realm whose purpose is not found in another, further one. And in that realm, wherever it is, it is this philosophy that holds.

That would not necessarily mean that this philosophy is to be followed now as well. It is theoretically possible that this present realm is simply a means to acquiring some trait, rather like a trip to the dentist, a realm where now to apply the appropriate final philosophy would curtail the extent of its later application. That philosophy would be right for us sometime – just not now. However, the holiness of everyday life ... is a holiness of the present realm. Whether or not there is any further realm in the future, the realm that is present and current is an appropriate arena for living one's final philosophy, for the fullest engagement within the spiral of activities and the pursuit of reality. Some who prize reality have been led by this world's defects to seek reality elsewhere – the Gnostics and some Platonists are examples – but reality here is reality enough. That is what the very greatest works of art, by their own reality, show us, even when this is not what some say. The philosophy developed here is not for the final realm alone, though this present realm may be exactly that. It is to be followed and lived in any realm that is holy.

[This means] offering responses as something due, or rather offering the acts of responding, exploring and creating as a celebration of reality, as a love of it. Love of this world is coordinate with love of life. Life is our being in this world. And love of life is our fullest response to being alive, our fullest way of exploring what it is to be alive.

This love of life is continuous with an appreciation of life's energy in its various forms, with the variety and balance and interplay of life in nature. Appreciating this, we will not wantonly exploit animal or plant life; we will take some care to minimize the damage we do. Would an appreciation of the complicated developmental history of the living things we encounter prevent us from making any use of them at all? We cannot survive without doing so – we are part of nature too – but it would be too glib simply to say we also appreciate our lives and their imperatives, and this warrants our using and killing other life forms as a means. Yet as part of nature and its cycles, we can repay our debt for what we take, nourishing and strengthening life, fertilizing the soil with the products of our eating, eventually having the material of our own body, after death, re-circulated. What constitutes us is had on loan.

It calms the spirit to see ourselves as part of a vast and continuing natural process. (Recall, for example, sitting beside the ocean, seeing and listening to wave after wave never ending, knowing the ocean's immensity.) To see yourself as a small part of a vast process makes your own death seem not so very significant, unworrisome even. When we identify ourselves with the totality of the vast (apparently) never-ending processes of existence through time, we can find our significance in (being part of) that, and our own particular passing comes to seem to us of passing importance.

But can such significance accrue to us through being part of a vast process, unless we are a necessary or irreplaceable part? How can the significance of that process help us if we are superfluous to it? However, if you take away from the vastness of existence everything that is unnecessary or replaceable, the truncated existence that remains is not nearly as wonderful. The totality of existence and its processes over time is wonderful in part because of its great superfluity, and so our existence, the existence of kinds of things like us, is a characteristic and valuable part. This existence of ours, moreover, is permeated by the very same scientific laws and ultimate physical material that constitute all the rest of nature; a representative piece of nature, we encapsulate its sweep.

I see people descended from a long sequence of human and animal forebears in an unnumbered train of chance events, accidental encounters, brutal takings, lucky escapes, sustained efforts, migrations, survivings of wars and disease. An intricate and improbable concatenation of events was needed to yield each of us, an immense history that gives each person the sacredness of a redwood, each child the whimsy of a secret. It is a privilege to be a part of the ongoing realm of existing things and processes. When we see and conceive of ourselves as a part of those ongoing processes, we identify with the totality and, in the calmness this brings, feel solidarity with all our comrades in existing. We want nothing other than to live in a spiral of activities and enhance others' doing so, deepening our own reality as we come into contact and relation with the rest, exploring the dimensions of reality, embodying them in ourselves, creating, responding to the full range of the reality we can discern with the fullest reality we possess, becoming a vehicle for truth, beauty, goodness and holiness, adding our own characteristic bit to reality's eternal processes. And that wanting of nothing else, along with its attendant emotion, is – by the way – what constitutes happiness and joy.

Specimen Questions

1 Do you find the Epicurean argument that we have nothing to fear in death convincing? Explain why or why not.

2 Critically discuss the Stoic recipe for tranquillity of mind.

3 'My soul is to you like a land without water: it cannot enlighten itself, and it cannot satisfy itself' (Augustine). Expound and evaluate the Augustinian ideal of finding meaning by serving God and obeying his commandment to help others in need.

4 'The finest lives, in my view, are those which conform to the ordinary human model, in an orderly way, without marvels and extravagances.' Does Montaigne's view represent a sound recipe for a meaningful and worthwhile life, or is it simply a piece of complacency?

5 'Our condition affords no true or solid satisfaction, and all our pleasures are mere vanity, while our ills are infinite.' Critically examine Pascal's characterization of the human plight and his proposed solution for it.

6 'Human life must be some kind of mistake ... man is a compound of needs and necessities hard to satisfy; and ... even when they are satisfied, all he obtains is a state of painlessness, where nothing remains to him but abandonment to boredom.' Does Schopenhauer have good grounds for his pessimistic verdict on human life?

7 'Lo, I teach you the Superman!' Explore Nietzsche's vision of what humanity must become following the 'death of God'. Is his vision an attractive one, or a dangerous jettisoning of traditional frameworks of value and meaning?

8 How plausible do you find Russell's claim that in a universe without God we can 'build a temple for the worship of our ideals'?

9 'We must imagine Sisyphus happy.' Explain what Camus means by the 'victory of the absurd', and set out how far you find it convincing.

10 What is Nagel's diagnosis for the feeling that life is absurd, and do you agree that the problem can be overcome by having a sense of irony?

11 Does Craig succeed in showing that human life without God must lack meaning, value and purpose?

12 Critically evaluate Nozick's claim that we can find meaning by 'identifying ourselves with the totality of the vast ... processes of existence through time'.

Suggestions for Further Reading

Valuable collections of papers on the topic of life's meaning are: D. Benatar (ed.), *Life, Death and Meaning* (Totowa, NJ: Rowman & Littlefield, 2004), which has a good editorial introduction; E. D. Klemke (ed.), *The Meaning of Life* (Oxford: Oxford University Press, 2nd edn, 2002); and J. Young (ed.), *The Death of God and the Meaning of Life* (London: Routledge, 2003).

For an accessible monograph on the topic see J. Cottingham, *On the Meaning of Life* (London: Routledge, 2003).

Influential discussions include K. Baier, 'The Meaning of Life' [1957], repr. in Klemke (ed.), *The Meaning of Life*; R. Taylor, 'The Meaning of Life' (from his *Good and Evil* [1967]), repr. in Klemke (ed.), *The Meaning of Life*; D. Wiggins, 'Truth, Invention and the Meaning of Life', in Wiggins, *Needs, Values, Truth* (3rd edn, Oxford: Blackwell, 1998); and B. Williams, 'The Makropoulos Case: Reflections on the Tedium of Immortality', in Williams, *Problems of the Self* (Cambridge: Cambridge University Press, 1981).

See also P. Edwards, 'Meaning and the Value of Life', in Edwards (ed.), *The Encyclopaedia of Philosophy* (New York: Macmillan, 1967).

The following works are also well worth consulting: A. Gewirth, *Self-fulfilment* (Princeton: Princeton University Press, 1998); J. Hick, 'The Religious Meaning of Life', in J. Runzo and N. Martin (eds), *The Meaning of Life in the World's Religions* (Oxford: Oneworld, 2000); J. Kekes, *The Art of Life* (Ithaca, NY: Cornell University Press, 2002); M. Nussbaum, *Love's Knowledge* (Oxford: Oxford University Press, 1990); E. J. Wielenberg, *Value and Virtue in a Godless Universe* (Cambridge: Cambridge University Press, 2005).

Notes on the Philosophers

An asterisk prefixed to a name indicates that a separate entry is devoted to the philosopher in question. The numbers in square brackets at the end of each entry refer, by Part and extract number, to the items in the present volume which are by the author being discussed (thus, 'II 7' refers to Part II, extract 7). The notes below provide basic information, but the reader should consult the commentary which precedes every extract for discussion of the ideas and concepts involved in each case.

Adams, Robert Merrihew (1937–). American philosopher whose interests include metaphysics, history of philosophy, religion and morality. He has taught at the University of California at Los Angeles and at Yale University, and is a fellow of Mansfield College, Oxford. His best-known works are *The Virtue of Faith* (1987), *Leibniz: Determinist, Theist, Idealist* (1994) and *Finite and Infinite Goods* (1999). [VI 11]

Anselm of Canterbury (1033–1109). Born at Aosta, he left home at the age of 23 and in 1060 entered the Benedictine monastery of Bec, near Rouen, where he eventually rose to be Prior and then Abbot. In 1093 he became Archbishop of Canterbury. He was the author of numerous philosophical-cum-theological works, including *De Veritate* ('On Truth'), *De Libertate Arbitrii* ('On Freedom of the Will') and *De Grammatico* ('On the Literate', dealing with logic and language). His best-known works are the *Monologion* ('Soliloquy', 1076) and the *Proslogion* ('Discourse', 1077–8); in the former he argues that God is the good which is the source of all good things and the self-existent being through whom all things exist; the latter contains his famous 'ontological' argument for the existence of God, defined as 'that than which no greater can be thought'. The term 'ontological argument' is not Anselm's, but became current much later, after *Kant had distinguished this special type of proof of God where 'abstraction is made from all experience' and the existence of a supreme being is 'inferred...from concepts alone'. [VI 1]

Aquinas, Thomas (1225–74). Born at Rocasecca near Aquino in Italy, St Thomas Aquinas was educated by Benedictine monks but later joined the Dominican order; he studied at universities in Naples, Paris and Cologne. He was the most prolific and widely respected philosopher and theologian of the medieval period, and of his voluminous works the best known are his two massive compendia of philosophy and theology, the *Summa contra Gentiles* and the *Summa Theologiae*. Aquinas's thought was strongly influenced by Aristotle, and his commentaries on the latter's works were influential in securing widespread acceptance for Aristotelian ideas in the universities of Western Europe. Aquinas's principal aim was to reconcile the philosophical teachings of Aristotle with Christian doctrine, and the resulting system which he inaugurated is known as scholasticism. In the philosophy of religion Aquinas is perhaps best known for his 'five ways' or proofs of the existence of God. Though a firm advocate of the use of philosophical reason in theology, he made a clear separation between the province of reason and that of faith, arguing that the conclusions of each were compatible, but independent. [IV 3; VI 2; IX 2; X 2]

Aristotle (384–322 BC) was born in Stagira, in the Chalcidic peninsula in northern Greece, and entered *Plato's Academy in Athens at the age of 18, where he remained, first as a student and then as a teacher, until Plato's death, twenty years later. After a spell in Macedonia to supervise the education of the king's son, Alexander, he returned to Athens to found his own philosophical and scientific school, the Lyceum. The range and versatility of Aristotle's thought is almost unbelievable, and quite apart from his prolific writings in the natural sciences he can fairly be said to have laid the foundations for most of the philosophical disciplines in the Western tradition. Perhaps his most famous achievement was in formal logic, where his theory of the syllogism remained dominant right up until the advent of the 'new' symbolic logic at the turn of the twentieth century. (The theory of the syllogism codified certain standard patterns of valid argument, for example 'All *A*s are *B*; all *B*s are *C*; therefore all *A*s are *C*.') But Aristotle also produced work of enormous significance in metaphysics, ethics, the philosophy of mind and the philosophy of science. His influence on European thought during the Middle Ages and Renaissance was so great that he was known simply as 'the philosopher'; even today the power of his ideas (particularly in ethics and the philosophy of mind) is far from exhausted. [I 3; II 2; IV 2; VII 1; VIII 2; IX 1; XI 2]

Augustine of Hippo (354–430) was born in North Africa, and taught rhetoric at Carthage; after visiting Rome and teaching in Milan (where he was baptized in 386), he eventually returned to Africa, where he became Bishop of Hippo (now Annaba, Algeria). St Augustine is regarded as the greatest of the 'Church fathers' who shaped the early development of Christianity. Of his voluminous writings, the best known are the *Confessions* (397–400) and *The City of God* (413–26). His interpretations of Christian teaching were strongly influenced by Platonic and neo-Platonic ideas. Among theologians he is perhaps best known for his rejection of the Pelagian doctrine of the perfectibility of man: Augustine insisted on the fallen nature of man and the need for salvation by divine grace. Of particular interest to philosophers are his analysis of the nature of time, his discussions of scepticism (and partial anticipation of *Descartes's Cogito), and his account of the relationship between divine foreknowledge and human freedom. [III 2; V 7; XII 3]

Austin, J[ohn] L[angshaw] (1911–60). Influential Oxford philosopher whose name is associated with the 'ordinary language' movement in philosophy. He was the author of *Sense and Sensibilia*, which criticized the notion of 'sense-data' as employed by many philosophers, and *How to Do Things with Words*, based on the William James Lectures he gave at Harvard. His *Philosophical Papers* (1961) are published by Oxford University Press. [III 10]

Bacon, Francis (1561–1626). Born in London, Bacon was a successful lawyer and politician who rose to become Lord Chancellor under James I and later Viscount St Albans; he was, however, disgraced in 1621 following charges of bribery and corruption. His philosophical writings, notably the *Advancement of Learning* (1605) and the *Novum Organum* (1620), exerted a powerful influence in the seventeenth-century transition from traditional to 'modern' ways of thinking. He was a fervent believer in the possibility of progress in the sciences, and is particularly famous for his formulation of precise inductive methods for the investigation of the physical world. [VII 2]

Bentham, Jeremy (1748–1832). The son of a London lawyer, Bentham studied law and later wrote extensively on the philosophical foundations of law. A leading champion of utilitarianism, the principle of the greatest happiness of the greatest number, Bentham developed a 'hedonic calculus' for determining the amounts of pleasure involved in any given course of action. He is best known for his *Introduction to the Principles of Morals and Legislation* (1798), the first chapter of which opens with the famous sentence, 'Nature has placed mankind under the governance of two sovereign masters, pain and pleasure'. His vision was of an ideal legal and social system all elements of which were to be rationally justified by reference to their role in promoting the greatest possible happiness of all concerned. [IX 7]

Berkeley, George (1685–1753). Born in Kilkenny, Ireland, and educated at Trinity College, Dublin, Berkeley became Dean of Derry in 1724, and subsequently (after an ill-fated attempt to found a college in Bermuda) Bishop of Cloyne. In 1709 he published his *Essay towards a New Theory of Vision*, which attacks the notion that we directly see external objects. His most famous works, the *Principles of Human Knowledge* (1710) and the *Three Dialogues between Hylas and Philonous* (1713), develop a form of radical idealism according to which nothing exists outside the mind. Berkeley regarded the corpuscularian science of his day as leading to scepticism (since there was no guaranteed route from our ideas or impressions to the supposed 'external world'), and also as tending to support a mechanistic atheism. His own immaterialist views were often attacked as defying common sense, but Berkeley insisted that he did not deny the existence of ordinary phenomena, only the existence of the 'material substance' which was supposed to be the basis of such phenomena. For Berkeley, the existence of objects consists in their being perceived; and the ultimate cause of our perceptions is not material objects, but the supreme immaterial Spirit, God. In his *De Motu* ('On Motion'), published in Latin in 1721, Berkeley articulates a philosophy of science consistent with his thoroughgoing immaterialism. [II 6; III 6; VII 4]

Brentano, Franz (1838–1917). German philosopher who taught at the University of Würzburg; he was ordained a priest in 1864. Though he wrote on many philosophical topics, his best-known work is *Psychologie vom Empirischen Standpunkt* (*Psychology* *from an Empirical Standpoint*, 1874), where he defines mental phenomena in terms of 'reference to a content, direction towards an object'. This notion of 'intentionality' as the hallmark of the mental has exerted a considerable influence on subsequent philosophy of mind. [IV 9]

Butler, Joseph (1692–1752). English theologian and moral philosopher, who became Bishop of Bristol and (in the last year of his life) of Durham. His *Fifteen Sermons* were published in 1726 and *The Analogy of Religion* in 1736. In the former work, Butler argues that conscience is a divinely bestowed voice of authority on matters of morality, but that the demands of conscience are consistent with our natural impulses of self-love and benevolence. In *The Analogy of Religion*, he defends the claims of revealed religion, and in the famous appendix he criticizes Locke's view of personal identity. [V 2]

Camus, Albert (1913–60). French novelist and philosopher. He was born in Algeria, and during the Second World War he was active in Paris in the resistance to the German occupation. His novel *L'Etranger* (*The Stranger* or *The Outsider*) appeared in 1942, and his philosophical essay *The Rebel* (*L'Homme révolté*) in 1951. His novel *The Fall* (*La Chute*) was published in 1956, and the following year he won the Nobel prize for literature. He was for some time closely associated with *Sartre, but himself repudiated the label 'existentialist'. [XII 9]

Carnap, Rudolf (1891–1970). One of the most influential of the group of philosophers known as 'logical positivists', Carnap taught in Vienna and later in the United States. His main works are *Der Logische Aufbau der Welt* (1928, known in English as 'The Logical Structure of the World', trans. 1967), *Logische Syntax der Sprache* ('Logical Syntax of Language', 1937), *Introduction to Semantics* (1942) and *Logical Foundations of Probability* (1950). Carnap saw the main function of philosophy as that of providing a precise logical analysis of the concepts of science. [II 10]

Craig, William Lane (1949–). American philosopher who has written widely on the philosophy of religion and in defence of the Christian worldview. His books include *Apologetics: An Introduction* (Chicago: Moody Press, 1984), *The Kalam Cosmological Argument* (New York: Barnes & Noble, 1979) and *God, Time and Eternity: The Coherence of Theism II* (Dordrecht: Kluwer, 2001). [XII 11]

Descartes, René (1596–1650). Often called the 'father of modern philosophy', Descartes was one of the key figures in the overthrow of the traditional 'scholastic' philosophy based on *Aristotle. In its place, he aimed to lay the foundations for a new approach to the sciences, based on 'clear and distinct' mathematical ideas. Born near Tours and educated by the Jesuits at the College of La Flèche in Anjou, Descartes lived for most of his adult life in Holland. His first major work, the *Rules for the Direction of our Native Intelligence* (written in the late 1620s) outlines the plan for a universal science based on indubitable principles of the kind hitherto found only in mathematics. His early treatise on physics and cosmology, *Le Monde*, was cautiously withdrawn in 1633 following the condemnation of Galileo for defending the heliocentric hypothesis (which Descartes too advocated). His philosophical masterpieces were the *Discourse on the Method*, written in French in 1637 as an introduction to a selection of scientific essays, and the *Meditations* (written in Latin in 1641), an examination of the foundations of knowledge, the existence of God and the nature of the human mind. The *Principles of Philosophy*, a comprehensive textbook of Cartesian metaphysics and science, appeared in 1644, and the *Passions of the Soul*, dealing with physiology, psychology and ethics, in 1649. Descartes died of pneumonia contracted during a visit to Stockholm at the invitation of Queen Christina of Sweden. [I 4; II 3; III 4; IV 4; VI 3; VII 3]

Dworkin, Ronald (1931–). Influential legal and political philosopher, who has taught at Yale, Oxford and London. His *Taking Rights Seriously* (1977) argues that the law contains principles which cannot be derived from a system of rules; it also puts forward the view of rights as political 'trumps'. His collections of essays *Life's Dominion* (1993) and *Freedom's Law* (1996) develop a version of liberalism which gives a central place to the idea of equality. [X 12]

Engels, Friedrich (1820–95). Friend and collaborator of Karl *Marx, Engels wrote extensively on politics, history and philosophy; he was the son of a wealthy cotton manufacturer, and spent many years in Manchester working with a branch of the family firm. His chief philosophical works are the *Anti-Düring* (1877–8) and *Ludwig Feuerbach and the End of Classical German Philosophy* (1886). Much of his writing was an elaboration and defence of Marx's views, though he made significant contributions in his own right to the doctrine now known as 'dialectical materialism'. He collaborated with Marx on *The Holy Family* (1844), *The German Ideology* (1845–6) and *The Communist Manifesto* (1848). [X 8]

Frankfurt, Harry G. (1929–). American philosopher who taught at Princeton, Yale and Rockefeller Universities. He published significant work on Descartes, including *Demons, Dreams and Madmen* (1970), and is especially known for his philosophical views in the philosophy of action, and his arguments concerning freedom, responsibility and autonomy. His philosophical essays, *The Importance of What We Care About* appeared in 1988, and a further collection, *Necessity, Volition and Love*, in 1999. [V 12]

Frege, Gottlob (1848–1925). German mathematician, logician and philosopher, considered, together with Bertrand *Russell, to be one of the founders of modern analytic philosophy. Frege's *Concept Script* [*Begriffsschrift*, 1879] and his *Foundations of Arithmetic* [*Die Grundlagen der Arithmetik*, 1893] developed a formal symbolic system which forms the basis for modern 'quantificational' logic. In his philosophy of logic, Frege was strongly opposed to 'psychologism' – the view that logic is reducible to an empirical study of how our thinking actually operates. In addition to his work on logic and the foundations of mathematics, Frege made important contributions in the philosophy of language; his influential paper 'On Sense and Reference' (*Über Sinn und Bedeutung*) was published in 1892. [III 8]

Freud, Sigmund (1856–1939). Physician and founder of psychoanalysis, Freud was born in Freiburg, Moravia, but spent almost all of his life in Vienna; he became a medical student at the University of Vienna in 1873, qualified as a doctor in 1881 and was appointed to a professorship in 1902. He published continuously throughout his long subsequent career, and the standard edition of his *Psychological Works* runs to twenty-four volumes. His central ideas are presented in *The Interpretation of Dreams* (*Die Traumdeutung*, 1900), *The Psychopathology of Everyday Life* (1904), *Totem and Taboo* (1913) and *Introductory Lectures on Psychoanalysis* (1916–17). Freud developed an account of human motivation according to which significant amounts of human behaviour derive from desires and beliefs of which the subject is only very imperfectly, if at all, aware. He argued, however, that the unconscious contents of the mind could be at least partly recovered by analysis of the patient's early childhood, and in particular of the sexual aspects of early experience which were characteristically repressed in later life. [V 4]

Gauthier, David (1932–). North-American moral and political philosopher who has taught at the Universities of Toronto and Pittsburgh. His *Practical Reasoning*, a study of the structure and foundations of prudential and moral arguments, appeared in 1963, and his best-known work, *Morals by Agreement*, in 1986. [X 11]

Gettier, Edmund (1927–). American philosopher whose reputation rests on his three-page paper 'Is Justified True Belief Knowledge?', published in the journal *Analysis* in 1963. [I 12]

Godwin, William (1756–1836). A prolific writer, author of numerous essays and many political novels, Godwin became famous for his *Enquiry concerning Political Justice* (1793), which maintains that all government is inevitably corrupt. The moral basis of Godwin's anarchist vision is utilitarian, and he argues that to maximize human happiness what is required is impartial benevolence – a virtue which is incompatible with the ingrained partialities and prejudices of the existing social and political order. In 1797 Godwin married Mary *Wollstonecraft. [IX 5]

Goodman, Nelson (1906–98). American philosopher who taught at the University of Pennsylvania and at Harvard. In his *Fact, Fiction and Forecast* (1955) he produced a 'new riddle of induction' which raised important issues about the confirmation of scientific theories. He also wrote on aesthetics (in his *Languages of Art*, 1968) and on epistemology and metaphysics (in his *Ways of Worldmaking*, 1978). [XI 12]

Grice, H[erbert] Paul (1913–88). British analytic philosopher who taught at St John's College, Oxford, and later at the University of California at Berkeley. He made important contributions to the philosophy of language and the theory of meaning; many of his influential papers are reprinted in his *Studies in the Ways of Words* (1989). [III 11]

Hegel, Georg Wilhelm Friedrich (1770–1831). Hegel was born in Stuttgart and followed an academic career, culminating in his appointment as Professor of Philosophy in Berlin, where he taught from 1818 till his death. His principal writings are the *Phenomenology of Mind* (*Phänomenologie des Geistes*, 1807), the *Encyclopedia of Philosophical Sciences* (*Encyclopädie der philosophischen Wissenschaften im Grundrisse*, 1817) and the *Philosophy of Right* (*Grundlinien der Philosophie des Rechts*, 1821). He is perhaps best known for the theory according to which all actual events in the world can be seen as stages in the progressive development of full self-conscious rationality – the absolute Mind, or 'self-positing' Spirit which Hegel calls *Geist*. Self-knowledge is the goal or end towards which the entire world system is moving, and the self-conscious cognitive activities of human beings are in a certain sense the culmination of that process. Throughout Hegel's philosophy there is a characteristic stressing of the importance of the historical dimension. The development of human thought has to be understood as a continuous dynamic process, in which each stage arises from the struggle to overcome the limitations of what has gone before. [I 9; X 7]

Heidegger, Martin (1889–1976). German philosopher who taught at Marburg and Freiburg and became Rector of Freiburg University in 1933. He was banned from teaching from 1945–51 on the grounds of his links with Nazism, though the extent of his ideological involvement with that movement is still the subject of controversy. He is generally regarded as one of the founders of the existentialist movement in philosophy. His magnum opus is *Sein und Zeit* (*Being and Time*, 1927), in which he develops his famous account of *Dasein* – a view of the human subject as a being who finds himself thrown into existence, but able nonetheless to find meaning in the world through participation and involvement in purposive activities and projects. [II 9]

Hempel, Carl G[ustav] (1905–97). Originally associated with the Vienna Circle of logical positivist philosophers, Hempel studied under Rudolph *Carnap, and emigrated to the USA in the 1930s, where he became one of the country's most influential philosophers of science. His *Aspects of Scientific Explanation* was published in 1965, and his *Philosophy of Natural Science* in 1966. He later became a colleague of Thomas *Kuhn at Princeton. [VII 10]

Hobbes, Thomas (1588–1679). Major English philosopher who had an important influence both on political philosophy in particular and on the general philosophical agenda of the early modern period. He was born in Wiltshire and educated at Oxford; his later career was supported by the patronage of William Cavendish, first Earl of Devonshire. He fled to France during the English civil war, where he wrote a set of objections to *Descartes's *Meditations*; he later published a trilogy of Latin works expounding his theories of the state, of physics and of physiology: *De Cive* ('Concerning the Citizen', 1642), *De Corpore* ('Concerning Body', 1655), *De Homine* ('Concerning Man', 1658). His masterpiece is the *Leviathan*, written in English and published in 1651. Hobbes took a firmly materialist view of the nature of the universe, including human nature, and attempted to explain all phenomena, including sensation and cognition, in terms of the movements of the particles of the body. Consistently with this materialistic approach, he held that such human freedom as we enjoy is compatible with universal causal necessity. In political theory he made a major contribution through his account of the nature of sovereignty and the grounds of political authority, advancing an early version of what has come to be known as the 'social contract' theory of the relationship between citizens and the government. [V 8; X 3]

Hume, David (1711–76). Scottish philosopher and historian, and leading thinker of the eighteenth-century 'enlightenment', Hume was born and educated in Edinburgh, but went to France in 1734, where he composed his first masterpiece, *A Treatise of Human Nature*; this was first published in 1739–40, after his return to Britain. The work attracted little or no attention at the time, but Hume's reputation began to grow with the publication of his *Essays Moral and Political* (1741–2). The ideas of the *Treatise* were later reworked in what are now known as the First and Second Enquiries – *An Enquiry concerning Human Understanding* (1748) and *An Enquiry concerning the Principles of Morals* (1751). Hume's highly successful multi-volume *History of England* appeared between 1754 and 1762; his *Dialogues concerning Natural Religion* (in all probability best interpreted as a powerful reflection of Hume's own atheistical outlook) was published the year after his death. Hume is unusual among great philosophers in having made major contributions to both the philosophy of knowledge and to moral philosophy. His general starting-point is the empiricist one that all knowledge derives ultimately from the impressions of the senses, and he aimed to develop a science of human nature, based on experience and observation. Perhaps the most widely studied parts of his philosophy are his discussions of the limits of scientific knowledge, and in particular his account of the problem of induction and the nature of causation. In moral philosophy he is famous for the doctrine that moral distinctions are derived from sentiment, not from reason; but he goes on to develop a complex and subtle account of the virtues, which gives pride of place to our natural feelings of human sympathy. [I 7; II 7; V 3; VI 6, 7; VII 5, 6; VIII 4; IX 3; X 5; XI 4]

Hutcheson, Francis (1694–1746). Scottish philosopher who became Professor of Moral Philosophy at Glasgow in 1729. In his *Inquiry into the Original of our Ideas of Beauty and Virtue* (1725), Hutcheson aimed to develop a theory of moral and aesthetic judgement based on the notion of an inner sense; his broadly empiricist approach to this project, emphasizing the role of sentiment as opposed to rational demonstration, strongly influenced the ideas of his compatriot David *Hume. [XI 3]

James, William (1842–1910). American philosopher and psychologist (brother of the novelist Henry James); he studied at Harvard, where he later taught anatomy, and subsequently became Professor of Philosophy and then Psychology. His *Principles of Psychology* appeared in 1890, his collection of essays, *The Will to Believe* in 1897 and his *Varieties of Religious Experience* in 1902. In his *Pragmatism* (1908) James argues that the truth of ideas consists in their usefulness, either in predicting experience or in promoting valuable behaviour. One of James's chief philosophical preoccupations was the nature of consciousness: his writings on the role of introspection and his famous metaphor of the 'stream of consciousness' have influenced many subsequent thinkers. [VI 9]

Kant, Immanuel (1724–1804) was born and lived all his life in Köningsberg, in East Prussia, where he became Professor of Logic and Metaphysics in 1770. Kant's thought represented a landmark in the history of philosophy, being both a culmination of the debates of the early modern period over the source and foundations of human knowledge, and also a powerful influence on subsequent conceptions of the scope and nature of philosophical inquiry. Kant's three massive critiques, the *Critique of Pure Reason* (*Kritik der reinen Vernunft*, 1781), the *Critique of Practical Reason* (*Kritik* *der praktischen Vernunft*, 1788) and the *Critique of Judgement* (*Kritik der Urteilskraft*, 1790), deal respectively with the foundations of scientific knowledge, morals and aesthetics. In the first *Critique*, Kant argues that no knowledge can transcend the bounds of experience, but that the very possibility of experience presupposes the possession of certain basic concepts or categories of the understanding. In the second *Critique*, and in his *Groundwork of the Metaphysic of Morals* (*Grundlegung der Metaphysik der Sitten*, 1785), Kant presents his celebrated 'categorical imperative': 'act only on that maxim which you can at the same time will to become a universal law.' The *Critique of Judgement* deals with the foundations of aesthetics, and also with 'teleological' judgements (the identification of purposiveness in nature). Kant's writing style and methods of argumentation are extremely complex, and his work prefigures the 'professionalization' of philosophy as a specialized academic subject. The *Prolegomena*, intended as a more accessible presentation of the intricate arguments of the first *Critique*, appeared in 1783. [I 8; II 8; VII 7; VIII 5; IX 6; XI 5]

Kass, Leon (1939–). Professor at the University of Chicago, who has published a number of influential books in the field of bioethics. His numerous writings include *Toward a More Natural Science: Biology and Human Affairs* (1984), *The Hungry Soul: Eating and the Perfecting of our Nature* (1994), *The Ethics of Human Cloning* (1998, with James Q. Wilson) *and The Challenge for Bioethics* (2002). [IX 12]

Kierkegaard, Søren (1813–55). Danish philosopher and religious writer, widely regarded as a precursor of the existentialist movement. Kierkegaard was educated at the University of Copenhagen, and many of his subsequent writings are highly polemical critiques of the *Hegelian ideas that then dominated Danish academic culture. His *Either–Or* was published in 1843, *Philosophical Fragments* in 1844 and the *Concluding Unscientific Postscript* in 1846. The chief themes of Kierkegaard's books are the nature of religious faith, and individual choice; many of his writings are anguished in tone, and the concepts of dread and despair play a prominent role. [VI 8]

Kripke, Saul Aaron (1940–) American philosopher of logic and language who has taught at Harvard, Cornell and Princeton. His influential views on naming and identity are presented in *Naming and Necessity* (1980), and his *Wittgenstein on Rules and Private Language* appeared in 1982. [III 12]

Kuhn, Thomas (1922–96). Professor of Philosophy at the Massachusetts Institute of Technology. Kuhn's best-known work, *The Structure of Scientific Revolutions* (1962), has had an important influence on contemporary philosophy of science. [VII 12]

Laplace, Pierre Simon, Marquis de (1749–1827). French philosopher and mathematician, author of the *Exposition du système du monde* ('Explanation of the World System', 1798) and *Essai philosophique sur les probabilités* ('Philosophical Essay on Probability', 1814). The latter work is famous as laying down some of the foundations for modern probability theory. In the philosophy of science Laplace's name is almost synonymous with the deterministic thesis that it is possible in principle to predict every future event in the universe from a complete specification of its state at any given time. [V 9]

Leibniz, Gottfried Wilhelm (1646–1716). German polymath, born in Leipzig, whose wide-ranging intellectual interests, in law, science, mathematics, logic, ethics, metaphysics and religion, were pursued in tandem with a life of courtly and diplomatic service to the house of Hanover. He left no magnum opus, but wrote numerous short pamphlets, booklets and articles (mainly in French), in which his philosophical views are developed; these include the *Discourse on Metaphysics* (1686), the *New System* (1695) and the *Monadology* (1714). Two fuller-length volumes, the *New Essays on Human Understanding* (*c*.1705) and the *Theodicy* (1710), examine, respectively, the origins of human knowledge, and theological problem of the existence of evil. Leibniz devised an elaborate metaphysical system (motivated partly by scientific, partly by logical and partly by theological considerations) in which the ultimate units of reality are infinitesimal simple immaterial substances, the monads, each of which contains within itself a reflection of the entire universe. Of all the possible sets of monads, God brings into actual existence the set that constitutes the 'best of all possible worlds'. Though Leibniz's philosophy is deterministic (he holds that there is a 'sufficient reason' for every true proposition), he attempts nonetheless to find a place in his system for genuine contingency, and, in particular, for human freedom. [I 6; II 5; VI 5]

Leopold, Aldo (1887–1949) was Professor of Wildlife Management at the University of Wisconsin from 1933 to 1949. His widely admired *A Sand County Almanac* (1949) had an important influence on the later rise of environmental ethics. [IX 8]

Locke, John (1632–1704). One of England's greatest philosophers, Locke was born in Somerset and educated at Christ Church, Oxford. His philosophical masterpiece is the *Essay concerning Human Understanding*, on which he worked for some twenty years before it was published in 1690 (when he was in his late fifties). The book advances the empiricist thesis that sensory experience is the original source of all our ideas; subsequent knowledge is a matter of the mind's reflecting on, and abstracting from, these primary data. Locke also made a famous distinction between primary qualities (such as shape) and secondary qualities (such as colour), arguing that our ideas of the latter do not resemble anything really existing in the objects. In addition to his work on the philosophy of knowledge and the nature of language and meaning, Locke made influential contributions to political theory, in his *Two Treatises of Government* (also published in 1690), which discuss the nature of civil society and the basis of governmental authority. Locke's own view of the nature of philosophical inquiry was a modest one: he considered the philosopher to be an 'under-labourer', clearing the ground and removing some of the rubbish that lies in the way of knowledge. [I 5; II 4; III 5; V 1; X 4]

Lucretius [Titus Lucretius Carus] (98– *c*.55 BC). Roman poet and philosopher, whose only known work is the long didactic poem *De Rerum Natura* ('The Nature of the Universe', or, literally, 'On the Nature of Things'). This presents a passionate and eloquent defence of the philosophical system of the Hellenistic philosopher Epicurus (born 341 BC). Lucretius' six-book poem, written in Latin hexameters, gives a detailed account of Epicurean physics: all existing things are held to have originated from the collisions of atoms in the void, and nothing exists beyond the material realm. Religion is dismissed by Lucretius as base superstition, and the poet aims to free mankind from the fear of death by showing that our nature is entirely corporeal and that any idea of the after-life is groundless. Lucretius also defends Epicurean moral philosophy, based on the pursuit of pleasure and the avoidance of pain; the goal, however, is not physical indulgence, but achieving tranquillity of mind. [XII 1]

MacIntyre, Alasdair (1929–) A strong influence on the development of moral philosophy in the late twentieth century, MacIntyre was born and educated in Britain, and taught at a number of universities, mostly in the USA. His early work *Marxism: An Interpretation* (1953) included a critical examination of the relationship between the Marxist and the Christian worldviews, and his *Short History of Ethics* (1967) emphasized the culturally embedded nature of moral reasoning. His best-known work, *After Virtue* (1981), was an important stimulus for the revival of virtue ethics. [VIII 11]

Malebranche, Nicolas (1638–1715). Malebranche was born in Paris and attended the Sorbonne; he joined the Oratorians and was ordained priest in 1664. His principal works are the *Search after Truth* (*Recherche de la Vérité*, 1674–5), and the *Dialogues on Metaphysics and Religion* (1688), both of which show the influence of *Augustine. Malebranche supported many aspects of *Descartes's philosophy, but drew a strong distinction between subjective sensations and clear and distinct ideas, arguing that the latter subsist in the mind of the Deity, so that 'we see all things in God'. Malebranche also advanced the theory known as occasionalism: no created body (or mind) has the power to cause changes in another; what we take to be causal interactions are merely the 'occasions' for God, the sole true cause, to exercise his efficacious will. There is evidence that Malebranche's conception of the role of God had a considerable influence on *Berkeley; and his discussions of causality opened up discussion of what kind of 'necessity' was involved in the causal relation, thus paving the way for the work of *Hume. [IV 6]

Marx, Karl (1818–83). The son of a wealthy Jewish lawyer, Marx studied in Bonn and Berlin, and later went to Paris where he formed a strong friendship with Friedrich *Engels, with whom he published the *Manifesto of the Communist Party* in 1848. After being expelled from France, and subsequently from Belgium and Germany, he settled in London in 1849, where he spent the rest of his life. The first volume of his monumental work *Das Kapital* ('Capital') was published in Hamburg in 1867; the two remaining volumes (edited by Engels) were published posthumously. Marx advanced a view of society according to which economic conditions control the direction of history, and the entire superstructure of religious, philosophical and artistic ideas is determined by the economic base. The dominant force in history is the struggle between economic classes, a struggle to be resolved only with the advent of communism. [X 8]

Maxwell, Grover (1918–81). Noted American philosopher of science, and author of several important papers including 'Scientific Methodology and the Causal Theory of

Perception' (1968), 'Structural Realism and the Meaning of Theoretical Terms' (1970) and 'Theories, Perception, and Structural Realism' (1971). Co-editor of the influential series 'Minnesota Studies in the Philosophy of Science'. [VII 11]

Mill, John Stuart (1806–73). The greatest British philosopher of the nineteenth century, J. S. Mill was born in London, son of the Scottish philosopher and historian James Mill, who was an enthusiastic supporter of *Bentham. Much of J. S. Mill's own thinking was strongly influenced by the utilitarian tradition, and his famous essay *Utilitarianism* (1863) is a detailed defence of the greatest-happiness principle in ethics; it nonetheless departs from the Benthamite views in some important respects, notably by introducing the idea that pleasures can be ranked by quality as well as quantity, and hence that the 'higher' pleasures of the intellect are to be preferred above the 'lower' bodily pleasures. Mill is perhaps best known nowadays as the great champion of Victorian liberalism; his *On Liberty* (1859) advances the thesis that the only justification for interfering with individual liberty is to prevent harm to others. Mill's monumental *System of Logic* (1843), written in the empiricist tradition of *Bacon and *Hume, covers a wide range of issues in the theory of knowledge and meaning, and presents a systematic defence of inductive methods in science. His *Examination of Sir William Hamilton's Philosophy*, an attempt to reduce statements about the external world to statements about actual or possible states of consciousness, appeared in 1865. [III 7; IV 8; VII 8; VIII 6; X 9]

Montaigne, Michel Eyquem de (1533–92). French humanist philosopher and brilliant essayist. His essays are loosely reasoned and discursive treatments of many different subjects, and are noted for their classical learning, as well as being full of amusing anecdotes and philosophical insights. His *Apology for Raymond Sebond* (1580) examines some of the ancient sceptical arguments of Sextus Empiricus, and also casts a doubtful eye on the supposed evidence for the superiority of human reason over animal instinct. [XII 4]

Moore, G[eorge] E[dward] (1873–1958). British philosopher who taught for many years at the University of Cambridge and was an influential figure in the rise of modern analytic philosophy. Moore's *Principia Ethica* (1903) argues that goodness is an indefinable 'non-natural' property. Of his many philosophical papers, the most famous are 'The Refutation of Idealism' (1903) and 'A Defence of Common Sense' (1925). [I 10]

Nagel, Thomas (1937–). Distinguished American philosopher, widely known for his work in philosophy of mind, and also in ethical and political philosophy. Born in Belgrade, he studied at Harvard and Oxford, and taught at Princeton and at New York University. His books include *The Possibility of Altruism* (1970), *Mortal Questions* (1979), *The View from Nowhere* (1986) and *Equality and Partiality* (1991). [IV 12; XII 10]

Nietzsche, Friedrich (1844–1900). Born in Saxony, the son of a Lutheran minister, Nietzsche had a brilliant career as a student and became Professor of Classics at the University of Basel at the age of 24, a post he was forced to abandon because of illness in 1879; he became insane in 1889. In his prolific and often poetic writings, Nietzsche developed not so much a philosophical system as a passionate rhetorical critique of traditional ethics, religion and metaphysics. His most significant works are *The Birth of Tragedy* (1872), *Untimely Meditations* (*Unzeitgemässe Betrachtungen*, 1873–6), *Beyond Good and Evil* (1886), *The Genealogy of Morals* (1887) and *The Antichrist* (1895). His most famous literary achievement is *Thus Spake Zarathustra* (1883–92), part poetry and part prose, an extraordinary mixture of anguished and affirmatory declarations on the human condition and how it may be 'overcome'. His *The Joyful Science* (*Die Fröhliche Wissenschaft*, 1882) contains the famous story of a madman who goes round the market-place at midday with a lighted lantern, crying that 'God is dead'. [VIII 8; XI 7; XII 7]

Nozick, Robert (1938–2002). Professor of Philosophy at Harvard University. His most celebrated contribution to philosophy was in political theory, through his *Anarchy, State and Utopia* (1974), a vigorous defence of libertarianism. His other writings include *Philosophical Explanations* (1981), *The Examined Life* (1989) and *The Nature of Rationality* (1993). [X 10; XII 12]

Ockham, William of (1285–1347). English scholastic philosopher and Franciscan friar. His philosophical writings cover a wide range of topics in metaphysics, epistemology, philosophy of language and philosophy of action. He is best known for his championing of 'nominalism' – a rejection of the doctrine that universals are real things – and for his principle (known as 'Ockham's razor') that 'entities are not to be multiplied beyond necessity'. [III 3]

Parfit, Derek (1942–). Fellow of All Souls College, Oxford since 1967, Parfit is best known for his book *Reasons and Persons* (1984), which covers many important issues in moral philosophy and the philosophy of mind, and whose main result is to undermine the concept of 'identity' as something of crucial importance for the continued survival of persons. [II 12; V 5]

Pascal, Blaise (1623–62). Pascal was noted in his lifetime for his work on a wide range of mathematical and scientific projects, including contributions to hydrodynamics and to the mathematical theory of probability (still in its infancy at the time); he invented a calculating machine, and performed a series of experiments on the vacuum and atmospheric pressure. On the night of 23 November 1654 Pascal had an intense mystical experience as a result of which he devoted himself to a life of religious piety. He became intimately associated with the Catholic Jansenist sect, whose community at Port Royal his sister Jacqueline had joined in 1652. His celebrated *Lettres provinciales*, a series of letters attacking the moral theology of the Jesuits, were written in 1655–7. His last few years were overshadowed by the illness that led to his premature death; his most famous work, the *Pensées*, is a compilation of notes and aphorisms which were to form the nucleus of a planned defence of the Christian faith. [VI 4; XII 5]

Plantinga, Alvin (1932–). Leading American philosopher of religion and professor at the University of Notre Dame. He is noted for his construction of a modern modal version of the ontological argument for God's existence, and for his defence of theism against the argument from evil. He is best known for his writings on the epistemology of religious belief, which centre around his thesis that religious belief is 'properly basic'. His *Warranted Christian Belief* appeared in 2000. [VI 12]

Plato (*c.*428–*c.*348 BC) is rightly regarded as the founder of Western philosophy. In his early career, he was closely associated with his teacher Socrates (469–399 BC), who was executed when Plato was 29 or 30; later, Plato established in Athens a philosophical school known as the Academy. He wrote over two dozen dramatic dialogues which systematically examine the nature of human understanding, the foundations of knowledge and the way to achieve excellence in our lives. The Platonic corpus covers the full range of what we now think of as philosophical inquiry, from logic and metaphysics to ethics, aesthetics and political theory. Though the precise order in which Plato's works were written is unknown, they are normally grouped into three presumed phases: an early period (including the *Protagoras, Gorgias, Crito* and *Euthyphro*), a middle period (including the *Meno, Symposium, Phaedo* and *Republic*) and a later period (including the *Parmenides, Theaetetus* and *Sophist*). Plato was evidently inspired by the ideas of Socrates, whom he makes the chief spokesman in his dialogues; but since Socrates himself wrote nothing, it is impossible to say with certainty how many of the ideas presented come directly from him. The general consensus is that the doctrines developed in the middle and later dialogues (most notably the famous Theory of Forms – see Part I, extract 2) represent Plato's own distinctive philosophical views, while the earlier writings more closely reflect the influence of Socrates. The Socratic project is to shake us out of our comfortable preconceptions, by challenging us to give a rational account, or *logos*, of the concepts and categories we employ, often unreflectively, in our ordinary lives. Socrates' chief technique was the *elenchus* – a kind of gruelling cross-examination designed to bring out instabilities or inconsistencies in an opponent's position. Many of the earlier dialogues are aimed at showing the difficulty of providing clear definitions of what is meant by such notions as justice, friendship, piety, temperance or courage; as a result of Socrates' remorseless logical probing, the other participants in the dialogues are often left in a state of *aporia* – a kind of numbed confusion, which forces them to admit that they are unable to give a clear rational account of their ordinary beliefs and convictions. So far, the exercise is largely a negative, or critical one. But it prepares the ground for the more ambitious project which is prominent in Plato's mature philosophy: to replace the uncertainties and confusions of ordinary opinion with something more solid and reliable, and to provide a clear account of what makes the results of the exercise qualify as genuine knowledge. [I 1, 2; II 1; III 1; IV 1; VIII 1; X 1; XI 1]

Popper, Karl (1902–94). Austrian-born philosopher who was Professor of Logic and Scientific Method at the London School of Economics from 1949 to 1969. His greatest work is the *Logik der Forschung* (1935; translated into English in 1959 as *The Logic of Scientific Discovery*), where he proposed falsifiability (the possibility of being refuted by empirical evidence) as the distinguishing mark of genuine science. This idea is developed further in *Conjectures and Refutations* (1963). Popper's *The Open Society and its Enemies* (1945) contains a powerful defence of individualism against political theorists who would offer fixed solutions based on their supposed knowledge of the principles of social and historical development. [VII 9]

Putnam, Hilary (1926–) Distinguished American philosopher whose work has been influential in several fields, including philosophy of mind, philosophy of language, metaphysics and philosophy of science. He championed, but later abandoned, a functionalist theory of mental states, and was a strong supporter of metaphysical realism, though he later became a strong critic of that view. Two volumes of his papers, *Mathematics, Matter and Method*, and *Mind, Language and Reality*, were published in 1975, and subsequent books have included *Reason, Truth and History* (1981), *Representation and Reality* (1988) and *Pragmatism: An Open Question* (1995). [IV 11]

Quine, Willard Van Orman (1908–2000). Highly influential American philosopher and logician and professor at Harvard University. He is famous for his critique of the standard distinction between analytic and synthetic statements (in 'Two Dogmas of Empiricism', 1953), and later developed a 'naturalized epistemology', which aimed to replace traditional philosophically based accounts of knowledge with a purely empirical and scientific account of how our view of the world is acquired. His *Word and Object* appeared in 1960, and nine of his best-known essays are collected in *From a Logical Point of View* (2nd edn 1980). [II 11]

Rachels, James (1941–2003). Noted American moral philosopher, whose name is associated with the strong growth in applied ethics in the latter decades of the twentieth century. His anthology *Moral Problems* (1971) became a very influential teaching text, as did his introduction to ethics, entitled *The Elements of Moral Philosophy* (1986). [IX 11]

Rawls, John (1921–). Professor of Philosophy at Harvard and author of the highly influential *A Theory of Justice* (1971), which develops a theory of the just society based on the fundamental idea of fairness, requiring the greatest measure of freedom compatible with like freedom for all, and allowing social and economic inequalities only if they benefit the worst-off members of society. [VIII 10]

Ross, W[illiam] D[avid] (1877–1971). Celebrated Classical scholar and translator of Aristotle, Ross also made a substantial contribution to moral philosophy with his *The Right and the Good* (1930). Ross regarded certain moral propositions as self-evidently true, and argued for pluralism in ethics, maintaining that our various duties cannot be derived from a single principle of right action. [VIII 9]

Rousseau, Jean-Jacques (1712–78). Born in Geneva, Rousseau lived for many years in Paris, where he published the *Discourse on the Sciences and the Arts* (1750), the *Discourse on the Origin of Inequality* (1755) and, in 1762, his masterpiece *The Social Contract* (*Du contrat social*). Here he argued that the source of political legitimacy was the voluntary subjection of each individual to the 'general will'. The same year also saw the publication of *Emile*, a philosophical novel which charts the course of an ideal education, where the naturally good and noble individual can develop freely into a social being through guidance and encouragement rather than coercion and restraint. [X 6]

Russell, Bertrand (1872–1970). Famous British philosopher, logician and mathematician, who is recognized as one of the founders of analytic philosophy. His first book was a critical exposition of the philosophy of Leibniz (1900), and he made his name with the publication of *Principia Mathematica* (co-authored with Alfred North Whitehead), a three-volume work on the logical foundations of mathematics (1910–13). Russell's philosophical interests were wide, including epistemology and the theory of meaning and, later on, moral and political philosophy. He was an outspoken critic of religion, and his *Why I am not a Christian* appeared in 1927. Russell's *History of Western Philosophy*, renowned for its clarity and accessibility, has long been a bestseller. [III 9; XII 8]

Ryle, Gilbert (1900–76). Oxford philosopher who had a great influence on many areas of British philosophical life. He developed a view of philosophy according to which its function was to correct absurdities and misunderstandings arising from 'category mistakes'. His magnum opus was *The Concept of Mind* (1949), which mounted a systematic attack on the Cartesian notion of the mind as a private theatre accessible only to the subject. [IV 10]

Sartre, Jean-Paul (1905–80). French philosopher, novelist and playwright whose ideas have been a formative influence on twentieth-century culture. His existentialist outlook, derived partly from his study of *Heidegger, emphasizes the inescapable anguish of a human existence in which we are 'condemned to be free'. His novels include the semi-autobiographical *La Nausée* (*Nausea*) published in 1938, and the tetralogy *Les Chemins de la Liberté* ('The Roads to Freedom') of which the first volume appeared in 1945. His monumental *Being and Nothingness* (*L'être et le néant*, 1943) examines the nature of human self-consciousness and the relationship between the self and others, and develops the concept of 'bad faith' – a series of manoeuvres whereby humans attempt to escape their total responsibility for their lives. Sartre's later work, especially the *Critique of Dialectical Reason* (1960) is largely concerned with an examination of Marxist views of society. [V 10; XI 9]

Schopenhauer, Arthur (1788–1860). German philosopher and metaphysician, whose major work was his *The World as Will and Idea* (*Die Welt as Wille und Vorstellung*, 1818). The work was not a success at the time, and it was only much later, with his collection of essays *Parerga and Paralipomena* (1851), that his ideas attracted wide attention. Born into a wealthy merchant family, Schopenhauer tried but failed in his attempts to pursue an academic career; he taught for a term at Berlin in 1820, but insisted on scheduling his course at the same time as *Hegel was lecturing, as a result of which no students came to hear him. Schopenhauer's ideas owe much to those of *Kant, from whom he took the view that our very notion of the ordinary phenomenal world presupposes the conceptual apparatus of an experiencing subject. But Schopenhauer went on to argue that our inner awareness of ourselves gives us knowledge of reality as it is 'in itself' – the world as Will (see introduction to Part IV, extract 7). Although the general tenor of Schopenhauer's philosophy is pessimistic, in his influential writings on aesthetics he maintains that our awareness of beauty provides a realm of pure contemplation where we can escape from the dominion of the Will. [IV 7; XI 6; XII 6]

Sellars, Wilfrid (1912–89). Noted American philosopher who taught at several institutions, including, for the last twenty years of his life, the University of Pittsburgh.

His interests spanned epistemology, metaphysics and the philosophy of mind and language, and he was a strong critic of naturalized epistemology (see *Quine). He is best known for his seminal paper, 'Empiricism and the Philosophy of Mind' (1956). [I 11]

Seneca [Lucius Annaeus Seneca] (c.4 BC–AD 65). The son of a famous rhetorician, Seneca pursued a senatorial career, and under the Emperor Claudius was tutor to the young Nero; on Nero's accession as Emperor he became his political advisor. He later fell out of favour and retired from Rome, but was implicated in a political conspiracy and forced to commit suicide. Seneca was a prolific writer, and wrote many ethical treatises, including *De vita beata* ('On the Happy Life'), *De tranquillitate animi* ('On Tranquillity of Mind') and *De otio* ('On leisure'). His collection of 124 'moral letters' (*Epistulae morales*), written to his friend Lucilius, present his broadly Stoic outlook in a relaxed and undogmatic manner, and were widely read in the Middle Ages and Renaissance. [XII 2]

Sibley, Frank (1923–96). British philosopher of art, who taught at the University of Lancaster. He is best known for his seminal paper 'Aesthetic Concepts' (1959); other important articles include 'Aesthetic and Non-aesthetic' (1965), 'Colours (1967–8) and 'General Criteria in Aesthetics' (1983). [XI 11]

Sidgwick, Henry (1838–1900). English moral philosopher who became Fellow of Trinity College and Professor of Moral Philosophy at Cambridge. He is best known for his long and meticulous work *The Methods of Ethics* (1874), which is a systematic examination of three principal approaches – intuitionist, utilitarian and egoist – for arriving at a rational basis for human action. [VIII 7]

Singer, Peter (1946–). Professor of Philosophy at Princeton, who is particularly known for his application of moral philosophy to the evaluation of contemporary ethical problems. Author of *Animal Liberation* (1975), which argues, from a utilitarian standpoint, that many of the ways we treat animals are ethically indefensible. His other writings include *Practical Ethics* (1979). [IX 10]

Spinoza, Benedict (1632–77). One of the greatest yet most unorthodox philosophers of the early-modern period, Spinoza was born to an immigrant Jewish family in Amsterdam, but expelled from the Jewish community for heresy in his early twenties. He was influenced by the philosophy of *Descartes (though he strongly criticized many of his doctrines), and his first publication, in 1663, was an exposition of Descartes's *Principles of Philosophy*. In his monumental *Ethics* (*Ethica ordine geometrico demonstrata*), written during the 1660s, Spinoza argues that all mental and physical phenomena are modes of a single all-embracing substance, 'God or Nature'. Though Spinoza unfolds his metaphysical system through a series of meticulous geometrical demonstrations, his chief interest is in applying it to human life, and the bulk of the work describes how a rational understanding of the inescapable causes of all phenomena can enable us to master the passions and make the transition from servitude to freedom. Spinoza's *Tractatus Theologico-Politicus* (published anonymously in 1670) achieved great notoriety in its time for its denial of the supernatural origin of reported miracles, and its radical treatment of the Bible as a historical document rather than a sacred repository of revealed truth. [IV 5; VIII 3]

Strawson, Peter F. (1919–2006). Oxford philosopher noted for his work on metaphysics, philosophical logic and the philosophy of mind. His writings include *Individuals* (1959) and *Logico-Linguistic Papers* (1971). [V 11]

Taylor, Charles (1931–). Canadian philosopher who taught mainly at McGill University. Though trained in the analytic tradition, Taylor has a broad and humane conception of philosophy, and his work draws on the ideas of Continental as well as anglophone writers. His most famous work is *Sources of the Self* (1989), which rejects the idea of the 'punctual self', or pure rational conscious agent, found in some enlightenment thinkers, and instead invokes a rich ethical tradition going back to Augustine which conceives of the self in terms of its orientation to the good. [V 6]

Thomson, Judith Jarvis (1929–). American philosopher, Professor of Philosophy at the Massachusetts Institute of Technology, whose writings have been influential in contemporary moral philosophy, particularly in the debate over the ethical status of abortion. Her *The Realm of Rights* appeared in 1990. [IX 9]

Tolstoy, Leo (1828–1910). The celebrated Russian writer, author of many novels, including most famously *War and Peace* (1865–72) and *Anna Karenina* (1875–6). In addition to his works of fiction he wrote many moral and political essays including *What is Art?* (1898) and *What Must We Do?* (1886), a critique of social and economic conditions in Russia. [XI 8]

Williams, Bernard (1929–2003). Leading British moral philosopher who taught at London, Cambridge (where he was Provost of King's College) and Oxford (where he was White's Professor of Moral Philosophy); he also held a chair at the University of California at Berkeley. A writer of great subtlety and insight, Williams was a formidable critic of utilitarianism, and also of Kantianism; he attacked the claims to dominance of what he called the 'morality' system (based on the concepts of duty and obligation), and instead advocated a wider conception of ethics construed as an attempt to address the problem of how to live well. His books include *Moral Luck* (1981), *Ethics and the Limits of Philosophy* (1985), *Shame and Necessity* (1993) and *Truth and Truthfulness: An Essay in Genealogy* (2002). [VIII 12]

Wisdom, John (1904–93). British philosopher, Professor at Cambridge from 1952 to 1968; he later taught in the United States. His work was particularly concerned with the nature of meaning, the philosophy of language and the purpose of philosophical analysis. Author of *Other Minds* (1952), *Philosophy and Psychoanalysis* (1953) and *Paradox and Discovery* (1965). [VI 10]

Wittgenstein, Ludwig (1889–1951). One of the most influential philosophers of the twentieth century, Wittgenstein was born in Vienna but went to Cambridge in 1912 to study under Bertrand Russell. He fought in the Austrian army in the First World War, and after abandoning philosophy for a decade he returned to Cambridge, becoming

Professor of Philosophy in 1939. Wittgenstein's famous early work, the *Tractatus Logico-Philosophicus* (1921), discusses the relationship between language and the world. Elementary propositions are 'pictures' of states of affairs, and the truth of more complex propositions is a function of how they are built up out of the elementary ones; these are the proper limits of language, and philosophy can say nothing when it attempts to step outside them. In his later work, most famously in *Philosophical Investigations* (published posthumously in 1953), Wittgenstein developed a more flexible view of the possible functions of language, and insisted that its meaning has to be understood within the public context of various forms of social life; he also argued that many philosophical problems are due to conceptual confusions, and that the role of true philosophy was to free us from the 'bewitchment of the intellect by means of language'. [XI 10]

Wollstonecraft, Mary (1759–97). Noted as an early champion of the cause of feminism, Wollstonecraft was the author of *A Vindication of the Rights of Women* (1792), a book which gives vivid expression to her longing for a society in which women could be set free from the restrictions caused by ignorance and prejudice, and where the relationship between the sexes could be more honest and equal. She married the philosopher William *Godwin in 1797, but died in childbirth the same year; her daughter survived, later to become the novelist Mary Shelley. [IX 4]

Index